C0-ARW-642

communism
in the world since 1945

CLIO BIBLIOGRAPHY SERIES

Africa Since 1914
American Popular Culture
The American Presidency
The American South, Volume I
The American South, Volume II
Communism in the World Since 1945
European Immigration and Ethnicity in the United States and Canada
The History of Canada
Indians of the United States and Canada
Indians of the United States and Canada, Volume II
Labor in America
Latin American Politics
The Middle East in Conflict
Military History of the United States
Religion and Society in North America
Social Reform and Reaction in America
Urban America
Women in American History
Women in American History, Volume II

communism in the world since 1945

an annotated bibliography

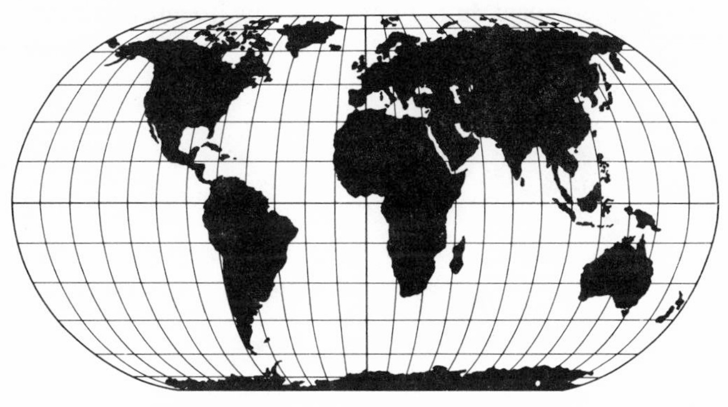

Susan K. Kinnell
Editor

Foreword by
Herbert J. Ellison

ABC-CLIO
Santa Barbara, California
Oxford, England

Library of Congress Cataloging-in-Publication Data

Kinnell, Susan K.
Communism in the world since 1945.

(CLIO bibliography series ; 25)
Includes index.
1. Communism—1945- —Bibliography. I. Title.
II. Series: Clio bibliography series ; no. 25.
Z7164.S67K52 1987 [HX73] 016.33543 86-28790
ISBN 0-87436-169-9

Cover design by Marci Siegel

ABC-Clio, Inc.
2040 Alameda Padre Serra, Box 4397
Santa Barbara, California

Clio Press Ltd.
55 St. Thomas Street
Oxford, England

Printed and bound in the United States of America.

TABLE OF CONTENTS

FOREWORD

World War II marked a dramatic turning point in the history of world communism. With the defeat of Germany and Japan, the Soviet Union emerged as the most powerful state on the Eurasian continent. The continued postwar growth of its military power and the rapid expansion of its influence abroad gave it new opportunities for the support of Communist revolution. Moreover, the Soviet Union, mainly as a result of the war, was joined by new Communist states in Eastern Europe and in East Asia. Both developments have had a profound impact on the postwar history of world communism.

Five main themes dominate the history of world communism since 1945: (1) continued failure to achieve power in the industrial states; (2) a wide range of revolutionary victories in the Third World; (3) severe division and conflict among governing parties; (4) continuity of the governing Leninist system and priorities of the major parties, governing and nongoverning; and (5) the continued dominance (in changed form) of the Soviet Union in the global movement.

Failure of the Communist Revolution in the Industrial States

The failure of communist revolution in the industrial countries was already an old story in 1945. The euphoric hopes generated by the Bolshevik Revolution had disappeared with the stabilization of European political life following World War I. In 1921 Lenin suggested a patient application of the United Front tactic as a long-term means of broadening the basis of Communist power until the appearance of the next "crisis of capitalism." The strategy produced a number of parliamentary parties—some quite powerful— and some major Communist-led trade unions and other mass organizations. But in the main revolutionary opportunity of the interwar years (depression-wracked Germany) the Communists lost the competition to a more powerful Nazi Party.

Political dislocation during World War II brought important opportunities in the wartime resistance movements in France and Italy, and postwar political turmoil brought new opportunities in both of those countries and in Japan. Yet Christian Democracy remained the dominant political power in the major continental states, and the Liberal Democratic Party in Japan. Except for France and Italy the major opposition parties were Democratic Socialist. The sole Communist successes in industrial countries during the early postwar years came in East Germany and Czechoslovakia—the former the result of political coercion under Soviet occupation and the latter the outcome of a coup d'etat.

The recovery of political stability and a long era of sustained economic growth reduced political opportunities and transformed postwar class structures, reducing the numerical importance of the very social class upon which communism relied—the industrial workers. In addition, the economic growth and general prosperity of the postwar democratic states raised workers' living standards and disinclined them to political radicalism. Meanwhile the anti-Communist demonstrations and revolts of the 1950's and 1960's—in East Germany, Czechoslovakia, Poland, and Hungary—greatly reduced the attractiveness of Soviet-style communism for many on the left.

The 1960's and 1970's brought a renewal of hope for communism in Western Europe. The United Front tactic used by the major parties (France, Italy and Spain) and by many of the smaller parties as well, helped to broaden the class base of Communist support and to allay or reduce fears that having Communists in power would lead inevitably to dictatorship. In Latin Europe at least, communism seemed to have acquired a broader support than at any time since the mid-1940's. But by the late 1970's and early 1980's, Communist electoral strength and hopes had collapsed in France and Spain and greatly weakened in Italy. The bid for power within the Portuguese revolution by the Portuguese Communists under the leadership of Alvaro Cunhal had failed, and both Portugal and Spain appeared to have made a successful transition from Fascism to parliamentary democracy.

In the early 1980's Soviet analysis suggested that opportunities for Communist political power were greatest in transitional (not yet fully industrialized) countries, and much attention and activity were concentrated on political opportunities in such countries, not only in Europe but in Latin America and Asia as well. Newly industrializing states, frequently destabilized by rapid social and economic change and by a difficult transition from authoritarian to representative political systems, were politically unstable and vulnerable to revolution. However, evidence to date suggests that communism has no inherently firmer guarantee of victory than a variety of other political forces, and that its recent successes have been mainly in the developing world.

Third World Revolutionary Victories

Following World War II, as in the early 1920's, declining opportunity for communist revolution in industrial countries was accompanied by expanded opportunity in Asia. As in post-World War II Europe (Yugoslavia, Greece, and Albania), so in Asia (Burma, Malaya, Indonesia, Indochina, and the Philippines) much of the opportunity derived from the wartime struggle against military occupation. The popular cause of liberation from Japanese occupation (to be followed by resistance to postwar reestablishment of European colonial power) was used by Communists to build a broad opposition front whose political and military organizations they dominated and the purpose of which was to provide postwar political power for themselves.

This strategy worked in Yugoslavia, Albania, and Vietnam but failed elsewhere, either because of the victory of the non-Communist political leadership (Burma, Indonesia, the Philippines) or because of foreign intervention (Greece and Malaya). The dramatic victory in China was the result of a Communist-Nationalist civil war lasting since the 1920's and only interrupted by Japanese military action in China during the 1930's and 1940's. Communist victory in China was aided by Soviet military and diplomatic support; the victory in North Korea was an "administered revolution" under the protection and supervision of Soviet military occupation.

By the time of Stalin's death in 1953, those Third World Communist parties that had not succeeded in their postwar revolutionary offensives had suspended them, recognizing the futility of further struggle and seeking alliance and cooperation with the very nationalist leaders they had opposed. The United Front strategy was again in vogue, and the appeal of Communist parties and of their Soviet patrons was for both internal political collaboration and a foreign policy hostile to the West. Of the many Asian Communist guerrilla risings (or, in the case of Korea, direct military invasion), only the Chinese and Vietnamese had succeeded, achieving a settlement at Geneva in 1954 that established formal Communist power in the north under Ho Chi-Minh. Elsewhere Communist efforts to acquire power by force had been blocked either by the new nationalist governments (India/Hyderabad, Burma, Indonesia, the Philippines) or by British (Malaya) or American/UN (Korea) intervention.

The return to the United Front tactic in the 1950's and 1960's brought little success (at least as measured by revolutionary victories) in the Third World. Communist success depended heavily on the attitudes and political fate of three non-Communist political leaders: Egypt's President Nasser, Indonesia's President Sukarno, and Cuba's Fidel Castro: the first two by design, the last by accident. The United Front tactic was based on close cooperation with government heads. The Communists and Soviet officials sought to win the confidence and support of government leaders and encourage them to provide legitimacy and freedom for Communist parties, and to undertake domestic policies leading to socialism and foreign policies hostile to the Western powers.

Impressive successes in both Egypt and Indonesia were abruptly reversed following the successful coup against President Sukarno in 1965 and the death of President Nasser in 1970. In Cuba, a political radical but non-Communist, Fidel Castro, came to power as the leader of the July 26 Movement in 1959, turning to communism both organizationally and personally after his victory, though previously scorned by the Cuban Communist Party.

Thus the 1960's was not a decade of outstanding successes for communist revolution, although Soviet diplomacy combined with the efforts of local Communists to expand the company of active parties, to encourage nationalist anticolonial and anti-Western sentiments from Latin America to East Asia, and to gain the confidence and cooperation of nationalist leaders of varied political persuasions. As they had done from the 1920's onward, Communists attempted to align with the powerful force of Third World nationalism as a means of broadening their own support.

The period from the renewal of the Communist (Vietminh) guerrilla offensive in South Vietnam in the 1960's to the end of the 1970's was one of many revolutionary offensives and revolutionary victories. The victories included South Vietnam, Laos, and Cambodia—all part of the long postwar struggle for revolutionary victory in Indochina; six countries of Africa—Angola, Benin, Congo, Ethiopia, Mozambique, and Zimbabwe; Nicaragua; South Yemen; and Afghanistan. The victories represented different models of political strategy and tactics, from the familiar political/military apparatus for overturn of an incumbent government to coups d'etat organized by radicalized military. The record might have been still more impressive but for the failure of the 1980 offensive in El Salvador, the U.S./OECS intervention in Grenada, and the coup against the Allende government in Chile in 1973.

Whatever the limits of success in the 1970's, it was a period that had begun to look like a golden age of revolution from the perspective of the 1980's when many of the new Communist Third World governments were faced with counter-revolutionary insurrections in Indochina, Afghanistan, Africa, and Nicaragua against which some three hundred thousand soldiers had been deployed.

Postwar Division between the States

Conflict between Communist states in the postwar era has consistently manifested a mix of two elements: (1) ideological differences between Communist parties; and (2) conflicts generated by efforts of one Communist state to control the state policy of another. Usually the two have been intertwined, as in postwar Eastern Europe. Stalin's concern with "Titoism" and with "national communism" more generally, was a combination of his claim to monitor the ideological orthodoxy of Soviet client parties and his concern that they not act independently of Soviet wishes. The result was the break with Tito and the servile application of the Soviet model in Eastern Europe which generated the popular revolts of the 1950's and the continuing reform pressures lasting still today, most powerfully in Poland.

Except for Stalinist Albania, in the East European context the deviant ideological positions have tended to be "rightist"—either a combination of traditional Soviet-style party dictatorship with revisions of social and economic policies in the Gomulka fashion, or an effort to achieve fundamental political-structural change in addition to other reforms, as with Imre Nagy, Alexander Dubček, and Polish Solidarity. From the Soviet ideological viewpoint, the policies of the latter three smacked of social democracy; hence the severity of the reaction. Conflict with Romania was chiefly over territorial claims (Moldavia) and an independent Romanian foreign policy, while Albania took a Stalinist position against Khrushchev's de-Stalinization and his foreign policy.

The ideological element of the Sino-Soviet conflict under Mao found the Chinese offering what the Soviets regarded as a "leftist" deviation—a rejection of de-Stalinization and of Khrushchev's foreign policy on the grounds that they led to "revisionism" in internal policy and unseemly dealings and compromise with the "imperialists" in foreign policy. Equally unacceptable from the Soviet viewpoint was Mao's radical Communist utopianism expressed in the Great Leap Forward of the 1950's and the Cultural Revolution of the 1960's.

Soviet efforts to maintain organizational and ideological direction of the postwar Communist world have had very mixed success.Dealing with governing Communist parties, military power was crucial in restoring an acceptable policy in Hungary in 1956 and Czechoslovakia in 1968, but it was of no use with Yugoslavia and Albania or with China, and it has bogged down in an immensely costly war in Afghanistan. It has also bequeathed a legacy of hostility and resistance that poses a significant barrier to cooperation within the Communist world today.

The use of Soviet military power against fellow Communist states (albeit in the guise of fraternal aid) has been bitterly attacked by both governing and nongoverning party leaders abroad; sometimes because of agreement with the reform developments Soviet intervention sought to suppress, sometimes because of fear that similar intervention under the Brezhnev Doctrine would be applied to themselves, and sometimes for both reasons. Yet the practice has also been given verbal support by both governing and nongoverning parties, and military cooperation by Warsaw Pact Allies. The Vietnamese invasions of Laos and Cambodia and the Chinese invasion of Vietnam suggest that neither of these states rejects military power as an acceptable policy instrument for dealing with fellow Communist states.

Continuity of Leninist Democratic Centralism

For all of the proliferation of Communist parties and states during the past forty years, there has been no significant modification of either the theory or the practice of their governance. All governing parties have retained dictatorial powers, and those that have come to power as the leaders of resistance coalitions, combining representatives of various political viewpoints and organizations, have quickly established full Communist control following the acquisition of power. Imre Nagy and Alexander Dubček sought restoration of a multiparty political system in their respective countries; some Eurocommunist intellectuals advocated intraparty democracy during the 1970's; and in Poland in 1981 important (albeit short-lived) elements of intraparty democracy were actually introduced. But all efforts were in vain, and the pattern of one-party dictatorship and intraparty governance within the Leninist tradition of democratic centralism remains.

Continuing Dominance of Soviet Leadership

Soviet leadership of world communism has met formidable challenges during the past forty years, and many would deny that it still exists or indeed that a coherent movement survives, since there has been no comprehensive international meeting of Communist parties since 1969 and none is in prospect. Yet the continuity of organization and ideology is impressive; the preeminence of the Soviet Union continues, and its role is superbly organized through the structure of the International Department of the Central Committee. Impressive too is the collaboration of many Communist states in each new revolutionary action, a collaboration illustrated remarkably by the documents of the Grenada government seized in 1983. In this context no recent trend has greater significance for the future of world communism than the developing reconciliation between the Soviet Union and China, for that division has greatly hampered the unity and the influence of the movement globally for most of the postwar era.

Looking to the Future

What a more united or less disunited and conflict-ridden Communist movement can achieve in the future will depend on many forces beyond the control of Communist parties and states. Past experience suggests that the primary revolutionary opportunities will still be found in the Third World. But the costs of such revolutionary enterprise are mounting, in particular the support of new revolutionary governments. Meanwhile the pressures for economic and political reform within Communist states grow, in some cases to crisis or near-crisis levels. Setting priorities between external revolutionary activities and internal reforms may well be the central challenge of Communist political leadership of the next generation.

HERBERT J. ELLISON
University of Washington

EDITORS' NOTE

COMMUNISM IN THE WORLD SINCE 1945 covers historical scholarship on communism in all parts of the world since the end of World War II. Here, in a single source, are developments within the major Communist countries and organizations, as well as the smaller movements and splinter groups in Western and developing nations. The majority of the entries deal with the political history of the larger Communist and socialist nations, but a substantial number cover such topics as the McCarthy era in the United States and the impact of communism in Southeast Asia. The substantial coverage of journals published in Communist countries will be of real value to researchers looking for a balanced and comprehensive approach to the subject.

The 4151 entries in this volume, selected from the *America: History and Life* and *Historical Abstracts* databases, were evaluated for their relevancy to all facets of Communist studies. Coverage includes informative abstracts of journal articles published between 1974 and 1985 along with book and dissertation citations. Book coverage is selective rather than comprehensive. All books cited have been reviewed in one or more of the major historical review journals. The dissertations included (from Dissertations Abstracts International) point out the depth of research being done in the field, and will allow the individual researcher to determine those areas in need of further study.

The classification scheme used is a broad, geographical one that provides the most complete framework for the variety of entries that fell within the selection criteria.

LIST OF ABBREVIATIONS

A. .... Author-prepared Abstract
Acad. .... Academy, Academie, Academia
Agric. .... Agriculture, Agricultural
AIA .... Abstracts in Anthropology
Akad. .... Akademie
Am. .... America, American
Ann. .... Annals, Annales, Annual, Annali
Anthrop. .... Anthropology, Anthropological
Arch. .... Archives
Archaeol. .... Archaeology, Archaeological
Art. .... Article
Assoc. .... Association, Associate
Biblio. .... Bibliography, Bibliographical
Biog. .... Biography, Biographical
Bol. .... Boletim, Boletin
Bull. .... Bulletin
c. .... century (in index)
ca. .... circa
Can. .... Canada, Canadian, Canadien
Cent. .... Century
Coll. .... College
Com. .... Committee
Comm. .... Commission
Comp. .... Compiler
DAI .... Dissertation Abstracts International
Dept. .... Department
Dir. .... Director, Direktor
Econ. .... Economy, Econom-.
Ed. .... Editor, Edition
Educ. .... Education, Educational
Geneal. .... Genealogy, Genealogical, Genealogique
Grad. .... Graduate
Hist. .... History, Hist-.
IHE .... Indice Historico Espanol
Illus. .... Illustrated, Illustration
Inst. .... Institute, Institut-.
Int. .... International, Internacional, Internationaal, Internationaux, Internazionale
J. .... Journal, Journal-prepared Abstract
Lib. .... Library, Libraries
Mag. .... Magazine
Mus. .... Museum, Musee, Museo
Nac. .... Nacional
Natl. .... National, Nationale
Naz. .... Nazionale
Phil. .... Philosophy, Philosophical
Photo. .... Photograph
Pol. .... Politics, Political, Politique, Politico
Pr. .... Press
Pres. .... President
Pro. .... Proceedings
Publ. .... Publishing, Publication
Q. .... Quarterly
Rev. .... Review, Revue, Revista, Revised
Riv. .... Rivista
Res. .... Research
RSA .... Romanian Scientific Abstracts
S. .... Staff-prepared Abstract
Sci. .... Science, Scientific
Secy. .... Secretary
Soc. .... Society, Societe, Sociedad, Societa
Sociol. .... Sociology, Sociological
Tr. .... Transactions
Transl. .... Translator, Translation
U. .... University, Universi-.
US .... United States
Vol. .... Volume
Y. .... Yearbook

Abbreviations also apply to feminine and plural forms.
Abbreviations not noted above are based on *Webster's Third New International Dictionary* and the *United States Government Printing Office Style Manual.*

LIST OF ACRONYMS

Agitprop . . . . Agitation and Propaganda Department (USSR)
AKEL . . . . Anorthotiko Komma Ergazomenoy Laou [Progressive Party of the Working People] (Cyprus)
AKFM . . . . Antokon'ny Kongresin'ny Fahaleovantenan'i Madagariskara [Congress Party for Malagasy Independence]
ALP . . . . Australian Labor Party
ANC . . . . African National Congress (South Africa)
BCP . . . . Bulgarian Communist Party
CCP . . . . Communist Party of the People's Republic of China
CPA . . . . Communist Party of Australia
CPC . . . . Communist Party of Colombia
CPC . . . . Communist Party of China (Taiwan)
CPI . . . . Communist Party of India
CPK . . . . Communist Party of Kampuchea
CPL . . . . Communist Party of Lesotho
CPN . . . . Communistische Partij Nederland [Communist Party of the Netherlands]
CPNZ . . . . Communist Party of New Zealand
CPP . . . . Communist Party of the Philippines
CPSU . . . . Communist Party of the Soviet Union
CPUSA . . . . Communist Party—USA
DEFOSZ . . . . . . Dolgozo Parasztok es Foldmunkasok Orszagos Szovetsege [National Association of Working Peasants and Laborers] (Hungary)
DKP . . . . Danmarks Kommunistisk Parti [Communist Party of Denmark]
DKP . . . . Deutsche Kommunistische Partei [German Communist Party] (West Germany)
ECP . . . . Egyptian Communist Party
EYL . . . . Eureka Youth League
FDJ . . . . Freie Deutsche Jugend [Free German Youth] (East Germany)
GATT . . . . General Agreement on Tariffs and Trade
ICP . . . . Iraqi Communist Party
JCP . . . . Japan Communist Party
JVP . . . . Janatha Vimukhti Peramuna [People's Liberation Front] (Sri Lanka)
KGB . . . . Committee of State Security (USSR)
LSSP . . . . Lanka Samasamaja Party [Ceylon Equal Society Party] (Sri Lanka)
MDP . . . . Magyar Dolgozók Pártja [Communist Party of Hungary]
MPLA . . . . Popular Movement for the Liberation of Angola
MPRP . . . . Mongolian People's Revolutionary Party
NOT . . . . Scientific Organization of Labor (USSR)
Obkom . . . . Regional Committee (USSR)
PASOK . . . . Panellinion Sosialistikon Kinema [Pan-Hellenic Socialist Movement] (Greece)
PCA . . . . Partido Comunista de Argentina [Communist Party of Argentina]
PCB . . . . Partido Comunista de Bolivia [Communist Party of Bolivia]
PCB . . . . Partido Comunista do Brasil [Brazilian Communist Party]
PCC . . . . Partido Comunista Cubano [Communist Party of Cuba]
PCCh . . . . Partido Comunista de Chile [Chilean Communist Party]
PCE . . . . Partido Comunista de España [Communist Party of Spain]
PCF . . . . Parti Communiste Français [French Communist Party]
PCH . . . . Partido Comunista de Honduras [Communist Party of Honduras]
PCI . . . . Partito Comunista Italiano [Italian Communist Party]
PCP . . . . Partido Comunista Paraquayano [Paraguayan Communist Party]
PCP . . . . Partido Comunista Portugues [Portuguese Communist Party]
PCU . . . . Partido Comunista del Uruguay [Communist Party of Uruguay]
PCV . . . . Partido Comunista Venezolana [Venezuelan Communist Party]
PDP . . . . Partido Democrata Popular [People's Democratic Party] (Argentina, Dominican Republic, Spain)
PKI . . . . Partai Komunis Indonesia [Indonesian Communist Party]
PPS . . . . Parti du Progres et du Socialisme [Party of Progress and Socialism] (Morocco)
PSL . . . . Polskie Stronnictwo Ludowe [Polish Peasant Party]
RAKAH . . . . New Communist List (Israel)
ROK . . . . Republic of Korea
SACP . . . . South Africa Communist Party
SCP . . . . Sudanese Communist Party
SCP . . . . Syrian Communist Party
SED . . . . Sozialistische Einheitspartei Deutschlands [Socialist Unity Party of Germany] (East Germany)
SL . . . . Sendero Luminoso [Shining Path] (Peru)
SPD . . . . Sozialdemokratische Partei Deutschlands [Social Democratic Party of Germany] (West Germany)
TPK . . . . Territorial Industrial Complex (USSR)
UTC . . . . Uniunea Tineretului Comunist [Union of Communist Youth] (Romania)
WLTBU . . . . Watermen's, Lightermen's, Tugmen's and Bargemen's Union

compiled by ÇARL MOODY, Ph.D.
Assistant Editor, *Historical Abstracts*

1. COMMUNISM IN THE SOVIET UNION

General

1. Abosch, Heinz. VERLUST DER INTERNATIONALEN VORHERRSCHAFT DER KPDSU [The CPSU's loss of international predominance]. *Frankfurter Hefte [West Germany] 1976 31(7): 15-22.* The Communist Party of the USSR was the leader of the world's Communists, but now faces challenges not only from the Chinese but from the Eurocommunists as well.

2. Alekseev, B. A. and Ivanov, V. I. KPSS—ORGANIZATOR POBEDY SOTSIALIZMA V SSSR (K VYKHODU V SVET VTOROI KNIGI CHETVERTOGO TOMA "ISTORII KOMMUNISTICHESKOI PARTII SOVETSKOGO SOIUZA") [The CPSU, organizer of the victory of socialism in the USSR: the publication of the second book of the fourth volume of *The History of the Communist Party of the Soviet Union]. Voprosy Istorii KPSS [USSR] 1972 (5): 36-53.* Edited by P. N. Pospelov, the contribution of *Istoriia Kommunisticheskoi partii Sovetskogo Soiuza. Tom 4-i Kommunisticheskaia partiia v bor'be sa postroenie sotsializma v SSSR (1921-1937 gg.). Kniga 2 (1929-1937 gg.)* [The history of the Communist Party of the Soviet Union, Vol. 4 The Communist Party in the struggle for the building of socialism in the USSR, 1921-37. Book 2: 1929-37] (Moscow: Politizdat, 1971) lies in its rejection of Western falsifications of Party history.

3. Alekseev, V. V. and Pashkov, N. M. PARTIINOE RUKOVODSTVO SOZDANIEM I RAZVITIEM NEFTEGAZOVOGO KOMPLEKSA ZAPADNOI SIBIRI [Communist Party leadership in building the oil and gas energy complex in Western Siberia]. *Voprosy Istorii KPSS [USSR] 1983 (6): 55-67.* The construction of the oil and gas complex in Western Siberia from 1962 to 1982 improves energy distribution in the USSR. The Communist Party makes every effort to coordinate and control this development, which is of national importance. 77 notes. R. Kirillov

4. Alekseeva, G. D. ISTPART: OSNOVNYE NAPRAVLENIIA I ETAPY DEIATEL'NOSTI [The Commission on the History of the October Revolution and the Communist Party (Istpart): main trends and stages of development]. *Voprosy Istorii [USSR] 1982 (9): 17-29.* Examines the role of the first scientific centers of the Soviet state, the Commission on the History of the October Revolution and the Communist Party, of which Lenin was the initiator in 1920. Scientific work carried out by the commission, its organizational and coordinating role vis-à-vis collection and publication of materials by local Commissions on the October Revolution and the Communist Party and their scientific and popularizing activity which have laid the foundation of the modern scientific work in this field are discussed. J

5. Aleksanov, P. A. RAZVITIE SOTSIALNOGO OBESPECHENIIA SOVETSKOGO KRESTIANSTVA [The development of the system of social security for the Soviet peasantry]. *Voprosy Istorii [USSR] 1974 (9): 18-32.* Outlines "the origin and development of the system of social security for the Soviet peasantry. It clearly reveals the policy consistently pursued by the Communist Party and the Soviet government in the sphere of improving and extending the system of social security for the toiling peasantry from the earliest decrees adopted by Soviet power to the system of social security for the collective farmers in the conditions of developed socialism. The author traces the principal stages and organizational forms of developing the system of social security for the Soviet peasantry. Particular attention is given in the article to the state of the social security system applied to the working population of the Soviet countryside in the 1950's and 1960's." J

6. Arinin, A. N. IZMENENIE V CHISLENNOSTI I SOSTAVE RABOCHIKH V PROMYSHLENNOSTI BASHKIRSKOI ASSR V 1971-1975 GG. [Changes in the number and composition of workers in industry in the Bashkir ASSR between 1971 and 1975]. *Vestnik Leningradskogo U.: Seriia Istorii, Iazyka i Literatury [USSR] 1982 (3): 114-117.* As noted at the 26th Party Congress, the working class is now not only the biggest class, but also an absolute majority of workers, being 57.4% of the population in 1970. This holds for the Bashkir Autonomous Soviet Socialist Republic. The types of jobs in the republic are described, and the movement between heavy and light industries, the growth of technological jobs, and the food sector are analyzed. The success of Leninist nationalities policies means that there is complete harmony among the peoples. New developments are taking place in metals, energy, oil, and machine tools. Based on materials of the 26th Party Congress; 26 notes. A. J. Evans

7. Atsarkin, A. N. ROZHDENIE KOMSOMOLA [Birth of the Young Communist League]. *Prepodavanie Istorii v Shkole [USSR] 1982 (3): 13-17.* Describes the history of the formation and activity of the Young Communist League (Komsomol) in the USSR.

8. Avetissian, V. A. and Garibdzhaian, G. B. PO LENINSKOMU PUTI [Following in Lenin's path]. *Voprosy Istorii KPSS [USSR] 1970 (11): 60-70.* Traces the history of the Armenian Communist Party and Republic since 1920, and examines early Armenian Marxist organizations.

9. Avtorkhanov, Abdurakhman. THE SOVIET TRIANGULAR DICTATORSHIP: PARTY, POLICE AND ARMY: FORMATION AND SITUATION. *Ukrainian Q. 1978 34(2): 135-153.* A shifting balance among Party, policy, and army characterizes the Soviet power system. Denounced after Stalin's death, police power receded but rose with Khrushchev's fall and now infiltrates the affairs of all Soviet citizens. The army, always subordinate to Party and policy in the past, has risen since Khrushchev to a powerful policymaking role within the Politburo. The equilibrium among the three is unstable, however, and must inevitably fail, perhaps with radical changes throughout Soviet society. 28 notes. K. N. T. Crowther

10. Azovtsev, N. and Gusarevich, S. V. I. LENIN, KPSS O SUSHCHNOSTI MILITARIZMA I PUTIAKH BOR'BY S NIM [V. I. Lenin and the CPSU on the principles of militarism and the means of resisting them]. *Voenno-Istoricheskii Zhurnal [USSR] 1976 (4): 13-21.* Examines Lenin's writings on militarism and shows that his ideas and principles form the basis of Soviet Communist Party policy.

11. Babko, Iu. V. SLAVNYI SHLIAKH LENINS'KOHO KOMSOMOLU [The glorious path of the Leninist Young Communist League (Komsomol)]. *Ukrains'kyi Istorychnyi Zhurnal [USSR] 1968 (10): 33-41.* Retraces the development of the Communist youth movement in the USSR, 1918-68, stressing the importance V. I. Lenin attributed to young people in the Communist movement and their help in bringing about revolutionary change.

12. Bakumenko, P. VOPLOSHCHENIE LENINSKIKH IDEI V EKONOMICHESKOI POLITIKE KPSS (K 70-LETIIU II S"EZDA RSDRP) [The fulfillment of Lenin's ideas in the economic policy of the Soviet Communist Party: the 70th anniversary of the Second Congress of the RSDRP]. *Ekonomika Sovetskoi Ukrainy [USSR] 1973 15(7): 2-10.* Shows that the continuing growth of the Soviet economy is the result of the application of V. I. Lenin's principles.

13. Bakunin, A. V. KPSS VO GLAVE NAUCHNO-TEKHNICHESKOGO PROGRESSA [The Communist Party of the Soviet Union (CPSU) as leader of scientific and technological progress]. *Voprosy Istorii KPSS [USSR] 1982 (10): 123-132.* Since its very inception, the CPSU has consistently paid great attention to the development of science and technology, regarding them as vital in the battle with capitalism, for enhanced productivity and for satisfying the growing material and cultural needs of the working

class. The Party has been the guiding light of scientific progress, dictating its direction by the Five-Year Plans it has drawn up. A particular boost was given to the development of science and technology in the late 1950's, and in recent years a big impetus was provided by the resolutions of the 26th Party Congress in 1981. This laid down concrete guidelines on how best to harness the benefits of science to increase production. 38 notes. J. Bamber

14. Barsukov, N. A.; Shaikullin, A. P.; and Iudin, I. N. KPSS—PARTIIA INTERNATSIONAL'NAIA [The Communist Party of the Soviet Union: an international party]. *Voprosy Istorii KPSS [USSR] 1966 (7): 3-15.* Discusses Communist internationalism related to nationalities within the USSR, 1917-66.

15. Bäskau, Heinz and Meger, Jutta. DER ANTEIL DES LENINSCHEN KOMSOMOL, DER PIONIERORGANISATION "W.I. LENIN" UND DER JUGEND- UND KINDERORGANISATIONEN SOZIALISTISCHER BRUDERLÄNDER AN DER ENTWICKLUNG DER SPORTLICHEN, TOURISTISCHEN UND WEHRSPORTLICHEN BETÄTIGUNG DER SCHULJUGEND [The role of the Young Communist League (Komsomol) and the Young Pioneers and the youth and children's organizations of socialist countries in developing students' sports, travel, and military activities]. *Wissenschaftliche Zeitschrift der U. Rostock. Gesellschafts- und Sprachwissenschaftliche Reihe [East Germany] 1975 24(7): 635-642.* The USSR's Young Communist League initiated more than 100 million young people into communist society, stressing physical, military, as well as ideological training, and sponsoring the Spartakiads as proletarian athletic events; 1920-75.

16. Belonosov, I. I.; Novopashin, I. G.; Shalaginova, L. M.; and Shostak, I. F. DOKUMENTY O SOTSIALISTICHESKOM SOREVNOVANII V 1959-1972 GODAKH [Documents on socialist competition, 1959-72]. *Sovetskie Arkhivy [USSR] 1973 (5): 32-44.* Demonstrates the contribution of socialist competition to the formulation of Communist Party economic policy and the work-consciousness of the workers. Discusses the mechanization of industry, the automatization of production, the completion of new enterprises, and the fulfillment of five-day programs in four days. Based on 19 previously unpublished documents in the Central State Archive of the October Revolution of the USSR and the Central Archive of the All-Union Central Trade Union Council; 10 notes. C. R. Pike

17. Belonosov, I. I. TRADITSII VELIKOGO POCHINA [Traditions of great initiative]. *Sovetskie Arkhivy [USSR] 1973 (3): 56-59.* The tradition of Communist Saturdays began during the Russian civil war in 1919. The author analyzes the effect of this innovation, 1919-20. Statistical material from labor union sources shows that 3.31 billion extra man hours were contributed by the workers for no extra pay. Subsequent efforts, 1921-72, are recorded, but in less detail. Today free labor is regarded as part of man's socialist responsibilities, and not as time voluntarily given. Based on archives, published documents, and newspaper accounts; table, 40 notes. D. N. Collins

18. Berkhin, I. B. ISTORICHESKOE ZNACHENIE OBRAZOVANIIA I RAZVITIIA SOIUZA SOVETSKIKH SOTSIALISTICHESKIKH RESPUBLIK [The international significance of the formation and development of the Union of Soviet Socialist Republics]. *Novaia i Noveishaia Istoriia [USSR] 1982(6): 44-59.* The formation of the Soviet state is a result of the consistent implementation of the Leninist nationalities policy of the Communist Party and the Soviet Government, and of the development of fraternal relations between the independent Soviet socialist republics. J/S

19. Beyme, Klaus von. A COMPARATIVE VIEW OF DEMOCRATIC CENTRALISM. *Government and Opposition [Great Britain] 1975 10(3): 259-277.* Discusses the principles of democratic centralism in the governmental and economic structure of the USSR and other socialist nations, 1950's-70's, including aspects of organizational theory.

20. Bezborodov, A. B. KOMSOMOL V STUDENCHESKHIKH STROITEL'NYKH OTRIADAKH (1958-1975 GG.) [The Komsomol among student construction brigades]. *Sovetskie Arkhivy [USSR] 1981 (1): 35-40.* Extracts from 10 documents relating to student construction brigades in the USSR in the period 1958-75. They are taken from a wide variety of archives and deal with various aspects of collaboration between young people of Russia and the Soviet republics, especially Kazakhstan. The extracts emphasize the importance of such work and its beneficial effect on the physical and ideological development of the participants. Based on central and local state, Party, and Komsomol archives; 11 notes. C. J. Read

21. Blackwell, Robert E., Jr. THE SOVIET POLITICAL ELITE—ALTERNATIVE RECRUITMENT POLICIES AT THE OBKOM LEVEL. *Comparative Pol. 1973 6(1): 99-122.*

22. Blagikh, B. M and Vazhnov, M. Ia. IZ OPYTA NORIL'SKOI GORODSKOI PARTIINOI ORGANIZATSII PO RUKOVODSTVU PROMYSHLENNYM RAZVITIEM KRUPNOGO REGIONA NA KRAINEM SEVERE [From the experience of the Party organization of Norilsk in the guidance of the industrial development of the great region of the extreme North]. *Voprosy Istorii KPSS [USSR] 1981 (7): 18-29.* The Norilsk industrial region, which has grown rapidly since the early 1960's, is one of the most important for the supply of light industry products in the USSR and is the nucleus of the planned Northern Enisei territorial and industrial complex. The local Communist Party organization has been of unceasing aid in the industrial development of the region, providing guidance on political, social, and economic problems, and the experience of organizers and workers in Norilsk can provide valuable guidance for extensive development under the harsh conditions of the Far North, where specialists in all fields are combining efforts to achieve the aims of the next Five-Year Plan. Based on material from 23d-26th Party Congresses and newspaper articles; 37 notes. L. Smith

23. Bociurkiw, Bohdan R. THE ORTHODOX CHURCH AND THE SOVIET REGIME IN THE UKRAINE, 1953-1971. *Can. Slavonic Papers [Canada] 1972 14(2): 191-212.* During the post-Stalin era, the rapport between the Ukrainian Orthodox Church and the Soviet regime was typical of church-state relations throughout the USSR. In 1946-56 the patriarchy of Moscow, supported by the government, aimed at reestablishing control over the Ukrainian church and at resisting such illegal groups as Greek Catholics, Jehovah's Witnesses, and Unitarians. This period of relative calm ended with Nikita Khrushchev's (1894-1971) antireligious campaign. After his deposition in the 1960's, authorities limited themselves to suppressing the most important of the local dissident sects, yet this apparent equilibrium between church and state did not last. Frustrated by the lack of success of its antireligious activities, the Communist Party initiated massive antireligious propaganda, especially in the Ukraine in 1969. J/S

24. Bogdenko, M. L. KOMMUNISTICHESKAIA PARTIIA—ORGANIZATOR I VDOKHNOVITEL' MASSOVOGO OSVOENIIA TSELINNYKH I ZALEZHNYKH ZEMEL' [The Communist Party: organizer and inspirer of the mass development of the virgin and fallow lands]. *Voprosy Istorii KPSS [USSR] 1984 (3): 113-124.* Discusses the state of Soviet historical writing about the campaigns to cultivate the virgin and fallow lands of the USSR initiated by Khrushchev 30 years ago. In the early years much of the histories produced were of low quality. Later, the detailed histories of the Communist Party threw new light on events, particularly the Leninist side of the policy. Recently, using voluminous research sources, historians have been able to demonstrate how the Party was always at the forefront in solving all the complex problems raised. Regional matters have been covered, yet so far no decent work on Siberia and the Far East has been written. Based on published works; 38 notes. D. N. Collins

25. Bohodyst, I. P. and Tertyshnyk, N. M. ZMITSNENNIA INTERNATSIONALNYKH ZVIAZKIV MIZH TRUDOVYMY KOLEKTYVAMY DONBASU I BRATNIKH SOTSIALISTYCHNYKH KRAIN: 1959-1971 [The strengthening of international

links between the labor collectives of the Donets Basin and those of fraternal socialist countries]. *Ukrains'kyi Istorychnyi Zhurnal [USSR] 1976 (2): 94-97.* Miners of the Donets Basin maintained close social and working relations with their colleagues in East Germany, Poland, Hungary, Bulgaria, and Rumania, 1959-71.

26. Bondar', V. Ia. MASSOVYI KHARAKTER KPSS I CHISTOTA PARTIINYKH RIADOV [The mass character of the CPSU and the purity of Party ranks]. *Voprosy Istorii KPSS [USSR] 1979 (6): 33-46.* Following the instructions of V. I. Lenin (1870-1924), the Communist Party struggled to become a popular party by increasing its numbers and by adhering to Marxist-Leninist principles. Changing economic and political conditions, often determined by Party policy, contributed to the Party's growth. Strict requirements on admission and the purge kept the Party free of harmful elements. Since the 1950's, Party leadership has emphasized the recruitment of workers, Komsomol members, and working women and insisted on continued ideological training of all Communists. Based on the published works of Marx, Engels, Lenin, and Brezhnev and on published Party documents; 68 notes.
L. E. Holmes

27. Borcke, Astrid von. DER UMTAUSCH DER PARTEIDOKUMENTE IN DER SOWJETUNION 1973/74 [The exchange of party documents in the Soviet Union 1973-74]. *Österreichische Osthefte [Austria] 1974 16(2): 164-179.* After the 24th congress of the Communist Party of the USSR membership books were exchanged for the sixth time since 1920. Based on printed documents and secondary sources; 128 notes. R. Wagnleitner

28. Brazhnik, I. I. VAZHNYI UCHASTOK IDEOLOGICHESKOI RABOTY KPSS [An important sector of the Communist Party of the Soviet Union's ideological work]. *Voprosy Istorii KPSS [USSR] 1965 (1): 10-19.* Describes the Leninist attitudes to religion, which hold that developed Soviet society must remove all traces of past ideology, including religion.

29. Bromlei, N. Ia. DUKHOVNAIA KUL'TURA—VAZHNYI KOMPONENT SOTSIALISTICHESKOGO OBRAZA ZHIZNI [Spiritual culture is an important component of the socialist way of life]. *Novaia i Noveishaia Istoriia [USSR] 1984 (6): 18-32.* Studies the radical changes in the intellectual life of people in socialist countries which have taken place as a result of the Russian Revolution and of the socialist revolutions in central and southeast Europe.
J

30. Brown, Archie. THE POWER OF THE GENERAL SECRETARY OF THE CPSU. Rigby, T. H.; Brown, Archie; and Reddaway, Peter, ed. *Authority, Power and Policy in the USSR: Essays Dedicated to Leonard Schapiro* (New York: St. Martin's Pr., 1980): 135-157. Discusses the changing relationship between the General Secretary and other political institutions, distinctions between different areas of policy, and the relationship between style of government and power and authority in the eras of Joseph Stalin, Nikita Khrushchev, and Leonid Brezhnev. Secondary sources; 60 notes.
J. Powell

31. Bruchis, Michael. *One Step Back, Two Steps Forward: On the Language Policy of the Communist Party of the Soviet Union in the National Republics (Moldavian: A Look Back, a Survey, and Perspectives, 1924-1980).* (East European Monographs, no. 109.) Boulder, Colo.: East European Q., 1982. 371 pp.

32. Burtiak, H. Ia. ROZVYTOK KOMUNISTYCHNOIU PARTIIEIU LENINS'KYKH IDEI PRO PARTIINO-POLITYCHNU INFORMATSIIU [The development by the Communist Party of Lenin's ideas about Party political information]. *Ukrains'kyi Istorychnyi Zhurnal [USSR] 1973 (4): 37-45.* Describes the difficult path traversed by Party propaganda workers in trying to adhere to V. I. Lenin's principles, from the first Marxist underground groups in the 1890's to the present.

33. Bykov, A. N. SSSR I EKONOMICHESKOE RAZVITIE SOTSIALISTICHESKOGO SODRUZHESTVA [The USSR and the socialist community's economic development]. *Voprosy Istorii [USSR] 1983 (2): 3-22.* The international significance of the Soviet economic experience, the range and specific features of its application in other socialist countries at different stages of their development, the importance of the Soviet assistance to these countries in the period of postwar economic rehabilitation on the socialist basis, in mastering socialist methods of economic management are the subjects of the article. The author underlines the current importance of mutual exchange of the experience accumulated in the fraternal countries for the intensification of Soviet socioeconomic development. The role of the Soviet Union, of Soviet principles of practically tested foreign trade relations in the emergence and consolidation of the international socialist division of labor, in implementing the socialist economic integration is also discussed. Concludes with a critique of anti-Marxist views on the role of the USSR and its economic experience in the development of the socialist community. J

34. Cary, Charles D. THE GOALS OF CITIZENSHIP TRAINING IN AMERICAN AND SOVIET SCHOOLS. *Studies in Comparative Communism 1977 10(3): 281-297.* Soviet and American styles of citizenship training differ in that the Soviets attempt to inculcate more values relating to political life than Americans. The Soviet concept is in line with the traditional Russian idea of upbringing. Soviet goals are to instill the Communist world view, good attitudes toward education, labor, morality, esthetics, and physical culture. Americans see citizenship as a relationship to the state while the Soviets think of it as a membership in a society that coincides with the political community. 25 notes.
D. Balmuth

35. Casstevens, Thomas W. and Ozinga, James R. THE SOVIET CENTRAL COMMITTEE SINCE STALIN: A LONGITUDINAL VIEW. *Am. J. of Pol. Sci. 1974 18(3): 559-568.* "The negative exponential model of attrition, XXXXXX, is a statistically acceptable model of continuous tenure on the Central Committee of the Communist Party of the Soviet Union. Applications of the model include 1) deductive predictions about future continuous service, 2) an estimate of the number of members 'purged' in 1957-61, and 3) comparative documentation of the relatively low rate of turnover on recent Central Committees." J

36. Chamberlin, William Henry. FIFTY YEARS OF COMMUNIST POWER. *Modern Age 1967 11(4): 364-373.* The test of a revolution is the stability of the institutions it creates, the well-being of the people living under those institutions, and the revolution's effect on those living outside the country. Against this test, the author surveys the Bolshevik seizure of power, the consolidation of its gains, and expansion in Eastern Europe after World War II. Analyzes postwar changes in Soviet policy and the present government by terror and propaganda. Lists the regime's crimes against humanity and notes the material progress it has presided over.
R. V. Ritter

37. Charlton, Michael. *The Eagle and the Small Birds. Crisis in the Soviet Empire: From Yalta to Solidarity.* Chicago: University of Chicago Press, 1985. 192 pp.

38. Chekharin, E. M. O NEKOTORYKH TEORETICHESKIKH PROBLEMAKH POLITICHESKOI SISTEMY SOVETSKOGO OBSHCHESTVA [The political system of Soviet society: some theoretical aspects]. *Sovetskoe Gosudarstvo i Pravo [USSR] 1970 (9): 3-14.* Considers the political system of socialist society, its functioning and organization during the stage of proletarian dictatorship and of the people's state. The Communist Party of the USSR has constantly advanced its political, ideological, organizational, and economic position. Scientific consideration has characterized its approach to state problems. It has endeavored to improve methods for guiding the social process, and has supported further mass participation in managing industrial units, agricultural firms, collective farms, and state government and administration in order to safeguard against bureaucratization. J/S

39. Chernev, A. D. VOPROSY POSTANOVKI I SOVERSHENSTVOVANIIA INFORMATSII V KPSS V ISTORIKO-PARTIINOI LITERATURE 60-70-KH GODOV [Questions of the organization and perfection of information on the Communist Party in historical

Party literature of the 1960's-70's]. *Vestnik Moskovskogo U., Seriia 8: Istoriia [USSR] 1979 (4): 3-14.* Historical analysis of early works on questions of Party information shows a lack of factual material. The exchange of information between fraternal Communist parties has long existed. After the Revolution the Party started collecting information. Now it is used by those who run the main party organs. What is needed is the study of Party information in relation to democratic centralism and collective leadership. 61 notes. D. Balmuth

40. Chernyshev, G. I. PARTIINYE ORGANIZATSII I PROTSESS INTEGRATSII NAUKI I PROIZVODSTVA [Party organizations and the process of the integration of science and production]. *Voprosy Istorii KPSS [USSR] 1983 (9): 77-87.* The experience of Moscow, Sverdlovsk, and other regions, 1965-83, indicates that conferences are one of the most effective forms of local Party organizational work on the scientific and technical policies of the Communist Party of the Soviet Union. However, this form of work has not yet been discussed sufficiently in Party literature, and this has held back the campaigns of organizers and collectives. In order to achieve maximum effectiveness in implementing the unified scientific and technical policies of the Communist Party, the creation of a coordinating body to act as liaison between Party committees and local organizations is necessary. Secondary sources; 52 notes. G. Dombrovski

41. Cherviakova, R. I. DOSVID ROZVYTKU UNIVERSYTETS'KOI OSVITY V SRSR [The development of higher education in the USSR]. *Ukrains'kyi Istorychnyi Zhurnal [USSR] 1981 (1): 69-75.* Traces the Communist Party's experience since 1918 in developing university level education as one of the three groups in the Soviet system of higher education, the other two being polytechnical and specialized institutions, called upon to train the people's intelligentsia. Based on Lenin's works and primary and secondary sources; table, 26 notes. I. Krushelnyckyj

42. Chigrinov, G. A. O METODIKE ISPOL'ZOVANIIA V LEKTSIIAKH MEMUARNOI LITERATURY (NA PRIMERE XII-XIII TEM VUZOVSKOGO KURSA ISTORII KPSS) [The use of memoirs in lectures: topics 12 and 13 of the higher education course in the history of the Communist Party of the Soviet Union as an example]. *Voprosy Istorii KPSS [USSR] 1980 (7): 114-122.* The publication of Leonid Brezhnev's memoirs focused the attention of Party history lecturers on the use of memoirs in their work. It is important to select correct works. Especially useful are the works of close collaborators of V. I. Lenin. The author indicates which works are of particular significance in Party history. Based on memoirs published in the USSR and Party documents; 82 notes. V. Sobell

43. Chiriaev, G. I. O RABOTE OBLASTNOI PARTIINOI ORGANIZATSII PO VOSPITANIIU TRUDIASHCHIKHSIA NA PRIMERE ZHIZNI I DEIATEL'NOSTI V. I. LENINA [On the regional Party organization of the education of the working people after the example of the life and activity of V. I. Lenin]. *Voprosy Istorii KPSS [USSR] 1981 (6): 15-30.* The Communist education of the workers is one of the most important tasks in the struggle for Communism since it governs the progress of economic, sociopolitical, and cultural development of the country. One of the most valuable means of ideological and political education of workers is using the life and activity of V. I. Lenin as an example. In recent years the Yakutsk regional Party organization has adopted an approach that demonstrates such methods, stressing Lenin's links with the people of Yakutia and thus providing a strong and successful example for the people's struggle for Communism. Based on material from the 26th Party Congress, articles in newspapers and journals, and secondary sources; 32 notes. L. Smith

44. Chuikov, V. MARSHAL BRONETANKOVYKH VOISK, P. P. POLUBOIAROV [Marshal of armored tank forces, Pavel P. Poluboiarov]. *Voenno-Istoricheskii Zhurnal [USSR] 1981 23(6): 93-96.* In honor of the 80th anniversary of his birth, an account of the life and work of Pavel Pavlovich Poluboiarov. Born in Tula in 1901, he entered the Red Army as a volunteer in 1919, attended military academies, made valuable contributions to the defeat of German fascism in the Great Patriotic War as a member of the armored tank forces, served the USSR in a succession of important positions in the tank forces in the postwar years, was appointed military inspector-adviser in the General Inspectors Group of the Soviet Army Ministry, and made contributions as a Party member and delegate to Party congresses. 2 notes. L. Smith

45. Churbanov, Iu. M. DEIATEL'NOST' KPSS PO FORMIROVANIIU I VOSPITANIIU KADROV SOVETSKOI MILITSII [The CPSU's activity in the formation and education of cadres in the Soviet militia]. *Voprosy Istorii KPSS [USSR] 1981 (8): 20-35.* The Communist Party of the Soviet Union has consistently devoted much effort to the formation and improvement of the forces of law and order. Even before the revolution, Lenin pointed out the need for a people's militia made up of workers and peasants. When such a force was eventually set up, each individual member was assessed for honesty, political suitability, aptitude for police work, and administrative qualities. In 1918 the Party took a firm hand in militia cadre formation with the establishment of a "cultural-educational department" under the Party's auspices within the militia. This became responsible for training. In recent years, now that socialism is maturing, the Soviet militia is still faced with the task of stamping out criminality. Training has been improved with the establishment of a militia workers' institute and political education departments have been set up in all militia organs to instruct the militia in Marxist-Leninist theory. 61 notes. J. Bamber

46. Currie, Kenneth. SOVIET GENERAL STAFF'S NEW ROLE. *Military Review 1984 64(10): 61-74.* From the time of Stalin to that of Khrushchev the Communist Party asserted itself in determining Soviet military doctrine. Since Khrushchev's ouster, however, the Party has only ratified doctrines already determined by an elite cadre of military spokesmen, the military general staff. This body, headed by Chief of Staff Nikolai V. Ogarkov, attempts to evaluate objectively evolving technical military trends and formulate appropriate responses. However, due to its increasing power, the general staff molds not only military and technical but also political aspects of Soviet military doctrine. By granting such autonomy to military leadership the Communist Party will endow the general staff with even more power. Reprinted from *Problems of Communism,* March-April 1984. Based on official Soviet publications; 52 notes. J. Powell

47. Deane, Michael J. THE MAIN POLITICAL ADMINISTRATION AS A FACTOR IN COMMUNIST PARTY CONTROL OVER THE MILITARY IN THE SOVIET UNION. *Armed Forces and Soc. 1977 3(2): 295-325.* Because of its unique structure and functions, the Main Political Administration, which is the agent of the Communist Party of the USSR in exerting political control over the military, has developed along lines separate from either the military or the Party. In recent years, this administration has been racked by political cleavages within its leadership cadres. These cleavages will almost certainly continue. 87 notes. J. P. Harahan

48. Dement'ev, V. and Kalinchuk, L. KRITIKA I SAMOKRITIKA V PARTIINYKH ORGANIZATSIIAKH ARMII I FLOTA [Criticism and self-criticism in the Party organizations of the army and navy]. *Voenno-Istoricheskii Zhurnal [USSR] 1976 (3): 79-84.* Explains the importance of criticism and self-criticism in the Communist Party organization of the armed forces, and includes excerpts from a number of Party documents published since the revolution, demonstrating its concern to foster a critical approach.

49. Demochkin, N. N. POVYSHENIE AKTIVNOSTI NARODNYKH DEPUTATOV SOVETOV NA SOVREMENNOM ETAPE [Increasing the activity of deputies to the people's soviets]. *Istoriia SSSR [USSR] 1983 (2): 21-34.* The system of the soviets, in which representatives of the people guaranteed the dictatorship of the proletariat, was established in 1917 with the Bolshevik revolution. It was strengthened in 1936 with the introduction of the Soviets of Workers' Deputies. They have played a vital role in the USSR's economic and social development by coordinating and checking on the work of local enterprises and other organizations. In the past 10 years the Communist Party of the Soviet Union (CPSU) has adopt-

ed a number of measures to boost the effectiveness of deputies. Their accountability to the electorate has been increased; they are obliged to attend more public meetings and conduct correspondence with individuals; and they are encouraged to do more to check that the administration implements their decisions. 49 notes, 6 tables.
J. Bamber

50. Demochkin, N. N. and Kulikova, G. B. SOVETY V PERIOD KOMMUNISTICHESKOGO STROITELSTVA V ISTORIOGRAFII 1956-1970 GODOV [The Soviets in the period of Communist construction as reflected in Soviet historiography, 1956-70]. *Voprosy Istorii [USSR] 1971 (11): 3-15.* "The authors examine the fundamental Leninist principles underlying the functioning of the Soviets, the progressive development of these principles and their practical implementation by the Communist Party of the Soviet Union, the Party's consistent policy of improving the activity of the Soviets of Working People's Deputies and enhancing their role in communist construction. They show the utter insolvency of a number of conceptions concocted by bourgeois 'Sovietologists' who are trying to distort the essence of Soviet socialist democracy, to play down the role of the Soviets as the organs of popular government. Analyzing a number of works produced by Soviet historians and lawyers over the past fifteen years, the article graphically shows how by dint of persevering efforts on the part of a large group of researchers new light is being shed on the history of the Soviets, on the process of all-round development and strengthening of the Soviet state at the present stage, the improved methods of exercising Party leadership of the Soviets, and the formation of closer ties between the Soviets and the masses." J

51. d'Encausse, Hélène Carrère. PARTY AND FEDERATION IN THE USSR: THE PROBLEM OF THE NATIONALITIES AND POWER IN THE USSR. *Government and Opposition [Great Britain] 1978 13(2): 133-150.* Examines Soviet policies regarding ethnic minorities from 1917 to 1977 and concludes that Lenin permitted the establishment of federal republics and national cadres of the Communist Party only as temporary compromises with ethnic minorities within the USSR until socialism might develop to the stage when national differences and ethnic identities would no longer be significant considerations. But all Soviet leaders from Lenin to Brezhnev have had to allow this same compromise nationalities policy to survive, although some of the centralizing measures and the tendency toward Russification of the minorities have made considerable inroads.

52. Denisov, S. G. KOMMUNISTICHESKAIA PARTIIA V BOR'BE ZA OSUSHCHESTVLENIE KUL'TURNOI REVOLIUTSII V SSSR [The Communist Party in the struggle for the realization of the Cultural Revolution in the USSR]. *Voprosy Istorii KPSS [USSR] 1981 (10): 101-114.* Stressing Lenin's insistence that the realization of the Cultural Revolution was one of the most important tasks of socialist construction in the USSR, discusses the practical and theoretical role of the Communist Party of the Soviet Union (CPSU) in the achievement of the Cultural Revolution during the transition from capitalism to socialism. Describes first the Leninist conception of cultural revolution, then the specific struggle of the CPSU toward cultural revolution in the transition period, finally evaluating the general conformity of the aims and achievements of the Cultural Revolution with the past and future aims of the construction of socialism and Communism. Based on the works of Marx, Engels, Lenin, and Brezhnev and secondary material; 55 notes.
L. Smith

53. Dinerstein, Herbert S. THE SOVIET UNION AND THE COMMUNIST WORLD. *Survey 1973 19(2): 140-150.* Almost from the first the Soviet leadership was misled by its own myth that the October Revolution was the paradigm of all future revolutions. This lasted until World War II when the Red Army became the surrogate for the proletariat in Eastern Europe. When there were no more wars, the national liberation model was asserted, but many nationalist leaders (Nkrumah, Ben Bella, Sukarno) collapsed. Now the USSR's main effort "will probably be concentrated on keeping existing socialist states socialist... rather than on looking for new socialist revolutions." Part of a special issue on the future of Soviet foreign policy. 2 notes.
R. B. Valliant

54. Dobrodumov, P. O. and Klapchuk, S. M. DIIAL'NIST' KPRS PO ZDIISNENNIU NAUKOVO-TEKHNICHNOI POLITYKY V UMOVAKH ROZVYNUTOHO SOTSIALIZMU (ISTORIOHRAFIIA PROBLEMY) [Activities of the CPSU in implementing the scientific-technical policy in conditions of developed socialism: historiography of the problem]. *Ukrains'kyi Istorychnyi Zhurnal [USSR] 1979 (4): 104-110.* Examines the literature on the work of the Communist Party of the USSR to accelerate scientific and technical advance in the period between the 21st (1959) and 25th (1976) Party congresses. 26 notes.
I. Krushelnyckyj

55. Dolepší, Antonín. EPOCHÁLNÍ VÝZNAM VZNIKU SSSR [The epochal significance of the rise of the USSR]. *Slovanský Přehled [Czechoslovakia] 1983 69(1): 89-97.* With the emergence of the USSR there came into existence, for the first time in history, a new sense of brotherly cooperation and development of nations and nationalities oriented to the progress and well-being of all peoples. The question of the rights of nationalities has been solved by the Communist Party of the USSR in its just and equal treatment of the many different peoples that inhabit the USSR. The 19 autonomous republics of the USSR have created a harmonious federation following the principles of Lenin and Stalin and have concentrated on the building of socialism as a supranational priority. 5 notes.
B. Reinfeld

56. Drizulis, A. RAZVITIE DUKHOVNOI ZHIZNI TRUDIASHCHIKHSIA LATVIISKOI SSR V USLOVIIAKH ZRELOGO SOTSIALISTICHESKOGO OBSHCHESTVA [Development of spiritual life of the Latvian SSR working people under the conditions of mature socialist society]. *Latvijas PSR Zinātņu Akadēmijas Vēstis [USSR] 1977 (7): 3-14.* Discusses the development of intellectual life in Latvia since the establishment of socialism in 1940. The decisive factor was the indoctrination of a Marxist-Leninist ideology throughout the population. Great successes were achieved in the field of education and higher education is now accessible to all sections of the population. In 1946 the Academy of Sciences of the Latvian SSR was established, and during 1945-75 the number of published books increased 20 times, both in Russian and Latvian languages. The number of translations also increased significantly. The author describes the internationalization of cultural life through the exchange of dramatic and musical performances between the states of the USSR. Under Soviet rule Latvian customs and traditions also changed. The Communist Party made every effort to introduce a high communist morale and to eradicate the influence of religion. As the result a new community is arising—a Soviet nation. 34 notes.
R. Vilums

57. Efimov, S. KOMSOMOL-SHEF FLOTA (K 50-LETIIU SHEFSTVA KOMSOMOLA NAD VOENNO-MORSKIM FLOTOM SSSR) [The Komsomol as patron of the navy: the 50th anniversary of Komsomol's patronage of the Soviet navy]. *Voenno-Istoricheskii Zhurnal [USSR] 1972 (10): 69-74.* Demonstrates the ties between the Young Communist League and the Soviet navy and stresses the positive role which this Communist youth organization has played in naval matters, 1920's-70's.

58. Epishev, A. A. O VOZRASTAIUSHCHEI ROLI KPSS V RUKOVODSTVE VOORUZHENNYMI SILAMI [The growing role of the CPSU in the leadership of the armed forces]. *Voprosy Istorii KPSS [USSR] 1963 (2): 3-14.* Focuses on the growing role of the Soviet Communist Party in the affairs of the army, 1917-63, drawing attention to the increasingly tense international situation and the ever greater responsibilities of the USSR as a world power.

59. Eremin, V. G. NEKOTORYE VOPROSY ISTORIOGRAFII DEIATEL'NOSTI KOMSOMOLA KAK BOEVOGO POMOSHCHNIKA PARTII V SOVETSKOM TYLU V GODY VELIKOI OTECHESTVENNOI VOINY [Some questions of the historiography of the activity of the Young Communist League (Komsomol) as a military aid to the Party in the Soviet rear during the Great Patriotic War]. *Voprosy Istorii KPSS [USSR] 1980 (6): 61-71.* The his-

torical work on the role of the Young Communist League in the Soviet rear during World War II has been divided into three stages: between 1941 and 1945 documents were collected; between 1945 and 1955 these documents were published together with writings of a somewhat schematic character; and between 1955 and the mid-1960's research of a higher standard was undertaken. The historical work of the last 15 years is of even higher quality, though further research is necessary on the role of the Communist Party and the reasons for the Soviet victory. Secondary sources; 38 notes.
G. Dombrovski

60. Es'kov, I. M. IZ OPYTA BOR'BY PARTIINYKH ORGANIZATSII ZA POVYSHENIE KACHESTVA PRODUKTSII (PO MATERIALAM SARATOVSKOI OBLASTI) [From the experience of the struggle of party organizations for a rise in the quality of production (based on materials of the Saratov region)]. *Voprosy Istorii KPSS [USSR] 1974 (6): 21-32.* The Communist Party has made possible significant industrial achievements in the Soviet Union. This has been accomplished through an extensive propaganda campaign, coordinated leadership of economic institutions, and by Party sponsorship of training, mechanization, scientific innovation, and socialist competition. Based on Soviet periodical literature, especially *Kommunist*, and materials in the Archive of the Saratov Regional Committee of the Communist Party; 74 notes.
L. E. Holmes

61. Faminski, I. ENTWICKLUNGSLINIEN IN DEN ÖKONOMISCHEN BEZIEHUNGEN ZWISCHEN DER UDSSR SOWIE DEN ANDEREN SOZIALISTISCHEN STAATEN UND DEN LÄNDERN DES KAPITALISTISCHEN WELTSYSTEMS [Lines of development in the economic relations between the USSR and other socialist countries and between Communist and capitalist countries]. *Wissenschaftliche Zeitschrift der Humboldt-Universität zu Berlin: Gesellschafts- und Sprachwissenschaftliche Reihe [East Germany] 1975 24(6): 723-729.* Illustrates with many concrete examples the increasingly frequent economic exchanges between capitalist and Communist countries, examining the impact of industrialization in the USSR and the decision of Comecon nations to trade with capitalist countries; the influence of detente and peaceful coexistence; the impact of Communist planning on international commerce; the influence of government policies on capitalist trade policies; and the relations of Communist countries with the European Economic Community. 2 tables, 12 notes.
M. Faissler

62. Fedirko, P. S. IZ OPYTA KRAEVOI PARTIINOI ORGANIZATSII PO RUKOVODSTVU KOMPLEKSNYM RAZVITIEM PROIZVODITEL'NYKH SIL [The experience of regional Party organization in the management of the combined development of productive forces]. *Voprosy Istorii KPSS [USSR] 1981 (3): 3-18.* Describes the experiences of the Party organization in Territorial Industrial Complexes (TPK), a new method of work in an advanced socialist economy, and especially in the Krasnoyarsk complex in Siberia. 23 notes.
A. J. Evans

63. Fejto, François. L'URSS ET LA STRATÉGIE DU MOUVEMENT COMMUNISTE INTERNATIONAL [USSR and the strategy of the international communist movement]. *Études Int. [Canada] 1975 6(3): 307-317.* Discusses the evolution of Soviet strategy from Khrushchev through Brezhnev and identifies a rising neo-Stalinism despite party support for collegiality. Détente has not forced the Soviets to abandon their revolutionary goals, apparent in the behavior of the national Communist parties in Portugal and France. 19 notes.
J. F. Harrington, Jr.

64. Filimonov, N. P. OSUSHCHESTVLENIE PARTIEI LENINSKOGO PRINTSIPA MATERIAL'NOI ZAINTERESOVANNOSTI NA SOVREMENNOM ETAPE [The Party's realization of Lenin's principle of material incentive]. *Voprosy Istorii KPSS [USSR] 1966 (4): 3-15.* Discusses the Soviet system of material incentives in view of Leninist principles and the decisions of the 23d Party Congress.

65. Fimin, D. N. OSVESCHENIE VOPROSOV PARTIINO-GOSUDARSTVENNOGO KONTROLIA V LITERATURE 1923-1966 GODOV [Studies on problems of party and state control published during 1923-66]. *Voprosy Istorii [USSR] 1969 (10): 150-154.* Review article. Some 200 studies on this subject appeared 1923-ca. 1935, and more than 300, mid-1950's-1966, only 20 having been published in the interim. Better researched, the later studies deal primarily with Lenin's plans for a unified control apparatus and the de facto control exercised by the Central Control Commission (TsKK) and the Workers' and Peasants' Inspection (RKI) during the early New Economic Policy period, 1921-25. 19 notes.
N. Frenkley

66. Forgus, Silvia P. NATIONALITY QUESTION IN THE RESOLUTIONS OF THE COMMUNIST PARTY OF THE SOVIET UNION 1898-1964. *Nationalities Papers 1977 5(2): 183-201.* Resolutions on the nationalities question in the Communist Party of the USSR from its founding went through three distinct phases. Before the October Revolution it accepted the right to secede but warned against splitting the proletariat into national units. After the Russian Revolution, with the responsibilities of preserving a newly created state, it made the right to secession contingent upon the level of social development, which in effect meant total integration into the Soviet Union. Under Khrushchev, after 1956, concessions were made to investment in nationality areas, but this in fact meant ignoring national boundaries in favor of development planning imperatives. Based on English translations of Soviet Communist Party and other documents; 71 notes.
M. K. Palat

67. Fortescue, Stephen. PARTY MEMBERSHIP IN SOVIET RESEARCH INSTITUTES. *Soviet Union 1984 11(2): 129-156.* A somewhat discriminatory policy in recruitment among the scientific community has produced a lower level of Communist Party membership than might have been expected. An apparent stress in recruitment on more senior managerial (cadre) rather than junior (mass leadership) personnel may be a realistic recognition of where power lies. Factors making Party membership attractive to scientists may include better job security, more opportunities to travel abroad, better access to scientific equipment and resources, and greatly increased promotion prospects. Party membership is a definite career asset, and current levels promise to insure sufficient Party presence to assure Party control of science. 5 tables, 88 notes.
H. S. Shields

68. Fortescue, Stephen. PARTY SECRETARIES IN SOVIET RESEARCH INSTITUTES: DIVIDED LOYALTIES? *Politics [Australia] 1983 18(1): 73-83.* Discusses the internal political struggles in Soviet research institutions, where research usually suffers because of bureaucratic pressures and the tension between Party loyalty and research.

69. Frelek, Ryszard. KRYZYS ZIMNEJ WOJNY [The crisis of the Cold War]. *Sprawy Międzynarodowe [Poland] 1971 24(9): 21-36.* The turning point of the Cold War was the 20th Congress of the Soviet Communist Party in 1956 which assumed a new policy of peaceful coexistence between countries of different social, economic, and political systems. The author describes the period of the Cold War beginning with the bombing of Hiroshima in 1945. He blames Harry S. Truman, Dwight D. Eisenhower, George Kennan and John Foster Dulles for the international tension. America pursued a policy of brinkmanship verging on atomic war in its attempt to liberate nations around the world. Based on published Polish, Russian, and American official documents; 27 notes.
J. M. Wilczek

70. Ganin, N. I. BOR'BA KPSS ZA EDINSTVO SVOIKH RIADOV [The CPSU's struggle for the unity of its ranks]. *Voprosy Istorii KPSS [USSR] 1965 (5): 104-110.* A study guide on the theme of unity in the workers' movement in the USSR and worldwide.

71. Gaponenko, L. S. ISTORICHESKAIA PREEMSTVENNOST' I RAZVITIE LENINSKIKH TRADITSII V PODGOTOVKE KADROV V PARTIINYKH UCHEBNYKH ZAVEDENIIAKH [The historical continuity and development of Leninist traditions in training specialists in Party educational establishments]. *Voprosy Istorii KPSS [USSR] 1981 (1): 62-75.* Lenin first opened a school for training Party specialists in Paris in 1911 but it was not until June

1917 that courses for agitators were organized legally in Russia. A central school for soviet and Party work was formed in 1919 and evolved into the Sverdlova Communist University. By 1921 there were four Communist universities in Russia. The Institute of Marxism-Leninism played a major role in training skilled personnel and the 1930's saw great emphasis laid on agricultural skills. In the post-war era the majority of people in responsible Party and government posts has been through the higher education system of the Soviet Union. 41 notes. A. Brown

72. García Garrido, José Luis. LENIN Y LA EDUCACIÓN [Lenin and education]. *Nuestro Tiempo [Spain] 1970 33(192): 5-24.* The Second Program of the Russian Communist Party, written mainly by V. I. Lenin in 1919, had as its main objective the creation of a "new man," generous and altruistic in a classless society. In spite of the efforts made in education by the Russian government the objectives have not yet been achieved.

73. Gladkov, I. A. VSEMIRNO-ISTORICHESKOE ZNACHENIE OPYTA POSTROENIIA SOTSIALIZMA V SSSR [The universal-historical significance of the experience of building socialism in the USSR]. *Voprosy Istorii KPSS [USSR] 1962 (1): 3-22.* Surveys the importance to other socialist countries of the Soviet experience in building socialism since 1917.

74. Grechko, A. A. RUKOVODIASHCHAIA ROL' KPSS V STROITEL'STVE ARMII RAZVITOGO SOTSIALISTICHESKOGO OBSHCHESTVA [The leading role of the CPSU in the construction of an army of a developed socialist society]. *Voprosy Istorii KPSS [USSR] 1974 (5): 30-47.* During the Civil War, World War II, Cold War and contemporary period the Communist Party has superbly led the Soviet Armed Forces. The Party has coordinated military with political and economic needs and assured the armed forces of the prerequisites for repelling aggression. Based on Lenin's *Collected Works* and published party documents; 27 notes. L. E. Holmes

75. Gregory, Eugene Richard. "Political Change in Revolutionary One-Party Systems: The Soviet Case." Vanderbilt U. 1982. 668 pp. *DAI 1983 44(2): 568-A.* DA8312567

76. Griffith, Samuel B. and Erickson, John. ZHUKOV, KHRUSHCHEV AND THE RED ARMY. *Marine Corps Gazette 1958 42(11): 48-51.* Explains why Nikita Khrushchev dismissed Marshal Georgi Zhukov as Russian Minister of Defense in 1957 and considers previous instances of tension between illustrious Russian officers and the Soviet Communist Party leaders.

77. Grigor'ev, N. ZABOTA KPSS O PODDERZHANII VYSOKOI DISTSIPLINY, BDITEL'NOSTI I BOEVOI GOTOVNOSTI V VOORUZHENNYKH SILAKH [The concern of the Soviet Communist Party to maintain a high standard of discipline, vigilance, and battle readiness in the Armed Forces]. *Voenno-Istoricheskii Zhurnal [USSR] 1971 (1): 3-8.* Shows how the Soviet Communist Party has always had special regard for conditions in the military, charting this involvement from the early days of the October Revolution up to the eve of the 24th Party Congress in 1971.

78. Gromyko, A. A. VNESHNIAIA POLITIKA SOVETSKOGO GOSUDARSTVA—MOGUCHEE ORUZHIE KOMMUNISTICHESKOI PARTII V BOR'BE ZA MIR I SOTSIAL'NYI PROGRESS [The foreign policy of the Soviet state is the Communist Party's mighty weapon in the struggle for peace and social progress]. *Novaia i Noveishaia Istoriia [USSR] 1978 (5): 3-15.* The USSR's Leninist foreign policy, whose basic principles, major achievements, and main lines are discussed in this article, has made a weighty contribution to the Soviet people's building of a new society. The author emphasizes the Peace Program adopted at the 24th and developed at the 25th congresses of the CPSU, and the new Constitution of the USSR which contains new tasks and guidelines of Soviet foreign policy. J

79. Groshev, I. I. OSUSHCHESTVLENIE KOMMUNISTICHESKOI PARTIEI LENINSKOI NATSIONAL'NOI POLITIKI [The Communist Party's implementation of V. I. Lenin's nationalities policy]. *Voprosy Istorii KPSS [USSR] 1982 (4): 18-31.* Examines the postrevolutionary abolition of the repression of nationalities, the establishment of national equality, the formation of the voluntary association of Soviet republics, the advancement of previously backward peoples, and the brotherly community of Soviet nations. Lenin insisted on the importance of political, economic, and cultural equality and on giving equality of opportunity to all nationalities. The Soviet state's first acts were to eliminate all colonial and racist repression. National languages and cultures were assured of support. Industrial growth, health care, and education facilities were widespread. The contrast between the USSR and Tsarist Russia shows how the Communist Party has consistently followed a Leninist policy in this as in other matters. Based on Lenin's works, Brezhnev's works, and on the press, especially *Pravda;* 54 notes. A. J. Evans

80. Gvozdev, I. I. V AVANGARDE BORIUSHCHEGOSIA NARODA: OBZOR LITERATURY O DEIATEL'NOSTI KPSS V GODY VELIKOI OTECHESTVENNOI VOINY, 1941-45. [In the avant-garde of the struggling people: a survey of literature on the activity of the Communist Party of the USSR during World War II]. *Voprosy Istorii KPSS [USSR] 1970 (5): 110-119.* Surveys literature appearing, 1956-70, concerning World War II which emphasizes the decisive role of the Communist Party organizers in achieving victory over the Germans.

81. Hammond, Thomas T. A SUMMING UP. *Studies on the Soviet Union [West Germany] 1971 11(4): 591-596.* A summary of methods and tactics used by Communists to achieve power, of which the most successful is an invading Red Army. Other techniques include urban revolution, rural revolution, legal takeovers through free elections, and the adoption of Communism by a non-Communist leader. Not all takeovers have been successful. The use of military force, geographical propinquity, war, free elections, and ability to camouflage actual goals and methods determine the success of a Communist takeover. Secondary sources; 5 notes. V. L. Human

82. Hanson, Philip. SOVIET STATE AND SOCIETY. ALEXANDER ZINOVIEV: TOTALITARIANISM FROM BELOW. *Survey [Great Britain] 1982 26(1): 29-48.* Studies two books by Alexander Zinoviev: *Ziiaiushchie Vysoty* (1976), translated into English as *Yawning Heights* (1979), and *Kommunizm kak Real'nost'* [Communism as reality] (1981). The first is a book of satire about social conditions in the USSR. The second is an exposition of Zinoviev's view of Communism. He sees the working collectives themselves as the root of Soviet totalitarianism. 12 notes. R. Grove

83. Harasymiw, Bohdan. PARTY RECRUITMENT IN SIBERIA. *Nationalities Papers 1983 11(2): 256-282.* Siberia contains a smaller proportion of Communist Party members than does the Soviet population as a whole. More than 80% of Siberians are Russian. They are represented in the Party in almost exact proportion to their percentage of the population in that region. In regard to the other nationalities, those with the highest levels of educational attainment tend to be overrepresented, while those of more modest attainment tend to be underrepresented. 17 tables, 11 notes. M. R. Yerburgh

84. Harasymiw, Bohdan. POLITICAL MOBILITY IN SOVIET UKRAINE. *Canadian Slavonic Papers [Canada] 1984 26(2-3): 160-181.* In the USSR one of the most important contextual factors of political recruitment is ethnicity, which gives the composition of the political elites a significance that goes beyond mere demographic statistics to fundamental questions of legitimacy and integration. The mobility of Communist Party members is a key element in inhibiting the formation of an indigenous, nationally-conscious political elite in the Ukraine. The introduction of a steady flow of outsiders into the pool of Party eligibles in the Ukraine is part of the larger strategy of nation-building and system maintenance worked out in Moscow. The formation of a Ukrainian elite based

on the intelligentsia is therefore extremely unlikely. Based on a paper presented at the 1982 annual meeting of the Canadian Association of Slavists, Ottawa; 2 graphs, 5 tables, 35 notes.
G. J. Bobango

85. Hill, Ronald J. PARTY-STATE RELATIONS AND SOVIET POLITICAL DEVELOPMENT. *British J. of Pol. Sci. [Great Britain] 1980 10(2): 149-165.* Examines changes within the Soviet political system between 1953 and 1978 with special emphasis on the development of party-state relations.

86. Hoffmann, Hans. ENTWICKLUNGSTENDENZEN DER SOWJETISCHEN ARBEITERKLASSE IN DEN LETZTEN ZWEI JAHRZEHNTEN [Trends in the evolution of the Soviet working class in the past two decades]. *Beiträge zur Gesch. der Arbeiterbewegung [East Germany] 1984 26(2): 147-157.* Chronicles the social conditions of the working class of the USSR under developed socialism. Focuses on the role of the Communist Party and of regionalism in development. The working class became the majority of the population. With changes in technology, more and more workers came to work in large, centralized industries. Qualifications for jobs were raised. Through all these changes, the working class of the USSR remained the vanguard of revolutionary movements striving to achieve communism. 29 notes. R. Grove

87. Holubova, H. H. VIDOMYI DIIACH KOMUNISTYCHNOI PARTII I RADIANS'KOI DERZHAVY (DO 80-RICHCHIA Z DNIA NARODZHENNIA L. R. KORNIITSIA) [A renowned activist of the Communist Party and the Soviet nation: dedicated to the 80th anniversary of the birth of L. R. Korniiets]. *Ukrains'kyi Istorychnyi Zhurnal [USSR] 1981 (8): 119-121.* Chronologically presents details of the life of Leonid R. Korniiets (1901-69), born in the Kherson region (now Kirovograd) of the Ukraine. Focuses on his work for the Communist Party, his positions and awards.
L. Djakowska

88. Hough, Jerry F. SOVIET POLICYMAKING TOWARD FOREIGN COMMUNISTS. *Studies in Comparative Communism 1982 15(3): 167-183.* After the abolition of the Comintern the Soviet Communist Party developed various organs for dealing with foreign communists; a foreign policy commission in 1945; a foreign relations section in the Central Committee in 1948, subdivided in 1949; and an international department after 1953 which split and produced a department for relations with socialist countries. Probably six different groups in the CPSU deal with foreign affairs: the international department, the Institute of the International Workers' Movement, and other institutes. It is likely that policy lines are established after representatives of these groups meet with representatives of ministries. 24 notes. D. Balmuth

89. Iarvel'ian, V. I. DVIZHENIE ZA KOMMUNISTICHESKII TRUD I EGO ROL' V POVYSHENII POLITICHESKOI AKTIVNOSTI RABOCHIKH (NA MATERIALAKH PARTIINOI ORGANIZATSKII G. LENINGRADA MEZHDU XXII I XXIII S'EZDAMI KPSS) [The movement for a Communist attitude toward labor and its role in the increasing political activities of the workers. Based on materials of the Leningrad Party organization between the 22d and 23d meetings of the CPSU]. *Vestnik Leningradskogo Universiteta [USSR] 1974 (14): 5-12.* The history of the building of socialism in the USSR is above all the history of the development of the creative initiative of workers. The Communist Party has repeatedly stated that the workers must realize that they are working, not for the exploiters, but for themselves and their society. "The growth of the working masses' activities in the building of the new life is the law of the epoch of socialism." This examination of the ways in which the Leningrad Party organization strengthened the influence of the Communist attitude toward labor details the various approaches utilized by party cadres to achieve their goals. Working through the schools, press, and factory organizations, the Party gained success in raising the social and political activities of the workers in the period between the 22d and 23d meetings of the CPSU. 34 notes. G. F. Jewsbury

90. Ierkhov, H. P. KPRS U BOROT'BI ZA ZMITSNENNIA I ROZVYTOK SOTSIALIZMU (DO VYKHODU U SVIT DRUHOI KNYHY P'IATOHO TOMU SHESTYTOMNOI *ISTORII KOMMUNISTICHESKOI PARTII SOVETSKOGO SOIUZA)* [The struggle of the CPSU to strengthen and advance socialism: in anticipation of the publication of the second book of the fifth volume of the six-volume *History of the Communist Party of the Soviet Union*]. *Ukrains'kyi Istorychnyi Zhurnal [USSR] 1981 (3): 43-50.* Reviews a newly published volume of the *History of the Communist Party of the Soviet Union,* which details the activities of the Communist Party during World War II and up to 1959 and shows how its leading role in the life of Soviet Communists was greatly enhanced during these years.

91. Ignatovskii, P. A. XXIV S'EZD KPSS I MERY PARTII PO REALIZATSII AGRARNOI POLITIKI [The 24th Congress of the Communist Party of the Soviet Union and Party measures for the realization of agrarian policy]. *Voprosy Istorii KPSS [USSR] 1974 (11): 68-79.* The Communist Party's 24th Congress guaranteed an improving agriculture. It provided the capital, technology, equipment, specialists, chemicals, and organizational changes necessary for expanding production and a higher, more cultured, standard of living in rural areas. Based on published resolutions of the Communist Party of the Soviet Union, speeches of Leonid Brezhnev, and materials in Soviet periodical literature; 49 notes.
L. E. Holmes

92. Ignatow, Assen. THE OLD AND NEW MARXISMS. *Studies in Soviet Thought [Netherlands] 1974 14(1-2): 93-98.* The asceticism, discipline, and self-effacement of Soviet Communism contrast with the flamboyant individualism, self-expression, and sexual liberation of the New Left. The two versions of Marxism clash ideologically over Freudianism and modernism in the arts. Nevertheless there are similarities, including a messianic spirit and an ecclesiastical logomachy. R. Stromberg

93. Ishchenko, F. and Chernov, V. O SOVERSHENSTVOVANII FORM I METODIKI MARKSISTSKO-LENINSKOI PODGOTOVKI OFITSEROV [Perfecting the Marxist-Leninist training of officers]. *Voenno-Istoricheskii Zhurnal [USSR] 1977 (4): 89-97.* Discusses the political education of officers of the Soviet armed forces since the revolution, analyzing the role of Party directives and the changing methods of education.

94. Iudin, I. N. KPSS: PARTIIA RABOCHEGO KLASSA, AVANGARD VSEGO NARODA [CPSU: Party of the working class, vanguard of all the peoples]. *Voprosy Istorii KPSS [USSR] 1973 (7): 32-49.* The 1903 second Party congress resolved that although the party would lead all exploited peoples in a revolution of liberation, it would strive primarily for the creation of a dictatorship of a particular class, the proletariat. By 1961 the achievement of social and political unity in the USSR enabled the 22d congress to declare that the Party now was the vanguard of all the Soviet people. This unity and the continuing need for firm leadership precludes the possibility of the development of political pluralism in the USSR. Based on V. I. Lenin's *Collected Works* and published party documents; 53 notes. L. E. Holmes

95. Iudin, I. N. and Cherniak, E. V. KRITIKA SOVREMENNYKH FAL'SIFIKATOROV MARKSISTSKO-LENINSKOGO UCHENIIA O ROLI PARTII V STROITEL'STVE SOTSIALIZMA I KOMMUNIZMA [Criticism of contemporary falsifiers of Marxist-Leninist study on the Party's role in the building of socialism and communism]. *Voprosy Istorii KPSS [USSR] 1975 (10): 97-107.* A critique of the views of bourgeois ideologues and revisionists that the notions of Marx and Engels on the historical role of a political party clash with those of Lenin; that Communist Party leadership is not necessary for political and socioeconomic progress; that the Communist Party maintains a monopoly of power by suppressing the people and Soviet organizations; and that the continuing technological revolution will bring about the convergence of the Communist and capitalist systems. Marx, Engels, and Lenin all recognized the necessity of a workers' party to the historical process. More than ever before in the Soviet Union the Communist

Party must coordinate the work of social, economic, and cultural organizations. Based on Western studies of the Soviet Communist Party and published documents; 55 notes. L. E. Holmes

96. Iuzzhalina, V. Iu. SEMINAR PO AKTUAL'NYM PROBLEMAM ISTORIKO-PARTIINOI NAUKI [A seminar on topical problems of historico-party science]. *Voprosy Istorii KPSS [USSR] 1979 (1): 148-150.* A summary of papers and reports delivered at a seminar held at the end of 1978 in Chelyabinsk and attended by scholars, heads of Party history departments of colleges and universities, and teachers from the Chelyabinsk area. Speakers called upon scholars and teachers to relate their work to recent decisions of the 25th Party Congress, to resolutions of the Party's Central Committee, and to Leonid Brezhnev's speeches and writings. L. E. Holmes

97. Iuzzhalina, V. Iu. SOVESHCHANIE-SEMINAR MOLODYKH ISTORIKOV PARTII [Seminar for young Party historians]. *Voprosy Istorii KPSS [USSR] 1981 (8): 155-158.* Describes the proceedings at a seminar held in the Black Sea resort of Sochi, 18-25 April 1981, on "Topical problems of the ideological and politico-didactic work of the CPSU in the light of the 26th Party Congress." Note. J. Bamber

98. Ivanov, O. F. NESPROMOZHNIST' BURZHUAZNYKH FAL'SYFIKATSII PRYNTSYPU INTERNATSIONALIZMU V ORHANIZATSIINII BUDOVI KPRS [The impossibility of bourgeois falsification destroying the principle of internationalism in the organization of the CPSU]. *Ukrains'kyi Istorychnyi Zhurnal [USSR] 1981 (9): 42-52.* Discusses the nature of Soviet proletarian internationalism, a feature both of the USSR and of the Communist Party of the Soviet Union. Bourgeois ideologues have attempted to undermine the leading role of the Soviet Union, but the author presents ways in which the Soviet Union has exposed the bourgeois ideological fabrications. L. Djakowska

99. Ivanov, R. F. OSVESHCHENIE ISTORII SOTSIALISTICHESKIKH STRAN TSENTRAL'NOI I IUGO-VOSTOCHNOI EVROPY V 11-13 TOMAKH "VSEMIRNOI ISTORII" (1945-70GG.) [Interpretations of the history of the socialist countries of Central and Southeastern Europe in volumes 11-13 of *World History* (1945-70)]. *Southeastern Europe 1980 7(2): 127-146.* A review essay of the recently published volumes 11-13 of *Vsemirnaia Istoriia*, the first attempt by Soviet scholars to write a history of the world. Volume 11 covers the immediate post-World War II years, 1945-50; volume 12 covers the decade of the 1950's and volume 13 the decade of the 1960's. All three volumes deal with the foreign and domestic political transformations of the socialist countries of Central and Southeastern Europe. J. M. Lauber

100. Ivashyn, V. H. and Meleshko, V. I. U SUZIR'I BRATNIKH RESPUBLIK [In the constellation of the fraternal republics]. *Ukrains'kyi Istorychnyi Zhurnal [USSR] 1978 (12): 29-36.* Describes the problems facing the Belorussian Communist Party, 1919-39, including Polish oppression and intervention by the Entente forces through Lithuania. The Party's real success was achieved after World War II as one of the Soviet republics. 16 notes. V. Packer

101. Jamgotch, Nish, Jr. ALLIANCE MANAGEMENT IN EASTERN EUROPE (THE NEW TYPE OF INTERNATIONAL RELATIONS). *World Pol. 1975 27(3): 405-429.* The theory of international relations of a new type characterizes Soviet-East European relations. Six functional aspects include pragmatic adjustments to polycentric communism; theoretical provisions for a transitional phase prior to the realization of communism on an international level; emphasis upon the East European subsystem as an indispensable core of Soviet national security; organizational efforts toward economic and political integration through Comecon and the Warsaw Pact; Communist summit conferences to forge and publicize unity; and the internationalist duty of socialism with special military obligations toward the territorial defense and security of Marxist-Leninist regimes. Faced with the unacceptable costs and military risks in forcibly expanding the international socialist system, the Soviets have concentrated on the maintenance of their East European subsystem: for as long as the Soviet Union maintains its exclusivist Marxist-Leninist doctrine, Eastern Europe will constitute the only dependable source of regime security and ideological fulfillment for the CPSU. J

102. Jepišev, A. A. VOJENSKÁ POLITIKA KSSS [Military policy of the Soviet Communist Party]. *Hist. a Vojenství [Czechoslovakia] 1979 28(4): 26-31.* Soviet military policy has been tied to the development of the economy and to the domestic and foreign policies of the USSR. The goal of this policy is a strong military in which the working class plays a leading role. 2 notes. G. E. Pergl/S

103. Jones, Christopher D. THE "REVOLUTION IN MILITARY AFFAIRS" AND PARTY-MILITARY RELATIONS, 1965-70. *Survey [Great Britain] 1974 20(1): 84-100.* Discusses the primacy of the Communist Party in USSR military command matters and of the establishment, role, and function of the political officer in the command structure. The Party reorganized the Army in 1960 and again in 1967, each time placing more emphasis on "moral-political factors." The quality of the political officers is not good, and some in the Army are growing restive with the increasing politicization. Based on magazines and books; 62 notes. R. B. Valliant

104. Jones, Christopher D. SOVIET HEGEMONY IN EASTERN EUROPE: THE DYNAMICS OF POLITICAL AUTONOMY AND MILITARY INTERVENTION. *World Pol. 1977 29(2): 216-241.* Most Western observers have concluded that in the conflicts between the USSR and the Communist regimes of Eastern Europe, the Soviets resorted to military intervention only when certain ideological or strategic issues were at stake. This study suggests that in the conflicts between the leaders of the CPSU and the leaders of the Communist Parties of Yugoslavia, Poland, Albania, Rumania, and Czechoslovakia there was only one real issue at stake: control over the local East European party. The adversaries in these struggles have been factions dependent on Soviet support and ultimately loyal to Moscow and domestic factions seeking to base their rule on genuine popular support. What determined whether the Soviets intervened militarily was not the ideological or strategic issue publicly raised by the Soviets, but whether the domestic faction had demonstrated to Moscow the capacity and will to mobilize its country for armed resistance against the Soviets. J

105. Kachurina, A. V., Timofeev, E. A.; and Zarubin, A. I. LITERATURA PO ISTORII KPSS, PARTIINOMU STROITEL'STVU I MEZHDUNARODNOMU KOMMUNISTICHESKOMU DVIZHENIIU V 1981 G. [Literature on the history of the CPSU, Party construction, and the international movement, 1981]. *Voprosy Istorii KPSS [USSR] 1981 (5): 134-139.* The Publishing House of Political Literature published many of V. I. Lenin's works, reports of the 26th Congress of the Communist Party of the Soviet Union (CPSU), and discussions of historical Party problems. It shows the CPSU's leading role in the struggle for socialism. Economic progress and new activities at the regional and national levels are examined. The Military Publishing House of the Ministry of Defense of the USSR published books on Lenin's military ideas and their relationship to modern conditions. The relations between the CPSU and Soviet armed forces and the latters' relations with Soviet society as a whole are given great attention. A. J. Evans

106. Kalashnik, M. Kh. ISTORICHESKII OPYT KPSS V OSUSHCENSTVLENII LENINSKIKH IDEI O ZASHCHITE SOTSIALISTICHESKOGO OTECHESTVA [The historical experience of the CPSU in implementing Lenin's ideas on the defense of the socialist homeland]. *Voprosy Istorii KPSS [USSR] 1969 (11): 34-48.* Retraces the USSR's military history since the 1917 Revolution in the light of V. I. Lenin's defense theories, highlighting the role of the Communist Party at every stage.

107. Kalinchuk, L. POSTWAR YEARS. *Soviet Military Rev. [USSR] 1977 (6): 57-59.* Describes Party political work in the armed forces in the postwar years which the author considers the most reliable means of education for servicemen. Photo.
D. G. Law

108. Kamenka, Eugene. PHILOSOPHY: THE BOLSHEVIK PERIOD. *Survey [Great Britain] 1967 (64): 80-98.* "Religious and political oppression amid general backwardness in Russia tended to produce an indirect threat to philosophy and rational thinking. The conditions of nineteenth-century Russia produced intellectuals: philosophy became ideology, more often the object of uncritical enthusiasm than of careful and critical study.... Bolshevik philosophy in the years from 1919 to 1956 earned nothing but contempt from serious philosophers of all nationalities. Bolshevik theory and Bolshevik practice openly proclaimed goals that amounted to the complete politicalisation, dogmatisation, and vulgarisation of philosophy. Dialectical materialism became the official philosophy of the Communist Party and the Bolshevik State consistently invoked as the ultimate ideological foundation of all communist political activity and as the only correct foundation for all science, whether social or natural." 8 notes.
D. D. Cameron

109. Kamins'ki, Anatol'. IAKA EVOLIUTSIA? [What kind of evolution?]. *Sučasnist [West Germany] 1976 (1): 76-91, (2): 86-103, (3): 83-93.* Part I. Analyzes the strength of potential national forces in the Ukraine on the basis of demographic changes in favor of ethnic Russians since 1959. Part II. Discusses the membership and development of the Communist Party of the USSR, 1953-76, and the possibilities for a movement toward democracy, with particular reference to the Ukraine. Part III. Considers the political platforms and organization of Russian dissidents and their attitude toward Ukrainian independence.

110. Kanet, Roger E. and Ziegler, Charles E. DIE OSTEUROPÄISCHEN STAATEN UND DIE INTERNATIONALE POLITIK: NEUE ENGLISCHSPRACHIGE BÜCHER ZUR SOWJETISCHEN AUSSENPOLITIK [The Eastern European countries and international politics: new English-language books on Soviet foreign policy]. *Osteuropa [West Germany] 1979 29(2): 165-173, (3): 251-261.* Part I. Reviews eight US and British publications on Soviet foreign policy toward the Comecon states, the Middle East, and South Africa, and the Soviet position in detente and naval expansion since World War II. Part II. Reviews 16 new US publications on East-West trade, the Sino-Soviet dispute, the domestic development of the Warsaw Pact states, and economic cooperation between Western multinational companies and the Communist countries since the 1950's.

111. Kanet, Roger E. SOWJETUNION, KOMMUNISTISCHE WELT UND ENTWICKLUNGSLÄNDER [USSR Communist countries, and developing nations]. *Osteuropa [West Germany] 1980 30(4): 358-365.* Reviews new English and American publications on Soviet relations with the Warsaw pact states and Third World countries since World War II.

112. Karawajew, W. DIE SOZIALISTISCHE ÖKONOMISCHE INTEGRATION ALS FAKTOR DER ÖKONOMISCHEN BEZIEHUNGEN ZWISCHEN STAATEN DER BEIDEN WELTSYSTEME [Socialist economic integration as one factor in the expansion of economic relations between countries of the two world systems]. *Wissenschaftliche Zeitschrift der Humboldt-Universität zu Berlin: Gesellschafts- und Sprachwissenschaftliche Reihe [East Germany] 1975 24(6): 744-747.* Socialism in Communist countries and the USSR has been a basic factor in their rapidly increasing participation in economic relations with the capitalist world. Their close ties with each other have not precluded economic exchanges with other lands. As their own economies have become more sophisticated they have found it easier to trade with capitalist countries, while their socialism has protected them from many evils of western capitalism. Socialist integration itself has greatly encouraged scientific-technological advance, the concentration of industries in favorable areas, and the establishment of banking facilities.
M. Faissler

113. Karkarashvili, Sh. V. POLVEKA SLUZHENIIA DELU PARTII (RESPUBLIKANSKOI GAZETE GRUZII "ZARIA VOSTOKA"—50 LET) [A half century of service to Party affairs: 50 years of the republican newspaper of Georgia *Zaria Vostoka]. Voprosy Istorii KPSS [USSR] 1972 (6): 108-111.* Surveys the publishing and editorial history of *Zaria Vostoka* [Dawn of the East], official paper of the Communist Party and government of the Georgian SSR.

114. Kartunova, A. I. NEISSIAKAEMYI ISTOCHNIK [A boundless source]. *Voprosy Istorii KPSS [USSR] 1963 (8): 117-120.* Studies the writings of Lenin on the international significance of the history of the Soviet Communist Party and illustrates how the Party's example has inspired the peoples of the USSR to struggle for peace, democracy, and socialism.

115. Kas'ianenko, V. I. LENINSKIE IDEI O SOTSIALISTICHESKOM OBRAZE ZHIZNI I IKH OSUSHCHESTVLENIE V SSSR [Lenin's ideas on the socialist way of life and its realization in the USSR]. *Voprosy Istorii KPSS [USSR] 1980 (4): 65-77.* Examines the development of socialism in the USSR from the revolution to the present. V. I. Lenin saw the proletariat as the instrument for destroying the old order and establishing the socialist way of life, based on material production and ideals of scientific socialism. Now, in the stage of a developed socialism, the Communist Party is dedicated to the full realization of Lenin's ideas. Based on Lenin's complete works and secondary sources; 64 notes.
S. J. Talalay

116. Khalmukhamedov, M. Kh. NAUCHNO-PRAKTICHESKAIA KONFERENTSIIA, POSVIASHCHENNAIA INTERNATSIONAL'NOMU VOSPITANIIU [A scientific-practical conference devoted to internationalist upbringing]. *Voprosy Filosofii [USSR] 1977 (4): 148-158.* Gives details of a conference held at Tbilisi in October 1976, organized by the Propaganda Section of the Soviet Communist Party and the Georgian Communist Party, on methods of educating national minority citizens of the USSR in internationalism, and fulfilling Lenin's nationality policies, 1920's-77.

117. Khanazarov, K. Kh. VAZHNOE NAPRAVLENIE POLITIKI KPSS V OBLASTI RESHENIIA NATSIONAL'NOGO VOPROSA I RAZVITIIA NATSIONAL'NYKH OTNOSHENII [An important political directive from the Communist Party concerning the nationalities question and the development of nationalities relations]. *Voprosy Istorii KPSS [USSR] 1978 (1): 44-55.* Traces the development of a language policy in the USSR from the first Declaration of the Rights of the Russian peoples, 15 November 1917, to the present day. This declaration and subsequent policy directives reversed tsarist insistence on the supremacy of Russian; and, while underlining its continuing value as a unifying factor, encouraged the development of other languages spoken within the Soviet Union.

118. Kharmandarian, S. V. SSHM KAZMAVORUMĚ EV NRA HAMASHKHARHAYIN PATMAKAN NSHANAKUTYUNĚ [The formation of the USSR and its world-wide historic significance]. *Patma-Banasirakan Handes. Istoriko-Filologicheskii Zhurnal [USSR] 1972 (4): 21-28.* Contrasts the bourgeois solution to the national problem, characterized by the separation of nations into small states under capitalist exploitation and national and racial discrimination, with the Soviet concept of the free union of peoples in a big and powerful state.

119. Khelemendyk, V. S. Z ISTORII VZAIEMODII PRESY, RADIO I TELEBACHENNIA U SPRAVI PIDVYSHCHENNIA TRUDOVOI I SUSPILNO-POLITYCHNOI AKTYVNOSTI TRUDIASHCHYKH 1924-1967 [The interaction between the press, radio, and television and the encouragement of the labor and sociopolitical activities of working people, 1924-67]. *Ukrains'kyi Istorychnyi Zhurnal [USSR] 1974 (4): 84-92.* The mass media has been, and remains, the Communist Party's main instrument in promoting the efficiency and loyalty of Soviet workers.

120. Khrobostov, V. V. I. LENIN, KPSS O SOVETSKOI VOINSKOI DISTSIPLINE [V. I. Lenin and the Communist Party of the Soviet Union on Soviet military discipline]. *Voenno-Istoricheskii*

Zhurnal [USSR] 1977 (7): 3-9. Examines the ideas of V. I. Lenin and the Soviet Communist Party on the importance of military discipline to the defense of the USSR.

121. Khromov, S. S. AKTUAL'NYE PROBLEMY IZUCHENIIA OTECHESTVENNOI ISTORII V SVETE RESHENII XXVI S'EZDA KPSS [Urgent problems of the study of Soviet history in the light of the decisions of the 26th Congress of the Communist Party of the Soviet Union]. *Istoriia SSSR [USSR] 1981 (3): 3-24.* The decisions of the 26th Congress of the Communist Party of the Soviet Union emphasized the need to enhance the role of the social sciences including history. Historical science must educate workers in the spirit of Soviet patriotism and socialist internationalism while at the same time waging a systematic struggle against bourgeois and revisionist historiography. Published sources; 53 notes. J. W. Long

122. Khromov, S. S. KPSS—REVOLIUTSIONNYI AVANGARD SOVIETSKOGO NARODA [The Communist Party, revolutionary vanguard of the Soviet nation]. *Voprosy Istorii KPSS [USSR] 1981 (11): 92-100.* Discusses decisions taken at the 26th Party Congress. 48 notes. L. Smith

123. Khromov, S. S. VEDUSHCHII KLASS SOVETSKOGO OBSHCHESTVA [The leading class of Soviet society]. *Voprosy Istorii [USSR] 1983 (12): 3-18.* Studies the place held by the working class in the social structure, its role in the revolutionary-liberation struggle of the working masses, in the victory of the socialist revolution and the consolidation of the new order. The author dwells, in particular, on the hegemony of the Russian proletariat in the revolutionary struggle, on its winning political power and becoming the leading force of Soviet society, on the fact that under the guidance of the Communist Party its role has been enhanced in the period of the emergence and development of mature socialism. Contains brief account of the multi-volume work *History of the Soviet Working Class* prepared by the Institute of the History of the USSR, USSR Academy of Sciences. J

124. Khromov, S. S. VOZRASTANIE ROLI KPSS—RUKOVODIASHCHEI SILY SOVETSKOI DERZHAVY [The growing role of the CPSU, the leading power of the Soviet State]. *Prepodavanie Istorii v Shkole [USSR] 1972 (6): 5-13.* Describes the growth and consolidation of the Communist Party guided by the dogmatic principles and teachings of V. I. Lenin. Includes general data on socioeconomic and cultural progress in the USSR, 1917-71. 15 notes. N. Frenkley

125. Khromushin, G. B. NESOSTOIATEL'NOST' BURZHUAZNYKH FAL'SIFIKATSII SOTSIAL'NOI POLITIKI KPSS [The bankruptcy of bourgeois falsifiers of the Communist Party of the Soviet Union's social policies]. *Voprosy Istorii KPSS [USSR] 1982 (3): 76-87.* The Soviet people support the Party's social policies and its leading role in the USSR's industrial, material, and social welfare. Bourgeois critics argue that the USSR relegates consumers' interests behind those of heavy industry and the military. This is untrue. Soviet consumption and living standards are unrivalled. Critics charge Soviet centralism with repression. This is false, as Soviet centralism is the synthesis of the wishes of all Soviet workers, of all Soviet citizens. That the USSR is immobile is untrue, as the Party is its prime mover. Nor is there inequality in the USSR, as the country enjoys real socialism, which guarantees equality. Freed from capital's exploitation, Soviet workers uninterruptedly improve their living standards. Based on Lenin's and Brezhnev's works; 49 notes. A. J. Evans

126. King, Marshall Roland. "Political Recruitment in a Mono-Organizational Setting: The Soviet Central Party Leadership in the Post-Stalin Period." State U. of New York, Buffalo 1980. 211 pp. *DAI 1980 41(1): 384-A.* 8016202

127. King, Robert R. RELIGION AND COMMUNISM IN THE SOVIET UNION AND EASTERN EUROPE. *Brigham Young U. Studies 1975 15(3): 323-347.* Discusses the basis for communism, its stand on religion, the effect which tradition and religious beliefs have had in the USSR and the countries of Eastern Europe, 1917-60.

128. Kitrinos, Robert W.; addenda by Spaulding, Wallace. INTERNATIONAL DEPARTMENT OF THE CPSU. *Problems of Communism 1984 33(5): 47-75.* It is now clear that the International Department of the CPSU Central Committee plays a far more significant role in the formulation and implementation of Soviet foreign policy than previously realized. As well as handling relations with nonruling Communist parties, the International Department seems to be responsible for channeling information and recommendations on foreign policy issues, based on inputs from the various ministries and intelligence services, to the CC Secretariat and Politburo. Based on numerous Soviet and Western secondary sources as well as Western intelligence reports; fig., table, appendix, 110 notes. Includes 2 addenda on ID organization with 96 and 20 notes respectively. J. M. Lauber

129. Klokov, Ie. V. 30-RICHCHIA ZAKONU PRO ZAKHYST MYRU [The 30th anniversary of the law on the defense of peace]. *Ukrains'kyi Istorychnyi Zhurnal [USSR] 1981 (2): 132-135.* On the occasion of the 30th anniversary of the law on the defense of peace passed by the USSR's Supreme Soviet on 12 March 1951, praises the USSR's peace policy as reflected in the latest Communist Party program and supported by such important instruments in the preservation of peace as the Warsaw Pact. 10 notes. I. Krushelnyckyj

130. Knapp, Vincent J. THE COMMUNIST PARTY AND THE SOCIAL CLASSES OF RUSSIA. *J. of Social and Pol. Studies 1977 2(4): 297-306.* The USSR, inspired by the elitist ideology of Leninism and the Communist Party, peopled with officials from the upper and middle classes, has essentially been molding a society run by elites with no basic understanding of the needs of common people, 1917-77.

131. Kneen, Peter. WHY NATURAL SCIENTISTS ARE A PROBLEM FOR THE CPSU. *British J. of Pol. Sci. [Great Britain] 1978 8(2): 177-198.* Analyzes how and why the Communist Party of the USSR has tried to control those natural scientists who have opposed monolithic Party control, 1960-76.

132. Kolesnikov, A. K. LENINSKII PRINTSIP EDINSTVA POLITIKI I ORGANIZATSIONNOGO RUKOVODSTVA PARTII [Lenin's principle of the unity of the party's policy and organizational leadership]. *Voprosy Istorii KPSS [USSR] 1969 (7): 12-25.* Discusses V. I. Lenin's idea that the Communist Party should play an important part not only in gaining power, but also in building socialism and communism.

133. Kolesnikov, A. K. RAZVITIE I SOVERSHENSTVOVANIE PARTIINOGO KONTROLIA NA PREDPRIIATIIAKH [The development and perfection of Party control at enterprises]. *Voprosy Istorii KPSS [USSR] 1963 (6): 52-65.* Describes the views of V. I. Lenin on the relationship between the Soviet Communist Party and industry, and examines congress decisions and the changing policy of the Party, 1917-63.

134. Kolisher, T. M. and Kryzhanivs'kyi, V. P. SERAFYMA ILLIVNA HOPNER (DO 100-RICHCHIA Z DNIA NARODZHENNIA) [Serafima Hopner: on the 100th anniversary of her birth]. *Ukraïns'kyi Istorychnyi Zhurnal [USSR] 1980 (3): 54-65.* Illuminates the life and multifaceted activities of Serafima I. Hopner (1880-1966), a Bolshevik, Leninist, noted member of the Communist Party and the international Communist movement, active participant in the Russian revolutions, and one of the people who worked under the direct leadership of V. I. Lenin. 57 notes. Russian summary. I. Krushelnyckyj

135. Kolomiichenko, I. I. KOMUNISTYCHNA PARTIIA UKRAINY V BOROT'BI ZA ZDIYSNENNIA LENNINS'KOHO PLANU BUDIVNYTSTVA SOTSIALIZMU [The Communist Party of the Ukraine in the struggle for the completion of Lenin's plan for the building of socialism]. *Ukrains'kyi Istorychnyi Zhurnal*

[USSR] 1978 (6): 23-35. To carry out Lenin's Socialist plan the Central Committee of the Communist Party used to send influential members such as Feliks Dzerzhinski, Mikhail Kalinin, Anastas Mikoyan and others to the Ukraine to oversee the work of the Party machinery. It also required the liquidation of the *kurkulian* or middle classes, and three purges of Ukrainian Party members. Based on the *History of the Communist Party of Ukraine* and Party archives; 32 notes. H. M. Diuk

136. Koloskov, A. G. VAZHNAIA VEKHA V STANOVLENII, RAZVITII SHKOL'NOGO ISTORICHESKOGO OBRAZOVANIIA (K 50-LETIIU POSTANOVLENIIA SNK SSSR I TSK VKP(B) "O PREPODAVANII GRAZHDANSKOI ISTORII V SHKOLAKH SSSR") [An important landmark in the establishment and development of school history teaching: the 50th anniversary of the resolution of the SNK of the USSR and the TsIK RCP(b) "On the Teaching of Civil History in the Schools of the USSR"]. *Prepodavanie Istorii v Shkole [USSR] 1984 (3): 2-9.* Discusses the role of the Communist Party in the development of history teaching in Soviet schools.

137. Kölsch, Hans and Schulze-Wollgast, Harald. PROBLEME DER AUSARBEITUNG DER KONZEPTION VON DER ENTWICKELTEN SOZIALISTISCHEN GESELLSCHAFT IN DEN 60ER UND 70ER JAHREN [Problems of the elaboration of the conception of the developed socialist society during the 1960's and 1970's]. *Wissenschaftliche Zeitschrift der Humboldt-Universität zu Berlin. Gesellschaftswissenschaftliche Reihe [East Germany] 1983 32(5): 477-483.* Discusses the political theory of the development of socialism in the USSR and other Communist countries.

138. Komkov, V. I. PIDHOTOVKA KADRIV MASOVYKH PROFESII NA SHAKHTAKH DONBASU (1959-1970 RR.) [Training cadre workers to direct mass employment in the Donbass mines, 1959-70]. *Ukraïns'kyi Istorychnyi Zhurnal [USSR] 1980 (3): 109-111.* The Central Committee of the Communist Party of the Soviet Union directed the training of skilled workers for mass employment and thus changed significantly the structure of the working class in the coal industry. 9 notes. I. Krushelnyckyj

139. Kondrats'ki, A. A. ROL' PROFSPILOK U POSYLENNI SUSPIL'NO-POLITYCHNOI AKTYVNOSTI ROBITNYCHOHO KLASU (1959-1970 RR) [Labor unions' role in increasing working-class activity, 1959-70]. *Ukrains'kyi Istorychnyi Zhurnal [USSR] 1974 (10): 10-18.* Considers the role of Soviet labor unions and organizations in the Communist Party's efforts to engage workers in higher production, and social and political life.

140. Kop'ev, N. Ia. OPYT KONKRETNO-ISTORICHESKOGO PODKHODA KPSS K ORGANIZATSII IDEINOGO VOSPITANIIA [The Soviet Communist Party's positive historical approach to the organization of ideological education]. *Voprosy Istorii KPSS [USSR] 1976 (6): 57-68.* Studies improvements in the Communist Party's ideological education in the USSR, 1920's-76.

141. Kornienko, S. I. and Iakovlev, Ia. R. GLASHATAI IDEI PARTII, ORGANIZATOR MASS [Herald of the ideas of the Party, organizer of the masses]. *Voprosy Istorii KPSS [USSR] (9): 145-149.* Seminars were held throughout the country in May 1982 to mark the 70th anniversary of the Soviet Communist Party newspaper, *Pravda.* 3 notes. J. Bamber

142. Korsch, Boris. THE ROLE OF READERS' CARDS IN SOVIET LIBRARIES. *J. of Lib. Hist. 1978 13(3): 282-297.* Readers' cards are used by librarians in the USSR to record the reading habits of clients and to guide them into reading Communist Party literature. They are also used by the Committee of State Security (KGB) to monitor the loyalty of readers. The use of readers' cards began in 1895 in V. I. Lenin's illegal libraries and expanded during the Stalinist period. It continues today. Previously published in Hebrew in *Yad Lakore* 1976 15(3): 135-145. 93 notes, appendix.

143. Kostikow, Wjatscheslaw. DER SOZIALISMUS UND DIE MORAL DES SOWJETISCHEN MENSCHEN [Socialism and the morals of Soviet man]. *Frankfurter Hefte [West Germany] 1980 35(2): 47-52.* Despite the introduction of collectivism in most spheres of social organization in Soviet society since the 1920's, the development of new forms of communist morals only slowly begins to show in the field of work.

144. Koval'ov, I. Ia. VIIS'KOVO-PATRIOTYCHNA ROBOTA SERED MOLODI: VAZHLYVYI NAPRIAM DIIAL'NOSTI LENINS'KOHO KOMSOMOLU [Military and patriotic work among youth: an important trend in the activities of the Leninist Young Communist League]. *Ukrains'kyi Istorychnyi Zhurnal [USSR] 1979 (6): 25-33.* Discusses various aspects of the military and patriotic work of the Young Communist League in the moral, political, military, technical, and physical preparation of young people for the defense of the USSR. Primary Communist Party and Young Communist League sources; 37 notes. Russian summary.
I. Krushelnyckyj

145. Kozlov, N. DEIATEL'NOST' KPSS PO SOZDANIIU I RAZVITIIU SOVETSKOI VOENNOI SHKOLY [The activity of the Communist Party in creating and developing the Soviet military school]. *Voenno-Istoricheskii Zhurnal [USSR] 1978 (7): 78-82.* The first of many Soviet military schools was opened in December 1917 in Moscow by order of V. I. Lenin. Red Army officers were recruited from the working and peasant classes to ensure unity between officers and soldiers. The author discusses the growth of the military school system and the consequent improvement in the army's educational standards. 27 notes. V. Sobeslavsky

146. Kozlova, G. N. IZ OPYTA IDEINO-POLITICHESKOGO VOSPITANIIA STUDENCHESKOI MOLODEZHI NA KAFEDRAKH MARKSIZMA-LENINIZMA KHUDOZHESTVENNYKH VYZOV (NA MATERIALAKH LENINGRADA 1959-1965 GG.) [On the experience of educating students in the spirit of communism in the departments of Marxism-Leninism in Leningrad art schools, 1959-65]. *Vestnik Leningradskogo Universiteta [USSR] 1974 (2): 38-44.* Discusses problems and challenges in the teaching of communism in the departments of Marxism-Leninism in art schools. Creative workers must be educated in the social sciences and in the spiritual and material richness of the state so they will make their proper contribution to the fatherland. 39 notes.
G. F. Jewsbury

147. Krancberg, Sigmund. CONTROLLING INDIVIDUAL DEVELOPMENT AND BEHAVIOR. *Studies in Soviet Thought [Netherlands] 1984 27(4): 319-334.* Describes the Soviet moral code as dictated by Communist Party philosophy. The author discusses the interpretations, purposes, policies, and impact of such leaders as Josef Stalin and Leonid Brezhnev on the Soviet state and its citizenry. Based on Communist Party and Soviet government documents; 55 notes. R. B. Mendel

148. Krasnov, A. V. BOR'BA KPSS ZA OSUSHCHESTVLENIE MARKSISTSKO-LENINSKOGO UCHENIIA O DIKTATURE PROLETARIATA V KHODE STROITEL'STVA SOTSIALIZMA V SSSR [The CPSU's struggle for the implementation of Marxist-Leninist teaching on the dictatorship of the proletariat in the course of the building of socialism in the USSR]. *Voprosy Istorii KPSS [USSR] 1981 (8): 113-125.* The concept of the dictatorship of the proletariat is one of the basic principles of Marxist-Leninist thought. It is the fulfillment of a revolutionary party's debt to the working class. The Communist Party of the Soviet Union is the first Marxist-Leninist party under whose leadership the dictatorship of the proletariat has been implemented, and the creative power of the concept vindicated. It has enabled the Soviet people to overcome backwardness, to build a socialist society, and move toward the establishment of Communism. 37 notes. J. Bamber

149. Kravchenko, L. V. UCHAST' KOMSOMOLU UKRAINY U ROZVYTKU I ZMITSNENNI INTERNATSIONAL'NYKH ZVIAZKIV RADIANS'KOI MOLODI [The participation of the Young Communist League (Komsomol) of the Ukraine in developing and strengthening Soviet youth's international relations]. *Ukrains'kyi Istorychnyi Zhurnal [USSR] 1979 (6): 15-24.* Reviews the participation of the Leninist Young Communist League of the Ukraine in the development and strengthening of Soviet youth's in-

ternational relations from the time of the league's inception. Gives examples of these relations and of the main forms of international cooperation. Based on Communist Party and Young Communist League publications; 22 notes. Russian summary.
I. Krushelnyckyj

150. Kress, John H. REPRESENTATION OF POSITIONS ON THE CPSU POLITBURO. *Slavic Rev. 1980 39(2): 218-238.* Analyzes positional data as a variable in its own right rather than as evidence explaining other variables. Discusses "entitlement," interrelationships among positions and institutions represented; explores the increasing institutionalism and "patterning of interests" within and without the Politburo. Cites government statistics (1953-76). Primary sources; 57 tables, 48 notes.
R. B. Mendel

151. Krivoručenko, V. ZU DEN BEZIEHUNGEN ZWISCHEN DER KPDSU UND DEM LENINSCHEN KOMSOMOL [On the relations between the Communist Party of the Soviet Union (CPSU) and the Leninist Komsomol]. *Wissenschaftliche Zeitschrift der Wilhelm-Pieck-Universität Rostock, Gesellschafts- und Sprachwissenschaftliche Reihe [East Germany] 1976 25(1): 13-20.* The basic character and function of the Young Communist League (Komsomol) in the USSR remains Leninist. In particular, the leading role of the Communist Party is acknowledged in determining the nature of the Komsomol's work and in ensuring that its activities accord with the overall needs of society. However, over the course of time, and especially with the victory of socialism in the Soviet Union, the relationship between the Party and the Komsomol has undergone considerable change. Based on the works of Lenin and documents of party congresses. 15 notes. English summary.
J. A. Perkins

152. Krivoruchenko, V. K. SOVETSKAIA MOLODEZH'—AKTIVNYI UCHASTNIK STROITEL'STVA MATERIAL'NO-TEKHNICHESKOI BAZY KOMMUNIZMA (1959-1975 GG.) [Soviet youth—an active participant in the construction of the material and technological base of Communism, 1959-75]. *Istoricheskie Zapiski Akad. Nauk SSSR [USSR] 1980 (105): 5-44.* Soviet youth, imbued with revolutionary fervor, are increasingly involved in building Communism; in 1969 24 million young people worked in industry and construction, in 1970 30 million participated. Many well educated and politically aware youth are working in high technology areas. In addition, youth brigades, comprising 3, 943,000 workers in 1975 (almost a 10-fold increase compared to 1959) are helping to open up Siberia. Based on Soviet government and Party statistics; 9 tables, 156 notes. A. J. Evans

153. Krivoruchenko, V. K. VAZHNYI ISTORICHESKII ISTOCHNIK [An important historical source]. *Sovetskie Arkhivy [USSR] 1968 (4): 16-23.* The collection of documents concerning the Young Communist League (Komsomol) was started in 1924 with a decree from the organization's central committee, and now a special index facilitates the use of the documents. Notwithstanding close cooperation between the Komsomol activists and the Party archivists, the importance of gathering documentary evidence is not always appreciated by all Komsomol bureaucrats. 10 notes. W. Kowalski

154. Krivoruchenko, V. K. VLKSM NA ETAPE ZRELOGO SOTSIALIZMA: ZAKONOMERNOSTI RAZVITIIA, NAPRAVLENIIA DEIATEL'NOSTI [The Komsomol under developed socialism: laws of development and direction of activities]. *Istoriia SSSR [USSR] 1978 (5): 21-37.* Reviews the history and present status of the Young Communist League (Komsomol). During the past 60 years the Young Communist League has directly participated in the education of the new Soviet man, the construction of the economic foundations of communism, and the development and consolidation of communist society. Based on published and archival sources; 2 tables, 80 notes. J. W. Long

155. Krukhmalev, A. E. VYDAIUSHCHIISIA VKLAD V NAUKU O KOMMUNIZME: K 50-LETIIU RABOTY V. I. LENINA "VELIKII POCHIN" [An outstanding contribution to the science of communism: the 50th anniversary of V. I. Lenin's work *The Great Beginning*]. *Voprosy Istorii KPSS [USSR] 1969 (6): 3-17.* Describes how this work contributed to developing the theory of scientific communism and clarified the ways of putting the theory into practice.

156. Kukin, D. M. PIATILETKI I SOTSIAL'NO-EKONOMICHESKII PROGRESS SOVETSKOGO OBSHCHESTVA [The five-year plans and the socioeconomic progress of Soviet society]. *Voprosy Istorii [USSR] 1981 (4): 3-20.* The five-year plans, which cover both socioeconomic and cultural development, have been key factors in the work of the Communist Party and the Soviet people in implementing Lenin's plan of building socialism and communism in the USSR. Considers the main tasks and results of the 10 five-year plans, 1928-80, and the guidelines for the social and economic development of the USSR in the present, 11th five-year plan, 1981-85, adopted by the 26th Communist Party Congress. J

157. Kul'chyts'kyi, S. V. and Nekora, S. I. POLITYKA KPRS PO PIDNESENNIU NARODNOHO DOBROBUTU V PERIOD ROZVYNUTOHO SOTSIALIZMU [The policy of the CPSU on raising the people's well-being in the period of advanced socialism]. *Ukrains'kyi Istorychnyi Zhurnal [USSR] 1974 (8): 12-22.* Explains the directives of the 24th Soviet Communist Party Congress with reference to economic development during the preceding two Five-Year Plans (1961-70), showing them to be integrated, all-embracing measures to raise the standard of living and reduce wastage.

158. Kurochkin, P. GLAVNYI MARSHAL BRONETANKOVYKH VOISK P. A. ROTMISTROV [The chief marshal of the armored tank forces, Pavel A. Rotmistrov]. *Voenno-Istoricheskii Zhurnal [USSR] 1981 23(6): 90-92.* In honor of the 80th anniversary of his birth, a brief account of the life and work of Pavel Alekseevich Rotmistrov (1901-75). Considers his entry in 1919 into the Red Army and involvement in the Civil War, his military and academic career in the peaceful years of the construction of socialism, his valuable contribution to the defeat of German fascism as a chief marshal of armored tank forces in the Great Patriotic War, his military pedagogical work in the postwar years, and involvement in the Communist Party as a delegate at Party congresses. 2 notes. L. Smith

159. Kutiiel', I. IULII MARGOLIN: DO DESIATYRICHCHIA Z CHASU SMERTY [Iuli Margolin: on the 10th anniversary of his death]. *Sučasnist [West Germany] 1981 (12): 60-71.* Biographical sketch devoted to the life and work of Iuli Margolin (1900-71), doctor of philosophy, Zionist, publicist, and litterateur, who made a valuable contribution to directing the struggle of Jews and Ukrainians alike against Russian Communist oppression.

160. Kuz'min, N. F. KRUPNAIA VEKHA NA PUTI STROITEL'STVA SOTSIALIZMA (K 50-LETIIU XI SEZDA RKP(B)) [A major landmark on the path of the construction of socialism: the 50th anniversary of the 11th congress of the RCP(B)]. *Voprosy Istorii KPSS [USSR] 1972 (4): 40-57.* Discusses the deliberations and actions of the 1922 congress, which made significant advances in laying the foundations of a socialist economic structure under the New Economic Policy while consolidating the development of a socialist government.

161. Kuzmina, T. THE INTELLIGENTSIA AND THE REVOLUTION: THE 20TH CENTURY. *Social Sci. [USSR] 1982 13(3): 202-205.* Reports on the proceedings of a scientific conference on "The History of the Great October Socialist Revolution," and "The History of Socialist and Communist Construction in the USSR," held in November 1981 in Tbilisi.

162. Kuznetsov, D. SHEFSTVO, PROVERENNOE ZHIZN'IU (K 50-LETIIU SHEFSTVA VLKSM NAD VOZDUSHNYM FLOTOM SSSR) [Patronage, proved by life: on the 50th anniversary of Komsomol's patronage of the Air Force of the USSR]. *Voenno-Istoricheskii Zhurnal [USSR] 1981 23(1): 79-81.* Traces the patronage of the Soviet Air Force by the Young Communist League (Komsomol) from the beginning of the connection in 1931. One aspect of this patronage is the several Komsomol-run aviation

activities such as aero-clubs and parachute-jumping training centers. Through these activities the Komsomol helps prepare young people for careers in aviation. Many former Komsomol members became famous wartime pilots, and one of the Komsomol's projects during World War II was to raise money for the purchase of military aircraft. Based on documents from the Komsomol Central Archive; 9 notes. A. Brown

163. Kuznetsov, D. and Akchurin, R. VOENNO-PATRIOTICHESKAIA I OBORONNO-MASSOVAIA RABOTA PROFSOIUZOV KOMSOMOLA, DOSAAF [Military-patriotic and civil defense work by labor unions, the Young Communist League, and the Voluntary Society for Assistance to the Army, Air Force, and Navy]. *Voenno-Istoricheskii Zhurnal [USSR] 1978 (6): 94-101.* From 1919 Soviet labor unions and organizations took a leading part in military and civil defense education for the masses and in forming reserve regiments. This was of particular significance during World War II, when the labor unions and related organizations trained nurses, first-aid teams, and air-raid wardens. In 1951 many of these functions were brought under the control of the Voluntary Society for Assistance to the Army, Air Force, and Navy (DOSAAF), which continued this vital work after the war. 27 notes. R. J. Ware

164. Kvashuk, L. P. BORETS ZA VELIKOE DELO LENINA [A fighter for Lenin's great work]. *Voprosy Istorii KPSS [USSR] 1984 (5): 147-151.* On 20 February 1984 a special session of the Institute of Marxist-Leninism of the Soviet Communist Party celebrated Aleksei Kosygin's 80th birth date. Kosygin joined the Party in 1927 and progressed through its ranks. He served with distinction in the Great Patriotic War and held several positions in the Soviet government, with a top position from 1964 to 1980. He was a great economist who sought industrial efficiency. In addition, he was exacting, democratic, and polite. 8 notes. A. J. Evans

165. Kvok, D. G. VAZHNOE NAPRAVLENIE POLITIKI KPSS PO POD"EMU ZHIZNENNOGO UROVNIA SOVETSKIKH LUDEI [An important aim of CPSU policy: raising the living standards of the Soviet people]. *Voprosy Istorii KPSS [USSR] 1982 (1): 41-50.* The documents of Soviet Communist Party congresses over the last 60 years are witness to the constant attention given to the questions of living standards, in particular the housing problem. At the 14th Party Congress, 1926, housing construction plans were debated at length; 20 years later, at the 20th Party Congress (1956), a resolution was passed to double the housing program; at the 26th Party Congress (1981), a decision was taken to build 540 million cubic meters of accommodation during the 11th Five-Year Plan. Based on secondary sources; 64 notes. G. Dombrovski

166. Laboor, Ernst. Z DĚJIN BOJŮ O VOJENSKÉ UVOLŇOVÁNÍ VE STŘEDNÍ EVROPĚ (K TRADICÍM A AKTUÁLNÍMU PŮSOBENÍ SOCIALISTICKÝCH MÍROVÝCH MYŠLENEK) [History of the struggle for military détente in Central Europe: traditions and present effects of socialist ideas on peace]. *Československý Časopis Hist. [Czechoslovakia] 1979 27(1): 19-44.* Since the Genoa Conference of 1922, the USSR has supported a general disarmament policy that emphasized arms reduction in equal proportions. The Soviet proposals of the 1920's and 1930's established the traditions on which socialist states are still building, and which inform the Conference on Security and Cooperation in Europe in Helsinki (1973-75) and the continuing great-power negotiations in Vienna. The NATO powers in the 1950's used German unification as a pawn in confrontation politics and still resist efforts of the Warsaw Pact countries to secure European peace. 64 notes. R. E. Weltsch

167. Laktionova, N. K. OHLIAD LITERATURY PRO KOMSOMOL, SHCHO VYISHLA PISLIA XXV Z'IZDU KPRS [A review of literature about the Young Communist League, published after the 25th CPSU Congress]. *Ukrains'kyi Istorychnyi Zhurnal [USSR] 1978 (10): 133-136.* Reviews literature published in the USSR, 1977-78, on the origins and development of the Young Communist League at all stages of the building of socialism. 14 notes.

168. Lavrushina, Iu. V.I. LENIN, KPSS O DISTSIPLINE KAK VAZHNEISHEM SLAGAEMOM BOEVOI GOTOVNOSTI VOORUZHENNYKH SIL [V. I. Lenin and the Communist Party of the Soviet Union (CPSU) on discipline as a most important component in the military preparedness of the armed forces]. *Voenno-Istoricheskii Zhurnal [USSR] 1983 (9): 3-9.* Demonstrates Lenin's concern for the development of discipline among Bolshevik troops during the Russian Civil War, 1918-22. Shows how this emphasis was continued by his successors in the Soviet Communist Party during World War II, and urges present day soldiers to continue the tradition. About 90% of the armed forces are members of the Communist Party or the Young Communist League. Their influence and that of the patriotic movement all contribute to raising levels of discipline. Based on published documents; 10 notes. D. N. Collins

169. Lebedev, N. I. LENINSKIE IDEI FUNDAMENTAL'NOI PERESTROIKI MEZHDUNARODNYKH OTNOSHENII [Lenin's ideas on the fundamental restructuring of international relations]. *Novaia i Noveishaia Istoriia [USSR] 1976 (5): 3-27.* Describes the Soviet state's consistent struggle for the realization of the Leninist principles of peaceful coexistence with differing states and social systems, discusses various stages of this struggle, and emphasizes the significance of the program of the struggle for peace and security and for the freedom and independence of peoples adopted at the 25th Congress of the CPSU. J

170. Lediaev, N. F. K VOPROSU O PERIODIZATSII ISTORII KPSS [The periodization of history in relation to the Communist Party of the USSR]. *Voprosy Istorii KPSS [USSR] 1970 (9): 87-91.* Details five separate stages in the historical development of the Communist Party of the USSR.

171. Leonova, L. S. PODGOTOVKA PARTIINYKH KADROV V PARTIINYKH UCHEBNYKH ZAVEDENIIAKH [Preparation of Party cadre at Party schools]. *Voprosy Istorii KPSS [USSR] 1983 (5): 123-133.* The author reviews studies on the education and training of Communist Party members at all levels in the USSR from 1917 to 1983. Based on secondary sources; 54 notes. R. Kirillov

172. Léontin, L. L'ARMÉE SOVIÉTIQUE ET LE PARTI COMMUNISTE DE L'URSS [The Soviet army and the Communist Party of the USSR]. *Rev. Militaire Générale [France] 1972 (4): 489-502.* Since the formation of the Red Army in 1918, political commissars controlled military leaders, thus weakening the army, but in 1942 their role was reduced to morale and ideological education. Today, political leadership is exercised by officers at every level. They organize party activities and supervise the political indoctrination of the troops, 80% of whom belong to the Communist Party or to a Komsomol. Communist soldiers are expected to be models of discipline. Political cadres have to take the lead in combating formalism and bourgeois thinking. Since the 24th Party Congress, the army has been represented in the highest party institutions. As a result of the close integration of the army with the Party, the army is no problem at all for the Kremlin. Based on Soviet publications. J. S. Gassner

173. Levesque, Jacques. MODELES DE CONFLITS ENTRE L'URSS ET LES AUTRES ETATS SOCIALISTES [Patterns of conflict between the USSR and other socialist states]. *Can. J. of Pol. Sci. [Canada] 1974 7(1): 135-142.* Divides eight conflicts between the USSR and other Communist countries, 1948-68, into two types: 1) conflicts arising from grave internal crises produced by bungled application of the Soviet model (Hungary, Poland, Czechoslovakia) and 2) conflicts precipitated by the Soviet Union's attempts to impose its will on its allies.

174. Levin, Dov. ZIMAN (ZIMANAS): DEREKH HAYIM SHEL MANHIG KOMONISTI YEHUDI BE'LITA [Ziman (Zimanas): the life of a Jewish Communist leader in Lithuania]. *Shvut [Israel] 1973 1: 95-100.* Born in 1910 Genia Ziman was one of the few influential Jews in top posts in the World War II period. The author compiles all available biographical data on Ziman, including his role as a partisan leader, his political activities in his native Lithua-

nia, and his influential job as editor of *Tiesa,* the Party newspaper. Since 1964 his career has deteriorated rapidly; he was not elected to the Party's presidium and was dismissed as editor of the newspaper. For the most part the Soviets manipulate him in their campaign against Israel and Zionism. Based on secondary sources; 93 notes. M. Feingold

175. Levytskyi, Borys. RADIANSKYI BIUROKRATYCHNYI MODEL PANUVANNIA [The Soviet bureaucratic model of domination]. *Sučasnist [West Germany] 1979 (10): 58-71.* Part I. Most studies of the functioning of the Soviet system and the Party's coercion tactics by Western Sovietologists lack personal experience, and contributions on this subject by Soviet dissidents are more revealing and convincing. Part II. Describes how the Party supervises state organs, administrative bodies, and public organizations.

176. Lewytzkyj, Borys. DIE FÜHRUNGSGREMIEN DER KPDSU IN SOZIOLOGISCHER SICHT [The leadership groups of the CPSU from a sociological perspective]. *Osteuropa [West Germany] 1973 23(11): 881-888.* Analysis of 558 leading Communist Party functionaries in Moscow and in the Union Republics shows an aging "generation," of whom 95% were Party members before Stalin's death, and many of whom rose in the wake of the Stalin purges. This self-recruited group faces the pressure of an excluded younger generation. 3 tables. R. E. Weltsch

177. Libman, A. B. and Maamagi, V. A. BORBA TRUDIASHCHIKHSIA ESTONII ZA VKHOZHDENIE V SOSTAV SOIUZA SSR [The Estonian workers' struggle for their republic's entry into the USSR]. *Voprosy Istorii [USSR] 1972 (5): 23-41.* "Traces the history of the Estonian workers' struggle for Soviet power, for Estonia's political union with the close-knit family of Soviet nations. The author's research is based on hitherto unpublished sources, primarily on a number of documents shedding light on the role played by the Estonian Communist Party in guiding the struggle of the masses and on the extensive participation of the working people in this struggle in the years of the civil war and foreign armed intervention as well as in the period of the domination of the bourgeoisie in Estonia. [Describes] incorporation of the Estonian Republic in the Union of Soviet Socialist Republics as a full-fledged member of the fraternal community of Soviet peoples. Much attention is given by the authors to the Republic's postwar development, to the generous and all-round fraternal assistance rendered the Estonian people by the other Soviet nations and nationalities in the effort to ensure their rapid economic and cultural advancement." J

178. Lin'kov, I. A. RAZVITIE USTAVNYKH POLOZHENII OB OBIAZANNOSTIAKH I PRAVAKH CHLENA KPSS [The development of statute provisions on the obligations and rights of a member of the CPSU]. *Voprosy Istorii KPSS [USSR] 1973 (8): 55-65.* Communist Party members are required to submit to the Party's decisions and moral code and, in general, lead an active political, economic, and cultural life. The Party guarantees equal treatment of all members and the right of appeal of decisions made by lower Party organs. Based on published party documents; 49 notes. L. E. Holmes

179. Liubimova, S. T. IZ ISTORII DEIATEL'NOSTI ZHENOTDELOV [The activity of women's organizations]. *Voprosy Istorii KPSS [USSR] 1969 (9): 68-77.* Describes the history and development of Soviet women's organizations, which were founded in 1919 as a part of the Communist Party apparatus.

180. Löwenhardt, John. *The Soviet Politburo.* Clark, Dymphna, transl. New York: St. Martin's, 1982. 151 pp.

181. Löwenthal, Richard. THE LIMITS OF INTRA-BLOC PLURALISM: THE CHANGING THRESHOLD OF SOVIET INTERVENTION. *Int. J. [Canada] 1982 37(2): 263-284.* During the Stalin era Soviet bloc states at first enjoyed a degree of autonomy, only to be forced into uniformity as Soviet fears of Titoism and the Marshall Plan increased. Khrushchev tolerated the growth of autonomy and undermined Soviet authority by attacking Stalin. The Sino-Soviet split led to further autonomy for bloc countries. Yet this autonomy has always been kept within limits as witnessed in the 1968 intervention in Czechoslovakia and the imposition of martial law in Poland. J. Powell

182. Lund, Caroline. COMMUNIST PARTY APPALLED BY SEXUAL POLITICS. *Int. Socialist Rev. 1971 32(3): 33-37.* Criticizes the review by Communist Party spokeswoman Carmen Ristorucci in the January 1971 issue of *Political Affairs* of Kate Millett's *Sexual Politics* (1970), praising Millett's attack on the family as the oppressive economic unit of society, her criticism of women's position in the USSR in the 1940's, and the relation between the women's and blacks' liberation movements of the 1960's.

183. L'vova, K. F. VOZRASTANIE ROLI SOVETSKIKH PROFSOIUZOV V PERIOD RAZVERNUTOGO STROITEL'STVA KOMMUNIZMA [Growing role of Soviet trade unions in the era of full-scale construction of communism]. *Vestnik Leningradskogo U.: Seriia Istorii, Iazyka i Literatury [USSR] 1962 17(14): 20-33.* Discusses V. I. Lenin's trade union principles and their violation during Joseph Stalin's rule from the 1930's and the resurgence of trade unionism (1957-61) under Nikita S. Khrushchev. Following the 20th Communist Party Congress, the trade unions were reorganized, their cadres reduced and purged of bureaucratic elements, and their economic, social, administrative, and educational functions enlarged. 55 notes. N. Frenkley

184. Lynch, G. J.; Karaska, J. J.; and Hamilton, F. E. I. OTSENKA KONTSEPTSII TERRITORIAL'NO-PROIZVODSTVENNOGO KOMPLEKSA, RAZRABOTANNOI V SOVETSKOM SOIUZE [An evaluation of the concept, pioneered in the Soviet Union, of the territorial-industrial complex]. *Izvestiia Sibirskogo Otdeleniia Akademii Nauk SSSR. Seriia Obshchestvennykh Nauk [USSR] 1981 (2): 26-33.* Territorial industrial complexes are areas of production covering a part or the whole of more than one Soviet republic or autonomous region. Local authorities must therefore coordinate financial, political and social policies on a supraregional or suprarepublic basis to ensure success. The Soviet Communist Party developed the concept after 1945 and emphasized their importance since 1971. Products, labor, and specialities can be used locally with minimal bureaucracy, saving time and transportation costs. A. J. Evans

185. Mackintosh, Malcolm. SOLDIERS OF THE PARTY. *Military Rev. 1963 43(5): 27-31.* Chronicles the physical, administrative, and ideological incorporation of the military into the Communist Party of the USSR, 1917-58.

186. Maher, Janet E. THE SOCIAL COMPOSITION OF WOMEN DEPUTIES IN SOVIET ELECTIVE POLITICS: A PRELIMINARY ANALYSIS OF OFFICIAL BIOGRAPHIES. Yedlin, Tova, ed. *Women in Eastern Europe and the Soviet Union* (New York: Praeger, 1980): 185-211. Examines patterns of recruitment of male and female deputies. Although fewer women are recruited than men, evidence suggests that a selection process favoring women may be in effect. Relative to men, women deputies are younger, have less formal education, are less frequently engaged in nonmanual occupations, and are less likely to have affiliations with the Communist Party. 10 tables, 18 notes.

187. Malov, Iu. K. KRITIKA BURZHUAZNYKH FAL'SIFIKATSII ROLI KPSS V POLITICHESKOI SISTEME SOTSIALISTICHESKOGO OBSHCHESTVA [The criticism in bourgeois falsification on the role of the CPSU in the political system of socialist society]. *Voprosy Istorii KPSS [USSR] 1978 (5): 78-89.* A response to Western critics who accuse the Communist Party of creating in the USSR a totalitarian regime, an "administrative society," or a one-party system based historically on the elimination of all other political parties. These theories ignore the necessity of the Party's leadership as a prerequisite for the development of communism, the importance of the Soviet constitution, and the active role of such organizations as the soviets, trade unions, and cooperatives. These critics refuse to recognize that after the October Revolution

the Menshevik Party and Left Socialist Revolutionaries opposed the interests of the Soviet peoples. Based on a critique of recent Western historiography of the Soviet political system; 37 notes.
L. E. Holmes

188. Malov, Iu. K. REGULIROVANIE ROSTA I SOSTAVA KPSS V TRAKTOVKE "SOVETOLOGOV" [The control over the growth and composition of the Soviet Communist Party in the interpretation of Sovietologists]. *Voprosy Istorii KPSS [USSR] 1976 (6): 69-80.* Attacks Western writing about the development of the Soviet Communist Party membership and includes statistics to rebut false claims.

189. Marcou, Lilly. *L'Internationale après Staline* [The International after Stalin]. Paris: Bernard Grasset, 1979. 316 pp.

190. Marcou, Lilly, ed. *L'U.R.S.S.: Vue de Gauche* [USSR: view from the Left]. (Politique d'Aujourd'hui series.) Paris: Pr. U. de France, 1982. 296 pp.

191. Mark, Jonathan Greenfield. "The Private Zone: A Development in Soviet Political Communication since Stalin." U. of Oklahoma 1981. 247 pp. *DAI 1982 42(7): 3286-3287-A.* 8129403

192. McAuley, Mary. THE HUNTING OF THE HIERARCHY: RSFSR OBKOM FIRST SECRETARIES AND THE CENTRAL COMMITTEE. *Soviet Studies [Great Britain] 1974 26(4): 473-501.* Recent attempts have been made to suggest a hierarchy within the total group of first secretaries of the Communist Party regional committees *(obkoms)* in the Russian Soviet Federated Socialist Republic. The author studies the Party congresses for 1956, 1961, 1966, and 1971, and other sources of data on the regions, to quantitatively analyze and test the hypothesis that membership in the Party Central Committee is awarded to important *obkom* first secretaries. Results show that size of the region's population, Party, and economic importance is one significant criterion for promotion to the Central Committee, 1956-71. Other factors are relevant, however, and new criteria may emerge. 4 tables, 20 notes, appendix.
D. H. Murdoch

193. McAuley, Mary. PARTY RECRUITMENT AND THE NATIONALITIES IN THE USSR: A STUDY IN CENTRE-REPUBLICAN RELATIONSHIPS. *British J. of Pol. Sci. [Great Britain] 1980 10(4): 461-487.* Examines the relationship in the USSR between central Party authorities and the Republican Party organizations by looking at the recruitment of the different nationalities between the years 1959 and 1979.

194. McNeal, Robert H. THE REVIVAL OF SOVIET ANTI-TROTSKYISM. *Studies in Comparative Communism 1977 10(1-2): 5-17.* Trotskyism has again become one of the chief enemies of Marxism-Leninism. Trotskyism is now considered an ideology of the left, a version of "ultraleftism" which underestimates the revolutionary role of the peasantry and aids the growth of fascism. However, the Soviets make vague instead of specific accusations and do not even mention the "show trials." Maoism is associated with Trotskyism and Trotskyism is also seen as influencing the New Left. Thus the Soviets see Trotskyism as more revolutionary than orthodox communism. 27 notes, biblio. D. Balmuth

195. McNeal, Robert H. RUDOLF SCHLESINGER'S HISTORY OF THE C. P. S. U. *Soviet Studies [Great Britain] 1978 30(2): 270-274.* Rudolf Schlesinger's *History of the Communist Party of the USSR, Past and Present* (1977) has no particular bias. There is a recognition of Joseph Stalin's terror, but the basic ethical argument is utilitarian: that the CPSU will ultimately provide the greatest good for the greatest number, and that so far it has generally been a force for good. Schlesinger's unique interpretation of the Party does not conform to traditional stereotypes.

196. Medvedev, M. F. and Ustinov, V. M. OBZOR LITERATURY PO ISTORII PARTIINYKH ORGANIZATSII SREDNEI AZII I KAZAKHSTANA [Survey of literature on the history of Party organizations of Central Asia and Kazakhstan]. *Voprosy Istorii KPSS [USSR] 1971 (11): 102-109.*

197. Medvedev, Roy. THE DEATH OF THE "CHIEF IDEOLOGUE." *New Left Rev. [Great Britain] 1982 (136): 55-65.* Discusses the political career of the USSR's "chief ideologue," Mikhail Suslov (1902-82), a member of the Communist Party Central Committee since 1939.

198. Mehnert, Klaus. IDEOLOGISCHER KRIEG TROTZ KOEXISTENZ, SAGT MOSKAU [Ideological warfare despite coexistence, proclaims Moscow]. *Osteuropa [West Germany] 1973 23(1): 1-8.* Soviet leaders caution Communists to resist such concepts as convergence of systems, polycentrism, consumer society, alienation, and "the end of ideology" which are dangerous importations from the West. Religion and nationalism are also alien imports, as is "revisionism." Since freedom and prosperity remain outstanding Western attractions among Soviet citizens, the West can strengthen its ideological influence by solving its social proglems. 15 notes.
R. E. Weltsch

199. Mehnert, Klaus. MOSKAU UND DIE NEUE LINKE [Moscow and the New Left]. *Osteuropa [West Germany] 1973 23(9): 645-756.* Neither the Marxist classics nor Party ideology prepared the USSR for the student movements of the 1960's in the United States and elsewhere. Soviet discussions of New Left and other American social criticism have become more frequent and perceptive, but the Communist Party keeps them channeled and imposes its own terms: The New "Left" lacks authenticity and is dangerous because of its rejection of Soviet communism; the intelligentsia, which carries the movement, has no standing as a social class; Herbert Marcuse, its prophet, errs in seeing the Third World, not the USSR, as the coming revolutionary force. As the USSR is moving toward a consumer society, it shows signs of the same stress, alienation and ennui that have given rise to the New Left in the West. Based on a systematic survey of the Soviet periodical press 1960-72; 236 notes, additional documentation, biblio.
R. E. Weltsch

200. Meissner, Boris. DER ENTSCHEIDUNGSPROZESS IN DER KREML-FÜHRUNG UND DIE ROLLE DER PARTEIBÜROKRATIE. DER WANDEL IN DER HERRSCHAFTSSTRUKTUR DER SOWJETUNION UND IM ENTSCHEIDUNGSMECHANISMUS DER KREML-FÜHRUNG [Decisionmaking in the Kremlin leadership and the role of the Party bureaucracy. Changes in the Soviet power structure and in the decisionmaking mechanism of the Kremlin leadership]. *Osteuropa [West Germany] 1975 25(2): 86-103; (3): 165-180.* Part I. (1945-64). Stalin's one-man rule in the USSR was followed by an uneasy balance between state functionaries and Communist Party leaders. Nikita Khrushchev succeeded once more in concentrating state and Party functions in his hands, but he neglected to maintain the necessary contact with the competing groups within the power elite. By reaching out to a wider constituency he lost consensus and control at the center. Part II. (1965-74). After Khrushchev's fall, as Party Secretary trying to enlarge his hold on state functions. Though the elite has become more differentiated, the oligarchical top-level bureaucracy heavily dominates policymaking at the expense of the leading economic-technical and scientific-cultural personnel. Table, 85 notes. R. E. Weltsch

201. Meissner, Boris. DER FÜHRUNGSWECHSEL IM KREML [Change of leadership in the Kremlin]. *Osteuropa [West Germany] 1983 33(3-4): 169-182.* Describes the history of the Soviet Communist Party and the power politics that surrounded the anticipated departure of Leonid Brezhnev from office, as well as developments in the Party after his death.

202. Meissner, Boris. DIE ERGEBNISSE DES XXV. PARTEIKONGRESSES DER KOMMUNISTISCHEN PARTEI DER SOWJETUNION [The results of the 25th Party Congress of the Communist Party of the Soviet Union]. *Europa Archiv [West Germany] 1976 31(9): 291-302.* Reviewing the results of the 25th Communist Party Congress, held during 1976, the author concludes that a change in leadership in the Kremlin during the next few years is unavoidable regardless of the state of Brezhnev's health.

203. Meissner, Boris. NEUE DATEN ZUR SOZIALEN STRUKTUR DER KPDSU [New data on the social structure of the Communist Party of the Soviet Union]. *Osteuropa [West Germany] 1979 29(9): 709-730.* Since 1927 the Communist Party of the Soviet Union went through major social changes, in its age structure, educational composition, and national ethnic structures.

204. Mel'nikov, Iu. XXVI S'EZD KPSS I SOTSIALISTICHESKOE SOREVNOVANIE V SOVETSKIKH VOORUZHENNYKH SILAKH [The 26th Congress of the Communist Party of the Soviet Union and socialist competition in the Soviet armed forces]. *Voenno-Istoricheskii Zhurnal [USSR] 1981 23(7): 3-11.* The 26th Party Congress stressed socialist competition as a clear manifestation of the new relationship of Soviet peoples to labor. The Party and its organs will allow no shortcomings in labor discipline. Lenin instituted socialist competition. Defense Minister D. F. Ustinov supports socialist competition, which will be maximized in the armed forces. It has been used in three stages in the past: from 1917-1930's, 1930's-50's and 1950's-80's. Based on Soviet printed sources and archives; 23 notes. P. R. Taylor

205. Mel'shin, A. ZA LENINYM, ZA BOL'SHEVIKAMI [In the footsteps of V. I. Lenin and the Bolsheviks]. *Morskoi Sbornik [USSR] 1982 (4): 57-62.* Describes the victory of Communist forces in the Russian Far East in the revolution and civil war and subsequent Soviet interest in the region development there. 12 notes.

206. Metelitsa, L. V. OBSHCHEE I OSOBENNOE V ISTORICHESKOM OPYTE KPSS PO RAZRESHENIIU NATSIONAL'NOGO VOPROSA V SSSR [The general and the particular in the historical experience of the CPSU in resolving the nationalities question in the USSR]. *Voprosy Istorii KPSS [USSR] 1972 (11): 34-47.* Traces the realization of Lenin's principles in building a multinational state through liquidating national antagonisms by insuring full sovereignty and equal rights for all nationalities, 1917-70.

207. Miasnikov, A. S. LENINSKII PRINTSIP PARTIINOSTI LITERATURI I ISKUSSTVA [The Leninist principle of the Party-orientation of literature and art]. *Voprosy Istorii KPSS [USSR] 1963 (8): 41-53.* Outlines V. I. Lenin's ideas on the relationship between the Communist Party, literature, and art, and argues that subsequent Soviet governments have honored his teaching, 1905-63.

208. Mickiewicz, Ellen. REGIONAL SOCIAL CLASS RECRUITMENT IN THE CPSU: INDICATORS OF DECENTRALIZATION, POWER, AND POLICY. *Soviet Union 1978 5(1): 101-125.* Identifies long- and short-term trends in social class and occupational recruitment for regional Party membership in the USSR, 1921-73. Soviet society is divided into working, peasant, and white collar classes. The methodology of this study includes analysis of the tendency to deliberately equate the social composition of the regional Party with the regional population, the extent to which regional recruitment follows the national leadership's policies and directives, and the correlation between aggregate, national level Party recruitment policies and those in the regional organizations. Based on Communist Party membership data from various regions in the USSR; 9 tables in text, 30 notes, appendix.

H. S. Shields

209. Mickiewicz, Ellen. REGIONAL VARIATION IN FEMALE RECRUITMENT AND ADVANCEMENT IN THE COMMUNIST PARTY OF THE SOVIET UNION. *Slavic Rev. 1977 36(3): 441-454.* It is very difficult to get data that will give an accurate idea of the relative mobility of women into full membership in the Communist Party of the USSR. Researchers must consider changes in policy under Stalin, Khrushchev, and Brezhnev, in addition to variations by region. The regional variations may reflect recording and reporting variations, but the opportunities and expectations of women can be understood only on a regional basis. 5 tables, 25 notes.

R. V. Ritter

210. Mies, Herbert. THE OCTOBER REVOLUTION AND OUR TIME. *World Marxist Rev. 1975 18(11): 3-13.* Hails the anniversary of the October Revolution of 1917 in the light of Marxist progress, notably that of the German Communist Party.

211. Mikeshin, N. P. TROTSKIZM NA VOORUZHENII IMPERIALISTICHESKOI PROPAGANDY [Trotskyism as an arm of imperialist propaganda]. *Voprosy Istorii KPSS [USSR] 1965 (12): 42-52.* Demonstrates how imperialist propaganda agents in the United States, and in Britain and elsewhere in Europe use the false doctrines of Trotskyism to attack the magnificent achievement of Soviet socialism.

212. Miller, John H. CADRES POLICY IN NATIONALITY AREAS: RECRUITMENT OF CPSU FIRST AND SECOND SECRETARIES IN NON-RUSSIAN REPUBLICS OF THE USSR. *Soviet Studies [Great Britain] 1977 29(1): 3-36.* The systematic and highly centralized policy on personnel deployment in the USSR is particularly important in the government of ethnic minority areas. Examination of the political biographies of Party first and second secretaries in union republics and autonomous republics, 1954-76, permits analysis of the functions of these posts, recruitment and duration of service, previous office held, and subsequent careers of the incumbents. The appointment of a Russian and a native of the local nationality is a practice designed to provide a system of mutual checks. The Russian presence is political; appointees are not drawn from local settler communities and have rapid turnover. Since 1953 the pattern of native first secretary and Russian second secretary in charge of cadres has emerged. The career background of Russians tends to be in production, that of natives in media and communications. Russians are moved frequently but natives are almost always employed in their home areas; there is some evidence for "a profession of nationality affairs specialists based on the Central Committee Cadres Department." 9 tables, 76 notes, appendix.

D. H. Murdoch

213. Mills, Richard M. THE SOVIET LEADERSHIP PROBLEM. *World Pol. 1981 33(4): 590-613.* Analyzes the question of leadership in the USSR's political system, the roles and functions of the top leaders within the collective leadership, and the problematic relationship of the leadership of the Communist Party elite and other functional elites in adopting and implementing major policies calculated to make more efficient the operation of highly bureaucratized administrative structures. There is a reciprocal impact of these issues on public attitudes and motivations as both are perceived by the leadership. The conflict between the requirements of modernization and the imperatives of the political culture is discussed, and matters for the research agenda are noted. J/S

214. Minagawa, Shugo. REGIONAL FIRST SECRETARIES IN SOVIET PARLIAMENTARY COMMITTEES. *Soviet Union 1979 6(1): 1-40.* Regional first secretaries play a prominent role in the USSR Federal Supreme Soviet standing committees, as well as other Supreme Soviet organs. By the eighth convocation of the Supreme Soviet, 1970-74, 66% of the deputies were members of these committees. Since 1965, regional first secretaries enjoyed a greatly disproportionate representation in the standing committees. The author reviews the political role and activities of the regional first secretaries in four areas: competition for resources and position, establishment of authority relations and roles, formalization of functional values of committee operations, and attempts to establish identity. Regional first secretaries were of key importance in Supreme Soviet activities and mobilized economic administrative activities. 7 tables, 43 notes, 2 appendixes. H. S. Shields

215. Mirovitski, A. I. and Raibov, K. M. ISSLEDOVANIE PO ISTORII PARTIINOI PROGRAMMY [Research on the history of the Party program]. *Voprosy Istorii KPSS [USSR] 1963 (10): 129-132.* Examines the three programs of the Soviet Communist Party and stresses their importance for historians and propagandists, 1903-63.

216. Mishakov, V. P. VOPROSY DVIZHENIIA ZA KOMMUNISTICHESKOE OTNOSHENIE K TRUDU V SOVETSKOI ISTORIOGRAFII [Questions of the movement for a Communist at-

titude to labor in Soviet historiography]. *Istoriia SSSR [USSR] 1982 (4): 71-87.* The Communist Party in the Soviet Union has constantly striven to develop more responsible attitudes to labor in the working class. The article discusses recent moves to heighten Communist awareness as expressed in published documents. From 1962 to 1965 around 300 books and brochures were printed calling on people to join the movement actively. In the 1970's the numbers of inventors and rationalizers of production methods grew steadily as the masses responded to the Party's call for a Communist work ethic. Based on published sources; 72 notes. D. N. Collins

217. Mitiaeva, O. I. KOMMUNISTICHESKAIA PARTIIA—ORGANIZATOR KUL'TURNO-PROSVETITEL'NOI RABOTY SREDI KREST'IANSTVA V GODY KOLLEKTIVIZATSII [The Communist Party, organizer of cultural educational work among the peasantry in the years of collectivization]. *Voprosy Istorii KPSS [USSR] 1981 (3): 68-78.* The general and political education of the peasants had always been a Soviet priority, and after the 1917 revolution village soviets introduced literacy classes into the villages. By 1930 compulsory education was a reality, and collectivization brought libraries and cinemas to an ever more enlightened peasantry, which enthusiastically endorsed the 1936 constitution. The Party's leading role is seen in its encouragement of political consciousness, the harnessing of socialist development to the improvement of village life, and the importance of agriculture in Soviet policy. 83 notes. A. J. Evans

218. Molchanov, I. G. DOKTORSKIE DISSERTATSII PO ISTORII KPSS V 1963 GODU [Doctoral dissertations for 1963 on the history of the Soviet Communist Party]. *Voprosy Istorii KPSS [USSR] 1964 (3): 149-158.* A review of main conclusions of some Soviet dissertations of 1963 on the history of the Party followed by a list of about 200 such dissertations.

219. Moliboshko, V. A. NESOSTOIATEL'NOST' BURZHUAZNYKH FAL'SIFIKATSII ROLI KRITIKI I SAMOKRITIKI V DEIATEL'NOSTI KPSS [The failure of bourgeois falsification of the role of criticism and self-criticism in the activity of the CPSU]. *Voprosy Istorii KPSS [USSR] 1977 (6): 68-82.* Historians in the West assert that the Communist Party in the USSR has acted as a conservative bureaucratic force which does not permit genuine freedom of discussion and criticism. Such views ignore the essence of V. I. Lenin's democratic centralism; the necessity of forbidding destructive criticism and fractions; the Party's criticism of its own policies such as collectivization in 1931 or later the cult of personality; and the Party's encouragement of criticism from Party and non-Party members alike. Based on recent Western secondary publications, published Party documents, and Lenin's *Collected Works;* 68 notes. L. E. Holmes

220. Monin, M. V. I. LENIN, KPSS O VOENNO-POLITICHESKOM SOTRUDNICHESTVE BRATSKIKH SOTSIALISTICHESKIKH STRAN [V. I. Lenin and the Communist Party of the Soviet Union on the military and political cooperation of fraternal socialist countries]. *Voenno-Istoricheskii Zhurnal [USSR] 1981 23(5): 3-11.* For 26 years the Warsaw Pact has successfully defended the revolutionary struggle of the workers for friendship, peace, and security in Europe, having arisen as a defense against the imperialist NATO organization formed in 1949 and led by the United States. In the military union of European socialist countries, the Soviet Communist Party and other Marxist-Leninist parties are guided by the ideas of V. I. Lenin. The politics of NATO have become increasingly hostile to the Warsaw Pact, as is shown by the decision to base American missiles in Western Europe, the Carter Doctrine, Reagan's anti-Soviet policies, and US cooperation with Peking, so that Warsaw Pact maintenance of peace with readiness for defense is vital. Based on the works of Lenin, Warsaw Pact Organization documents, and newspaper articles; 24 notes. L. Smith

221. Morgunov, V. Ia. OB OPYTE PARTII PO PRAVLENIIU RUKOVODIASHCHIKH KADROV K AGITATSIONNO-MASSOVOI RABOTE V PERVYE GODY SOVETSKOI VLASTI [On the Party's experience in drawing leading cadres into mass agitational work in the first years of Soviet power]. *Voprosy Istorii KPSS [USSR] 1980 (12): 37-49.* Discusses how high-ranking Bolshevik Party activists were called into the propaganda and agitation effort during the first years after the seizure of power in 1917. Much of the material is drawn from Moscow Province, but attention is also given to the Volga and the Northwest. Agitprop trains traveled great distances throughout the Russian Republic. Elsewhere wagon trains crossed the steppes spreading literature and speeches. A postscript details the vast extent of agitational work in the 1970's. Based on archive materials in the Moscow Party Archive (fond 3), PASO (fond 594), and on press sources; 88 notes. D. N. Collins

222. Morhaienko, O. P. ZHYTTIA, HIDNE KOMUNISTA: DO 90-RICHCHIA Z DNIA NARODZHENNIA A. V. MOKROUSOVA [A life worthy of a communist: the 90th anniversary of the birth of A. V. Mokrousov]. *Ukrains'kyi Istorychnyi Zhurnal [USSR] 1977 (5): 129-131.* Describes the life and work of the prominent Crimean activist whose pseudonym was SAVIN.

223. Moses, Joel C. THE IMPACT OF *NOMENKLATURA* IN SOVIET REGIONAL ELITE RECRUITMENT. *Soviet Union 1981 8(1): 62-102.* Communist Party Regional Committee Bureau (OBKOM) leaders can be divided into agriculture, industrial, ideological, cadre, and mixed generalist specialties. These career types are important in understanding the *nomenklatura* process. The careers of 614 OBKOM members are examined by statistical profiles according to regional and geographical origins, variations in career patterns 1953-79, Party/OBKOM tenure, and political mobility. The distinct career specializations marking local Soviet cadres are a determining factor in their future positions and tenure. Rural or urban career origin is also important. As a result, these cadres may come to identify with their specialist subgroups rather than polarize along more traditional ideological, ethnic, generational, or factional lines. 40 notes, 16 tables. H. S. Shields

224. Mosolov, V. G. VERNYI SYN PARTII [A true son of the Party]. *Voprosy Istorii KPSS [USSR] 1984 (2): 148-151.* A conference was held at the Institute of Marxism-Leninism in Moscow in November 1983 to mark the 80th anniversary of the birth of Nikolai A. Voznesenski (1903-50). Voznesenski was an important official in the Communist Party and state economic apparatus. His early death prevented the appearance of his magnum opus on Communist political economy. D. N. Collins

225. Musaev, A. M. OPYT KPSS V SOVERSHENSTVOVANII STRUKTURY SEL'SKIKH PARTIINYKH ORGANIZATSII [The experience of the CPSU in perfecting the structure of rural Party organizations]. *Voprosy Istorii KPSS [USSR] 1979 (7): 47-58.* Surveys the organization, growth, and responsibilities of the Communist Party in rural areas of the Soviet Union from 1919 to 1979. With collectivization, rural Party cells were created on the collective farms. Transfer of Party members during the early 1950's strengthened these cells. Since then, Party committees appeared in collective farms with many smaller Party units organized within a single collective. Recent integration of industry and agriculture has led to a number of changes in order to coordinate the work of rural and urban Party organizations in a given area. Based on published documents and on recent periodical literature; 38 notes. L. E. Holmes

226. Mzhavanadze, V. P. NEKOTORYE VOPROSY IDEOLOGICHESKOI RABOTY KOMPARTII GRUZII [Ideological work by the Georgian Communist Party]. *Voprosy Istorii KPSS [USSR] 1961 (2): 28-42.* Surveys the history of Marxist thought in Georgia since the 1890's and the ideological and cultural leadership given by the Georgian Communist Party in the Soviet period.

227. Nachinkin, N. POLITICHESKIE ORGANY I IKH ROL' V STROITEL'STVE I UKREPLENII SOVETSKIKH VOORUZHENNYKH SIL [The political organs and their role in the construction and strengthening of the Soviet Armed Forces]. *Voenno-Istoricheskii Zhurnal [USSR] 1969 (5): 18-28.* The creation of a regular army and draft increased the rural army contingent, and made widespread political education in the army a must. The decree of the Central Committee dated 25 October 1918 described the role and place of the Party organizations in the military. The Institute of

Military Commissars was created in 1918 for the purpose of securing the Communist Party a leading role in the army. In the period between the world wars a great deal was done in improving the political and moral outlook of army personnel.The army political staff was trained in the military academies and military political schools. During the war years a restructuring of the army political organs took place and the Central Political Administration of the Red Army was formed, headed by the secretary of the Central Committee. In the postwar period, the Central Committee of the CPSU continued to oversee the political work in the armed forces. Primary sources; 9 notes. L. Kalinowski

228. Naik, J. A. *Russia and the Communist Countries.* Atlantic Highlands, N.J.: Humanities, 1980. 367 pp.

229. Nikolaev, I. I. DEIATEL'NOST' KPSS PO IDEINO-TEORETICHESKOI PODGOTOVKE RUKOVODIASHCHIKH KADROV [The Soviet Communist Party's activity in the ideological-theoretical preparation of leading cadres]. *Voprosy Istorii KPSS [USSR] 1982 (12): 98-106.* Expounds the Party's system for assuring the political maturity of its cadres, stressing 1) the organization and the history of the Party's own study institutions; 2) the founding in 1978 of the Academy of Social Sciences, attached to the Central Committee of the CPSU, as the leading center for the preparation of all Party and Soviet ideological cadres; 3) the establishment since 1967-68 of permanent courses for the training of higher cadres, with the aim of raising the qualifications of Party and Soviet workers; 4) the Party's general system of education, with its universities of Marxism-Leninism, schools for the Party-economic activists, permanent seminars, periodic conferences, etc. F. A. K. Yasamee

230. Nikolaev, N. I. V. I. LENIN, KPSS O PODBORE I VYDVIZHENII RUKOVODIASHCHIKH KADROV [V. I. Lenin and the Soviet Communist Party on selection and promotion of cadres]. *Voprosy Istorii KPSS [USSR] 1984 (6): 101-111.* Discusses the Leninist principle of selection of Party cadres as developed in the USSR. Systematic recruiting work, first begun in 1928-29, produced a type of politically and socially motivated Party worker, born organizer and community leader. There is a need to involve more women cadres at higher levels. 33 notes. M. Hernas

231. Nurullin, R. A. NAUCHNO-PRAKTICHESKAIA KONFERENTSIIA V SAMARKANDE [A scholarly and practical conference in Samarkand]. *Voprosy Istorii KPSS [USSR] 1979 (1): 155-156.* Summarizes papers and the work of four sections at a conference on the strengthening and perfecting of Party leadership of socialist competition organized by the Party's Samarkand Regional Committee and the Institute of Party History of the Uzbek Communist Party. L. E. Holmes

232. Nusupbekov, A. N. and Ustinov, V. V. KNIGA PO ISTORII KOMPARTII KAZAKHSTANA [A book on the history of the Communist Party of Kazakhstan]. *Voprosy Istorii KPSS [USSR] 1963 (10): 124-129.* Describes the economic development of Kazakhstan since the Revolution, 1917-63, showing how industrialization and collectivization have affected the area.

233. Oìnas, Felix J. THE POLITICAL USES AND THEMES OF FOLKLORE IN THE SOVIET UNION. *J. of the Folklore Inst. 1975 12(2/3): 157-175.* Discusses the Communist Party's political use of folklore research in the USSR, 1920's-50's, including folk songs, poems, and propaganda.

234. Oleinikov, V. E. O PARTIINOM RUKOVODSTVE PROMYSHLENNYM OSVOENIEM NOVYKH RAIONOV [On the Party leadership of industrial development in new regions]. *Voprosy Istorii KPSS [USSR] 1981 (11): 19-32.*

235. Ol'sevich, Iu. Ia. EKONOMICHESKII KURS KPSS I BANKROTSTVO EGO BURZHUAZNYKH KRITIKOV [The economic policy of the Communist Party of the Soviet Union (CPSU) and the bankruptcy of its bourgeois critics]. *Voprosy Istorii KPSS [USSR] 1975 (10): 70-83.* Presents arguments and information to reject interpretations of Western sovietologists regarding the Soviet economy. Heavy industry has not developed at the expense of improvement of the general welfare; economic growth has not produced social differentiation; the convergence theory is mistaken; planning and the Party's leadership have contributed to greater industrial production; and the Soviet centralized economy has made substantial technological progress possible. Based on recent Western studies of the Soviet economy and on Soviet periodical literature; 54 notes. L. E. Holmes

236. Orlik, I. I. SSSR I VOZNOKNOVENIE MEZHDUNARODNYKH OTNOSHENII NOVOGO TIPA [The USSR and formation of a new type of international relations]. *Istoriia SSSR [USSR] 1973 (5): 17-32.* Describes how Western writers try to discredit and falsify Soviet foreign policy. A new type of international relations has been emerging among socialist states, based on the end of capitalist exploitation and the victory of new production relations of mutual trust, aid, and cooperation which are characteristic of socialism. The author describes the Soviet liberation of Eastern Europe from fascism and the subsequent good relations established between the USSR and Eastern Europe. He also discusses how the Soviet Union helped China in its revolution. The formation of the new type of international relations has been a long and complex historical process. The author describes Soviet aid to various liberation struggles and opposes the imperialist policies of war, aggression, and conquest. 50 notes. L. Kalinowski

237. Ovcharenko, N. E. IZ ISTORII BOR'BY KPSS PROTIV PRAVOGO I "LEVOGO" OPPORTUNIZMA [The struggle of the CPSU against Right and "Left" opportunism]. *Voprosy Istorii KPSS [USSR] 1978 (7): 109-120.* A survey of the 1) significance of the Communist Party's struggle against all forms of opportunism; 2) the fundamental stages of the Party's efforts in Russia and the Soviet Union against opportunism, especially against Economism, Legal Marxism, Menshevism, and Trotskyism; and 3) the importance of the Party's attacks on such international forms of opportunism as social chauvinism, the convergence theory, and the alleged need for political pluralism. The Communist Party has successfully defended at home and abroad revolutionary theory and the unity of the Communist movement. Based on V. I. Lenin's *Collected Works,* published speeches and articles by Leonid Brezhnev, and secondary materials; 56 notes. L. E. Holmes

238. Palishko, V. K. ROL' KRYTYKY I SAMOKRYTYKY V DIIAL'NOSTI PARTORHANIZATSII [The role of criticism and self-criticism in the work of Party organization]. *Ukrains'kyi Istorychnyi Zhurnal [USSR] 1974 (5): 22-30.* Following Marx's beliefs, the Communist Party of the USSR has encouraged criticism in the period 1920-74. The author cites examples of how the Party deals with those who suppress or persecute critics.

239. Pashuto, V. T. ZA TVORCHESKOE SODRUZHESTVO ISTORIKOV I PISATELEI [Creative collaboration of historians and writers]. *Voprosy Istorii [USSR] 1973 (4): 191-195.* Communist Party unity has demanded the close cooperation of all scientists and artists, including historians and writers.

240. Pavliuk, P. I. and Klimko, M. S. KOORDINATSIIA: VAZHNEISHEE ZVENO ORGANIZATSII NAUCHNOI RAZRABOTKI ISTORII KPSS [Coordination: the most important link in organizing the scientific working out of the CPSU's history]. *Voprosy Istorii KPSS [USSR] 1965 (11): 156-158.* Discusses the role of the All-Union and Republican Councils for the coordination of scientific work on the history of the Communist Party of the Soviet Union, CPSU, which were set up on the advice of the Central Committee Secretariat.

241. Pavliv, Omelian. CHYSTKA U VIRMENS'KII KOMPARTII I SHCHO VONA ZAPOVIDAIE [A purge in the Armenian Communist Party and its consequences]. *Sučasnist [West Germany] 1975 (9): 79-81.* Analyzes the consequences of Karin Demirchan's appointment as First Secretary of the Armenian Communist Party, comparing the Armenian situation with the Ukrainian one.

242. Pavlov, V. I. VOZRASTANIE ROLI PARTII V STROITEL'STVE KOMMUNIZMA [Growing role of the Party in building communism]. *Prepodavanie Istorii v Shkole [USSR] 1962 17(1): 9-18.* Discusses the socioeconomic and ideological reasons for the steadily growing importance of the Communist Party in the historical development of the Soviet Union since 1917. The program of the 22d Communist Party Congress of 1961 reaffirms Party dedication to ideals of Marxism-Leninism, and shows the way for a practical resolution of contemporary problems. 7 notes.

N. Frenkley

243. Pegov, A. M. 60 JAHRE ARCHIVWESEN DER USSR [Sixty years of archives in the USSR]. *Archivmitteilungen [East Germany] 1978 28(4): 121-127.* Discusses the organization and centralization of the Soviet archives from the decree of 1 June 1918 to their subordination to the Council of Ministers of the USSR in 1960. The archives preserve the history of the USSR and the Communist Party since the October Revolution.

244. Perepelov, Leonid. SOVIET SOCIETY: CHANGES IN THE SOCIO-CLASS STRUCTURE. *Co-existence [Great Britain] 1974 11(2): 140-145.* Describes the changes in the USSR's class structure that resulted from economic development directed by the Communist Party between 1917 and 1973.

245. Perevedentsev, V. I. VOSPROIZVODSTVO NASELENIIA I SEM'IA [Reproducing the population and the family]. *Sotsiologicheskie Issledovaniia [USSR] 1982 (2): 80-88.* After the remarkable increase during the preceding 60 years, the demographic situation in the USSR changed dramatically from 1960 to 1980; the program established by the 26th Party Congress called for strengthening the moral influence of communism on family and marriage.

246. Petrenko, V. S. PIDNESENNIA KOLHOSPNOHO VYROBNYTSTVA UKRAINSKOI RSR V UMOVAKH ROZVYNUTOHO SOTSIALISTYCHNOHO SUSPILSTVA, 1959-1973 [The upsurge of collective farm production in the Ukrainian SSR under the conditions of developed socialism, 1959-73]. *Ukrains'kyi Istorychnyi Zhurnal [USSR] 1974 (5): 31-42.* In 1965 the Central Committee of the Communist Party of the USSR introduced more effective moral and material incentives for workers which increased agricultural production to new heights.

247. Petrov, I. I. KOMMUNISTICHESKAIA PARTIIA I OKHRANA SOVETSKIKH GRANITS [The Communist Party and the protection of Soviet borders]. *Voprosy Istorii KPSS [USSR] 1963 (5): 78-83.* Considers the role of Party propaganda and political work in the history of the Soviet border guards since the revolution.

248. Petrov, P. S. KPSS V BOR'BE ZA UPROCHENIE I RAZVITIE SOTSIALIZMA [The CPSU and its role in the consolidation and development of socialism]. *Voprosy Istorii KPSS [USSR] 1981 (1): 103-117.* Publishes guidelines for Soviet teachers on the topic of the activities of the Communist Party in the first 15 years after World War II. The Party could no longer refer to the parameters extant during the third, unfinished Five-Year Plan, faced as it was with devastation on a vast scale. Other factors for the Party to consider were the new territories absorbed into the union and the changing face of the political map of Eastern Europe. The main post-war task of the Party was to rebuild a shattered economy and the fourth Five-Year Plan was devised with this aim in mind. The fifth Five-Year Plan, 1951-55, witnessed a Party-inspired new challenge: the opening up of the virgin territories. 27 notes.

A. Brown

249. Pilotovich, S. A. SEKRETAR' TSK KPB-BOEVOI AVANGARD NARODA (K 50-LETIIU OBRAZOVANIIA KOMPARTII BELORUSSII) [The Secretary of the Central Committee of the Communist Party of Belorussia: the fighting vanguard of the people: the 50th anniversary of the formation of the Belorussian Communist Party]. *Voprosy Istorii KPSS [USSR] 1968 (12): 3-15.* Traces the history of the Belorussian Communist party over the 50 years of its existence and explains its importance for the Belorussian Soviet Republic.

250. Platkovski, V. V. TORZHESTVO LENINSKIKH PROGRAMMNYKH PRINTSIPOV PARTII [The triumph of the Party's Leninist programmatic principles]. *Voprosy Istorii KPSS [USSR] 1961 (4): 29-48.* Reviews the achievments of the Soviet Communist Party since its present political program was adopted in 1919 and the background to that program.

251. Plokhi, V. S. KOMSOMOL: VIRNYI POMICHNYK KOMUNISTYCHNOI PARTII [The Young Communist League: loyal helper of the Communist Party]. *Ukrains'kyi Istorychnyi Zhurnal [USSR] 1978 (10): 8-19.* Discusses the Young Communist League (Komsomol) on the 60th anniversary of its founding, demonstrating its role in implementing the Party's plans at all stages of the construction of Communism. Highlights the role of the Party and V. I. Lenin in strengthening the Komsomol. Traces the Komsomol's history, describes various conferences, and stresses its important work in war and peacetime. Primary sources; 15 notes.

V. A. Packer/S

252. Plysiuk, V. P. and Semkiv, O. I. ROZVYTOK KPRS LENINS'KYKH IDEI SHEFSTVA MISTA NAD SELOM [The development by the Soviet Communist Party of Lenin's idea of the patronage of a town over a village]. *Ukrains'kyi Istorychnyi Zhurnal [USSR] 1979 (12): 42-52.* In 1922 Lenin wrote to the Central Committee of the Communist Party in Moscow, suggesting that every town Communist Party organization adopt villages in its area to encourage regional cooperation. The idea spread and in recent years the town parties have sent not only technical help in the repair of tractors, provision of machinery for drainage and irrigation, but also hundreds of lecturers and ideological workers to explain the resolutions of Communist Party congresses. Based on Soviet Communist Party archives; 53 notes. H. Diuk

253. Pol'ova, N. A. PROPAHANDA KOMUNISTYCHNOIU PARTIEIU ZAKHIDNOI UKRAINY OSNOVNOHO ZAKONU KRAINY RAD [Propaganda by the Communist Party in the western Ukraine in support of the basic law of the USSR]. *Ukrains'kyi Istorychnyi Zhurnal [USSR] 1973 (1): 80-84.* Describes Party activities promoting the Soviet Union and its 1936 constitution.

254. Polozov, G. P. PARTIINOE RUKOVODSTVO DEIATEL'NOST'IU INTELLIGENTSII V GODY VELIKOI OTECHESTVENNOI VOINY (ISTORIOGRAFICHESKII OBZOR) [Party control of the work of the intelligentsia during World War II: a historiographical review]. *Voprosy Istorii KPSS [USSR] 1976 (9): 116-125.* Discusses increasing Communist Party influence over the work of the intelligentsia, 1941-76.

255. Pomazanov, S. I. SSSR I SOZDANIE TIAZHELOI INDUSTRII V STRANAKH SOTSIALISTICHESKOGO SODRUZHESTVA [The USSR and the creation of heavy industry in the countries of socialist cooperation]. *Voprosy Istorii [USSR] 1979 (3): 102-116.* Describes the important role played by the Soviet Union in developing heavy industry in communist countries. In the less developed countries, such as Bulgaria and Romania, Soviet help has consisted of materials and expertise. In the more developed countries, such as East Germany and Czechoslovakia, it has provided raw materials, and guided specialized development, such as shipbuilding in Poland. There have been successful joint projects such as the Darkhan industrial complex in Mongolia. Cuba has also been assisted. Cooperation within Comecon continues in the field of nuclear energy. 57 notes. B. Holland

256. Ponomaryov, B. N. ON THE THEORETICAL WORK OF THE CPSU IN THE 60 YEARS SINCE THE OCTOBER REVOLUTION. *World Marxist Rev. [Canada] 1977 20(9): 5-21.* Remaining loyal to the ideas and conclusions of the theory created by Marx, Engels, and Lenin, the Communist Party of the Soviet Union (CPSU) proceeds from the fact that Marxism is not a dogma but a guide, and has made great strides in such areas as the theory of the transitional period, analysis of economic processes, cultural revolution, perfecting Soviet socialist democracy, upholding national rights, banishing world war, and defining the relationship between détente and the class struggle.

257. Popadiuk, Roman. PARTY-MILITARY RELATIONS IN THE SOVIET UNION. *Ukrainian Q. 1976 32(4): 393-408.* Party-military relations in the USSR have passed through three eras. In the first period, 1918-53, the Party came to dominate the military with Stalin's military purge of 1937 marking the high point of his control. During World War II military prestige grew, so that after 1941 a transition phase was entered during which the military had to be treated more circumspectly. With Stalin's death the second stage, 1953-64, was entered. The political power of the military grew as they moved into positions in the government and Party hierarchy. After 1957 Khrushchev concentrated on limiting the growing independence of the military. Following Khrushchev the third stage, 1964 to the present, is characterized by a partnership between Party and military for mutual benefit. 23 notes.
K. N. T. Crowther

258. Pospelov, P. N. O ZADACHAKH NAUCHNO-ISSLEDOVATEL'SKOI RABOTY PO ISTORII PARTII V SVETE RESHENII XXII S'EZDA KPSS [The tasks of scientific research work on the history of the Party in the light of the decisions taken at the 22d Congress of the CPSU]. *Voprosy Istorii KPSS [USSR] 1962 (2): 9-25.* Reviews the current state of the history of the Soviet Communist Party, the incorrect interpretation of Party history promoted by Stalin, and the analysis of his decisions during World War II.

259. Pospelov, P. N. V. I. LENIN O GEGEMONII PROLETARIATA I O PARTII NOVOGO TIPA [V. I. Lenin on the hegemony of the proletariat and a new kind of party]. *Novaia i Noveishaia Istoriia [USSR] 1970 !(3): 8-17.* Describes the Marxist origins and the significance for world history of the formation of the Russian Communist Party under the leadership of V. I. Lenin, and outlines the Party's many unprecedented successes for the working class since 1917. 25 notes. L. Smith/S

260. Pospielovsky, Dmitry. SOME REMARKS ON THE CONTEMPORARY RUSSIAN NATIONALISM AND RELIGIOUS REVIVAL. *Canadian Review of Studies in Nationalism [Canada] 1984 11(1): 71-85.* Two forms of nationalism exist in the contemporary Soviet Union. One is a patriotism of the soil-bound and neo-Slavophile orientation, based primarily on the Russian Orthodox Church as institution and religion and on an appreciation of the Russian land and prerevolutionary history. The other is the national socialist, national-Bolshevism brand of nationalism cultivated by the government, which incorporates international communism with Russian patriotism. 47 notes. R. Aldrich

261. Povch, M. P. V. I. LENIN PRO TAKTYKU IEDYNOHO FRONTU, IAK ZASIB MOBILIZATSII MAS U BOROT'BI PROTY VLADY KAPITALU [V. I. Lenin on the tactics of a united front as a means of mobilizing the masses against the power of capital]. *Ukrains'kyi Istorychnyi Zhurnal [USSR] 1969 (1): 32-39.* Stresses the importance and universality of Lenin's ideas on the united front as a powerful mass weapon against capitalism and expoitation and discusses how his ideas have been demonstrated at various international Communist Party congresses since 1921.

262. Priezzhev, S. I. and Cherniavski, Ia. A. O SERII BROSHIUR *S'EZDY I KONFERENTSII KPSS* [The series of brochures: *The Congresses and Conferences of the CPSU*]. *Voprosy Istorii KPSS [USSR] 1962 (1): 179-184.* Discusses a recently reissued series of 36 historical brochures on the congresses and conferences of the Communist Party of the Soviet Union, *S'ezdy i konferentsii KPSS* (1955-61), finding that though they filled a gap in material available to the general reader, the series is in some respects inadequate.

263. Prokop, Myroslav. NASTUP NA DRUHII FRONT SAMOOBORONY NARODU [Attack on the second line of self-defense of the nation]. *Sučasnist [West Germany] 1973 (9): 93-105.* Discusses the differing Soviet interpretations of the history of the Ukrainian nation as determined by the nationalities policy of the Communist Party of the USSR, 1920-73.

264. Pykha, D. D. 50-RICHCHIA TSYVIL'NOI OBORONY SRSR [The 50th anniversary of the civil defense of the USSR]. *Ukrains'kyi Istorychnyi Zhurnal [USSR] 1982 (10): 142-145.* Celebrates 50 years of the Soviet military and discusses its development under the guidance and leadership of the Communist Party.
L. Djakowska

265. Radziejowski, Janusz; Himka, John-Paul, transl. ROMAN ROSDOLSKY: MAN, ACTIVIST AND SCHOLAR. *Sci. and Soc. 1978 42(2): 198-210.* An economic and political historian and analyst of Marxian thought, Roman Rosdolsky was a political activist during his earlier years in Europe. He supported Marxist revolution in a Ukrainian setting, in particular the cause of Ukrainian Communists to retain an ethnic identity rather than be submerged in Poland's Communist Party. He did, however, realize the need for collaboration with the Poles and thus opposed the intransigent nationalist stand of some fellow Ukrainian Communists. During the 1920's Rosdolsky became deeply involved in the polemics generated by the various attitudes toward Russian cultural influences held by sharply different Ukrainian Party factions. His works published before World War II reflect on nationalism, the peasant question, and the development of the thought of Marx and Engels. Based on personal observation. N. Lederer

266. Rakowska-Harmstone, Teresa. THE DIALECTICS OF NATIONALISM IN THE USSR. *Problems of Communism 1974 23(3): 1-22.* Examines the growth and development of an increasingly assertive ethnic nationalism among the non-Russian minorities of the USSR. This development is on a collision course with Communist Party policy, and the present leadership seems to lack a clear consensus on how to proceed. Such a circumstance will be increasingly disruptive to the existing political system. Based on primary and secondary sources; map, 3 tables, 2 figs., 70 notes.
J. M. Lauber

267. Ramazanova, B. R. DOKUMENTY O NERASTORZHIMOM BRATSTVE [Documents on an indissoluble brotherhood]. *Sovetskie Arkhivy [USSR] 1981 (6): 17-21.* Russian-Kazakh friendship had an important progressive influence on the Kazakh people. In particular the Russian proletariat under the guidance of the Communist Party had a powerful revolutionary influence on the development of Kazakhstan. Reviews documents in the archives of the Kazakh SSR supporting this thesis. Based on manuscript and published documents from the state archive of Kazakhstan.
D. H. Watson

268. Reiman, Pavel. O PRIMENENII OPYTA KPSS V KHODE STROITEL'STVA SOTSIALIZMA V STRANAKH VOSTOCHNOI I TSENTRAL'NOI EVROPY [The application of the experience of the CPSU while building socialism in the countries of Eastern and Central Europe]. *Voprosy Istorii KPSS [USSR] 1961 (5): 73-90.* Reviews ways in which the historical experience of the Soviet Communist Party has been applied to the construction of socialism in Eastern and Central Europe, 1948-60.

269. Reshetar, John S., Jr. ON RESOLUTIONS: SOVIET COMMUNIST PARTY HISTORY AND POLITICS AS REFLECTED IN OFFICIAL DOCUMENTS. *Slavic Rev. 1977 35(2): 321-325.* A review essay on *Resolutions and Decisions of the Communist Party of the Soviet Union,* 4 vols., Robert H. McNeal, general editor (U. of Toronto Pr., 1974). This Toronto edition is based on the standard Soviet collection, *Kommunisticheskaia Partiia Sovetskogo Soiuza v rezoliutsiiakh i resheniiakh s'ezdov, konferentsii i plenumov TsK (1898-1970),* 8th ed., 10 vols. (Moscow, 1970-72), but eliminates the trivia and includes important documents not in the Soviet edition. A fifth volume covering the Brezhnev period is in preparation. 6 notes. R. V. Ritter

270. Revutsky, Valerian. A SURVEY OF THE UKRAINIAN POST-WAR DRAMA. *Can. Slavonic Papers [Canada] 1972 14(2): 251-268.* Ukrainian drama after the war was controlled by the Communist Party's varying ideological interpretations. The brief existence of a patriotic drama (1944-46) was restricted in 1946-53. Official critics pointed to the insufficient number of Russian or Soviet non-Russian dramas in the Ukrainian theater repertoire. They

condemned non-Soviet dramas' lack of artistic value and denounced cosmopolitan tendencies. The late 1950's brought a lessening of controls, and many playwrights varied their subjects and style to those of the 1920's. Restrictions were reinitiated in 1965 with the celebration of the 50th anniversary of the Soviet Union (1967) and the Lenin centenary (1970). J/S

271. Rigby, T. H. POLITICAL PATRONAGE IN THE USSR FROM LENIN TO BREZHNEV. *Politics [Australia] 1983 18(1): 84-89.* Examines the advantage of friendship and loyalty among Party leaders in the Soviet Union.

272. Riishøj, Søren. FRA OKTOBERREVOLUTIONEN TIL DET UDVIKLEDE SOCIALISTISKE SAMFUND [From the October Revolution to the developed socialist society]. *Økonomi og Politik [Denmark] 1977 51(4): 341-354.* The 60th anniversary of the Russian Revolution recalled the original concepts of the Bolshevik uprising: democratic centralism and Communist Party leadership. Democracy is to be found within the economic and social structures; discussion and criticism are only possible within the Party. USSR historians and theorists have defended War Communism and NEP as necessary steps in the development of a socialist society in the light of capitalist threats. R. E. Lindgren/S

273. Rønneberg, Harald B. M. SOVJETSAMVELDETS EKPANSJON: TRUSELENS RETNING OG ANVENDELSEN AV SJØMILITAER MAKT [The expansion of the USSR: the direction of the threat and the use of sea power]. *Norsk Militaert Tidsskrift [Norway] 1973 143(8): 369-374.* The USSR's aim is to spread Communism over the entire globe, and since 1950 the expansion of its naval power has been seen as the best way of bringing this about.

274. Rudyk, P. A. ZROSTANNIA I ZMITSNENNIA RIADIV KPRS NA SUCHASNOMU ETAPI [The growth and consolidation of the cadres of the CPSU in the contemporary era]. *Ukrains'kyi Istorychnyi Zhurnal [USSR] 1982 (1): 38-48.* Describes the growth, composition, and unifying mission of the Communist Party of the USSR. 61 notes. N. M. Diuk

275. Rybecký, Vladislav. KSSS A OTÁZKA VÁLKY A MÍRU (1945-1980) [The Soviet Communist Party and the problem of war and peace, 1945-80]. *Hist. a Vojenství [Czechoslovakia] 1981 30(2): 16-36.* Problems of war and peace are the central issues of foreign policy, for the Communist Party as well as for the USSR, which seeks maximum advantage in international affairs for the socialist and communist growth. Soviet foreign policy has served the Marxist-Leninist movement and sought to prepare for the advance of the three main revolutionary powers of the world, the global socialist system, the international working class, and national liberation movements. Based on official publications; 43 notes.
G. E. Pergl

276. Rywkin, Michael. BLACK AMERICANS: A RACE OR NATIONALITY? SOME COMMUNIST VIEWPOINTS. *Can. Rev. of Studies in Nationalism 1975 3(1): 89-96.* Different code words applied to American blacks have reflected uncertainty on the US race problem in Soviet Marxist thinking, beginning with Lenin, and have signaled Soviet policy changes toward the United States.

277. Ryzhenko, F. D. STANOVLENIE I RAZVITIE VNESHNEI POLITIKI KPSS [Rise and development of the foreign policy of the CPSU]. *Voprosy Istorii [USSR] 1973 (8): 3-14.* Examining the CPSU activity in the sphere of foreign policy over the 70-year period of the existence of Lenin's Party, the author divides it into three major historical stages. In the first stage (1903-17) the Party under V. I. Lenin's leadership worked out its foreign policy program in the conditions of struggle against the tsarist autocracy and capitalism, for the establishment of the dictatorship of the proletariat. The second stage embraces the period 1917-45, when the CPSU became the ruling party of the world's first socialist state. The third stage set in after the end of the second world war and is characterized by the formation of the socialist world system, the breakdown of the colonial system of imperialism and the new powerful upsurge of the working-class and communist movement throughout the world. Analyzing the foreign policy of the CPSU, the author emphasizes its strictly scientific character, internationalism, democratism and consistent striving for peace. Particular attention is devoted in the article to the Peace Program adopted by the 24th Congress of the CPSU, which accords with the interests of all nations, and to the indefatigable efforts of the Party and the Soviet government to implement it. J

278. Ryzhova, M. D. ROL' MOSKOVSKOI PARTIINOI ORGANIZATSII V SOTSIALISTICHESKOM STROITEL'STVE [The role of the Moscow Party organization in the building of socialism]. *Voprosy Istorii KPSS [USSR] 1981 (3): 156-158.* Describes the role of the Party in taking over the heights of the economy, the rapid expansion of industry, the electrification of the USSR, and the expulsion from the Party of anti-Leninist groups. The Moscow Party has had a particularly important role in publishing and the press. Based on conference proceedings, the works of Lenin and Brezhnev, and the press, especially *Pravda;* 4 notes. A. J. Evans

279. Sadykov, F. B. DIALEKTICHESKAIA ZAKONOMERNOST' RAZVITIIA KOMMUNISTICHESKOI PARTII [The dialectical regularity of the development of the Communist Party]. *Voprosy Istorii KPSS [USSR] 1960 (6): 27-43.* Discusses specific disagreements within the Party, emphasizing that differences, and the capacity for self-criticism, are essential for the health of the Party.

280. Salem, Norma. NOTES ON ISLAM AND COMMUNISM: MUSLIMS IN THE SOVIET UNION. *Search: J. for Arab and Islamic Studies 1981 2(1): 390-409.* Though politically and religiously suppressed in the early 20th century, Moslems in the USSR are currently prospering due to the compatibility of Islam and Marxism (as a method to power rather than an inspiring ideology), rapid population growth, the creation of a Moslem political and economic elite, and the rise of the Uzbeks as Soviet leaders.

281. Samsonova, T. V. LENINSKAIA PROGRAMMA KOMMUNISTICHESKOGO VOSPITANIIA PODRASTAIUSHCHIKH POKOLENII [Lenin's program for communist education of rising generations]. *Prepodavanie Istorii v Shkole [USSR] 1970 (5): 2-7.* Discusses the everlasting importance of V. I. Lenin's speech *The Tasks of the Youth Leagues,* delivered at the Third All-Russia Congress of the Russian Young Communist League, 2 October 1920. Its ideological maxims on morality and materialist philosophical teachings have shaped generations of Soviet youth and remain fundamental principles for the development of Communist discipline and true Marxist-Leninist education. 7 notes. N. Frenkley

282. Sapargaliev, G. S. and Binder, M. A. RAZVITIE SOVETSKOI NATSIONAL'NOI GOSUDARSTVENNOSTI KAZAKHSKOGO NARODA [The Kazakh national Soviet state and communist construction]. *Sovetskoe Gosudarstvo i Pravo [USSR] 1970 (9): 24-31.* Examines the achievements of the Kazakhstan Soviet Socialist Republic, 1920-70, its role in the development of communism in the USSR, and its relationship both with the central Soviet government and other autonomous republics. J/S

283. Saveliev, V. L. and Spirin, O.A. NESPROMOZHNIST' BURZHUAZNYKH FALSYFIKATSII KADROVOI POLITYKY KPRS [The failure of bourgeois falsifications of the cadre policy of the Communist Party of the Soviet Union]. *Ukraïns'kyi Istorychnyi Zhurnal [USSR] 1980 (1): 36-44.* Distorting facts and reality, some Western sovietologists present the CPSU as an "elite," which can be easily refuted by the class composition of the Party and its ruling bodies.

284. Schapiro, Leonard. THE GENERAL DEPARTMENT OF THE CC OF THE CPSU. *Survey [Great Britain] 1975 21(3): 53-65.* Established in 1919 as one of the five original central committee departments, the General Department was later known as the Secret Department and also as the Special Section. Joseph Stalin used the head of the Secret Department/Special Section as his personal secretary. By 1954 the Special Section had assumed its original title of General Department; however, this transformation took until the late 1960's in the various republics. Nikita Khrushchev

chose not to appoint one of his supporters as head of the General Department. The General Department's role as the Politburo's secretariat makes it a key link in the political command structure; recognizing this Leonid Brezhnev appointed one of his own nominees as head of the department. Based on newspaper reports and secondary sources; 37 notes. D. R. McDonald

285. Schapiro, Leonard. THE INTERNATIONAL DEPARTMENT OF THE CPSU: KEY TO SOVIET POLICY. *Int. J. [Canada] 1976-77 32(1): 41-55.* Foreign policy formulation in the USSR is not characterized by Party-state rivalry, but is unified and well-coordinated. 14 notes. R. V. Kubicek

286. Schapiro, Leonard. THE REAL STALIN. *Survey [Great Britain] 1977-78 23(3): 131-133.* Pays tribute to Boris Souvarine who was a socialist and a founder of the Communist Party of the USSR. Souvarine quickly saw the direction in which the Party was going. He objected and was expelled. His literary efforts to portray the true face of Stalinism won him few favors in political and literary circles dominated by leftists. Soviet participation on the side of the Allies during World War II further delayed acceptance. Only recently has Souvarine been recognized as the author who has given us the most accurate account of the policies and character of Joseph Stalin. V. L. Human/S

287. Scott, D. J. R. RESISTANCE AND OPPOSITION. *Survey [Great Britain] 1967 (64): 34-44.* Analyzes political resistance and opposition in the USSR. The Soviet Union looks to the outside world, as from the first it always has done, for many of the useful services of an opposition. The countries officially styled capitalist, and especially the United States, provide a stimulating threat and a justification for the siege regime, as well as offering a standard for the comparison of achievements.... Since the one clear and distinctive principle which the Soviet system of government has carried forward from Lenin to Brezhnev is the power of the central leadership of the party to take, and secure compliance with, the crucial decisions in all aspects of the national life—which in the terminology of any other system would be described as exercising the power of government—the possibility suggests itself that the body designated in the written constitution as the government—the Council of Ministers—and the corresponding bodies at the lower levels of administration, with the departmental apparatus answering to them, may be allowed to exercise some of the functions of an opposition." D. D. Cameron

288. Seliger, Kurt. DER PROLONGIERTE SOZIALISMUS [The prolonged socialism]. *Osteuropa [West Germany] 1977 27(7): 573-582.* In 1961, the 22d Party Congress of the Communist Party of the USSR proclaimed that by 1980 the transition from socialism to communism would begin, but it has not happened.

289. Selunskaia, V. M. LENINSKII KOOPERATIVNYI PLAN I EGO DAL'NEISHEE RAZVITIE V DOKUMENTAKH KPSS [The Leninist cooperative plan and its further development in documents of the CPSU]. *Voprosy Istorii KPSS [USSR] 1979 (4): 12-26.* V. I. Lenin insisted that agricultural cooperatives in Russia contributed to a transition from capitalism to socialism. During the 1920's, the Communist Party defended Lenin's views first against the Trotskyists who rejected agricultural cooperatives and then against those opposed to the next stage in the cooperative movement, collectivization. From the inception of collectivization, the Party sought the most effective methods to enhance agricultural production. Beginning in the 1960's, the Party concentrated on integrating industrial and agricultural production by forming agroindustrial combines. Based on Lenin's *Collected Works* and published documents; 64 notes. L. E. Holmes

290. Semenov, V. G. GUMANIZM LENINSKOI MEZHDUNARODNOI POLITIKI KPSS [The humanism of the Communist Party of the Soviet Union's Leninist international policies]. *Voprosy Istorii KPSS [USSR] 1982 (8): 63-74.* Marxism-Leninism is the world's most humane ideology. The USSR, a Marxist-Leninist state, is therefore the world's most humane state. The foundations of the USSR's policies are 1) the Great October Socialist Revolution; 2) Lenin's peace decree; 3) peaceful coexistence between capitalism and socialism; and 4) proletarian internationalism. The USSR has attained nuclear parity with the United States, which is a triumph for peace. Imperialism can no longer wage aggression with impunity. The USSR stands ready to reduce arms and reduce world tension by fair and mutually advantageous policies. It stands ready, however, to rebuff threats to itself and the socialist community. Based on the works of Lenin and Brezhnev and *Pravda;* 59 notes. A. J. Evans

291. Seniavski, S. L. IZMENENIIA V SOTSIAL'NOI STRUKTURE SOVETSKOGO OBSHCHESTVA (1938-1970 GG.) [Changes in the social structure of Soviet society, 1938-70]. *Voprosy Istorii [USSR] 1973 (4): 3-17.* Examines the basic regularities and some specific features of the process of changes taking place in the social and class structure of Soviet society in the period of consummating the building of socialism and going over to the building of communism. Singles out five groups of the principal social and class distinctions in the conditions of victorious socialism and analyzes the process of their gradual elimination during the period of transition to a classless, socially homogeneous communist society: distinctions between classes; between classes and intermediate social strata and groups; between town and country; between mental and physical labour; inter-class distinctions. Highlights the decisive influence exerted by the quantitative and qualitative growth of the working class on progressive changes in the social structure of Soviet society. J

292. Sen'kin, I. I. PARTIINAIA GRUPPA V SOVREMENNYKH USLOVIIAKH [The party group in contemporary conditions]. *Voprosy Istorii KPSS [USSR] 1974 (8): 36-44.* The smallest party organization, the party group, has recently enjoyed greater popularity and strength in the Soviet Karelian Republic. The party group has especially contributed to greater and more efficient industrial production. Based on published party documents; 5 notes. L. E. Holmes

293. Serebrianykov, V. V. PARTIIA TA NAROD U BOROT'BI ZA ZMITSNENNIA RADIANS'KYKH ZBROINYKH SYL [The Party and people in the struggle to strengthen the Soviet armed forces]. *Ukrains'kyi Istorychnyi Zhurnal [USSR] 1968 2(83): 14-22.* Describes the growth of the Soviet armed forces, both in equipment and personnel, 1917-68, stressing how the Party and people have contributed morally and practically to this cause.

294. Sergeev, S. V. ISTORIOGRAFIIA ISTORII KPSS: PROBLEMY METODOLOGII [Historiography of the history of the Communist Party of the Soviet Union (CPSU): methodological issues]. *Voprosy Istorii KPSS [USSR] 1984 (6): 146-149.* Summarizes proceedings of a conference organized by the history department of the Academy of Social Sciences for the Central Committee of the CPSU in 1984 on the subject of methodology in the historiography of the history of the CPSU. Issues under discussion included typology of sources, problems of historical reality, and refuting falsifications of Western historians. M. Hernas

295. Serishchev, Ia. M. V. I. LENIN I KOMUNISTYCHNYI INTERNATSIONAL MOLODI (DO 50-RICHCHIA KIM) [V. I. Lenin and the Communist Youth International: the 50th anniversary of the Communist Youth International]. *Ukrains'kyi Istorychnyi Zhurnal [USSR] 1969 (10): 3-10.* Traces the history of the Communist youth movement in the USSR and places it in the context of the international Communist youth movement. Stresses the importance of the first congress of the International Union of Socialist Youth Organizations in Berlin in 1919, at which the Communist Youth International was founded.

296. Shapiro, Jane P. CANDIDATE MEMBERSHIP IN THE CPSU CENTRAL COMMITTEE: STEPPING-STONE TO GLORY OR OBSCURITY? *Comparative Pol. 1974 6(4): 606-616.*

297. Shapiro, Jane P. THE POLITICIZATION OF SOVIET WOMEN: FROM PASSIVITY TO PROTEST. *Can. Slavonic Papers [Canada] 1975 17(4): 596-616.* Equality of the sexes, guaranteed by Article 122 of the Soviet Constitution, has been encouraged by the Soviet government, as well as by the scarcity of male work-

ers following World War I and the Civil War and then again following the great purge and World War II. Yet only 23% of Party members in the USSR are women, perhaps because of the New Soviet Woman, expected to be both worker and housewife, has little time for the additional demands of Communist Party membership. Inequality between men and women is, however, less pronounced than that between rulers and ruled, and it is accordingly on the latter that women dissidents have focused their attention. Husbands or male relatives have drawn most women into activism. Based on *Khronika tekushchikh sobytii,* other primary sources, and secondary materials; 63 notes. L. W. Van Wyk

298. Shapko, V. M. V. I. LENIN O LICHNOM PRIMERE KOMMUNISTA V VYPOLNENII OBSHCHESTVENNOGO DOLGA [V. I. Lenin on the personal example of the Communist in fulfilling social duty]. *Voprosy Istorii KPSS [USSR] 1963 (1): 66-75.* Notes the high ethical standards required by Lenin of Communists and quotes Communist Party circulars, 1918-62, disapproving of nepotism and the taking of bribes.

299. Shapoval, Iu. I. VYKRYTTIA FAL'SYFIKATSII BURZHUAZNOIU ISTORIOHRAFIIEIU FRN LENINS'KOHO VCHENNIA PRO KERIVNU ROL' KPRS U BUDIVNYTSTVI NOVOHO SUSPIL'STVA [An exposition of the falsifications of bourgeois historiography in West Germany on Lenin's teachings about the leading role of the Communist Party in the construction of the new society]. *Ukrains'kyi Istorychnyi Zhurnal [USSR] 1982 (3): 29-37.* The West German school of "sovietology" has based its attacks on the Soviet Union on the contention that Lenin did not follow the works of Marx in the formation of the Communist Party. The author surveys the statements of the West German scholars and constructs a counterargument using V. I. Lenin's writings. 40 notes. N. M. Diuk

300. Sharapov, G. V. LENINSKIE PRINTSIPY PARTIINOGO RUKOVODSTVA PROFSOIUZAMI [Lenin's principles of the Party guidance of trade unions]. *Voprosy Istorii KPSS [USSR] 1981 (11): 3-18.* Examines the work of Soviet trade unions and their place in Soviet society, with reference to Lenin's statement that "the trade unions should have no rights without obligations." Considers unions' duties to Soviet society, the concomitant need for Party leadership, the principles on which such leadership should be based, and the methods it must adopt to further the cause of socialist construction. 49 notes. L. Smith

301. Sharlet, Robert. SOVIET LEGAL POLICY MAKING: A PRELIMINARY CLASSIFICATION. *Sociol. Inquiry [Canada] 1977 47(3-4): 209-230.* Explores legal policymaking of the Communist Party in the USSR which bears on the Soviet social regulation process, 1930-76.

302. Shelest, P. E. BOEVOI OTRIAD KPSS [A fighting unit of the Communist Party of the Soviet Union]. *Voprosy Istorii KPSS [USSR] 1968 (7): 7-20.* Commemorates the 50th anniversary of the founding of the Communist Party of the Ukraine by evaluating its achievements, 1918-68, and by stressing the Party's role within the broad framework of the Soviet Communist Party.

303. Shevardnadze, E. A. UTVERZHDENIE LENINSKIKH PRINTSIPOV SOTSIALISTICHESKOGO GUMANIZMA [The consolidation of the Leninist principles of socialist humanism]. *Voprosy Filosofii [USSR] 1981 (6): 3-19.* Discusses methods of consolidating Leninist principles of socialist humanism and the Soviet way of life in the economic and social structure of Georgian life and examines the evolution of the Georgian Communist Party and of the republic itself from 1921 to 1981.

304. Shevchenko, V. F. Z'IZD—VERKHOVNII ORHAN KOMUNISTYCHNOI PARTII [The Congress: the supreme organ of the Communist Party]. *Ukrains'kyi Istorychnyi Zhurnal [USSR] 1981 (3): 5-17.* Discusses how the leading role of Communist Party congresses evolved from their inception to the 26th Party Congress (1981) and includes a short history of the Communist Party.

305. Shevtsov, V. S. TVORCHESKOE RAZVITIE KPSS UCHENIIA O FEDERATIVNOM USTROISTVE MNOGONATSIONAL'NOGO SOTSIALISTICHESKOGO GOSUDARSTVA [The creative development by the CPSU of the teaching on the federal organization of the multinational socialist state]. *Voprosy Istorii KPSS [USSR] 1979 (9): 38-49.* In the 60 years since the October Revolution the conception of a single, united, multinational state has taken shape as a result on the one hand of the theoretical development of Leninist ideas by the Communist Party, and on the other of the practical experience of constructing a national state in the USSR. The unity of the country is based on the interchange between the union and the republics of which it consists. The further development of the socialist federation will lead to a more centralized state and at the same time to the flowering of democracy. Secondary sources; 45 notes. L. Waters

306. Shinkarenko, V. V. OB IZUCHENII TEORETICHESKOGO NASLEDIIA V. I. LENINA V OBLASTI KOMMUNISTICHESKOI PROPAGANDY [On the study of V. I. Lenin's theoretical legacy in the area of Communist propaganda]. *Voprosy Istorii KPSS [USSR] 1981 (11): 122-126.* Communist propaganda is one of the most important areas of Party work, since it regulates both the level of the Party's ideological influence on the masses and the entire progress of communist construction. Lenin was a great theoretician and master of propaganda, and his work has provided vital guidelines. Reviews research on the subject and its detailed and illuminating picture of Lenin's contribution. 8 notes. L. Smith

307. Shirokov, A. I. LITERATURA PO METODIKE PREPODAVANIIA ISTORII KPSS, IZDANNAIA V 1957-1974 GG. [Literature on the methods of teaching the history of the CPSU, 1957-74]. *Vestnik Moskovskogo U. Seriia 9: Istoriia [USSR] 1976 (3): 23-35.* A resolution of the Central Committee of the Communist Party of the Soviet Union (CPSU), 5 June 1974, called for raising the ideological and theoretical level of teaching social sciences in higher schools. The relatively large number of publications on methodology since 1967 have been concerned with the theoretical level of lectures and the clarification of the history of the CPSU. One question is whether a separate lecture on the defeat of anti-Leninist forces in the Party is necessary. Lecturing on anti-Marxist theories does not seem an appropriate task in a course on the CPSU since the errors may not be refuted. Partisanship must be observed to oppose right and left views. 43 notes.
D. Balmuth

308. Shitarev, G. I. VYSOKAIA ROL' PARTIINYKH S"EZDOV V DEIATEL'NOSTI KPSS [The superior role of Party congresses in activities of the CPSU]. *Voprosy Istorii KPSS [USSR] 1966 (2): 3-13.* Discusses the important policymaking role of Party congresses, 1903-66.

309. Shmeleva, M. Iu. PARTIINYE ORGANIZATSII LENINGRADSKIKH TEKSTIL'NYKH PREDPRIATII V BOR'BE ZA VYPOLNENIE PIATOGO PIATILETNEGO PLANA (1951-1955) [The Party organization of the Leningrad textile enterprises in the struggle for the fulfillment of the fifth five-year plan (1951-55)]. *Vestnik Leningradskogo Universiteta [USSR] 1976 (8): 19-26.* In the drive to improve both the output and the quality of the Leningrad textile enterprises, it was decided in 1951 to blend the proper degree of economic, trade union, and Communist Party activities. The Party would increase its efforts to improve political activity and to emphasize the avant-garde role of each Communist in the attempt to upgrade textile productivity. The Party took the lead in bringing new methods to bear and in improving the training of the workers. 18 notes. G. F. Jewsbury

310. Shmorhun, P. M. SPIVVIDNOSHENNIA ZAHAL'NOISTORYCHNOHO TA ISTORYKO-PARTIINOHO MATERIALU V DOSLIDZHENNIAKH Z ISTORII KPRS [The correlation between general historical and Party historical material in research on Communist Party history]. *Ukrains'kyi Istorychnyi Zhurnal [USSR] 1977 (11): 30-36.* Explains the importance of achieving a balance between general historical and Party historical

material for scientific research on the history of the Communist Party and for teaching Party history in institutions of higher education.

311. Shul'ha, I. V. DOPOMOHA MIS'KYKH PARTORHANIZATSII SIL'S'KYM U IKH ORHANIZATSIINOMU ZMITSNENNI (1952-70) [The strengthening of organizational links within the Party through assistance given to village Party organizations by town Party organizations]. *Ukrains'kyi Istorychnyi Zhurnal [USSR] 1970 (10): 3-10.* Assesses the directives of Party Congresses in the USSR, 1940-64, (16th-23d) concerning the organization and mutual assistance between Party cadres in agriculture and industry, detailing their realization, 1952-70.

312. Skorupa, V. K. PARTIIA V PERIOD RAZVITOGO SOTSIALIZMA [The Party in the period of developed socialism]. *Voprosy Istorii KPSS [USSR] 1981 (2): 102-117.* Publishes guidelines for lecturers in the Soviet educational system on the role of the Party in the period of developed socialism. The lecture can be usefully divided into five parts: 1) the Communist Party of the Soviet Union (CPSU) as the Party of the working class and the Soviet people; 2) the growth of the role played by the Party in society; 3) the scientific basis of CPSU policies; 4) organizational and ideological work; 5) the perfection of internal Party work as a prerequisite for improving the leadership qualities of the Party. 53 notes.
A. Brown

313. Slepov, L. A. AZ SZKP TORTÉNETE A PÁRTPROGRAMOK TÜKRÉBEN [The history of the CPSU through Party programs]. *Párttörténeti Közlemények [Hungary] 1974 20(3): 169-194.* In the history of the Russian labor movement three dates and the three corresponding programs possess worldwide implications: firstly, the second Social Democratic congress and its program of 1903; secondly, the October Revolution and the Leninist program of 1918; and thirdly, the program of 1961 in conjunction with the 22d to 24th CPSU congresses. P. I. Hidas

314. Slepov, L. A. NEKOTORYE ZAMECHANIIA K VOPROSU OB IZUCHENII ISTORII KPSS I EE PERIODIZATSIIA [A few remarks on the question of the study of the history of the CPSU and its periodization]. *Voprosy Istorii KPSS [USSR] 1971 (10): 68-72.* Discusses critically the outline periodization of history of the Communist Party of the USSR proposed by A. F. Kostin (see *Voprosy Istorii KPSS* 1969 9: 55-67).

315. Slepov, L. A. O NEKOTORYKH METODOLOGICHESKIKH PROBLEMAKH PARTIINOGO STROITEL'STVA [Some methodological problems of party development]. *Voprosy Istorii KPSS [USSR] 1969 (6): 75-86.* Discusses some of the problems encountered by the Communist Party of the USSR in applying theory to practice, with special reference to the Party's recent experiences.

316. Slomp, J. ELITEN IN DE SOWJET-UNIE [Elites in the Soviet Union]. *Acta Politica [Netherlands] 1974 9(4): 365-378.* Next to the party elite of the Communist Party, there are several policy elites in the Soviet Union. They consist of officials in every field of policy and have their basis of power in the resources that are allocated in the government budget. Most resources flow to the economy, the scientific and cultural sector, the military and the administrative apparat. So elites in these sectors can be seen as most influential in the policymaking process. J/S

317. Sobolev, M. BOEVOI OTRIAD LENINSKOGO KOMSOMOLA (K 60-LETIIU VLKSM) [Battle detachment of Lenin's Komsomol: 60th anniversary of the All-Union Leninist Young Communist League]. *Voenno-Istoricheskii Zhurnal [USSR] 1978 20(10): 10-19.* Describes the formation, November 1918, of the Russian (later All-Union) Young Communist League (*Komsomol*) and its military prowess. It was the mainstay of the Red Army and Navy during the Civil War and World War II. It continues to provide men and leadership to the armed forces, initiates new and advanced technological improvements, helps raise military moral and political standards. The importance of the Komsomol was particularly apparent in World War II: the number of Komsomol members in front-line service rose from 34.8% in 1942 to 57.1% in 1945. 18 notes. N. Frenkley

318. Soldatenko, V. F. KONSUL'TATSII Z PROBLEMY "ISTORYCHNYI DOSVID KPRS": BOROT'BA PARTII BIL'SHOVYKIV ZA PEREMOHU VELYKOI ZHOVTNEVOI SOTSIALISTYCHNOI REVOLIUTSII [Consultations on the problem of the historical experience of the CPSU: the Bolshevik Party's struggle for the triumph of the Great October Socialist Revolution]. *Ukrains'kyi Istorychnyi Zhurnal [USSR] 1981 (12): 115-124.* The Communist and workers' parties and the progessive forces in the world see in the revolutionary achievements of the Communist Party of the Soviet Union (CPSU) a brilliant example to follow and a model for creative application in practical activities. In contrast, apologists of anti-Communism try by all means to falsify the historical events. The author suggests a plan for studying the theme of the historical experience of the Bolshevik party from the period of the October Revolution to the present. Based on Lenin's works and Communist party history; 14 notes. I. Krushelnyckyj

319. Solonitsyn, G. KOMSOMOLETS—NA SAMOLET!: K 40-LETIIU SHEFSTVA KOMSOMOLA NAD AVIATSIEI [Young Communist, onto the airplane!: the 40th anniversary of the Young Communist League's sponsorship of aviation]. *Voenno-Istoricheskii Zhurnal [USSR] 1971 (1): 89-93.* Discusses the involvement of Communist youth in the development of a Soviet Air Force, March 1923-71, with particular reference to the official involvement of the Young Communist League from 1931 onwards.

320. Sorokin, A. I. RUKOVODSTVO KPSS: ISTOCHNIK MOGUSHCHESTVA VOORUZHENNKH SIL SSSR I PROCHNOSTI OBORONY STRANY [The leadership of the Communist Party of the Soviet Union (CPSU): source of the might of the armed forces of the USSR and the strength of the country's defense]. *Voprosy Istorii KPSS [USSR] 1980 (5): 62-73.* The present military might of the armed forces of the USSR is the result of the efforts of the CPSU in the period since the Russian Revolution. Communists must play a leading role in military matters in time of war, as the history of World War II illustrates, and in time of peace. The organizational and ideological work of the CPSU ensures that the Soviet army and navy serve not only as a weapon of defense, but as a school for the education of youth. Secondary sources; 25 notes. G. Dombrovski

321. Soshnev, V. IZ ISTORII STROITEL'STVA PARTIINYKH ORGANIZATSII V SOVETSKIKH VOORUZHENNYKH SILAKH [From the history of the construction of Party organizations in the Soviet armed forces]. *Voenno-Istoricheskii Zhurnal [USSR] 1973 (6): 3-12.* Discusses Party organization in the Soviet military since 1917 in connection with the 24th Soviet Communist Party Congress and the recent issuing of a Party directive on Party organs and instruction in the Soviet armed forces.

322. Sredin, G. OSNOVY OSNOV SOVETSKOGO VOENNOGO STROITEL'STVA [The foundations of Soviet military development]. *Voenno-Istoricheskii Zhurnal [USSR] 1978 (2): 3-15.* The first deputy chief of the Main Political Administration of the Soviet army and navy pays tribute to the Communist Party of the USSR which implemented V. I. Lenin's ideals, created a new army for the defense of socialism, forged the Soviet Armed Forces, inspired troops to rout imperialist interventionists during the Civil War, and led the Soviet people to victory over fascism in World War II. The Soviet Armed Forces owe their military success, advanced technology, and spiritual strength to the leadership of the Party which is the basis of Soviet military power. Photo, 16 notes.
N. Frenkley

323. Sredin, G. V. BOEVYE ORGANY PARTII [The Party's military organs]. *Voprosy Istorii KPSS [USSR] 1979 (5): 31-43.* Surveys the organizational history and activity of political organs and political officers of the Communist Party in the Soviet armed forces from 1918 to 1978. Party organizations and their official representatives in the armed forces have contributed to close cooperation between the Party and the military leadership within the army

and navy and in the Soviet communities where military units may be stationed. Through its organs and representatives, the Party provides military, ideological, and political instruction. Based on published documents; 35 notes. L. E. Holmes

324. Stepanov, A. DIPLOMATIC PRACTICE: FORMS AND METHODS. *Int. Affairs [USSR] 1972 (12): 43-49.* Discusses the Marxist ideological aspects of the foreign policies of the USSR and other communist countries and their diplomatic methods in dealing with capitalist and developing nations, 1920's-70's.

325. Stepanov, V. P. BOEVOE ORUZHIE LENINSKOI PARTII: K PIATIDESIATILETIIU GAZETY *PRAVDA* [The battle-weapon of Lenin's party: the 50th anniversary of the newspaper *Pravda]. Voprosy Istorii KPSS [USSR] 1962 (2): 26-42.* Surveys the history of the newspaper *Pravda,* 1912-61, and its revival of the tradition established by V. I. Lenin's *Iskra,* 1900-03.

326. Stetsko, Slava. NATIONAL PERSECUTION IN THE USSR. *Ukrainian Rev. [Great Britain] 1976 22(1): 31-55.* The Communist Party of the USSR has persecuted ethnic groups and intellectuals in the Ukraine in the 1970's. Accounts of nationalists' imprisonment and mistreatment in the Ukraine since the 1950's.

327. Storozhenko, G. A. 26. S''EZD KPSS I PROBLEMY SOVETSKOGO OBRAZA ZHIZNI: ROL' POLITIKI PARTII V STANOVLENII I RAZVITII SOTSIALISTICHESKIKH FORM ZHIZNEDEIATEL'NOSTI [The 26th Congress of the Communist Party of the Soviet Union and the problems as to the Soviet way of life: the role of Party policy in the establishment and development of the socialist forms of vital activity]. *Latvijas PSR Zinātņu Akad. Vēstis [USSR] 1982 (1): 10-26.* Discusses material and intellectual changes in the way of living of the population of Soviet Latvia since the establishment of the Soviet regime in Latvia and the influence of policies of the Communist Party on the development of a socialist society. Based on documentary materials of the 26th Congress of the Communist Party of the Soviet Union and on primary sources; 66 notes. R. Vilums

328. Suprunenko, M. I. ZMINY U SOTSIAL'NII STRUKTURI SOTSIALISTYCHNOHO SUSPIL'STVA I PIDNESENNIA KERIVNOI ROLI ROBITNYCHOHO KLASU [The changes in the social structure of a socialist society and the advancement of the leading role of the working class]. *Ukrains'kyi Istorychnyi Zhurnal [USSR] 1972 (8): 3-11.* Outlines the changes that have taken place in the social structure of the working class in the Soviet Union according to the postulates of the 24th Congress of the Communist Party, which were published 1971.

329. Surovtsev, Iu. I. RUKOVODSTVO KPSS LITERATURNO-KHUDOZHESTVENNOI ZHIZN'IU SOVETSKOGO OBSHCHESTVA: ISTORICHESKAIA PREEMSTVENNOST' I RAZVITIE [Leadership of the Communist Party of the Soviet Union in the literary and artistic life of Soviet society: historical continuity and development]. *Voprosy Istorii KPSS [USSR] 1984 (6): 18-32.* Elaborates the Soviet Communist Party's stance on the role of literature and the arts in Soviet society since V. I. Lenin's doctrine of *partiinost'* as the necessary quality in artistic production. In the 1920's and 30's the issue of positive hero occupied one of the central places in the debate. Since the 1960's the emphasis has been on the educative role of art and its moral and ideological responsibility. 42 notes. M. Hernas

330. Suslov, Iu. P. IZ ISTORII PARTIINYKH ORGANIZATSII POVOLZH'IA [From the history of Party organizations of the Volga region]. *Voprosy Istorii KPSS [USSR] 1981 (7): 131-134.* The 1970's formed a particularly active decade for the historians of the Volga region, producing collections of historical Party documents, detailed work on the history of local Party organizations, and studies of regional problems, especially in relation to the spreading of Marxism in Russia and information about the early life and revolutionary activity of V. I. Lenin and his struggle to create a new type of party. Such study of Party history aids the contemporary Party in the realization of Lenin's plans for the construction of socialist society in the USSR by outlining the problems involved and the various areas of organization and ideological and political work necessary for the development of socialism. Based on published works on Volga region Party history; 19 notes. L. Smith

331. Suvorov, K. I. O NEKOTORYKH VOPROSAKH I ISSLEDOVANIIA ISTORII PERVICHNYKH ORGANIZATSII KPSS [Issues in historical research on local organizations of the Soviet Communist Party]. *Voprosy Istorii KPSS [USSR] 1979 (7): 123-130.* A survey of the history of the activity of Party members and workers of Moscow's Rublev Waterworks demonstrates the potential of the study of local Party organizations. The Party unit of the waterworks contributed to the Bolshevik victory during the Civil War, the reconstruction of the Soviet economy during the 1920's, recruitment of new Party members, the struggle against opposition groups within the Party, collectivization, the defeat of Germany during World War II, and economic improvements after the war. Based on materials in the Moscow Party Archive; 44 notes. L. E. Holmes

332. Suvorov, K. I. VSEMIRNO-ISTORICHESKOE ZNACHENIE OPYTA KPSS [The global historical significance of the experience of the CPSU]. *Voprosy Istorii KPSS [USSR] 1980 (1): 87-99.* The history of the Communist Party of the USSR reveals the struggle against all forms of reformism, application of theory to practice, flexible development of strategy and tactics, creation of a dictatorship of the proletariat, and the building of a socialist society. Based on published documents and V. I. Lenin's *Collected Works;* 37 notes. L. E. Holmes

333. Sverdlovtsev, M. B. PODGOTOVKA TEORETICHESKIKH KADROV KPSS [The training of theoretical cadres of the CPSU]. *Voprosy Istorii KPSS [USSR] 1972 (1): 89-98.* Surveys the history of the Institute of Red Professors, 1921-38, and the Academy of Social Sciences of the Party's Central Committee, 1946-70, in educating a new socialist intelligentsia, for which Lenin saw a need in 1918.

334. Svoboda, Ludvik. 50TH ANNIVERSARY USSR: BULWARK OF SOCIALISM, PEACE AND FREEDOM. *World Marxist Rev. [Canada] 1972 15(12): 5-54.* Testimonials to the USSR from world Communist Party leaders on the occasion of the USSR's 50th anniversary, outlining the world development of socialism, 1920's-70's.

335. Sweezy, Paul M. ON SOCIALISM. *Monthly Rev. 1983 35(5): 35-39.* According to Karl Marx in his *Critique of the Gotha Program* (1875), only true socialists aspire to communism: the USSR purports to follow this dictum, but according to its critics it has not succeeded.

336. Szydlak, Jan. GLĘBOKI PROCES HISTORYCZNY [Deep historical process]. *Nowe Drogi [Poland] 1976 (10): 21-24.* Emphasizes the role of the USSR and its Communist leadership in bringing about the economic integration of Soviet bloc countries.

337. Tadevosian, E. V.; Dubinin, A. B.; Zhiromskaia, I. P.; and Mnatsakanian, M. O. RAZVITOI SOTSIALIZM I AKTUAL'NYE PROBLEMY NAUCHNOGO KOMMUNIZMA [Developed socialism and topical problems of scientific communism]. *Voprosy Filosofii [USSR] 1981 (1): 170-173.* Reviews a 1979 collection of essays on scientific communism prepared by the Institute of Philosophy of the Academy of Sciences of the USSR, which tackles a range of issues including agriculture, collectivism, and problems of the periodization of developed socialism.

338. Tadevosian, E. V. XXVI S''EZD KPSS OB INTERNATSIONALISTSKOI SUSHCHNOSTI SOVETSKOI GOSUDARSTVENNOSTI I EE NATSIONAL'NYKH FORM [The 26th Congress of the Communist Party of the Soviet Union on the internationalist essence of Soviet statehood and its national forms]. *Istoriia SSSR [USSR] 1982 (4): 3-19.* Declares the Communist Party of the Soviet Union's undying allegiance to the principles of internationalism and the equal development of the national regions of the USSR, restated at the 26th Congress. From the beginning the Soviet state, unlike bourgeois countries, was eager to help the na-

tional minorities. Thus at the height of the famine in the early 1920's the Bolshevik government resolved to irrigate parts of Turkestan. Membership in the Party is open to all nationalities. Soviet federalism is democratic because it recognizes and does not strive to quash national self-expression. Based on Party documents and Lenin's writings; 50 notes. D. N. Collins

339. Tang, Peter S. H. SOVIET POLEMICS: AGAINST MAO ZEDONG THOUGHT: THEMES AND MOTIVATIONS. *Asian Thought and Soc. 1980 5(13): 81-84.* Soviet analysis of Mao Zedong's (Mao Tse-tung) thought concentrates on what is perceived as a cult of personality, sinicization of Marxism, anti-Sovietism, and chauvinism; the Soviet critique is inaccurate.

340. Tangepera, Rein and Chapman, Robert Dale. A NOTE ON THE AGEING OF THE POLITBURO. *Soviet Studies [Great Britain] 1977 29(2): 296-305.* Documents and discusses the trend toward an increasing age for members of the Politburo of the Communist Party of the USSR. Data show the average age of members has risen from 36.3 in 1917 to 66.6 in 1975. However, the recent steep rise in the mean age, and of the advanced age of members recruited in 1973, is a temporary phenomenon due to the long tenure of power by the current political leadership. These trends can be compared with parallel age data for members of the US presidential cabinet, 1789-1974. Here the mean age curve is much more uneven than that for the Politburo, and is subject to drastic rejuvenations after presidential elections. Though the present very high average age of the Politburo may drop slightly after the retirement of the current leadership, the long-range trend will hold its average age in the mid-60's, with consequent conservatism, caution, and rigidity in decisionmaking. 4 tables, 2 fig., 8 notes.
D. H. Murdoch

341. Tarasenko, N. I. FORMIROVANIE I RAZVITIE PARTIEI OBSHCHENATSIONAL'NOI GORDOSTI SOVETSKOGO CHELOVEKA [The formation and development by the party of national pride in the Soviet person]. *Voprosy Istorii KPSS [USSR] 1974 (10): 3-17.* Since 1917 the Communist Party of the Soviet Union has pursued a policy of proletarian internationalism, political, economic and military cooperation of the Soviet peoples, and pride in the USSR and one's own nationality. This policy has resulted in the continuing gradual abolition of national differences in the USSR. Based on V. I. Lenin's *Collected Works* and published materials of the Communist Party of the Soviet Union; 25 notes.
L. E. Holmes

342. Tarasenko, N. I. INTERNATSIONALIZM VNUTRENNEI I VNESHEI POLITIKI KPSS [The internationalism of the CPSU's domestic and foreign policy]. *Voprosy Istorii KPSS [USSR] 1977 (2): 3-17.* The 25th Party Congress continues to direct party and state policy along the internationalist lines pursued since 1917. Genuine internationalism stems from a rejection of a narrowly nationalist approach to class interests, a general emulation of the political, economic, and cultural policies of the USSR, the economic and military cooperation of socialist countries, and the support of national liberation struggles as well as detente. Based on published Party documents, periodical literature *(Pravda),* and Lenin's *Collected Works;* 42 notes. L. E. Holmes

343. Tarschys, Daniel. *The Soviet Political Agenda: Problems and Priorities, 1950-1970.* White Plains, N.Y.: M. E. Sharpe, 1979.

344. Timmermann, Heinz. SOVIET TREATMENT OF WESTERN COMMUNISTS: A COMPARATIVE ANALYSIS. *Studies in Comparative Communism 1982 15(3): 288-307.* In the 1920's leaders of factions in the Soviet Union tried to strengthen their position by securing allies among foreign communists. Now the Soviets can rely on the support of Third World movements and are less dependent on western communists. Soviet maneuvers against opposition include: raising the rank and file against the leaders, encouraging splits if appropriate, attacking leaders or cultivating local socialists; mistranslation or omissions in printed versions of agreements. The Soviets did have to concede in 1976 a veto to member Parties on resolutions. They have also allowed Western communists to address Soviet institutes. It is doubtful however, that Soviet leaders consider anything other than power in their decisions. 47 notes.
D. Balmuth

345. Timmermann, Heinz. ZUR INTERNATIONALISMUS-KONTROVERSE ZWISCHEN SOWJETKOMMUNISTEN UND AUTONOMISTEN [The internationalism-controversy between Soviet Communists and autonomists]. *Osteuropa [West Germany] 1982 32(5): 414-420.* In 1920 Lenin differentiated between proletarian internationalism and the petit bourgeois pacifist internationalism of the Second International, a distinction that Stalin used to establish the principle that the attitude of any Communist party toward the USSR was the major test of orthodoxy, a dogma that has been challenged by the Yugoslavian, French, Italian, and Spanish Communists.

346. Titarenko, S. L. KPSS: AVANGARD SOVETSKOGO NARODA [The Communist Party of the Soviet Union: vanguard of the Soviet people]. *Voprosy Istorii KPSS [USSR] 1961 (5): 20-37.* Discusses the historical background to the projected transformation of the Soviet Communist Party from a party of the working class to a party of the whole Soviet people, with particular reference to the tremendous growth in the Party since 1917.

347. Titarenko, S. L. V. I. LENIN O ZNACHENII EDINSTVA PARTII V BOR'BE ZA POBEDU SOTSIALIZMA I KOMMUNIZMA [V. I. Lenin on the importance of party unity for the victory of socialism and communism]. *Voprosy Istorii KPSS [USSR] 1960 (3): 159-169.* Criticizes the Cult of Personality and the activities of the anti-party group formed after the 20th Communist Party Congress by Malenkov, L. M. Kaganovich, Y. M. Molotov, N. A. Bulgarian, and Shepilov.

348. Tkachenko, V. K. 25 LET ZHURNALU "VOPROSY ISTORII KPSS" [25 years of the journal *Voprosy Istorii KPSS*]. *Voprosy Istorii KPSS [USSR] 1982 (9): 149-157.* A special meeting was held at the Institute of Marxism-Leninism at the Soviet Communist Party (CPSU) Central Committee in Moscow on 14 July 1982 to mark the 25th anniversary of the journal *Voprosy Istorii KPSS.* The main speaker was the Institute's Director, A. G. Egorov, who stressed the contribution made by the publication to the development of the study of Party history. The journal was founded after directives of the CPSU Central Committee issued on 12 June 1957. Since then it has published 267 issues carrying more than 5, 600 articles. They have covered all aspects of Party history and, like the CPSU itself, the journal has been involved in the whole range of economic and social affairs. 2 notes. J. Bamber

349. Topornin, B. THE STRONGHOLD OF PEACE AND PROGRESS. *Int. Affairs [USSR] 1973 (2): 6-12.* Discusses the application of Marxist-Leninist ideology and the principle of socialist internationalism in the USSR's foreign policy toward Communist countries, 1922-70's.

350. Toshchenko, Zh. T. AKTUALNYE VOPROSY IDEOLOGICHESKOGO OBESPECHENIIA KHOZIAISTVENNOGO STROITEL'STVA V SOVREMENNYKH USLOVIIAKH [Guaranteeing an ideological basis for economic development in contemporary conditions]. *Voprosy Istorii KPSS [USSR] 1982 (1): 28-40.* From the first years of Soviet power the Communist Party has regarded the problems of economic development as directly connected with the tasks of ideological struggle. The Party carries out propaganda to raise productivity and improve quality. Practice shows that the success of ideological work depends on the skillful use of agitational methods and the ability to respond to the creative initiatives of the working masses. Based on secondary sources; 62 notes.
G. Dombrovski

351. Trukhanovski, V. G. MIRNOE SOSUSHESTVOVANIE V DEISTVII [Peaceful coexistence in action]. *Voprosy Istorii [USSR] 1974 (10): 3-32.* "Examines the elaboration by V. I. Lenin and the Soviet Communist Party of the cardinal principles of Soviet foreign policy—the principle of proletarian internationalism and the principle of the peaceful co-existence of states with different social sys-

tems, as well as the basic content of the Peace Program put forward by the 24th Congress of the CPSU. The author focuses attention on graphically illustrating the unflagging efforts made by the Soviet Union to implement this far-reaching program."
J

352. Trush, M. I. RAZVITIE LENINSKIKH IDEI BOR'BY ZA MIRNOE SOSUSHCHESTVOVANIE V PROGRAMME KPSS [The development of the Leninist idea of struggle for peaceful coexistence in the program of the Soviet Communist Party]. *Voprosy Istorii KPSS [USSR] 1962 (4): 143-154.* Argues that the principle of peaceful coexistence between states of differing social structure was evolved by V. I. Lenin and became fundamental to Soviet policy, 1917-62.

353. Trushchenko, N. V. LENINSKII KOMSOMOL—VOEVOI POMOSHCHNIK PARTII V PODGOTOVKE MOLODEZHI K ZASHCHITE RODINY NA OSNOVE IDEI XVIII S"EZDA VKP(B) [The Lenin Komsomol: the fighting assistant of the Party in the training of youth for the defense of the homeland on the basis of the ideas of the 18th Congress of the All-Russian Communist Party (Bolshevik)]. *Voprosy Istorii KPSS [USSR] 1981 (6): 64-74.* Outlines and discusses recent documents and research work on the varied efforts of the Communist Party in preparing young people for active participation in work for the furthering of socialism in the USSR. Considers the efforts of the Komsomol in the prewar years, giving detailed accounts of the involvement with the Party from 1938 onwards, shows how the Komsomol supported the Party during World War II, and notes its continued efforts in cooperation with other organizations to further the cause of Soviet socialism. Based on archive material in Komsomol Central Archives and secondary sources; 48 notes. L. Smith

354. Ukraintsev, V. V. POLITIKA KPSS V OBLASTI PODGOTOVKI I VOSPITANIIA KADROV SPETSIALISTOV S VYSSHIM OBRAZOVANIEM [The CPSU's policies in the fields of the preparation and training of specialist cadres with higher education]. *Voprosy Istorii KPSS [USSR] 1976 (10): 41-52.* Charts the impact of the policy decisions of the Communist Party on expanding the numbers and quality of technical specialists in the 1960's-70's.

355. Urum, Valentin. LE MOUVEMENT DES PAYS NON-ALIGNÉS: PROLOGUES HISTORICO-DIPLOMATIQUES [The movement of the nonaligned nations: historical and diplomatic prologues]. *Rev. Roumaine d'Hist. [Rumania] 1977 16(1): 135-153.* The postwar struggle against imperialism and neocolonialism meant that the cardinal principle of the independence of each nation became the guiding force of a new international configuration. Progressive states sought an end to the division of the world into blocs; instead mutual collaboration of all peoples was to be the rule. Analyzes the foundations and evolution of these ideas after the 1955 Bandung Conference, the 1956 Brioni Declaration of Yugoslavia, India, and Egypt, and the affirmations of the 20th Party Congress of the Soviet Union. Based on published documents and secondary sources; 37 notes. G. J. Bobango

356. Usatov, M. V. I. LENIN I KOMMUNISTICHESKAIA PARTIIA O REVOLUTSIONNOI BDITEL'NOSTI [V. I. Lenin and the Communist Party on revolutionary vigilance]. *Voenno-Istoricheskii Zhurnal [USSR] 1972 (2): 3-10.* Discusses Soviet countermeasures against Western infiltration, espionage, and subversion in the USSR since the revolution.

357. Ushakov, N. A. MEZHDUNARODNO-PRAVOVYE PROBLEMY POSLEVOENNOGO MIROVOGO RAZVITIIA [International legal problems of the postwar world development]. *Sovetskoe Gosudarstvo i Pravo [USSR] 1980 (5): 59-68.* The victory over fascism in World War II began establishment of the world international socialist system which is regulated by principles of noninterference and national sovereignty as well as close cooperation and brotherly assistance. Alongside the socialist system a new system of developing countries struggling against all forms of colonialism and neo-colonialism has been emerging. The USSR (and other socialist countries) pursue a policy of detente with the capitalist countries and the USSR has signed a number of treaties regulating mutual relations. Based on resolutions of the 1971 and 1976 Congresses of the Communist Party of the Soviet Union and on statements by L. Brezhnev quoted in *Pravda;* 7 notes.
V. Sobeslavsky

358. Ustinov, D. F. RUKOVODIASHCHAIA ROL' KPSS V STROITEL'STVE SOVETSKIKH VOORUZHENNYKH SIL [The leading role of the CPSU in the building of the Soviet armed forces]. *Voprosy Istorii KPSS [USSR] 1979 (2): 14-34.* A survey of the history of the Soviet army. The Communist Party encouraged its members to join the armed forces, sponsored industrialization and, after World War II, rapid economic recovery, understood the need for new weapons, and provided for the moral and political education of troops. Based on V. I. Lenin's *Collected works* and articles in *Pravda;* 34 notes. L. E. Holmes

359. Usubaliev, T. PARTIINOE RUKOVODSTVO PODEMOM KUL'TURNO-TEKHNICHESKOGO UROVNIA TRUDIASHCHIKHSIA [The Party's leadership in raising the cultural and technical level of the workers]. *Voprosy Istorii KPSS [USSR] 1972 (12): 17-33.* Surveys the growth and improvement of the educational system and level of the Kirghiz SSR, 1925-72.

360. Varhatiuk, P. L. DO 100-RICHCHIA Z DNIA NARODZHENNIA G. I. PETROVS'KOGO: VYDATNYI DERZHAVNYI I PARTIINYI DIIACH [The 100th anniversary of the birth of G. I. Petrovski: a prominent statesman and Party activist]. *Ukrains'kyi Istorychnyi Zhurnal [USSR] 1978 (1): 32-42.* A biography of Grigori Ivanovich Petrovski, prominent revolutionary and founding member of the Ukrainian Soviet state. Examines in particular his work as a Bolshevik in close union with V. I. Lenin, and later his role as a talented statesman. He made noteworthy contributions to the Soviet legislative system and socialist construction. 37 notes.
V. A. Packer/S

361. Varhatiuk, P. L. LENINS'KE VCHENNIA PRO PARTIIU NOVOHO TYPU I VTILENNIA IOHO V DIIATEL'NOSTI KPRS [Leninist teaching about a party of the new type and its embodiment in the work of the CPSU]. *Ukrains'kyi Istorychhyi Zhurnal [USSR] 1978 (7): 5-17.* V. I. Lenin's analysis of the problems of 19th-century Russia and the social contradictions of imperialism show the necessity and logic of forming a new type of party made up from the union of workers' groups. The history of the Soviet Communist Party forged thus from small underground groups in Russia and the Ukraine and pioneering Marxist-Leninist theory in action, is unique. The steady development of the Party and growth in international authority confirm the correctness of the path chosen. 20 notes. V. Packer

362. Varshavchik, N. A. K VOPROSU OB OTBORE ISTORIKO-PARTIINIKH ISTOCHNIKOV [The selection of sources for Party history]. *Voprosy Istorii KPSS [USSR] 1966 (3): 112-117.* Discusses the problems of historical sources on both the state and the Communist Party.

363. Varshavchyk, M. Ia. MATERIALY PARTIINYKH Z'IZDIV IAK DZHERELO VYVCHENNIA ISTORII KPRS [Materials from the Party Congresses as sources for studying the history of the CPSU]. *Ukrains'kyi Istorychnyi Zhurnal [USSR] 1971 (1): 3-12.* Discusses the publication of materials from Soviet Communist Party Congresses, 1902-71, and their value as reference works for the correct interpretation of Marxist-Leninist political theory.

364. Varshavchyk, M. Ia. OSNOVNI ETAPY ROZVYTKU DZHERELOZNAVSTVA ISTORII KPRS [The main stages of the development of the source study for a history of the Soviet Communist Party]. *Ukrains'kyi Istorychnyi Zhurnal [USSR] 1973 (11): 25-36.*

365. Vasil'ev, G. V. and Il'in, Iu. K. ISPYTANNYI POMOSHCHNIK PARTII: K 50-LETIIU GAZETY *PRAVDY* [The Party's trusty helper: the 50th anniversary of *Pravda*]. *Voprosy Istorii KPSS [USSR] 1962 (4): 225-229.* Discusses aspects of the history of the

Soviet Communist Party newspaper *Pravda* raised at a conference dedicated to its 50th anniversary, held at Kharkov, USSR, in April 1962.

366. Verkhovtsev, I. P. VELIKAIA PARTIIA LENINA [The great Party of Lenin]. *Voprosy Istorii KPSS [USSR] 1963 (11): 125-128.* Summarizes two books published in 1963 to mark the 60th anniversary of the Second Party Congress, *The great Party of Lenin* and *At the roots of the Party.* The author criticizes the first for its dry style and the latter for inaccuracies.

367. Vezirov, Kh. G. VERNAIA DOCH' KOMMUNISTICHESKOI PARTII (K 90-LETIIU SO DNIA ROZHDENIIA N. N. KOLESNIKOVOI) [Faithful daughter of the Communist Party: on the 90th birthday of N. N. Kolesnikova]. *Voprosy Istorii KPSS [USSR] 1972 (9): 116-119.* Reflects on the teaching, research, and welfare activity during 1904-57 of Nadezhda Kolesnikova, who was a leading figure in the Baku underground of 1907-17.

368. Vianu, Alexandru. CONSTITUIREA ŞI DEZVOLTAREA STATULUI SOVIETIC. 1922-1972 [The constitution and development of the Soviet state, 1922-72]. *Anale de Istorie [Rumania] 1972 18(6): 117-134.* Reviews the creation of the USSR, 1917-22, the unification of various Soviet republics, the impressive economic development of the Soviet state under its five-year plans since the 1920's, the 1936 Soviet constitution, the cult of personality era under Joseph Stalin, and the immense contribution of the Russian people to the defeat of Hitler. Summarizes the directives of the Party congresses, 1952-66. Secondary sources; 12 notes.
G. J. Bobango

369. Vigne, Éric. URSS: LES INGÉNIEURS PRENNENT LE POUVOIR [USSR: the technocrats take power]. *Histoire [France] 1980 (26): 88-90.* Nearly 80 of the 100 members of the Politburo of the Communist Party of the USSR for the past 30 years have belonged to the technical intelligentsia: engineers, agronomists, technicians, and scientists.

370. Vilkova, V. P. LENIN, PARTIIA I RABOCHII KLASS [Lenin, the Party, and the working class]. *Voprosy Istorii KPSS [USSR] 1984 (5): 61-71.* At the 30th Congress of the Russian Communist Party, which took place in May 1924, Lenin emphasized that socialist construction was impossible without full worker participation and enthusiasm. The Party must have a high percentage of working class members. The congress rallied around Lenin's line. Throughout the Soviet period the Party has displayed concern for the workers. For example, between 1961 and 1981 the percentage of workers in the Party rose from 33.9% to 43.4%. Between the 25th and the 26th Party Congresses, the Party admitted 1,500,000 workers. Based on Lenin's work and CPSU documents and Congresses; 46 notes.
A. J. Evans

371. Vinogradov, N. N. LENINSKAIA KONTSEPTSIIA PARTIINOGO RUKOVODSTVA SOVETAMI [The Leninist conception of the Party guidance of the soviets]. *Sovetskoe Gosudarstvo i Pravo [USSR] 1980 (4): 13-21.* Describes V. I. Lenin's views on the character, content, and style of the Party work in the soviet organs.
J/S

372. Vinokurova, R. F. LENINSKII KOMSOMOL—AKTIVNYI POMOSHCHNIK I REZERV PARTII [Lenin's Komsomol, an active helper of the Party and its reserve pool]. *Prepodavanie Istorii v Shkole [USSR] 1978 (4): 24-34.* Sketches, with selected statistical data, the growth of the Young Communist League (Komsomol) since 1922 and its expanding role within the last 40 years. The author discusses its rising membership ratio among students, political cadres, and local government bodies, contributions to industrial and agricultural development of frontier lands, and educational and political activist work to strengthen the labor effort. At present, the Komsomol numbers almost 38 million members versus 260,000 in 1922 and 3.9 million in 1936. 7 notes, biblio. N. Frenkley

373. Virnyk, D. RASTSVET I SBLIZHENIE SOTSIALISTICHESKIKH NATSII SSSR [The flowering and communion of socialist nations of the USSR]. *Ekonomika Sovetskoi Ukrainy [USSR] 1972 14(3): 17-26.* Emphasizing the Leninist principles which underlie the national policies of the Soviet Communist Party, the author describes the harmonious economic commonwealth of the Soviet republics and the important role played by the Ukraine in the economy of the USSR, 1913-71.

374. Vitruk, L. D.; Pliushch, M. R.; and Talan, Ie. P. POLITYCHNA AKTYVNIST' TRUDIASHCHYKH RADIANS'KOI UKRAINY U ZV'IAZKU Z VIDZNACHENNIAM 50-RICHCHIA SRSR [Political activity by the working people of Soviet Ukraine to celebrate the 50th anniversary of the USSR]. *Ukrains'kyi Istorychnyi Zhurnal [USSR] 1973 (12): 61-68.* Describes propaganda work carried out by the Communist Party, Young Communist League and cultural organizations in the Ukraine, in cooperation with other republics, 1970-72, to ensure a fitting celebration of the 50th anniversary of the creation of the USSR, in 1972.

375. Voigt, Gerd. HISTORIOGRAPHIE UND KOMMUNISMUSFORSCHUNG [Historiography and research on communism]. *Zeitschrift für Geschichtswissenschaft [East Germany] 1976 24(5): 501-515.* Imperialist research on communism uses the theory of pluralism, the theory of the Russian renunciation of proletarian internationalism, and the ideological wear and tear of Marxism-Leninism as arguments for the downfall of the socialist system. Based on Western works on Russian history and secondary literature. 54 notes. R. Wagnleitner

376. Volin, Ia. R. K 60-LETIIU X S''EZDA RKP(B) [The 60th anniversary of the 10th Russian Communist Party (Bolshevik) Congress]. *Voprosy Istorii KPSS [USSR] 1981 (6): 151-153.* Conferences took place in various academic centers in Moscow, Leningrad, Saratov, Omsk, and Perm on the theme of V. I. Lenin and Local Party Organizations in connection with the anniversary of the 10th Communist Party Congress, organized by the Ministry of Higher and Middle Special Education of the Russian Federation. Papers were presented by 37 participants on topics including the 10th Party Congress and its decisions, the Leninist conception of the transition from capitalism to socialism, the significance of the New Economic Policy in the building of socialism, and the 10th Party Congress and the strengthening of international links of the working class of the USSR. L. Smith

377. Volkov, I. M.; Vyltsan, M. A.; and Zelenin, I. E. VOPROSY PRODOVOL'STVENNOGO OBESPECHENIIA NASELENIIA SSSR (1917-1982 GG.) [Problems of food supply for the population of the USSR, 1917-82]. *Istoriia SSSR [USSR] 1983 (2): 3-20.* Guaranteeing adequate food stocks for the population has always been one of the prime tasks of the Communist Party of the Soviet Union (CPSU). In 1917, the country was in the grip of Civil War and famine. Lenin introduced a flexible system of agricultural production and distribution, allowing some capitalist methods to be retained so as to boost productivity. The CPSU's efficient Five-Year Plans improved food supplies consistently until World War II, educating farmers in new techniques and modernizing the USSR's technological base. This has been continued since the war, and the resolutions of the 1982 CPSU Congress laid firm foundations for further improvement until 1990. 4 tables, 78 notes.
J. Bamber

378. VonBorcke, Astrid. DILEMMAS OF SINGLE-PARTY RULE IN THE SOVIET UNION. *Problems of Communism 1982 31(3): 60-65.* A review of Ronald J. Hill and Peter Frank's *The Soviet Communist Party* (1981), Michael S. Voslensky's *Nomenklatura: Die Herrschende Klasse der Sowjetunion* (1980), and Helene Carrère d'Encausse, *Le Pouvoir Confisqué: Gouvernants et Gouvernés en U.R.S.S.* (1980). The Communist Party of the Soviet Union, the dominant and most pervasive of all Soviet bureaucracies, faces the still unresolved dilemma of balancing modernization-rationalization with maintenance of political power. 18 notes. J. M. Lauber

379. Vorozheikin, I. E. BOEVOI ORGAN LENINSKOI PARTII (K 70-LETIIU GAZETY *PRAVDA*) [The fighting organ of Lenin's Party: on the 70th anniversary of *Pravda*]. *Voprosy Istorii KPSS*

[USSR] 1982 (5): 34-46. Pravda began publication on 5 May 1912. Since the beginning under V. I. Lenin it has kept a resolutely Marxist-Leninist line. Its history is inseparable from that of the Communist Party of the Soviet Union. During the Russian Revolution, *Pravda* informed workers about the advance of Soviet power and the machinations of the imperialists. *Pravda* has always striven for the advancement of the workers, and now in the era of advanced socialism it tirelessly explains the duties of the educated and sophisticated socialist masses. *Pravda's* principal role in the 1970's was to elucidate the decisions of the 24th and 25th Party Congresses. At least 10,700,000 copies are published daily in 48 cities, and it is one of the most authoritative newspapers in the world. Based on the works and speeches of Lenin and Brezhnev and on *Pravda;* 43 notes. A. J. Evans

380. Walther, Arne Roy. GRETSJKO OG DEN 24. PARTIKONGRESS [Grechko and the 24th Party Congress]. *Norsk Militaert Tidsskrift [Norway] 1971 141(7): 341-344.* Provides a biography of Andrei Grechko, reproduces parts of his speech to the 24th Party Congress on 3 April 1971, and assesses the increasing influence of the military sector in the USSR.

381. Wessely, Kurt. DIE ENTDECKUNG DES KONSUMENT. ÖSTLICHE DISKUSSIONEN ÜBER MARKTFRAGEN UND GÜTERWAHL [The discovery of the consumer: eastern discussions on questions of the market and selection of goods]. *Österreichische Osthefte [Austria] 1962 4(1): 36-42.* At the 22d congress of the Communist Party of the USSR, the consumer was promised the fulfillment of his requirements. In contrast to the Western system of manipulating the consumer by private interests, the consumer in Eastern European countries is manipulated by state economic planning. Secondary sources; 15 notes. R. Wagnleitner

382. White, Stephen. CONTRADICTION AND CHANGE IN STATE SOCIALISM. *Soviet Studies [Great Britain] 1974 26(1): 41-55.* One of the most favored elite and elite conflict theories that have been postulated by Western scholars in relation to the USSR argues a split between party officials and the managerial elite or "technocrats." This disguises a more serious if latent cleavage between party and managerial elites as a single group and other sections of society, particularly the industrial worker. In addition, it obscures and minimizes the important sources of stability in the system: socialization, party recruitment policy, and ideology. These factors may well produce greater stability and cohesion in the Soviet Union than is possible under a Western capitalist regime. 48 notes. L. Brown

383. White, Stephen. POLITICAL COMMUNICATIONS IN THE USSR: LETTERS TO PARTY, STATE AND PRESS. *Pol. Studies [Great Britain] 1983 31(1): 43-60.* The Soviet authorities have been devoting increasing attention to the "link with the masses" provided by letters sent by citizens to Party and state bodies and to the press since the late 1960's. An examination of the extent and nature of such communications shows that their total number has increased significantly since ca. 1960, and that more constructive and general proposals have been increasing at the expense of particular individual grievances, although this change is less apparent at the local level. Critics are sometimes victimized and frequently ignored, but the evidence suggests that a considerable groundswell of opinion as reflected in letters can have some influence upon public policy and that particular cases of maladministration or abuse of position can be relatively readily corrected in this way. 2 tables, 93 notes. D. J. Nicholls

384. Wiles, Peter J. D.; Smith, Alan; Zafiris, Nicos; Lynch, Barry; and Chudo, Yukimasa. THE COMMERCIAL POLICIES OF THE COMMUNIST THIRD WORLD. *Millennium: J. of Int. Studies [Great Britain] 1980-81 9(3): 197-214.* Investigates the economic policy of the USSR and Eastern European countries toward those developing nations that have proclaimed a Marxist-Leninist form of government to determine the effects on the internal economic and social structure of the developing countries and to discover the nature of their economic relations with the Eastern bloc and the developed capitalist nations.

385. Yudin, I. N. O NEKOTORYKH VOPROSAKH RAZVITIIA SOTSIAL'NOI BAZY KPSS [The development of the social basis of the Communist Party of the USSR]. *Voprosy Istorii KPSS [USSR] 1971 (10): 16-32.* Outlines the changes that have affected the working class, peasantry, and intelligentsia in the USSR since 1917, and notes the impact on CPSU membership.

386. Zachariacisová, L. Z HISTORIE A SOUČASNOSTI KOMSOMOLŮ (K VYROCI 60 VLKSM) [From the history and the present of the Komsomol: honoring the 60th anniversary of the ALCYO]. *Slovanský Přehled [Czechoslovakia] 1983 69(6): 448-462.* The Young Communist League (Komsomol) was formally established at the first All-Soviet Congress in 1918 with a membership of 22,100. For the last 60 years it has served an important function in nurturing the young in the ideals of socialism. Komsomol members have participated in brigades, sport events, and cultural events; they were also partisans in World War II. Today, the leaders of the Communist Party have all come up through the Komsomol and most new party members had been Komsomol participants in their youth. 35 notes. B. Reinfeld

387. Zagladin, V. V. VELIKII OKTIABR'I KOMMUNISTICHESKOE DVIZHENIE: PROSHLOE I NASTOIASHCHEE [Great October and the Communist movement: past and present]. *Voprosy Istorii KPSS [USSR] 1980 (11): 13-30.*

388. Zamlyns'kyi, V. O. KOMUNISTYCHNA PARTIIA: ORHANIZATOR PEREMOHY SOTSIALIZMU V ZAKHIDNYKH OBLASTIAKH UKRAÏNY [The Communist Party, organizer of the victory of socialism in the western Ukraine]. *Ukraïns'kyi Istorychnyi Zhurnal [USSR] 1979 (9): 16-28.* The Communist Party of the Soviet Union supported by all means the struggle of the working people in West Ukraine under Polish and Romanian occupation, for the reunification with Soviet Ukraine and for the triumph of the socialist order after the West Ukrainian lands were incorporated with the Soviet Union in 1939. 40 notes. Russian summary. I. Krushelnycky

389. Zatulin, A. F. O NEKOTORYKH VOPROSAKH PERIODIZATSII ISTORII KPSS [The periodization of history of the CPSU]. *Voprosy Istorii KPSS [USSR] 1971 (12): 91-97.* Suggests that Soviet Communist Party history may be divided into five stages: 1) the emergence of the Bolshevik Party, 1883-1903; 2) the struggle for victory in the bourgeois-democratic revolution, 1903-February 1917; 3) the organization of victory after the socialist revolution and the formation of the proletarian dictatorship, February-October 1917; 4) during the construction of socialism in the USSR, October 1917-58; 5) the transition to the Communist construction of the USSR, 1959-70's.

390. Zibarev, V. A. LENINSKAIA NATSIONAL'NAIA POLITIKA KPSS I MALYE NARODY SEVERA [The Leninist nationality policy of the CPSU and the minority peoples of the north]. *Istoriia SSSR [USSR] 1981 (3): 44-59.* Describes the impact of the Leninist nationalities policy of the Communist Party of the Soviet Union (CPSU) on the national minorities of the northern USSR. During the prerevolutionary era, the 26 minorities of the north were backward and downtrodden. As a result of Soviet policies these peoples have now made the transition from patriarchal-clan relations to modern socialism. This phenomenon represents one of the most brilliant achievements of the nationality policy of the Communist Party. Published sources; 36 notes. J. W. Long

391. Zlatopol'ski, D. L. PROGRAMMA KPSS PO NATSIONAL'NOMU VOPROSU I STROITEL'STVO SOVETSKOI FEDERATSII [The program of the CPSU on the national question and the building of the Soviet Federation]. *Sovetskoe Gosudarstvo i Pravo [USSR] 1972 (11): 10-17.* Discusses the principles of the theory and practice of Soviet federalism, which unites more than 100 nationalities and ethnic groups at different stages of economic and political development. All are bound together by a single economic structure and the Russian language. Describes the constant process

of convergence and merger occurring between these constituent groups of the multinational USSR. Based on V. I. Lenin's writings; 17 notes. S. P. Dunn

392. Zuvojic, Zoran. DE GESHIEDENIS VAN DE COMMUNISTISCHE PARTIJ DER SOVJETUNIE [The history of the Communist Party of the Soviet Union]. *Internationale Spectator [Netherlands] 1970 24(18): 1672-1696.* Translation of a series by the Moscow correspondent of the Yugoslavia journal *Politica.* In this third edition, the point of view has changed from the two earlier editions (1959, 1963) in that Stalin is no longer the hero, but many of the failures of the Russian Communist forces to deal with problems is attributed to Stalin. Refers in particular to the German capture of Moscow and the break between Russia and Yugoslavia. W. S. Reid

393. —. [DEFINITION OF THE SOCIAL NATURE OF THE SOVIET UNION]. *Critique [Great Britain] 1979-80 (12): 117-137.*

Mandel, Ernest. ONCE AGAIN ON THE TROTSKYIST DEFINITION OF THE SOCIAL NATURE OF THE SOVIET UNION, *pp. 117-126.* Contends that Soviet society has yet to advance from capitalism to socialism but still has a latent capacity to effect that transition.

Ticktin, Hillel. THE AMBIGUITIES OF ERNEST MANDEL, *pp. 127-137.* The USSR has no capacity to advance toward socialism in its present state.

394. —. DEIATEL'NOST' KPSS PO STROITEL'STVU RAZVITOGO SOTSIALIZMA V 60-E GODY [The activity of the Communist Party of the Soviet Union in constructing developed socialism in the 1960's]. *Voprosy Istorii [USSR] 1984 (4): 3-14.* Deals with Party policy in upgrading the Soviet economy, perfecting social relations, and raising living standards in the 1960's-70's. In the 1960's positive qualitative shifts in social development were observed despite objective and subjective difficulties. The essence of the tasks confronting the Party today aimed at at the further acceleration of Soviet economic development and the improvement of all sides of the life of Soviet society are also examined. J

395. —. DOKUMENTY I STAT'I PO ISTORII KPSS I MEZHDUNARODNOGO KOMMUNISTICHESKOGO I RABOCHEGO DVIZHENIIA, OPUBLIKOVANNYE V ZHURNALAKH, UCHENYKH ZAPISKAKH, SBORNIKAKH I TRUDAKH V NOIABRE-DEKABRE 1962 GODA [Documents and articles on the history of the CPSU and the international communist and workers' movement, published in journals, scholarly notebooks, collections, and works, in November and December, 1962]. *Voprosy Istorii KPSS [USSR] 1963 (2): 147-150.* Provides a comprehensive list of documents and articles relating to the history of the Soviet Communist Party and the international communist movement published in the USSR, November and December 1962.

396. —. FIFTY YEARS OF UNION OF SOVIET SOCIALIST REPUBLICS (1922-72). *World Marxist Rev. [Canada] 1972 15(10): 3-143.*

—. SOVIET EXPERIENCE OF BUILDING SOCIALISM AND ITS WORLD-HISTORIC SIGNIFICANCE, *p. 3.*

Zarodov, K. I. MILESTONE IN MANKIND'S SOCIAL PROGRESS, *pp. 4-5.*

Ponomaryov, Boris. INTERNATIONAL SIGNIFICANCE OF FORMATION AND DEVELOPMENT OF USSR, *pp. 5-19.*

Tellalov, Konstantin. SOCIALIST INTERNATIONALISM IN ACTION, *pp. 19-22.*

Guyot, Raymond. OUTSTANDING CONTRIBUTION TO REVOLUTIONARY EXPERIENCE, *pp. 22-25.*

Sen, Bhawani. SOVIET EXPERIENCE AND THE NATIONAL QUESTION IN INDIA, *pp. 26-29.*

Pessi, Ville. USSR AND NATIONAL INTERESTS OF FINNISH PEOPLE, *pp. 29-32.*

Abdel-Hamid, Abu Aitah. LENINIST PRINCIPLE OF UNITY, *pp. 32-24.*

Ashimov, Baiken. ELIMINATING ECONOMIC AND CULTURAL INEQUALITY, *pp. 34-37.*

Cox, Idris. BEACON OF PEOPLE'S STRUGGLE, *pp. 37-40.*

Luvsanravdan, Namsarai. MATERIALIZATION OF THE OBJECTIVE LAWS OF SOCIALISM, *pp. 41-44.*

Bouhali, Larbi. FLOURISHING SOCIALIST REPUBLICS, *pp. 44-46.*

Ashhab, Naim. POWERFUL SPUR TO NATIONAL LIBERATION, *pp. 46-48.*

Werblan, Andrzej. MODEL OF NEW INTERNATIONAL RELATIONS, *pp. 49-52.*

Savvidis, Georgos. THE ONLY ROAD TO FRATERNITY OF NATIONS, *pp. 52-54.*

Gensini, Gastone. SOME ASPECTS OF THE ITALIAN COMMUNISTS' FIGHT FOR DEMOCRACY AND SOCIALISM, *pp. 54-57.*

Bagdash, Khaled. FIDELITY TO PROLETARIAN INTERNATIONALISM, *pp. 57-60.*

Constantinescu, Miron. THE RCP IN REVOLUTION AND SOCIALIST BUILDING, *pp. 60-63.*

Peter, Alois. NO COMPROMISE IN IDEOLOGICAL STRUGGLE, *pp. 63-65.*

Heyden, Guenter. INTERNATIONAL RELATIONS OF A NEW TYPE, *pp. 66-69.*

Demir, Yakub. INDESTRUCTIBLE FRATERNAL UNION, *pp. 69-71.*

Junttila, Lars. RISE OF A MULTINATIONAL CULTURE, *pp. 71-74.*

Szabo, Josef. LESSONS OF SOCIALIST CONSTRUCTION IN THE USSR, *pp. 74-76.*

Fuchs, Jaime. BULWARK OF THE WORLD REVOLUTIONARY MOVEMENT, *pp. 76-79.*

Kulichenko, M. I. THE SOVIET PEOPLE: A NEW HISTORICAL COMMUNITY, *pp. 79-83.*

Bart, Philip. THE COMMUNIST PARTY IN THE FIGHT AGAINST RACIALISM, *pp. 83-86.*

Noibert, Harald. CRITERION OF LOYALTY TO MARXISM-LENINISM, *pp. 86-88.*

Yata, Ali. THE MAIN FORCE CONFRONTING IMPERIALISM, *pp. 88-90.*

Van Geit, Louis. THE ANTI-PEOPLES' POLICY OF THE MONOPOLY BOURGEOISIE, *pp. 90-93.*

Harmel, Mohamed. FROM FEUDALISM TO SOCIALISM, BYPASSING CAPITALISM, *pp. 93-95.*

Iskenderi, Iraj. POWERFUL FACTOR FOR PEACE AND PROGRESS, *pp. 95-97.*

Mendez, Pedro. A SOURCE OF REVOLUTIONARY ENERGY, *pp. 98-101.*

Nagy, Laszlo. SOVIET SOCIALIST DEMOCRACY, *pp. 101-104.*

Harmel, Michael. THE POWER OF PROLETARIAN SOLIDARITY, *pp. 104-105.*

Ahmed, Kerim. AGAINST BOURGEOIS NATIONALISM AND CHAUVINISM, *pp. 106-108.*

Fojtik, Jan. THE SOVIET UNION'S GROWING PRESTIGE AND AUTHORITY, *pp. 109-112.*

Venetsanopoulos, Vasilis. TRIUMPH OF THE LENINIST NATIONAL POLICY, *pp. 112-114.*

Bagramov, E. A. APROPOS THE FALSIFICATION OF NATIONAL RELATIONS IN THE USSR, *pp. 115-118.*

Ohman, Rodney. THE ROAD TO WOMEN'S EMANCIPATION, *pp. 118-121.*

Mruhe, Kerim. THE ARAB LIBERATION MOVEMENT, *pp. 121-123.*

Buschmann, Martha. TRIUMPH OF SOCIALIST IDEAS, *pp. 123-126.*

Mendes, Catarina. PORTUGUESE COMMUNISTS BATTLE COLONIALISM, *pp. 126-128.*

Norlund, Ib. THE FUNDAMENTAL SIGNIFICANCE OF SOVIET EXPERIENCE, *pp. 128-131.*

Jaroszewski, Tadeusz. THE GENERAL AND SPECIFIC IN SOCIALIST CONSTRUCTION, *pp. 132-134.*

Foster, John. NATIONAL PROBLEMS IN BRITISH WORKING-CLASS MOVEMENT, *pp. 134-137.*

Dix, Rudolf. CREATIVE APPROACH TO CPSU EXPERIENCE, *pp. 137-139.*

Fedoseev, P. N. INTERNATIONALISM, AN INALIENABLE PART OF COMMUNIST IDEOLOGY AND POLICY, *pp. 139-143.* Presentations from a conference in Prague, Czechoslovakia, in 1972 concerning the significance of the creation and social development of the USSR since 1922 for the international Communist and national liberation movements.

397. —. ÎNSEMNĂTATEA ISTORICĂ A CELUI DE-AL XXI-LEA CONGRES EXTRAORDINAR AL P. C. U. S. [The historical significance of the 21st Extraordinary Congress of the Communist Party of the USSR]. *Studii: Rev. de Istorie [Rumania] 1959 12(2): 5-12.* An appreciation of Soviet achievements as presented at the 21st Party congress in Moscow, January-February 1959.

398. —. LENINSKIE NORMY PARTIINOI ZHIZNI, IKH OSUSHCHESTVLENIE V DEIATEL'NOSTI KPSS [Leninist norms of Party life: their realization in the activity of the CPSU]. *Voprosy Istorii KPSS [USSR] 1981 (12): 101-114.* The Communist Party of the Soviet Union follows guidelines established by V. I. Lenin in its organization and work. The Party insures that the best people are admitted as members and encourages their active participation. Furthermore, the Leninist principles of democratic centralism, responsible leadership, accountability, conscious discipline, and self-criticism govern the Party's activity. Based on Lenin's *Collected Works;* 27 notes. L. E. Holmes

399. —. [THE METHODOLOGY OF THE HISTORY OF THE RUSSIAN COMMUNIST PARTY].

Varshavchik, M. A. VOPROSY METODOLOGII ISTORIKO-PARTIINOI NAUKI [Questions on the methodology of Party historical science]. *Voprosy Istorii KPSS [USSR] 1976 (4): 85-97.* Discusses the meaning of methodology and how it should be applied in the study of the Soviet Communist Party's history to raise and develop Marxist theory.

Maslov, N. N. and Mogilnitski, B. G. O NEKOTORYKH VOPROSAKH METODOLOGII ISTORII KPSS [Some aspects of the methodology of the history of the Russian Communist Party]. *Voprosy Istorii KPSS [USSR] 1976 (6): 106-111.* Considers problems raised by M. A. Varshavchik in his discussion on methodology and the Russian Communist Party, and points out deficiencies in his methodological concepts.

400. —. MIKHAIL ANDREEVICH SUSLOV [Mikhail A. Suslov]. *Voprosy Istorii KPSS [USSR] 1982 (12): 55-61.* Commemorates the 80th birthday of the Kremlin's leading ideologist. A Young Communist League activist at age 16, Suslov joined the Party in 1921, and held a number of responsible posts in the Party apparat before the war. During World War II he was a member of the Military Council of the Northern Group of Armies on the Caucasus Front, and led the partisan movement in the Stavropol region. He became a secretary of the Communist Party Central Committee in 1947, and since 1952 he has been a member of the Presidium and of the Politburo. As a leading theoretician of Marxism-Leninism, he has contributed to the preparation of Party Congresses and to the 1977 constitution, and has made key recommendations in the field of propaganda and ideology. He has also contributed to the history of the Party. F. A. K. Yasamee

401. —. [THE PERIODIZATION OF THE HISTORY OF THE CPSU].

Kostin, A. F. K VOPROSU O METODE IZUCHENIIA ISTORII KPSS I KRITERIIAKH EE PERIODIZATSII [The question of a method for studying the history of the CPSU and criteria for its periodization]. *Voprosy Istorii KPSS [USSR] 1969 (9): 55-67.* Outlines various shortcomings in the different approaches to periodizing the history of the Communist Party of the USSR.

Sekerin, A. I. O NEKOTORYKH VOPROSAKH PERIODIZATSII POSLEOKTIABR'SKOI ISTORII KPSS [Concerning some questions of periodizing the post-October history of the CPSU], *Voprosy Istorii KPSS [USSR] 1969 (12): 76-81.* Criticizes Kostin's approach and offers a new periodization scheme.

402. —. PIĘĆDZIESIĘCIOLECIE CZASOPISMA "KOMMUNIST" [Fifty years of the journal *Communist]. Nowe Drogi [Poland] 1974 4: 88-94.* Surveys the work and achievements of the theoretical and political organ of the Central Committee of the Communist Party of the USSR, now called *Kommunist* but which was entitled the *Bolshevik,* 1924-52.

403. —. RESOLUTION OF THE CPSU CENTRAL COMMITTEE OF JANUARY 31, 1977 ON THE 60TH ANNIVERSARY OF THE GREAT OCTOBER SOCIALIST REVOLUTION. *Int. Affairs [USSR] 1977 (3): 3-16.*

404. —. S"EZDY PARTII O FLOTE, FLOT—S"EZDAM PARTII [Party congresses about the navy, the navy to Party congresses]. *Morskoi Sbornik [USSR] 1981 (1): 57-61.* Outlines the history of the fleet and its integration in the Soviet defense system from 1917 to the present, emphasizing the USSR's self-sufficiency in military technology and supplies. Based on various CPSU congresses and documents; 16 notes.

405. —. S"EZDY PARTII O FLOTE, FLOT—S"EZDAM PARTII [Party conferences on the fleet; the fleet and Party conferences]. *Morskoi Sbornik [USSR] 1981 (2): 52-56.* The history of the relationship between the Soviet Navy and Soviet Communist Party Congresses shows that the Party is the originator and organizer of the navy's success.

406. —. SLAVNYM TRADITSIIAM KREPNUT' [Keeping to the glorious traditions]. *Morskoi Sbornik [USSR] 1982 (10): 3-7.* Reviews the strong links between the Young Communist League (Komsomol) and the Soviet Navy since 1922; Komsomol branches have provided naval cadets and they have also "adopted" ships, writing to the crew and sending them food parcels and other presents.

407. —. SOVETSKIE ISTORIKI—K 60-LETIIU OBRAZOVANIIA SSSR (OBZOR LITERATURY ZA 1981-1983 GG.) [Soviet historians: a tribute on the 60th anniversary of the founding of the USSR—survey of literature published in 1981-83]. *Istoriia SSSR [USSR] 1984 (4): 60-80.* A survey of some 300 books, including bibliographies, monographs, collections of papers, and revised editions, and criticizes the shortage of publications devoted exclusively to the role of Lenin's party in building the USSR. Most studies deal with the past and present of Soviet minorities, contributions of the Communist Party to the rise of an international socialist fraternity of nations, Soviet economic policy contributing to socioeconomic and cultural progress of socialist countries, and call for an intensified struggle against bourgeois ideology. 46 notes. N. Frenkley

408. —. TEMY DISSERTATSII, ZASHCHISHCHENNYKH V 1968 G. NA SOISKANIE UCHENOI STEPENI KANDIDATA ISTORICHESKIKH NAUK PO RAZDELU "ISTORIIA KOMMUNISTICHESKOI PARTII SOVETSKOGO SOIUZA" [The dissertations concerning the history of the Communist Party of the USSR receiving the degree of Candidate of History in 1968]. *Voprosy Istorii KPSS [USSR] 1968 (11): 155-157.* Lists over 100 theses concerning the history of the Communist Party, 1894-1967. The list is divided into 12 sections devoted to the anti-Tsarist struggle, Russian Revolution, Civil War, economic reconstruction, industrialization, collectivization, *kolkhoz* building, completion of socialist reconstruction, World War II, postwar reconstruction, national economic development during the 1950's, and the development of Communism in the 1960's. N. Dejevsky

409. —. VELIKAIA POBEDA SOVETSKOGO NARODA [The great victory of the Soviet people]. *Morskoi Sbornik [USSR] 1981 (5): 3-8.* As during World War II, the Soviet people, army, and fleet stand united around the party of Lenin.

410. —. VELIKII ZNAMENOSETS KOMMUNIZMA (K 60-LETIIU II S"EZDA RSDRP) [The great standard bearer of communism: the 60th anniversary of the Second Party Congress]. *Voprosy Istorii KPSS [USSR] 1963 (7): 3-16.* Evaluates the significance of the second congress of the Russian Social Democratic Workers' Party for the development of Bolshevism and the USSR.

411. —. VO SLAVU RODINY, NA BLAGU NARODA (K VYKHODU V SVET IZBRANNYKH RECHEI I STATEI CHLENA POLITBIURO TSK KPSS, PREDSEDATELIA SOVETA MINISTROV SSSR N. A. TIKHONOVA) [For the glory of the homeland, for the good of the people (on the occasion of the publication of the collected speeches and articles of N. A. Tikhonov, member of the CPSU Politburo and Council of Ministers)]. *Voprosy Istorii KPSS [USSR] 1981 (2): 3-12.* Discusses the collection of speeches and articles published by N. A. Tikhonov, chairman of the USSR Council of Ministers. The speeches cover the period 1949-80 and were given at the various Party conferences, international forums, and sessions of the Supreme Soviet that Tikhonov attended. The major part of the work is devoted to the 1970's, with particular attention being given to the Communist Party's economic strategy and the utilization of recent scientific and technical achievements. 11 notes. A. Brown

412. —. 60 YEARS OF RUSSIAN COMMUNISM. *Can. Dimension [Canada] 1977 12(7): 14-23.* Journal's editors chronicle the growth and ideological evolution in the USSR's Communist Party, 1917-77.

1945-1953

413. Abramenko, T. F. and Simonian, M. N. ELENA FEDEROVNA ROZMIROVICH (K 80-LETIIU SO DNIA ROZHDENIIA) [Yelena Federovna Rozmirovich: the 80th anniversary of her birth]. *Voprosy Istorii KPSS [USSR] 1966 (3): 98-102.* A biography of the Russian revolutionary and Party activist Elena F. Rozmirovich (1886-1953).

414. Abramov, B. A. ORGANIZATSIONNO-PARTIINAIA RABOTA KPSS V GODY CHETVERTOI PIATILETKI [The organizational work of the CPSU during the fourth five-year plan]. *Voprosy Istorii KPSS [USSR] 1979 (3): 55-65.* During 1946-50 the Communist Party improved the quality of its membership by the recruitment of workers and an aggressive campaign of political and ideological training in special Party establishments from short-term evening schools to the Academy of Social Sciences. The Party carefully distributed its personnel, reorganized its own structure, and stimulated improved performance from its members and from state agencies in order to support the fulfillment of the five-year plan. Published documents; 16 notes. L. E. Holmes

415. Abramsky, Chimen. THE RISE AND FALL OF SOVIET YIDDISH LITERATURE. *Soviet Jewish Affairs [Great Britain] 1982 12(3): 35-44.* Discusses the cultural life of Soviet Jewry in three periods corresponding to the policies of the Soviet Communist Party.

416. Agafanenkov, E. F. PODGOTOVKA I PEREPODGOTOVKA PARTIINYKH I SOVETSKIKH KADROV (1946-1950 GG) [The preparation and renewed preparation of Party and Soviet cadres, 1946-50]. *Voprosy Istorii KPSS [USSR] 1970 (11): 101-109.* Discusses how, after World War II, a campaign was launched to raise the standard of political education of Communist Party workers, especially in Marxist theory.

417. Albright, David E. ON EASTERN EUROPE: SECURITY IMPLICATIONS FOR THE U.S.S.R. *Parameters 1984 14(2): 24-36.* Eastern Europe has created security problems for the USSR since World War II. Economic growth in the area had blunted opposition to the USSR right after the war, but growth slowed by the 1970's. The USSR responded with increased economic assistance, thus straining its own economy. Nevertheless, workers became critical of Communist regimes in several countries such as Poland. A Soviet fear is that such political opposition could spread to other countries or even to the USSR itself. The USSR has experienced internal worker unrest from time to time and has a growing ethnic minority population with which to contend. Many of these minority groups have ties to Eastern Europe. The Soviets have had to weigh the dangers of allowing worker opposition to continue against the economic and political costs of intervention. Based on Eastern European Statistical Yearbooks, US agency reports, Soviet news reports, and secondary sources; 28 notes. L. R. Maxted

418. Armstrong, John A. THE UKRAINIAN APPARATUS AS A KEY TO THE STUDY OF SOVIET POLITICS. *Ann. of the Ukrainian Acad. of Arts and Sci. in the U.S. 1961 9(1-2): 225-233.* Suggests several areas of study, 1917-58, in Ukrainian Communist Party politics that remain to be explored by scholars in order to understand Soviet internal politics and foreign relations.

419. Avrich, Paul H. THE *SHORT COURSE* AND SOVIET HISTORIOGRAPHY. *Pol. Sci. Q. 1960 75(4): 539-553.* Discusses Soviet historiography on the history of the Communist Party and the reign of Joseph Stalin, 1931-53.

420. Borisov, O. THE CHINESE REVOLUTIONARY FORCES' MIGHTY BRIDGEHEAD (35TH ANNIVERSARY OF THE ESTABLISHMENT OF THE MANCHURIAN REVOLUTIONARY BASE). *Far Eastern Affairs [USSR] 1980 (4): 26-38.* The presence of Soviet troops in Northeast China and the rout of Japanese militarism in 1945 enabled the Chinese people and their Communist Party to carry out a number of measures to establish and strengthen the Manchurian revolutionary base—the main bridgehead for the achievement of final victory for the Communist cause.

421. Bozhko, H. I. DIIAL'NIST' PARTIINYKH ORHANIZATSII DONBASU PO ROZVYTKU TRUDOVOI AKTYVNOSTI HIRNYKIV (1946-1950) [The work of Party organizations in the Donets Basin in stimulating the miners' productivity, 1946-50]. *Ukrains'kyi Istorychnyi Zhurnal [USSR] 1975 (6): 110-113.* Describes the work of Communist Party organizations, 1946-50, creating incentives, increasing labor resources, reconstructing the Donets mining industry, and politically educating young miners.

422. Bradley, John F. N. LE SYSTEME ET LA VIE POLITIQUE EN TCHECOSLOVAQUIE DE 1945 AU COUP DE PRAGUE EN 1948 [The political system and political life in Czechoslovakia from 1945 to the 1948 coup in Prague]. *Can. J. of Pol. Sci. [Canada] 1982 15(3): 471-501.* Analyzes Czechoslovakia's political development during the liberalization period. Centers on the policies of Czech President Eduard Beneš (1884-1948) and his relations with Czechoslovakia's Communist Party and Soviet leader Josef Stalin, which were harmonious and in accordance with the Communist model of peaceful transition from bourgeois democracy to people's democracy. But a change in Czechoslovakian Communist and Soviet policy brought about a Communist plot to seize power, beginning in 1947 and achieved easily in February 1948. Based on British Foreign Office documents, Prague Academia archives, and other Communist primary sources; 54 notes. G. P. Cleyet

423. Bromberg, L. M. and Shirokov, V. G. BOR'BA PARTII ZA VOSSTANOVLENIE I RAZVITIE SOTSIALISTICHESKOGO NARODNOGO KHOZIAISTVA V POSLEVOENNYI PERIOD (1945-1953 GG) [The struggle of the Party to restore and develop the socialist national economy in the post-war period, 1945-53]. *Voprosy Istorii KPSS [USSR] 1963 (1): 76-85.* Summarizes the main changes in the international situation, 1945-53, and the work of the Communist Party to restore and develop the Soviet economy.

424. Buchta, Bruno. DIE ÖKONOMISCHE HILFE DER UDSSR FÜR DIE VOLKSDEMOKRATISCHEN LANDER EUROPAS 1944-1950 [Soviet economic aid for European socialist countries, 1944-50]. *Jahrbuch für Geschichte der Sozialistischen Länder Europas [East Germany] 1974 18(1): 115-138.* Quantitative survey of the economic cooperation between the USSR and the people's democracies in Europe. Soviet aid helped create a new type of economic relations between sovereign countries.

425. Cherniavs'kyi, F. F. PROVIDNA ROL' ROBITNYCHOHO KLASU V KOLEKTYVIZATSII SIL'S'KOHO HOSPODARSTVA ZAKHIDNYKH OBLASTEI URSR (1939-1950 RR.) [On the leading role of the working class in the collectivization of agriculture in the western Ukraine, 1939-50]. *Ukrains'kyi Istorychnyi Zhurnal [USSR] 1980 (11): 77-86.* Examines the organizational and political

work by the Communist Party aimed at strengthening the leading role of the working class in the task of collectivizing agriculture in the western Ukraine. Based on the official history of the Communist Party of the Ukraine and other sources; 39 notes.

I. Krushelnyckyj

426. Danilov, P. P. U ISTOKOV SHIROKOGO TORCHESKOGO SODRUZHESTVA [Sources of fruitful cooperation]. *Vestnik Leningradskogo U.: Seriia Istorii, Iazyka i Literatury [USSR] 1964 19(8): 138-141.* Discusses research conducted in Leningrad, 1948-49, to aid postwar industrial development, and programs originated by the Leningrad Communist Party organization to strengthen cooperation between research institutes and industry. 22 notes.

N. Frenkley

427. Danowitz, Edward F. PARTY CONTROL OF THE SOVIET ARMY. *Marine Corps Gazette 1957 41(9): 19-22.* Describes the development of the Red Army from the time of Leon Trotsky and the first political commissars, to the present day control by the Ministry of Defense and the Military Department of the Central Committee of the Party. 6 illus., graph. S. Bonnycastle

428. Endler, Brunhild. "ICH STEHE IM POLITISCHEN TAGESKAMPF": GERTRUD ALEXANDER ["I am in the daily political struggle": Gertrud Alexander]. *Beiträge zur Gesch. der Arbeiterbewegung [East Germany] 1982 24(4): 588-594.* Traces the life, career, and political activities of German Communist and writer Gertrud Alexander (1882-1967). Traces the development of Alexander's political ideas during her studies at Jena University, through the influence of her father-in-law, and in her friendship with leading German Communists such as Karl Kautsky, Rosa Luxemburg, and Franz Mehring. Assesses the impact of her meeting with Clara Zetkin and her joining the Communist Party in 1918. Discusses her work as editor of the Communist newspaper *Die Rote Fahne,* 1920-25. In 1925 she traveled to Moscow and became involved in the international women's movement. Despite some serious illness she continued to work in Moscow and retired in 1949. Based on documents in Susanne Alexander's possession in Moscow and secondary sources; 21 notes. G. L. Neville

429. Fitzpatrick, Sheila. CULTURE AND POLITICS UNDER STALIN: A REAPPRAISAL. *Slavic Rev. 1976 35(2): 211-231.* Examines the evidence for a departure from the common assumption of an absolute totalitarian model as expressive of the relation of those in authority to the scholars and intelligentsia of the Stalin period. "The old Russian intelligentsia maintained its traditions and sense of identity right through the Stalin period." They became a privileged group holding high status in Soviet society even though few were Communists. The Communist intelligentsia, on the other hand, quickly lost authority, influence, and identity in the 1930's. The party required conformity but this was above all "conformity to *professional* norms established within each profession through a process of negotiation between professionals, cultural bureaucrats, and party leadership." 48 notes. R. V. Ritter

430. Grigorjanc, T. J. KSZTAŁTOWANIE SIĘ SYSTEMU UKŁADÓW POMIĘDZY ZSRR A KRAJAMI DEMOKRACJI LUDOWEJ EUROPY ŚRODKOWEJ I POŁUDNIOWO-WSCHODNIEJ W LATACH 1945-1947 [The formation of a system of agreements between the USSR and the countries of peoples' democracy in central and southeastern Europe, 1945-47]. *Przegląd Zachodni [Poland] 1978 34(1): 63-80.* Outlines the evolution of a common anti-fascist defense system, initiated by the USSR during World War II and implemented, 1945-47. Analyzes defense pacts between Poland, Czechoslovakia, Yugoslavia, and the USSR, and outlines Soviet support for defensible and equitable frontiers and the elimination of fifth column minorities in postwar Poland and Czechoslovakia. Also emphasizes the USSR's desire to extend its defense system across the continent and to demilitarize, democratize, and denazify Germany after the war. 39 notes. M. A. Zurowski

431. Hein, Manfred. ZUR HILFE UND UNTERSTÜTZUNG DER SMAD BEI DER POLITISCH-IDEOLOGISCHEN ERZIEHUNG DER JUNGEN GENERATION IN MECKLENBURG IN DEN JAHREN DER ANTIFASCHISTISCH-DEMOKRATISCHEN UMWÄLZUNG [The assistance and support given by the Soviet Military Administration in the political and ideological education of the younger generation in Mecklenburg during the antifascist democratic upheaval]. *Wissenschaftliche Zeitschrift der Wilhelm-Pieck-Universität Rostock. Gesellschafts- und Sprachwissenschaftliche Reihe [East Germany] 1977 26(1): 47-52.* Gives examples of the development of relations between youth in the USSR and members of the Free German Youth organization in Mecklenburg during their joint struggle with the Soviet Military Authorities to overcome anti-communism, 1945-48.

432. Hortschansky, Günter. NOVEMBERREVOLUTION UND GRÜNDUNG DER KPD [The November Revolution and the foundation of the German Communist Party]. *Beiträge zur Gesch. der Arbeiterbewegung [East Germany] 1983 25(6): 777-785.* Discusses the November Revolution of 1918 in Germany and the founding of the German Communist Party on the occasion of its 65th anniversary. Celebrates the founding and achievements of the Socialist Unity Party in East Germany, which has carried on the work of the Communist Party since the foundation of the German Democratic Republic in 1948. The author traces the main events of the November Revolution, discusses the activities of the leading personalities of the revolution, and demonstrates how the Russian October Revolution influenced both the workers and the soldiers in Germany. In addition he describes the suppression of the revolution in April 1919. The revolution demonstrated the need for a revolutionary party, and the author traces the evolution of the Communist Party in Germany, 1919-48. Based on German Communist Party documents held in Berlin and secondary sources; 16 notes.

G. L. Neville

433. Iatseniuk, F. S. PARTIINA PRESA PRO BRATERS'KU DOPOMOHU NARODIV SRSR ZAKHIDNYM OBLASTIAM UKRAINY (1945-1950 RR.) [The Party press on the fraternal assistance from the peoples of the USSR to the western Ukraine, 1945-50]. *Ukrains'kyi Istorychnyi Zhurnal [USSR] 1980 (11): 111-116.* After the defeat of Nazi Germany in World War II, the rebuilding and further development of the economy and social and cultural services in the western Ukraine were carried out with the assistance of other parts of the USSR. The scope and forms of this assistance were reflected in the Communist Party press of that period. Based on Soviet newspapers; 29 notes.

I. Krushelnyckyj

434. Iatsenko, I. O. VIDRODZHENNIA I DIIAL'NIST' PARTIINYKH ORHANIZATSII KRYMU V 1944-1948 [The rebirth and activity of Party organizations in the Crimea, 1944-48]. *Ukrains'kyi Istorychnyi Zhurnal [USSR] 1973 (2): 89-93.*

435. Ijiri, Hidenori. CHKA JINMIN KYŌWAKOKU SEIRITSU ZENYA NO KOKUSAI KANKEI [Foreign relations on the eve of the establishment of the People's Republic of China]. *Ajia Kenkyū [Japan] 1981 28(1): 30-53.* Within the Communist Party of China in 1948-49, the moderates, led by Zhou Enlai (Chou En-lai), advocated rebuilding the nation by obtaining aid from capitalist countries. The radicals, led by Liu Shaoqi (Liu Shao-ch'i), desired aid solely from the USSR. The latter faction won. Meanwhile, the United States, which had intensified tension with the Soviet Union in Europe, did not dare to support the Chinese Communist Party. China was forced to adopt a pro-Soviet policy, but the Soviet Union under Stalin's leadership was not friendly to the new China. The alliance between the two countries became strained. Based on published US official documents; 68 notes. E. Motono/S

436. Kaplan, Cynthia S. THE COMMUNIST PARTY OF THE SOVIET UNION AND LOCAL POLICY IMPLEMENTATION. *J. of Pol. 1983 45(1): 2-27.* In the period of mature Stalinism (1946-53) the Soviet regime emphasized the reestablishment of institutions and the administration of society rather than social transformation. The role of the Communist Party was transformed from implementation to coordination. In industry, technical managers assumed greater importance because of their stronger qualifications than those possessed by local Party cadres, industry's higher national priority, the nature of industrial production, and the grant of limited

autonomy. In agriculture, the low levels of education and political reliability, the eclipsing of technical by political issues, the need for flexible administration, and political distrust of the rural sector led to greater Party control, contributing to agricultural inefficiency and failure. Illus., 5 tables, 6 notes, biblio. A. W. Novitsky

437. Kaplan, Cynthia Sue. "The Communist Party of the Soviet Union in the Implementation of Industrial and Agrarian Policy: Leningrad, 1946-1953." Columbia U. 1981. 458 pp. *DAI 1981 42(6): 2836-A.* 8125319

438. Karaljuns, V. LATVIJAS KOMPARTIJAS DARBĪBA REPUBLIKAS LAUKSAIMIECĪBAS ELEKTRIFIKĀCIJĀ (1940-1953) [The activity of the Latvian Communist Party in the electrification of agriculture in the republic, 1940-53]. *Latvijas PSR Zinātņu Akadēmijas Vēstis [USSR] 1976 (6): 37-56.* All significant private electric power plants in Latvia were nationalized in 1940 when the Communist Party of Latvia launched a campaign to bring electricity to the countryside and eliminate differences between urban and rural areas in the availability of electrical power. The power capacity developed during the bourgeois period was very small, and even that was almost totally destroyed during the occupation. Before the victory of the state and collective farm system, the necessary socioeconomic conditions for developing a widespread power network did not exist. In 1946, however, the use of electrical power in rural areas of the Latvian SSR was six times greater than it had ever been in the bourgeois period. Small hydroelectric plants serving only one or a small group of agricultural enterprises were producing more than a third of all rural electric power requirements by 1953. 137 notes. C. Moody

439. Kolychev, V. PARTIINO-POLITICHESKAIA RABOTA V VOISKAKH [Party political work among troops]. *Voenno-Istoricheskii Zhurnal [USSR] 1975 (9): 35-41.* Examines the methods of the Communist Party's political work during the war with Japan, which led to a significant growth in the number of Young Communist League and party members in the army.

440. Kortkotsenko, D. I. BOR'BA PARTII ZA VOSSTANOVLENIE I RAZVITIE NARODNOGO KHOZIAISTVO V POSLEVOENNII PERIOD [The Party's struggle to rebuild the economy in the postwar period]. *Voprosy Istorii KPSS [USSR] 1966 (5): 85-95.* Describes the Communist Party's economic policy, 1946-50.

441. Kutulas, Judy. THE "SCIENTIFIC MORALITY": INDEPENDENT MARXISTS AND STALIN'S RUSSIA, 1935-1940. *UCLA Hist. J. 1983 4: 66-91.* Traces the disillusionment of American independent Marxists with the Stalinist USSR in the 1930's. Viewing the party line of the Communist Party of the USA as lacking in what they termed "scientific morality," independent Marxists became embittered by what they witnessed in the Soviet Union during Stalin's purge trials. By 1940, they no longer distinguished between Stalinist Russia and Marxist Russia, but considered Marxism there a failed experiment. The anti-Stalinist views of such critics as Sidney Hook, Max Eastman, and Edmund Wilson grew into a rationale for Cold War anticommunism by the 1950's. 60 notes. A. Hoffman

442. Kuznetsov, N. G. VIDNYI POLITRABOTNIK ARMII I FLOTA [An outstanding Communist Party worker in the army and the navy]. *Voenno-Istoricheskii Zhurnal [USSR] 1969 11(8): 42-47.* Pays tribute to General I. V. Rogov (1899-1949), former member of the Military Council of the Belorussian Special Military District, member of the Central Committee of the Communist Party and head of the Army and Navy Propaganda Office.

443. Labedz, Leopold. ISAAC DEUTSCHER'S "STALIN": AN UNPUBLISHED CRITIQUE. *Encounter [Great Britain] 1979 52(1): 65-82.* Publishes the author's 1962 manuscript critique of Isaac Deutscher's *Stalin, A Political Biography* (1960) with a new introduction discussing the vicissitudes of Communist historiography, especially the treatment of the Stalin era.

444. Leonetti, Alfonso. ITALIANI VITTIME DELLO STALINISMO IN URSS [Italian victims of Stalinism in the USSR]. *Ponte [Italy] 1975 31(2-3): 222-227, (6): 655-660.* Part I. GIUSEPPE RIMOLA, pp. 222-227. Giuseppe Rimola, called Micca Carmelo (1904-47), was an Italian victim of Stalinism who while working as a functionary of the Communist Youth International in Moscow was arrested and never reappeared but was eventually "rehabilitated" by the Soviet state in 1956. Part II. EDMUNDO PELUSO, pp. 655-660. A communist militant, Edmundo Peluso, was an exile living in Russia when he was arrested at the direction of Stalin, 4 October 1940; he was imprisoned and disappeared after 1946.

445. Līdace, E. KOMUNISTISKĀS PARTIJAS PIRMORGANIZĀCIJU IZVEIDOŠANĀS UN NOSTIPRINĀŠANĀS REPUBLIKAS RPNIECĪBAS UZŅĒMUMOS (1944 G. JLIJS-1950. G. DECEMBRIS) [The formation and consolidation of local Party organizations in industrial enterprises of the Latvian Republic, July 1944-December 1950]. *Latvijas PSR Zinātņu Akadēmijas Vēstis [USSR] 1976 (6): 22-35.* The formation of local Communist Party organizations began immediately after the partial liberation of Latvia from military occupation. Since the nucleus of the working class was found in industry, efforts were concentrated there. The central committee of the Communist Party of Latvia sent the most effective organizers and propagandists to fulfill organizational duties in industry. Local Party organizations grew as a result of recruitment as well as through the demobilization of Communist soldiers from the Soviet Army. In addition, many Communists were sent to Latvia from fraternal republics. This work was basically completed by the end of 1948, when there were 377 organizations at large industrial enterprises and 5,487 Communists working in industry. At the end of 1950, 18 percent of Communists in the republic were working in industry. 2 tables, 49 notes. C. Moody

446. Mackintosh, J. Malcolm. STALIN'S POLICIES TOWARDS EASTERN EUROPE, 1939-1948: THE GENERAL PICTURE. *Studies on the Soviet Union [West Germany] 1971 11(4): 200-214.* The Soviet takeover of Eastern Europe was motivated by considerations of nationalism, establishment of a buffer zone between Russia and the West, and prevention of a resurgent militarism in Germany. The pattern was much the same everywhere. Local Communist parties were set up in government by the Red Army and in coalition with other nationalist groups, single-party elections were staged and purges soon followed. Stalin indeed wished for Communization, but was much more interested in the pursuit of traditional Russian expansionist aims. Secondary sources; 20 notes. V. L. Human

447. Mackintosh, Malcolm. THE TECHNIQUE OF TYRANNY. *J. of the Royal United Services Inst. for Defence Studies [Great Britain] 1974 119(4): 78-79.* A review article of Ronald Hingley's *Joseph Stalin: Man and Legend* (London: Hutchinson, 1974). Hingley is "as near to finding an explanation of Stalin's achievement as is feasible without access to his and the Kremlin's archives." Particularly significant is the portrayal of the interaction between Stalin and the Communist Party as helping to explain Stalin both as a tyrant and successful war leader. Nevertheless, most of what Stalin achieved could have been done by "less wasteful and brutal, more acceptable and more efficient methods." D. H. Murdoch

448. Maistrenko, Ivan. STORINKY Z ISTORII KOMUNISTYCHNOI PARTII UKRAINY: KP(B)U PISLIA DRUHOI SVITOVOI VIINY [A page from the history of the Communist Party of the Ukraine after World War II]. *Sučasnist [West Germany] 1974 (3): 75-88.* Analyzes the changes in policy and structure of the postwar Ukrainian Communist Party against the background of growing national resistance movements and Stalinist purges.

449. Mikeshin, N. P. PROTIV BURZHUAZNOI FAL'SIFIKATSII BOR'BY KPSS ZA VOSSTANOVLENIE I RAZVITIE NARODNOGO KHOZIAISTVA V POSLEVOENNYE GODY [Against bourgeois falsification of the CPSU struggle for the reestablishment and development of the national economy during the postwar years]. *Voprosy Istorii KPSS [USSR] 1969 (12): 59-68.*

A critical analysis of mainstream bourgeois historiography about the leadership provided by the Communist Party of the USSR during the postwar national reconstruction of the economy.

450. Mor, N. M. MIKHAIL IVANOVICH KALININ: PARTIINYI PROPAGANDIST [Mikhail Ivanovich Kalinin: a Party propagandist]. *Voprosy Istorii KPSS [USSR] 1965 (11): 66-75.* Episodes from the life of the Soviet Communist Party and government worker Mikhail Kalinin (1875-1946) are used to exemplify the good Communist propagandist and to inspire the younger generation.

451. Nikolaev, V. V. O GLAVNYKH ETAPAKH RAZVITIIA SOVETSKOGO SOTSIALISTICHESKOGO GOSUDARSTVA [Main stages in the development of the Soviet socialist state]. *Voprosy Filosofii [USSR] 1957 (4): 10-25.* Traces the development of the Soviet Union through the initial transition from capitalism to socialism, 1917-30, a period characterized by the multi-layered nature of the economy and the gradual extinction of the exploiting classes, to the second stage, 1930-56, that of the transition to full communism.

452. Nikolaevskaia, Z. S. PLAMENNYI BORETS ZA KOMMUNIZM [An ardent fighter for communism]. *Voprosy Istorii KPSS [USSR] 1976 (6): 154-156.* Reports on a session held to commemorate the 80th anniversary of the birth of Andrei Aleksandrovich Zhdanov (1896-1948) with reference to his life's work.

453. Oleinik, K. E. OTCHETY TSENTRAL'NOGO KOMITETA KOMMUNISTICHESKOI PARTII MOLDAVII KAK ISTORICHESKII ISTOCHNIK [The transcripts of the Central Committee of the Moldavian Communist Party as a historical source]. *Sovetskie Arkhivy [USSR] 1972 (5): 105-109.* The transcripts of the early meetings of the Central Committee of the Moldavian Communist Party, especially those of 1949 and 1951, are extremely important for studying the development of the Modavian Communist Party in government.

454. Osichkina, G. A. SOREVNOVANIE KOMSOMOL'TSEV I MOLODEZHY MOSKVY: 1946-1950 GODY [Competition among Komsomol members and youths in Moscow, 1946-50]. *Sovetskie Arkhivy [USSR] 1977 (3): 31-36.* The youth and Young Communist League groupings of Moscow concentrated their energy on the fundamental tasks posed by the Fourth Five-Year Plan, and after training were able to contribute to the overfulfillment of goals.

455. Parinov, M. P. ROL' PRESY V BOROT'BI PARTIINYKH ORHANIZATSII DONBASU ZA TEKHNICHNYI PROHRES U CHETVERTII P'IATYRICHTSI: 1946-1950 [The role of the press in the struggle of Communist Party organizations of the Donets basin for technical progress during the 4th Five-Year Plan, 1946-50]. *Ukrains'kyi Istorychnyi Zhurnal [USSR] 1973 (5): 62-66.* Discusses the role of newspapers in disseminating Party propaganda in the Donets area, 1946-50, to encourage the reconstruction of industry and facilitate the introduction of new technology.

456. Paul, Diane B. A WAR ON TWO FRONTS: J.B.S. HALDANE AND THE RESPONSE TO LYSENKOISM IN BRITAIN. *J. of the Hist. of Biol. 1983 16(1): 1-37.* J. B. S. Haldane, who united classical Darwinism and Mendelian genetics, was a member of the British Communist Party. During the Lysenko controversy (a Soviet effort to increase grain production by ignoring Mendelian genetics and by stressing the inheritance of acquired characteristics), Haldane was editor of the British *Daily Worker.* As the evidence against Lysenko's theory increased, Haldane resigned from the Party in 1950. Lysenkoism functioned for over 30 years in the USSR but scientists such as Haldane defended it until the gross error was apparent to all, including the Soviet authorities. 67 notes.
D. K. Pickens

457. Perezhogin, M. A.; Ugarov, I. F.; Chernomorski, M. N.; and Shipova, G. M. NA STARYKH POZITSIIAKH [An outdated standpoint]. *Voprosy Istorii KPSS [USSR] 1961 (6): 199-205.* Attacks *Obzor istochnikov istorii KPSS* (1961), a survey of sources for the history of the Soviet Communist Party, for its insufficiently critical attitude toward Joseph Stalin and its failure to identify the extent of his departure from Leninist principles in the 1930's and 1940's.

458. Petrov, I. F. OSVESHCHENIE NEKOTORYKH PROBLEM OKTIABR'SKOI REVOLIUTSII V ISTORIKO-PARTIINOI LITERATURE [The illumination of certain problems concerned with the October Revolution in Party-historical literature]. *Voprosy Istorii KPSS [USSR] 1962 (5): 5-26.* Surveys Soviet Communist Party histories of the October Revolution of 1917, published 1920's-50's, finding that the serious distortions of the Stalin period have been corrected to a large extent, but much work still remains to be done on Bolshevik tactics during the summer and fall of 1917.

459. Rakitina, I. S. IZ ISTORII PARTIINOGO RUKOVODSTVA POLITICHESKIM OBRAZOVANIEM KOMMUNISTOV (1946-1950 GG.) [The Communist Party's direction of the political education of Communists, 1946-50]. *Voprosy Istorii KPSS [USSR] 1978 (11): 100-109.* Archival material throws more light on the reorganization of the system of political education and propaganda within the Communist Party organization of the Russian Soviet Federated Socialist Republic.

460. Ramazani, Rouhollah K. THE AUTONOMOUS REPUBLIC OF AZERBAIJAN AND THE KURDISH PEOPLE'S REPUBLIC: THEIR RISE AND FALL. *Studies on the Soviet Union [West Germany] 1971 11(4): 401-427.* A review of the brief histories of two Communist regimes in northern Iran. The governments were established by occupying Soviet troops. Great Britain and the United States opposed these states from the beginning. Conquest of the whole of Iran was the Soviet goal, but pressure to achieve this goal was successfully resisted. The Red Army pulled out because the United States stood firm in opposition. A year later the puppet governments fell having no further bases of support. Secondary sources; 78 notes. V. L. Human

461. Rybalko, V. A. ORHANIZATSIINA ROBOTA PARTIINYKH ORHANIZATSII DONBASU V 1946-1950 RR [The organizational work of Party organizations in Donets, 1946-50]. *Ukrains'kyi Istorychnyi Zhurnal [USSR] 1974 (8): 44-50.* Describes important work done in the post-war period to restructure and improve Communist Party organization, quoting membership figures and giving details of meetings and plenums.

462. Semiriaga, M. I. POLITIKA KOMMUNISTICHESKOI PARTII I SOVETSKOGO PRAVITEL'STVA V OTNOSHENII STRAN TSENTRAL'NOI I IUGO-VOSTOCHNOI EVROPY V 1944-1945 GG. I EE IZVRASHCHENIE V BURZHUAZNOI ISTORIOGRAFII [The policy of the Communist Party and the Soviet government toward Central and Southeastern Europe, 1944-45, and its distortion in bourgeois historiography]. *Voprosy Istorii KPSS [USSR] 1981 (6): 96-107.* An account of Soviet government and Party foreign policy toward Central and Southeastern Europe at the end of World War II, giving details of the aid provided by the USSR. Bourgeois literature of the last decade falsifies and distorts the benevolent democratic nature of the Party's and Soviet government's policies. Based on archival and Soviet, Western, and East European secondary sources; 46 notes. L. Smith

463. Shirinia, K. K. VYDAIUSHCHIISIA DEIATEL' MEZHDUNARODNOGO KOMMUNISTICHESKOGO DVIZHENIIA [A prominent figure in the international Communist movement]. *Voprosy Istorii KPSS [USSR] 1982 (6): 43-55.* Commemorates the centenary of the birth of the Bulgarian Communist leader Georgi Dimitrov (1882-1949). Particularly notes his role in placing the Bulgarian Social Democratic movement on the Leninist path, his leading role in the antifascist struggle between the wars, symbolized by his triumphant defense at the Reichstag Trial (1934), his contribution at the Comintern to the development of the strategy of the Popular Front, his role in leading Bulgarian resistance to fascism during World War II, and his ceaseless emphasis on the strengthening of the revolutionary party of the working class and on the role of the USSR within the international workers' movement.
F. A. K. Yasamee

464. Sokhan, P. S. HEORHII DYMYTROV PRO MIZHNAROD-NE ZNACHENNIA LENINIZMU I DOSVIDU SOTSIALISTY-CHNOHO BUDIVNYTSTVA V SRSR [Georgi Dimitrov on the international significance of Leninism and on the experience of socialist construction in the USSR]. *Ukrains'kyi Istorychnyi Zhurnal [USSR] 1982 (6): 39-48.* Almost from his initial revolutionary and trade union activities Dimitrov was governed in all organizational work by the directives formulated by Lenin. His brilliant knowledge of Lenin's heritage was especially vividly shown during the trial in Leipzig in 1934 when he, a defendant, acted as an accuser of Hitler and Nazism. A strict disciple of Leninism, he frequently added new and highly relevant elements to Communist tactics, especially after becoming chairman of the Comintern. His formulation of proletarian internationalism as "favoring the USSR and CPSU everywhere and at all times" still serves as a means to separate the friend from the foe. V. Bender

465. Suh, Dae-Sook. A PRECONCEIVED FORMULA FOR SOVIETIZATION: THE COMMUNIST TAKEOVER OF NORTH KOREA. *Studies on the Soviet Union [West Germany] 1971 11(4): 428-442.* The Communist regime in North Korea has proved remarkably stable in view of the fact that its creation was haphazard and unplanned. The techniques used were identical with those in Eastern Europe. A genuine coalition government was set up by the invading Red Army, which was gradually undermined until the Communist Party occupied all key positions. Then a rigid, centralized government was set up, which immediately proceeded to eliminate all rivals. Secondary sources; 27 notes. V. L. Human

466. Utenkov, A. Ia. NEKOTORYE VOPROSY ISTORIOGRAFII SOTSIALISTICHESKOGO SOREVNOVANIIA V POSLEVOEN-NYE GODY [The historiography of socialist competition in the postwar period]. *Voprosy Istorii KPSS [USSR] 1966 (6): 110-115.* Analyzes Soviet historiography on the role of the Communist Party in organizing socialist competition in industry, 1945-55.

467. Vashchenko, N. I. and Kozybaev, M. K. VOENNYE OTDE-LY PARTIINYKH ORGANOV V GODY VELIKOI OTECHEST-VENNOI VOINY [Military sections of Party organs during World War II]. *Voprosy Istorii KPSS [USSR] 1982 (6): 63-73.* Military units were formed at all levels of the Communist Party in May-June 1939 and given the task of preparing for defense and promoting a patriotic spirit. After the outbreak of war in 1941 they were charged with coordinating the work of mobilization, the formation of reserves, and training. They also participated in the organization of self-defense, antiaircraft and firefighting, and in the Red Cross and the Red Crescent. After 1945 they assisted in the task of demobilization; they were abolished in 1948.
F. A. K. Yasamee

468. Zelenin, I. E. OBSHCHESTVENNO-POLITICHESKAIA ZHIZN' SOVETSKOI DEREVNI V PERVYE POSLEVOENNYE GODY [Sociopolitical life of the Soviet village in the first postwar years]. *Istoriia SSSR [USSR] 1974 (2): 27-48.* Examines sociopolitical conditions in Soviet villages during the first five years after World War II, describing the condition and activity of local Communist Party organizations, the village Communist Youth League (Komsomol), the professional unions of workers on the state farms, the participation of the peasantry in the work of the Soviets of workers' deputies and their reactions to the most important events that were occurring inside the country and beyond its borders. Statistical data is also given on the number of village Communists and Komsomols, 1941-51. Primary and secondary sources; 2 tables, 69 notes. L. Kalinowski

469. Zelenkov, I. A. and Kholopova, S. P. DEIATEL'NOST' MOSKOVSKOI PARTIINOI ORGANIZATSII V USLOVIIAKH PEREKHODA K MIRNOMU STROITEL'STVU: 1945-1946 [The work of the Moscow Party organization under conditions of the transition to peacetime construction, 1945-46]. *Voprosy Istorii KPSS [USSR] 1982 (2): 66-78.* Much valuable work was done by Moscow Party organizations for the reconstruction of industry and agriculture, the development of workers' labor and political activity, and improving the standard of living and forms and methods of Party work in the postwar period. Data on the growth of individual factories and farms show that conditions necessary for the successful fulfillment of the 4th Five-Year Plan were created during this period. Primary sources; 37 notes. V. A. Packer

470. —. KOMMUNISTICHESKAIA PARTIIA V USLOVIIAKH PEREKHODA OT VOINY K MIRU [The Communist Party in the transition from war to peace]. *Voprosy Istorii KPSS [USSR] 1977 (3): 81-93.* A survey of successful efforts from 1945 to 1946 by the Soviet Communist Party to reconstruct the war-ravaged agriculture and industry of the USSR. From the official *History of the Communist Party of the Soviet Union.* Based on published documents and Communist Party archival materials; 28 notes. Article to be continued. L. E. Holmes

471. —. LENINISM AND THE PROBLEMS OF CHINA. *Far Eastern Affairs [USSR] 1980 (3): 3-16.* The USSR has followed the scientific principles of Leninist foreign policy in its relations with China, but the Communist movement in China has experienced continuous struggle between Marxist-Leninist internationalism and the petit borgeois nationalism.

1953-1964

472. Aleksandrov, P. A. and Lezhepekov, V. Ia. IZ OPYTA PAR-TIINOI RABOTY PO ULUCHSHENIIU PROIZVODSTVENNOI DEIATEL'NOSTI SOVKHOZOV V BELORUSSII (1956-1962) [Party work on improving the productive activity of state farms in Belorussia, 1956-62]. *Voprosy Istorii KPSS [USSR] 1963 (11): 18-31.* Summarizes the changes made in the structure of the Belorussian Communist Party organizations, 1956-63.

473. Alekseev, G. M. DEIATEL'NOST' PARTIINYKH ORGAN-IZATSII PO RAZVITIIU MASSOVOGO DVIZHENIIA RAT-SIONALIZATOROV I IZOBRETATELEI V PROMYSHLENNOSTI (1959-1961 GODY) [Activities of Party organizations in the development of a mass movement of efficiency experts and inventors in industry, 1959-61]. *Vestnik Moskovskogo U. Seriia 9: Istoriia [USSR] 1963 18(6): 8-30.* Deals with Communist Party programs to raise industrial production and neutralize harmful aftereffects of Joseph Stalin's cult of personality. Inventors and efficiency experts, encouraged by the Party to submit suggestions on technical development and social reforms, played a major role in raising labor productivity, promoting political motivation of workers, and introducing advanced technology. Selected statistical data, 1958-61, are included. Table, 113 notes. N. Frenkley

474. Andrianov, V. I. IZUCHENIE ISTORII MESTNOI PARTI-INOI ORGANIZATSII V STUDENCHESKOM KRUZHKE [The investigation of local Party history in a student circle]. *Voprosy Istorii KPSS [USSR] 1965 (3): 149-151.* The Iaroslavl' Pedagogical Institute organized a student group to study the local history of the Communist Party; some results have been printed.

475. Balakiriev, V. P. VYKHOVANNIA VOINIV U DUSI RADI-ANS'KOHO PARTIOTYZMU I SOTSIALISTYCHNOHO IN-TERNATSIONALIZMU (1956-1961) [The education of soldiers in the spirit of Soviet patriotism and socialist internationalism, 1956-61]. *Ukrains'kyi Istorychnyi Zhurnal [USSR] 1975 (7): 51-57.* Discusses the achievements of the Kiev and other Party organizations between the 20th and 21st Party congresses in improving the internationalist and patriotic education of soldiers and officers in the army and navy, giving details of subjects taught and results of socialist competition between the groups.

476. Barsukov, N. A. and Petriakov, G. V. POLNEE OT-VECHAT' NASUSHCHNYM ZADACHAM PARTIINOI PROPA-GANDY [Let us serve more fully the urgent tasks of Party propaganda]. *Voprosy Istorii KPSS [USSR] 1961 (3): 186-195.* Discusses 18 brochures concerning the history of the Soviet Communist Party, 1917-60, and published by the Znanie publishing house, 1959-60, finding serious errors in the presentation of historical material.

477. Beliaev, Edward and Butorin, Pavel. THE INSTITUTIONALIZATION OF SOVIET SOCIOLOGY: ITS SOCIAL AND POLITICAL CONTEXT. *Social Forces 1982 61(2): 418-435.* The development of sociology in the USSR must be seen as shaped by the interplay of various important state and party institutions—the Central Committee of the Communist Party of the USSR, the Academy of Sciences, the Soviet Sociological Association, the Ministry of Education, and the major universities. The part played by the Communist Party, as active promoter and supporter of sociology, is underlined, as is the important influence of the "universities of Marxism-Leninism" (organized by the Party) in preparing cadres of sociologists throughout the country. This was especially crucial since such professional education was lacking in the more traditional schools. The evolution of these various interlocking influences during two periods of the development of sociology (1956-60 and 1960-68) is traced. The analysis of the revival of Soviet sociology leads to the recognition of two major differences between Soviet and American sociology: the mode of thinking (hence the nature of social research itself) and the character of the organization and development of a community of sociologists. Soviet sociology is distinguished from any Western brand by its propensity for measuring everything from a collectivistic rather than individualistic point of view. An analysis of the employment of members of the Soviet Sociological Association shows a large proportion of party officials among the sociologists. Soviet sociology has close and multiple connections with the establishment. It is essential to recognize the practical functions of Soviet sociology, its intricate connection to the power system, and its particular pragmatic and ideological orientation. J

478. Blank, A. S. MIROVOE KOMMUNISTICHESKOE DVIZHENIE: SAMAIA VLIIATEL'NAIA POLITICHESKAIA SILA NASHEGO VREMENI [The world Communist movement: the most influential political power of our times]. *Prepodovanie Istorii v Shkole [USSR] 1961 16(6): 19-27.* The ideological struggle of the Communist Party of the USSR against revisionism, dogmatism, and sectarianism was given new life by Nikita Khrushchev (1894-1971). His foreign and domestic policy since the mid-1950's and his denunciation of war, aggression, colonialism, and American imperialism deserve great credit for the worldwide expansion of Communism and, especially, its spread to the developing nations. 25 notes. N. Frenkley

479. Chotiner, Barbara Ann. INSTITUTIONAL INNOVATION UNDER KHRUSHCHEV: THE CASE OF THE 1962 REORGANIZATION OF THE COMMUNIST PARTY. *Soviet Union 1982 9(2): 154-188.* The most significant reform introduced by Nikita Khrushchev during his first secretaryship was the bifurcation of the Communist Party in 1962. Of the two hierarchies created, one was to supervise the industry and construction sector of the economy, and the second the agricultural. The Party's chief concern was economic and productional efficiency, with ideology becoming less significant. The background and enactment of the proposal are discussed, as well as Khrushchev's tactics to gain its acceptance by a hostile Party organization. To build a supporting majority, he arranged trade-offs involving other issues before the Party policymaking bodies. This process is presented through tables showing the position of prominent presidium and central committee officials on the various issues and their relationship to the bifurcation issue. 6 tables, 54 notes. H. Shields

480. Colton, Timothy J. THE ZHUKOV AFFAIR RECONSIDERED. *Soviet Studies [Great Britain] 1977 29(2): 185-213.* The standard interpretation of the fall of Marshal Georgi Zhukov (1895-1974) in 1957, which stressed a power struggle between the Army and the Party in the USSR, needs major modification. Examination of the assertions made by Soviet leaders, particularly the charges brought against Zhukov, shows that key portions of the indictment are contrived and fraudulent. The most serious charge, that Zhukov was preparing a coup and dismantling the Communist Party apparatus in the Army, was without foundation. The author concludes that Zhukov's fall was not a frontal confrontation between Army and Party but a single episode in the developing relationship between the two. Criticizes the self-justificatory rhetoric of Western observers who have uncritically accepted analyses of Soviet elite politics. 105 notes. D. H. Murdoch

481. Degras, Jane. REVISITING THE COMINTERN. *Survey [Great Britain] 1960 (33): 38-47.* Critically reviews recent Soviet historiography of the Communist International, 1929-39.

482. DeVries, Paul T. KHRUSHCHEV AND THE MILITARY: A STUDY OF PARTY-MILITARY RELATIONS, 1955-64. *Military Rev. 1977 57(5): 73-81.* The military community of the USSR is also a powerful political force. Any attempts to enforce strict controls by the Communist Party, as during the Nikita Khrushchev regime, will be met by stiff resistance. Because of the Party's reliance on the military during times of crisis it is unlikely that the Party leadership will be able to maintain absolute control over the military. 24 notes. D. J. Kommer

483. Duevel, Christian. THE WAY OF "OBLITERATION": A PROGRESS REPORT AND SOME PERSPECTIVES. *Problems of the Peoples of the USSR [West Germany] 1963 (20): 3-16.* The USSR's Communist Party Program adopted in 1961 seems to indicate an unstated policy of elimination of national differences through Russification.

484. Enenko, M. P. MATERIALY O SHEFSTVE KOMSOMOLA NAD UDARNYMI STROIKAMI [Komsomol's supervision over the highest priority industrial construction sites]. *Sovetskie Arkhivy [USSR] 1968 (4): 24-26.* The Young Communist League (Komsomol) has under its patronage many of the priority sites of industrial development throughout the USSR. Documents concerning this activity are kept in the central Komsomol archive in Moscow. 8 notes. W. Kowalski

485. Ermakov, F. I. PARTIIA I SOTRUDNICHESTVO SOVETSKIKH NATSII V SOZDANII MATERIAL'NO-TEKHNICHESKOI BAZY KOMMUNIZMA [The Party and the cooperation of the Soviet nations in the creation of the material and technical base of communism]. *Voprosy Istorii KPSS [USSR] 1963 (7): 46-60.* Traces the growing cooperation between the different nationalities within the USSR in economic and other spheres, 1957-63, and insists on the Soviet Union's internationalist mission.

486. Erykalov, E. F. OSVESHCHENIE OKTIABR'SKOGO VOORUZHENNOGO VOSSTANIIA V PETROGRADE V ISTORIKOPARTIINOI LITERATURE 1956-1966 GG [Discussion of the October armed uprising in Petrograd in the Party's historical literature, 1956-66]. *Voprosy Istorii KPSS [USSR] 1966 (5): 120-128.*

487. Evseev, I. F. VYKORYSTANNIA BRATNIMY SOTSIALISTYCHNYMY KRAINAMY DOSVIDU SRSR U PERETVORENNI SIL'S'KOHO HOSPODARSTVA [The utilization of the USSR's experience in the transformation of agriculture by fraternal socialist countries]. *Ukrains'kyi Istorychnyi Zhurnal [USSR] 1971 (10): 12-20.* Details the role of the Communist Party of the Soviet Union in furthering the development of socialist relations to change the peasant classes to working classes, to reconstruct the agricultural system and to construct a new community.

488. Fadeev, A. D. PARTIINAIA RABOTA NA STROITEL'STVE VOLZHSKOI GES IMENI V. I. LENINA [Party work in the construction of the Volga hydroelectric power station named in honor of V. I. Lenin]. *Voprosy Istorii KPSS [USSR] 1961 (3): 94-105.* Describes the contribution of the Kuibyshev Communist Party to the construction of the Lenin Hydroelectric Power Station on the Volga, 1951-58.

489. Frolov, K. M. TVORCHESKOE RAZVITIE MARKSISTSKO-LENINSKOGO UCHENIIA O STROITEL'STVE SOTSIALIZMA I KOMMUNIZMA [The creative development of Marxist-Leninist teaching on the construction of socialism and communism]. *Voprosy Istorii KPSS [USSR] 1963 (9): 3-14.* With reference to the proceedings of the 20th and 21st Party Congresses,

argues that over the last decade the Soviet Communist Party has made a new and valuable contribution to the development of the theory of scientific communism, 1953-63.

490. Grebennikov, G. I. and Luniakov, P. I. KPSS V BOR'BE ZA DAL'NEISHII POD'EM SEL'SKOGO KHOZIAISTVA SSSR [The CPSU in the struggle for the further development of agriculture in the USSR]. *Voprosy Istorii KPSS [USSR] 1963 (1): 120-126.* Deals with the agricultural successes of the USSR in the post-Stalin period, quoting various Party directives and emphasizing the important role of Nikita Khrushchev.

491. Grishin, V. M. BOR'BA PARTII ZA MOSHCHNYI POD'EM NARODNOGO KHOZIAISTVA, ZA ZAVERSHENIE STROITEL'STVA SOTSIALIZMA (1953-1958 GG) [The struggle of the Party for the powerful upsurge of the national economy, and for the completion of the construction of socialism, 1953-58]. *Voprosy Istorii KPSS [USSR] 1963 (3): 70-82.* Summarizes the political struggle waged after Stalin's death against the anti-Party group, 1953-58, and the decisions of the 20th Party Congress.

492. Gubarev, G. D. OPYT MESTNYKH PARTIINYKH ORGANIZATSII V SOZDANII NOVYKH FORM PROIZVODSTVENNO-TEKHNICHESKOGO OBSLUZHIVANIIA KOLKHOZOV (1953-1958 GODY) [Experience of local Party organizations in supplying collective farms with new kinds of industrial and technological aid, 1953-58]. *Vestnik Moskovskogo Universiteta, Seriia 9: Istoriia [USSR] 1963 18(1): 3-22.* Describes local Party organizations' initiative in cooperating with the collective farm and the machine and tractor station administrations to implement the agricultural engineering program decreed after the collectivization of 1953. The prime goals were to improve the efficient use of existing farm machinery and acquisition of new technology, and to raise agricultural production and labor productivity. The reorganization of the machine and tractor station administration and the permanent assignment of technical personnel and agricultural experts to farms were some of the most important reforms of 1956-58. 60 notes. N. Frenkley

493. Harasymiw, Bohdan. HAVE WOMEN'S CHANCES FOR POLITICAL RECRUITMENT IN THE USSR REALLY IMPROVED? Yedlin, Tova, ed. *Women in Eastern Europe and the Soviet Union* (New York: Praeger, 1980): 140-184. Reviews data on Soviet recruitment policy to establish levels of women's political participation. These include party-political management positions, representation in the elected councils (soviets) and their executive bodies; fulltime staff positions, general membership in the Party and on elected committees; candidate membership in the Communist Party; and representation in the Young Communist League. Comparison of the percentage of women in the labor force and in the Communist Party is used as a reference point for assessing women's opportunities. 14 tables, 9 fig., 39 notes.

494. Hodnett, Grey. THE *OBKOM FIRST SECRETARIES. Slavic Rev. 1965 24(4): 636-652.* Presents a profile of the government workers (some 240 individuals) who served as *obkom* first secretaries prior to, during, and following Nikita Khrushchev's reorganization of agricultural and industrial administration in the USSR, 1962-64.

495. Il'ina, L. I. and Nikiforova, V. I. LENINGRADSKAIA PARTIINAIA ORGANIZATSIIA V BOR'BE ZA TEKHNICHESKII PROGRESS V PROMYSHLENNOSTI (1959-1962 GG) [Leningrad Party organization in the struggle for technological progress in industry, 1959-62]. *Voprosy Istorii KPSS [USSR] 1965 (12): 118-122.* Refers to documents from the Leningrad Party Archive which describe the local Party's efforts to increase technological advance in the province's industry, 1959-62.

496. Kabanova, I. D. PARTIINYE I KOMSOMOL'SKIE ORGANIZATSII G. MOSKVY V BOR'BE ZA POVYSHENIE OBSHCHEOBRAZOVATEL'NYKH ZNANII RABOCHEI MOLODEZHI (1959-1963 GODY) [The struggle of Party and Komsomol organizations of Moscow to improve the general education level of young workers, 1959-63]. *Vestnik Moskovskogo Universiteta, Seriia 9: Istoriia [USSR] 1964 19(3): 3-18.* Describes the activities of Moscow Party organs, labor unions, and the Young Communist League (Komsomol) to promote enrollment of working youth in the so-called *rabfak* (secondary evening schools attached to industrial plants) after the school reform of 1959. Includes statistical data on student enrollment. 51 notes. N. Frenkley

497. Karałuns, V. LATVIJAS KOMPARTIJAS RPES PAR PADOMJU LATVIJAS LAUKSAIMNIECĪBAS ELEKTRIFIKĀCIJU 50. GADOS [The concern of the Latvian Communist Party for the electrification of rural Latvia in the 1950's]. *Latvijas PSR Zinātņu Akadēmijas Vēstis [USSR] 1976 (8): 6-17.* The second stage in the electrification program for rural Latvia began in 1953, when the newly reorganized Party and government brought both collective and state farms into the state energy system. The need was based on difficulties associated with the rapid increase in urban and industrial power demands. Party and government organizations at all levels participated in the campaign, and collective and state farm workers were mobilized for the construction of electrical stations and the stringing of power lines. At the end of the period under examination, 91% of state farms and 56% of collective farms had electric power, as well as 24% of rural farm homes. Due to the special concern of the Central Committee of the Communist Party of the Soviet Union and of the Soviet government, rural electrification of Latvia developed at a faster rate than it did in the country overall. Nevertheless, by 1958 Latvia still did not achieve the average level of the USSR as a whole. 55 notes. C. Moody

498. Kharchuk, Teodor. UKRAINIAN NATIONALISM AND THE FALL OF PETRO SHELEST. *Internat. Socialist R. 1973 34(10): 14-17, 34-37.* Reconstructs the decade of factional conflict preceding the expulsion of Ukrainian Party First Secretary Petro Shelest from the CPSU Politburo (1973) and Shelest's attempt to manipulate Ukrainian nationalist sentiment to his benefit.

499. Khyzhniak, I. I. ROBITNYKY ELETROTEKHNICHNOI PROMYSLOVOSTI RESPUBLIKY (1959-1965) [The workers of the electro-technical industry of the republic, 1959-65]. *Ukrains'kyi Istorychnyi Zhurnal [USSR] 1974 7: 66-72.* Describes work of primary party organizations of the electrical industry in mobilizing workers to improve production methods.

500. Kniazev, S. P. VOPROSY KOMMUNISTICHESKOGO STROITEL'STVA V TRUDAKH LENINGRADSKIKH ISTORIKOV PARTII (1953-1969 GG) [Questions of Communist construction in the works of Leningrad Party historians, 1953-63]. *Voprosy Istorii KPSS [USSR] 1964 (1): 153-156.* Shows how Leningrad historians of the Soviet Communist Party have been correcting distortions from the Stalin period and raising the intellectual level of discussions of the development of socialism in the Soviet Union.

501. Kocherova, L. S. POVYSHENIE POLITICHESKOI AKTIVNOSTI RABOCHIKH-KOMMUNISTOV LENINGRADA V PERIOD MEZHDU XXII I XXIII S"EZDAMI KPSS [The increase in the political activity of Communist workers in Leningrad between the 22d and 23d congresses of the CPSU]. *Vestnik Leningradskogo U.: Seriia Istorii, Iazyka i Literatury [USSR] 1980 (3): 30-33.* Between the 22d and 23d Party congresses, 47.6% of the men and women accepted into the Party as candidates and members were workers. This percentage has subsequently risen; the proportion of workers in the Party is particularly high in the industrial regions of the USSR. Many workers hold responsible positions in the Communist Party of the Soviet Union as members of committees and bureaus and the number delegated to regional and national conferences has increased. Secondary sources; 20 notes.

L. Waters

502. Kogai, P. KOMSOMOL KAZAKHSTANA—POMOSHCHNIK KOMMUNISTICHESKOI PARTII V OSUSHCHESTVELENII KOMPLEKSNOI MEKHANIZATSII KHLOPKOVODSTVA (1959-1965 GG.) [The Komsomol of Kazakhstan—an aid to the Communist Party in the promotion of the complex mechanization of cotton production, 1959-65]. *Vestnik Leningradskogo U.: Seriia Istorii, Iazyka i Literatury*

[USSR] 1977 (8): 138-140. An examination of the effective combination of the Young Communist League (Komsomol) and Communist Party efforts to develop more efficient cotton production. 23 notes. G. F. Jewsbury

503. Korkotsenko, D. I. and Ushakov, V. S. IZ OPYTA RABOTY MESTNYKH PARTIINYKH ORGANIZATSII PO RUKOVODSTVU ELEKTRIFIKATSIEI SEL'SKOGO KHOZIAISTVA (1959-1962 GG) [From the experience of the work of local Party organizations in supervising the electrification of agriculture, 1959-62]. *Voprosy Istorii KPSS [USSR] 1963 (6): 76-86.* Using specific examples, examines how electrification has helped strengthen the technical base of agriculture and improve standards of living, 1959-62.

504. Korolev, A. M. RUKOVODSTVO PARTII: ZALOG USPEKHOV LENINSKOGO KOMSOMOLA [The Party leadership: the guarantor of the success of Lenin's Komsomol]. *Voprosy Istorii KPSS [USSR] 1965 (12): 15-28.* Discusses the role of the Soviet Young Communist League, the Komsomol, in the 1960's stressing the importance always given to youth work by the Communist Party leadership.

505. Kostrikin, V. I. and Perezhogin, M. A. PIAT' LET OBSHCHENARODNOGO DVIZHENIIA ZA KOMMUNISTICHESKII TRUD [Five years of the Public Movement for Communist Labor]. *Prepodavanie Istorii v Shkole [USSR] 1963 18(5): 9-18.* Describes the so-called movement for communist labor begun in 1958 by competing workers' teams and among shockworkers. Over 23 million industrial and agricultural workers and millions of people employed in trade, health, cultural and scientific organizations participate now in these labor competitions contributing to technological progress, heightened labor productivity, and economic growth. 10 notes. N. Frenkley

506. Kretov, F. D. O MESTE ISTORII KPSS V SISTEME OBSHCHESTVENNYKH NAUK [CPSU history in the system of social sciences]. *Voprosy Istorii KPSS [USSR] 1963 (12): 131-135.* Discusses the importance of Soviet Communist Party history and affirms its status as an independent branch of the social sciences, 1962-63.

507. Kulikov, V. I. ISTORICHESKII OPYT PARTII PO RUKOVODSTVU MASSOVYM OSVOENIEM TSELINY I SOVREMENNOST' [The Party's historical experience in directing the mass exploitation of the virgin soils, and the present]. *Voprosy Istorii KPSS [USSR] 1984 (4): 108-118.* World War II delayed Soviet plans to exploit the virgin lands for agriculture. The 1954 plenum of the Central Committee of the Soviet Communist Party ordered the creation of the material and technological base for the exploitation of virgin lands in Siberia, Kazakhstan, the Urals, and the Volga region. Newly created Sovkhozes, staffed by workers from all over the USSR, began to tame the virgin lands. The main historical lessons are that the Soviet Communist Party can alone mobilize the people's creative energies. Based on the Soviet press, especially Pravda and *Sel'skaia Zhizn';* 36 notes. A. J. Evans

508. Kultyshev, S. S. K IZUCHENIIU OPYTA PARTIINOGO RUKOVODSTVA KHOZIASTVENNYM STROITEL'STVOM [The experience of Party leadership in economic construction]. *Voprosy Istorii KPSS [USSR] 1963 (4): 133-137.* A critical look at the literature published in the USSR on the role of the Communist Party in the country's economic development since the 20th Party Congress in 1956.

509. Lalaj, Petro. VEPËR E SHKËLQYER MARXISTE-LENINISTE—LIBRI I SHOKUT ENVER HOXHA *HRUSHOVIANËT (KUJTIME)* [Brilliant Marxist-Leninist work: Comrade Enver Hoxha's book *The Khrushchevians (Memoirs)]. Studime Hist. [Albania] 1980 34(4): 3-24.* Describes the origin and causes of revisionism in the USSR and identifies the leading revisionists. The Albanian Communist Party opposed this trend, especially the rehabilitation of Josip Tito. Nikita Khrushchev, backed later by China, tried to stop the industrialization of Albania. Based on Enver Hoxha's *Khrushchevians (Memoirs)* (1980). French summary. G-D. L. Naci

510. Latkin, V. R. and Usikov, R. A. ZA VYPOLNENIE RESHENII SENTIABRSKOGO PLENUMA TS.K. KPSS (1953-1958 GG) (OBZOR FONDOV KRASNODARSKOGO PARTARKHIVA) [Fulfilling the decisions of the September plenum of the Communist Party Central Committee, 1953-59: a survey of the Krasnodar Party archives]. *Voprosy Istorii KPSS [USSR] 1964 (7): 99-103.* Attempts to carry out the Communist Party Central Committee decisions of September 1953 on the collective farms of the Krasnodar region were so successful that considerable increases in agricultural production were made possible.

511. Lewandowski, Józef. "TAJNY" REFERAT CHRUSZCZOWA: OKOLICZNOŚCI WYGŁOSZENIA I UJAWNIENIA [Khrushchev's "secret" speech: the circumstances of its delivery and disclosure]. *Zeszyty Hist. [France] 1977 (41): 197-209.* Describes the circumstances in which Nikita Khrushchev's speech of 25 February 1956, exposing the nature of the Soviet system under Stalin, was made and the manner of its disclosure to the Communist Parties in Western Europe.

512. Lewytzkyj, Borys. WANDLUNGSPROZESS DER SOWJETISCHEN FÜHRUNGSSCHICHT [The process of transformation of the Soviet leadership]. *Österreichische Osthefte [Austria] 1966 8(6): 463-468.* The division of tasks between the Party and state apparatus in the USSR was purely functional in the 1960's and of minor importance compared to the actual relationship between Party, economic, and state bureaucracy. The alliance between these three widened the social basis of the Soviet ruling class so that intellectuals and technological experts are now on a par with Party officials. R. Wagnleitner

513. Maiorov, S. M. IZDANIE KNIG PO ISTORII VELIKOGO DESIATILETIIA [The publication of books on the history of the great decade]. *Voprosy Istorii KPSS [USSR] 1963 (10): 152-156.* Surveys a number of books which deal with the role of the Communist Party in the socioeconomic development of the USSR, 1953-63.

514. Maistrenko, Ivan. STORINKY Z ISTORII KOMUNISTYCHNOI PARTII UKRAINY: KPU PISLIA SMERTY STALINA (DOBA KHRUSHCHOVA) [Pages from the history of the Communist Party of the Ukraine after the death of Stalin: the Khrushchev era]. *Sučasnist [West Germany] 1974 (5): 63-77.* Assesses the real consequences of the "thaw" on the Ukraine, revealing great centralization and Russification policies beneath the veneer of liberalism.

515. Maneli, Mieczysław. REFLECTIONS ON THE TWENTIETH CONGRESS. *Polish Rev. 1980 25(2): 89-95.* A review of the conclusions of a colloquium held on the twentieth anniversary of the 20th Congress of the Communist Party of the Soviet Union in 1956. The death of Stalin had shaken the system; it became less monolithic but also more stable. In Poland, the main problems have been state legitimacy, anti-Semitism, and church-state relations. The 20th Congress seemed to augur a new era of liberalism, but events were to prove that the changes were matters of theory rather than fact. Internal problems in Hungary and Czechoslovakia helped reinstitute a mood of conservatism and repression, not unusual after a liberal advance. V. L. Human

516. Medvedev, S. A. and Tymchenko, V. V. ORHANIZATSIINO-PARTIINA ROBOTA NA PROMYSLOVYKH PIDPRYIEMSTVAKH DONBASU V ROKY SEMYRICHKY [Party organizational work at industrial enterprises in the Donets Basin during the Seven-Year Plan]. *Ukrains'kyi Istorychnyi Zhurnal [USSR] 1972 (9): 87-91.* Discusses the Communist Party's effort to improve leadership at all levels of production.

517. Mel'kov, I. D. NEKOTORYE VOPROSY ORGANIZATSIONNO-PARTIINOI RABOTY POSLE XXIII S'EZDA KPSS [Some questions of organizational party work following the 23d

Congress of the Communist Party of the USSR]. *Voprosy Istorii KPSS [USSR] 1969 (7): 79-90.* Shows the effect of the decisions of the 23d CPSU congress on the Moldavian Communist Party, whose leadership improved in quality as a result.

518. Mezhenin, M. M. and Titenko, M. P. MASOVO-POLITYCHNA DIIAL'NIST' PARTORHANIZATSII PROMYSLOVYKH PIDPRYIEMSTV DONBASU (1951-1958) [Mass political work by Communist Party organizations in industry in the Donets Basin, 1951-58]. *Ukrains'kyi Istorychnyi Zhurnal [USSR] 1974 (1): 80-85.*

519. Mnatsakanian, M. O. DEIATEL'NOST' KPSS PO RASSHIRENIIU PRAV SOIUZNYKH RESPUBLIK (1953-1962) [The work of the CPSU in extending the rights of the union republics, 1953-62]. *Voprosy Istorii KPSS [USSR] 1963 (10): 3-15.* Explores the achievements of the Soviet Communist Party in the political life of the union republics in the period since the 20th Party Congress and considers the rejection of the personality cult, 1953-62.

520. Modestov, V. V. PARTIIA V BOR'BE ZA RAZVITIE SOTSIALISTICHESKOGO OBSHCHESTVA V SSSR I UPROCHNENIE MIROVOI SISTEMY SOTSIALIZMA (1952-1961 GG.) [The Party in the struggle for the development of socialist society in the USSR and the strengthening of the world system of socialism, 1952-61]. *Voprosy Istorii KPSS [USSR] 1980 (5): 111-119.* The concept of developed socialism should be discussed as part of the 17th theme in the history course of the Communist Party of the Soviet Union. Two lectures should be devoted to this subject. The first lecture should cover the five-year plan, 1951-55, and the 20th Party Congress, 1956. The second lecture should cover the 21st Party Congress, 1959, the complete and final victory of socialism in the USSR, and the Party's third program. Lecturers should explain the economic and social transformations of the decade and make use of Party documents. Secondary material; 71 notes.
G. Dombrovski

521. Monakhov, V. S. PARTIIA—ORGANIZATOR POD''EMA OBSHCHESTVENNOGO ZHIVOTNOVODSTVA SEVERO-ZAPADNOI ZONY RSFSR V 1953-1960 GODAKH [The Party as organizer of the rise in livestock husbandry in the Northwestern zone of the RSFSR, 1953-60]. *Vestnik Leningradskogo U.: Seriia Istorii, Iazyka i Literatury [USSR] 1962 17(20): 51-61.* Deals with political mass education conducted during 1954-60 by the Communist Party to raise lagging cattle production in northwest European Russia. Though overall growth rates improved, production on some farms remained low and in some instances such as sheep raising fell below 1953 averages. Regional management of farm production was introduced by the agrarian reform of 1962 to alleviate shortcomings of local farm administration. 51 notes. N. Frenkley

522. Nakanishi, Osamu. SOREN NI OKERU SHIN-ROSEN-STALIN HIHAN NO KEISEI KATEI, 1952-1956 [The policymaking process of the new course and de-Stalinization in the USSR, 1952-56]. *Rekishigaku Kenkyū [Japan] 1980 (477): 2-15, 30.* The new policy line and the de-Stalinization at the 20th Congress of the Soviet Communist Party in February 1956 were not the abrupt events often portrayed but had been formulated gradually after the 19th Congress in October 1952. After analyzing Stalin's papers presented before and at the 19th Congress, reexamines the policy change after the death of Stalin, the political struggles among Malenkov, Molotov, and Khrushchev, and in this context the shift in the evaluation of Stalin. Discusses the adoption of the new policy line and the de-Stalinization at the 20th Congress. Primary sources; 92 notes. Y. Imura

523. Nikiforov, Iu. N. KPSS: ORGANIZATOR STROITEL'STVA NEFTEKHIMICHESKOI PROMYSHLENNOSTI V BASHKIRSKOI ASSR [CPSU: the organizer of the building of the oil and chemical industry in the Bashkir ASSR]. *Voprosy Istorii KPSS [USSR] 1963 (10): 16-25.* Traces the development of the oil and chemical industries in Bashkir since the May plenum of 1958 and the 21st Communist Party Congress.

524. Norwid, T. GENERATIONSBYTE I DET SOVJETRYSKA PARTIET [A generation change in the Soviet Party]. *Svensk Tidskrift [Sweden] 1961 48(4): 233-240.* Nikita Khrushchev failed to place production under adequate Party control and an agricultural crisis ensued, 1958-60. The crisis was due to the generation gap within the Party for the better educated and less regimented youth was less motivated to follow the Party leadership.
U. G. Jeyes/S

525. Opryshchenko, H. P. VYKHOVANNIA MOLODYKH ROBITNYKIV DONBASU V DUSI RADIANS'KOHO PATRIOTYZMU I PROLETARS'KOHO INTERNATSIONALIZMU (1956-1961 RR.) [Educating young workers in the Donets Basin region in the spirit of Soviet patriotism and proletarian internationalism, 1956-61]. *Ukrains'kyi Istorychnyi Zhurnal [USSR] 1972 (11): 100-107.* Reviews Communist Party and the Young Communist League initiatives and activities.

526. Panchenko, P. P. and Haivoroniuk, B. O. PRYKORDONNI ZVIAZKY TRUDIASHCHYKH URSR I ZARUBIZHNYKH SOTSIALISTYCHNYKH KRAIN 1956-1959 [The contact of the working masses of the USSR with their socialist neighbors, 1956-69]. *Ukrains'kyi Istorychnyi Zhurnal [USSR] 1969 (12): 50-57.* Relates the experience of various exchanges of workers from the USSR and other communist countries, citing books and newspaper reports, 1956-69.

527. Pchelin, V. G. UKREPLENIE I RAZVITIE SVIAZEI PARTII S MASSAMI (1953-1962 GG) [The strengthening and development of the Party's ties with the masses, 1953-62]. *Voprosy Istorii KPSS [USSR] 1963 (3): 3-17.* Deals with the growing political activism of the masses in the period since the death of Stalin and describes the changes that have taken place in the organization and functioning of the Communist Party, 1953-62.

528. Petrenko, F. F. and Shapko, V. M. VAZHNOE NACHINANIE [An important start]. *Voprosy Istorii KPSS [USSR] 1961 (1): 193-199.* Reviews two books on the Soviet Communist Party, 1953-58: V. I. Ignat'ev's *Partiia na puti k razvernutomu stroitel'stvu kommunizma v SSSR (1953-1958)* [The Party on the path to the detailed construction of communism in the USSR, 1953-58] (1960) and F. V. Nosov's *Bor'ba kommunisticheskoi partii za moshchynyi pod'em narodnogo khoziaistva, za zavershenie stroitel'stva sotsializma v SSSR (1953-1958)* [The struggle of the Communist Party for strong growth in the national economy and for the completion of the construction of socialism in the USSR, 1953-58] (1960).

529. Polner, L. S. KOMMUNISTY RUDNOGO ALTAIA V BOR'BE ZA TEKHNICHESKII PROGRESS (1956-1965 GG) [The Communists of the Altai mining region in the struggle for technological progress, 1956-65]. *Voprosy Istorii KPSS [USSR] 1965 (12): 69-77.* Details the successes of the Communist Party organizations of the Soviet mining district in the Altai mountains in modernizing their zinc, lead, and other ore extraction industries, 1956-65.

530. Popov, K. I. DER AUSSENHANDEL ALS FAKTOR DER WIRTSCHAFTLICHEN ENTWICKLUNG IN DEN SOZIALISTISCHEN STAATEN [Foreign trade as a factor in the economic development of socialist states]. *Österreichische Osthefte [Austria] 1966 8(4): 330-338.* Analyzes the position of the USSR's foreign trade in international economic relations and the aims of the foreign trade of socialist countries during the 1960's.

531. Prusanov, I. P. POVYSHENIE ORGANIZUIUSHCHEGO I NAPRAVLIAIUSHCHEGO VLIIANIIA PARTII V VOORUZHENNYKH SILAKH (1956-1964) [Increasing the organizing and governing influence of the Communist Party in the armed forces, 1956-64]. *Voprosy Istorii KPSS [USSR] 1965 (2): 3-13.* Outlines means adopted after the denouncement of Joseph Stalin in 1956 to restore Leninist norms in the military, including the restoration of the Soviet Communist Party's leading ideological role.

532. Rudych, F. M. ZDIISNENNIA LENINS'KOHO PRYNTSYPU MASOVOSTI KONTROLIU I ZALUCHENNIA TRUDIASHCHYKH DO UPRAVLINNIA VYROBNYTSTVOM [The realization of Lenin's principle of mass control and the inclusion of workers into the direction of production]. *Ukrains'kyi Istorychnyi Zhurnal [USSR] 1965 (4): 63-70.* Describes the formation, function, and operation of the system of groups to aid Party and government control in the Ukraine, 1961-65, according to the guidelines put forward at the 22d Congress of the Communist Party of the Soviet Union (1961).

533. Rybecký, Vladislav. DVACÁTÉ VÝROČÍ MOSKEVSKÉ PORADY KOMUNISTICKÝCH A DĚLNICKÝCH STRAN [The 20th anniversary of the Moscow meeting of Communist and workers' parties]. *Historie a Vojenství [Czechoslovakia] 1978 27(1): 91-112.* Evaluates the meaning of the 1957 Moscow congress as a clear expression of Party unity and also explains the changes in the Communist movement since the Seventh Comintern Congress in 1935. In that year there were 61 Communist parties with 3 million members; in 1957 there were 33 million members of 75 workers' parties in the world. G. E. Pergl

534. Safronova, G. P. and Slivina, A. P. KRASNOIARSKAIA PARTIINAIA ORGANIZATSIIA V BOR'BE ZA POD'EM SEL'SKOGO KHOZIAISTVA V 1953-1958 GG (OBZOR FONDOV KRASNOIARSKOGO PARTIINOGO AKTIVA) [The Krasnoyarsk Party organization in the stuggle to improve agriculture, 1953-58: a survey of the holdings of the Krasnoyarsk Party archive]. *Voprosy Istorii [USSR] 1963 (6): 102-107.* Looks at the developments in agriculture in the five years following the death of Stalin, 1953-58.

535. Savichenko, N. V. and Levykin, K. G. IZ OPYTA NAUCHNOI SPETSIALIZATSII STUDENTOV NA KAFEDRE ISTORII KPSS ISTORICHESKOGO FAKUL'TETA MGU [The scientific specialization of students in the department of CPSU history of Moscow University's history faculty]. *Voprosy Istorii KPSS [USSR] 1963 (9): 149-152.* Evaluates the success of the program taught by the Communist Party history department at Moscow University, 1953-63.

536. Schultz, Eberhard. KOMMUNISMUS UND FRIEDEN [Communism and peace]. *Martin-Luther-U. Halle-Wittenberg. Wissenschaftliche Zeitschrift. Gesselleschafts- und Sprachwissenschafliche Reihe [East Germany] 1962 11(11): 1397-1411.* Analyzes the development of Soviet military theory and foreign policy as reflected in the decisions of the Soviet Communist Party in the 1950's. 38 notes.

537. Shapko, V. M. PARTIIA I GOSUDARSTVO NA SOVREMENNOM ETAPE KOMMUNISTICHESKOGO STROITEL'STVA: ISTORIOGRAFICHESKII OBZOR [The Party and state at the present stage of communist construction: an historiographical survey]. *Voprosy Istorii KPSS [USSR] 1961 (6): 182-191.* Discusses Soviet historiography, 1956-61, devoted to the relationship between the Communist Party and the State in the period since 1953. Asserts that the topic has not been examined sufficiently.

538. Shepeta, M. T. ROL' ROBITNYCHYKH ZBORIV V UPRAVLINNI BYROBNYTSTVOM (1951-1958 RR.) [The role of workers' meetings in production management, 1951-58]. *Ukrains'kyi Istorychnyi Zhurnal [USSR] 1975 (2): 82-89.* Labor unions and the Communist Party sponsored shop and factory meetings in the Ukraine of workers, engineers, and other technical workers in production management as well as implementation of worker participation and communist education during the culminating phase of socialist construction.

539. Shkliar, E. E. OB IZUCHENII RESHENII XX S"EZDA KPSS [On studying the decisions of the Communist Party's 20th Congress]. *Voprosy Istorii KPSS [USSR] 1965 (1): 86-93.* After Nikita Khrushchev's fall from grace, Soviet Communists received guidance as to how to interpret the decisions of the 20th Congress of the CPSU (1956), which Khrushchev had dominated.

540. Shmidt, S. O. K VOPROSU O PREPODAVANII ISTOCHNIKOVEDENIIA ISTORII KPSS [Teaching the study of sources concerning the history of the CPSU]. *Voprosy Istorii KPSS [USSR] 1963 (2): 101-104.* Discusses the methods of teaching the study of sources on the Soviet Communist Party, emphasizing the contact between teachers and researchers, 1957-62.

541. Smerychevs'ki, F. H. PRO FORMUVANNIA MARKSYSTS'KOHO-LENINS'KOHO SVITOHLIADU MOLODYKH ROBITNYKIV (1959-1965 RR.) [The formation of a Marxist-Leninist outlook among young workers, 1959-65]. *Ukrains'kyi Istorychnyi Zhurnal [USSR] 1976 (10): 102-107.* Examines the activities of the Communist Party of the Soviet Union in educating the entire population in scientific Marxism-Leninism. Pays particular attention to such political education among young workers in the Ukraine.

542. Startsev, V. I. and Shkaratan, O. I. PARTIINYE ORGANIZATSII VO GLAVE DVIZHENIIA BRIGAD KOMMUNISTICHESKOGO TRUDA: PO MATERIALAM LENINGRADA [Party organizations at the head of the Communist labor brigade movement: materials on Leningrad]. *Voprosy Istorii KPSS [USSR] 1961 (4): 95-106.* Describes the organization by the Soviet Communist Party, starting in the fall of 1958, of a new form of socialist competition under the title of the Communist Labor Brigade.

543. Stepanov, V. P. NACHALA RAZVERNUTOGO STROITEL'STVA KOMMUNIZMA (K PIATILETIIU VNEOCHEREDNOGO XXI S"EZDA KPSS) [The beginning of the full-scale construction of Communism: on the fifth anniversary of the extraordinary 21st Congress of the Communist Party of the Soviet Union]. *Voprosy Istorii KPSS [USSR] 1964 (1): 13-22.* Recalls, on the occasion of its fifth anniversary, the extraordinary 21st Congress of the Communist Party, 27 January-5 February 1959, which, under the supervision of Nikita Khrushchev, approved the Seven-Year Plan and proclaimed the goal of catching up with and overtaking the United States.

544. Taborsky, Edward. THE REVOLT OF THE COMMUNIST INTELLECTUALS. *Rev. of Pol. 1957 19(3): 308-329.* Analysis of the revolt of intellectuals within the Soviet Communist Party emphasizes its spread, persistence, hierarchical effect, and the occupations of those involved.

545. Topuzlu, G. N. SOTRUDNICHESTVO MOLDAVSKOI SSR S BRATSKIMI SOIUZNYMI RESPUBLIKAMI V RAZVITII SEL'SKOGO KHOZIAISTVA NA ZAVERSHAIUSHCHEM ETAPE STROITEL'STVA SOTSIALIZMA [The cooperation of the Moldavian SSR with the fraternal union republics in the development of agriculture in the final stage of the construction of socialism]. *Istoricheskie Zapiski Akad. Nauk SSSR [USSR] 1982 (107): 5-30.* Especially since the 19th and 20th Congresses of the Communist Party of the Soviet Union, Moldavia has received great help from other Soviet republics. This help was very necessary from 1950 to 1957. Fraternal republics provided technology, tractors, combines, road construction equipment, and electrification expertise. Many young Moldavians were educated outside their home republic. Moldavia repays its debt with food products and gratitude. Based on material in the Central State Archive of the Moldavian SSR; 97 notes. A. J. Evans

546. Ugriumov, A. L. K VOPROSU O METODIKE PREPODAVANIIA SEMINARSKIKH ZANIATII PO ISTORII KPSS [Ways of teaching seminars on the history of the Communist Party of the USSR]. *Voprosy Istorii KPSS [USSR] 1968 (11): 144-148.* Discusses the best ways for a teacher in higher education to prepare for seminars on the history of the Communist Party. Emphasizes the importance of a stimulating syllabus to command the students' interest while presenting them with a truthful account of the Party's history. Comments on various aspects of teacher-student relations which demand careful attention in order that a seminar prove successful. N. Dejevsky

547. Voronovich, A. A.; Donskoi, V. M.; and Shapkarin, A. V. NOVOE IZDANIE UCHEBNIKA [A new edition of a textbook]. *Voprosy Istorii KPSS [USSR] 1963 (4): 120-129.* Praises one of the new textbooks on the history of the Soviet Communist Party published in 1962 for its detailed examination of the personality cult.

548. Vovchyk, A. F. and Niemchenko, M. O. VYKORYSTANNIA PRATS' TOVARYSHA L. I. BREZHNEVA "MALA ZEMLIA", "VIDRODZHENNIA" I "TSILYNA" U VUZIVS'KOMU KURSI ISTORII KPRS [Using comrade L. I. Brezhnev's *Malaia Zemlia, Rebirth,* and *The Virgin Land* for the study of the history of the CPSU in higher education]. *Ukrains'kyi Istorychnyi Zhurnal [USSR] 1979 (7): 113-125.* Leonid Brezhnev's three volumes of memoirs describe the heroism of the Soviet peoples and are an ideological weapon of great force. Suggests how they can be used for the study of the history of the Communist Party of the USSR in Soviet higher educational establishments. 71 notes. I. Krushelnyckyj

549. Willetts, H. T. DYNAMIC CONFORMITY: THE PUBLIC IMAGE OF THE CPSU. *Survey [Great Britain] 1961 (35): 69-75.* Discusses the image of the Communist Party of the USSR in the period of Nikita Khrushchev's leadership, 1954-61, as portrayed in the journal *Partiinaia zhizn'.*

550. Zaitsev, V. S. PARTIIA—VDOKHNOVITEL' I ORGANIZATOR RAZVERNUTOGO STROITEL'STVA KOMMUNISTICHESKOGO OBSHCHESTVA (1959-1961 GG) (K IZUCHENIIU 18-I TEMY KURSA ISTORII KPSS) [The Party, inspirer and organizer of the advanced construction of Communist society, 1959-61: the 18th theme of the course of the history of the CPSU]. *Voprosy Istorii KPSS [USSR] 1963 (4): 70-80.* Describes the proceedings of the 21st Communist Party Congress, outlines the main points of the Seven-Year Plan and emphasizes the role of the Party in strengthening the world socialist system and internationalism, 1959-61.

551. Zelenin, I. E. IZ ISTORII OBSHCHESTVENNO-POLITICHESKOI ZHIZNI SOVETSKOY DEREVNI V 50-E GODY [Soviet villages in the 1950's: their society and politics]. *Istoriia SSSR [USSR] 1976 (4): 30-53.* Examines important sociopolitical developments in Soviet villages during the 1950's, a particularly important decade for Soviet rural life. The developments include the work of local Communist Party organizations, civic participation in the latter, and the peasants' reactions to domestic and international affairs. The author gives special attention to the organizational and political activities of village Party organizations. Public participation in Party work increased sharply in the 1950's, and rural life generally became richer and more substantial than in the prewar period. 4 tables, 110 notes. N. Dejevsky

552. Zhelezin, V. I. OBSHCHESTVENNYE NACHALA V PARTIINOI RABOTE NA SOVREMENNOM ETAPE [The social bases of Party work in the contemporary period]. *Voprosy Istorii KPSS [USSR] 1965 (6): 11-22.* With the imminent creation of communism, the Party in the Soviet Union has begun to widen its social net, using technical experts to solve problems and wide-ranging initiatives in contrast to the dry bureaucratic methods of the Stalin era.

553. Zykov, A. N. K IZUCHENIIU ISTORII PARTIINOI RABOTY NA STROITEL'STVE BRATSKOI GES (OBZOR FONDOV PARTIINOGO ARKHIVA IRKUTSKOGO OBKOMA KPSS) [The study of the history of Party work during the construction of the Bratsk hydroelectric power station: a review of the Party archives of the Irkutsk district committee of the Communist Party of the USSR]. *Voprosy Istorii KPSS [USSR] 1971 (10): 115-120.* Emphasizes the role of the Irkutsk Party committee in guiding construction work, 1955-67.

1964-1982

554. Aksionenko, P. H. DEIAKI PYTANNIA VDOSKONALENNIA VNUTRIPARTIINOI DEMOKRATII: 1966-1971 [On some questions concerning the improvement of intraparty democracy, 1966-71]. *Ukraïns'kyi Istorychnyi Zhurnal [USSR] 1980 (6): 95-100.* Lenin taught that the Communist Party is the property of the whole membership and should be run directly by members or through elected bodies. Hence, intraparty democracy should be looked upon as a guarantee that functionaries at all levels constantly report back to the rank-and-file. And the more developed socialism becomes, the higher becomes the degree of intraparty democracy.

555. Alakhverdov, G. G. and Kas'ianenko, V. I. O NEKOTORYKH BURZHUAZNYKH FAL'SIFIKATSIIAKH ROLI I ZNACHENIIA IDEINO-VOSPITATEL'NOI RABOTY KPSS [On some bourgeois falsifications of the role and significance of the ideological-educational work of the CPSU]. *Voprosy Istorii KPSS [USSR] 1974 (4): 46-55.* Western authors such as L. Schapiro, M. Fainsod, and Z. Brzezinski have argued that the Communist Party and its propaganda have become increasingly ineffective. Such a conclusion ignores the growth in party membership, economic development, cultural achievements, coordination of interests by the Party, and the expansion of Party education. Based on Western studies and recent Party publications; 37 notes.
L. E. Holmes

556. Alekseev, V. K. PARTIINOE RUKOVODSTVO SREDSTVAMI MASSOVOI INFORMATSII I PROPAGANDY G. MOSKVY (1966-1970 GG) [Party management of mass information and propaganda in Moscow, 1966-70]. *Sovetskie Arkhivy [USSR] 1978 (6): 44-47.* Examines materials illustrating Moscow Communist Party management of mass information, using press, radio, and television, during the eighth Five-Year Plan, 1966-70.

557. Alekseev, V. K. PARTIINOE RUKOVODSTVO PECHAT'IU I RADIOVESHCHANIEM V PROIZVODSTVENNYKH KOLLEKTIVAKH G. MOSKVY V GODY VOS'MOI PIATILETKI [Party direction of the press and radio broadcasting in production collectives in the city of Moscow during the 8th Five-Year Plan]. *Voprosy Istorii KPSS [USSR] 1980 (12): 71-79.* During the 8th Five-Year Plan period, 1966-70, in Moscow there were 200 large-circulation newspapers, around 50,000 wall newspapers, and over 100 local radio broadcasting systems, mostly in production collectives. The author examines the importance of these in assisting production, given the Party Central Committee's 1979 declaration via ideologist Mikhail A. Suslov, that they were a powerful ideological weapon. In the 8th plan period the city Party organization was careful not to let control over these means of information slip from its grasp. Based on Moscow Party Archive, local newspapers from Moscow, and secondary sources; 62 notes. D. N. Collins

558. Anikeev, V. V. NAUCHNAIA OSNOVA SOZDANIIA DOKUMENTAL'NOI BAZY PO ISTORII KPSS [The creation of a documentary base for the history of the CPSU]. *Voprosy Istorii KPSS [USSR] 1965 (8): 150-153.* Discusses shortcomings and achievements in the storage and use of Soviet Communist Party documents in the 154 archives used for the purpose.

559. Anikeev, Vasili Vasil'evich, and Iudin, G. V. O RABOTE MESTNYKH PARTIINYKH ARKHIVOV V 1966-1970 GODAKH [The local archives of the Communist Party and work completed, 1966-70]. *Sovetskie Arkhivy [USSR] 1971 (5): 28-35.* Reviews the work of regional and district Party archives in various Soviet republics, as well as their publications concerning all periods of Soviet history. Particular attention is given to works commemorating the 50th anniversary of the October Revolution and the Red Army, the 25th anniversary of the victory over Germany, and the 100th anniversary of Lenin's birth. It notes the lack of books generalizing on the experience of the Party's regional organization, and it stigmatizes insufficient professionalism in a few archives, as well as defects in reader services. C. I. P. Ferdinand

560. Åslund, Anders. SOVJETKOMMUNISMENS LEGITIMETSKRIS [Soviet communism's legitimacy crisis]. *Svensk Tidskrift [Sweden] 1982 69(3): 150-153.* The economic and ideological bases for Soviet communism have been weakened, causing the most serious legitimacy crisis that the USSR has ever faced. Political concessions are impossible, although terror and military power remain as means for the regime to defend itself if economic conditions in Eastern Europe do not improve. L. B. Sather

561. Bartsch, Günther. DER TROTZKISMUS ALS INTERNATIONALE SONDERBEWEGUNG [Trotskyism as a separate international movement]. *Osteuropa [West Germany] 1976 26(5): 369-381.* Trotskyism, represented today by the Fourth International and three splinter groups, remains the prisoner of Leon Trotsky's insistence that the USSR is still a workers' state; Trotskyites are torn between this analysis and their affection for the old Soviet Union of Lenin and the fact that the Soviet Union murdered Trotsky and is their determined enemy.

562. Beglov, S. A PEACEFUL FUTURE FOR EUROPE. *Int. Affairs [USSR] 1973 (11): 3-9.* Discusses the USSR and Communist countries' role in the 1973 Conference on Security and Cooperation in Europe and alleges that some Western observers still articulating Cold War attitudes are preventing detente between East and West.

563. Beliaev, R. K. and Luk'ianenko, V. I. IZ OPYTA RABOTY NABEREZHNO-CHELNINSKOGO GORKOMA KPSS PO FORMIROVANIIU I UKREPLENIIU PERVICHNYKH PARTIINYKH ORGANIZATSII [From the experience of the Naberezhno-Chelninsk Communist Party City Committee in the formation and strengthening of primary Party organizations]. *Voprosy Istorii KPSS [USSR] 1980 (11): 31-41.* The city of Naberezhno-Chelninsk was built after a decision in 1969 to construct the Kama automotive plant (KamAZ) on the Kama River near the Ural mountains in the USSR. Details the progress of the city Communist Party Committee in establishing primary Party cells among the new inhabitants of this automobile workers' city. During 1976-77, 3,442 cell meetings were held. The city organization has set up 433 commissions to control the activities of the administration, with 1,800 Communists participating in them. Based on published sources; 13 notes. D. N. Collins

564. Bērziņš, I. POVYSHENIE UROVNIA PARTIINOGO RUKOVODSTVA: RESHAIUSHCHEE USLOVIE VYPOLNENIIA RESHENII MARTOVSKOGO (1965 G.) PLENUMA TSK KPSS (1965-1971 GG.) [Advancement in the level of the Party leadership: a decisive precondition for the execution of the March (1965) resolution of the plenary session of the CPSU Central Committee (1965-71)]. *Latvijas PSR Zinātņu Akadēmijas Vēstis [USSR] 1984 (10): 10-20.* The resolution of the March (1965) plenary session of the Central Committee of the Communist Party of the Soviet Union demanded urgent improvements in the development of agricultural productivity. Describes the efforts of the Latvian Communist Party to upgrade the quantitative and qualitative leadership of Party members in Latvia's state and collective farms. Based on archival data; 48 notes. R. Vilums

565. Beschastni, L. SOVERSHENSTVOVANIE SISTEMY UPRAVLENIIA I MEKHANIZMA KHOZIAISTVOVANIIA: UZLOVOI VOPROS EKONOMICHESKOI POLITIKI PARTII [Improving the system of control and the mechanism of management: a central question of the economic policy of the Party]. *Ekonomika Sovetskoi Ukrainy [USSR] 1972 14(3): 70-75.* Examines the growing role of the systems of economic control following the decisions of the 23d and 24th Congresses of the Soviet Communist Party and underlines the importance the Party attached to the democratic control of the socialist economy.

566. Bezik, I. V. OB OPYTE PARTORGANIZATSII PRIMORSKOGO I KHABAROVSKOGO KRAEV PO VOSPITANIIU MOLODEZHI V KHODE SOTSIALISTICHESKOGO SOREVNOVANIIA V GODY DESIATOI PIATILETKI [On the experience of Party organizations in the Primorsk and Khabarovsk regions in the education of young people in the trend of socialist competition in the years of the 10th Five-Year Plan]. *Vestnik Leningradskogo U.: Seriia Istorii, Iazyka i Literatury [USSR] 1981 (3): 91-93.* One of the most important tasks of the Party organizations is to inculcate socialist values in the young. On a trip to the Far East in 1978 L. I. Brezhnev emphasized the importance of a correct moral attitude to work and the nation. The Khabarovsk and Primorsk Party organizations instituted the system of socialist competition. The best worker in each profession is chosen, and others invited to follow his example. The Party organization gives Komsomol organizations carefully chosen, responsible jobs which, successfully accomplished, give a feeling of solid, socialist achievement. Yearly Komsomol meetings, Lenin hours, and Lenin tests provide educational amusement for young people. Based on items from *Komsomolskaia Pravda,* and works and speeches of L. I. Brezhnev; 20 notes. A. J. Evans

567. Bezik, I. V. PARTIINOE RUKOVODSTVO NASTAVNICHESTVOM: IZ OPYTA PARTORGANIZATSII PRIMORSKOGO I KHABAROVSKOGO KRAEV V GODY VOS'MOI PIATILETKI [Party leadership of tutoring: from the experience of the Party organizations of the Primorski and Khabarovsk regions during the eighth Five-Year Plan]. *Vestnik Leningradskogo U.: Seriia Istorii, Iazyka i Literatury [USSR] 1980 (4): 95-98.* The tutorship movement which began in Leningrad in the early 1960's proved to be an effective method of Communist education and of apprenticeship for participation in socialist society. The Communist Party and Komsomol issued a number of resolutions and recommendations on this subject which were successfully implemented in the Primorski and Khabarovsk regions, where organizational, economic, and ideological work was fully integrated. Both individual and collective methods of tutoring have been practiced and have helped to raise standards of productivity and reduce absenteeism. Communists and heroes of labor have played an important role in the movement. Based on Soviet archival and secondary sources; 17 notes. L. Waters

568. Bialer, Seweryn and Gustafson, Thane, ed. *Russia at the Crossroads: The 26th Congress of the CPSU.* London: Allen & Unwin, 1981. 223 pp.

569. Biddulph, Howard L. LOCAL INTEREST ARTICULATION AT CPSU CONGRESSES. *World Pol. 1983 36(1): 28-52.* Soviet regional leaders of the USSR were modestly successful in their attempts to add local projects to the agenda of forthcoming Five-Year Plans at Party Congresses during the Brezhnev era. The volume of local demands expressed in Congress speeches steadily increased from the 24th to the 26th Congresses, as did the frequency of speaker participation in petitioning for investment. This seems to reflect the gradual legitimation of regional consultation in long-range planning and the sharpening politics of stringency of the latter Brezhnev era. While the vast majority of requests were purely provincial in scope, broader regional interests were articulated to an increasing extent at the 25th and 26th Congresses. Requests respecting agriculture were the most frequent, followed by energy and fuels, water resources, and transportation. J

570. Birons, A. K. MEZHDUNARODNYI SIMPOZIUM, POSVIASHCHENNYI ISTORIOGRAFII VELIKOGO OKTIABRIA [International symposium devoted to the historiography of the Great October]. *Latvijas PSR Zinātnu Akademijas Vestis [USSR] 1977 (2): 136-138.* Report on the International Symposium in Bucharest, 26-28 October 1976, on the international significance of the October Revolution and its reflections in contemporary historiography. Representatives of the USSR, Bulgaria, Hungary, East Germany, Mongolia, Poland, Rumania, and Czechoslovakia participated. Includes authors and summaries of the most important presentations. Stresses the creative character of the studies and the interest displayed by historians of the socialist countries in the problems of the October Revolution. R. Vilums

571. Blinkin, A. Ia. "KRITIKA"—AMERIKANSKII ZHURNAL PO ISTORII SSSR [*Kritika,* an American journal of Soviet history]. *Voprosy Istorii [USSR] 1983 (4): 162-168.* Discusses the 1970-81 content of *Kritika: A Review of Current Soviet Books on Russian History,* a Harvard University journal reflecting the views of Richard Pipes and similar anti-Soviet and anti-Communist spokesmen.

Its review articles deal primarily with publications of source materials, memoirs, and books on prerevolutionary Russian history. Criticisms of Soviet methodology and Soviet analyses of historical processes and the journal's attacks on Leninism verge on disinformation and tendentious distortion of historical facts. 16 notes.
N. Frenkley

572. Bohodyst, I. P. DIIAL'NIST' PARTIINYKH ORHANIZATSII DONBASU PO VYKHOVANNIU TRUDIASHCHYKH U DUSI INTERNATSIONALIZMU TA DRUZHBY NARODIV SRSR: 1966-70 [The work of Party organizations in the Donets Basin with regard to educating working people in the spirit of internationalism and friendship of peoples of the USSR, 1966-70]. *Ukraïns'kyi Istorychnyi Zhurnal [USSR] 1980 (1): 78-82.* Since the Donets region is populated by representatives of 74 nationalities, the party has done a great deal in drawing working people together, instilling them with Soviet patriotism, and developing closer cultural ties with various union republics.

573. Bokarev, N. N. OB OPYTE ISSLEDOVANIIA RABOTY PERVICHNYKH PARTIINYKH ORGANIZATSII PO POVYSHENIIU SOTSIAL'NOI AKTIVNOSTI KOMMUNISTOV [Research on the work of primary Party organizations for increasing the social activity of Communists]. *Voprosy Istorii KPSS [USSR] 1978 (4): 94-105.* Surveys the activity of members of primary Party organizations in industrial enterprises in the Moscow region, 1970-75. An increasing number of Party members assumed leading roles in raising the quality and quantity of production, achieving labor discipline, assisting socialist competition, and participating in the activity of professional and social organizations as well as in the management of industry. Based on published documents, periodical literature, and the research of the Sector for Sociological Research of the Academy of Sciences; 19 notes. L. E. Holmes

574. Bokarev, N. N. SOTSIOLOGICHESKIE ISSLEDOVANIIA V DEIATEL'NOSTI PARTIINYKH KOMITETOV [Sociological research in the activity of Party committees]. *Sotsiologicheskie Issledovaniia [USSR] 1982 (1): 44-51.* Describes the use of sociological research to strengthen ideological activity as well as control functions of Party committees.

575. Borcke, Astrid von. DAS APRIL-PLENUM 1973 DES ZENTRALKOMITEES DER KPDSU UND DIE UMBESETZUNGEN IM POLITBÜRO [The plenary session of the Central Committee of the CPSU in April 1973 and the shifts in Politburo membership]. *Osteuropa [West Germany] 1973 23(12): 917-929.* The plenary meeting confirmed the Soviet policy of detente while underscoring internal security and military strength. The promotions of KGB Chief Yuri Andropov, Foreign Minister Andrei A. Gromyko, and Marshal Andrei Grechko to the Politburo express the new tendency and strengthen Leonid Brezhnev's leadership without giving him one-man rule. The meeting spelled a hardening of ideological lines and resistance to reforming tendencies. 55 notes.
R. E. Weltsch

576. Borisov, E. F. REALIZATSIIA USTANOVOK XXV S'EZDA KPSS NA USKORENIE NAUCHNO-TECKHNICHESKOGO PROGRESSA [The realization of the purposes of the 25th Congress of the CPSU for the acceleration of scientific-technical progress]. *Voprosy Istorii KPSS [USSR] 1980 (1): 100-109.* The Soviet government and Communist Party successfully promoted the development, coordination, and application of science and technology. This progress was due to a planned economy, utilization of new equipment, reliance on economic stimuli, and the training of workers. Based on published materials of the 25th Party Congress (1976); 52 notes. L. E. Holmes

577. Borodin, O. A.; Mingazutdinov, O. F.; and Sliusarenko, A. G. Z DOSVIDU VYKLADANNIA ISTORII KPRS NA HUMANITARNYKH FAKUL'TETAKH KYIVS'KOHO UNIVERSYTETU [Teaching the history of the CPSU in the Humanities Departments of Kiev University]. *Ukrains'kyi Istorychnyi Zhurnal [USSR] 1976 (5): 114-120.* Relates the experiences gained in teaching the history of the Communist Party of the USSR at Moscow's M. E. Bauman Institute and Saratov's M. G. Chernishevsky State University, and how the methods used there were applied at Kiev's T. G. Shevchenko State University, 1974-76.

578. Breslauer, George W. IS THERE A GENERATION GAP IN THE SOVIET POLITICAL ESTABLISHMENT?: DEMAND ARTICULATION BY RSFSR PROVINCIAL PARTY FIRST SECRETARIES. *Soviet Studies [Great Britain] 1984 36(1): 1-25.* Detailed analysis of articles and speeches by 24 Communist Party leaders at the provincial level reveals attitudinal patterns that cannot yet be explained satisfactorily in the literature on Soviet politics. In terms of current Soviet policy and performance, provincial first secretaries who began their careers during the Stalin era are, on the average, much more patient and less demanding than their post-Stalin equivalents. The younger political generation is more polarized, less homogeneous; its representatives include disproportionate numbers of those who are most and least demanding. 21 notes, 2 appendixes.
M. E. Yerburgh

579. Brinkley, George. HISTORY IN THE USSR—A PERSONAL MEMOIR. *Hist. Teacher 1967 1(1): 25-31.* Discusses history teaching in Moscow as observed in a visit to Moscow schools and in discussions with Moscow historians. Contacts and discussions with history scholars revealed programming in Communist Party ideology as a basis for historical interpretation. There was a little encouragement, however, in discussions with historians at the Academy of Science's Institute of History, where some genuine intellectual exchange was still possible. R. V. Ritter

580. Bulkina, V. P. and Shtepa, O. F. TRUDOVI ZVERSHENYIA KOMSOMOLU UKRAINY (1971-1975 RR.) [The labor achievements of the Komsomol of the Ukraine, 1971-75]. *Ukrains'kyi Istorychnyi Zhurnal [USSR] 1976 (2): 49-60.* Reviews contributions by members of the Young Communist League to fulfillment by workers of the Ukrainian SSR of the Ninth Five-Year Plan.

581. Bulygina, T. A. and Shirokov, A. I. IZ OPYTA PARTIINOI RABOTY PO ULUCHSHENIIU PREPODAVANIIA OBSHCHESTVENNYKH NAUK V MGU (1966-1970) [Party work on improving the teaching of social sciences at Moscow State University, 1966-70]. *Vestnik Moskovskogo U., Seriia 8: Istoriia [USSR] 1979 (6): 7-18.* Between the 23d and 24th Congresses of the Communist Party, efforts to improve the teaching of social sciences included observation of lectures, consideration of texts, an increase in the number of Party historians, and the preparation of courses in criticism of anticommunism and of bourgeois ideologies. The passing rate in social sciences increased at Moscow State University from 1972 to 1974. Based on Moscow Party Archive; 62 notes.
D. Balmuth

582. Bulyshkin, A. D. DEIATEL'NOST' LENINGRADSKOI PARTIINOI ORGANIZATSII PO RAZVITIIU NAUCHNO-TEKHNICHESKOGO TVORCHESTVA RABOCHIKH V 9-I PIATILETKE [The work of the Leningrad Party organization to develop the scientific and technical creativity of the workers during the 9th Five-Year Plan]. *Vestnik Leningradskogo U.: Seriia Istorii, Iazyka i Literatury [USSR] 1982 (2): 109-112.* During the 9th Five-Year Plan, 1971-75, the Leningrad Communist Party organization paid particular attention to increasing the role of workers in the rationalization movement. Communists took the initiative, and through their own individual examples they were able to encourage the broad masses of working people to contribute their own suggestions. The economic savings achieved by the implementation of rationalization projects in the course of the Five-Year Plan totalled 794 million rubles, 28.4% more than in the 8th Five-Year Plan. Secondary sources; 26 notes. G. Dombrovski

583. Butenko, R. K. ROL' MISTSEVOI PRESY U POSHYRENNI PEREDOVOHO DOSVIDU V SIL'S'KOHOSPODARS'KOMU VYROBNYTSTVI V ROKY VOS'MOI P'IATYRICHKY [The role of the local press in spreading advanced experience in agricultural production during the 8th Five-Year Plan]. *Ukrains'kyi Istorychnyi*

Zhurnal [USSR] 1975 (10): 73-81. Shows that during the eighth Five-Year-Plan, Soviet provincial press explained to agricultural workers the tasks set by the Communist Party.

584. Chernenko, K. U. XXV S'EZD KPSS O DAL'NEISHEM RAZVITII LENINSKOGO STILIA V PARTIINOI RABOTE [The 25th Congress of the CPSU and the further development of a Leninist style in Party work]. *Voprosy Istorii KPSS [USSR] 1976 (12): 22-39.* The 24th and especially the 25th Party Congresses have contributed to achieving, in the spirit of Leninism, the development of agriculture. Scientific problem-solving in many areas, including the use of the complex method whereby individual problems are viewed in their relation to major tasks before the party, has advanced. Organizational efficiency, including an encouragement of socialist competition and control mechanisms, intelligent selection, training, and assignment of cadres, and the principle of collective leadership were studied. Based on Lenin's *Collected Works* and published speeches and articles by Leonid Brezhnev; 26 notes.
L. E. Holmes

585. Chernov, B. V. ZABOTA PARTII O POVYSHENII ROLI SOVETOV NA SOVREMENNOM ETAPE [The party's concern for raising the role of soviets in the contemporary period]. *Voprosy Istorii KPSS [USSR] 1974(11): 45-57.* The Communist Party, especially its 23d and 24th Congresses, has provided the soviets (councils) with a more secure financial base, given them more carefully defined responsibilities, increased the Party's role in the selection and education of soviet leaders, and shown greater concern for the efficient functioning of the soviets. Based on government periodicals, notably *Izvestiia*, and published materials of the Communist Party of the Soviet Union; 66 notes. L. E. Holmes

586. Cocks, Paul. COMMENT. *Survey 1973 19(2): 151-159.* In breaking out of Stalinist simplicities, avoiding Khrushchev's harebrained schemes, and in response to growing institutionalization in the USSR, the Soviet leadership has shifted from revolution to organization, from adventurism to administration, and from struggle to stability in dealing with the Third World. The Soviets have realized that socialist states can decay and that they are backward in more than just missiles. This new awareness will probably only confuse them more. Part of a special issue on the future of Soviet foreign policy. R. B. Valliant

587. Demochkin, N. N. DEIATEL'NOST' KPSS PO SOVERSHENSTVOVANIIU DEMOKRATICHESKIKH OSNOV RABOTY SOVETOV V USLOVIIAKH ZRELOGO SOTSIALIZMA [Activities of the Communist Party in perfecting the democratic principles of the soviets in the period of mature socialism]. *Voprosy Istorii KPSS [USSR] 1979 (12): 8-17.* Discusses the developing role of the soviets and deputies, emphasizing that successful communist construction depends on the widening of their activities and initiatives. Under the guidance of the Communist Party and following the principles of the new constitution, the democratic bases of the soviets' work are being perfected, the soviets developed and strengthened, and legislation developed to improve their work. 60 notes.
J. S. S. Charles

588. Denysov, A. F. DEIAKI PYTANNIA PARTIINOHO KERIVNYTSTVA PROMYSLOVISTIU U ROKY VOS'MOI P'IATYRICHKY [Party leadership of industry in the years of the eighth Five-Year Plan]. *Ukrains'kyi Istorychnyi Zhurnal [USSR] 1978 (3): 64-73.* Important work was carried out by Communist Party organizations in setting up a broad system of economic education for workers, to give them the knowledge and stimulus to increase productivity during the eighth Five-Year Plan. More effective use was made of people's creativity and innovatory talents. Scientific-technical progress was stressed and ties between scientists and production workers strengthened. Primary sources; 36 notes.
V. Packer

589. Dimitrov, Dimitur. NAUCHNA KONFERENTSIIA PO SLUCHAI 50 GODINI OT SUZDAVANETO NA KIM [Scholarly conference on the 50th anniversary of the Communist Youth International]. *Izvestiia na Inst. po Istoriia na BKP [Bulgaria] 1970 24: 523-527.* Reports on the conference, held in Moscow in November 1969, attended by representatives from 19 countries, including veterans of the Communist Youth International.

590. Dumachev, A. P. PARTIINYE ORGANIZATSII I PROIZVODSTVENNYE OB'EDINENIIA [Party organizations and production cooperatives]. *Voprosy Istorii KPSS [USSR] 1974 (9): 3-15.* Party organizations have helped organize and lead production cooperatives, 1970-73, to improve and coordinate the use of technology, education of workers, and allocation of financial resources so that industrial production will serve state interests. 4 notes.
L. E. Holmes

591. Efimov, V. P. MEROPRIIATIIA PARTII PO EKONOMICHESKOMU STIMULIROVANIIU SEL'SKOKHOZIAISTVENNOGO PROIZVODSTVA [The Party's measures toward the economic stimulation of agricultural production]. *Voprosy Istorii KPSS [USSR] 1965 (9): 3-13.* Discusses decisions adopted at the March 1965 plenum of the Soviet Communist Party's Central Committee to increase agricultural production in the USSR in view of conditions evident from 1963 onwards.

592. Elantseva, O. P. VOSPITATEL'NAIA RABOTA PARTIINYKH ORGANIZATSII PO ZAKREPLENIIU KADROV STROITELEI BAMA [The educational work of Party organizations in strengthening the cadres of Baikal-Amur Railroad construction workers]. *Vestnik Leningradskogo U.: Serii Istorii, Iazyka i Literatury [USSR] 1982 (3): 109-111.* Deals with problems arising from movements among the trained construction personnel on the Baikal-Amur Railroad, one of the great projects for the development of the Soviet Far East. The percentage figures of Communists involved in individual jobs is given. The difficult conditions mean that workers, who in any case often stay for only part of the project, must be highly qualified technically and highly motivated politically. The Communist Party organization attends to political education, social conditions, and ensuring as good a life as is possible in such remote conditions. Entertainment such as films and libraries is plentiful and there are good facilities for children. Based on Party documents and the press; 24 notes. A. J. Evans

593. Epishev, A. A. PARTIINYE ORGANIZATSII SOVETSKIKH VOORUZHENNYKH SIL [Party organizations of the Soviet Armed Forces]. *Voprosy Istorii KPSS [USSR] 1973 (6): 3-16.* Party organizations in the Soviet Armed Services contribute to the military preparedness of the USSR by directing ideological, cultural, technical, and political training of the troops. They also recruit members for the Communist Party. Based on the author's experience as Chief of the Main Political Administration of the Soviet Armed Services and on Communist Party resolutions; 11 notes.
L. E. Holmes

594. Fartushniak, A. K. ZALUCHENNIA KOMSOMOL'TSIV I MOLODI DO UPRAVLINNIA DERZHAVOIU CHEREZ RADY DEPUTATIV TRUDIASHCHYKH (1966-1970) [The involvement of members of the Young Communist League (Komsomol) and youth in governing the state through Councils of Workers' Deputies, 1966-70]. *Ukrains'kyi Istorychnyi Zhurnal [USSR] 1975 (7): 43-51.* Discusses the Communist Party's involvement with youth, describes the electoral system, and gives data from elections in various areas, 1966-70.

595. Farukshin, M. Kh. PO POVODU BURZHUAZNYKH FAL'SIFIKATSII KLASSOVOI PRIRODI KPSS I ROLI IDEOLOGII V SOTSIALISTICHESKOM OBSHCHESTVE [On bourgeois falsifications of the CPSU and the role of ideology in a socialist society]. *Voprosy Istorii KPSS [USSR] 1975 (2): 73-83.* Bourgeois Sovietologists have recently propagated several myths about the functions of the Party and its ideology in the USSR. They have mistakenly maintained four views: 1) The Communist Party lacks a social base and has thereby become a privileged elite; 2) the Party as a vanguard is a retreat from Marxism; 3) modernization and detente preclude the need for ideology; and 4) the Party has become a mere administrative organ. Based on a critique of

articles and books on the USSR by such Western authors as Alfred Meyer, Bertram Wolfe, Samuel Huntington, and especially Zbigniew Brzezinski; 35 notes. L. E. Holmes

596. Fedan, V. I. SHLIAKHOM INTENSYFIKATSII SIL'S'KOHO HOSPODARSTVA: 10-RICHCHIA BEREZNEVOHO (1965) PLENUMU TSK KPRS [Intensifying agriculture: the 10th anniversary of the March 1965 Plenum of the Central Committee of the Soviet Communist Party]. *Ukrains'kyi Istorychnyi Zhurnal [USSR] 1975 (4): 44-51.* The 1965 plenum marked a new, successful stage in the Party's agricultural policy, as tables of productivity and other economic data, 1965-75, show.

597. Feshbach, Murray. SOVIET HEALTH PROBLEMS. *Society 1984 21(3): 79-81.* Comments on the Accountability Report of the general secretary of the Party, Leonid Brezhnev, delivered at the 26th Congress of the Communist Party of the Soviet Union held in February and March of 1981, delineating the problems of insufficient medical supplies, outdated medical equipment, inadequate facilities, a lack of ethics when dealing with patients, and the problem of alcoholism.

598. Fortescue, Stephen. RESEARCH INSTITUTE PARTY ORGANIZATIONS AND THE RIGHT OF CONTROL. *Soviet Studies [Great Britain] 1983 35(2): 175-195.* In 1971, the 24th Soviet Party Congress granted increased powers to the primary party organizations (PPO's) of all research institutions. Among other things, those powers included the right to receive reports from management, the right to establish commissions, and the right to make recommendations to management. Since the Party Congress decision, the PPO's have attempted to control productivity and social environment within the research institutions, but management and researchers have not acquiesced readily. 83 notes.
M. R. Yerburgh

599. Galiguzov, I. F. LENINSKIE PRINTSIPY UPRAVLENIIA EKONOMIKOI V PRAKTICHESKOI DEIATEL'NOSTI KPSS [Leninist principles of directing the economy in the practical activity of the CPSU]. *Vestnik Moskovskogo U., Seriia 8: Istoriia [USSR] 1979 (3): 3-11.* In 1965 the Communist Party dealt with economic questions involving the five-year plans. Specialists and economic leaders have technical training. Nationally 73% of the workers have had at least some secondary education. Some have had college education. About 650,000 groups supervise production. 36 notes.
D. Balmuth

600. Gelman, Harry. *The Brezhnev Politburo and the Decline of Detente.* Ithaca, N.Y.: Cornell U. Pr., 1984. 268 pp.

601. Gorbachev, M. S. PARTIINOE RUKOVODSTVO VOSPITANIEM MOLODEZHI [Party guidance in the education of youth]. *Voprosy Istorii KPSS [USSR] 1971 (3): 40-54.* Outlines the work of the Stavropol Party district committee in this field, 1966-70.

602. Gorokhov, A. BOR'BA SOVETSKOGO SOIUZA ZA LIKVIDATSIIU VOENNYKH OCHAGOV ZA MEZHDUNARODNUIU BEZOPASNOST' [The struggle of the Soviet Union for the liquidation of military hotbeds and for international security]. *Mezhdunarodnaia Zhizn' [USSR] 1971 18(6): 3-13.* Gives an analysis of the foreign policy decisions taken at the 24th Communist Party Congress, 1971.

603. Gorshkov, L. A. VO GLAVE DVIZHENIIA ZA BEREZHLIVOST': IZ OPYTA RABOTY OBLASTNOI PARTIINOI ORGANIZATSII PO EKONOMII TOPLIVNO-ENERGETICHESKIKH RESURSOV [At the head of the movement for thrift: from the experience of one oblast Party committee in economizing fuel and energy resources]. *Voprosy Istorii KPSS [USSR] 1984 (2): 3-16.* Presents an account of methods used by the Kemerovo Oblast Communist Party organization in the USSR to preserve fuel and energy resources by increased productivity. The central Party organizations insisted in 1983 that the five-year plan could only be fulfilled if all elements in the economy increased efficiency by lowering costs. Means used in Kemerovo include discipline of workers in the coal and electricity industries, centralization of plant to increase efficiency, and promoting socialist competition between workers and between enterprises. Based on published materials; 24 notes. D. N. Collins

604. Gotun, M. Iu. PARTIINE KERIVNYTSTVO DOBOROM, ROZSTANOVKOIU I NAVCHANNIAM KOMSOMOL'S'KYKH KADRIV (1966-1971 RR) [Party leadership in the selection, distribution, and education of Komsomol cadres, 1966-71]. *Ukrains'kyi Istorychnyi Zhurnal [USSR] 1978 (2): 82-90.* Examines Communist Party work, 1966-71, which was designed to increase the number of Party members within the Young Communist League, in accordance with the directives of the 23d Congress of the Communist Party of the Soviet Union. Quotes extensive data from various regions on increases in Party members amongst the Young Communist League, and especially its leadership. As Party membership increased, so its leadership became more stable. Several regions set up special evening classes for league workers at local universities. Throughout, there were substantial improvements in the education and organization of Young Communist groups. 2 tables, 36 notes.
V. A. Packer/S

605. Gradov, K. L. VAZHNEISHIE ISTORIKO-PARTIINYE PROBLEMY PERIODA RAZVITOGO SOTSIALIZMA [The most important historical and Party-centered problems in the period of developed socialism]. *Voprosy Istorii KPSS [USSR] 1981 (2): 146-151.* Discusses the proceedings and papers presented at a conference of the all-Union Council for the Coordination of Research into the History of the Communist Party of the Soviet Union (CPSU) held at the Institute of Marxism-Leninism in Moscow, November 1980. Two main papers examined the "theoretical and methodological treatment of developed socialism in historical and Party literature" and current problems in Party structuring. Other reports dealt with CPSU agricultural policy under conditions of developed socialism and the CPSU and technological change. 6 notes.
A. Brown

606. Gramov, M. V. DEIATEL'NOST' KPSS PO POVYSHENIIU ROLI TRUDOVYKH KOLLEKTIV V KOMMUNISTICHESKOM VOSPITANII TRUDIASHCHIKHSIA [The activity of the CPSU on increasing the role of labor collectives in the Communist training of laborers]. *Voprosy Istorii KPSS [USSR] 1975 (2): 3-19.* The Communist Party of the USSR encourages greater activity of labor collectives within industry. These collectives serve as agents of cultural, technical, and ideological education of the workers, as vehicles for greater efficiency in production and management, and as levers of Party control over the industrial economy. Based on published Party documents; 31 notes. L. E. Holmes

607. Gruzdeva, V. P. NIAKOI PROBLEMI V SUVETSKATA ISTORIOGRAFIIA NA KOMUNISTICHESKIIA INTERNATSIONAL [Problems in Soviet historiography of the Communist International]. *Izvestiia na Inst. po Istoriia na BKP [Bulgaria] 1980 42: 135-170.* Examines the sources of information available to historiographers in particular about Lenin's works and works about Lenin's contribution to the construction of the Comintern, as well as slanderous writings in bourgeois, reformist, and Maoist publications. Russian, French, and German summaries.

608. Gurkin, A. B. DEIATEL'NOST' LENINGRADSKOI PARTIINOI ORGANIZATSII PO OKAZANIIU TEKHNICHESKOI POMOSHCHI GORODA SELU (1966-1970 GG.) [The Leningrad Party organization's technical assistance to villages, 1966-70]. *Vestnik Leningradskogo U.: Seriia Istorii, Iazyka i Literatury [USSR] 1979 (1): 102-105.* Examines the Party's role in the rendering of technical assistance, both planned and supplemental, from the city to the agricultural enterprises of Leningrad oblast during the eighth Five-Year Plan. Directed by joint plans between industrial enterprises and agricultural institutions, this technical assistance included efforts at mechanization, construction, machine and spare part production, student construction brigades and direct worker assistance in agricultural tasks. Based on Leningrad party archives; 23 notes. R. E. Glatfelter

609. Gusev, K. V. XXIV S"EZD KPSS I OTECHESTVENNAIA ISTORIOGRAFIIA [The 24th Congress of the Communist Party of the Soviet Union and Soviet historiography]. *Istoriia SSSR [USSR] 1971 (3): 3-12.* The Communist Party congresses of the USSR are historical landmarks which reflect the main stages of revolutionary reorganization of the Soviet people and help interpret the past. The 24th Party Congress determined that it was the social sciences' responsibility to strengthen the ties between theory and practice in the construction of Communism. Describes the themes of history books published between the 23d and 24th Party Congresses. 34 notes. L. Kalinowski

610. Gvishani, D. MEZHDUNARODNYE NAUCHNO-TEKHNICHESKIE SVIAZI SSSR I PERSPEKTIVY IKH RAZVITIIA [Soviet international technological and scientific links and the prospects of their development]. *Mezhdunarodnaia Zhizn' [USSR] 1971 18(6): 30-42.* Surveys economic and technological exchanges between the USSR and Comecon countries, the Third World, and the West in the contemporary period in the light of decisions taken at the 24th Party Congress, 1971.

611. Hammer, Darrell P. BREZHNEV AND THE COMMUNIST PARTY. *Soviet Union 1975 2(1): 1-21.* It is characteristic of Leonid Brezhnev's wardship of the Party that he has not perceived himself as a reformer or innovator. Rather he seems to have played the role of power broker among the great bureaucracies which manage the USSR, and the essence of his internal policy has been to maintain a balance of power by calling on old established cadres—especially those with "ideological" functions—rather than on younger men. G. E. Snow

612. Hammond, Thomas T. MOSCOW AND COMMUNIST TAKEOVERS. *Problems of Communism 1976 25(1): 48-67.* Analyzes the attitude of the USSR toward Communist takeovers in the world today, attempting to cast light on the traditional duality of Soviet foreign policy: establishing peaceful relations with non-Communist states while promoting Communist revolutions in these same states. In deciding whether or not to promote (or support) a Communist takeover, Politburo members will presumably make a rough cost-benefit analysis relative to Soviet foreign policy goals. Primary and secondary sources; 61 notes. J. M. Lauber

613. Harasymiw, Bohdan. LES DÉTERMINANTES SOCIALES DU RECRUTEMENT ET DE L'APPARTENANCE AU PARTI COMMUNISTE DE L'UNION SOVIÉTIQUE [Social determinants of recruitment into and membership in the Communist Party of the Soviet Union]. *Rev. d'Études Comparatives Est-Ouest [France] 1978 9(2): 43-87.* Communist Party recruiters during the 1960's-70's gave preference to highly skilled manual workers and to those belonging to the nominal nationality of union republics which had low levels of economic development and which are located far from Moscow.

614. Harding, Ted. KIEV WORKERS PROTEST TO THE CENTRAL COMMITTEE. *Critique [Great Britain] 1973 1(2): 71-77.* Presents an introduction to, and the first English translation of, a letter of 10 June 1969 from the workers of the Kiev hydroelectric power station to the Central Committee of the Soviet Communist Party, protesting management's illegal actions.

615. Heerdegen, Helga. DIE SOWJETISCHE POLITIK ZUR ÜBERWINDUNG DER WESENTLICHEN UNTERSCHIEDE ZWISCHEN STADT UND LAND IN DEN SIEBZIGER JAHREN [Soviet policies for overcoming the essential differences between town and country in the 1970's]. *Zeits. für Geschichtswissenschaft [East Germany] 1982 30(9): 771-776.* The Soviet Communist Party had two main tasks in the 1970's: to secure a stable supply of foodstuffs and agricultural produce; to close the gap in cultural and material living conditions between workers in the town and country. Agricultural productivity, like industrial output, had increased between 1965 and 1975. The Communist Party's policies were directed to overcoming the essential differences between the working class and the peasants by improving living and working conditions in the country, providing higher incomes and health and social security for peasants, improving housing, giving agricultural training and a career structure to peasants. Secondary sources; 30 notes. G. L. Neville

616. Holubkov, M. Ie. ZROSTANNIA ROLI HROMADS'KYKH ORHANIZATSII U ZHYTTI TRUDOVOHO KOLEKTYVU [The increased role of public organizations in the life of the working collective]. *Ukrains'kyi Istorychnyi Zhurnal [USSR] 1975 (3): 80-88.* Discusses the composition and activities of labor unions and organizations, the Young Communist League and councils of workers' deputies during transition from socialism to communism, 1967-72.

617. Il'ichev, L. F. and Rakhmaninov, Iu. N. SSSR V BOR'BE ZA REALIZATSIIU PROGRAMMY MIRA NA 80-E GODY [The USSR in the struggle for the implementation of the Peace Program for the 1980's]. *Novaia i Noveishaia Istoriia [USSR] 1982 (6): 3-25.* The entire 65-year history of the Soviet state—from Lenin's Decree on Peace to the Peace Program advanced by the 24th CPSU Congress and further developed by the 25th and 26th Congresses—serves as a demonstration of the peaceful nature of the Soviet foreign policy aimed at preserving and strengthening peace, deepening international cooperation, and curbing the arms race. J/S

618. Ipatova, A. S. VSESOIUZNAIA KONFERENTSIIA KITAEVEDOV [The All-Union Conference of Sinologists]. *Narody Azii i Afriki [USSR] 1972 (4): 210-212.* Describes the proceedings of a conference of Soviet Sinologists held in Moscow, 29 November-1 December 1971, and organized by the Soviet Academy of Sciences, Far East Institute. The participants, who adopted a strictly Marxist-Leninist view of contemporary China under Maoist chauvinism, described topics of current study by Soviet Sinologists.

619. Iskrov, M. V. K OBSUZHDENIIU TEMATIKI DOKTORSKIKH DISSERTATSII [The themes of doctoral dissertations]. *Voprosy Istorii KPSS [USSR] 1965 (12): 143-147.* The Secretary of the USSR All-Union Coordinating Council on the Scientific Study of Communist Party History draws some conclusions from discussions carried on in the pages of this journal, about the correct themes for doctoral dissertations about the Soviet Communist Party.

620. Izmailov, A. F. PARTIINOE RUKOVODSTVO GAZETAMI PROIZVODSTVENNYKH OB'EDINENII LENINGRADA (1967-1977) [The Party direction of the newspapers of the industrial combines of Leningrad, 1967-77]. *Vestnik Leningradskogo U.: Seriia Istorii, Iazyka i Literatury [USSR] 1977 (4): 144-147.* Both information and propaganda necessary to achieve industrial goals have been provided by the Party direction of the newspapers of Leningrad's large industrial amalgamations. The problem of precise information to specific layers of authority has been solved. 12 notes. G. F. Jewsbury

621. Kapitonov, Ivan. DEVELOPMENT OF INNER-PARTY DEMOCRACY IN THE CPSU. *World Marxist R. [Canada] 1973 16(11): 17-26.*

622. Kas'ianenko, V. I. NEKOTORYE VOPROSY VOZRASTANIIA RUKOVODIASHCHEI ROLI KPSS V RAZVITOM SOTSIALISTICHESKOM OBSHCHESTVE: OBZOR LITERATURY VYSHEDSHEI MEZHDU XXIV I XXV S"EZDAMI KPSS [A few questions on the growth of the CPSU's leading role in developed socialist society: a review of the literature published between the 24th and 25th congresses of the CPSU]. *Voprosy Istorii [USSR] 1976 (10): 121-129.* Examines material published on the Communist Party's role during the transition from socialism to communism, 1972-77.

623. Kim, G. F. and Kaufman, A. S. XXV S'EZD KPSS I PROBLEMY NATSIONAL'NO-OSVOBODITEL'NYKH REVOLIUTSII [The 25th party congress of the CPSU and the problems of the national liberation revolutions]. *Narody Azii i Afriki [USSR] 1976 (3): 3-16.* Analyzes the decrees, conclusions, and problems formulated by the 25th Party Congress of the Communist Party of the Soviet Union on national liberation movements and on developments in the liberated states. The authors examine the great political and

economic changes that took place in the liberated states during the period between the 24th and 25th Party congresses, and cite the foreign policy objectives of the 25th Party Congress that have yet to be achieved. The authors criticize Peking's outlook and discuss other anti-Marxist influences. Based on primary sources; 17 notes. L. Kalinowski

624. Kim, M. P. and Seniavski, S. L. RABOCHII KLASS SSSR V GODY DEVIATOI I DESIATOI PIATILETOK [Soviet working class during the ninth and tenth Five-Year Plans]. *Voprosy Istorii [USSR] 1980 (11): 3-18.* The working class acquired maturity with the growth of developed socialism. Its numbers and share in the population of the USSR has grown and its cultural and technical level has been enhanced. It exerts a stronger influence on the development of production, higher productivity, and the formation of the new, communist personality. The working class is replenished chiefly by school leavers. This tendency, already apparent in the 1950's and 1960's, has become a cardinal social process promoted by the Communist Party's social policy. J/S

625. Kireev, E. P. PROBLEMA VOZRASTANIIA RUKOVODIASHCHEI ROLI KPSS V ISTORIKO-PARTIINOI LITERATURE POSLEDNEGO DESIATILETIIA [The problem of the growth of the leadership role of the CPSU in the Party historical literature in the past ten years]. *Vestnik Leningradskogo U.: Seriia Istorii, Iazyka i Literatury [USSR] 1977 (8): 5-14.* A survey of important works dealing with the growth in the leadership role of the CPSU. 24 notes. G. F. Jewsbury

626. Kirichenko, N. K. PARTIINOE RUKOVODSTVO USKORENIEM NAUCHNO-TEKHNICHESKOGO PROGRESSA V SEL'SKOM KHOZIAISTVE [Party leadership of the acceleration of scientific-technical progress in Agriculture]. *Voprosy Istorii KPSS [USSR] 1974 (3): 34-46.* In accordance with the program adopted by its 24th Congress, the Communist Party stimulated increased agricultural and livestock production by assisting essential industry, educational institutions, research institutes, and experimental stations. Table. L. E. Holmes

627. Kirichenko, V. STRATEGIIA POSTUPATEL'NOGO ROSTA EKONOMIKI [The strategy of progressive growth of economy]. *Mirovaia Ekonomika i Mezhdunarodnye Otnosheniia [USSR] 1981 (3): 25-37.* Stresses the attention paid by the delegates to the 26th CPSU Congress to the problems of economic policy and long-term planning.

628. Kitaeva, T. B. DEIATEL'NOST' PARTIINYKH ORGANIZATSII PREDPRIIATII PISHCHEVOI PROMYSHLENNOSTI G. MOSKVY V 1966-1975 GG. [The activity of Party organizations of enterprises of the food industry of Moscow, 1966-75]. *Sovetskie Arkhivy [USSR] 1983 (3): 44-48.* Communist Party documents demonstrate that under the leadership of Party organizations many enterprises of the food industry of Moscow fulfilled the targets of the 8th and 9th five-year plans ahead of schedule. Party organizations were responsible for significant increases in production, improvement in quality and technical progress. In this respect ideological and educational work was very important and successful. 41 ref. D. H. Watson

629. Kladina, M. A. PARTIINE KERIVNYTSTVO IAK VYRISHAL'NA UMOVA ORHANIZATSIINOHO ZMITSNENNIA TOVARYSTVA "ZNANNIA" URSR (1966-1970) [The leadership of the party as the decisive factor in strengthening the organization of the Znanie society in the USSR, 1966-70]. *Ukrains'kyi Istorychnyi Zhurnal [USSR] 1982 (7): 78-84.* The organization Znanie was formed to encourage the study of Marxism-Leninism in the USSR. It has always sought a close relationship with the Communist Party, as this study of the period 1966-70 shows. Party organizations have taken advantage of the intellectual output from Znanie and have ensured a continual flow of members of high caliber into the organization. 39 notes. N. M. Diuk

630. Koch, Ute. ZU DEN BEZIEHUNGEN UND ZUR ZUSAMMENARBEIT ZWISCHEN FDJ UND LENINSCHEM KOMSOMOL IM 50. JAHR DER GROSSEN SOZIALISTISCHEN OKTOBERREVOLUTION [The relations and cooperation between the Free German Youth Organization (FDJ) and the Young Communist League in 1967, the 50th anniversary of the Russian October Revolution]. *Wissenschaftliche Zeitschrift der Wilhelm-Pieck-Universität Rostock. Gesellschafts- und Sprachwissenschaftliche Reihe [East Germany] 1977 26(1): 71-75.* Describes the furthering of friendship and cooperation between the Free German Youth Organization and the Young Communist League, reflected in their political activities in the mid-1960's in preparing for and organizing the 50th anniversary of the October Revolution.

631. Kocherova, L. S. and Romanov, Iu. G. O RAZVITII SOTSIAL'NOI AKTIVNOSTI MOLODYKH RABOCHIKH V GODY 9-I I 10-I PIATILETKI [On the development of social activities of young workers during the 9th and 10th Five-Year Plans]. *Vestnik Leningradskogo U.: Seriia Istorii, Iazyka i Literatury [USSR] 1983 (1): 5-10.* Communist Party conferences, 1968-79, expressed growing concern for the youth of the labor force of the USSR, urging the local Party and Young Communist League (Komsomol) organizations as well as the trade unions to work more closely with the young and to involve them in the life of their communities. As statistic analysis shows, many factory collectives have taken the Party directive to heart and have organized courses giving their prospective employees ideological training. Based on primary sources; 21 notes. English summary. M. Hernas

632. Kolomiitsev, V. F. V AVANGARDE REVOLIUTSIONNOGO PROTSESSA [In the vanguard of the revolutionary process]. *Prepodavanie Istorii v Shkole [USSR] 1974 (3): 2-11.* Describes trends in the international Communist movement and the official policies adopted at the 24th Congress of the Communist Party of the Soviet Union, 1971.

633. Kolotukha, I. I. DIIAL'NIST' RAD DEPUTATIV TRUDIASHCHYKH URSR U ROKI DEV'IATOI P'IATYRICHKY [The activities of the Soviets of Working Peoples' Deputies during the Ninth Five-Year Plan period]. *Ukrains'kyi Istorychnyi Zhurnal [USSR] 1976 (2): 14-26.* Points out positive qualitative changes which took place 1971-75 in the work of local Councils of Workers' Deputies in the Ukraine; relates the activities of the organs of the people's authority in the struggle to fulfill the Ninth Five-Year Plan; and shows the CPSU's concern for increasing the role and authority of local councils in Communist construction, the advancement of social democracy, and increasing the efficiency of state guidance and management.

634. Kolpakova, O. V. ZROSTANNIA ROLI BIBLIOTEK U KOMUNISTYCHNOMU VYKHOVANNI TRUDIASHCHYKH (1971-1975 RR.) [Increased role of libraries in the Communist education of the working class, 1971-75]. *Ukrains'kyi Istorychnyi Zhurnal [USSR] 1981 (12): 108-114.* Public libraries in the USSR have played an important role in the Communist upbringing and political education of the working people. Their main task is to transmit the policy of the Communist Party and the Soviet state and to help accelerate the scientific and technological advance of Soviet society. The work of public libraries in the Ukraine during the 9th Five Year Plan is described. 31 notes. I. Krushelnyckyj

635. Konashevych, A. P. SOTSIALISTYCHNA DERZHAVA: POLITYCHNA OSNOVA NOVOI ISTORYCHNOI SPIL'NOSTI LIUDEI [The socialist state: the political basis of the new historic community of people]. *Ukrains'kyi Istorychnyi Zhurnal [USSR] 1974 6: 13-21.* Examines the work of the Party in strengthening the political organization of the Soviet people, according to the directives of the 24th Communist Party Congress in 1970.

636. Kondratiuk, V. O. OKREMI PYTANNIA KOMUNISTYCHNOHO VYKHOVANNIA STUDENTS'KOI MOLODI: 1966-1971 [The communist education of student youth, 1966-71]. *Ukrains'kyi Istorychnyi Zhurnal [USSR] 1976 (11): 108-115.* Outlines the post-23rd Party congress program for improving ideological work among youth.

637. König, Gerd. GLEICHARTIGE AUFGABEN [Homogeneous tasks]. *Einheit [East Germany] 1971 26(10): 1092-1103.* Examines the tasks and meanings of Party congresses in several socialist countries in 1971. Notes the economic goals of future socialist planning. The Soviet five-year plan presumes to raise the workers' real income 30 percent between 1971 and 1975. Constructive cooperation between socialist states creates strong bases for the common tasks of socialist society. 4 notes. G. E. Pergl

638. Konnik, I. I. LENINSKIE IDEI O KHOZIAISTVENNOM MEKHANIZME I IKH RAZVITIE NA SOVREMENNOM ETAPE [Leninist ideas on the economic mechanism and their development in the contemporary stage]. *Voprosy Istorii KPSS [USSR] 1981 (4): 51-61.* Summarizes V. I. Lenin's (1870-1924) concern for centralized economic planning and recent efforts by the Communist Party of the Soviet Union, especially its 26th Congress (1981), to implement Leninist economic principles. Lenin advocated and the Party continues to practice economic planning as determined mainly by the Communist Party, efficiency and profitability, cooperation among chief elements of the economy, and the use of wages to reward superior achievement. Based on Lenin's *Collected Works;* 59 notes. L. E. Holmes

639. Korolev, S. A. ANTIREVOLIUTSIONNAIA SUSHCHNOST' TROTSKISTSKOI "KONTSEPTSII" MIROVOGO REVOLIUTSIONNOGO PROTSESSA [The antirevolutionary essence of the Trotskyist concept of a global revolutionary process]. *Voprosy Istorii KPSS [USSR] 1981 (4): 87-97.* Followers of Leon Trotsky (1879-1940) in the 4th International rely on Trotsky's notion of the impossibility of socialism in one country as a platform for their anti-Sovietism. They falsely insist on the bureaucratization of Soviet society, call for a political revolution in socialist countries, and reject cooperation with national-democratic forces in developing nations. They oppose detente and hope for an attack on the USSR by imperialist states. Maoists, extremists, and all kinds of anti-Communist elements benefit from the propaganda and support of Trotskyists. Based on recent secondary works; 47 notes.
L. E. Holmes

640. Kosolapov, V. V. and Shishkin, V. F. O NEKOTORYKH VOPROSAKH METODOLOGII ISTORII KPSS [A few questions of the methodology of the history of the CPSU]. *Voprosy Istorii KPSS [USSR] 1976 (10): 87-95.* Attempts to construct a hierarchical structure of categories of understanding or knowledge for the history of the Communist Party of the Soviet Union.

641. Kovalenko, A. V. PARTIINAYA ORGANIZATSIIA I POD'EM SEL'SKOGO KHOZIAISTVA [Party organization and the development of agriculture]. *Voprosy Istorii KPSS [USSR] 1971 (3): 29-39.* Outlines the work of the Orenburg regional committee in encouraging the development of agriculture, 1968-70.

642. Krivoruchenko, V. K. PARTIINOE RUKOVODSTVO ORGANIZATSIONNYM UKREPLENIEM KOMSOMOLA (1961-1978 GG.) [Party management of the organizational strengthening of the Young Communist League (Komsomol), 1961-78]. *Voprosy Istorii KPSS [USSR] (11): 104-114.* Examines the role of the Communist Party in developing the principle of democratic centralism in the Young Communist League (Komsomol). The Party strengthened the Komsomol by increasing its activity and independence and broadening the activity of the main Komsomol organizations. The leading role of the Leninist Young Communist League has been strengthened, and increased importance placed on administrative organization and the training of activists. Based on central and regional Communist Party and Komsomol archival material; 54 notes. J. S. S. Charles

643. Kukin, D. M. and Spirin, L. M. ISTORIKO-PARTIINAYA NAUKA K XXIV S'EZDU KPSS [The science of Party history prepares for the 24th congress of the Communist Party of the USSR]. *Voprosy Istorii KPSS [USSR] 1971 (3): 3-16.* Outlines the main trends of historical research on the Communist Party of the USSR, 1966-70.

644. Kul'chytskyi, S. V. PIDVYSHCHENIIA MATERIAL'NOHO DOBROBUTU RADIANS'KOHO NARODU V DEV'IATII P'IATYRICHTSI [Improvement of the material well-being of the Soviet people during the ninth Five-Year Plan period]. *Ukrains'kyi Istorychnyi Zhurnal [USSR] 1976 (2): 36-48.* Summarizes Communist Party activities designed to improve the standard of living of the Soviet people, 1971-75.

645. Kulish, N. POVYSHAT' EFFEKTIVNOST' UPRAVLENIIA KRUPNYMI SEL'SKOKHOZIAISTVENNYMI PREDPRIIATIIAMI [To raise the effectiveness of the control of large agricultural enterprises]. *Ekonomika Sovetskoi Ukrainy [USSR; 1972 14(3): 27-34.* Analyzes research undertaken to improve the planning and control of agricultural production in the Pugachev region, 1970-71, and notes the contribution made by the regional branch of the Communist Party.

646. Kul'pins'kyi, V. L. and Motorniuk, M. M. DIIAL'NIST' PARTIINYKH ORHANIZATSII RESPUBLIKY PO TRUDOVOMU VYKHOVANNIU UCHNIV (1966-1975 GG) [The work of Party organizations of the republic in the labor training of pupils, 1966-75]. *Ukrains'kyi Istorychnyi Zhurnal [USSR] 1978 (1): 43-50.* Recapitulates Marxist-Leninist teachings on the importance of the vocational training of youth and examines the resolution on improving secondary education adopted by the Communist Party and government in 1966. Demonstrates how this was put into practice, 1966-75, and shows how the profession distribution became more even and balanced as a result of giving secondary schools the important function of vocational guidance. 31 notes.
V. A. Packer

647. Kulski, W. W. THE TWENTY-SIXTH CONGRESS OF THE COMMUNIST PARTY OF THE SOVIET UNION. *Polish Rev. 1983 28(1): 47-63.* A summary of the proceedings of the 26th Congress with particular emphasis on speeches made by foreign guests. The content of these speeches, grouped by geographical area, graphically demonstrates the spread of Soviet external influence. The principal event of the congress was Leonid Brezhnev's speech. Brezhnev's leading position was stressed by all the speakers. Regarding Poland, Brezhnev, in assuring Polish Communists of support against "antisocialist" anarchy, alluded to possible Soviet intervention. Stanisław Kania, first secretary of the Polish Communist Party, suggested, in effect, that Soviet intervention was unnecessary. Giancarlo Pajetta, a leader of the Italian Communist Party, objected to Soviet intervention in Afghanistan and asked that Polish independence be respected. Based on speeches reported in *Pravda* 23 February-4 March, 1981. W. F. Young

648. Kutuzov, O. P. NA DOPOMOHU VYKLADACHU ISTORII: ZASTOSUVANNIA NAOCHNOSTI PRY PROBLEMNOMU VYVCHENNI ISTORII KPRS [Aids to the lecturer in history: the application of visual aids in the teaching of the history of the Communist Party of the Soviet Union (CPSU)]. *Ukraïns'kyi Istorychnyi Zhurnal [USSR] 1980 (8): 125-134.* Discusses the role of education in Soviet high schools and its tasks and methods in producing young specialists who are the future builders of Communism.

649. Kuz'minets', O. V. DIIAL'NIST' PARTIINYKH ORHANIZATSII U SPRAVI IDEINO-POLITYCHNOHO VYKHOVANNIA UCHYTEL'S'KYKH KADRIV V UMOVAKH ROZVYNUTOHO SOTSIALIZMU [The work of Party organizations in the matter of the ideological and political education of teaching cadres under conditions of developed socialism]. *Ukrains'kyi Istorychnyi Zhurnal [USSR] 1978 (11): 67-73.* V. I. Lenin stressed the importance of training teaching specialists to effect social change in the USSR. Following the decisions of the 23d and 25th Communist Party Congresses, the Party worked to raise the ideological and theoretical level of teachers and teaching methods, organizing many seminars and conferences. Primary sources; 36 notes. V. Packer

650. Kvasov, Iu. P. MELIORATSIIA ZEMEL'-VAZHNOE ZVENO AGRARNOI POLITIKI KPSS [Land improvement: an important factor in the agricultural policy of the Communist Party

of the USSR]. *Vestnik Leningradskogo U.: Seriia Istorii, Iazyka, i Literatury [USSR] 1978 2(1): 135-139.* A discussion of the efforts made to improve the land of the Soviet Union since 1966 in order to increase agricultural output. 22 notes. G. F. Jewsbury

651. Lahav, Yehuda. HA-M'DINIYUT HA-SOVIETIT B'MIZRAH HA-TIKHON 1964-1967 B-ASPAKLARIA SHEL YAHAS BRIT HA-MOATSOT L'SHNAI HA-PLAGIM HA-KOMUNISITIM B-YISRAEL [Soviet policy in the Middle East and the Soviet attitude toward the two communist factions in Israel]. *Shvut [Israel] 1981 8: 42-67.* A split in the philosophy of the Israeli Communist Party in 1964 created two splinter groups, a Jewish faction (Maki) and a pro-Arab faction (Rakah). Between 1964 and 1966 the USSR found it politically expedient to avoid making a choice between the two, but the Ba'ath revolution in Syria in 1966 and the prospects of greater Soviet influence in the Middle East threw the balance toward an extreme anti-Israel stance, and Rakah received Soviet support. All ties with Maki were broken at the outbreak of the 1967 war. Based primarily on Israeli and Soviet Communist Party publications; 192 notes. T. Koppel

652. Laptev, V. B. MELKOBURZHUAZNYE NATSIONALISTICHESKIE TENDENTSII V KPK I FORMIROVANIE ANTISOVETSKOGO KURSA PEKINA [Petit bourgeois nationalist tendencies in the Chinese Communist Party and the emergence of China's anti-Soviet course]. *Voprosy Istorii [USSR] 1981 (7): 59-73.* The objective conditions under which the Communist Party of China was formed and acted predetermined the prevalence of petit bourgeois tendencies and the advancement to its leadership of political figures like Mao Zedong who strove to establish his individual rule over the Party, consolidate its anti-Soviet, anti-Communist positions, and turn it into an instrument for achievement of his great-power, hegemonistic aims. After a bitter struggle the Maoists managed to remove from the Party, and political life in general, Communists who, guided by Marxism-Leninism, supported friendly relations with the USSR and cooperation with the world Communist movement. The Maoists imposed upon the Party and the state their own anti-popular course fraught with danger for the cause of peace. Their break with Marxism-Leninism and their anti-Sovietism stimulated a turn to the right in the 1970's. In foreign policy and the drive for modernization the Beijing leaders are cooperating with the United States and other capitalist countries. J

653. Leonhard, Wolfgang. DAS ENDE EINER ÄRA [The end of an era]. *Osteuropa [West Germany] 1983 33(3-4): 183-193.* Describes the reaction to Leonid Brezhnev's death within the Communist Party, among Soviet citizens, and among politicians abroad, and analyzes the background of the internal Party politics concerning his succession.

654. Lewytzkyj, Borys. DER XXIV. PARTEITAG DER KOMMUNISTISCHEN PARTEI DER SOWJETUNION [The 24th congress of the Communist Party of the USSR]. *Österreichische Osthefte [Austria] 1971 13(2): 105-112.* While the 24th congress of the USSR's Communist Party opened a new phase in Soviet relations with the United States and especially with West Germany, the Soviet government continued to demand a leading role among socialist states. Dissidents were warned not to continue their anti-Soviet activities. The stability and continuity of the leading Party group was a visible expression of the basically conservative tendency of the 24th party congress. Based on newspapers; 6 notes. R. Wagnleitner

655. Liu, William H. THE MAKING OF A COMMUNIST PARTY SECRETARY-GENERAL. *Issues and Studies [Taiwan] 1977 13(4): 80-85.* Reviews John Dornberg's *Brezhnev, the Masks of Power* (London: Andre Deutsch, 1974), which chronicles the rise to power of Leonid Brezhnev in the USSR, 1959-76.

656. Liuliukin, V. V. IZ OPYTA RUKOVODSTVA PSKOVSKOI OBLASTNOI PARTIINOI ORGANIZATSII SHKOLAMI KOMMUNISTICHESKOGO TRUDA [The experience of the Pskov region Party organization in the guidance of schools of Communist labor]. *Vestnik Leningradskogo U.: Seriia Istorii, Iazyka i Literatury [USSR] 1980 (1): 108-110.* Discusses the history of Communist Party workers' schools in the Pskov region from their inception in 1966 up to the present. Attendance in these schools has a positive influence on the productivity and sociopolitical activities of the workers, increases their ideological and cultural awareness and strengthens work discipline, thus promoting a greater understanding of the Party's contemporary economic policies. Based on the Pskov region Party Archives; 12 notes. A. Brown

657. Loginova, A. A. ROL' SOTSIALISTICHESKOGO SOREVNOVANIIA V RAZVITII TRUDOVOI AKTIVNOSTI MODOLEZHI [The role of socialist competition in the development of the Communist labor activities of youth]. *Vestnik Leningradskogo Universiteta [USSR] 1974 (14): 13-20.* Examines the content and forms of socialist competition and outlines the successful approaches and results in the improvement of the proper Communist attitude toward work among young people. The Party has always emphasized the importance of a proper Communist relationship to work by young people. One way of achieving this has been through the encouragement of meaningful labor competitions. 35 notes. G. F. Jewsbury

658. Lomakin, M. N. DEIATEL'NOST' KPSS PO RAZVITIIU ORGANIZATSIONNO-TEKHNICHESKOI POMOSHCHI KOLKHOZAM I SOVKHOZAM V 1966-1970 GG (NA MATERIALAKH LENINGRADSKOI, NOVGORODSKOI I PSKOVSKOI OBLASTEI) [The activity of the CPSU in developing technical assistance organizations for collective and state farms, 1966-70, based on materials from the Leningrad, Novgorod, and Pskov regions]. *Vestnik Leningradskogo U.: Istoriia, Iazyk, Literatura [USSR] 1975 (14): 44-49.* Agricultural policies have been at the center of the CPSU's political attention. This was especially the case during the eighth five-year plan and in the decisions of the 23d congress of the Communist Party. The Party and the government worked closely to enable the Leningrad, Novgorod, and Pskov area agricultural enterprises to increase their output. 31 notes. G. F. Jewsbury

659. Loventhal, Milton and McDowell, Jennifer. THE STALIN RESOLUTIONS AND THE ROAD TO WORLD WAR II. *San José Studies 1980 6(3): 78-104.* Discusses five briefings and 242 deliberations and decisions by Joseph Stalin and the Politburo of the Central Committee of the Communist Party of the Soviet Union, and some correspondence, obtained by German intelligence agents between 1934 and 1936, which shed light on "the inner workings of the Politburo, the Politburo's private perspectives, its methods, its strategy and tactics, and its psychology," in light of the 1979 Soviet invasion of Afghanistan. Article to be continued.

660. Lu Lu. THE SOVIET UNION IN THE YEAR 1970. *Issues and Studies [Taiwan] 1970 6(7): 35-42.* Analyzes the first ten years of the USSR's transition-to-Communism campaign, with its goals of creating the material and technical base for communism and cultivating the new communist man. The 1960-65 five-year plan produced industrial development but agricultural output, labor productivity, and real income lagged. The 1965-70 five-year plan will not be a total success because of the failure to develop the new communist man free of errors which now plague Soviet planning. Based on published Soviet documents and newspaper reports. L. J. Stout

661. Lutsenko, V. K. DEIATEL'NOST' PARTII V OBLASTI SOVERSHENSTVOVANIIA NOT NA SOVREMENNOM ETAPE [Party activity in the field of the perfection of the scientific organization of labor (*NOT*) in the contemporary stage]. *Voprosy Istorii KPSS [USSR] 1974 (7): 28-39.* The Soviet Communist Party from its local party cells to its Central Committee has provided the leadership necessary for a more efficient and mechanized production and for improved working conditions. The Party encourages the use of new industrial methods such as self-supporting brigades. Based on Soviet periodical literature and published materials of the Communist Party of the Soviet Union; 55 notes. L. E. Holmes

662. Maistrenko, Ivan. STORINKY Z ISTORII KOMUNISTYCHNOI PARTII UKRAINY (XIII): KPU V DOBU BREZHNIEVA [A page out of the history of the Communist Party of the Ukraine (XIII): the CPU in the Brezhnev era]. *Sučasnist [West*

Germany] 1975 (7-8): 118-128. Analyzes the development of the Ukrainian Communist Party since the revolution, concentrating in particular on the effects of the transition from Nikita Khrushchev to Leonid Brezhnev and from Petr Shelest to Vladimir Shcherbitski.

663. Maksimov, Nikolai. ROLIIATA NA KPSS I SSSR V SVETOVNOTO REVOLIUTSIONNO DVIZHENIE [The role of the Communist Party of the Soviet Union and the USSR in the world revolutionary movement]. *Izvestiia na Inst. po Istoriia na BKP [Bulgaria] 1972 28: 245-269.* Emphasizes the role of the CPSU and the USSR in the world socialist movement and the struggle for peace and collective security, based on the reports and decisions made at the 24th Congress of the CPSU, April 1971.

664. Malov, Iu. K. KRITIKA SOVREMENNYKH FAL'SIFIKATSII RUKOVODIASHCHEI ROLI KPSS V RAZVITOM SOTSIALISTICHESKOM OBSHCHESTVE: K ISTORIOGRAFII PROBLEMY [Criticism of contemporary falsifiers of the Communist Party of the Soviet Union's leading role in developed socialist society: the historiography of the problem]. *Voprosy Istorii KPSS [USSR] 1982 (3): 62-75.* During the 1970's more than 200 books and 20 candidate dissertations were published in the USSR on themes rebutting and generally countering the accusations and slanders of bourgeois critics against socialism and the USSR. Chief among these defenses of the USSR were 1) Party documents, especially of the 24th, 25th, and 26th Party Congresses, which presented the truth about the USSR's industrial, social, and military activity; 2) the works of Leonid Il'ich Brezhnev, an unrivalled interpreter of Marxist-Leninism; and 3) the works and speeches of other members of the politburo, especially P. N. Fedoseev. All the works emphasize that the Party is the leading force in Soviet society, trusted by all Soviet people. Where the Party leads, the people willingly follow. Based on published works and the speeches of L. I. Brezhnev; 34 notes. A. J. Evans

665. Matkovski, N. V. PROLETARSKII INTERNATSIONALIZM—OSNOVOPOLAGAIUSHCHII PRINTSIP DEIATEL'NOSTI KPSS [Proletarian internationalism: a basic principle of the CPSU's work]. *Voprosy Istorii KPSS [USSR] 1976 (11): 3-17.* Outlines the characteristics of proletarian internationalism as a definition of a basic principle of the Soviet Communist Party's activities in the 1970's.

666. Matveeva, L. A. DEIATELNOST PARTIINYKH ORGANIZATSII SREDNEGO POVOLZHIA PO FORMIROVANIIU NAUCHNOGO MIROVOZZRENIIA RABOCHEI MOLODEZHI V GODY VOSMOI PIATILETKI [The moves by the Middle Volga Communist Party organizations to instill a scientific outlook in young workers during the eighth Five-Year Plan]. *Vestnik Leningradskogo U.: Seriia Istorii, Iazyka i Literatury [USSR] 1978 (4): 126-129.* Discusses the indoctrination of the labor force in Marxist-Leninist ideology and describes the progress made by propaganda workers in the Middle Volga region, 1965-66, and 1970-71.

667. Mehnert, Klaus. FROM MAO AND MARCUSE TO MARX. *Encounter [Great Britain] 1974 42(2): 39-42.* Discusses the reactions of Soviet journalism to the emergence of the New Left in the United States—at first ignoring the movement, then condemning it, finally and ponderously examining it seriously—and compares it with the inflexible hostility of Soviet press commentators to Maoism. Illus. D. H. Murdoch

668. Meissner, Boris. DIE SOWJETUNION ZWISCHEN DEM XXIV. UND XXV. PARTEIKONGRESS DER KPDSU [The Soviet Union between the 24th and 25th Party Congresses of the CPSU]. *Osteuropa [West Germany] 1975 25(11): 897-915, (12): 987-1007; 1976 26(1): 11-33.* Surveys the development of the USSR as reflected by Communist Party decisions between June 1971 and August 1975. The Party's collective leadership has been very stable but rigid. The ninth Five-Year Plan underlines the need for consumer goods but continues to favor heavy industry. Detente abroad has led to greater repression at home. These contradictions and the accompanying cultural stagnation impede the growth of a modern industrial society. 299 notes. R. E. Weltsch

669. Meissner, Boris. THE 26TH PARTY CONGRESS AND SOVIET DOMESTIC POLITICS. *Problems of Communism 1981 30(3): 1-23.* The recent 26th Congress of the Communist Party of the Soviet Union showed that the USSR is undergoing a crisis of leadership as the Brezhnev era nears its end. The current leadership took no significant initiative to alleviate growing domestic and foreign difficulties. The congress ritual merely represented a substitute for actions needed to close the growing gap between the regime and Soviet society. 3 tables, 59 notes. J. M. Lauber

670. Mezhenin, N. M. and Alekseeva, G. D. O NEKOTORYKH VOPROSAKH METODOLOGII ISTORII KPSS [The methodology of the history of the CPSU]. *Voprosy Istorii KPSS [USSR] 1976 (11): 74-81.* Attempts to define a theory of historical science as both historical process and historical understanding based on Marxist-Leninist dialectical materialism.

671. Mitchell, R. Judson. PARTY AND SOCIETY IN THE SOVIET UNION. *Current Hist. 1972 63(374): 170-174, 186.* Discusses the suppression of dissent and political power struggles within the Communist Party and Politburo in the USSR, 1964-70's.

672. Mol'kov, L. M. OCHERKI ISTORII MESTNYKH PARTIINYKH ORGANIZATSII: NEKOTORYE VOPROSY METODOLOGII I METODIKI ISSLEDOVANIIA, SOSTOIANIE RAZRABOTKI [Essays on the history of local Party organizations: some questions of methodology, research methods, and the finished product]. *Voprosy Istorii KPSS [USSR] 1980 (6): 144-150.* Reports on a session of the All-Union Council on Coordination of Scientific Research on the history of the Communist Party of the Soviet Union (CPSU) and Party construction on problems of methodology in local party history. M. V. Iskrov spoke about the importance of local party history and addressed some questions of sources and exposition. L. M. Spirin analyzed the quality of research and discussed the weight to be given to the history of the early years of social democracy in Russia. G. Dombrovski

673. Morgun, V. L. SOVERSHENSTVOVANIE RUKOVODSTVA PERVICHNYMI PARTORGANIZATSIIAMI PROMYSHLENNYKH PREDPRIIATII VOSTOCHNOI SIBIRI V 1971-1975 GG. [The perfection of the leadership of primary Party organizations of industrial enterprises of Eastern Siberia, 1971-75]. *Vestnik Leningradskogo U.: Seriia Istorii, Iazyka i Literatury [USSR] 1979 (4): 101-104.* Primary Party organizations for the Communist Party of the Soviet Union in industrial enterprises are crucial institutions in plan fulfillment. This was especially true in Krasnoyarsk Krai and Irkutsk Oblast during the ninth Five-Year Plan, 1971-75. During those years the Party, in order to increase the efficiency of the primary party organizations, emphasized the improvement of forms and methods of work such as passing informational reports to the lowest levels, the preparation and training of primary Party organization secretaries, and various methods of long-term planning, the length of which varied from one to three years. Based on some material from Krasnoyarsk and Irkutsk party archives and published sources; 19 notes. R. E. Glatfelter

674. Morgunov, V. Ia. IZ OPYTA PARTIINYKH ORGANIZATSII PO POVYSHENIIU EFFEKTIVNOSTI UCHEBY KOMMUNISTOV V USLOVIIAKH RAZVITOGO SOTSIALIZMA [From the experience of party organizations on increasing the effectiveness of the training of communists in conditions of developed socialism]. *Voprosy Istorii KPSS [USSR] 1981 (12): 70-81.* Surveys recent training and activity of Communist Party propagandists in the USSR. Based on periodical literature; 64 notes. L. E. Holmes

675. Motylev, A. S. DEITAL'NOST' KPSS PO SOVERSHENSTVOVANIIU UPRAVLENIIA SOTSIALISTICHESKOI EKONOMIKOI [The activity of the Communist Party in perfecting the management of the socialist economy]. *Voprosy Istorii KPSS [USSR] 1974 (11): 30-44.* The Communist Party exercises leadership over Soviet agriculture and industry to coordinate supply and demand, insure the use of the latest technology and methods, create

production associations, and encourage worker initiative. Based on *Pravda* and published material of the Communist Party of the Soviet Union; 74 notes. L. E. Holmes

676. Murphy, Paul J. *Brezhnev, Soviet Politician.* Jefferson, N.C.: McFarland, 1981. 363 pp.

677. Nezhinski, L. N. AKTUAL'NYE PROBLEMY EDINSTVA STRAN SOTSIALISTICHESKOGO SODRUZHESTVA V OSVESHCHENII SOVREMENNOI SOVETSKOI ISTORIOGRAFII [Topical problems of unity of the countries of socialist cooperation in the light of contemporary Soviet historiography]. *Novaia i Noveishaia Istoriia [USSR] 1980 (3): 3-20.* Examines topical problems of unity and cohesion of the socialist community countries, demonstrates Soviet historiography's contribution to the elaboration of these problems, and stresses the need to highlight some urgent questions. J

678. Nicholson, Martin. THE NEW SOVIET CONSTITUTION: A POLITICAL ANALYSIS. *World Today [Great Britain] 1978 34(1): 14-20.* Examines the history of the writing of the newest Soviet constitution, the "constitution of developed socialism," and describes its chapters on the place of the Communist Party in Soviet life, the system of soviets, economic provisions, the status of the Union Republics, the rights and duties of citizens, and foreign policy. The true importance of the constitution is not the social functions it outlines but that it is a document of Party doctrine emerging during the Leonid Brezhnev era.

679. Nikolayev, Y. SOVIET FOREIGN POLICY: BASIC IDEOLOGICAL PRINCIPLES. *Int. Affairs [USSR] 1973 (11): 63-70.* Discusses the application of the ideology of Marxism-Leninism in the USSR's foreign policy, especially the peace program of the 24th Congress of the Communist Party of the Soviet Union, 1971.

680. Nikulin, V. V. RAZVITIE TEKHNICHESKOGO TVORCHESTVA TRUDIASHCHIKHSIA V GODY VOS'MOI PIATILETKI (NA MATERIALAKH PARTIINYKH ORGANIZATSII PROMYSHLENNYKH PREDPRIIATII VORONEZHSKOI, LIPETSKOI, TAMBOVSKOI OBLASTEI) [Development of workers' technical initiative during the eighth five-year plan (Based on materials of Party organizations of industrial enterprises in Voronezh, Lipetsk, and Tambovsk oblasts)]. *Vestnik Leningradskogo U.: Seriia Istorii, Iazyka i Literatury [USSR] 1979 (2): 99-102.* Under conditions in the USSR during the eighth five-year plan, a major aid to socioeconomic progress was the technical initiative of the workers themselves. The Communist Party organization of the three Central Black Earth oblasts—Voronezh, Lipetsk, and Tambovsk—actively encouraged that initiative. Methods of mobilization included Socialist competition, the creation of rationalization funds (which were in place in all three oblasts by April 1970), the conducting of reviews, and the holding of specific competitions. Significant increases in the introduction of rationalization suggestions and inventions into the productive process are claimed, as well as a significant increase in the economic value of such actions. Based partly on regional archival materials; 27 notes. R. E. Glatfelter

681. Novikova, A. A. and Fedorov, A. G. LICHNYE ARKHIVY I VEDOMSTVA [Personal archives and records]. *Sovetskie Arkhivy [USSR] 1970 (3): 37-43.* In 1962 the Central State Archives of the USSR National Economy started collecting documents referring to the activities of state officials: ministers, senior Party officials, managers of the large industrial enterprises, and staff at the science and technical institutions. W. Kowalski

682. Novosel'tsev, E. and Khomutov, N. OTNOSHENIIA SSSR S GLAVNYMI KAPITALISTICHESKIMI STRANAMI [Soviet relations with the main capitalist countries]. *Mezhdunarodnaia Zhizn' [USSR] 1968 15(4): 98-107.* Surveys the implementation of resolutions at the 23d Party Congress, 1966, and the attempts to improve relations with the major Western European states.

683. Novyts'kyi, Ie. A. KONTROL' I ORHANIZATSIIA VYKONANNIA IAK ZASIB PARTIINOHO KERIVNYTSTVA [Control, organization, and the fulfillment of plans as facets of Party leadership]. *Ukrains'kyi Istorychnyi Zhurnal [USSR] 1975 (12): 14-24.* Describes the functions and obligations of the Communist Party apparatus in the Soviet Union, as set out by the Party leadership, 1972-75.

684. Odom, William E. THE SOVIET MILITARY: THE PARTY CONNECTION. *Problems of Communism 1973 22(5): 12-26.* Explores traditional western assumptions that the party-military boundary in the USSR marks a potential cleavage that affects military efficiency. Instead, an alternative conceptualization should be investigated centering on the historical closeness of Russian-Soviet military-political relations. Primary and secondary sources; 45 notes. J. M. Lauber

685. Orlik, I. I. SSSR I UKREPLENIE SOTSIALISTICHESKOGO SODRUZHESTVA [The strengthening of the world socialist community]. *Voprosy Istorii [USSR] 1975 (4): 3-26.* Examines the main problems of promoting united action by the countries of the socialist community in the 1970's and the outstanding role played by the USSR in this process. The main trends in strengthening the ideological and political unity of the socialist countries are developing and deepening economic integration, joint activity in the international arena in the interests of peace and socialism, and combating bourgeois ideology. The constant improvement and perfection of the various links binding the socialist countries results in the systematic expansion and deepening of their mutual relations and gives rise to new forms of cooperation. Based on documents of the CPSU and other parties. J

686. Ostapenko, F. P. and Feshchenko, M. T. ORHANIZATSIINE ZMITSNENNIA PERVYNNYKH PARTORHANIZATSII NA SELI (1966-1970) [Organizational strengthening of primary Party organizations in rural areas, 1966-70]. *Ukrains'kyi Istorychnyi Zhurnal [USSR] 1974 7: 15-21.* Considers the work of the Communist Party with youth, in rural areas in particular, 1966-70.

687. Patock, Coelestin. ORTHODOXE KIRCHE IN DER UDSSR: BERICHT DES ZUSTÄNDIGEN KOMMISSARIATS AN DAS ZK DER KPSS [The Orthodox Church in the USSR: a report of the authorized commissariat to the Central Committee of the Soviet Union's Communist Party]. *Ostkirchliche Studien [West Germany] 1980 29(4): 311-333.* Discusses in detail the 1974-75 report on matters concerning the Russian Orthodox Eastern Church, which confirms the suppression of the church in the Soviet Union.

688. Pecheritsa, V. F. ORGANIZATSIONNO-PARTIINAIA RABOTA V KHABAROVSKOI PARTORGANIZATSII (1966-1967) [Party and organizational work in the Khabarovsk Party organization, 1966-67]. *Vestnik Leningradskogo U.: Seriia Istorii, Iazyka i Literatury [USSR] 1977 (4): 136-141.* One of the most important endeavors in the area of Party structure is the elaboration of problems of internal Party development, especially as it pertains to the work involved with industrial activities. The author deals with these activities in the Khabarovsk area. 43 notes. G. F. Jewsbury

689. Pelikán, Dragutin. ROZVINUTÁ SOCIALISTICKÁ SPOLEČNOST V SSSR A DĚJINY SOVĚTSKÉHO STÁTU A PRÁVA [Developed socialist society in the USSR and the history of the Soviet state and law]. *Právněhistorické Studie [Czechoslovakia] 1980 (23): 51-66.* In the USSR the 1970's represent a watershed in the history of socialist development, when the dictatorship of the proletariat was superceded by a people's state, as is seen by the new Soviet constitution. The function of the new state is the full development of the social, economic, and political levels of communism. The earlier goals of the dictatorship of the proletariat, such as the elimination of the exploitative bourgeoisie, have been accomplished and by its new constitution of 1977 the USSR became the chief component of the great world communist movement. 10 notes. B. Reinfeld

690. Petrov, A. A. RAZVITIE SOTSIAL'NOI AKTIVNOSTI MOLODYKH RABOCHIKH V 1966-1970 GG. (NA MATERIALAKH IVANOVSKOI OBLASTNOI PARTORGANIZATSII) [The development of social activities among working youth in 1966-70, based on Ivanovo district Party organization materials]. *Vestnik*

Leningradskogo U.: Istoriia, Iazyk, Literatura [USSR] 1975 (8): 40-49. As part of the process of bringing the working youth into the avant-garde of Soviet society, the Communist Party in the Ivanovo district worked to encourage the young proletariat into various parts of public life during the eighth five year plan. The Party used a number of methods, including slogans such as "five days' tasks done in four" and "Ivanovo work means excellent work." More young workers entered Party functions during this time, in response to Party urging. 46 notes. G. F. Jewsbury

691. Petrov, F. KPSS—ORGANIZATOR POBED SOVETSKOGO NARODA (OBZOR KNIG) [The CPSU: organizer of the Soviet people's victories: a survey]. *Voenno-Istoricheskii Zhurnal [USSR] 1980 22(12): 57-60.* A review article on several recent Soviet books on the relationship between the armed forces and the Communist Party. The Party always controls the armed forces, and takes the initiative in all political work among the troops. The value of the books under discussion lies in their broad coverage of all aspects of party-army relations, and particularly the field of ideological work. 3 notes. D. N. Collins

692. Petrov, F. ZABOTA KPSS OB EKONOMICHESKOM, OBORONNOM MOGUSHCHESTVE NASHEI RODINY I SOKHRANENII MIRA [The CPSU's concern for the national economic and defensive power and for the preservation of peace]. *Voenno-Istoricheskii Zhurnal [USSR] 1981 23(8): 75-79.* Examines published documents of the Central Committee of the Communist Party for the period 1978-80, noting their emphasis upon the need to overcome technology and energy problems, improve the rural sector, and develop the extractive industries of the east, and their parallel emphasis upon the need to develop Soviet defensive strength. Also notes efforts for the Communist education of the Soviet people, for fraternal cooperation with socialist countries, and references to the problem of China. F. A. K. Yasamee

693. Petrov, S. N. DEIATEL'NOST' LENINGRADSKOI PARTIINOI ORGANIZATSII PO VOENNO-PATRIOTICHESKOMU VOSPITANIIU TRUDIASHCHIKHSIA V GODY DEVIATOI PIATILETKI [The Leningrad Party organization's activity toward the military-patriotic education of the workers during the years of the 9th Five-Year Plan]. *Vestnik Leningradskogo U.: Seriia Istorii, Iazyka i Literatury [USSR] 1981 (1): 100-103.* Discusses the Leningrad Communist Party's work in connection with training the working population for military and patriotic purposes during the late 1960's and early 1970's. Stress is laid on the ties between factories and army units, and on visits by soldiers to places of work. Over 70 industrial enterprises have connections with military or naval units in the region. Based on Leningrad Party Archive (LPA fondy 32, 415, 2315) and published documents; 24 notes. D. N. Collins

694. Petrov, V. T. SOVETSKAIA SHKOLA K XXVI S'EZDU KPSS [Soviet schools approach the 26th Congress of the Communist Party of the Soviet Union]. *Prepodavanie Istorii v Shkole [USSR] 1981 (1): 2-7.* Soviet secondary education underwent a steady expansion and improvement during the 10th Five-Year Plan, and all its personnel are ready to carry out the decisions of the approaching 26th Congress of the Communist Party.

695. Pogudin, V. I. IDEINO-VOSPITATEL'NAIA RABOTA PARTII V SOVREMENNYKH USLOVIIAKH [Education in Communist Party ideals in contemporary conditions]. *Voprosy Istorii KPSS [USSR] 1977 (12): 114-119.* An examination of the work of the All-Union Scientific Practical Conference held in 1975-76 in republic capitals and some other large towns, dealing with political education in Communist Party ideals. J. P. H. Myers

696. Poliakov, E. M. UKREPLENIE TRUDOGO SOTRUDNICHESTVA RABOCHEGO KLASSA SOVETSKIKH RESPUBLIK V GODY DEVIATOI PIATILETKI: NA MATERIALAKH LENINGRADSKOI PARTIINOI ORGANIZATSII [The improvement of labor cooperation among the working class of the Soviet republics during the ninth Five-Year Plan: the evidence of the Leningrad Party organization]. *Vestnik Leningradskogo U.: Seriia Istorii, Iazyka i Literatury [USSR] 1978 (4): 119-123.* Discusses the coordination of labor forces from different national republics of the USSR by Communist Party policies and describes the economic, social, and political implications. Also gives examples of interrepublic planning and production in a multinational economy and the operation of socialist competition in the early 1970's, with particular reference to the Leningrad Metal Factory. Secondary sources; 35 notes. E. R. Sicher

697. Poliakov, Iu. A. and Pisarenko, E. E. ISTORICHESKIE ASPEKTY IZUCHENIIA SOVETSKOGO OBRAZA ZHIZNI [Historical aspects of studying the Soviet daily life]. *Voprosy Istorii [USSR] 1978 (6): 3-14.* Emphasizes the synthetic character of the concept "way of life," which organically demands both the systemic and historic approach. The Soviet way of life is viewed by the authors as a concrete historical phenomenon. They stress the need of studying its emergence in the early years of Soviet power as well as the main stages of its development and perfection during the period of transition and in the era of mature socialism. The Soviet way of life is a dynamic phenomenon which is in the process of uninterrupted development and perfection under the influence of both objective and subjective factors, the most important of which is the single-minded, constantly expanding and deepening activity of the Communist Party. J

698. Polsky, M. P. and Khvostov, V. M. XXIV S'EZD KPSS I ZADACHI SOVETSKOI ISTORICHESKOI NAUKI [The 24th Congress of the CPSU and the tasks of Soviet historical science. A conference of coordination in the Department of History of the Academy of Sciences of the USSR]. *Istoriia SSSR [USSR] 1972 (2): 178-183.* The study of history must be as close as possible to the ideological work of the Party and to the solution of great state problems connected with the construction of communism. The main goal of the conference was to direct the efforts of historians to the solution of problems that were put forth by the Party congress. A very important part of this was the preparation for the celebration of the 50th anniversary of the USSR. Conference held 10-12 November 1971. Primary sources; 3 notes. L. Kalinowski

699. Polurez, V. I. and Turivnyi, V. P. DIIAL'NIST' KPRS PO VDOSKONALENNIU UPRAVLINNIA EKONOMIKOIU [The activity of the Communist Party of the Soviet Union (CPSU) in administering the economy]. *Ukraïns'kyi Istorychnyi Zhurnal [USSR] 1980 (7): 30-43.* Reviews V. I. Lenin's economic principles and their implementation by the Communist Party and the Communist leadership, who have developed a far-sighted economic and political plan designed to aid the building of developed socialism, whose foundations require a highly developed economic system.

700. Prazsky, Jan. LOST STAKE IN ANTI-SOVIET GAME; COMMENTARY. *World Marxist R. [Canada] 1974 17(4): 133-122.* The prominence given in Western capitalist countries to the publication of Alexander Solzhenitsyn's *The Gulag Archipelago* is part of a new anti-Soviet propaganda campaign.

701. Prusanov, I. P. VVEDENIE K IZUCHENIIU KURSA ISTORII KPSS [Introductory course in the history of the CPSU]. *Voprosy Istorii KPSS [USSR] 1981 (9): 115-123.* The 26th Congress of the Communist Party of the Soviet Union stressed the need for strengthening ideological-political education, and a consolidation of knowledge of the history of the CPSU is of paramount importance to this concept. Outlines which parts of the *Communist Manifesto* should always be covered in introductory lectures. 36 notes. J. Bamber

702. Prutski, A. A. PARTIINAIA ZHIZN': TSIFRY I FAKTY O SBORNIKAKH STATISTICHESKIKH MATERIALOV MESTNYKH PARTIINYKH ORGANIZATSII [Party life: figures and facts on collections of statistical materials of local party organizations]. *Voprosy Istorii KPSS [USSR] 1984 (5): 72-82.* Analyzes membership of the Soviet Communist Party in the Ukraine, Armenia, Belorussia, Moldavia, Kazakhstan, Estonia, Arkhangelsk, and Rostov between 1966 and 1981. It details the types of ideological, theoretical, propagandist, and scientific tasks that the members do for the Party. It shows in particular that young people of all nationalities are joining the Leninist Party. Their educational

achievements are high. The development of the Party reflects changes in Soviet society. Based on statistics from a wide variety of Soviet Communist Party publications; 63 notes. A. J. Evans

703. Rigby, T. H. THE SOVIET GOVERNMENT SINCE KHRUSHCHEV. *Politics [Australia] 1977 12(1): 5-22.* Shows how the Soviet premier Nikita Khrushchev's successors in 1965 reversed most of his innovations in the structure of the Council of Ministers. Since then turnover in its membership has been very low, but has lately accelerated owing to age-related deaths and retirements. Also, other places have been created to head new agencies so that the Council of Ministers is again becoming an important arena for competition for high office. New government members are of two types: career specialists, who have worked mainly in the field concerned, and Party generalists, who have risen mainly through the regional Party machine. Discusses a recent increase in party tutelage over the government machine. Also notes the significance of continued delays in the long-promised constitutional revision. 33 notes, three appendixes. A. W. Howell

704. Rigby, T. H. THE SOVIET REGIONAL LEADERSHIP: THE BREZHNEV GENERATION. *Slavic Rev. 1978 37(1): 1-24.* Focuses on the first secretaries of regional and Party committees of the Russian Federation (RSFSR), one portion of the second most important category of officials in the USSR. Details the pre-Soviet and Soviet roots of this bureaucracy, its bases of support, patronage, the educational and career background of the first secretaries, and bureaucratic and reorganizational obsessions. Compares the Nikita Khrushchev era (reforms, bureaucratic training ground) to that of the present Leonid Brezhnev era. 10 tables, 47 notes. R. B. Mendel

705. Romanov, A. R. O KOMMUNISTICHESKOM VOSPITANII SEL'SKOI MOLODEZHI V GODY 9-I PIATILETKI (NA MATERIALAKH LENINGRADSKOI OBLASTNOI PARTIINOI ORGANIZATSII) [On the Communist education of village youth during the 9th Five-Year Plan: based on material from the Leningrad regional Party organization]. *Vestnik Leningradskogo U.: Seriia Istorii, Iazyka i Literatury [USSR] 1982 (2): 112-114.* The increase in the migration of village youth to the towns in the 1970's can be explained on the one hand by industry's need for labor and on the other by the subjective desire of rural youth for greater opportunities in life. By employing a complex approach to the education of youth, the rate of migration has been reduced during the 9th Five-Year Plan; the organization of cultural and educational facilities has been improved, the network of social services has been extended, and Party leadership over the education program increased. However, despite a certain degree of success in stemming the exodus of youth from the villages, the situation remains complex. Based on Leningrad regional Party archives and secondary sources; 20 notes. G. Dombrovski

706. Ruble, Blair A. ROMANOV'S LENINGRAD. *Problems of Communism 1983 32(6): 36-48.* While Grigori Romanov was first secretary of the Leningrad Oblast Party Committee from 1970 to 1983, he fostered pragmatic but basically conservative solutions to problems relating to manpower supply, urban planning, and the promotion of technological innovation. His experiences and management style are likely to be relevant to his new responsibilities in Moscow as a secretary of the Communist Party Central Committee. Based on the speeches and articles by Romanov as well as official Soviet publications; 3 tables, 63 notes. J. M. Lauber

707. Rudkovskaia, E. V. PARTIINOE RUKOVODSTVO SOVETAMI (POMATERIALAM LENINGRADA) [Party leadership of the soviets: based on Leningrad materials]. *Vestnik Leningradskogo U.: Istoriia, Iazyk, Literatura [USSR] 1975 (8): 16-22.* The soviet source of strength and power is the leadership of the Communist Party, especially after the 23d and 24th Party congresses. In the past few years the Party has given concrete directives to the soviets on the achievement of basic political goals. One of the major thrusts of the Party has been to increase worker participation in the political life of the country, and in Leningrad the percentage of workers in the various soviets has risen from 46% in 1967 to almost 60% in 1973. The Party direction to the Soviets will aid the attainment of the Communist society. 16 notes. G. F. Jewsbury

708. Rudyk, P. A. ROZVYTOK VNUTRIPARTIINOI DEMOKRATII V SUCHASNYKH UMOVAKH [The development of intraparty democracy under present-day conditions]. *Ukrains'kyi Istorychnyi Zhurnal [USSR] 1976 (2): 27-35.* Reports those activities of the Ukrainian Party organizations during the Ninth Five-Year Plan, 1971-75, which supported intra-Party democracy and emphasizes the view that implementation of the decisions of the 24th Congress of the Communist Party of the Soviet Union was a result of increased activity by Communists and the aggressiveness of Party organizations.

709. Rudyk, P. A. ZROSTANNIA AVANHARDNOI ROLI KOMUNISTIV V UMOVAKH ROZVYNUTOHO SOTSIALIZMU [The growth of the leading role of Communists in conditions of developed socialism]. *Ukraïns'kyi Istorychnyi Zhurnal [USSR] 1980 (2): 31-42.* The role of the Communist Party of the Soviet Union, its prestige, and its influence on the masses depend on the active position of Communists and on the successful implementation of their role as a vanguard of the working people. CPSU publications and other sources; 54 notes. I. Krushelnyckyj

710. Rybakov, O. K. DEIATEL'NOST' KPSS V OBLASTI POVYSHENIIA EFFEKTIVNOSTI VNESHNEEKONOMICHESKIKH SVIAZEI SSSR [The CPSU's activities toward increasing the efficiency of Soviet external economic links]. *Voprosy Istorii KPSS [USSR] 1980 (12): 24-36.* A discussion of means used by the Soviet Communist Party to increase the range and effectiveness of trade links between the USSR and the countries of Comecon and the world. Rational planning, long-term decisions, and the isolation of the most important strategic economic decisions have been essential. Government agencies have been made more accountable for adequate performance, and new items for export are being developed. Based on published documentary and statistical sources; 58 notes. D. N. Collins

711. Sahai, Nisha. SOVIET SPECIALISTS ON SOUTH ASIA. *Int. Studies [India] 1980 19(1): 87-109.* Examines the interaction between Soviet scholars and other types of specialists, such as diplomats and journalists, on South Asia in the Communist Party and in the Soviet government. The high priority the USSR has placed on relations with India and South Asia in the last decade is reflected in the increased importance of scholars in the formation of policy for that area. 43 notes. T. P. Linkfield

712. Sarbei, B. H. and Shapata, V. F. NA DOPOMOHU VYKLADACHU ISTORII: DYPLOMNI ROBOTY—VAZHLYVYI ZASIB PIDHOTOVKY SPETSIALISTIV-ISTORYKIV [Aids for the lecturer in history: academic theses—a vital means of preparation for specialist historians]. *Ukraïns'kyi Istorychnyi Zhurnal [USSR] 1980 (7): 117-123.* Higher education should not only produce specialists but should also provide idelogical and political education, which is of particular importance for historians, who should become the active leaders in political education of the Communist Party, defenders of Marxism-Leninism, and the unmaskers of the evil insinuations of bourgeois falsifiers, as exemplified by some cited works.

713. Savel'iev, V. L. and Shevchuk, V. P. KRYTYKA BURZHUAZNYKH FALSYFIKATSII KERIVNOI ROLI KPRS V POLITYCHNI SYSTEMI ROZVYNUTOHO SOTSIALISTYCHNOHO SYSPIL'STVA [Bourgeois falsification and criticism of the leading role played by the CPSU in the political system of advanced socialism]. *Ukrains'kyi Istorychnyi Zhurnal [USSR] 1976 (9): 47-57.* Describes the increasingly hostile East-West ideological struggle, 1965-75, and the continual bourgeois denigration of the role of the Communist Party of the Soviet Union.

714. Schwartz, Joel J. POLITICAL SOCIALIZATION: THE ELUSIVE "NEW SOVIET MAN." *Problems of Communism 1973 22(5): 39-50.* Concentrates on the major factors which limit the political socialization efforts carried on by the Soviet Young Commu-

nist League (Komsomol) in molding the New Soviet Man. The basic problems result from the infrastructure of the organization itself as well as from basic systemic features of the USSR. Primary and secondary sources; 31 notes. J. M. Lauber

715. Sdobnov, S. I. ZABOTA KPSS O NEUKLONNOM POD"EME SELSKOGO KHOZIAISTVA [The CPSU's concern with the firm ascent of agriculture]. *Voprosy Istorii KPSS [USSR] 1981 (10): 18-32.* Discusses Soviet agriculture's development and achievements, and Party policy for improving the rural standard of living. Based on material from the 26th CPSU Congress, the works of Lenin and Brezhnev, and newspaper articles; 63 notes. L. Smith

716. Seliger, Kurt. FRIEDLICHE KOEXISTENZ UND PROLETARISCHER INTERNATIONALISMUS [Peaceful coexistence and proletarian internationalism]. *Osteuropa [West Germany] 1973 23(12): 930-940.* The great-power interests of the USSR frequently involve the cultivation of foreign governments which have persecuted and outlawed their domestic Communist parties. Between 1964 and 1973 Soviet relations with several Arab governments, the Greek Junta, and the Franco regime in Spain have exemplified the one-sided Soviet understanding of proletarian internationalism as unconditional support of Soviet policy by all Communist parties. 48 notes. R. E. Weltsch

717. Seliger, Kurt. KOMINFORM—DER UNGEBETENE GAST. DISKUSSION UM EIN NEUES KOMMUNISTISCHES WELTZENTRUM [Cominform, the unbidden guest: discussions about a new worldwide Communist center]. *Osteuropa [West Germany] 1974 24(7): 534-542.* Since 1968 the Communist Party of the USSR has sought some coordinating device that would enable it to guide world communism. At the same time many non-Soviet Communist parties have emphasized their support of polycentrism and rejected the idea of a joint Moscow-imposed discipline. As a result, Soviet leaders find it politic to disavow any intention to revive the former Cominform in a new guise. 48 notes. R. E. Weltsch

718. Seliger, Kurt. KPDSU: UNBEWÄLTIGTER TROTZKISMUS [CPSU: unconquered Trotskyism]. *Osteuropa [West Germany] 1976 26(5): 357-368.* The Communist Party of the USSR still feels threatened by Trotskyism and denounces it periodically with fervor, though it appears that none of the dissident groups inside the Soviet Union has Trotskyite tendencies.

719. Semerov, A. M. PARTIINOE RUKOVODSTVO SOVERSHENSTVOVANIEM SISTEMY POLITICHESKOGO PROSVESHCHENIIA KOMMUNISTOV LENINGRADA POSLE XXIII S'EZDA KPSS [Party guidance in the perfection of the Leningrad Communist system of political education after the 23d congress of the CPSU]. *Vestnik Leningradskogo U. [USSR] 1974 (20): 5-12.* To improve the cultural and political level of the people and to better all aspects of contemporary life, an increased effort is essential in the realm of political education. The Leningrad Party organization, one of the most powerful in the country, in 1965-66 adopted a new system of political education which divided the students into three levels. The author describes the various instructional strategies for each level and gives statistical tables enumerating the students, both Party and non-Party, at each level. 35 notes. G. F. Jewsbury

720. Shabel'nykov, V. I. DIIALNIST' PARTORHANIZATSII DONBASU PO FIZYCHNOMU VYKHOVANNIU TRUDIASHCHYKH (1966-1970) [The work of Party organizations of the Donets Basin on the physical education of the working class, 1966-70]. *Ukrains'kyi Istorychnyi Zhurnal [USSR] 1973 (11): 92-97.*

721. Shapko, V. M. KPSS—BOEVOI AVANGARD SOVETSKOGO NARODA [The CPSU: the fighting avant-garde of the Soviet people]. *Voprosy Istorii KPSS [USSR] 1965 (3): 5-19.* Refutes Leonard Schapiro's assertions about the Communist Party of the USSR.

722. Shcheprov, B. S. VOZRASTANIE RUKOVODIASHCHEI ROLI KPSS V PERIOD RAZVITOGO SOTSIALIZMA [The rise of the Communist Party of the Soviet Union's leading role in the period of developed socialism]. *Voprosy Istorii KPSS [USSR] 1982 (3): 143-147.* From 8 to 10 December 1981 the Ministry of Secondary and Higher Education of the USSR held a symposium on the decisions of the 23d to the 26th Party Congresses. It had six sections: 1) the growing role of the CPSU in directing the Soviet economy, 2) criticism of bourgeois falsifications of the theory, history, and policies of the CPSU, 3) ideological and political educational work of the CPSU, 4) the CPSU's leadership of state and social organizations, 5) the improvement of the Party's organizational work under conditions of developed socialism, and 6) historical and source problems of the growth of the CPSU's leading role under conditions of developed socialism. A. J. Evans

723. Shevchenko, A. N. XXIV S'EZD KPSS I PROBLEMA RAZORUZHENIIA [The 24th Congress of the CPSU and disarmament problems]. *Sovetskoe Gosudarstvo i Pravo [USSR] 1972 (4): 11-20.* Outlines the initiatives toward world disarmament put forward by the Soviet Communist Party at its 24th Congress in 1971, stressing the relevance of this for experts in international law.

724. Shevchenko, F. P. DO PYTANNIA PRO VYKORYSTANNIA KINODOKUMENTIV V ISTORYCHNIY NAUTSI [The use of film documentaries in historical sciences]. *Ukrains'kyi Istorychnyi Zhurnal [USSR] 1976 (6): 64-72.* Discusses the importance of using historical film documentaries to educate the people in Communist ideology.

725. Shul'ha, I. V. and Vlasenko, O. V. ROL' SOTSIALISTYCHNOHO ZMAHANNIA TRUDOVYKH KOLEKTYVIV BRATNIKH RESPUBLIK U ZMITSNENNI INTERNATSIONAL'NOI IEDNOSTI RADIANS'KOHO SUSPIL'STVA (1971-1975 RR.) [The role of the socialist struggle of proletarian collectives of fraternal republics in the strengthening of the international unity of Soviet society, 1971-75]. *Ukrains'kyi Istorychnyi Zhurnal [USSR] 1982 (10): 28-36.* Discusses the work conducted among the Communist parties and workers of the Russian Federation, the Ukraine, and Belorussia, in particular their attempts to strengthen proletarian internationalism. Gives details of meetings, exchange visits, delegations, and other contacts between workers' and farmers' collectives, industries, and work brigades on town, regional, national, and individual levels. Concentrates on the period following the 31 August 1971 decree on the strengthening of the international unity of Soviet society, issued by the Central Committee of the Communist Party of the Soviet Union. L. Djakowska

726. Shumakov, V. P. DEIATEL'NOST' LENINGRADSKOI PARTIINOI ORGANIZATSII PO PODBORU I RASSTANOVKE RUKOVODIASHCHIKH KADROV PROIZVODSTVENNYKH OB"EDINENII V PERIOD IKH STANOVLENIIA (1962-1970 GG.) [The work of the Leningrad Party organization in the selection and assignment of trained personnel in production concerns in their first years 1962-70]. *Vestnik Leningradskogo U.: Seriia Istorii, Iazyka i Literatury [USSR] 1983 (1): 98-101.* Discusses the Leningrad Communist Party committee's decisions on the concentration of production and assignment of specialists. The production concerns in and around Leningrad have profited from the mergers, which have resulted in higher productivity and growth rates, ensured proper distribution of the managerial staff, and strengthened the position of Party organizations within each concern. Based on materials from the Leningrad Party Archive; 18 notes. English summary. M. Hernas

727. Šik, Ota. THE SHORTCOMINGS OF THE SOVIET ECONOMY AS SEEN IN COMMUNIST IDEOLOGIES. *Government and Opposition [Great Britain] 1974 9(3): 263-276.* Discusses the Soviet economy and bureaucracy from the point of view of Maoist and Trotskyite ideologies, which see the Communist Party of the USSR as betraying socialism.

728. Silin, V. A. VYPOLNENIE ZADANII XXIII S'EZDA KPSS V OBLASTI POVYSHENIIA MATERIAL'NOGO BLAGOSOSTOIANIIA NARODA [The fulfilment of the tasks of the 23d CP-

SU congress in raising the material well-being of the people]. *Voprosy Istorii KPSS [USSR] 1971 (3): 55-69.* Reviews the achievements of the Communist Party of the USSR in raising the standard of living of the Soviet people, 1966-70.

729. Silkova, N. P. IZ OPYTA IDEOLOGICHESKOGO OBESPECHENIIA KOMPLEKSNOGO RAZVITIIA PROIZVODITEL'NYKH SIL KRAIA [From the experience of the ideological provision for the complex development of the region's productive forces]. *Voprosy Istorii KPSS [USSR] 1982 (11): 105-115.* Discusses the contribution of ideological work to the development of the Krasnoyarsk Region. A territorial industrial complex established on the basis of electricity supplied by new dams required combining economic, sociopolitical, demographic, geographic and other data to provide an outcome which would develop the area in the most productive way. The Communist Party regional committee's ideological work assisted in the task by promoting socialist emulation, morale boosting, and the brigade system. 12 notes. D. N. Collins

730. Skleznev, E. V. and Pavlikov, K. F. NESOSTOIATEL'NOST' SOVREMENNYKH BURZHUAZNYKH KONTSEPTSII ROLI KPSS V SOVETSKOM VOENNOM STROITEL'STVE [The bankruptcy of contemporary bourgeois conceptions on the role of the Communist Party in Soviet military construction]. *Voprosy Istorii KPSS [USSR] 1982 (5): 95-106.* As the balance of forces has shifted in favor of socialism, Western Sovietologists have increased their slanders against the USSR, accusing it of building up aggressive military forces and moving toward military dictatorship. They call for a Western military buildup to counter this imagined threat. The imperialists describe Lenin's defensive military policy as aggressive. The Soviet Union is ruled by the Communist Party and there exists no internal military threat to its stability. The Party and the armed forces are in complete agreement. The USSR is invincible, and will counter any threat to it from outside. It seeks peace, relying on Lenin's dictum, "The most dangerous thing is to underestimate the enemy, and to rest, thinking that we are stronger." Based on Lenin's works, Brezhnev's works and speeches, Communist Party congresses, and Western studies; 56 notes. A. J. Evans

731. Smolianski, V. G. EKONOMICHESKAIA POLITIKA KPSS I IDEOLOGI ANTIKOMMUNIZMA [The economic policy of the Communist Party of the USSR and anti-Communist ideologists]. *Voprosy Istorii KPSS [USSR] 1966 (1): 18-29.* Defends the record of the USSR, especially the economic reforms of 1965, against charges of monopoly capitalism.

732. Sokolov, I. MAGISTRAL'NYI PUT' MIROVOGO RAZVITIIA [The main path of world development]. *Mirovaia Ekonomika i Mezhdunarodnye Otnosheniia [USSR] 1974 (7): 4-18.* Describes the achievements and influence on subsequent international political developments of the decisions taken at the 1969 Conference of Communist and Workers' Parties in Moscow.

733. Soroka, P. O. DIIAL'NIST' PARTIINYKH ORHANIZATSII PO DOBORU, ROZSTANOVTSI TA VYKHOVANNIU SPETSIALISTIV SIL'S'KOHO HOSPODARSTVA (1966-1970) [The work of Party organizations in the selection, allocation, and education of agricultural specialists, 1966-70]. *Ukrains'kyi Istorychnyi Zhurnal [USSR] 1975 (5): 76-84.* Stresses the role of Soviet Communist Party organizations in implementing agricultural policy during the 8th Five-Year Plan, focusing on the training of specialists.

734. Spaulding, Wallace. NEW HEAD, OLD "PROBLEMS OF PEACE AND SOCIALISM." *Problems of Communism 1982 31(6): 57-62.* The appointment this year of Iuri Skliarov as Editor-in-Chief of *Problems of Peace and Socialism* highlights the firm control that the USSR has maintained over this important symbol of world Communist unity since its inception in 1958. This control has been challenged by Albanian and Chinese Communists who have left the editorial council, and by other, nonruling Communist parties in Europe and the Far East. Based on official publications of the *Problems of Peace and Socialism;* 2 tables, 31 notes. J. M. Lauber

735. Spirin, L. M. SUSTOIANIE I PERSPEKTIVI NA RAZVITIE NA ISTORIKO-PARTIINATA NAUKA V SSSR [Composition and development perspectives in Party scholarship in the USSR]. *Izvestiia na Inst. po Istoriia na BKP [Bulgaria] 1972 28: 7-36.* Analyzes the ideological and thematic content of Soviet Communist Party historiography, 1967-71, when ca. 3,000 books and brochures were published.

736. Staruns'ka, N. V. LEKTSIINA PROPAGANDA TOVARYSTVA "ZNANNIA" URSR (1970-1975 RR.) [Propaganda lectures by the Znanie society in the Ukraine, 1970-75]. *Ukrains'kyi Istorychnyi Zhurnal [USSR] 1981 (1): 119-124.* Reviews the work in the Ukraine of the voluntary Znanie [Knowledge] society, whose tasks include the implementation of the Communist Party program through propaganda lectures among the masses. Party archives and other sources; 33 notes. I. Krushelnyckyj

737. Stepanov, A. I. SSSR I SOVESHCHANIE PO BEZOPASNOSTI I SOTRUDNICHESTVU V EVROPE [The USSR and the Conference on Security and Cooperation in Europe]. *Voprosy Istorii [USSR] 1976 (2): 3-21.* Highlights the diplomatic struggle around the All-European Conference on Security and Cooperation, beginning with the initiative displayed by the Soviet Union and the other socialist countries in 1966 in proposing the convocation of such a conference and ending with its proceedings and successful conclusion in 1975. Holding the conference marked the fulfillment of one of the paramount tasks formulated in the peace program mapped out by the 24th Congress of the CPSU. The steadily developing and deepening process of international detente is determined above all by the continuously growing might of the socialist world system, the active and constructive foreign policy steadfastly pursued by the USSR, and the other member countries of the socialist community, and the militant actions by the peace loving forces and the broadest segments of progressive minded people everywhere. The author draws attention to the fact that the struggle for peace and security in Europe and on the international arena is continuing unabated because the opponents of detente have neither laid down their arms nor abandoned their attempts to switch international relations back to the period of the Cold War. J

738. Stewart, Philip D.; Warhola, James W.; and Blough, Roger A. ISSUE SALIENCE AND FOREIGN POLICY ROLE SPECIALIZATION IN THE SOVIET POLITBURO OF THE 1970S. *Am. J. of Pol. Sci. 1984 28(1): 1-22.* Explores the roles played by individual members of the Soviet Politburo in the 1970's regarding the policy process and substance of foreign policy. The method employed is systematic, thematic content analysis of public speeches and writings by Politburo members. Three distinct patterns of foreign policy issue salience exist, and responsibility for the pursuit of each pattern is generally assumed by different segments of the leadership. The three patterns of issue salience are support for detente (Brezhnev, Gromyko, Ponomarev), support for national liberation movements and worldwide class struggle (Suslov, Ponomarev), and support for military and security issues (Andropov, Grechko, Ustinov). Although the findings indicate some degree of overlapping patterns of issue support, the evidence also points to role differentiation such that leading spokesmen for each group appear to express contrasting images regarding the appropriate priorities, objectives, and content of Soviet foreign policy. The analysis also lends credence to the image of a leadership divided on basic issues, yet "settling" these conflicts through simultaneous pursuit of potentially conflicting policy lines by different groupings of elites. J

739. Suslov, I. KOLKHOZY V SISTEME NARODNOGO KHOZIAISTVA [Collective farms in the national economy]. *Voprosy Ekonomiki [USSR] 1982 (12): 23-29.* Examines the development of agriculture since the March 1965 Plenum of the Central Committee of the Communist Party of the Soviet Union, and lists the measures taken by collective farms to eliminate obstacles to the planned rate of production. Based on secondary sources; table, 2 notes.

740. Tabeev, F. A. BOR'BA ZA POVYSHENIE EFFEKTIVNOSTI PROMYSHLENNOGO PROIZVODSTVA V TATARII V SVETE RESHENII XXIV S'EZDA KPSS [The struggle for improv-

ing the effectiveness of industrial production in the Tatar Republic in light of the decisions of the XXIV Congress of the CPSU]. *Voprosy Istorii KPSS [USSR] 1975 (4): 17-31.* Concentrates on the Party's efforts in the Tatar Republic to improve the quantity and quality of industrial production, especially in the petroleum industry, 1971-75. Through the Party's leadership, science, education, rational administration, socialist competition, and popular initiative contributed to the desired increases in industrial production. Based on periodical literature, primarily *The Soviet Tatar Republic*; 30 notes. L. E. Holmes

741. Talan, A. H. PRO RUKH ZA KOMUNISTYCHNE STAVLENNIA DO PRATSI (1976-1980 RR.) [The Communist approach to work, 1976-80]. *Ukrains'kyi Istorychnyi Zhurnal [USSR] 1981 (3): 104-110.* Discusses the evolution of the socialist-communist approach to labor by the workers of the Soviet Union, and in particular in the Ukrainian SSR, and considers their approach as a vital contribution to Soviet socioeconomic development.

742. Tannenbaum, Aron G. SOVIET PARTY APPARATCHIKI ATTITUDES TOWARD CHANGE. *Comparative Pol. Studies 1976 9(1): 93-106.* Discusses Communist Party members' attitudes toward allowing industrial management a greater role in economic affairs and politics in the USSR, 1965-67.

743. Taratuta, V. N. O RABOTE S PARTIINYMI KADRAMI I PARTIINYM AKTIVOM V SOVREMENNYKH USLOVIIAKH [Work with Party cadres and the Party active in contemporary conditions]. *Voprosy Istorii KPSS [USSR] 1979 (1): 10-23.* Following the example set by V. I. Lenin and past congresses of the Communist Party of the Soviet Union, the Party continues efforts to improve the selection, training, and performance of its members. Based on Lenin's *Collected Works,* published speeches of Leonid Brezhnev, and Party periodical literature; 24 notes.
L. E. Holmes

744. Titarenko, S. L. MARKSISTSKO-LENINSKOE UCHENIE O PARTII I EGO DAL'NEISHEE RAZVITIE V SOVREMENNYKH USLOVIIAKH [Marxist-Leninist teaching about the Party and its further development in contemporary conditions]. *Voprosy Istorii KPSS [USSR] 1965 (9): 87-98.* A guide for Soviet teachers on conducting seminars on the subject of Marxist-Leninist teachings about the role of the Communist Party, applying these concepts to modern conditions.

745. Tomilin, Iu. NERASPROSTRANENIE IADERNOGO ORUZHIIA—VELENIE VREMENI [Nuclear nonproliferation—the dictates of an epoch]. *Mirovaia Ekonomika i Mezhdunarodnye Otnosheniia [USSR] 1980 (12): 48-56.* Discusses the efforts of the USSR and other socialist countries to neutralize the menace of spreading nuclear arms since the Nuclear Nonproliferation Treaty (1968), analyzing the results of the second nonproliferation treaty review conference, the dangers emerging from military nuclear programs in Israel and South Africa, and the problem of the conclusion of a treaty on complete and general prohibition of nuclear weapons tests.

746. Tomilin, Iu. RAZORUZHENIE—KLIUCHEVAIA PROBLEMA MIROVOI POLITIKI [Disarmament: a key problem of world politics]. *Mirovaia Ekonomika i Mezhdunarodnye Otnosheniia [USSR] 1977 (2): 3-13.* At its 24th and 25th Congresses the Soviet Communist Party made numerous appeals for the renunciation of the "utilization of force in solving conflicts in international relations"; the UN has adopted several proposals directed at improving international relations put forth by the USSR.

747. Trukhanovski, V. G. PROGRAMMA MIRA: GENEZIS I REALIZATSIIA [The peace program: its origin and realization]. *Istoriia SSSR [USSR] 1976 (1): 3-33.* Reviews the efforts made by the USSR to realize the peace program adopted at the 24th Congress of the Communist Party of the Soviet Union in 1971. During the past five years, the leaders of the Communist Party and the Soviet state have worked tirelessly in both bilateral negotiations and international conferences on arms control and disarmament to promote the cause of detente and peaceful coexistence. Although these efforts have encountered opposition from elements in some capitalist countries and from the leadership of China, the USSR will continue to work for the strengthening and development of detente. Primary and secondary sources; 56 notes. J. W. Long

748. Trukhanovski, Vladimir G. PROGRAM POKOJU: OPRACOWANIE, ROZWÓJ I PIERWSZE WYNIKI REALIZACJI [Peace program: conceptions, development, and first results]. *Kwartalnik Hist. [Poland] 1977 84(4): 1071-1088.* Discusses the Soviet Communist Party's foreign policy program, prepared at the 24th Congress and further developed at the 25th Congress. Presents the attempts of the Soviet bloc to introduce it and analyzes the closing act of the Helsinki Conference characterizing contemporary international relations and the attitudes of the opponents and adherents of the program. 13 notes. H. Heitzman-Wojcicka

749. Tsaliuk, M. Ia. and Klymenko, P. P. SIL'S'KE BUDIVNYTSTVO—VAZHLYVA SKLADOVA CHASTYNA AHRARNOI POLITYKY PARTII [Agricultural construction: an important component of the Party's agrarian policy]. *Ukrains'kyi Istorychnyi Zhurnal [USSR] 1981 (1): 33-42.* Discusses Communist Party and government policies and work on the establishment and development of agriculture as an important component of general Party policy, 1965-80. Based on works by Marx, Lenin, and Brezhnev and Party and government documents; 60 notes.
I. Krushelnyckyj

750. Tsekhmistro, N. Ia. ZMITSNENNIA BRATERSKOHO SPIVROBITNYTSVA TRUDIASHCHYKH RRFSR I URSR V KHODI SOTSIALISTYCHNOHO ZMAHANNIA V ROKY VOSMOI PIATYRICHKY [Strengthening fraternal cooperation between the working people of the RSFSR and the Ukraine during socialist competition in the 8th Five-Year Plan]. *Ukrains'kyi Istorychnyi Zhurnal [USSR] 1982 (9): 15-23.* During the period of mature socialism the development and improvement of economic cooperation among fraternal republics has taken place, particularly in socialist competition. Opportunities for this movement were initiated by the September 1965 plenary session of the Communist Party Central Committee, which decided upon a new approach to organizing such activities, especially between the working collectives of different republics. Numerous initiatives and innovations in the Ukraine were emulated by plants in other republics. This constructive labor rivalry has become intense between industrial plants of the Russian Federation and the Ukraine. V. Bender

751. Tuvaiev, V. I.; Hus'kevych, B. O.; and Ivanova, V. O. KRYTYKA SUCHASNYKH REVIZIONISTS'KYKH PEREKRUCHEN' LENINS'KOHO VCHENNIA PRO PARTIIU [A criticism of contemporary revisionist distortions of Lenin's teachings about the Party]. *Ukrains'kyi Istorychnyi Zhurnal [USSR] 1973 (2): 26-34.* Reviews works of various foreign revisionists who cast doubt on the Soviet Communist Party and Marxism-Leninism as a basis for a Communist state, correcting their vision of revolution, in accordance with the directives of the 24th Party Congress (1971).

752. Upadyshev, A. N. DEIATEL'NOST' LENINGRADSKOI OBLASTNOI PARTIINOI ORGANIZATSII PO PEREVODU OBSHCHESTVENNOGO ZHIVOTNOVODSTVA NA PROMYSHLENNUIU OSNOVU (1965-1970) [The activities of the Leningrad regional Party organization toward industrialization of cattle-breeding on collective farms, 1965-70]. *Vestnik Leningradskogo U.: Seriia Istorii, Iazyka, i Literatury [USSR] 1976 (14): 24-31.* The Communist Party organization emphasized the necessity of putting cattle-breeding on a scientific, highly mechanized, efficient basis. Such policies resulted in vastly increased productivity. 29 notes.
G. F. Jewsbury

753. Urban, Joan Barth. CONTEMPORARY SOVIET PERSPECTIVES ON REVOLUTION IN THE WEST. *Orbis 1976 19(4): 1359-1402.* Although Salvador Allende's accession to the presidency of Chile in 1970 took the USSR by surprise, his victory did serve to "set in motion a broad-gauged re-evaluation of revolutionary prospects in the West." This process is an on-going one although not as noisy as before, and there are indications "that the silencing of the revolutionary viewpoint triggered a top-level party fight cul-

minating in the ouster of Politburo member Alexander Shelepin in April 1975." Soviet leaders have drawn certain and very definite parameters to control Soviet public differences regarding revolution in Western nations. 132 notes. A. N. Garland

754. Usenko, E. INTERNATIONAL LEGAL PRINCIPLES OF RELATIONS BETWEEN SOCIALIST COUNTRIES. *Int. Affairs [USSR] 1973 (8): 46-52.* Discusses the attempt to apply Marxist-Leninist ideology to international law and to Soviet foreign relations with communist countries, 1969-70's.

755. Val'chuk, B. A. VNUTRIPARTIINA ROBOTA PARTORHANIZATSIINA PROMYSLOVYKH PIDPRYIEMSTVAKH URSR (1966-1970 RR) [Internal Party work by Party organizations in industry in the USSR, 1966-70]. *Ukrains'kyi Istorychnyi Zhurnal [USSR] 1973 (8): 81-85.* Discusses sources emanating from the 23d and 24th Communist Party Congresses of 1966 and 1971 respectively in the Ukraine especially on the subject of the organization of labor.

756. Valerov, V. A. PARTIINOE RUKOVODSTVO PERSPEKTIVNYM PLANIROVANIEM IDEINO-POLITICHESKOGO VOSPITANIIA STUDENCHESTVA (NA MATERIALAKH LENINGRADSKIKH VUZOV 1966-1971) [Party leadership in the planning of the ideological-political education of students (based on materials from Leningrad higher schools, 1966-71)]. *Vestnik Leningradskogo Universiteta [USSR] 1974 (8): 29-36.* The 23rd congress of the Communist Party of the Soviet Union commanded Party organizations among institutions of higher learning in Leningrad to upgrade ideological-political education. The previous programs lacked coordination and duplicated work. Inefficient use was made of the Komsomol groups and other youth affiliated organizations. The 24th congress noted the educational improvements. 12 notes. G. F. Jewsbury

757. Vinogradov, I. I. DEIATEL'NOST' LENINGRADSKOI PARTIINOI ORGANIZATSII PO RAZVITIIU SHEFSKOI POMOSHCHI GORODA SELU (1966-1970 gg.) [The Leningrad party organization's activity in developing the guiding role of the city toward the countryside, 1966-70]. *Vestnik Leningradskogo Universiteta [USSR] 1973 14: 13-20.* Following Leninist principles, the Communist Party continually encourages the close interaction of the city with the countryside, of the proletariat with the peasantry. From 1966 to 1970 the Leningrad working class directed special efforts toward the countryside to increase production, improve political education, and enhance cultural development. Major advances were made in all areas. 24 notes. G. F. Jewsbury

758. Vinogradov, N. N. VOPROSY PARTIINOGO RUKOVODSTVA SOVETAMI V SOVREMENNOI ISTORIOGRAFII [Questions of Party leadership of the Soviets in contemporary historiography]. *Voprosy Istorii KPSS [USSR] 1982 (3): 110-120.* Many books and studies deal with the Communist Party of the Soviet Union (CPSU) and its leading role in Soviet society, which began with the Great October Socialist Revolution in 1917. *The CPSU in the Resolutions and Decisions of Congresses, Conferences, and Plenums of the Central Committee* and the works of L. I. Brezhnev, Iu. V. Andropov, A. A. Gromyko, and K. Chernenko are basic reading, as are B. N. Morozov on Leninist theory and F. M. Burlatski on Soviet leadership. All deal with central planning, agriculture, education, and Party control in town and village, where Party workers check the people's reactions to each Party decision. 40 notes. A. J. Evans

759. Volkov, I. M. and Vyltsan, M. A. SOVETSKAIA DEREVNIA NA SOVREMENNOM ETAPE: NEKOTORY ITOGI I ZADACHI ISSLEDOVANIIA [The soviet countryside in its modern phase: some results of and aims for research]. *Istoriia SSSR [USSR] 1979 (2): 3-19.* Sums up research on the history of the soviet countryside since the March 1965 plenary at the 22d Party congress and draws the attention of investigators to insufficiently studied problems such as the formulation of current agricultural policy, with special attention to the role of the Communist Party. The effect of the scientific revolution on farming is a relatively new area for research. The population in the countryside has been the subject of many books, pamphlets, and articles. Their psychological and material situation deserves as much in-depth study as agricultural production. 73 notes. L. J. Feintuck

760. Voronina, H. I. DIIALNIST' KPRS PO ZMITSNENNIU TVORCHYKH ZVIAZKIV VCHENYKH BRATNIKH RESPUBLIK [The work of the Communist Party of the Soviet Union among scientists of the fraternal republics]. *Ukraïns'kyi Istorychnyi Zhurnal [USSR] 1979 (5): 79-86.* Reviews the Party's activities to establish stronger ties between science and production through cooperation agreements between research establishments and enterprises.

761. Vorozheikin, I. E. XXIV S'EZD KPSS I DAL'NEISHEE RAZVITIE NARODNOGO OBRAZOVANIIA [The 24th Party congress and the subsequent development of public education]. *Voprosy istorii KPSS [USSR] 1973 (5): 24-38.* Under the direction of the Communist Party, public education in the USSR continues to meet the needs of society and the individual. Since the 24th Party congress 10 years of primary and secondary schooling has become universal, vocational institutions and universities have trained needed specialists, night and correspondence course offerings have increased, and updated curricula, texts, and methods have been introduced. Based on published and recent newspaper reports; 50 notes. L. E. Holmes

762. Wolodarski, L. DER XXIV PARTEITAG DER KPDSU: EIN WICHTIGER SCHRITT AUF DEM WEGE ZUM KOMMUNISMUS [The 24th party congress of the CPSU: an important step on the road to communism]. *Dokumentation der Zeit [East Germany] 1971 (14): 3-7.* Discusses the 24th party congress in Moscow (1971), outlining its resolutions on economic problems, the anti-imperialist struggle for peace, the development of the united socialist system, and continuing solidarity with the working class of capitalist countries. G. E. Pergl

763. Wysozki, V. DER XXIV. PARTEITAG DER KPDSU UND DIE PROBLEME DER EUROPÄISCHEN SICHERHEIT [The 24th Party Congress of the CPSU and the problems of European security]. *Dokumentation der Zeit [East Germany] 1971 (12): 3-10.* Discusses the meaning and the resolution of the 24th Communist Party Congress in Moscow (March-April 1971). Stresses that Europe has experienced its longest period of peace, 1945-70's, yet the struggle for peaceful coexistence presents a difficult task. The resolutions of the 24th Congress presented concrete actions toward a durable peace. 32 notes. G. E. Pergl

764. Zaborov, M. A. ISTORIIA MEZHDUNARODNOGO RABOCHEGO I KOMMUNISTICHESKOGO DVIZHENIIA [A history of the international working-class and Communist movement: a brief survey of Soviet literature]. *Voprosy Istorii [USSR] 1978 (6): 41-57.* Systematizes up-to-date Soviet literature (monographs and collections of articles) according to the more conspicuous dominant trends in the history of the class struggle of the international proletariat in modern times: the working class as a social category, its socioeconomic and political struggle at the different stages of capitalism's development, the trade union movement. The Social Democratic and Communist parties, their international organizations, the crucial events in the destinies of the international working-class and Communist movement (the Paris Commune of 1871, the three Russian revolutions, 1905-1917) and proletarian internationalism. The consistent application of the principle of historicism by Soviet scientists, with due attention being given to the theoretical aspect of the question, the systematic broadening and deepening of the themes—all this is bound to help the working class to realize more clearly the various aspects of the process of fulfilling its world-historic mission. J

765. Zabortseva, L. P. SOVERSHENSTVOVANIE SISTEMY POLITICHESKOGO OBRAZOVANIIA KOMI OBLASTNOI PARTIINOI ORGANIZATSIEI V PERIOD MEZHDU XXIII I XXIV S'EZDAMI KPSS [The perfection of the political education system of the Komi ASSR Party organization between the 23d and 24th Soviet Communist Party Congresses]. *Vestnik Leningradskogo U.: Seriia Istorii, Iazyka i Literatury [USSR] 1978 (4): 123-126.*

Describes the effects of the reform of the propaganda system, 1965-66, in the Komi ASSR and discusses the successful results achieved. The educational level of the Party workers has been raised and propaganda work intensified. Archive and primary sources; 13 notes. E. R. Sicher

766. Zadorozhnaia, L. A. DEIATEL'NOST' POSTOIANNYKH KOMISSII SOVETOV NARODNYKH DEPUTATOV LENINGRADA V GODY 9-I PIATILETKI [The activity of the permanent committees of the Leningrad Councils of People's Deputies during the 9th Five-Year Plan]. *Vestnik Leningradskogo U.: Seriia Istorii, Iazyka i Literatury [USSR] 1982 (2): 105-109.* Between 1971 and 1974 the Leningrad Communist Party organization sought to increase the role of the Councils of People's Deputies by deepening and extending the work of their committees and having them focus their attention on the priority areas of the economy and culture and on the question of raising living standards. During the 9th Five-Year Plan the number of deputies engaged in committee work increased and Communist members such as A. A. Laktiushkin provided able leadership. The extension of the committees' rights in the field of economic, social, and cultural construction has helped to increase their influence on the operation of enterprises, economic organizations, and the service sector. Secondary sources; 28 notes. G. Dombrovski

767. Zagladin, V. V. NA NOVOM ISTORICHESKOM ETAPE (K PIATILETIIU MEZHDUNARODNOGO SOVESHCHANIIA KOMMUNISTICHESKIKH I RABOCHIKH PARTII 1969 G.) [At a new historical stage (toward the fifth anniversary of the International Conference of Communist and Workers Parties, 1969)]. *Voprosy Istorii KPSS [USSR] 1974 (6): 3-20.* The International Conference of Communist and Workers Parties held in Moscow in 1969 assisted the cause of world communism and peace. In particular, it contributed to the struggle against opportunism, the convergence theory, and the escalating anti-Communist campaign of rightist groups in this period of detente. Based on international communist periodical literature; 10 notes. L. E. Holmes

768. Zairov, Sh. Sh. VKLAD KOMSOMOLU UKRAINY V LIKVIDATSIIU NASLIDKIV TASHKENTSKOHO ZEMLETRUSU: 1966-68 [The Ukrainian Komsomol's contribution to the elimination of the consequences of the Tashkent earthquake, 1966-68]. *Ukrains'kyi Istorychnyi Zhurnal [USSR] 1982 (9): 57-61.* The earthquake of 1966 destroyed in Tashkent 2 million square meters of housing, leaving 100,000 families homeless. To help the city, all union republics undertook to form 35 special construction trains, 10 of which originated in the Ukraine. By 1967, nearly 5,100 construction workers from the Ukraine were engaged in reconstructing the city, 75% of this workforce belonging to the Communist Youth League (Komsomol). V. Bender

769. Zaretski, Iu. I. DEIATEL'NOST' PARTIINYKH ORGANIZATSII PO POVYSHENIIU OBSHESTVENNO-POLITICHESKOI AKTIVNOSTI SEL'SKOI INTELLIGENTSII (1966-1970 GG.) [Party organization activity in the increased social and political activity of the village intelligentsia, 1966-70]. *Voprosy Istorii KPSS [USSR] 1980 (9): 50-61.* The Communist Party of the Soviet Union (CPSU) always attached great importance to cultural as well as professional development of the rural intelligentsia, but a qualitatively new era began in March 1965 after a plenary session of the Central Committee. The experiences of the Party organizations of the Russian Republic (RSFSR) in implementing the program of intensifying the social and political activities of the village intelligentsia are discussed. The overall aim of the Party is to minimize cultural differences between towns and villages. 48 notes. V. Sobell

770. —. DOKUMENTATION. ZUM 100. GEBURTSTAG WLADIMIR ILJITSCH LENINS [Documentation on the 100th birthday of Vladimir Il'ich Lenin]. *Zeitschrift für Geschichtswissenschaft [East Germany] 1970 18(3): 366-402.* Includes 21 theses on the political works of V. I. Lenin by the Central Committee of the Communist Party of the Soviet Union.

771. —. DOKUMENTY I STAT'I PO ISTORII KPSS I MEZHDUNARODNOGO KOMMUNISTICHESKOGO I RABOCHEGO DVIZHENIA, OPUBLIKOVANNYE V ZHURNALAKH, UCHENYKH ZAPISKAKH, SBORNIKAKH I TRUDAKH [Documents and articles on the history of the Soviet Communist Party and the international Communist and labor movement, published in journals, scientific notes, collections, and works]. *Voprosy Istorii KPSS [USSR] 1978 (11): 144-149.* Selects the most important Soviet and foreign publications of 1978 concerning the Communist Party of the USSR and the international Communist and Labor movement.

772. —. A GENERAL "POGROM." *Ukrainian Rev. [Great Britain] 1976 22(3): 59-84.* Examines the course taken in the Ukraine in the 1970's by the Communist Party of the USSR, including the policy of Russification, the purge of Party cadres in the Ukrainian Communist Party, the prohibition of Ukrainian culture and science, the persecution of the local intelligentsia and Christians, and the destruction of Ukrainian national monuments and churches.

773. —. K 20-LETIIU VELIKOI POBEDY (V NAUCHNYKH KOLLEKTIVAKH ISTORIKOV PARTII) [On the 20th anniversary of the great victory: in the scientific collectives of Party historians]. *Voprosy Istorii KPSS [USSR] 1965 (5): 147-152.* Lists six separate celebrations of the 20th anniversary of the Soviet victory in World War II in institutions where historians of the Communist Party of the Soviet Union are active.

774. —. LENINSKII KURS XXIV S'EZDA KPSS V DEISTVII [The Leninist course of the XXIV Congress of the CPSU in action]. *Voprosy Istorii KPSS [USSR] 1974 (8): 3-20.* The fourth volume of *The Leninist Course* (Moscow, 1974) contains speeches and articles by Leonid Brezhnev for the period from June 1972 to March 1974. Brezhnev focuses on the history, theory, and policies of the Communist Party and on issues germane to the economic, scientific, educational, cultural, and international objectives and achievements of the Soviet Union. Based on the fourth volume of Leonid Brezhnev's *Leninskii kurs* (1974); 48 notes. L. E. Holmes

775. —. NAUCHNYI SOVET GLAVARKHIVA SSSR, POSVIASHCHENNYI 60-LETIIU VELIKOI OKTIABR'SKOI SOTSIALISTICHESKOI REVOLIUTSII [The meeting of the Soviet Archive Control Office's scientific board dedicated to the 60th anniversary of the Great October Revolution]. *Sovetskie Arkhivy [USSR] 1978 (1): 59-64.* Describes a special meeting of the board of the organization responsible for overseeing all state archives in the USSR, held on 23 November 1977 in commemoration of the October Revolution; it was decided that one of the principal tasks of Soviet archive keepers is to help propagandize the achievements of communist construction.

776. —. [PARTY MEMBERSHIP UNDER BREZHNEV].

Rigby, T. H. SOVIET PARTY MEMBERSHIP UNDER BREZHNEV. *Soviet Studies [Great Britain] 1976 28(3): 317-337.* By 1964 the Communist Party of the USSR faced the problem of a party enlarged to fullfil its various roles, yet suffering erosion of its status and authority because of its broad membership. During 1965-76 Leonid Brezhnev's regime instituted policies to limit party growth in line with population increases, to avoid fluctuations through maintenance of "trauma-free conditions," and to maintain recruitment of workers. The author concludes that persistence of these patterns will ensure unprecedented stability of party membership and a more precise adjustment of its composition to its functions than has been achieved previously. 7 tables, 38 notes.

Unger, Aryeh L. SOVIET PARTY MEMBERSHIP UNDER BREZHNEV: A COMMENT. *Soviet Studies [Great Britain] 1977 29(2): 306-316.* Adds comment on developments overlooked by T. H. Rigby. Net growth figures for the Communist Party of the USSR (CPSU) after 1964 show a marked decline, 1962-75; estimates suggest that more than half of the membership loss was due to deaths, and less than half to exclusions. The author discusses the composition of the Party, its "vanguard" role, and the significance of the increase of members with higher education, which does not indicate an intention to proletarianize the CPSU. Unlike Rigby, the author does not believe that the CPSU is solving its membership problems, but still "faces the fundamental dilemma of a ruling party which also aspires to the image of a proletarian vanguard." 4 tables, 16 notes.

Rigby, T. H. SOVIET PARTY MEMBERSHIP UNDER BREZHNEV: A REJOINDER. *Soviet Studies [Great Britain] 1977 29(3): 452-453.* Increase in CPSU members with higher educational qualifications can be explained by the growth of young industrial workers with specialist training, a target group for recruitment, and the upgrading of qualifications of persons already in the Party. The author otherwise agrees with Unger's emphasis on the internal determinants of CPSU recruitment policy and on anticipation of a relatively high recruitment rate in the near future. 3 notes. D. H. Murdoch

777. —. PID PRAPOROM LENINSKOI DRUZHBY NARODIV (DO VYKHODU V SVIT KNYHY V. V. SHCHERBYTSK'KOHO "IZBRANN'IEE RECHI I STAT'I") [Under the flag of the Leninist friendship of nations: a preview of V. V. Shcherbitski's *Collected materials and articles]. Ukraïns'kyi Istorychnyi Zhurnal [USSR] 1979 (2): 15-21.* Comments on the increasing role played by the Communist Party, the Central Committee, and the Politburo in realizing Communism. From the forthcoming collected works of Ukrainian Communist Party First Secretary Vladimir Shcherbitski. L. Djakowska

778. —. [POLITICAL SCIENCE TEXTBOOKS ON THE SOVIET UNION]. *Studies in Comparative Communism 1975 8(3): 211-247.*

Tokes, Rudolf L. INTRODUCTION: COMPARATIVE COMMUNISM: THE ELUSIVE TARGET, *pp. 211-229.* Comparative studies of Communism in the United States have relied too much on the behavioristic approach that is popular among students of American politics. They consequently have ignored the character of communism. However, individual scholarly monographs have been excellent. 28 notes.

Hoffman, Erik P. THE SOVIET UNION: CONSENSUS OR DEBATE? *pp. 230-244.* Textbooks on the politics of the Soviet Union lack new theoretical approaches to the subject. No particular approach is indispensable although each has a special emphasis: economic and social policies, political culture, or socialization. R. Medvedev's *On Socialist Democracy* (New York, 1975) is the best study of Soviet politics because it combines new evidence with a definite point of view. 19 notes.

Dallin, A. COMMENT, *pp. 245-247.* Textbooks in fact differ on important questions such as whether communism is influenced by Russian history, whether a developmental or mobilization model is most apt for the USSR, whether there has been continuity or change in the Soviet era, whether pluralism exists, and whether Stalinism was an aberration. D. Balmuth

779. —. XXV SEZD KPSS I ZADACHI IZUCHENIIA PROBLEM NATSIONAL'NO-OSVOBODITEL'NYKH REVOLUTSII [The 25th Party Congress of the Communist Party of the Soviet Union and the problems of study dealing with the national liberation revolutions]. *Narody Azii i Afriki [USSR] 1976 (2): 1-8.* An important link in the world revolutionary process is the national liberation movements. The 25th Party Congress paid serious attention to the analysis of changes that are taking place in the internal affairs of the developing nations and in their foreign policies. The first half of the 1970's is the concluding stage of destruction of the colonial system, the crash of the last colonial empire, that is, Portugal's. In his report, Leonid Brezhnev found the following progressive tendencies to be occurring in the liberated countries: the switch to state development of industry, liquidation of feudal land ownership, nationalization of foreign enterprises in order to establish effective sovereignty over national resources, and the formation of national cadres. Primary sources. L. Kalinowski

780. —. THE 24TH CONGRESS OF THE COMMUNIST PARTY OF THE SOVIET UNION. *New World Rev. 1971 39(3): 3-192.* Presents texts of reports and speeches made at the 24th Congress of the Communist Party of the USSR and summarizes the meaning of the Congress.

1982-1985

781. Babakov, A. A. RUKOVODSTVO KPSS STROITEL'STVOM VOORUZHENNYKH SIL SSSR V SOVREMENNYKH USLOVIIAKH [The directing role of the Soviet Communist Party over the formation of the armed forces in modern conditions]. *Voprosy Istorii KPSS [USSR] 1984 (5): 107-121.* Since 1978 the tensions between capitalism and socialism have increased. The Soviet Communist Party, though trying to maintain world peace, maintains defenses adequate to protect the USSR. The Party provides the Soviet military with all necessary weaponry. It trains young people to defend the USSR. It educates Soviet youth in Soviet patriotism and proletarian internationalism. Soviet young people consider the defense of the USSR to be a duty and an honor. Thus the Party and military cooperate. Based on the speeches of Chernenko and Ustinov; 66 notes. A. J. Evans

782. Beichman, Arnold and Bernstam, Mikhail S. *Andropov: New Challenge to the West; a Political Biography.* New York: Stein & Day, 1983. 255 pp.

783. Chernenko, A. M. and Ahapov, P. V. Z DOSVIDU PIDHOTOVKY NAUKOVO-PEDAHOHICHNYKH KADRIV Z ISTORII KPRS [The preparation of educated cadres in the history of the Communist Party of the Soviet Union (CPSU)]. *Ukrains'kyi Istorychnyi Zhurnal [USSR] 1982 (3): 128-131.* Discusses procedures and guidelines of the faculty of history at the University of Dnepropetrovsk in the selection of students in the history of the CPSU. 3 notes. N. M. Diuk

784. Karaliun, V. Iu. RESHENIIA MAISKOGO (1982 G.) PLENUMA TSK KPSS I RAZRABOTKA PROBLEM TEORII I ISTORII RAZVITIIA AGRARNO-PROMYSHLENNYKH OTNOSHENII [Decisions of the May 1982 Plenary Session of the Central Committee of the Communist Party of the Soviet Union and elaboration of the problems of theory and history of the development of agrarian-industrial relations]. *Latvijas PSR Zinātņu Akad. Vēstis [USSR] 1982 (11): 63-74.* Discusses problems connected with the integration of agricultural and industrial production under a socialist system and recent decisions of the Communist Party in order to improve the manufacture of farm machinery and to enchance the exchange of produce between urban and rural communities. Primary sources; 3 charts, 29 notes. R. Vilums

785. McCauley, Martin. A CHANGE OF GUARD AT THE KREMLIN: FROM ANDROPOV TO CHERNENKO. *Soviet Jewish Affairs [Great Britain] 1984 14(2): 3-17.* Reviews the succession of political leadership in the USSR and the process by which Konstantin Chernenko replaced Yuri Andropov as head of the Communist Party, focusing on its implications for Soviet Jews.

786. Schneider, Eberhard. JURIJ WLADIMIROWITSCH ANDROPOW [Yuri Vladimirovich Andropov]. *Osteuropa [West Germany] 1983 33(3-4): 194-200.* Describes Yuri Andropov's life and the phases of his activity in the Communist Party.

787. Zlobin, V. I. VELIKII PODVIG (K 80-LETIIU VTOROGO S''EZDA RSDRP) [A great exploit: 80th anniversary of the 2d Congress of the Russian Social Democratic Workers' Party]. *Vestnik Moskovskogo U. Seriia 8: Istoriia [USSR] 1983 (3): 3-12.* The role of the Party has grown and it now is made up of 43.4% industrial workers, 12.8% peasants, and 43.8% service workers. Women are now 25% of the Party's members. The yearly growth of new members is now about 360,000. 33 notes. D. Balmuth

788. Zlotnik, Marc D. CHERNENKO SUCCEEDS. *Problems of Communism 1984 33(2): 17-31.* The selection of Konstantin Chernenko to succeed Yuri Andropov as general secretary of the Soviet Communist Party proceeded amidst unusual signs of division in the Soviet leadership between the Brezhnev group and those promoted by Andropov. This indicates a transitional and weak rule, unless Chernenko is able to surmount this division and work with both factions to make important and needed changes. Based on Soviet periodical publications, primarily *Pravda;* 104 notes.
J. M. Lauber

789. —. NESGIBAEMYI BORETS ZA KOMMUNISTICHESKIE IDEALY [The unflagging fighter for Communist ideals]. *Voprosy Istorii KPSS [USSR] 1984 (6): 3-17.* Obituary of Yuri Andropov (1914-84), First Secretary of the Soviet Communist Party since 1982. First elected to the Central Committee in 1951, he spent the subsequent few years (1954-57) as USSR's ambassador to Hungary. Having headed the KGB between 1967-73, he became a member of the Politburo in 1973. 11 notes. M. Hernas

2. COMMUNISM IN EUROPE

General

790. Boggs, Carl. *The Impasse of European Communism.* Boulder, Colo.: Westview, 1982. 181 pp.

791. Byrnes, Robert F. THE CLIMAX OF STALINISM. *Ann. of the Am. Acad. of Pol. and Social Sci. 1958 (317): 8-11.* Josef Stalin succeeded in strengthening communism, 1950-53, by reshaping cultural values, developing heavy industry, promoting agricultural collectivism, and exploiting the entire area of Eastern Europe so as to place pressure on Tito and Western Europe.

792. Cohen, Gerry. COMMUNISTS AND THE LABOR MOVEMENT. *World Marxist R. [Canada] 1973 16(11): 98-107.* Discusses Communists' position and goals in British trade union and Labour Party politics.

793. Fögl, Hans-Jochen. P'IATDESIATA RICHNYTSIA ZASNUVANNIA KOMUNISTYCHNOI PARTII NIMECHCHYNY [The 50th anniversary of the formation of the German Communist Party]. *Ukrains'kyi Istorychnyi Zhurnal [USSR] 1968 (12): 14-23.* Outlines the history of the German Communist Party and its links with the Communist Party of the Soviet Union from its formation in December 1918 to its accession to power within East Germany. Indicates the continuing obligations of the Party to workers in West Germany.

794. Gerber, John Paul. "Anton Pannekoek and the Socialism of Workers' Self-Emancipation, 1873-1960." U. of Wisconsin, Madison 1984. 715 pp. *DAI 1984 45(5): 1495-A.* DA8414237

795. Gozzano, Francesco. RAPPORTI DELLA COMUNITÀ ECONOMICA EUROPEA COL MONDO SOCIALISTA [Relations between the European Economic Community and the socialist world]. *Problemi di Ulisse [Italy] 1974 12(77): 163-170.* The EEC went from the Cold War with socialist Europe to a general lack of initiative, 1961-69. West Germany's Willy Brandt launched a detente with the USSR in 1970, but the EEC remains limited since it has no alternative to NATO, its defense. It is too disunited to create its own defense policy to counterbalance the clout of the United States and USSR. C. Bates

796. Grabowski, Tadeusz. EWG JAKO PARTNER HANDLOWY KRAJÓW SOCJALISTYCZNYCH [The Common Market as a trade partner of the socialist bloc]. *Przegląd Zachodni [Poland] 1969 25(5): 1-25.* Examines economic relations, particularly trade between Western Europe and the Eastern bloc, 1949-57, and focuses on trends in exports from Communist countries to members of the European Economic Community, 1957-66.

797. Hotz, Robert. DIE OSTPOLITIK DES HEILIGEN STUHLS [The Holy See's eastern policy]. *Civitas [Switzerland] 1980 35(9-10): 320-335.* Contemplates the diplomatic entanglements between the Communist countries in Eastern Europe and the Vatican, in its attempts to further the interests of the Catholic Church in these countries.

798. Hüfner, Klaus. DIE FREIWILLIGEN FINANZLEISTUNGEN AN DAS VN-SYSTEM [Voluntary financial contributions to the UN system]. *German Yearbook of International Law [West Germany] 1983 26: 299-342.* Surveys varying levels of financial support for seven UN organs and programs, focusing on the disproportionately large contributions of West Germany, Scandinavia, and the Netherlands and on the disproportionately small contributions of the Eastern European Communist countries.

799. Jaśica, Roman. ZACHODNIONIEMIECKA USTAWA O WYPĘDZONYCH I UCIEKINIERACH A PROGRAM NORMALIZACJI STOSUNKOW MIĘDZY PRL I RFN [The West German Expelled and Refugees Act and the question of normalizing relations between Poland and West Germany]. *Państwo i Prawo [Poland] 1974 29(3): 59-67.* The Expelled and Refugees Act (1953) has incited hatred against Communist countries, particularly Poland and the USSR, and until it is repealed relations between Poland and West Germany cannot be normalized.

800. Jelisejew, M. G. ZUR FRAGE DER IDEOLOGISCHEN DIVERSION UND DER PRAXIS DES KAMPFES DES IMPERIALISMUS IN DER BRD GEGEN DIE DDR [The question of the ideological diversion and the imperialist West German struggle against East Germany]. *Wissenschaftliche Zeitschrift der Friedrich-Schiller-U. Jena. Gesellschafts- und Sprachwissenschaftliche Reihe [East Germany] 1971 20(6): 77-92.* Analyzes the impact of the West German Hallstein Doctrine on the development of East German foreign relations and the political cooperation of the West German Christian Democratic Union (CDU) and Social Democratic Party (SPD) 1961-69. 81 notes.

801. Kanet, Roger E. OST-WEST-BEZIEHUNGEN [East-West relations]. *Osteuropa [West Germany] 1980 30(2): 161-167.* Reviews new English and American publications on detente, the Berlin Wall, West German *Ostpolitik,* the strategic relations between the United States and the Soviet Union, and the trading relations between the East and the West since 1945.

802. Kolbe, Hellmuth. ZU EINIGEN VERÄNDERUNGEN IM INHALT UND IN DEN FORMEN DES KAMPFES DER ARBEITERKLASSE GEGEN DAS STAATSMONOPOLISTISCHE SYSTEM [Some changes in the substance and forms of the working-class struggle against the state monopoly system]. *Beiträge zur Geschichte der Arbeiterbewegung [East Germany] 1975 17(3): 402-413.* In recent years socialist countries have shown stable economic growth, while economic crises have beset capitalist countries. In capitalist and developing capitalist countries the working class has expressed its dissatisfaction through strikes. Even fascist Spain has been affected. These actions have strengthened the working-class movement because they have been uniquely worker-caused and directed at the basic capitalist structure. They have been the concrete expression which Lenin knew was the most important step for communism in Western Europe and the Americas. Table, 27 notes.
G. H. Libbey

803. Kousoulas, D. George. THE TRUMAN DOCTRINE AND THE STALIN-TITO RIFT: A REAPPRAISAL. *South Atlantic Q. 1973 72(3): 427-439.* The prevailing view in the West was, and still is, that the Communist guerrilla campaign unleashed in Greece in 1946 was merely part of a Soviet plan to extend Moscow's control to the shores of the eastern Mediterranean. However, the evidence now indicates that Joseph Stalin did not favor another round of armed conflict initiated by the Communist Party in Greece. Josip Tito supported Communist operations in Greece in accordance with traditional cooperation between Athens and Belgrade. "A friendly government in Greece appeared to be almost a matter of survival for Tito's regime. The Truman Doctrine with its prospect of American presence in Greece made Stalin concerned with Tito's adventure. Stalin's effort however to split the Central Committee failed, most of the members siding with Tito. The American Government offered economic assistance in ways that would not compromise Tito." E. P. Stickney

804. Kramer, John M. THE VATICAN'S *OSTPOLITIK. Rev. of Pol. 1980 42(3): 283-308.* Since 1960 the Vatican has utilized a variety of policies to achieve at least limited religious freedom in the Communist countries. The Communist governments have made concessions to the Vatican when it has been politically convenient. Giv-

en the internal problems facing the USSR, the ascendency of the Polish-born John Paul II to the Papacy at this time may be most propitious for the Catholic Church. Table, 64 notes.
L. E. Ziewacz

805. Lacoste, Raymond. LA DÉPOSITION DU CARDINAL MINDSZENTY ET L'OSTPOLITIK DU VATICAN [The deposing of Cardinal Mindszenty and the "Ostpolitik" of the Vatican]. *Écrits de Paris [France] 1974 (334): 17-28.* Raises objections to the deposing of Cardinal Josef Mindszenty by Pope Pius VI in 1974 and criticizes the Vatican for its policy of accommodation toward the Communist countries.

806. Lombardo Radice, Lucio. ERNST FISCHER NEL MARXISMO EUROPEO [Ernst Fischer and European Marxism]. *Ponte [Italy] 1973 29(2-3): 228-247.* Outlines the life and thought of Ernst Fischer (1899-1972), the Austrian Communist leader who broke with the Communist Party over the Soviet invasion of Czechoslovakia, and who can be considered a Marxist, but not a Marxist-Leninist.

807. Mitev, Dimiter. ZA STRATEGIATA I TAKTIKATA NA SUVREMENNOTO KOMUNISTICHESKO DVIZHENIE [The strategy and tactics of the contemporary Communist movement]. *Istoricheski Pregled [Bulgaria] 1962 18(1): 3-31.* Survey of the strategy of the Italian, French, Spanish, West German, Yugoslav, Greek, and Bulgarian Communist parties in organizing the masses for revolution since the first world war.

808. Pryor, Frederic L. THE DISTRIBUTION OF NONAGRICULTURAL LABOR INCOMES IN COMMUNIST AND CAPITALIST NATIONS. *Slavic Rev. 1972 31(3): 639-650.* A comparative statistical analysis of the distribution of nonagricultural labor incomes in communist and capitalist nations as a means of testing various, sometimes contradictory hypotheses regarding such distributions. The method used separates two major factors: labor-income differences in various branches of manufacturing and mining, and overall size distributions of nonagricultural labor incomes of full-time male workers. The author concludes that "labor incomes in the non-agricultural sector are more evenly distributed in Eastern Europe than in Western Europe, other things being equal. 2 tables, 15 notes, statistical appendix giving sources, comments, and regressions.
R. V. Ritter

809. Puja, Frigyes. THE POLITICAL SITUATION IN EUROPE TODAY. *New Hungarian Q. [Hungary] 1971 12(42): 23-36.* A communist view of contemporary European politics. Relative calm prevails, but only because the Communist bloc is so powerful that the capitalists fear further adventures. The primary problems created by World War II remain unsolved, particularly the German question. American imperialist policy is now planned and carried out on a worldwide scale. European stability is fragile, perhaps illusory; too much reliance should not be placed on it. Based on secondary sources.
V. L. Human.

810. Schebera, Jürgen. KOMMUNIST, PUBLIZIST, POLITIKER: GERHART EISLER [Communist, political writer, politician: Gerhart Eisler]. *Beiträge zur Gesch. der Arbeiterbewegung [East Germany] 1983 25(5): 724-736.* Traces the life, career, political and journalistic activities of the German political writer Gerhart Eisler (1897-1968). He was born in Leipzig, but his family moved to Vienna in 1901 and most of his education took place there. As a young man Eisler was deeply affected by the horrors of war and joined the Red Guard in Vienna in 1918. His journalistic career began in 1919 and in 1921 he went to Berlin to work as a political journalist for the German Communist Party (his sister was the Communist Ruth Fischer). His political activities continued, and in 1925 he became involved in the party's bureau of information. The author considers Eisler's career in the Communist Party, his extensive travels to the USSR, China, Sweden, Spain, France, and the United States. During World War II he worked as a political journalist in the United States and was imprisoned in 1948 for Communist activities and was deported to Germany in 1949. In Leipzig he continued his writings and political activities until his death in 1968. (See also other articles about Eisler in the US chapter, 1945-1965.) Secondary sources; 49 notes.
G. L. Neville

811. Schlesinger, Rudolph. OSSERVAZIONI SUI FONDAMENTI FILOSOFICI DELL'ESTREMISMO DI SINISTRA [Observations on the philosophical basis of leftist extremism]. *Annali dell'Istituto Giangiacomo Feltrinelli [Italy] 1972 14: 7-54.* Presents the philosophical approach to leftist thought as opposed to communism, notably in the ideology of the Soviet Communist Party. Centers on Dutch pamphleteer and political philosopher Herman Gorter (1864-1927), who replied to Lenin's *Left-Wing Communism: An Infantile Disorder.* His views led to the formation of the German Workers' Communist Party (KAPD) as an offshoot of the German Communist Party (KPD). The former African colonies are attracted by extremist communism. Secondary sources; 41 notes.
C. Bates

812. Seifert, O. DIE ENTWICKLUNG DER WISSENSCHAFTSBEZIEHUNGEN ZWISCHEN SOZIALISTISCHEN UND IMPERIALISTISCHEN STAATEN EUROPAS [The development of scientific relations between socialist and imperialist European states]. *Wissenschaftliche Zeitschrift der Karl-Marx U. Leipzig [East Germany] 1976 25(1): 67-72.* Scientific progress in the Soviet Union, Poland, and East Germany since the 1950's increased the interest of Swedish, French, West German, and American scientists in the exchange of technological know-how with their colleagues in Eastern Europe.
R. Wagnleitner

813. Stites, Richard. KOLLONTAI, INESSA, AND KRUPSKAIA: A REVIEW OF RECENT LITERATURE. *Can.-Am. Slavic Studies 1975 9(1): 84-92.* Review of Aleksandra Kollontai, *Izbrannye stat'i i rechi* (Moscow: Izdatel'stvo Politicheskoi literatury, 1972); Alexandra Kollontai, *The Autobiography of a Sexually Emancipated Communist Woman*, edited by Irving Fetscher, translated by Salvator Attanasio, foreword by Germaine Greer (New York: Herder and Herder, 1971); Alexandra Kollontai, *Sexual Relations and the Class Struggle; Love and the New Morality* translated with an introduction by Alix Holt (Bristol, England: Falling Wall Press, 1972); Polina S. Vinogradskaia, *Pamiatnye vstrechi* (Moscow: Sovetskaia Rossiia, 1972); and Robert H. McNeal, *Bride of the Revolution: Krupskaia and Lenin* (Ann Arbor: U. of Michigan Press, 1972). Based on published sources; 27 notes.
G. E. Munro

814. Sułek, Jerzy and Wojna, Ryszard. THE PROBLEM OF POLAND'S NATIONAL SECURITY AND RELATIONS BETWEEN THE POLISH PEOPLE'S REPUBLIC AND THE FEDERAL REPUBLIC OF GERMANY. *Polish Western Affairs [Poland] 1980 21(2): 165-183.* There is ample evidence that the primary political goal of West Germany is reunification with East Germany, a nation with which Poland and its socialist allies have worked out peaceful terms of coexistence. Such reunification would endanger Poland by recreating a German nation that has been hostile to Poland for a thousand years. In particular, Poland fears that a new, unified Germany would attempt to regain Polish territory east of the current Oder and Lusatian boundaries and upset the peace that now exists in Europe.
D. Powell

815. Terzuolo, Eric Robert. "Relations Between the Communist Parties of Italy and Yugoslavia, 1941-1960." Stanford U. 1980. 371 pp. *DAI 1980 41(5): 2255-2256-A.* 8024747

Eurocommunism

816. Amyot, Grant. *The Italian Communist Party.* New York: St. Martin's, 1981. 252 pp.

817. Antonian, Armen Bedros. "Eurocommunism, Eurogauche and the French Left." U. of California, Riverside 1983. 319 pp. *DAI 1984 44(7): 2231-2231-A.* DA8324899

818. Aspaturian, Vernon V.; Valenta, Jiri; and Burke, David P., ed. *Eurocommunism between East and West.* Bloomington: Indiana U. Pr., 1980. 373 pp.

819. Bernstein, Sarah and Lawrence, Stewart. EUROCOMMUNISM AS CURRENT EVENTS AND CONTEMPORARY HISTORY: A CRITICAL BIBLIOGRAPHY. *Radical Hist. Rev. 1980 (23): 165-190.* Survey of English-language works on Eurocommunism published during the late 1970's.

820. Birnbaum, Norman and Laqueur, Walter. EURO-COMMUNISM SYMPOSIUM. *Partisan Rev. 1979 46(1): 9-42.* Transcript of a 1977 discussion led by William Phillips at the Carnegie International Center, New York City. Walter Laqueur distrusted the Communist Parties of Western Europe for their Stalinist ways and their ties to the Soviet Union. Norman Birnbaum took the position that Eurocommunism might be a sincere development of the ultraleft to accommodate parliamentary democracy and the desire for an independent national culture and policies.
D. K. Pickens

821. Boffa, Giuseppe. 1956: ALCUNE PREMESSE DELL'"EUROCOMUNISMO" [1956: some antecedents of Eurocommunism]. *Studi Storici [Italy] 1976 17(4): 211-224.* The year 1956 was a watershed for world communism. At the 20th Congress of the Communist Party of the Soviet Union, Nikita Khrushchev denounced Joseph Stalin as a tyrant. In the fall, new liberal leaderships came to power in Poland and Hungary; the first retreated under Soviet pressure, the second was crushed with Soviet tanks. Seeing their erstwhile hero Stalin unmasked was a tremendous disillusionment to many Western Communists; the sight of the armies of the USSR repressing a people's revolution in Hungary caused more to lose faith in Soviet infallibility. In these disillusioning events, the seeds of Eurocommunism, with its acceptance of Western democracy and critical attitude toward Soviet dictatorship, were sown among the parties of Western Europe. 55 notes.
J. C. Billigmeier

822. Boggs, Carl. GRAMSCI AND EUROCOMMUNISM. *Radical Am. 1980 14(3): 7-24.* Antonio Gramsci (1891-1937) has been used (and misused) by some postwar leaders of the Left and particularly by the Eurocommunists since 1975 to validate a strategy of taking over capitalist institutions and gradual revolution. Gramsci recognized the possibilities of tactical working from within, but never lost sight of the strategic objective of the overthrow of bourgeois political institutions. Gramsci's work in the Italian Communist Party in the 1920's bears out this distinction from the present approach, which claims descent from his writings through Palmiro Togliatti. Drawn from the author's *Gramsci's Marxism;* 39 notes.
C. M. Hough

823. Brey, Thomas. ZU DEN GRUNDLAGEN DES EUROKOMMUNISMUS: DER JUGOSLAWISCHE MARXISMUS [The foundations of Eurocommunism: Yugoslavian Marxism]. *Donauraum [Austria] 1978 23(4): 125-153.* On the basis of presumed links between the Yugoslavian interpretation of Marx, Engels, and Lenin, and Eurocommunism, examines three points of contact which permit a deeper analysis of Marxist ideology in Yugoslavia. Describes the political situation directly after World War II, considers the genesis of Yugoslavia's move from capitalism to socialism, including the role of the state in this development, and discusses the growing rift since 1960 in Yugoslavian Marxism. Special attention is devoted to the conflict between party and socialist humanists after 1968-69. Secondary sources; 144 notes.
A. A. Strnad

824. Brunello, Anthony Raymond. "The Dilemmas of Deradicalization and Democracy in Western European Communist Parties: The Emergence of Eurocommunism in the 1970s in the Italian Case." U. of Oregon 1983. 308 pp. *DAI 1984 44(7): 2232-A.* DA8325257

825. Caccamo, Domenico. GLI EUROCOMUNISTI ITALIANI E IL PCUS [Italian Eurocommunists and the Communist Party of the USSR]. *Storia e Pol. [Italy] 1979 18(2): 215-241.* It was the Italian journalist Frane Barbieri who first spoke of Eurocommunism in June 1975, referring to resistance to the centralizing and authoritarian line of the Soviet Communist Party on the part of the Italian and Spanish parties. The most important differences between the Eurocommunists and the USSR centered on the Portuguese situation. The Italian Communist leader, Enrico Berlinguer, supported the Socialist Mario Soares more than the Communist Alvaro Cunhal, asserting the importance of "national ways" to communism. Based on secondary sources; 64 notes.
A. Canavero

826. Childs, David. EUROCOMMUNISM: ORIGINS AND PROBLEMS. *Contemporary Rev. [Great Britain] 1978 232(1344): 1-6, (1345): 66-71.* Part I. Discusses aspects of the development of Western European Communist Parties since 1918 and compares Communist support in different countries. Part II. Examines the support European Communist Parties have received since 1945 and influential events in the formulation of Eurocommunist strategies, 1956-77.

827. Colbert, James G., Jr. EUROCOMMUNISM AND THE ITALIAN MARXIST TRADITION. *Studies in Soviet Thought [Netherlands] 1982 23(3): 205-228.* Views Eurocommunism as a theory. Discusses leftist and socialist reservations and Catholic objections. Examines the impact of Antonio Gramsci on Eurocommunist organization. Compares Gramscian ideas to those of Machiavelli. Based extensively on the works of Santiago Carrillo, Norberto Bobbio, Scritti Giovanili; 80 notes.
R. B. Mendel

828. Denitch, Bogdan. EUROCOMMUNISM AND THE RUSSIAN QUESTION. *Dissent 1979 26(3): 326-330.* The invasion of Czechoslovakia by the Warsaw Pact countries in 1968 has led the Communist parties of Western Europe to act independently of the USSR, which the Eurocommunists still consider socialist because of its collective property relations, although a ruling bureaucracy divorced from the ideals and needs of the working class is responsible for actions which have been increasingly criticized by Western European Communists.

829. Devlin, Kevin. THE CHALLENGE OF EUROCOMMUNISM. *Problems of Communism 1977 26(1): 1-20.* Describes the events that culminated in the "institutionalization of diversity" at the Conference of European Communist and Workers' Parties held in East Berlin in June of 1976. Based on European Communist newspaper accounts; 83 notes.
J. M. Lauber

830. Duhamel, Luc. LÉNINE, LA VIOLENCE ET L'EUROCOMMUNISME [Lenin, violence, and Eurocommunism]. *Can. J. of Pol. Sci. [Canada] 1980 13(1): 97-120.* Examines the attitudes of the Communist parties of France, Italy, and Spain toward violence and its role in the revolutionary movements in Western Europe in order to learn if these positions are consistent with the theories of V. I. Lenin. Emphasizes the evolution of Lenin's views on violence as they related to the real condition of the working-class movement and the revolutions in Russia. Outlines agreement and disagreement between the theories of Lenin and those of European Party leaders Georges Marchais, Enrico Berlinguer, and Santiago Carrillo. 53 notes.

831. Foner, Eric. THE DILEMMAS OF EUROCOMMUNISM. *Monthly Rev. 1980 32(7): 39-45.* Reviews Carl Marzani's *The Promise of Eurocommunism* (Westport, Conn.: Lawrence Hill, 1980), which examines Communist parties in the European democratic countries.

832. Glejdura, Stefan. EL *EUROCOMUNISMO* [Eurocommunism]. *Rev. de Politica Int. [Spain] 1977 (149): 121-135, (150): 183-190.* Part I. Studies the early development of Eurocommunism, the reasons why it has proved successful, and the way that it is regarded by Yugoslavia. Part II. Discusses Italy's experience with Eurocommunism, particularly her relationship with the USSR.

833. Glejdura, Stefan. EL *EUROCOMUNISMO* [Eurocommunism]. *Rev. de Pol. Int. [Spain] 1977 (151): 181-188.* Continued from a previous article. Part III. Discusses Eurocommun-

ism in light of contradictory policies of the USSR since 1969 of seeking peaceful coexistence with the West while seemingly attempting to resurrect the International. Part IV. Discusses US reaction to Eurocommunism.

834. Goldsborough, James O. EUROCOMMUNISM AFTER MADRID. *Foreign Affairs 1977 55(4): 800-814.* Since their recent summit meeting in Madrid, the French, Italian, and Spanish Communist Parties have referred to themselves as "Eurocommunists." They stress their common interests and seem willing to work for change within the framework of traditional democracy. "Inevitably, one of these parties, if not all of them, will someday reap the harvest of its new policy. Probably it is best for everyone, and certainly for Western Europe, that the experiment be tried out before long, for the present feeling is one of waiting for the other shoe to drop." 2 notes. M. R. Yerburgh

835. Gosztony, Peter. UNGARN 1956: VOLKSAUFSTAND IN EINER VOLKSREPUBLIK [Hungary 1956: people's rebellion in a people's democracy]. *Schweizer Monatshefte [Switzerland] 1976 56(7): 597-606.* The Hungarian rebellion of 1956 ended in immediate defeat, but it made possible a special Hungarian form of communism that strengthened tendencies to the emancipation of the Eastern European Communist states and initiated the development of Eurocommunism.

836. Hassner, Pierre. "EUROCOMMUNISME" ET "EUROSTRATÉGIE" [Eurocommunism and Eurostrategy]. *Défense Natl. [France] 1980 36(8): 27-40.* Discusses the ideas on defense of the French, Italian, and Spanish Communist Parties between 1975 and 1980 in the light of their relations with the USSR.

837. Huyn, Hans. EUROCOMMUNISM AND POPULAR FRONT MOVEMENTS. *J. of Social and Pol. Studies 1977 2(4): 247-258.*

838. Insulza, José Miguel. EUROCOMUNISMO Y SOCIALISMO EUROPEO EN LA SITUACIÓN CHILENA [Eurocommunism and European socialism in the Chilean situation]. *Foro Int. [Mexico] 1981 21(3): 289-303.* Examines the European Left's interpretation of the Chilean coup d'état of 1973 and how that interpretation affected its policies. 22 notes. D. A. Franz

839. Jenson, Jane. ONE ROBIN DOESN'T MAKE SPRING: FRENCH COMMUNIST ALLIANCE STRATEGIES AND THE WOMEN'S MOVEMENT. *Radical Hist. Rev. 1980 (23): 57-75.* Discusses how the French Communist Party came to accept the French women's liberation movement as an ally with the party's broad political coalition, and how the party altered its analysis of women's subordination in capitalism during the 1970's as Western European Communist parties Eurocommunized.

840. Kapur, Harish. EUROCOMMUNISM AND THE ALLIANCES. *Ann. d'Études Int. [Switzerland] 1979 10: 83-96.* Eurocommunism, the movement within the Communist parties of Western Europe (particularly in Spain, Italy, and France) for independence from Moscow, is seen by both the United States and the USSR as a threat to their alliance systems.

841. Kautsky, John H. KARL KAUTSKY AND EUROCOMMUNISM. *Studies in Comparative Communism 1981 14(1): 3-44.* The Communism of the French, Italian and Spanish Communist Parties, with its emphasis on the importance of bourgeois democratic safeguards against tyranny, exhibits the same acceptance of political liberty that Karl Kautsky defended in his polemic with Lenin. The remarks of the Eurocommunists correspond to Kautsky's position in the late German Empire and the Weimar Republic. This parallel is a result of economic changes. Increased industrialization in France, Italy, and Spain has brought these countries to the industrial level of Germany just before 1914 and as in Germany, have influenced the labor movement to abandon the stage of revolutionary anarchosyndicalism. Now, having passed that stage and the subsequent stage of revolutionary reformism, they have entered the stage of reformist social democracy. 85 notes. D. Balmuth

842. Kimmel, Adolf. ZWISCHEN STALINISMUS UND EUROKOMMUNISMUS [Between Stalinism and Eurocommunism]. *Neue Politische Literatur [West Germany] 1977 22(2): 244-257.* Analyzes the ideological blindness of Western European Communist intellectuals toward Stalinism in the 1950's, the break with dogmatic Stalinism in the 1960's, and the development of new forms of socialist ideologies in the 1970's.

843. Kindersley, Richard, ed. *In Search of Eurocommunism: Based on Papers from Two Seminars Given at St. Antony's College, Oxford, in 1978.* New York: St. Martin's, 1981. 218 pp.

844. König, Helmut. MOSKAU UND DIE EUROKOMMUNISTEN [Moscow and the Eurocommunists]. *Osteuropa [West Germany] 1978 28(10): 892-910.* Discusses Moscow's attitudes to the Italian Communist Party since Palmiro Togliatti's criticism of Soviet politics in 1956, Santiago Carrillo's independent course, and Yugoslavia and France's Eurocommunism.

845. Lahav, Yehuda. "EURO-KOMUNIZM": HA-ETGAR HA-DEMOKRATI [Eurocommunism: the democratic challenge]. *Int. Problems [Israel] 1978 17(1): 37-45.* Shows that Eurocommunism has presented a dilemma for the USSR by insisting on democratic freedoms which the USSR has suppressed at home and in its satellites.

846. Laqueur, Walter. "EUROCOMMUNISM" AND ITS FRIENDS. *Commentary 1976 62(2): 25-30.* Sir Harold Wilson warned recently of the danger of collaboration between democratic socialists and communists. However, in the US many have proposed cooperation with western European communism or Eurocommunism. It has been asserted that Italian communism is at heart moderate and reformist and can be encouraged to increase those tendencies by an accommodating American foreign policy. There are definite differences between the Western European Communist parties of France, Italy, and Spain and the Russians. It is impossible, however, to assess the democratic statements issued by Western European Communists. It is hard to conceive of these essentially authoritarian and nondemocratic party structures' defending the cause of democracy in national politics. It may be that Western observers have overreacted to recent ideological variations in Western European Communism, perhaps out of their own desire for such change. Based on primary and secondary sources. S. R. Herstein

847. LeGloannec, Anne-Marie. LES RELATIONS ENTRE LA SOCIAL-DEMOCRATIE ALLEMANDE (SPD) ET LES PARTIS EUROCOMMUNISTES (NOTE DE RECHERCHE) [Relations between the German Social Democrats (SPD) and the Eurocommunist parties: research note]. *Études Int. [Canada] 1980 11(1): 133-144.* Discusses the relations between the German Social Democratic Party and the Communist parties in Spain, Italy, and France. In alliances between socialists and Communists relations with the Russian Communist Party are of paramount importance. 44 notes. J. F. Harrington

848. Leonhard, Wolfgang. *Eurocommunism: Challenge for East and West.* Vecchio, Mark, transl. New York: Holt, Rinehart & Winston, 1980. 430 pp.

849. Liehm, A. J. THE PRAGUE SPRING AND EUROCOMMUNISM. *Int. J. [Canada] 1978 33(4): 804-819.* Discusses the Soviet invasion of Czechoslovakia in 1968, and the effect it had on Eurocommunist parties.

850. Lowenthal, Richard. MOSCOW AND THE "EUROCOMMUNISTS." *Problems of Communism 1978 27(4): 38-49.* Examines the Soviet perspective on Eurocommunism. There is friction between Moscow and the major nonruling Communist Parties in the industrial countries, but this has not led to schism because

Moscow recognizes the continued usefulness of these parties to Soviet foreign policy. The situation would be different if one of the Eurocommunist parties came to power. 32 notes.
J. M. Lauber

851. Macleod, Alex. THE PCI'S RELATIONS WITH THE PCF IN THE AGE OF EUROCOMMUNISM, MAY 1973-JUNE 1979. *Studies in Comparative Communism 1980 13(2-3): 168-196.* Through Georges Marchais, the Communist Party of France (PCF) announced in 1975 that henceforth it would determine its own policies. The PCF takes issue with the Communist Party of Italy (PCI) on questions of domestic policy, proletarian internationalism, and relations within the Communist movement. The policies of the PCF have differed from those of the PCI, and the Italians see the French as too rigid in their analyses. From 1973 and especially 1975, relations between the two parties have improved despite the differences. 58 notes. D. Balmuth

852. Mandel, Ernest. A CRITIQUE OF EUROCOMMUNISM. *Marxist Perspectives 1979-80 2(4): 114-142.* Critical analysis of gradualist policies of Eurocommunism during the 1960's and 1970's.

853. Maravall, J. M. SPAIN: EUROCOMMUNISM AND SOCIALISM. *Pol. Studies [Great Britain] 1979 27(2): 218-235.* Analyzes political competition between the Communist Party (PCE) and the Socialist Party (PSOE) in Spain since the 1930's. The main decisions taken by the PCE traditionally followed a policy of broad alliances, moderate strategies, and attempts to minimize Socialist influence. In the 1960's the Socialists' influence seemed to be limited; there was however a Socialist renaissance in the last years of Franco. The general elections of 1977 demonstrated remarkable political continuity with the Second Republic, with a strong vote to the PSOE in the historical leftist areas. The trade union elections of 1978 qualified this Socialist predominance on the left. Here, recent militancy at the shop floor level, represented by the Communist-oriented Workers' Commissions, seemed more important than historical memory. Theoretical-ideological convergence between the political programs of the PSOE and the PCE may paradoxically maximize political competition between communism and socialism in Spain. J/S

854. Marcou, Lilly. LA CONFÉRENCE DE BERLIN DE JUIN 1976: ANALYSE DU DISCOURS COMMUNISTE [The Berlin Conference of June 1976: analysis of Communist public statements]. *Études Int. [Canada] 1979 10(3): 439-470.* The Berlin Conference was the last of the series of congresses that began in 1975 with the World Congress of Communist Parties in Moscow. It represented a turning point in the history of the Communist movement, especially as regards Europe. The density and contradictory nature of its proceedings provided a new image of European Communism in crisis. Bringing together a variety of Communist parties, some in power and others underground, the congress was the theater of heated debates. It stabilized Eurocommunism, a phenomenon that had its origins in the 1969 World Congress of Communist Parties. 81 notes.
J. V. Coutinho

855. Marzani, Carl. A MARXIST VARIANT? *Monthly Rev. 1979 31(5): 55-64.* Review article on Eurocommunism based on Santiago Carrillo's *Eurocommunism and the State* (Westport, Conn.: Lawrence Hill, 1978), Ernest Mandel's *From Stalinism to Eurocommunism* (London: New Left Books, 1978), and Ralph Miliband's *Marxism and Politics* (Oxford: Oxford U. Pr., 1977).

856. Marzani, Carl. *The Promise of Eurocommunism.* Westport, Conn.: Lawrence Hill, 1980.

857. Morgan, Annette. SCHISMATICS AND SCEPTICS. *West European Pol. [Great Britain] 1979 2(2): 268-277.* Reviews Santiago Carrillo's *'Eurocommunisme' et Etat* (Paris: Flammarion, 1977), Fernando Claudin's *L'eurocommunisme* (Paris: Francois Maspero, 1977), Annie Kriegel's *Un autre communisme?* (Paris: Hachette, 1977), G. R. Urban's *Euro-communism. Its roots and future in Italy and elsewhere* (London: Maurice Temple Smith, 1978), and Hermann Vogt's *Eurokommunismus. Ein Reader* (Berlin: Berlin Verlag, 1978); 1970's.

858. Mortimer, Edward; Story, Jonathan; and DellaTorre, Paolo Filo. WHATEVER HAPPENED TO "EUROCOMMUNISM"? *Int. Affairs [Great Britain] 1979 55(4): 574-585.* Reviews developments in the Eurocommunist parties of Italy, France, and Spain, 1970's.

859. Mujal-León, Eusebio. CATALUÑA, CARRILLO, AND EUROCOMMUNISM. *Problems of Communism 1981 30(2): 25-47.* The Catalan challenge to Eurocommunism that surfaced in January 1981 is in many respects symptomatic of the problems facing the Spanish Communist Party (PCE) and other West European Communist parties today. At the same time, there are unique aspects to the Catalan Party's status within the PCE, and there is some resentment toward the heavy-handed leadership style of PCE Secretary-General Santiago Carrillo. For now, the threat to Carrillo seems manageable, but the future is by no means certain. Based on publications of the Spanish left-wing political parties; 55 notes.
J. M. Lauber

860. Nilsson, K. Robert. THE EUR ACCORDS & THE HISTORIC COMPROMISE: ITALIAN LABOR & EUROCOMMUNISM. *Polity 1981 14(1): 29-50.* Discusses the Italian Communist Party (PCI), its Eurocommunism, the contradiction in its strategic goals, the "Convention Hall" of Rome (EUR) accords prepared by a three-union federation of organized Italian labor, their internal contradictions, and the agreement on tripartite negotiations among government, unions, and management, an agreement which raises the specter of neocorporatism. The deadlock between union members and leaders combined with the immobilism of the PCI make the proclaimed goal of Italian social transformation impossible. J

861. Ochocki, Kazimierz. LENIN, GRAMSCI I "EUROKOMUNIZM" [Lenin, Gramsci, and Eurocommunism]. *Z Pola Walki [Poland] 1982 25(1-2): 3-25.* Analyzes those currents in the thought of V. I. Lenin and Antonio Gramsci which contributed to the rise of Eurocommunism and the roots of Soviet antipathy toward Gramsci as the founding father of European Communism. The hostility to Gramsci in the Eastern bloc is due to lack of good knowledge of his writings, resulting in the fallacious opposition of Lenin's and Gramsci's brands of Communism. 45 notes. Russian and English summaries. M. Hernas

862. Owens, J. B. SPANISH EUROCOMMUNISM AND THE COMMUNIST PARTY ORGANIZATION IN MURCIA. *Iberian Studies [Great Britain] 1979 8(1): 3-12.* Shows how the institutions of Spanish Eurocommunism, below the level of the Central Committee, function by presenting the results of detailed observation of the party at work in the region of Murcia, 1977-79.

863. Pasquino, Gianfranco. EUROCOMMUNISM: CHALLENGE TO WEST AND EAST. *Problems of Communism 1979 28(5-6): 85-91.* A review of six recent studies on Eurocommunism and the challenge presented to both the West because it threatens European integration and defense, and to the East because it undermines the legitimacy of the Soviet model and suggests an alternate that could promote dissent if not political change in the Soviet bloc. 4 notes.
J. M. Lauber

864. Popoff, Stephane. EUROCOMMUNISM. *Bulgarian Rev. [Brazil] 1977 17: 3-9.* Examines the history of communism in Western Europe from 1956 to 9 May 1977 (the "birthday" of Eurocommunism) to discover why Europe lost communism to Russia.

865. Popov, Milorad. "EUROCOMMUNISM" AND THE PAN-EUROPEAN CONFERENCE. *World Today [Great Britain] 1976 32(10): 387-392.* Western European Communist Parties object to the 18-month effort to hammer out a common line for the heterogeneous parties that participated in the 1976 European conference of Communist parties in East Berlin.

866. Prevost, Gary. EUROCOMMUNISM AND THE SPANISH COMMUNISTS. *West European Pol. [Great Britain] 1981 4(1): 69-84.* Describes the growth and development of the Spanish Communist Party (PCE) since 1921 and how, after nearly 40 years of underground existence during the rule of Francisco Franco, it has firmly established itself in the post-Franco political scene in Spain.

867. Priester, Karin. EUROKOMMUNISMUS UND PLURALISMUS [Eurocommunism and pluralism]. *Frankfurter Hefte [West Germany] 1980 35(3): 13-22.* The development of the Eurocommunist model in the 1960's and 1970's can easily be traced back to concepts of political pluralism especially in the Spanish and Italian Communist parties in the 1920's and 1930's.

868. Priester, Karin. EUROKOMMUNISMUS: KONTINUITÄT UND WANDEL WESTEUROPÄISCHER KOMMUNISTISCHER PARTEIEN [Eurocommunism: continuity and change of Western European Communist parties]. *Neue Politische Literatur [West Germany] 1979 24(4): 425-445.* Although based on a long ideological transformation since 1945, Eurocommunism became a prominent political concept after the Common Program of French Communists and Socialists in 1972, the historical compromise in Italy of 1973 and new program proposals of the Spanish, Italian, and French Communist parties in 1975. These theories hark back to the theory of the historical bloc of the Italian Communist Antonio Gramsci. 32 notes. R. Wagnleitner

869. Priklmajer, Zorica. EVROKOMUNIZAM I NESVRSTANOST [Eurocommunism and nonalignment]. *Medjunarodni Problemi [Yugoslavia] 1980 32(3): 385-404.* In the 1970's the Communist Parties of Western Europe showed an increasing affinity with the nonaligned countries of the Third World. They shared a desire to dismantle the current international economic structure dominated by the capitalist countries and to transcend the division of the world into blocs.

870. Pütz, Karl Heinz. ATLANTISCHE BEZIEHUNGEN UND EUROKOMMUNISMUS: DIE KPI IN DER AUSSENPOLITIK DER USA [Transatlantic relations and Eurocommunism: the place of the Italian Communist Party in American foreign relations]. *Politische Vierteljahresschrift [West Germany] 1980 21(1): 20-42.* Since World War II, American policy toward Communism has changed only superficially, alternating between the attempt to control it by a policy of containment and that of dividing the international Communist movement through a more relaxed coexistance with Eurocommunism. While mistrusting nationalist and Communist movements alike, the US government has been forced to accept the Communist Party of Italy, while it, in turn, has softened its attitude to the United States. Despite the appearance of a more liberal trend, the Carter administration has returned to policies of containment. 2 notes, biblio. S. Bonnycastle

871. Revel, Jean Francois. THE MYTHS OF EUROCOMMUNISM. *Foreign Affairs 1978 56(2): 295-305.* Observers on both sides of the Atlantic misunderstand the concept of Eurocommunism. Simply stated, Eurocommunism is the result of two phenomena that have occurred over the last 20 years: the realization in Western Europe of the economic and human failure of Soviet socialism; and the adaption of the Communist parties to advanced industrial societies. M. R. Yerburgh

872. Rosa, Luigi. DER EUROKOMMUNISMUS DER KPI UND DIE ITALIENISCHEN KATHOLIKEN [The Eurocommunism of the CPI and the Italian Catholics]. *Stimmen der Zeit [West Germany] 1978 196(3): 147-157.* The Eurocommunist strategy of the Communist Party of Italy (CPI) is to convince Catholics that their faith is separable from politics. But once Catholicism is reduced to a private faith it will dwindle away to nothing, so Catholics must become conscious of this Communist plan and resist it.

873. Ross, George. *Workers and Communists in France: From Popular Front to Eurocommunism.* Berkeley: U. of California Pr., 1981. 368 pp.

874. Schapiro, Leonard B. THE SOVIET REACTION TO "EUROCOMMUNISM." *West European Pol. [Great Britain] 1979 2(2): 160-177.* Discusses the ideological similarities and differences between Soviet communism and Eurocommunism, and the extent to which the USSR continues to rely on the latter for support of Soviet policies.

875. Schlesinger, Arthur, Jr. SOVIET RELATIONS WITH WESTERN EUROPE. *Marxist Perspectives 1979 2(2): 140-144.* Both the United States and the USSR fear Eurocommunism, the first because it might weaken NATO, the second because it would further undermine Soviet hegemony over Western Communist parties and, eventually, Eastern Europe.

876. Schwab, George, ed. *CUNY Conference on History and Politics (3d: 1978). Eurocommunism: The Ideological and Political-Theoretical Foundations.* Contributions in Political Science, no. 60. Westport, Conn.: Greenwood, 1981. 325 pp.

877. Seliger, Kurt. EUROKOMMUNISMUS IN ZWIESPALT [Eurocommunism in discord]. *Osteuropa [West Germany] 1977 27(10): 848-859.* Examines the divergent views of the USSR and its policies as expressed by various Western European Communist leaders.

878. Sherman, Howard. EUROCOMMUNISM, SOCIALISM, & DEMOCRACY. *Marxist Perspectives 1980 3(1): 158-172.* Reviews Santiago Carrillo's *Eurocommunism and the State* (Westport, Conn.; Laurence Hill, 1978), comparing it with works by V. I. Lenin, Ernest Mandel, and Fernando Claudin. Carrillo demolishes all excuses for one-party dictatorship and shows how socialism in Western Europe and the United States will be more compatible with political democracy than capitalism has been.

879. Sodaro, Michael J. WHATEVER HAPPENED TO EUROCOMMUNISM? *Problems of Communism 1984 33(6): 59-65.* A review of 12 recent publications on the Communist parties of France, Italy, and Spain. These parties have distanced themselves from the Soviet Union, but have not developed viable alternative economic policies to capitalism, have not solidified their democratic identities, or become more democratic internally. J. M. Lauber

880. Spieker, Manfred. DEMOKRATIE ODER DIKTATUR? ZUR IDEOLOGIE DES EUROKOMMUNISMUS [Democracy or dictatorship? The ideology of Eurocommunism]. *Pol. Vierteljahresschrift [West Germany] 1978 19(1): 23-48.* Summarizes events, 1936-77, affecting the rise of Eurocommunism, particularly in Italy, Spain, and France. Socialism is favored by all Western Communist Parties controlled by a multiparty system, and by party elections, not by the dictatorship of the proletariat. They regard their current ideology as based in past history: notably the resistance to Fascism in Italy; the Republic of 1936 in Spain; and events in France after 1936. However, the objective in each case was not the establishment of an "advanced democracy," but the introduction of Stalinistic regimes or military dictatorships. Changes in Marxist-Leninist philosophy following growing independence in Yugoslavia, the cooling of relations between the USSR and China, and the unmasking of Joseph Stalin's activities by Nikita Khrushchev paved the way for Eurocommunism. 102 notes. S. Bonnycastle/S

881. Spieker, Manfred. EUROCOMMUNISM AND CHRISTIANITY: ON THE LIMITS OF THE DIALOGUE. *Rev. of Pol. 1983 45(1): 3-19.* Since the mid 1960's, European Marxist theorists have provided a new critique of Christianity which has emphasized its revolutionary fervor and protest function while de-emphasizing its opiate appeal. While the new Marxist critique is not religious in a Christian sense, it has found a counterpart in Christian liberation theology prevalent in Latin America which champions political and revolutionary collaboration through the Marxist theory of class war. While the Eurocommunists have appeared to be more accommodating toward Christianity and liberation theology, their approach toward religious freedom and respect for plurality has been

contradictory. Enmeshed in Marxist-Leninist heritage, Eurocommunists would not abandon their religious belief in the authoritarian state, or share power with Christians in any manner. 78 notes.
G. A. Glovins

882. Timmermann, Heinz. AKTUELLE PROBLEME DES EUROKOMMUNISMUS [Present problems of Eurocommunism]. *Schweizer Monatshefte [Switzerland] 1979 59(2): 125-133.* While the Italian and Spanish Communists have developed democratic models for their parties since the early 1970's, the French Communists returned to a strategy of establishing a countersociety in the mid-1970's.

883. Timmermann, Heinz. DER "EUROKUMMUNISMUS" IN MEHRZAHL [Eurocommunism in the plural]. *Schweizer Monatshefte [Switzerland] 1977 57(4): 277-293.* The political and ideological developments within the Communist Parties of Spain, Italy, and France, though structurally of different origins and strength, demonstrate similar characteristics in their adoption of democratic pluralism, independent foreign policy, and the support of detente—long range attempts for the establishment of a democratic socialism.

884. Timmermann, Heinz. MOSKAU UND DIE LINKE IN WESTEUROPA. ASPEKTE UND PERSPEKTIVEN DES VERHÄLTNISSES ZU DEN EUROKOMMUNISTEN UND ZU DEN DEMOKRATISCHEN SOZIALISTEN [Moscow and the Western European left: aspects and perspectives of the relationship with the Eurocommunists and the democratic socialists]. *Osteuropa [West Germany] 1980 30(5): 389-400, (6): 494-509.* Part I. While Soviet policies in the 1970's have been characterized by attacks on the Italian, French, and Spanish Eurocommunist policies, the European socialists, though different in their ideological positions from communism, have been seen as partners who advocate realistic positions for cooperation on some limited concrete issues. Part II. The growth of the importance of the Socialist International in the 1970's made the Soviet leadership realize that the Communist parties had been wrong in their policies toward democratic socialism in the 1920's and 1930's.

885. Urban, George R. A CONVERSATION WITH ANTONIN LIEHM: "EUROCOMMUNISM" AND THE PRAGUE SPRING. *Survey [Great Britain] 1979 24(1): 1-31.* Responding to the author's questions on the theme of the impact of the Czechoslovak reform movement on Eurocommunism, Liehm argues that, in the eyes of Western European Communist parties, already restive and working in an essentially Social-Democratic milieu, the Prague Spring offered the first opportunity for the de-Russification of socialism without getting into conflict with Moscow, an expectation that was eventually shattered. Based on a radio broadcast.
V. Samaraweera

886. Valenta, Jiri. EUROCOMMUNISM AND CZECHOSLOVAKIA. *East Central Europe 1980 7(1): 17-38.* Given certain similarities between them, a study of the development of Czechoslovak communism throws light on the nature of Eurocommunism. Czechoslovakia, like Western Europe, has a strong democratic tradition. The legacy of early Party leader Bohumir Šmeral is one of pluralistic communism, resisting the universality of the Soviet experience. In the 1930's, Stalinist elements took control of the Party, depriving it of its mass character. After World War II, only the naked power of the USSR maintained a Stalinist government. Dubček's reforms were in the Czechoslovakian tradition and had great relevance to communism all over Europe. Based largely on Czechoslovakian sources.
R. V. Layton, Jr.

887. Valenta, Jiri. THE USSR AND CZECHOSLOVAKIA'S EXPERIMENT WITH EUROCOMMUNISM: REASSESSMENT AFTER A DECADE. Brisch, Hans and Volgyes, Ivan, ed. *Czechoslovakia: The Heritage of Ages Past* (New York: Columbia U. Pr., 1979): 201-212. Considers the motives and consequences of Soviet military intervention in Czechoslovakia after the Prague Spring of 1968. The USSR needed to control the unpredictable course of events in its satellite. East German and Polish Communist leaders warned that they would not be able to guarantee stability in their countries if order was not restored by force. Like Eduard Beneš in 1938 and 1948, the Czech leaders did not resist. The immediate impact was adverse for the USSR's international position, caused a setback for the Nonproliferation Treaty in the US Senate, and enhanced NATO, but the long-term significance was slight. For the Italian, French, and Spanish Communist parties, Soviet intervention signaled the end of proletarian internationalism and the inspiration for pluralistic socialism. 6 notes.
S

888. Wagner, Wolfgang. KOMMUNISTEN IM WESTLICHEN BÜNDNIS? ATLANTISCHE ALLIANZ UND EUROPÄISCHE GEMEINSCHAFT VOR EINEM NEUEN PROBLEM [Communists in the Western alliance? Atlantic alliance and European Community facing a new problem]. *Europa Archiv [West Germany] 1976 31(10): 315-324.* The French, Italian, and Spanish Communist parties have adopted Eurocommunism since the early 1970's, but Communist participation in the governments of Italy, Spain, or France could endanger the unity and cohesion of NATO and the European Economic Community.

889. Wang Chien-hsün. COMMUNIST CHINA AND EUROCOMMUNISM. *Issues & Studies [Taiwan] 1980 16(11): 13-29.* Serious alienation of Western European Communist parties from the USSR began with the Russian invasion of Czechoslovakia in 1968. In March 1977 the French, Italian, and Spanish Communist parties proclaimed independence for all Communist parties and for Eurocommunist policies that are contrary to those of the Communist Party of the Soviet Union. There are also disagreements among Eurocommunists that threaten their solidarity. The Chinese Communists have begun to court this group of parties as allies against Russia. Many differences between China and the Eurocommunists remain to be resolved. 23 notes.
J. A. Krompart

890. Webb, Carole. EUROCOMMUNISM AND THE EUROPEAN COMMUNITIES. *J. of Common Market Studies [Great Britain] 1979 17(3): 236-258.* Clarifies the discussion of the complex issue of Eurocommunism, focusing on the role of Communist parties in their national governments and integration of the entire movement, 1970's.

891. Wolffsohn, Michael. EUROCOMMUNISM. *Issues and Studies [Taiwan] 1978 14(8): 44-71.* Examines the background of Eurocommunism and European Communist parties from 1930 to 1977.

892. —. ON THE ROAD TO EUROCOMMUNISM. *Can. Dimension [Canada] 1978 3(4): 25-29.* The history of the move toward Communism in Europe beginning with Joseph Stalin's leadership of the Soviet Communists in 1928.

Eastern Europe

General

893. Alexandrescu, Ion. SEMINARUL ROMÂNO-BULGAR PRIVIND ROLUL PARTIDELOR COMUNISTE DIN CELE DOUĂ ȚĂRI ÎN LUPTA PENTRU INSTAURAREA ȘI CONSOLIDAREA PUTERII POPULARE [A Rumanian-Bulgarian seminar on the role of the Communist Party in the struggle to establish and consolidate popular power in both countries]. *Anale de Istorie [Rumania] 1970 16(2): 141-152.* Summarizes the papers of a joint conference in Sofia, 22-27 December 1969, dedicated to the Communist Party's leadership, 1944-48. Presentations dealt with the parties' organizational, theoretical, and economic participation in the peoples'revolutions: 23 August in Rumania and 9 September 1944 in Bulgaria. Speakers included Iordan Iotov, Petar Ostoici, Minka Trifonova, and Gh. Zaharia, Gheorghe Țuțui, Paraschiva Nichita, and the author. All agreed that the phenomenal economic and democratic development in the two countries after 1944 was due to the wisdom, dedication, and tireless activity of the Marxist-Leninist ideologies of the two parties.
G. J. Bobango

894. Alexandrescu, Ion. SIMPOZION ROMÂNO-BULGAR PRIVIND POLITICA DE ALIANŢE PROMOVATĂ DE PARTIDELE COMUNISTE DIN CELE DOUĂ ŢARI IN PERIOADA 1944-1948 [A Rumanian-Bulgarian symposium to examine the policy of alliances promoted by the Communist Parties of the two countries, 1944-48]. *Anale de Istorie [Rumania] 1971 17(4): 146-155.* Summarizes the contributions to this joint conference on the role of the Communist Parties in the installation of People's Republics, held by the Institute for Historical and Sociopolitical Studies at the Central Committee of the Rumanian Communist Party, 15-22 November 1970. Delegates from the Bulgarian Communist Party's Historical Institute presented papers on economic policy, the Patriotic Front, the intelligentsia, the collaboration between Bulgaria's Communist Party and its Popular Agrarian Union, while papers by delegates of the Rumanian Institute covered the Rumanian Communist Party's alliance policy, the United Workers' Front, and the worker-peasant alliance. The symposium helped emphasize the similarity of problems and policies of the first years of popular revolution. 3 notes. R. O. Khan

895. Brada, Josef C. *Technology Transfer between the United States and the Countries of the Soviet Bloc.* Trieste: Istituto di Studi e Documentazione sull'Est Europeo, 1981. 122 pp.

896. Budavári, János. AZ EURÓPAI SZOCIALISTA ORSZÁGOK MEZŐGAZDASÁGI ÉS ÉLELMISZERIPARI FEJLŐDÉSÉRŐL [The development of agriculture and the food industry in the European socialist states]. *Társadalmi Szemle [Hungary] 1978 33(1): 45-50.* Analyzes the development of European socialist agriculture and the food industry compared to certain tendencies in Denmark and the United States.

897. Bushkoff, Leonard. REVOLUTION AND NATIONALISM: TWO STUDIES ON THE HISTORY OF COMMUNISM IN EASTERN EUROPE. *World Pol. 1963 15(3): 495-529.* Joseph Rothschild's *The Communist Party of Bulgaria: Origin and Development 1883-1936* (1959), a pioneering study in the history of Eastern Europe, is flawed by its attempt at encyclopedic inclusiveness, its anti-Communist invective, and its compartmentalized treatment of national groups, obscuring their dynamic interaction; M. K. Dziewanowski's *The Communist Party of Poland: An Outline History* (1959), a balanced study of Polish Communism, 1863-1958, views nationalism as the primary force behind Poland's rebirth in 1918 and revival in 1956.

898. Conner, Cliff. THE TWILIGHT OF BUREAUCRATIC REFORMISM IN EASTERN EUROPE. *Int. Socialist Rev. 1972 33(6): 20-31.* Discusses the reform policies of oppositionist leaders of the Communist Party in Poland, Hungary, and Czechoslovakia, 1953-70's, emphasizing Wladyslaw Gomulka, Imre Nagy, and Alexander Dubček's conflicts with the USSR.

899. Domke, Martin. ASSETS OF EAST EUROPEANS IMPOUNDED IN THE UNITED STATES. *Am. Slavic and East European Rev. 1959 18(3): 351-360.* Discusses American legal statutes governing the proper and complete dispersal of testate funds to beneficiaries residing in Communist countries, 1939-59.

900. Feldbrugge, F. J. M. THE UNTAPPED POTENTIAL IN THE STUDY OF SOVIET AND EAST EUROPEAN LAW. *Studies in Comparative Communism 1982 15(4): 384-390.* Legal studies which offer insight into the operation of Communist states are most closely followed in West Germany. The work is concentrated in law schools and so tends to be ignored by political and social scientists. D. Balmuth

901. Fischer-Galati, Stephen, ed. *The Communist Parties of Eastern Europe.* East European Monographs. New York: Columbia U. Pr., 1979. 393 pp.

902. Georgescu, Titu. BILANŢ ŞI INVĂŢĂMINTE LA FINELE CELUI DE-AL DOILEA RĂZBOI MONDIAL [The balance sheet and lessons by the end of World War II]. *Anale de Istorie [Rumania] 1969 15(6): 110-119.* World War II demonstrates the role of the masses and of communist groups everywhere in defeating fascism and aggression, and in the worldwide struggle for peace and democratic liberty. The author catalogs Rumania's sacrifices in lives, and material and money given to the UN, and shows how the war produced in Rumania new foreign policy alignments and a new internal order, 23 August 1944. Since 1945 Communist Countries have fought for world peace and against imperialism, the former threatened in particular by the Middle East conflict and US aggression in Vietnam. Rumania and all peace-loving countries have called for a new European collective security arrangement, based on recognition of the postwar boundaries in Europe and the inviolability of frontiers. G. J. Bobango

903. Gornyi, V. A. and Masich, V. F. IUBILEIAM BRATSKIKH PARTII POSVIASHCHAETSIA [The jubilees of fraternal parties]. *Voprosy Istorii KPSS [USSR] 1979 (4): 143-151.* Summarizes papers delivered on 14 December 1978 at the Institute of Marxism-Leninism and on 19 December 1978 at a conference sponsored by the Institute of Marxism-Leninism and the Academy of Social Sciences celebrating the 30th and 60th anniversaries of the Polish United Workers' Party and Polish Communist Party, respectively, and of papers read on 9 January 1979 at a meeting honoring the 60th anniversary of the German Communist Party. 12 notes.
L. E. Holmes

904. Gura, Vladislav. NIAKOI PROBLEMI NA AGRARNITE PREOBRAZOVANIIA V POLSHA I BULGARIIA PREZ PERIODA 1944-1948 G. [Some problems of agrarian reform in Poland and Bulgaria, 1944-48]. *Izvestiia na Instituta po Istoriia na BKP [Bulgaria] 1970 24: 45-67.* A comparison of land reform in Poland and Bulgaria in 1944-48 reveals how differing social, economic, and political circumstances can lead to varying agrarian policies in socialist countries experiencing similar revolutions. Poland experienced vast redistribution of large estates and land abandoned by German refugees. Polish peasants had a stronger belief in private land than Bulgarians, and were more influenced by right-wing parties. The Aleksandr Stamboliski regime in Bulgaria had experimented with mild land reforms such as the maximum size of farms. The major agrarian problems in both countries were stagnation, low yields, minute land parcels, overcrowding, and bank credit. The Bulgarian Communists had more peasant allies than the Polish Communists because of their successful Fatherland Front. Organization of productive cooperatives began immediately in Bulgaria, even before land redistribution. The parties of the Left were weaker in the Polish countryside, so the village bourgeoisie was allowed to take part in the formation of new farms along with the poor. Bulgaria collectivized, but Poland did not. Central Party Archives, Central State Archives; 2 charts, 34 notes. C. S. Masloff

905. Habuda, Miklós. CSEHSZLOVÁK ÉS MAGYAR PÁRTTÖRTÉNÉSZEK TANÁCSKOZÁSA [Conference of Czechoslovakian and Hungarian party historians]. *Párttörténeti Közlemények [Hungary] 1973 19(4): 172-178.* Czechoslovakian and Hungarian party historians met at Bratislava in March 1973. Discussed were: the preconditions of proletarian dictatorship in Hungary, the impact of external factors on the Czechoslovak revolution, the periodization of the Czechoslovak revolution (1944-48), the nature and phases of the Hungarian popular democratic revolution, and the role of class struggle in Slovakia during the revolution.
P. I. Hidas

906. Hámori, Laszlo. AVSPÄNNINGENS PRIS [The price of detente]. *Svensk Tidskrift [Sweden] 1973 60(7): 314-317.* Assesses the importance of Radio Free Europe and Radio Liberty for the people of the Eastern bloc in light of Senator J. William Fulbright's 1973 proposal to abolish them.

907. Ivaničková, Edita. ČESKOSLOVENSKÝ FEBRUÁR A VYCHODNÉ NEMECKO V ROKU 1948 [Czechoslovak February and East Germany in 1948]. *Slovanské Štúdie [Czechoslovakia] 1983 24(2): 63-71.* The people's victory in February 1948 in Czechoslovakia affected the future of the East German state on its way toward socialism. Its revolutionary forces led by the Socialist

Unity Party of Germany (SED) accepted and developed the strategy of revolution for typical conditions in Germany and created a socialist state. Based on official records and printed items; 28 notes. G. E. Pergl

908. Kanet, Roger E. DIE KOMMUNISTICHEN STAATEN IN DER INTERNATIONALEN POLITIK: NEUE ENGLISCHSPRACHIGE PUBLIKATIONEN ÜBER DIE AUSSENBEZIEHUNGEN DER OSTEUROPÄISCHEN LÄNDER [The Communist countries in international politics: new English language publications on the foreign relations of the Eastern European countries]. *Osteuropa [West Germany] 1979 29(9): 771-778.* Reviews 12 new publications on the foreign relations of the Comecon states with Western Europe, the United States, Asia, and Africa and within the Warsaw Pact.

909. Klein, George and Reban, Milan J. *The Politics of Ethnicity in Eastern Europe.* (East European Monographs, no. 93.) Boulder, Colo.: East European Monographs, 1981. 279 pp.

910. Koleva, Tatiana. NOVA PROIAVA NA NAUCHNO SUTRUDNICHESTVO MEZHDU RUMUNSKI I BULGARSKI ISTORITSI [New manifestation of scholarly cooperation between Rumanian and Bulgarian historians]. *Izvestiia na Inst. po Istoriia na BKP [Bulgaria] 1975 32: 489-495.* The Rumanian and Bulgarian Institutes for Communist Party History held a joint seminar in Bucharest on 16-18 May 1974, the theme of which was the transformation of the two countries' socialist parties into Communist Parties.

911. Kołomejczyk, Norbert. POLSKA PARTIA ROBOTNICZA A PARTIE KOMUNISTYCZNE I ROBOTNICZE EUROPY ŚRODKOWEJ I POŁUDNIOWO-WSCHODNIEJ W REWOLUCJI LUDOWEJ (1944-1948) [The Polish Workers' Party and the Communist and Workers' parties of Central and Southeastern Europe in the people's revolution, 1944-48]. *Z Pola Walki [Poland] 1976 19(4): 57-78.* Communist parties of Central and Southeastern Europe in the postwar period continued the policy of democratic national fronts. Events produced a consolidation of revolutionary forces around Communist parties and simultaneous class and political polarization, with varying scope, tempo, and forms. In Poland there was a sharp division between the working class and bourgeoisie. The bourgeoisie retained in the early postwar period some relatively strong influences. This caused class struggle in Poland to take specifically sharp forms, including armed struggle and elements of civil war. The main link in the strategy of democratic national fronts was the unity of the working class and the worker-peasant alliance. For the Party, the most important question in all countries was consolidation of its position and influence, and unity with the Social Democratic left and the radical popular movement. An important influence was exerted by foreign policy, particularly unity with the Soviet Union. The rapid formation Marxist-Leninist parties was the most important component of the political activization of the working class. J/S

912. Lewin, Erwin. BRIEFE DER FREUNDSCHAFT: WILHELM PIECK AN GEORGI DIMITROFF [Letters of friendship: Wilhelm Pieck to Georgi Dimitrov]. *Beiträge zur Gesch. der Arbeiterbewegung [East Germany] 1982 24(3): 370-376.* Reproduces a selection of letters written by the German Socialist Wilhelm Pieck to the Bulgarian Communist leader Georgi Dimitrov (1882-1949), 1945-48. These letters reveal Pieck's deep admiration and friendship for Dimitrov and provide an insight into the cooperation between the German and Bulgarian Communists. Based on Wilhelm Pieck's letters in the Institute for Marxism-Leninism, Berlin and secondary sources; 14 notes. G. L. Neville

913. Lundgreen-Nielsen, Kay. USA, ØSTEUROPA OG DEN KOLDE KRIGS OPRINDELSE: EN FORSKNINGSOVERSIKT [USA, Eastern Europe and the origins of the Cold War: a research overview]. *Historisk Tidsskrift [Denmark] 1984 84(1): 58-85.* Until about 1970 views on postwar US policy in Europe tended to be either traditionalist or revisionist. Postrevisionist ideas were more unified. The United States wanted to maintain influence in Europe and thus feared confrontation between Eastern Europe and Western Europe under British leadership. Communist takeovers from 1946-47 led America to see Communism as the main enemy and to view the European situation in black-and-white terms. Secondary sources, 19 notes. D. F. Spade

914. Mančev, Krstú and Penčikov, K.. FEBRUÁR 1948 A BULHARSKO [February 1948 and Bulgaria]. *Slovanské Štúdie [Czechoslovakia] 1979 (20): 121-138.* Reaction of Bulgaria to the February 1948 Communist takeover in Czechoslovakia was positive. Both countries went through similar political development, building a new socialist society and closely cooperating with Moscow. Bulgarian support for Czechoslovakia against reactionary forces led finally to a mutual aid and cooperation treaty signed in April 1948. 59 notes. G. E. Pergl

915. Manchev, Krust'o and Penchikov, Kos'o. FEVRUARSKITE SUBITIIA V CHEKHOSLOVAKIIA PREZ 1948 G. I BULGARSKIIAT PECHAT [The February events in Czechoslovakia during 1948 and the Bulgarian press]. *Istoricheski Pregled [Bulgaria] 1978 34(2): 51-60.* Describes the Bulgarian press coverage of the Czechoslovakian Communist Party's coming to power in February 1948. The action of the party was applauded by the Bulgarian Communist press and that of allied parties. Bulgarian support of these February events laid the foundation for friendship between Czechoslovakia and Bulgaria afterwards. Based chiefly on contemporary press and secondary works; 49 notes. F. B. Chary

916. Mates, Pavel. POZEMKOVÉ REFORMY V ZEMÍCH STŘEDNÍ A JIHOVÝCHODNÍ EVROPY 1944-1948—VÍTĚZSTVÍ POLITICY KOMUNISTICKÝCH STRAN [Land reform in central and southeastern Europe, 1944-48: the victory of the Communist parties]. *Právněhistorické Studie [Czechoslovakia] 1979 22: 177-202.* The land reforms carried out in Czechoslovakia, Hungary, and Yugoslavia, 1944-48, represent a victory for the Communist movements of these lands. In each case the land reform strengthened the working class. 95 notes. B. Reinfeld

917. Mietkowska-Kaiser, Ines. ZUR BRÜDERLICHEN ZUSAMMENARBEIT ZWISCHEN POLNISCHEN UND DEUTSCHEN KOMMUNISTEN UND ANTIFASCHISTEN NACH DEM SIEG ÜBER DEN DEUTSCHEN FASCHISMUS (1945-1949) [Brotherly cooperation between Polish and German Communists and antifascists after the victory over German fascism 1945-49]. *Jahrbuch für Geschichte dur Sozialistischen Länder Europas [East Germany] 1979 23(1): 49-67.* The spirit of proletarian internationalism, forged in the antifascist struggle, 1933-45 allowed the proletarian parties of Poland and Germany to create a new relationship between the nations in the socialist community. When East Germany was instituted, one of the first statements of its leaders declared that the Oder-Neisse borderline had to be a line of mutual trust and friendship for both nations. 67 notes. G. E. Pergl

918. Moysov, Lazar. ON THE SOUTH SLAV FEDERATION. *Macedonian Review [Yugoslavia] 1984 14(3): 237-269.* Traces the evolution of the idea for a South Slav federation from the 19th century to 1948 and examines in detail the attitude of both Yugoslav and Bulgarian Communists to such a federation during the period 1941-48.

919. Ostoich, Petur. POLZOTVORNA SRESHTA MEZHDU BULGARSKI I RUMUNSKI ISTORITSI [A useful meeting between Bulgarian and Rumanian historians]. *Izvestiia na Inst. po Istoriia na BKP [Bulgaria] 1970 24: 535-537.* Reports a joint seminar held in Sofia in December 1969 on the theme "The Leading Role of the Bulgarian and Rumanian Communist Parties in founding and consolidating popular power in Bulgaria and Rumania, 1944-48."

920. Pell, Claiborne. THE CHALLENGES. *Foreign Service J. 1972 49(5): 16-19, 29-31.* Surveys the evolution of Communism in Eastern Europe and US foreign policy toward it. From *Power and Policy: America's Role in World Affairs* (New York: Norton, 1972).

921. Peterson, James W. POLITICAL ELITES AND POLITICAL ADAPTATION: A COMPARATIVE STUDY OF THE GERMAN DEMOCRATIC REPUBLIC AND CZECHOSLOVAKIA. *Michigan Academician 1979 11(3): 283-296.* Comparison of the political adaptation of Communist political elites to broad socioeconomic changes in East Germany and Czechoslovakia, 1954-62, shows that in both countries persons entering the Party after World War II were successful in becoming members of the central committee. They overwhelmingly had experience in economic affairs.

922. Schlauch, Wolfgang. DISSENT IN EASTERN EUROPE: RUDOLF BAHRO'S CRITICISM OF EAST EUROPEAN COMMUNISM. *Nationalities Papers 1981 9(1): 105-116.* In the wake of the Helsinki Accords, the Communist Parties of Eastern Europe have had to face growing human rights movements. Most significant is Rudolf Bahro's book entitled *The Alternative: A Contribution to the Critique of Actually Existing Socialism,* published in West Germany in 1977. Bahro, a respected party member, philosopher, propagandist, editor, trade union official, and industrial research director, shows his affinity with the humanistic aspect of Marx's theory and demonstrates the gap between Marxist theory and actual practice in Eastern Europe. He was accused of covert intelligence activities and arrested by the secret police. 20 notes.
J. V. Coutinho

923. Schlögl, Ludwig. KIRCHLICHE PRESSE NATIONALER MINDERHEITEN IN DEN KOMMUNISTISCHEN LÄNDERN [The ecclesiastical press of the national minorities in the Communist countries]. *Europa Ethnica [Austria] 1978 35(4): 164-166.*

924. Schoenberg, Hans W. THE PARTITION OF GERMANY AND THE NEUTRALIZATION OF AUSTRIA. *Studies on the Soviet Union [West Germany] 1971 11(4): 321-337.* Germany, greatly feared and harshly treated, was the primary target of Soviet military and political adventurism. The takeover pattern was otherwise similar to that used in other captive nations. Germany's eastern provinces were divided between Poland and the USSR and the German population driven out. Only military intervention by the other Allied powers could have prevented this development. Austria escaped Soviet rule because its Communist Party was weak and the Red Army controlled only a small part of its territory. Secondary sources; 22 notes. V. L. Human

925. Seeber, Eva. DIE VOLKSDEMOKRATISCHEN STAATEN MITTEL- UND SÜDOSTEUROPAS IN DER INTERNATIONALEN KLASSENAUSEINANDERSETZUNG ZWISCHEN IMPERIALISMUS UND SOZIALISMUS (1944-1947) [The people's republics of central and southeast Europe in the international class struggle between imperialism and socialism, 1944-47]. *Jahrbuch für Geschichte der Sozialistischen Länder Europas [East Germany] 1972 16(2): 39-90.* Reviews the process of the formation of the people's republics in central and southeast Europe, in particular the first parliamentary elections, the international treaties of Poland, Yugoslavia, and Czechoslovakia with the USSR, and the peace treaties with Bulgaria, Rumania, and Hungary. In the years 1944-47 the diplomatic successes of the USSR created a favorable situation for the founding of the people's republics. The USSR pursued a foreign policy aimed at peaceful coexistence and the strengthening of the socialist camp in the face of imperialist expansion from the West. Secondary works; 163 notes. J. B. Street

926. Staar, Richard F. *Communist Regimes in Eastern Europe.* 4th ed. Stanford: Hoover Inst. Pr., 1982. 375 pp.

927. Street, David P. THE BREAK-UP OF THE SOVIET MONOLITH IN EASTERN EUROPE: DOMESTICISM, POLYCENTRISM, AND NATIONAL COMMUNISM. *J. of Int. and Comparative Studies 1971 4(2): 37-55.* Attempts to define and make useful concepts of the terms "monolith," "domesticism," "polycentrism," and "national Communism" as they apply to Eastern Europe, 1946-56 in the movement away from monolithic Communism.

928. Tampke, Jürgen. *The People's Republics of Eastern Europe.* New York: St. Martin's, 1983. 178 pp.

929. Ţuţui, Gheorghe. COLOCVIU AL INSTITULUI DE STUDII ISTORICE ŞI SOCIAL-POLITICE DE PE LÎNGĂ C. C. AL P. C. R. ŞI INSTITULUI DE MARXISM-LENINISM DE PE LÎNGĂ C. C. AL P. S. U. G. (BERLIN) [The colloquium of the Rumanian Communist Party Central Committee's Institute for Historical and Sociopolitical studies, and the German United Socialist Party's Institute of Marxist-Leninism, Berlin]. *Anale de Istorie [Rumania] 1971 17(6): 167-172.* Reviews this East German-Rumanian Conference held for the first time, in Berlin, on 10-12 November 1971, and its three themes 1) the struggle of the two countries' Communist Parties to unify working-class activism, 2) the development of single Marxist-Leninist parties in the two countries, and 3) the present role of both countries' Communist Parties. The Rumanian papers were given by Gheorghe Matei, Gheorghe Ţuţu, and Gheorghe Surpat, and the German ones by Heinz Karl, G. Benzer, and Eckhard Trümpler. The colloquium speakers emphasized the indispensability of working-class unity for successful socialist revolution. R. O. Khan/S

930. Vasetski, N. A. KRITIKA TROTSKISTSKIKH FAL'SIFIKATOROV REAL'NOGO SOTSIALIZMA [Criticism of Trotskyite falsifiers of real socialism]. *Voprosy Istorii KPSS [USSR] 1982 (2): 104-115.* Critical analysis of methods and theories used by today's Trotskyites to slander real socialism and substitute Trotskyism for Marxism-Leninism in socialist and potentially socialist countries. Following an outline of the rise of the Trotskyist movement in the 1930's, asserts that Trotskyism was responsible for the troubles in Hungary in 1956, in Czechoslovakia in 1968, and now in Poland. Bourgeois propaganda in capitalist countries uses Trotskyism as a weapon against true socialism in the USSR. Primary sources; 67 notes. V. A. Packer

931. Voráček, Emil. VĚDECKÉ KOLOKVIUM O PROBLEMATICE IMPERIALISTICKÉHO "VÝCHODNÍHO BADÁNÍ A VÝZKUMU KOMUNISMU" [A scholarly colloquium on the problem of imperial Eastern Europe and Communist studies]. *Slovanský Přehled [Czechoslovakia] 1984 90[i.e., 70](2): 160-165.* An abstract of the proceedings of a colloquium held jointly by representatives of Czechoslovak and East German universities dealing with the study of Eastern Europe under Communism in the West. It includes the history of such institutes as the Hoover Institution in California and the Russian Institute at Columbia University, with an overview of the ideological swings as they have coincided with changes in the progress of the cold war and detente between the superpowers. B. Reinfeld

Albania

932. Agolì, Nesti. DELLE COSE ALBANESI [Albaniana]. *Balcanica [Italy] 1983 2(4): 31-38.* Reviews the politics and foreign policy of Albania, as well as the political leadership of Enver Hoxha's Communist Party.

933. Atanasova, Elena. GEORGII DIMITROV I ALBANSKOE KOMMUNISTICHESKOE DVIZHENIE [Georgi Dimitrov and the Albanian communist movement]. *Études Balkaniques [Bulgaria] 1972 (1): 63-78.* Discusses the role of Georgi Dimitrov (1882-1949), secretary of the Presidium of the Balkan Communist Federation, head of the West European office of Comintern and general secretary of the Third International, in the formation of the Albanian Communist Party. Dimitrov's conduct at the Leipzig trial became so well known that a Soviet film on the subject was banned in Albania at the request of the German ambassador. Provides a full account of international communist activity, particularly in Albania, up to the early 1940's. 74 notes. E. R. Sicher

934. Banja, Hasan. MENDIMI TEORIK I PPSH MBI KRIJIMIN E PRONËS SOCIALIST MBI MJETET E PRODHIMIT NË ETAPËN E NDËRTIMIT TË BAZËS EKONOMIKE TË SOCIALIZMIT NË SHQIPËRI [The theoretical thinking of the Albanian Party of Labor on the formation of socialist ownership of the means of production during the phase of the foundation of the economic bases of socialism in Albania]. *Studime Historike [Albania]*

1984 38(1): 17-32. Marxist theory enables the Albanian Party of Labor to establish the bases of socialism. Even before the complete liberation of the country the party decided on the nationalization of private and industrial property. The nationalization of the property of foreigners followed in 1946, despite Sejfulla Malëshova's opportunism. Industry and capital were in the hands of the proletariat. At the same time the agrarian reform was completed, ushering in the collectivization of rural property, which was achieved in stages: first by the theoretical preparation of the peasants in 1956 and then the collectivization of small farms which was completed in 1967. Based on Albanian state archives, *The History of the Albanian Party of Labor,* works by Stalin and Hoxha, and the official gazette; 57 notes. French summary. G.-D. L. Naçi

935. Belegu, Mentar. MBI LUFTEN A KLASAVE NË VENDIN TONË NË VITËT E PARA TË ÇLIRIMIT (1945-1947) [The outbreak of class warfare in the aftermath of our country's liberation, 1945-47]. *Studime Hist. [Albania] 1968 22(1): 189-197.* An account of the various measures of the Albanian communist government shortly after it took power in November 1944. All Italian industrial concerns and banks were nationalized; agricultural reform was introduced in August 1945; the property of political emigrés was confiscated; and new taxes levied on profits made by businessmen during the war. Relying on Albanian official sources, the author claims that these measures fostered a class struggle between the supporters of the régime and the landowners and other reactionary elements who were supported by the western powers. 52 notes.
A. Logoreci

936. Bihiku, Koço. DE L'ESSOR ULTÉRIOR DES ÉTUDES LITTÉRAIRES A LA LUMILRE DES DÉCISIONS DU VIIe CONGRÈS DU PTA [On the further scope of literary studies in the light of the decisions of the seventh congress of the Albanian Communist Party]. *Studia Albanica [Albania] 1977 14(2): 51-59.* Refers to contemporary studies on socialist realism in Albanian literature in the past 30 years. Traces the role of the Communist Party, especially the seventh congress, in promoting literature and the arts in the political education of the working class.
P. J. Taylorson

937. Birch, Julian. THE ALBANIAN POLITICAL EXPERIENCE. *Government and Opposition [Great Britain] 1971 6(3): 361-380.* Discusses the influence of Maoism in the political system of Albania, 1945-70's, including elections and the role of the military.

938. Bollano, Priamo. DISA ÇËSHTJE TË PËRSOSJES SË MARRËDHËNIEVE TË KËMBIMIT NË ETAPËN E NDËRTIMIT TË PLOTË TË SOCIALIZMIT NË SHQIPËRI [The improvement of exchange relations in the phase of the complete building of socialism in Albania]. *Studime Hist. [Albania] 1981 35(1): 3-24.* Inspired by the principles of Marxism-Leninism, the Albanian Party of Labor undertook the gradual improvement of relations between town and village to improve the people's living standards. A constant effort was made to reduce differences of income, stabilize prices between industry and agriculture, and improve the exchange of goods and services. Agricultural cooperatives were gradually organized on commercial lines and exchanges were based on money to allow the peasants to buy what they needed from industry. Prices were often reduced by good economic management. The process continues on the road to communism, without ignoring the fact that the abolition of private property is a slow process. Based on various Enver Hoxha reports; 4 tables, 51 notes. French summary. G-D. L. Naci

939. Çaushi, Tefik. ZHVILLIMI I MËTEJSHËM I MENDIMIT ESTETIK MARKSIST-LENINIST NË DOKUMENTAT E PPSH DHE NË VEPRAT E SHOKUT ENVER HOXHA NË VITET 1944-1960 [The further development of Marxist-Leninist aesthetics in the documents of the Albanian Party of Labor and in the work of Enver Hoxha, 1944-60]. *Studime Filologjike [Albania] 1980 34(2): 3-32.* A review of the ideological guidance provided for literature and the arts in the documents of the Albanian Party of Labour and the works of Enver Hoxha. 55 notes. French summary.

940. Delcheva, Greta. VNESHNIAIA POLITIKA ALBANII 1944-1948 [Albania's foreign policy, 1944-48]. *Etudes Balkaniques [Bulgaria] 1984 20(4): 15-37.* After the political change in the fall of 1944, which made the Albanian government part of the nation's anti-Nazi movement, the Communist Party took a leading role in the creation of a new Albania. Chronicles the new state's relations with the United States, Great Britain, and the USSR, as Albania began to establish a people's democracy. 111 notes.
R. Grove

941. Dyrmishi, Demir. VEPRIMTARIA REAKSIONARE E ORGANIZATËS TRADHTARE 'GRUPI I DEPUTETËVE, ZBULIMI DHE LIKUIDIMI I SAJ NË VITET 1945-1947 [The reactionary activities of the treacherous Deputies Group, its unmasking and liquidation, 1945-47]. *Studime Hist. [Albania] 1980 34(1): 57-83.* The great reforms undertaken by the Party after liberation provoked a strong reaction by the bourgeoisie. Aided and abetted by the Americans, British, and Greeks, reactionary groups committed sabotage and murder. Among the most important opposition groups was the Deputies Group formed by deputies, elected in the 1946 elections, who immediately put themselves at the service of the Americans. The Party launched the class struggle and mobilized the people. The traitors were arrested and condemned. Reforms were carried out, but the class struggle continues, because the reactionaries have not abandoned their treacherous objectives. Based on Party Archives, Enver Hoxha's works, and secondary sources; 103 notes. French summary. G-D. L. Naci

942. Fishta, Iljaz and Toçi, Veniamin. PPSH—ARKITEKTE E ZHVILLIMIT EKONOMIKO-SHOQËROR TE SHQIPERISE NE RRUGËN E SOCIALIZMIT [The Albanian Party of Labor, architect of Albania's socioeconomic development on the road to socialism]. *Studime Hist. [Albania] 1981 35(4): 29-49.* French summary.

943. Frashëri, Xhemil. OEUVRE MARXISTE-LENINISTE REMARQUABLE—A PROPOS DU LIVRE DU CAMARADE ENVER HOXHA *LES TITISTES* (NOTES HISTORIQUES) [A remarkable Marxist-Leninist work: Enver Hoxha's book *Les Titistes* (Historical notes)]. *Studia Albanica [Albania] 1983 20(2): 3-20.* An assessment of the Albanian Communist leader Enver Hoxha's (b. 1908) *Les Titistes* (1982), which constitutes a study of Albanian Marxist-Leninist historiography. The main emphasis of the work is the different aspects of the struggle between the Albanian Party of Labor and the Titoists between 1945 and 1948, when the Titoists tried to impose their revisionist policies on Albania and destroy its independence. In addition, the work places the struggle against Titoism within the framework of the general struggle against modern revisionism. 5 notes. G. L. Neville

944. Frashëri, Xhemil. ORGANIZIMI DHE ZHVILLIMI I KRYENGRITJES SË ARMATOSUR NË SHQIPËRI [The organization and development of the Albanian revolutionary army]. *Studime Hist. [Albania] 1976 30(1): 21-49.* The Communist Party of Albania, under the direction of Enver Hoxha, organized, inspired, and guided Albania's revolutionary army in the 1940's. The author discusses three distinct phases in the army's development, its composition, and its role in the struggle for national liberation. 52 notes. A. Logoreci/S

945. Frashëri, Xhemil. VEPËR E SHQUAR MARKSISTE-LENINISTE, ME VLERA TË MËDHA E TË SHUMANSHME (RRETH LIBRIT TË SHOKUT ENVER HOXHA *"TITISTËT" SHËNIME HISTORIKE)* [A valuable Marxist-Leninist work: Comrade Enver Hoxha's *The Titoites: Historical Notes]. Studime Hist. [Albania] 1983 37(1): 3-16.*

946. Gjilani, Feti. RRUGA HISTORIKE E LINDJES DHE E ZHVILLIMIT TË LEGJISLACIONIT TË PUNËS NË RPSH [The historical path of the birth and development of labor legislation in the People's Republic of Albania]. *Studime Hist. [Albania] 1971*

25(4): 125-144. Labor legislation in Albania developed very rapidly in the context of socialism. It has been the juridical expression of the fundamental directives of the Communist Party. 28 notes.

J. C. Billigmeier

947. Hysi, Gramos. KRIJIMI I APAPATIT TË RI SHTETËROR GJATË LUFTËS NACIONALÇLIRIMTARE [The creation of a new state apparatus during the national liberation war]. *Studime Hist. [Albania] 1970 24(1): 65-77.* A study of the formation of a new state apparatus conducted by the Albanian Communist Party at the close of World War II. The principles of this apparatus were fully articulated at the Communist Party-sponsored historical congress of Permët held in May of 1944. The principles of government were put into practice when the Albanian republic was proclaimed on 11 January 1946. 43 notes.

948. Kambo, Enriketa. ASPEKTE TË LUFTËS SË PKSH PER FORMIMIN E VETËDIJES POLITIKE SOCIALISTE TË KOMUNISTËVE E TË PUNONJËSVE NË VITET 1944-1948 [Aspects of the struggle of the Communist Party of Albania for the formation of political socialist awareness in the Communists and workers, 1944-48]. *Studime Hist. [Albania] 1983 37(1): 17-38.* Parallel with the fight for liberation, the Communist Party of Albania undertook to educate its cadres in the party school founded in 1945. Short courses were organized for the education of the Communists. The education of the entire population followed, special attention being given to developing a Communist awareness in the peasants. The press played a special role in popularizing Marxist-Leninist doctrine. Based on the Communist Party Central Archives and Enver Hoxha's works; 61 notes. French summary.

G.-D. L. Naçi

949. Kambo, Enriketa. CERTAINS ASPECTS DE LA LUTTE DU PCA POUR LA CREATION ET LA PROPAGATION DE LA CULTURE SPIRITUELLE SOCIALISTE AU COURS DES ANNEES 1944-48 [Certain aspects of the struggle of the Albanian Communist Party (ACP) for the creation and propagation of socialist culture from 1944 to 1948]. *Studia Albanica [Albania] 1981 18(1): 25-50.* To complement the achievement of the antifascist liberation in 1945 Albania had to abandon preliberation cultural values, essentially those of the bourgeoisie, and establish new values based on the socialist principles of Marxism-Leninism. The 5th Plenum of the ACP approved the construction of 23 cultural institutes and 200 lecture halls in 1946. By 1948 the works of Marx, Engels, and Lenin had been translated into Albanian. The principal aim of the new movement was to relate art to the struggles of the working class; but to avoid narrowness of outlook it was decided to translate the world's classics into Albanian. A. Alcock

950. Kambo, Enriketa. DISA ASPEKTE NGA LUFTA E PKSH PËR KRIJIMIN DHE PËRHAPJEN E KULTURËS SHPIRTËRORE SOCIALISTE NË VITET 1944-1948 [Aspects of the Communist Party of Albania's struggle for the creation and spread of socialist spiritual culture from 1944-48]. *Studime Hist. [Albania] 1980 34(3): 3-30.* Assuming power in 1944 the Communist Party undertook the creation of a Marxist-Leninist state. It conducted a long and intense struggle against feudal and bourgeois values and Malëshova's counterrevolutionary tendencies. The democratization of culture was achieved by the founding of Homes of Culture and public reading rooms. The Party adopted a nationalist attitude with regard to Albanian traditions and customs and cultural developments abroad. Based on the Central state archives; 64 notes. French summary. G-D. L. Naci

951. Koka, Viron. SESION SHKENCOR NË VLORË KUSHTUAR 90-VJETORIT TË LINDJES SË HEROIT TË POPULLIT HALIM XHELO [Scientific session marking the 90th anniversary of the birth of the people's hero Halim Xhelo]. *Studime Historike [Albania] 1984 38(3): 194-196.* On 2 June 1924 in the Vlora school Halim Xhelo a conference was organized in which the people's hero Vehbi Hoxha gave a brief biography of Halim Xhelo, who devoted all his life to the interest of the underdog, and especially the peasants. Viron Koka described the evolution of the hero's thoughts from democratic bourgeois ideas to Communist beliefs, especially during his 1925-37 exile, and said that he had been not only an active fighter but also a revolutionary journalist.

G.-D. L. Naçi

952. Kraja, Musa. ASPEKTE TË ZBATIMIT TË POLITIKËS ARSIMORE TË PKSH (1944-1948) [Aspects of the implementation of the educational policy of the Communist Party of Albania, 1944-48]. *Studime Hist. [Albania] 1984 38(2): 33-49.* At the time of the revolution, Albanian education was geared to the support of the reactionary regime and was in a state of complete anarchy. The aim of the Communist Party of Albania (CPA) was to establish a system of secular democratic and socialist education and abolish illiteracy. The first task was to politically and technically educate the existing teachers and to train new ones. Since all had to work within a unified Marxist system, it was necessary to fight Malëshova's opportunism and Xoxe's Trotskyism. In 1946 the Plenum of the CPA carried out this reform. Based on Hoxha's works and the central Party and state archives; 22 notes. French summary.

G-D. L. Naçi

953. Lalaj, Petro. PROBLEMI I REVOLUCIONIT POPULLOR NË VEPRAT E SHOKUT ENVER HOXHA TË VITËVE TË PARA PAS ÇLIRIMIT (NENTOR 1944-QERSHOR 1948) [The problem of the popular revolution in the works of Enver Hoxha in the first years after liberation]. *Studime Hist. [Albania] 1978 32(4): 3-28.* After Albanian liberation, the important problem was the defense of the ideology and experience of the liberation struggle against Berat deviationists and against hostile Yugoslav revisionists. Enver Hoxha believed that the struggle was the apotheosis of national tradition and true patriotism, liberating not only the country but also the people from social oppression, and enabling them, guided by the Communist Party, to take power. The Party was able rapidly to construct integral socialism. Only scientific Marxist-Leninist principles enabled the Communist Party to achieve socialism despite the Yugoslav revisionists. Based on Enver Hoxha's works; 46 notes. G-D. L. Naci

954. Lange, Klaus. ALBANIAN MARXISM'S NOTION OF REVISIONISM. *Studies in Soviet Thought [Netherlands] 1979 20(1): 61-66.* The struggle against revisionism is a constant theme in post-1945 Albanian thought. It is a matter of legitimizing the Albanian Communist Party's rule, in a country lacking almost all the classical Marxist conditions for revolution. The chief goal has been the creation of an Albanian "nation." Any opposition to this is condemned as "revisionism." 13 notes. R. N. Stromberg

955. Liess, Otto Rudolf. ALBANIEN—EIN NEUES "MODELL" IM WELTKOMMUNISMUS [Albania, a new "model" in world communism]. *Schweizer Monatshefte [Switzerland] 1978 58(4): 249-254.* After Albania severed relations with Yugoslavia in 1948 and with the Soviet Union in 1960, it closely cooperated with China until 1977. In 1977 the Albanian Communist leadership denounced the relevance of Mao Tse-tung's theory of the three worlds, marking the beginning of the split with their former ally.

R. Wagnleitner

956. Madhi, S. LUFTA E PPSH KUNDËR OPORTUNIZMIT TË DJATHTË NË VITET 1949-1955 [The struggle of the Albanian Communist Party against right-wing opportunists, 1949-55]. *Studime Hist. [Albania] 1967 21(3): 43-54.* Surveys the measures taken between 1949 and 1955 against right-wing elements in the ranks of the Albanian Communist Party.

957. Maksutovici, Gelcu. TREI DECENII DE LA ELIBERAREA ALBANIEI DE SUB DOMINAŢIA FASCISTĂ ŞI VICTORIA REVOLUŢIEI POPULARE [Three decades since the liberation of Albania from fascist domination and the victory of the people's revolution]. *Anale de Istorie [Rumania] 1974 20(6): 151-155.* Celebrating thirty years from the final victory over the Italian and German occupation armies, with the liberation of Shkodër by the Albanian Army of National Liberation on 29 November 1944, summarizes the chronology of the military efforts which led to the reconquest of independence, the leading role played by the Albanian Communist Party in the victory, and the great economic, social,

and political strides made in all areas of the national life since the victory, which produced the nationalization and collectivization of all land and industry. Based on Archives of the Party Institute of History. G. J. Bobango

958. Mara, H. MBI ZHVILLIMIN EKONOMIK E SHOQËROR TË RP TE SHQIPËRISË [The economic and social development of the People's Republic of Albania]. *Studime Hist. [Albania] 1967 21(2): 15-25.* Summarizes Albania's economic and social achievements during the first 20 years of Communist rule, 1945-65.

959. Marjani, Stavri; Malindi, Nevrus; and Shtëpani, Tefta. KRIJIMI DHE ZHVILLIMI I NDERMARRJEVE BUJQESORE SOCIALIST NË SHQIPERI (1944-1960) [The founding and development of socialist agriculture in Albania, 1944-60]. *Studime Hist. [Albania] 1982 36(2): 15-34.* Following Marxist ideas and policies the Albanian Party of Labor immediately after taking power decided to form big state farms and collectives to show the peasants the advantages of large-scale exploitation. Big landowners were expropriated to form the socialist sector; foreign landowners' lands belonging to the Italian and German states as well as to internal enemies were also expropriated. By 1956 the socialist sector had been modernized and mechanized. By 1960 14.22% of all arable lands belonged to that sector. Its great successes provided the basis for the collectivization of all land. Based on Hoxha's reports and the Central state archives. Summary in French.

G.-D. L. Naçi

960. Naçi, S. N. LUFTA E PUNONJËSVE TË BAZËS PËR SHPEJTIMIN E RITMIT TË KOLEKTIVIZIMIT TË FSHATIT NË VITET 1956-1959 [The campaign of Party workers to speed up collectivization, 1956-59]. *Studime Hist. [Albania] 1969 23(4): 175-184.* By 1955, 318 cooperative farms had been set up in Albania, comprising 14.48% of the arable land. In December of that year, the government decided to extend collectivization to 70% of the arable land in the plains and up to 15% in the mountain areas. Communist Party propagandists had instructions to use persuasion and not pressure in the campaign. After the uprising in Hungary and the disturbances in Poland in 1956, there was some peasant opposition to the collectivization campaign, but the campaign reached a turning point by 1957. 42 notes. A. Logoreci

961. Omari, Luan. PROBLEMI I PUSHTETIT NË LUFTËN ANTIFASHISTE NACIONALÇLIRIMTARE TË POPULLIT SHQIPTAR [The problem of political power in the antifascist and national liberation struggle of the Albanian people]. *Studime Hist. [Albania] 1974 28(4): 71-88.* Describes how the councils of the Communist national liberation movement of World War II gradually evolved from purely guerrilla and military units to become representative and executive political bodies which replaced the prewar political and administrative structure. Although the monarchical regime had, for all practical purposes, come to an end by late 1944, the formal replacement of the monarchy by a republic was decided by the Albanian constituent assembly in January 1946. 11 notes.

A. Logoreci

962. Prifti, Peter R. THE ALBANIAN PARTY OF LABOR AND THE INTELLIGENTSIA. *East European Q. 1974 8(3): 307-335.* An account of the attempt by the Albanian Communist Party leadership both to encourage and use the intellectuals and ensure their loyalty to the party. The problem of allowing adequate creative freedom while maintaining party discipline has led to four confrontations since 1945, all of which are described in detail. 97 notes.

C. R. Lovin

963. Prifti, Peter R. THE ALBANIAN WOMEN'S STRUGGLE FOR EMANCIPATION. *Southeastern Europe 1975 2(2): 109-129.* In prerevolutionary Albania, a woman's position was oppressive in the extreme; she was often regarded as property, not as a person. The Albanian Party of Labor sees the elevation of the status of women as an integral part of the revolution. Their program has had some degree of success. Women now have equality under the law, but the attitudes of Albanian men, and women, has been slow to change. Published primary and secondary sources; 87 notes.

E. M. McLendon

964. Rusi, Deko. SHNDËRRIMI SOCIALIST I EKONOMIVE TË VOGLA FSHATARE: FITORE E MADHE E VIJËS SË PPSH [The socialist transformation of small village economies: the great victory of the line of the Albanian Party of Labor]. *Studime Hist. [Albania] 1981 35(4): 145-173.* Albania's agriculture in the interwar period was backward, and the practices of the big landowners and King Zog's policies worsened the situation. In 1945 the Party introduced agrarian reform on the principle that the land belongs to the toilers. But small farms persisted, impeding the adoption of new techniques. Following Lenin, the Party launched the cooperative movement. Cooperativization was gradual and took into consideration the psychology of the peasant. By 1960 cooperatives were established in the lowlands and by 1967 in the mountains, when the change was completed and mechanization introduced everywhere. The results amply justify the Party's policies. Based on Enver Hoxha's works and official publications; 28 notes. G.-D. L. Naçi

965. Sadikaj, Dilaver. DISA ASPEKTE TË RRITJES SË PJESËMARRJES SË GRUAS NË JETËN POLITIKE SHOQËRORE TË VENDIT (1967-70) [Some aspects of the greater participation of women in the political and social life of the country, 1967-70]. *Studime Hist. [Albania] 1977 31(4): 21-48.* Reviews the progress achieved, 1967-70, in the campaign for the greater involvement of Albanian women in the social and political activities of the Communist Party and in the work of the country's local and central administration. The campaign was launched at the fifth congress of the Albanian Communist Party in November 1966. As a result of complex and intense propaganda and agitation, by 1970 the participation of women in social and political work at all levels had increased. They made up 22% of the party members, 27% of the national assembly members, and nearly 46% of local government officials. 2 tables, 64 notes. A. Logoreci

966. Sadikaj, Dilaver. RRITJA E ROLIT TË GRUAS NË PRODHIMIN SHOQËROR FAKTOR VENDIMTAR I EMANCIPIMIT TË SAJ TË PLOTË (NËNDOR 1966-DHJETOR 1968) [The growth of women's role in social production, a decisive factor for their total emancipation, November 1966-December 1968]. *Studime Hist. [Albania] 1976 30(4): 11-50.* Although women in Albania have enjoyed legal equality since 1948, they are far from being totally emancipated. A new stage in the revolutionary movement for the qualitative emancipation of women began in August 1967 at the fifth Congress of the communist Albanian Party of Labor (PPSH) when the participation of women in the work force and in all social and political life was presented as a political imperative. The activity undertaken, 1966-68, to destroy the remnants of patriarchy, elevating women in the professions, and eliminating their domestic subjugation, brought considerable results. Women's participation in the labor force increased from 33.6% to 38.4%, with a qualitative improvement as well. By 1968 more than 600 women were managers of businesses, factories, and social and cultural institutions. 109 notes.

967. Shapo, Petro. BOTIMI I DYTË I HISTORISË SË PPSH—GJARJE ME RËNDËSI TË MADHE NË JETËN IDEOLOGJIKE E SHKENCORE TË VENDIT [The second edition of the history of the Albanian Party of Labor: event of great importance in the ideological and scientific life of the country]. *Studime Hist. [Albania] 1981 35(4): 3-24.* The second edition of the history of the Albanian Workers Party contains some abbreviations of and amendments to the first edition. The last three chapters, covering 1966-80, are the most important and show how the Party followed and developed by continuous revolution the Marxist-Leninist principles it had adopted from the start. Mass participation was consolidated, the class struggle intensified, and defense against aggressors strengthened. Cultural and economic progress without foreign aid characterizes this period, which also saw the intensification of the ideological line against all revisionists, a new scientific

constitution, and the proclamation of the atheist state. Based on published Party documents and Enver Hoxha's reports; 20 notes. French summary. G.-D. L. Naçi

968. Sinani, Petrit. "DISA ÇËSHTJE TË POLITIKËS AGRARË TË P. K. SH. NË VITET 1941-1948" [Questions on the agrarian policy of the Albanian Communist Party, 1941-48]. *Studime Historike [Albania] 1972 26(4): 235-238.* Reviews Apostol Kotani's *Questions on the Agrarian Policy of the Albania Communist Party 1941-1948,* which covers the national liberation movements against Nazi and Fascist military occupations, 1941-44, and the postwar era until the Soviet-Yugoslav break of 1948. Includes the approval of a new Agrarian Reform Law on 27 May 1946.

J. C. Billigmeier

969. Tase, Alfreda. ASPEKTE TË LUFTËS PËR EMANCIPIMIN E PLOTË TË GRUAS NË RRETHIN E TIRANËS NË VITET 1961-1970 [Aspects of the struggle in the Tiranë region during the 1960's for the complete emancipation of women]. *Studime Historike [Albania] 1984 38(3): 15-31.* Women's participation and sacrifices during the liberation struggle proved that the Party policy of complete economic and political emancipation of women was right. Enver Hoxha's advice to the 5th Congress and the decisions of 2d Plenum in 1967 were followed by the Tiranë Party which fought for women's equality in social production and management and helped them to acquire the necessary skills and education. It also encouraged them to participate in politics and administration and reach the highest positions in the Party and government. Based on documents of the Tiranë Women's Union and secondary sources; 46 notes. French summary. G.-D. L. Naçi

970. Thomas, John I. COMMUNIST EDUCATION IN THE SCHOOLS OF THE PEOPLE'S REPUBLIC OF ALBANIA. *Paedagogica Historica [Belgium] 1973 13(1): 107-119.* Though it is difficult to ascertain how well entrenched the political principles of communism are in Albanian schools, education for communism seems deeply rooted. The heavy stress placed by the present regime on ideological and political education of teachers and students has clearly shaped their character and direction. 32 notes.

J. M. McCarthy

971. Toçi, Veniamin. KRYERJA E PROCESIT TE KALIMIT TË KOOPERATIVAVE TË ARTIZANATIT NË PRONË TË TË GJITHË POPULLIT (1968-1969) [The completion of the transformation process of craft cooperatives into people's property, 1968-69]. *Studime Hist. [Albania] 1981 35(2): 3-17.* The first craft cooperatives were founded in 1946. By 1968 they were producing 29 times more than craftsmen in 1938 and only 7% of the craftsmen continued to be independent. The movement had become an important economic factor, and it became obvious that some changes were necessary to avoid duplication and difficulties with the state sector. A general debate among members was conducted and its conclusions studied by the Communist Party, which decided to incorporate the cooperatives in the state sector. That decision reflected the craftsmen's wishes; they had become workers. The incorporation was completed by May 1969. Albania was the first country to transform cooperative property into people's property with great success and on the initiative of those concerned. Based on the Central State Archives and secondary sources; 30 notes. French summary. G-D. L. Naçi

972. Tönnes, Bernhard. EINIGE GRUNDZÜGE DER ALBANISCHEN POLITIK: AUS ANLASS DES VI. PARTEITAGS IN TIRANA [Some basic traits of Albanian policy (on the occasion of the 6th Party Congress in Tirana)]. *Osteuropa [West Germany] 1972 22(4): 287-297.* Though Communist Albania supports the Chinese People's Republic, its domestic political posture has evolved independently. The cultural revolution proceeds under firm Party control, but has not reached its goal of rejuvenating and proletarizing the party cadres. It has sharpened Albania's isolation, to the regret of many intellectuals. 31 notes. Additional documentation on pp. A274-A275. R. E. Weltsch

973. Tsiovaridou, Theanō N. Ē EXELIXĒ TĒS DOMĒS TĒS ALVANIKĒS OIKONOMIAS (1939-1978) [The development of the Albanian economy, 1939-78]. *Valkanika Symmeikta [Greece] 1981 1: 229-291.* Sketches Albanian manufacturing and economic growth during the military occupation by Italy, World War II, and the political change under communism.

974. Tuli, Jonuz. POLITIKA E PARTISË SË PUNËS TË SHQIPËRISË PËR NGRITJEN E MIRËQENIES MATERIALE E KULTURALE NË RPS TË SHQIPËRISË (1944-1980) [The policy of the Albanian Party of Labor for improving the well-being and the cultural progress of the People's Socialist Republic of Albania, 1944-80]. *Studime Hist. [Albania] 1983 37(2): 17-38.* To stop the decline in the standard of living of the working population following World War II, the Party inaugurated a policy based on increasing production and productivity without foreign aid, credits, or loans. Using only national resources living standards of the working class have improved: prices have remained stable or fallen, taxes have been abolished and social services have been created. In addition differences between life in the villages and cities have been reduced. Based on Enver Hoxha's reports to Party congresses; 8 tables, 39 notes. French summary. G-D. L. Naçi/S

975. Xhaxhiu, Muzafer. VEPRIMTARIA LETRARE E NONDA BULKËS [The literary activity of Nonda Bulka]. *Studime Filologjike [Albania] 1979 33(1): 63-92.* A review of the work of Nonda Bulka (who occasionally wrote under the pseudonymn Chri-Chri), a Communist journalist and translator who began his career in 1932. French summary.

976. Xholi, Zija. LA RÉVOLUTION CULTURELLE SOCIALISTE ET LA CULTURE ARTISTIQUE SOCIALISTE [The socialist cultural revolution and socialist artistic culture]. *Studia Albanica [Albania] 1976 13(2): 59-82.* Evaluates the achievement of the Communist Party in creating a new culture in Albania in the 35 years since its foundation. The cultural revolution has developed in close association with the socialist revolution and the dictatorship of the proletariat. Aspects of the new culture are the Albanian language, moral and spiritual formation, education, abandonment of retrogressive customs and religious practices, and improved living conditions. P. J. Taylorson

977. Zanga, Louis. DAS AUSSENPOLITISCHE MODELL ALBANIENS [The pattern of Albania's foreign policy]. *Osteuropa [West Germany] 1977 27(9): 767-780.* Surveys the foreign policy of Albania outlined by First Secretary Enver Hoxha at the Seventh Congress of the Communist Party. Based on issues of *Zeri i Popullit.*

978. —. KONGRES HISTORIK, ANALIZË MARKSISTE-LENINISTE E ARRITHEVE DHE E PERSPEKTIVAVE TË NDËRTIMIT SOCIALIST NË SHQIPËRI [Historical congress, a Marxist-Leninist analysis of the achievements and projections for socialist construction in Albania]. *Studime Hist. [Albania] 1982 36(1): 3-8.* Reviews the work of the 8th Congress of the Albanian Party of Labor in November 1981 on the 40th anniversary of the Party's founding. Enver Hoxha reported the country's economic, social, and educational successes, and the congress approved Central Committee acts and the 7th Five-Year Plan, which became law in January 1982. 8 notes. G.-D. L. Naci

979. —. L'ANALYSE DU TRAVAIL DE L'INSTITUT DE L'HISTOIRE A LA LUMIERE DES MATERIAUX DU 8e PLENUM DU CC DU PTA [Analysis of the work of the Historical Institute in the light of the proceedings of the 8th Plenum of the Central Committee of the Albanian Party of Labor]. *Studia Albanica [Albania] 1981 18(1): 211-217.* Recognizing the importance of scientific developments for socialism, particularly in history writing, Enver Hoxha has encouraged Albanian historians to collaborate more closely in the writing of history, especially at a local level. For example, the history of the hydroelectric plant of Vau i Dejës should be confined to one or two local historians at

Shkodër. Historians of all periods are urged to conduct their investigations as vigorously as possible, always using as their basis principles fundamental to the ideals of the proletariat.
A. Alcock

Bulgaria

980. Istoricheski Pregled Editors. EDINADESETIAT KONGRES NA BKP I BULGARSKITE ISTORTSI [The 11th BCP congress and Bulgarian historians]. *Istoricheski Pregled [Bulgaria] 1976 32(3): 3-15.* Examines the directives given by the 11th Congress of the Bulgarian Communist Party, 29 March-2 April 1976 in Sofia, concerning the work of Bulgarian historians. Based on articles in the Party paper *Rabotnichesko Delo;* 11 notes. B. R. Pach

981. Aleksieva, Tsvetana. ORGANIZATSIONNATA I MASOVO-POLITICHESKATA RABOTA NA BKP ZA VŬZSTANOVIAVANETO I RAZVITIETO NA ZHELEZOPŬTNIIA TRANSPORT (9 SEPTEMVRII 1944-DEKEMVRI 1948) [The organizational and mass political work of the Bulgarian Communist Party in the reconstruction and development of rail transport, 9 September 1944-December 1948]. *Izvestiia na Inst. po Istoriia na BKP [Bulgaria] 1975 32: 247-272.* The need to transport Russian troops through Bulgaria after the coup and occupation of September 1944 led the Bulgarian Communist Party to concentrate special effort on the political organization, mobilization, and indoctrination of railroad workers, long a center of Socialist Party influence. There were, however, problems of inertia and opposition among engineers. Soviet specialists were vital to the reorganization and reconstruction of lines in the immediate postwar years. Errors in administration, slowness in taking command of existing unions, and the lack of sufficient economic stimulation of rail workers were continuing problems in the postwar period. Central Party and State Archives, local Party archives; 84 notes.
C. S. Masloff

982. Amort, Čestmír. BUDOVÁNÍ ZÁKLADŮ SOCIALISMU V BULHARSKU [Building the foundations of Socialism in Bulgaria]. *Slovanský Přehled [Czechoslovakia] 1980 66(5): 389-396.* The first two Five-Year Plans in Bulgaria effected the country's modernization and its solid partnership with the USSR and other People's Republics. The most outstanding achievements of the Five-Year Plans were the electrification of the countryside and the mechanization and collectivization of the farms. Orchestrating these efforts were the Communist Party of Bulgaria with the USSR providing technical advisors and training Bulgarians in the USSR. 22 notes.
B. Reinfeld

983. Amort, Čestmír. CESTA K SOCIALISTICKÉ REVOLUCI V BULHARSKU [The road to socialist revolution in Bulgaria]. *Hist. a Vojenství [Czechoslovakia] 1979 28(4): 32-52.* The August 1944 entry into the Balkans by the Soviet Army created favorable conditions for the Communist takeover of Bulgaria. On 9 September 1944 a popular uprising led by the Bulgarian Fatherland Front began in coordination with Soviet troop movements into Bulgaria. This development allowed the Bulgarian Army to enter the war against Germany. 35 notes. G. E. Pergl

984. Apostolova, Veneta. PO NIAKOI VŬPROSI NA RAZVITIETO NA SPETSIALNATA RETROSPEKTIVNA BIBLIOGRAFIIA PO ISTORIIA NA BKP RABOTNICHESKOTO I MLADEZHKOTO DVIZHENIE V BŬLGARIIA [Some problems in the development of a specialized retrospective bibliography of the history of the Bulgarian Communist Party (BKP) and labor and youth movements in Bulgaria]. *Izvestiia na Inst. po Istoriia na BKP [Bulgaria] 1974 31: 57-85.* A survey and evaluation of bibliography on specialized topics of the history of the Bulgarian Communist Party, the inadequacies of standard reference works, and various types of specialized literature. Theoretical studies have not given enough attention to such faults in the existing bibliography. Only direction and guidance by deeper work on Party theory can solve the problem of improving the quality of individual historical studies. Secondary sources; 66 notes. C. S. Masloff

985. Atanasov, Atanas. PODOBRIAVANE NA MATERIALNO-BITOVOTO POLOZHENIE NA RABOTNICHESKATA KLASA V BULGARIIA (1948-1958 G.) [Improving the material living standard of the working class in Bulgaria (1948-58)]. *Izvestiia na Instituta po Istoriia na BKP [Bulgaria] 1983 (48): 155-195.* Describes the policies of the Bulgarian Communist Party aimed at improving the material living conditions and the general life of Bulgarian workers between 1948 and 1958. Working conditions, industrial expansion, productivity, governmental revenue, and personal incomes improved. In addition, the provision of social benefits, free medical care, cultural and sports facilities, and educational opportunities increased during this period. Based on a wide variety of Bulgarian statistical, economic, and political literature; 92 notes.
A. J. Evans

986. Atanasov, Atanas. POLITIKATA NA BKP I RŬKOVODNATA ROLIA NA RABOTNICHESKATA KLASA V PREDSTAVITELNITE ORGANI NA DŬRZHAVNATA VLAST (1948-1958 G.) [The policy of the Bulgarian Communist Party and the leading role of the working class in the representative organs of the state, 1948-58]. *Izvestiia na Inst. po Istoriia na BKP [Bulgaria] 1975 32: 195-221.* A study of the policies of the Bulgarian Communist Party aimed at widening workers' participation in local popular councils during the first two five-year plans, 1948-58. Turning points occurred at the fifth Party congress in 1948 which approved local self-administration and at the April plenum of the Central Committee in 1956 which corrected the errors concerning worker participation in local government stemming from the personality cult of Vŭlko Chervenkov. Permanent advisory committees attached to the popular councils drew in specialized workers to connect local government with the Fatherland Front, labor unions, and specialized organizations on social, economic, and cultural projects. Based on central Party and state archives, published sources; 62 notes. C. S. Masloff

987. Auersperg, Pavel, et al. FRIENDS LOOK AT BULGARIA; THE LIFE AND DESTINY OF A COUNTRY AND PEOPLE THAT HAVE CHOSEN SOCIALISM. *World Marxist R. [Canada] 1974 17(9): 82-112.* Report on socialist life in Bulgaria since the Communist Party came to power 30 years ago.

988. Avramov, Ruben. VSTUPITELNO SLOVO NA SESIIATA, POSVETENA NA 60-GODISHNINATA OT RAZTSEPLENIETO (1903 G) I 40-GODISHNINATA OT SEPTEMVRIISKOTO VUSTANIE (1923 G) [The opening address at the symposium dedicated to the 60th anniversary of the 1903 split and the 40th anniversary of the 1923 September Rising]. *Izvestiia na Inst. po Istoriia na BKP [Bulgaria] 1964 11: 4-12.* The symposium, organized by the Institute of History of the Bulgarian Communist Party and other official bodies, met at the Bulgarian Academy of Sciences on 10 and 11 October 1963; the opening discourse assesses the importance of the 1903 split in the Bulgarian Social Democratic Party and the 1923 September Rising for the development of Bulgaria's labor movement and Communist Party.

989. Baichinski, Kostadin. PRODULZHITEL NA TEORETICHESKOTO I REVOLUTSIONNOTO DELO NA DIMITER BLAGOEV I GEORGI DIMITROV (IZBRANI SUCHINENIA NA TODOR ZHIVKOV) [The continuer of the theoretical and the revolutionary work of Dimitur Blagoev and Georgi Dimitrov: selected works by Todor Zhivkov]. *Izvestiia na Inst. po Istoriia na BKP [Bulgaria] 1977 36: 5-31.* An appraisal of the work of Bulgarian Communist Party leader Todor Zhivkov on the publication of a new edition of his selected works in 1975.

990. Baichinski, K. GEORGI DIMITROV—STROITEL' MARKSISTSKO-LENINSKOI PARTII V BOLGARII [Georgi Dimitrov: builder of a Marxist-Leninist party in Bulgaria]. *Voprosy Istorii KPSS [USSR] 1972 (6): 46-55.* Discusses Dimitrov's organizational and theoretical work as the leader of the Bulgarian Communist Party, 1919-49.

991. Baichinski, K. INTERNATSIONAL'NOE EDINSTVO—OSNOVA VZAIMOOTNOSHENII MEZHDU BKP I KPSS [International unity, the foundation of the mutual relations

between the Bulgarian Communist Party and the Communist Party of the Soviet Union]. *Voprosy Istorii KPSS [USSR] 1981 (3): 79-87.*

992. Baichinski, K. PARIZHKATA KOMUNA I NASHATA SURVREMENNOST [The Paris Commune and our present]. *Izvestiia na Inst. po Istoriia na BKP [Bulgaria] 1971 26: 371-388.* Relates the 1871 Paris Commune to the problems of the contemporary Communist movement, and sees the victory of the Bulgarian revolution as a continuation of the Paris Commune and the Russian October Revolution.

993. Baichinski, K. VOZRASTANIE RUKOVODIASHCHEI ROLI BOLGARSKOI KOMMUNISTICHESKOI PARTII [The increasingly prominent role of the Bulgarian Communist Party]. *Voprosy Istorii KPSS [USSR] 1969 (7): 62-78.* Outlines the formation and development of the Bulgarian Communist Party and shows the increasing importance of its leadership in a developing socialist country.

994. Baichinski, Kostadin and Zarchev, Iordan. PREOBRAZUVASHTATA SILA NA APRILSKIIA KURS [The transforming of the April Plenum]. *Izvestiia na Inst. po Istoriia na BKP [Bulgaria] 1981 45: 13-37.* Extended review of Party leader Todor Zhivkov's two-volume collection of speeches and articles on the April Plenum, the reorientation of Party policy at the plenum of the Central Committee in April 1956.

995. Baichinski, Kostadin. GEORGI DIMITROFF UND DER AUFBAU DES SOZIALISMUS IN BULGARIEN [Georgi Dimitrov and the foundation of socialism in Bulgaria]. *Beiträge zur Gesch. der Arbeiterbewegung [East Germany] 1982 24(3): 323-333.* Assesses the important role played by the Bulgarian Communist leader Georgi Dimitrov (1882-1949) in establishing socialism in Bulgaria, and considers his contribution to the international Communist movement. Dimitrov's most important activities in Bulgaria were: to make the Bulgarian Communist Party into a Marxist-Leninist Party; and to unite the Bulgarian people in order to bring about the Socialist revolution which occurred 9 September 1944. In addition, as Bulgarian leader, Dimitrov established the foundations of the Bulgarian Socialist Republic. On an international level Dimitrov came to symbolize the cooperation of antifascist powers throughout the world as the result of his work as a theorist and strategist in the fight against fascism. Secondary sources; 9 notes.
G. L. Neville

996. Berov, Ljuben. THE ECONOMIC DEVELOPMENT OF BULGARIA UNDER SOCIALISM 1944-1984. *Etudes Balkaniques [Bulgaria] 1984 20(3): 15-25.* Chronicles the economic and social change following the political change in Bulgaria at the end of World War II. Socialist economic planning guided by the Communist Party and in concert with that of other Communist countries accomplished much agricultural reform and industrialization.
R. Grove

997. Boev, Boris. APREL'SKII PLENUM TSK BKP 1956 GODA I EGO ZNACHENIE V RAZVITII PARTII I STRANY [The April 1956 Plenum of the Central Committee of the Bulgarian Communist Party and its significance in the development of Party and country]. *Études Balkaniques [Bulgaria] 1981 17(4): 13-26.* Resolutions reached at this plenum would not have been endorsed without the political courage, adherence to Lenin's principles, and farsightedness of Todor Zhivkov, First Secretary of the Central Committee. He denounced factional dogmatism and subjectivism inherent in the cult of personality and endorsed the creative Marxist-Leninist program adopted at the 20th Congress of the Communist Party of the USSR. The plenum decreed basic reforms of national economy, administration, party ideology, cadre selection, cooperative farming, trade unionism, education, and socioeconomic development, while preserving the political traditions of Bulgarian Communist leader, Georgi Dimitrov (1882-1949). 35 notes.
N. Frenkley

998. Boev, Boris. APRILSKATA LINIIA NA BKP I RAZVITIETO NA SŬIUZA NA RABOTNICHESKATA KLASA I SELIANITE [The April Plenum of the Bulgarian Communist Party and the development of the alliance of the working class and the peasants]. *Izvestiia na Inst. po Istoriia na BKP [Bulgaria] 1981 45: 41-90.* Traces the processes through which the working class and the Communist Party have strengthened their predominant role in their alliance with the peasantry and the Agrarian Popular Union since 1956. French, German, Russian summaries.

999. Bozhinov, V. DVE DESETILETIIA RAVNI NA VEK [Two decades equal a century]. *Istoricheski Pregled [Bulgaria] 1964 20(2-3): 21-44.* Examines the tremendous changes in Bulgaria since the 1944 uprising which laid the basis of socialism. An important step in the consolidation of the people's power was the victory of the Communist Party in the elections to the people's assembly, 1946. This facilitated the nationalization of industry, the state takeover of external trade, and the destruction of the power of the exploiting classes. An important political change was the establishment of voting rights for all citizens over 18. Bulgaria's international authority rests on its faithfulness to its peaceloving policy, its aid to underdeveloped nations, its participation in world organizations, and its friendship with the USSR and the other socialist countries. Internally industrialization has advanced rapidly, and this has produced constantly rising living standards. Based on materials in Party archives, and on the records of national institutions; 45 notes, table.
A. J. Evans

1000. Canev, Petăr. VASIL KOLAROV ET LES PROBLÈMES BALKANIQUES [Vasil Kolarov and the Balkan question]. *Études Balkaniques [Bulgaria] 1977 (3): 8-16.* Commemorates the centenary of Vasil Kolarov (1877-1950), a leading figure in the revolutionary workers' movement and the Bulgarian Communist Party, close associate of Georgi Dimitrov, and a renowned militant of the international Communist movement. Outlines Kolarov's career and examines his writings to summarize his views of questions affecting the Balkans. Pays tribute to Kolarov's role in promoting friendly relations among the Balkan nations. Based mainly on Kolarov's writings; 21 notes.
P. J. Taylorson

1001. Chernii, A. I. PROBLEMY SOTSIALISTYCHNOI INDUSTRIALIZATSII NRB U RADIANS'KII I BOLHARS'KII LITERATURI [Problems of socialist industrialization of Bulgaria as reflected in Soviet and Bulgarian literature]. *Ukrains'kyi Istorychnyi Zhurnal [USSR] 1981 (6): 139-145.*

1002. Chizhevski, N. T. DEINOSTTA NA BKP ZA RAZPROSTRANIAVANE OPITA NA SUVETSKITE NOVATORI PO SNIZHAVANE SEBESTOINOSTTA NA PROMISHLENATA PRODUKTSIIA PREZ PURVATA PETILETKA (1949-1952 G) [The activity of the Bulgarian Communist Party in spreading the experience of Soviet innovators in lowering the prime cost of industrial production during the first Five-Year Plan, 1949-52]. *Istoricheski Pregled [Bulgaria] 1962 18(4): 54-65.* To raise the efficiency and quality of industrial production the Bulgarian Communist Party followed the example of innovators in the USSR by introducing the principle of socialist emulation, which it propagated through the press, in resolutions implemented by lower Party echelons, by agitating in factories, and by the appointment of Communists to production planning bodies. Many enterprises used the method successfully, but in some it was unsatisfactorily applied. Based on contemporary newspapers, material in the Central Party Archive, and statistical data; 64 notes.
G. S. Tulloch

1003. Čingo, Nikola. SUKOB IZMEDJU BRP(K) I BURŽOASKE OPOZICIJE I NJIHOV ODNOS PREMA MAKEDONSKOM PITANJU U RAZDOBLJU 1944-1948 GODINE [The conflict between the Bulgarian Communist Party and the bourgeois opposition and their attitude toward the Macedonian question, 1944-48]. *Medjunarodni Problemi [Yugoslavia] 1978 30(3-4): 119-137.* Notes that the Bulgarian Communist Party came into conflict with the bourgeoisie, 1944-48, over Macedonia and suggests that the Party's political attitude was part of the overall strategy for accomplishing the socialist revolution, and did not represent the genuine Party view.

1004. Dimitrov, Georgi V. KOMUNITE V BLAGOEVGRADSKIIA OKRUG (1919-1923 G.) [Communes in the Blagoevgrad district, 1919-23]. *Izvestiia na Inst. po Istoriia na BKP [Bulgaria] 1976 34: 267-285.* The Communists scored their first successes in the district's local elections in December 1919, and up to 1923 controlled one town council and 24 village councils; analyzes their electoral tactics and policies in power.

1005. Dimitrov, Mircho. PROPAGANDSKATA RABOT NA BKP ZA KOMUNISTICHESKOTO VUZPITANIE NA TRUDESHTITE SE (1962-1966 G) [The Bulgarian Communist Party's propaganda work for the Communist education of the workers, 1962-66]. *Izvestiia na Inst. po Istoriia na BKP [Bulgaria] 1971 26: 247-295.* Discusses Communist Party activity, at national and local level, in reorganizing propaganda work in line with the decisions of the Eighth Party Congress concerning the construction of a developed socialist society.

1006. Dolapchieva, Iordanka and Minkova, Tsveta. ISTORIIA NA BKP, NA MLADEZHKOTO I RABOTNICHESKOTO DVIZHENIE V BULGARIIA [The history of the Bulgarian Communist Party and of the youth and workers' movement in Bulgaria]. *Izvestiia na Inst. po Istoriia na BKP [Bulgaria] 1966 15: 448-473; 1967 16: 410-418, 17: 375-415.* Continued from previous articles (see *Izvestiia na Inst. po Istoriia na BKP* vols. 12 and 13). These three bibliographies include books, articles, and memoirs published in 1965 and 1966 in Bulgaria, the USSR, and the East European socialist countries concerning the Marxist and Communist movement in Bulgaria ca. 1880-1965. Bibliographies continued (see abstracts 27B:1989 and 2038).

1007. Dolapchieva, Iordanka and Minkova, Tsveta. ISTORIIA NA BKP, NA MLADEZHKOTO I RABOTNICHESKOTO DVIZHENIE V BULGARIIA [History of the Bulgarian Communist Party and the youth and workers' movement in Bulgaria]. *Izvestiia na Inst. po Istoriia na BKP [Bulgaria] 1969 22: 379-425.* A bibliography of books, articles, and memoirs, published in Bulgaria, the USSR, and the European socialist countries during 1968 concerning the Marxist and Communist movement in Bulgaria, ca. 1880-1969.

1008. Donev, Doniu. OTNOSNO BORBATA PROTIV SUVREMENNIIA REVIZIONIZUM (IZ OPITA I PRINOSA NA BKP) [On the struggle against contemporary revisionism, from the experience and contributions of the Bulgarian Communist Party]. *Izvestiia na Instituta po Istoriia na BKP [Bulgaria] 1975 33: 115-151.* A historical-ideological study of the main factors that hardened the Bulgarian Communist Party (BKP) against infection by left- or right-wing Marxist revisionism. The strong antibourgeois attitudes were due to the quality of the Party leadership and national characteristics of the Bulgarian revolution. Since the 1930's there have been no dissident factions, only individual cases of ideological deviation. However, the dangers of infiltration of liberalism or radicalism as a mask for intellectual elitism remain. Based on official documents; 54 notes. C. S. Masloff

1009. Dragoicheva, Ts. THE ORIGINS OF THE FATHERLAND FRONT. *World Marxist Rev. [Canada] 1976 19(10): 47-58.* History of Bulgaria's Fatherland Front, 1946-76.

1010. Dragoliubov, Petur. IZBORNITE BORBI I RABOTATA NA BKP V NARODNOTO SUBRANIE (1945-1949 G) [The electoral struggle and work of the Bulgarian Communist Party in the National Assembly, 1945-49]. *Izvestiia na Inst. po Istoriia na BKP [Bulgaria] 1965 13: 209-268.* Examines the elections of 1945 and 1946, the Communist Party's campaigning parliamentary tactics, and relations with other political parties up to 1949.

1011. Elazar, D. CHETVURT VEK V SLUZHBA NA ISTORIKO-PARTIINATA NAUKA [A quarter of a century in the service of the Party's history]. *Izvestiia na Inst. po Istoriia na BKP [Bulgaria] 1978 39: 7-26.* Views the achievements of the scientific collective of the History Institute of the Bulgarian Communist Party at the Central Committee of the BKP, 1944-69.

1012. Enchev, Stefan. NIAKOI VUPROSI NA POLITIKATA NA BKP ZA PREUSTROISTVOTO NA OBRAZOVANIETO (1944-1958) [Some questions about the policy of the Bulgarian Communist Party (BCP) concerning the reorganization of education, 1944-56]. *Izvestiia na Inst. po Istoriia na BKP [Bulgaria] 1981 44: 43-77.* Describes Communist policy toward education in Bulgaria during the transitional period 1944-58, before the thorough Marxist-Leninist reorganization of 1959. Based on materials from the BCP and State archives, Sofia municipal and the Ministry of National Education archives.

1013. Firsov, F. I. GEORGII DIMITROV—VYDAIUSHCHIISIA REVOLIUTSIONER-LENINETS [Georgi Dimitrov, an outstanding revolutionary Leninist]. *Novaia i Noveishaia Istoriia [USSR] 1982 (3): 73-91.* Describes three periods in Dimitrov's life as Comintern chief in the 1930's, in the Soviet Union during World War II, and as postwar leader of Bulgaria. 2 photos, 100 notes. A. J. Evans

1014. Gain, Nicole. LE CONTRÔLE DE L'ÉTAT ET DU PEUPLE EN BULGARIE (LOI DU 12 JUILLET 1974) [The state and popular control in Bulgaria: the act of 12 July 1974]. *Rev. d'Études Comparatives Est-Ouest [France] 1978 9(4): 129-145.* Analyzes the popular control of the state administration in Bulgaria, its efficiency, the functions of the citizens' general inspection, and the power of control exercized by state organizations.

1015. Genchev, Nikolai. OKONCHATELNOTO UKREPIAVANE NA NARODNODEMOKRATICHNATA VLAST V BULGARIIA (1947-1948) [The final consolidation of popular democratic power in Bulgaria, 1947-48]. *Izvestiia na Inst. za Istoriia [Bulgaria] 1966 (16-17): 25-64.* Studies the defeat of the bourgeois opposition parties, chiefly the Agrarian Popular Union, and their attempt to unite against the Bulgarian Communist Party and the Fatherland Front. Also examines the nationalization of industry, and the changes in the national political structure symbolized by the 1947 constitution and the transformation of the role of the Fatherland Front. F. A. K. Yasamee

1016. Georgieva, Elena. SUZDAVANE I UKREPVANE NA TKZS NA TERITORIIATA NA DNESHNIIA PAZARDZHISHKI OKRUG PREZ PERIODA 1945-1950 G. [The creation and strengthening of the worker-production agricultural cooperatives]. *Godishnik: Natsionalen Muzei na Revoliutsionnoto Dvizhenie [Bulgaria] 1980 9: 179-191.* The Bulgarian Communist Party charged the cooperatives, founded in 1945, with overseeing the fulfillment of agricultural plans, enforcing work norms, monitoring inventories, and educating the masses in collectivization.

1017. Gesheva, Iordanka. DEVETDESETGODISHNIIAT IUBILEI NA PARTIIATA [The 90th anniversary of the Party]. *Istoricheski Pregled [Bulgaria] 1981 37(5): 178-183.* Describes July-August 1981 anniversary celebrations of the founding of the Bulgarian Communist Party (1891) and the simultaneous observations of the 78th anniversary of the Ilinden Uprising. Secondary sources. A. J. Evans

1018. Gesheva, Iordanka. NAUCHNA SESIIA ZA 100-GODISHNINATA OT ROZHDENIETO NA GEORGI DIMITROV [A scholarly session on the 100th anniversary of the birth of Georgi Dimitrov]. *Istoricheski Pregled [Bulgaria] 1982 38(4): 147-153.* The Bulgarian Academy of Sciences, the Academy of Social Sciences, and the Social Directorate of the Central Committee of the Communist Party of Bulgaria held a congress, 19-21 May 1982, to commemorate the 100th anniversary of Georgi Dimitrov's birth. It attracted more than 140 contributions about Dimitrov. Foreign contributions were few and time was too short. Based on the records of the session. A. J. Evans

1019. Goranova, Margarita. NACHALNI STUPKI V ORGANIZATSIONNOTO UKREPVANE NA BULGARSKATA KOMMUNISTICHESKA PARTIIA (IX. 1944-II. 1948) [Initial steps in the organizational strengthening of the Bulgarian Communist Party, September 1944-February 1948]. *Izvestiia na Inst. po Istoriia na*

BKP [Bulgaria] 1969 21: 331-367. Reproduces 14 Party documents concerning the Party's organization and membership, broken down by region and enterprise.

1020. Grigorew, Bojan. GEGEN DIE BÜRGERLICHEN VERFÄLSCHUNG DER BULGARISCHEN KOMMUNISTISCHEN UND ARBEITERBEWEGUNG [Against the bourgeois falsification of the Bulgarian Communist and workers' movement]. *Beiträge zur Geschichte der Arbeiterbewegung [East Germany] 1974 16(5): 812-816.* Bourgeois historians have presented a false image of the Communist and workers' movements in Bulgaria, most often attacking these popular movements as antinational phenomena. Anti-Soviet feeling is at the center of much of this anti-Communist attack. Bulgarian Communists must defend themselves by a complete depiction of events and a defense of the Soviet Union as a friend and mentor of Bulgaria. The youth must not be allowed to forget its socialist heritage. Primary and secondary materials; 4 notes.
G. H. Libbey

1021. Grigorov, Boian. KOMMUNISTICHESKOE I RABOCHEE DVIZHENIE V BOLGARII V KRIVOM ZERKALE BURZHUAZNYKH FAL'SIFIKATOROV [The Communist and labor movement in Bulgaria through the eyes of bourgeois falsifiers]. *Voprosy Istorii KPSS [USSR] 1976 (7): 83-90.* Criticizes the works of J. Rothschild (1883-1936), Oren Nissen, 1971-73, and R. Burns, 1967, which attacked Bulgarian Communism.

1022. Grigorov, Boian. PROMINENT FIGURES OF THE INTERNATIONAL SOCIALIST MOVEMENT AND THE BULGARIAN WORKER'S SOCIAL-DEMOCRATIC PARTY (UNITED), 1923-1931. *Bulgarian Hist. Rev. [Bulgaria] 1975 3(2): 3-23.* Discusses contacts made by the Bulgarian Social Democratic Party (BSDP) with other European Socialist Parties, 1923-31. Although the BSDP temporarily joined the government after the coup d'état of 1923, the European left-wing parties and organization continued their support for the Party. Left-wing forces within the BSDP led to the formation of a Popular Front with the Bulgarian Workers' Party (Communist) in 1936 which resulted in their final fusion into the Bulgarian Communist Party in 1948. Based on Bulgarian press reports.
J. P. H. Myers

1023. Gruzdeva, V. P. RUKOVODIASHCHAIA SILA BOLGARSKOGO NARODA [The Bulgarian people's leading force]. *Voprosy Istorii KPSS [USSR] 1981 (8): 99-102.* August 1981 marked the 90th anniversary of the Buzludzha Congress, which laid the foundations for the creation of a revolutionary Marxist party of the Bulgarian proletariat. The roots of such a party were formed in the 1880's and 1890's when a Bulgarian industrial proletariat came into being. This proletariat was influenced by the experience of the workers' movement in other capitalist countries. Its aspirations were channelled by Dimitur Blagoev. He organized the meeting at Buzludzha in 1891 at which Bulgaria's socialist forces joined to set up a Bulgarian Social Democratic Party. In 1919 this became the Bulgarian Communist Party. 13 notes.
J. Bamber

1024. Gurova, Svoboda. BORBATA NA PLEVENKATA OBLASTNA ORGANIZATSIA NA BKP PROTIV OPOZITSIIATA PO VREME NA REFERENDUMA I IZBORITE ZA VELIKO NARODNO SUBRANIE: 1946 [The fight of the Pleven district Communist Party organization against the opposition during the referendum and the elections for a Grand National Assembly: 1946]. *Izvestiia na Inst. po Istoriia na BKP [Bulgaria] 1977 36: 333-365.* Reviews the gradual liquidation of middle-class institutions in Pleven up to the elections for a Grand National Assembly on 27 October 1946.

1025. Gurova, Svoboda. BORBATA PROTIV OPOZITSIONNITE SILI V PLEVENSKATA OBLAST, (1946-1947) [The fight against the opposition forces in the district of Pleven, 1946-47]. *Izvestiia na Inst. po Istoriia na BKP [Bulgaria] 1981 44: 344-370.* Opposition forces in the Pleven district in northern Bulgaria were gradually liquidated between 27 October 1946 and December 1947, after the elections for the Grand National Assembly and up to the disbanding of the opposition parties. Based on published and unpublished Bulgarian materials.

1026. Holub, V. I. ROL' BKP U ZMITSNENNI SOIUZU ROBITNYCHOHO KLASU TA SELIANSTVA V PERIOD BUDIVNYTSTVA SOTSIALIZMU [The role of the Bulgarian Communist Party in strengthening the alliance of the working class and the peasants during socialist construction]. *Ukrains'kyi Istorychnyi Zhurnal [USSR] 1970 (8): 51-58.* Discusses the Party's role in the collectivization of rural Bulgaria, 1944-69.

1027. Hoppe, Hans-Joachim. TUDOR SHIWKOW: EINE POLITISCHE BIOGRAPHIE [Todor Shivkov: a political biography]. *Osteuropa [West Germany] 1978 28(5): 399-408.* Discusses the beginning of the political career of the Bulgarian communist leader Todor Shivkov (b. 1911). Considers his role in the destalinization of Bulgaria, his problems after Khrushchev's fall, and his role in the reforms of the 1960's.

1028. Horner, John E. THE ORDEAL OF NIKOLA PETKOV AND THE CONSOLIDATION OF COMMUNIST RULE IN BULGARIA. *Survey [Great Britain] 1974 20(1): 75-83.* Discusses the trial and execution of the Bulgarian Agrarian Union leader, Nikola Petkov, by the Bulgarian Communist Party in 1947. The Communists would accept no local opposition nor free elections. Based on unpublished archives, published documents and memoirs; 40 notes.
R. B. Valliant

1029. Horner, John E. TRAICHO KOSTOV: STALINIST ORTHODOXY IN BULGARIA. *Survey [Great Britain] 1979 24(3): 135-142.* The execution of the Party Secretary Traicho Kostov has yet to be fully explained. While no simple explanation is possible, attention would have to be paid to the background of the times which saw the relentless struggle between the Muscovites and local factions among the East European Communists and the exacerbation of the Cold War as well as to personal factors relating to Stalin and the personal standing of Kostov among his comrades. 16 notes.
V. Samaraweera

1030. Ignat'eva, T. V. BOR'BA DEMOKRATICHESKIKH SIL PROTIV OPPOZITSIONNOI GRUPPIROVKI N. PETKOVA V B.Z.N.S. ZA OSUSHCHESTVLENIE SOTSIAL'NO-EKONOMICHESKIKH PREOBRAZOVANII V BOLGARII V PERVYE GODY NARODNOI VLASTI [The struggle of the democratic forces against N. Petkov's opposition grouping in the Bulgarian Agrarian Popular Union for the realization of socioeconomic reforms in Bulgaria during the first years of the people's power]. *Sovetskoe Slavianovedenie [USSR] 1976 (2): 16-32.* After the successful armed national uprising on 9 September 1944, the Fatherland Front government directed its economic programs against the exploiters of the peasants. The author discusses various governmental measures, including liquidation of private monopolies, establishment of government monopolies, liquidation of private property, and land distribution together with the arguments and struggles that occurred within the Bulgarian Agrarian Popular Union and between it and Bulgarian Communists. The reactionary faction of the Agrarians, led by Nikola Petkov, opposed most of the governmental measures. This struggle reached its peak when the government tried to pass a law concerning workers' land ownership. Though the law passed, the opposition was able to delay its application, which gave landowners a chance to sell their lands. 106 notes.
L. Kalinowski

1031. Ignatovski, Dimitur. UCHASTIETO NA MLADEZHTA V OSUSHTESTIAVANE POLITIKATA NA BKP ZA SOTSIALISTICHESKA INDUSTRIALIZATSIIA NA STRANATA (1944-1958 G.) [The participation of youth in realizing the Bulgarian Communist Party's policy of socialist industrialization, 1944-58]. *Izvestiia na Inst. po Istoriia na BKP [Bulgaria] 1978 38: 137-172.* Studies the Dimitrov Union of Popular Youth and its contribution to industrialization during the period of the transition from capitalism to socialism in Bulgaria, 1944-58.

1032. Iliescu, Crişan. ETAPELE CONSTRUIRII SOCIETĂŢII SOCIALISTE ÎN REPUBLICA POPULARĂ BULGARIA [The stages in building a socialist society in the People's Republic of Bulgaria]. *Anale de Istorie [Rumania] 1971 17(5): 129-137.* Describes the development of socialism in Bulgaria since 1945 see-

ing the insurrection led by the communist dominated Fatherland Front as the beginning of the socialist transformation. Analyzes the Fatherland Front's program and administration, particularly its land reform, and its abolition of the monarchy, discussing the ascendancy of the Communist Party in the Great Popular Assembly and its suppression of opposition. Considers the nationalization of industry, and the creation of cooperatives, which followed the proclamation of a Peoples' Republic in 1947, as well as the new emphasis on economic independence and a planned economy. Records subsequent five year plans, Communist Party congresses, the modernization of heavy industry, Party reorganization after 1956, and improvements in production, administration, and living standards. Based on Bulgarian Communist Party documents; 37 notes.
R. O. Khan/S

1033. Iordanov, Boris. PARTIIATA I RABOTNICHESKIIAT KONTROL NAD KAPITALISTICHESKATA PROMISHLENOST V BULGARIIA (1944-1947 G.) [The Party and workers' control over capitalist industry in Bulgaria, 1944-47]. *Istoricheski Pregled [Bulgaria] 1969 25(2-3): 106-121.* Discusses and analyzes the methods of workers' control over Bulgarian factories after the Communist-led Fatherland Front government came to power in September 1944. Compares this to the workers' control in Russia after the Bolshevik Revolution. In Bulgaria, unlike Russia, capitalist owners remained in positions of authority several years after the socialist revolution. However their ability to control the economy was limited by law. Furthermore, Bulgaria in 1944 had the example and experience of the Soviet Union on which to rely. In Bulgaria many government and Communist Party institutions directed the workers' control in contrast to the factory committees which had operated in Russia in 1917-18. The Communist Party, in fact, played the decisive role in instituting workers' control in Bulgaria. Based on documents from several Bulgarian archives; 91 notes.
F. B. Chary

1034. Iotov, I. et al. DVADESET I PET GODINI ISTORIKO-PARTIINA NAUKA [Twenty-five years of historical-Party scholarship]. *Izvestiia na Inst. po Istoriia na BKP [Bulgaria] 1969 21: 5-47.* Describes the work of Bulgarian Party historians since 1944, noting their major publications and fields of activity, and considering certain weaknesses, notably deficiency of analysis in work so far achieved.

1035. Isusov, Mito. IZBORITE ZA KONSTITUTSIONNO SUBRANIE I RAZPOLOZHENIETO NA POLITICHESKITE SILI V BULGARIIA PREZ 1946 GODINA [The elections for the constituent assembly and the distribution of political power in Bulgaria in 1946]. *Istoricheski Pregled [Bulgaria] 1976 32(4): 3-30.* Analyzes the political situation in Bulgaria, July-November 1946, when the Fatherland Front government introduced a law facilitating a referendum about abolishing the monarchy, and organized elections for a constituent assembly to prepare a new constitution. The elections were fought by a government coalition of five parties against four opposition parties, and the Bulgarian Workers' Party (Communist) came out strongest with 275 seats. Based on Bulgarian state and Party documents, and newspaper articles; 153 notes.
B. R. Pach/S

1036. Isusov, Mito. THE SOCIALIST REVOLUTION IN BULGARIA: PREMISES, LAW-GOVERNED PROCESSES AND DIMENSIONS. *Bulgarian Hist. Rev. [Bulgaria] 1981 9(1-2): 9-24.* Surveys the economic and political background in pre-World War II Bulgaria, which contributed to the emergence of socialism in the 1940's, and to its consolidation in the later years. The mildly reformist rule of the Bulgarian National Agrarian Union in 1920-23 ended with a coup staged by totalitarian dictatorship, which developed strong links with rising German fascism. This led to the strengthening of the Bulgarian Communist Party, which took the leading part in the formation of socialist Bulgaria in the years 1944-56. After Stalin's death the Party reviewed many issues, criticizing the cult of strong political personality, dominant in the Bulgarian Politburo, and denounced dogmatism and subjectivism. Based on Central Party Archives; 28 notes. M. Hernas

1037. Isusov, Mito. SOTSIAL'NAIA DEMOKRATIIA I NAROD-NO-DEMOKRATICHESKAIA REVOLIUTSIIA V BOLGARII (1944-1948 GG) [Social democracy and national democratic revolution in Bulgaria, 1944-48]. *Études Balkaniques [Bulgaria] 1972 (1): 41-62.* Describes the multiparty structure of the national democratic system in Bulgaria after the September 1944 rebellion. Provides an account of the political initiatives taken by the Bulgarian Communist Party, and the various political factions prior to the unification of the Bulgarian Social-Democratic Workers' Party with the Bulgarian Workers' Party in May 1948. Based on Bulgarian Communist Party archives sources; 121 notes. E. R. Sicher

1038. Itshenskaja, Doris. DER WEG ZUR EINHEITLICHEN SOZIALISTISCHEN JUGENDORGANISATION IN BULGARIEN 1944-47 [The road toward uniform socialist organization of the youth in Bulgaria, 1944-47]. *Jahrbuch für Geschichte der Sozialistischen Länder Europas [East Germany] 1979 23(1): 103-126.* Surveys Bulgaria's youth organizations during the interwar period, focusing on the attempts of the Communist Youth International to unify all nonfascist youth groups. The many-faceted youth movements and organizations in prewar Bulgaria after liberation became a more unified system under the leadership of the ruling Communist Party. Primary sources; 65 notes. G. E. Pergl

1039. Ivanoski, Orde. BUGARSKA KOMUNISTIČKA PARTIJA O PRAVIMA MAKEDONACA U PIRINSKOJ MAKEDONIJI: KRATAK ISTORIJSKI OSVRT [The Bulgarian Communist Party on the rights of Macedonians in Pirin, Macedonia: a brief historical review]. *Medjunarodni Problemi [Yugoslavia] 1978 30(3-4): 205-216.* Discusses the allocation to Bulgaria of the Pirin area of Macedonia when the latter was partitioned after World War I, and describes how the Bulgarian Communist Party supported Macedonian national rights, 1919-78, such as the teaching of Macedonian in schools.

1040. Ivanov, Kiril. THE GUIDING FORCE. *World Marxist R. [Canada] 1975 18(1): 98-107.* The Communist Party has been the guiding force in Bulgaria, 1945-75.

1041. Ivanov, Mitko. SPISANIE *NOVO VREME:* BELEZHIT VOIN NA REVOLIUTSIONNATA TEORIIA [The journal *New Time:* a remarkable combatant of revolutionary theory and practice]. *Istoricheski Pregled [Bulgaria] 1977 33(2): 3-7.* In 1897 Dimitur Blagoev, the founder of the Bulgarian Social Democratic Workers' Party, published the journal *Novo Vreme* in Plovdiv. Between 1916 and 1919 the journal was prohibited by the government, because of Blagoev's negative stand concerning Bulgaria's entry into World War I. After the reactionary coup d'état in June 1923 it was prohibited again. In 1947 it was revived by such famous contributors as Georgi Dimitrov, Vasil Kolarov, and Vladimir Poptomov. It is now the official theoretical organ of the Bulgarian Communist Party. 9 notes. S. Troebst

1042. Ivantsev, I. D. RADIANS'KA ISTORYCHNA LITERATURA PRO VPLYV VELYKOI ZHOVTNEVOI SOTSIALISTYCHNOI REVOLIUTSII NA PARTIIU TISNYKH SOTSIALISTIV BOLHARII [Soviet historical literature on the influence of the Russian Revolution (October) on the Narrow Socialists in Bulgaria]. *Ukrains'kyi Istorychnyi Zhurnal [USSR] 1980 (11): 149-153.* Reviews Soviet and Bulgarian publications that shed light on the influence of the Russian Revolution on activities of the Bulgarian Workers' Social Democratic Party (Narrow Socialists), which, after its emergence in 1903, maintained close relations with the Russian Social Democratic Workers' Party. Based on Soviet and Bulgarian publications; 23 notes. I. Krushelnyckyj

1043. Kait, L. A REVOLUTIONARY OF THE LENINIST SCHOOL. *Int. Affairs [USSR] 1972 (7): 50-55.* Chronicles the political career of Georgi M. Dimitrov, a Leninist member of the Communist Party and founder of the Bulgarian Communist Party, 1921-48.

1044. Kanatsieva, Rimka. BKP I POVISHAVANE SOTSIALNATA AKTIVNOST NA SELIANITE-KOOPERATORI (1958-1970 G.) [The Bulgarian Communist Party and raising the social activity of the peasant cooperativists, 1958-70]. *Izvestiia na Inst. po Istoriia na BKP [Bulgaria] 1978 38: 211-250.* Examines the role of peasant cooperativists in political, state, and professional organizations and argues that the Communist Party's political aims and its mechanization of agriculture have transformed rural labor and abolished the division between peasants' and workers' labor.

1045. Khadzhinikolov, Veselin. DRUGARIAT TODOR ZHIVKOV I BULGARSKATA ISTORICHESKA NAUKA [Comrade Todor Zhivkov and Bulgarian economic science]. *Istoricheski Pregled [Bulgaria] 1981 37(5): 16-38.* Discusses Todor Zhivkov's practical and philosophical works on economic, social, political and cultural matters, particularly his speech to the April 1956 Plenum of the Bulgarian Communist Party. 65 notes. A. J. Evans

1046. Khadzhinikolov, Veselin. OSMIIAT KONGRES NA BULGARSKATA KOMUNISTICHESKA PARTIIA I NIAKOI VAZHNI ZADACHI NA NASHATA ISTORICHESKA NAUKA [The Eighth Congress of the Bulgarian Communist Party and some important tasks for our study of history]. *Istoricheski Pregled [Bulgaria] 1962 18(6): 3-28.* Todor Zhivkov assessed the eighth Party conference of 5-14 November 1962 as of the utmost importance, and reviewed the Bulgarian people's achievements showing their solidarity of aims and opinions, and their support of the USSR. He emphasized the importance of the consolidation of socialist democracy, and the transition to Communism and stressed that historians must explain these concepts to the people by: 1) presenting solutions to theoretical problems; 2) describing the inevitability of socialist development; 3) analyzing the differences between capitalist and socialist Bulgaria; and 4) underlining the cooperation in Bulgaria between workers and peasants. Based on Todor Zhivkov's speech at the eighth Party conference, 1962; 51 notes. A. J. Evans/S

1047. Khalachev, Kiril. ZA MORIASHKOTO I VOINISHKOTO VUSTANIE V BELOMORIETO PREZ SEPTEMVRI 1944 G. [The sailors' and soldiers' uprising in the Belomorea during September 1944]. *Istoricheski Pregled [Bulgaria] 1972 28(4): 81-88.* Reprints and analyzes seven documents on the uprising and trial of a group of Bulgarian Communist soldiers and sailors in occupied Greece (Thrace) in September 1944. Although the group was antifascist, they defied the Anglo-American military command and the Bulgarian ministry of war, under the Zvenarist Colonel Damian Velchev, in the antifascist coalition established 9 September 1944. The leaders of the uprising were tried and convicted, despite protests of Communist leaders, because of the presence of fascists in the ministry of war at that time. Based on documents in various Bulgarian archives and museums and in the contemporary press; 3 notes. F. B. Chary

1048. Khristov, Khristo A. INTERNATSIONALIZMUT NA BKP I BORBATA ZA EDINSTVO NA MEZHDUNARODNOTO REVOLIUTSIONNO DVIZHENIE [The internationalism of the Bulgarian Communist Party and the struggle for the unity of the international revolutionary movement]. *Istoricheski Pregled [Bulgaria] 1964 20(6): 3-14.* When the First International met, Bulgaria was struggling to free itself from Turkish domination, but the country's working class nevertheless took great interest in the workers' movement throughout Europe. Dimitur Blagoev, the first Bulgarian proponent of scientific socialism, founded the Bulgarian revolutionary socialist party which intended to destroy capitalism and to introduce socialism in Bulgaria. As members of the Third International, the Bulgarian socialists supported Soviet Russia. The Bulgarian Communist Party fought for the unity of the Balkan proletariat, joined the Balkan Federation in 1924 and between the wars Bulgarian Communists were active both at home and abroad. After the 9 September 1944 uprising in Bulgaria, the Communist Party led the workers against reaction and the international bourgeoisie, and has since shaped Bulgaria into an advanced socialist state, a member of Comecon and an active participant in world politics. 5 notes. A. J. Evans

1049. Khristov, Pasko. BULGARSKATA RABOTNICHESKA PARTIIA (KOMUNISTI) I REZERVNATA MILITSIIA (1944-1948 G.) [The Bulgarian Workers' Party (Communist) and the reserve militia, 1944-48]. *Istoricheski Pregled [Bulgaria] 1980 36(2): 43-51.* Describes and analyzes the role of the reserve militia in preserving the victory against fascism in Bulgaria after 9 September 1944 until the establishment of popular power by the Dimitrov Constitution of 1947. The reserve militia was disbanded in 1948. The reserve militia's chief organizer was the Bulgarian Communist Party. Based chiefly on documents from several Bulgarian archives; 62 notes. F. B. Chary

1050. Kiracow, Peniu. POLITYKA EKONOMICZNA BPK W OKRESIE BUDOWY ROZWINIETEGO SPOLECZENSTWA SOCJALISTYCZNEGO [The economic policy of the Bulgarian Communist Party in the period of construction of a developed socialist society]. *Nowe Drogi [Poland] 1976 (3): 98-106.* Recounts the successes of the economy in Bulgaria.

1051. Klejn, Zbigniew. W STULECIE URODZIN GEORGI DYMITROWA (1882-1949): IDEE PRZETWORZONE W CZYN [The centenary of Georgi Dimitrov: ideas transformed into action]. *Nowe Drogi [Poland] 1982 (6): 83-95.* Georgi Dimitrov, active in the Comintern and chairman of the Communist Party of Bulgaria, contributed to the solution of many problems posed by the theory and practice of socialism.

1052. Kolář, Josef. ČTYŘICET LET OD VÍTĚZSTVÍ BULHARSKÉHO LIDU NAD FAŠISMEM [Forty years since the victory of the Bulgarian people over fascism]. *Slovanský Přehled [Czechoslovakia] 1984 90[i.e., 70](4): 273-283.* At the outset of World War II, Bulgaria, led by King Boris, was allied with the Nazi powers, but when that alliance demanded an invasion of the USSR, a country that was traditionally a friend of Bulgaria, tensions arose. By the end of 1943, not only had the king died, but the Allied bombing of Sofia had taken its toll and under the leadership of the Communist Party, a United Patriotic Front emerged. By October 1944, thousands of partisans were fighting against the Germans and Bulgaria was supporting the Russians. On 15 September 1946, the Patriotic Front, with the full support of the Bulgarian people, declared the creation of the People's Republic of Bulgaria. 42 notes. B. Reinfeld

1053. Koleva, Tatiana and Boev, Boris. NAUCHNO-TEORETICHNA KONFERENTSIIA ZA GEORGI DIMITROV V MOSKVA [A theoretical conference on Georgi Dimitrov in Moscow]. *Izvestiia na Instituta po Istoriia na BKP [Bulgaria] 1983 (48): 513-522.* At a conference held 1 and 2 June 1982 in Moscow to celebrate the 100th anniversary of Georgi Dimitrov's birth, participants discussed Dimitrov's role in, and influence on, the international Communist movement between 1930 and 1948. A. J. Evans

1054. Kosev, Dimitur. ZA SUSTOIANIETO I ZADACHITE NA BULGARSKATA ISTORICHESKA NAUKA [The condition and tasks of Bulgarian historical science]. *Istoricheski Pregled [Bulgaria] 1964 20(4): 3-39.* The Eighth Congress of the Bulgarian Communist Party held in 1962 included three sessions where the role of Bulgarian historians was examined. The first dealt with their achievements before and after the April Plenum, the role of Dimitur Blagoev, and the congresses of 1948 and 1949 which, held under Party auspices, enabled historians to identify their mistakes. The second session concentrated on historians' weaknesses which included a lack of analysis, unskilled evaluation of Marxist-Leninist theory, dogmatism, schematicism and sociologism. The third session suggested ways of coordinating historians' activities and organizing cadres while avoiding an excess of bureaucracy. Based on documents from the Eighth Congress of the Bulgarian Communist Party; 3 notes. A. J. Evans

1055. Kosev, K. BKP: ORGANIZATOR I RUKOVODITEL' VOORUZHENNOI BOR'BY BOLGARSKOGO NARODA PROTIV MONARKHO-FASHISTSKOGO REZHIMA [The BKP: the organizer and leader of the armed struggle of the Bulgarian nation against the monarcho-fascist regime]. *Voenno-Istoricheskii Zhurnal [USSR] 1977 (9): 72-78.* Studies the revolutionary role of the Bulgarian Communist Party (BKP) and the decisions taken by it concerning the formation of military forces, ca. 1891-1977.

1056. Kostov, Mladen. PARTIINITE ARKHIVI PRED 25-GODISHNINATA OT 9. IX. 1944 G [The Party archives before the 25th anniversary of 9 September 1944]. *Izvestiia na Inst. po Istoriia na BKP [Bulgaria] 1969 21: 49-68.* Discusses the history of the central and regional Party archives and plans for the reorganization of the central Party archive.

1057. Kotsev, Venelin. 25-RICHCHIA SOTSIALISTYCHNOI REVOLIUTSII V BOLHARII [The 25th anniversary of the socialist revolution in Bulgaria]. *Ukrains'kyi Istorychnyi Zhurnal [USSR] 1969 (8): 24-34.* Sketches the history of the Bulgarian Communist Party since the communist takeover in September 1944.

1058. Kovachev, Velcho. DISERTATSII PO ISTORIIA NA BKP, ZASHTITENI V BULGARIIA [Dissertations on the history of the Bulgarian Communist Party defended in Bulgaria]. *Izvestiia na Inst. po Istoriia na BKP [Bulgaria] 1967 16: 419-436.* Surveys papers presented between March 1961 and the end of February 1966.

1059. Kovachev, Velcho. DISERTATSII PO ISTORIIA NA BULGARSKATA KOMUNISTICHESKA PARTIIA ZASHTITENI V SSSR OT BULGARI. [Dissertations on the history of the Bulgarian Communist Party defended by Bulgarian graduates in the USSR]. *Izvestiia na Inst. po Istoriia na BKP [Bulgaria] 1967 17: 417-427.* Covers work completed during 1954-66.

1060. Kuzova, Olga and Dimitrova, Liubov. MEZHDUNARODNO RABOTNICHESKO I KOMUNISTICHESKO DVIZHENIE: BIBLIOGRAFIIA NA LITERATURA, IZLIAZLA I POLUCHENA V BULGARIIA PREZ 1980 G. [The international workers' and communist movement: a bibliography of literature published and received in Bulgaria in 1980]. *Izvestiia na Inst. po Istoriia na BKP [Bulgaria] 1982 (47): 444-498.* Presents a list of works on the international worker and communist movement, trade unionism, and the Asian, African and Latin American revolutionary process published or received in Bulgaria in 1980.

1061. Lapteva, Zlatka. 35-GODISHNINATA NA SOTSIALISTICHESKATA REVOLIUTSIIA V BULGARIIA I DEINOSTTA NA MUZEIA [The 35th anniversary of the socialist revolution in Bulgaria and the activity of the National Museum]. *Godishnik: Natsionalen Muzei na Revoliutsionnoto Dvizhenie [Bulgaria] 1980 9: 214-219.* The National Museum of the Revolutionary Movement of Bulgaria mounted special exhibits to celebrate 35 years of socialism in Bulgaria, most of which emphasized the role of the Communist Party.

1062. Larrabee, F. Stephen. NEUE TENDENZEN IN DER BULGARISCHEN INNENPOLITIK [New tendencies in Bulgarian domestic policy]. *Osteuropa [West Germany] 1973 23(3): 174-184.* Close integration with Soviet economic and foreign policy remains the basic guideline of Bulgarian politics. Since December 1972 economic planners have emphasized increased production of consumer goods. Vast agricultural-industrial complexes are now in their first (agricultural) phase of integration. The Communist Party has reasserted control over cultural life. Its Secretariat seems to be gaining in power at the expense of the aging Politbureau. 35 notes.
R. E. Weltsch

1063. Lilov, Aleksandr. KOMMUNISTICHESKAIA PARTIIA—RUKOVODIASHCHAIA SILA V SOTSIALISTICHESKOI REVOLIUTSII I STROITEL'STVE SOTSIALISTICHESKOGO OBSHCHESTVA V BOLGARII [The Communist Party: leading force in the socialist revolution and construction of a socialist society in Bulgaria]. *Voprosy Istorii KPSS [USSR] 1974 (9): 16-28.* The Bulgarian Communist Party emerged as the most important subjective factor organizing and directing the revolutionary and democratic movement in Bulgaria. The Party led the struggle against monarchist-fascist and bourgeois forces. It created the Fatherland Front which engineered the revolt of 9 September 1944. Since then, in the context of a multiparty system, the Communist Party has transformed the nation's economy and culture. Based on writings of Bulgarian Communist Party leaders, V. I. Lenin, and Leonid Brezhnev; 9 notes. L. E. Holmes

1064. Marinov, Vylo. LENINIZM - IDEINAIA OSNOVA RAZVITIIA BOLGARSKOI KOMMUNISTICHESKOI PARTII [Leninism, the ideological base for the development of the Bulgarian Communist Party]. *Voprosy Istorii KPSS [USSR] 1968 (10): 18-31.* Outlines the important role Lenin and his works played in the political development of the Bulgarian Communist Party and in its success in establishing communism.

1065. Markov, Iulian Georgiev. BORBATA NA BKP ZA LIKVIDIRANE NA NEGRAMOTNOSTTA SRED TURSKOTO NASELENIE V BULGARIIA (9.IX. 1944-1953) [The struggle of the Bulgarian Communist Party to eliminate illiteracy among the Turkish population, 9 September 1944-53]. *Izvestiia na Inst. po Istoriia na BKP [Bulgaria] 1969 21: 147-172.* In 1946, the Turkish minority, 9.8% of the total population, enjoyed only 10-20% literacy, but the Bulgarian Communist Party (BKP) instituted an educational campaign, and illiteracy had been largely eradicated by 1953.

1066. Melamed, Ana. PREUSTROISTVO NA OTECHESVENIIA FRONT V EDINNA OBSHTESTVENO-POLITICHESKA ORGANIZATSIIA [The reconstruction of the Fatherland Front into a united sociopolitical organization]. *Istoricheski Pregled [Bulgaria] 1978 34(6): 3-21.* After 9 September 1944, the Fatherland Front became one of the fundamental parts of the new political system in Bulgaria. It consisted of members from all the political parties, and unified them into a mass sociopolitical organization with a democratic program. After Bulgaria became a republic in September 1946, and the Peace Treaty was signed with the Allies in February 1947, the Bulgarian government began to prepare the country for socialism. On 2 February 1948, the Second Congress of the Fatherland Front decided to turn the organization into a unified body, and with the participation of all democratic forces in the country, to prepare the people for public service. B. R. Pach

1067. Mevorah, Barouh. DARKHO HA-YEHUDIT-BULGARIT SHEL PROFESOR NISIM MVORAKH [Nissim Mevorah's Jewish-Bulgarian life]. *Shvut [Israel] 1982 9: 102-103.* Outlines the life of Nissim Mevorah (1891-1968), a Bulgarian diplomat and a founder of the Bulgarian Communist Party. He was also a committed Zionist and active in resistance groups. He remained a fervent Zionist and died under house arrest because of his views. 21 notes.
T. Koppel

1068. Mičev, Dobrin. GEORGI DIMITROV UND DIE INTERNATIONALE KOMMUNISTISCHE BEWEGUNG [Georgi Dimitrov and the international Communist movement]. *Bulgarian Historical Review [Bulgaria] 1982 10(2): 3-20.* Traces the life and career of the Bulgarian Communist leader Georgi Dimitrov (1882-1949) on the occasion of the centenary of his birth. The author examines his work and organizational activities for the Communist Party and trade union movement in Bulgaria, 1909-20, and emphasizes the development of his ideas and activities with the international communist movement, 1919-40's. During the 1920's and 1930's he paid many visits to Moscow where he met Lenin and travelled extensively throughout Europe where he undertook a great deal of work for the Communist International. Between 1932 and 1945 he helped to organize antifascist resistance in Europe and became famous for his alleged involvement in the burning of the Reichstag in Berlin in 1933, for which he was brought to trial and imprisoned by Hitler. The author also discusses Dimitrov's theories concerning the strategy and tactics of the international Communist movement. Secondary sources; biblio. G. L. Neville

1069. Migev, Vladimir. DVANADESETIIAT KONGRES NA BULGARSKATA KOMUNISTICHESKA PARTIIA [The 12th Congress of the Bulgarian Communist Party]. *Istoricheski Pregled [Bulgaria] 1981 37(5): 49-66.* Delegates to the 12th Bulgarian Party Congress (1971) warmly praised the 1956 Party Congress. Between 1970 and 1980, Bulgarian GNP rose from 33 to 77 billion levs. Per capita personal income rose from 879 levs to 1,336, public sector per capita income from 285 levs to 619. Some 600,000 dwellings were built, 148,000 nurseries. More than a million people received higher education. External trade quadrupled. Economic cooperation with the USSR offset Bulgaria's smallness. Steps were decided upon to correct the balance between goods for export and home consumption. 45 notes. A. J. Evans

1070. Migev, Vladimir. THE SEPTEMBER 9TH, 1944 UPRISING: A CULMINATING POINT IN THE REVOLUTIONARY STRUGGLE AND THE BEGINNING OF THE HISTORICAL ADVANCE OF THE BULGARIAN PEOPLE. *Bulgarian Hist. Rev. [Bulgaria] 1974 2(3): 3-24.* Examines the development of revolutionary movements in Bulgaria and the great international significance of the 9th September anti-fascist uprising, which opened the way for socialism and communism in Bulgaria. Stresses the importance of class contradictions in Bulgarian society and the high level of political awareness among the working class and the progressive intelligentsia. Traces the growth of the Bulgarian Communist Party following the 1923 uprising and its struggle to shape a popular antifascist movement and describes 30 years of socialist construction following the 1944 uprising. Based on documents in the state archives, Sofia, and secondary sources; 89 notes. A. Armstrong

1071. Migev, Vladimir. SOFIISKA OKRUZHNA PARTIINA ORGANIZATSIA I SOTSIALISTICHESKOTO PREUSTROISTVO NA SELSKOTO STOPANSTVO (1949-1958) [The Sofia district Party organization and the socialist transformation of the village economy, 1949-58]. *Izvestiia na Inst. po Istoriia na BKP [Bulgaria] 1981 44: 371-396.* Describes the collectivization of private agriculture in the villages of the Sofia district of Bulgaria during the period 1949-58, and the organization and introduction of agricultural mechanization on the new collective farms. Based on published Bulgarian materials.

1072. Minchev, D. VIDNYI DEIATEL' BOLGARSKOGO I MEZHDUNARODNOGO KOMMUNISTICHESKOGO DVIZHENIIA (K 100-LETIIU SO DNIA ROZHDENIIA G. M. DIMITROVA) [A prominent member of the Bulgarian and international Communist movement: on the 100th anniversary of the birth of Georgi Dimitrov]. *Voenno-Istoricheskii Zhurnal [USSR] 1982 (6): 94-96.* Georgi M. Dimitrov was born in 1882 in the Bulgarian village of Kovachevitsy. He joined the Social Democratic Party (later renamed the Communist Party) in 1902, and two years later became a member of its central committee. After his acquittal in the Reichstag trial, he moved to the USSR, where he conducted agitational work during World War II. In 1945 he returned to Bulgaria, and in 1948, the year before his death, became the general secretary of the Bulgarian Communist Party. Secondary sources; note. G. Dombrovski

1073. Minkova, Tsveta and Dolapchieva, Iordanka. ISTORIIA NA BKP, NA MLADEZHKOTO I RABOTNICHESKOTO DVIZHENIE V BULGARIIA [History of the Bulgarian Communist Party, and the youth and workers' movements in Bulgaria]. *Izvestiia na Inst. po Istoriia na BKP [Bulgaria] 1968 19: 310-370.* An extensive bibliography of books, articles, memoirs and other works on the above themes, published in Bulgaria, the USSR, and other Communist countries during 1967.

1074. Minkova, Tsveta and Apostolova, V. ISTORIIATA NA BKP, NA MLADEZHKOTO I RABOTNICHESKOTO DVIZHENIE V BULGARIIA [The Bulgarian Communist Party, youth and workers' movements in Bulgaria]. *Izvestiia na Inst. po Istoriia na BKP [Bulgaria] 1971 26: 391-461.* Lists monographs and articles on the above themes published in Bulgaria, the USSR, and the European Socialist countries during 1970: the bibliography is divided by subject and period.

1075. Monov, Tsviatko. DEINOSTTA NA BKP ZA LIKVIDIRANETO NA NEGRAMOTNOSTTA I MALOGRAMOTNOSTTA V STRANATA (1944-1953 G.) [The activity of the Bulgarian Communist Party in liquidating illiteracy and semiliteracy, 1944-53]. *Izvestiia na Instituta po Istoriia na BKP [Bulgaria] 1975 33: 83-111.* A primary goal of the Fatherland Front when it came to power in September 1944 was to abolish the 23% illiteracy rate in Bulgaria. Concerted efforts of the Party, state, and mass organizations led to success. There were increased funds for special courses after 1946, and greater attention was paid to more backward country and mountain areas and the Turkish and Gypsy minorities. There was slow progress until 1948 due to lack of resources, war damage, minority distrust, and religious problems with Moslems. A big step forward came in 1947 with centralization and tight coordination of previously scattered efforts and campaigns. By 1953, illiteracy had disappeared for the 15-50 age group. Based on Party archives, state archives, and official statistics; 3 charts, 124 notes.
C. S. Masloff

1076. Moysov, Lazar. THE VICIOUS CIRCLE OF NATIONALIST PRETENSIONS. *Macedonian Rev. [Yugoslavia] 1982 12(2): 207-220.* Examines the attitude of the Bulgarian Communist Party toward the Macedonian national question as expressed in a Party treatise published in 1948 and its subsequent effect on Yugoslav-Bulgarian relations.

1077. Natan, Zhak. BULGARSKATA KOMUNISTICHESKA PARTIIA I ISTORICHESKATA NAUKA [The Bulgarian Communist Party and historical science]. *Istoricheski Pregled [Bulgaria] 1971 27(5): 11-21.* Analyzes and interprets the influence of Bulgarian Communist authors on Bulgarian historiography. Discusses the particular achievements of Dimitur Blagoev, Georgi Dimitrov, Vasil Kolarov, and Todor Zhivkov. The two major types of contribution that Communist writers made to historiography are the Marxist interpretation of the past and their commentary on contemporary events which serve as a rich documentary source for future historians. Based on the works of Bulgarian communist authors, chiefly Blagoev and Kolarov; 11 notes. F. B. Chary

1078. Natan, Zhak. DESETIIAT KONGRES NA BKP I NASHATA ISTORICHESKA NAUKA [The 10th congress of the BCP and our historical science]. *Istoricheski Pregled [Bulgaria] 1971 27(3): 3-18.* An analysis of the effects of the resolutions of the tenth congress of the Bulgarian Communist Party (1971) on historiography in Bulgaria. The congress's commitment to building socialism in the Marxist-Leninist fashion encourages Bulgarian historians to develop their interpretation of the past and present on the principles of Marxism-Leninism. The most direct outcome for historians from the congress is the resolution calling for a multivolume history of Bulgaria in connection with the 1300th anniversary of the founding of the state. Based on speeches at the 10th congress; 10 notes.
F. B. Chary

1079. Natan, Zhak. PETNADESET GODINI "ISTORICHESKI PREGLED" [Fifteen years of *Istoricheski Pregled*]. *Istoricheski Pregled [Bulgaria] 1960 16(1): 3-11.* Distinguishes three periods in the history of this periodical, corresponding to the three main periods of Communist rule in Bulgaria: 1945-48, when the periodical's outlook, though antifascist, was not fully Marxist-Leninist; 1948-56, characterized by rapid development, guided and aided by the Communist Party; and 1956-60, when progress was freed from the burdensome cult of personality. Evaluates some major historical and historiographical problems tackled by *Istoricheski Pregled* during this time, noting continuing weaknesses. F. A. K. Yasamee

1080. Nenchovski, Georgi. IDEOLOGICHESKATA I POLITICHESKATA RABOTA NA PARTIIATA V PERIODA NA PODGOTOVKATA ZA MASOVO KOOPERIRANE NA ZEMIATA (1944-1948 G.) [The ideological and political work of the Party during the preparation for mass collectivization of the land, 1944-48]. *Izvestiia na Instituta po Istoriia na BKP [Bulgaria] 1974 31: 189-226.* Survey of the ideological struggle of the Bulgarian Communist Party for the victory of its concept of cooperation over that of the Agrarian Party and various smallholder views. Bulgarian peasants had strong ties to private land, and, although 80% of Bulgarian farmers were already in mutual aid cooperatives, few saw them as future units of production. Communists attempted to isolate large landholders through redistribution and there were battles for control of older cooperatives and splits in agrarian ranks. Machine Tractor Stations were important in inducing collectivization. The united opposition to collectivization by both rich and poor in some villages led to concessions to cooperatives over land ownership in

the 1947 constitution, and serious errors in methods of collectivization led to modifications. Based on Central Party Archives, the agrarian press, and official statistics; 150 notes.
C. S. Masloff

1081. Niederhauser, Emil. A BOLGÁR PÁRTTÖRTÉNETI FOLYÓIRAT 1972-1975-ÖS SZÁMAIRÓL [The 1972-75 volumes of the Bulgarian Party history periodical]. *Párttörténeti Közlemények [Hungary] 1976 22(4): 214-221.* Reviews the articles published in the journal of the Institute for the History of the Bulgarian Communist Party between 1972 and 1975. Sums up two articles on theory and methodology, reviews 23 more in chronological order, and discusses a 1972 conference on the role of the Bulgarian Communist Party during World War II. CK-AU

1082. Nikolov, Tsanko. DESET GODINI PO PUTIA, NACHERTAN OT APRILSKIIA PLENUM [Ten years along the route mapped out by the April plenum]. *Istoricheski Pregled [Bulgaria] 1966 22(2): 3-9.* The April 1956 plenum of the Bulgarian Communist Party condemned the cult of personality, reaffirmed the correctness of the Party's general approach, and called for increased vigilance against petit bourgeois tendencies and those who denigrated the Party. It reemphasized the importance of Leninist norms and of democratic centralism in Party life, urged members to involve themselves more directly with the masses, and recommended that the Party take more power in the development of industry. Great success crowned the 10 years following this call, and the greater discipline and involvement in all spheres of life increased the people's material and spiritual standard of living. Based on Lenin's writings and Todor Zhivkov's speeches; 4 notes. A. J. Evans

1083. Nikonov, G. V. VYDAIUSHCHIISIA RUKOVODITEL' SOTSIALISTICHESKOI BOLGARII [The distinguished leader of socialist Bulgaria]. *Voprosy Istorii KPSS [USSR] 1981 (9): 95-98.* Todor Zhivkov, Secretary General of the Central Committee of the Bulgarian Communist Party and President of the Council of State of the People's Republic of Bulgaria, was born on 7 September 1911 in the village of Pravets near Sofia. In 1928, during his early career as a printer, he joined the Bulgarian Communist Youth Union and entered the Communist Party in 1932. He worked as a Party activist in Sofia until the outbreak of World War II, when he became a partisan commander. His wartime efforts made a great contribution to the eventual victory of the dictatorship of the proletariat over fascism. Todor Zhivkov became head Party leader in 1951, and since then has worked to further the class struggle of the Bulgarian people, to strengthen the hegemony of the working class, to consolidate the union of workers and peasants and heighten the leading role of the Bulgarian Communist Party in Bulgarian society. 6 notes. J. Bamber

1084. Ognianov, Liubomir. DRUGARIAT TODOR ZHIVKOV ZA APRILSKATA LINIIA NA PARTIIATA [Comrade Todor Zhivkov on the Party's April line]. *Istoricheski Pregled [Bulgaria] 1981 37(5): 39-48.* Todor Zhivkov formulated the Party's 1956 April policies, denouncing the cult of personality and mapping Bulgaria's socialist development. Since 1956 he has chronicled Bulgaria's economic success, which rests on the full implementation of socialist policies, high technological efficiency, education, the Party's April 1956 line, and friendship with the USSR. Zhivkov has also emphasized the necessity for friendship with other Balkan nations and amicable relations with the capitalist countries. Based on the Party congresses and on *On the April Line: Speeches, Treatises, Articles, Pronouncements on the April Plenum and the Party's April Course,* 2 vol.; 3 notes. A. J. Evans

1085. Ognianov, Liubomir. ISTORICHESKITE ZAVOEVANIIA NA SOTSIALISTICHESKA BULGARIIA SLED APRILSKIIA PLENUM NA TSK NA BKP (1956 G.) [The historical achievements of socialist Bulgaria after the April Plenum of the CC of the BKP (1956)]. *Istoricheski Pregled [Bulgaria] 1981 37(2): 20-37.* Describes and analyzes the development of Bulgarian society and the economy after the decisions taken by the central committee of the Bulgarian Communist Party at its historic plenary session in April 1956. In the years after the Plenum the country was led by Party General Secretary Todor Zhivkov. Economic progress advanced as the country remained completely loyal to the Soviet Union and economically integrated with the other socialist countries but expanded trade, diplomatic, and cultural relations with capitalist countries as well. Concludes that the April Plenum was a major turning point for Bulgarian history, setting the country on a beneficial path. Based on published documents of the Bulgarian Communist Party, published statistics, and secondary works; 98 notes.
F. B. Chary

1086. Oren, Nissan. A REVOLUTION ADMINISTERED: THE SOVIETIZATION OF BULGARIA. *Studies on the Soviet Union [West Germany] 1971 11(4): 292-309.* The Communist takeover in Bulgaria was a product of the Red Army invasion. Bulgaria lacked a strong, well-organized Communist Party, and a suitable one was quickly invented. The Red Militia spread a reign of terror, causing mass revulsion and the rise of opposition parties. This new opposition proved to be quite vociferous and anti-Communist. The Soviet Union loosed a wholesale purge once the peace treaty was signed in 1947. Secondary sources; 27 notes. V. L. Human

1087. Ostoich, Petur. BRSDP (AVGUST 1945-AVGUST 1948 G) [The Bulgarian Social Democratic Party, August 1945-August 1948]. *Izvestiia na Inst. po Istoriia na BKP [Bulgaria] 1971 26: 181-246.* Examines the Workers' Social Democratic Party's role in the Fatherland Front and the consolidation of popular power from the expulsion of Lulchev's rightists in 1945 to its fusion with the Bulgarian Workers' Party (Communist) in 1948.

1088. Petkov, Vladislav. DEINOSTTA NA BKP ZA VNEDRIAVANE I RAZVITIE NA OBSHTESTVENOTO NACHALO V RABOTATA NA NARODNITE SUVETI (1958-1971 G.) [The activity of the Bulgarian Communist Party for the introduction and development of the social principle in the work of the People's Councils, 1958-71]. *Izvestiia na Inst. po Istoriia na BKP [Bulgaria] 1980 43: 219-242.* After the 7th Congress of the Bulgarian Communist Party in 1958 the municipalities in Bulgaria were reorganized in order to meet the requirements for mass participation in the work of the local authorities.

1089. Petrov, Kostadin. POLITIKATA NA BKP ZA USKORIAVANE NA TEKHNICHESKIIA PROGRES V PROMISHLENOSTTA (1956-1960 G.) [The Bulgarian Communist Party's policy on accelerating technological progress in industry, 1956-60]. *Izvestiia na Inst. po Istoriia na BKP [Bulgaria] 1967 17: 161-198.* After the Bulgarian Party Plenum in April 1956 and the Party's 7th Congress in 1958, a policy was implemented which increased productivity and intensified economic development.

1090. Petrov, O. V. DIIAL'NIST' BKP I PORP PO ROZVYTKU BOLHARO-POL'S'KOHO SPIVROBITNYTSTVA (1966-1975) [The work of the Bulgarian Communist Party and the Polish United Workers' Party in development of Bulgarian-Polish cooperation, 1966-75]. *Ukraïns'kyi Istorychnyi Zhurnal [USSR] 1979 (8): 123-129.* Cooperation between Bulgaria and Poland in the years 1966-75 was an example of the effectiveness of the multifaceted bilateral relations of countries of socialist unity. Interparty relations between the Bulgarian Communist Party and the Polish United Workers' Party (PUWP) has been at the core of such cooperation, which has extended to ideology, international detente, collective security, disarmament, economy, sciences, trade unionism, trade, and public life. 32 notes. I. Krushelnycky

1091. Petrov, Stojan. UN CENTENAIRE MEMORABLE: GEORGES DIMITROV ET LA DEMOCRATIE POPULAIRE [Georgi Dimitrov and popular democracy]. *Etudes Balkaniques [Bulgaria] 1982 18(2): 3-20.* On the birthday of Georgi Dimitrov (1882-1949), analyzes the origin and rationale of the people's democracy. Dimitrov's theoretical explication played an important role in the struggle against fascism and in the building of socialism, particularly after the 7th Comintern Congress in 1935. A people's democratic government was established in Bulgaria on 9 September 1944, under the leadership of the working class and the Communist Party. Based on official Bulgarian archives and Dimitrov's works; 43 notes. G. P. Cleyet

1092. Popov, Georgi N. DEINOSTTA NA BKP ZA OSUSHTESTIAVANE NA ZADULZHITELNO SEDEMGODISHNO OBRAZOVANIE (SEPTEMVRI 1944-IUNI 1958 G) [The efforts of the Bulgarian Communist Party in support of compulsory seven-year education]. *Izvestiia na Inst. po Istoriia na BKP [Bulgaria] 1965 13: 177-208.* Seven years' education was made compulsory by Alexander Stamboliski's government in 1921, but was not comprehensively enforced until 1944-58, when it was extended throughout the country by the Communist Party.

1093. Popov, Georgi N. DEINOSTTA NA BKP ZA PREUSTROIVANE NA UCHEBNO-VUZPITATELNIIA PROTSES V UCHILISHTETO PREZ PURVITE GODINI NA NARODNATA VLAST (SEPTEMVRI 1944G-DEKEMVRI 1948 G) [The activity of the Bulgarian Communist Party in reorganizing school education in the first years of the national government, September 1944-December 1948]. *Istoricheski Pregled [Bulgaria] 1964 20(1): 63-78.* After assuming power in 1944 the Government of the Patriotic Front began to change Bulgaria's educational system according to the progressive traditions of Bulgarian reformers since Dimitur Blagoev. In 1945 the Russian language was made a compulsory subject, and logic, psychology, history, and geography courses were revised. In 1945 the Higher Education Council was set up, and in October 1947 the National Committee of the Patriotic Front founded a youth movement modeled on the Soviet Pioneer organization. Reactionary elements attempted to sabotage these reforms, but the government pursued its policy with determination and the benefits of socialist education soon became apparent. Based on records of speeches, Bulgarian archive material, and government records; 137 notes. A. J. Evans

1094. Pulova, Violeta. ARKHIVEN FOND "BULGARSKA RABOTNICHESKA SOTSIALDEMOKRATICHESKA PARTIIA" 1944-1948 G. [The archives of the Bulgarian Workers' Social Democratic Party, 1944-48]. *Izvestiia na Inst. po Istoriia na BKP [Bulgaria] 1971 25: 349-358.* The Party's ideological, political and organizational records are indispensable to the study of modern Bulgarian history.

1095. Radkov, Ivan. SUZDAVANE NA TKZS V RUSENSKA OBLAST (1944—1948 G.) [The creation of TKZS in the Ruse region, 1944-48]. *Istoricheski Pregled [Bulgaria] 1971 27(4): 74-87.* Discusses the creation of cooperative farms (TKZS—*Trudovo-kooperativno zemedelsko stopanstvo*) in the Ruse region during 1944-48. The Bulgarian Communist Party and the progressive wing of the Bulgarian Popular Agrarian Union were responsible for propagandizing the value of such farms. They were resisted by reactionary elements opposed to the cooperative movement and had to combat Communists and government officials who forced farmers onto the farms when participation was voluntary. Through mechanization, the cooperative farms produced more than private farms in 1948. Based on regional state archives from Ruse, other archives, and contemporary press; 3 tables, 117 notes. F. B. Chary

1096. Rusakov, K. V. K 100-LETIIU SO DNIA ROZHDENIIA GEORGIIA DIMITROVA: VYDAIUSHCHIISIA BORETS ZA MIR I SOTSIALISM [The 100th anniversary of the birth of Georgi Dimitrov: an outstanding fighter for peace and socialism]. *Voprosy Istorii KPSS [USSR] 1982 (7): 20-32.* Georgi Dimitrov (1882-1949) joined the Bulgarian Marxist party in 1902 and in 1909 became a member of the central committee of the Bulgarian Social Democratic Party. He rose to be general secretary of the Comintern by 1935. His conviction, organizational skill, and determination were put to the twin aims of achieving social change in Bulgaria and friendship with the USSR. He is renowned for his analysis of fascism, his demonstration of the link between proletarian internationalism and genuine patriotism, his stress on the importance of the USSR to the working people of the world, and his recognition of the anti-Soviet nature of Chinese politics. Based on speeches and secondary sources; 25 notes. N. S. T. Pentland

1097. Samokovliev, Nikola. KUM VUPROSA ZA PERIODIZATSIIATA NA ISTORIIATA V RAMKITE NA KOMMUNISTICHESKATA FORMATSIIA [The problem of the periodization of history within the framework of the Communist formation]. *Izvestiia na Instituta po Istoriia na BKP [Bulgaria] 1970 24: 285-317.* Attempts a Marxist periodization of Bulgarian contemporary history since the revolution of 9 September 1944. This has been the least discussed period in problems of setting historical boundaries and epochs. Discussions held in 1966 and 1969 on periodization for a new multivolume history of the Bulgarian Communist Party have not been published, and arguments continue over the characterization of transitional eras from capitalism to socialism to communism. Uses Russian, East German, and Bulgarian philosophical and historical sources to label and delimit the three basic stages which follow a socialist revolution. Socioeconomic formations are the base for identifying types of society, general historical periods, and transitional phases. 118 notes. C. S. Masloff

1098. Samokovliev, Nikola. OSMIYAT KONGRES NA BULGARSKATA KOMUNISTICHESKA PARTIYA [The Eighth Congress of the Bulgarian Communist Party]. *Izvestiia na Inst. po Istoriia na BKP [Bulgaria] 1963 10: 5-25.* Reviews the activities and decisions of the Eighth Congress of the Bulgarian Communist Party (BKP), in November 1962, stressing its importance for historians and historical interpretation, particularly of the contemporary period, 1956-62. C. S. Masloff

1099. Schliewenz, Birgit and Schulze, Joachim. ERGEBNISSE UND ERFAHRUNGEN BEI DER ERHÖHUNG DER FÜHRENDEN ROLLE DER ARBEITERKLASSE IN DER VOLKSREPUBLIK BULGARIEN (1958-1981) [The leading role played by the working class in the People's Republic of Bulgaria, 1958-81]. *Beiträge zur Gesch. der Arbeiterbewegung [East Germany] 1982 24(3): 359-369.* Describes the economic advances which have been achieved in Bulgarian industry and agriculture: increases in industrial production; an increase in the number of workers; the development of strong workers' sections in all spheres of industry; an increase in agricultural production; economic development in all areas of Bulgaria; and an increase in the educational qualifications of the workers. In addition there has been a rise in the numbers of working-class members of the Communist Party and an increase in political education and local party organizations, as well as the development of greater social and cultural activities. Based on Bulgarian Communist Party documents held in Sofia and secondary sources; 42 notes. G. L. Neville

1100. Schultz, Lothar. BULGARIENS NEUE VERFASSUNG [Bulgaria's new constitution]. *Osteuropa [West Germany] 1972 22(4): 280-286.* The constitution of May 1971 reflects Bulgaria's entry into the mature socialist phase. The new personal union between the leaderships of State Council and Communist Party strengthens the Party. The concentration of production units resembles Soviet practice. A decentralizing trend appears in the role given to People's Councils at the local level. 18 notes. Additional documentation on pp. A270-A274. R. E. Weltsch

1101. Semerdjiev, Petar. THIRTY YEARS OF THE TRIAL OF TRAITCHO KOSTOV: 7-12 DECEMBER 1949. *Bulgarian Rev. [Brazil] 1979 19: 3-6.* Traicho Kostov, political secretary of the Bulgarian Communist Party, 1908-48, was executed in 1949, indicating that the Bulgarian Party had completely fallen under the domination of the USSR.

1102. Sharova, Krumka. *IZVESTIIA* INSTITUTA ISTORII BOLGARSKOI KOMPARTII [The Institute for the History of the Bulgarian Communist Party *Izvestiia]. Voprosy Istorii KPSS [USSR] 1961 (1): 230-233.* Surveys the contents of the journal of the Institute for the History of the Bulgarian Communist Party, 1957-60.

1103. Smilianov, Iordan V. APRILSKIIAT PLENUM NA TSK NA BKP OT 1956 G. I SOTSIALISTICHESKOTO PREUSTROISTVO NA SELSKOTO STOPANSTVO V BLAGOEVGRADSKI OKRUG [The April 1956 Plenum of the Central Committee of the Bulgarian Communist Party and socialist reconstruction of the village economy in the Blagoevgrad region]. *Istoricheski Pregled [Bulgaria] 1981 37(5): 130-140.* The Blagoevgrad region felt the results of the decisions of the 1956 April Plenum immediately, and in 1956 alone 204 agricultural units were built at a cost of 10.5

million levs. By 1957 high productivity rates were the norm, and in 1955 worker productivity rose by more than half in the two years 1955-57. 64 notes. A. J. Evans

1104. Sobolev, A. I. G. M. DIMITROV: VYDAIUSHCHIISIA DEIATEL' I TEORETIK KOMMUNISTICHESKOGO DVIZHENIIA [G. M. Dimitrov: an outstanding activist and theoretician of the Communist movement]. *Novaia i Noveishaia Istoriia [USSR] 1972 (2): 3-20.* Georgi Dimitrov played a major role in both the Bulgarian and international Communist movements. A consistent Leninist, he helped the Bulgarian Party overcome the mistakes of its socialist past. He was one of the first communist leaders to understand fascism as a terrorist dictatorship of the bourgeoisie. Dimitrov developed the conception, realized in practice after World War II, of the democratic anti-fascist revolutions growing into socialist revolution and called for the formation of national anti-fascist fronts. In Bulgaria he created the Patriotic Front, led by the Communist Party, and presided over the country's transition to socialism. Secondary sources; 19 notes. J. H. H. Presland

1105. Sobolev, A. I. PROBLEMUT ZA LENINIZATSIIATA NA KOMUNISTICHESKITE PARTII V ISTORICHESKI I TEORETICHESKI ASPEKT [The historical and theoretical problems of the Leninization of the Communist Parties]. *Izvestiia na Inst. po Istoriia na BKP [Bulgaria] 1976 35: 269-286.* A paper given by a Soviet historian at a joint Bulgarian-Soviet symposium on the theme "The Comintern and the Bulgarian Communist Party," held in Sofia 3-5 June 1975 which surveys the question of Leninization, 1903-75.

1106. Sokhan', P. S. BOLHARS'KA KOMUNISTICHNA PARTIIA I KOMINTERN [The Bulgaria Communist Party and the Comintern]. *Ukrains'kyi Istorychnyi Zhurnal [USSR] 1969 (5): 58-67.* Reviews the history of the Bulgarian Communist Party, formed in 1919, outlining its relationship with the Comintern in Moscow.

1107. Stoianov, Kostadin. ROLIATA NA RMS ZA UTVURZHDAVANE NA NARODNODEMOKRATICHNATA VLAST (1944-1947 G.) [The role of the Working Youth Union (RMS) in confirming popular democratic power, 1944-47]. *Istoricheski Pregled [Bulgaria] 1969 25(2-3): 122-146.* Describes the activities of the Bulgarian Communist youth organization, the Rabotnicheskiiat Mladezhki Suiuz (RMS), in the first years after the Communist-led Fatherland Front came to power. The RMS helped to transmit and put in practice the policies of the Bulgarian Communist Party's central committee and worked together with and sometimes against youth organizations of the other parties of the Fatherland Front. It mobilized the youth to work on the home front in the last months of World War II and in economic brigades for the postwar reconstruction of the country. It helped to educate Bulgarian youth in the principles of socialism. Based on documents in several Bulgarian archives, contemporary newspapers, and published material; 143 notes. F. B. Chary

1108. Stoianova, Penka. RABOTATA NA BKP VUV VARNENSKA OBLAST ZA PREUSTROISTVO NA OBRAZOVANIETO NA MARKSISTKO-LENINSKI OSNOVI (1944-1948) [The work of the Bulgarian Communist Party in the Varna district on educational reform according to Marxist-Leninist principles, 1944-48]. *Izvestiia na Inst. po Istoriia na BKP [Bulgaria] 1981 44: 313-343.* Surveys changes in education in Varna, in northeast Bulgaria, between 9 September 1944 and the summer of 1948, including the purge of fascist teachers from the schools and universities and the cleansing of textbooks of chauvinist ideas and religion.

1109. Surpionova, Kirilka. POLITIKATA NA BKP ZA RAZSHIRIAVANE NA SUTRUDNICHESTVOTO MEZHDU EVROPSKITE SOTSIALISTICHESKI STRANI (1966-1973 G.) [The policy of the Bulgarian Communist Party for broadening cooperation between the European socialist countries, 1966-73]. *Izvestiia na Inst. po Istoriia na BKP [Bulgaria] 1976 34: 205-240.* Reviews the development of various forms of bilateral and multilateral economic, political and cultural cooperation among European communist countries.

1110. Tanchev, P. EDINODEISTVIETO NA BZNS I BKP V REVOLIUTSIONNOTO MINALO I V SOTSIALISTICHESKOTO STROITELSTVO [The cooperation of the Bulgarian Agrarian Popular Union and the Bulgarian Communist Party in the revolutionary past and in socialist construction]. *Istoricheski Pregled [Bulgaria] 1975 31(3): 12-28.* The Bulgarian Agrarian Popular Union (BAPU) was formed in 1900 to express the political voice of the rural peasant population. It was inspired by the Russian Revolution and wished to emulate the achievements of the Soviet people. When the BAPU government was overthrown in 1923, some sections of the BAPU cooperated with the Bulgarian Communist Party (BCP) to rid Bulgaria of fascism. This was achieved in 1944, and since then the BAPU and the BCP have remained staunch allies. The BAPU helped the BCP in the collectivization of agriculture, and in narrowing the gap between town and country. The BAPU has also promoted and explained the policies of the BCP to the peasants.
A. J. Evans

1111. Tanchev, Petr. VERNYI SOIUZNIK RABOCHEGO KLASSA: K 80-LETIIU BOLGARSKOGO ZEMLEDEL'CHESKOGO NARODNOGO SOIUZA [A true ally of the working class: on the 80th anniversary of the Bulgarian Agrarian Popular Union]. *Voprosy Istorii KPSS [USSR] 1979 (12): 115-120.* The period of proletarian revolution in Bulgaria engendered both the Bulgarian Social Democratic Party and the Bulgarian Agrarian Popular Union (BAPU), formed in 1899. The history of BAPU is traced from its inception to the present, emphasizing its constant solidarity with the Bulgarian Communist Party in the process of socialist construction. Highlights the life and political thoughts and activities of Aleksandr Stamboliski (1879-1923), revolutionary leader and fierce opponent of the monarchy and capitalist oppression. 12 notes.
J. S. S. Charles

1112. Tanev, Stoian. BULGARSKATA KOMUNISTICHESKA PARTIIA V ISTORICHESKATA SUDBA NA RABOTNICHESKA KLASA I NARODA [The Bulgarian Communist Party in the historical destiny of the working class and the people]. *Istoricheski Pregled [Bulgaria] 1981 37(5): 67-91.* With the October Revolution the Bulgarian Revolutionary Social Democratic Party, founded in 1891, became more Leninist, and in 1919 was renamed the Bulgarian Communist Party. Between 1919 and 1939 ultra-revolutionaries and opportunists were routed. The BCP inspired the September 1944 uprising. At the Party's 1956 April Plenum Todor Zhivkov opened the road to real socialism. Based on the 1971 program of the BCP, and on the works of Blagoev, Dimitrov, and Zhivkov; 119 notes. A. J. Evans

1113. Topencharov, Vladimir. PUBLITSISTICHNOTO KREDO NA GEORGI DIMITROV [The publishing creed of Georgi Dimitrov]. *Izvestiia na Inst. po Istoriia na BKP [Bulgaria] 1982 (47): 7-21.* Describes Georgi Dimitrov's journalistic skills, his brilliant analysis of the dangers of fascism at the 1935 Comintern congress, and his post-1944 role as Bulgarian Prime Minister.

1114. Traikov, Georgi. ALLIANCE WITH THE COMMUNISTS. *World Marxist Rev. [Canada] 1972 15(8): 47-52.* Discusses the alliance between the Bulgarian Agrarian People's Union (BAPU) and the Communist Party in Bulgaria since the 1923 uprising and BAPU's participation in postwar governments.

1115. Trifonov, D. DVIZHENIETO NA TRUDOBOKULTURNITE BRIGADI 1945-1948 G [The worker-cultural brigades' movement, 1945-48]. *Istoricheski Pregled [Bulgaria] 1964 20(2-3): 184-199.* The brigades were formed in the harsh conditions of 1945 to strengthen the political unity of the working class and peasants. Reactionaries wishing to destroy the brigades had to be countered and on 2 September 1945 Georgi Dimitrov sent the Sofia Regional Committee a telegram stating that the brigades were a vital part of the revolutionary struggle. All type of work was tackled, including medical and scientific assignments, but they were mainly engaged in agriculture. Although the brigades had weaknesses, for example they sometimes undertook non-essential projects, they were extremely important. The workers were educated in the socialist concept of work and it taught them collectivism and discipline; the peasants' awareness and education were heightened in all spheres, agriculture, medicine, music, and literature; and the economy was helped. The author analyzes the brigades and differentiates them from the Soviet Subbotnik. Based on Bulgarian Communist Party materials and documents in the Central State Archive; 109 notes, 2 tables. A. J. Evans/S

1116. Trifonova, Minka. BKP I MATERIALNO-TEKHNICHESKATA BAZA NA TKZS SLED PRELOMA V KOOPERIRANETO (1951-1955 G.) [The Bulgarian Communist Party and the material and technical base of collective farms after the turning point of cooperative formation, 1951-55]. *Izvestiia na Inst. po Istoriia na BKP [Bulgaria] 1975 32: 157-191.* The Communist Party of Bulgaria, borrowing from the experience of the Soviet Union in devising the methods and forms of agricultural collectivization, learned from mistakes and made many practical corrections in its programs in 1951-55. Too much land for individual cooperators and many quarrels over land between collective farms and their members resulted from lack of attention to details. The Party succeeded in defeating smallholder tendencies from the past, while also broadening the rights of cooperators within their collectives. Based on Central Party Archives, Central State Archives, and the records of the Ministry of Agriculture; 2 tables, 97 notes.
C. S. Masloff

1117. Trifonova, Minka. BKP I POSLEDNIAT ETAP NA SOTSIALISTICHESKOTO PREUSTROISTVO NA SELSKOTO STOPANSTVO [The Bulgarian Communist Party and the last stage in the socialist transformation of the agrarian economy]. *Izvestiia na Inst. po Istoriia na BKP [Bulgaria] 1977 37: 281-314.* Surveys the last stage of the socialist transformation of agriculture in Bulgaria, 1955-58.

1118. Trifonova, Minka. ZNACHENIETO NA NOEMVRIISKIIA PLENUM NA TS.K. NA B.K.P. V BORBATA ZA PULNOTO LIKVIDIRANE NA OSTATUTSITE OT KULTA KUM LICHNOSTTA I VREDNITE POSLEDITSI OT NEGO [The significance of the November plenum of the Central Committee of the Bulgarian Communist Party in the struggle to liquidate the remains of the personality cult and its bad effects]. *Izvestiia na Inst. po Istoriia na BKP [Bulgaria] 1963 10: 26-45.* Until the November 1961 plenum of the Central Committee, many Party members failed to realize that the effects of the Bulgarian version of Stalinism continued under First Secretary Valko Chervenkov. The Plenum blamed Chervenkov's subjectivism and personal faults and ambitions for Bulgaria's economic failures, and new information of his crimes was revealed at large Party meetings and secret conferences in 1961: in 1962 Chervenkov was removed from office. 42 notes.
C. S. Masloff

1119. Tsanev, Petur. ISTORIKO-PARTIINATA NAUKA V BULGARIIA PREZ PERIODA 1944-1948 G. [Party historical science in Bulgaria, 1944-48]. *Izvestiia na Inst. po Istoriia na BKP [Bulgaria] 1979 41: 349-369.* A chronological-bibliographical review of the first steps in the development of the Party historical science in Bulgaria during 1944-48.

1120. Tsolov, Georgi T. IZ DEINOSTA NA SHUMENSKATA OKRUZHNA PARTIINA ORGANIZATSIA ZA ISPULNENIE APRILSKATA LINIIA NA PARTIIATA (1956-1958) [The activities of the Shumen district Party organization in applying the April decisions of the Party, 1956-58]. *Izvestiia na Inst. po Istoriia na BKP [Bulgaria] 1977 36: 367-399.* Surveys the transitional period in the district of Shumen during the change to socialism after the Communist Party plenum in April 1956.

1121. Tsutsov, Marin. NAUCHNA SESSIA, POSVETENA NA 60-GODISHNINATA OT PURVIIA KONGRES NA BULGARSKATA KOMUNISTICHESKA PARTIIA [Research session devoted to the 60th anniversary of the first congress of the Bulgarian Communist Party]. *Izvestiia na Inst. po Istoriia na BKP [Bulgaria] 1980 42: 551-556.* Report on a 1979 conference on the history of the Bulgarian Communist Party.

1122. Tsvetanski, Stoian. DEINOSTTA NA BKP ZA REGULIRANE NA SOTSIALNIIA I SŬSTAV (1944-1958 G.) [The Bulgarian Communist Party's action to regularize its social composition, 1944-58]. *Izvestiia na Inst. po Istoriia na BKP [Bulgaria] 1981 45: 207-248.* Examines the Party's campaigns to expand and improve its membership, and in particular, to increase the proportion of working class members. French, German, Russian summaries.

1123. Tsvetanski, Stoian. ROLIATA NA PARTIINATA CHLENSKA KNIZHKA ZA ORGANIZATSIONNOTO UKREPVANE I RASVITIE NA BKP (1944-1978) [The role of the Party membership card in the organizational strengthening and development of the BKP, 1944-78]. *Izvestiia na Inst. po Istoriia na BKP [Bulgaria] 1980 42: 349-384.* Analyzes the use made by the Bulgarian Communist Party of the membership card as a means to organize, control, and promote the avant-garde role of communism. Based on archival sources.

1124. Valev, L. B. VIDNYI DEIATEL' BOLGARSKOGO I MEZHDUNARODNOGO KOMMUNISTICHESKOGO I RABOCHEGO DVIZHENIIA [An eminent statesman of the Bulgarian and international Communist and workers' movement]. *Voprosy Istorii KPSS [USSR] 1977 (7): 116-119.* A biographical sketch of Vasil Kolarov, Bulgarian Communist, one of the founders of the Bulgarian Communist Party, Comintern official, participant in the 1923 Bulgarian revolution, and prominent official in the Bulgarian government after 1945. Based on Kolarov's publications; 10 notes.
L. E. Holmes

1125. Valev, Liubomir B. NOVAIA I NOVEISHAIA ISTORIIA BOLGARII V TRUDAKH SOVREMENNYKH BOLGARSKIKH ISSLEDOVATELEI (1944-1966) [Modern and current Bulgarian history in the works of contemporary Bulgarian historians, 1944-66]. *Sovetskoe Slavianovedenie [USSR] 1967 3(4): 99-106.* Since 1944 there have been three stages in the development of modern Bulgarian historiography. In the first stage the small cadre of Marxist historians reinterpreted Bulgarian history from earliest times, and contemporary history was neglected. In 1948 a discussion by historians focused on eliminating remnants of fascist distortions, bourgeois formalism, and objectivism from some Marxist historians such as D. Kazasov. The second period, 1949-58, saw the publication of many monographs and collective works as historians mastered Marxist methodology. However, the false theory of the infallibility of Josef Stalin and V. Chervenkov hampered progress. The third stage began after the April Plenary Session of the Central Committee, 1956, and the 7th Congress of the Bulgarian Communist Party, June 1958. Since then the historical process and the role of the popular masses have been studied. 44 notes. L. C. Moody

1126. Volkov, A. A SENSE OF THE TIMES. *World Marxist R.[Canada] 1973 16(3): 107-115.* The Communist Party must continue to improve its political organization and policy coordination.

1127. Volokitina, T. ORGANIZATSIONNO-POLITICHESKOE RAZVITIE OTECHESTVENNOGO FRONTA V PERIOD STANOVLENIIA I UKREPLENIIA NARODNO-DEMOKRATICHESKOI VLASTI V BOLGARII (9 SENTIABRIA 1944-OKTIABR' 1946 GG.) [Organizational and political development of the Fatherland Front during the period of establishment and consolidation of the people's democratic power in Bulgaria, 9 September 1944-October 1946]. *Sovetskoe Slavianovedenie [USSR] 1981 (6): 25-36.* An important vehicle for the Bulgarian Communists' formation of the system of people's democracy was the establishment of the Fatherland Front as a bloc of Leftist political forces. With the Communists the Front included, the Bulgarian Agrarian Union, the Bulgarian Social Democratic Party, and Zveno—a bourgeois antifascist party. Due to international circumstances, the first Fatherland Front government was a coalition, with Kimon Georgiev of the Zveno as Premier. The Fatherland Front established nationwide committees, which under the leadership of the Communists carried out a purge of nonprogressive elements in the Front. S. Liptai

1128. Zakharieva, I. and Petrov, M. NAUCHNO-TEORETICHNA KONFERENTSIIA ZA 75 GODISHINATA NA BZNS [A scientific-theoretical conference on the 75th anniversary of the Bulgarian Agrarian Popular Union]. *Istoricheski Pregled [Bulgaria] 1975 31(3): 165-168.* On 24 and 25 February 1975 a conference, organized by the Bulgarian Agrarian Popular Union (BAPU), was held in Sofia. Its theme was the cooperation of the union and the Bulgarian Communist Party in the revolutionary past and in socialist construction. Many foreign delegations attended the conference which discussed the unity of the two parties, their common struggle against fascism, their postwar cooperation, the international links of the BAPU with agrarian parties, and their continuing efforts both to promote friendship between the Bulgarian and Soviet peoples and to strengthen peace throughout the world. A. J. Evans

1129. Zakharieva, Iordanka. NAUCHNA SESIIA PO SLUCHAI 35 GODINI OT POBEDATA NA SOTSIALISTICHESKATA REVOLIUTSIIA V BULGARIIA [Conference on the 35th anniversary of the victory of the socialist revolution in Bulgaria]. *Istoricheski Pregled [Bulgaria] 1979 35(6): 165-168.* The conference, organized by the Bulgarian Academy of Sciences, the Institute for the History of the Bulgarian Communist Party, and other bodies, was held in Sofia on 4 September 1979. Summarizes papers on the Bulgarian revolutionary process and the political system, 1944-48, agrarian policy in the 1970's, the Communist Party in socialist society, the Bulgarian working class, and socialist life and contemporary ethnography. F. A. K. Yasamee

1130. Zarchev, Iordan. DVADESET GODINI OT APRILSKIIA PLENUM NA TSENTRALNIIA KOMITET NA BULGARSKATA KOMUNISTICHESKA PARTIIA [Twenty years of the April Plenum of the Central Committee of the Bulgarian Communist Party]. *Istoricheski Pregled [Bulgaria] 1976 32(2): 3-14.* Analyzes the effect of the April Plenum of 1956 on the subsequent development of Bulgarian history. The plenum successfully eliminated the negative effects of the cult of personality in the country. Bulgaria has since shown great progress in economic, social, cultural, and political areas. Based on writings of Bulgarian Communist leaders, published documents of the Bulgarian Communist Party, and the Bulgarian statistical yearbook; 30 notes. F. B. Chary

1131. Zhekov, Ivan. DMYTRO BLAHOIEV I RADIANS'KA ROSIIA [Dimitur Blagoev and the Soviet Ukraine]. *Ukrains'kyi Istorychnyi Zhurnal [USSR] 1968 (7): 75-79.* Discusses the life and works of Dimitur Blagoev (d. 1924), founder of the Communist Party in Bulgaria, with special reference to his activities in the Ukraine.

1132. Zhivkov, Todor. FROM THE SUMMIT OF 30 YEARS. *World Marxist R. [Canada] 1974 17(9): 3-7.* Examines factors contributing to the Communist Party's social reform achievements in Bulgaria since it came to power 30 years ago.

1133. Zhivkov, Todor. L'OEUVRE DE GEORGES DIMITROV ET LE MONDE CONTEMPORAIN [The work of Georgi Dimitrov and the contemporary world]. *Etudes Balkaniques [Bulgaria] 1982 18(4): 3-16.* The Secretary of the Central Committee of the Bulgarian Communist Party and President of the State Council of the People's Republic of Bulgaria pays tribute to Georgi Dimitrov, Bulgarian statesman and prime minister, a Marxist-Leninist theorist who had the ability to ensure historical responsibility with spiritual force and skill. Stresses the problems brought about by capitalist militarism and sets forth Communist policies for struggling against the United States while averting a nuclear holocaust. G. P. Cleyet

1134. Zlateva, Anka. KHUDOZHESTVENO-TVORCHESKITE SUIUZI I PODGOTOVKATA NA PETIIA PARTIEN KONGRES [The unions of the creative arts and the preparation for the fifth Party congress]. *Istoricheski Pregled [Bulgaria] 1979 35(4-5): 155-169.* The fifth congress of the Bulgarian Workers' Party (Communist), held in December 1948, was intended to set guidelines for Bulgaria's socialist transformation, and was preceded by intensive campaigns of preparation among the intelligentsia conducted by the Union of Writers, the Union of Artists, the Union of Film Workers and other bodies. From September 1948, artists, writers and other cultural workers were mobilized for agitprop activities in preparation for the Congress. F. A. K. Yasamee

1135. Żmigrodzki, Marek. SYSTEM PARTYJNY LUDOWEJ REPUBLIKI BUŁGARII [The party system of the People's Republic of Bulgaria]. *Z Pola Walki [Poland] 1975 18(4): 117-134.* Analyzes the problem of political forces in Bulgaria in 1944-48 and the stages in the development of the political system just after the war. Reflects on the leading role of the Bulgarian Communist Party within the political and juridical system of Bulgaria. Discusses the mechanism of interparty collaboration between the Bulgarian Communist Party and the Bulgarian Agrarian People's Union. J/S

1136. —. NOV ETAP V POLITIKATA NA PARTIIATA ZA POVISHAVANE ZHIZNENOTO RAVNISHTE NA NARODA [A new stage in the Party's policy to increase the people's standard of living]. *Istoricheski Pregled [Bulgaria] 1973 29(2): 3-8.* The 11-13 December 1972 plenum of the central committee of the Bulgarian Communist Party (BCP) unanimously approved Todor Zhivkov's report on the success of Party policy in raising the people's living standards. The 1956 Party plenum fostered the development of industry, enabling increases in the average wage. The disparity between living standards in town and country decreased, free medical provisions were extended, social welfare payments augmented, and the level of public services improved. Zhivkov's speech traced national development since 1944, emphasized the role of the Party, and provided the workers with greater goals. The plenum agreed on methods to secure wider public support. Based on Todor Zhivkov's speech at the 1972 plenum of the BCP; 3 notes. A. J. Evans

1137. —. PRIVETSTVIE NA TSENTRALNIIA KOMITET NA BULGARSKATA KOMUNISTICHESKA PARTIIA DO BULGARSKIIA ZEMEDELSKI NARODEN SUIUZ [The greetings of the central committee of the Bulgarian Communist Party to the Bulgarian Agrarian Popular Union]. *Istoricheski Pregled [Bulgaria] 1975 31(3): 5-10.* The Bulgarian Agrarian Popular Union (BAPU), formed in 1900, was the only non-Marxist party to oppose Bulgaria's participation in World War I. The BAPU government after 1920 led by Aleksandr Stamboliski strove to help the poor and to establish good relations with the USSR, but failed to combat the fascist forces which overthrew it in 1923. Thereafter, some sections of the BAPU cooperated with the Bulgarian Communist Party to eradicate fascism, and this cooperation continued after the 9 September 1944 uprising which marked a new era in Bulgarian history. A. J. Evans

Czechoslovakia

1138. Aleksandrov, A. N. VAZHNYI POLITICHESKII DOKUMENT [An important political document]. *Voprosy Istorii KPSS [USSR] 1971 (3): 133-137.* Discusses the significance of the document *The Lessons of the Crisis Development in the Czechoslovak Communist Party and Society after the Eighth Congress of the Czechoslovak Communist Party,* which was adopted by the Central Committee of the Party in December 1970, and which was intended to explain the Soviet intervention in Czechoslovakia in 1968.

1139. Amort, Čestmír. G. DIMITROV A NÁRODNĚ OSVOBOZENECKÉ HNUTÍ ČECHŮ A SLOVÁKŮ [Georgi Dimitrov and the national liberation movement of Czechs and Slovaks]. *Hist. a Vojenství [Czechoslovakia] 1982 31(3): 111-127.* Discusses Dimitrov's role in the support of the Czechoslovak liberation movement during World War II. As Comintern secretary general Dimitrov stressed the basic duty of Czech Communists to create and lead the anti-Nazi resistance, and after 1941 he endeavored to unify the actions of Right and Left with the single goal of the defeat of Nazism. Dimitrov also organized special training for resistance fighters sent from abroad into occupied areas to lead the resistance of Czech and Slovak patriots. Based on writings of Dimitrov and some published items; 43 notes. G. E. Pergl

1140. Andersson, John E. FRA GOTTWALD TIL HUSAK [From Gottwald to Husak]. *Samtiden [Norway] 1972 81(6): 339-347.* The conflict between national and Moscow-oriented leaders in the Czechoslovak Communist Party dates from the 1920's. Both Klement Gottwald (1896-1953) and Gustav Husak (b. 1913) represent Moscow-oriented groups. R. G. Selleck

1141. Babincová, Marie; Barala, Jaroslav; and Gawrecki, Dan. VÝSLEDKY VÝZKUMU DĚJIN DĚLNICKÉHO HNUTÍ, KSČ A BUDOVÁNÍ SOCIALISMU V SEVEROMORAVSKÉM KRAJI (1971-1980) [Results of a historical survey of the workers' movement, the Communist Party, and the building of socialism in Northern Moravia, 1971-80]. *Slezský Sborník [Czechoslovakia] 1981 79(3): 186-214.* Traces the development of the workers' movement from about 1870 to 1948, especially 1917-48, when the Communist Party led the workers' efforts. Examines the historiography of the labor movement in Czechoslovakia and the Northern Moravian region. 20 notes. B. Reinfeld

1142. Barnard, F. M. THE PRAGUE SPRING AND MASARYK'S HUMANISM. *East Central Europe 1978 5(2): 215-231.* The aspirations for a "democratic socialism" in 1968 in Czechoslovakia were inspired in part by the heritage of Tomáš Masaryk. Three strands in his thought assumed special importance: his acceptance of the Enlightenment idea of autonomous man and its political implication of democratic citizenship, the belief in pluralism, and the postulate of abiding values in a world of change and imperfection. Masaryk's thought was attractive to Communist intellectuals tired of the personal insecurity, mutual distrust, loss of truthfulness, and erosion of citizenship, all so characteristic of socialist democracy. 44 notes. R. V. Layton

1143. Barnovský, Michal. GUSTÁV HUSÁK A NAŠA CESTA K FEBRUÁRU 1948 [Gustáv Husák and our way toward February 1948]. *Hist. Časopis [Czechoslovakia] 1983 31(1): 3-13.* Uses the anniversary of Communist coup of February 1948 in Czechoslovakia to evaluate the political and organizational work of Czech President Gustáv Husák. From 1944 to 1948, Husák was able to unite and coordinate revolutionary demands of different groups of working people and cope with reactionary intrigues of the defeated bourgeoisie. In this way he enhanced the political influence of the Communists in Slovakia and throughout the whole state. Based on published sources; 16 notes. G. E. Pergl

1144. Barnovský, Michal. 30 YEARS OF ECONOMIC DEVELOPMENT OF SLOVAKIA. *Studia Hist. Slovaca [Czechoslovakia] 1978 10: 207-254.* A statistical survey of economic development in Slovakia, 1945-75. Considers industrialization and the development of agricultural production in particular, and analyzes the economic policy of the Communist Party of Czechoslovakia. Also compares the development with that of Slovakia before 1945 and the general economic progress of European socialist countries since 1945. Based on the statistical yearbooks of the Czechoslovak Socialist Republic and minutes of the congresses of the Communist Party; 3 tables, 80 notes. G. L. Neville

1145. Beran, Jiří. PŘEDÚNOROVÁ VĚDNÍ POLITIKA KOMUNISTICKÉ STRANY ČESKOSLOVENSKA A OTÁZKA ZŘÍZENÍ ČESKOSLOVENSKÉ AKADEMIE VĚD [The science policy of the Communist Party of Czechoslovakia before February 1948 and the question of establishing a Czechoslovak Academy of Sciences]. *Československý Časopis Historický [Czechoslovakia] 1985 33(2): 212-241.* After World War II, the Communist Party of Czechoslovakia, though preoccupied with the political power struggle, recognized the need for a scientific program, established a Research Section in the Party, and sought support for a Czechoslovak Academy of Sciences that would coordinate and promote research. It met half-hearted approval among Social Democrats and resistance among the academic establishment, which was still attached to the bourgeois intellectual traditions of prewar Czechoslovakia. Nevertheless, the Party worked out a new higher education program for the sciences and planned for a national research center. Though belatedly, Czechoslovakia joined the scientific revolution. Based on materials in the Central Archives of the Czechoslovak Academy of Sciences and the Central State Archives, Prague, and on published sources; 76 notes. Russian and German summaries. R. E. Weltsch

1146. Bianchi, Leonard. SOCIALISTICKÉ KODIFIKACIE V CESKOSLOVENSKU [Socialist codification in Czechoslovakia]. *Právněhistorické Studie [Czechoslovakia] 1984 26: 161-179.* Traces the development of civil law and criminal law under the direction of the Communist Party with the goal of creating a truly socialist country. The most important right, protected by law, in Czechoslovakia, is the right to work, guaranteed by the state. 33 notes. B. Reinfeld

1147. Bilak, Vasil. THE GENERAL AND THE SPECIFIC IN REVOLUTION. *World Marxist R. [Canada] 1975 18(1): 20-28.* Assesses the achievements of Communism in Czechoslovakia in the past 30 years.

1148. Bílek, Jiří. VZNIK, VÝSTAVBA A ÚLOHA LIDOVÝCH MILICÍ V LETECH 1948-1955 [The birth, build-up and the mission of People's Militia in the years 1948-55]. *Hist. a Vojenství [Czechoslovakia] 1983 32(4): 32-50.* An important role in the process of national and democratic revolution in Czechoslovakia since 1944 was carried by armed groups created by national committees as a powerful instrument of the revolution. During the early 1948 crisis the future position of the Army and the Internal Security units was to be balanced by forces of the Left. This is why the Communists instituted the People's Militia. These units challenged the attempts of disruption and civil disobedience carried on by reactionary groups. Based on official documents; 46 notes. G. E. Pergl

1149. Biliak, Vasil. PROTIV OPPORTUNISTICHESKOI PASSIVNOSTI: ZA BOL'SHEVISTSKUIU AKTIVNOST' [Against opportunist passivity: for Bolshevik activity]. *Voprosy Istorii KPSS [USSR] 1973 (7): 50-60.* Throughout its 50-year history, the Communist Party of Czechoslovakia has been attacked by reformists and revisionists of all types. In 1968 Right Opportunist elements led by Alexander Dubček rejected the principles of class solidarity, dictatorship of the proletariat, and friendship with the Soviet Union. Based on V. I. Lenin's *Collected Works* and published documents of the Czechoslovak and Soviet Communist Parties; 33 notes. L. E. Holmes

1150. Bjørnflaten, Jan Ivar. ERFARINGER PÅ VEIEN MOT EN MENNESKELIG SOSIALISME [Experiences on the way toward a humanist socialism]. *Samtiden [Norway] 1979 88(1): 50-54.* Discusses the development of the Communist Party of Czechoslovakia from 1948 through 1968 on the basis of recent books by former party members Jiří Hájek, Zdeněk Hejzlar, Zdeněk Mlynář, and Jiří Pelikán.

1151. Borodovčák, Viktor. PERSPEKTIVY POVOJNOVÉJ CŠL-POL'SKEJ SPOLUPRÁCE V PŘEDSTAVÁCH POKROKOVÝCH SLOŽIEK ODBOJA NA SLOVENSKU (1939-1945) [Perspectives of postwar cooperation as conceived by the progressive units of the resistance movement in Slovakia]. *Slovanský Přehled [Czechoslovakia] 1981 67(1): 31-44.* Communist elements in the resistance movement in Slovakia during World War II formulated a program of cooperation with the Poles against the imperialism of the Germans in the Košice program. But the real problem lay in convincing the masses that the relationship between the Poles and the Czechs would in the socialist world be built on the bonds of friendship and past wrongs and resentment would be cast aside. The memory of official Polish anti-Czech policy in 1937-38 had to be slowly eradicated by the demonstrations of good faith by the Poles of the new Communist Poland. 76 notes. B. Reinfeld

1152. Bouček, M. and Klimeš, M. DIE VEREINIGUNG DER ARBEITERBEWEGUNG IN DER TSCHECHOSLOWAKEI [The unification of the labor movement in Czechoslovakia]. *Beiträge zur Geschichte der Arbeiterbewegung [East Germany] 1976 18(2): 226-239.* The Czechoslovak working class had carried through spontane-

ous action between Communists and Social democrats in the 1930's. But a common program for the organization of a popular front was not achieved until the final stage of the Slovak resistance against the Germans in 1944. While the Slovak Communists and Social Democrats had negotiated a common platform in September 1944, the Czech parties were not united until June 1948. Based on published documents and secondary literature; 15 notes.
R. Wagnleitner

1153. Bowers, Stephen R. THE RE-IMPOSITION OF ORTHODOXY IN CZECHOSLOVAKIA. *J. of Pol. Sci. 1983 10(2): 70-82.* Nationalism is a strong unifying force in Poland; in Czechoslovakia, by contrast, it has contributed to divisions within the country. Attacks on Slovak nationalism find a receptive audience in Czechoslovakia. While orthodoxy was eroding in Poland in the 1970's, it was quietly reimposed and the Party's authority reestablished in Czechoslovakia. Table, biblio. T. P. Richardson

1154. Brabec, Antonín. ÚNOROVÉ VÍTĚZSTVÍ A NAŠE ARMÁDA [The February victory and the army]. *Historie a Vojenství [Czechoslovakia] 1978 27(1): 3-13.* Recalls the events of February 1948 in Czechoslovakia and the role of the army in that final struggle for power. The opponents of the Communist Party tried unsuccessfully to use the army; but the role of the army in the bloodless outcome cannot be denied. G. E. Pergl

1155. Brabec, Václav. MÍSTO A VÝZNAM XI. SJEZDU KSČ V DĚJINÁCH SOCIALISTICKÉ VÝSTAVBY V ČESKOSLOVENSKU [The place and significance of the 11th Communist Party Congress in the history of socialist construction in Czechoslovakia]. *Československý Časopis Hist. [Czechoslovakia] 1984 32(1): 1-26.* Czechoslovakia's Communist Party saw the Party Congress of June 1958 as a marker between the transitional decade of socialist construction and a new phase of "completion of socialist construction." The Congress stressed the further "upward development of a developed socialist society" without elaborating specific programs in this direction. Based on Communist Party publications and some material from the Central Committee Archives; 58 notes. Russian and German summaries. R. E. Weltsch

1156. Bradley, John F. N. PRAGUE SPRING 1968 IN HISTORICAL PERSPECTIVE. *East European Q. 1982 16(3): 257-276.* A straightforward description of the various events, particularly within the Communist Party, which occurred in Czechoslovakia in 1967 and 1968. The various votes within the Central Committee and the Politburo are emphasized, and the changing positions of the top Party officials are outlined. Based on published materials; 22 notes.
C. R. Lovin

1157. Brett, Vladimír. BOJ O REALIZACI KULTURNÍHO PROGRAMU KSČ ROKU 1945 [The struggle for the realization of the cultural program of the Czechoslovak Communist Party in 1945]. *Slovanský Přehled [Czechoslovakia] 1983 69(1): 11-19.* In 1945 the debate about the direction and control of culture, including the press, the theater, film, and publishing, was fought largely between two periodicals, *Tvorba* and *Kritický Měsíčník. Tvorba,* the Communist Party journal, insisted on bridging the gap between the intellectuals and the masses and on state ownership of cultural enterprises. *Kritický Měsíčník,* on the other hand, wanted to serve the class interests of the middle classes and follow a prowestern orientation in cultural interests and exchanges. Because of the elitist nature of the latter, the Communist Party's *Tvorba* won the confidence of both the artists and the people. 28 notes.
B. Reinfeld

1158. Broué, Pierre. SUR L'HISTOIRE DU PARTI COMMUNISTE TCHECOSLOVAQUE [On the history of the Czechoslovakian Communist Party]. *Rev. Française de Sci. Pol. [France] 1982 32(2): 270-274.* Discusses the censorship of names and ideas in M. Rupnik's *Histoire du Parti Communiste Tchécoslovaque* and discusses the requisites of a historiography of communism.

1159. Bruegel, J. W. DR. BENEŠ ON HIS POSITION AFTER FEBRUARY, 1948. *East Central Europe 1981 8(1-2): 103-105.* Conversations between Eduard Beneš of Czechoslovakia and British diplomats reveal that in 1948 before the Communist coup President Beneš was optimistic about the possibility of preserving a democratic state; after the coup he blamed himself and his ministers for not comprehending the extent of the Communist plot. Based mostly on communications from British Ambassador Dixon to Foreign Minister Bevin in the Public Record Office, London; 5 notes.
R. V. Layton

1160. Brügel, Johann Wolfgang. DIE KPČ UND DIE JUDENFRAGE [The Communist Party of Czechoslovakia and the Jewish question]. *Osteuropa [West Germany] 1973 23(11): 874-880.* In contrast with their behavior before World War II, Czechoslovak Communist spokesmen took up anti-Semitic positions after 1945, resisting restitution of Jewish property and, in the 1950's, following the anti-Zionist line laid down by Moscow. The Prague Spring and subsequent Soviet intervention of 1968 have brought on a new wave of anti-Jewish accusations, which dovetail with anti-Israeli propaganda. 14 notes. R. E. Weltsch

1161. Brügel, Johann Wolfgang. GEDANKEN ZUM SLÁNSKÝ-PROZESS—ZWANZIG JAHRE DANACH [Reflections on the Slánský trial—20 years after]. *Osteuropa [West Germany] 1972 22(12): 916-920.* Contrasts the show trial of November 1952 with the proceedings against Communist dissenters after 1968 in Czechoslovakia. The trial of 1952, which was marked by trumped-up charges, forced confessions, and anti-Semitic agitation, resulted in the execution of Party Secretary Rudolf Slánský, Foreign Minister Vladimír Clementis, and nine other completely loyal Communist leaders. In 1963 and 1968 the condemned were officially rehabilitated. 5 notes. R. E. Weltsch

1162. Bušek, Vratislav. PRÄSIDENT BENEŠ UND DER PRAGER FEBRUAR-PUTSCH VON 1948 [President Beneš and the Prague coup of February 1948]. *Osteuropa [West Germany] 1973 23(2): A120-A123.* A deputy of President Eduard Beneš's National Socialist Party maintains that the Czechoslovakian governmental crisis of 1948 involved the resignation of 14 ministers (a majority), and that it was Beneš who missed his opportunity to enforce a constitutional solution, thus giving the Communists an uncontested victory. R. E. Weltsch

1163. Cambel, Samuel. KOŠICKÝ VLÁDNY PROGRAM A SITUÁCIA NA SLOVENSKEJ DEDINE [The Košice government program and the situation in the Slovak countryside]. *Československý Časopis Hist. [Czechoslovakia] 1976 24(1): 22-54.* The agricultural part of the Košice program liquidated the power of capitalist German and Magyar landowners in Slovakia and created rural democracy, unknown for centuries to the Slovak agricultural population. Based on documents; 72 notes. G. E. Pergl

1164. Cambel, Samuel. XVI. ZJAZD KOMUNISTICKEJ STRANY ČESKOSLOVENSKA A ÚLOHY NAŠEJ HISTORIOGRAFIE [The 16th Congress of the Czechoslovak Communist Party and the tasks of our historiography]. *Hist. Časopis [Czechoslovakia] 1981 29(5): 617-627.* Since its 1929 Congress, the Czechoslovak Communist Party has strived to achieve the complete political leadership of the working class. Since the early 1970's, the Party has been able to lay the groundwork for the development of an advanced socialist society. The 16th Congress expressed the basic tasks of socialist historiography, which are to mold the ideological, political, and moral characteristics of the younger generation on the bases of socialist consciousness and proletarian internationalism while continuing research on Party history. G. E. Pergl

1165. Čarvaga, Vladimír. K PROBLEMATIKE POZEMKOVEJ REFORMY ZO ZVLÁŠTNYM ZŘETELOM NA SITUACIU NA SLOVENSKU [The problem of land reform with special emphasis on Slovakia]. *Právněhistorické Studie [Czechoslovakia] 1980 (23): 93-125.* The question of land reform in Slovakia came up before the end of World War II, when Eduard Beneš, in his 1943 negotiations with the USSR agreed that the land of collaborators, traitors, and enemies of the people should be seized. Although this plan was carried out in Bohemia, in Slovakia land hunger and poverty were such that, before the conclusion of the war, many rural poor simply moved on to abandoned land and possessed it. Much land in Slovakia was actually owned by Hungarians, which complicated the question of ownership by the people. In 1946 the Communist Party worked out the so-called Hradecký plan, which stated that land belonged to those who worked it. The workers and the farmers formed a strong force that no one could stop; they dispossessed reactionary landowners and after the 1948 victory of the Communist Party land was nationalized. 47 notes. B. Reinfeld

1166. Chňoupek, B. UNITY, SOLIDARITY AND COOPERATION: THE BASIS OF OUR SUCCESSES. *Int. Affairs [USSR] 1973 (5): 8-13.* Discusses the Communist Party of Czechoslovakia's interest in maintaining friendly relations with the USSR, 1968-73, and considers the attempt of counterrevolutionaries to dissolve Czechoslovakia's ties with the USSR.

1167. Čierny, Ján. JURAJ DIMITROV A KOMUNISTICKÁ STRANA ČESKOSLOVENSKA [Georgi Dimitrov and the Communist Party of Czechoslovakia]. *Hist. Časopis [Czechoslovakia] 1982 30(3): 369-376.* On the 100th anniversary of Dimitrov's birth, evaluates his connection with Czech Communists. In 1925 Dimitrov lived in exile in Prague. During the Reichstag fire trial in Leipzig in 1933, he became a hero of the international workers' movement. In Moscow during World War II, Dimitrov was able to help with some problems dealing with the future of Communists in liberated Czechoslovakia. His advice on the equality of Czech and Slovak populations later became law. G. E. Pergl

1168. Čierný, Ján. LENINSKÁ CESTA REVOLÚCIE V ČESKOSLOVENSKU V ROKOCH 1944-1948 [The Leninist road of the revolution in Czechoslovakia, 1944-48]. *Československý Časopis Hist. [Czechoslovakia] 1979 27(6): 801-827.* Surveys the years between Czechoslovakia's liberation by the Red Army and the communist takeover of February 1948. Because the Communists had carefully prepared their dominant positions in most key sectors, they could promptly seize the revolutionary opportunity which the bourgeois-created government crisis offered to them. 40 notes. R. E. Weltsch

1169. Činčar, J. 30 LET SOTSIALISTICHESKOI CHEKHOSLOVAKII [Thirty years of socialist Czechoslovakia]. *Voenno-Istoricheskii Zhurnal [USSR] 1978 (2): 106-110.* The military attaché of the Czechoslovak Embassy in the USSR describes the rehabilitation of the Czechoslovak army and economy since the liberation of the country by Soviet troops. He considers the military, social, and political programs of the National Front government set up in spring 1945, the futile attempts of reactionary forces to scuttle national democracy, and the final victory of the workers' socialist revolution. The new constitution, adopted in May 1949 at the 9th Communist Party Congress, consolidated the general Party line based on Leninism and led to steady industrial, economic, and social progress, briefly interrupted in 1968 by the abortive right-wing opportunist counterrevolution. The crisis was averted by the timely help of the USSR and other socialist countries. 5 notes. N. Frenkley

1170. Clark, Joseph. CZECHOSLOVAKIA: 1918-1968: A RECORD OF NATIONAL MARTYRDOM. *Dissent 1968 15(6): 523-538.*

1171. Cviij, Christopher. CZECHOSLOVAKIA. *World Survey [Great Britain] 1974 (68): 1-16.* Describes how the Communist Party took power in Czechoslovakia, 1945-48, the Party's policies which led to the military intervention by the USSR in 1968, and its effects through 1973.

1172. Deli, Peter. THE SOVIET INTERVENTION IN CZECHOSLOVAKIA AND THE FRENCH COMMUNIST PRESS. *Survey [Great Britain] 1976 22(2): 96-117.* The Soviet intervention in Czechoslovakia in 1968 produced a difficult dilemma for the French Communist Party (PCF). On the one hand the PCF could not disassociate itself from the Dubček experiment to produce "Socialism with a Human Face" for it had been trying to convince socialists of France's distinctive path to communism. Conversely, the Party could not reject Soviet communism for this would also have meant the rejection of the Russian Revolution and a whole series of symbols and slogans built up over the previous half century. The PCF solution was a compromise, the evolution of which is illustrated by extensive quotations from the French Communist press. Primary sources; 53 notes. R. G. Neville

1173. Dočkal, Miloslav. KSČ V ČELE ÚSILÍ O POKROKOVOU ORIENTACI MLÁDEŽE PŘED ÚNOREM 1948 [The Czechoslovak Communist Party heading the struggle for a progressive orientation of youth before February 1948]. *Československý Časopis Hist. [Czechoslovakia] 1978 26(3): 363-383.* From May 1945 until the Communist victory of February 1948, the Czechoslovak Communist Party deployed its younger members as leaders in the unified Czech and Slovak youth organizations of the National Front. By this method the Communists assured themselves of nationwide influence and outlasted the slump in youth membership caused by non-Communist disaffection during 1946-47. Based on Communist Party archives in Prague; 29 notes. R. E. Weltsch

1174. Doležal, Miloslav and Pelikán, Dragutin. 30. VÝROČÍ VYVRCHOLENÍ NÁRODNĚ-OSVOBOZENECKÉHO BOJE ČESKOSLOVENSKÉHO LIDU A OSVOBOZENÍ ČESKOSLOVENSKA SOVĚTSKOU ARMÁDOU [The 30th anniversary of the climax of the Czechoslovak people's national liberation struggle and of the liberation of Czechoslovakia by the Soviet Army]. *Pravněhistorické Studie [Czechoslovakia] 1975 (19): 9-13.* Czech national survival throughout the German occupation cannot be attributed to the servile policy of bourgeois class collaboration but was the result of the active antifascist struggle organized and led by Czech Communists. G. E. Pergl

1175. Dresler, Jaroslav. KAFKA AND THE COMMUNISTS. *Survey [Great Britain] 1961 (36): 27-32.* Describes the partial rehabilitation and discussion of Franz Kafka's work in his native Czechoslovakia in the "brief thaw" of the late 1950's.

1176. Drška, Pavel. KOŠICKÝ VLÁDNÝ PROGRAM A BUDOVANIE NOVEJ ČESKOSLOVENSKEJ ARMÁDY [The Košice government program and the buildup of the new Czechoslovak army]. *Hist. a Vojenství [Czechoslovakia] 1975 (1): 66-78.* Basic ideas for the buildup of the army were delineated in the third chapter of the 5 April 1945 program of the Czechoslovak National Front government. The author explains the historical and political background of this document, worked out by Moscow-based Czech Communists against the bourgeois conceptions of the London exile government. 15 notes. G. E. Pergl

1177. Duchacek, Ivo. A "LOYAL" SATELLITE: THE CASE OF CZECHOSLOVAKIA. *Ann. of the Am. Acad. of Pol. and Social Sci. 1958 (317): 115-122.* Czechoslovakia, 1948-58, proved to be a politically quiet, seemingly loyal Communist satellite due to its relatively high standard of living, pragmatic leadership, tradition of democracy, and nonviolent method of actions.

1178. Eidlin, Fred. THE TWO FACES OF CZECHOSLOVAK COMMUNISM. *East Central Europe 1983 10(1-2): 185-190.* Reviews Jacques Rupnik's *Histoire du Parti Communiste Tchécoslovaque, des origines à la Prise du Pouvoir* [History of the Czechoslovak Communist Party, from its origins to the taking of power] (1981) and Zdenek Suda's *Zealots and Rebels: A History of the Ruling Communist Party of Czechoslovakia* (1980). These books trace the two traditions in the Czechoslovak Communist Party, the one stressing subordination to Moscow, the other noting Czechoslovak ideas of pluralism and democracy. The reviewer considers Rupnik's book the more completely documented, but Suda's book carries the story into the late 1970's, whereas Rupnik's stops at 1948. Both books fill an important gap in the historiography. R. V. Layton

1179. Evanson, Robert K. REGIME AND WORKING CLASS IN CZECHOSLOVAKIA 1948-1968. *Soviet Studies [Great Britain] 1985 37(2): 248-268.* For two decades prior to the Soviet-led occupation of 1968, the Communist Party of Czechoslovakia enjoyed considerable success in restraining and pacifying that nation's industrial working class. Methods included the provision of certain material benefits, coercion, inter-class levelling, and selective

opportunities for upward mobility. Though this policy of worker appeasement had a negative economic effect, major disruptions of the type that developed in Poland after 1976 were avoided. This article is a revision of a paper presented at the 15th Annual Convention of the American Association for the Advancement of Slavic Studies in Kansas City, Missouri, on 23 October 1983; 106 notes.
M. R. Yerburgh

1180. Faltys, Antonín and Klimeš, Jan. HISTORICKÝ VÝZNAM KVĚTNOVÉHO POVSTÁNÍ ČESKÉHO LIDU PRO NÁRODNĚ OSVOBOZENECKÝ BOJ NAŠICH NÁRODŮ [The historical significance of the May uprising of the Czech people for the liberation struggle of our nations]. *Československý Časopis Historický [Czechoslovakia] 1985 33(1): 1-24.* The popular uprising that accompanied the liberation of Czechoslovakia in May 1945 must be seen primarily as a fruit of the previous antifascist resistance led by the Czech Communists. This leadership and the decisive liberating role of the Red Army expressed revolutionary changes in Czech society and pointed to a Soviet alliance as the only safeguard of Czechoslovakia's future. R. E. Weltsch

1181. Faltys, Antonin and Krempa, Ivan. ZUM SIEG DER ARBEITERKLASSE IM FEBRUAR 1948 IN DER CSR [The victory of the working class in February 1948 in Czechoslovakia]. *Zeitschrift für Geschichtswissenschaft [East Germany] 1979 27(3): 226-230.* The Communist Party of Czechoslovakia proved its effectiveness and maturity in February 1948 by peacefully completing the transformation from a popular democratic to a socialist revolution. An important step forward was the nationalization of key industries and financial institutions in 1945. In February 1948, the working class united to thwart the bourgeois counterrevolutionary coup, initiated by the resignation of the bourgeois ministers. Subsequently, the new cabinet, led by Klement Gottwald, began to carry out the dictatorship of the proletariat. 9 notes. J. T. Walker

1182. Felcman, Ondřej. PODÍL KRAJSKÝCH KONFERENCÍ KSČ NA ZÁPASE O PŘERŮSTÁNÍ NÁRODNÍ A DEMOKRATICKÉ REVOLUCE V SOCIALISTICKOU [The role of regional conferences of the Czechoslovak Communist Party in the struggle to transform the national and democratic into a socialist revolution]. *Československý Časopis Hist. [Czechoslovakia] 1978 26(3): 330-362.* The Czechoslovak Communist Party between May 1945 and February 1948 used its regional organizations and meetings to strengthen its popular base, recruit members, involve itself in distinctively regional concerns, and publicize its own qualifications for nationwide political leadership. Based on Party archives and published sources; 7 tables, 90 notes. R. E. Weltsch

1183. Ftoreková, Terézia. BUDOVANIE JEDNOTNÉHO SYSTÉMU SPOLOČENSKÝCH ORGANIZÁCIÍ A ICH ZAČLEŇOVANIE DO POFEBRUÁROVÉHO SLOVENSKÉHO NÁRODNÉHO FRONTU [Building a unified system of social organizations and their incorporation into the post-February Slovak National Front]. *Hist. Časopis [Czechoslovakia] 1984 32(1): 24-50.* Discusses the problem of social organizations in the policy of the Communist Party of Slovakia with regard to events in Czechoslovakia in February 1948 and the Communist assumption of power.
J/S

1184. Furtak, Robert K. EL "INTERNACIONALISMO-SOCIALISTA" A LA LUZ DE LA CRISIS CHECOSLOVACA DE 1968 ["Socialist internationalism" in light of the Czechoslovak crisis of 1968]. *Foro Internacional [Mexico] 1971 11(3): 444-459.* Surveys the concept of international socialism from the Second International Communist Congress (1920) to presentation of the Brezhnev Doctrine (1968). Indicates that with the Czechoslovak crisis came a redefinition of socialist internationalism. Primary and secondary sources; 36 notes. D. A. Franz

1185. Gawrecki, Dan. REVIZIONISTICKÉ FALZIFIKACE VÝZNAMU V. SJEZDU KSČ A JEJICH KRITIKA [Revisionist falsification of the Fifth Congress of the Czechoslovak Communist Party and their criticism]. *Slezský Sborník [Czechoslovakia] 1980 78(2): 88-113.* In the 1960's, culminating in 1968, there appeared a number of revisionist interpretations of the Fifth Party Congress (1929), at which the Leninist-Stalinist model of party structure and discipline was adopted. Jan Mlynarík in the *Literární listy* (Literary Gazette) was the foremost proponent of this interpretation and claimed that at the Fifth Congress of the Czechoslovak Party in 1929 a purge of the social democrats took place and a dogmatic leftist leadership assumed control. This is a falsification of the party's history; in fact, strongly influenced by the Sixth Congress of the Comintern in 1928, the Czechoslovak Party became a truly revolutionary organ. In the last 10 years Marxist historiography has severely criticized the revisionist positions which approached the bourgeois West German historical account of the Czechoslovak Communist Party. 78 notes. B. Reinfeld

1186. Gawrecki, Dan and Výtiska, Josef. Z HISTORIE KSČ V N.P. VAGÓNKA STUDÉNKA (1921-1948) [The Czechoslovak Communist Party in the National Enterprise Vagonka in Studenka, 1921-48]. *Prmyslové Oblasti [Czechoslovakia] 1978 6: 257-332.* Studies the birth and development of Communist organization in one of the largest Czechoslovak railway factories. Examines the first organizational attempts before World War I, the aims after the Party's formation in 1921, the German occupation, and the seizure by the state in February 1948. Based on industrial archives of the factory and personal papers; 272 notes. G. E. Pergl

1187. Glejdura, Stefan. ESLOVAQUIA, EN ERUPCIÓN REVOLUCIONARIA (1945-1975) [Slovakia, in revolutionary uproar, 1945-75]. *Rev. de Política Int. [Spain] 1976 (143): 115-137.* Examines the role of small states in a great power system, and considers the Communist takeover of Czechoslovakia since 1948.

1188. Gorshkov, A. I. IZMENENII V STRUKTURE RABOCHEGO KLASSA CHEKHOSLOVAKII V GODY STROITEL'STVE OSNOV SOTSIALIZMA (1948-1960) [Changes in the structure of the Czechoslovak working class during the years of the construction of the foundations of socialism, 1948-60]. *Sovetskoe Slavianovedenie [USSR] 1975 (2): 21-33.* Discusses qualitative and quantitative changes in the composition of the working class, and the role of the working class and the Communist Party in the construction of socialism. Notes the developed nature of the national economy in 1948, and offers a demographic portrait of the changing composition of the working class during the 1950's. Based on various statistical publications of the government of Czechoslovakia; 56 notes.
J. W. Kipp

1189. Gradilak, Zdenek. PROBLEMY ISTORIKO-PARTIINOI NAUKI V CHEKHOSLOVAKII I ZHURNAL "MATERIALY K ISTORII KPCH" [Problems of Party history in Czechoslovakia and the journal *Materials for the History of the Communist Party of Czechoslovakia]. Voprosy Istorii KPSS [USSR] 1965 (1): 115-120.* Discusses the contents of *Příspěvky k dějinám KSČ* with reference to the history of the Czech Communist movement, Comintern, and the antifascist movement.

1190. Grešík, Ladislav. VÝCHOVA VYSOKOŠKOLSKEJ INTELIGENCIE NA SLOVENSKU V ROKOCH 1956-1960 [Education of the university intellectuals in Slovakia, 1956-60]. *Hist. Časopis [Czechoslovakia] 1983 31(6): 891-911.* In the continuity with the line of the 9th Congress of the Communist Party, construction of socialism in Czechoslovakia was carried on with its claim to educate a new, socialist intelligentsia. J

1191. Grobelný, Andělín. HISTORICKÉ VĚDOMÍ DĚLNICKÉ TŘÍDY V PRŮMYSLOVÝCH OBLASTECH ZA KAPITALISMU [Historical consciousness of the working classes in the industrial regions under capitalism]. *Slezský Sborník [Czechoslovakia] 1980 78(4): 258-289.* During the capitalist era, the consciousness of the working classes was totally subordinated to the bourgeois conception of history as worked out by Palacký. Within the workers' own definition of national awareness, there was an affinity with the idea of Slavdom, but this was understood in the form of an international proletariat. Only after the formation of the Communist Party in 1921 do some progressive works on the evolution of a national consciousness among the workers appear. These are the works of Šmeral, Šverma, Čejchan, and Nejedlý. They show that instead of a passive acceptance of the bourgeois view of Czech history, the workers, though at different paces in different industrial areas, identified their true enemy, the middle class, as well as the national enemy, the Germans. Secondary sources; 108 notes.

B. Reinfeld

1192. Hájek, Hanuš. 30 YEARS OF COMMUNISM: A STUDY IN DISILLUSION. *Bohemia. Jahrbuch des Collegium Carolinum [West Germany] 1978 19: 331-342.* Political illusions and opportunism during and after World War II smoothed the path for communism in Czechoslovakia. They also characterized the years of Communist rule after 1948. Even the high hopes for democratization in 1968 rested on unrealistic assumptions and inadequate political strategies. R. E. Weltsch

1193. Hartmann, Eva. INNENPOLITISCHE VORAUSSETZUNGEN FÜR DIE MACHTÜBERNAHME DER KOMMUNISTISCHEN PARTEI IN DER TSCHECHOSLOWAKEI [Domestic political preconditions for the Communist Party's seizure of power in Czechoslovakia]. *Bohemia. Jahrbuch des Collegium Carolinum [West Germany] 1978 19: 197-246.* Czechoslovak politics, 1918-38, had relied excessively on government by committee and interparty deals, at the expense of firm party principles and vigorous parliamentarism. By overemphasizing Czechoslovak leadership in a unitary nation state, the Czech politicians neglected the more genuine leadership of conciliation in what was really a multinational country. Their habit of overestimating external guarantees of their national frontiers led them to overlook factors of internal strength. Handicapped by the Munich Agreement and operating in exile during World War II, the traditional party leaders could not break out of their old patterns and were defenseless against the Communist Party, which in 1945 utilized the mass expulsion of national minorities to create a revolutionary climate and could claim that its subsequent takeover in February 1948 was constitutional. 77 notes.

R. E. Weltsch

1194. Havelka, Jan. KOMMUNISTICHESKAIA PARTIIA CHEKHOSLOVAKII V BOR'BE ZA SOTSIALISTICHESKOE PEREUSTROISTVO SEL'SKOGO KHOZIAISTVA CHSSR [The Czech Communist Party's struggle for the socialist reconstruction of Czech agriculture]. *Voprosy Istorii KPSS [USSR] 1965 (9): 40-51.* Follows the Czech Communist Party's efforts to reconstruct agriculture along socialist lines, 1948-65, and presents statistical data.

1195. Hejl, František and Kolejka, Josef. ŘEŠENÍ NÁRODNOSTNÍ OTÁZKY V ČESKOSLOVENSKU V LETECH 1944-1945: OBNOVENÍ ČS. REPUBLIKY JAKO STÁTU ČECHŮ A SLOVÁKŮ [Solving the nationality question in Czechoslovakia, 1944-45: the renewal of the Czechoslovak Republic as a state of the Czechs and Slovaks]. *Sborník Prací Filosofické Fakulty Brněnské University: Řada Historická [Czechoslovakia] 1974-75 23-24(21-22): 21-52.* Analyzes the Communist Party of Czechoslovakia's views on national minorities, especially the Slovak question, from the prewar Republic to 1948.

1196. Hendrych, Jiří. KOMMUNISTICHESKAIA PARTIIA CHEKHOSLOVAKII VO GLAVE BOR'BY ZA POBEDU SOTSIALISTICHESKOGO STROIA [The Communist Party of Czechoslovakia in the vanguard of the struggle for the victory of a socialist order]. *Voprosy Istorii KPSS [USSR] 1961 (3): 59-76.* Reviews the first 40 years of the Czechoslovak Communist Party, 1921-61, and its achievement in fighting for socialism, especially in the post-war period.

1197. Heumos, Peter. BETRIEBSRÄTE, EINHEITSGEWERKSCHAFT UND STAATLICHE UNTERNEHMENSVERWALTUNG: ANMERKUNGEN ZU EINER PETITION MÄHRISCHER ARBEITER AN DIE TSCHECHOSLOWAKISCHE REGIERUNG VOM 8. JUNI 1947 [Shop councils, trade union and governmental administration of enterprises: comments on a petition of Moravian workers to the Czechoslovak government of 8 June 1947]. *Jahrbücher für Geschichte Osteuropas [West Germany] 1981 29(2): 215-245.* Free articulation of the interests of the workers, promised by the Czechoslovak government in the Košice Program of 5 April 1945, had been circumscribed and suppressed long before the Communist coup in February 1948. A 1947 petition by the Moravian workers of the Bat'a shoe factory in Zlín, published for the first time, demonstrates the high degree of integration of union leadership into the sociopolitical power structure of the state between 1945-47. Following shop council elections in the spring of 1947, which threatened continued Communist hegemony of the industrial sector, the Party intensified its campaign of political terrorism in the factories. Based on journals, trade union newspapers, and documentary collections; illus., 2 tables, 268 notes.

S. A. Welisch

1198. Heumos, Peter. GESCHICHTSWISSENSCHAFT UND POLITIK IN DER TSCHECHOSLOWAKEI [Historiography and politics in Czechoslovakia]. *Jahrbücher für Geschichte Osteuropas [West Germany] 1978 26(4): 541-576.* Divides Czechoslovak historiography into the periods 1945-48, 1948-62, 1962-69, and 1970, and traces the relationship between historical interpretation and politics in each. Historiography 1945-48 reflected the national liberal tradition of the First Czechoslovak Republic as well as the broad spectrum of opinion typical of a pluralistic society. Thereafter, except for 1962-69, the Central Committee of the Czechoslovak Communist Party assumed a dominant role in directing the writing of history according to Marxist-Leninist principles. The earlier emphasis on "baroque Prague" shifted to "Lenin's Prague" as the course of Czechoslovak history since 1918 became closely linked to political developments in the USSR. Based on contemporary historical literature; 290 notes. S. A. Welisch

1199. Hlavova, Viera. XI. ZJAZD KSČ A ÚLOHY POL'NOHOSPODÁRSTVA NA SLOVENSKU [The 11th Congress of the Communist Party of Czechoslovakia and the tasks of agriculture in Slovakia]. *Hist. Časopis [Czechoslovakia] 1983 31(3): 415-436.*

1200. Hříbek, Bruno. HRADECKÝ PROGRAM A JEHO VÝZNAM V ZÁPASE KOMUNISTICKÉ STRANY ČESKOSLOVENSKA O DALŠÍ UPEVNĚNÍ A PROHLOUBENI DĚLNICKO-ROLNICKÉHO SVAZKU (JARO 1947-ÚNOR 1948) [The program of Hradec Králové and its significance in the struggle of the Czechoslovak Communist Party for the further strengthening and deepening of the worker-peasant alliance, Spring 1947-February 1948]. *Československý Časopis Hist. [Czechoslovakia] 1978 26(2): 177-202.* The Czechoslovak government of Klement Gottwald on 4 April 1947 proclaimed a reform program designed to speed up the revolutionary process in the village by a sweeping redistribution of land. Its 17 points aimed at a rapid rural democratization without as yet alienating the wealthier peasantry. By appealing to the mass of cotters, smallholders, and middle peasants, the Communist-led government gained adherents in the stepped-up class struggle and provoked the resistance of the agrarian bourgeoisie. After the Communist coup of February 1948 the land legislation was quickly enacted. Based on published sources; 65 notess

R. E. Weltsch

1201. Hrnko, Anton and Žatkuliak, Jozef. UNIVERZITA KOMENSKÉHO NA ROZHRANÍ PAŤDESIATYCH A ŠESŤDESIATYCH ROKOV [Comenius University of Bratislava, late 1950's and early 1960's]. *Hist. Časopis [Czechoslovakia] 1984 32(4): 593-619.* Comenius University played an important role in the formation of a socialist school system and socialist intelligentsia in the 1950's. The conclusions of the 11th Congress of the Communist Party of Czechoslovakia in 1958 and the resolutions of the Central Committee of the Communist Party of Czechoslovakia in April 1959 represented significant changes in the increase of the standard of education. Efforts were made to realize the connection of school and life as well as the deepening of its socialist features in order that its educational process and scientific capacities could keep up with the social and economic development of Czechoslovakia. J

1202. Hruby, Peter. *Fools and Heroes: The Changing Role of Communist Intellectuals in Czechoslovakia.* Oxford: Pergamon, 1980. 265 pp.

1203. Hrzalová, Hana. OSOBNOST A DÍLO LADISLAVA ŠTOLLA [The personality and work of Ladislav Štoll]. *Česká Literatura [Czechoslovakia] 1982 30(6): 487-492.* Ladislav Štoll (1902-81) was an antiformalist, antineostructuralist Marxist-Leninist literary critic, and for many years the Czechoslovak Communist Party's theoretical representative on literature.

1204. Hubernák, Ladislav. KOMMUNISTICKÁ STRANA ČESKOSLOVENSKÁ V NOVODOBÝCH DĚJINAĆH ČESKOSLOVENSKÉHO STÁTU A PRÁVĚ [The Czechoslovak Communist Party in the contemporary history of the Czechoslovak state and law]. *Právněhistorické Studie [Czechoslovakia] 1978 (21): 27-48.* The working class of Czechoslovakia, under the leadership of the Czechoslovak Party, has been a progressive force in the history of the Czechoslovak state. Since its founding in 1921, the Czechoslovak Communist Party has been the vanguard of revolutionary ideas and social integration. It led the country to victory in 1948. Since then the Party has continued its role of integration and socialist construction. 32 notes. B. Kimmel

1205. Hurley, V. J. A NEW PHASE IN THE SOCIALIST ECONOMIC REFORM. *Slovakia 1973 23(46): 57-65.* Analyzes recent developments in economic planning in Czechoslovakia. Following a brief period of liberalization in 1968, the subject of economic reform has generally been avoided by Czech economic planners. However, in 1970 Andrej Lantay, director of the Economic Institute of the Slovak Academy of Sciences, published an important restatement of the issues involved in economic reform in the socialist countries. Whereas most socialist planners support a model with the decisionmaking powers vested in the central planning authority, the Lantay model proposed that decisionmaking be shared by both the individual firms and by the central planning authority. Since the model outlined by Lantay is not congruent with the economic thinking of the central planning authority, it does not appear likely that they will support it. The author notes a number of rigidities that impede economic development in socialist countries: neither profitability nor productivity are viewed as significant determinants in the allocation of resources to industry; and socialist managers do not always support technological improvements that will increase productivity because they will be required to meet expanded quotas.
J. Williams

1206. Husak, Gustav. GREAT LANDMARK IN WORLD HISTORY. *World Marxist R. 1975 18(5): 4-14.* Celebrates the success of the Communist Party and socialism in Czechoslovakia since 1945.

1207. Husak, Gustav. TRUE TO THE BEHESTS OF OCTOBER. *World Marxist Rev. 1977 20(11): 16-24.* Surveys the victory of socialism in 1917 through the concerted efforts of the workers, peasantry, and the Leninist Party, the spread of Communist politics to Czechoslovakia in 1935, and the revolutionary aims of Communist Parties and movements, 1935-75.

1208. Jager, Janine. TSJECHOSLOWAKIJE IN BEWEGING [Czechoslovakia in motion]. *Kleio [Netherlands] 1977 18(5): 355-361.* Reports on Czechoslovakia's totalitarian state under Antonín Novotný, his confrontations with the more liberal elements in the Communist Party, and the rising opposition of intellectuals, West-oriented youth, and Slovaks, which led to his downfall and replacement as first party secretary by Alexander Dubček. 9 notes.

1209. Jelinek, Yeshayahu. THE COMMUNIST PARTY OF SLOVAKIA AND THE JEWS: TEN YEARS (1938-48). *East Central Europe 1978 5(2): 186-202.* The Slovak Communist Party, which was independent from 1938 until 1948, chose an opportunistic line toward Jews, reflecting propaganda and pragmatic needs of the Communists in the struggle for supremacy. Moreover, anti-Semitism affected both leaders and rank and file. When the Holocaust began in Slovakia, Communists aided victims on an individual basis, but the Party itself did nothing to hinder the Germans, regarding the Jews as ineffective fighters against the Germans. Even after the war, high Party officials urged the use of stringent criteria when admitting Jews. Nevertheless, Jews flocked to the Party. However, once the Communists were firmly in power in 1948, about 70% of the Jews emigrated. 90 notes. R. V. Layton

1210. Jelinek, Yeshayahu A. *The Lust for Power: Nationalism, Slovakia, and the Communists, 1918-1948.* (East European Monographs series, no. 130.) Boulder, Colo.: East European Monographs, 1983. 185 pp.

1211. Jones, Christopher D. AUTONOMY AND INTERVENTION: THE CPSU AND THE STRUGGLE FOR THE CZECHOSLOVAK COMMUNIST PARTY, 1968. *Orbis 1975 19(2): 591-625.* Discusses political factors in the USSR's military intervention in Czechoslovakia in 1968, including Leonid Brezhnev's accusations of ideological revisionism against Czechoslovakia's Communist Party and First Secretary Alexander Dubček.

1212. Kadnár, Milan. CZECHOSLOVAKIA SINCE HELSINKI. *Int. Affairs [USSR] 1977 (2): 74-78.* In the past few years, Czechoslovakia has devoted much effort to implementing the Final Act of the Conference on Security and Cooperation in Europe in Helsinki. In 1975, Czechoslovakia had important consultations with 17 Western states, and concluded a total of 305 treaties. Czechoslovakians have greater access to books, television programs, and plays, from England, France, West Germany, and the United States than citizens of these countries have to Czechoslovakian productions. In these and many other ways, Czechoslovakia is endeavoring to make Helsinki work, and to aid in the creation of a lasting peace.
L. W. Van Wyk

1213. Kirschbaum, J. M. JESUITS FIND A HOME IN CANADA. *Jednota Ann. Furdek 1977 16: 107-109.* Jesuits from Czechoslovakia came to Canada in 1950 following the dissolution of religious communities under Communism.

1214. Kirschbaum, J. M. SLOVAK LANGUAGE UNDER COMMUNISM. *Jednota Ann. Furdek 1975 14: 83-93.* In spite of Communist political pressure since the war, the Slovak language successfully resisted Russification and a Czechoslovak literary language, as it has done since the 18th century.

1215. Kirschbaum, Stanislav J. FEDERALISM IN SLOVAK COMMUNIST POLITICS. *Can. Slavonic Papers [Canada] 1977 19(4): 444-467.* Discusses the difficulties involved in solving the national question in a multinational state. In Czechoslovakia the problem has been compounded by the Slovak declaration of independence in 1939, which was almost immediately recognized by the USSR, but reversed during World War II. The author traces the steps taken by the Communist Party, directed from Moscow to achieve a federalism consonant with the requisites of their ideology and describes the obstacles and the results. A major contradiction remains. The present regime seems to support federalism while simultaneously pursuing a policy of centralization and of depriving Slovakia as well as Bohemia-Moravia of the political and economic autonomy granted in 1968. 103 notes. R. V. Ritter

1216. Kolesnikov, S. I. KLEMENT GOTVAL'D: K 80 LETIIU SO DNIA ROZHDENIIA [Klement Gotwald (1895-1953): on the 80th anniversary of his birth]. *Voprosy Istorii KPSS [USSR] 1976 (11): 107-110.* Charts the history of the Czech Communist Party and Klement Gottwald's activities in the Czech labor movement and government, 1921-53.

1217. Kolesnikov, S. I. SLAVNYI PUT' BOR'BY I POBED POD ZNAMENEM MARKSIZMA-LENINIZMA (K 60-LETIIU KOMMUNISTICHESKOI PARTII CHEKHOSLOVAKII) [A glorious journey of struggle and victories under the banner of Marxism-Leninism: the 60th anniversary of the Communist Party of Czechoslovakia (CPCz)]. *Voprosy Istorii KPSS [USSR] 1981 (5): 102-106.* The CPCz has had sixty years of hard but glorious struggle. The author reviews its opposition to the Munich betrayal and fascism, its wartime leadership, the 1946 election and the formation of a government under Klement Gottwald, the 1948 taking of power, the crisis years to 1968, and the subsequent normalization with So-

viet help. The country now has a sound economy, high living standards, and a lively cultural life, and relations between the CPCz and the CPSU are a model of inter-Party relations. 6 notes.
A. J. Evans

1218. Kollár, Ján. BOJ KSČ PROTI BURŽOÁZNEJ IDEOLÓGII A OPORTUNIZMU V ROKOCH 1948-1949 [The fight of the Communist Party of Czechoslovakia against bourgeois ideology and opportunism, 1948-49]. *Československý Časopis Hist. [Czechoslovakia] 1983 31(6): 801-833.* The quick Communist victory of February 1948 did not mean the immediate end of Czechoslovakia's bourgeoisie. Bourgeois attitudes lingered on and infiltrated the rapidly growing Communist Party. Among their earmarks were exaggerated war scares, excessive nationalism or cosmopolitanism, and even open antisocialist manifestations. At the 9th Party Congress, Party leaders emphasized the ideological struggle against these elements as part of the continuing class struggle. Based on materials in the Slovak Central State Archives and the Slovak Institute of Marxism-Leninism and on published sources; 99 notes. German and Russian summaries. R. E. Weltsch

1219. Kollár, Ján. NIEKTORÉ METODOLOGICKÉ OTÁZKY STRATEGIKOTAKTICKEJ ORIENTÁCIE KSČ V ROKOCH 1944-1948 [Some methodological questions in the strategic and tactical orientation of the Communist Party of Czechoslovakia, 1944-48]. *Československý Časopis Hist. [Czechoslovakia] 1981 29(5): 641-669.* Emphasizes the distinction between the Czechoslovak national and democratic revolution before February 1948, and the subsequent dictatorship of the proletariat. When Communists during 1944-48 spoke of a "specific Czechoslovak road to socialism" they were merely referring to their organizing tactics, which were to achieve a socialist revolution by gradual, peaceful means. Revisionist historians in the 1960's distorted the true meaning of the phrase by maintaining that a democratic socialist revolution had already begun in 1944-45, only to be overlaid by a Stalinist coup d'état in 1948. Such non-Marxist interpretations are now a thing of the past. 75 notes. Russian and English summaries.
R. E. Weltsch

1220. Kollár, Ján. ZÁPAS KSS ZA JEDNOTU REVOLUČNÝCH SÍL V ROKOCH 1947-1948 [The struggle of the Communist Party of Slovakia for the unity of revolutionary forces, 1947-48]. *Hist. Časopis [Czechoslovakia] 1980 28(2): 181-209.* The Communist Party of Slovakia was successful in fulfilling the demand of the Communist Party of Czechoslovakia to gain a majority of the nation. The weakened position of the bourgeoisie and a deep differentiation of the non-Communist parties were important factors. The February events in Slovakia represented a proof of the Marxist-Leninist approach of the Communist Party of Slovakia toward the question of the socialist revolution. J/S

1221. Kopejtková, Drahomíra. ZEMĚDĚLSKÁ POLITIKA KSČ V POČÁTCÍCH SOCIALISTICKÉ VÝSTAVBY ČESKOSLOVENSKA (1948-1950) [The agrarian policy of the Communist Party in the beginnings of socialist production in Czechoslovakia, 1948-50]. *Slovanský Přehled [Czechoslovakia] 1981 67(6): 484-492.* The agrarian policy of the Communist Party in the first two years after the victorious 1948 revolution was that of collectivization through education and persuasion of the farming population. In this two-year period, farmers became convinced that collectivization would be advantageous to them in that it would bring about mechanization. Farm machinery would be bought by the collectives and decisions dealing with the administration of each collective would be communal. In all four different types of collectives formed in this period, landowners did not lose title to their land and joined voluntarily. 22 notes. B. Reinfeld

1222. Kopejtková, Prahomíra. UPLATNOVÁNÍ PRINCIPŮ LENINOVA DRUŽSTEVNÍHO PLÁNU PŘI VYTVÁŘENÍ KONCEPCE SOCIALISTICKÉ PŘESTAVBY ČESKOSLOVENSKÉHO ZEMĚDĚLSTVÍ V LETECH 1948-1949 [The application of Lenin's principles of collectivization in the transformation of Czechoslovakian agriculture into a socialist form, 1948-49]. *Slovanský Přehled [Czechoslovakia] 1979 65(6): 469-482.* Immediately after the Communist victory in Czechoslovakia in February 1948, the Party turned to the problem of land reform and dedicated itself to Lenin's principles in transferring land ownership from the bourgeoisie, especially rich kulaks, to collectives through initial division of land into small parcels that could be privately maintained until collectivization was finalized. While there was opposition to this within the Party, especially from those who saw Czechoslovakia as primarily an industrial country in which small landholdings would be a step backward, the successful operation of collectivization vindicated the majority opinion. The formal dedication to Leninist principles at the Ninth Party Congress in May 1949 was the right decision. 75 notes. B. Reinfeld

1223. Kovanda, Karel. WORKS COUNCILS IN CZECHOSLOVAKIA, 1945-47. *Soviet Studies [Great Britain] 1977 29(2): 255-269.* Previous studies of the Czechoslovak Communist Party's struggle against its right-wing opponents, 1945-48, have noted its campaign to control all working class political institutions, but have not examined the mechanism involved. The Party proceeded by stages to bring the works councils within the organizational structure of the originally independent Revolutionary Labor Movement (ROH) and then introduced democratic centralism to bring the ROH under Communist control. By 1947 workers were no longer interested in the works councils but they survived, devoid of content, until merged with ROH locals in March 1948. 33 notes.
D. H. Murdoch

1224. Kozák, Jan. ÜBER DEN KAMPF UM DIE DIKTATUR DES PROLETARIATS IN DER TSCHECHOSLOWAKISCHEN REPUBLIK (1945-1948) [On the struggle for the dictatorship of the proletariat in the Czechoslovakian republic, 1945-48]. *Jahrbuch für Geschichte der UdSSR und der Volksdemokratischen Länder Europas [East Germany] 1961 5: 95-110.* Because of specific historical preconditions in Czechoslovakia the dictatorship of the proletariat was realized peacefully through the power of the revolutionary masses. Though several political parties were in existence, all decisive class conflicts outside the parliament were decided by the mobilization of the working population and the intervention of national mass organizations. Their quick and purposeful actions under the leadership of the Communist Party secured the transition to socialism without civil war.

1225. Kožnar, Vlastimil. SOCIALISTICKÉ SOUTĚŽENÍ V ČSLA 1955-1981 [Socialist competition in the Czechoslovakian Army, 1955-81]. *Hist. a Vojenství [Czechoslovakia] 1981 30(6): 13-41.* Socialist competition became a part of life in Czechoslovakia to increase military readiness and political and cultural activity. The build-up of the army in the late 1950's included socialist competition on the recommendation of the Communist Party. Based on official papers; 53 notes. G. E. Pergl

1226. Král, Václav. VELKÁ ŘÍJNOVÁ SOCIALISTICKÁ REVOLUCE A REVOLUČNÍ PROCES V ČESKOSLOVENSKU [The October Revolution and the revolutionary process in Czechoslovakia]. *Slovanský Přehled [Czechoslovakia] 1977 63(4-5): 257-275.* The October Revolution in Russia prepared the change in 1948 Czechoslovakia. Immediately after the revolution in Russia, the Czech working class was still too much under the influence of nationalist propaganda to fully understand the revolutionary process. In 1948, however, the situation had changed because the workers and peasants no longer had any faith in the nationalist leadership which betrayed them at Munich and then collaborated with the Nazi occupiers. The Communist leadership showed courage against the invaders and presented a united front throughout the war. Its behavior during the occupation won many intellectuals and the petite bourgeoisie. Under the leadership of Klement Gottwald, Czechoslovakia committed itself to the goals of the October Revolution: peace, security, and cooperation among nations, with the USSR at the head of the socialist community.
B. Kimmel

1227. Krejci, Jaroslav. LES ÉVÉNEMENTS IMPRÉVUS DE L'HISTOIRE TCHÉCOSLOVAQUE MODERNE—DES SUJETS D'ÉTUDE POUR LA SOCIOLOGIE POLITIQUE [Unexpected events in modern Czechoslovak history: a case for political sociology]. *Rev. d'Études Comparatives Est-Ouest [France] 1977*

8(3): 25-36. Explains the Communist Party electoral success in 1946 and the reform movement in 1968 in terms of changing political attitudes due to external and internal circumstances or causes.

1228. Krempa, Ivan. CSKP KB MARXIZMUS-LENINIZMUS INTÉZETÉNEK TÍZ ÉVE [Ten years of the Marxist-Leninist Institute of the Central Committee of the Czechoslovakian Communist Party]. *Párttörténeti Közlemények [Hungary] 1981 27(1): 183-195.* The Marxist-Leninist Institute of the Czechoslovakian Communist Party's Central Committee was established in 1970. It has a sister organization in Bratislava. In the past 10 years interdisciplinary working committees have conducted research in Party ideology, history, the impact of anti-Communist ideologies, and Communist education. Based on official publications; 3 notes.
P. I. Hidas

1229. Krempa, Ivan. REVOLUČNÍ ODKAZ KLEMENTA GOTTWALDA [Klement Gottwald's revolutionary legacy]. *Československý Časopis Hist. [Czechoslovakia] 1982 30(2): 161-172.* As the Communist Party of Czechoslovakia has emerged victoriously from the dangerous attempts at disintegration in the 1960's, the Leninist leadership of Klement Gottwald (1896-1953), both before and after World War II, is being once more duly appreciated. 20 notes. R. E. Weltsch

1230. Kropilák, Miroslav. PŘEDPOKLADY A DOSIÁHNUTIE FEBRUÁROVÉHO VÍŤAZSTVA 1948 [Assumptions and achievement of the February 1948 victory]. *Československý Časopis Historický [Czechoslovakia] 1973 21(4): 485-497.* Evalutes the coup d'etat of February 1948 in Czechoslovakia. Explains the meaning of this revolutionary solution to the political crisis, where the reactionary parties were defeated by the constitutional actions of the people on their way toward socialism. 5 notes. G. E. Pergl

1231. Kroupa, Vlastislav. K NĚKTERÝM OTÁZKÁM VZNIKU A VÝVOJE SBORU NÁRODNÍ BEZPEČNOSTI V LETECH 1945-1948 [Some questions concerning the rise and development of the National Security Corps in 1945-48]. *Sborník Historický [Czechoslovakia] 1974 (22): 201-231.* In liberated Czechoslovakia the Communists insisted on controlling the interior and defense ministries, which enabled them to reshape the security services (SNB). By recruiting anti-fascist and revolutionary elements and merging them with existing police forces, the Communists created a loyal support for a people's democracy, though at the cost of increasing interparty tensions. After 1948 the security forces were rebuilt on socialist principles. Based on various Prague archives; 68 notes. R. E. Weltsch

1232. Kutnohorská, Jana. ÚSILÍ KSČ O UPEVNĚNÍ SVAZKU DĚLNÍKŮ A ROLNÍKŮ PŘI REALIZACI KOŠICKÉHO VLÁDNÍHO PROGRAMU V OBLASTI EXPOZITURY ZNV OSTRAVA (1945-1948) [The Czechoslovakian Communist Party's endeavor to strengthen the unity of workers and peasants during the realization of the Košice government program in the area of the Land National Committee of Ostrava, 1945-48]. *Prmyslové Oblasti [Czechoslovakia] 1980 7: 7-107.* The Leninist line of worker-peasant unity became Communist policy in liberated Czechoslovakia after 1945. Examines events in the Ostrava region 1945-48, during the realization of the Košice Program. The goal of Communist policy was establishing a strong bond between peasants and the working class to prevent the disorientation of the agricultural population by bourgeois intrigues. Based on archival and secondary sources; map, 12 tables. G. E. Pergl

1233. Kvaček, Robert. OD LIDOVÉ FRONTY K FRONTĚ NÁRODNÍ [From the Popular Front to the National Front]. *Acta U. Carolinae Philosophica et Hist. [Czechoslovakia] 1975 (2): 65-76.* Surveys the actions of the Czechoslovak Communist Party in defense of the state before 1938 and the Party's transformation of the pre-World War II Popular Front into the National Front during and after the war. 34 notes. G. E. Pergl

1234. Lavrik, E. G. BOR'BA KOMMUNISTICHESKOI PARTII SLOVAKII ZA SOZDANIE EDINOGO SOIUZA SLOVATSKIKH KREST'IAN 1945-1947 GG. [The struggle of the Communist Party of Slovakia for the creation of the General Union of Slovak Peasants, 1945-47]. *Sovetskoe Slavianovedenie [USSR] 1973 1(1): 16-28.* Describes the 17 March 1945 creation of the General Union of Slovak Peasants within the framework of the Preparatory Committee of the National Front. The committee contained eight members of the Slovak Communist Party and their rivals, the Democratic Party. The Democratic Party opposed the liquidation of the Peasant Chamber, supposedly controlled by landowners and the food industry. At a 2 March 1946 meeting of the Slovak government, the Communists forced the Democratic Party to vote for a cessation of the Peasant Chamber's activities, but only after the General Union of Slovak Peasants had been voted for in the Czechoslovak National Assembly. The Communists wanted members from the National Front elected to the General Union of Slovak Peasants, but as a minority in the agricultural commission, the Communists had to vote for the principle of forced participation in and political elections to the peasant organization. This vote of 11 July 1947 helped solve the tasks of the national democratic revolution. Based on Czech documents, newspapers, and secondary sources; 51 notes.
E. Dunn

1235. Lenart, Jozef. LENINISM AND THE LESSONS OF THE SLOVAK UPRISING. *World Marxist R. [Canada] 1974 17(8): 20-29.* The Slovak National Uprising of August 1944 was part of the continuing struggle of Czechoslovakia's Communist Party against capitalistic imperialism.

1236. Levine, Herbert M. and Gilderdale, Susie. GENETICS AND COMMUNISM. *Colorado Q. 1975 24(1): 17-24.* Describes the imposition of Stalinist genetics in Czechoslovakia after 1948 and the recovery in the 1960's up to the reimposition of orthodoxy in 1968.

1237. Liptak, Ia. and Spicak, M. BOR'BA KOMMUNISTICHESKOI PARTII CHEKHOSLOVAKII ZA ARMIIU V 1945-1948 GG. [The struggle by the Communist Party of Czechoslovakia for the army in 1945-48]. *Voenno-Istoricheskii Zhurnal [USSR] 1974 (10): 74-80.*

1238. Lipták, Ján and Čejka, Eduard. A CSEHSZLOVÁK NÉPHADSEREG A NÉPI DEMOKRATIKUS FORRADALOM SZOCIALISTA FORRADALOMMÁ VALÓ ÁTNÖVÉSE IDŐSZAKÁBAN (1945 ÁPRILIS-1948 FEBRUÁR) [The Czechoslovak People's Army during the period when the people's democratic revolution developed into a socialist revolution]. *Hadtörténelmi Közlemények [Hungary] 1982 29(4): 615-637.* The difficulties of the Czechoslovakian army after 1945 were solved by the help offered by the USSR and the work of the Communist Party in the political education of the lower ranks as well as the officers. During the open attacks by the bourgeoisie in 1948, the parading of the army in the streets discouraged the reactionaries. 35 notes. T. Kuner

1239. Lipták, Ján and Špičák, Milan. FEBRUAR 1948—REVOLUTIONÄRE TRADITIONEN DER TSCHECHOSLOWAKISCHEN STREITKRÄFTE [February 1948: revolutionary traditions of the Czechoslovak army]. *Militärgeschichte [East Germany] 1975 14(1): 44-52.* After the Communist takeover in 1948 the Czechoslovak army was loyal to the new government despite attempts by the bourgeoisie to use the army for its own ends, and the anti-Communist sentiments of the lower-ranking officers.

1240. Lipták, Ján and Špičák, Milan. KSČ A ČS. LIDOVÁ ARMÁDA 1945-1948 [Czechoslovak Communist Party and the Czechoslovak People's Army 1945-48]. *Československý Časopis Hist. [Czechoslovakia] 1975 23(2): 190-216.* Examines the military policy of Czech communists during the era of gradual change from national and democratic revolution to socialism. The bourgeois influence on the ideological profile of the Czechoslovak Armed Force ended in 1948 with the defeat of rightist parties. Based on news reports; 41 notes. G. E. Pergl

1241. Lipták, Ján. KSČ A OSVĚTOVÝ APARÁT V ČSLA V LÉTECH 1945-1948 [The Czechoslovakian Communist Party and political education in the Czechoslovak People's Army, 1945-48].

Historie a Vojenství [Czechoslovakia] 1975 19(5): 27-48. The political education system in the Czech army has been carried on by Communists since the institution of armed units in exile. The army, which did not participate in the February 1948 events, afterwards became totally subordinate to the ruling Communist Party. Secondary sources; 38 notes. G. E. Pergl

1242. Lipták, Ján. VÍTĚZNÝ ÚNOR A ČS. ARMÁDA: K POČÁTKŮM VÝSTAVBY ČSLA JAKO SOCIALISTICKÉ ARMÁDY [Victorious February of 1948 and the Czechoslovak Army: beginnings of the construction of the Czechoslovak People's Army as a socialist army]. *Hist. a Vojenství [Czechoslovakia] 1983 32(1): 3-24.* The aggressive policy of NATO forced Czechoslovakia after 1948 to extraordinary measures for defense. The building of the Czechoslovak People's Army was guided by the vast experience of the Soviet Union. The Czechoslovak Communist Party's work within the army was enlarged and deepened; political officers were given a special training and dispersed to individual units. From February 1948 to the end of 1949 bourgeois-inclined career officers, 40% of staff officers, were discharged. New armaments came with Soviet help to enhance the fighting power of the new socialist army. Based on official statements and bulletins; 38 notes.
G. E. Pergl

1243. Lipták, Ján. VÝSTAVBA ČSLA V PRVNÍM POVÁLEČNÉM DESETILETÍ [The development of the Czechoslovak Popular Army in the first postwar decade]. *Historie a Vojenství [Czechoslovakia] 1974 (5): 64-81.* Describes the growth of the Communist Party within the Czechoslovakian armed forces, 1945-55. Published sources; 25 notes.

1244. Luža, Radomir V. FEBRUARY 1948 AND THE CZECHOSLOVAK ROAD TO SOCIALISM. *East Central Europe 1977 4(1): 44-55.* The Czechoslovak Communist Party in World War II, in exile in Moscow, worked out a formula for a special Czechoslovakian road to socialism. It was a politically moderate strategy, concentrating on winning popular confidence under the banner of national liberation and cooperation with democratic parties within a parliamentary context. The Party was aided by the national mood of sympathy for democratic socialism and warm friendship for the Russian liberators. The Party's large vote in the free election of May, 1946, confirmed the correctness of the Party's strategy. The Cold War put an end to these developments, as Stalin turned to a policy of complete internal and external subservience of Czechoslovakia to the USSR. The Czechoslovak Communists switched to undemocratic practices, thereby alienating the noncommunist parties. The democratic parties struck back in February 1948 through parliamentary maneuvers, and the Communists were forced to carry out a takeover earlier than they had intended. Using mass demonstrations and violence, backed by the threat of Soviet military intervention, the Communist coup succeeded. Once in power, the Czechoslovak party soon succumbed completely to Stalinist techniques and Soviet overlordship. Based on Czech sources; 41 notes. R. V. Layton

1245. Margolius-Kovaly, Heda. FROM AUSCHWITZ TO PRAGUE: A MEMOIR. *Commentary 1972 54(6): 47-54.* A memoir of Heda Margolius-Kovaly written during the Nazi occupation of Czechoslovakia and the Communist takeover.

1246. Marzo, Alberto. BENES E IL COLPO DI PRAGA [Beneš and the Prague coup]. *Riv. di Studi Politici Int. [Italy] 1976 43(4): 559-574.* Czechoslovakia belonged culturally to the West but for reasons of national interest its policy tended to look to Russia for protection against German attack. At the end of World War II the Communists in Czechoslovakia had gathered only about a third of the votes, but they obtained important ministerial posts influencing internal policy decisions. In response to the resignation of liberal ministers protesting the transfer or dismissal of a number of non-Communist police officers, the Communists took over all the major administrative branches of government. Secondary sources; 7 notes.
A. Sbacchi

1247. Mel'kov, Iu. D. RABOTA PARTIINOI ORGANIZATSII MOLDAVII S KHOZIAISTVENNYMI KADRAMI [The work of the Moldavian party organization with economic personnel]. *Voprosy Istorii KPSS [USSR] 1973 (4): 19-33.* Since 1945 significant economic achievements resulted in Moldavia from the Communist Party's efforts to provide specialized education at factories, technical schools, and universities; to encourage the mechanization of agriculture; and to stimulate private initiative and political consciousness. Based on undocumented statistics; 6 notes.
L. E. Holmes

1248. Michnovič, Imrich. K NIEKTORÝM OTÁZKAM POLITICKOORGANIZÁTORSKEJ PRÁCE STRANY NA VÝCHODOSLOVENSKEJ DEDINE V ROKOCH 1949-1953 [Some questions of the agricultural policies of the Communist Party of Czechoslovakia, 1949-53]. *Hist. Časopis [Czechoslovakia] 1983 31(6): 871-890.* After the 9th Congress of the Communist Party of Czechoslovakia the agricultural policies of the Party were realized. They followed the change from agricultural small industry to the socialist wholesale manufacture in east Slovakia. J/S

1249. Mikhniak, A. RAZVITIE CHEKHOSLOVATSKOI NARODNOI ARMII POSLE FEVRALIA 1948 GODA [The development of the Czechoslovak army after February 1948]. *Voenno-Istoricheskii Zhurnal [USSR] 1976 (10): 54-60.* Describes how the Communist Party, supported by the Soviet army, helped develop Czechoslovakia's army after the February 1948 coup.

1250. Mlýnský, Jaroslav. DVACETPĚT LET CÍRKEVNÍCH ZÁKONŮ V ČESKOSLOVENSKU [Twenty five years of church laws in Czechoslovakia]. *Československý Časopis Hist. [Czechoslovakia] 1974 22(5): 663-671.* Examines the meaning of the church laws (1949) in Czechoslovakia, which reflected the desire of the ruling Communist Party for a practical solution of the relationship between church and state. This conception respected religious freedom and the Marxist-Leninist requirement that religion be a private matter. Secondary sources; 25 notes.
G. E. Pergl

1251. Mlýnský, Jaroslav. HISTORICKÝ VÝZNAM VIII. SJEZDU KSC [Historical significance of the 8th Congress of the Communist Party of Czechoslovakia]. *Československý Časopis Hist. [Czechoslovakia] 1976 24(3): 341-358.* The 1946 Congress of Czech Communists advocated peaceful transition from national and democratic revolution to socialism and accepted the policy of the National Front in the new Czechoslovakia. 38 notes. G. E. Pergl

1252. Mlýnský, Jaroslav. KOMUNISTICKÁ STRANA ČESKOSLOVENSKA A NÁRODNÍ FRONTA [The Communist Party of Czechoslovakia and the National Front]. *Československý Časopis Hist. [Czechoslovakia] 1981 29(3): 321-349.* Harking back to the Popular Front of the mid-1930's, the Czechoslovak Communists from 1938 through World War II promoted an antifascist National Front in which the Communist Party acted as the most dynamic element. In February 1945 the Košice government program specified the National Front as an exclusive alignment of left-of-center parties that would control postwar Czechoslovak politics. After February 1948 the Communists kept the National Front alive as a means to coordinate all mass organizations under their leadership. When revisionists in the late 1960's threatened a return to bourgeois pluralism, the Party had to reassert the closed character of the National Front and to return it to its socialist purpose. Based on published Party documents and some archival sources; 60 notes. Russian and English summaries. R. E. Weltsch

1253. Mlýnský, Jaroslav. KRITICKY K ZÁPADONĚMECKÉ HISTORIOGRAFII O DĚJINÁCH KSČ [A critique of West German historiography on the Czech Communist Party]. *Československý Časopis Hist. [Czechoslovakia] 1976 24(6): 801-820.* Rejects contemporary West German historiography on the history of the Czechoslovak Communist Party. The author sees it as a negative evaluation of the Czechoslovak endeavor toward a socialist society. 62 notes. G. E. Pergl

1254. Mlýnský, Jaroslav. ÚNOR 1948 A BURŽOAZNÍ HISTORIOGRAFIE [February 1948 and bourgeois historiography]. *Československý Časopis Hist. [Czechoslovakia] 1978 26(5): 641-656.* Before 1960 most Western histories either belittled or condemned the Communist seizure of power in Czechoslovakia. Under the influence of detente and Marxist histories, this negative approach changed to a more objective appreciation of the political skill of the Communists, the bankruptcy of the bourgeois parties, and the constitutional correctness of the takeover. This trend is significant in view of Czechoslovakia's international importance as a model for peaceful change to socialism of an industrialized society. 29 notes. R. E. Weltsch

1255. Müller, Adolf. ZUR LAGE IN DER TSCHECHOSLOWAKEI [The situation in Czechoslovakia]. *Osteuropa [West Germany] 1973 23(8): 599-617.* Surveys the "normalization" pursued by the Communist Party leadership in Czechoslovakia since the Soviet intervention of August 1968. Though the Soviet-inspired repression by 1972 had reached into all aspects of public life, the situation appears "permanently unstable." 36 notes.
R. E. Weltsch

1256. Myant, M. R. *Socialism and Democracy in Czechoslovakia, 1945-1948.* (Soviet and East European Studies.) New York: Cambridge U. Pr., 1981. 302 pp.

1257. Neborezov, A. I. ROL' K. GOTVAL'DA V OSUSHCHESTVLENII REVOLIUTSIONNOI LINII CZECHOSLOVATSKOVO RABOCHEVO DVIZHENIIA [The role of Klement Gottwald in the establishment of the revolutionary line of the Czechoslovak workers' movement]. *Sovetskoe Slavianovedenie [USSR] 1967 (1): 28-31.* Traces the revolutionary activity and career of Klement Gottwald, who began as a simple Communist Party worker in 1921 and rose quickly to a responsible position in the press, thence through party ranks to national preeminence and international influence. Details his role as party organizer and spokesman throughout the depression and his successful wartime efforts to create the basis for the postwar Communist Czechoslovakia, however incomplete at the time of his death in 1953. Secondary sources; 8 notes.
R. P. Fritze

1258. Nedorezov, A. I. KLEMENT GOTVAL'D I REVOLIUTSIONNOE PREOBRAZOVANIE CHEKHOSLOVATSKOGO OBSHCHESTVA [Klement Gottwald and the revolutionary reorganization of Czechoslovak society]. *Sovetskoe Slavianovedenie [USSR] 1977 (1): 9-15.* Political biography of Klement Gottwald (1896-1953). An early supporter of the Soviet Union and a leader of Czech resistance, he opposed the post-World War II bourgeois government of Eduard Beneš, and strove to convert it into a socialist revolution. He advocated a closer union with the USSR, endorsed the communist program of socialist reconstruction and, in 1948, became president of Communist Czechoslovakia, a post he held until death. 10 notes. N. Frenkley

1259. Nedorezov, A. I. VEDUSHCHAIA ROL' RABOCHEGO KLASSA CHEKHOSLOVAKII V STROITEL'STVE SOTSIALIZMA [The leading role of the Czechoslovak Communist Party in the construction of socialism]. *Voprosy Istorii KPSS [USSR] 1976 (4): 59-71.* Discusses the directing hand played by the Czechoslovak Communist Party in the development of socialism in Czechoslovakia, 1930-76.

1260. Nedorezov, A. N. KSČ—ORGANIZÁTORKA VÍTĚZSTVÍ SOCIALISTICKÉ REVOLUCE [The Czechoslovak Communist Party as the organizer of the victory of the socialist revolution]. *Československý Časopis Hist. [Czechoslovakia] 1975 23(4): 461-470.* Analyzes the role of the Czech Communist Party in planning and organizing the development of Czechoslovakia from a national democracy into a socialist state after 1945. The Party foiled the plans of bourgeois politicians for a return to a capitalist system by developing swift, offensive countermeasures in a peaceful revolution. Secondary sources; 9 notes. G. E. Pergl

1261. Nikitin, G. N. VERNYI SYN TRUDOVOGO NARODA [A true son of the working people]. *Voprosy Istorii KPSS [USSR] 1964 (12): 81-84.* Recounts the political career of Antonín Novotný from the time of his activities as a founder member of the Czech Communist Party when he was 16 until his reelection as president of Czechoslovakia in 1964.

1262. Nováčková, Eva. SOCIALISTICKÁ KOLEKTIVIZACE VESNICE NA TŘEBÍČSKU A MORAVSKO-BUDĚJOVICKU V LETECH 1949-1960 [Socialist collectivization of villages in the Třebíč and Moravské Budějovice districts, 1949-60]. *Časopis Matice Moravské [Czechoslovakia] 1981 100(3-4): 207-217.* In 1949 Třebíč and Moravské Budějovice districts had 81 and 88 parishes and 51, 992 and 58,536 hectares of agricultural land respectively. The latter was more completely agricultural, with better soil conditions, while Třebíč was a partly industrialized district where the process of collectivization went more slowly. The process was hampered by labor shortages (part-time farmers preferring industrial employment) and by the unwillingness of middle-sized farmers to become involved. Two progressions to "higher types" of collectives, in 1951 and 1955, did not resolve all the problems. After 1957 concerted action by the Communist Party and the trade union organization brought more land under state or cooperative control. By 1959 approximately 91% of Třebíč and 96% of Moravské Budějovice was so controlled. Based mainly on documents in the Třebíč archives; 21 notes, tables. L. Short

1263. Novotný, Ladislav. INTERNACIONÁLNÍ CHARAKTER BOJE PROTI SOUČASNÉ BURŽOASNÍ A REVIZIONISTICKÉ [International character of the struggle against contemporary bourgeois and revisionist ideology]. *Historie a Vojenství [Czechoslovakia] 1975 19(6): 17-42.* A critical review of different waves of leftist and rightist revisionism focusing on the case of Czechoslovakia in 1968, when the attempt of counterrevolution got active support from all anti-Communist elements. G. E. Pergl

1264. Ostoich, Petŭr. KONFERENTSIIA ZA FEVRUARSKITE SUBITIIA V CHEKHOSLOVAKIIA PREZ 1948 G [The conference on events in Czechoslovakia February 1948]. *Izvestiia na Inst. po Istoriia na BKP [Bulgaria] 1974 30: 489-492.* The conference, held to mark the 25th anniversary of the Communist accession to power in Czechoslovakia, was held in Prague 30-31 January 1973 and organized by the Institute for Marxism-Leninism and other Czechoslovak Party organizations; 80 delegates from the Socialist countries attended.

1265. Pelikan, Jiri. WORKERS' COUNCILS IN CZECHOSLOVAKIA. *Critique [Great Britain] 1973 1(1): 7-19.* Describes the creation and activities of workers' councils, 1968-69, in strengthening socialism, the necessity of combining political reform with economic reform, and the repression of these successful councils by the USSR.

1266. Peša, Václav. KLEMENT GOTTWALD A ČESKOSLOVENSKÉ DĚJINY [Klement Gottwald and Czechoslovak history]. *Časopis Matice Moravské [Czechoslovakia] 1977 96(1-2): 24-36.* Reviews Klement Gottwald's (1896-1953) lifelong association with the Czechoslovak Communist Party, referring in particular to his early revolutionary activities and his role in the Bolshevization of the Party, the struggle against fascism during World War II, and the February 1948 victory over the middle classes. Based on Gottwald's published writings and secondary sources; 27 notes. M.-M. Petrzilkova

1267. Pešek, Jan. PRÁCE STRANY V ARMÁDĚ PO ÚNORU 1948 [Communist Party work in the Czech armed forces after February 1948]. *Hist. a Vojenství [Czechoslovakia] 1980 29(2): 3-22.* The ninth Party congress created the general line for the building of socialism in Czechoslovakia and thus basic conditions for forming socialist armed forces of a new type. At the end of 1948 around 80% of the leadership in the armed forces was organized in the Communist Party (against 20% before February 1948). Organizing work among soldiers from high commands down to every unit made possible the dismissal of unworthy elements from the service. Based on official documents; 54 notes. G. E. Pergl

1268. Pešek, Jan. STRANICKÝ ŽIVOT V ČS. ARMÁDĚ V OBDOBÍ PO CELOSTÁTNÍ KONFERENCI KSČ (1952) DO X. SJEZDU KSČ [The life of the Communist Party in the Czechoslovak Army between the all-state conference of 1952 and the 10th Congress of the Party]. *Hist. a Vojenství [Czechoslovakia] 1982 31(4): 91-104.* The December 1952 high-level meeting of Czech Communists prepared the way for further realization of a speedy build-up of the Czechoslovak army and the improvement and political education of the commanding officers. At the same time the political educational work of the party became an indivisible part of preparation of the units for the defense against possible imperialist aggression. Party members in the army with their organizational network were the decisive force in the political preparation of the soldier. The quality of Party leadership in the army was visible in the fact that in January 1954 61.7% of officers were Party members. Based on official documents of the party; 35 notes. G. E. Pergl

1269. Pešek, Thomas G. "MULTI-PARTY SOCIALISM" AND *LITERÁRNÍ LISTY:* AN ASPECT OF CZECHOSLOVAK REVISIONISM. *East Central Europe 1978 5(2): 232-244. Literární Listy,* organ of the Czechoslovak Writers Union, in 1968 called for a new governmental system based on the principle of pluralism. The writers attacked political monolithism as unjustifiable, if not legally, then in a broader human sense, and charged that control by one party, even if justifiable, had never worked. They did not wish to abandon socialism but objected to the Communist Party's domination and abuse of decisionmaking power, recognizing a truth well understood in the West: power acts responsibly only when those who exercise it take into account the possibility of losing it. When the Soviet Union and its allies intervened in Czechoslovakia, *Literární listy* ceased publication rather than submit to the new censorship. 46 notes. R. V. Layton

1270. Pleva, Ján. BOJ MARXISTICKO-LENINSKÝCH SÍL ZA SPLNENIE UZNESENÍ PLÉNA ÚV KSČ Z NOVEMBRA 1968 [The Marxist-Leninist struggle for the fulfillment of the Central Committee's decision of November 1968]. *Historické Štúdie [Czechoslovakia] 1977 22: 5-32.* Describes problems within the Czech Communist Party in the late 1960's and how they were coped with by a November 1968 Central Committee resolution. There were also external questions needing rapid solutions; a deeply disturbed national economy and the reorganization of Czechoslovakia into a federal state. The struggle for Party unity continued until April 1969 when right-wing and antisocialist elements were expelled. Printed sources; 50 notes. G. E. Pergl

1271. Pleva, Ján; Kozic, Jan; and Kázmerová, L'uba. K NIEKTORÝM OTÁZKAM IDEOVÝCHOVNEJ PRÁCE KSČ OD OSLOBODENIA DO VIII. ZJAZDU (1945-1946) [Some problems in the ideological training conducted by the Communist Party of Czechoslovakia between the liberation and the 8th Congress, 1945-46]. *Československý Časopis Hist. [Czechoslovakia] 1983 31(3): 321-337.* The rapid growth of Communist Party membership in Czechoslovakia immediately after World War II led the Party leaders to intensify the ideological preparation of new members. A Party-sponsored instructional network quickly spread to factories and homes. It emphasized the teaching of Soviet revolutionary experience and its applicability to Czechoslovakia. Based on the archives of the Institute of Marxism-Leninism, Prague; 25 notes. Russian and German summaries. R. E. Weltsch

1272. Pleva, Ján and Jiřičková, Mária. K NIEKTORÝM OTÁZKAM IDEOVO-VÝCHOVNEJ PRÁCE V KOMUNISTICKEJ STRANE SLOVENSKA V ROKOCH 1945-1948 [Some problems of ideological training by the Communist Party of Slovakia, 1945-48]. *Hist. Časopis [Czechoslovakia] 1983 31(1): 14-34.* Ideological training by the Communist Party of Slovakia in 1945-48 followed the existence of new conditions of the national-democratic development. The Communist Party held respectable position in the political life of the country. In coincidence with its efforts in building up a new life the ideal-education work was developed. Marxist-Leninist ideology helped the members of the party to take active part in the historical-formational process and to explain its policy to working people. J

1273. Pleva, Ján. K NIEKTORÝM OTÁZKAM VÝVOJA NA SLOVENSKU V PRVEJ POLOVICI ROKU 1968 [Some aspects of the development of the Communist Party of Czechoslovakia in Slovakia during the first half of 1968]. *Hist. Časopis [Czechoslovakia] 1983 31(4): 598-613.*

1274. Plevza, Viliam. AZ 1948. FEBRUÁRI FORDULAT ÉS CSEHSZLOVÁKIA SZOCIALISTA FEJLŐDÉSÉNEK NÉHÁNY TAPASZTALATA [The February 1948 change and experiences of socialist development in Czechoslovakia]. *Párttörténeti Közlemények [Hungary] 1983 29(4): 131-152.* The workers of Czechoslovakia made their wishes very clear when in 1948 they demanded the removal of all reactionary politicians from the current bourgeois government, and their replacement by members of the Communist Party. Although the new government had considerable difficulties, with the help of every honest person and every true Communist they managed to win their fight against representatives of opportunism and creators of constant discord. After 1968 there was a considerable increase in the Party's prestige in the country. 57 notes. T. Kuner

1275. Plevza, Viliam. GUSTÁV HUSÁK A SPOLOČENSKÉ VEDY (K 70. NARODENINÁM) [Gustáv Husák and the social sciences: on his 70th birthday]. *Československý Časopis Hist. [Czechoslovakia] 1983 31(1): 1-23.* Gustáv Husák (b. 1913), First Secretary of the Communist Party of Czechoslovakia, became a Party member in 1933, while attending the University of Bratislava. Aside from his leading role in the resistance during World War II, his leadership in postwar Slovakia, and his solution of the Czechoslovak troubles in the 1960's, he maintained a lively interest in history and the social sciences. The current Czechoslovak emphasis on Marxist-Leninist methodology owes something to his direction. 56 notes. Russian and German summaries. R. E. Weltsch

1276. Plevza, Viliam. NA CESTE K SOCIALISTICKEJ REVOLÚCII (K 35. VÝROČIU VÍŤAZNÉHO FEBRUÁRA) [On the road to socialist revolution: the 35th anniversary of victorious February]. *Československý Časopis Hist. [Czechoslovakia] 1983 31(2): 161-176.* The Communist takeover in Czechoslovakia, February 1948, ensured the postwar social gains already achieved under Communist leadership and foiled the plans of bourgeois politicians to exploit the government crisis which they had engineered. 41 notes. Russian and English summaries. R. E. Weltsch

1277. Pospelov, P. N. and Nedorezov, A. I. REVOLIUTSIONNYI PUT' K. GOTVAL'DA [The revolutionary road of K. Gottwald]. *Novaia i Noveishaia Istoriia [USSR] 1972 (2): 21-34.* During the 1920's Klement Gottwald fought to Bolshevize the Czechoslovak Communist Party. After the defeat of the opportunists at the Party's Fifth Congress he became its leader. In the 1930's he sought the formation of a national front against fascism, but the Social-Democratic leaders blocked this attempt. During the German occupation Gottwald led the party from exile in the USSR. He played a major role in the victory over counterrevolution in February 1948, and as president presided over the building of socialism in Czechoslovakia. Secondary sources; 31 notes. J. H. H. Presland

1278. Pravda, Alex. CZECHOSLOVAKIA: THE LEGACY OF 1968. *World Today [Great Britain] 1976 32(8): 282-286.* Discusses ways in which the current Czechoslovakian political situation is still affected by the events of August 1968, showing that dissent within the Czechoslovakian Communist Party still exists, although the crisis period is over.

1279. Prunytsia, S. Iu. ROL' RADIANS'KOHO SOIUZU U VYZVOLENNI CHEKHOSIOVACHCHYNY VID FASHYSTS'KYKH ZAHARBNYKIV TA VIDRODZHENNI II NEZALEZHNOSTI I SUVERENITETU [The USSR's role in liberating Czechoslovakia from the fascist invaders and renewing its independence and sovereignty]. *Ukrains'kyi Istorychnyi Zhurnal [USSR] 1975 (4): 87-94.* Describes German oppression in Czechoslovakia from the Munich agreement in 1938 through the atrocities perpetrated during World War II, and recounts the activities of the resistance led by the Czechoslovak Communist Party, which with Soviet aid paved the way for the liberating Red Army in 1945 and the eventual establishment of socialism.

1280. Pstolovski, R. M. IDEINO-POLITYCHNA ROBOTA SOTSIALISTYCHNOI SPILKY MOLODI CHSSR 1970-1977 RR [Ideological and political work of the Socialist Youth Association of the Czechoslovak SSR]. *Ukrains'kyi Istorychnyi Zhurnal [USSR] 1978 (5): 62-66.* The anti-socialist forces in Czechoslovakia succeeded by 1968 in disbanding the Czechoslovak Youth Association, and forming some 60 different youth organizations free from Communist Party control. The Communist Party reestablished its control over the Socialist Youth Association and its membership rose to nearly two million, 1970-76. The teams of socialist youth and students worked without pay on many projects in Czechoslovakia and the USSR to raise funds for the youth of Vietnam, Chile, and the Arab countries. Based on documents of the Czech Communist Party and newspaper articles; 37 notes. H. M. Diuk

1281. Radouchová, Jaroslava. ČESKOSLOVENSKÝ STÁT A KATOLICKÁ CÍRKEV PO ÚNORU 1948 [The Czechoslovak state and the Catholic Church after February 1948]. *R. Dějin Socialismu [Czechoslovakia] 1969 9(1): 37-62.* Examines the roughly three-year test of strength between the post-February 1948 Czechoslovak regime and the Catholic Church which ended in the subjugation of the Church. The regime's policies toward the Catholic Church were influenced not only by the Communist Party's antipathy toward religion, but also by the fact that, as a universal church with its center outside the boundaries of the socialist camp, it had a strong claim on the loyalties of over 70% of the population. The Catholic Church pursued its traditional aim of seeking to protect its interests while refusing to tie itself to any particular regime. Although the Catholic Church was eventually subjugated, all attempts failed of transforming it into a national church, independent of the Vatican. 31 notes. F. H. Eidlin

1282. Renner, Hans. DE COMMUNISTISCHE STAATS-GREEP IN TSJECHOSLOWAKIJE [The Communist coup d'état in Czechoslovakia]. *Kleio [Netherlands] 1977 18(5): 353-354.* Traces the rise to power of the Czech Communist Party, abetted by Moscow, from the end of the Nazi occupation to its victorious confrontation with President Eduard Beneš in 1948. 10 notes.

1283. Rice, Condoleezza. "The Politics of Client Command: Party-Military Relations in Czechoslovakia: 1948-1975." U. of Denver 1981. 373 pp. *DAI 1982 43(5): 1678-A.* DA8216695

1284. Richter, Karel. VÝCHOVNÝ VÝZNAM TRADIC [Educational significance of traditions]. *Historie a Vojenství [Czechoslovakia] 1974 (2): 63-78.* The military traditions of the Czechoslovak People's Army are those of the nation and the international revolutionary traditions of the Communist Party. Tradition became a part of the ideological education in the armed forces by rejecting the falsification of historical facts by bourgeois historiography. 15 notes. G. E. Pergl

1285. Richter, Karel and Rosa, Alfonz. VYUŽÍVÁNÍ NOVODOBÉ HISTORIE VE VÝCHOVĚ K SOCIALISTICKÉMU VLASTENECTVÍ A INTERNACIONALISMU: IDEOLOGICKÁ PRÁCE V ČSLA A VÝZNAM VLASTENECKÉ A INTERNACIONALNÍ VÝCHOVY [Evaluation of modern history for a patriotic and internationalist education: ideological work in the Czechoslovakian Army and the significance of a patriotic and internationalist education]. *Hist. a Vojenství [Czechoslovakia] 1981 30(5): 43-65.* Fulfilling the goals of Czechoslovakia's military defense is unthinkable without the ideological education of the soldier. Resistance against outdated nationalist or religious slogans is on the rise among soldiers of socialist Czechoslovakia. Continuing education in socialist patriotism and proletarian internationalism is part of the ideological work proclaimed by the Communist Party for the socialist armed forces. 11 notes. G. E. Pergl/S

1286. Robrieux, Philippe. VOYAGE À L'INTÉRIEUR DU PARTI COMMUNISTE TCHÉCOSLOVAQUE [Journey into the interior of the Czech Communist Party]. *Histoire [France] 1979 (10): 88-90.* Karel Kaplan, a member of the Central Committee of the Communist Party of Czechoslovakia, explored the archives in order to rehabilitate the victims of the Stalin era at the time of the Prague Spring, 1968; his findings were published as *Dans les archives du Comité central: trente ans de secrets du bloc soviétique* (Paris: Albin Michel, 1978).

1287. Rupnik, Jacques. *Histoire du Parti Communiste Tchécoslovaque: Des Origines á la Prise du Pouvoir* [The history of the Communist Party of Czechoslovakia: from its origins to the taking of power]. Paris: Presses de la Fondation Nationale des Sciences Politiques, 1981. 288 pp.

1288. Schröder, Sibylle. DIE LÖSUNG DER MACHTFRAGE IN DER TSCHECHOSLOWAKEI IM FEBRUAR 1948 [The solution of the power question in Czechoslovakia, February 1948]. *Jahrbuch für Geschichte der Sozialistischen Länder Europas [East Germany] 1973 17(1): 9-32.* The Communist Party's leadership ensured the victory of the revolutionary Czechoslovakian working class, which in February 1948 transformed the country into a constituent part of the socialist world system.

1289. Schröder, Sybille. DER WANDEL IM CHARACTER DER TRADITIONELLEN NATIONALAUSSCHÜSSE IN DER TSCHECHOSLOWAKEI 1918 UND 1945 [Changes in the character of the traditional national assemblies in Czechoslovakia 1918 and 1945]. *Jahrbuch für Geschichte [East Germany] 1984 (30): 205-234.* Describes the fundamental differences in composition and function that separate the Czechoslovakian national assembly of 1945 from that of 1918. In 1918, the Czech and Slovakian peoples' revolutionary movements against the Hapsburg government lost the fight for national independence to the capitalist bourgeois government's fear of revolution, shared by the Social Democrats, that led to the national assembly's liquidation. In 1945, the newly reformed national assembly, representing in the majority the workers led by the Communist Party with the Soviet Union's support succeeded in defeating the reactionary elements in the government to become the true power organ in the peoples' democratic state. Based on Czech and Slovakian national assembly records and other primary sources; 90 notes. G. Herritt

1290. Schütz, Hans. MARTIN K. BACHSTEIN: WENZEL JAKSCH UND DIE SUDETENDEUTSCHE SOZIALDEMOKRATIE [Martin K. Bachstein: Wenzel Jaksch and Sudeten German Social Democracy]. *Sudetenland [West Germany] 1974 16(4): 263-267.* Reviews Martin K. Bachstein's book on Wenzel Jaksch (Munich, 1974). Jaksch, a native of Bohemia, of German parentage, a bricklayer's son, was an apprentice to a stucco-worker in Vienna. He grew up in the Socialist Youth Organization and became a member of the editorial staff of *Sozial Demokrat* of Prague. He came into prominence in 1936 with his election as Chairman of the Czech Social Democratic Party, but he held no office during the presidency of Eduard Beneš, 1935-38. When Hitler took over Czechoslovakia in March 1939, Beneš had already resigned. Jaksch was important among Social Democratic exiles at London, with Beneš. He was part of the revived Beneš Social Democratic Czechoslovakia after World War II, but when the Communists took over, Beneš resigned and was succeeded by Klement Gottwald. Again, Jaksch went into exile. He died in a traffic accident in November 1966. R. E. Penney

1291. Selucky, Radoslav. CZECHS RESPOND TO NORMALIZATION WITH CONSUMPTION AND APATHY. *Int. Perspectives [Canada] 1975 Mar-Apr: 31-35.* Examines political and economic affairs in Czechoslovakia, 1969-75, following Communist Party leader Gustav Husák's normalization program designed to revive Party unity, consolidate the economy, and restore ties with other communist and socialist countries.

1292. Skoupá, Dana. K ÚSILÍ KSČ O DEMOKRATIZACI VEŘEJNÉ SPRÁVY NA STŘEDNÍ A SEVERNÍ MORAVĚ (1945-1948) [The Czechoslovak Communist Party's democratization of public administration in central and northern Moravia, 1945-48]. *Slezský Sborník [Czechoslovakia] 1980 78(4): 289-294.* In accordance with the Košice program introduced immediately after World War II, the Czechoslovak Communist Party decentralized power and put many of the tasks of regional administration in areas such as central and northern Moravia into the hands of the people themselves. The most important role in this transfer of power was played by the Party's propaganda section, which was responsible for the dissemination of information in general and for acquainting the people at large with their new responsibilities. True democratization took place after the victory of the working classes in February 1948. Secondary sources; 24 notes. B. Reinfeld

1293. Sladecek, Josef. LES COMMUNISTES ET LES AUTRES: LE PRINTEMPS ET LA NORMALISATION [The Communists and the others: Prague Spring and normalization]. *Esprit [France] 1979 (1): 105-121.* Analyzes Czechoslovakia's economic situation following Prague Spring (1968), and centers on the attitude of the Communists, the Reformist-Communists, and the non-Communists.

1294. Slavkovská, Eva. SLOVENSKÝ NÁRODNÝ FRONT—ŠPECIFICKÁ SÚČASŤ POLITICKÉHO SYSTÉMU V PÄŤDESIATYCH ROKOCH [Slovak National Front: a specific part of the political system in Czechoslovakia in the 1950's]. *Hist. Časopis [Czechoslovakia] 1983 31(2): 204-230.* The victory of the working class in February 1948 conditioned the origin of the socialist political system in Czechoslovakia. It represented suppressive as well as democratic features of the dictatorship of the proletariat. The National Front represented a specific part of the Czechoslovak political system. Marxist-Leninist principles were accepted in its activities from the very beginning: the principle of the leading role of the Communist Party of Czechoslovakia in the National Front, the principle of democratic centralism, the principle of collective membership in political and social organizations of the National Front and the principle of proletarian democracy. J

1295. Smirnova, Nina Dmitrievna. POLITIKA SSHA V OTNOSHENII GRETSII (1943-1945). [American policy toward Greece, 1943-45]. *Novaia i Noveishaia Istoriia [USSR] 1984 (1): 44-62.* In 1943, US political aims in Greece began to diverge from the British and grew apart in late 1944, during Britain's overt support of Greek reactionary forces against the workers' liberation movement. However, while professing nonintervention in Greek internal affairs, America, too, continued to obstruct Greek democratic aspirations. The Truman Doctrine of March 1947 was, in fact, a defiant challenge to world socialism and, under the guise of economic aid, converted Greece into a major American military base. Based mainly on published US State Department documents; 65 notes. N. Frenkley

1296. Smoleja, František. VOJENSKOPOLITICKÁ LINIE XI. SJEZDU KSČ [Military and political line of the 11th Congress of the Czechoslovak Communist Party]. *Hist. a Vojenství [Czechoslovakia] 1982 31(5): 40-55.* Among important parts of the work of the 11th Congress (1958) was the decision to evaluate the meaning of national defense and security in view of further development of socialist construction. The congress accepted the line of action focusing on full unity of the Czechoslovak armed forces with the people and stressed the need to adopt the products of the scientific and technical revolution in the army's training, armament and equipment. Based on official records; 37 notes. G. E. Pergl

1297. Snítil, Zdeněk. DAS REVOLUTIONÄRE VERMÄCHTNIS KLEMENT GOTTWALDS—LEBENDIGER BESTANDTEIL DER SECHZIGJÄHRIGEN GESCHICHTE DER KPTSCH [The revolutionary legacy of Klement Gottwald: a lively component of the 60-year history of the Czechoslovak Communist Party]. *Beiträge zur Gesch. der Arbeiterbewegung [East Germany] 1981 23(3): 339-344.* Assesses the Czechoslovak Communist leader Klement Gottwald's (1896-1953) importance in establishing the Communist Party in Czechoslovakia, and considers his role within the Party, particularly as its leader, 1948-53. Under his leadership the Czechoslovak Communist Party established close links with the USSR and other socialist states including East Germany. Gottwald—revolutionary, politician, and statesman—began his political activities in 1917, joined the Czechoslovak Communist Party in 1921, gained a reputation as a politician during the 1920's and 1930's, was active in Moscow during World War II continuing the work of the Party, participated in the Slovak uprising of 1945, was nominated as Party chairman in 1946, and served as president of the Czechoslovak Republic, 1948-53. G. L. Neville

1298. Snítil, Zdeněk. LENINISMUS A REVOLUČNÍ ZKUŠENOSTI KSČ [Leninism and the revolutionary experiences of the Communist Party of Czechoslovakia]. *Československý Časopis Hist. [Czechoslovakia] 1982 30(5): 641-643.* At the 16th Czechoslovak Communist Party Congress in 1981, Gustav Husák and Leonid Brezhnev reminded Czechoslovak Communists of the revolutionary schooling their party had undergone during its 60 years. Drawing on this accumulated experience, they could contribute to the continuing struggle of the world's working masses. 4 notes. R. E. Weltsch

1299. Snítil, Zdeněk. O NĚKTERÝCH OTÁZKACH DĚJIN BUDOVÁNÍ ROZVINUTÉ SOCIALISTICKÉ SPOLEČNOSTI V ČESKOSLOVENSKU VE SVĚTLE XV. SJEZDU KSČ [The building of a developed socialist society in Czechoslovakia as seen by the 15th Party Congress]. *Československý Časopis Hist. [Czechoslovakia] 1977 25(1): 6-24.* Points out problems related to the history of socialist construction in Czechoslovakia in the 1970's and the history of the Communist Party itself. 24 notes. G. E. Pergl

1300. Snitil, Zdenek. VERNOST' LENINSKIM PRINTSIPAM PROLETARSKOGO INTERNATSIONALIZMA [Allegiance to the Leninist principles of proletarian internationalism]. *Voprosy Istorii KPSS [USSR] 1981 (12): 59-69.* Surveys the history of the Communist Party of Czechoslovakia, 1921-81. During this period, the Party overcame right opportunist and leftist errors, struggled for a united front against Nazi Germany, completed the development of the democratic revolution into a socialist revolution in February 1948, led efforts toward socialist construction including industrialization of all parts of the country, and with the assistance of other socialist countries defeated counterrevolutionary and opportunist forces in 1968. Based on published works of Klement Gottwald and Gustav Husak; 18 notes. L. E. Holmes

1301. Špičák, Milan. KE VZNIKU STRANICKOPOLITICKÉHO APARÁTU ČSLA [On the origin of the political and party apparatus of the Czechoslovak People's Army]. *Historie a Vojenstvi [Czechoslovakia] 1975 (2): 99-109.* After 1948 the Communist Party of Czechoslovakia was oriented to building a socialist armed force and required the creation of party organization in every military unit for the purpose of supporting and spreading the party's ideology among the troops. Political workers received special education in the Military Political Academy, instituted in 1953. 4 notes. G. E. Pergl

1302. Špičák, Milan and Liptak, Jan. VOJENSKÁ POLITIKA KSČ V ÚDOBÍ URYCHLENÉ VÝSTAVBY ARMÁDY SOCIALISTICKÉHO TYPU (1948-1954) [The military policy of the Czechoslovak Communist Party in the period of the accelerated buildup of a socialist army, 1948-54]. *Československý Časopis Hist. [Czechoslovakia] 1975 23(5): 641-664.* The buildup of Czech armed forces after 1948 was reinforced by the political situation of the world and the state itself. The socialist state needed the support of a socialist army which would protect Czechoslovakia against possible outside imperialist aggression. The authors examine the Communist Party's policy and its attempt to create armed forces of the socialist type. Secondary sources; 16 notes. G. E. Pergl

1303. Štaigl, Jan. VÝVOJ ODBOJOVÝCH SVAZŮ NA SLOVENSKU OD R. 1945 DO VYPUKNUTÍ POLITICKÉ KRIZE NA PODZIM 1947 [Development of resistance veterans' organizations in Slovakia from 1945 to the outbreak of political crisis in the fall of 1947]. *Hist. a Vojenství [Czechoslovakia] 1981 30(3): 73-92.* After the liberation of Czechoslovakia the Slovak resistance fighters created no fewer than five organizations between April and September 1945. Political parties courted their support, and when reactionary forces took the nation toward crisis in search of political power in Slovakia, Slovak Communists sought the total unification of resistance associations. This was achieved in the National Front, embracing all groups to give them full participation in the socialist building of a new Slovakia. Based on published documents and reports; 63 notes. G. E. Pergl

1304. Štefanský, Václav. PREHLBOVANIE SOCIALISTICKÉHO CHARAKTERU ČSLA V OBDOBÍ XI. ZJAZDU KSČ. ZÁKLADNÉ VÝCHODISKÁ VOJENSKEJ POLITIKY KSČ V OBDOBÍ PRÍPRAV STRANY A SPOLOČNOSTI NA XI. ZJAZD KSČ [The deepening of the socialist character of the Czechoslovak People's Army at the time of the 11th Congress of the Czechoslovak Communist Party: basic outlook on the Czechoslovak Communist Party's military policy at the time of the preparations of the Party and the people for the 11th Congress of the Communist Party of Czechoslovakia]. *Hist. a Vojenství [Czechoslovakia] 1980 29(4): 83-105.* Facing the constant imperialist menace and the emergent technical and scientific revolution in modern warfare, the 20th Congress of the Soviet Communist Party gave an impulse for a review of the situation of the armed forces of the socialist camp. The Czechoslovak Communist Party accepted the challenge for a deeper socialization of armed units after a national discussion of the modern needs of defense. This became the main ideological issue of the Party's 11th Congress in 1958. Congress resolutions made possible a new approach and total upgrading of army organization and armament. Based on published resolutions of Communist Party congresses; 62 notes. G. E. Pergl

1305. Suda, Zdeněk L. *Zealots and Rebels: A History of the Ruling Communist Party of Czechoslovakia.* Histories of Ruling Communist Parties. Stanford: Hoover Inst., 1980. 412 pp.

1306. Suško, Ladislav. K OTÁZKE RIADENIA EKONOMIKY V POLITIKE KSČ V PRVEJ POLOVICI ŠEST'DESIATYCH ROKOV [The problem of economic management in the policy of the Czechoslovak Communist Party in the first half of the 1960's]. *Hist. Štúdie [Czechoslovakia] 1981 25: 5-24.* Economic reform became the central political goal of an emerging group of opportunists and revisionists. Newly introduced principles of leadership made the production area of the economy stronger with greater returns and effectiveness. Based on Party sources; 33 notes. G. E. Pergl

1307. Suško, Ladislav. ORIENTÁCIA XII. ZJAZDU KSČ NA INTENZIFIKÁCIU EKONOMIKY A ZAČIATKY REVIZIONISTICKÉHO POKRIVENIA PROJEKTU EKONOMICKEJ REFORMY [Orientation of the 12th Congress of the Czechoslovak Communist Party on intensification of the economy and the beginnings of revisionist distortion of economic reform]. *Hist. Štúdie [Czechoslovakia] 1980 24: 7-41.* Aggravated economic problems in the 1960's forced an open investigation into several sectors of Czechoslovakia's economic system in 1962. The results were first discussed and evaluated at the 12th Party Congress. It became clear that the goals of the 3d Five-Year Plan were unrealistic and not based on the conditions and possibilities of the Czechoslovak economy at that time. The congress revealed the false conceptions of E. Löbl's economic theories and those of his supporters and followers such as O. Šik and others. Based on official documents; 70 notes. G. E. Pergl

1308. Svoboda, Vaclav. EFFECTIVENESS OF MARXIST-LENINIST AGRARIAN POLICY. *World Marxist Rev. [Canada] 1972 15(11): 50-57.* Discusses the Communist Party's agrarian policy in Czechoslovakia, 1945-72.

1309. Taborsky, Edward. PRESIDENT EDVARD BENEŠ AND THE CRISES OF 1938 AND 1948. *East Central Europe 1978 5(2): 203-214.* In the two crises of 1938 and 1948, Eduard Beneš at first resolved on armed resistance if necessary, and yet he gave in when threatened with force. His decision not to go to war in 1938 was due to his feeling that it would be utterly irresponsible to risk a war that was bound to be lost. His decision not to resist the Communist takeover of Czechoslovakia rested upon his conviction that resistance would lead to Soviet military intervention. Beneš tended to be overly optimistic until too late. He believed a statesman could not consider just the happiness of one generation, but must keep in mind future generations. Hence preservation of the Czechoslovak people and land was his prime responsibility. 41 notes. R. V. Layton

1310. Taborsky, Edward. TRAGEDY, TRIUMPH AND TRAGEDY: CZECHOSLOVAKIA 1938-1948. Brisch, Hans and Volgyes, Ivan, ed. *Czechoslovakia: The Heritage of Ages Past* (New York: Columbia U. Pr., 1979): 113-134. The Czechs survived a world war and dictatorship of the extreme Right only to face a dictatorship of the extreme Left. Eduard Beneš believed in 1938 that to go to war with the support only of the USSR would play into the hands of Nazi propagandists and give the Western allies the alibi they needed for their failure to help Czechoslovakia. The Allies also did not honor their guarantee of the truncated Czech state after Munich. The author discusses wartime diplomacy, repressive conditions with the German protectorates, and the behavior of the Russians as they moved into the country, 1944-45. In a three-year struggle with the Communists, who had control of the media and national police, Beneš again capitulated in order to avoid a bloodbath.

1311. Tigrid, Pavel. THE PRAGUE COUP OF 1948: THE ELEGANT TAKEOVER. *Studies on the Soviet Union [West Germany] 1971 11(4): 352-385.* Czechoslovakia in 1947 was the only Balkan state that had a coalition government not directly installed by the Red Army. Promulgation of the Marshall Plan and intensification of the Cold War rendered this situation intolerable to the Soviet Union. Action to eliminate non-Party coalition members was undertaken. Single-slate elections were attempted, but balked. The Soviets forced the coalition government to step down. The non-Communist politicians failed, despite strong popular support, because they were unable to develop an effective, unified plan of action. Secondary sources; 98 notes. V. L. Human

1312. Tomčík, Miloš. ZÁVEREČNÉ SLOVO [A word in conclusion]. *Česká Literatura [Czechoslovakia] 1981 29(6): 525-527.* The conference on the history of Czech and Slovak socialist literature in Smolenice, 22-24 April 1981 threw light on the relations between the Communist Party of Czechoslovakia and literature from both Czech and Slovak points of view and prepared the ground for future projects, including more comparativist work, to be followed by the respective institutes of literature.

1313. Topornin, B. N. OSNOVNYE CHERTY KONSTITUTSIONNOGO RAZVITIIA CHEKHOSLOVAKII (POSLE 9 MAIA 1945 G.) [Basic features of constitutional development in Czechoslovakia after May 1945]. *Sovetskoe Slavianovedenie [USSR] 1967 3(4): 58-67.* Czechoslovakia's peaceful revolution and the existence of a bourgeois democratic constitution permitted the participation of the middle classes in the postwar government and continued use of certain provisions of the 1920 constitution. National committees composed of rural and urban workers were established in 1945 to replace the pre-Munich system of self-government. The Communist Party presented a draft constitution in 1946, but prior to February 1948 various bourgeois parties tried to substitute their own constitutional projects. On 9 May 1948 the National Assembly adopted a constitution which nationalized natural resources and provided for the later nationalization of the means of production. A unified economic plan was instituted and the rights of citizens were defined. The government structure was maintained, but the National Assembly became unicameral. In 1960, a revised constitution was adopted preserving features of the 1948 constitution but eliminating all vestiges of bourgeois laws. 28 notes. L. C. Moody

1314. Urban, George R. A CONVERSATION WITH OTA SIK. *Survey 1973 19(2): 250-270.* Ota Sik was Director of the Economic Institute of the Czech Academy of Sciences and a member of the Central Committee of the Czech Communist Party. Comments on

Stalinism, the role of bureaucracy and the manipulation of man, worker management, egalitarianism, the use of leisure time, morality and the Czech reform movement of the mid-1960's.
R. B. Valliant

1315. Valenta, Jiri. SOVIET DECISIONMAKING AND THE CZECHOSLOVAK CRISIS OF 1968. *Studies in Comparative Communism 1975 8(1/2): 147-173.* The moderates, Suslov, Kosygin, Shelepin and Ponamaev, were more tolerant of changes in Czechoslovakia than the security police and men like Shelest. Brezhnev's role was to offer moderate criticism of the Czechs and of similar arguments in the USSR to the effect that economic reforms were necessary. As the crisis developed, Brezhnev undermined Kosygin's public position. While in mid-July, 1968, a substantial number of Politburo members preferred a political solution, pressure from the regional party apparatus, Party groups in the western parts of the USSR, and army and police elements forced the invasion. Brezhnev may have joined this group because he feared that the moderates would undermine his position in the Politburo. 93 notes.
D. Balmuth

1316. Varholik, Juraj and Cmolik, Otto. COMMUNIST PARTY AND YOUTH OF CZECHOSLOVAKIA. *World Marxist R. [Canada] 1973 16(11): 114-121.*

1317. Vávra, Vlastimil and Drška, Pavel. K VOJENSKOPOLITICKÉMU ODKAZU KLEMENTA GOTTWALDA [Military and political legacy of Klement Gottwald]. *Hist. a Vojenství [Czechoslovakia] 1981 30(5): 33-42.* Klement Gottwald, a leading personality in the history of the Czech Communist movement, struggled against fascism in all of its mutations. This struggle was led first from the platform of the Czech Parliament and the Communist Party press. After the Munich disaster, Gottwald escaped to Moscow to continue the fight. After liberation, his participation in the development of a modern socialist army made it a dependable tool in the hands of workers and peasants in the socialist state. Based on Gottwald's writings; 12 notes.
G. E. Pergl

1318. Verbík, Antonín. PRŮMYSL BRNĚNSKÉHO KRAJE NA POČÁTKU PRVNÍ PĚTILETKY [The industry of the Brno region at the beginning of the 1st Five-Year Plan]. *Časopis Matice Moravské [Czechoslovakia] 1982 101(3-4): 211-233.* Most branches of industry were represented in the Brno region. Except for various clays, limestone, marble and gravel, and the raw materials for the food industry, most industries suffered from a lack of local raw materials. The 1st Five-Year Plan saw nationalization completed, production of previously imported items introduced, and further industrialization to reduce commuting. The program suffered from investment problems, the continuing lack of raw materials, and absenteeism. Nevertheless the leadership of the Communist Party and its policy of socialist competition brought moderate success, despite some shortfalls. Statistical tables, 50 notes. L. Short

1319. Vidnians'ki, S. V. KERIVNA I ORHANIZUIUCHA ROL' KPCH V KONSOLIDATSII PROFSPILKOVOHO RUKHU CHEKHOSLOVACHCHYNY (KVITEN' 1969-CHERVEN' 1972) [The leading and organizing role of the Communist Party in consolidating the labor union movement in Czechoslovakia, April 1969-June 1972]. *Ukrains'kyi Istorychnyi Zhurnal [USSR] 1975 (6): 69-76.*

1320. Vidnians'kyi, S. V. ROBITNYCHYI KLAS CHEKHOSLOVACHCHYNY V UMOVAKH BUDIVNYTSTVA ROZVYNUTOHO SOTSIALIZMU [The working class of Czechoslovakia in conditions of building developed socialism]. *Ukraïns'kyi Istorychnyi Zhurnal [USSR] 1979 (8): 66-76.* The working class in Czechoslovakia had a decisive role in overcoming crises in Czech society and economy and in the construction of developed socialism after the entry of Warsaw Pact troops. Construction of developed socialism demands further increases in the role of the Communist Party and improvements in its organizational, ideological, and political work. The Czechoslovakian Party strives to strengthen the leading role of the working class. 57 notes. I. Krushelnycky

1321. Vondrášek, Václav. KSČ A MOCENSKOPOLITICKÝ ZÁPAS V ČESKOSLOVENSKU V PRŮBĚHU ROKU 1947 [The Communist Party of Czechoslovakia and the struggle for political power in Czechoslovakia during 1947]. *Československý Časopis Hist. [Czechoslovakia] 1981 29(4): 481-514.* Surveys the confrontations between the Communist Party and its three major political adversaries, the National Socialists, the People's Party, and the Slovak Democratic Party. The Czech anti-Communists could not equal the Communists' dynamic leadership in the national reconstruction programs; they therefore concentrated on destructive public criticism and made feeble yet damaging attempts to cultivate the Western Allies. The Slovak Democrats combined an anti-Soviet outlook with outright separatism. Spurred on by the incipient cold war, this domestic conflict culminated in the government crisis of February 1948. Based on material in the Military Historical Archives, Prague, and on the press; 139 notes. Russian and English summaries.
R. E. Weltsch

1322. Vondrášek, Václav. KSČ A MOCENSKOPOLITICKÝ ZÁPAS V PŘEDVEČER ÚNORA 1948 [The Communist Party of Czechoslovakia and the struggle for political power on the eve of February 1948]. *Československý Časopis Hist. [Czechoslovakia] 1983 31(5): 645-673.* Between November 1947 and February 1948, Czechoslovakia's three major non-Communist parties intensified their political campaign designed to represent the Communists as enemies of democracy and to hamper the Communist-led program of reconstruction and nationalization. In mid-February this bourgeois bloc denied its votes to needed constitutional enactments and provoked a crisis by the resignation of 12 of its ministers. The working people and armed forces of Czechoslovakia responded by backing the Communists in their resolution of this crisis. Attempts to misrepresent this constitutional changeover as a Communist coup lack any foundation. Based on material in the Military Historical Archives, Prague, and on newspapers; 115 notes. Russian and German summaries. R. E. Weltsch

1323. Voráček, Emil. KONCEPCE HOSPODÁŘSKÉ SPOLUPRÁCE S SSSR ÚVAHÁCH ČESKOSLOVENSKÉ EMIGRACE ZA DRUHÉ SVĚTOVÉ VÁLKY [The conception of economic cooperation with the USSR in the consideration of the Czechoslovak emigration during World War II]. *Slovanský Přehled [Czechoslovakia] 1982 68(6): 493-503.* President Eduard Beneš signed a treaty of friendship with the Soviet Union December 1943. Immediately after the signing he held discussions with Czechoslovakians resident in Moscow, all future leaders of the Communist Party. In their views the most important aspect of the postwar situation was to be tight political, social, and economic ties with the Soviet Union. In 1945 they included such conditions in the Košice Program, on which a new government was based. Klement Gottwald, the leader of the Communist Party, was especially responsible for this fruitful collaboration with the USSR, which brought about a brisk revival of the national economy. 42 notes. B. Reinfeld

1324. Voráček, Emil. KSČ A ČESKOSLOVENSKO-SOVĚTSKÁ HOSPODÁŘSKÁ SPOLUPRÁCE 1945-1947 [The Communist Party and Czechoslovak-Soviet economic cooperation, 1945-47]. *Slovanský Přehled [Czechoslovakia] 1981 67(3): 200-212.* Describes how before 1948 the Czechoslovakian Communist Party broadened the scope of economic cooperation between the USSR and Czechoslovakia. Long-term economic plans were in the planning stages in 1947 when the bourgeois government flirted with the idea of accepting the Marshall Plan, which would have changed the internal development of the country. Instead, close partnership with the USSR emerged, especially after the USSR sent massive relief, following the disastrous crops of 1947. 55 notes. B. Reinfeld

1325. Voráček, Emil. ÚNOR 1948 A ČESKOSLOVENSKO-SOVĚTSKÉ VZTAHY [February 1948 and Czechoslovak-Soviet relations]. *Slovanský Přehled [Czechoslovakia] 1983 69(1): 28-37.* In February 1948 the working class of Czechoslovakia, led by the Communist Party, rose up against the last attempt by the middle classes to reinstate class rule. Preceding the events of February, there was a deliberate policy of the bourgeoisie to neglect the Košice program and the 1943 treaty of alliance with the USSR. Trade with the Soviet Union, 1945-48, declined steadily, which would have led to a weakening of the Czechoslovak economy. In defeating the bourgeoisie, an important role was played by the Congress of Czech-Soviet Friendship Union, which was a manifestation of the strong traditional ties between the two peoples, expressed by Klement Gottwald's slogan: "With the Soviet Union Forever." 38 notes. B. Reinfeld

1326. Vošahlíková, Pavla. IDEOVÝ A POLITICKÝ VÝVOJ ČESKOSLOVENSKÉ SOCIÁLNÍ DEMOKRACIE V DOBĚ NÁRODNÍ A DEMOKRATICKÉ REVOLUCE (KVĚTEN 1945—LISTOPAD 1947) [Ideological and political development of Czechoslovak Social Democracy during the national and democratic revolution, May 1945-November 1947]. *Československý Časopis Hist. [Czechoslovakia] 1981 29(4): 515-545.* The Social Democratic Party was included in the National Front, the postwar party system in Czechoslovakia. As many Social Democrats had joined the Communist Party, and the Social Democratic left wing led by Zdeněk Fierlinger favored close cooperation with Communists, the old right-wing party leaders countered this revolutionary trend by emphasizing formal democracy in their program. The party's losses in the May 1946 elections combined with political maneuvering at the 21st Social Democratic Congress, November 1947, to give the right-wingers a short-lived control, which could not reverse the general pro-Communist trend. Based on the archives of the Institute of Marxism-Leninism, Prague, and other archival and published sources; 86 notes. Russian and English summaries. R. E. Weltsch

1327. Westers, Gerard. HET BUITENGEWONE XIVe CONGRES VAN DE CPTSJ [The extraordinary XIVth congress of the Czech Communist Party]. *Kleio [Netherlands] 1977 18(5): 386-387.* Planned for September, the 14th Congress met secretly shortly after the Soviet intervention to elect a new Central Committee without the conservatives in the old, and to demand withdrawal of the invading troops. The Moscow Protocol declared it invalid. 3 notes.

1328. Wightman, Gordon. THE CHANGING ROLE OF CENTRAL PARTY INSTITUTIONS IN CZECHOSLOVAKIA, 1962-67. *Soviet Studies [Great Britain] 1981 33(3): 401-420.* Examines the changes in central Party institutions in Czechoslovakia, December 1962 to January 1968, particularly in the leadership and the roles of the Central Committee and Congress. Though less obvious than those occurring in other institutions and less dramatic than those of 1968, these changes were significant. Reformist tendencies were visible in 1963 and some movement observable by 1966, leading to a generalized opposition to First Secretary Antonin Novotny, an important factor in forcing his resignation. 53 notes, 4 tables. D. H. Murdoch

1329. Wightman, Gordon. MEMBERSHIP OF THE COMMUNIST PARTY OF CZECHOSLOVAKIA IN THE 1970'S: CONTINUING DIVERGENCE FROM THE SOVIET MODEL. *Soviet Studies [Great Britain] 1983 35(2): 208-222.* The collapse of the Dubček government (1968) led to a major purge of reformist elements within the Communist Party of Czechoslovakia. In attempting to rebuild the Party during the 1970's, the Czechoslovak leadership generally mirrored the aims of its Soviet counterpart—to develop a strong working-class profile, but with substantial representation of technical and administrative elites. Despite similarities, the Czech Party "diverged from the Soviet model in encouraging a level of recruitment which brought the size of the party closer to that in the 1960's when the proportion of the population in the CPC had been much higher than that of Soviet citizens represented in the CPSU." 4 tables, 82 notes. M. R. Yerburgh

1330. Wightman G. and Brown, A. H. CHANGES IN THE LEVELS OF MEMBERSHIP AND SOCIAL COMPOSITION OF THE COMMUNIST PARTY OF CZECHOSLOVAKIA, 1945-73. *Soviet Studies [Great Britain] 1975 27(3): 396-417.* Examines changes in level and social composition of the Czechoslovakian Communist Party and their relation to party policy. Size of membership has fluctuated as it has alternately been desirable and dangerous for the party to have full-scale membership. However, attempts to alter social composition and to extend working-class representation, have not been so successful. Primary and secondary sources; 2 tables, 102 notes. L. Brown

1331. Wolchik, Sharon L. ELITE STRATEGY TOWARD WOMEN IN CZECHOSLOVAKIA: LIBERATION OR MOBILIZATION? *Studies in Comparative Communism 1981 14(2-3): 123-142.* Communist control led to changes in the access of women to education and employment, although Czechoslovakia had a strong feminist movement before World War II. Women were encouraged to move into the labor force as Communists saw women primarily as a labor resource. The traditional identification of women with children was maintained. After 1952 women's organizations were disbanded but revived in the 1960's. Opinion polls indicate a diversity of opinion on women's roles. Equality has not been a primary goal of the Party elite. 51 notes. D. Balmuth

1332. Žatkuliak, Jozef. NÁRODNÉ VÝBORY NA SLOVENSKU OD VYHLÁSENIA KOŠICKÉHO VLÁDNEHO PROGRAMU DO VOLIEB ROKU 1946 [National committees in Slovakia from the proclamation of the Košice Governmental Program to the elections in 1946]. *Hist. Časopis [Czechoslovakia] 1983 31(5): 749-775.* Chronicles the struggle between the representatives of the Communist Party of Slovakia and the Democratic Party. J

1333. Zdycha, Pavol. PROBLÉM KOVOROLNÍKOV V PROCESE KOLEKTIVIZÁCIE POLNOHOSPODÁRSTVA NA SLOVENSKU [The problem of "metal farmers" in the collectivization of agriculture in Slovakia]. *Hist. Časopis [Czechoslovakia] 1984 32(5): 781-805.* In the period of socialist collectivization in Slovakia there were numerous strata of "metal farmers." They were employed in industry, the building industry, and forestry. They were owners of the two-hectare plots of farmland, which represented their food supply. These farms were not equally spread over the territory of Slovakia, but depended on the possibility of work outside of agriculture. This group of peasants supported the Communist Party of Czechoslovakia in its struggle against capitalism. J

1334. Zorin, V. A. "S SOVETSKIM SOIUZOM NA VECHNYE VREMENA" (O RAZVITII SOVETSKO-CHEKHOSLOVATSKIKH OTNOSHENII V 1945-1948 GG.) ["With the Soviet Union for ever and ever": development of Soviet-Czechoslovak relations, 1945-48]. *Novaia i Noveishaia Istoriia [USSR] 1978 (2): 83-92, (3): 79-89.* Part I. Describes the USSR's negotiations after 1941 with the London-based Czechoslovak government-in-exile, liberation of Czechoslovakia by Soviet troops, and the formation in April 1945 of a Czech and Slovak coalition government headed by President Eduard Beneš (1884-1948), Prime Minister Zdeněk Fierlinger, and Deputy Prime Minister Klement Gottwald. Acceding to Ukrainian demands for national reunification, Trans-Carpathian Ukraine (Ruthenia) was ceded to the USSR on 29 June 1945. Personal recollections of the author's meetings with Czech and Slovak leaders enliven the account. 15 notes. Part II. The class struggle that erupted in the wake of liberation failed to weaken the Czechoslovak Communist Party, skillfully led by Klement Gottwald, Secretary General of its Central Committee. The elections held in May 1946 gave a plurality to the Communist Party and a National Front government comprising the Communist and several socialist parties was formed by Eduard Beneš with Gottwald as Premier. The US Marshall Plan, aimed at economic subjugation of Europe, was rejected, a separatist Slovak movement fomented by France and Britain was suppressed, and in 1948, Gottwalt became president by a peaceful constitutional process. 17 notes. N. Frenkley

1335. Zubek, Theodoric. REMINISCENCES AND REFLECTIONS OF A SLOVAK REFUGEE PRIEST IN AMERICA. *Jednota Ann. Furdek 1978 17: 259-267.* The author, a Franciscan, recounts Communist persecution of religion in Czechoslovakia, his escape in 1951, his arrival in the United States in 1952, and his ministry in America. Discusses social and spiritual occurrences affecting religious thought in the United States, 1960's-78.

1336. ZumFelde, Lubica. DIE STELLUNG UND FUNKTION DES JOURNALISTEN IN DER GEGENWÄRTIGEN TSCHECHOSLOWAKISCHEN GESELLSCHAFT [The journalist's position and function in contemporary Czechoslovak society]. *Bohemia [West Germany] 1980 21(2): 303-324.* Since 1948, the Leninist conception of journalists as engaged Communists has come to dominate the schools of journalism at the universities of Prague and Bratislava, which refined their ideological and professional curricula from 1952 on. After 1969 the Communist Party achieved a complete purge and total control of the media. Studies and surveys of mass communication have been undertaken since the 1970's and are still in progress. 67 notes. R. E. Weltsch

1337. —. DIE PROZESSE IN DER CSSR UND DIE WESTLICHEN KPS [The trials in Czechoslovakia and the Western Communist parties]. *Osteuropäische Rundschau [West Germany] 1972 18(10): 11-17.* Describes the reaction of West European Communist parties to the trials in Czechoslovakia of communists associated with the Dubček government and the Prague Spring of 1968. Most West European Communist parties were highly critical about the overthrow of the Dubček government. Only such small parties as those in Portugal and Luxembourg approved the Moscow approach. In 1971, despite earlier assurances by Gustáv Husák that there would be no such trials, 32 Communists were charged. These trials, four years after the 1968 invasion, have provoked a new spate of criticism. Only the Austrian Communist Party has revised its stand. Others, especially large parties in a position to hope for actual early participation in government, such as the French and Italian, are particularly outspoken. Based on press and radio accounts mostly from Czechoslovak and West European Communist sources; 44 notes. P. R. Taylor

1338. —. HISTORIOGRAFIE K DĚJINÁM MEZINÁRODNÍHO A KOMUNISTICKÉHO HNUTÍ. PUBLIKAČNÍ ČINNOST ÚML A VSP ÚV KSČ [Historiography on the international and communist movement: publications issued by Central Committee of the Communist Party of Czechoslovakia]. *Acta U. Carolinae Phil. et Hist. [Czechoslovakia] 1981 (5): 129-131.* Surveys the publications of original works on history sponsored by the Communist Party of Czechoslovakia. These papers were a result of the Central Committee's decision in 1974 to "enhance the level of political education for the future of socialist society." More than 20 significant publications appeared between 1977-80. Based on official reports; biblio.

G. E. Pergl

1339. —. K DĚJINÁM VOJENSKÉ POLITIKY KSČ: VÝBĚROVÁ BIBLIOGRAFIE ZA LÉTA 1970-1980 [The history of military policy and the Czechoslovak Communist Party: a selected bibliography, 1970-80]. *Hist. a Vojenství [Czechoslovakia] 1981 30(3): 162-176.* A selected bibliography of documents and publications connected with the Party's military policy and published since 1970, listing 279 works. The beginnings of Party military policy may be traced from actions of militant revolutionary groups between 1917 and 1920. After the founding of the Czechoslovak Communist Party, military policy became an indivisible part of its mission. Prepared by the bibliographic-documentation group in the Military Historical Institute in Prague. G. E. Pergl

1340. —. [SOVIET BUREAUCRACY AND THE INVASION OF CZECHOSLOVAKIA]. *Studies in Comparative Communism 1975 8(1/2): 174-182.*

Simes, Dimitri. THE SOVIET INVASION AND THE LIMITS OF KREMLINOLOGY, *pp. 174-180.* Although some Soviet Politburo representatives may have been hesitant about the military intervention in Czechoslovakia in 1968, their ability to act in concert was displayed by the actual events. The author equates bureaucratic politics with Soviet politics, demonstrating the bureaucratic self-image of Politburo members. 2 notes.

Valenta, Jiri. REJOINDER, *pp. 181-182.* Argues that Politburo opposition to the invasion was stronger than Simes supposed. Cites the opposition of Boris Ponamarev as an example. Note.

D. Balmuth/S

1341. —. TSJECHOSLOWAKIJE TUSSEN TWEE WINTERS: [Czechoslovakia between two winters: Outside reactions to the events in Czechoslovakia]. *Kleio [Netherlands] 1977 18(5): 389-397.*

Hullegie, Bert and Kroeze, Arend. DE DDR EN DE PRAAGSE LENTE [The DDR and the Prague Spring], *pp. 389-390.* Fear of the effects of Czechoslovakia's planned economic relations with the West, and of losing its prestige in international affairs, led to East Germany's hard stand against the Czech reformers, expressed in open criticism supported by a one-sided and unjust press.

Westers, Gerard. DE HOUDING VAN POLEN EN HONGARIJE TEGENOVER DE "PRAAGSE LENTE" [The attitude of Poland and Hungary toward the "Prague Spring"], *p. 390.* Poland's support of the Russian attitude served to strengthen Gomulka's position as Party leader against internal nationalist movements sympathetic to the Czech reforms. Hungary, itself intent on liberalizing, was the most sympathetic of the Eastern bloc to the reformers, though advising caution.

Sietsema, Luit. DE REACTIES VAN JOEGOSLAVIE EN ROEMENIE OP DE GEBEURTENISSEN IN TSJECHOSLOWAKIJE [The reactions of Yugoslavia and Rumania to the events in Czechoslovakia], *pp. 391-392.* Having supported Dubček's policies from the beginning, both countries were highly critical of the invasion of Czechoslovakia and not intimidated by Soviet accusations of imperialism.

Galama, Annemieke. DE REACTIE VAN CUBA, ALBANIE EN CHINA OP DE INVAL [Cuba's, Albania's, and China's reactions to the invasion], *pp. 392-393.* Fidel Castro condemned the Russian intervention as against international law, yet found it understandable as directed against counterrevolutionaries and their bourgeois-liberal practices. Albania declared itself both against Russia's barbarian aggression and against Dubček's "revisionist" regime as the cause for the Czech people's passive resistance. Chou En-lai condemned the intervention, calling it a manifestation of fascist dictatorship by Soviet revisionists.

Hart, Marjolein 't. REACTIE VAN WESTEUROPESE COMMUNISTISCHE PARTIJEN EN VAN LINKSRADICALEN IN WEST-DUITSLAND OP DE GEBEURTENISSEN IN TSJECHOSLOWAKIJE [Reactions of West European Communist parties and of the left-wing radicals in West Germany to the events in Czechoslovakia], *pp. 393-395.* Although the great majority of Western Communist parties, following the Italian example, favored the Czech reforms, believing a more democratic image to be of advantage to themselves, and condemned Russia's intervention, the Prague Spring movement led to increasing dissension between the parties' more conservative and more radical members. It also provoked controversy among non-Communist left-wing radicals, as in West Germany between Rudi Dutschke and Ulrike Meinhof.

Otten, Marko and Ijzerdreef, Wim. NEDERLANDSE REACTIES [Reactions in the Netherlands], *pp. 395-397.* While the Russian invasion was unanimously condemned by the Dutch people, its government, and all political parties' opinions differed on the Prague Spring movement and its political consequences for the West, with the Dutch Communist Party strongly in favor of imitating Dubček's policies. G. Herritt

1342. —. TSJECHOSLOWAKIJE TUSSEN TWEE WINTERS: TSJECHOSLOWAKIJE OP DE NIEUWE WEG EN DE REACTIE VAN DE SOVJETUNIE [Czechoslovakia between two winters: Czechoslovakia on the new road and the reaction of the Soviet Union]. *Kleio [Netherlands] 1977 18(5): 377-383.*

Galama, Annemieke. I. DE ONTWIKKELINGEN JANUARI-APRIL 1968 [The developments of January-April 1968], *pp. 377-379.* Although the Soviet Union's hopes for an end to the Czech rebellion were not realized with the replacement of Party secretary Novotný by Alexander Dubček on 5 January, it did not become alarmed about the new Černik-government's reform policies until the Central Committee's approval of the Czech Communist Party's Action Program, 5 April.

Hart, Marjolein 't. HET ACTIEPROGRAMMA VAN DE COMMUNISTISCHE PARTIJ VAN TSJECHOSLOWAKIJE [The Action Program of the Communist Party of Czechoslovakia], *pp. 379-380.* This progressive Marxist program outlined the basic social and economic reforms necessary for the democratization process advocated by Dubček as condition for Czechoslovakia's own form of socialism.

Galama, Annemieke. II. MEI EN JUNI 1968 [May and June, 1968], *pp. 380-381.* During this period Russia, supported by Poland and East Germany, took ever sharper repressive measures against Czechoslovakia, without, however, stemming the democratization and reforms demanded by the Czech people, as expressed in Ludvík Vakulík's Manifesto of 2,000 Words.

Wassenaar, Karel-Jan. DE HETE ZOMER [The hot summer], *pp. 382-383.* Pressured by the Communist Eastern bloc to take counterrevolutionary measures, and by the Czech people for more reforms, the Czech government proceeded cautiously with plans for secret balloting, not realizing that the invasion was already being prepared. G. Herritt

East Germany

1343. Aleksievets, M. M. DIIAL'NIST' SEPN SHCHODO PIDVYSHCHENNIA DOBROBUTU NASELENNIA NDR [The activity of the Socialist Unity Party of East Germany in raising the standard of living of the population]. *Ukrains'kyi Istorychnyi Zhurnal [USSR] 1976 (9): 98-103.*

1344. Arendt, Hans-Jürgen. ZUR ENTWICKLUNG DER BEWEGUNG DER HAUSFRAUENBRIGADEN IN DER DDR 1958 BIS 1961-62: EINE BESONDERE FORM DER EINBEZIEHUNG NICHTBERUFSTÄTIGER FRAUEN IN DIE LÖSUNG VOLKSWIRTSCHAFTLICHER AUFGABEN BEIM AUFBAU DES SOZIALISMUS [The development of the housewife brigade movement in East Germany 1958 to 1961-62: a special form of mobilizing nonprofessional women for the solution of national economic tasks during the construction of socialism]. *Jahrbuch Für Wirtschaftsgeschichte [East Germany] 1979 (1): 53-70.* The first Housewives' Brigade was formed in 1956 to work in agriculture. In 1958 the Socialist Unity Party (SED) endorsed the movement as a way to assist agricultural and industrial units meet production goals, to bring women into the work force, and to promote equal status for women. By 1961, 70,000 housewives were members, 3/4 in agriculture. Before the movement declined in the mid-1960's, 30,000 housewives had become permanent laborers. Based on dissertations, archives of the SED, government statistics and secondary sources; table, 59 notes. E. L. Turk

1345. Arlt, Wolfgang. DIE JUGENDPOLITIK DER SED IN DER ÜBERGANGSPERIODE VOM KAPITALISMUS ZUM SOZIALISMUS IN DER DDR [The youth policy of the Socialist Unity Party in the period of transition from capitalism to socialism in East Germany]. *Beiträge zur Geschichte der Arbeiterbewegung [East Germany] 1978 20(2): 183-200.* Analyzes the Party's youth policy, 1945-63. The Party was successful in molding the youth organization, Free German Youth, into a socialist institution inculcated with antifascist democratic consciousness and capable of playing an important role in building a Communist society. Based on published documents, Party conference reports, documents in the archives of the Institute for Marxism-Leninism, Berlin, and journals; 83 notes. J. B. Street

1346. Arlt, Wolfgang; Drewes, Uwe; and Jahnke, Karl Heinz. ZUM PROZESS DER AUSARBEITUNG DER JUGENDPOLITIK DER SED BEI DER GESTALTUNG DER ENTWICKELTEN SOZIALISTISCHEN GESELLSCHAFT IN DER DDR [The process of the working out of youth policy of the Socialist Unity Party of Germany in the formation of a developed socialist society in East Germany]. *Beiträge zur Geschichte der Arbeiterbewegung [East Germany] 1979 21(5): 690-702.* The final introduction of socialist means of production and the securing of the East German border with West Berlin enabled the Socialist Unity party of Germany to adopt a new phase in policies toward East German youth. The main task was to motivate as many young people as possible for the further development of socialism as stated in the sixth party meeting in 1963. The main organizational work was carried through by the Free German Youth (FDJ) in its socialist organization of work, study, and leisure time. Based on printed documents and secondary literature; 58 notes. R. Wagnleitner

1347. Arlt, Wolfgang. ZUR JEGENDPOLITIK DER SED VON DER ERRICHTUNG DER ARBEITER-UND-BAUERN-MACHT BIS ZUM SIEG DER SOZIALISTISCHEN PRODUKTIONSVERHÄLTNISSE IN DER DDR (1949-1961) [The youth policy of the Socialist Unity Party from the foundation of the worker-peasant state to the triumph of socialist production in East Germany, 1949-61]. *Wissenschaftliche Zeitschrift der Wilhelm-Pieck-Universität Rostock, Gesellschafts- und Sprachwissenschaftliche Reihe [East Germany] 1976 25(1): 29-35.* From 1949 relations between the Socialist Unity Party (SED) and the Free German Youth (FDJ) movement became increasingly close. With the decision of the Second Party Congress in 1952 to place primary emphasis on the creation of a socialist state, attention was directed toward the integration of youth into this task. At the same time, the FDJ came to be viewed as the major source of recruits to the party and efforts were made to widen participation in the youth movement beyond functionaries and activists. Based on published party documents; 27 notes. English summary. J. A. Perkins

1348. Auer, D.; Beitz, W.; and John, E. ZUR FÜHRENDEN ROLLE DER PARTEI AUF KULTURELLEM GEBIET UND ZUR HERAUSBILDUNG EINES NEUEN VERHÄLTNISSES VON ARBEITERKLASSE UND KULTUR [The role of the Party in culture and the development of a new relationship between the working class and culture]. *Wissenschaftliche Zeitschrift der Karl-Marx U. Leipzig [East Germany] 1971 20(2): 245-262.* Suggests that the practical work of the Socialist Unity Party of Germany, 1946-71, shows the universal efficacy of socialist cultural revolution. Emphasizes that the establishment of socialist politics and economy are impossible without the introduction and development of a socialist culture. 33 notes. R. Wagnleitner

1349. Badstübner, Rolf. HISTORISCHE PROBLEME DER VOLKSDEMOKRATISCHEN REVOLUTION [Historical problems of the people's democratic revolution]. *Jahrbuch für Geschichte [East Germany] 1974 12: 51-80.* World War II destroyed the state apparatuses of most European countries. In France, Italy, and other Western European countries, the influence of the US and Great Britain prevented a people's democratic revolution led by Communists. In Eastern Europe, however, under the protection of Soviet occupation forces, the Communist Parties were able to establish people's democratic revolutionary regimes. In East Germany, the key event in this process was the formation of the Socialist Unity Party (SED) by fusion of the Communists and Social Democrats in April 1946. 37 notes. J. C. Billigmeier

1350. Badstübner, Rolf. ZUM PROBLEM DES EINHEITLICHEN REVOLUTIONÄREN PROZESSES AUF DEM GEBIET DER DDR [On the problem of a unitary revolutionary process in the area of East Germany]. *Zeitschrift für Geschichtswissenschaft [East Germany] 1973 21(11): 1325-1341.* Analyzes the role of the USSR and of the Socialist Unity Party of Germany for the continuous development of socialism in East Germany. Based on printed documents and secondary literature; 40 notes. R. Wagnleitner

1351. Badstübner-Peters, Evemarie. KULTURDEBATTEN IM VORFELD DES ZWEIJAHRPLANS 1948 [Cultural debates in the forefront of the Two Year Plan of 1948]. *Zeitschrift für Geschichtswissenschaft [East Germany] 1982 30(4): 304-321.* Describes the cultural debates that took place at the Socialist Unity Party's (SED) 11th Party Congress in 1948 in Berlin, East Germany. The cultural tasks resolved at the congress and integrated into the Two Year Plan for 1949-50 were: to raise the general educational and cultural level of the people; to develop learning, research, and art; to strengthen the alliance of the working class and workers with the intelligentsia; and to evolve a new democratic intelligentsia. Based on documents relating to the SED's 11th Party Congress, Berlin, and secondary sources; 76 notes. G. L. Neville

1352. Badstübner-Peters, Evemarie. ZU DEN ANFÄNGEN GEWERKSCHAFTLICHER KULTURARBEIT NACH 1945 [The beginnings of trade-union cultural work after 1945]. *Zeitschrift für Geschichtswissenschaft [East Germany] 1984 32(7): 573-585.* Surveys the cultural activities of Free Germany and of the Communist Party of Germany after World War II. The trade unions of the Free German Trade Union Federation coordinated the development of the popular culture of the working classes. They needed to begin a cultural revolution to extinguish the roots of Nazism. 55 notes. R. Grove

1353. Bălănica, Emilia. 25 DE ANI DE LA PROCLAMAREA REPUBLICII DEMOCRATE GERMANE [Twenty-five years since the proclamation of the German Democratic Republic]. *Anale de Istorie [Rumania] 1974 20(5): 127-132.* The German Communist Party laid the foundation for profound transformations in social relations in the immediate postwar years in East Germany in establishing the Antifascist Parties Bloc and (in 1946) the union with the Social Democrats which produced the Socialist Unity Party (SED). Traces East Germany's passage from capitalism to socialism by 1960 and observes its current high levels in every branch of industry, agriculture, education, and social and cultural production. The eighth SED congress in 1971 set new goals for a multilateral socialist development and by nationalizing the remaining "mixed enterprises" in the country placed 99.9% of total industrial output in state hands. The SED's nearly two million members continue to be the most advanced force for progress. Secondary works; 13 notes. G. J. Bobango

1354. Bartel', Kh. OSNOVANIE I ZNACHENIE GDR—PERVOGO SOTSIALISTICHESKOGO GOSUDARSTVA NA NEMETSKOI ZEMLE [The establishment and significance of the GDR: the first socialist state on German soil]. *Voprosy Istorii [USSR] 1979 (10): 14-24.* The Soviet Union's victory in the Great Patriotic War and the liberation of the peoples from fascism have radically altered the alignment of forces in the world. Relying on the Soviet Union's assistance and creatively applying the experience of the CPSU, the working class in the Soviet occupation zone of Germany carried out an anti-fascist democratic coup under the leadership of its party in the difficult conditions of struggle against the restoration and splitting policies of the imperialist forces operating in the Western zones. Acting in alliance with the peasantry and other segments of the toiling population in this part of Germany, the working class established a state in which the power wielded by the workers and peasants was a form of the dictatorship of the proletariat. The founding of the GDR marked a turning point in the history of the German people as well as in the history of Europe as a whole. J

1355. Barthel, Horst. DER SCHWERE ANFANG. ASPEKTE DER WIRTSCHAFTSPOLITIK DER PARTEI DER ARBEITERKLASSE ZUR ÜBERWINDUNG DER KRIEGSFOLGEN AUF DEM GEBIET DER DDR VON 1945 BIS 1949/50 [The difficult beginning: the economic policy of the party of the working class in overcoming the consequences of the war in East Germany, 1945-50]. *Jahrbuch für Geschichte [East Germany] 1977 16: 253-282.* Outlines the economic policy of the Communist Party of Germany (KPD) and of the Socialist Unity Party (SED) for the reconstruction of the country in the five years after the war. The SED insisted on state planning, nationalization, and cooperation with the USSR and other Communist countries as the bases for economic reconstruction. 92 notes. J. C. Billigmeier

1356. Bartl, Wilhelm; Braun, Albert; and Hergert, Hans-Jürgen. WIRTSCHAFTSWACHSTUM UND ZUNAHME DER EFFEKTIVITÄT DER GESELLSCHAFTLICHEN ARBEIT—HAUPTENTWICKLUNGSRICHTUNGEN DER ÖKONOMISCHEN STRATEGIE DER SED [Economic growth and increasing the efficiency of social labor: the main path of development in the economic strategy of the Socialist Unity Party of Germany]. *Wissenschaftliche Zeitschrift der Wilhelm-Pieck-Universität Rostock. Gesellschaftswissenschaftliche Reihe [East Germany] 1984 33(1): 44-48.* Analyzes the economic theory motivating the economic policy of East Germany, designed to increase the efficiency of production.

1357. Bauerfeind, Alfred; Buske, Heinz; and Hümmler, Heinz. DIE BÜNDNISPOLITIK DER SED MIT KOMPLEMENTÄREN PRIVATEN UNTERNEHMERN, HANDWERKERN UND GEWERBETREIBENDEN (1963 BIS 1973) [The SED's policy for an alliance between the Party, private business, craftsmen, and manufacturers, 1963-73]. *Jahrbuch für Wirtschaftsgeschichte [East Germany] 1978 (2): 7-27.* Discusses the gradual integration of private business, craftsmen, and manufacturers with the workers' movement in East Germany through craft production cooperatives and joint state involvement in industry. This policy of integration, which was implemented by the Socialist Unity Party (SED), culminated in the formation of state-owned enterprises known as Volkseigene Betriebe (VEB's) and a socialist transformation of the economy. 25 notes. S. G. Jackson/S

1358. Bauerfeind, Alfred. DIE UMWANDLUNG DER BETRIEBE MIT STAATLICHER BETEILUNG UND PRIVATBETRIEBE IN VOLKSEIGENE BETRIEBE. ZUR ENTWICKLUNG DER BUNDNISPOLITIK IN DER DDR NACH DEM VIII. PARTEITAG DER SED [Transformation of enterprises with state participation and private businesses into state-owned enterprises: developing the policy of alliance in the German Democratic Republic after the eighth party congress of the Socialist Unity Party (SED)]. *Zeitschrift für Geschichtswissenschaft [East Germany] 1975 23(1): 5-16.* The 1970's began a new stage in the transformation of East Germany into a socialist state. The policy of state ownership of the means of production was modified in practice by a movement toward state participation in private businesses. This was an intermediate step toward actual government ownership. Annual production increases of 25 percent have been common in the 1970's. Primary and secondary sources; 33 notes. G. H. Libbey

1359. Becher, J. and Richter, H. DIE SCHÖPFERISCHE ANWENDUNG DER LENINSCHEN LEHRE VOM STAAT BEI DER PLANUNG IM ÖKONOMISCHEN SYSTEM DES SOZIALISMUS IN DER DDR [The creative application of the Leninist doctrine of the state and socialist economic planning in East Germany]. *Wissenschaftliche Zeitschrift der Karl-Marx U. Leipzig [East Germany] 1970 19(6): 819-842.* The central Leninist principles of planning, the principle of the scientific plan and democratic centralism, were creatively applied by the Socialist Unity Party of Germany for the building of a socialist state. Primary and secondary sources; 63 notes. R. Wagnleitner

1360. Becker, Gerhard et al. KONFERENZ ZUM 25. JAHRESTAG DER GRÜNDUNG DER SED [Conference on the occasion of the 25th anniversary of the founding of the Socialist Unity Party of Germany]. *Zeitschrift für Geschichtswissenschaft [East Germany] 1971 19(9): 1178-1183.* Reviews the lectures and discussions of the 18th conference of the Commission of Historians of the Soviet Union and East Germany, which analyzed the political and economic policies of the Socialist Unity Party of Germany since its founding in 1946.

1361. Becker, Inge. DER 50. JAHRESTAG DER GROSSEN SOZIALISTISCHEN OKTOBERREVOLUTION IN DER POLITISCH-IDEOLOGISCHEN ARBEIT DER SED [The 50th anniversary of the October Revolution in the political-ideological work of the Socialist Unity Party of Germany]. *Beiträge zur Geschichte der Arbeiterbewegung [East Germany] 1976 18(4): 579-592.* Discusses the propaganda work and preparation of publications on the October revolution in East Germany on the occasion of the 50th anniversary of the revolution in 1967. Based on printed documents, secondary literature, and newspapers; 54 notes. R. Wagnleitner

1362. Bednareck, Horst. DIE KOMMUNISTISCHE PARTEI DER SOWJETUNION UND DIE GRÜNDUNG DER SOZIALISTISCHEN EINHEITSPARTEI DEUTSCHLANDS [Communist Party of the Soviet Union and the foundation of the Socialist Unity Party of Germany]. *Zeits. für Geschichtswissenschaft [East Germany] 1981 29(4): 304-313.* Two events were of high importance for the birth of the modern revolutionary party of the German working class: the liberation of the German people through the defeat of fascism, and the unification of Communists and Social Democrats into the Socialist Unity Party of Germany (April 1946). This act of workers' unification took place with the full support of Soviet Communists. *Pravda* stressed the fact that "the class-conscious workers of Germany took their lesson now from the fateful split in their ranks which made possible the rule of Nazism." Based on official publications and secondary sources. G. E. Pergl

1363. Behrendt, Albert. DER FDGB UND DIE VEREINIGUNG VON KPD UND SPD ZUR SED [The FDGB and the unification of the KPD in the SED]. *Zeitschrift für Geschichtswissenschaft [East Germany] 1976 24(10): 1131-1144.* The Free German League of Trade Unions (FDGB) was founded in 1945-46 with the support of the Soviet Military Administration (SMAD), as well as the Communist Party (KPD) and the Social Democratic Party (SPD). The first Congress of the FDGB, in February 1946, gave further impetus to the movement to unify the KPD and the SPD, a goal attained the following April, despite the opposition of reformists and right-wing Social Democrats. 48 notes. J. T. Walker

1364. Behrendt, Albert and Heitzer, Heinz et al. NEUE FORSCHUNGEN ÜBER DIE GESCHICHTE DER DEUTSCHEN DEMOKRATISCHEN REPUBLIK [New Research on the history of the German Democratic Republic]. *Jahrbuch für Geschichte [East Germany] 1969 4: 321-373.* Surveys current historiography from and on East Germany. Aspects covered include social, economic, cultural, and political history, with discussion of the historiography of the Socialist Unity Party (SED), as well as that of the minor parties. Emphasizes military developments. 161 notes. J. C. Billigmeier

1365. Behrendt, Albert. PROBLEME DER ARBEIT DES FREIEN DEUTSCHEN GEWERKSCHAFTSBUNDES BEIM ÜBERGANG ZUM PLANMÄSSIGEN AUFBAU DES SOZIALISMUS IN DER DDR [Problems in the work of the Confederation of Free German Trade Unions during the planned building of socialism in East Germany]. *Jahrbuch für Geschichte [East Germany] 1974 ll: 243-269.* The Free German Labor Union Federation played a key role in building socialism in East Germany. Not only did it represent the interests of industrial workers, but under the leadership of the Socialist Unity Party (SED), had to learn to run both the state and industry. It played an important role in the cultural and ideological development of the working class; it could truly be called a school for socialism. With the active participation of members of the Labor Federation, the power of workers and peasants in the German Democratic Republic was secured. Table, 56 notes. J. C. Billigmeier

1366. Beier, Günter. 25 JAHRE SOZIALISTISCHE EINHEITSPARTEI DEUTSCHLANDS: 25 JAHRE SOZIALISTISCHE MILITÄRPOLITIK [25 years of the Socialist Unity Party of Germany and 25 years of socialist military policy]. *Wissenschaftliche Zeitschrift der Wilhelm-Pieck-U. Rostock. Gesellschafts- und Sprachwissenschaftliche Reihe [East Germany] 1971 20(1-2): 53-59.* Analyzes the development of the East German army and military expenditure in the Cold War and détente periods.

1367. Benser, Günter. BÜRGERLICHE UND SOZIALDEMOKRATISCHE LITERATUR ÜBER DIE VEREINIGUNG VON KPD UND SPD ZU SED [Bourgeois and social democratic literature on the union of the Communist Party (KPD) and the Social Democratic Party (SPD) in the Socialist Unity Party of Germany]. *Zeitschrift für Geschichtswissenschaft [East Germany] 1976 24(4): 431-441.* The West German publications on the formation of the Socialist Unity Party of East Germany neglect the historical role of the working class and the necessity of its unity. Based on West German historical works and secondary literature; 40 notes. R. Wagnleitner

1368. Benser, Günter. DIE ANFÄNGE DER DEMOKRATISCHEN BLOCKPOLITIK. BILDUNG UND ERSTE AKTIVITÄTEN DES ZENTRALEN AUSSCHUSSES DER ANTIFASCHISTISCH-DEMOKRATISCHEN PARTEIEN [The political beginnings of the democratic bloc: the formation and initial activities of the central committee of the antifascist democratic parties]. *Zeitschrift für Geschichtswissenschaft [East Germany] 1975 23(7): 755-768.* In accord with the Popular Front policy of the seventh Congress of the Communist International in 1935, the Communist Party (KPD) of the Soviet Zone joined the Social Democratic Party (SPD), the Christian Democratic Union (CDU), and the Liberal Democratic Party (LDPD) to create a democratic order in Germany. In July 1945 these parties formed a central committee to undertake multiple tasks, including the gathering of the harvest, the punishment of Nazi leaders, and the implementation of the Potsdam Declaration. 63 notes. J. T. Walker

1369. Benser, Günter; Hortzschansky, Günter; and Mammach, Klaus. DIE GROSSE SOZIALISTISCHE OKTOBERREVOLUTION UND DIE ANWENDUNG IHRER LEHREN FÜR DEN WEG ZUM SOZIALISMUS IN DER DDR [The great socialist October Revolution and the application of its lessons to the path toward socialism in the German Democratic Republic]. *Zeitschrift für Geschichtswissenschaft [East Germany] 1967 15(6): 966-996.* Describes the founding of the Socialist Unity Party of Germany (SED) after World War II, and the application of the lessons of the Russian Revolution to the conditions prevailing in Germany in 1945. The SED represented a new type of party which called for a unitary, peaceful, anti-Fascist, democratic German republic in 1945. The SED in 1945 set the stage for the later change from a democratic to a socialist revolution in East Germany. Based on Lenin's writings, published documentary collections of the SED, and secondary works; 104 notes. J. B. Street

1370. Benser, Gűnter. DIE REVOLUTIONÄRE EINHEITSPARTEI DER ARBEITERKLASSE UND DIE POLITISCHE MACHT [The revolutionary unity party of the working class and the political power]. *Beiträge zur Geschichte der Arbeiterbewegung [East Germany] 1979 21(5): 663-667.* The cooperation of German Communist and Socialist trade unionists and political functionaries immediately after the liberation from Nazi dictatorship in 1945 was based on the common struggle against Nazism since 1933. The radical antifascist democratic transformation of the Soviet occupation zone and the founding of East Germany in 1949 were only achieved because of the cooperation of these two groups. Based on published documents and secondary literature; 11 notes. R. Wagnleitner

1371. Benser, Günter. POWSTANIE SOCJALISTYCZNEJ PARTII JEDNOŚCI NIEMIEC (SED) [The formation of the Socialist Unity Party of Germany (SED)]. *Z Pola Walki [Poland] 1971 14(2): 75-89.* Describes the formation of the SED from the fusion of the German Communist Party (KPD) and the German Social Democratic Party (SPD) at the Congress in Berlin on 22 April 1946 and claims that the decision was not imposed but freely arrived at.

1372. Benser, Günter. SED UND SOZIALISTISCHE STAATSMACHT: IHRE ROLLE UND IHRE WECHSELWIRKUNG BEI DER ERRICHTUNG DER GRUNDLAGEN DES SOZIALISMUS IN DER DDR [The Socialist Unity Party and the power of the socialist state: its role and mutual effect on the establishment of the basis of socialism in the German Democratic Republic]. *Zeits. für Geschichtswissenschaft [East Germany] 1982 30(10-11): 869-883.* Examines the establishment of the basic principles of socialism in the German Democratic Republic, particularly the role and responsibility of the Marxist-Leninist party within the state and the inner functions of state socialism. Considers: the development, function and role of the Socialist Unity Party (SED); the establishment of a developed socialist society with reference to institutions and traditions; the essential characteristics of the political system; the foundation of the state as the result of class struggle; the role and importance of the SED in all spheres of social life; and the establishment of the political and economic socialist system in East Germany during this period. Based on SED documents in Berlin and secondary sources; 17 notes. G. L. Neville

1373. Benser, Günter; Fiedler, Helene; and Krusch, Hans-Joachim. ZUR HISTORISCHEN BEDEUTUNG DER VEREINIGUNG VON KPD UND SPD ZUR SOZIALISTISCHEN EINHEITSPARTEI DEUTSCHLANDS [The historical importance of the

union of the German Communist Party and the German Social Democrats into the Socialist Unity Party of Germany]. *Beiträge zur Geschichte der Arbeiterbewegung [East Germany] 1976 18(2): 195-214.* East German Communists and Social Democrats negotiated a treaty of action in June 1945, and at the conference of 20-21 December 1945 they prepared for the union of their parties. Unification of the parties in April 1946 was the basis for the creation of East Germany's revolutionary party organization. Based on published documents and secondary literature; 41 notes.
R. Wagnleitner

1374. Bensing, Manfred and Heilhecker, Elly. DIE ARBEITERKLASSE DER DDR AN DER SCHWELLE DER ENTWICKELTEN SOZIALISTISCHEN GESELLSCHAFT. PROBLEME IHRES WACHSTUMS IN DER JAHREN 1961/1962 [The working class of the German Democratic Republic on the threshhold of a developed socialist society: problems of growth, 1961-62]. *Jahrbuch für Geschichte [East Germany] 1972 6: 397-416.* The triumph of socialist production in East Germany was proof that the working class there was capable, under the leadership of the Socialist Unity Party (SED), to overcome capitalism. The working class grew in numbers during these two years; this was a sign of progress, for the working class gives the socialist order of society its political and moral quality. With the growth of East Germany's working class, the historical advantage of socialism as the most progressive form of social organization became increasingly clear. 39 notes.
J. C. Billigmeier

1375. Bensing, Manfred and Keller, Dietmar. DIE ENTFALTUNG DES HISTORISCHEN, SCHÖPFERTUMS DER ARBEITERKLASSE IN DER DDR—DIE VERWIRKLICHUNG DER LENINSCHEN ERKENNTNISSE VON DER GESCHICHTLICHEN MISSION DES PROLETARIATS [The development of the historical creativity of the working class in East Germany: the realization of Leninist perceptions on the historical mission of the proletariat]. *Jahrbuch für Geschichte [East Germany] 1970 5: 263-301.* The working class of East Germany has, in two revolutions and in the building of socialism, demonstrated the universal applicability of Lenin's theory of revolution and socialist development. The working class and its political party have mastered the complicated problems of an industrial scientific-technological society, showing the creativity of the emancipated working class, as posited by Lenin. Based on Lenin's writings, published statistics, published documents of the Socialist Unity Party of East Germany, and secondary works; 107 notes. J. B. Street

1376. Berg, Lene. ZUM KAMPF UM DIE VERWIRKLICHUNG DER LINIE DER MOSKAUER BERATUNG VOM JUNI 1969 UND ZUR INTERNATIONALEN TÄTIGKEIT DER SED [The fight for the realization of the line of the Moscow conference of June 1969 and the international activities of the Socialist Unity Party of Germany]. *Beiträge zur Geschichte der Arbeiterbewegung [East Germany] 1972 14(4): 531-547.* The success of the policy of the world conference of Communist Parties is inseparably connected with the realization of the decisions of national party conferences, especially the 24th conference of the CPSU. The following will have a prominent place in the research of the social scientists of East Germany: 1) the new phase of development of the socialist community of states and the activities of the Socialist Unity Party of Germany, 2) problems of the struggle against imperialism, 3) problems of the strengthening of the Communist world movement. Report at the founding meeting of the Commission of Scientists of the USSR and the GDR for Research in the History and Theory of the International Workers' Movement; 9 notes.
R. Wagnleitner

1377. Berthold, Rudolf and Hombach, Wilfried. 25 JAHRE SOZIALISTISCHE EINHEITSPARTEI DEUTSCHLANDS: 25 JAHRE MARXISTISCH-LENINISTISCHE AGRARPOLITIK [25 years of the Socialist Unity Party of Germany and 25 years of Marxist-Leninist agrarian policies]. *Wissenschaftliche Zeitschrift der Wilhelm-Pieck-U. Rostock. Gesellschafts- und Sprachwissenschaftliche Reihe [East Germany] 1971 20(1-2): 29-37.* Analyzes the land reforms in East Germany after World War II and the socialization of East German agriculture in the 1950's and 1960's. 27 notes.

1378. Bock, Helmut and Kintscher, Harald. ANTIIMPERIALISTISCHE DEMOKRATIE UND KULTURENTWICKLUNG IN DER SOWJETISCHEN BESATZUNGSZONE DEUTSCHLANDS 1945/1946 [Anti-imperialist democracy and cultural development in the Soviet occupation zone of Germany, 1945-46]. *Jahrbuch für Wolkskunde und Kulturgeschichte [East Germany] 1975 18: 9-50.* After World War II, the German proletariat, protected and encouraged by Soviet occupation troops, began the task not only of rebuilding cities and factories, but also of renewing German culture, corrupted by 12 years of Nazi racism and anti-Communism. The formation of the Socialist Unity Party (SED) was a crucial step in safeguarding and promoting these gains made by the working people of East Germany. 162 notes.
J. C. Billigmeier

1379. Bogisch, Manfred. DER BEITRAG DER LDPD ZUM AUFBAU DES SOZIALISMUS IN DER DDR [The contribution of the Liberal Democratic Party of Germany to the building of socialism in East Germany]. *Zeitschrift für Geschichtswissenschaft [East Germany] 1979 27(12): 1126-1128.* The imperialist elements among the Liberal Democrats were not able to turn the party against the Socialist Unity Party (SED) of Germany in 1948, when the socialist majority mobilized craftsmen and other workmen for socialist construction, lasting friendship with the USSR, and cooperation with the SED. Modern Liberal Democrats are the co-builders of socialist East Germany. G. E. Pergl

1380. Bogisch, Manfred. DIE LDPD UND DIE GRÜNDUNG DER DDR. ZUM PROBLEM DER KONTINUITÄT DES PARTEIENBÜNDNISSES IN DER DDR UNTER FÜHRUNG DER PARTEI DER ARBEITERKLASSE [The LDPD and the foundation of the GDR. The problem of the continuity of the alliance of parties in GDR under the leadership of the party of the working class]. *Jahrbuch für Geschichte [East Germany] 1974 12: 183-204.* The positions taken by the Liberal Democratic Party of Germany (LDPD) and by most of its members during the period of the formation of the German Democratic Republic (GDR) show that the LDPD had overcome numerous prejudices against the working class and its party, the Socialist Unity Party (SED). The Liberals conceived of the founding of the GDR as a patriotic act whose legitimacy sprang from the right of self-determination, the obligations of the Potsdam Agreements, and the continuation of the party alliance system under leadership of the SED. 85 notes.
J. C. Billigmeier

1381. Bogisch, Manfred. DIE LDPD UND DIE REVOLUTION VON 1848/49. ZUR ENTWICKLUNG DES TRADITIONS-VERSTÄNDNISSES IN DER LDPD 1945 BIS 1948 [The Liberal Democratic Party (LDPD) and the Revolution of 1848-49: the development of the understanding of the tradition in the LDPD, 1945-48]. *Jahrbuch für Geschichte [East Germany] 1973 8: 353-377.* The Liberal Democratic Party of Germany was formed after World War II in the Soviet occupation zone as a successor to various middle-class liberal parties of the Weimar Republic and as a counterpart to the Free Democrats of West Germany. At first its ideology was traditionally liberal in the European sense; it stood for free enterprise and a limited role for government. But as its members realized that the working class and the Socialist Unity Party (SED) were the dominant force in East Germany's political life, the LDPD adjusted its platform to the new realities, calling for nationalization of some industries, and for a third way between capitalism and socialism. Later, the LDPD saw that this was impossible, and embraced socialism wholeheartedly, guided by the traditions of 1848. 96 notes. J. C. Billigmeier

1382. Böhme, Walter and Griese, Rosemarie. DIE ENTWICKLUNG DER BETRIEBSGRUPPEN DER SED IN SACHSEN 1946-1950 [The development of the shop groups of the Socialist Unity Party of Germany in Saxony, 1946-50]. *Zeitschrift für Geschichtswissenschaft [East Germany] 1973 21(12): 1489-1503.* The establishment of shop groups in Saxony between 1946-50 was the fundamental strategy of the Socialist Unity Party (SED) to transform society into a Marxist-Leninist state. These groups became the

organizational basis to activate the East German working class. Based on documents in the Bezirksparteiarchiv, Dresden, printed documents and secondary literature; 55 notes.
R. Wagnleitner

1383. Bouvier, Beatrix W. ANTIFASCHISTISCHE ZUSAMMENARBEIT, SELBSTÄNDIGKEITSANSPRUCH UND VEREINIGUNGSTENDENZ. DIE ROLLE DER SOZIALDEMOKRATIE BEIM ADMINISTRATIVEN UND PARTEIPOLITISCHEN AUFBAU IN DER SOWJETISCHEN BESATZUNGSZONE 1945 AUF REGIONALER UND LOKALER EBENE [Antifascist cooperation, claim to independence and unifying tendency: the role of Social Democracy in the administrative and party-political reconstruction on regional and local levels in the Soviet occupation zone in 1945]. *Archiv für Sozialgeschichte [West Germany] 1976 16: 417-468.* Describes the political activities of the Social Democrats in the first months after the Soviet occupation and compares them with Communist activities at regional and local levels. Local "Antifas"—antifascist committees, born of the whole labor movement—dominated early activities. After political parties were allowed, the Social Democratic Party (SPD) followed the German Communist Party (KPD) in the reconstruction of an independent party. The SPD resorted to Weimar traditions and officials, but were often open to a unified labor movement too. After the KPD's apparatus had grown strong and the SPD's membership had surpassed the KPD's, the KPD took the initiative toward unification. Based on unpublished sources, and primary and secondary works; 291 notes. H. W. Wurster

1384. Bowers, Stephen R. CONTRAST AND CONTINUITY: HONECKER'S POLICY TOWARD THE FEDERAL REPUBLIC AND WEST BERLIN. *World Affairs 1976 138(4): 309-335.* Discusses the foreign policy of the First Secretary of East Germany's Socialist Unity Party, Erich Honecker, and his negotiations with West Germany, 1971-75, including the influence of the USSR.

1385. Bowers, Stephen R. EAST GERMAN NATIONAL CONSCIOUSNESS: DOMESTIC AND FOREIGN POLICY CONSIDERATIONS. *East European Q. 1979 13(2): 145-182.* Discusses the efforts of the East German Socialist Unity Party (SED) to develop a sense of nationhood. This is necessary because the party leadership has accepted the fact that German reunification is unlikely. The presence of tension is still necessary to create a strong national identity in East Germany, and this tension will continue to be directed against West Germany. Based primarily on current East German newspapers and journals; 132 notes. C. R. Lovin

1386. Bowers, Stephen R. LAW AND LAWLESSNESS IN A SOCIALIST SOCIETY: THE POTENTIAL IMPACT OF CRIME IN EAST GERMANY. *World Affairs 1982 145(2): 152-176.* Discusses the form and causes of crime in East Germany from 1950 to 1978, the special threat of crime in a socialist society, and the efforts of the Socialist Unity Party to contain crime through ideological education and adjustments of the legal system.

1387. Brühl, Reinhard. ZUR MILITÄRGESCHICHTSWISSENSCHAFTLICHEN ARBEIT IN DER NATIONALEN VOLKSARMEE [On military history in the National People's Army]. *Zeitschrift für Geschichtswissenschaft [East Germany] 1977 25(8): 942-945.* Military historians play an important role in the German Democratic Republic in educating the soldiers of the National People's Army, thereby increasing its strength and readiness. Since the Eighth Party Congress of the Socialist Unity Party, military historians have intensified their efforts to investigate the class struggle in its revolutionary context. Discusses the research interests and methodological concerns of military historians, such as the need to present both facts and historical-materialist generalizations. J. T. Walker

1388. Burtsev, M. UCHASTIE GERMANSKIKH ANTIFASHISTOV V IDEOLOGICHESKOI BOR'BE SOVETSKOI ARMII PROTIV GITLEROVSKIKH ZAKHVATCHIKOV [The participation of German Anti-Fascists in the Soviet Red Army's ideological struggle against the Hitlerite aggressors]. *Voenno-Istoricheskii Zhurnal [USSR] 1969 11(10): 41-49.* Describes the cooperation of the German Communist Party with the USSR prior to the establishment of the German Democratic Republic.

1389. Carr, G. A. THE BIRTH OF THE GERMAN DEMOCRATIC REPUBLIC AND THE ORGANIZATION OF EAST GERMAN SPORT. *Can. J. of Hist. of Sport and Physical Educ. [Canada] 1976 7(1): 1-21.* Discusses athletics and sports organizations sponsored by the Socialist Unity Party in East Germany, 1945-70's.

1390. Childs, David. EAST GERMAN FOREIGN POLICY: THE SEARCH FOR RECOGNITION AND STABILITY. *Int. J. [Canada] 1977 32(2): 334-351.* Reviews developments in East German politics, its foreign policy initiatives, and its recent relations with West Germany. Notes that under Erich Honecker, first secretary of the ruling Socialist Unity Party (SED), its foreign policy has become even more closely tied to that of the USSR. 33 notes.
R. V. Kubicek

1391. Croan, Melvin. REGIME, SOCIETY, AND NATION: THE GDR AFTER THIRTY YEARS. *East Central Europe 1979 6(2): 137-151.* Describes the impact of West Germany on the people of East Germany in the 1970's through visits, telephone calls, television, and the like. The Communist regime has been forced by this impact to resort to "consumeristic authoritarianism"—meaning that the regime, aware of its precarious hold on power, seeks to maintain the utmost discipline and control, but it also seeks to gain acceptance by satisfying consumers' demands for goods and services. Given the ease with which West German culture makes a strong impact, relations between the Communist regime and the increasingly self-assertive East German society are destined to be strained. The GDR's problems are thus likely to remain "intractable." 39 notes. R. V. Layton

1392. Deutschland, Heinz; Polzin, Hans; and Thoms, Günter. GEWERKSCHAFTER FORDERN: "SCHAFFT DIE EINHEITSPARTEI!" [Trade unionists demand: "Create the United Party!"]. *Beiträge zur Geschichte der Arbeiterbewegung [East Germany] 1981 23(2): 255-264.* Letters and resolutions submitted by various trade unions from different parts of the Soviet occupied zone in support of the Socialist Unity Party (SED). Based on several trade union archives; 27 notes. A. Schuetz

1393. Devulder, Catherine. L'HISTOIRE EN RÉPUBLIQUE DÉMOCRATIQUE ALLEMANDE [History in East Germany]. *Rev. d'Allemagne [France] 1979 11(4): 597-604.* According to the directives of the Socialist Unity Party (SED), historiography's responsibilities are to promote the development of a socialist awareness in the population, especially in the youth, to justify the continuity and legitimacy of the SED, and to base history upon the ideology of the SED. As the prime social science, history must be subordinated to philosophy. Historical periodization must be controlled by social and economic criteria. The integrating principle of history is the dialectic of world social progress. 18 notes.
J. S. Gassner

1394. Dick, Wolfgang and Golub, Arno. AUFGABEN AUF DEM GEBIET DER GESCHICHTE DER ÖRTLICHEN ARBEITERBEWEGUNG UND BETRIEBSGESCHICHTE IN VORBEREITUNG DES X. PARTEITAGES DER SED [Studies in the field of the history of the local working-class movement and industrial history in preparation for the 10th SED Party conference]. *Beiträge zur Gesch. der Arbeiterbewegung [East Germany] 1980 22(5): 746-750.* Examines the 10th SED Party conference, held in February 1980 in Berlin, whose theme was the history of the local working-class movement and industrial history. The following points were considered: the political and ideological function of this field of history since 1945; the study of regional history, German history, the world revolutionary process, and the worldwide class struggle; the link between research and propaganda; the use of this field of history to unmask the reactionary and aggressive existence of imperialism; the history of the Leuna works before 1945 and an examination of class struggle; the relationship between economic and social policies in industrial history; and the management and leadership of industry. 3 notes. G. L. Neville

1395. Diehl, Ernst. ALS DIE GRUNDMAUERN DES BUNDES VON KPDSU UND SED ENTSTANDEN [The foundations of the alliance between the CPSU and SED]. *Beitraäge zur Geschichte der Arbeiterbewegung [East Germany] 1971 13(5): 707-717.* The union of the German Communist Party and the Social Democratic Party in the Soviet zone after 1945 was the foundation of the victory of the working class in the German Democratic Republic. Russian Communist activists who served in the Red Army were a great asset in the fight against reaction. In contrast to the anti-Soviet policy of the right-wing Social Democratic group of Kurt Schumacher in the Western zones, the Socialist Unity Party declared its solidarity with the Soviet Union. Based on published documents and secondary material; 11 notes. R. Wagnleitner

1396. Diehl, Ernst; Wimmer, Walter; and Zimmermann, Fritz. ERFAHRUNGEN UND ERFORDERNISSE. ZUR ARBEIT DER PARTEIHISTORIKER BEI DER DURCHFÜHRUNG DER BESCHLÜSSE DES VIII. PARTEITAGES DER SED [Experiences and requirements: the work of the Party historians in the realization of the decision of the eighth congress of the Socialist Unity Party]. *Beiträge zur Geschichte der Arbeiterbewegung [East Germany] 1972 14(3): 355-370.* The historian has to improve the theoretical level and scientific value of his work. The work of the historian must be popularized and used to combat bourgeois historiography, anti-communism and social democracy in order to prove the scientific basis of Marxism-Leninism. It was decided at the eighth congress of the Socialist Unity Party that the social sciences, including history, are of great theoretical and practical importance for the development of socialism in East Germany. Based on published documents and secondary material; 27 notes. R. Wagnleitner

1397. Dietrich, Gerd. DIE INTERNATIONALISTISCHE ARBEIT DER SED 1947 [The internationalist work of the Socialist Unity Party of Germany 1947]. *Zeitschrift für Geschichtswissenschaft [East Germany] 1976 24(4): 415-430.* The basis for the internationalist work of the Socialist Unity Party of East Germany was the development of close relations with the Soviet Communist Party. In various conferences in 1947 the party documented that it had developed a new concept of international cooperation. Based on printed documents and secondary literature; 84 notes. R. Wagnleitner

1398. Dietrich, Gerd. ZUR INTERNATIONALISTISCHEN ARBEIT DER SED 1948-49 [Internationalist activities of the Socialist Unity Party (SED), 1948-49]. *Zeitschrift für Geschichtswissenschaft [East Germany] 1979 27(9): 820-834.* The Socialist Unity Party (SED) promoted international solidarity, which enabled it to benefit from the experience of other Communist parties, especially from that of the USSR, and to facilitate the international recognition of the SED. To this end, the party sent delegations to Communist countries, promoted the study of the history of the Soviet Communist Party, published information about other Communist countries, and received visits from foreign Communist leaders. 75 notes. J. T. Walker

1399. Dietrich, Gerd. ZUR PROPAGIERUNG VON ERFAHRUNGEN DER VOLKSDEMOKRATISCHEN LÄNDER IN DER SOZIALISTICHEN PRESSE DER SOWJETISCHEN BESATZUNGSZONE DEUTSCHLANDS (SEPTEMBER 1947 BIS SEPTEMBER 1949) [On the propagation of experiences of the people's democratic countries in the socialist press of the Soviet Occupation Zone of Germany, September 1947-September 1949]. *Beiträge zur Geschichte der Arbeiterbewegung [East Germany] 1974 16(Supplement): 137-154.* From 1947 to 1949 the press effectively spread the message of the Socialist Unity Party of Germany throughout the Soviet Occupation Zone. The Soviet victory over fascist-imperialistic Germany marked a new step in the revolutionary world process; Eastern European countries appeared ready to discard the old state system and establish workers' governments. It was clear during these years that two opposing international camps had been established. East Germany's Socialist Unity Party led in establishing a consolidated workers' democracy. Primary and secondary materials; 68 notes. G. H. Libbey

1400. Dillwitz, Sigrid. DIE ENTWICKLUNG DER ARBEITSRECHTS FÜR JUGENDLICHE LANDARBEITER IM GEBIET DER HEUTIGEN DDR 1945 BIS 1949 [The development of the employment code for young agricultural laborers in East Germany, 1945-49]. *Jahrbuch für Wirtschaftsgeschichte [East Germany] 1972 (1): 41-64.* Land reform and increasing agricultural output received primary emphasis after 1945 in the countryside of the Soviet zone. However, under the leadership of the Socialist Unity Party, a campaign was instituted to raise the condition of agricultural workers to the level of industrial workers and provide adequate protection for young agricultural workers. This culminated in the law of December 1949, which was the last to specifically regulate employment conditions in agriculture. Primary sources; 82 notes. J. A. Perkins

1401. Dillwitz, Sigrid. ZWEITE ROSTOCKER HISTORIKERWOCHE [The Second Historians Week at Rostock]. *Zeitschrift für Geschichtswissenschaft [East Germany] 1971 19(1): 101-104.* Reviews the lectures and discussions of the Second Historians Week at the University of Rostock in May 1970, which analyzed the development of the German working classes and the Communist Party in the 19th and 20th centuries.

1402. Dittrich, Gottfried. DIE II. PARTEIKONFERENZ DER SED UND DER ÜBERGANG ZU HÖHEREN FORMEN DER WIRTSCHAFTSLEITUNG UND DES WETTBEWERBS IM JAHRE 1952 [The Second Party Conference of the Socialist Unity Party (SED) and the transition to higher forms of economic planning and competition during 1952]. *Jahrbuch für Geschichte [East Germany] 1973 9: 439-466.* The Second Party Conference of the Socialist Unity Party (SED) in 1952 determined to take up the task of building socialism in the German Democratic Republic, and to do this in a well-planned and systematic way. This meant, among other things, accelerated industrialization on socialist lines. New socially owned industries were to be started and would compete with capitalistic ones, which would not be nationalized. During the rest of the year, East German workers achieved the goals of the Five-Year Plan, and more than met their quotas, in many cases, as they set themselves to the task of reaching the industrial goals and thus contributing to building socialism in East Germay. 100 notes. J. C. Billigmeier

1403. Dittrich, Gottfried. DIE SED UND DIE AKTIVISTEN- UND WETTBEWERBSBEWEGUNG IN DEN JAHREN 1948 BIS 1950 [The Socialist Unity Party (SED) and the activists' and competition movement during 1948-50]. *Jahrbuch für Geschichte [East Germany] 1972 6: 343-369.* In the aftermath of World War II, the East German masses experienced hunger and want. The way out was higher production. A small group of activist workers committed themselves to work harder, to a socialist competition to see who could produce the most. The result was that increased production led to better living standards for the people of the German Democratic Republic. The period 1948-50 represents the breakthrough years, in which, due to the heroic labors of relatively few men and women, the shortages of the postwar era were overcome. 115 notes. J. C. Billigmeier

1404. Dittrich, Gottfried. ZU DEN REPRODUKTIONSQUELLEN UND EINIGEN VERÄNDERUNGEN IN DER SOZIALEN STRUKTUR DER ARBEITERKLASSE DER DDR WÄHREND DER ÜBERGANGSPERIODE VOM KAPITALISMUS ZUM SOZIALISMUS (1945 BIS 1961) [Sources of reproduction and certain changes in the social structure of the working class of the German Democratic Republic during the period of transition from capitalism to socialism, 1945-61]. *Jahrbuch für Wirtschaftsgeschichte [East Germany] 1981 (2): 243-279.* Unlike most of the other people's democracies, the German Democratic Republic was a complex industrial society before the transition to socialism. The working class was broad-based, but without solidarity. Led by the Socialist Unity Party, the workers' government socialized the major sectors of the economy, extending and strengthening the structure and consciousness of the working class. The process is not total; some private enterprises remain. However, they are also run by workers and support mutual development goals. Based on government statistics and reports, Party protocols, and Soviet and German secondary sources; 116 notes, 7 tables. E. L. Turk

1405. Dlubek, Rolf and Steinke, Monika. ZUR ROLLE DES THEORETISCHEN ERBES VON MARX UND ENGLES IM RINGEN UM DIE SOZIALISTISCHE EINHEITSPARTEI DEUTSCHLANDS [The role of the theoretical heritage of Marx and Engels in the struggle for the Socialist Unity Party of Germany]. *Beiträge zur Geschichte der Arbeiterbewegung [East Germany] 1971 13(6): 883-910.* The heritage of Karl Marx and Friedrich Engels served as a theoretical basis for the unification of the workers' movement in East Germany. It was the task of the ideological clearing process to keep Marxism free from falsifications, to spread Marxism to the working class, especially to youth, and to base the struggle against fascism and militarism on Marxism. One of the most important educational programs was the publication of the theoretical works of Marxism-Leninism to secure far-reaching distribution of Marxist doctrines. Based on documents in the Institute for Marxism-Leninism, Archiv des Dietz Verlags, published documents, newspapers, and secondary literature; 84 notes. R. Wagnleitner

1406. Doernberg, Stefan and Schirmeister, Helga. 25 JAHRE SED—25 JAHRE KAMPF FÜR FRIEDEN UND SICHERHEIT IN EUROPA [25 years of SED: 25 years of struggle for peace and security in Europe]. *Dokumentation der Zeit [East Germany] 1971 (9): 3-12.* Reviews the 25 year history of the East German Socialist Unity Party (SED), which was instituted 21 April 1946. Describes the struggle for peace in Europe after 1945 and since 1955 and the background of different party congresses. The SED developed a clear conception of a socialist state of Germans in Europe. 13 notes. G. E. Pergl

1407. Drewes, Uwe. AKTIVITÄTEN DER ARBEITERJUGEND: AUSDRUCK DER JUGENDPOLITIK DER SED (1971 BIS 1976) [Activities of the workers' youth: an expression of the youth policies of the Socialist Unity Party of Germany, 1971-76]. *Beiträge zur Gesch. der Arbeiterbewegung [East Germany] 1981 23(1): 18-28.* Includes extensive statistics on the East German youth movement, its importance within the state and the party, and the contributions of the Free German Youth (FDJ) and other youth organizations to the state's economy. Based on statistical yearbooks, archival material, and other sources; 65 notes. A. Schuetz

1408. Drewes, Uwe. KOMMUNISTISCHE ERZIEHUNG ALS GRUNDLINIE DER JUGENDPOLITIK DER SED NACH DEM VIII. PARTEITAG [Communist education as the basis of the youth policy of the Socialist Unity Party after the 8th party congress]. *Wiss. Zeits. der Wilhelm-Pieck-Universität Rostock. Gesellschafts- und Sprachwissenschaftliche Reihe [East Germany] 1981 30(1): 75-78.*

1409. Drewes, Uwe. ZU EINIGEN ASPEKTEN DER ROLLE DER FDJ BEI DER VERWIRKLICHUNG DER AGRARPOLITISCHEN KONZEPTION DES VIII. PARTEITAGES DER SED (1971-1976) [Aspects of the role of Free German Youth in implementing the agricultural policy of the 8th Congress of the Socialist Unity Party of Germany, 1971-76]. *Wissenschaftliche Zeitschrift der Wilhelm-Pieck-Universität Rostock. Gesellschaftswissenschaftliche Reihe [East Germany] 1982 31(1-2): 35-40.* Labor and other contributions by the official Communist youth organization of East Germany helped rural areas of the country achieve Party goals in agricultural production.

1410. Dreyfus, François-Georges and Losser, Alphonse. LA SITUATION POLITIQUE DE LA REPUBLIQUE DEMOCRATIQUE ALLEMANDE AU DEBUT DES ANNEES 1980 [The political situation in the German Democratic Republic at the beginning of the 1980's]. *Revue d'Allemagne [France] 1984 16(1): 2-19.* The policies of East Germany (GDR) are evolving in reaction to world economic and political conditions. In the area of domestic policies, the two major trends are: the promotion of the stability, continuity, and authority of the SED (Socialist Unity Party); and the increasing militarization of society. Opposing the latter is a growing peace movement supported by both the Evangelical and the Catholic Churches as well as by young people who condemn both American and Soviet nuclear arms expansion. As a result, relations between the government and the churches have become difficult. In regard to foreign policy, the cardinal feature is loyalty to the USSR. The GDR supported the hard-liners in Poland but closer relations are developing between the GDR and West Germany. The GDR is cultivating certain socialist states of the Third World through increased trade, military aid, and cultural exchanges. Table, 11 notes. J. S. Gassner

1411. Ebert, Friedrich. SO THAT WAR SHALL NEVER AGAIN START FROM GERMAN SOIL. *World Marxist R. [Canada] 1975 18(4): 4-12.* Discusses the development of the Socialist Unity Party in East Germany, 1945-75.

1412. Effenberger, Willi. DIE WEITERENICKLUNG DER SOZIALISTISCHEN WEHRERZIEHUNG IN DER DDR IN DER ZWEITEN HÄLFTE DER SECHZIGER JAHRE [The further development of socialist defense education in East Germany, 1965-70]. *Militärgeschichte [East Germany] 1978 17(6): 645-655.* Under the leadership of the Socialist Unity Party and with the active cooperation of different social forces, the system of socialist defense education shaped itself more and more in this period. The author shows the increased demands and how, corresponding to the new directions, the tasks were fulfilled. Soviet experiences were applied creatively and the defense policy initiatives of the masses were a helpful influence on the process of defense education. 2 illus., 23 notes. H. D. Andrews

1413. Effenberger, Willi. DIE ENTWICKLUNG DER SOZIALISTISCHEN WEHRERZIEHUNG IN DER DDR ZU BEGINN DER SECHZIGER JAHRE [The development of Socialist defense education in the German Democratic Republic at the beginning of the 1960's]. *Militärgeschichte [East Germany] 1978 17(5): 553-563.* Shows how the policy of the Socialist Unity Party on this topic helped to advance the defensive ability of socialism. The especially tense international situation in the summer of 1961 and the revolution in military organization were part of the complicated conditions which socialist defense education had to take into account in the comprehensive construction of socialism. The efforts undertaken under the Free German Youth motto "The Fatherland calls! Defend the Socialist Republic," in the Society for Sports and Technology, as well as in the introduction of the new defense law, drew in the different social forces in ever stronger measure. 4 illus., 22 notes. J/T (H. D. Andrews)

1414. Eichhofer, Sonja. DAS KARL-MARX-JAHR 1953—EIN HÖHEPUNKT DER REVOLUTION AUF DEM GEBIET DER IDEOLOGIE UND KULTUR IN DER ERSTEN HÄLFTE DER FÜNFZIGER JAHRE [The 1953 Karl Marx Year: a climax to the revolution in ideology and culture in the early 1950's]. *Beiträge zur Gesch. der Arbeiterbewegung [East Germany] 1983 25(2): 187-199.* The Socialist Unity Party in Germany had three main aims for the Karl Marx celebrations in 1953: to honor the historic occasion by taking decisive measures; to make full use of recent historic experiences to make theoretical generalizations concerning these experiences; and to mobilize the Party and the working class to secure peace, social progress and a socialist society. With the establishment of the German Democratic Republic and the beginning of the first Five-Year Plan, the antifascist democratic transformation of society had succeeded. Based on Party documents in Berlin and secondary sources; 66 notes. G. L. Neville

1415. Eichhofer, Sonja and Möschner, Günter. DER KAMPF DER SED UM DIE VERBREITUNG DES MARXISMUS-LENINISMUS IN DER DDR 1950 BIS 1954/1955 [The struggle of the Socialist Unity Party of Germany for the spread of Marxism-Leninism in East Germany, 1950-55]. *Beiträge zur Geschichte der Arbeiterbewegung [East Germany] 1976 18(5): 826-842.* Reviews the propaganda strategy of the Socialist Unity Party of Germany to spread Marxist-Leninist ideology, 1950-55. Based on printed documents and secondary literature; 58 notes. R. Wagnleitner

1416. Eichhofer, Sonja. DER 8. MAI 1945 UND DIE GEISTIGE BEWÄLTIGUNG DER IMPERIALISTISCHEN VERGANGENHEIT [8 May 1945 and the intellectual comprehension of the imperialist past]. *Zeitschrift für Geschichtswissenschaft [East Germany] 1970 18(4): 480-496.* Although there were no major differences between the Communists and Social Democrats in East Germany on the responsibility of German imperialism and militarism for World War II, the ideological development of the East German Social Democrats initiated a new understanding of the socioeconomic background to German fascism; one of the most important and difficult tasks of the Communist Party was educating the German people about their responsibility for the war. Based on secondary literature and printed documents; 52 notes.

1417. Eichhofer, Sonja. DIE IDEOLOGISCHE OFFENSIVE DER SED IM KARL-MARX-JAHR 1953 [The ideological offensive of the German Socialist Unity Party in the Karl Marx Year, 1953]. *Beiträge zur Geschichte der Arbeiterbewegung [East Germany] 1972 15(2): 262-282.* The year 1953, the 70th anniversary of Karl Marx's death and the 135th anniversary of his birth, was the occasion for the Socialist Unity Party of Germany to solidify its position of Marxist theory in East Germany. To this end, it sponsored educational programs in the districts, factories, and various institutions, including exhibitions, lectures, and seminars. Based on documents in the Bezirksparteiarchiv Karl-Marx-Stadt, Bezirksparteiarchiv Gera, the Institute for Marxism-Leninism, published documents, newspapers, and secondary sources; 82 notes. R. Wagnleitner

1418. Fabritzek, Uwe G. DIE SED ZWISCHEN MOSKAU UND PEKING [The Socialist Unity Party (SED) between Moscow and Peking]. *Osteuropa [West Germany] 1973 23(3): 185-192.* Reviews the fluctuations in the attitude of East Germany's Communist leaders to the People's Republic of China, primarily in the years 1964-72. Although closely dependent on Moscow in their rejection of the Chinese Communist Party line, the East Germans are susceptible to recent Chinese sponsorship of the "interests of the German people" and seem reluctant to attack Peking severely. 40 notes.
R. E. Weltsch

1419. Fahlbusch, Lutz. ZU EINIGEN PROBLEMEN DER AUSARBEITUNG EINER WISSENSCHAFTLICH FUNDIERTEN STRATEGIE UND TAKTIK DER KPD ZUR HERSTELLUNG DES BÜNDNISSES ZWISCHEN ARBEITERKLASSE UND WERKTÄTIGER BAUERNSCHAFT [The formulation of the scientific strategy and tactics of the German Communist Party for the creation of an alliance between the working class and peasants]. *Wissenschaftliche Zeitschrift der Friedrich-Schiller-Universität Jena. Gesellschafts- und Sprachwissenschaftliche Reihe [East Germany] 1976 25(4-5): 585-588.* After 1945 the German Communist Party in the Soviet Zone applied its experience in the Weimar Republic in tactics toward the rural population, especially those of the peasants aid program of 1931, to be able to create a united political platform of workers and peasants. R. Wagnleitner

1420. Falk, Waltraud. DER BEGINN DES PLANMÄSSIGEN AUFBAUS DES SOZIALISMUS IN DER DDR—BESTANDTEIL DES REVOLUTIONÄREN WELTPROZESSES. PROBLEME DER WERTUNG DER HISTORISCHEN UMWÄLZUNGEN IN DER DDR [The beginning of the planned construction of socialism in the GDR—part of the world revolutionary process: problems in connection with the evaluation of the historic changes in the GDR]. *Beiträge zur Geschichte der Arbeiterbewegung [East Germany] 1972 14(6): 956-969.* At the second conference of the Socialist Unity Party of Germany it was decided to plan socialism within the frame of the socialist world economic system, to destroy exploitation, and to transform agriculture through socialism. The transition from capitalism to socialism in East Germany had two phases, the antifascist democratic phase and the socialist phase within the world evolutionary process. Based on published documents and secondary literature; 36 notes. R. Wagnleitner

1421. Falk, Waltraud; Müller, Hans; and Reissig, Karl. DIE HISTORISCHE BEDEUTUNG DER II. PARTEIKONFERENZ DER SED: DIE ÜBERGANGSPERIODE VOM KAPITALISMUS ZUM SOZIALISMUS IN DER DDR. BESTANDTEIL DES REVOLUTIONÄREN WELTPROZESSES [The historical significance of the second party conference of the Socialist Unity Party: the period of transition from capitalism to socialism in East Germany, part of the world revolutionary process]. *Jahrbuch für Wirtschaftsgeschichte [East Germany] 1972 (2): 11-42.* Describes the preparations for the transition to socialism in East Germany from 1945 to 1950, and analyzes the historical importance of the actions of the second party conference of the Socialist Unity Party in the summer of 1952 in bringing about the transition from capitalism to socialism. Outlines the ideological principles and economic plans of the conference. Shows how the socialist revolution in East Germany was part of the world revolutionary process and how the East German economy developed within the world socialist economy. Emphasizes the lessons learned from the Soviet Union's experiences in establishing socialism. Based on published party reports, government statistics, and secondary works; 3 tables, 103 notes.
J. B. Street

1422. Falk, Waltraud. DIE SCHAFFUNG DER ÖKONOMISCHEN GRUNDLAGEN DES SOZIALISMUS IN DER DDR [The creation of the economic foundations of socialism in the German Democratic Republic]. *Zeitschrift für Geschichtswissenschaft [East Germany] 1979 27(10): 915-925.* The third Party Assembly of the Socialist Unity Party in 1950 sought to increase the percentage of the gross national product produced by state-owned enterprises and to construct the material basis of a modern socialist society. Guided by the First Five-Year Plan (1950-55), East Germany made significant progress toward these ends even though it was handicapped by a lack of investment capital and hostile measures by West Germany. 39 notes. J. T. Walker

1423. Falk, Waltraud. ZUR GENESIS DER SOZIALISTISCHEN INTENSIVIERUNG [The genesis of socialist intensification]. *Beiträge zur Gesch. der Arbeiterbewegung [East Germany] 1984 26(4): 451-464.* Chronicles Communist economic policy in East Germany aimed at increasing production. Focuses on political economy and technology. 53 notes. R. Grove

1424. Feige, Hans-Uwe. DER AUFBAU DER SED-BETRIEBSGRUPPE AN DER UNIVERSITÄT LEIPZIG (1945-1948) [The structure of the trade group of the Socialist Unity Party of Germany at the University of Leipzig, 1945-48]. *Beiträge zur Gesch. der Arbeiterbewegung [East Germany] 1984 26(2): 247-256.* Colleges and universities as fields for the labor movement were loci for organization in East Germany after World War II. The author describes labor unions and organizations under the auspices of the Socialist Unity Party of Germany at the University of Leipzig. 48 notes. R. Grove

1425. Fiedler, F. DIE MARXISTISCH-LENINISTISCHEN GRUNDLAGEN DER WISSENSCHAFTSPOLITIK DER SED [The Marxist-Leninist principles of the scientific policy of the Socialist Unity Party of Germany]. *Wissenschaftliche Zeitschrift der Karl-Marx U. Leipzig [East Germany] 1971 20(2): 263-280.* Discusses the importance of sciences in the foundation of the social system of socialism, and the development of sciences in East Germany, 1946-71. Demonstrates that social sciences, natural sciences, and technical sciences are promoted in East Germany and used for the improvement of socialist society. 39 notes.
R. Wagnleitner

1426. Fiedler, Helene. DIE POLITIK DER SED ZUR WEITERENTWICKLUNG DER ANTIFASCHISTISCH-DEMOKRATISCHEN STAATLICHEN MACHTORGANE VON 1947 BIS MITTE 1948 [The policy of the Socialist Unity Party of Germany in connection with the further development of the antifascist-democratic state organs of power from 1947 until the middle of 1948]. *Beiträge zur Geschichte der Arbeiterbewegung [East Germany] 1973 15(4): 663-667.* When the Socialist Unity Party of Germany was given more rights by the Soviet Military Administration of Germany in 1947, the development of a new democratic administration and the founding of central and coordinated economic planning machinery were greatly accelerated. In a series of party conferences the Socialist Unity Party of Germany worked out the guidelines for the application of democratic centralism. In 1948 the Socialist Unity Party of Germany concentrated on the development of central political machinery by establishing committees for the peace treaty, the constitution, the economy, culture, social policy, communal policy, and agriculture. Based on documents in the Institute for Marxism-Leninism, printed documents, and secondary literature; 75 notes. R. Wagnleitner

1427. Fiedler, Helene. DIE SED UND DER HUNDERTSTE JAHRESTAG DER MÄRZREVOLUTION VON 1848 IN DEUTSCHLAND [The Socialist Unity Party (SED) and the 100th anniversary of the March Revolution of 1848 in Germany]. *Jahrbuch für Geschichte [East Germany] 1973 8: 323-352.*

1428. Fiedler, Helene. RUNDSCHREIBEN DER SED ZUM VOLKSENTSCHEID IN SACHSEN [The circular of the Socialist Unity Party of Germany on the plebiscite in Saxony]. *Beiträge zur Geschichte der Arbeiterbewegung [East Germany] 1976 18(3): 463-471.* Publication of a 16 May 1946 circular of the Socialist Unity Party of Germany in which the committee of the Party in Saxony discussed political strategy for expropriating the wealth of Nazis and war profiteers. 4 notes.

1429. Fiedler, Helene. WALKA KLASY ROBOTNICZEJ I NSPJ O UTWORZENIE WŁADZY ROBOTNIKÓW I CHŁOPÓW (1945-1949) [Struggle of the working class and of the German Socialist Unity Party for workers' and peasants' rule, 1945-49]. *Z Pola Walki [Poland] 1980 23(2): 177-190.* Marx and Lenin affirmed that the proletariat can fulfill its historical role only after it has gained political power and control over the society. The creation of the German Democratic Republic on 6 July 1950 was an expression of anti-imperialist and democratic forces under the leadership of the working class and its Marxist-Leninist party. Based on German secondary sources; 57 notes. I. Lukes

1430. Fiedlerová, Soja. K NĚKTERÝM OTÁZKÁM VYTVÁŘENÍ SPOJENECTVÍ DĚLNICKÉ TŘÍDY S PŘÍSLUŠNÍKY STARŠÍ INTELIGENCE PROSTŘEDNICTVÍM KOMUNISTICKÉ STRANY NĚMECKA, PŘÍPADNĚ JEDNOTNÉ SOCIALISTICKÉ STRANY NĚMECKA (1945-1949) [Some problems in the formation of an alliance between the working class and members of the older intelligentsia through the Communist Party and the Socialist Unity Party of Germany, 1945-49]. *Československý Časopis Hist. [Czechoslovakia] 1981 29(3): 366-388.* Lenin showed, and practical experience confirmed, that prerevolutionary specialists and intellectuals are needed for the work of postrevolutionary socialist construction. In East Germany the Communist Party followed this approach in the face of sectarian criticism on the Left and in spite of the many ex-Nazis on the university faculties. Assurance of material security and respect for intellectual achievement created a climate of confidence, which enabled the Party to appeal to these professionals for more positive ideological cooperation later on. Based on Lenin's works and East German published sources; 78 notes. Russian and German summaries.
R. E. Weltsch

1431. Findeisen, Otto. DIE FREUNDSCHAFT ZUR SOWJETUNION—ECKPFEILER DER POLITIK DER SOZIALISTISCHEN EINHEITSPARTEI DEUTSCHLANDS UND DER DEUTSCHEN DEMOKRATISCHEN REPUBLIK [Friendship with the USSR: cornerstone of the policy of the Socialist Unity Party of Germany and East Germany]. *Wissenschaftliche Zeitschrift der Humboldt-U. zu Berlin. Gesellschafts- und Sprachwissenschaftliche Reihe [East Germany] 1970 19(5): 645-654.* The cooperation between the USSR and East Germany after 1949 derives from the former's support of Communists during the Weimar Republic and later serving in the Anti-Nazi underground; German Communists who emigrated to the USSR during World War II had also been well-treated.

1432. Finzelberg, Sigtraut and Trümpler, Eckhard. ZUR AUSARBEITUNG DER WIRTSCHAFTSPOLITISCHEN KONZEPTION DER SED IN VORBEREITUNG DES VIII. PARTEITAGES [The elaboration of the political and economic ideology of the Socialist Unity Party in preparation for the 8th Party Conference]. *Beiträge zur Gesch. der Arbeiterbewegung [East Germany] 1981 23(3): 323-338.* Examines the presentation of economic and political ideology by the Socialist Unity Party (SED) Central Committee in preparation for the 8th party conference of the SED in Germany, 15-19 June 1971. East Germany had undergone important changes during the 1960's, particularly with regard to cooperation with other socialist countries, progress in scientific and technical spheres, and improvements in the material and cultural life of its inhabitants. The important aims for 1970-71 were to increase productivity and production. Therefore the SED Central Committee put forward an economic plan concerning production, industrial costs, workers' productivity, and wages. These measures were subsequently endorsed at the 8th Party Conference and were aimed at strengthening workers' confidence in party policies. Based on conference reports and secondary sources; 41 notes. G. L. Neville

1433. Foitzik, Jan. KADERTRANSFER. DER ORGANISIERTE EINSATZ SUDETENDEUTSCHER KOMMUNISTEN IN DER SBZ 1945/46 [Transfer of cadres: the organized assignment of Sudeten German Communists to the Soviet Zone of Occupation]. *Vierteljahrshefte für Zeitgeschichte [West Germany] 1983 31(2): 308-334.* As part of the post-World War II expulsion of Sudeten Germans from Czechoslovakia, some 17,000 German Communists (about 50,000 people with families) were resettled in East Germany. This cadre of Communists was an important addition to the decimated ranks of remaining and emigrant functionaries available to the East German Party. They helped insure the Communist predominance in the newly merged Socialist Unity Party and later held important positions in the diplomatic service (Foreign Minister Oskar Fischer for example), military, and secret service. Brief biographies of some 40 functionaries are included in this article. Based on Czech and German press, memoirs, and biographical dictionaries; 104 notes. D. Prowe

1434. Foske, Heinz. IZ ISTORII ORGANIZATSIONNOGO STROITEL'STVA SOTSIALISTICHESKOI EDINOI PARTII GERMANII [The history of the organizational construction of the Socialist Unity Party of Germany]. *Voprosy Istorii KPSS [USSR] 1971 (4): 99-106.* Describes the growth, doctrinal development, and organizational changes of the Party from its formation in 1946, after the unification of the Communist and Social Democratic Parties, to the mid-1960's.

1435. Fosske, Heinz. OTTO GROTEVOL': ODIN IZ OSNOVATELEI SEPG, PERVYI PREM'ER-MINISTR NEMETSKOGO GOSUDARSTVA RABOCHNIKH I KREST'IAN [Otto Grotewohl: one of the founders of the Socialist Unity Party, first prime minister of the German workers' and peasants' state]. *Novaia i Noveishaia Istoriia [USSR] 1981 (3): 82-107.* Traces the career of Otto Grotewohl (1894-1964). He became a printer in his home town of Brunswick, joined the Social Democratic Party, saw military service, was a member of the Landtag, was arrested and imprisoned, 1938-39, and emerged in 1945 as proponent of unity with the Communists. By 1949 he was president of the Council of Ministers of East Germany. 4 illus., 39 notes. J. P. H. Myers

1436. Franz, Werner. ZUR ENTWICKLUNG DES SOZIALISTISCHEN WETTBEWERBS IN DEN KAMPFGRUPPEN DER ARBEITERKLASSE [On the development of socialist competition in the task forces of the working class]. *Militärgeschichte [East Germany] 1979 18(6): 687-695.* The members of the task forces of the working class always fulfilled the missions assigned to them by the Central Committee of the Socialist Unity Party within the framework of defense and security policy. The author investigates the role and significance which socialist competition thus acquired. He recounts the competition goals and explains by what means competition initiatives were developed and used effectively for increasing productivity. 10 notes. J/T (H. D. Andrews)

1437. Friedrich, Gerd. LEITUNGSWISSENSCHAFT UND VERVOLLKOMMUNG DER SOZIALISTISCHEN WIRTSCHAFTSFÜHRUNG [The science of management and the realization of socialist management of the economy]. *Einheit [East Germany] 1973 28(5): 573-584.* Discusses the reasons for the increasing interest in scientific management of the economy and its practical application since the 8th Congress of the Socialist Unity Party of East Germany. Generalizes from the practical experiences of well-managed combines and enterprises, identifying successful management methods. Addresses questions relating to the management of social processes in enterprises and ways of increasing the rationality and effectiveness of the system of management. 20 notes.
F. H. Eidlin

1438. Gambke, Heinz and Stöckigt, Rolf. DIE BÜNDNISPOLITIK DER SED BEIM AUFBAU DER ENTWICKELTEN SOZIALISTISCHEN GESELLSCHAFT [The alliance policy of the Socialist Unity Party of Germany for building a developed socialist society]. *Zeitschrift für Geschichstwissenschaft [East Germany] 1976 24(4): 400-414.* The creation of a developed socialist society makes a coalition of working class, commercial classes, and private factory owners necessary. Based on printed documents and secondary literature; 70 notes. R. Wagnleitner

1439. Gambke, Heinz; Hümmler, Heinz; and Stöckigt, Rolf. DIE BÜNDNISPOLITIK IN DER STRATEGIE UND TAKTIK DER SED [Alliance policy in the strategy and tactics of the Socialist Unity Party of Germany]. *Zeitschrift für Geschichtswissenschaft [East Germany] 1969 17(10): 1265-1282.* Karl Marx and Friedrich Engels emphasized the need for the working class to free the entire society of which it was only a part. The Socialist Unity Party of Germany accepted this as its goal, seeking union with other parties which shared at least part of its ideology. Its combined opposition to fascism and imperialism provided common political ground for farmers and workers. Based on Marxist theoretical works and secondary sources; 11 notes. G. H. Libbey

1440. Glazer, G. RUKOVODIASHCHAIA ROL' SEPG V VOENNOM STROITEL'STVE GDR [The leading role played by the SED in the war industry of the GDR]. *Voenno-Istoricheskii Zhurnal [USSR] 1977 (2): 68-75.* Describes the close links formed in the 1950's between the Socialist Unity Party (SED) of East Germany and the USSR for the defense of socialism and peace against NATO, 1950-76.

1441. Goldmann, Sonja and Welker, Peter. ZUR GESCHICHTSPROPAGANDA NACH DEM VIII. PARTEITAG DER SED [Concerning the historical propaganda after the 8th Party Congress of the Socialist Unity Party of Germany]. *Beiträge zur Gesch. der Arbeiterbewegung [East Germany] 1981 23(1): 29-38.* History is being conveyed to the populace as ideological fortification of the political system of the state. The state does so by making use of anniversaries and similar occasions, including the 25th anniversary of the founding of the German Democratic Republic. Based on articles, party documents, and other sources; 29 notes.
A. Schuetz

1442. Graffunder, Siegfried. DAS BÜNDNIS DER ARBEITERKLASSE MIT DER WERKTÄTIGEN BAUERNSCHAFT IN DER ANTIIMPERIALISTISCH-DEMOKRATISCHEN AGRARREVOLUTION UND IHRER HINÜBERLEITUNG IN DIE SOZIALISTISCHE UMGESTALTUNG DER LANDWIRTSCHAFT IN DER DDR [The union of the working class with the working-class peasants in the anti-imperialist democratic agrarian revolution and its role in the socialist transformation of agriculture in the German Democratic Republic]. *Beiträge zur Gesch. der Arbeiterbewegung [East Germany] 1980 22(1): 48-58.* Examines how the German Communist Party (KPD) and the Socialist Unity Party (SED) helped agriculture in its transition from capitalism to socialism, 1945-55. The author discusses the ways in which the working-class peasants were won over to the cause of the working class and thus helped to strengthen the power base of the working class. Considers changes in agriculture and village life. Based on documents belonging to the KPD and the SED concerning agriculture and secondary sources; 24 notes. G. L. Neville

1443. Greese, Karl and Hamisch, Wilfried. DER 13. AUGUST 1961—EIN ERFOLG DER SICHERHEITS- UND MILITÄRPOLITIK DER SED [13 August 1961: a success for the defense and military policy of the Socialist Unity Party of Germany]. *Militärgeschichte [East Germany] 1981 20(4): 389-398.* Securing the boundaries of East Germany with West Berlin in August 1961 made illusory the plans for a march of the Bundeswehr through the Brandenburg Gate "with drums beating and trumpets sounding." The authors show the urgent necessity for national security measures and the solidarity of the Warsaw Pact countries manifested on that occasion. They prove that the coordinated employment of task forces of the working class, the border police, the mobile police, and the military defense by units of the National People's Army and the Soviet Armed Forces Group in East Germany contributed in essential ways to carrying out the policy of peaceful coexistence. 2 photos, 21 notes. J/T (H. D. Andrews)

1444. Grenkov, V. P. STOIKII BORETS ZA DELO SOTSIALIZMA I MIRA [A staunch fighter for the cause of socialism and peace]. *Voprosy Istorii KPSS [USSR] 1983 (6): 103-106.* Commemorates the life and work of Walter Ulbricht, former East German leader who served as General Secretary of the United Socialist Party, 1950-71. Based on primary sources; 4 notes.
R. Kirillov

1445. Grenkov, V. P. 30 LET PO MARKSISTSKO-LENINSKOMU PUTI [Thirty years on the path to Marxism-Leninism]. *Voprosy Istorii KPSS [USSR] 1976 (4): 105-110.* Celebrates the 30th anniversary of the founding of the East German Socialist Unity Party, briefly detailing its achievements since 1946.

1446. Griebenow, Helmut and Meyer, Kurt. DIE EINBEZIEHUNG DER GROSSBAUERN IN DIE SOZIALISTISCHE UMGESTALTUNG DER LANDWIRTSCHAFT IN DER DDR [The involvement of the upper peasantry in the socialist transformation of agriculture in the German Democratic Republic]. *Jahrbuch für Geschichte [East Germany] 1972 6: 371-396.* One of the great theoretical and practical contributions of the Socialist Unity Party (SED) is that, in the course of the socialist transformation of East German agriculture, it recognized that the peasants with large land holdings could be won over and integrated into cooperatives. This was possible in good part because these richer peasants were being ruined by competition with latifundia owners, whether Junkers or capitalists. The SED showed them that a socialist system of agriculture was their only salvation, and it saw to it that the transition to a socialist means of agricultural production was made easier for these owners of larger farms. 9 tables, 78 notes.
J. C. Billigmeier

1447. Grosser, G.; Gustmann, N.; and Pfretzschner, R. DIE SOZIALISTISCHE EINHEITSPARTEI DEUTSCHLANDS: FÜHRENDE KRAFT IM SYSTEM DER POLITISCHEN ORGANISATION DER SOZIALISTISCHEN GESELLSCHAFT IN DER DDR [The Socialist Unity Party: a leading force in the political organization of socialist society in East Germany]. *Wissenschaftliche Zeitschrift der Karl-Marx U. Leipzig [East Germany] 1971 20(2): 165-181.* The Socialist Unity Party is the highest form of political organization in East Germany. As a Marxist-Leninist party it has to fulfill the tasks of political leadership, political education, and social organization. Secondary sources; 36 notes. R Wagnleitner

1448. Grümmert, Jurgen. DIE WAFFENBRÜDERSCHAFTSBEZIEHUNGEN EINES PANZERVERBANDES DER NVA ZU SEINEM PARTNERVERBAND DER GSSD 1970-1976 [The comradeship-in-arms between a tank unit of the National People's Army and its partner unit of the Group of Soviet Forces in Germany]. *Militärgeschichte [East Germany] 1980 19(2): 169-177.* In order to strengthen the socialist community, especially under the threat of nuclear warfare, units of the Group of

Soviet Forces in Germany and the National People's Army engaged in cooperative meetings and maneuvers on the basis of the 1969 East German comradeship-in-arms decree. The Soviet units, being more highly trained, provided the German units with worthwhile information and training, especially on the role of the individual, because NPA personnel overemphasized the importance of technology. Stress was placed on political ideas, and NPA members were encouraged to join the Socialist Unity Party. Socialist competition among army units was encouraged, and friendship with the Soviet Union was strengthened. 3 photos, 17 notes.

H. D. Andrews

1449. Grützmacher, Irmgard. DER BESTAND MARX-ENGELS-ARCHIV IM ZENTRALEN PARTEIARCHIV DER SED: SEINE BEDEUTUNG, ENTWICKLUNG UND ARCHIVWISSENSCHAFTLICHE ERSCHLIESSUNG [The Marx-Engels Archive within the central party archives of the SED: its meaning, development, and archival handling]. *Archivmitteilungen [East Germany] 1983 33(1): 2-5.* Describes the efforts of the Socialist Unity Party's (SED) central Party archives in Berlin to gather and house Karl Marx's and Friedrich Engels's works since 1949.

1450. Gulin, V. I. BOR'BA SOTSIALISTICHESKOI EDINOI PARTII GERMANII ZA VYBORNYE ORGANY VLASTI OSEN'IU 1946 GODA [The fight of the Socialist Unity Party of Germany for elective government bodies, Fall 1946]. *Vestnik Moskovskogo U., Seriia 9: Istoriia [USSR] 1963 18(4): 15-33.* Describes the economic ruin of East Germany, social conditions in the wake of World War II defeat, the political unification goals of the Socialist Unity Party (SED), and the elections for municipal and local councils in the Fall of 1946. Discusses the electoral campaign of the SED, and its antifascist and antibourgeois program for economic rehabilitation and social reforms. Tabulates the results of the local elections by province and party affiliation. The SED averaged over 57% of the total vote. Table, 98 notes.

N. Frenkley

1451. Haack, Hanna and Schucany, Gudrun. DAS PRODUKTIONSAUFGEBOT 1961/1962 IN DEN BETRIEBEN DER SEEWIRTSCHAFT [The 1961-62 production effort in the shipbuilding industry]. *Wissenschaftliche Zeitschrift der U. Rostock. Gesellschafts- und Sprachwissenschaftliche Reihe [East Germany] 1973 22(6): 577-585.* In the shipbuilding industries around Rostock productivity had not reached world standards in the late 1950's. In 1961 productivity campaigns were started by the Socialist Unity Party of Germany and by the East German labor unions (FDGB) which, by organizing working collectives and new work programs, were able to increase production within one year. Based on documents in the FDGB-Bezirksvorstand Rostock-Archiv and secondary literature; 65 notes. R. Wagnleitner

1452. Hagen, Gerd. DIE DDR UND DER MOSKAUER VERTRAG [East Germany and the Treaty of Moscow]. *Aussenpolitik [West Germany] 1970 21(11): 661-667.* Analyzes the negative reaction of the East German Socialist Unity Party toward the talks initiated by West Germany and the USSR in 1969, particularly the connection between the Treaty of Moscow, 1970, and detente on the Berlin question.

1453. Hager, Kurt. EIN BEDEUTENDER MEILENSTEIN AUF DEM WEG ZUM SOZIALISMUS [An important milestone on the road to socialism]. *Einheit [East Germany] 1972 27(7): 872-875.* The 2d Party Conference of the Socialist Unity Party (SED) of East Germany in Berlin in July 1952 abolished all remaining capitalist economic structures and established state power as the main instrument of the working class.

1454. Hagerty, James J. LA LIQUIDACION DE LA SOCIAL DEMOCRACIA EN ALEMANIA ORIENTAL, 1945-1946 [The liquidation of social democracy in East Germany, 1945-46]. *Estudios sobre la Unión Soviética [West Germany] 1971 11(37): 22-37.* Explains how Communists destroyed the East German Social Democratic Party by fusing their party with the Communists to form the Socialist Unity Party.

1455. Halbauer, Günter. 30 JAHRE MARXISTISCH-LENINISTISCHES GRUNDLAGENSTUDIUM [Thirty years of Marxist-Leninist basic studies]. *Wiss. Zeits. der Wilhelm-Pieck-Universität Rostock. Gesellschafts- und Sprachwissenschaftliche Reihe [East Germany] 1981 30(9): 3-8.* Reports on efforts of the Communist Party in postwar East Germany to influence and direct research and teaching at the country's universities and gives an insight into the methods of basic studies in Marxism-Leninism.

1456. Handel, Gottfried. ZUM LEBEN UND WIRKEN VON GEORG MAYER: EIN VERMÄCHTNIS FÜR DIE SOZIALISTISCHE UNIVERSITÄT [The life and influence of George Mayer: a testimony to the socialist university]. *Wissenschaftliche Zeitschrift der Karl-Marx U. Leipzig. Gesellschafts- und Sprachwissenschaftliche Reihe [East Germany] 1977 26(6): 505-611.* Traces the life and career of Georg Mayer (1892-1973), Vice-Chancellor of the Karl Marx University, Leipzig, 1950-63. Discusses his student days in Tübingen, his membership of the German Social Democratic Party in 1919, his relationship with the USSR, his anti fascism, 1929-33, his expulsion from Giessen University because of his views in 1933, his war service, and his decision to become a member of the Socialist Unity Party of Germany (SED) in 1947. Also examines his career and major achievements at Leipzig University, 1948-63, and includes memories and anecdotes of Georg Mayer by his contemporaries. Based on Georg Mayer's writings, letters from friends and acquaintances, university reports, and secondary sources; 240 notes, 44 illus. G. L. Neville

1457. Harder, G. and Maiwald, M. DIE GRUNDBEZIEHUNGEN ZWISCHEN ÖKONOMISCHEM GRUNDGESETZ, BEDÜRFNISSEN, INTERESSEN UND IDEOLOGIE IM SOZIALISMUS. IHRE ANWENDUNG IN DER POLITIK DER SED BEI DER SCHAFFUNG DES ENTWICKELTEN GESELLSCHAFTLICHEN SYSTEMS DES SOZIALISMUS IN DER DDR [The basic relations between economic laws, needs, interests, and ideology in socialism: their application in the policy of the Socialist Unity Party of Germany for the creation of socialism in East Germany]. *Wissenschaftliche Zeitschrift der Karl-Marx U. Leipzig [East Germany] 1971 20(2): 219-244.*

1458. Harnisch, Karla. DIE POLITIK DER SED ZUR ENTWICKLUNG DER LANDWIRTSCHAFT DER DDR 1966 BIS 1968 [The policy of the Socialist Unity Party of Germany on the development of agriculture in East Germany, 1966-68]. *Beiträge zur Gesch. der Arbeiterbewegung [East Germany] 1984 26(3): 356-364.* The main object of East German agricultural policy was to supply sufficient foodstuffs for domestic consumption and sufficient raw materials for domestic industry. Chronicles attempts to accomplish those ends by means of cooperation with the seventh party conference of the Socialist Unity Party of Germany. 37 notes.

R. Grove

1459. Hartmann, Ulrich. DIE PARTEIORGANISATION DER MAXHÜTTE ORGANISIERT DIE ERSTEN ÖKONOMISCHEN KONFERENZEN [The Maxhütte party organization organizes the first economic conferences]. *Beiträge zur Gesch. der Arbeiterbewegung [East Germany] 1983 25(1): 123-129.* The economic successes of the first Five-Year Plan in the German Democratic Republic, 1950-55, caused the Socialist Unity Party to examine very closely the economic laws of socialism as well as the efficient planning and organization of the economy. The author pays particular attention to the three economic conferences which were organized by the Party organization in the metallurgical factory of Maxhütte, November 1954-January 1955. Based on local factory archives and secondary sources; 22 notes. G. L. Neville

1460. Hegler, Harry. ZUM WIRKEN DER NDPD IN DER GESCHICHTE DER DDR [The activities of the National Democratic Party of Germany in the history of East Germany]. *Zeitschrift für Geschichtswissenschaft [East Germany] 1979 27(12): 1129-1133.* Through the institution of the National Democratic Party of Germany the petite bourgeoisie of the towns and cities found a political institution with a close alliance to the working class and its revolutionary party, the Socialist Unity Party (SED). National Democrats acknowledged the leading role of the working class and the SED as well as friendship with the USSR. They also confirmed at their 11th Party Congress in 1977 their readiness to support the path toward socialism. 4 notes. G. E. Pergl

1461. Heider, Paul. MILITÄRISCHE TRADITIONEN DER DDR UND IHRER STREITKRÄFTE: PROBLEME IHRER KONTINUITÄT UND IHRES ENTSTEHENS [Military traditions of East Germany and its armed forces: problems of their continuity and origins]. *Militärgeschichte [East Germany] 1979 18(4): 440-449.* Military traditions which are related to the struggle of the masses, especially the revolutionary labor movement, have been nurtured in East Germany. Forces that have shaped the new traditions include the role of the Socialist Unity Party, the alliance with the Soviet army and the other allied armies and the unity of people and army. 29 notes. J/T (H. D. Andrews)

1462. Heinz, Helmut. DIE ERSTE ZENTRALE TAGUNG DER HISTORIKER DER DDR 1952 [The first central meeting of the historians of East Germany, 1952] *Zeitschrift für Geschichtswissenschaft [East Germany] 1978 26(5): 387-399.* Maintains that historiography is an organic part of the German Democratic Republic and as such should be directed by the Socialist Unity Party, the party of the government. The purpose of this first meeting was to discuss the requirements of a Marxist-Leninist society and to establish a dialog with Western historians. It was the feeling of the meeting that the study of Russian history is indispensable for East German historians, and it stimulated cooperation between the Historical Institutes in Berlin, Leipzig and Halle and the Museum for German History in adopting Marxist-Leninist principles. Based on secondary works; 62 notes. A. Alcock

1463. Heinz, Helmut and Sumpf, Fredi. ZUR ENTWICKLUNG DER PARTEIGESCHICHTSSCHREIBUNG IN DER DDR: 1976 bis 1980 [Development of the historiography of the Party in East Germany: 1976-80]. *Beiträge zur Geschichte der Arbeiterbewegung [East Germany] 1981 23(2): 208-217.* A bibliography of monographs and document collections on the history of East Germany's ruling Socialist Unity Party and its antecedents, 1848-1961. 4 notes. A. Schuetz

1464. Heitzer, Heinz. ALLGEMEINES UND BESONDERES DER ÜBERGANGSPERIODE VOM KAPITALISMUS ZUM SOZIALISMUS IN DER DDR [General and specific information on the transitional period between capitalism and socialism in the German Democratic Republic]. *Jahrbuch für Geschichte [East Germany] 1974 ll: 7-57.* The dialectic between the general and the specific is at the core of Marxist-Leninist methodology. In the case of the transition in East Germany from capitalism to socialism, this doctrine can be observed in practice. The situation in East Germany after World War II was peculiar in many respects. The country was in ruins, militarily defeated. The conditions for a socialist revolution were not present, so the Marxist-Leninist forces had to proceed slowly, starting with the merger of the two workers' parties, the Communists and Social Democrats, into the Socialist Unity Party (SED). 53 notes. J. C. Billigmeier

1465. Heitzer, Heinz. DIE AUSARBEITUNG DER DEUTSCHLANDPOLITIK DER DDR 1949/1950 [The formulation of East Germany's German policy, 1949-50]. *Jahrbuch für Geschichte [East Germany] 1969 4: 233-257.* Describes the policy of East Germany, dominated by the Communist-led Socialist Unity Party (SED), toward the question of German unity. The East German position was that German unity was destroyed through the imperialist actions of Nazi Germany. Unity could not be restored as long as West Germany continued to be allied with the West and had a capitalist social system. 61 notes. J. C. Billigmeier

1466. Heitzer, Heinz. DIE WEITERENTWICKLUNG DER STRATEGIE UND TAKTIK DER SED IM KAMPF GEGEN DEN WESTDEUTSCHEN IMPERIALISMUS 1954/55 [The further development of the strategy and tactics of the Socialist Unity Party of Germany (SED) in the struggle against West German imperialism 1954-55]. *Zeitschrift für Geschichtswissenschaft [East Germany] 1967 15(4): 595-620.* After the conservative victory in the West German elections of 1953, the SED worked out a new program for the unification of a democratic antifascist Germany. The SED proposed the formation of a provisional government for the whole of Germany which would hold free elections in all occupied zones. It also demanded the formation of a bloc against West German militarism by Communists, Social Democrats, trade unionists, Christian workers, and non-party workers. After the integration of West Germany into NATO in 1955, the East German government changed this strategy and entered the Warsaw Pact. 94 notes. R. Wagnleitner

1467. Heitzer, Heinz. GRUNDPROBLEME DES ÜBERGANGS VON DER ANTIFASCHISTISCHDEMOKRATISCHEN ORDNUNG ZUR SOZIALISTISCHEN REVOLUTION IN DER DDR 1949/50 [Basic problems in the transition from the antifascist democratic order to the socialist revolution in East Germany, 1949-50]. *Zeitschrift für Geschichtswissenschaft [East Germany] 1968 16(6): 715-738.* Discusses the role of the Socialist Unity Party and political developments leading to a socialist East Germany.

1468. Heitzer, Heinz. HAUPTETAPPEN DER KAMPFGEMEINSCHAFT VON SED UND KPDSU [Principal stages of the united struggle of the Socialist Unity Party of East Germany and the Communist Party of the USSR]. *Zeitschrift für Geschichtswissenschaft [East Germany] 1976 24(9): 973-991.* The Socialist Unity Party of Germany and the Communist Party of the Soviet Union have long been allied in the struggle for the worldwide spread of socialism. Leonid Brezhnev's 1976 remarks at a party congress, echoed by those of Erich Honecker, emphasize the brotherhood of the Soviet and German parties as shown by their unity of goals, outlook, and operations. This community of interests began with the founding of the German Democratic Republic in 1949, with roots in the earliest writings of Karl Marx and Friedrich Engels. Primary and secondary materials; 54 notes. G. H. Libbey

1469. Heitzer, Heinz. PARTEI, ARBEITERKLASSE, MASSENAKTIVITÄT IN DER ÜBERGANGSPERIODE VOM KAPITALISMUS ZUM SOZIALISMUS IN DER DDR: VOM ANFANG DER SECHSIGER JAHRE BIS ZUR GEGENWART [Party, working class, and mass activity in the transitional period from capitalism to socialism in the German Democratic Republic: from the beginning of the sixties to the present]. *Zeitschrift für Geschichtswissenschaft [East Germany] 1977 25(10): 1239-1256.* After the defeat of fascism the German Communist Party and the Socialist Unity Party (SED) strove to organize the masses and raise their revolutionary consciousness. Although numerous objective factors favored a socialist revolution in Soviet-occupied Germany, important subjective factors were lacking. With the founding of the German Democratic Republic the working class obtained the instrument necessary to lay the foundations for socialism, a process begun in 1952 and completed in the early sixties. Based on 21 theses presented at the Sixth Historical Congress of the German Democratic Republic, 1977; 5 notes. J. T. Walker

1470. Hellborn, Rudolf. HISTORISCHE ERFAHRUNGEN DER SED ÜBER DIE VERBINDUNG SOZIALISTISCHER VOLKSWIRTSCHAFTSPLANUNG MIT DEN PRINZIPIEN SOZIALISTISCHER WARENPRODUKTION [Historical experiences of the Socialist Unity Party (SED) with socialist economic planning and the principles of socialist production of goods]. *Jahrbuch für Geschichte [East Germany] 1969 4: 295-320.* The SED's experience with socialist economic planning and the socialist production of goods shows that socialism is not a brief transitional period between capitalism and communism, but a relatively stable socioeconomic system occupying the historical epoch between capitalism and communism. 52 notes. J. C. Billigmeier

1471. Herold, Manfred. ARBEITERKLASSE UND WISSENSCHAFTLICH-TECHNISCHER FORTSCHRITT [Workers' class and scientific-technical progress]. *Einheit [East Germany] 1971 26(10): 1104-1113.* The working class plays an important role in socialist society, the main productive power. Soviet research states that a 75 percent increase in production can be achieved by skillfully oriented mass production. Intensification of production requires the full use of scientific and technical progress on all levels of socialist society. 15 notes. G. E. Pergl

1472. Hertzfeldt, Gustav. AUSSENPOLITISCHE BILANZ IM 17. JAHR UNSERER REPUBLIK [The foreign policy balance in the 17th year of our republic]. *Deutsche Aussenpolitik [East Germany] 1966 11(10): 1169-1178.* Reviews East German cooperation with Communist countries and its efforts to overcome diplomatic isolation since 1949.

1473. Heuer, U. J. DIE LENINISCHEN PRINZIPIEN DER STAATLICHEN LEITUNG DER SOZIALISTISCHEN WIRTSCHAFT UND IHRE ANWENDUNG IM ÖKONOMISCHEN SYSTEM DES SOCIALISMUS IN DER DDR [The Leninist principles of state leadership of the socialist economy and its application in the socialist economic system in East Germany]. *Wissenschaftliche Zeitschrift der Karl-Marx U. Leipzig [East Germany] 1970 19(6): 843-855.* According to V. I. Lenin the dictatorship of the proletariat was the necessary political organization for the revolutionary abolition of private ownership of the means of production. The Socialist Unity Party of Germany used this principle as the basis for central state planning. Primary and secondary sources; 30 notes. R. Wagnleitner

1474. Heyden, Günter. VOR DEM 60. JAHRESTAG DES GROSSEN OKTOBER [Before the 60th anniversary of the great October]. *Beiträge zur Geschichte der Arbeiterbewegung [East Germany] 1976 18(6): 963-973.* Analyzes the impact of the October Revolution and the building of the Soviet Union on the development of the German Communist Party since 1917. Based on printed documents and secondary literature; 21 notes.

R. Wagnleitner

1475. Hoffmann, Heinrich. ÜBER DIE AKTIONSGEMEINSCHAFT ZUR VEREINIGUNG [To union via the action community]. *Beiträge zur Geschichte der Arbeiterbewegung [East Germany] 1976 18(2): 313-319.* Personal recollections of the conflicts between East German Communists and revisionist Social Democrats over unification of the German Communist Party and the German Social Democratic Party, 1945-46.

1476. Höhn, Hans. ZU PROBLEMEN DER ENTWICKLUNG DES MILITÄRTHEORETISCHEN DENKENS IN DEN LANDSTREITKRÄFTEN DER NVA [On problems of the development of military-theoretical thought in the land forces of the NVA]. *Militärgeschichte [East Germany] 1976 15(2): 168-178.* Describes the successful efforts of the forces of the National People's Army (NVA) of East Germany to solve the problems of national defense in the era of atomic weapons and the clash of socialism and imperialism (1955-75). Drawing on Soviet military theory and practice the Socialist Unity Party and the NVA have undertaken scientific research and used military publications and conferences to keep abreast of modern technical means of war and to coordinate defense measures with the Soviet Union and other Warsaw Pact countries. Based on documents in the military history institute of East Germany and secondary works; 19 notes.

J. B. Street

1477. Honecker, Erich. MEZHDUNARODNOE ZNACHENIE ISTORICHESKOGO OPYTA VELIKOGO OKTIABRIA [The international significance of the historical consequences of the great October Revolution]. *Voprosy Istorii KPSS [USSR] 1977 (4): 13-24.* Notes the significance of the October revolution on the occasion of its 60th anniversary. The October revolution and the subsequent development of the Soviet Communist Party as well as the Socialist Unity Party of East Germany demonstrate the need of the international working class for a Leninist party, the importance of achieving a new socialist society, and the possibilities for genuine international peace. Based on the published works of Marx, Engels, and Lenin; 20 notes. L. E. Holmes

1478. Honecker, Erich. ON THE ROAD OF SOCIALIST REVOLUTION. *World Marxist R. [Canada] 1974 17(10): 3-15.* Announces East Germany's 25th anniversary and describes the progress toward socialism made by the country's Communist Party, 1945-74.

1479. Horn, Werner. DIE FÜHRENDE ROLLE DER MARXISTISCH-LENINISTISCHEN PARTEI: EINE OBJEKTIVE GESETZMÄSSIGKEIT UNSERER ZEIT [The leading role of the Marxist-Leninist party: a contemporary example of a historical law]. *Zeitschrift für Geschichtswissenschaft [East Germany] 1969 17(1-2): 80-86.* The leading role of the Socialist Unity Party in East Germany's transition to socialism after 1946 illustrates the strategic function of Communist and workers' parties in the historical development of a socialist world system.

1480. Hornbogen, Lothar. EIN KÄMPFERISCHES LEBEN FÜR DEN SOZIALISMUS: FRITZ GÄBLER [A life as a fighter for socialism: Fritz Gäbler]. *Beiträge zur Geschichte der Arbeiterbewegung [East Germany] 1981 23 (2): 284-291.* Fritz Gäbler (1897-1974) joined the Social Democratic Party (SPD) in 1914 and the newly formed German Communist Party (KPD) in 1919. During the Weimar period he was repeatedly incarcerated. In 1931 he became a Reichstag deputy for Thuringia. After the Reichstag fire he was again arrested and remained jailed until his liberation by Soviet troops. He then joined the editorial staff of the *Deutsche Volkszeitung,* the official KPD newspaper; he participated in the founding congress of the Socialist Unity Party (SED) and attained various local, regional, and national positions in East Germany. Based on Party archives; 26 notes. A. Schuetz

1481. Hübner, Christa. DAS ABKOMMEN VON ZGORZELEC UND DIE POLITISCH-IDEOLOGISCHE ARBEIT DER SED 1950/51 [The Zgorzelec agreement and the political-ideological work of the Socialist Unity Party of Germany, 1950-1951]. *Beiträge zur Gesch. der Arbeiterbewegung [East Germany] 1981 23(1): 39-50.* The Zgorzelec Agreement has turned the border between the German Democratic Republic and the People's Republic of Poland into a border of "peace and friendship." However, some East German refugees, inspired by West German revisionists, still do not recognize the validity of the Oder-Neisse border. There is also still prejudice among some East Germans against Poland, due to ignorance of Polish history. Based on diplomatic documents, newspaper articles, and other printed sources; 66 notes. A. Schuetz

1482. Hümmler, Heinz. DIE GESTALTUNG DER ENTWICKELTEN SOZIALISTISCHEN GESELLSCHAFT ALS EIN PROZESS REVOLUTIONÄRER WANDLUNGEN [The formation of the developed socialist society as a process of revolutionary changes]. *Zeits. für Geschichtswissenschaft [East Germany] 1982 30(10-11): 884-898.* Discusses the basic questions of state and socialist revolution, socialist democracy, and political organization in East Germany: the international military, political, and economic problems which have helped to strengthen socialism and have led to closer cooperation with other socialist states; the development of socialist society; the concept of the formation of the developed socialist society as a process of revolutionary change; the character of the socialist state and socialist democracy; the leading role of the working class; the Socialist Unity Party's cooperation with other mass organizations and parties in eastern Europe. Based on Socialist Unity Party documents in Berlin and secondary sources; 57 notes.

G. L. Neville

1483. Ianivets, A. M. TEORETICHESKIE VOPROSY SOTSIAL'NOI POLITIKI V OBSHCHESTVENNO-POLITICHESKOI LITERATURE GDR (60-70-E GG.) [Theoretical questions of social policy in the social-political literature of East Germany, 1960's-70's]. *Vestnik Moskovskogo U., Seriia 8: Istoriia [USSR] 1981 (1): 40-50.* The Socialist Unity Party has tried to improve the standard of living by means of planned and differentiated improvements. In the process the income of middle levels of workers and peasants have approached each other. In the future, expenses for public functions will grow more quickly than the fund for wages. The East German government has increased expenditures for chil-

dren and encouraged the birthrate. Theorists must try to improve their ability to predict developments and also establish quantitative indices for measuring the social effectiveness of measures. 46 notes.
D. Balmuth

1484. Jahn, Wolfgang. ZUR ENTWICKLUNG VON LEHRE UND FORSCHUNG AN DER MILITÄRAKADEMIE "FRIEDRICH ENGELS" [On the development of teaching and research in the Friedrich Engels Military Academy]. *Militärgeschichte [East Germany] 1979 18(6): 676-687.* The founding of the Friedrich Engels Military Academy on 5 January 1959 was a result of national and international requirements for the military defense of socialism. The author deals with the initial problem of obtaining a competent faculty and shows that it was solved through cooperation with Soviet military academies and East German universities. He goes into detail about the evolution of the Academy's faculty and the expansion of its teaching and research programs, emphasizing especially the indoctrination of its students in the ideals of socialist cooperation and its success in meeting the goals established by the Socialist Unity Party. 3 illus., 20 notes. H. D. Andrews

1485. Jahnke, Karl Heinz. ZUM VERHÄLTNIS VON WILHELM PIECK ZUR FREIEN DEUTSCHEN JUGEND [On the relationship of Wilhelm Pieck to Free German Youth]. *Wiss. Zeits. der Wilhelm-Pieck-Universität Rostock. Gesellschafts- und Sprachwissenschaftliche Reihe [East Germany] 1979 28(1-2): 3-8.* Reports on Wilhelm Pieck's major role in devising and implementing the youth policies of the Communist Party of East Germany, concentrating on his work from 1945 to 1949.

1486. Jahnke, Karl Heinz. ZUR ENTWICKLUNG DER BEZIEHUNGEN VON FDJ UND KOMSOMOL VON 1946 BIS ZUR GEGENWART [The development of the relations between the Free German Youth (FDJ) and the Young Communist League (Komsomol) between 1946 and the present]. *Wissenschaftliche Zeitschrift der U. Rostock. Gesellschafts- und Sprachwissenschaftliche Reihe [East Germany] 1973 22(6): 551-557.* In 1947 the first official delegation of the Free German Youth (FDJ) was invited to the USSR. In 1948 the FDJ was accepted into the World League of Democratic Youth. In the 1950's and 1960's continuous exchanges between the FDJ and the Soviet Komsomol strengthened the understanding between the youth of both countries. Based on documents in the Zentralarchiv der FDJ, Berlin, and secondary literature; 24 notes. R. Wagnleitner

1487. Jahnke, Karl Heinz. ZUR ROLLE UND ZUM PLATZ DER FDJ BEI DER GESTALTUNG DER ENTWICKELTEN SOZIALISTISCHEN GESELLSCHAFT IN DER DDR [The role and place of Free German Youth in shaping the developed socialist society in East Germany]. *Wissenschaftliche Zeitschrift der Wilhelm-Pieck-Universität Rostock. Gesellschaftswissenschaftliche Reihe [East Germany] 1983 32(9): 13-16.* Eulogizes the achievements of Free German Youth, the official youth organization of the Socialist Unity Party of Germany, in advancing the economic policy of East Germany.

1488. Janicki, Lech. PRAWNE ZAŁOŻENIA SYSTEMU PARTII POLITYCZNYCH W NRD [Legal aspects of the political parties system in East Germany]. *Państwo i Prawo [Poland] 1974 29(6): 57-74.* Examines the legal institutionalization of a uniform coalition party system in East Germany since 1948. The Marxist-Leninist Socialist Unity Party had held a predominant position.

1489. Jarvie, Grant. SCIENTIFIC SOCIALISM THROUGH SPORT. *Canadian Journal of History of Sport [Canada] 1984 15(2): 5-18.* Examines factors which have made East Germany one of the top sporting nations in the world, including the example of the USSR.

1490. Jehser, Werner. ASPECKTE DES KLASSENCHARAKTERS UND DER PARTEILICHKEIT IN DER LITERATURENTWICKLUNG DER SECHZIGER JAHRE [Aspects of the class-character and party-consciousness in the development of literature in the sixties]. *Beiträge zur Geschichte der Arbeiterbewegung [East Germany] 1974 16(Supplement): 83-99.* The literary production of the German Democratic Republic in the 1960's reflects the change from the fascist and imperialist to the socialist environment. At a writers' congress in 1961 Anna Seghers stressed the appropriateness of this change, following the cultural policies of the Socialist Unity Party of Germany. The greatest writers of previous decades were those who had broken away from their imperialistic society and had become part of the truly humanistic tenor of the new socialist society. Primary and secondary materials; 11 notes.
G. H. Libbey

1491. Jensen, Jens-Jørgen. TYSKLAND SOCIALISTISKE ENHEDSPARTI [The German Socialist Unity Party]. *Økonomi og politik [Denmark] 1973 47(3): 247-273.* Of the several models available for analysis of East Germany the most applicable is a modified industrial society model. East Germany experienced a period of mass organization until 1949, followed by the development of socialism until 1961, and a broader development of socialism into state, culture, economy, and foreign policy after that. The Socialist Unity Party (SED), created in 1946 by the union of the Social Democrats and Communists, is a mass party. Bourgeois parties—Christian Democrats and the Farmers Party—have been allowed to persist. East Germany moved toward a Soviet style Communist system after 1949 with collectivization, creation of both state and Party apparatuses, and five-year plans. Walter Ulbricht's departure in 1971 marked a change in emphasis to technological rather than ideological goals. Centralization and legitimization have accompanied economic growth and improved living standards.
R. E. Lindgren

1492. Kahrs, Karl H. THE THEORETICAL POSITION OF THE INTRA-MARXIST OPPOSITION IN THE GDR. *East Central Europe 1979 6(2): 250-265.* Reviews the varieties of political dissent, which has a long tradition in the GDR. The opposition holds itself to be adhering to communism, which it feels has been distorted by "bureaucratic-dictatorial rule." Many critics lament the "mindless desire for consumption and affluence" which the regime has encouraged without being able really to compete in these areas with the capitalist countries. Not too much should be made of the impact of the Communist opposition, for the USSR will not tolerate a dramatically different development in East Germany. 31 notes.
R. V. Layton

1493. Kaiser, Monika; Klose, Christel; and Münch, Ursula. ZUR BLOCKPOLITIK DER SOZIALISTISCHEN EINHEITSPARTEI DEUTSCHLANDS VON 1955 BIS 1961 [The bloc policies of the Socialist Unity Party, 1955-61]. *Zeits. für Geschichtswissenschaft [East Germany] 1982 30(12): 1059-1071.* Examines decisions made by the Socialist Unity Party and other democratic bloc parties in East Germany concerning the foundations of socialism in the German Democratic Republic: the struggle for the maintenance of peace and the strengthening of the German Democratic Republic; the success of the socialist means of production in essential spheres of society; the importance of establishing the material and technological basis of socialism; the continuation of the socialist revolution in the areas of ideology and culture; socialist change in agriculture; and socioeconomic change in business as well as in the private sector of industry. Based on the Statistical Yearbook of the German Democratic Republic, Party documents in Berlin, and secondary sources; 61 notes. G. L. Neville

1494. Kanzig, Helga. DIE ANWENDUNG SOWJETISCHER ERFAHRUNGEN UND DIE ZUSAMMENARBEIT MIT DER UDSSR BEIM AUFBAU DES SOZIALISMUS IN DER DDR [The use of Soviet experience and cooperation with the USSR in socialist construction in East Germany]. *Jahrbuch für Wirtschaftsgeschichte [East Germany] 1977 (4): 9-25.* Traces the growing dimensions of political, economic, and scientific-technical cooperation between East Germany and the Soviet Union, 1945-70's. In a spirit of proletarian internationalism and through multilateral and bilateral treaties and agreements the two states have cooperated in building a socialist society in East Germany. Based on protocols of conferences of the Socialist Unity Party of Germany and secondary works; 33 notes. J. B. Street

1495. Kanzig, Helga. DIE POLITIK DER SED ZUR HERAUSBILDUNG UND FESTIGUNG ÖKONOMISCHER GRUNDLAGEN DER ANTIFASCHISTISCH-DEMOKRATISCHEN UMWÄLZUNG IM ZWEITEN HALBJAHR 1946 [The policy of the Socialist Unity Party (SED) on the growth and stabilization of the economic base in the antifascist revolution in the second half of 1946]. *Zeitschrift für Geschichtswissenschaft [East Germany] 1979 27(9): 805-819.* In July 1946 the people of Saxony passed a referendum to confiscate the factories of Nazis and war criminals. After overcoming the opposition of monopoly capital, the Socialist Unity Party led the workers in efforts to increase production by coordinating efforts in these factories, enlarging the plant factory organizations, establishing factory councils, and training new cadres of plant managers. 43 notes. J. T. Walker

1496. Kanzig, Helga and Rolfs, Klaus. ZUM STUDIEN DER ERFAHRUNGEN DES SOZIALISTISCHEN AUFBAUS IN DER UDSSR DURCH DIE SED IN DEN ERSTEN JAHREN DER HERAUSBILDUNG DER SOZIALISTISCHEN PRODUKTIONSWEISE IN DER DDR [The study of the experiences of socialist construction in the USSR by the Socialist Unity Party of Germany during the first years of the formation of the socialist mode of production in the German Democratic Republic]. *Beiträge zur Geschichte der Arbeiterbewegung [East Germany] 1975 17(2): 306-322.* On the 25th anniversary of the founding of East Germany, the friendship and support of the Soviet Union was recognized as the key factor in the success of this new socialist state. German workers received instruction in Marxist-Leninist doctrine, Soviet history, and methods of production in the Soviet Union. Study of the Soviet experience in production and government enabled the Socialist Unity Party of Germany to provide effective leadership and growth. Primary and secondary materials; 53 notes. G. H. Libbey

1497. Kanzig, Helga. ZUR GESCHICHTE DER ÖKONOMISCHEN POLITIK DER SED IN DER ERSTEN HÄLFTE DER SECHZIGER JAHRE [The history of the economic policy of the Socialist Unity Party of Germany in the first half of the 1960's]. *Zeitschrift für Geschichtswissenschaft [East Germany] 1971 19(12): 1483-1503.* In the early 1960's, East Germany reached the stage of realization of socialism. The production program of the Socialist Unity Party guaranteed improvement in the material and political condition of the East German people and at the same time stabilized the national economy. Based on printed documents and secondary literature; 49 notes. R. Wagnleitner

1498. Kanzig, Helga and Rolfs, Klaus. ZUR ZUSAMMENARBEIT ZWISCHEN DER DDR UND DER UDSSR 1949-1974 [On cooperation between the GDR and USSR 1949-74]. *Zeitschrift für Geschichtswissenschaft [East Germany] 1974 22(9): 933-949. 1974 22(9): 933-949.* The political and ideological closeness of the Socialist Unity Party of Germany (SED) and the Communist Party of the Soviet Union (KPdSU) was the core of their cooperation in carrying through socialist revolution and construction in East Germany. The founding of the GDR on 7 October 1949, the establishment of diplomatic relations between East Germany and the Soviet Union on 15 October 1949, the Warsaw Pact of 14 May 1955, and the state treaty of friendship, mutual assistance, and cooperation of 12 June 1964 were based on proletarian internationalism and socialist equality. The political, economic, and military aid of the Soviet Union was of the highest importance for the economic and political stability of East Germany. Primary and secondary sources; 65 notes. R. Wagnleitner

1499. Keller, Dietmar. DIE ENTWICKLUNG DER PRODUKTIONSDEMOKRATIE IN DER VOLKSEIGENEN INDUSTRIE IN DEN JAHREN DER ALLSEITIGEN FESTIGUNG DER ANTIFASCHISTISCH-DEMOKRATISCHEN ORDNUNG [The development of the democracy of production in the nationalized industries during the all-around strengthening of the antifascist democratic order]. *Jahrbuch für Geschichte [East Germany] 1969 4: 207-231.* During the immediate postwar period in East Germany, many industries were nationalized by order of the Soviet occupation authorities, or, later, by the East German government itself. These industries were governed by workers' councils dominated by the Socialist Unity Party (SED). This method of industrial government constitutes part of the gradual creation of the dictatorship of the proletariat. 82 notes. J. C. Billigmeier

1500. Keller, Dietmar. ZU DEN HOCHSCHULPOLITISCHEN GRUNDSÄTZEN DER SED IN DER ÜBERGANGS PERIODE VOM KAPITALISMUS ZUM SOZIALISMUS [On the principles of higher education policy of the Socialist Unity Party of Germany during the period of transition from capitalism to socialism]. *Beiträge zur Geschichte der Arbeiterbewegung [East Germany] 1976 18(5): 811-825.* Parallel to the denazification of the East German universities, 1945-49, the bourgeois education monopoly was broken. Between 1949 and 1961 the sciences were incorporated into the central planning of the state. Based on printed documents and secondary literature; 55 notes. R. Wagnleitner

1501. Kessel, Werner. DIE ÖKONOMISCHEN KONFERENZEN 1955/56 IM BEZIRK KARL-MARX-STADT [The 1955-56 economic conferences in the region of Karl Marx Stadt]. *Beiträge zur Gesch. der Arbeiterbewegung [East Germany] 1984 26(3): 395-402.* Shows the contributions of conferences in Karl Marx Stadt, 1955-56, to the economic policy of the Socialist Unity Party of Germany and to the development of East Germany. 37 notes. R. Grove

1502. Khager, K. 30 LET GERMANSKOI DEMOKRATICHESKOI RESPUBLIKI [The 30th anniversary of the German Democratic Republic]. *Novaia i Noveishaia Istoriia [USSR] 1979 (5): 3-13.* Highlights the outstanding successes achieved for the past 30 years by the working class of the German Democratic Republic in alliance with other working people under the leadership of the Marxist-Leninist party, the Socialist Unity Party (SED), successes scored thanks to the joint efforts of all parties and social forces united in the National Front. The cornerstone of the successful development is the fraternal alliance with the Soviet Union and the inviolable friendship between the people of the GDR and the Soviet people. J

1503. Khasenov, M. NEKOTORYE ASPEKTY DEIATEL'NOSTI SEPG PO RAZVERTYVANIIU TVORCHESKOI INITSIATIVY TRUDIASHCHIKHSIA SOTSIALISTICHESKOI PROMYSHLENNOSTI GDR V 1959-1963 GG. [Aspects of SED activity in developing creative initiative in socialist industrial labor of East Germany, 1959-63]. *Vestnik Moskovskogo U., Seriia 9: Istoriia [USSR] 1973 28(1): 33-46.* Examines the socioeconomic program of the East German seven-year plan, 1959-65, and the principle of the active participation of the working class in economic rehabilitation promulgated at the fifth conference of the Socialist Unity Party (SED). Discusses proposals advanced by factory workers to raise labor productivity, increase industrial output, and stimulate labor-management cooperation, as well as SED labor reform legislation. Includes selected statistical data. Table, 78 notes. N. Frenkley

1504. Khvostov, V. M. and Tsapanov, V. I. SOTRUDNICHESTVO KPSS I SEPG-VOPLOSHCHENIE PRINTSIPOV PROLETARSKOGO INTERNATSIONALIZMA [The collaboration of the CPSU and the SEPD: an embodiment of the principles of proletarian internationalism]. *Novaia i Noveishaia Istoriia [USSR] 1971 (5): 3-14.* Considers the cooperation between the Communist Parties of the USSR and East Germany. Emphasizes Soviet contributions in helping the German people to overcome their lethargy and despair in 1945 and in carrying out socialist changes. Notes subsequent economic, military, and cultural collaboration, and refers to the close ties between regional Party organizations in both countries. 21 notes. C. I. P. Ferdinand

1505. Kirchner, Jürgen. ZUR BEDEUTUNG DER BETRIEBSFRAUENAUSCHÜSSE FÜR DIE GLEICHBERECHTIGTE TEILNAHME DER FRAUEN AM PLANMÄSSIGEN AUFBAU DER GRUNDLAGEN DES SOZIALISMUS IN DER DDR (1952 BIS 1955) [The significance of the women's industrial committees for the equal participation of women in the systematic construction of the foundations of socialism in East Germany, 1952-55]. *Jahrbuch für Wirtschaftsgeschichte [East Germany] 1976 (2): 33-52.*

In the early 1950's it was decided that women should be admitted to all occupations for which they were physically fitted. Some resistance on the part of the defenders of tradition had to be overcome before women could be completely integrated into a socialist labor force. In 1952 the Politburo of the Socialist Unity Party (SED) encouraged women to form their own industrial committees. Since then, women have graduated from these committees to responsible positions in the bureaucracy, and the committees themselves have helped to improve working conditions for women. Primary and secondary sources; 59 notes. R. J. Bazillion

1506. Kirste, Peter and Pellmann, Dietmar. DIE BÜNDNISPOLITIK DER SED MIT DER WISSENSCHAFTLICH-TECHNISCHEN INTELLIGENZ. FORSCHUNGSGEGENSTAND, ETAPPEN UND REIFESTUFEN [Alliance policy of the Socialist Unity Party of Germany with scientific-technical intellectuals: subject of research, stages, and mature steps]. *Beiträge zur Gesch. der Arbeiterbewegung [East Germany] 1984 26(3): 304-312.* Scientists and technicians in East Germany are united with the working class by means of the Socialist Unity Party of Germany. The interests of the working class and the distinction between socialism and imperialism govern research policies. Explores the implications of these principles for historians. 23 notes. R. Grove

1507. Kittner, Klaus and Wätzig, Alfons. ZUR ENTSTEHUNG DER EINHEITLICHEN GEWERKSCHAFT DER EISENBAHNER 1945 [The origins of a unified railroad workers union, 1945]. *Beiträge zur Geschichte der Arbeiterbewegung [East Germany] 1976 18(1): 112-119.* Communists and Socialists met in Dresden on 17 May 1945 to create a main committee for railroad labor unions. The agreement between Communist and Socialist unionists became the basis for cooperation within a united trade union, the main task of which was reorganization of the traffic system and motivation of the workers. Based on documents in the Archiv des RAW, Dresden, Archiv des Ministeriums für Verkehrswesen, Berlin, interviews, and secondary literature; 23 notes. R. Wagnleitner

1508. Klein, Ingomar. DIE ENTWICKLUNG DES SOZIALISTISCHEN EIGENTUMS [Development of socialist property]. *Wissenschaftliche Zeitschrift der Humboldt U. zu Berlin [East Germany] 1974 23(1): 31-37.* In a fully communist state all property is nationalized, while in precommunist socialism cooperatives still exist. Although socialism presupposes an already high economic-technological level, the transition to communism is long and difficult. A steady increase in nationalization is required along with upgrading of cooperatives. Businesses of a single type must be concentrated in nearby areas best suited to their needs, there must be central planning and leadership, and at the same time democratic centralism involving workers in planning. Movement in these directions has been rapid in East Germany since 1950. Tables, 7 notes. M. Faissler

1509. Kobr, Jaroslav. HLAVNÍ TENDENCE VÝVOJE NĚMECKÉ DEMOKRATICKÉ REPUBLIKY DO POČÁTKU ŠEDESÁTÝCH LET [Principal trends of development in the German Democratic Republic until the 1960's]. *Slovanský Přehled [Czechslovakia] 1982 68(4): 303-316.* The development of East German socialism differed from other countries in that in East Germany the national liberation was not connected with the antifascist struggle. After the Soviet occupation, the Social Democratic Party became dominant. Most important changes were the land reforms which completely eliminated the old Junker class. Well into the 1950's East Germany had to contend with the image of the West German economic "miracle." East Germany suggested several peace treaties and submitted proposals for making Berlin a free city, all rejected by the West. The Berlin Wall, erected in 1961, has secured East Germany as has her membership in the Warsaw Pact. 43 notes. B. Reinfeld

1510. Kobr, Jaroslav. ROZVOJ SOCIALISTICKÉ SPOLEČNOSTI NDR V 60. LETECH [The development of socialist society in East Germany in the 1960's]. *Slovanský Přehled [Czechoslovakia] 1981 67(3): 223-234.* In the early 1960's, East Germany rejected the possibility of union with West Germany as long as it remained under imperialist control. The socialist program adopted by the 6th Party Congress (1963) stressed increased productivity, to be achieved by more scientific methods. By 1967 the plans brought results, and the German people agreed to a new constitution, which was mailed to all residents and was widely read and debated for two months before adoption. 45 notes. B. Reinfeld

1511. Koch, Ute. ZU MERKMALEN UND ERGEBNISSEN DER BEZIEHUNGEN VON FDJ UND LENINSCHEM KOMSOMOL IN DEN 60ER UND 70ER JAHREN [Features and consequences of relations between the Free German Youth and Lenin's Young Communist League, 1960's-70's]. *Wissenschaftliche Zeitschrift der Wilhelm-Pieck-Universität Rostock. Gesellschaftswissenschaftliche Reihe [East Germany] 1983 32(9): 20-23.* Relates relations between the official Communist youth movements of East Germany and of the USSR to broader issues of foreign relations and cooperation between the two countries within the context of Comecon.

1512. Kohlsdorf, Fred and Opitz, Heinrich. WISSENSCHAFTLICHE WELTANSCHAUUNG UND BEWUSSTES HÄNDELN DER ARBEITERKLASSE [Scientific *weltanschauung* and conscious acting of the workers' class]. *Einheit [East Germany] 1971 26(10): 1081-1091.* Considers the connection of everyday life and the systematic formation of a socialist society. Discusses the essence and recognition of objective social laws and the new relationship of man to law in a society in which Party, working class, and *weltanschauung* are an indivisible unit. Revealing the nature of imperialism is a prime duty of socialist philosophy. 20 notes. G. E. Pergl

1513. Kopp, Fritz. GERMAN HISTORY AND THE SED. *Survey [Great Britain] 1960 (34): 52-57.* Outlines campaigns in East Germany by the Communist Party for a more socialist orientation in historical studies, 1950-60.

1514. Köppen, Peter. ZU EINIGEN AUFGABEN UND ERGEBNISSEN REGIONALGESCHICHTLICHER FORSCHUNG [On some tasks and results of research in regional history]. *Wiss. Zeits. der Wilhelm-Pieck-Universität Rostock. Gesellschafts- und Sprachwissenschaftliche Reihe [East Germany] 1981 30(9): 47-53.* Reports on research on the historical development of the Socialist Unity Party's Rostock county organization conducted by the Department of Marxism-Leninism at the University of Rostock.

1515. Köppen, Peter. ZUR KONSTITUIERUNG DER BEZIRKSPARTEIORGANISATION ROSTOCK DER SED IM JAHRE 1952 [Constituting the Rostock organization of the Socialist Unity Party of Germany, 1952]. *Wissenschaftliche Zeitschrift der Wilhelm-Pieck-Universität Rostock. Gesellschaftswissenschaftliche Reihe [East Germany] 1983 32(7): 27-32.* East Germany created national districts in 1952, and along with them district chapters of the Socialist Unity Party of Germany. The chapter from Rostock concentrated on shipbuilding as the region's main contribution to the development of socialism.

1516. Kozlov, A. P. KRUPNOE SOBYTIE V ZHIZNI KOMMUNISTOV [A great event in the life of Communists]. *Voprosy Istorii KPSS [USSR] 1981 (6): 127-131.* A conference of European Communist and workers' parties took place in East Berlin at the end of June 1976. Delegates were present from 29 fraternal parties, representing 29 million Communists, to discuss their united struggle on the international field, and accepted unanimously the motto "For peace, security, cooperation, and social progress in Europe." Questions discussed included detailed plans for antimilitary action, the problems encountered by Communist and workers' parties in capitalist European countries, and the greater unified effort of all parties toward European socialist progress and the strengthening of fraternal ties by means of such conferences. Based on conference and Party congress material; 11 notes. L. Smith

1517. Krause, Manfred. DER VI. PARTEITAG DER SED UND DIE ZUSAMMENARBEIT DER PARTEIEN IN DER DDR [The Sixth Congress of the Socialist Unity Party of Germany (SED) and the cooperation of parties in East Germany]. *Zeitschrift für Gesch-*

ichtswissenschaft [East Germany] 1967 15(2): 224-239. The decisions of the sixth congress of the SED consolidated the cooperation of the various parties in East Germany. Based on secondary literature and printed documents; 48 notes. R. Wagnleitner

1518. Krause, Manfred. ZUR ZUSAMMENARBEIT DER SED MIT DEN ANDEREN PARTEIEN DES DEMOKRATISCHEN BLOCKS NACH DER GRÜNDUNG DER DDR BIS MITTE 1952 [Cooperation of the Socialist Unity Party with other parties of the Democratic Bloc from the founding of East Germany up to 1952]. *Jahrbuch für Geschichte [East Germany] 1979 20: 111-142.* The Socialist Unity Party of East Germany declared its goals for the democratic coalition during 1949-52: strengthening the antifascist-democratic system and consolidation of democratic reforms. With the aid of the working class, reactionaries within the middle-class democratic parties, such as Hickmann and Moog, were eventually forced out, facilitating closer cooperation between the parties. Following the election in 1950, the 400 seats in the parliament were distributed proportionally to all the democratic-socialist parties. Based on Socialist Unity Party documents, Berlin, Union archives, Central Party Archives, Berlin, and other East German archives; table. T. Parker

1519. Krisch, Henry. NATION BUILDING AND REGIME STABILITY IN THE DDR. *East Central Europe 1976 3(1): 15-29.* Analyzes the efforts of the German Democratic Republic (DDR) since 1971 to develop a separate national self-image by examining the East German constitution, the party program of the Socialist Unity Party (SED), and the USSR-DDR Treaty of 1975. Political development in the DDR differs from the historical pattern because it seeks to overcome the cultural, ethnic, and linguistic similarities which impelled Germans to unite in the 19th century. DDR nationalism is not "a societal force but... a political decision"; it implies the rejection of "all-German ambitions" by the East German government. West Germany is regarded as a foreign country and a different society, and closer ties are sought with the Soviet bloc. Primary and secondary sources; 70 notes. R. J. Bazillion

1520. Krisch, Henry. POLITICS IN THE GERMAN DEMOCRATIC REPUBLIC. *Studies in Comparative Communism 1976 9(4): 389-419.* West German and American literature on East Germany shows the central position of Peter C. Ludz's *Changing Party Elite in East Germany* (MIT Pr., 1968) which posited a conflict between Party leaders and the new scientific and technical elite. Other studies have noted the appearance of separate national identities in East and West Germany indicating that political loyalties are susceptible to rewards. East Germany has performed better than the Soviets in placing women in important positions; its agricultural productivity has increased and educational opportunities are more open in the East than in the West. Apparently the GDR has created a loyal and skilled officer corps. Work must still be done in economics, culture, national feeling, and the role of experts. 35 notes. D. Balmuth

1521. Krusch, Hans Joachim. POWSTANIE I ROZWÓJ NIEMIECKIEJ SOCJALISTYCZNEJ PARTII JEDNOŚCI 1946-1949 [The origins and development of the German Socialist Unity Party, 1946-49]. *Z Pola Walki [Poland] 1979 22(4): 163-179.* The German Socialist Unity Party was created on 21 and 22 April 1946 out of the Communist Party of Germany and the Socialist Party of Germany, in the Russian sector of occupied Germany. For three years, it paved the way for the formation in 1949 of the workers' state of East Germany. E. Jaworska

1522. Krusch, Hans-Joachim. AUF DEM WEGE ZUR GRÜNDUNG DER SED: DER 15. PARTEITAG DER KPD [On the road to founding the Socialist Unity Party (SED): the 15th German Communist Party Congress]. *Beiträge zur Geschichte der Arbeiterbewegung [East Germany] 1981 23(2): 194-207.* The 15th German Communist Party Congress, the first on German soil since 1929, worked toward implementing the Party platform of 11 June 1945: unite all working class parties; continue the fight against fascism; help create conditions in all of Germany and Europe that would open the doors for socialism. In all of Germany, the Party acted as a tightly knit revolutionary party. In the Soviet zone, a united Party, trade union, and youth organization was being created. In the western zones, imperialism prevailed. In the east, membership statistics demonstrate the great attraction of the newly united Party on all segments of the working class as well as on the intelligentsia. Based on congress proceedings and holdings of the central Party archives; 31 notes. A. Schuetz

1523. Krusch, Hans-Joachim. OKTOBERJUBILÄUM IN UNSEREM LANDE IM JAHR DER BEFREIUNG VOM FASCHISMUS [The October jubilee in our country in the year of liberation from fascism]. *Beiträge zur Geschichte der Arbeiterbewegung [East Germany] 1977 19(5): 862-876.* Describes the programs and celebrations in honor of the 28th anniversary of the Russian Revolution prepared by the Communist Party of Germany in 1945. This first legal celebration after 12 years of fascist dictatorship aimed at strengthening the Communist Party, professing true friendship with the Soviet Union, and furthering the political, economic, and social transformation in the Soviet zone of occupation in East Germany. Based on documents in the archives of the Institute for Marxism-Leninism, Berlin, newspapers, and secondary works; 20 notes. J. B. Street

1524. Kubatzki, Rainer. DAS PARTEILEHRJAHR DER SED VON 1971 BIS 1975: EIN BEITRAG ZUR ERFÜLLUNG DER BESCHLÜSSE DES VIII. PARTEITAGES DER SED [The SED's years of apprenticeship from 1971 to 1975: a contribution to the accomplishment of the resolution of the SED's 8th Party Conference]. *Beiträge zur Gesch. der Arbeiterbewegung [East Germany] 1980 22(4): 513-525.* Examines how the resolutions of the 8th Party Conference of the Socialist Unity Party (SED) were fulfilled in East Germany, 1971-75, with particular reference to the further development of ideological unity and determination within the Party. The most important developments occurred in the study of Marxist Leninist theories, the study of the history and policies of the SED, the systematic study of Party resolutions and their ideological basis, the creation of a fully developed socialist society, and the study of the history and theory of communism and its opposition to imperialism, opportunism, revisionism, and Maoism. Based on SED conference reports and secondary sources; 32 notes. G. L. Neville

1525. Kuczynski, Jürgen. DIE DURCHSETZUNG DER FREUNDSCHAFTSIDEE ZUR SOWJETUNION IN UNSEREM VOLKE [The establishment of the idea of friendship with the USSR in our people]. *Beiträge zur Geschichte der Arbeiterbewegung [East Germany] 1979 21(5): 678-681.* When the Soviet troops liberated Eastern Germany, the Soviet administration and German Communist politicians were confronted by an extreme anti-Soviet spirit, the result of Nazi anti-Communist propaganda since 1933. Until 1949 the reeducation was mainly accomplished in thousands of meetings and discussions led by functionaries of the Socialist Unity Party of Germany (SED). Based on printed documents and secondary literature; 3 notes. R. Wagnleitner

1526. Kuhne, Lutz. DIE WIRTSCHAFTSPOLITIK DER SED ZUR VORBEREITUNG ZER ZENTRALEN WIRTSHAFTSPLANUNG (ANFANG BIS MITTE 1948) [The economic policy of the Socialist Unity Party of Germany for the preparation of central economic planning; 1948]. *Jahrbuch für Wirtschaftsgeschichte [East Germany] 1978 (3): 9-30.* While the western zones of Germany were preparing for the introduction of the Marshall Plan from the beginning of 1948, the creation of a new administration, land reform, and the nationalization of the main banks, insurance companies, and industries resulted in deep social and economic changes in the Soviet occupied zone. The continuous training of the members of more than 30,000 factory committees for the modernization and coordination of production assisted the advancement of central planning. Only the cooperation of the Soviet Military Administration with the administration of the nationalized industries and the labor unions could guarantee the success of a central economic plan. Based on documents in the Central State Archive, Potsdam, and the Institute for Marxism-Leninism central Party archive; 2 tables, 18 notes. R. Wagnleitner/S

1527. Kulinych, I. M. 30 ROKIV NIMETS'KIY DEMOKRATYCHNIY RESPUBLITSI [30 years of the German Democratic Republic]. *Ukraïns'kyi Istorychnyi Zhurnal [USSR] 1979 (9): 132-135.* Views East Germany's existence as testimony to Marxism-Leninism and the superiority of socialism to capitalism. Describes some of East Germany's notable economic achievements under the leadership of the Socialist Unity Party in unity with the USSR and other Comecon members. 14 notes. I. Krushelnycky

1528. Laboor, Ernst. TRADITIONEN DEUTSCH-SOWJETISCHER ARBEITERSOLIDARITÄT [Traditions of German and Soviet worker solidarity]. *Zeitschrift für Geschichtswissenschaft [East Germany] 1969 17(9): 1148-1154.* The October 1917 Russian Revolution is the most compelling model for the German workers' movement. V. I. Lenin fostered better Soviet-German relations, recognizing Germany's key role in the socialist struggle against imperialism. During the German Third Reich many individual Germans and Russians worked together, and Soviet Communists aided the outlawed German Communists in their fight for survival. Opposition to communism and enmity toward the Soviet Union have precipitated Germany's worst catastrophes of the century. Based on contemporary documents and secondary sources; 14 notes. G. H. Libbey

1529. Lebedel, Claude. LA POLÍTICA DE PRECIOS EN LAS ECONOMÍAS SOCIALISTAS [Price policy in socialist economies]. *Investigación Econ. [Mexico] 1971 31(124): 827-837.* Examines the role of price policy in Communist countries, especially in East Germany, including the way prices are determined.

1530. LeGloannec, Anne-Marie. LA RDA DANS LE MONDE SOCIALISTE [The German Democratic Republic in the socialist world]. *Rev. d'Allemagne [France] 1979 11(4): 554-569.* East Germany is caught in the dilemma between involuntary dependence upon the USSR and national independence. Close economic ties with the USSR guarantee the economic viability of the GDR but also increase its dependence on the USSR. Situated between the western and eastern European systems, the GDR serves as a bridge which strengthens it in dealing with the USSR and provides economic opportunities in the Council for Mutual Economic Assistance (Comecon) states. The Mutual Aid Treaty of 1975, while confirming Soviet domination of the GDR, increases GDR influence in eastern Europe. The Socialist Unity Party (SED) has been able to mediate between the Communist Party of the USSR and those of western Europe. In regard to Third World countries, while aid given by the GDR implements Soviet policies, it also enhances the international status of the GDR. 34 notes. J. S. Gassner

1531. Lemmnitz, Alfred. LERNENDER LEHRER. AUS DEN ANFÄNGEN MEINER ARBEIT AN DER PARTEIHOCHSCHULE [Student teacher: the beginnings of my work at the Party college]. *Beiträge zur Gesch. der Arbeiterbewegung [East Germany] 1984 26(3): 347-355.* Prints an excerpt from the memoirs of Alfred Lemmnitz, who contributed to higher education in East Germany under the auspices of the Socialist Unity Party of Germany. He taught political economy at the Karl Marx Party College in Berlin. R. Grove

1532. Leonhardt, Rolf. DIE POLITIK DER SED ZUR FESTIGUNG DES DEMOKRATISCHEN BLOCKS NACH DER GRÜNDUNG DER DDR OKTOBER 1949 BIS FRÜHJAHR 1950 [The politics of the Socialist Unity Party regarding the consolidation of the Democratic Block after the founding of the German Democratic Republic, October 1949 to early 1950]. *Zeitschrift für Geschichtswissenschaft [East Germany] 1978 26(6): 483-496.* Surveys the various political parties in East Germany immediately after the founding of the republic, of which the Socialist Unity Party was always the largest. Maintains that the most notable achievement of the consolidation process was the decision concerning the program of the National Front and the declaration of the Democratic Block of 16 May 1950 concerning the common preparations for the October elections. Argues that the successful liaison between the workers of the various parties led to their merging in the Socialist Unity Party. Archival sources; table, 49 notes. A. Alcock

1533. Leonhardt, Rolf. ZUR BÜNDNISPOLITIK DER SED BEIM AUFBAU DER ENTWICKELTEN SOZIALISTISCHEN GESELLSCHAFT 1961-1970 [The alliance policy of the Socialist Unity Party in the building of a developed socialist society]. *Zeits. für Geschichtswissenschaft [East Germany] 1981 29(4): 291-303.* Since the 1960's the socialism in East Germany has achieved the capability of developing independently out of its own political, economic, and ideological foundation. The Socialist Unity Party (SED), at the 6th Party Congress (1963), accepted the new strategic task of a broad advance of socialism, accentuating the basic problems of maintaining the successful alliance of the working class with other friendly parties in the democratic bloc. But the cooperation of the Democratic Farmers' Party, Christian-Democratic Union, Liberal Democratic Party, and National Democratic Party, allied in the National Front and led by the SED, made possible the fulfillment of the task of building a developed socialist society. Based on official publications; 52 notes. G. E. Pergl

1534. Lieck, Steffen. DIE ANEIGNUNG WIRTSCHAFTSPOLITISCHER ERFAHRUNGEN DER KPDSU DURCH DIE SED 1963-64 [The assimilation of economic and political experiences of the CPSU by the SED in 1963-64]. *Zeitschrift für Geschichtswissenschaft [East Germany] 1977 25(6): 645-655.* With the consolidation of the socialist system in the German Democratic Republic the Socialist Unity Party (SED) studied Soviet economic policies and production techniques more intensively and systematically, beginning in 1963. Delegations from the Central Committee of the SED visited the Soviet Union, SED district organizations exchanged information with their counterparts in the USSR, the German press reported Soviet experiences and techniques, and Soviet lecturers visited East Germany. As a result, Soviet experiences were successfully applied to the economy of the GDR. 28 notes. J. T. Walker

1535. Liening, Rudi. JAHRESTAGE DES ROTEN OKTOBER IN BERLIN [Anniversary of Red October in Berlin]. *Archivmitteilungen [East Germany] 1977 27(5): 173-176.* Charts the solidarity shown by the German working class movement with the USSR, 1917-77, with special reference to the response of the German Communist Party to the possibility of a repeated imperialist intervention in the USSR, in 1927.

1536. Linder, Bertrand. LA POLITIQUE DE DEFENSE DE LA RDA [GDR defense policy]. *Revue d'Allemagne [France] 1984 16(1): 43-59.* The National People's Army of East Germany (GDR) grew steadily by gradual stages from the police force in the Soviet occupation zone in 1945 until the consolidation in the defense establishment in the 1970's. The armed forces are controlled by the National Defense Council, except that the mobile forces of the NPA are under the Warsaw Pact Unified Command. Political control of the armed forces has been achieved through close integration with the SED (Socialist Unity Party). Popular support for the military establishment has been strengthened by military training provided by the educational system and through the growing militarization of society. The mission of the armed forces is determined by their position within the Warsaw Pact organization. Special emphasis is placed upon the protection of socialism against the aggressive intentions of NATO. 32 notes. J. S. Gassner

1537. Lozek, Gerhard. ZÁKLADNÍ OTÁZKY SOUČASNÉ KRITIKY BURŽOAZNÍ HISTORIOGRAFIE [Fundamental questions about contemporary criticism of Bourgeois historiography]. *Československý Časopis Hist. [Czechoslovakia] 1980 28(6): 888-911.* West German manipulations of general and German history have become increasingly sophisticated during the 1970's. The new bourgeois social history operates with materialist or reformist conceptions that obscure or deny the inevitability of socialism. West German historiography tends to harness all Germans to nationalist West German claims and attacks the legitimacy of the East German Socialist Unity Party (SED). Against this, Marxist historians

must assert the continuity of the democratic-socialist development that is now embodied in East Germany, but is applicable to all of Germany. 67 notes. Russian and German summaries.
R. E. Weltsch

1538. Lozek, Gerhard. ZU NEUEREN BÜRGERLICHEN DARSTELLUNGEN DER GESCHICHTE DER DDR [On recent bourgeois works on the history of East Germany]. *Zeitschrift für Geschichtswissenschaft [East Germany] 1973 21(5): 509-523.* Review essay on recent American and West German publications on the formation of the Socialist Unity Party of Germany and the social, economic, and political development of East Germany since World War II. 65 notes. R. Wagnleitner

1539. Lück, Hansjürgen. ZUM BESCHLUSS DES POLITBÜROS DES ZK DER SED VOM 14. JANUAR 1958 "ÜBER DIE ROLLE DER PARTEI IN DER NATIONALEN VOLKSARMEE" [On the decree of the Politburo of the Central Committee of the Socialist Unity Party of 14 January 1958 "On the Role of the Party in the National People's Army]. *Militärgeschichte [East Germany] 1983 22(2): 186-188.* Demonstrates that the leadership of the Socialist Unity party has devoted great attention to Party organizations within the army for a long time. The focus is on the special responsibility of Party members and candidates for the effectiveness of political work and the success of military training as well as for a constantly high combat readiness. 10 notes.
J/T (H. D. Andrews)

1540. Lux, Gerhard and Nelles, Toni. DER AUFBAU UND DIE ENTWICKLUNG DER NVA—SCHÖPFERISCHE ANWENDUNG DES LENINSCHEN MILITÄRPROGRAMMS DURCH DIE SED [Creation and development of the National People's Army through the creative application of Lenin's military program by the Socialist Unity Party]. *Zeitschrift für Militärgeschichte [East Germany] 1970 9(6): 659-673.* Continued from a previous article (see abstract 17B:1813). Part II. The social and state system of socialism is a stable base for the achievement of larger and qualitatively new military-political and military tasks. The character of the relationship among socialist states made possible Soviet military aid to other socialist states. The training of the socialist soldier and the formation of a strong socialist collective in the Army has a natural ideological basis. 30 notes. G. E. Pergl

1541. Mai, Joachim. DIE UNIVERSITÄT GREIFSWALD IM RINGEN UM EIN NEUES VERHÄLTNIS ZUR SOWJETUNION 1945-1949 [Greifswald University in the struggle for a new relationship with the USSR, 1945-49]. *Jahrbuch für Geschichte der Sozialistischen Länder Europas [East Germany] 1976 20(2): 211-225.* Greifswald University was the only university in East Germany to survive the war completely undestroyed. It closed down on 30 May 1945 in order to purge the teaching staff, the teaching material, and the curricula of all fascist and militarist influences. After reopening in February 1946, there were only germs of a progressive attitude toward the USSR because of the lingering influences of fascism, the withdrawal by the staff and students into academic work, and anti-Soviet propaganda from the imperialist side. On the other hand, progressive attitudes could be found among the new professors, members of the Institute for Slavic Studies, and the new pedagogical faculty. The leading role was played by the Socialist Unity Party (SED), which had had its own section in the university since August 1946. Starting in January 1948, courses were given, in which the staff studied thoroughly the classics of Marxism-Leninism. After the SED had developed into a party of the "new type," a systematic study of the history of the Communist Party was begun. The unfolding and deepening of German-Soviet friendship needed extensive effort. The lack of qualified cadres was considerable, therefore the commitment and work of the existing progressive forces of those days are to be valued even more highly. 52 notes. L. H. Schmidt

1542. Marcou, Gérard. LE PARTI ET L'ÉTAT EN R.D.A. [Party and state in East Germany]. *Rev. d'Allemagne [France] 1974 6(4): 73-114.* Discusses the growth of responsibility of the organs of the state and the reinforcing role of the Socialist Unity Party (SED). This double relation is "concretized by the presence at nearly every important political post" which guarantees that the activity of the organs of the state, as all other organizations, follows the party line. Analyzes the direction of the political system by the SED, its functions and functional liaisons, the determination of the party line, specifically decision-making, and ideological action and activities. Emphasizes the modalities of political direction of state agencies by the party. Primary and secondary sources; 62 notes.
L. S. Frey

1543. Masich, V. F. VERNYI SYN NEMETSKOGO RABOCHEGO KLASSA: K 70-LETIIU SO DNIA ROZHDENIIA GENERAL'NOGO SEKRETARIA TSK SEPG ERIKHA KHONEKKERA [A true son of the German working class: on the 70th birthday of Erich Honecker, general secretary of the Socialist Unity Party of East Germany]. *Voprosy Istorii KPSS [USSR] 1982 (8): 86-89.* Erich Honecker was born on 25 August 1912 into a workers' family, and early knew deprivation. He entered the Young Communist League in 1926 and the German Communist Party in 1927. From 1930 to 1933 he studied in Moscow. He was imprisoned in Germany in 1935 and freed by the Soviet army in 1945. He performed signal services for the Socialist Unity Party of Germany, becoming its general secretary in 1971. He has been chief of East Germany's defense committee since 1971. He combats imperialism. He fights for peace and progress and is a true friend and ally of the USSR. Based on *Protocols of the Activities of the 10th Party Congress of the Socialist Unity Party of Germany,* Berlin, 1981; 12 notes.
A. J. Evans

1544. Matern, G. BOR'BA SEPG ZA KONSOLIDATSIIU DEMOKRATICHESKIKH SIL V GDR [The struggle of the Socialist Unity Party of Germany for the consolidation of democratic forces in East Germany]. *Voprosy Istorii KPSS [USSR] 1966 (4): 29-42.* Describes the events preceding the formation in East Germany in 1946 of the Socialist Unity Party, and subsequent party policies.

1545. Mattausch, Antje. ZUR JUGENDPOLITIK DER SED BEI DER GESTALTUNG DER ENTWICKELTEN SOZIALISTISCHEN GESELLSCHAFT IN DER DDR [On the youth policy of the Socialist Unity Party of Germany (SED) in the formation of the development of the socialist society in East Germany]. *Wissenschaftliche Zeitschrift der U. Rostock. Gesellschafts- und Sprachwissenschaftliche Reihe [East Germany] 1974 23(2): 183-189.* Since the middle of the 1950's, when the period of the development of the socialist East Germany was arrived at, the Free German Youth became one of the most important party organizations to prepare the young people for an advanced socialist society. Based on documents in the Zentralarchiv der FDJ, Berlin, and secondary literature; 43 notes. R. Wagnleitner

1546. Meissner, Klaus-Peter. EIN KÄMPFERISCHER KOMMUNIST IM DIENSTE DER ARBEITERKLASSE: ZUM 90. GEBURTSTAG VON WALTER ULBRICHT [A fighting Communist in the service of the working class: on the 90th birthday of Walter Ulbricht]. *Militärgeschicte [East Germany] 1983 22(3): 349-352.* A veteran of World War I, Ulbricht joined the new Communist Party of Germany in 1919 and rose in the ranks during the 1920's. He left Germany in 1933 but continued his active involvement in Communist activities in the Soviet Union as a founder of the National Committee "Free Germany." In 1945 he returned to Germany and helped to found the Socialist Unity Party and the German Democratic Republic. Photo; 5 notes. H. D. Andrews

1547. Meske, Werner. WECHSELBEZIEHUNGEN ZWISCHEN WISSENSCHAFT UND PRODUKTION UND DIE ENTWICKLUNG DES SOZIALISTISCHEN FORSCHUNGSPOTENTIALS [The correlation between science and production and the development of socialist research potential]. *Wissenschaftliche Zeitschrift der Friedrich-Schiller-Universität Jena. Gesellschafts- und Sprachwissenschaftliche Reihe [East Germany] 1980 29(5): 555-561.* Discusses the importance of the scientific and technological research that has been carried out in East Germany, 1965-78, and shows that the rate of growth in the field of research and development slowed in the 1970's. Identifies the most important problems in the development of research potential under socialism and suggests fundamental changes in the system of developing and utilizing research potential to increase the efficiency and social effectiveness of labor, facilities, and finance in scientific research. Secondary sources; 11 notes. G. L. Neville

1548. Meusel, Hans. DIE IDEOLOGISCHE TÄTIGKEIT DER PARTEI ZUR VERWIRKLICHUNG IHRER WIRTSCHAFTSPOLITIK VOM JULI 1958 BIS SOMMER 1961 [The ideological work of the Party for the realization of its economic policies, July 1958 to the summer of 1961]. *Beiträge zur Gesch. der Arbeiterbewegung [East Germany] 1982 24(1): 53-65.* Considers how the ideological work of the Socialist Unity Party (SED) in East Germany, 1958-61, contributed to the realization of the economic policy that had been decided on at the 5th Party Congress in July 1958. The political and ideological work of the Party during this period stressed the links between socialist reconstruction and the need for an increase in productivity and efficiency and the importance of scientific and technical progress. Based on documents relating to the 5th Party Congress held in Berlin and secondary sources; 51 notes. G. L. Neville

1549. Meusel, Hans. PROBLEME DER AUSARBEITUNG UND DER VERWIRKLICHUNG DES ZWEITEN ZENTRALEN PERSPEKTIVPLANS ZUR ERFORSCHUNG UND DARSTELLUNG DER REGIONALEN GESCHICHTE DER ARBEITERBEWEGUNG DURCH DIE GESCHICHTSKOMMISSIONEN DER SED (1971-1975) [Problems of the composition and realization of the second central plan of perspective for the research and presentation of the regional history of the workers' movement by the Commissions for History of the German Socialist Unity Party, 1971-75]. *Beiträge zur Geschichte der Arbeiterbewegung [East Germany] 1971 13(5): 846-850.*

1550. Minnerup, Günter. EAST GERMANY'S FROZEN REVOLUTION. *New Left Rev. [Great Britain] 1982 (132): 5-32.* The creation of East Germany in 1949 has done little to fulfill the aspirations of the international communist movement of a German state in which socialism would prosper in more than an economic sense.

1551. Möschner, Günter and Gabert, Josef. DER HISTORISCHE PLATZ DER 3. PARTEIKONFERENZ DER SED IM KAMPF FÜR FRIEDEN UND SOZIALISMUS [The Third Conference of the Socialist Unity Party of Germany in the struggle for peace and socialism]. *Beiträge zur Gesch. der Arbeiterbewegung [East Germany] 1984 26(3): 291-303.* Studies the effects of the Party conference of 24-30 March 1956 on the development of East Germany. It articulated the conflict between socialism and imperialism and the unity of peace and socialism. It laid the foundation for 1957 laws detailing the rights and duties of local governments. 49 notes. R. Grove

1552. Möschner, Günter. DIE POLITIK DER SED FÜR DEN AUFBAU UND DIE ENTWICKLUNG DES SOZIALISTISCHEN AUSSENHANDELS DER DDR (1949 BIS 1955) [The policy of the Socialist Unity Party for the building and development of the socialist foreign trade of East Germany, 1949-55]. *Jahrbuch für Wirtschaftsgeschichte [East Germany] 1979 (3): 27-48.* The ruling party of East Germany has realized since the birth of the state that foreign trade would present an important instrument for strengthening the country's economy, improving the standard of living, and realizing foreign policy concepts corresponding to the interests of the socialist camp. Imperialist embargo policies against East Germany became ineffective when trade with the USSR and other socialist states made friendly trade relations with other states possible. Based on published works; 3 tables, 41 notes. G. E. Pergl

1553. Mückenberger, Erich. 35. JAHRESTAG DER GRÜNDUNG DER SED: ERINNERUNGEN UND GEDANKEN [35th anniversary of the founding of the Socialist Unity Party (SED): memories and thoughts]. *Beiträge zur Geschichte der Arbeiterbewegung [East Germany] 1981 23(2): 163-171.* The emergence of a unified party corresponded to the desire of the large majority of the working class. Unification became possible through the legacy of the common battle against fascism. It was attained in hard struggle against the representatives of revisionism with their anti-Soviet propaganda. Based on published sources, including minutes of Party meetings; 10 notes. A. Schuetz

1554. Müller, Gerhard. EINIGE ASPEKTE DER ENERGIEPOLITIK DER SED SEIT DEM VIII. PARTEITAG [Some aspects of the energy policies of the Socialist Unity Party (SED) since the 8th Party Conference]. *Zeitschrift für Geschichtswissenschaft [East Germany] 1982 30(7): 609-620.* Describes the measures taken by the SED during the 1970's to produce a rational energy policy in East Germany. This was important because the prices of all types of fuel increased dramatically during tnis period and the high energy costs affected industry and industrial investment. An energy commission was set up to look into the problems, and an annual review of energy resources and use in industry was introduced. Based on SED documents and secondary sources; 33 notes. G. L. Neville

1555. Müller, Hans and Reissig, Karl. ZUR GESCHICHTE DER ÖKONOMISCHEN POLITIK DER SED [The economic policy of the Socialist Unity Party]. *Zeitschrift für Geschichtswissenschaft [East Germany] 1967 15(1): 5-19.* Between 1949 and 1963 the economic policy of the SED created the preconditions for the transformation of the existing social and economic structures of East Germany into a socialist system. Based on printed documents and secondary literature; 23 notes. R. Wagnleitner

1556. Müller, Klaus and Wessel, Karl-Friedrich. MARXISTISCH-LENINISTISCHE PHILOSOPHIE UND DIE EINZELWISSENSCHAFTEN: 25 JAHRE WISSENSCHAFTSPOLITIK DER SED [Marxist-Leninist philosophy and the sciences: 25 years of science and politics in the Socialist Unity Party]. *Wissenschaftliche Zeitschrift der Humbolt-U. zu Berlin. Gesellschafts- und Sprachwissenschaftliche Reihe [East Germany] 1971 20(4): 357-371.* Discusses the influence of Marxism-Leninism on the development of the humanities and natural sciences in East Germany 1949-71. Based on secondary literature; 61 notes.

1557. Müller, Roland. EIN NEUER AUFSCHWUNG IN DER TÄTIGKEIT DER FDJ NACH DEM IV. PARTEITAG DER SED (FRÜHJAHR 1954 BIS FRÜHJAHR 1955) [A new upsurge in the activities of the Free German Youth (FDJ) movement after the Fourth Party Congress of the Socialist Unity Party, spring 1954 to spring 1955]. *Wissenschaftliche Zeitschrift der Wilhelm-Pieck-Universität Rostock, Gesellschafts- und Sprachwissenschaftliche Reihe [East Germany] 1976 25(1): 37-43.* The decision of the Fourth Party Congress of early April 1954 to press ahead in the creation of a socialist state gave an important impetus to the development of the FDJ as a socialist mass organization. Youth brigades and youth projects were established, particularly in the machine tool and power industries, to assist in the achievement of record levels of production. Emphasis was placed on increasing working-class membership of the FDJ, the economic and political education of youth, and the political participation of youth. Overall substantial achievements were made, especially in the industrial sector and in distribution. But the results in the agricultural sector left much to be desired. Based on documents in the central archives of the FDJ and secondary sources; 68 notes. English summary. J. A. Perkins

1558. Müller, Roland. IM KAMPF UM DIE EINHEIT DER ARBEITERKLASSE WURDE DIE FDJ GESCHAFFEN [The Free German Youth (FDJ) was created in the struggle for the unity of the working class]. *Wissenschaftliche Zeitschrift der U. Rostock. Gesellschafts- und Sprachwissenschaftliche Reihe [East Germany] 1974 23(2): 157-163.* Immediately after the end of World War II antifascist youth committees were formed in the Soviet occupation zone of Germany which prepared the formation of a uniform youth movement. After the founding of the Socialist Unity Party of Germany (SED) in the spring of 1946, the political conditions for the formation of the Free German Youth (FDJ) were set. Based on documents in the Institute for Marxism-Leninism, Leipzig, Zentralarchiv der FDJ, Berlin, and secondary literature; 17 notes. R. Wagnleitner

1559. Muschalle, Adelheid and Dittrich, Gottfried. VERÄNDERUNGEN IM QUALIFIKATIONSNIVEAU DER ARBEITER IN DER SOZIALISTISCHEN INDUSTRIE 1958-1962 UND IHRE ROLLE IM WACHSTUM DER ARBEITERKLASSE DER DDR IN DER ENDPHASE DER ÜBERGANGSPERIODE [Changes in the level of qualifications of workers in socialist industry, 1958-62, and their role in the growth of the working class of East Germany in the last phase of the transition period]. *Jahrbuch für Geschichte [East Germany] 1983 (28): 235-264.* Chronicles the work of the Socialist Unity Party of Germany in establishing qualifications for industrial workers. Advances in technology necessitated rising qualifications, which were met, especially by women workers. Reflects on the effects in terms of social conditions and the growth of the working class. 6 tables, 137 notes. R. Grove

1560. Naumann, Gerhard. DIE AUSWERTUNG DER BESCHLÜSSE DES VIII PARTEITAGES IN DEN LEITUNGEN UND GRUNDORGANISATION DER SED [Evaluating the resolutions of the 8th Party Congress in the administration and basic organization of the Socialist Unity Party (SED)]. *Beiträge zur Gesch. der Arbeiterbewegung [East Germany] 1982 24(2): 163-172.* Examines the importance of the resolutions passed at the 8th SED Party Congress in 1971 for the evolution of socialist society in East Germany, 1971-75. One of the main tasks was to make all Party members familiar with the resolutions taken at the conference through meetings, seminars, and further education. These resolutions and objectives concerned the political, ideological, economic, cultural, and military strengthening of the German Democratic Republic. Based on reports of the 8th Party Conference held in Berlin and secondary sources; 40 notes. G. L. Neville

1561. Naumann, Gerhard. DIE SOZIALISTISCHE EINHEITSPARTEI DEUTSCHLANDS IN DER ZEIT DER VORBEREITUNG IHRES VIII. PARTEITAGES [The Socialist Unity Party (SED) of Germany during the preparation for the 8th Party Congress]. *Beiträge zur Gesch. der Arbeiterbewegung [East Germany] 1981 23(1): 3-17.* Preparations for the 8th Party Congress in June 1971, included party elections, seminars, and membership drives, and local, regional, and national meetings, starting with the 14th meeting of the Central Committee of the SED in December 1970. Of special importance was the 16th meeting of the Central Committee, where Walter Ulbricht resigned as First Party Secretary, and Erich Honecker was elected as his successor. The Central Committee meetings dealt heavily with the problems in fulfilling the five-year economic plan. Based largely on minutes of party meetings; 75 notes. A. Schuetz

1562. Nehrig, Christel and Piskol, Joachim. ZUR FÜHRENDEN ROLLE DER KPD IN DER DEMOKRATISCHEN BODENREFORM [The leading role of the German Communist Party in democratic land reform]. *Zeitschrift für Geschichtswissenschaft [East Germany] 1980 28(4): 324-339.* During the process of land reform in East Germany, the German Communist Party used the teachings of Marxism and Soviet experience to create a strong bond between workers and peasants. Agricultural workers were once the most exploited laborers in Germany, but eventually even the middle-class farmers accepted the ideas of democratic land reform and rejected the intrigues of large landowners. The needs of the industrial centers and their workers were soon fulfilled through the reorganization of agricultural production on a Marxist basis. 91 notes. G. E. Pergl

1563. Nehrig, Christel. ZUR WEITERENTWICKLUNG DER AGRARPOLITISCHEN KONZEPTION DER SED VOR DER 1. PARTEIKONFERENZ 1949 [The further development of the conception of the agrarian policy of the Socialist Unity Party (SED) before the 1st Party Conference in 1949]. *Zeitschrift für Geschichtswissenschaft [East Germany] 1982 30(6): 483-497.* Examines the formulation by the SED, in preparation for its 1st Party Conference in 1949, of its agricultural policy and considers the strategies it used to strengthen socialism in rural areas and to repulse capitalist powers. A transitional process to socialism was taking place in East Germany, 1948-49, with regard to agriculture and the farming communities. The reeducation of the farmers was aided by the working class in this process. Particular attention is paid to the need for increasing the efficiency of agriculture as a central theme of economic planning, the problem of land ownership, and the need to strengthen links between the industrial workers and the farmers. Based on Party conference documents held in Berlin and secondary sources; 69 notes. G. L. Neville

1564. Norden, Albert. A DECISIVE CONDITION FOR VICTORY. *World Marxist R. [Canada] 1975 18(1): 29-38.* Discusses the emergence of the Socialist Unity Party in East Germany in 1946.

1565. Otto, Wilfriede and Sellin, Gerhard. KONFERENZ AN DER PARTEIHOCHSCHULE ANLÄSSLICH DES 25. JAHRESTAGES DER GRÜNDUNG DER SED [Conference at the party college on the occasion of the 25th anniversary of the founding of the Socialist Unity Party of Germany]. *Zeitschrift für Geschichtswissenschaft [East Germany] 1971 19(10): 1289-1291.* Reviews the lectures and discussions of the conference at the party college in Berlin in March 1971 which analyzed the role of the Socialist Unity Party of Germany in the political and economic development of East Germany.

1566. Parson, Walter. ASPEKTE DER PROGRAMMATIK DER FDJ IN DER ERSTEN HÄLFTE DER FÜNFZIGER JAHRE [Program of the Free German Youth in the first half of the 1950's]. *Wissenschaftliche Zeitschrift der Wilhelm-Pieck-Universität Rostock [East Germany] 1976 25(9): 715-721.* The revolutionary program of the Free German Youth worked out between 1949 and 1952 was based on the close cooperation with all other organizations of the Socialist Unity Party of Germany and attempted the formation of the social, economic, cultural, and political basis of socialist society in East Germany.

1567. Parson, Walter. DIE ROLLE DER ARBEITERJUGEND BEI DER ENTWICKLUNG DER FDJ ZU EINER SOZIALISTISCHEN JUGENDORGANISATION [The role of working-class youth in the development of the Free German Youth into a socialist youth organization]. *Beiträge zur Geschichte der Arbeiterbewegung [East Germany] 1973 15(4): 678-691.* The political education of working-class youth by the Free German Youth in the fifties was a central task of the youth policy of the Socialist Unity Party of Germany. The systematic study of Marxism-Leninism and education in the spirit of proletarian internationalism were the two bases of the educational work of the Free German Youth. In the fifties the Free German Youth developed from an antifascist-democratic movement to a socialist mass organization. Based on documents in the FDJ archive Berlin, published documents. and secondary literature; 81 notes. R. Wagnleitner

1568. Parson, Walter. PROBLEME DER JUGENDPOLITIK DER SED WÄHREND DER SOZIALISTISCHEN REVOLUTION IN DER DDR [Problems of youth policy in the Socialist Unity Party of Germany (SED) during the socialist revolution in East Germany]. *Wissenschaftliche Zeitschrift der U. Rostock. Gesellschafts- und Sprachwissenschaftliche Reihe [East Germany] 1972 21(2): 189-198.* The aims of Party youth policy in Germany immediately after the war were the winning of the sympathies of German youth after years of fascist indoctrination, the creation of an antifascist democratic youth organization that was able to win the majority of the German youth, and the socialist transformation of this organization.

1569. Pawula, G. and Pawula, H. ZUR SCHÖPFERISCHEN ANWENDUNG DER MARXISTISCH-LENINISTISCHEN PRINZIPIEN DER BÜNDNISPOLITIK DER SED [The creative application of the Marxist-Leninist principles of alliance policy by the Socialist Unity Party of Germany]. *Wissenschaftliche Zeitschrift der Karl-Marx U. Leipzig [East Germany]. 1971 20(2): 183-200.* The basic principle of Marxist-Leninist alliance policy is the promotion of the leading role of the working class and its Marxist-Leninist party. The Socialist Unity Party of Germany collected important experience through a combination of alliance policy with

socialist democracy. Agricultural cooperatives and production groups in the industries are prominent in securing the development of Marxist-Leninist alliance policy. Secondary sources; 34 notes.
R. Wagnleitner

1570. Pellmann, Dietmar and Gässner, Wolfgang. DIE BÜNDNISPOLITIK DER SED BEI DER ENTWICKLUNG ENGER BEZIEHUNGEN ZWISCHEN ARBEITERKLASSE UND WISSENSCHAFTLICH-TECHNISCHER INTELLIGENZ ENDE DER FÜNFZIGER/ANFANG DER SECHZIGER JAHRE [The alliance policies of the Socialist Unity Party (SED) to develop closer relations between the working class and scientific and technical intellectuals in the late 1950's and early 1960's]. *Beiträge zur Gesch. der Arbeiterbewegung [East Germany] 1982 24(2): 173-184.* Examines the importance of developing the alliance between the working class and scientific and technical specialists for the SED's policies in East Germany, 1957-61. The SED's task was to get the scientists, engineers, and technicians from the old capitalist system to accept socialist reconstruction and to improve their living and working conditions. At the same time a new socialist scientific and technical intelligentsia was being educated from the ranks of the working class. Secondary sources; 52 notes. G. L. Neville

1571. Peter, Willy. ZUR HERAUSBILDUNG DER KONZEPTION DES ENTWICKELTEN SOZIALISMUS: ÜBER EINIGE HISTORISCHE ABSCHNITTE IM PROZESS DER THEORIE- UND STRATEGIE- ENTWICKLUNG IN DER DDR 1961/1962-1971 [Growth of the concept of developed socialism: historic phases in the process of theory and strategy development in East Germany, 1961-71]. *Jahrbuch für Geschichte [East Germany] 1979 20: 269-322.* As socialism advanced, changes occurred and new strategies had to be worked out, always focusing on the correlation between socialism and communism. The progress and result of this development are reflected in the documents from the yearly conferences of the German Socialist Unity Party and the Communist Party in the USSR. No longer considered a short phase between capitalism and communism, socialism, by the end of the 1960's, was expected to cover a much longer time and was deemed an important step toward fully developed communism. Based on the program for the Socialist Unity Party of East Germany and other primary sources. T. Parker

1572. Picaper, Jean Paul. WALTER ULBRICHT, OU LA FIN D'UNE ÉPOQUE [Walter Ulbricht, or the end of an epoch]. *Documents [France] 1973 28(5): 113-122.* Views the transformation in opinion by East Germany's Communist leaders and officials about the policies of Walter Ulbricht, which are respected as those of the founder of the German Communist Party but seen as outdated today.

1573. Pietsch, Wolfgang and Willisch, Jürgen. ZUR FÜHRENDEN ROLLE DER SED BEI DER ENTWICKLUNG DER LUFTSTREITKRÄFTE/LUFTVERTEIDIGUNG ZU EINER MODERNEN TEILSTREITKRAFT DER NVA [On the leading role of the Socialist Unity Party in developing the air force and air defense into a modern part of the forces of the National People's Army]. *Militärgeschichte [East Germany] 1981 20(2): 133-144.* Describes Party activities among the troops of the air force and air defense forces, especially the delegate conferences of the Party organizations. Discusses the air forces' development through three phases: 1956-61, 1961-70, and 1971-79. Illus., 20 notes.
J/T (H. D. Andrews)

1574. Pikarski, Margot and Voigtländer, Annelies. ZUR STELLUNG DER REVOLUTIONÄREN PARTEI DER DEUTSCHEN ARBEITERKLASSE ZUR GROSSEN SOZIALISTISCHEN OKTOBERREVOLUTION [The position of the revolutionary party of the German working class on the Great Socialist October Revolution]. *Jahrbuch für Geschichte [East Germany] 1977 17: 521-542.* Introduces and reproduces five documents issued by the leadership of the Communist Party of Germany (KPD) and the Socialist Unity Party (SED) in 1927, 1937, 1947, 1957, and 1967 to celebrate the Russian Revolution and to set new directions for the class struggle in Germany. The documents show the continuous application of the lessons of the Russian Revolution to the struggle of the German working class and reflect the stages of development of the KPD and the SED. 17 notes. J. B. Street

1575. Plener, Ulla. ZUM IDEOLOGISCH-POLITISCHEN KLÄRUNGSPROZESS IN DER SPD DER SOWJETISCHEN BESATZUNGSZONE 1945 [The ideological-political clarification in the German Social Democratic Party in the Soviet zone of occupation, 1945]. *Beiträge zur Geschichte der Arbeiterbewegung [East Germany] 1972 14(1): 35-59.* The defeat of Germany, the completely changed power situation, the assurance of the democratic transformation of state and economy under the Russian administration and the German Communists, and the experience of the fascist dictatorship forced many Social Democrats to the realization of the superior importance of the unity of the working class. The social-political changes in the Soviet zone resulted in the strengthening of the German Communist Party which profited from the ambiguous policy of the Social Democrats. Based on documents in the Institute of Marxism-Leninism, published documents, and secondary sources; 74 notes. R. Wagnleitner

1576. Pletsch, Carl. "THE SOCIALIST NATION OF THE GERMAN DEMOCRATIC REPUBLIC" OR THE ASYMMETRY IN NATION AND IDEOLOGY BETWEEN THE TWO GERMANIES. *Comparative Studies in Soc. and Hist. [Great Britain] 1979 21(3): 323-345.* The Socialist Unity Party (SED) of East Germany developed an ideology that recognized that the two Germanies had irreconcilable differences. Like the Austrians, East Germans were Germans who were not German, 1947-78.

1577. Reinert, Fritz. DER BEFEHL NR. 209 DER SMAD. DIE ZUSAMMENARBEIT ZWISCHEN SOWJETISCHER MILITÄRADMINISTRATION UND ANTIFASCHISTISCH-DEMOKRATISCHEN STAATSORGANEN BEI DER ERFÜLLUNG DES NEUBAUERN-PROGRAMMS [Order No. 209 of the Soviet military government in Germany: cooperation between the Soviet military administration and antifascist democratic state institutions in realizing the new farmers program]. *Zeitschrift für Geschichtswissenschaft [East Germany] 1975 23(5): 504-515.* Order No. 209 of September 1947 of the Soviet military administration in Germany (SMAD) was designed to provide houses and agricultural buildings for over 200,000 new farmers who had recently received land as a result of the land reform of 1946. The SMAD and the Communist Party of the USSR worked closely with German officials, mass organizations, and the Socialist Unity Party to meet the goals set by the order and to tighten the alliance between the workers and agricultural labor. Consequently, both the democratic, antifascist society in Germany and German-Soviet friendship were strengthened. Based on documents in the Central State Archives in Potsdam; 71 notes. J. T. Walker

1578. Reinhold, Otto. DIE SED—BEWUSSTER UND ORGANISIERTER VORTRUPP DER ARBEITERKLASSE UND DES WERKTÄTIGEN VOLKES [The Socialist Unity Party of Germany: the conscious and organized vanguard of the working class and the working people]. *Beiträge zur Geschichte der Arbeiterbewegung [East Germany] 1976 18(3): 387-402.* The condition for the unification of the German Communist Party and the German Social Democrats in April 1946 was the complete break with opportunism. Already in the 1920's and 1930's the German Communists under Ernst Thälmann had asserted that only a policy of commitment to proletarian class interest could achieve working-class unity. Based on published documents, journals, newspapers, and secondary literature; 22 notes. R. Wagnleitner

1579. Reissig, Karl and Uhlmann, Georg. DIE FESTIGUNG UND ENTWICKLUNG DES SOZIALISMUS IN DER DDR (1961-1965) [The strengthening and development of socialism in the German Democratic Republic, 1961-65]. *Beiträge zur Geschichte der Arbeiterbewegung [East Germany] 1974 16(S): 64-82.* The years 1961-65 were a period of consolidation for the socialist movement in East Germany. The transformation from the capitalist to the socialist structure was essentially complete by 1960. The Socialist Unity Party of Germany (SED) stressed the need for communal social and economic goals set by the workers with the guidance of the Party. Comparison of the years 1961-65 with the 1950's shows that the GDR had become a true socialist state by the mid-1960's. Primary and secondary materials; 43 notes. G. H. Libbey

1580. Reissig, Karl. DIE WACHSENDE ROLLE DER MARXISTISCH-LENINISTISCHEN PARTEI DER ARBEITERKLASSE UND DER BEWUSSTHEIT DER VOLKSMASSEN BEI DER GESTALTUNG DER ENTWICKELTEN SOZIALISTISCHEN GESELLSCHAFT IN DER DDR: VOM ANFANG DER SECHZIGER JAHRE BIS ZUR GEGENWART [The increasing role of the Marxist-Leninist party of the working class and of the consciousness of the popular masses during the formation of the developed socialist society in the German Democratic Republic: from the beginning of the sixties to the present]. *Zeitschrift für Geschichtswissenschaft [East Germany] 1977 25(10): 1257-1271.* After the victory of the socialist revolution in East Germany in the beginning of the sixties, the Socialist Unity Party (SED) molded the development of socialist society. The Sixth (1963), Seventh (1967), Eighth (1971) and Ninth (1976) Party Congresses coordinated both theory and practice in a period unique in human history in that subjective and conscious factors formed society more than did those over which man had no control. Based on 22 theses presented at the Sixth Historical Congress of the German Democratic Republic. 17 notes. J. T. Walker

1581. Reissig, Karl and Schmidt, Walter. ZUR GESCHICHTE DER ENTWICKELTEN SOZIALISTISCHEN GESELLSCHAFT IN DER DDR [On the history of developed socialist society in the German Democratic Republic]. *Zeitschrift für Geschichtswissenschaft [East Germany] 1977 25(4): 389-410.* The ninth Congress of the Socialist Unity Party of Germany in May 1976 gave new impetus to the study of recent German history. By 1918 Lenin had noted the importance of historical instruction in achieving Communist goals. A comprehensive and uniform view of history is essential to the growth of a developed socialist society in the German Democratic Republic. Based on primary and secondary sources; 52 notes. G. H. Libbey

1582. Reissig, Karl. ZUR VERWIRKLICHUNG DER BESCHLÜSSE DES VIII. PARTEITAGES DER SED [On the realization of the decisions of the 8th congress of the Socialist Unity Party of Germany]. *Zeitschrift für Geschichtswissenschaft [East Germany] 1976 24(4): 381-399.* Analyzes the impact of decisions made during the 1971 congress on social, economic, and political development in East Germany. Based on printed documents and secondary literature; 57 notes. R. Wagnleitner

1583. Řezanková, Ivona. KULTURNÍ REVOLUCE NA ÚZEMÍ SOVĚTSKÉ OKUPAČNÍ ZÓNY V NĚMECKU (1945-1949) [The cultural revolution in the Soviet-occupied zone of Germany, 1945-49]. *Sborník Historický [Czechoslovakia] 1984 30: 187-218.* Surveys the steps by which the progressive forces in the Soviet zone of occupied Germany achieved an ideological realignment that rested on both Marxism-Leninism and the German democratic tradition. Far-reaching educational reforms and systematic use of mass communication, which enlisted all of the arts, enabled the Socialist Unity Party (SED) to lay a solid foundation for the German Democratic Republic. The Soviet Military Administration supplied guidance and assistance. Published sources; 57 notes. Russian and German summaries. R. E. Weltsch

1584. Richter, H. DAS ÖKONOMISCHE SYSTEM DES SOZIALISMUS IN DER DDR: SCHÖPFERISCHE ANWENDUNG UND WEITERENTWICKLUNG DER POLITISCHEN ÖKONOMIE DES SOZIALISMUS DURCH DIE SED [The socialist economic system in East Germany: the creative application and development of the political economy of socialism by the Socialist Unity Party of Germany]. *Wissenschaftliche Zeitschrift der Karl-Marx U. Leipzig [East Germany] 1971 20(2): 201-217.* Discusses Leninist principles for the running of a socialist economy as applied to the political leadership of the Socialist Unity Party, 1946-71.

1585. Richter, Hans-Joachim. POLITISCH-IDEOLOGISCHE PROBLEME BEI DER ENTWICKLUNG DES WISSENSCHAFTLICHEN NACHWUCHSES FÜR DIE HOCHSCHULLEHRERSCHAFT DER DDR IN DEN JAHREN 1956/1957 [Political and ideological problems in the development of the new generation of scientists among university teachers in East Germany, 1956-57]. *Jahrbuch für Geschichte [East Germany] 1969 4: 261-294.* Colleges and universities have the duty of developing socialism in East Germany under the conditions of the scientific-technological revolution. In 1956-57, this meant an increasing role for the Socialist Unity Party (SED) and the Freie Deutsche Jugend [Free German Youth] among the students and teachers of science. The SED was much stronger among economists than among members of the mathematics, physical science, medical, and agriculture faculties. 56 notes. J. C. Billigmeier

1586. Riege, Gerhard. L'ÉVOLUTION DU DROIT PUBLIC EN RDA APRÈS LE VIIIe CONGRÈS DU SED (PARTI SOCIALISTE UNIFIÉ D'ALLEMAGNE) [The evolution of administrative law in East Germany after the Eighth Congress of the Socialist Unity Party of Germany]. *Rev. d'Études Comparatives Est-Ouest [France] 1979 10(3): 185-207.* Since the beginning of the seventies there has been a notable evolution in administrative law, characterized by legislative acts pertaining to the prerogatives of central and local state organs and also to the citizen's place in the German socialist state. The author analyzes modifications made in 1974, the Constitution of 1968, and collateral laws. Also discusses the problem of international relations with the USSR and with West Germany. J/S

1587. Rigby, T. H. SOME RECENT BOOKS ON EAST GERMAN POLITICS. *Politics [Australia] 1981 16(2): 303-306.* Reviews several books on politics in East Germany: Eberhard Schneider's *The G. D. R.: The History, Politics, Economy and Society of East Germany* (1978); Martin McCauley's *Marxism-Leninism in the German Democratic Republic. The Socialist Unity Party (SED)* (1979); John Steele's *Socialism with a German Face: The State that Came in from the Cold* (1977); *Politics in the German Democratic Republic* (1975) by John M. Starrels and Anita M. Mallinckrodt; *The Government and Politics of East Germany* (1975) by Kurt Sontheimer and Wilhelm Bleek; Thomas A. Baylis's *The Technical Intelligentsia and the East German Elite: Legitimacy and Social Change in Mature Communism* (1974); Gero Neugebauer's *Partei und Staatsapparat in der DDR. Aspekte der Instrumentalisierung des Staatsapparats durch die SED* (1978); Gert-Joachim Glaessner's *Herrschaft durch Kader. Leitung der Gesellschaft und Kaderpolitik in der DDR* (1977); and *Macht durch Wissen: Zum Zusammenhang von Bildungspolitik, Bildungssystem und Kaderqualifierung in der DDR* (1978) by Gert-Joachim Glaessner and Irmhild Rudolf.

1588. Rodovich, Iu. V. DOKUMENTY O SOTRUDNICHESTVE KPSS I SEPG [Documents on the cooperation between the Communist Party of the Soviet Union and the German Socialist Unity Party]. *Voprosy Istorii [USSR] 1982 (6): 160-164.* The documents were prepared by the Institute of Marxism-Leninism of the Central Committee of the Socialist Unity Party. They show the attention given to uniting agriculture and material resources in East Germany and the USSR through the joint agreements and projects of 1972-74. Joint efforts for peace were crowned by the four-party agreement on Berlin. Problems of the transition from socialism to Communism, the development of a socialist consciousness, and the fight against bourgeois and Maoist ideology are illustrated. Cultural links are also shown. N. S. T. Pentland

1589. Roesler, Jörg. ERFORDERNISSE DER WIRTSCHAFTSENTWICKLUNG UND AUFGABEN DER WIRTSCHAFTSPLANUNG. ZUR WIEDERSPIEGELUNG NEUER ENTWICKLUNGSTENDENZEN DER PRODUKTIVKRÄFTE IN DER PERSPEKTIVPLANUNG 1956 BIS 1959 [The requirements of economic development and the tasks of economic planning: the reflection of new developmental tendencies of productive energies in extended planning, 1956-59]. *Jahrbuch für Wirtschaftsgeschichte [East Germany] 1976 (4): 9-29.* Assesses the economic position of East Germany in the late 1950's. Postwar recovery was virtually complete and the task of building a socialist industrial society lay ahead. As economic planning became more complicated, the Socialist Unity Party (SED) developed more sophisticated techniques to enhance the "productivity, quality, profitability and effectiveness" of industry. The planning mechanism functioned smoothly during the second Five Year Plan and the Seven Year Plan. Primary and secondary sources; 65 notes. R. J. Bazillion

1590. Rohlfs, Dietmar. HEINZ HOFFMANN—FÜNF JAHRZEHNTE IM DIENSTE DER PARTEI UND DES VOLKES [Heinz Hoffmann: five decades in the service of the party and people]. *Militärgeschichte [East Germany] 1980 19(6): 645-666.* A biographical sketch commemorating the 70th birthday of Heinz Hoffman, member of the Politburo of the Central Committee of the Socialist Unity Party and Minister for National Defense of East Germany. 9 photos, 23 notes. J/T (H. D. Andrews)

1591. Rosman, Gerhard. OTNOSNO ETAPITE NA REVOLIUTSIONNOTO PREUSTROISTVO V GDR PREZ PERIODA OT 1945 G. DO VI KONGRES NA GESP 1963 G [The stages of the revolutionary reconstruction in East Germany from 1945 to the Fifth Congress of the Socialist Unity Party in 1963]. *Izvestiia na Inst. po Istoriia na BKP [Bulgaria] 1972 28: 227-242.* Divides the process of reconstruction in East Germany into two stages: the liquidation of fascism, militarism, and imperialism 1945-51, and the appearance of the general features of a socialist structure, 1951-63.

1592. Roth, Heidi; Dittrich, Gottfried; and Funkner, Jutta. ZUR GESCHICHTE DES SOZIALISTISCHEN WETTBEWERBS IN DER DDR ZWISCHEN DEM VIII. UND DEM IX.PARTEITAG DER SED [Socialist competition in East Germany between the eighth and ninth conferences of the Socialist Unity Party (SED)]. *Zeitschrift für Geschichtswissenschaft [East Germany] 1980 28(1): 5-22.* The SED 1976 conference evaluated the results of socialist competition as "the largest rise in production achieved in the history of GDR five-year plans since 1971." Workers' participation was supported by material incentives and also by political and moral recognition. Based on published official documents; 92 notes. G. E. Pergl

1593. Rothe, Lya. DIE WIDERSPIEGELUNG DER GROSSEN SOZIALISTISCHEN OKTOBERREVOLUTION UND IHR EINFLUSS AUF DIE REVOLUTIONÄRE DEUTSCHE ARBEITERBEWEGUNG IN DEN DOKUMENTEN UND MATERIALIEN DES ZENTRALEN PARTEIARCHIVES DER SED [The great socialist October Revolution and its influence on the German revolutionary working class movement as reflected in the documents and materials of the central Party archive of the Socialist Unity Party]. *Archivmitteilungen [East Germany] 1977 27(5): 167-172.* The Socialist Unity Party archive contains documents demonstrating the German response to the October Revolution by Wilhelm Liebknecht, Clara Zetkin, Rosa Luxemburg, and Ernst Thälmann, 1917-24, showing that there is only one model for socialist revolution, that of Marxism-Leninism.

1594. Rothe, Lya. DU BIST IMMER DEN GERADEN WEG EINES REVOLUTIONÄRS GEGANGEN. HERMANN MATERN [You always went the straight way of a revolutionary: Hermann Matern]. *Beiträge zur Geschichte der Arbeiterbewegung [East Germany] 1973 15(3): 485-496.* Returning from the western front in 1918 where he had been a member of a soldiers' council, Hermann Matern joined the Independent Socialist Party of Germany in Magdeburg and in 1920 became a member of the Communist Party. In the twenties and early thirties he established himself as a leading party official in Magdeburg-Anhalt and East Prussia. In 1934 he went into exile, residing in Czechoslovakia, France, Belgium, the Netherlands, Norway, Sweden, and finally the Soviet Union. During the war he worked in Soviet antifascist schools. After the defeat of fascism he returned to Germany where he became political secretary in Saxony. Matern devoted all his energies to the establishment of a common political platform of the working class. In 1946 he was elected to the central secretariat of the Socialist Unity Party of Germany. He was a member of the people's chamber from the founding of the GDR and served as First Deputy to the chamber president. Based on documents in the Institute for Marxism-Leninism, published documents, and secondary literature; 19 notes. R. Wagnleitner

1595. Rothe, Lya. 30 JAHRE SOZIALISTISCHE EINHEITSPARTEI DEUTSCHLANDS [Thirty years of the Socialist Unity Party of Germany]. *Archivmitteilungen [East Germany] 1976 26(2): 41-44.* Celebrates the 30th anniversary of the founding of the Socialist Unity Party in 1946, formed by a merger of the Communists (KPD) and Social Democrats (SPD) of East Germany; expresses pride over the contributions of archivists to the building of socialism in East Germany.

1596. Sanderson, Paul Wayne. "Policy and Decision-Making Processes in an Industrially Advanced Communist System: The Case of the Economic Policy Realm in East Germany, 1953-1963." U. of Toronto (Canada) 1979. *DAI 1980 40(10): 5578-A.*

1597. Schmidt, Peter and Schwanengel, Thomas. DIE KONZEPTIONEN VON KPD UND SED ZUR UMGESTALTUNG DES MONOPOLISTISCHEN BANKWESENS IN EIN MACHTINSTRUMENT DER ARBEITERKLASSE UND IHRER VERBÜNDETEN IN DEN JAHREN VON 1945 BIS ZUR GRÜNDUNG DER DDR [The German Communist Party and the Socialist Unity Party of Germany's concept of transforming monopolist banks into an instrument of power for the working class and its allies, between 1945 and the foundations of East Germany]. *Wissenschaftliche Zeitschrift der Humboldt-Universität zu Berlin. Gesellschafts- und Sprachwissenschaftliche Reihe [East Germany] 1977 26(2): 267-272.* According to the Potsdam Agreement, the nationalization of banks in the Soviet occupied zone in Germany was begun immediately after World War II, to avoid inflation and to block the funds of industrialists and landowners.

1598. Schneider, K. ZUR GESETZMÄSSIGKEIT DER WACHSENDEN FÜHRUNGSROLLE DER MARXISTISCH-LENINISTISCHEN PARTEI BEIM AUFBAU DES SOZIALISMUS UND IHRER VERWIRKLICHUNG DURCH DIE SED IN DER DDR [The role of leadership of the Marxist-Leninist Party in the building of socialism and its realization by the Socialist Unity Party of Germany in East Germany]. *Wissenschaftliche Zeitschrift der Karl-Marx U. Leipzig [East Germany] 1971 20(2): 151-164.* The history of the Socialist Unity Party of Germany has shown the correctness of the Marxist-Leninist working class as the most revolutionary and progressive force in society. The activities of the Socialist Unity Party of Germany demonstrate the conscious and planned cooperation of all social classes in the perfection of socialism. Secondary sources; 39 notes. R. Wagnleitner

1599. Scholz, Hans. DER ÜBERGANG ZUR GENOSSENSCHAFTLICH-SOZIALISTISCHEN LANDWIRTSCHAFT IM BEZIRK HALLE (1952 BIS 1961) [The transition to cooperative-socialist agriculture in the district of Halle, 1952-61]. *Jahrbuch für Wirtschaftsgeschichte [East Germany] 1979 (2): 87-116.* In 1952 the Socialist Unity Party (SED) called for the formation of agricultural producers' cooperatives (LPG). Farm labor was augmented after 1953 by rotating industrial workers in from the cities. As bourgeois farmers fled west, their land was added to the cooperative holdings. Cooperative tractor stations (MTS) were established, and socialist competition raised consciousness and stimulated production. Between 1952 and 1962 the number of agricultural cooperatives in Halle rose from 329 to 1,141, and the use of arable land increased from 27 to 81.1%. Based on government and Party statistics and reports; 8 tables, 35 notes. E. L. Turk

1600. Schröder, Stefanie. DIE IDEOLOGISCHE ARBEIT DER SED ZUR ENTWICKLUNG DER KOOPERATION IN DER LANDWIRTSCHAFT MITTE DER SECHZIGER JAHRE [The ideological work of the Socialist Unity Party (SED) to develop cooperation in agriculture during the mid-1960's]. *Beiträge zur Gesch. der Arbeiterbewegung [East Germany] 1980 22(1): 95-108.* At the 11th Plenary Session of the SED, December 1965, the Central Committee examined the role of agriculture and devised a five-year plan. The author pays particular attention to SED efforts to inform all agricultural workers about these ideas and to develop coopera-

tion in agriculture during this period. At the 9th Agricultural Congress in 1966 all these plans were discussed and adopted. Based on official SED and Agricultural Congress documents; 45 notes.
G. L. Neville

1601. Schultze, Renate. DER VERSCHÄRFTE KLASSENKAMPF AUF WIRTSCHAFTSPOLITISCHEM GEBIET IN DER DDR UNMITTELBAR NACH IHRER GRÜNDUNG [The intensified class struggle over economic policy in East Germany immediately after its founding]. *Jahrbuch für Wirtschaftsgeschichte [East Germany] 1977 (2): 45-63.* Describes the struggle of the working class and the Socialist Unity Party in East Germany against the corporate bureaucracy and the capitalist forces which attempted to prevent the building of a democratic socialist economy after World War II. The Party and state had to take political, educational, and economic countermeasures to defeat reactionary efforts to sabotage the economy. The cooperation of Party and state organs of popular control and supervision helped establish law and order in the East German economy. Based on documents in the Central State Archive at Potsdam and secondary works; 2 tables, 63 notes.
J. B. Street

1602. Schultze, Renate. DIE AUSARBEITUNG DES FÜNFJAHRPLANES DER DDR 1951 BIS 1955: DIE REAKTION DER WERKTÄTIGEN UND DER KLASSENGEGNER AUF SEINE VERKÜNDUNG [The formulation of East Germany's five-year plan, 1951-55: the reaction of the workers and the class enemies to its announcement]. *Jahrbuch für Wirtschaftsgeschichte [East Germany] 1980 (2): 31-54.* East Germany, led by the Socialist Unity Party, the labor confederation, and the government, followed this model in developing the 1st Five-Year Plan in 1951. The workers responded enthusiastically, establishing competitions and developing new technology to reach and exceed quotas. The success of the plan belies capitalist criticism of it as authoritarian. Based on East German government statistics, Socialist Unity Party reports, and secondary sources; 96 notes, 2 tables.
E. L. Turk

1603. Schultze, Renate. ZUR HERAUSBILDUNG DER WIRTSCHAFTLICH-ORGANISATORISCHEN FUNKTION DER ARBEITER-UND-BAUERN-MACHT NACH DER GRÜNDUNG DER DDR [The creation of the economic organizational function of workers' and peasants' power after the founding of the German Democratic Republic]. *Zeitschrift für Geschichtswissenschaft [East Germany] 1980 28(7): 609-623.* The internal development of the German socialist state after October 1949 was focused on the building of the workers' and peasants' power into state power, the dictatorship of the proletariat. This most important process of that era ended in the middle of 1950, when the 3d Party Congress created means for further strengthening the workers' alliance with other progressive elements. Reactionary political groups who attempted to undermine the position of the working class were finally defeated. The National Front of progressive forces opened the way to the building of socialism in the 1950's. 53 notes. G. E. Pergl

1604. Schulz, Dieter. ZUR ENTWICKLUNG VON STÄNDIGEN PRODUKTIONSBERATUNGEN IN SOZIALISTISCHEN INDUSTRIEBETRIEBEN DER DDR VON 1957-1958 BIS 1965 [Development of Permanent Production Conferences in socialist industrial enterprises in East Germany from 1957-58 to 1965]. *Zeitschrift für Geschichtswissenschaft [East Germany] 1980 28(9): 842-848.* In 1958 the Socialist Unity Party (SED) and the Free German Trade Union Federation (FDGB) organized Permanent Production Conferences in factories throughout the country, in order to increase the workers' leadership in production. These conferences, modeled after those of the Soviet Union, have proven most valuable in promoting scientific progress, while contributing to the further development of the socialist character of the working class. 54 notes. J. T. Walker

1605. Schulz, Eberhart. UM DEN SCHUTZ DER DDR: ASPEKT DER IDEOLOGISCHEN ARBEIT DER SED IN THÜRINGEN 1952 [The defense of East Germany: aspects of the ideological work of the Socialist Unity Party (SED) in Thuringia in 1952]. *Beiträge zur Gesch. der Arbeiterbewegung [East Germany] 1982 24(4): 595-603.* The ideological work of the SED in East Germany since 1949 has been concerned with the development of the economy, the establishment and strengthening of democratic state organs, the transformation of ideology and culture, and the defense of the GDR. The author considers the ideological work of the local Party organization in Thuringia in 1952, concerning defense, which demonstrated that ideological work, aimed principally at young people, could be successful only if it was combined with efforts to develop national consciousness among all workers. Based on local Party documents in the Bezirksparteiarchiv in Erfurt and SED documents held in Berlin; 51 notes. G. L. Neville

1606. Schulz, Eberhart. UM DIE FREUNDSCHAFT ZUR UDSSR: DER IDEOLOGISCHE KAMPF DER LANDESORGANISATION THÜRINGEN DER SED 1948/1949 [Concerning friendship with the USSR: the ideological struggle of the Thuringian organization of the Socialist Unity Party (SED), 1948-49]. *Beiträge zur Gesch. der Arbeiterbewegung [East Germany] 1980 22(4): 599-607.* Traces the development of cooperation between the Soviet Communist Party and the German SED Party between the summer of 1948 and October 1949, when the German Democratic Republic was established, with particular attention to the ideological work of the local SED organization in Thuringia. The local party organization was successful in informing both its members and workers of the necessity of maintaining friendly relations with the USSR and of the close relationship between SED members and those of the Soviet Communist Party. In addition it succeeded in supporting the ideologies of Soviet communism in its disputes with anti-Soviet elements. Based on local Party documents in Berlin and secondary sources; 51 notes. G. L. Neville

1607. Schwank, Monika and Göttlicher, Franz. KPD UND DEMOKRATISCHE BODENREFORM [The Communist Party of Germany and the democratic land reform]. *Beiträge zur Geschichte der Arbeiterbewegung [East Germany] 1975 17(5): 848-861.* Publishes for the first time five documents on land reform in East Germany. Dated 1945 and 1946, the documents trace the history of land ownership in Germany and outline the need for reforms and the means of their implementation. The documents, including two signed by Wilhelm Pieck and one by Walter Ulbricht, are unedited. G. H. Libbey

1608. Schwarzbach, Helmut. ZUR GESCHICHTE DER ÖRTLICHEN ARBEITERBEWEGUNG: DIE IDEOLOGISCHE TÄTIGKEIT DER SEDKREISPARTEIORGANISATION ZITTAU ZUR VERTIEFUNG DES SOZIALISTISCHEN INTERNATIONALISMUS [Concerning the history of local worker movements: the ideological activities of the Socialist Unity Party's local organization in Zittau for the deepening of socialist internationalism]. *Beiträge zur Gesch. der Arbeiterbewegung [East Germany] 1981 23(1): 101-109.* The party organization at Zittau established good relations with the Communist parties in neighboring Czechoslovakia as well as Poland. Some people still harbored reservations about Poland in the early 1960's because of the annexation of Bogatynia, formerly Reichenau, through the establishment of the Oder-Neisse border. Effective ideological work had to overcome this problem. Such work improved economic production in the area and caused the populace to welcome the construction of the Berlin wall with enthusiasm. The Soviet space flight of 1961 produced a new peak in relations between the USSR and East Germany. Based on regional party archives, newspapers, and other sources; 40 notes.
A. Schuetz

1609. Sebisch, Claude. LA RDA ET L'AFRIQUE NOIRE: BILAN D'UN VOYAGE [The German Democratic Republic and black Africa: the balance sheet of a journey]. *Rev. d'Allemagne [France] 1979 11(4): 570-576.* In February 1979, Erich Honecker, General Secretary of the Socialist Unity Party (SED) and President of the Council of State, set out on a long journey through Africa with a delegation representing both the party and the government of East Germany. They traveled from Libya to Mozambique, Angola, and Zambia. The journey, which appears as the culmination of GDR policies in Africa, provided contacts with the leaders of national liberation movements, demonstrated GDR opposition to South African racism, and increased cooperation between the GDR and African socialist states. 3 notes. J. S. Gassner

1610. Seeber, Eva. ZU DEN BEZIEHUNGEN ZWISCHEN DER DDR UND DEN EUROPÄISCHEN VOLKSDEMOKRATISCHEN STAATEN BIS 1950 [On the relations between East Germany and Eastern Europe until 1950]. *Zeitschrift für Geschichtswissenschaft [East Germany] 1973 21(2): 141-163.* One of the most delicate tasks of the Socialist Unity Party of Germany after World War II was to establish friendly relations with the countries in which the German army had murdered millions. The analysis of the class origin of the fascist system helped the SED to show these nations that not all Germans were guilty of war crimes. The USSR assisted the German antifascist groups and promoted the establishment of contacts with Eastern Europe. Based on printed documents and secondary literature; 71 notes.
R. Wagnleitner

1611. Seifert, Helmut. DIE BEDEUTUNG DER II. PARTEIKONFERENZ DER SED FÜR DIE ANEIGNUNG, ANWENDUNG UND ENTWICKLUNG DER POLITISCHEN ÖKONOMIE DES SOZIALISMUS IN DER DDR [The significance of the second party conference of the SED for the adoption, application, and development of political economy of socialism in the DDR]. *Jahrbuch für Wirtschaftsgeschichte [East Germany] 1972 (2): 155-182.* Describes the building of socialism in East Germany as a continuous process of applying Marxist-Leninist principles of political economy. Analyzes the role of the second party conference in 1952 in formulating the economic principles leading to the transition from democracy to socialism and setting economic goals for further development. Discusses the general economic laws of socialism and how they have been applied to East Germany. Based on party reports and programs and secondary works; 66 notes.
J. B. Street

1612. Seifert, Helmut. ZUR ROLLE DER POLITISCHEN ÖKONOMIE IN DER ANTIFASCHISTISCH-DEMOKRATISCHE UMWÄLZUNG BIS ZUR GRÜNDUNG DER DEUTSCHEN DEMOKRATISCHEN REPUBLIK [The role of political economy in the antifascist-democratic revolution until the founding of the German Democratic Republic]. *Jahrbuch für Wirtschaftsgeschichte [East Germany] 1975 (2): 117-136.* The transformation of East Germany into a socialist state was due to the successful application of Leninist principles by the East Germans themselves, with assistance from the USSR. The Soviets did not impose revolution on their occupation zone; socialism's roots lay in the prewar program of the German Communist Party and in the wartime pronouncements of its exiled leaders. During the transition from capitalism to socialism, the KPD (later the SED) played the essential role of guide and director of the revolution. The antifascist-democratic revolution is to be distinguished from the socialist revolution presided over by the SED after 1949. Primary and secondary sources; 20 notes. R. J. Bazillion

1613. Sergeeva, V. V. PROBLEMY GERMANSKOI ISTORII V NOVOE I NOVEISHEE VREMIA V "EZHEGODNIKE GERMANSKOI ISTORII" [The problems of German history in the modern and contemporary period in the *Yearbook of German History*]. *Novaia i Noveishaia Istoriia [USSR] 1982 (3): 169-174.* The *Ezhegodnik Germanskoi Istorii,* published by the Academy of Sciences of the USSR and the Commission of Historians of the USSR and East Germany, examines Germany's 1,000-year history, especially the Nazi and postwar periods. It emphasizes the friendly relations between the Soviet and German workers' movements, and the role of German thinkers and activists in the world revolutionary movement. The German movement had a hard struggle against debilitating social democratic elements. Describes the development of fascist Germany, especially working-class resistance to militarism, postwar development, the success of the GDR, and the problems of the FRG. 4 notes. A. J. Evans

1614. Shumeiko, I. M. and Shtern, V. Iu. TRUDOVI ZV'IAZKY VLKSM I SPILKY VIL'NOI NIMETS'KOI MOLODI: 1966-1971 [Working ties between the Young Communist League and the Union of Free German Youth, 1966-71]. *Ukrains'kyi Istorychnyi Zhurnal [USSR] 1978 (10): 80-87.* As economic cooperation between the USSR and East Germany increased in the sixties, so did ties between youth organizations. Exchanges were organized, conferences held, and exhibitions of scientific and cultural achievements mounted. Socialist competition motivated building teams from both youth organizations to work better and faster on projects in the USSR and East Germany. Primary sources; 29 notes.
V. A. Packer

1615. Sieber, Horst. ZUR ERFORSCHUNG DER GESCHICHTE DER FDJ IN DEN SECHZIGER JAHREN [Research into the Free German Youth in the 1960's]. *Wissenschaftliche Zeitschrift der Wilhelm-Pieck-Universität Rostock. Gesellschaftswissenschaftliche Reihe [East Germany] 1982 31(1-2): 27-33.* The official Communist youth organization of East Germany contributed to the construction of an oil refinery at Schwedt and a nuclear power station "Kernkraftwerk Nord" and participated in other ways in shaping the developed socialist society under the guidance of the Socialist Unity Party of Germany.

1616. Smelov, Nikolai. DIE AUSEINANDERSETZUNG DER KPD MIT DEN REAKTIONÄREN KRÄFTEN IN DER CDU IM KAMPF UM DIE DURCHSETZUNG DER DEMOKRATISCHEN BODENREFORM (2. HALBJAHR 1945) [The debate of the KPD with the reactionary forces in the CDU during the struggle for the accomplishment of democratic agrarian reform: July-December 1945]. *Jahrbuch für Wirtschaftsgeschichte [East Germany] 1977 (2): 27-43.* Describes the political struggle between the reactionary wing of the Christian Democratic Union and the Communist Party over land reform in the eastern provinces of Germany in fall, 1945. The Communist Party, the working class, and the peasantry were able to push through democratic agrarian reform despite the numerous attempts of reactionary forces to divert and subvert true reform. The agrarian reform was an important step in the postwar revolution in East Germany. Based on official East German documentary publications, documents in the Historical Archive of the CDU and in the State Archive of Schwerin, newspapers, and secondary works; 74 notes. J. B. Street

1617. Starrels, John M. COMPARATIVE AND ELITE POLITICS. *World Pol. 1976 29(1): 130-142.* Reviews Thomas Arthur Baylis's *The Technical Intelligentsia and the East German Elite* (U. of California Pr., 1974) and Peter Christian Ludz's *The Changing Party Elite in East Germany* (MIT Pr., 1972), which represent new trends in the evolution of American scholarship on East German politics. In moving away from the previously one-sided emphasis in the field of German affairs, both authors analyze the broad evolution of Communist Party recruitment and the emergence of a new political elite to replace the old elite which established itself after World War II.

1618. Stein, Udo. HISTORISCHE BEDINGUNGEN UND ERFORDERNISSE DER INTENSIVIERUNG DES ERWEITERTEN REPRODUCTIONS-PROZESSES DER INDUSTRIE DER DDR IN DER ERSTEN HÄLFTE DER SIEBZIGER JAHRE [Historical conditions and requirements for intensification of the extended industrial production processes in East Germany during the first half of the 1970's]. *Jahrbuch für Wirtschaftsgeschichte [East Germany] 1979 (1): 7-31.* In 1966 the Socialist Unity Party (SED) and the government of East Germany agreed to plan for increased industrial production by combining the extension of industry with intensification of production. The plan implemented in 1971 included increased research and development, application of new technology, increased investment, automation, and extension and training of workers to utilize modern technology. Economic planning was coordinated with other European socialist nations. There has been measurable progress in all planned areas. Based on SED archives, official statistics, and secondary sources; 9 tables, 53 notes.
E. L. Turk

1619. Steinke, Volker and Trümpler, Eckhard. DIE ENTWICKLUNG DER BRÜDERLICHEN BEZIEHUNGEN VON KPDSU UND SED SEIT DEM FREUNDSCHAFTSVERTRAG VOM 7. OKTOBER 1975 [The development of fraternal relations between the Soviet Communist Party and the Socialist Unity Party (SED) in East Germany since the friendship treaty of 7 October 1975]. *Beiträge zur Gesch. der Arbeiterbewegung [East Germany] 1982 24(5): 643-656.* In 1971 the two Party congresses examined the need for new links, considering the need to create a developed socialist society, to realize policies of peace and security, and to support popular freedom struggles, as well as the need for coordination of foreign and defense policies, increased economic, scientific, and technical cooperation, the development of economic integration, and the furtherance of ideological relationships. Based on German documents; 39 notes. G. L. Neville

1620. Steinke, Volker. HERAUSBILDUNG UND ENTWICKLUNG DER BEZIRKSBEZIEHUNGEN ZWISCHEN DER SED UND DER KPDSU [The origins and development of regional contacts between the Socialist Unity Party and the Soviet Communist Party]. *Beiträge zur Gesch. der Arbeiterbewegung [East Germany] 1981 23(3): 398-406.* The period of the late 1950's and early 1960's was important in the development of international cooperation between the Socialist Unity Party and the Communist Party of the USSR. Links were established between party leaders at both central and regional levels as well as in the industrial, agricultural, scientific, and cultural spheres. The author pays particular attention to the contacts and exchanges of ideas that were made at the regional level between 1960 and 1971 and notes the progress that was made because of this cooperation in ideological, intellectual, industrial, scientific, and technical areas. Based on local party archives in Dresden, Socialist Unity Party documents in Berlin, and secondary sources; 19 notes. G. L. Neville

1621. Stempel, Fred. ERINNERUNGEN: MITARBEITER OTTO GROTEWOHLS [Reminiscences by a collaborator of Otto Grotewohl]. *Beiträge zur Geschichte der Arbeiterbewegung [East Germany] 1981 23(2): 266-276.* Stempel completed the Party academy training in 1951 and immediately received a position with Otto Grotewohl, first as his personal secretary at the Central Committee of the Socialist Unity Party (SED), then as his personal assistant at the Office of the Prime Minister. He accompanied him during domestic and international travels and remembers him in the fondest terms possible, both in his private and public life. A. Schuetz

1622. Stepanov, L. L. STROITEL'STVO SOTSIALIZMA V GDR [The building of socialism in East Germany]. *Novaia i Noveishaia Istoriia [USSR] 1976 (1): 154-165.* After the war only the Communist Party had a clear and realistic program, outlined to the German nation on 11 June 1945. This called for the extirpation of fascism, confiscation of property from all active Nazis and war criminals, and agrarian reform. When the East German state was officially proclaimed in 1949, economic restoration was begun under a new constitution giving priority to industrialization and cooperative farming. Comecon and Soviet assistance helped the country in the 1960's, and by the 1970's it had become a successful and universally recognized state. 12 notes, biblio. V. A. Packer

1623. Stöckigt, Rolf. ZUR BÜNDNISPOLITIK DER SED [On the alliance policy of the Socialist Unity Party of Germany]. *Zeitschrift für Geschichtswissenschaft [East Germany] 1979 17(12): 1115-1120.* The German Democratic Republic was born only through the effort of the working class in alliance with a wide range of other working segments of the population. This alliance required the removal of the imperialist bourgeoisie from political and financial power, the unity of democratic elements, the rejection of demagogy and false reformism, and the defeat of chauvinism, racism, and ultranationalism. Finally, the separation of church and state and the equality of all citizens made East German statehood a fact. 12 notes. G. E. Pergl

1624. Stöckigt, Rolf. ZUR POLITIK DER SED BEI DER FESTIGUNG DES BLOCKS DER ANTIFASCHISTISCH-DEMOKRATISCHEN PARTEIEN (1948 BIS ZUR GRÜNDUNG DER DDR) [On the policy of the Socialist Unity Party of Germany in connection with the strengthening of the bloc of the antifascist democratic parties (1948 until the founding of the German Democratic Republic)]. *Beiträge zur Geschichte der Arbeiterbewegung [East Germany] 1974 16(Supplement): 120-136.* In the two years preceding the founding of the German Democratic Republic, the Socialist Unity Party of Germany sought to ally all democratic antifascist elements in Germany. Campaigns to involve workers in politics weakened the obstructionist leaders of center parties. Exchanges of delegations with the Soviet Union strengthened ties with the international socialist movement. The successful founding of the German Democratic Republic resulted from the careful planning and concerted efforts of the Socialist Unity Party and its alliance with other workers' parties. Primary and secondary materials; 113 notes. G. H. Libbey

1625. Stoljar, Margaret. CULTURAL POLITICS AND LITERARY THEORY IN THE GERMAN DEMOCRATIC REPUBLIC. *J. of European Studies [Great Britain] 1982 12(2): 130-149.* Since its foundation in 1949, East Germany has pursued the Soviet idea of socialist realism in literature and art under the control of its single political party, the German Socialist Unity Party (SED), against a background of close cooperation with the USSR on the one hand and the propinquity of West Germany on the other. There have, however, been local variations, notably the Bitterfield Way, launched in 1959 to encourage the growth of popular culture, and the publication of *Zur Theorie de Sozialistischen Realismus* (On the Theory of Socialist Realism) (1974) under the auspices of the SED's Institute for Social Sciences, which cautiously recognized the work of such Western writers as Proust, Joyce, and Kafka. Since then, there has been a turning away from theoretical discussion of socialist realism and more emphasis on the sociology of literature and the concept of appropriation of reality in the aesthetics of realism. 28 ref. A. E. Standley

1626. Streber, Jannek. VON DEN "GRUNDPRINZIPIEN" ZUM "KOMPLEXPROGRAMM." ZUR VERTIEFUNG DER WIRTSCHAFTLICHEN ZUSAMMENARBEIT DER RGW - LÄNDER [From the "fundamental principles" to the "complex program." The deepening of the economic cooperation of the Comecon countries]. *Beiträge zur Geschichte der Arbeiterbewegung [East Germany] 1972 14(4): 548-565.* The fundamental principles which were worked out at the Moscow conference of the communist and workers parties in 1962 were the basis for the strengthening of the economic cooperation and the building of socialism and communism in the socialist countries. The creative use of these fundamental principles led to the further development of a complex program for which the Socialist Unity Party of Germany contributed 1) the consideration of the objective conditions of the socialist international division of labor after 1960, 2) the deepening of the international division of labor on the basis of the fundamental principles, and 3) the further development of the process of reproduction and development of a complex program. Based on published documents and secondary literature; 39 notes. R. Wagnleitner

1627. Suckut, Siegfried. DOKUMENTATION: ZU KRISE UND FUNKTIONSWANDEL DER BLOCKPOLITIK IN DER SOWJETISCH BESETZTEN ZONE DEUTSCHLANDS UM DIE MITTE DES JAHRES 1948 [Documentation: crisis and shift in the function of bloc politics in the Soviet Occupied Zone of Germany around the middle of 1948]. *Vierteljahrshefte für Zeitgeschichte [West Germany] 1983 31(4): 674-718.* Publication, with commentary, of the minutes of the meeting of the Joint Committee of the Anti-Fascist-Democratic Parties of the Soviet Zone of Germany on 5 August 1948. It shows the almost completed capitulation of the non-Marxist Christian Democratic and Liberal Parties to the Communist Socialist Unity Party (SED) with the intensification of the Cold War during the Berlin blockade. Although some criticisms of the Communist monopolization of power were still voiced, the SED was no longer willing to engage in substantial discussions with its bloc partners and clearly anticipated the establishment of a Communist East German state. Based on the archive of the East German Christian Democratic Union executive committee; 88 notes. D. Prowe

1628. Teller, Hans and Thomas, Siegfried. DIE STELLUNG DER SOZIALDEMOKRATISCHEN FÜHRUNG ZUR GRÜNDUNG UND ENTWICKLUNG DER DDR [The attitude of the Social Democratic leadership toward the foundation and development of the German Democratic Republic]. *Beiträge zur Geschichte der Arbeiterbewegung [East Germany] 1974 16(5): 155-172.* Wilhelm Pieck viewed the founding of the German Democratic Republic as the beginning of an independent workers' state. Konrad Adenauer, speaking for the Federal Republic of Germany, declared that only his West German state was legitimate. The Social Democratic Party supported Adenauer's position from 1940 to 1969, claiming that Germany could be free only if united. By 1969 Willy Brandt, Federal Chancellor and leader of the Social Democrats, began to move toward a new political structure which included two German states. Primary materials; 74 notes. G. H. Libbey

1629. Teresiak, Manfred. DIE GESCHICHTE DER SED UND IHRE BÜRGERLICHEN VERFÄLSCHER [The history of the Socialist Unity Party (SED) and its bourgeois falsifiers]. *Beiträge zur Gesch. der Arbeiterbewegung [East Germany] 1980 22(4): 526-538.* Examines work in West Germany, 1970-80, concerning the history of the SED, particularly on the treatment of the class characteristics of the socialist state and the SED's supremacy. The researchers' evident political motives for falsifying SED history reflect the growing crisis of bourgeois ideology within West Germany. 40 notes.
G. L. Neville

1630. Thiele, Gisela. ANTIKOMMUNISTISCHE REAKTIONEN AUF DIE ENTWICKLUNG DER VOLKSWIRTSCHAFT DER DDR [Anti-Communist reactions to East German economic development]. *Wissenschaftliche Zeitschrift der Friedrich-Schiller-Universität Jena. Gesellschafts- und Sprachwissenschaftliche Reihe [East Germany] 1976 25(6): 699-709.* Western propaganda and boycott tactics have hindered East German economic development, 1949-75.

1631. Tidke, Kurt. SEPG—ORGANIZATOR STROITEL'STVA SOTSIALIZMA V GERMANSKOI DEMOKRATICHESKOI RESPUBLIKE [The Socialist Unity Party of Germany: the organizer of the construction of socialism in the German Democratic Republic]. *Voprosy Istorii KPSS [USSR] 1965 (1): 34-42.* An investigation of the Socialist Unity Party of East Germany's role in the socialist transformation of the national economy, 1950-65.

1632. Tiulpanov, Sergei Ivanovich. GEDANKEN ÜBER DEN VEREINIGUNGSPARTEITAG DER SED 1946 [Thoughts on the unification congress of the Socialist Unity Party of Germany, 1946]. *Zeitschrift für Geschichtswissenschaft [East Germany] 1970 18(5): 617-625.* Personal recollections of the creation by the East German Communists and Social Democrats of the SED in April 1946.

1633. Tkachenko, I. V. V VOPROSY ISTORII KPSS V ZHURNALE GDR *BEITRAGE ZUR GESCHICHTE DER ARBEITERBEWEGUNG* (1971-1975) [The history of the CPSU in the East German journal *Beiträge zur Geschichte der Arbeiterbewegung*, (1971-75)]. *Vestnik Leningradskogo U.: Seriia Istorii, Iazyka, Literatury [USSR] 1976 (14): 32-38.* One of the most important and least studied aspects of the history of the Communist Party of the Soviet Union (CPSU) is the question of the international character of its activities. The author surveys various East German publications on the history of the CPSU, including publications of Lenin's works and important Bolshevik documents. Such publications aid East Germany and other countries in solving the problems they face in the construction of socialism. 29 notes.
G. F. Jewsbury

1634. Truger, Wolf. AMERIKANISCHE GLOBALSTRATEGIE UND PSYCHOLOGISCHE KRIEGFÜHRUNG DER USA GEGEN DIE DDR [US global strategy and psychological warfare against East Germany]. *Deutsche Aussenpolitik [East Germany] 1968 13(Sonderheft 2): 173-189.* Because of the immense economic, political, and strategic importance of Germany for US hegemony in Europe in the 1950's and 1960's, US propaganda has concentrated on East Germany trying to falsify the socialist ideology, isolate East Germany from the other Communist countries, create riots and provocations, and destroy the unity between party, government, and population.

1635. Trümpler, Eckhard. KONFERENZ ZUM 30. JAHRESTAG DER GRÜNDUNG DER SED [Conference the occasion of the 30th anniversary of the foundation of the Socialist Unity Party of Germany (SED)]. *Beiträge zur Geschichte der Arbeiterbewegung [East Germany] 1976 18(3): 525-526.* Reviews the proceedings of the March 1976 meeting in Berlin on the occasion of the 30th anniversary of the founding of the Socialist Unity Party of Germany. Analyzes the role of the SED in transforming East Germany into a socialist country since 1946. R. Wagnleitner

1636. Tsapanov, V. I. ERIKH KHONEKKER [Erich Honecker]. *Voprosy Istorii KPSS [USSR] 1972 (8): 108-110.* Reviews the political career of Erich Honecker, a prominent member of the East German Socialist Unity Party, 1926-71.

1637. Tsitson, N. S. TVORCHESKOE PRIMENENIE SEPG ISTORICHESKOGO OPYTA KPSS PO VOVLECHENIIU STARYKH SPETSIALISTOV V STROITEL'STVO SOTSIALIZMA (1949-1955 GG.) [The creative application by the SED of the historical experience of the CPSU pertaining to the involvement of the old specialists in the construction of socialism, 1949-55]. *Voprosy Istorii KPSS [USSR] 1974 (1): 74-85.* From 1949 to 1955 the Socialist Unity Party of East Germany forged an alliance of the working class and intellectuals. The party provided the intelligentsia with material benefits, new and reorganized research and educational institutes, ready access to essential literature, and special courses for their moral and ideological reeducation. Based on published documents, periodical literature, and archival materials; 67 notes.
L. E. Holmes

1638. Uhlemann, Manfred. DIE FÜHRUNGSROLLE DER SED-BEZIRKSPARTEIORGANISATION BEI DER SOZIALISTISCHEN UMGESTALTUNG DER LANDWIRTSCHAFT IM BEZIRK POTSDAM (1952-1955) [The leading role of the Socialist Unity Party's regional organization in the socialist transformation of agriculture in the Potsdam area, 1952-55]. *Beiträge zur Gesch. der Arbeiterbewegung [East Germany] 1981 23(3): 428-438.* The 2d Socialist Unity Conference of July 1952 established the guidelines for the transformation of agriculture through a five-year plan. The power of local organizations was strengthened in 1953 and was able to play a greater part in organizing the agricultural transformations which occurred. The author discusses the establishment of farmworkers' unions in the Potsdam area, the growing relationship between workers and farmers, and the increase in farm machinery and production during this period. Based on statistical reports from the Potsdam area and secondary sources; 34 notes.
G. L. Neville

1639. Uhlig, Ch. DIE AUFGABENSTELLUNG DER SED ZUR INTERNATIONALISTISCHEN ERZIEHUNG DER SCHULJUGEND IN DER DDR IN DEN JAHREN 1946 BIS 1971 [The responsibility of the Socialist Unity Party of Germany (SED) for the internationalist education of East German school-youth between 1946 and 1971]. *Wissenschaftliche Zeitschrift der Karl-Marx U. Leipzig [East Germany] 1975 24(4): 389-400.* After the nationalist education of German fascism, the education toward internationalism and democratic patriotism was a prominent but, especially in the first years, very difficult task of the East German authorities.
R. Wagnleitner

1640. Uhlmann, Maria. ZUR HERAUSGABE UND VERBREITUNG VON LENIN-ARBEITEN IN DEUTSCHER SPRACHE NACH DER ZERSCHLAGUNG DES FASCHISMUS BIS ZUR GRÜNDUNG DER SED [The publication and distribution of Lenin's works in German after the destruction of fascism until the founding of the Socialist Unity Party of Germany]. *Beiträge zur Geschichte der Arbeiterbewegung [East Germany] 1976 18(2): 332-337.* The publishing company of the East German Communist Party, Neuer Weg, was founded in the summer of 1945. It published important works of V. I. Lenin by late autumn 1945 and in early 1946. Based on documents in the Archiv des Dietz Verlags, published documents, newspapers, and secondary literature; 41 notes.
R. Wagnleitner

1641. Ulbricht, Walter. DER LENINISMUS UND DIE BÜNDNISPOLITIK DER SOZIALISTISCHEN EINHEITSPARTEI DEUTSCHLANDS [Leninism and the alliance policy of the Socialist Unity Party of Germany]. *Zeitschrift für Geschichtswissenschaft [East Germany] 1970 18(4): 445-463.* The Leninist principle of a strong, unified workers' movement became the dominant political strategy of the German Communists after World War II. The basis for the formation of the Socialist Unity Party of Germany (SED) was the unity platform between Communists and Social Democrats and the establishment of free trade unions. According to Lenin's theory that the dictatorship of the proletariat did not necessarily demand a one-party system, the East German Communists allied themselves with progressive political groups in East Germany to build a socialist system. Based on Lenin's works, personal recollections, and secondary literature; 9 notes.

R. Wagnleitner

1642. Vogl, Dieter. ZU DEN ERGEBNISSEN DES VIII. PARTEITAGES DER SED: DIE BEZIEHUNGEN DER DDR ZU DEN NATIONAL BEFREITEN STAATEN SEIT 1967 [On the results of the Eighth Party Congress of the SED: Relations of East Germany with the nationally liberated states since 1967]. *Dokumentation der Zeit [East Germany] 1971 (22): 3-10.* Stresses that since 1967 East Germany has achieved notable results in the economic, scientific, technical, and trade fields in mutual cooperation with the nations of the Third World. Includes a statistical evaluation of trade with the developing nations. Based on statistics and printed sources. G. E. Pergl

1643. Vogt, G. NNA: ARMIIA SOTSIALISTICHESKOGO NEMETSKOGO GOSUDARSTVA [GPA: the army of the German socialist state]. *Voenno-Istoricheskii Zhurnal [USSR] 1975 (6): 51-55.* Demonstrates the important role played by the German Communist Party in the formation of the German People's Army and emphasizes the close cooperation between the armies of East Germany and the USSR.

1644. Vogt, Roy. THE COURSE OF ECONOMIC REFORMS IN EAST GERMANY: IMPLICATIONS FOR SOCIAL CHANGE. *Can. Slavonic Papers [Canada] 1976 18(2): 168-177.* Economic reforms introduced in East Germany, 1963-70, had two major objectives: the creation of a more efficient economic system based on more rational prices and incentives and the development of a more decentralized planning system, based on greater decisionmaking powers for the collective enterprises. It was believed for some time that these objectives could be realized simultaneously by the creation of larger units of production and by the integration proposed for these larger units in the associations of Kombinaten. In giving decisionmaking power to the associations, but not to individual enterprises, a partial form of decentralization was created at the intermediate level, avoiding the supposedly anarchist dangers of a radical decentralization. However, the economic results were very disappointing and the process of decentralization was reversed in 1971 by the 8th Congress of the Socialist Unity Party under the new direction of Erich Honecker. J/S

1645. Voroshilov, S. I. KHARAKTER ANTIFASHISTSKOGO EDINSTVA V NACHAL'NYI PERIOD ANTIFASHISTSKO-DEMOKRATISCHESKIKH PREOBRAZOVANII V VOSTOCHNOI GERMANII [The character of antifascist unity at the beginning of the antifascist-democratic changes in East Germany]. *Vestnik Leningradskogo U.: Seriia Istorii, Iazyka i Literatury [USSR] 1981 (3): 19-25.* Antifascist democratic changes in East Germany resulted from the united front of antifascist forces headed by the German Communist Party. The Party had always maintained a principled stand against fascism, while other forces, notably monopoly capitalism, were opportunist. They joined the antifascist bloc only after the defeat of Hitler, hoping to salvage their position. But the German Party, supported by the CPSU, was able to convince the people that it alone could provide fundamental, structural, real socialist change, and the transition from antifascism to socialist construction. 21 notes. A. J. Evans

1646. Voroshilov, S. I. O KHARAKTERE SOIUZA RABOCHEGO KLASSA I TRUDIASHCHEGOSIA KREST'IANSTVA V VOSTOCHNOI GERMANII V NACHALNYI PERIOD ANTIFASHISTSKO-DEMOKRATICHESKIKH PEREOBRAZOVANII (1945-1946 GG.) [On the character of the workers' and peasants' union in East Germany at the time of the early antifascist democracy, 1945-46]. *Vestnik Leningradskogo U.: Seriia Istorii, Iazyka i Literatury [USSR] 1983 (2): 32-38.* Surveys the political scene in East Germany in 1945-46, when the democratic parties of workers and the union of peasants grew closer in their interests and aims, until they merged into a single party, facilitating East Germany's fast progress toward socialism. Based on secondary material; 29 notes. English summary. M. Hernas

1647. Vosske, Heinz, ed. AUS OTTO GROTEWOHLS BRIEFWECHSEL MIT KÜNSTLERN UND SCHRIFTSTELLERN [From Otto Grotewohl's correspondence with artists and authors]. *Beiträge zur Gesch. der Arbeiterbewegung [East Germany] 1984 26(2): 197-206.* Introduces and prints letters between Otto Grotewohl (1894-1964) and artists and writers such as Gottfried Röhrer, Willi Bredel, Ernst Busch, Erich Engel, Stephan Hermlin, Lea Grundig, Bertolt Brecht, Martin Andersen Nexö, Lion Feuchtwanger, Bert Heller, and Otto Nagel. An official of the Socialist Unity Party of Germany, Grotewohl was also a friend of art, who saw the need for culture to express the aspirations of the working class of East Germany. 10 notes. R. Grove

1648. Vosske, Heinz. DER KAMPF DER SED UM DIE DURCHSETZUNG DES MARXISMUS-LENINISMUS ALS DIE HERRSCHENDE IDEOLOGIE IN DER DDR (ENDE 1949 BIS ANFANG 1952) [The struggle of the Socialist Unity Party (SED) for the triumph of Marxism-Leninism as the dominant ideology of the GDR (late 1949-early 1952)]. *Jahrbuch für Geschichte [East Germany] 1974 11: 99-122.* The foundation of the German Democratic Republic on 7 October 1949 marked the triumph of socialism and of the working masses of East Germany. In order to consolidate this victory, it was necessary for the ruling Socialist Unity Party to educate the masses ideologically, and to win them over for a Marxist-Leninist approach to life and politics. In carrying out this task, the SED set up Party schools around the country in which first Party members, then other citizens, were taught Marxist-Leninist fundamentals. By 1952, the SED leadership could report that the ideological education of the working masses had gone so far in East Germany that it could move to the next task, that of building socialism. 42 notes. J. C. Billigmeier

1649. Vosske, Heinz. FÜR IMMER MIT DEM WERDEN UND WACHSEN DER DDR VERBUNDEN. FRIEDRICH EBERT [Forever linked with the creation and growth of the German Democratic Republic: Friedrich Ebert]. *Beiträge zur Gesch. der Arbeiterbewegung [East Germany] 1982 24(1): 104-113.* Traces the life, career, and political activities of the East German leader Friedrich Ebert (1894-1979). The author pays particular attention to his role in establishing and developing the Socialist Unity Party, strengthening its ideological unity, and establishing and strengthening the East German state, as well as his role in rebuilding Berlin. He also considers Ebert's contribution to establishing a socialist society in East Germany and his work for peace and international cooperation. Based on Ebert's writings and secondary sources; 23 notes.

G. L. Neville

1650. Vosske, Heinz. MATERIALIEN WILHELM PIECKS ZUM ENTWURF DER "GRUNDSÄTZE UND ZIELE DER SED" [Wilhelm Pieck's papers pertaining to the drafting of *Principles and Goals of the SED*]. *Beiträge zur Geschichte der Arbeiterbewegung [East Germany] 1981 23(2): 240-254.* Previously unpublished notes of meetings, speeches, and related materials pertaining to the Socialist Unity Party (SED) document *Principles and Goals of the SED,* passed on 21 and 22 April 1946. Based on Party archives and *Deutsche Volkszeitung;* 18 notes. A. Schuetz

1651. Vosske, Heinz. SEIN LEBEN WAR TREUE ZUM MARXISMUS-LENINISMUS UND AUFOPFERUNGSVOLLE ARBEIT FUR UNSEREN SOZIALISTISCHEN STAAT. WALTER ULBRICHT [His life was loyalty to Marxism-Leninism and devoted work for our socialist state: Walter Ulbricht]. *Beiträge zur Gesch. der Arbeiterbewegung [East Germany] 1983 25(1): 109-122.* Traces the life, career and political influence of the first secretary general of the Socialist Unity Party, Walter Ulbricht (1893-1973). Describes his school life and early political involvement in the working-class youth movement in Germany. In 1919 he became actively involved in founding the German Communist Party and his political development and activities were then closely linked to the Party. His ambition was achieved with the founding of the German Democratic Republic in 1949. Secondary sources; 18 notes.

G. L. Neville

1652. Vosske, Heinz. ÜBER DIE ENTWICKLUNG DER BEZIEHUNGEN DER SED ZUR INTERNATIONALEN ARBEITERBEWEGUNG IN DEN ERSTEN JAHREN NACH DER GRÜNDUNG DER PARTEI [On the development of the relations of the SED to the international workers' movement in the first years after the foundation of the party]. *Beiträge zur Geschichte der Arbeiterbewegung [East Germany] 1972 14(2): 222-234.* The revolutionary antifascist and antimilitarist transformation in East Germany under the German Socialist Unity Party (SED) was a condition for the establishment of good contacts with Communist parties in other formerly occupied countries. The most important link was with the CPSU. As the international links were established, intensive education of the party members in the spirit of proletarian internationalism was initiated and SED delegations led by Wilhelm Pieck, Walter Ulbricht, Franz Dahlem, Anton Ackermann, and Otto Grotewohl went to Bulgaria, Hungary, Rumania, Poland, and Czechoslovakia. Based on documents in the Institute of Marxism-Leninism, published documents, and secondary sources; 35 notes. R. Wagnleitner

1653. Vosske, Heinz. ÜBER DIE ENTWICKLUNG DER PARTEISTATUTEN DER SED [On the development of the party statutes of the Socialist Unity Party of Germany]. *Zeitschrift für Geschichtswissenschaft [East Germany] 1971 19(4): 497-509.* Although the first party statute of the Socialist Unity Party of Germany (SED) was based on Marxist-Leninist principles of organization, the workshop group *(betriebsgruppe)* was not yet accepted as the basis of party organization. After intensive ideological discussions within the party, the statutes of 1950 based the organization on the principle of democratic centralism, which established the SED as a revolutionary party. 22 notes. R. Wagnleitner

1654. Vosske, Heinz. ÜBER DIE POLITISCH-IDEOLOGISCHE HILFE DER KPDSU, DER SOWJETREGIERUNG UND DER SMAD FÜR DIE DEUTSCHE ARBEITERKLASSE IN DEN ERSTEN NACHKRIEGSJAHREN (1945 BIS 1949) [The political-ideological aid of the CPSU, the Soviet government, and the Soviet military administration (SMAD) for the German working class in the first years after the war, 1945-49]. *Beiträge zur Geschichte der Arbeiterbewegung [East Germany] 1972 14(5): 725-739.* In the situation of complete defeat the USSR tried hard to assist the German Communists in their fight for a reorientation of the German people and for the development of a class consciousness of the working class. The forms of political and ideological aid for the development of the Socialist Unity Party of Germany toward a revolutionary Marxist-Leninist party were numerous. Very important for the ideological reorientation was the publication of numerous books and articles which dealt with the best traditions of German humanitarianism and progressivism. Based on documents in the Institute for Marxism-Leninism, published documents, and secondary literature; 34 notes. R. Wagnleitner

1655. Warning, Elke. DIE TÄTIGKEIT DER SED IM BRANDENBURGISCHEN LANDTAG [The actions of the Socialist Unity Party of Germany in the Brandenburg legislature]. *Beiträge zur Geschichte der Arbeiterbewegung [East Germany] 1975 17(5): 887-901.* Since 1945 the Socialist Unity Party of East Germany has sought to consolidate its position in the Brandenburg legislature and to establish a democratic society which would prevent the recurrence of fascist rule. To achieve these goals, committees and agencies for all aspects of political and social life were established to eliminate the inequities of the old fascist and capitalist system and to promote the socialist aim of equality. 50 notes.

G. H. Libbey

1656. Weber, Bernd. SED-IDEOLOGIE: ANNÄHERUNG UND ABGRENZUNG [SED-ideology: rapprochement and demarcation]. *Aussenpolitik [West Germany] 1971 22(12): 705-712.* As East Germany became integrated into the detente process during the 1960's, the Socialist Unity Party (SED) advocated the theory of two German nations (bourgeois and socialist) but maintained its differentiation from social democracy, pluralism, and convergence.

1657. Wille, Manfred. DER KAMPF DER SOZIALISTISCHEN EINHEITSPARTEI DEUTSCHLANDS IM LAND SACHSEN-ANHALT UM DIE DURCHSETZUNG DES BEFEHLS NR. 234 DER SMAD VOM 9. OKTOBER 1947 (ZUR VERTIEFUNG DES REVOLUTIONÄREN UMWÄLZUNGSPROZESSES IN OSTDEUTSCHLAND NACH DEM II. PARTEITAG) [The struggle of the Socialist Unity Party (SED) in Sachsen-Anhalt in carrying out Order No. 234 of SMAD (9 October 1947) on deepening the process of revolutionary transformation in East Germany]. *Jahrbuch für Geschichte [East Germany] 1974 11: 59-97.* On 9 October 1947, the Soviet Military Administration in Germany (SMAD) issued its Order No. 234, which called for the deepening of the revolutionary process of transformation which was changing East Germany from a capitalist country to a socialist. This order was carried out with the aid of the Socialist Unity Party (SED), whose cadres gave indispensable help to the Soviet occupation authorities. In the province of Sachsen-Anhalt, the SED cadres distinguished themselves in applying Order No. 234 and the resolutions of the SED Second Party Congress. 199 notes. J. C. Billigmeier

1658. Willisch, Jürgen. DIR JAGDFLIEGERKRÄFTE DER NATIONALEN VOLKSARMEE BIS ZUM ANFANG DER ACHTZIGER JAHRE [The fighter airplane forces of the National People's Army to the beginning of the 1980's]. *Militärgeschichte [East Germany] 1984 23(1): 18-26.* Describes the development of the fighter airplane forces since the mid-1950's in terms of capabilities of airplanes, weaponry, tactics, and personnel and shows that that development was related to the political goals of the Socialist Unity Party, the plans for common air defenses of the Warsaw Pact members, and the perceived concomitant development in the air forces of potential opponents. Included are basic descriptions of seven airplanes successively assigned to the fighter forces. 2 tables, 35 notes. H. D. Andrews

1659. Winzer, Helmut. ZUR FÜHRENDEN ROLLE DER PARTEIORGANISATION BEI DER ENTWICKLUNG DER LANDWIRTSCHAFTLICHEN PRODUKTIONSGENOSSENSCHAFTEN UND IHRE DARSTELLUNG IN DER AGRAREN BETRIEBSGESCHICHTSSCHREIBUNG [On the leading role of the party organization in the development of agricultural productive cooperatives and its presentation in agrarian history writing]. *Jahrbuch für Wirtschaftsgeschichte [East Germany] 1972 (2): 137-154.* Outlines the socialist transformation of agriculture in East Germany after 1952, and describes in detail the role played and methods employed by local party units in encouraging and organizing agricultural productive cooperatives in certain rural districts. Reviews past efforts and future goals in the writing of agrarian history, with special reference to the leadership role of party units in the villages and cooperatives. Based on party documents, and secondary works; table, 43 notes. J. B. Street

1660. Wörfel, Erhard. ALS DAS BANNER DER EINHEIT DER ARBEITERKLASSE IN THÜRINGEN ENTROLLT WURDE [When the banner of the unity of the working class was unrolled in Thuringia]. *Wissenschaftliche Zeitschrift der Friedrich-Schiller-Universität Jena. Gesellschafts- und Sprachwissenschaftliche Reihe [East Germany] 1976 25(4-5): 603-609.* In spring and summer 1945 German Communists and Social Democrats who had cooperated in the resistance, formed action committees in Thuringia, which negotiated a common political platform for the formation of the Social-

ist Unity Party of Germany (SED), which was founded on 6 April 1946 at Gotha. Based on documents in the Institute of Marxism-Leninism, Berlin, and secondary sources; 14 notes.
R. Wagnleitner

1661. Yosske, Heinz. WILHELM PIECK—VORKÄMPFER FÜR DIE DEUTSCH-SOWJETISCHE FREUNDSCHAFT [Wilhelm Pieck: a pioneer of German-Soviet friendship]. *Beiträge zur Geschichte der Arbeiterbewegung [East Germany] 1975 17(6): 963-975.* Wilhelm Pieck is an outstanding example of international socialist brotherhood. Active from the 1890's to the 1940's-50's, Pieck was an early and consistent supporter of German-Soviet socialist cooperation. Pieck was an active leader of the Communist Party of Germany, officially during the period of the Weimar Republic and unofficially when the party was illegal during the Wilhelmine and Nazi eras. As the first leader of the German Democratic Republic, founded in 1949, he was a major designer of modern Europe. 26 notes.
G. H. Libbey

1662. Zav'ialov, A. S. KRITIKA RABOT ZAPADNOGERMANSKIKH BURZHUAZNYKH ISTORIKOV O SEPG I EE POLITIKE SOIUZOV [Critique of the work of West German bourgeois historians on the Socialist Unity Party and its alliance policy]. *Vestnik Moskovskogo U., Seriia 8: Istoriia [USSR] 1977 (4): 3-16.* West German historiography on East Germany in its first stage presented East Germany as a country doomed to collapse, and the aim of the Socialist Unity Party as one-party dictatorship. More moderate works appeared with less obvious distortions in the mid-1960's when detente was forced on the imperialist powers. West German historians then saw the Party as totalitarian, but perceived that, in its industrialization policy, East Germans used a national form of communism. They also noted the value of the other East German political parties to that state's foreign policy. They became more willing to acknowledge the achievements of East Germany, although they sometimes presented them as the result of the innate qualities of the German people. Thus, many old views remain in the new form of "mobilization" and "industrialization" theory. 63 notes.
D. Balmuth

1663. Zimmermann, Fritz. 25 JAHRE BZG [25 years of *Beiträge zur Geschichte]. Beiträge zur Gesch. der Arbeiterbewegung [East Germany] 1984 26(1): 3-12.* Commemorates the first quarter century of *Beiträge zur Geschichte der Arbeiterbewegung* [Contributions to the history of the labor movement]. Sets it in the context of East German historiography of Communist parties and movements and of the working class. 9 notes.
R. Grove

1664. —. DER KAMPF DER SED UM DIE SCHAFFUNG UND FESTIGUNG DER SOZIALISTISCHEN GESELLSCHAFT IN DER DDR: AUSWAHLBIBLIOGRAPHIE VON LITERATUR DER DDR OKTOBER 1979 BIS MÄRZ 1984 [The struggle of the Socialist Unity Party of Germany to shape and establish socialist society in the German Democratic Republic: selected bibliography of literature of the German Democratic Republic, October 1979-March 1984]. *Beiträge zur Gesch. der Arbeiterbewegung [East Germany] 1984 26(4): 567-576.* Prints a bibliography of documents and studies relating to the Socialist Unity Party of Germany and the politics, culture, and social conditions of East Germany. Note.
R. Grove

1665. —. IM ZEICHEN DES SIEGES DER SOZIALISTISCHEN PRODUKTIONSVERHÄLTNISSE (1961 BIS 1965) [A token of the victory of socialist production rates, 1961-65]. *Wissenschaftliche Zeitschrift der Ernst-Moritz-Arndt-Universität Greifswald [East Germany] 1974 23(3-4): 137-139.* During 1961-65 the staff of the Ernst-Moritz-Arndt University, Greifswald promoted cooperation with universities in other Communist countries, working out a program to coordinate research with practical needs.

1666. —. KARL-MARX-UNIVERSITÄT UND ENTWICKELTE SOZIALISTISCHE GESELLSCHAFT 1961/62-1976 [Karl Marx University and the developed socialist society, 1961-76]. *Wissenschaftliche Zeitschrift der Karl-Marx U. Leipzig. Gesellschafts- und Sprachwissenschaftliche Reihe [East Germany] 1978 27(1): 112-181.* Considers the University's place in a socialist society and the effects of the Communist Party's educational goals.

1667. —. REALITY OF THE FASCIST MENACE. *World Marxist R. [Canada] 1973 16(5): 41-67.* At an international Marxist symposium in Essen, East Germany, representatives from the Communist parties of 21 capitalist countries discussed the dangers posed by new forms of fascism.

Hungary

1668. Ács, Tibor. KONFERENCIA AZ MSZMP HONVÉDELMI POLITIKÁJÁRÓL ÉS A MAGYAR NÉPHADSEREG 25 ÉVES FEJLŐDÉSÉRŐL [Conference on Hungarian Socialist Workers Party defense policy and development of the armed forces during the past 25 years]. *Párttörténeti Közlemények [Hungary] 1982 28(3): 211-215.* Under appropriate political guidance the new Hungarian armed forces, whose leadership has come to be largely of working-class background, have stood ready to work within the framework of the Warsaw Pact, prepared to suppress any act of aggression, whether from within or external.
T. Kuner

1669. Airapetov, A. G. OBSHCHESTVENNO-POLITICHESKIE VZGLIADY ERVINA SABO V OSVESHCHENENII SOTSIAL-DEMOKRATICHESKOI I KOMMUNISTICHESKOI LITERATURY VENGRII [Social political views of Erwin Szabo in the interpretations of Social Democratic and Communist literature of Hungary]. *Vestnik Moskovskogo U. Seriia 9: Istoriia [USSR] 1976 31(3): 36-53.* Erwin Szabo (1877-1918) was one of the most important leaders of the Hungarian Marxist movement. From 1903 he began to work in the Hungarian Sociological Society and defended historical materialism in its publications. Objective analysis of Szabo's views was prevented by Stalin's 1931 negative evaluation of the role of the left German Social Democrats. Szabo struggled against the opportunism of the Hungarian Social Democrats, whose historians have presented Szabo as an opponent of the dictatorship of the proletariat. Communist historians have shown him as a supporter of the Communist Party and the dictatorship of the proletariat. 109 notes.
D. Balmuth

1670. Apro, Antal. SUPREME ORGAN OF POPULAR RULE. *World Marxist R. [Canada] 1974 17(10): 27-35.* Analyzes democracy and parliamentary authority under Communism in Hungary (1949-74).

1671. Balogh, Sándor. A BALOLDALI ERÖK KÜZDELME A KÖZIGAZGATÁS DEMOKRATIZÁLÁSÁÉRT. AZ 1946. ÉVI BÉLISTA VÉGREHAJTÁSA ÉS REVIZIÓJA [The struggle of leftist forces for the democratization of public administration: the execution and revision of the 1946 "B" list]. *Párttórténeti Kózlemények [Hungary] 1974 20(2): 55-87.* After 1945 the Hungarian Communist Party (HCP) aimed at purging the civil service of rightist elements rather than a fundamental transformation of the public administration. The Independent Smallholder Party (ISP), the largest political party in Hungary, in constantly frustrating this effort, demanded an equal share with the HCP in the control of the police before the government established a "B" list, a blacklist of unwanted administrators. The HCP Minister of Interior, Imre Nagy, was to replace purged administrators with Communist Social Democratic, and union cadres, which the ISP attempted to counter. Eventually 60,000 civil servants, mainly right wingers, were laid off. Soon the ISP and even the non-Communist leftist parties clamored for a revision of the "B" list. In agreeing to a revision the HCP made certain that only the leftist groups benefited. The purge within the armed forces and the police reinforced the dominance of the Communists. 114 notes.
P. I. Hidas

1672. Balogh, Sándor. A POLITIKAI PÁRTOK ÉS A SZÖVETKEZETEK KÉRDÉSE MAGYARORSZÁGON 1945-1946-BAN [The question of political parties and cooperatives in Hungary in 1945-46]. *Párttörténeti Közlemények [Hungary] 1975 21(4): 51-82.* Immediately following the end of World War II all

Hungarian political parties had their own program on the land question and the future of cooperatives. The Communist Party (MKP) advocated respect for private property, and as a result there was a political consensus on land reform measures. There was less agreement and collaboration on the question of cooperatives, as the parties contended for political control of the cooperative movement, by early 1947 securely won by the MKP. 116 notes.

P. I. Hidas

1673. Bango, Jenö F. KOMMUNIKATIONSSTRUKTUREN UND VERHALTENSWEISEN IM SOZIALEN WANDEL DES UNGARISCHEN DORFES [Communication structures and behavioral patterns in the social transformation of the Hungarian village]. *Osteuropa [West Germany] 1977 27(11): 962-977.* Examines the impact of the Communist Party, the churches, and social change on traditional Hungarian country life, 1944-75.

1674. Belényi, Gyula. A SZEGEDI TANYÁK 1949-BEN [Isolated farms around Szeged in 1949]. *Agrártörténeti Szemle [Hungary] 1981 23(1-2): 223-235.* Due to obsolete production systems that demanded excessive manpower, the Hungarian Communist Party decided to liquidate all isolated small farms in Hungary and replace them with centralized communities. Contrary to the Party's high hopes for immediate changes and improvement, this process took more than a decade to accomplish. 47 notes, 2 tables.

T. Kuner

1675. Benke, József. A SZOCIALISTA AGRÁRVISZONYOK KIALAKULÁSA ÉS FEJLŐDÉSE SOMOGYBAN, 1948-1970 [The socialist transformation of agrarian conditions and the development of socialist production conditions in Somogy county, 1948-70]. *Agrártörténeti Szemle [Hungary] 1976 18(1-2): 75-114.* The formation of agricultural cooperatives in 1948 was prescribed by the Communist Party. In Somogy county most cooperative farm members were also Party members. Despite a campaign of forced delivery, 1949-53, and the imprisonment of defaulters crop production remained low. In the 1950's the membership of the cooperatives fluctuated according to political pressure, but the introduction of a system of state bonuses in 1957 made membership more attractive. By the 1970's the Somogy agricultural cooperatives were reported to be both politically and economically stable. 10 tables, 149 notes.

T. Kabdebo/S

1676. Blaskovits, János. BÉKÉS ÁTMENET ÉS SZÖVETSÉGI POLITIKA (A MKP HARMINC ÉV ELŐTTI III. KONGRESSZUSÁRÓL) [Peaceful transition and the policy of alliance: on the 3d Congress of the Hungarian Communist Party 30 years ago]. *Társadalmi Szemle [Hungary] 1976 31(10): 50-58.* The 3d Congress of the Hungarian Communist Party in the fall of 1946 did not concentrate on the ultimate alternatives of socialism versus capitalism or dictatorship of the proletariat versus bourgeois democracy, but followed the correct line of allying Communists with the Social Democrats and small peasants for a gradual transition to people's democracy. The Cold War, however, contributed to the acceleration of the process leading to socialism in Hungary.

1677. Blaskovits, János. A PÁRT ÉS A MUNKÁSOSZTÁLY (1956. NOVEMBER - 1957. FEBRUÁR) [The Party and the working class, November 1956-February, 1957]. *Párttörténeti Közlemények [Hungary] 1975 21(1): 166-196.* In November 1956 the main task of the Hungarian government was maintaining a proletarian dictatorship through armed presence. For tactical reasons the government allowed the operation of independent workers' councils and unions. The majority of the working class momentarily opposed the government. The Soviet army had to safeguard Hungary's independence and socialist achievements. The counterrevolutionary mood was strongest among youth and low wage earners, especially women, printers, transport, textile, and ironworkers. Miners and construction workers were less affected. Under the circumstances the rebuilding of the Communist Party was most difficult. Workers' wages were raised several times. Many adamant Social Democrats were expelled from the labor unions and the workers' councils were dissolved. Communists reassured the masses that they would not return to the mistakes of the Rakosi regime. In 1957 the Party began to regain the trust of the workers. 40 notes. P. I. Hidas

1678. Čierná, Dagmar. MAĎARSKÁ EKONOMIKA ROKU 1946 A III. SJAZD KSM [Hungarian economics in 1946 and the third Congress of Hungarian Communists]. *Slovanský Přehled [Czechoslovakia] 1976 62(6): 440-444.* Recounts the development of Hungarian economic policy after World War II. The September congress of the 1946 Communist Party of Hungary adopted a new policy calling for the gradual elimination of the capitalist agricultural system through peaceful transition. 42 notes. G. E. Pergl

1679. Čierná, Dagmar. MAĎARSKO V ROKU PŘELOMU 1947-48 [Hungary at the turning point 1947-48]. *Slovanský Přehled [Czechoslovakia] 1975 61(1): 58-63.* Reflects on the political development of Hungary after World War II. The unification of the workers' parties became a fact in March 1948. In June 1948, the Hungarian Workers' Party was founded. This was the beginning of the socialist era in Hungary. 54 notes. G. E. Pergl

1680. Čierna, Dagmar. ZÁKLADNÉ PROBLÉMY MAD'ARSKEJ L'UDOVEJ DEMOKRACIE A PRELOM 1947-1948 V INTERPRETÁCII BURŽOÁZNEJ HISTORIOGRAFIE [Fundamental problems of Hungarian people's democracy and the break of 1947-48 in bourgeois historiography]. *Slovanské Štúdie [Czechoslovakia] 1981 22: 197-220.* Compares the results of Marxist historiographical research on problems of postwar developments in Hungary with the evaluation of those events in bourgeois historiography. Bourgeois views of the revolutionary process are distorted. This era of political development in Hungary cannot be described as a "liquidation" of the Social Democratic Party. The trend toward socialist revolution in Hungary was a logical outcome of the nation's will and desire. Based on official papers and published material; 107 notes. G. E. Pergl

1681. Csikesz, Mrs. József. A KÖZTÁRSASÁG TÉRI PÁRTHÁZBAN [In the Party center on Köztársaság Square]. *Társadalmi Szemle [Hungary] 1981 36(10): 57-63.* In 1950, the standard of living of workers in Hungary declined and in 1953 the leadership was still hesitant and ambiguous. On 23 October 1956, terror activities erupted, directed at Party activists. The center was attacked and occupied on 30 October. Restoration of order began in November. Part of a special issue. R. Hetzron

1682. Csikós-Nagy, Béla. LIQUIDITY PROBLEMS AND ECONOMIC CONSOLIDATION. *New Hungarian Q. [Hungary] 1984 25(94): 42-54.* Predicts changes in the state management of the Hungarian economy. Outlines economic policy and the establishment of a Consultative Body to suggest reforms by the Political Committee of the Hungarian Socialist Workers' Party. Summarizes Hungary's trade with Comecon and western nations.

R. Grove

1683. Csurdi, Sándor. TUDOMÁNYOS EMLÉKÜLÉS DR. RÓNAI ZOLTÁN SZÜLETÉSÉNEK CENTENÁRIUMÁN [Scholarly memorial conference on the centennial of the birth of Zoltán Rónai]. *Párttörténeti Közlemények [Hungary] 1981 27(1): 196-202.* On 14 November 1980 the Historical Institute of the Hungarian Academy of Sciences and the Institute of Party History sponsored a conference dedicated to the life and work of the Social Democratic politician and journalist, Zoltán Rónai.

P. I. Hidas

1684. Czigler, Róbert. A MAGYAR KOMMUNISTA PÁRT TÖREKVÉSEI A FALUSI LAKOSSÁG KÖNYVTÁRI ELLÁTÁSÁÉRT A KOALÍCIÓS KORSZAKBAN (1945-1948) [Efforts of the Hungarian Communist Party to provide libraries for villages between 1945 and 1948]. *Magyar Könyvszemle [Hungary] 1984 100(4): 363-373.* Though the Hungarian Communist Party realized the importance of upgrading village cultural life early on, important political and economic matters took precedence. However, in the summer of 1945 the Party began a weekly intended for rural areas entitled *Szabad Föld* [Free land], with Gyula Kállai as editor-in-chief. In the winter of 1946 the Party began to encourage the building of collections, particularly of Communist propaganda and literature with rural themes. The third Party Congress, 29 September to 1 October 1946, developed a three-year economic plan that included cultural development. The first peoples' library opened on 30 March 1947 in Törökbálint. Primary sources; 59 notes. A. M. Pogany

1685. Derzhaliuk, N. TRUDY PO ISTORII STROITEL'STVA VENGERSKOI NARODNOI ARMII [Works on the history of the construction of the Hungarian People's Army]. *Voenno-Istoricheskii Zhurnal [USSR] 1981 23(6): 83-85.* Briefly outlines and assesses recent publications on the history of the Hungarian People's Army. Considers in detail the Hungarian involvement in World War II at the beginning of 1945, the liberation by the Soviet army of the entire territory of Hungary, and subsequent creation of favorable conditions for democratic and socioeconomic transformations. Describes the valuable efforts of the Hungarian Communist and Social Democratic Parties during the war and the eventual formation of the new People's Army, now an important member of the fraternity of armies of the Warsaw Pact for the defense of socialist nations. Based on Hungarian published materials; 5 notes. L. Smith

1686. Dimény, Imre. EGY ÉV MÉRLEGE A MEZŐGAZDASÁGBAN [One year's balance in agriculture]. *Társadalmi Szemle [Hungary] 1969 24(3): 34-42.* Discusses the agricultural policy of the Communist Party and government. The Party harmonized agricultural reforms with the building of socialism, achieving in 1968 all prescribed quotas. A. Mina

1687. Dimitrova, Stela. NAUCHNA KONFERENTSIIA PO SLUCHAI 50-GODISHNINATA NA UNGARSKATA SUVETSKA REPUBLIKA PREZ 1919 [Scholarly conference on the 50th anniversary of the Hungarian Soviet Republic, 1919]. *Izvestiia na Inst. po Istoriia na BKP [Bulgaria] 1969 22: 441-445.* Reports the proceedings of the conference, held in Budapest, 17-19 March 1969 to commemorate the 50th anniversary of the first Communist state in Hungary, and summarizes the major papers given.

1688. Door, Rochus. ZUR AUSARBEITUNG UND DURCHSETZUNG DER POLITISCHEN LINIE DER KOMMUNISTISCHEN PARTEI UNGARNS BEI DER HINÜBERLEITUNG DES ANTIFASCISTISCHEN WIDERSTANDS IN DIE VOLKSDEMOKRATISCHE REVOLUTION [On the formulation and implementation of the political line of the Hungarian Communist Party in the metamorphosis of the antifascist resistance into the People's Democratic Republic]. *Martin-Luther-U. Halle-Wittenberg. Wissenschaftliche Zeitschrift Gesellschafts- und Sprachwissenschaftliche Reihe [East Germany] 1976 25(3): 108-111.* Between 1944 and 1947 Communist-inspired factory committees were formed in Hungary to clear the ruins and restart production and by 1944 the Communists' Hungarian Front embraced all political parties. In the provisional National Assembly of 1944 the Communists held 71 of 230 seats and in the later provisional government of Bela Miklós there were three Communist ministers. A. Alcock

1689. El'ter, P. SOROK PIAT' LET BOR'BY I TRUDA [Forty-five years of struggle and labor]. *Voprosy Istorii KPSS [USSR] 1963 (12): 79-84.* Describes the development of Hungary's Communist Party, 1918-63, and demonstrates that despite the mistakes of the leadership and the counterrevolution of 1956, it is successfully accomplishing socialist construction.

1690. Eörsi, István. GYÖRGY LUKÁCS, FANATIC OF REALITY. *New Hungarian Q. [Hungary] 1971 12(44): 26-34.* Analyzes the life and works of Hungarian philosopher György Lukács who passed through several intellectual periods. He was always more interested in discovering truth than in proving the truth of his own assertions. Thus he shed his earlier theories and positions with cheerful ease. He never lost his unique talent for distinguishing between the objective and the subjective. This was his greatest achievement, the one facet of his thought which the changing, synthesis-resisting upheaval of his times failed to alter. V. L. Human

1691. Erez, Zvi. HA-YEHUDIM VE-HA-"OKTOBER" HA-HUNGARI, 1956: BE-TOKH HA-TSAMERET VE-NEGDAH [The Jews and Hungarians October 1956: the Communist Party leaders and the opposition]. *Shvut [Israel] 1976 4: 119-125.* The leaders of the Hungarian Communist Party, 1945-56, including the five at the top, Matyas Rakosi, Joszef Revai, Erno Gero, Mihaly Farkas, and Gabor Peter, were Jews. The 1956 opposition was also led predominantly by Jewish Communists. Despite efforts by Jews in both camps to suppress their origins, anti-Semites have accused Jews of subjecting Hungary to Soviet imperialism. 40 notes, appendix. T. Sassoon

1692. Fedoseev, P. N. VYDAIUSHCHIISIA RUKOVODITEL' NARODNOI VENGRII (K 70-LETIIU SO DNIA ROZHDENIIA IANOSHA KADARA) [The outstanding leader of People's Hungary: on the 70th birthday of János Kádár]. *Voprosy Istorii KPSS [USSR] 1982 (5): 107-111.* János Kádár was born 26 May 1912 into a worker's family and early knew the harsh conditions of capitalism. He joined the Communist Party in 1931 and was arrested many times. After the war he was elected to many political functions. He was arrested and imprisoned on false charges in 1951 and rehabilitated in 1954. He was elected to the Politburo in 1956. After the attempt at counterrevolution in 1956, Kadar became First Secretary of the Central Committee of the Hungarian Socialist Workers' Party and began the consolidation of socialism. He introduced successful reforms in industry and agriculture. Brezhnev and Kadar meet regularly. He is a staunch Marxist-Leninist, a great leader of his people, and a true friend of the USSR. Based on Kadar's works, *Pravda,* and other Soviet sources; 12 notes. A. J. Evans

1693. Felkai, Dénes. NEVELŐTISZTKÉPZŐ TANFOLYAM [The officers' training course]. *Hadtörténelmi Közlemények [Hungary] 1978 25(2): 237-247.* Surveys the development of officers' training courses at the Hungarian Officers' Educational Institution, founded in 1945. Six-month officer training courses were introduced in 1946 by Dénes Felkai. These courses included lectures on the democratic world view and Marxist education for trainee officers, but the reactionary elements in the Ministry of Defense attempted to hinder the courses. In 1948 the Hungarian Workers' Party was formed and chose Dénes Felkai to organize the Petőfi Academy which was opened in December 1948. Primary sources. Gy. and N. H. Foxcroft

1694. Fischer, Rudolf. REMEMBERED HISTORY. *New Hungarian Q. [Hungary] 1980 21(78): 174-177.* Foreign Minister Frigyes Puja's *A Felszabadult Battonya* [Liberated Battonya] (1979) describes how the village of Battonya was liberated in 1944 before any other Hungarian town, how the villagers then formed a Communist Party organization, and how they subsequently dealt with problems within the Party. Concludes with the local results of the August 1947 parliamentary elections. E. L. Keyser

1695. Földes, György. EGYSZERŰSÍTÉS, MECHANIZMUS ES IPARIRÁNYÍTÁS, 1953-1956 [Simplification, mechanism, and industrial management, 1953-56]. *Párttörténeti Közlemények [Hungary] 1984 30(2): 72-108.* Charts the progress of the limited economic reforms initiated by the Hungarian Workers' Party at the session of its central executive in June 1953 and analyzes the ensuing debates within the party about the necessary extent of the simplification of state administration and decentralization of the economy. Based on archives of the Institute of Party History in Budapest, contemporary newspaper articles, and secondary sources; 142 notes. I. Karacs

1696. Földes, Karoly. KÜLGAZDASÁGI TEVÉKENYSÉG ÉS SZOCIALISTA FEJLŐDÉS (A GAZDASÁGI NÖVEKEDÉS ALAPTÉNYEZŐI ÉS A KÜLKERESKEDELEM) [External economic activity and socialist development: the factors of economic growth and foreign trade]. *Közgazdasági Szemle [Hungary] 1984 31(11): 1281-1296.* Analyzes the interaction of external and internal economic activity in increasing resources: the level of the specific expenditures, the terms of trade, the competitiveness of goods, and the structural movement influenced by these components. Modes of operation must simultaneously guarantee dynamic balance, efficiency, and social objectives. The balance-maintaining function of the economy became weaker, the stimulating role of wages lost its importance, and economic performance did not sufficiently serve society. J/S

1697. Fry, Michael G. and Rice, Condoleezza. THE HUNGARIAN CRISIS OF 1956: THE SOVIET DECISION. *Studies in Comparative Communism 1983 16(1-2): 85-98.* There were several possible scenarios for Soviet action in Hungary in 1956. Khrushchev was willing to make concessions to the rebels while Molotov favored military intervention. The decisive events which led a united Politburo to approve invasion was Imre Nagy's promise to return to a multi-party system and his effort to purge the military command of officers loyal to the USSR. The pattern in Hungary was a precedent for action in Czechoslovakia in 1968. 23 notes.
D. Balmuth

1698. Gaál, Miklós. MAGYAR-NDK-BELI PÁRTTÖRTÉNÉSZ TALÁLKOZÓ [A meeting of Party historians from Hungary and East Germany]. *Párttörténeti Közlemények [Hungary] 1984 30(2): 185-188.* An account of a round-table conference held 6-7 December 1983 in Budapest organized by the Party History Institute of the Central Committee of the Hungarian Socialist Workers' Party and the Marxism-Leninism Institute of the Central Committee of the Socialist Unity Party of Germany. Lectures were delivered by Volker Steinke, Gerd Dietrich, Sándor Rákosi, Éva Standeisky, Sonja Eichofer, and János Botos; all dealt with the revolutionary processes that emerged in Hungary and East Germany after 1945.
I. Karacs

1699. Garai, George. RÁKOSI AND THE "ANTI-ZIONIST" CAMPAIGN OF 1952-53. *Soviet Jewish Affairs [Great Britain] 1982 12(2): 19-36.* Hungarian Jewish leader of the Hungarian Communist Party Mátyás Rákosi attempted to follow Stalin's anti-Zionist line for his own protection, 1952-53.

1700. Gergely, Ladislau. REVCOLUŢIA POPULARĂ ŞI PRINCIPALELE MOMENTE ALE CONSTRUCŢIEI SOCIALISTE ÎN REPUBLICA POPULARĂ UNGARĂ [The people's revolution and the principal moments in the building of socialism in the People's Republic of Hungary]. *Anale de Istorie [Rumania] 1971 17(5): 138-147.* Surveys political and economic developments in Hungary since 1945, particularly the role of the Hungarian Communist Party and its fusion with the Hungarian Social-Democratic Party to form the controlling Hungarian Workers' Party. Describes the establishment of socialism in 1945 following the liberation of Hungary by the USSR and the Party's 1944 reform program. A coalition of left and center parties, the Hungarian National Independence Front, held office initially, effecting agrarian and economic reform. In 1946 non-Marxist, nonworker political parties were eliminated, a republic was declared, the economy stabilized and largely nationalized, agriculture collectivized, and education secularized and placed under state control. Both the emphasis on industrialization which retarded the rise in living standards and shortages resulting from collectivization caused an uprising in 1956 which was suppressed by Soviet troops. 26 notes. R. O. Khan/S

1701. Gosztony, Peter I. THE HUNGARIAN WORKERS' MILITIA. *Military Rev. 1972 52(7): 54-58.* Since the 1956 rebellion, the Hungarian Workers' Militia, comprised mostly of Communist Party members, has assumed a public service role, but its main function is as a counterrevolutionary force.

1702. Gyarmati, György. POLITIKAI SZEMPONTOK ÉRVÉNYESÜLÉSE A TANÁCSRENDSZER ELŐKÉSZÍTŐ MUNKÁLATAIBAN [The predominance of political considerations in the formation of the council system]. *Történelmi Szemle [Hungary] 1981 24(2): 178-190.* Reviews the strategies of the Communist Party in Hungary at the conclusion of World War II, noting that the Communists aimed at establishing a system of soviets or councils that would unite the entire country in a single political system under a dictatorship of the proletariat that required the withdrawal of democracy. J/S

1703. Habuda, Miklós. A MAGYAR DOLGOZÓK PÁRTJA MUNKAPOLITIKÁJÁNAK NÉHÁNY KÉRDÉSE (1954-1956) [Some questions of the labor policy of the Hungarian Workers' Party, 1954-56]. *Párttörténeti Szemle [Hungary] 1978 24(4): 85-121.* Because of some sectarian and revisionistic trends, Hungary experienced economic difficulties in 1954. In 1955, some official distrust toward laborers manifested itself, but signs of improvement soon started to appear.

1704. Habuda, Miklós. A MAGYAR DOLGOZÓK PÁRTJA MUNKÁSPOLITIKÁJÁNAK NÉHÁNY KÉRDÉSE A KÖZPONTI VEZETŐSÉG 1953. JÚNIUSI HATÁROZATA UTÁN [Questions regarding political actions of the Hungarian Worker's Party after the June 1953 resolution of the Central Committee]. *Párttörténeti Közlemények [Hungary] 1980 26(1): 23-55.* The purpose of the Central Committee meeting was to rectify past mistakes, reexamine current activities, and evaluate political trends. Workers' living standards were unfavorably influenced by rapid industrialization, neglect of agriculture, and forced collectivization. Further difficulties were caused by an autocratic bureaucratic system and personal cults of past political leaders. It was decided to reduce production of heavy industry and increase food production, changes intended to regain for the Party the lost confidence of the working class. Although prices were reduced, general inertia and lack of organization made final results extremely unsatisfactory. 3 tables, 80 notes. T. Kuner

1705. Habuda, Miklós and Rákosi, Sándor. A MAGYAR KOMMUNISTA PÁRT ÉS A SZOCIÁLDEMOKRATA PÁRT MUNKÁSÖSSZE-TÉTELÉNEK ALAKULÁSA 1945-1948-BAN [The proportion of industrial workers in the Hungarian Communist Party and Social Democratic Party, 1945-48]. *Párttörténeti Közlemények [Hungary] 1976 22(3): 36-68.* At the end of World War II, the Hungarian Communist Party formerly underground, became an openly organized mass party, recruiting in competition with the Social Democratic Party, which had preserved its legal existence even during the war. The proportion of the organized industrial workers within the two mass parties, and the changes in that proportion, were connected with the changing political situation. One year before the fusion of the two parties in 1947, the number of Communist Party members among industrial workers grew noticeably faster. In the absence of reliable sources the authors do not discuss the proportion among agricultural workers. Based on material in the Party archives; 87 notes. CK-AU

1706. Habuda, Miklos. ZUR ENTSTEHUNG DER VOLKSREPUBLIK UNGARN [The foundation of the People's Republic of Hungary]. *Beiträge zur Geschichte der Arbeiterbewegung [East Germany] 1975 17(2): 249-259.* As in other Southern and Eastern European states, the socialist and democratic victory in Hungary was part of the international rise of the working class. Of the major world powers, only the USSR aided this expression of popular government. As the Soviet army drove German fascists from Hungary during World War II, the Communist Party of Hungary changed its emphasis from resistance to the postwar rebuilding. Socialist alliances assured that future governance would be popular and free of capitalistic interests which had suppressed democratic feelings before the war. Based on records of the Social Democratic Party of Hungary and the Communist Party of Hungary; 4 notes.
G. H. Libbey

1707. Háncs, Ernő. A POLITIKAI FŐCSOPORTFŐNÖKSÉG ÉS A POLITIKAI TISZTI INTÉZMÉNY LÉTREHOZÁSÁNAK ELŐZMÉNYEI A MAGYAR NÉPHADSEREGBEN (1948 ÁPRILIS-1949 FEBRUÁR) [Preliminaries to establish an institute for political leadership and political education for officers in the Hungarian People's Army (April 1948-February 1949)]. *Hadtörténelmi Közlemények [Hungary] 1984 31(1): 72-93.* To overcome disorganized and confusing political training methods, in 1948 the Military Board of the Hungarian Communist Party ordered the inauguration of a new nationwide political oriented educational program for all new officers. The curriculum was clearly defined and included several weekly sessions on folk dancing and singing. 43 notes. T. Kuner

1708. Haraszti, E. H. BRITISH REFLECTIONS ON THE DECISIVE YEAR OF POST-WAR HUNGARY: 1948. *Acta Hist. [Hungary] 1981 27(1-2): 189-204.* Outlines the political events in Hungary in 1948 and Great Britain's reaction to them. In March 1945 the Hungarian government decreed a land reform bill, which Britain felt might destroy the country, but still ought to be supported as a step toward democracy. The Communist Party program developed rapidly in 1948. Right-wing leaders in the Social Democratic Party were deposed and György Marosán and Mátyás Rákosi announced the merger of the two parties. The campaign against the kulaks, rich peasants, and the arrest of Cardinal József Mindszenty followed closely. In Britain there was fear of new totalitarian right-wing regimes in Hungary as well as dismay at the extent of Soviet control. At the same time substantial trade continued between the two countries. Based primarily on the Foreign Office files of the Public Record Office, Great Britain; 37 notes. A. M. Pogany

1709. Havasi, Ferenc. A GAZDASÁGIRÁNYÍTÁS TOVÁBBFEJLESZTÉSE [The continued developing of the system of economic control and management]. *Közgazdasági Szemle [Hungary] 1984 31(7-8): 769-785.* The reform of the system of economic management, decided by the Central Committee of the Hungarian Socialist Workers' Party (HSWP) in 1966, meant the control and direction of the economy predominantly by economic methods. By 1984, there remained three main fields where further improvements were needed: the central direction of the economy (the government level); the degree of independence of the individual firms and enterprises where there should be more room for initiative; and organizational and institutional economic methods enabling greater efficiency. Speech delivered in the Central Committee of the HSWP, 17 April 1984. G. Jeszenszky

1710. Havasi, Ferenc. GAZDASÁGUNK AZ ÚJ NÖVEKEDÉSI PÁLYÁN [The Hungarian economy on the new growth path]. *Közgazdasági Szemle [Hungary] 1982 29(7-8): 785-792.* Traces the antecedents of the present intensive economic development to 1973 when the first world market price explosion created a new international situation. For some time the Hungarian reaction was characterized by an underestimation of the external economic changes and an exaggeratedly optimistic judgment of its own situation. Necessary economic measures were made difficult by the political uncertainty from 1972 to 1974. The five-year plan for 1976-80, which called for increased competition, and higher production, and raising the standard of living proved unrealistic. The session of the Central Committee of the Hungarian Socialist Workers Party in December 1978 and the 12th Party Congress considered a balance of trade to be the highest priority, with the qualification that the standard of living must be maintained and living conditions improved.

J/S

1711. Havasi, Ferenc. POLITIKAI SZERVEZETEINK ÉS A VÁLTOZÓ VALÓSÁG (HOZZÁSZÓLÁS AZ ESZME-SZERVEZET-MOZGALOM CÍMŰ CIKKHEZ) [Our political organizations and changing reality: response to the article entitled "Idea-structure-movement"]. *Társadalmi Szemle [Hungary] 1972 27(12): 52-56.* Responds to Imre Poszgay's article, "Eszme-Szervezet-Mozgalom" [Idea-Structure-Movement], *Társadalmi Szemle* 1971 26(11), refuting its contention that Hungarian public life is overorganized by the Communist Party and noting that some new industries and even certain local governments lack the Party's unifying influence.

1712. Hedli, Douglas J. UNITED STATES INVOLVEMENT OR NON-INVOLVEMENT IN THE HUNGARIAN REVOLUTION OF 1956. *Int. Rev. of Hist. and Pol. Sci. [Great Britain] 1974 11(1): 72-78.* No US political or economic aid was provided or offered to the Hungarian people in their revolt against Russian authority in 1956. Prior to and during the revolution, US leaders acted under outdated and misguided understanding of the goals of Communism and insufficient information on the intent of the Hungarian people. Based on government documents and secondary sources; 10 notes, biblio. E. McCarthy

1713. Hedri, Gabriella. A GAZDASÁGFEJLESZTÉS MINT ELSŐDLEGES POLITIKAI CÉL: ITT ÉS MOST [Economic policy as a primary political objective: here and now]. *Közgazdasági Szemle [Hungary] 1984 31(6): 641-649.* One effect of the military menace to the socialist community is that while the community is a global factor in the political and military field, it has remained a regional factor in world economy. If, because of the simultaneous appearance of East-West tensions, the world economic crisis, and the requirements of transition to the stage of intensive development, the rising trend of living standards suffered a break in socialist society, economic development, the safeguarding of security, and the development of social consciousness achieved qualitatively new relationships with each other. It would be expedient to analyze the factory democracy in Hungary in the period 1945-49 and to increase the transparency of the economy. J/S

1714. Hegedüs, Sándor. BRAUN ÉVA (1917-1945) [Eva Braun (1917-45)]. *Párttörténeti Közlemények [Hungary] 1980 26(4): 187-198.* Growing up in an intellectual middle-class family, fluent in German, French, and English, Eva Braun joined the Young Workers' Movement at a very early age. Her group was successful in disturbing and interrupting several Fascist meetings and distributing socialist literature. Arrested in 1940 and severely tortured, she did not divulge the names of others in her organization. At this stage her social orientation changed to communism. After regaining freedom she resumed her political activities with even greater devotion. In 1945 she was arrested in Budapest by a Fascist patrol. The Communist literature which was found on her person was considered sufficient evidence for immediate execution without a hearing or trial. She was killed by a firing squad two weeks before Budapest was liberated by the Russian army. 44 notes. T. Kuner

1715. Hegedüs, Sándor. SZATON REZSŐ (1888-1957) [Rezső Szaton (1888-1957)]. *Párttörténeti Közlemények [Hungary] 1980 26(2): 142-159.* Szaton, one of the founding members of the Hungarian Communist movement spent his life in the service of the Party. A lathe operator, he was instrumental in organizing metal workers before World War I. In 1923 he escaped Hungary to live in the USSR, where he actively worked for the Party with Germans and Ukrainians. He returned to Budapest in 1946 and was put in charge of the personnel office of the newly established Hungarian-Soviet Airline. 39 notes. T. Kuner

1716. Hegedüs, Sándor. MEZŐ IMRE (1905-1956) [Imre Mező (1905-56)]. *Párttörténeti Közlemények [Hungary] 1981 27(3): 173-192.* Mezo, a tailor by profession, unable to find employment in Hungary, emigrated to Belgium in 1924. There he joined the Communist Party, which sent him to Spain in 1936 to fight against Franco in the International Brigade. After 1945 he returned to Hungary and was elected as a member of parliament and became a member of the Party committee in Budapest. He was shot in 1956 while protecting the entrance to his office against the counterrevolutionaries. 65 notes. T. Kuner

1717. Ignotus, Paul. THE FIRST TWO COMMUNIST TAKEOVERS OF HUNGARY: 1919 and 1948. *Studies on the Soviet Union [West Germany] 1971 11 (4): 338-351.* Hungary produced a short-lived Communist regime as early as 1919. This government was formed as a reaction to the policies of the Western powers, who whittled away Hungarian territory in the name of self-determination. The regime failed because of the united opposition of the Hungarian people and the Western powers. The post-World War II takeover followed the customary pattern of Red Army invasion, coalition government, power consolidation, and purge of dissidents. The 1919 revolution was intensely nationalistic, whereas the 1948 version was not. Secondary sources; 10 notes.

V. L. Human

1718. Izsák, Lajos. DIE WICHTIGSTEN FRAGEN DER GESCHICHTE DER UNGARISCHEN VOLKSDEMOKRATIE IN UNSERER MARXISTISCHEN GESCHICHTSLITERATUR [The most important questions in the history of the Hungarian People's Democracy in our Marxist historical literature]. *Ann. U. Sci. Budapestinensis de Rolando Eötvös Nominatae: Sectio Hist. [Hungary]*

1975 16: 255-293. Bibliographic article covering historical, economic, social, political, and cultural studies on the history of the Communist government of Hungary.

1719. Izsák, Lajos. OSZTÁLY-ÉS PÁRTHARCOK, POLITIKAI IRÁNYZATOK A FELSZABADULÁS UTÁN [Class and party struggles, political directions in the years after liberation]. *Társadalmi Szemle [Hungary] 1981 36(7): 52-65, (8-9): 53-66.* The first free elections in Hungary took place in 1945. Due in part to Cardinal Josef Mindszenty's negative attitude, the Communist Party gained only 42% of the votes. New laws, enacted in 1947, eliminated a great number of the electors and candidates but did not affect the democratic character of the next election, which in the same year produced a majority 61% for the left coalition. After Mindszenty's arrest, the Soviet format was adopted and all political parties were dissolved. In 1949 the newly created Hungarian Workers' Party received 95% of the votes. The fact that all previous parties were allowed to exist within the Hungarian Workers' Party had a strong effect on the outcome of the election. 21 notes.
T. Kuner

1720. Izsák, Lajos. A RADIKÁLIS DEMOKRATA PÁRTSZÖVETSÉG [The Radical Democratic Party federation]. *Párttörténeti Közlemények [Hungary] 1980 26(1): 56-89.* To gain support of the middle-class and intellectual voters, both the Citizen Democratic Party (PDP) and the Hungarian Radical Party (MRP) presented themselves as parties for individual freedom. In 1948, they merged as the Radical Democratic Party (RDP) for the 1949 elections, but 95% of the voters supported the People's Front (the only list presented), led by the Hungarian Workers' Party (MDP), and the Radical Democratic Party, together with other elements of the liberal bourgeois opposition, disappeared from the political scene. 121 notes. T. Kuner

1721. Izsák, Lajos. VYTESNENIE BURZHUAZNOI KONSERVATIVNO-LIBERAL'NOI OPPOZITSII IZ POLITICHESKOI ZHIZNI VENGRII (1947-1949 GG.) [The elimination of the conservative-liberal opposition from the political life of Hungary, 1947-49]. *Ann. U. Sci. Budapestinensis de Rolando Eötvös Nominatae: Sectio Hist. [Hungary] 1981 21: 417-439.* The 21 August 1947 elections gave the Communist-led coalition 61% of the votes, the Communist Party receiving 23%, making it the largest single party. The Hungarian Independence Party, largely preoccupied with internal problems, lost public support and was banned on 19 November 1947. This was a great victory for Hungarian democracy. The Democratic People's Party had no role in the era of proletarian dictatorship, and was suppressed. A party grouping patriotic non-Communists was formed 13 May 1948 and the bourgeois coalition, failing to respond to the people's wishes, was removed from political life after the formation of the new government on 2 September 1947. Based on newspapers and secondary sources; 102 notes. A. J. Evans

1722. Jemnitz, János. ADALÉKOK A MAGYARORSZÁGI SZOCIÁLDEMOKRATA PÁRT ÉS AZ ANGOL LABOUR PARTY KAPCSOLATAINAK TÖRTÉNETÉHEZ (1945-1947) [Contribution to the history of the relations between the Hungarian Social Democratic Party and the English Labour Party in the years 1945-47]. *Történelmi Szemle [Hungary] 1975 18(1): 107-118.* The English Labour Party had a prominent position in the foreign political plans and international relations of the Hungarian Social Democratic Party after 1945. The Labour Party had taken the initiative in the revival of the international social democratic movement toward the end of the war, and from 1946 on the party controlled the work of organization as well. The fact that the Labour Party had formed a government in London in 1945 gave the party special importance. There were, at the same time, some shades of difference between the Foreign Office, led by Bevin, and the Foreign Department of the party concerning the relationship with the Hungarian Social Democrats. The Foreign Department—at that time led by Denis Healey—showed a definite sensitivity toward the realities of Eastern Europe. Although Healey did not approve of the cooperation with the Communists either, he knew that this relationship could not be fully neglected, and realized that, at least in Hungary, there existed dangerous counterrevolutionary forces which justified anxiety among Social Democrats. Based on sources in the archives of the Labour Party and Hungarian archives.

1723. Jemnitz, János. PÁL JUSTUS AND THE BRITISH LABOUR PARTY. *New Hungarian Q. [Hungary] 1980 21(79): 137-144.* From the end of World War II until his trial on trumped-up charges and imprisonment in 1949 Pál Justus was a leading theoretician of the Hungarian Social Democratic Party. Justus, a firm believer in internationalism, worked to strengthen ties with other eastern European countries and with Socialists in France and Italy, and in the first issue of *Szocializmus* he heralded the success of Great Britain's Labour Party. Despite Justus's efforts to promote ties with the Labour Party, however, Hungarian Socialists severed relations when the Labour Party continued to oppose international cooperation. Note. E. L. Keyser

1724. Kadarkay, Arpad A. HUNGARY: AN EXPERIMENT IN COMMUNISM. *Western Pol. Q. 1973 26(2): 280-301.* Discusses the reform of Hungary's Communist Party and economy instituted by the regime of János Kádár following the national rebellion of 1956.

1725. Kallai, D. LENINSKIE PRINTSIPY INTERNATSIONALISMA V POLITIKE VENGERSKOI SOTSIALISTICHESKOI RABOCHEI PARTII [Leninist principles of internationalism in the policy of the Hungarian Socialist workers' party]. *Novaia i Noveishaia Istoriia [USSR] 1970 (2): 18-29.* Approximately 100,000 Hungarians participated in the 1917 Russian Revolution. The leaders of the Hungarian Internationalists returned home to organize the Hungarian Communist Party and under their guidance Hungary became the first country in Europe where socialist revolution triumphed after 1917. Soviet Hungary gave military help to the revolutionaries of Slovakia and the underground National Front Party, which aided the struggle against fascism during World War II, and became legal when the Soviet Red Army freed Hungary. By 1948 socialist Leninism had triumphed, and Hungary joined the USSR on the path to communism. The counterrevolution of 1956 showed the strength of the Communist Party and the force of Leninist internationalism. Note. L. Smith

1726. Katona, István. A KONSZOLIDÁCIÓ ÉS A MEGÚJULÁS FŐ VONÁSAI [The major features of consolidation and renewal]. *Társadalmi Szemle [Hungary] 1981 36(11): 3-16.* The four main causes of the counterrevolution of 1956 were: dogmatism and sectarianism, revisionism and opportunism, activities of the enemy within, and the open interference of international reactionaries. At times, the governing power is forced to resort to violent means to maintain order; this is what happened in the struggle for consolidation. This was not an act of revenge. The new Hungarian Socialist Workers' Party has been relying on the working class, but has also strengthened its alliance with the peasantry and regulated its connections with the intellectuals. Emphasis has been placed on the recognition of realities and on the setting of realistic goals.
R. Hetzron

1727. Kelen, Jolán. HIROSSIK JÁNOS A MAGYAR MUNKÁSMOZGALOMBAN [János Hirossik and the Hungarian labor movement]. *Párttörténeti Közlemények [Hungary] 1975 21(4): 104-122.* János Hirossik was born in Budapest in 1887. His father was in the transport business but sent his son to trade school. At an early age Hirossik became a construction worker and a social democratic activist. He wrote for and edited several socialist trade papers. By 1910 he became one of the leaders of the Left Opposition within the Social Democratic Party. During the war he served on the front. Following his discharge Hirossik continued his activities in the union movement. He participated in the founding of the Hungarian Communist Party. In 1919 he served the Soviet Republic as government commissioner in northern Hungary. In emigration Hirossik opposed Bela Kun. In the mid-1920's with Rakosi he led the underground movement in Hungary. During the early 1930's he worked in Berlin for the Soviet government. 19 notes.
P. I. Hidas

1728. Kende, János. SZAKASITS ÁRPÁD [Árpád Szakasits]. *Társadalmi Szemle [Hungary] 1982 37(12): 71-80.* Active in leftist politics and as editor of the newspaper *Nepszava* [The People's Voice], Arpad Szakasits (1888-1965) received several jail sentences between 1920 and 1923. After his final release he joined the Social Democratic Party. In 1938 he became executive secretary. As leader of his party, he was elected president of Hungary in 1948. Two years later he was jailed on the basis of false accusations and spent six more years in prison. During this time his wife died and his family was persecuted. After he regained his freedom he spent the remaining 10 years of his life in the service of his party. T. Kuner

1729. Knausz, Imre. ORSZÁGOS TANÁCSKOZÁS AZ MSZMP MŰVELŐDÉSPOLITIKAI IRÁNYELVEI MEGJELENÉSÉNEK 25. ÉVFORDULÓJA ALKALMÁBÓL [A national conference on the occasion of the 26th anniversary of the publication of the cultural policy guidelines of the Hungarian Socialist Workers' Party]. *Párttörténeti Közlemények [Hungary] 1984 30(2): 188-197.* An account of a conference held in Budapest, 15-16 December 1983, which analyzed developments in the cultural life of Hungary in the 25 years since the publication of the cultural policy guidelines of the Hungarian Socialist Workers' Party. Provides a summary of lectures delivered at the conference. I. Karacs

1730. Komlos, John. A CONVERSATION WITH A COMMUNIST ECONOMIC REFORMER: JOHN KOMLOS INTERVIEWS REZSŐ NYERS. *Hungarian Studies Rev. [Canada] 1982 9(2): 39-44.* Rezső Nyers, former secretary of the Central Committee of the Hungarian Socialist Workers Party, discusses the 1968 reforms of the Hungarian system which he helped to initiate. These reforms were intended to liberalize the society and eventually lead to socialist democracy but, although a measure of success was achieved, some reforms were dropped for practical and political reasons. D. Powell

1731. Komócsin, Zoltán. HAZÁNK FELSZABADULÁSÁNAK NEGYEDSZÁZÁDOS ÉVFORDULÓJA A LENINI CENTENÁRIUM ÉVÉBEN [The 25th anniversary of the liberation of our country in the Lenin centenary year]. *Társadalmi Szemle [Hungary] 1970 25(4): 3-15.* Remarks on the coincidence of the Lenin's centenary and the 25th anniversary of Hungarian liberation. A. Mina

1732. Köpeczi, Béla. MŰVELŐDÉSPOLITIKAI ALAPELVEINK DOKUMENTUMA, TÖRTÉNELMI KÖRÜLMÉNYEK ÉS TANULSÁGOK [A document of our principles of cultural policy: historical circumstances and lessons]. *Társadalmi Szemle [Hungary] 1982 37(4): 53-60.* The cultural policy of the Hungarian Socialist Workers Party has been realistic, aiming at renewal. The dogmatism of the early 1950's, followed by the events of 1956, which revived old illusions, could be efficiently done away with beginning with August 1958. Cooperation and discussion play a central role. Emphasis has been laid on examining the public consciousness of workers and peasants, on the independence and responsibility of creative workshops, on decentralization, and on a wider interpretation of progress. R. Hetzron

1733. Kořálko, Květa. LASZLO RAJK A JEHO PROCES [Laszlo Rajk and his trial]. *Slovanský Přehled [Czechoslovakia] 1969 55(5): 403-408.* Laszlo Rajk was one of the prominent members of the Hungarian Communist Party early in the 1930's and became minister of the interior after World War II. As minister of foreign affairs in May 1949, Rajk and his wife were surprised by their arrests on charges of treason. Falsely accused of treason, rightist leanings, and Trotskyite sympathies, the trial of Rajk and seven other Communist leaders became a model for other trials of the Stalinist period. In September, the brainwashed Rajk admitted to his crimes and the "judgment of the people." Not until October 1956 was he officially rehabilitated. 13 notes. B. Kimmel

1734. Korbuly, Dezsö. DER UNTERGANG DER UNGARISCHEN KLEINLANDWIRTEPARTEI NACH DEM ZWEITEN WELTKRIEG [The decline of Hungary's Smallholders' Party after World War II]. *Österreichische Osthefte [Austria] 1976 18(1): 44-54.* The Hungarian Communists who returned to Hungary from exile in Moscow in 1945 openly pronounced their aim of establishing a political system which would transcend bourgeois democracy. While Communists, Social Democrats and the National Peasant Party cooperated, the Smallholders' Party, which had won an absolute majority in the elections of 1945, created an atmosphere of conflict within the government of the people's front. After uncovering an alleged plot by a group of sympathizers of the Smallholders' Party, the Hungarian Communists took the initiative and overthrew the government. Based on published documents, secondary literature, and newspapers; 43 notes. R. Wagnleitner

1735. Korbuly, Dezsö. DIE UNGARISCHE SOZIALDEMOKRATISCHE PARTEI NACH DEM ZWEITEN WELTKRIEG (1945-1948) [The Hungarian Social Democratic Party after World War II, 1945-48]. *Donauraum [Austria] 1978 23(1): 5-25.* Describes the development of the Hungarian Social Democratic party from its reestablishment in the winter of 1944 to the so-called fusion with the Hungarian Communists in the spring of 1948. Explains the successful application by the Communists of the "salami"-method, which permitted the development of the Social Democratic-Communist unity party (Hungarian Workers' Party), despite opposition from within the party. Secondary sources; 121 notes. A. A. Strnad

1736. Kővágó, László. A NEMZETISÉGI KÉRDÉS MAGYARORSZÁGON [The question of national minorities in Hungary]. *Társadalmi Szemle [Hungary] 1982 37(5): 84-93.* The 1944 program of the Hungarian Communist Party declared all nationalities to be equal. The cult of personality distorted the program of 1948-49. It was thought that the minority question would be solved by itself. Since 1958, the government has regularly devoted its attention to this problem. The modified constitution of 1972 and the program of the 9th Congress of the Hungarian Socialist Workers' Party declared again the equal rights of all minorities. Schools, clubs, theatrical groups and radio broadcasts in minority languages have been established. R. Hetzron

1737. Kovrig, Bennett. *Communism in Hungary: From Kun to Kádár.* Stanford: Hoover Inst. Pr., 1979. 525 pp.

1738. Lackó, Miklós. RÉVAI-PROBLÉMÁK [Problems connected with the writings of Révai]. *Történelmi Szemle [Hungary] 1972 15(3-4): 454-470.* József Révai's writings in prison have often been incorrectly described as demagogical distortions of Communist ideology laid down in Moscow by Béla Kun. Nonetheless Révai's writings on Ervin Szabó do reveal traces of reformist, even bourgeois-radical ideas. Based on Révai's manuscripts and on secondary sources; 32 notes. H. Szamuely/S

1739. Lakos, Sándor. TÁRSADALMI, GAZDASÁGI VÁLTOZÁSOK AZ ELMÚLT 15 ÉVBEN MAGYARORSZÁGON [Social and economic changes in the last 15 years in Hungary]. *Magyar Tudomány [Hungary] 1975 20(10): 581-593.* The basis of the Hungarian socialist state was laid, 1960-61, with the socialist transformation of agriculture. The author illustrates economic growth, 1960-75, and suggests that this has been an outstanding period in the history of the Communist Party. 19 notes. R. Hetzron

1740. Lavergne, Bernard. LES TENDANCES DEMOCRATIQUES DU PARTI COMMUNISTE HONGROIS [Democratic tendencies in the Hungarian Communist Party]. *Année Pol. et Écon. [France] 1970 43(218): 416-420.* Discusses the July theses, which appeared in the Hungarian press and were subsequently approved in the form of a manifesto by the Hungarian Communist Party. While expressing many of the commonplaces of Communist doctrine, the document indicates that the Party is becoming truly democratized, at the same time steering a middle course between the temptations of left-wing and right-wing deviations. G. E. Orchard

1741. Lehav, Yehuda. HA'KOMUNISTIM HA'YEHUDIM, V'HA'MISHTARA B'HUNGARIA SHEL'AHAR HA'MILHAMA [The Jewish Communists and the police in Hungary after the war]. *Shvut [Israel] 1980 7: 83-90.* The four major Communist leaders in

Hungary just after World War II were Jews. Further, the chief of the political police was Jewish. Other Jews held high roles in the Hungarian Communist party, far beyond the proportion of their numbers in the population. This situation, together with substantial anti-Communist sentiment, made many Hungarians equate communism with Jews and provoked further anti-Semitism. Based on Hungarian newspapers and periodicals, and a few US and British government documents; 40 notes. T. Koppel

1742. Losonczi, Pal. ONWARD ALONG LENIN'S PATH. *World Marxist R. [Canada] 1975 18(4): 13-22.* Discusses developments in communism in Hungary, 1945-75.

1743. Makkai, László. THE DEVELOPMENT OF HUMAN RIGHTS IN HUNGARY FROM THE REFORMATION TO THE PRESENT. *Soundings (Nashville, TN) 1984 67(2): 154-164.* Hungarian conceptions of human rights developed from late medieval ideas of natural rights as modified during the Reformation, Enlightenment, and modern periods.

1744. Maróti, Lajos. THE BUILDING OF SOCIALISM ON A HIGHER LEVEL. *New Hungarian Q. [Hungary] 1971 12(44): 3-25.* The works of Marx, Engels, and Lenin laid the basis for socialism, but failed to provide for its future development. Each nation must proceed at its own pace and in its own manner. Hungary cannot hope to become a major industrial power, yet it must set priorities while establishing a viable framework for future development in low-priority areas. The human factor must not be forgotten in the chaotic welter of technological change. Socialism is established; its development must be planned now. 4 notes. V. L. Human

1745. Matveev, R. F. and Bedov, A. V. 60-LETIE BRATSKIKH PARTII [The sixtieth anniversary of fraternal parties]. *Voprosy Istorii KPSS [USSR] 1979 (1): 143-147.* A summary of papers presented at the Institute of Marxism-Leninism (Moscow) in November 1978 commemorating the sixtieth anniversary of the founding of the Communist Party of Austria and also of Hungary. Based on papers delivered at two sessions; 5 notes. L. E. Holmes

1746. Molnar, István. AZ IFJUMUNKÁS-MOZGALOM A KIALAKULÓ MUNKÁSHATALOMÉRT 1948 ELSŐ HÓNAPJAIBAN [The Labor Youth Movement for the growth of workers' power during the first months of 1948]. *Párttörténeti Közlemények [Hungary] 1979 25(4): 62-90.* The Labor Youth and Apprentice Movement existed between 1945 and 1950. Its leadership was always under Communist influence. The youth movement aided the Hungarian Communist Party in obtaining and consolidating power in Hungary. Based on Communist Party archives and secondary sources; 71 notes. P. I. Hidas

1747. Molnár, János. DOKUMENTUMOK A SZOCIÁLDEMOKRATA PÁRT ÉRTELMISÉGI ÉS OKTATÁSPOLITIKÁJÁRÓL (1945-1947) [Documents on the policy of the Social Democratic Party toward education and the intellectuals]. *Párttörténeti Közlemények [Hungary] 1984 30(3): 216-236.* Introduces and edits 12 documents (circulars, memoranda, speeches, reports, proposals, etc.) drawn up within the Hungarian Social Democratic Party, showing its efforts to formulate a determined and distinct approach to cultural and intellectual life. Documents held by the Archive of Party History; 12 notes. G. Jeszenszky

1748. Molnár, János. IRÁNYZATOK HARCA A SZOCIÁLDEMOKRATA PÁRTBAN 1946-1947-BEN [The struggle to determine policy in the Social Democratic Party, 1946-47]. *Párttörténeti Közlemények [Hungary] 1977 23(1): 3-68.* The Social Democratic Party of Hungary made important contributions to the victory of workers' in the struggle for power, yet it could not provide revolutionary leadership. Some rightist leaders, especially Károly Peyer, attempted to change its main orientation in 1947. This met with strong resistance and led to a union with the Communist Party. 191 notes. R. Hetzron

1749. Molnár, János. A SZOCIÁLDEMOKRATA PÁRT 1945 UTÁNI MŰVELŐDÉSPOLITIKÁJÁNAK NÉHÁNY VONÁSA [Characteristics of the Social Democratic Party's cultural policy after 1945]. *Párttörténeti Közlemények [Hungary] 1983 29(2): 50-90.* Afraid of ghettoization of Hungarian literature, where all Western accomplishments would be absent, the Social Democratic Party refused to enter into an agreement to follow cultural guidelines of the Communists, who believed that all artistic expressions should be politically oriented. The Social Democrats were also reluctant to offer entrance into the literary world to those who had made political mistakes before 1945 and had shown nationalistic and anti-Semitic tendencies. This attitude was in sharp contrast to the Communist Party's policy. 143 notes. T. Kuner

1750. Much, Sh. RUKOVODIASHCHAIA ROL' VENGERSKOI KOMMUNISTICHESKOI PARTII V ORGANIZATSII I STROITEL'STVE VENGERSKOI NARODNOI ARMII [Leading role of the Hungarian Communist Party in the organization and buildup of the Hungarian People's Army]. *Voenno-Istoricheskii Zhurnal [USSR] 1978 20(11): 74-79.* Describes the formation in spring 1945, of a true people's army through efforts of the Communist Party in Hungary, supported by the Soviet Union, its postwar consolidation, and the paralyzing blow inflicted by the counterrevolutionary coup of October 1956. Internal reorganization carried out by the Communist Party during 1960-75 has led to the political and military rehabilitation of the Hungarian People's Army. 10 notes. N. Frenkley

1751. Mucs, Sándor. A NEMZETI PARASZTPÁRT KATONAPOLITIKÁJÁRÓL 1944-1948 [On the military policy of the National Peasant Party, 1944-48]. *Hadtörténelmi Közlemények [Hungary] 1983 30(4): 637-650.* The radical Hungarian National Peasant Party was determined that the newly established army should be instrumental in advancing democratic education, and should be directed by officers coming from and representing the people, first of all the peasants, in contrast to the elitist and right-wing pre-1945 army. Despite its strong interest in the character of the army, the Peasant Party was most reluctant to accept the portfolio of defense in 1947, at first for fear of the strong Communist hold over the armed forces, then because the post was not prestigious enough. Finally it acquiesced; the noted populist writer Péter Veress, the president of the party, became minister of defense in the hope that Communist control of the army would ensure the desired democratic spirit to permeate the troops. Based on the Hungarian Military Archives, the Archive of Party History, and the press; 42 notes. G. Jeszenszky

1752. Mucs, Sándor. A SZOCIÁLDEMOKRATA PÁRT KATONAPOLITIKÁJA 1945-1947. [Military policy of the Social Democratic Party, 1945-47]. *Párttörténeti Közlemények [Hungary] 1982 28(3): 112-132.* Great efforts were made by the Social Democratic Party after the war to recruit members of the newly established armed forces to the Party. Their efforts were diminished by the dismal results of the 1947 election, in which they suffered considerable losses against the Communist candidates. By early 1948 the party gave up the attempt to organize the army and most soldiers joined the Communist Party. 26 notes. T. Kuner

1753. Nagy, Eta. BAJÁKI FERENC (1883-1946) [Ferenc Bajáki, 1883-1946]. *Párttörténeti Közlemények [Hungary] 1973 19(3): 162-172.* A biographical sketch of a lesser-known commissar of the 1919 Hungarian Soviet Republic. Bajáki, an industrial worker, became a union activist in 1911. He was soon the chief organizer at the giant Weisz Manfred Works. He joined the Social Democrats and in 1918 was elected to the Budapest Labor Council. For his part in the Soviet Republic, Bajaki was sentenced to life imprisonment in 1920. He was freed the following year under a prisoner exchange agreement, and retired in 1935. Three years later this veteran communist was arrested and sent to a labor camp, where he died in 1946. 36 notes. P. I. Hidas

1754. Nemes, D. LENIN IST MIT UNS [Lenin is with us]. *Études Hist. [Hungary] 1970 (1): 11-85.* Discusses the creation of the Hungarian Workers' Party by the fusion of the Communist Party and the Social Democrats, and vindicates Leninism as opposed to the revisionism which, it is alleged, led up to the revolution of 1956. Events subsequent to 1956 are seen as vindicating the Marxist-Leninist line. L. G. G. Twyman

1755. Nemes, Dezső. AZ OKTÓBERI FORRADALOM ÉS MAGYARORSZÁG ÚTJA A SZOCIALIZMUSHOZ [The October Revolution and Hungary's road to socialism]. *Századok [Hungary] 1967 101(5): 827-850.*

1756. Nemes, János. RÁKOSI MÁTYÁS [Mátyás Rákosi]. *Társadalmi Szemle [Hungary] 1983 38(1): 73-85.* Rákosi, founding member of the Hungarian Communist Party and absolute ruler of the country until 1956, was rejected and discharged by the Party shortly after Stalin's death. He was responsible for the gradual distortion of socialist progress and the initiation of a dogmatic sectarian despotic rule where lawlessness was accepted, together with an overwhelmingly distasteful personality cult. He left Hungary in 1956 and died in the USSR 15 years later. 23 notes. T. Kuner

1757. Nemet, K. DEIATEL'NOST' VSRP PO UKREPLENIIU IDEINO-POLITICHESKOGO EDINSTVA VENGERSKOGO OBSHCHESTVA [The activity of the Hungarian Socialist Workers' Party in strengthening the ideological-political unity of Hungarian society]. *Voprosy Istorii KPSS [USSR] 1981 (11): 58-68.* Describes the beginnings of socialism in Hungary and the vital role of the Hungarian Socialist Workers' Party in the creation, strengthening, and defense of socialist political unity in the Hungarian nation. Considers the postwar development of the party, its links with the CPSU, dedication to the cause of socialist construction, and achievements. Based on material from the 12th HSWP congress; 6 notes. L. Smith

1758. Nezhinski, L. N. SOZDANIE EDINOI PARTII RABOCHEGO KLASSA V VENGRII (1944-1948) [The creation of a single working-class party in Hungary, 1944-48]. *Voprosy Istorii KPSS [USSR] 1960 (4): 95-112.* Analyzes the course of the struggle for workers' unity with reference to the communist and social democrat organs Szabad Nep and Nepszava and Hungarian Social Democratic Party archives.

1759. Nezhinsky, L. N. TRI DESIATILETIIA, RAVNYE EPOKHE [The three decades encompassing a whole epoch]. *Voprosy Istorii [USSR] 1975 (4): 58-73.* Traces the historic path traversed by the Hungarian People's Republic during the postwar decades. Analyzes the significance of the country's liberation from fascism for the future of the Hungarian people and the results achieved by the working people of Hungary in the building of socialism under the leadership of the Hungarian Socialist Workers' Party. Sums up the results of the eleventh congress of the Hungarian Communists recently held in Budapest. J

1760. Novák, Zoltán. BEITRÄGE ZUM VERHÄLTNIS VON LUKÁCS UND KASSÁK [Contributions on the relationship of Lukács and Kassák]. *Annales Universitatis Scientiarum Budapestinensis de Rolando Eötvös Nominatae: Sectio Philosophica et Sociologica [Hungary] 1982 16: 111-128.* Studies the relationship in politics, political theory, aesthetics, and personal life of two leaders of the Communist Party of Hungary, Georg Lukács and Lajos Kassák. Traces their revolutionary movement through various political changes. Based on a presentation, "Georg Lukács und die Ungarische Kultur" [Georg Lukács and Hungarian culture], Institute for Literary Studies, Hungarian Academy of Sciences, 15 October 1980. R. Grove

1761. Ólmosi, Zoltán. TUDOMÁNYOS ÜLÉSSZAK A MAGYAR SZOCIALISTA MUNKÁSPÁRT 1957. JÚNIUSI ÉRTEKEZLETÉNEK 25. ÉVFORDULÓJÁRA [Scientific session on the 25th anniversary of the Hungarian Socialist Workers' Party meeting of June 1957]. *Párttörténeti Közlemények [Hungary] 1982 28(3): 186-200.* Report of a session at the Political Academy in 1982. Twelve speakers discussed economic, international, and internal aspects of the country. In closing it was established that the Party made great progress in offering guidance after the counterrevolution to a considerable number of disoriented individuals. T. Kuner

1762. Ölvedi, Ignác. EMLÉKEK ES ADALÉKOK NÉPHADSEREGÜNK SZÜLETÉSÉHÖZ [Memories and facts about the birth of our People's Army]. *Hadtörténelmi Közlemények [Hungary] 1980 27(3): 464-490.* A chronicle covering the period between 17 February 1945 and the end of 1948, interspersed with commentaries, sometimes argumentative, that contrast with the memoirs of Sándor Nógrádi and other military leaders of that ilk. Having joined the new army, the author became a training officer in 1945. He accompanied his unit to the Western front, where their involvement was preempted by the armistice in May 1945. The author analyzes the causes of the delay and the subsequent politicization of the army, which, by 1948, was in the hands of Communist generals and officers, 80% of whom were members of the Communist Party. Exponents of the personality cult period characterize this part of the Army's history differently. T. Kabdebo

1763. Orbán, Sándor. ADALÉKOK A FÖLDEREFORM UTÁNI FALUSI VISZONYOK TANULMÁNYOZÁSÁHOZ [Contributions to the study of rural conditions after the agricultural reforms]. *Történelmi Szemle [Hungary] 1966 9(1): 85-97.* Considers the results of a 1946 Hungarian census designed to examine rural conditions. Devastation caused by World War II slowed agricultural reform. Social problems included overpopulation, unemployment, and a lack of basic resources. The majority of those who had been in favor of agricultural reform belonged to left-wing parties, particularly the Communist Party. The conditions in villages were therefore auspicious for a left-wing takeover in the 1946 parliamentary elections. 25 notes. G. L. Neville

1764. Pataki, István. SZARVASI KOMMUNISTÁK KÜZDELME 1956-57-BEN [The struggle of the Communists of Szarvas in 1956-57]. *Társadalmi Szemle [Hungary] 1981 36(10): 69-71.* In late October, a truckful of armed men came from Békéscsaba and disarmed the local forces of order. But the local Communists applied good defensive strategy, and, allying themselves with non-party members, they restored order. Based on personal reminiscences, part of a series in the same issue. R. Hetzron

1765. Pécsi, Kálmán. A KELET-NYUGATI EGYÜTTMŰKÖDÉSRŐL AZ MSZMP KB 1977. OKTÓBER 20-I HATÁROZATÁNAK TÜKRÉBEN [On East-West cooperation in the light of the resolution of the Central Committee of the Hungarian Socialist Workers' Party of October 1977]. *Közgazdasági Szemle [Hungary] 1978 25(7-8): 781-795.* The resolution by the Central Committee on long-term foreign economic policy is an organic continuation of the strategic conception worked out in the late 1960's. It closely fits the process whereby the new foreign economic policies of the CMEA countries, first of all of the Soviet Union, are formulated. The author discusses the development of East-West relations in the light of the new foreign economic strategy. J

1766. Piazza, Hans. REVOLUTIONÄR, WISSENSCHAFTLER, INTERNATIONALIST: EUGEN VARGA [Revolutionary, scholar, internationalist: Eugen Varga]. *Beiträge zur Gesch. der Arbeiterbewegung [East Germany] 1983 25(6): 866-874.* Traces the life, academic career, and political activities of the Hungarian scholar and Communist Eugen Varga (1879-1964), and pays particular attention to his writings on political economy and his position as one of the leading early economic theoreticians of the world Communist movement. He joined the Hungarian Social Democratic Party in 1906 and between 1909 and 1916 wrote many articles on economics as well as examining the nationality question in Hungary. In 1918 he took an active part in the Hungarian revolution and in that same year became professor of economics at Budapest University. In 1920 he went to the USSR and in 1927 he became the director of the Institute for International Economics and Politics, a post that he

held until 1947. The author also pays tribute to Varga's extremely rich academic legacy, extracts of which were published in *Selected Writings, 1918-1964* (1982). Secondary sources; 26 notes.
G. L. Neville

1767. Racz, Barnabas A. THE CHANGING ROLE OF THE COMMUNIST PARTY IN HUNGARY. *Int. Rev. of Hist. and Pol. Sci. [India] 1975 12(1): 49-98.* Since the mid-1960's, and especially since the introduction in 1968 of the decentralizing New Economic Mechanism, the Hungarian political atmosphere has been liberalized. The Communist Party has permitted an ideological relaxation formally described as the "three plus one" formula. This means that the three dominant party groups, elitists, favored workers and peasant cadres, and conformist professionals and experts, will deemphasize the class struggle and cooperate with everyone else (the "plus one") not openly hostile to the regime. Outsiders rejecting this formula are treated with suspicion but not terrorized. There has emerged a rudimentary pluralism characterized by more humane administration and diminishing intellectual restraints, but at the same time political apathy, especially among the young, and increasingly bourgeois attitudes. The Hungarian Communist Party is characterized as the most liberal in the Soviet bloc. Based principally on personal observations and interviews in Hungary and Hungarian Communist publications; 4 tables, 189 notes.
D. M. Cregier

1768. Racz, Barnabas A. THE TWELFTH COMMUNIST PARTY CONGRESS AND THE POLITICS OF NEO-CONSERVATISM IN HUNGARY. *East European Q. 1981 15(4): 511-537.* The New Economic Mechanism established in 1968 was intended to strengthen the economy through decentralization. Beginning in 1974, the reform was modified, and since then the Hungarian Socialist Workers' Party has been moving toward recentralization. This trend continued at the 12th Party Congress in 1980. The main theme of 1980 was a call to hold on to past achievements and to try nothing new. The working out of this policy in all aspects of Hungarian life is discussed. Based on government documents, secondary works, and personal interviews; 114 notes.
C. R. Lovin

1769. Rácz, Béla. A BELÜGYMINISZTÉRIUM UJJÁSZERVEZÉSE [The reorganization of the Ministry of the Interior]. *Levéltári Közlemények [Hungary] 1970 41(1): 89-131.* During the Horthy era the gendarmerie, the police, and the organs of county and city administration all were under the control and supervision of the Ministry of Internal Affairs. The Provisional National Government initiated the first reorganization of the state and municipal administration in 1945, but made no basic structural changes. The parties of coalition government all realized the importance of the Ministry of the Interior; soon Ferenc Erdei, the first minister of the Peasant Party, was replaced by Communist László Rajk, in spite of the demands of the Smallholders Party, which was soon to receive 57% of the votes in general elections. Rajk took over the administration of the Ministry in March 1945. He successfully cleaned the organization of reactionary elements and increased the influence and proportion of Communist Party officials within the ministry. Centralization and the elimination of bureaucratic methods were some of his major goals. Rajk lived and worked as a real Communist; initiative, sensitivity to other people's reactions, and faith in Marxism-Leninism characterized his two years in the ministry. Detailed organizational descriptions supplement the article.
S. Szilassy

1770. Rákosi, Sándor. A MAGYAR DOLGOZÓK PÁRTJA II. KONGRESSZUSA A TÁRSADALMI-GAZDASÁGI FEJLŐDÉSRŐL [The 2d Congress of the Hungarian Workers' Party on socioeconomic development]. *Párttörténeti Közlemények [Hungary] 1984 30(2): 39-71.* Reviews the process by which socioeconomic policy and a stance on major international issues was formulated during the 2d Congress of the Hungarian Workers' Party (MDP) and establishes that the party leadership was aware of the main sources of tension but nevertheless developed a policy that further intensified these tensions. The congress thus became another step toward the distorted party policy personified by Mátyás Rákosi. Based on archives of the Hungarian Institute of Party History and secondary sources; 102 notes.
I. Karacs

1771. Reuland, James M. GATT AND STATE-TRADING COUNTRIES. *J. of World Trade Law [Switzerland] 1975 9(3): 318-340.* Hungary became the first East European country to negotiate its terms of accession to GATT primarily on the basis of most-favored nation tariff reciprocity rather than negotiated trade flows, the case for the other five socialist states already GATT members. This break from precedent was due primarily to Hungary's domestic economic reforms (New Economic Mechanism) of 1968. The author questions the extent to which the Hungarian protocol is viable, examining it in light of past history of accommodation of the most-favored nation clause to state-trading countries.
J

1772. Sabo, Balint. TRIDTSAT' LET BOR'BY I POBED NARODNOI VENGRII [Thirty years of struggle and victories for people's Hungary]. *Voprosy Istorii KPSS [USSR] 1975 (4): 46-56.* Traces the development of Hungary's socialist revolution, including the nationalization of industry, collectivization of agriculture, expansion of social services, and higher wages, all achieved with the assistance of the Soviet Union, 1945-75. In 1956, the Communist Party successfully defeated a counterrevolution waged by right revisionist and reactionary forces. Based on periodical literature; 6 notes.
L. E. Holmes

1773. Ságvári, Ágnes. NÉPFRONT ÉS PROLETÁRDIKTATÚRA [The National Front and the dictatorship of the proletariat]. *Történelmi Szemle [Hungary] 1966 9(2): 204-226.* The Truman Doctrine and the Marshall Plan provoked the setting up of the Information Bureau of the Communist and Socialist parties against the disruptive US plots in Eastern Europe. In the 1947 Hungarian election, the National Independence Front (NIF) had a 61.5% majority (including the Communist Party's 21.7%) against 39% cast for the opposition supporting the US doctrines. The NIF coalition expected to command sufficient mass support to put through its three-year program. The opposition attempted to split the NIF and form blocks against the Communist Party, particularly with the aid of the Independent Smallholders' Party. While unsuccessful in this respect, it received unexpected backing from the Social Democratic Party (SPD). Eventually the leftist elements prevailed in the internal debates of the SDP. The survival of the coalition and the Information Bureau's advice were the first steps toward the dictatorship of the Hungarian proletariat. Primary and secondary sources; 55 notes.
E. E. Soos

1774. Ságvári, Ágnes. ÜNNEPI ÜLÉSSZAK A KOMMUNISTA MOZGALOM MEGALAKULÁSÁNAK 50. ÉVFORDULÓJÁRA [Jubilee session celebrating the 50th anniversary of the foundation of the Communist movement]. *Történelmi Szemle [Hungary] 1968 11(4): 428-441.* Summarizes and discusses the three lectures and 18 discussion papers given at this conference organized by the Institute of Party History, attached to the Hungarian Socialist Workers' Party.
I. Hont

1775. Sagvari, Agnes. VORAUSSETZUNGEN UND BESONDERHEITEN DER REVOLTIONÄREN UMWALZUNG IN UNGARN 1945-1949 [The preconditions and peculiarities of the revolutionary transition in Hungary, 1945-49]. *Jahrbuch für Geschichte der Sozialistischen Länder Europas [East Germany] 1977 21(1): 59-80.* Discusses the abandonment of the national councils in Hungary as administrative organs, and the resurrection of the original, reformed administrative mechanisms. The 1945 election saw the victory of the Smallholders' Party, but the 1947 election gave a majority to the progressive National Independence Front, a heterogeneous coalition eventually dominated by the Communists. The new government prepared the transition to the dictatorship of the proletariat, but serious mistakes made during the transition had a damaging effect on the Party. 32 notes.
L. H. Schmidt/S

1776. Sánta, Ilona, interviewer. INTERJÚK AZ ELLENFORRADALOMRÓL ÉS A KONSZOLIDÁCIÓRÓL [Interviews on the counterrevolution and the consolidation]. *Társadalmi Szemle [Hungary] 1981 36(11): 17-37, (12): 44-61.* Part

1. Three persons related their memories of the counterrevolution of 1956 in Hungary: Ágnes Bakó, vice-director of the Institute of the History of the Party (Central Committee, Hungarian Socialist Workers' Party), János Brutyó (president of the Central Supervising Committee of the Hungarian Socialist Workers' Party), and Gyula Kállai, a member of the Central Committee of the Party and president of the Patriotic Popular Front. Part 2. Personal reminiscences of the events of 1956-57 in Hungary by Mrs. Ferenc Cservenka (member of the Central Committee of the Hungarian Socialist Workers' Party and First Secretary of the Party Committee of the County of Pest), Jenő Szirmai (General Director of the National Savings Bank), and László Eperjesi (Hungarian diplomat in Berlin). R. Hetzron

1777. Seewann, Gerhard. GESCHICHTSWISSENSCHAFT UND POLITIK IN UNGARN 1950-1980 [Historiography and politics in Hungary, 1950-80]. *Südost-Forschungen [West Germany] 1982 41: 261-323.* In the period immediately after World War II and the seizure of political power by the Communist Party, historiography was consciously and systematically bent to the service of the Party and its Marxist ideology. This produced aberrations that the Party itself recognized after approximately 1953, but was unwilling to change until the revolution of 1956. That crisis forced the state leadership to reformulate the function of historiography and to allow historians a considerably widened field of inquiry and publication. From at least as early as 1960, historiography has been granted a conditional release from the restrictions formerly imposed upon it by ideology, as the Party has come to realize the close dependency between informed sociopolitical practice and the freedom of scientific inquiry. 245 notes. P. J. Adler

1778. Sipos, Peter. A MAGYAR NEPFRONT TÖRTÉNETE: DOKUMENTUMOK, 1935-1970 [The history of the Hungarian People's Front: documents, 1935-70]. *Társadalmi Szemle [Hungary] 1978 33(3): 102-104.* Reviews the *History of the Hungarian People's Front: Documents, 1935-1970* (1977), which surveys the development of the Hungarian Communist Party, and the activities of the Hungarian National Independence Front after 1945 and of the Patriotic People's Front after 1954.

1779. Sipos, Péter. RAJK LÁSZLÓ [Laszlo Rajk]. *Társadalmi Szemle [Hungary] 1983 38(5): 76-86.* Fighting in Spain, working for the Communist Party in Hungary, or jailed for his activities, Laszlo Rajk's main concern was always the well-being of the Party. After 1945 he was elected first as minister of the interior and later as foreign minister. The leader of the country, the Russian-educated Rákosi, felt that home-grown Party members could interfere with his personal progress. For this reason Rajk and several other Party members were falsely accused as traitors to the country's interest. They were all executed, making mockery of all basic tenets of justice and law. The question how Rajk was convinced to publicly accept the role of traitor cannot be answered. T. Kuner

1780. Standeisky, Éva. A MUNKÁSPÁRTOK ÉS MUNKÁS KULTÚRSZÖVETSÉG 1945-1948 [The workers' parties and the Workers' Cultural Association, 1945-48]. *Párttörténeti Közlemények [Hungary] 1979 25(2): 32-71.* The Workers' Cultural Association (MKSZ, 1945-48) was jointly sponsored by the Communist and Social Democratic Parties. It was at first dominated by the latter, but the Communists recognized its potential in 1946. Its activities included theatrical performances, publications, exhibitions, radio programs and international relations. In 1947, the association had its financial problems solved, moved into a permanent quarters and elected a permanent board of directors. Its name was changed to Working People's Cultural Association (DKSZ). In 1948, new divisions were created. Soon it was dissolved. 75 notes. R. Hetzron

1781. Stolypine, Dimitri. LES GRANDS ENSEIGNEMENTS DE L'INSURRECTION HONGROISE [The great lessons of the Hungarian insurrection]. *Écrits de Paris [France] 1976 363: 5-10.* Commemorates the Hungarian rebellion of October-November 1956 on behalf of those who continue to suffer under the yoke of totalitarian communism throughout the world.

1782. Strassenreiter, Erzsébet. DIE VEREINIGUNGEN DER BEIDEN ARBEITERPARTEIEN IN UNGARN (JUNI 1948) [The union of the two workers' parties in Hungary, June 1948]. *Beiträge zur Geschichte der Arbeiterbewegung [East Germany] 1976 18(3): 418-430.* As early as October 1944, Hungarian Communists and left-wing Social Democrats began negotiations for a common platform. Although the right wing of the Social Democratic Party opposed the policy of a popular front, especially during preparations for the 1947 elections, a common party was created in June 1948. Based on documents in the archives of the Institute of Party History, Budapest, published documents, and secondary literature; 21 notes. R. Wagnleitner

1783. Strassenreiter, Erzsébet. A FORDULAT ÉVE ÉS A KÉT MUNKÁSPART EGYESÜLÉSE [The year of change and the union of the two labor parties]. *Párttörténeti Közlemények [Hungary] 1978 24(2): 3-40.* In 1947 new parliamentary elections were held in Hungary. Four left-wing parties, Communist (MKP), Social Democratic (SDP), Smallholder (MKGP), and Peasant (MPP), captured nearly 61% of the vote. The MKP gained 22.2% of the ballots. After the election the MKGP and the SDP refused to cooperate with the Communists, thus precipitating a cabinet crisis. In response the MKP began to demand the union of the two labor parties and the expulsion of right-wing SDP members. This aim was realized in 1948 when a new party, the Hungarian Workers' Party (MDP), was formed from the reformed membership of the former MKP and SDP. 70 notes. P. I. Hidas

1784. Strassenreiter, Erzsébet. A POLGÁRI ELLENZÉK OLDALÁN: PEYER KÁROLY POLITIKAI PÁLYAFUTÁSA 1944 UTÁN [On the side of the bourgeois opposition: Károly Peyer's political career after 1944]. *Párttörténeti Közlemények [Hungary] 1983 29(4): 84-130.* Peyer, a socialist member of the parliament for 22 years, could not adjust to the new and different political situation after 1945. As one of the leaders of the Social Democratic Party, he spoke endlessly about his opposition to the people's democracy and the occupying Soviet Union. His proposal for the establishment of a bourgeois socialist country with Western values where capitalist private properties would be permitted caused embarrassment and distress to other members of his party. By 1947 he was rejected by all political organizations and left Hungary. He died in 1956 in New York of a heart attack. 152 notes. T. Kuner

1785. Szabó, Ágnes and Varga, Lajos. GARBAI SÁNDOR (1879-1947) [Sándor Garbai (1879-1947)]. *Párttörténeti Közlemények [Hungary] 1979 25(3): 174-219.* The biography of the president of the Hungarian Soviet Republic's Governing Council can now be outlined with the aid of Sándor Garbai's memoirs, correspondence, and other papers recently donated to the Institute of Party History by Béla Riesz of France. Garbai became active in the labor movement at the turn of the century. He worked for the construction workers' union and later for the Social Democratic Party. His position during the revolutions of 1918-19 was mainly ceremonial. Based on Communist Party archives; 218 notes. P. I. Hidas

1786. Szabó, Bálint. AZ MDP POLITIKÁJA 1954 MÁSODIK FELÉBEN ÉS AZ 1955. MÁRCIUSI FORDULAT [The policy of the Hungarian Workers' Party in the second half of 1954 and the change in March 1955]. *Párttörténeti Közlemények [Hungary] 1984 30(3): 37-90.* Continued from an earlier article. While Imre Nagy tried to implement his "New Course" announced in the previous June by increasing agricultural output and cutting back on heavy industry, right-wing views, questioning all the results achieved after 1948 and thus the very foundations of the socialist system, also cropped up. At the end of 1954, Matyasi Rakosi arrived back from the Soviet Union and soon had the Central Directorate of the Party condemn Nagy for the deviations, without admitting the responsibility of Rakosi and his group for the economic difficulties. This new turn was not justified by the international situation, neither was it inspired by the international Communist movement. The return to the pre-1953 methods increased the distrust of the population in the Party leadership, and pushed the country toward a political crisis. Based on the Archive of Party History; 89 notes. Russian, French and English summaries. G. Jeszenszky

1787. Szabó, Bálint. AZ ÚJ SZAKASZ POLITIKÁJÁNAK KEZDETEI AZ MDP KÖZPONTI VEZETŐSÉGÉNEK 1953. JÚNIUSI ÜLÉSÉTŐL AZ OKTÓBERI PLÉNUMIG [Political beginnings of the new period: from the June 1953 session of the central management to the plenary session in October]. *Párttörténeti Közlemények [Hungary] 1983 29(2): 91-139.* The Hungarian delegation, on its return from Moscow in 1953, publicly announced that errors committed by Party leaders must be corrected. Overdevelopment of heavy industry and agriculture, unsatisfactory production of consumer goods, and illegalities in the judiciary system were all to be rectified. Other errors were seen in the fact that the Hungarian Workers' Party had permitted itself to masquerade in the role of government, producing an unacceptable cult of personality instead of collective leadership. The magnitude of reform proved overwhelming for all participants, and it took considerable time before all problems were solved. 95 notes. T. Kuner

1788. Szabó, Bálint. GAZDASÁGI, POLITIKAI VÁLTOZÁSOK AZ 1953. JÚNIUSI FORDULAT UTÁN ÉS AZ MDP III. KONGRESSZUSA [Economic and political changes following the turnabout of June 1953 and the 3d Congress of the Hungarian Workers' Party]. *Párttörténeti Közlemények [Hungary] 1984 30(1): 52-98.* Continued from a previous article. Evaluates the changes introduced when Imre Nagy (1896-1958) took over the premiership from Matyas Rakosi (1892-1971), the foremost exponent of Stalinism. While noting significant improvements, the author criticizes both the rearguard actions of the Rakosi group and some of the ideas of Nagy. Uses archival sources from the Institute of Party History; 102 notes. Russian, French, and English summaries. G. Jeszenszky

1789. Szabó, Bálint. A MAGYAR SZOCIALISTA MUNKÁSPÁRT POLITIKÁJÁNAK ALAPVETÉSE 1956. NOVEMBER-1957. JÚNIUS [The establishment of the political principles of the Hungarian Socialist Workers Party, November 1956-June 1957]. *Párttörténeti Közlemények [Hungary] 1982 28(1): 3-58.* From the date of its founding on 6 November 1956, the Hungarian Socialist Workers' Party (MSzMP) waged an ideological struggle against both its left wing, the Rákosi-Gerő group and its right, the Nagy-Losonczy group. This middle-of-the-road policy meant a return to Marxism-Leninism. There were few debates in the party after December 1956 because the MSzMP concentrated its efforts on consolidating the state apparatus, "the oppressive feature of the dictatorship of the proletariat became foremost." The cultural and economic policies of the party also followed this principle. Based on party archives and secondary sources; 123 notes. P. I. Hidas

1790. Szabó, Éva. ADALÉKOK BÖHM VILMOS POLITIKAI ÉLETRAJZÁHOZ [Additional information on the political biography of Vilmos (William) Böhm (1880-1949)]. *Történelmi Szemle [Hungary] 1980 23(2): 227-240.* After the liberation of Hungary, having been absent for 27 years as a political emigrant, Böhm returned to help the cause of the Social Democratic Party. As ambassador to Sweden he traveled constantly between Stockholm and Budapest, participating in the political life of his party. As a firm believer in collaboration with the USSR in every respect, he was alienated by political changes in Hungary and eventually gave up his position as ambassador. 44 notes. T. Kuner

1791. Szakács, Kálmán. A KÖZÉPPARASZT-KÉRDÉS ÉS A DEFOSZ 1949-BEN [The middle peasant question and the DEFOSZ]. *Párt-Történeti Közlemények [Hungary] 1972 18(4): 82-109.* Once the Communist Party (MDP) acquired power in Hungary in 1948, all peasant associations were ordered to form a new united organization, the DEFOSZ. The Party wanted to use the DEFOSZ to gain the support of the middle peasantry. The author discusses how the Communists eliminated the influence of other political parties and also alienated the peasants through mismanagement of the DEFOSZ. By 1950, the DEFOSZ was an instrument of local government officials rather than an organization for the protection of peasant interests. 59 notes. P. I. Hidas

1792. Tökés, Rudolf L. POLYCENTRISM: CENTRAL EUROPEAN AND HUNGARIAN ORIGINS. *Studies in Comparative Communism 1973 6(4): 414-428.* The treatment of opposition groups within the Communist parties has often reflected the culture and history of the nation. The Communist Party of Hungary, illegal 1919-45, was split between an Orthodox Muscovite group and a more pragmatic group led by Eugene Landler. Other factions developed in the late 1920's favoring either a leftist approach or a popular front strategy. Imre Nagy apparently was led by his own experiences in the 1920's to question the unrealistic dictates of Marxism. In power, 1955-56, Nagy defended his New Course as a Hungarian version of the New Economic Policy. His national communism was a non-Soviet solution to the transition to socialism. 22 notes. D. Balmuth

1793. Tomioka, Jiro. HANGARI HOKI TO IGIRISU KYOSANTO [The Hungarian uprising and the Communist Party of Great Britain]. *Shirin [Japan] 1977 60(4): 453-485.* The 20th Congress of the Communist Party of the USSR and the Hungarian uprising of 1956 were the most important events in the history of the international Communist movement. The author analyzes the impact of these two events on the Communist Party of Great Britain, especially on Communist intellectuals such as Christopher Hill. The Communist intellectuals criticized the leadership of the CPGB, which supported Soviet intervention in Hungary. The inflexibility of the leadership invited the British Party's greatest crisis, causing a 20% loss of membership. Based on the party's *Daily Worker,* the *Reasoner,* published by these intellectuals, and other newspapers and periodicals; 105 notes. Y. Aoki

1794. Turko, N. G. STROITEL'STVO RAZVITOGO SOTSIALIZMA V VENGERSKOI NARODNOI RESPUBLIKE [The building of developed socialism in Hungary]. *Novaia i Noveishaia Istoriia [USSR] 1985 (1): 41-54.* Describes the policy pursued by the Hungarian Socialist Workers' Party in the country's socioeconomic development and notes its efforts to extend socialist democracy. Also analyzes economic statistics and the main directions of Hungarian foreign policy. J

1795. Urbán, Károly. AZ 1953-AS FORDULAT ÉS A MAGYAR ÉRTELMISÉG [The turnabout of 1953 and the Hungarian intelligentsia]. *Párttörténeti Közlemények [Hungary] 1981 27(4): 30-83.* In Hungary a political turnabout followed the death of Stalin and the Berlin riots. The Communist Party and the new government headed by Imre Nagy changed their attitude toward the old intelligentsia. Attempts were made to involve the intellectuals in the management of the country, improve their living standard, and create an atmosphere for creative work. Based on the Party history archives, the Révai papers, and secondary sources; 121 notes. Russian and French summaries. P. I. Hidas

1796. Urbán, Károly. RÉVAI JÓZSEF (1898-1959) [József Révai (1898-1959)]. *Párttörténeti Közlemények [Hungary] 1978 24(3): 162-222.* A biography of the Marxist-Leninist theoretician József Révai. He joined the progressive students' association Galilei Circle in 1917, and was one of the founders of the Communist Party of Hungary. He was also an active journalist. In 1919 he emigrated to Vienna and participated in illegal Communist activities. After 1928 he was involved in fighting, and was arrested in 1930. He was in prison, 1931-34 and spent the period 1939-44 in the USSR where he accepted Mátyás Rákosi's leadership. After 1945, he became one of the most important leaders and the chief ideologist of the Communist Party, despite his occasionally controversial activities. Throughout his career he was involved in journalism and literary criticism. His weak heart caused his premature death in 1959. 97 notes. R. Hetzron

1797. Váli, Ferenc A. TWENTY YEARS AFTER: KÁDÁR AND HIS RULE ASSESSED, 1956-1976. *Can.-Am. Rev. of Hungarian Studies [Canada] 1976 3(2): 155-167.* An assessment of János Kádár's rule from 1956 to 1976. Allegedly, Kádár at first tried to reestablish order and Communist Party authority through persuasion, by attempting to rejuvenate the Party and purify socialism. By November 1957, Kádár resorted to repression of intellectuals and forced collectivization. Special courts levied onerous sentences. Relaxation followed four years later, heralding a peaceful coexistence between the regime and "the silent majority." This was Khrushchev's famous "goulash communism." The New Economic Mechanism of January 1968 placed the Hungarian economy on a solid and rational footing and decentralized decisionmaking. Most Hungarians today tolerate Kádár, although they resent Hungary's lack of national independence. 16 notes. T. Spira

1798. Varga, Sándor. A MAGYAR KÖNYVKIADÁS ÉS KÖNYVKERESKEDELEM A FORDULAT ÉVÉBEN [Hungarian book publishing and bookselling in 1948]. *Magyar Könyvszemle [Hungary] 1978 94(3-4): 291-302.* The large Hungarian publishing houses were nationalized on 25 March 1948. Under the auspices of the Hungarian Workers' Party, a National Book Bureau was created. New foundations were then laid for Hungarian publication policy, and new publishing houses were established. The lowering of prices was a major issue. Primary sources; 17 notes. R. Hetzron

1799. Vass, Henrik. JAK POWSTAWAŁ ZARYS HISTORII PARTII NA WĘGRZECH (Z DOŚWIADCZEŃ METODOLOGICZNYCH I PROBLEMÓW DYSKUSYJNYCH KOLEKTYWU AUTORSKIEGO) [The development of the outline of the history of the Party in Hungary: based on methodological experiments and discussion problems of an authors' collective]. *Z Pola Walki [Poland] 1969 12(1): 111-126.* Traces the work carried out on the research into the history of the Social Democratic Party and the Communist Party of Hungary before and after 1957, noting the setback suffered by the research as a result of the personality cult prior to 1957.

1800. Vass, Henrik. A KÖZELMÚLT PÁRTDOKUMENTUMAINAK PUBLIKÁLÁSÁRÓL [On the publication of Party documents of the recent past]. *Párttörténeti Közlemények [Hungary] 1979 25(2): 72-87.* On the publication policy and methods of the Institute of the History of the Party. 2 notes. R. Hetzron

1801. Vida, István. A FÜGGETLEN KISGAZDAPÁRT 1946 MÁSODIK FELÉBEN [The Independent Smallholders' Party during the second half of 1946]. *Párt-Történeti Közlemények [Hungary] 1973 19(2): 79-120.* The leaders of the Independent Smallholder's Party (ISP) considered their organization the leading force in Hungarian society. The influence of Zoltán Tildy, who favored a Finnish model and cooperation with local Communists, began to decline in early 1946. The other leaders wanted to serve the interests of both the peasantry and the urban middle classes and restrict communist participation in the coalition government to 17%, the percentage vote they had gained at the 1945 election. The Smallholders tried, unsuccessfully, to gain influence in the army and the police, institutions that were in communist hands. The ISP mobilized about 150,000 demonstrators for Budapest's National Peasant Days, 7-8 September, while conservative groups in the countryside and members of the National Assembly attempted to loosen the communist grip on Hungary. When the political leadership began to compromise with the Communists, dissident leaders formed new political parties. 97 notes. P. I. Hidas

1802. Záhorská, Dagmar. POČIÁTKY VÝVINU MAĎARSKEJ L'UDOVEJ DEMOKRACIE [Initial development of the Hungarian people's democracy]. *Slovanský Přehled [Czechoslovakia] 1972 58(6): 469-475.* Describes the role of the Communist Party in the creation of modern Hungary. After the liberation of Hungary, April 1945, the political struggle for a people's democracy against bourgeois reactionary forces continued through the crucial years 1947-48. Published sources; 57 notes. G. E. Pergl

1803. —. DIE UNGARISCHE VERFASSUNGS-REFORM VON 1972 [The Hungarian constitutional reform of 1972]. *Osteuropäische Rundschau [West Germany] 1972 18(10): 18-23.* Describes the adoption of a revision of the Hungarian constitution of 1949 by the Hungarian parliament at its spring meeting, 18-19 April 1972. The proposal passed unanimously with little debate. Since the early 1960's government figures had advocated such revisions. The 10th Congress of the Hungarian Socialist Workers' Party (1970) approved changes proposed by Janos Kadar, and in June 1971 a committee appointed to consider the question began work and had a draft ready by September. In several particulars the altered constitution reflected the changes in Hungarian society since 1949. Based on Hungarian press and radio; 43 notes. P. R. Taylor

1804. —. A MAGYAR KOMMUNISTA MOZGALOM HAT ÉVTIZEDES TÖRTÉNELMI ÚTJA [The 60-year history of the Hungarian Communist movement]. *Párttörténeti Közlemények [Hungary] 1978 24(3): 3-48.* The Communist Party of Hungary was founded on 24 November 1918. Among its founders were former soldiers who had witnessed the Russian Revolution. Following an intermediate bourgeois democratic revolution, a Hungarian Soviet Republic which lasted for 133 days was declared in 1919. After its fall, the Communist Party became illegal until 1944, but it remained active underground and in exile. Close cooperation with the Social Democratic Party was achieved in 1944 and the two parties merged in 1948 as the Hungarian Workers' Party. In 1956, a reorganization led to the establishment of the Hungarian Socialist Workers' Party which has instituted socialist development. R. Hetzron

1805. —. A MUNKÁSMOZGALOM TÖRTÉNETE KUTATÁSÁNAK NEGYEDSZÁZADA [Twenty-five years of research on the history of the labor movement]. *Párt-Történeti Közlemények [Hungary] 1973 19(3): 3-18.* In 1946 the Hungarian Communist Party formed a Party History Commission which by 1948 developed the Party History Institute, later called the Labor History Institute. During World War II many labor unions, Social Democratic Party, and illegal Communist documents were destroyed, but most of the relevant police records survived. Until 1957 the absence of trained and experienced staff and the negative features of Party policy lowered the quality of the institute's output. Since then trained Party historians have emerged, and a synthesis and several popular histories have been published. P. I. Hidas

1806. —. A MUNKÁSOSZTÁLY EGYSÉGE: GYŐZELMÉNEK ZÁLOGA: A KÉT MUNKÁSPÁRT EGYESÜLÉSÉNEK 30. ÉVFORDULÓJÁRA [The unity of the working class is the pledge of its victory: the 30th anniversary of the fusion of the two workers' parties]. *Társadalmi Szemle [Hungary] 1978 33(6): 12-21.* Views the events leading up to the fusion of the Communist Party and Social Democratic Party of Hungary in June 1948 emphasizing the activities of the Communists.

Poland

1807. Antoniuk, S. M. UCHAST' VOINIV VIIS'KA POL'S'KOHO U VIDBUDOVI NARODNOHO HOSPODARSTVA POL'SHCHI (1944-1949) [Participation by soldiers from the Polish army in rebuilding Poland's economy, 1944-49]. *Ukrains'kyi Istorychnyi Zhurnal [USSR] 1978 (11): 54-60.* Polish soldiers participated in land reforms, rebuilding industry and developing and settling Northern Poland. The Communist Party guided the political education of soldiers and youth to prevent counterrevolution. Based on documents from the military archives of the Polish Ministry of Defense and other primary sources; 63 notes. V. Packer

1808. Baranowski, Feliks. Z DZIEJÓW NURTU LEWICOWEGO POWOJENNEJ PPS [From the history of the Leftist current of the postwar Polish Socialist Party (PPS)]. *Z Pola Walki [Poland] 1974 17(67): 25-48.* The Polish Socialist Party (PPS) suffered from a clash of various internal political orientations and directions. During the Second World War, the Socialist left created an independent party. Nevertheless, in the reborn PPS serious divergences still appeared, resulting in the formation of three new currents: leftist, centrist and rightist. The author presents the struggle of the left in the party against the background of postwar political activities of the

PPS, and marks off several stages of the struggle: 1) from the Lublin Conference in 1944 to the 26th Congress (June 1945), during which the left socialists held a dominating position in the party's leadership; 2) 1945-46, which culminated in the defeat of the left by the centrist group; 3) from 1946 to the beginning of 1948, when attempts were made to establish a homogeneous front of the working class, with an increase of rightist pressure, and a growing consolidation of the socialist left; 4) from the beginning of 1948, the Leftists were gradually gaining broader influence within the party, the position of the centrists was weakened, and rightist influences were eliminated. In September 1948, the Chief Council condemned ideological and political misconceptions of the reborn PPS and voted for the unification of the Polish workers' movement. J/S

1809. Barcikowski, Andrzej. KONCEPCJE PATRIOTYZMU I JEDNOŚCI POLITYCZNEJ NARODU W DOKUMENTACH PROGRAMOWYCH PPR [Concepts of patriotism and the political unity of the nation in program documents of the Polish Workers' Party]. *Studia Nauk Politycznych [Poland] 1978 (6): 39-63.* Discusses the concept of patriotism and the political unity of the nation and defines relations between them. Stresses that patriotism is the part of national consciousness which is formed by the aim to create, to protect one's own state. Between patriotism and national political unity there is a causal link: similarity of patriotic attitudes causes a mutual identification of individuals who are characterized by such attitudes. Presents five models of relations between national and class aims of the proletariat in the history of socialist thought, and suggests that the presentation of national questions in program documents of the Polish Workers' Party follows the Leninist model. Gives a humanistic interpretation of the Polish model of patriotism and political unity and distinguishes two periods in the history of the Party: 1) January 1942-July 1944; and 2) July 1944-December 1948. J/S

1810. Bieliakov, H. F. 30-RICHCHIA UTVORENNIA POL'S'KOI OB'IEDNANOI ROBITNYCHOI PARTII [The 30th anniversary of the creation of the Polish United Workers' Party]. *Ukrains'kyi Istorychnyi Zhurnal [USSR] 1978 (11): 123-125.* Traces the formation of the Polish United Workers' Party (PZPR) in 1948 from the union of the Polish Workers' Party and the Polish Socialist Party and considers the resultant social change in Poland, in particular the expansion of the working class and the strengthening of ties among workers, peasants, and the intelligentsia. A number of features peculiar to Poland such as the absence of collective farms and an influential Catholic Church make the PZPR's tasks in building a developed socialist party more complex. Friendship with the USSR is a great help. 15 notes. V. Packer

1811. Bobrowski, Czesław. ZE WSPOMNIEN, 1945-1948 [Reminiscences, 1945-48]. *Kwartalnik Hist. [Poland] 1979 86(3): 701-732.* The author, an economist and politician, returned from the West to Poland in 1945, joined the Polish Socialist Party and was offered the post of president of the Central Planning Office from which he resigned in 1948 to become ambassador to Sweden. In his memoirs he deals with the problems of planning the economic recovery of postwar Poland according to the Marxist rules and discusses the personalities connected with that planning. Part of a larger unpublished work. H. Heitzman Wojcicka

1812. Borkowski, Jan. PERTRAKTACJE PRZEDWYBORCZE MIĘDZY POLSKĄ PARTIĄ ROBOTNICZĄ I POLSKĄ PARTIĄ SOCJALISTYCZNĄ A POLSKIM STRONNICTWEM LUDOWYM (1945-1946) [Pre-election negotiations between the Polish Labor Party, the Polish Socialist Party, and the Polish Peasant Party]. *Kwartalnik Hist. [Poland] 1964 71(2): 423-439.* After the recognition of the Provisional Government of National Unity at the Yalta Conference, general elections proved its popularity. To counteract the counterrevolutionary elements which tried to seize power, the Polish Workers' Party created an electoral coalition comprising the Polish Socialist Party, the Polish Peasant Party, the Polish Democratic Party, and the Polish Labor Party with the distribution of mandates at 20% each for the first three parties and 10% each for the others. The Polish Peasant Party's demand for 75% of the mandate proved that some clandestine factions were about to seize power. J. Wilczek

1813. Bromke, Adam. A NEW JUNCTURE IN POLAND. *Problems of Communism 1976 25(5): 1-17.* Analyzes the recent trends in the economic and political spheres that have led to current tensions in Poland. Communist chief Edward Gierek has adopted policies that have led to a polarization between the Communist Party and the people of Poland and made compromise increasingly difficult. A crisis is rapidly approaching. Based on primary and secondary Polish and English language sources; 56 notes. J. M. Lauber

1814. Brzeziński, Bogdan and Halaba, Ryszard. SPRAWOZDANIA KOMITETÓW WOJEWÓDZKICH POLSKIEJ PARTII ROBOTNICZEJ Z 1945 R [Reports of the Provincial Committees of the Polish Workers' Party in 1945]. *Z Pola Walki [Poland] 1971 14(4): 279-351.* A selection of 10 reports of Provincial Committees of the Polish Workers' Party submitted in 1945 and related to contemporary events and problems including resettlement, economic difficulties, and postwar reconstruction.

1815. Buchta, Bruno. POLNISCHE ARBEITEN ÜBER DIE DURCHSETZUNG DER EINHEIT DER ARBEITERKLASSE IN DER VOLKSDEMOKRATISCHEN REVOLUTION IN POLEN [Polish studies on the implementation of the unity of the working class in the people's democratic revolution in Poland]. *Jahrbuch für Geschichte der Sozialistischen Länder Europas [East Germany] 1978 22(2): 147-157.* Reviews new Polish works on the unification of the Polish Workers' Party and the Polish Socialist Party to the Polish United Workers' Party during world War II and thereafter under the influence of the USSR and during the Cold War.

1816. Buczek, Roman. PRL W 1946 ROKU [The Polish People's Republic in 1946]. *Zeszyty Hist. [France] 1975 31: 158-170.* Minutes of meetings of a committee of the National People's Council on 25 January and 1 February 1946 to consider the new electoral law and an electoral bloc of all democratic parties. The draft law was to be framed by an interparty committee including representatives from nonpolitical organizations. The Polish Peasants' Party (PSL) objected that nonpolitical organizations should not be represented in a purely political process and that if they were, then so must the cooperatives. The electoral bloc was again opposed by the PSL for fear of dominance by the Polish Workers' Party. But all the others were strongly in favor and accused the PSL of rupturing the democratic front at a time of grave crisis. Meanwhile, the participants resolved to initiate discussions at all levels on this issue. M. K. Palat

1817. Bukharin, N. I. and Iazhborovskaia, I. S. REVOLIUTSIONNO-INTERNATSIONALISTICHESKIE TRADITSII POL'SKOGO RABOCHEGO DVIZHENIIA [Revolutionary-internationalist traditions of the Polish labor movement]. *Voprosy Istorii [USSR] 1982 (10): 47-61.* Adherence to Marxism in the struggle against bourgeois ideology and petit bourgeois socialism, reformism, and revisionism: proletarian internationalism; close ties with the international labor movement; revolutionary union of the Russian and Polish proletariat—such are the main traditions of the revolutionary-internationalist forces of the Polish labor movement. Polish revolutionary parties of the working class were always guided by the basic interests of the Polish working people and drew on the revolutionary struggle of the masses. These glorious traditions are the source of ideological strengthening of the Polish United Workers' Party and of the cause of socialism in Poland. J

1818. Cave, Jane. LOCAL OFFICIALS OF THE POLISH UNITED WORKERS' PARTY, 1956-75. *Soviet Studies [Great Britain] 1981 33(1): 125-141.* The need for the Polish United Workers' Party, as for other Communist regimes, to solve the problem of obtaining the expertise required to direct modern industrial society, has been met by emphasizing specialist educational qualifications in the recruitment and training of Party officials. Analysis of PUWP policy in this area, 1956-75, shows a steady rise in the educational level of officials, with a further increase in the appointment of those with technical and managerial skills in the 1970's. Among the results is a growth of pragmatism in the attitude of officials. 77 notes, 5 tables. D. H. Murdoch

1819. Checinski, Michael. *Poland: Communism, Nationalism, Anti-Semitism.* Szafar, Tadeusz, transl. New York: Karz-Cohl, 1982. 300 pp.

1820. Chekalenko, L. D. SPILKA BOROT'BY MOLODYKH TA II ROL' U VIDBUDOVI NARODNOHO HOSPODARSTVA POL'SHCHI [The Union of Fighting Youth and its role in the reconstruction of the national economy in Poland]. *Ukrains'kyi Istorychnyi Zhurnal [USSR] 1973 (7): 101-104.* Discusses the activities of Communist youth organizations in Poland, May 1945-July 1948.

1821. Chołaj, Henryk. LENINIZM A POLITYKA ROLNA PZPR [Leninism and the agrarian policy of the Polish United Workers' Party]. *Kultura i Społeczeństwo [Poland] 1970 14(2): 39-60.* The current Polish agrarian policy, abandoned in 1948 and reinstituted in 1956, is harmonious with Leninism. It consists of pursuing the socialization of agriculture only in conjunction with technical developments that allow for the convergence of socialization and improved production. Points out that despite predominantly private ownership, Polish agriculture is part of the socialist economy through various influences of central planning, cooperatives, government farms, and public funding aid. This approach is a creative application of Marxism-Leninism that is suited to Polish conditions and strengthens the vital worker-peasant alliance. Based on primary and secondary sources, periodicals, newspapers; 23 notes.

L. A. Krzyzak

1822. Cieplak, Tadeusz N. SOME DISTINCTIVE CHARACTERISTICS OF THE COMMUNIST SYSTEM IN THE POLISH PEOPLE'S REPUBLIC. *Polish R. 1974 19(1): 41-66.* Examines the political system in Poland and compares it with its Soviet prototype.

1823. Čwik, Kazimierz. HISTORYCZNE PRZESŁANKI I KONSEKWENCJE ZJEDNOCZENIA POLSKIEGO RUCHU ROBOTNICZEGO [Historical circumstances and consequences of the unification of the Polish workers' movement]. *Studia Nauk Politycznych [Poland] 1979 (6): 11-33.* In December 1948 the Polish United Workers' Party was established from the unification of the Workers' Party and the Socialist Party. The founding of the Polish Workers' Party in January 1942 with a new program of working-class unity was an important precursor, as was the establishment of a left deviation in the socialist movement during the war, the Workers' Party of Polish Socialists. The left Socialists contributed to establishing the democratic popular front, the National People's Council, and the Polish Committee of National Liberation, and after the liberation also participated in reestablishing the Polish Socialist Party. The postwar cooperation of the Polish Workers' Party and the Polish Socialist Party led to an agreement on unity of actions in November 1946. J/S

1824. Czubiński, Antoni. ROLA KLASY ROBOTNICZEJ I RUCHU ROBOTNICZEGO W POLSKIM PROCESIE DZIEJOWYM [Role of the working class and workers' movement in Polish history]. *Z Pola Walki [Poland] 1972 15(57): 17-27.* The working class emerged rather late in Poland, in the middle of the 19th century. Slow industrial progress checked its growth and the political division of the country weakened its cohesion. Polish workers emigrated to look for work abroad. Foreign capital prevailed everywhere in Poland. Polish workers were socially exploited and nationally oppressed at the same time. Class conflicts interlocked with the growing national conflicts and the struggle for social liberation was carried on along the same lines as the struggle for national liberation. A complete fusion of the social struggle with the struggle for national rights took place during the Nazi occupation. Under the leadership of the Polish Workers' Party, the working class took over the state and shaped the present people's democratic system. Text of a lecture delivered in the Higher School of Social Sciences at the Central Committee of the Polish United Workers' Party in Warsaw on the occasion of inauguration of the 1971-1972 academic year. J/S

1825. Desanti, Dominique. POLSKA... POCZĄTEK WSZYSTKIEGO [Poland... the beginning of everything]. *Zeszyty Hist. [France] 1976 (35): 181-226.* Describes the strange political and intellectual atmosphere in Poland under the Communist government, 1944-56, which resulted from the clash between Stalinism and the democratic approach to Communism. At the World Peace Congress of Intellectuals in Wrocław in 1948 this led to open ideological disagreement and subsequently it produced the revolt of Polish workers in Poznań, the "Polish October" in 1956, and the return to power of Władysław Gomułka.

1826. DeWeydenthal, Jan B. *The Communists of Poland: An Historical Outline.* Histories of Ruling Communist Parties series. Stanford: Hoover Inst., 1979. 217 pp.

1827. deWeydenthal, Jan B. PARTY DEVELOPMENT IN CONTEMPORARY POLAND. *East European Q. 1977 11(3): 341-363.* Analyzes changes in membership and organization in the Polish United Workers' Party, 1960-75. The party more than doubled in size. Although recruitment was aimed primarily at workers and peasants, the main change was the increase in the proportion of white collar employees. Among the party functionaries, the emphasis has been on youth and education. This altered party has attempted to improve the management of Poland's economic and political systems without making any major structural changes. Based on government statistics and a wide variety of secondary sources; 52 notes. C. R. Lovin

1828. DeWeydenthal, Jan B. WORKERS AND PARTY IN POLAND. *Problems of Communism 1980 29(6): 1-22.* The strikes of July-August 1980 have brought about substantial changes in Poland, including a new Party leadership. However, the fundamental question remains: how can a lasting accommodation between society and the Communist Party be achieved? Efforts to overcome the mutual distrust are a central feature of the Party's current efforts to reestablish its authority. Resolution of this question, amid the uncertainties posed by economic difficulties and the threat of Soviet intervention, is crucial to future developments in Poland. Based on Polish newspaper and radio accounts; 80 notes.

J. M. Lauber

1829. Doroszewski, Jerzy. SYTUACJA SPOŁECZNO-POLITYCZNA NAUCZYCIELI NA LUBELSZCZYŹNIE W LATACH 1944-1948 [The sociopolitical situation of teachers in the Lublin region, 1944-48]. *Kultura i Społeczeństwo [Poland] 1980 24(3-4): 155-170.* The postwar period was difficult for teachers in Lublin. Most of them dutifully returned to work and complied with the regulations of the new government, but they suffered economically and politically. Although most were members of the Association of Polish Teachers, which assumed an apolitical role, many were subjected to pressures to join various political factions. In the early postwar years only a few joined the Polish Workers' Party. Based on Polish government sources and secondary materials; 3 tables, 72 notes. D. S. Lloyd

1830. Drewnowski, Jan. THE CENTRAL PLANNING OFFICE ON TRIAL: AN ACCOUNT OF THE BEGINNINGS OF STALINISM IN POLAND. *Soviet Studies [Great Britain] 1979 31(1): 23-42.* The trial of the Central Planning Office in Warsaw on 18-19 February 1948 may be seen as the beginning of Stalinism in Poland. The Central Planning Office was established in the autumn of 1945 to introduce a planned economy in Poland. By early 1948 its planning methods were being criticized, and the trial of the office by the Polish Workers' Party led to the abolition of the office in April 1949 and the dismissal of all economics professors from their chairs. Based mainly on the author's memory as one of the participants in the Central Planning Office trial; 27 notes.

F. P. Tudor

1831. Dymek, Benon. ALFRED FIDERKIEWICZ (1886-1972) [Alfred Fiderkiewicz (1886-1972)]. *Z Pola Walki [Poland] 1979 22(2): 141-152.* Alfred Fiderkiewicz, a Polish political activist, first encountered socialist ideas at school. From 1904 to 1922 he was in the United States, working, studying, and conducting political work among Polish and American socialists. On his return to Poland, he joined the Polish People's Party but soon moved to the Communist Party of Poland. During World War II, he joined the new Polish Workers' Party. After the war, he organized Polish embassies abroad. He retired in 1956 and died in 1972. Based on A. Fiderkiewicz's autobiographical writings, documents in the Central Archives of the Central Committee of the Polish United Workers' Party in Warsaw, and eyewitness accounts; 33 notes.
E. Jaworska

1832. Fijałkowska, Barbara. PPR WOBEC ŚRODOWISK TWÓRCZYCH (1944-1948) [The Polish Workers' Party and artistic circles, 1944-48]. *Z Pola Walki [Poland] 1981 24(3-4): 27-48.* The Polish Workers' Party took the task of stimulating the cultural life in Poland after World War II. Initially, artists enjoyed considerable freedom of expression and independence from the Party, but also suffered from shortages of financial resources from the state sponsor. From 1947 onward, ideological education at universities began, promoting close cooperation between Party members and academics. This led to universities' becoming dependent on the Party and artists' work being criticized for its lack of political concern. Based on contemporary press articles and documents held at the Central Archives of the Central Committee of the Polish United Workers' Party; 52 notes. Russian and English summaries.
E. Jaworska

1833. Fuks, Marian. PRASA PPR I PZPR W JEZYKU ŻYDOWSKIM *(FOŁKS-SZTYME,* 1946-1956) [The press of the Polish Workers' Party (PPR) and Polish United Workers' Party (PZPR) in Yiddish translation]. *Biuletyn Żydowkiego Instytutu Hist. w Polsce [Poland] 1979 (3): 21-36.* Founded in 1946, *Folks-Sztyme* was the Yiddish organ of the Polish Workers' Party and its successor, the Polish United Workers' Party.

1834. Gać, Stanislav. POLSKÁ LIDOVÁ ARMÁDA 1943-1978 [Polish People's Army, 1943-78]. *Hist. a Vojenství [Czechoslovakia] 1978 27(5): 66-94.* Divides the history of modern Polish army into five periods: 1942-45, People's Guard and People's Army, led by the Polish Workers' Party; 1945-49, the struggle for people's power in the state; 1950-55, cold war; 1955-60, the Warsaw Pact; and 1960 forward, continued modernization, with sophisticated weapons and services. 46 notes. G. E. Pergl

1835. Głowacki, Andrzej. WYDARZENIA GRUDNIA 1970 R.-STYCZNIA 1971 R. W SZCZECINIE [The events of December 1970-January 1971 in Szczecin]. *Zapiski Historyczne [Poland] 1981 46(4): 127-154.* A reconstruction of events during the strikes in the Polish port town based on interviews with local Party officials and striking workers, and on other sources. 89 notes.

1836. Goldfarb, Jeffrey C. *On Cultural Freedom: An Exploration of Public Life in Poland and America.* Chicago: U. of Chicago Pr., 1982. 173 pp.

1837. Golębiowski, Janusz W. and Góra, Wladyslaw. HAUPTPROBLEME IN DER ENTWICKLUNG UND TÄTIGKEIT DER PVAP (1948 BIS 1975) [The main problems in the development and activities of the PVAP (1948-75)]. *Beiträge zur Gesch. der Arbeiterbewegung [East Germany] 1980 22(1): 3-19.* The Polish United Workers' Party was formed in December 1948 in Warsaw as the amalgamation of the Communist and Socialist parties. Examines the changes in the Party's organization and structure, 1948-75, and considers the economic, social, and industrial progress in Poland due to Party activities and the closer links that have been formed with the USSR. Based on Party documents and secondary sources; 61 notes. G. L. Neville

1838. Golin, E. M. POL'S'KI ZAKHIDNI TA PIVNICHNI ZEMLI PISLIA ZOZZ'IEDNANNIA [West and north Polish territories after the reunification]. *Ukrains'kyi Istorychnyi Zhurnal [USSR] 1976 (6): 102-107.* Analyzes the achievements of the Polish People's Republic in the north and west territories, along the Oder and Neisse rivers, ceded to Poland from Germany in 1945.

1839. Gomułka, Władysław. Z PISM I PRZEMÓWIEŃ WŁADYSŁAWA GOMUŁKI: 1943-1948 [From the letters and speeches of Władysław Gomułka, 1943-48]. *Nowe Drogi [Poland] 1982 (9): 12-62.* A selection of Władysław Gomułka's speeches and open letters, 1943-48, among them a letter to the Sikorski government, an excerpt from the Polish Workers' Party Manifesto, a speech at an open meeting in Warsaw, and others.

1840. Góra, Władysław. KLĘSKA REAKCJI I ANTYLUDOWEGO PODZIEMIA (LIPIEC 1944-STYCZEŃ 1947) [Defeat of reaction and the antipopulist underground, July 1944-January 1947]. *Nowe Drogi [Poland] 1982 (12): 34-45.* Surveys the political spectrum and activities of the opposition to socialist rule in Poland operating between 1944-47 and eventually quashed in the 1947 elections won by the Democratic Bloc.

1841. Góra, Władysław. PRZEKSZTALCANIE SIĘ PARTII KLASY ROBOTNICZEJ W PARTIĘ NARODU [The transformation of the party of the working class into a party of the people]. *Z Pola Walki [Poland] 1970 13(4): 3-34.* Discusses how the political and national awareness of the working class matured into an active political force, and considers the creation and development of the Polish Workers' Party.

1842. Gora, Wladyslaw. REVOLUTIONÄRE VERÄNDERUNGEN UND KAMPF FÜR DIE FESTIGUNG DER VOLKSMACHT IN POLEN 1944-1948 [Revolutionary changes and the fight for the strengthening of the people's power in Poland, 1944-48]. *Beiträge zur Geschichte der Arbeiterbewegung [East Germany] 1975 17(2): 232-248.* After the imperialist Second World War, socialist organizations of Poland were able to assume power and make revolutionary changes in government operations and foreign relations. The Polish government-in-exile in London represented only bourgeois interests. The Polish Workers' Party, formed in 1942, represented the majority of the people. Its goals were socialist and humanitarian, including opposition to the genocide practiced by Adolf Hitler's government, reform of capitalist society with new freedoms for oppressed workers, and friendship with socialist nations, especially the Soviet Union. From 1944 to 1948 this party formed a provisional government; the 1947 plebiscite gave the democratic bloc, led by the Polish Workers Party, a clear majority. Primary materials; 18 notes. G. H. Libbey

1843. Góra, Władysław. REWOLUCJA LUDOWA W POLSCE 1944-1947, JEJ ROZWÓJ I CECHY CHARAKTERYSTYCZNE [The people's revolution in Poland 1944-47: its development and characteristic features]. *Z Pola Walki [Poland] 1974 17(67): 69-84.* Discusses the character of revolutionary change in Poland, 1944-47. Analyzes in detail three factors: 1) the apparatus of power after July 1944; 2) the basic changes in the field of socioeconomic transformations with special attention paid to the nationalization of industry; 3) the Polish Workers' Party and the Polish United Workers' Party as revolutionary vanguards of the working class and a driving force for all revolutionary change. J/S

1844. Góra, Władysław. WALKA O UTRWALENIE WŁADZY LUDOWEJ (1944-1948) [The struggle for the consolidation of popular power, 1944-48]. *Nowe Drogi [Poland] 1979 (5): 72-86.* Sees the consolidation of Communist rule in Poland in the context of different social and economic policies and the struggle with the London government-in-exile.

1845. Gross, Feliks. ADAM CIOŁKOSZ (1902-1978). *Polish Rev. 1978 23(4): 66-70.* Recalls the political activities and political and historical writings of Polish Socialist Party and Sejm member Adam Ciołkosz, who endured imprisonment by both Germans and Russians and lived the postwar years in London.

1846. Grzybowski, Leszek. ROZWÓJ LICZEBNY I KSZTAŁTOWANIE SIĘ SPOŁECZNEGO SKŁADU PZPR (1948-1975) [The social composition of the Polish United Workers' Party,

1948-75]. *Z Pola Walki [Poland] 1978 21(4): 33-57.* Analyzes the changes in the social composition of the PUWP, 1948-75, beginning with the merging of the Polish Workers' Party and the Polish Socialist Party in 1948 and leading up to the 7th Party Congress in 1975. 11 tables, 51 notes. M. A. Zurowski

1847. Gura, Vladislav. DVADTSAT' PIAT' LET NARODNOI POL'SHI [25 years of people's Poland]. *Voprosy Istorii KPSS [USSR] 1969 (7): 50-61.* Describes the achievements of Communist Poland, 1944-69, attained despite various difficulties, mistakes and opposition.

1848. Hillebrandt, Bogdan; with commentary by Hemmerling, Zygmunt et al. IDEOWA INSPIRACJA PARTII ROBOTNICZYCH W RUCHU MŁODZIEŻOWYM [Ideological inspiration of the worker parties in the youth movement]. *Z Pola Walki [Poland] 1984 27(1-2): 173-183.* Surveys the role of worker parties in the formation and development of progressive youth organizations in 20th-century Poland. The Polish Socialist Party (PPS) sustained close links with the Union of Polish Socialist Youth, although internal party dissent led to fragmentation of the socialist youth movement in the interwar period. During World War II the Fighting Youth Union collaborated with the Polish Workers' Party, whose merger with the Polish Socialist Party in 1948 created some dissatisfaction among youth leaders and splintered the movement. Post-1956 attempts to integrate youth organizations with the Polish United Workers' Party denied them freedom to develop free cooperation with the Party and caused the disintegration of the official unions during the 1980 crisis. Comments, pp. 215-256. Secondary sources. Russian and English summaries. M. Hernas

1849. Hillebrandt, Bogdan. PZPR I SOCJALISTYCZNE WYCHOWANIE MŁODZIEŻY (1948-1957) [PZPR and the socialist upbringing of youth, 1948-57]. *Z Pola Walki [Poland] 1977 20(2): 183-201.* The educative action of the Polish United Workers' Party (PZPR) aimed at the socialist upbringing of the country's youth was effected mainly through three channels: schools; the official youth organization ZMP (Polish Youth Union); and mass information media. The ZMP had a difficult task as it had originated from a conglomeration of youth organizations and it eventually succumbed to widespread criticisms and inner tensions among the three elements: rural youth; students; and young workers in towns. Eventually the ZMP was dissolved and the three groups set up their own organizations, the latter two combining later into the Socialist Youth Union while the former set up a Rural Youth Union. 49 notes. Z. K. L. Chojecki

1850. Hillebrandt, Bogdan. SYTUACJA POLITYCZNA NA WYŻSZYCH UCZELNIACH W LATACH 1956-1959 [Political climate at universities, 1956-59]. *Z Pola Walki [Poland] 1982 25(3-4): 103-123.* Views the political developments in Polish universities after the thaw of 1956 until 1959, focusing on the student movements to form unions independent of the Party, and the growing alienation of academic establishments from the Party's aims and policies. In 1957 the Party imposed the institution of the Socialist Youth Union, causing resentment and disillusionment among the academics, of whom very few were party members. Party Central Committee Central Archives, Warsaw Party Committee Archives; 35 notes. Russian and English summaries. M. Hernas

1851. Iazhborovskaia, I. S. O KHARAKTERE I ETAPAKH REVOLIUTSIONNOGO PROTSESSA V POL'SHE V 1944-1948 GODAKH [The character and stages of the revolutionary process in Poland, 1944-48]. *Voprosy Istorii [USSR] 1973 (12): 67-77.* Shows the interpretation given by Polish historiography to the question concerning the character and the principal stages of the revolutionary process in Poland in the early postwar years. Examines the views of Polish historians on the correlation of the democratic and socialist tasks of the revolutionary process, the efforts made by the Polish Workers' Party to strengthen the hegemony of the proletariat in the people's democratic revolution, paying particular attention to the general laws governing the development of the democratic revolution into the socialist revolution, which clearly manifested themselves in the specific conditions obtaining in Poland during the early postwar years. J

1852. Iazhborovskaia, I. S. SOTSIAL'NO-POLITICHESKIE ASPEKTY PROTSESSA NATSIONALIZATSII V NARODNOI POL'SHE [The sociopolitical aspects of nationalization in Poland]. *Sovetskoe Slavianovedenie [USSR] 1976 (3): 19-39.* The demand for the nationalization of heavy industry had appeared in the prewar period in Poland. It was reflected in 1943 in the party platforms of the Communist, Socialist, and Peasant parties, and appealed to the working masses. Medium and light industry was to remain in private hands. During the period of Poland's liberation from fascism, it was very difficult to introduce a new method of production or prepare the working class for the revolutionary breakdown of the old production relationships. The author describes the struggle of the Polish Workers' Party to achieve nationalization, democratization, and the institution of economic and political changes in the structure of Polish society. Shows the close connection between the process of nationalization and the spread of the revolutionary process in Poland, 1944-48. Often, the nationalization process was conditioned by the revolutionary process. 77 notes. L. Kalinowski

1853. Jabłoński, Henryk. HISTORYCZNE PRZESŁANKI POWSTANIA POLSKIEJ ZJEDNOCZONEJ PARTII ROBOTNICZEJ [Historical premises of the origin of the Polish United Workers' Party]. *Nowe Drogi [Poland] 1973 (12): 11-20.* Examines the political conditions of the Polish working-class movement, ca 1900-50.

1854. Jagiełło, Jerzy. DYSKUSJE NAD KONCEPCJAMI DOKTRYNALNYMI W PPR I PPS Z PERSPEKTYWY HISTORYCZNEJ [Discussions on doctrinal conceptions in the Polish Workers' Party and the Socialist Party of Poland in historical perspective]. *Z Pola Walki [Poland] 1981 24(3-4): 49-64.* In the Polish Workers' Party, one group spoke for a Soviet-like socialism in Poland and the other group spoke for a Polish road to socialism. The former was for a centralized economic system, while the latter recognized the significance of market laws and forces. The dominant idea in the Socialist Party of Poland was a state like the USSR of 1918-20. From today's point of view, the central problem is the ownership of means of production. A mixed economy seems preferable, where consumers' changing needs are satisfied by production in small private factories functioning alongside state-owned industry. Based on unpublished *Notatki Alfreda Lampego* [Notes by Alfred Lampe], minutes of the parties' meetings, and other documents held at the Central Archives of the Central Committee of the Polish United Workers' Party; 22 notes. E. Jaworska

1855. Jakubowska, Halina. UDZIAŁ ZWIĄZKÓW ZAWODOWYCH W ŻYCIU POLITYCZNYM I SPOŁECZNYM W PIERWSZYCH LATACH POLSKI LUDOWEJ (1944-1948) [The participation of trade unions in social and political life in the first years of the Polish People's Republic, 1944-48]. *Z Pola Walki [Poland] 1979 22(2): 153-172.* The new trade unions founded by the Polish Workers' Party in July 1944 in the Lublin region were subject to the political struggle between the Polish Workers' Party and the Polish Socialist Party. By the end of 1948, about 90% of the Polish work force was unionized, and the unions secured decent economic standards for the workers and looked after their cultural and intellectual development. The unions played an important role in promoting the ideas and actions of the new Polish state among the masses. Based on documents in the Central Archives of the Central Committee of the Polish United Workers' Party and the Archives of the Central Council of Trade Unions in Warsaw, contemporary press articles, and other sources; 3 tables, 76 notes. E. Jaworska

1856. Jakubowski, Józef. KONCEPCJE PPR W SPRAWIE ODBUDOWY I ORGANIZACJI SZKOLNICTWA W LATACH 1944-1948 [The concepts of the PPR regarding the reconstitution and organization of the school system, 1944-48]. *Z Pola Walki [Poland] 1971 14(4): 91-112.* Describes the plans of the Polish Workers' Party (PPR) concerning the future of the educational system in Poland, 1944-48.

1857. Jakubowski, Józef. PROBLEMY ODBUDOWY WARSZAWY W DZIAŁALNOŚCI STOŁECZNEJ ORGANIZACJI PPR (1945-1948) [The Problems of rebuilding Warsaw in the activities of the metropolitan organization of the Polish Workers' Party, 1945-48]. *Z Pola Walki [Poland] 1976 19(4): 79-105.* The rebuilding of the almost completely destroyed city of Warsaw was one of the main tasks facing Poland after World War II. It was both a political and an economic problem. Decisions on metropolitan status and on rebuilding were made at the central level, but realization of the project fell to the city itself and to the Warsaw organization of the Polish Workers' Party (PPR). Almost all undertakings of the Warsaw organization of the PPR were connected with the unusual situation of the town and its returning inhabitants. The PPR Warsaw Committee brigades performed an important role in the first phase of rebuilding. In March of 1945 the Warsaw Committee mobilized a broad popular movement and soon secured a group of skilled workers and architects to work out concepts for the rebuilding, many of which were realized. J/S

1858. Jakubowski, Józef. Z PROBLEMØW POLITYKI OŚWIATOWEJ PZPR W LATACH 1948-1960 [The educational policy of the Polish United Workers' Party, 1948-60]. *Z Pola Walki [Poland] 1980 23(1): 43-60.* Breaks Polish educational policy, 1948-60, into three periods: 1948-49, the adoption of a democratic ideal based on Soviet pedagogy; 1950-55, a six-year plan emphasized vocational education; and 1956-60, reforms were enacted to modernize education in line with domestic political and economic changes.

1859. Janowski, Andrzej. ARCHIWA POLSKIEJ ZJEDNOCZONEJ PARTII ROBOTNICZEJ [The archives of the Polish United Workers' Party]. *Archeion [Poland] 1964 (41): 275-286.* The party history archives, created in 1946, were enlarged by the inclusion of the archives of the Polish Socialist Party and the Archive for Research into the Contemporary History of Poland, previously held under the auspices of the Council of Ministers. Microfilmed documents illustrating the activities of the Polish Communist parties (SDKPiL and KPP), of which the originals remained in Moscow, also enhanced the collection. The archives contain records of the provincial offices of the former security service, and documents of the Polish government-in-exile, London, during World War II. 21 notes. W. Kowalski

1860. Janowski, Karol B. KSZTAŁTOWANIE SIĘ JEDNOŚCI RUCHU ROBOTNICZEGO NA DOLNYM ŚLĄSKU (1945-1948) [The development of unity in the workers' movement in Lower Silesia, 1945-48]. *Z Pola Walki [Poland] 1971 14(3): 59-81.* Discusses measures adopted to facilitate the fusion of the Polish Workers' Party (PPR) and the Polish Socialist Party (PPS) prior to the formation of the Polish United Workers' Party (PZPR) in 1948, in Lower Silesia; 1945-48.

1861. Jarecki, Edward. TRZY TRUDNE LATA W ORGANIZACJI PARTYJNEJ STOCZNI GDAŃSKIEJ IM. LENINA (1980-1983) [Three difficult years for the Party organization in the Lenin Shipyard in Gdańsk: 1980-83]. *Nowe Drogi [Poland] 1983 (9): 53-76.* Presents a report by a Party official at the Gdańsk shipyard about the state of the Party organization from the first strikes in August 1980 to the lifting of martial law in July 1983.

1862. Jaroszewicz, Piotr. THIRTY YEARS OF PEOPLE'S POWER. *World Marxist R. [Canada] 1974 17(7): 3-14.* Reviews achievements of the Communist Party in Poland since 1944 and the party's current programs and goals.

1863. Jesionek, Czesław. WSPOMNIENIA I RELACJE O PPR, PPS I PZPR WŁĄCZONE DO ZASOBU CENTRALNEGO ARCHIWUM KC PZPR W LATACH 1971-1977 [Memoirs and reports about the Polish Workers' Party, Polish Socialist Party, and Polish United Workers' Party (PUWP) in the archive of the Central Committee of the PUWP, 1971-77]. *Z Pola Walki [Poland] 1978 21(3): 336-349.* A bibliography of memoirs and reports of members of the Polish Workers' Party, Polish Socialist Party, and Polish United Workers' Party, 1940's-50's.

1864. Juchnowski, Jerzy and Kalicki, Wojciech. DZIAŁALNOŚĆ PROPAGANDOWA PPS DOLNEGO ŚLĄSKA (1945-1948) [The propaganda of the Polish Socialist Party (PPS) in Lower Silesia, 1945-48]. *Śląski Kwartalnik Hist. Sobótka [Poland] 1979 34(1): 71-93.* Surveys the presentation of topical issues in Polish Lower Silesia in the articles of the Polish Socialist Party daily *Naprzód Dolnośląski* in the period 1945-48, especially the problems of resettlement, the indigenous German population, and political unity.

1865. Kalashnik, M. DEIATEL'NOST' KPSS I POL'SKOI RABOCHEI PARTII PO UKREPLENIIU BOEVOGO SODRUZHESTVA SOVETSKOGO I POL'SKOGO NARODOV V GODY MINUVSHEI VOINY [The CPSU and Polish Workers' Party in strengthening the military community in the USSR and Poland during the past war]. *Voenno-Istoricheskii Zhurnal [USSR] 1973 (9): 61-68.* The elimination of the age-old heritage of nationalist tensions between Poland and the USSR was one of the main tasks of the Bolsheviks after their assumption of power in Russia. The author discussed the foundations and evolution of present Soviet-Polish cooperative relations.

1866. Khrenov, I. A. POL'SKAIA RABOCHAIA PARTIIA: ORGANIZATOR BOR'BY ZA SVOBODU I NEZAVISIMOST' NARODA [The Polish Workers' Party: organizer of the struggle for freedom and the independence of the nation]. *Voprosy Istorii KPSS [USSR] 1962 (1): 186-193.* Considers the activities of the Polish Workers' Party, 1942-62, especially during and immediately after World War II.

1867. Kolesnyk, V. P. SPIVROBITNYTSTVO MISTSEVYKH KOMITETIV KPRS I PORP PRYKORDONNYKH OBLASTEI RADIANS'KOHO SOIUZU I VOIEVODSTV POL'S'KOI NARODNOI RESPUBLIKY (1956-1975) [Cooperation between local committees of the Communist Party of the Soviet Union and the Polish United Workers' Party in the border regions of the USSR and voivodships of the Polish People's Republic, 1956-75]. *Ukrains'kyi Istorychnyi Zhurnal [USSR] 1976 (3): 83-91.* Describes the strengthening and development of fraternal relations between the USSR and Poland, 1956-75, when border exchanges began between Party committees in Lublin, Lvov, and Volhynia, giving details of socialist competition and conferences held between them.

1868. Kołodziej, Edward. ODRODZENIE ZWIĄZKU ZAWODOWEGO PRACOWNIKÓW POCZT I TELEKOMUNIKACJI W OKRESIE OD SIERPNIA 1944 R. DO STYCZNIA 1947 R. [Rebirth of the Postal and Telecommunication Workers' Union from August 1944 to January 1947]. *Kwartalnik Historii Ruchu Zawodowego [Poland] 1983 22(1-2): 43-62.* The formative years of the union in postwar Poland were dominated by the political struggle between supporters of the Polish Workers' Party and the Socialist Party of Poland. Based on documents held at the Archives for Recent Documents, Warsaw, the Archives of the General Board of the Communication Workers' Union, Warsaw, and the Archives of the Central Council of the Trade Unions, Warsaw; table, 75 notes.

1869. Kolomeichik, Norbert. V BOR'BE INTERESY TRUDIASHCHIKHSIA POL'SHY [In the struggle for the interests of the working class in Poland]. *Voprosy Istorii KPSS [USSR] 1968 (12): 45-55.* Traces the history of the organization of the Polish Communist Party from its foundation in 1918 through its subsequent political struggles.

1870. Kołomejczyk, Norbert; Szyszko, Mieczysław; and Hass, Ludwik. ODPOWIEDZI NA ANKIETĘ REDAKCJI 'KWARTALNIKA HISTORII RUCHU ZAWODOWEGO' DOTYCZĄCĄ PROBLEMATYKI BADAWCZEJ DZIEJÓW RUCHU ZAWODOWEGO [Replies to the research questionnaire of the editorial board of *Kwartalnik Historii Ruchu Zawodowego* on the history of the labor movement]. *Kwartalnik Hist. Ruchu Zawodowego [Poland] 1978 (3): 81-100.* Thematically considers differences between blue-collar and white-collar unions, interwar Communist Party participation in the Polish situations, and the labor unions and organizations supported by the government, 1948-78.

1871. Kołomejczyk, Norbert. POLITYKA PPR W DZIEDZINIE TERYTORIALNONARODOWEGO ZESPOLENIA LUDOWEGO PAŃSTWA [The policy of the Polish Workers' Party in the sphere of territorial and national integration of the people's state]. *Z Pola Walki [Poland] 1979 22(2): 19-43.* Political thought of Polish Workers' Party (PPR) assumed the formation of a homogeneous national state within its natural frontiers, assuring national security and creating favorable conditions for social and economic development and for European peace. J/S

1872. Kołomejczyk, Norbert and Kozik, Zenobiusz; with commentary by Iazhborovskaia, Inessa S. et al. STAN BADAŃ NAD POLSKIM RUCHEM ROBOTNICZYM 1918-1970 [Current research on the Polish labor movement, 1918-70]. *Z Pola Walki [Poland] 1984 27(1-2): 391-402.* Low credibility of Polish historiography dealing with the Polish labor movement of 1918-70 evoked criticism by the public and the more outspoken historians during the 1980 period of social upheaval in society and the Polish United Workers' Party. The Institute of Party History in the 1950's and 1960's published theoretical studies rather than sociohistorical research, thus causing potential researchers to choose other institutions and other fields of study. Some valuable work has been done under the auspices of the Central Council of the Trade Unions, but there are still many areas in the history of the Polish labor movement of the period which need thorough and frank academic treatment. Comments, pp. 403-432. Based on secondary sources; Russian and English summaries. M. Hernas

1873. Korcz, Władysław. ROZWØJ ŻYCIA POLITYCZNEGO W LATACH 1945-1950 NA ZIEMIACH DAWNEGO POGRANICZA [Political activity in Poland's ex-German territories in the west, 1945-50]. *Przegląd Zachodni [Poland] 1969 25(1): 123-139.* In the five years after the war, all the main Polish political parties became established in the newly-acquired ex-German borderlands; the parties included the Polish Workers' Party, the Polish Socialist Party, the People's Party, the Democratic Party, and the Polish People's Party.

1874. Kormanowa, Żanna. MELANIA KIERCZYŃSKA (1888-1962) Z DZIEJÓW INTELEKTUALNEJ LEWICY KOMUNISTYCZNEJ [Melania Kierczyńska (1888-1962) from the history of the intellectual communist left wing]. *Z Pola Walki [Poland] 1975 18(1): 133-153.* A biography of this communist intellectual of bourgeois origins, who was a teacher, poet, translator, and literary critic until her death in 1962.

1875. Kostiushko, I. I. POL'SKAIA NARODNAIA RESPUBLIKA. OSNOVNYE ETAPY RAZVITIIA [The Polish People's Republic: the main stages of its development]. *Novaia i Noveishaia Istoriia [USSR] 1975 (5): 158-170.* Outlines the national development of Poland as a socialist state, from 1939. Economic data is quoted to show the benefits of Comecon membership, and agreements with capitalist countries are seen as promoting detente. Results of various Polish Party congresses demonstrate ideological bonds existing with the Soviet Communist Party. 8 notes.
V. A. Packer

1876. Kostiushko, I. I. USPEKHI POL'SKOGO NARODA V STROITEL'STVE SOTSIALIZMA [The successes of the Polish nation in the building of socialism]. *Sovetskoe Slavianovedenie [USSR] 1975 (2): 11-20.* Considers the development of Poland during the three decades since its founding. Stresses the accomplishments of the new government as a triumph of the working class under the leadership of the United Polish Workers' Party. Taking note of the damages and loss of life inflicted upon Poland during the Nazi occupation, the author points to the successful reconstruction of the postwar period and the rapid development of the national economy since then. Stresses Poland's close political and ideological ties with the Soviet Union and the other members of the socialist commonwealth. Based on published documents and Party declarations; 33 notes. J. W. Kipp

1877. Kowalczyk, Jozef. BOLESŁAW BIERUT (1892-1956) [Bolesław Bierut (1892-1956)]. *Nowe Drogi [Poland] 1976 (3): 118-129.* A biographical contribution concerning the life of the Stalinist leader of Polish Communists.

1878. Kowalczyk, Józef. TRUDNE POCZĄTKI ROZBUDOWY OŚWIATY [Difficult beginnings in the development of education]. *Z Pola Walki [Poland] 1978 21(1): 179-195.* As Head of the Department of Education of the Central Committee of the Polish Workers' Party (PPR) and later of the Polish United Workers' Party, 1948-53, Józef Kowalczyk was in charge of Party policy in matters of education, culture, science, press, publishing, and propaganda. He initiated a number of measures to reorganize the system of education at all levels, and had to correct deviations in the application of new regulations, including the social class principle and ideological discipline. He also made efforts to reduce illiteracy. 16 notes. Z. K. L. Chojecki

1879. Kowalczyk, Stanisław. 125 LAT MANIFESTU KOMUNISTYCZNEGO [One hundred and twenty five years of the *Communist Manifesto*]. *Nowe Drogi [Poland] 1973 (4): 74-79.* Assesses the importance of the *Communist Manifesto* for the development of Marxism-Leninism in Poland.

1880. Kowalik, Anastazja and Pasierb, Bronisław. KONGRES ZJEDNOCZENIOWY WE WSPOMNIENIACH UCZESTNIKÓW [The alliance congress in the reminiscences of its participants]. *Śląski Kwartalnik Hist. Sobótka [Poland] 1973 28(4): 493-506.* A report from a meeting held in Wrocław on the 20th anniversary of the alliance between the Polish Workers Party (PPR) and the Polish Socialist Party (PPS), held on 15 December 1948, which established a new united party: the Polish United Workers' Party (PZPR). Out of 170 original delegates elected from Lower Silesia to the congress in 1948, only 13 were represented at the meeting in Wrocław. They all recalled the joyful moment and pointed out that the idea of alliance between PPR and PPS originated during the days of Nazi occupation. The idea was carried out in 1948 and was preceded by party and mass meetings across Lower Silesia.
C. M. Nowak

1881. Kozik, Zenobiusz. DIE VEREINIGUNG DER ARBEITERBEWEGUNG IN VOLKSPOLEN [The unification of the workers movement in Poland]. *Beiträge zur Geschichte der Arbeiterbewegung [East Germany] 1976 18(2): 215-225.* Between 1893 and 1948 the Polish working class movement was split into revolutionary and reformist wings. In the spring of 1948 leaders of the Polish Workers' Party and the Polish Socialist Party stressed the importance of a common platform for the working class. On 14 December 1948 both parties accepted a common program and unification was carried through at the congress of 15-20 December 1948. Based on documents in the Zentrales Parteiarchiv, Warsaw, published documents, and secondary literature; 24 notes.
R. Wagnleitner

1882. Kozik, Zenobiusz. FORMOWANIE SIE STRATEGII GOSPODARCZEJ PZPR (1953-1956) [The formation of the economic policy of the Polish United Workers' Party, 1953-56]. *Z Pola Walki [Poland] 1978 21(4): 7-31.* Discusses the formation of the economic policy of the PUWP, 1953-56, when greater emphasis was placed on raising the living standards of the population. Changes were, with difficulty, successfully implemented in the system of planning and management. 7 notes. M. A. Zurowski

1883. Kozik, Zenobiusz. PARTIA A RUCH ZAWODOWY I RUCH MŁODZIEŻY (1954-1957) [The Party and the trade union movement and youth organizations, 1954-57]. *Z Pola Walki [Poland] 1979 22(2): 47-70.* Deals with political aspects of trade union and youth movements against the background of problems faced in the period 1954-56 by the Party, state, and society in Poland. The wide discussion on trade unions resulted in an enlarged scope for the labor movement. The Polish Youth Union (ZMP) was dissolved in January 1957 and replaced by the Socialist Youth Union (ZMS) and the Peasant Youth Union (ZMW). The Party leadership allowed some tactical elasticity in its policy toward the youth movements, where antisocialist and revisionist elements were manifested. In both movements the Party held its leading and decisive role throughout the period. J/S

1884. Kozik, Zenobiusz. PARTIE ROBOTNICZE REGIONU KRAKOWSKIEGO U PROGU POLSKI LUDOWEJ (STYCZEŃCZERWIEC 1945 R.) [Workers' parties in the Cracow region on the eve of People's Poland (January-July 1945)]. *Z Pola Walki [Poland] 1974 17(66): 57-89.* Presents the organizational, ideological and political development of the Polish Workers' Party (PPR) and the Polish Socialist Party (PPS) in Cracow during the first months of People's Poland, 1945. Based on party and administrative archival records. J/S

1885. Kozik, Zenobiusz. PPR I PPS W KRAKOWSKIEM NA DRODZE DO ZJEDNOCZENIA. [The Polish Workers' Party and the Polish Socialist Party on their way to unification in Cracow voivodship]. *Z Pola Walki [Poland] 1975 18(71): 53-78.* Discusses the process of attaining organizational unity of the working class in Cracow, which began with the organized working class movement in Galicia which had never produced any deep divisions within the working class. This explains some subsequent achievements of the working class movement in spite of the relatively small number of proletarians involved in political struggles in the interwar years, especially in 1923 and 1936, and the agreement between the Polish Communist Party (KPP) and the Polish Socialist Party (PPS) in 1936. The creation of one working class party after 1948 is discussed against this background, noting, in addition to the KPP's and PPS's, the development, role, and place of the Polish Workers' Party (PPR) in this process. Attention is paid to details of the final phase of unification—i.e., the achievement of ideological unity. The unification of the working class movement concluded with the creation of the Polish United Workers' Party (PZPR). J/S

1886. Kozik, Zenobiusz. PRZEMIANY POLITYCZNE W POLSCE W ŚWIETLE VII I VIII PLENUM KC PZPR W 1956 R [Political developments in Poland in light of the 7th and 8th plenums of the Central Committee of the Polish United Workers' Party]. *Z Pola Walki [Poland] 1980 23(2): 69-95.* Makes clear that the political line of the Communist Party in Poland from 1953 to 1957 aimed to rapidly improve social standards, deepen socialist democracy, and develop heavy industry at a moderated rate of investment.

1887. Kozłowski, Czesław. DZIAŁALNOŚĆ ZWIĄZKU WALKI MŁODYCH NA RZECZ JEDNOŚCI MŁODZIEŻY (DO POWSTANIA ZWIĄZKU MŁODZIEŻY POLSKIEJ) [The activities of Fighting Youth Union in support of unity of the youth (until the birth of Polish Youth Union)]. *Z Pola Walki [Poland] 1978 21(2): 3-45.* Describes the organization and activities during World War II of the Fighting Youth Union (ZWM) as the youth wing of the Polish Workers' Party and its leadership in its unification with Socialist, Peasant, and Democratic youth movements into the Polish Youth Union (ZMP) in 1947. J/S

1888. Kozłowski, Ryszard. ODBUDOWA ORGANIZACJI PPS W WOJ. POMORSKIM (BYDGOSKIM) STYCZEŃ-MAJ 1945 R [The reconstruction of the organization of the PPS in Pomerania, January-May 1945]. *Z Pola Walki [Poland] 1977 20(2): 163-182.* The Polish Socialist Party (PPS) had organizational traditions in Pomorze before 1939 and, in conspiratorial form, under German occupation. As soon as the region was liberated some of the PPS members began reestablishing the organization. The Bydgoszcz and the Torun organizations set up a joint committee in March 1945 after the arrival of A. Przyboj-Jarecki from the Central Executive Committee. The provincial committee had a well-developed structure by April 1945 and its work was facilitated by its own press. In various areas of the province, organizations were set up and the First Provincial Congress held early in May 1945 established a permanent character for the Party organization. 99 notes.
Z. K. L. Chojecki

1889. Kozłowski, Ryszard. ROZWÓJ ORGANIZACYJNY POLSKIEJ PARTII ROBOTNICZEJ W WOJ. POMORSKIM (1945-1948) [Organizational development in the Polish Workers' Party in the Pomerania region, 1945-48]. *Z Pola Walki [Poland] 1979 22(2): 173-194.* The Polish Workers' Party in western Pomerania became legal in January 1945. Since the region did not have a history of revolutionary movements, the main task for the Party was to establish their ideas among the people. An intensive recruitment system failed to provide the Party with high quality members but it secured a large rank and file. At the time of the merger with the Polish Socialist Party in 1948, workers constituted just over 50% of the Workers' Party membership. Based on documents in the Central Archives of the Central Committee of the Polish United Workers' Party in Warsaw; 30 notes. E. Jaworska

1890. Kozminski, Andrzej J. LES ENTREPRISES PILOTES DANS LE NOUVEAU SYSTÈME DE GESTION DE L'ECONOMIE POLONAISE [Pilot firms in the new system of Polish economic management]. *Rev. de l'Est [France] 1974 5(4): 31-41.* The political and social crisis in Poland in 1970 brought the authorities to an analysis of the causes and the formulation of a series of measures to improve the standard of living and accelerate economic development. Their concern was exemplified by the resolutions of the Sixth Congress of the Polish United Workers' Party. Goals were set for the five-year period 1970-75. By 1973, it was already evident that prospects had been surpassed. Such an achievement would have been impossible had profound changes not been made in the system of management. Three major factors had been responsible for earlier inefficiency: the incoherence of economic calculations effected at different levels of the economy; a system of salaries, promotions, and fringe benefits which did not encourage labor to act in the interest of society; and fear of innovation at technological and organizational levels. Using the systems analysis approach, a new series of managerial techniques were set in motion, using "pilot" enterprises as the framework. Salary has become the most important source of encouragement. Profit in the new system is the source of wage benefits for management and the improvement fund. Finally, the central plan is no longer a directive but an "indicator" for the pilot firm. This experiment is too new for final conclusions to be drawn but the initial results seem promising. J/S

1891. Krawczyński, Zbigniew. ROLA MISTRZA W ROZWOJU SPOŁECZNO GOSPODARCZYM [The role of the foreman in social and economic development]. *Nowe Drogi [Poland] 1976 (5): 26-36.* Discusses the elevated position of foremen in the Communist working class.

1892. Król, Edmund. LITERATURA O PZPR W ZBIORACH BIBLIOTEKI WSNS [Literature on the Polish United Workers' Party in the collections of the library of the Higher School of Social Studies]. *Z Pola Walki [Poland] 1978 21(4): 241-257.* A bibliography on the Polish United Workers' Party, including archival sources, published scholarly works, and doctoral theses covering a wide range of subjects relating to the Party.

1893. Krupa, Julian. RUCH ZAWODOWY W POLSCE WOBEC ZJEDNOCZENIA PARTII ROBOTNICZYCH [The Polish trade union movement vis-à-vis the unification of the workers' parties]. *Kwartalnik Hist. Ruchu Zawodowego [Poland] 1979 18(1): 41-68.* Lists resolutions and circulars of the Central Committee of the Polish trade unions issued in 1948-49, which proclaim support for the newly merged Polish United Workers' Party.

1894. Kuciński, Jerzy. FRONT NARODOWY W KONCEPCJI PZPR (1951-1956) [The concept of the National Front of the Polish United Workers' Party (PZPR), 1951-56]. *Studia Nauk Pol. [Poland] 1980 (3): 157-173.* The Central Committee of the Polish United Workers' Party (PZPR) declared the National Front during its sixth congress in 1951. In his main speech before the congress, Bolesław Bierut proclaimed the National Front and defined its purpose as the struggle for peace and the Six-Year Plan. PZPR concluded in 1956 that the National Front played a positive role in uniting millions of Party members as well as others. Based on PZPR Archives in Warsaw and secondary sources; 40 notes.
I. Lukes

1895. Kuciński, Jerzy. KSZTAŁTOWANIE SIĘ PZPR-OWSKIEJ KONCEPCJI RAD NARODOWYCH JAKO TERENOWYCH ORGANÓW JEDNOLITEJ WŁADZY PAŃSTWOWEJ [Formation of the Polish United Workers' Party's concept of National Councils as local organs of the unified state power]. *Przegląd Hist. [Poland] 1979 70(2): 201-213.* Having evaluated the role of the National Councils in the late 1940's, the Polish United Workers' Party (PZPR) decided to further strengthen their impact on public life in Poland. The constutition of 20 March 1950 brought about such a change. National Councils were to rely more dramatically on the masses (more attention was to be paid to social backgrounds of the councils' members) and become a truly Leninist instrument of power. Based on party documents, *Trybuna Ludu* (newspaper), and other secondary sources; 30 notes.

I. Lukes

1896. Kuciński, Jerzy. MYŚL PROGRAMOWA PZPR NA TEMAT NIEKTÓRYCH ZAGADNIEŃ DYKTATURY PROLETARIATU W POLSCE [Programmatic thought of the Polish United Workers' Party on some problems of the dictatorship of the proletariat in Poland]. *Z Pola Walki [Poland] 1979 22(4): 93-120.* Traces the changes in official Party political theory, 1948-70. The distinction between dictatorship of the proletariat and people's democracy was abandoned in 1948, and the doctrine of the intensification of the class struggle was dropped between 1953 and 1956. After the 20th Soviet Party Congress in 1956 a new view of the role of the Party in socialist democracy was developed, formulated by the third congress of the Polish United Workers' Party (PZPR) in 1959. The weakening of democratic institutions in the mid-1960's led to the reform adopted by the seventh plenum of the PZPR in December 1970. 48 notes. Russian and English summaries.

J/S

1897. Kuciński, Jerzy. SEJM W POGLĄDACH I PRAKTYCE POLITYCZNEJ PZPR (1948-1970) [Sejm in concept and political activities of Polish United Workers' Party (1948-70)]. *Z Pola Walki [Poland] 1978 21(1): 71-98.* Attempts to reconstruct the concept of the Polish United Workers' Party (PZPR) on the role of the Polish Parliament (Sejm). The party's general concepts of the political system were the continuation of the political thought of the Polish Workers' Party, formed according to doctrinal assumptions of socialist parliamentarism as formulated by classics of Marxism-Leninism and traditions of Polish parliamentarism. The author outlines characteristics of the PZPR's thought on constitutional and political roles and activities of the Sejm, 1948-70. During 1961-70 the PZPR stressed the Sejm's work on economic planning and budget, with no accent on the necessity of parliamentary discussion of other important fields of Polish life. J/S

1898. Kuciński, Jerzy. UKSZTAŁTOWANIE SIĘ KONCEPCJI PZPR DOTYCZĄCEJ POLSKIEGO SYSTEMU PARTYJNEGO (1948-1957) [The formation of the concept of the Polish United Workers' Party in reference to the Polish party system, 1948-57]. *Państwo i Prawo [Poland] 1979 34(10): 58-70.*

1899. Kulykivs'ki, M. D. BOROT'BA POL'S'KOI ROBITNYCHOI PARTII ZA ZMITSNENNIA DYKTATURY PROLETARIATU V 1947-1948 RR [The struggle of the Polish Workers' Party for the strengthening of the dictatorship of the proletariat, 1947-48]. *Ukrains'kyi Istorychnyi Zhurnal [USSR] 1969 (7): 95-98.* Traces the acceptance of the policy of dictatorship of the proletariat and one-party rule in Poland, 1947-48, and the gradual loss of power by the Polish Socialist Party.

1900. Kuznetsov, A. V. O TEORETICHESKIKH KONTSEPTSIIAKH ODNOGO POL'SKOGO POLITOLOGA [On the theoretical concepts of one Polish political scientist]. *Voprosy Filosofii [USSR] 1983 (12): 26-39.* Denounces the views of Polish sociologist and political scientist Jerzy Wiatr, who, on the eve of martial law imposed in Poland in 1981, called on the Polish United Workers' Party to renounce the monopoly of power.

1901. Laeuen, Harald. IM ZEICHEN DES STARKEN STAATES; VERWALTUNGSREFORM IN POLEN [Under the sign of the strong state; administrative reforms in Poland]. *Osteuropa [West Germany] 1974 24(6): 434-441.* The reforms of 1950 had robbed Polish provincial and local government of any standing or initiative vis-à-vis the national authorities. In 1973 this situation was formally modified and provincial governorships were reestablished, but Communist Party secretaries now became chairmen of the provincial councils. The change typifies a tendency to concentrate power by merging state and party offices; it makes the Communist Party visibly responsible for the daily functioning of government. 20 notes.

R. E. Weltsch

1902. LeBihan, Adrien. DEUX MANIERES DE TRAITER AVEC LE DIABLE: DU CARDINAL WYSZYNSKI AU CARDINAL GLEMP [Two ways to negotiate with the Devil: from Cardinal Wyszyński to Cardinal Glemp]. *Esprit [France] 1984 (7): 51-61.* Compares the policy of the Polish primate, Cardinal Stefan Wyszyński, toward the Communist authorities with the more submissive position of his successor, Cardinal Józef Glemp.

1903. Lebioda, Józef. POLITYKA KULTURALNA PZPR W LATACH 1949-1955 [Cultural policy of the Polish United Workers' Party, 1949-55]. *Z Pola Walki [Poland] 1978 21(4): 147-167.* Analyzes the PUWP's cultural policies, 1949-55, which aimed to increase society's awareness of socialist ideology in culture. 27 notes.

1904. Legurov, E. I. DEIATEL'NOST' POL'SKOI RABOCHEI PARTII PO PRIVLECHENIIU INTELLIGENTSII K KUL'TURNOMY STROITEL'STVU (1944-1948 GG.) [The activities of the Polish Workers' Party in drawing the intelligentsia into the cultural development of the country, 1944-48]. *Vestnik Leningradskogo U.: Seriia Istorii, Iazyka, i Literatury [USSR] 1978 (2): 35-40.*

1905. Leinwand, Artur. DZIAŁALNOŚĆ POLITYCZNA TADEUSZA SZTURM DE SZTERMA [The political career of Tadeusz Szturm de Szterm]. *Z Pola Walki [Poland] 1979 22(4): 143-161.* J. T. Szturm de Szterm joined the Polish Socialist Party (PPS) in 1921. During World War I, he had organized subversive actions against the Russians; after the war, he tried to organize socialist groups within the Polish army. When World War II broke out, he joined the right wing organization within the Polish Socialist Party called Freedom-Equality-Independence (PPS-WRN), and took part in the Warsaw Uprising. He was imprisoned in 1946 for three months and in 1947 for 10 years, but was released in 1952. At the trial, he became disillusioned with the new Polish system and spent the rest of his life writing. Based on eyewitness accounts, J. T. Szturm de Szterm's notes and writings, and documents in his private archives; 50 notes. E. Jaworska

1906. Lewis, Paul G. OBSTACLES TO THE ESTABLISHMENT OF POLITICAL LEGITIMACY IN COMMUNIST POLAND. *British J. of Pol. Sci. [Great Britain] 1982 12(2): 125-147.* Discusses the historical roots of the weakness of popular support for the Communist regime in Poland, 1945-81.

1907. Loiko, L. V. ROST RIADOV POL'SKOGO RABOCHEGO KLASSA V GODY SOTSIALISTICHESKOI INDUSTRIALIZATSII STRANY (1950-1960) [The growth of the Polish working class during the years of the socialist industrialization of the country, 1950-60]. *Sovetskoe Slavianovedenie [USSR] 1974 (5): 35-48.* The development of the national economy brought about a fundamental change in the economic structure of Poland during the execution of the Six-Year-Plan, 1950-55, and the Five-Year Plan, 1956-60. Industry, construction, and transportation dominated in the economy, their part in the national income rising from 42% in 1949 to 56% in 1960. Central to Poland's economic development in the 1950's was the socialist industrialization of the country. The author describes the rapid growth of the Polish working class during socialist industrialization, a process which occurred systematically and which the Polish United Workers Party supervised. Peasants, city and country youth, and housewives were the new working-class cadres. The nucleus of the working class remained the industrial workers. Primary sources; 2 tables, 69 notes. L. Kalinowski

1908. Łopatka, Adam. WZNAWIANIE DZIAŁALNOŚCI SAMORZĄDU ZAŁOGI PRZEDSIĘBIORSTWA PAŃSTWOWEGO [On resuming the activities of worker self-management in state enterprises]. *Państwo i Prawo [Poland] 1982 37(11): 5-18.* Argues for the Polish United Workers' Party view of worker self-management in state enterprises in 1982, legalized in the 25 October 1981 act. Based on press articles and materials from the 9th Party Congress; 17 notes.

1909. Lötzsch, Dietmut. DIE VERÄNDERUNGEN DES POLITISCHEN KRÄFTEVERHÄLTNISSES IN VOLKSPOLEN VOM JULI 1944 BIS JANUAR 1947 [The changes in the political power structure in the People's Republic of Poland from July 1944 to January 1947]. *Jahrbuch für Geschichte der Sozialistischen Länder Europas [East Germany] 1971 15(2): 9-36.* Describes the development of the political and social groups in Poland, especially the struggles between the Communist and Socialist parties.

1910. Łukaszewicz, Bohdan. STRATY OBOZU LEWICY REWOLUCYJNEJ W WOJEWÓDZTWIE OLSZTYŃSKIM W LATACH 1945-1950 [The losses of the revolutionary leftist camp in the Olsztyn voivodeship, 1945-50]. *Komunikaty Mazursko-Warmińskie [Poland] 1982 (1-2): 17-49.* Provides a statistical treatment of the 145 supporters of the Polish Workers' Party (Communist) killed by the opposition during the establishment of communism in Poland. The article includes available biographical sketches of those killed. Based on archival sources from Olsztyn, other primary and secondary sources; 5 tables, 26 notes. German summary. L. A. Krzyzak

1911. Maciszewski, Jarema. IDEE W. I. LENINA PODSTAWĄ WSPÓŁPRACY PZPR I KPZR: HISTORIA I WSPÓŁCZESNOŚĆ [The ideas of V. I. Lenin as the basis of cooperation between the Polish United Workers' Party and the Communist Party of the Soviet Union: history and the present]. *Nowe Drogi [Poland] 1980 (5): 82-89.* Analyzes Polish-Soviet relations since the signing of the Treaty of Friendship, Mutual Assistance, and Cooperation in 1945 in the light of Lenin's ideas.

1912. Madajczyk, Czesław. IDEOWE ZRÓDLA WSPÓŁCZESNOŚCI (W TRZYDZIESTĄ ROCZNICĘ DEKLARACJI PROGRAMOWEJ PPR: "O CO WALCZYMY?") [The ideological sources for today: the 30th anniversary of the Polish Workers Party's declaration *What are we fighting for?]. Nowe Drogi [Poland] 1973 (11): 88-97.* Reviews the ideological disputes which accompanied the creation in 1942 of the Polish Workers' Party the forerunner of the present ruling Polish United Workers' Party i.e., Communist Party.

1913. Malinowski, Henryk. PROBLEMY HISTORIOGRAFII KPP [Problems of the historiography of the Polish Communist Party (KPP)]. *Z Pola Walki [Poland] 1969 12(1): 85-110.* Outlines the research into the history of the Polish Communist Party from its founding in 1918, assesses the works on the subject published in Poland and abroad, and notes the gaps in research.

1914. Malykhin, A. A. POLITICHESKAIA BOR'BA V POL'SHE NAKANUNE I V PERIOD REFERENDUMA 1946 G. [The political struggle in Poland on the eve of and during the referendum of 1946]. *Vestnik Moskovskogo U., Seriia 9: Istoriia [USSR] 1972 27(2): 36-46.* The questions in the referendum were whether to abolish the Senate, to include agrarian reform and nationalization of the basic branches of the economy in the new constitution, and to strengthen the western border on the Baltic, Oder, and Niesse. All progressive parties, led by the Polish Workers' Party (PWP), the Democratic Party, and the Peasant Party approved all three measures. The reactionary forces sought to distinguish themselves from the PWP and its allies and show their strength by calling for a no vote on the first question. Massive propaganda and agitation work in the last weeks before the referendum guaranteed the passage of all three proposals, by 68, 77, and 91 percent respectively. Based on archival sources; 90 notes. G. E. Munro

1915. Marczak, Tadeusz. PRASA PSL WOBEC REFERENDUM [The press of the Polish Peasant Party on the referendum]. *Śląski Kwartalnik Hist. Sobótka [Poland] 1976 31(1): 27-57.* Analyzes the Peasant Party (PSL) press and speeches of PSL leaders and contrasts the stance of leading members of the PSL, led by Stanisław Mikołajczyk, with that of the Polish Workers' Party on the three points raised in the June 1946 referendum.

1916. Markiewicz, Władysław. STATE AND SOCIETY: THE BUILDING OF SOCIALISM IN PEOPLE'S POLAND. *Polish Western Affairs [Poland] 1974 15(1): 3-17.* In People's Poland the working class, represented by the Polish United Workers' Party (PUWP), has advanced to the ruling class. The farmers are the second largest of the social classes. Poland is the only socialist country which has not carried out large-scale collectivization of agriculture. Radical changes have also taken place in the third largest social class, the intelligentsia, which has increased sevenfold. But even though Polish society has completely changed its face during the 30 years of socialist rule, its image is not uniform. M. A. J. Swiecicka

1917. Masewicz, Warley. TREŚĆ I FUNKCJA NIEZWŁOCZNEGO ROZWIĄZANIA UMOWY O PRACĘ [The essence and function of the immediate dissolution of labor contracts]. *Państwo i Prawo [Poland] 1965 20(2): 253-263.* Studies the development of the law concerning the dissolution of labor contracts, from early legislation in France and Germany in the 19th century to the situation in Communist countries, especially Poland, in 1965.

1918. Mason, David S. MEMBERSHIP OF THE POLISH UNITED WORKERS' PARTY. *Polish Rev. 1982 27(3-4): 138-153.* The membership of workers and peasants in the Polish United Workers' Party (PUWP) declined over the years, threatening to isolate the Party from the masses. Total membership growth has been historically cyclical with periodic purges and resumption in growth. From 1977 an unprecedented number of workers were brought into the Party, but the total expansion in membership raises the question of whether the PUWP can maintain its elite role and élan. The internal erosion of the Party was one factor contributing to the disturbances of 1980. Based on Polish United Workers Party documents and secondary sources; 30 notes. W. F. Young

1919. Mason, David S. THE POLISH PARTY IN CRISIS, 1980-1982. *Slavic Rev. 1984 43(1): 30-45.* Examines the policies of the Polish United Workers' Party, 1980-82, its membership demographic data, public attitudes of party and non-party members to the party, and its effective role in Polish society. Based on Polish government statistical sources and press sources; 3 tables, 59 notes. R. B. Mendel

1920. Matejko, Alexander. LA MODERNISATION EN EUROPE DE L'EST: L'EXEMPLE POLONAIS [The Polish case of modernization]. *Rev. d'Études Comparatives Est-Ouest [France] 1977 8(2): 157-182.* Studies the process of modernization under Polish conditions of Soviet-style state socialism, especially the effect of the Polish gentry tradition, and the extent to which the policies of Edward Gierek (Party Chairman, 1970-) have met the needs and aspirations of Poland.

1921. Matejko, Alexander J. THE PHENOMENON OF SOLIDARITY: AN ATTEMPT OF ASSESSMENT. *Nationalities Papers 1983 11(1): 77-92.* The legal abolition of the Polish workers' union Solidarity in 1982 demonstrates once again that, under current circumstances, peaceful transformations of the Communist system have little chance for success. 31 notes. M. R. Yerburgh

1922. Matwiejewa, Helena J. WALKA PPR O JEDNOŚĆ DZIAŁANIA KLASY ROBOTNICZEJ W RUCHU ZAWODOWYM W LATACH 1944-1948 [The Polish Workers' Party's struggle for working-class unity in the labor movement, 1944-48]. *Kwartalnik Hist. Ruchu Zawodowego [Poland] 1978 (4): 62-85.* Describes how the Polish United Workers' Party first saw labor unions as nonpartisan, then used them to explain to workers the causes of the 1947 strikes, strengthening union ideology.

1923. Melichor, Václav. ČERVENCOVÝ MANIFEST A VZNIK LIDOVÉHO POLSKA [The July Manifesto and the creation of People's Poland]. *Slovanský Přehled [Czechoslovakia] 1979 65(4): 273-283.* After the liberation of Polish territory by the Soviet Army in World War II, the Polish Left, led by the Communists, took over the administration of the country. In July 1944 the Polish Committee of National Liberation, which became the provisional government, issued the July Manifesto to the Polish nation. The importance of the document lies in its concrete proposals for achieving peace and stability. The expulsion of the Germans, the conquest of the Western Territories, the suppression of reactionary forces, and future security of Poland (the training of a strong army and the support of the USSR) are outlined in detail. 32 notes.
B. Reinfeld

1924. Michnik, Adam. THE NEW EVOLUTIONISM. *Survey [Great Britain] 1976 22(3-4): 267-277.* Two schools entertaining concepts of evolution, revisionists and neopositivists, emerged from the Polish October of 1956. The revisionists entertained the possibility of evolution from within the Polish Communist Party and were anti-Russian and pro-Marxist. The neopositivists believed evolution would come from without and were pro-Russian and anti-Marxist. The events of 1968 marked the end of revisionism in Poland.
D. R. McDonald

1925. Misztal, Jan. DZIAŁALNOŚĆ PROPAGANDOWA PODZIEMIA PONIEMIECKIEGO NA ŚLĄSKU OPOLSKIM W LATACH 1945-1949 [Propaganda activity of the post-German underground in Opole Silesia, 1945-49]. *Kwartalnik Hist. [Poland] 1978 85(1): 51-64.* The German underground had its beginnings before the collapse of Germany, following the plans of General Reinhard Gehlen. It consisted of loose groups of saboteurs, provocateurs, spies, and propagandists, as well as armed bands. The major groups were: Werwolf, Freies Deutschland, Edelweiss-Piraten, and Freikorps-Oberschlesien. During 1945-49 the fate of Silesia seemed uncertain, and the prospect of the Communist domination of Poland, and therefore of Opole Silesia, was played up by the German anti-Polish agitators. Leaflets, posters, and rumors aimed at spreading disorientation and encouraging discord between the population and the occupying Soviet army were usual and commonly included appeals to the local population to declare its German nationality. This activity decreased with the transfers of the Germans, 1945-50, and with a strict control of national verification. 63 notes.
H. Heitzman-Wojcicka

1926. Moldoveanu, Milică. 30 DE ANI DE LA RENAŞTEREA POLONIEI [Thirty years since the rebirth of Poland]. *Anale de Istorie [Rumania] 1974 20(4): 122-127.* Recalls the heroic struggles for freedom of the Polish people while recounting the process of national liberation waged by the Polish Workers' Party and its creation, early in 1944, of a coalition of democratic forces. With the help of the Union of Polish Patriots, based in the USSR, and coordinating their actions with the strong military sweep of the Soviet Army against the Germans, the Polish liberation forces created the Polish Committee of National Liberation by 22 July and issued a manifesto of resistance to the people, along with a political program calling for a complete economic and social reorganization once independence had been regained. After the war the coalescence of the Polish Communists and Social Democrats produced the Polish United Workers' Party, which led the nation to the progress and prosperity of a new socialist order. 18 notes.
G. J. Bobango

1927. Monasterska, Teresa. ADAM LEŚKIEWICZ (1894-1983) [Adam Leśkiewicz (1894-1983)]. *Kwartalnik Historii Ruchu Zawodowego [Poland] 1984 23(1-2): 169-171.* An obituary of a Party and union activist from the 1920's to retirement in 1969.

1928. Mroczkowski, Władysław and Sierocki, Tadeusz, ed. PROTOKOŁY POSIEDZEŃ RADY GOSPODARCZEJ PPS (1945-1946) [Minutes of the meetings of the economic council of the Polish Socialist Party (PPS), 1945-46]. *Z Pola Walki [Poland] 1982 25(1-2): 227-262.* Reprints, with an introduction, the minutes of the meeting of the Economic Council of the Polish Socialist Party, an advisory body created after the 26th Congress of the party, whose aim was to ensure the influence of socialist ideas on the economic life of post-war Poland. The minutes include assessment of the IMF, of the American aid to Poland through UNNRA, of the state of Polish industry as a result of change of eastern frontier and of the problem of the peasant-worker alliance in Poland. Central Archives of the Polish United Workers Party's Central Committee; 58 notes.
M. Hernas

1929. Naumiuk, Jan. MIEJSCE I ROLA RUCHU ZAWODOWEGO W POLITYCZNEJ ORGANIZACJI SPOŁECZEŃSTWA POLSKIEGO W LATACH 1944-1949 [The place and role of the labor movement in the political organization of Polish society, 1944-49]. *Z Pola Walki [Poland] 1979 22(4): 181-200.* The labor movement was an important component in the formation of the Polish People's Republic. The Polish Workers' Party was more firmly in control of trade unions than the Polish Socialist Party was when the unions' congress in 1944 pledged its loyalty to the new state, and the merger of the two parties into the Polish United Workers' Party in 1948 strengthened the Leninist foundations of the labor movement. The 1949 congress expressed its support for the new Party and stressed the necessity to rid the unions of social-democratic and opportunistic elements. Based on documents at the Central Archives of the Central Committee of the Polish United Workers' Party and at the History Bureau of the Central Council of the Trade Unions in Warsaw, and on published Party and union documents; 3 tables, 23 notes.
E. Jaworska

1930. Naumiuk, Jan. POWSTANIE ODRODZONYCH ZWIĄZKÓW ZAWODOWYCH JAKO ETAP NA DRODZE DO JEDNOŚCI RUCHU ROBOTNICZEGO W POLSCE LUDOWEJ [Emergence of the new trade unions as an advance toward the unity of the workers' movement in the Polish People's Republic]. *Kwartalnik Hist. Ruchu Zawodowego [Poland] 1979 18(1): 28-40.* The emergence of centralized trade unions in postwar Poland reflected the overall process of consolidation between the Polish Workers' Party and the Socialists, united into one party in 1948.

1931. Nazarewicz, Ryszard. CZOŁOWA SIŁA WALKI O WYZWOLENIE NARODOWE I SPOŁECZNE [The leading force in the struggle for national and social liberation]. *Nowe Drogi [Poland] 1977 332(1): 53-69.* Commemorates the 35th anniversary of the formation of the Polish Workers' Party (PPR), stressing the leading role of the PPR in the national liberation movement during World War II, in abolishing the capitalist system, and in beginning socialist construction. Domestic factors and the PPR's own efforts primarily explain the party's success in winning political power. The author describes the role of the USSR as very important but still of secondary significance. 8 notes.
W. J. Lukaszewski

1932. Nazarewicz, Ryszard. OBLICZE POLSKI POWOJENNEJ W KONCEPCJACH OBOZÓW BURŻUAZYJNEGO I LUDOWO-REWOLUCYJNEGO [The position of postwar Poland in the conceptual camps of the bourgeoisie and the revolutionaries]. *Nowe Drogi [Poland] 1979 (3): 80-101.* Assesses the role of the Polish Communist Party in ensuring the transformation of Polish society after 1945.

1933. Nelson, Daniel N. CHARISMA, CONTROL, AND COERCION: THE DILEMMA OF COMMUNIST LEADERSHIP. *Comparative Politics 1984 17(1): 1-16.* Discusses the dilemma of Communist leadership, focusing on the events in Poland, 1980-81. The authority to lead and the power to rule do not coincide in Communist systems. Leadership authority is sought through a combination of the strategies of charisma, coercion, and control. In the absence of leadership authority, the power to rule will erode and policy implementation may not be possible without the use of force. Based on newspapers; table, 57 notes.
M. A. Kascus

1934. Nikolaev, K. O. SLAVNYI SYN POL'SKOGO NARODA [A glorious son of the Polish people]. *Voprosy Istorii KPSS [USSR] 1965 (2): 93-96.* A biography of Wladyslaw Gomulka (b. 1905) the leader of the Polish United Workers' Party after the 1956 uprising, on the occasion of his 60th birthday.

1935. Ol'shanski, P. N. BOEVOI AVANGARD POL'SKOGO RABOCHEGO KLASSA [The militant avant-garde of the Polish working class]. *Voprosy Istorii KPSS [USSR] 1963 (12): 76-79.* Traces the history of the Communist Party of Poland (KKP), 1906-38, and its successor the Polish Workers' Party (PPR), 1938-63, and considers the decision of the Comintern in 1938 to disband the KKP.

1936. Olszewski, Edward. ROZWÓJ I DZIALALNOŚĆ PPR I PPS NA RZESZOWSZCZYŹNIE W LATACH 1944-1948 [Development and activity of the Polish Workers' Party and Polish Socialist Party in Rzeszów region, 1944-48]. *Z Pola Walki [Poland] 1975 18(1): 57-101.* Discusses the development of the Polish Workers' Party (PPR), the Polish Socialist Party (PPS), the formation of a front of both parties during 1944-48 in Rzeszów province, the unification of the workers' movement, and the creation of the Polish United Workers Party (PZPR). Analyzes the situation, activity, and achievements of workers' movements during the Nazi occupation. Outlines the organizational development of the PPR and PPS, 1944-48. This process together with collaboration between the PPR and the PPS after November 1946 led to abolition of dissent in the Polish labor movement and to creation of the Marxism-Leninism of the Polish United Workers Party. J/S

1937. Orzechowski, Marian; with commentary by Góra, Władysław et al. WIZJA SPOŁECZEŃSTWA SOCJALISTYCZNEGO W TEORII I PRAKTYCE POLSKIEGO RUCHU ROBOTNICZEGO [Vision of the socialist society in the theory and practice of the Polish labor movement]. *Z Pola Walki [Poland] 1984 27(1-2): 7-20.* Surveys the emergence and growth of the Polish visions of the ideal socialist society, first generated by the nationally-oriented Polish Socialist Party (PPS) and the more internationalist Communist Party of Poland (KPP) in the 1930's, and elaborated in the post-1945 period by the theoreticians of the Polish United Workers Party. Party ideology, motivated by its own manifestos, grew out of touch with the working class socialist ideals, leading to serious ideological discrepancies of the 1980 crisis. Comments, pp. 115-147. Secondary sources. Russian and English summaries. M. Hernas

1938. Orzechowski, Marian. WSPÓLNOTA SOCJALISTYCZNA W MYŚLI POLITYCZNEJ PZPR (1949-1979) [The socialist community in political thought of the Polish United Workers' Party, 1949-79]. *Z Pola Walki [Poland] 1979 22(2): 103-127.* Development of community of Socialist countries gives rise to series of practical problems connected with bringing to perfection its action and theory. These problems are at focus of research and studies of numerous branches of science. The article takes up the most important research problems mostly from the viewpoint of political sciences and the history of political thought. J/S

1939. P. T. O TAJEMNICZEJ ŚMIERCI M. NOWOTKI I B. MOŁOJCA [Concerning the mysterious deaths of M. Nowotko and B. Mołojec]. *Zeszyty Hist. [France] 1982 (59): 210-220.* The killing during World War II of two Polish Communist leaders, first Marceli Nowotko and the subsequent apparent execution by comrades of Bolesław Mołojec, the man accused of Nowotko's murder, remains in controversy, with the account of Franciszek Jóźwiak appearing more likely than that of Władysław Gomułka. Note. L. A. Krzyzak

1940. Parsadanova, V. IZ ISTORII SOZDANIIA EDINOI PARTII POL'SKOGO RABOCHEGO KLASSA (SOGLASHENIE O EDINSTVE DEISTVII PPR I PPS NOIABR' 1946 G) [On the history of the creation of the Polish United Workers' Party: the agreement for united action between the PWP and the PSP, November 1946]. *Sovetskoe Slavianovedenie [USSR] 1974 (1): 14-27.* Describes the steps that led to the November 1946 political action coalition between the Polish Workers' Party (PWP) and the Polish Socialist Party (PSP). The new leadership of the PSP stopped the anti-Communist policies of the prewar PSP, accepted USSR's role as the leader of the working class, and decided that Poland could be rebuilt only on the basis of friendship with the Soviet Union. The 26th Party Congress (1945) of the PSP resolved to cooperate with the PWP in order to achieve unity in the workers' movement and maintain a united national front. The author describes the difficulties that both parties encountered, and were able to overcome in their effort to cooperate and finally, in 1947, to agree on the creation of a single Marxist-Leninist party of the Polish working class. 30 notes. L. Kalinowski

1941. Parsadanova, V. S. POLITICHESKAIA BORBA V KRESTIANSKOM DVIZHENII POLSHI (1944-1949 GG.) [Political struggle in the Polish peasant movement, 1944-49]. *Voprosy Istorii [USSR] 1972 (2): 43-58.* Analyzes the peasant movement associated with the struggle for the consolidation of people's government in Poland. The process of political polarization of the class forces in the Polish countryside and the experience of implementing the agrarian reform convinced the Polish peasants that the sociopolitical and cultural backwardness of the countryside could be liquidated only on the basis of socialism, in close alliance with the working class and under the leadership of its party. The political and organizational growth of the left wing of the peasant movement, its active participation in all undertakings initiated by people's government, and close cooperation with the working class helped to overcome the division within the peasant movement. Marching shoulder to shoulder with the Polish Workers' Party in the struggle for national liberation, for the abolition of feudal landownership and the monopolies, for the restoration of the country's war-ravaged economy, the Polish peasantry, joined the nationwide effort to build socialism. J

1942. Pawłowicz, Jerzy; with commentary by Ermolaeva, Rozaliia et al. INTERNACJONALISTYCZNE TREŚCI W POLSKIM RUCHU ROBOTNICZYM CZASU WOJNY I POLSKI LUDOWEJ [Internationalist contents in the Polish labor movement during World War II and in People's Poland]. *Z Pola Walki [Poland] 1984 27(1-2): 269-280.* Discusses the balance of nationalist and internationalist trends in the Polish Workers' Party at the end of World War II and their evolution in the party theory and practice when the Polish United Workers' Party was formed in 1948. Deformations of the Workers' Party ideology came to light in the 1948 merger as "rightist and nationalist" deviations, and the Polish United Workers' Party developed a manifesto which emphasized the internationalist orientation of the worker movement. In the subsequent decades, the personality cult led to the distortions of party ideology and, despite the declarations of the W. Gomułka and E. Gierek governments, Polish party practice of the 1960's and 1970's led to a decline in the spirit of international socialism. Comments, pp. 281-332. Based on secondary sources; 4 notes. Russian and English summaries. M. Hernas

1943. Pienkos, Donald. THE POLISH PARTY ELITE. *East Europe 1974 23(1): 19-24.* Between 1948 and 1972 party leaders in successive administrations became more typical of the masses of Poland in terms of class, ethnic origin, education, and age. As the perceived differences between the elite and the masses decreased, political stability increased. Based on Polish newspapers and secondary sources; 5 tables, 20 notes. E. W. Jennison, Jr.

1944. Pilch, Andrzej; with commentary by Hemmerling, Zygmunt et al. RUCH ZAWODOWY W POLSCE [Labor movement in Poland]. *Z Pola Walki [Poland] 1984 27(1-2): 185-195.* Views the development of the Polish trade union movement from its beginnings in the 1850's. Originally splintered under the influence of interparty conflicts, they became more articulate and committed to socialist ideals under the influence of the Russian revolutions of 1905 and 1917. Creation of the Polish United Workers Party in 1948 subordinated unions to the Party and state apparatus and alienated them from the working class. The new trade unions, replacing the anti socialist Solidarity of the 1980-82 period, attempted to regain the confidence of the workers by representing their genuine interests. Comments, pp. 215-256. Secondary sources. Russian and English summaries. M. Hernas

1945. Pleśniarski, Bolesław. W SPRAWIE BADAŃ NAD PROGRAMEM I DZIAŁALNOŚCIĄ OŚWIATOWOWYCHOWAWCZĄ PPR W OKRESIE OKUPACJI HITLEROWSKIEJ [On the research into the program and educational activities of the Polish Workers' Party (PPR) during Hitler's occupation]. *Z Pola Walki [Poland] 1969 12(1): 141-*

144. Outlines briefly books and articles on the educational and pedagogical activities of the Polish Workers' Party (PPR) during the German occupation 1939-45 and immediately after the war.

1946. Przygoński, Antoni. PRZEGLĄD BADAŃ NAD DZIEJAMI PPR W LATACH OKUPACJI HITLEROWSKIEJ [Review of the research into the history of the Polish Workers' Party during Hitler's occupation of Poland]. *Z Pola Walki [Poland] 1969 12(2): 57-85.* Discusses postwar studies of the activities of the Polish Workers' Party (PPR), founded in January 1942, and lists aspects of it that require further investigation.

1947. Przywuski, Stanisław. PPS W WOJEWÓDZTWIE GDAŃSKIM 1945-1948: POWSTANIE, ORGANIZACJA I FORMY DZIAŁANIA [The Polish Socialist Party (PPS) in Gdańsk Province, 1945-48: its formation, organization, and activities]. *Z Pola Walki [Poland] 1978 21(1): 155-178.* In the 1930's the socialist movement in Gdańsk province developed mainly in Gdynia. The Polish Party was reorganized gradually as the Germans withdrew, toward the end of World War II. In Gdańsk itself the Committee of the PPS was set up in April 1945. The movement then underwent two stages: March 1945-June 1947 when the membership reached approximately 35,000 and June 1947-December 1948 when membership declined. In December 1948 the Party merged with the Polish Workers' Party to form the Polish United Workers' Party (PZPR). 109 notes. Z. K. L. Chojecki

1948. Raina, Peter. *Stefan Kardynał Wyszyński Prymas Polski* [Cardinal Stefan Wyszyński, Polish primate]. Vol. 1. London: Poets' and Painters' Press, 1979. 578 pp.

1949. Ratyński, Władysław. ZWIĄZKI ZAWODOWE W POLSCE W LATACH SIEDEMDZIESIĄTYCH A LENINOWSKA KONCEPCJA RUCHU ZAWODOWEGO [Trade unions in Poland in the 1970's and the Leninist conception of the labor movement]. *Kwartalnik Hist. Ruchu Zawodowego [Poland] 1982 21(3-4): 48-63.* Criticizes the limitations imposed on the role of the unions in Polish socioeconomic life by the Polish United Workers Party in the 1970's, in conflict with Lenin's ideas about trade unions. Based on Polish United Workers Party decrees and other published documents, press articles, and Lenin's works; 28 notes.

1950. Rodionov, Pëtr A.; with commentary by Góra, Władysław et al. INTERNACJONALISTYCZNE TRADYCJE I SOJUSZ SIŁ REWOLUCYJNYCH ZSSR I POLSKI [Internationalist traditions and the union of revolutionary powers between the USSR and Poland]. *Z Pola Walki [Poland] 1984 27(1-2): 49-60.* Surveys the collaboration between Russian and Polish revolutionary party activists from the 1890's. Ludwik Waryński, the founder of the Proletariat Party, had friends among the Russian revolutionaries, while such activists as Felix Dzerzhinsky and Julian Marchlewski became personal friends of V. I. Lenin during his stay in Polish territory, 1912-14. The decay of internationalism within the Polish United Workers Party led to the internal disturbances of 1980. Comments, pp. 115-147. Secondary sources; 11 notes. Russian and English summaries. M. Hernas

1951. Rozenbaum, Wlodzimierz. THE ANTI-ZIONIST CAMPAIGN IN POLAND, JUNE-DECEMBER 1967. *Can. Slavonic Papers [Canada] 1978 20(2): 218-236.* A study of the anti-Zionist campaign as one facet of a larger power struggle within the Polish United Workers Party between General Mieczysław Moczar and Władysław Gomułka. That it was an integral part becomes clear when one sees the maneuverings of the Gomułka regime and the involvement of the secret police. There was, in addition, a growing concern about revisionism and the extent of popular sympathy for Israel and pride in Israel's victory in the Six-Day War regardless of Soviet backing of the Arabs. The campaign secured the removal of many Zionists and other undesirable elements from Party ranks, and, shortly, from their jobs. 51 notes. R. V. Ritter

1952. Rybicki, Marian. POZYCJA USTROJOWA RZĄDU W SYSTEMIE POLITYCZNYM PRL W LATACH 1970-1980 [The place of government in the political system of the Polish People's Republic in the 1970's]. *Państwo i Prawo [Poland] 1982 37(10): 39-51.* Assesses the effect of the 1976 decree declaring the leading role of the Polish United Workers Party on the constitutional status of the government in relation to the Party Central Committee, which led to the diminishing in the effective power of the Ministerial Council.

1953. Sakwa, George. THE POLISH 'OCTOBER': A REAPPRAISAL THROUGH HISTORIOGRAPHY. *Polish Rev. 1978 23(3): 62-78.* A critical examination of the historiography of the Polish events of 1956 and the turn from Stalinism to national Communism, 1954-59. The areas for further study are seen to be 1) the extent to which Polish society came to be autonomous of Communist Party control and 2) what constitute the main pluralist and social checks to any subsequent attempt to reconvert Poland to a totalitarian political system. 60 notes. R. V. Ritter

1954. Sakwa, George and Crouch, Martin. SEJM ELECTIONS IN COMMUNIST POLAND: AN OVERVIEW AND A REAPPRAISAL. *British J. of Pol. Sci. [Great Britain] 1978 8(4): 403-424.* Analyzes Polish elections, 1952-76, stressing their plebiscitary function and their value in legitimizing Communist Party policies.

1955. Sałkowski, Jan and Szaflik, Józef; with commentary by Hemmerling, Zygmunt et al. KLASA ROBOTNICZA I RUCH ROBOTNICZY W PROGRAMACH I DZIAŁALNOŚCI RUCHU LUDOWEGO [The working class and the labor movement in the manifestos and activities of the peasant movement]. *Z Pola Walki [Poland] 1984 27(1-2): 197-205.* Views the evolution of rapprochement between the Polish worker and peasant movements from the 1880's to 1947. With little political awareness among peasants, the cooperation between the two was not possible until the emergence after 1918 of the peasant parties and groupings, of which the Polish Peasant Party-Liberation became a close ally of the Polish Socialist Party (PPS) until the rift in 1925 over the land reform proposals. The coup of 1926 achieved progressive radicalization of the peasant parties, whose members frequently voiced communist sentiments, which brought the peasant movement into ideological agreement with the Polish Workers' Party in the 1945-47 period. Comments, pp. 215-256. Based on secondary sources. Russian and English summaries. M. Hernas

1956. Sanford, George. *Polish Communism in Crisis.* New York: St. Martin's, 1983. 249 pp.

1957. Sanford, George. THE POLISH COMMUNIST LEADERSHIP AND THE ONSET OF THE STATE OF WAR. *Soviet Studies [Great Britain] 1984 36(4): 494-512.* In response to the defiance of Solidarity and the accompanying waves of popular unrest, the Polish government declared a state of war on 13 December 1981. Among other things, the government created a Military Council of National Salvation and ordered the immediate arrest of Solidarity leadership. Solidarity's fundamental error was its failure to negotiate with the authorities prior to the latter's realization that compromise was impossible. 73 notes. M. R. Yerburgh

1958. Sanness, John. SMITTEFARE FRA POLEN? [Danger of contamination from Poland?]. *Internasjonal Politikk [Norway] 1980 (3B): 609-622.* After surveying the factors playing a role this autumn in Poland and Eastern Europe, assesses the danger of contamination from the Communist regimes' point of view. J/S

1959. Sawicki, Jan Kazimierz. KSZTAŁTOWANIE UDZIAŁU INTELIGENCJI W STRUKTURZE SPOŁECZNEJ PZPR W WOJEWÓDZTWIE GDAŃSKIM W LATACH 1949-1974 [The shaping of the participation of the intelligentsia in the social structures of the Polish United Workers' Party in the Gdańsk region in 1949-74]. *Zapiski Hist. [Poland] 1980 45(1): 67-92.* Examines the statistics of the number of white-collar workers in the party ranks in the Gdańsk region for the period 1949-74, assessing the success of the policy of recruitment among the intelligentsia.

1960. Sawicki, Jan Kazimierz. ROLA SZKOLNICTWA PARTYJNEGO W KSZTAŁCENIU KADR POLITYCZNYCH PZPR (1949-1971) [The role of the Party educational system in the training of political cadres of the Polish United Workers' Party, 1949-71]. *Z Pola Walki [Poland] 1978 21(4): 59-84.* Analyzes the role of the educational system in the training of political cadres of the PUWP, 1949-71.

1961. Seeber, Eva. ZUM KAMPF DER ARBEITERPARTEIEN UM EIN NEUES VERHÄLTNIS ZWISCHEN DEN VÖLKERN POLENS UND DER DDR IM SPIEGEL DER PRESSE DER POLNISCHEN ARBEITERPARTEI 1945 BIS 1950 [The struggle of the workers' parties for a new relationship between the peoples of Poland and the GDR as reflected in the press of the Polish Workers' Party, 1945-50]. *Jahrbuch für Geschichte [East Germany] 1974 12: 205-243.* At the end of the war, the Polish people looked at Germany and the Germans with hate and fear. The Socialist Unity Party (SED) of the German Democratic Republic (GDR) and the Polish Workers' Party in Poland, as leaders of their respective working classes, in the spirit of proletarian internationalism, took positive steps to overcome both German revanchism and Polish resentment. Germans were taught that Poles were not inferior, but had achieved much culturally and artistically. Poles were shown that they should distinguish between the Nazis and the German people. The resultant lessening of resentment can be followed in the press of the Polish Workers' Party. 115 notes.
J. C. Billigmeier

1962. Shelton, Anita K. A BIBLIOGRAPHIC ESSAY ON NATIONAL COMMUNISM AND THE POLISH OCTOBER. *East European Q. 1983 17(3): 283-298.* Describes the points of view in several recent publications on the Polish revolution of 1956. Those who say that the changes in Poland in 1956 represented a victory for national communism are correct. Actually the Polish changes were more significant because they were more lasting than the more radical changes wrought temporarily by the Hungarians in 1956. 23 notes, biblio. C. R. Lovin

1963. Sierocki, Tadeusz. LENINOWSKA TAKTYKA SOJUSZÓW I POROZUMIEŃ A POLITYKA PPR [The Leninist strategy of alliances and agreements and the policies of the Polish Workers' Party (PPR)]. *Z Pola Walki [Poland] 1970 13(1): 201-206.* Examines the creative adaptation of Leninist directives by the Polish Workers' Party with reference to the periods 1942-43 and 1945-46.

1964. Sierocki, Tadeusz. PPR-OWSKA KONCEPCJA JEDNOŚCI RUCHU ROBOTNICZEGO W LATACH 1942-1948 [The PPR's concept of the unity of the workers' movement, 1942-48]. *Z Pola Walki [Poland] 1976 19(4): 3-28.* Describes five stages in the realization of the unity of the workers' movement in Poland from the preparatory era during the war and occupation to the final unification of the Polish Workers' Party (PPR) and the Polish Socialist Party (PPS) in 1948.

1965. Siniawski, Karol. WSPOMNIENIA Z DZIAŁALNOŚCI W ZWIĄZKU ZAWODOWYM PRACOWNIKÓW DROGOWYCH W LATACH 1927-1950 [Recollections of activities in the Union of Road Workers between 1927 and 1950]. *Kwartalnik Hist. Ruchu Zawodowego [Poland] 1982 21(1-2): 75-94.* Recollections of a road worker, union activist, and Communist, about working conditions, political struggle, and union activities before and after World War II in Poland. 14 notes.

1966. Skshipek, A. ETAPY POLITIKO-EKONOMICHESKOGO RAZVITIIA POL'SKOI NARODNOI RESPUBLIKI (1944-1971 GG.) [The main stages in the political and economic development of the Polish People's Republic, 1944-71]. *Voprosy Istorii [USSR] 1977 (12): 20-33.* The author characterizes the principal phases in the socioeconomic and political development of People's Poland during the thirty years of its existence. This period is divided into four stages. In the first stage, 1944-49, the factors of fundamental significance were the conquest of power by the revolutionary forces of society, the consolidation of popular rule and the gradual enlistment of the toiling masses in the work of effecting socialist transformations. Those years were marked by the restoration of the war-ravaged economy and by the great displacements of population, especially in connection with the need to settle and develop the regained lands. In the second stage, 1949-56, the chief stress was laid on consummating the process of Poland's industrialization and introducing the principle of planning in the national economy. The formation of the Polish United Workers' Party as the only party of the working class in the country, as well as the drafting and adoption of the constitution, became a reflection of the changes being effected in Poland in those years. The third stage, 1956-64, was keynoted by the laying of the foundations of socialism along the whole front. Already in those years the advantages offered by the socialist countries' economic integration became clearly apparent. At the same time there gradually emerged the forms of government by the people, organically connected with the socialist system. In the fourth stage, from 1969 to the present, the quantitative changes have been increasingly developing into qualitative changes determining the process of building a developed socialist society in Poland.
J

1967. Słabek, Henryk. CZŁONKOWIE CHŁOPSKICH KÓŁ PPR I PPS NA ZIEMIACH ODZYSKANYCH (W ŚWIETLE MATERIAŁOW ANKIETOWYCH) [Members of peasant circles of the Polish Workers' Party and the Polish Socialist Party (in the light of questionnaire materials)]. *Z Pola Walki [Poland] 1972 15(58): 71-101.* Questionnaire information, gathered in the 1960's from 3500 peasants, showed that about 600 persons were members of the Polish Workers' Party, the Polish Socialist Party, the Peasants' Party, and the Polish Peasants' Party. Verifies that repatriates are much less influenced by political parties in general and by the Polish Workers' Party in particular. The lower participation of Communists in party organizations of repatriates was compensated by the influence of Socialists. Prior to 1948, almost half of the repatriates and emigrants from other parts of Poland who belonged to different parties were members of both workers' parties.
J/S

1968. Słabek, Henryk. PRZESŁANKI SOJUSZU ROBOTNICZO-CHŁOPSKIEGO (1948-1959) [The premises of the worker-peasant alliance; 1948-59]. *Z Pola Walki [Poland] 1981 23[i.e., 24](2): 89-108.* Surveys the socioeconomic situation accompanying Poland's collectivization campaign in the 1950's in the context of the Leninist concept of the worker-peasant alliance. Although collectivization failed as a mode of efficient agricultural production in Poland, the ideological union of the Polish United Workers' Party and United Peasants' Party has not suffered. Russian and English summaries. M. Hernas

1969. Słabek, Henryk. WPŁYWY PARTII ROBOTNICZYCH WŚRÓD CHŁOPÓW ZIEM DAWNYCH (1944-1948) [The influences of worker parties among the peasants of Polish Old Territories, 1944-48]. *Z Pola Walki [Poland] 1974 17(66): 39-55.* The peasants, especially the poorest, were not able to adapt their own values and opinions to the changing social situation. Unlike the new farmers (the result of land-reform), a substantial part of the peasantry (owners of farms who did not profit directly from the postwar reforms) undertook activities and assumed unfriendly attitudes towards the worker parties. The author presents the scope and structure of worker parties' influence—particularly the Polish Workers' Party—among the peasants, and analyzes the participation of worker party members in village People's Councils against the background of political differentiation with the peasantry. J

1970. Sokolewicz, Wojciech. CHANGES IN THE STRUCTURE AND FUNCTIONS OF THE POLISH *SEJM*. *East Central Europe 1975 2(1): 78-91.* A process of adapting legal forms to political and socioeconomic aims has produced structural changes in the Sejm in recent years. The Sixth Congress of the United Polish Workers' Party in 1971 democratized the decisionmaking process by upgrading the role of the Sejm and its committees. Enhancement of the political role of the Sejm has increased its level of participation in legislative affairs. The legal position of the deputies has improved, partly because of their closer relations with the administration since the 1971 reforms. Based on newspapers, government documents and secondary sources; 39 notes. R. J. Bazillion

1971. Spadolini, Giovanni. IL CASO DELLA POLONIA [The case of Poland]. *Nuova Antologia [Italy] 1973 519(2076): 455-460.* Discusses the prospect of a concordat between Pope Paul VI and the Polish government of Edward Gierek, reviewing recent relations between the two in comparison with relations between Italian Catholics and the Italian Communist Party.

1972. Staar, Richard F. THE COMMUNIZATION OF A CAPTIVE NATION: POLAND, 1944-1947. *Studies on the Soviet Union [West Germany] 1971 11(4): 310-320.* The Communist takeover of Poland followed a familiar East European pattern. Soviet troops entered, a coalition government was formed and given official sanction, and the opposition parties were gradually eliminated. Poland differed from the other East European states in being populous, Catholic, anti-Communist, and anti-Russian. A pretext of free elections could not be permitted. The Soviet execution of 14, 000 Polish officers, and the German slaughter of 200,000 persons in the ill-timed Warsaw uprising did much to eliminate effective opposition to Communist rule. Secondary sources; 33 notes.
V. L. Human

1973. Staar, Richard F. POLAND: THE PRICE OF STABILITY. *Current Hist. 1976 70(414): 101-106, 133-134.* Despite unanimous ratification of official policies at the 1975 seventh Party congress, Poland's economic conditions remain difficult and a higher standard of living depends on loans from the West, repayment of which adds to the economic problems of the future.

1974. Stame, Nicoletta. POLAND: THE LOGIC OF TWO ANTI-SYSTEMIC MOVEMENTS. *Rev. (Fernand Braudel Center) 1983 7(1): 15-52.* Focuses on two popular movements in postwar Poland. The first movement favored socialist changes and provided a leading role to the Communist Party. The second movement (Solidarity) opposed these changes and promoted the "self-organization of society." The military coup of the "Communists in Uniform" intervened to guarantee that the Party need not negotiate with society. 24 notes.
L. V. Eid

1975. Stembrowicz, Jerzy. Z PROBLEMATYKI GŁOWY PAŃSTW W POLSCE [The problems connected with the head of state in Poland]. *Kultura i Społeczeństwo [Poland] 1977 21(2): 42-68.* The Polish office of the first secretary corresponds to that of chairman of the Communist Party in other socialist countries and to that of heads of state elsewhere. The first secretary signs political documents and international agreements in the name of the Polish People's Republic with both socialist and capitalist countries.
M. Swiecicka-Ziemianek

1976. Swiatkowski, Lucja Urszula. "The Imported Communist Revolution and Civil War in Poland, 1944-47." Columbia U. 1981. 469 pp. *DAI 1982 42(12): 5238-A.* DA8211136

1977. Symonenko, O. R. VAZHLYVA PODIIA V ISTORII POL'S'KOHO NARODU: DO 35-RICHCHIA UTVORENNIA KRAIOVOI RADY NARODOVOI [An important event in the history of the Polish people: the 35th anniversary of the creation of the National Council]. *Ukrains'kyi Istorychnyi Zhurnal [USSR] 1978 (12): 114-116.* The formation of the National Council, December 1943-January 1944, in the apartment of Czesław Blicharski was important in renewing Poland's statehood and creating a new democratic Poland. Attempts by Polish Communists to form a broad front against Hitler were rejected by middle-class and reactionary Poles in London, and such initiatives were successful only when links were established with the USSR in 1944 and the National Council was able to unite all democratic forces in Poland. After creating the preconditions for a new Polish state, the National Council transferred its functions to the Sejm in 1947. 13 notes.
V. Packer

1978. Syzdek, Bronisław. PPR—DECYDUJĄCA SIŁA JEDNOŚCI KLASY ROBOTNICZEJ [The Polish Workers' Party: the decisive force of the unity of the working class]. *Nowe Drogi [Poland] 1974 (2): 61-70.* Examines the emergence of the Communist Polish Workers' Party in 1942, and its unification with the Polish Socialist Party in December 1948 to form the Polish United Workers' Party, emphasizing the leading role of the former in this process.

1979. Syzdek, Bronislaw. PROGRAM BUDOWY LUDOWEJ POLSKI NA I ZJÉZDIE PPR W 1945 R [Program of People's Poland at the 1st Congress of the Polish Workers' Party in 1945]. *Z Pola Walki [Poland] 1980 23(4): 25-45.* Treats problems concerning the policy of the Polish Workers' Party (PPR) in the first years of People's Poland, discussed by the 1st Party Congress in December 1945.
J/S

1980. Syzdek, Bronisław. W TRZYDZIESTOLECIE I ZJAZDU PPR [The 30th anniversary of the first meeting of the Polish United Workers' Party]. *Nowe Drogi [Poland] 1975 (12): 81-89.* Summarizes the proceedings of the first conference of the Polish United Workers' Party in Warsaw in December 1945, the decisions of which formed the basis of the radical socialist transformation of Polish society, 1945-48.

1981. Syzdek, Bronisław. ZJEDNOCZENIE PPR I PPS—POWSTANIE PZPR (SPORY IDEOWE I ETAPY PRZYGOTOWAŃ) [Unification of the Polish Workers' Party (PPR) and Polish Socialist Party (PPS): the creation of the Polish United Workers' Party (PZPR)]. *Z Pola Walki [Poland] 1968 11(4): 93-120.* Accomplished in spite of some internal differences, the 1948 unification ended 50 years of division in the labor movement; the new party became the leading force in the development of a new Poland.

1982. Syzdek, Eleonora. O WANDZIE WASILEWSKIEJ [Wanda Wasilewska]. *Nowe Drogi [Poland] 1975 (7): 74-86.* Biography of Wasilewska, a writer and leading member of the left-wing Polish Socialist Party in Cracow and Warsaw in prewar Poland who did much between 1943 and 1946 to lay the foundations of Polish-Soviet cooperation.

1983. Szajkowski, Bogdan. REPORT ON THE SESSION ON POLAND AT THE 1981 ANNUAL CONFERENCE OF THE NATIONAL ASSOCIATION FOR SOVIET AND EAST EUROPEAN STUDIES IN GREAT BRITAIN. *Studies in Comparative Communism 1981 14(1): 94-98.* The rank-and-file members of Solidarity expect much of their leaders. The Catholic Church, in particular the Episcopate, whose power has grown recently, has used its influence over Solidarity in negotiations with the elite. The Communist Party itself changed after 1970. In 1972, members of the ruling elite were guaranteed financial security and some official position to accept scapegoat roles in a political crisis. In 1974, the election system to the Central Committee was changed, and as a result almost half of the members are members of the *apparat.* A third development was the Party's decision to overlook the use of public office for private gain. Now a movement has developed in the Party to allow formulation of different platforms within the Party. The future will see further economic crises and integration into the Soviet economy as a substitute for military intervention.
D. Balmuth

1984. Szczeblewski, Jan. WYBRANE PROBLEMY ROZWOJU ORGANIZACYJNEGO PZPR W OKRESIE MIĘDZY I A II JEJ ZJAZDEM [Problems of organizing the Polish United Workers' Party between the first two Party congresses]. *Z Pola Walki [Poland] 1968 11(4): 121-141.* Discusses the Party's revision of its Party register, its expulsion of undesirable members, its social composition, and the introduction of collective farms, 1949-54.

1985. Szlachcic, Waldemar and Tarnowska, Maria. AKTA ORGANIZACJI MŁODZIEŻOWYCH Z LAT 1945-1948 W ARCHIWUM KOMITETU WOJEWÓDZKIEGO POLSKIEJ ZJEDNOCZONEJ PARTII ROBOTNICZEJ W OLSZTYNIE [The records of youth organizations, 1945-48, in the archives of the provincial committee of the Polish United Workers Party in Olsztyn]. *Komunikaty Mazursko-Warmińskie [Poland] 1980 (2): 197-212.* Describes the state of conservation and the quality of the archives. The organizations concerned are the Union of Fighting Youth for Olsztyn province, the Masurian Union of Rural Youth, the Union of Democratic Youth, the Youth Organization of the Society of the

Workers University for the province, and the provincial committee of the Polish United Youth. Documents of political youth organizations in Olsztyn province in the period 1945-48.
M. A. Zurowski

1986. Szlachcic, Waldemar and Tarnowska, Maria. AKTA POLSKIEJ PARTII ROBOTNICZEJ W ZASOBIE AKTOWYM ARCHIWUM KOMITETU WOJEWÓDZKIEGO POLSKIEJ ZJEDNOCZONEJ PARTII ROBOTNICZEJ W OLSZTYNIE [Documents of the Workers' Party in the archival collection of the Provincial Committee of the Polish United Workers' Party in Olsztyn]. *Komunikaty Mazursko-Warmińskie [Poland] 1977 (3-4): 429-446.* Founded in 1956, this archival collection covers the years 1945-48 and contains records of the Provincial Committee and district committees of the Polish Workers' Party, the Polish Socialist Party, youth organizations, city and county committees, memoirs of 143 activists, photos, posters, and materials sent by the Central Committee of the Polish Workers' Party and other organizations. The collection is incomplete, but the most valuable documents concern provincial committees, plenary sessions, meetings of party activists, and monthly reports. 113 notes. R. Seitz

1987. Tang, Peter S. H. EXPERIMENTS IN COMMUNISM: POLAND, THE SOVIET UNION, AND CHINA—PART 1: THE POLISH EXPERIENCE. *Studies in Soviet Thought [Netherlands] 1983 26(4): 287-370.* Traces the development of Polish Communism from Rosa Luxemburg's early influence to the emergence of Solidarity. Based on governmental reports, newspaper accounts, and secondary sources; 295 notes. Article to be continued.
R. B. Mendel

1988. Taras, Ray. DEMOCRATIC CENTRALISM AND POLISH LOCAL GOVERNMENT REFORMS. *Public Administration [Great Britain] 1975 53(4): 403-426.* Analyzes the workings of the system of dual subordination—both to the central Communist Party and to the local government structure—in Poland, 1945-75.

1989. Topolski, Jerzy. CREATIVE PROCESSES OF THE FORMATION OF SOCIALIST SOCIETY IN POLAND (1944-1974). *Acta Poloniae Hist. [Poland] 1975 31: 5-32.* A sociological analysis of social changes in Poland under communism.
H. Heitzman-Wojcicka

1990. Tóth, Béla. A LENGYEL EGYESÜLT MUNKÁSPÁRT VI. KONGRESSZUSA UTÁN [After the 6th Congress of the Polish United Workers' Party]. *Társadalmi Szemle [Hungary] 1972 27(1): 41-46.* Examines the work of the 6th Congress of the Polish United Workers' Party, 1971.

1991. Unger, Leopold. THE PEOPLE VERSUS THE PARTY. *Wilson Q. 1983 7(2): 50-68.* Examines the isolation of the Polish Communist Party from Polish public opinion, emphasizing the Party's favorable view of the USSR and noting the Party's policies toward religion and the universities.

1992. Vaughan, Michalina. A MULTIDIMENSIONAL APPROACH TO CONTEMPORARY STRATIFICATION. *Survey [Great Britain] 1974 20(1): 62-74.* Prewar sociology failed because it offered only a dichotomous view of society—privileged and nonprivileged. This outlook neglected urban-rural differences, the weakness of the industrial sector, and the originality and prestige of the intelligentsia. The new Polish regime set out to undermine the old class structure and introduce a planned society. Now it must justify its resultant "inegalitarian classlessness." The new categories are skilled/unskilled and ruler/ruled. The prewar structure remains, and the new ruling class has been merely recruited to an ideologically acceptable criterion. 33 notes. R. B. Valliant

1993. Verblian, Andzhei. ISTORICHESKOE ZNACHENIE OB'EDINENIIA RABOCHEGO DVIZHENIIA DLIA STROITEL'STVA SOTSIALIZMA V POL'SHE [Historical significance of the unification of the workers' movement for the construction of socialism in Poland]. *Voprosy Istorii KPSS [USSR] 1979 (4): 63-76.* Surveys the history of the Polish Communist Party founded in 1918, the Polish Workers' Party organized in 1942, and its unification in 1948 with the Polish Socialist Party to form the Polish United Workers' Party, and the economic and foreign policies of this new Party and the government. Published documents; 12 notes.
L. E. Holmes

1994. Verblian, Andzhei. PORP: VEDUSHCHAIA SILA STROITEL'STVA SOTSIALIZMA V POL'SHE [PUWP (United Workers Party of Poland): the leading force for the construction of socialism in Poland]. *Voprosy Istorii KPSS [USSR] 1974 (7): 17-27.* Since 1944 the Polish United Workers Party, of which the Communist Party is the dominant element, has helped Poland achieve significant advances in industrial and agricultural production, education, science, culture, urbanization, political unity, and foreign policy. Based on Polish periodical literature; 5 notes. L. E. Holmes

1995. Walichnowski, Tadeusz. BOR'BA ZA USTANOVLENIE I UKREPLENIE NARODNOI VLASTI V POL'SHE [The struggle for the establishment and consolidation of people's power in Poland]. *Novaia i Noveishaia Istoriia [USSR] 1984 (5): 19-33.* Treats of Polish people's struggle, led by the Polish Workers' Party set up in 1942, for the liberation of the country from the fascist invaders and for carrying out initial popular-democratic reforms. Shows also the fierce struggle of the Western reactionary forces and internal counterrevolution against people's power, as well as consolidation and strengthening of the democratic forces of Polish society.
J

1996. Walichnowski, Tadeusz. ZU DEN BEWAFFNETEN AUSEINANDERSETZUNGEN IN POLEN IN DER ERSTEN ETAPPE DER VOLKSDEMOKRATISCHEN REVOLUTION (1944-1947) [Armed conflicts in Poland during the first stage of the socialist revolution, 1944-47]. *Jahrbuch für Geschichte der Sozialistischen Länder Europas [East Germany] 1975 19(1): 23-33.* The most reactionary factions of the London-based Polish government-in-exile, 1944-47, considered a civil war to be the only way of regaining power in Poland. This even included a military conflict with the USSR, as the so-called "Burza" plan shows. The execution of this plan attempted to demonstrate the exiled government's claim for the eastern Polish territories. Furthermore the refusal of the nationalist Polish *Armia Krajowa* to hand over their arms to the Polish Committee of National Liberation at Lublin after the end of the German occupation, led straight into an armed conflict between the reactionary and Communist forces. More than 30,000 Poles died in this civil war. 24 notes. S. Boehnke

1997. Ważniewski, Władysław. ROZWÓJ PZPR W WOJEWÓDZTWIE RZESZOWSKIM W LATACH 1949-1970 [The development of the Polish United Workers' Party in Rzeszów Province, 1949-70]. *Z Pola Walki [Poland] 1978 21(4): 169-185.* There was a general shift in Party membership from the peasantry to the urban proletariat and a slow but steady increase in the educational standards of Party cadres. The percentage of middle class members also grew, though to a lesser extent. 6 tables, 58 notes.
M. A. Zurowski

1998. Ważniewski, Władysław. VERÖFFENTLICHUNGEN ZUM 30. JAHRESTAG DER GRÜNDUNG DER POLNISCHEN ARBEITERPARTEI [Publications on the occasion of the 30th anniversary of the founding of the Polish Workers' Party]. *Beiträge zur Geschichte der Arbeiterbewegung [East Germany] 1973 15(4): 700-705.* Reviews new publications on the difficulties of the organization of the Polish Workers Party during the occupation (1941), the foreign policy and relations of the Party, and the development of the resistance movement. 29 notes. R. Wagnleitner

1999. Werblan, Andrzej. NIEKTÓRE PROBLEMY ROLI KLASY ROBOTNICZEJ I JEJ PARTII W BUDOWIE SOCJALISTYCZNEJ POLSKI [Some problems of the working class and the Communist Party's role in building a socialist Poland]. *Nowe Drogi [Poland] 1973 (7): 78-98.* Discusses the relationship between the working class and the Communist Party during the transition to socialism in Poland, 1945-73.

2000. Werblan, Andrzej. POLSKA LUDOWA—URZECZYWISTNIENIE CELÓW SPOŁECZNYCH I NARODOWYCH [People's Poland, fulfillment of social and national purposes]. *Z Pola Walki [Poland] 1979 22(4): 3-19.* Polish revolutionary socialist organizations always linked the objectives of national liberation and revolution, both realized in the unification of the workers' movement in the Polish United Workers' Party and the 1952 constitution. Russian and English summaries. J/S

2001. Werblan, Andrzej. PZPR: PRZEWODNIA SIŁA KLASY ROBOTNICZEJ I NARODU POLSKIEGO [The Polish United Workers' Party: the leading strength of the working class and the Polish nation]. *Nowe Drogi [Poland] 1979 (1): 47-64.* Reviews the social, political, economic, and ideological role of the Polish United Workers' Party in the development of Polish society since 1948 and affirms the ideological basis for its leading role.

2002. Weydenthal, Jan B. de. ACADEMIC DISSENT AS A CATALYST FOR POLITICAL CRISIS IN A COMMUNIST SYSTEM. *Polish R. 1974 19(1): 17-40.* Analyzes political development in Poland, 1956-70.

2003. Winczorek, Piotr. FUNKCJE STRONNICTW SOJUSZNICZYCH W SYSTEMIE POLITYCZNYM Z PERSPEKTYWY 30-LECIA PRL [The allied parties in the 30 years of the Polish People's Republic's political system]. *Państwo i Prawo [Poland] 1974 29(7): 67-77.* The United Peasants' Party and the Democratic Party have for 30 years been in close alliance with the leading force in the system—the Polish United Workers' Party. The author examines their functions by the methods of the school of functional analysis in sociology and systems analysis in political sciences. In 1945-49 they considered their main task to be a representation of interests of the strata which constitute their social basis—peasants and the intelligentsia, and the middle class. In 1949-56 both parties focused on political training of these strata. After 1956 these tasks were balanced by those of the representation of interests. Toward the end of the 1960's the balance was in favor of the latter task. J/S

2004. Wisniewski, Leszek. PODSTAWOWE PRAWA, WOLNOŚCI I OBOWIĄZKI OBYWATELI PRL NA TLE NOWYCH KONSTYTUCJI SOCJALISTYCZNYCH [Fundamental rights, liberties, and duties of Polish citizens against the background of socialist constitutions]. *Państwo i Prawo [Poland] 1977 32(12): 12-25.* Describes the present state of fundamental rights, liberties, and duties of Polish citizens after the latest amendments to the constitution of 10 February 1976 against the background of constitutional rights and duties of Communist countries which modified their constitutions between 1960 and 1977.

2005. Wójcik, Stanisław. NA 30-LECIE WYBORÓW W POLSCE [The 30th anniversary of the general election in Poland]. *Zeszyty Hist. [France] 1978 (43): 16-43.* Suggests that on the orders of Joseph Stalin, acts of terrorism were used by the Polish Workers' Party (PPR) to prevent the Polish People's Party (PSL) from gaining the expected majority in the general election in Poland in 1947.

2006. Wolański, Marian S. PROBLEM NIEMIECKI W POLSKIEJ MYŚLI POLITYCZNEJ W LATACH 1944-1948 [The German question in Polish political calculations, 1944-48]. *Śląski Kwartalnik Hist. Sobótka [Poland] 1975 30(1): 59-77.* The Polish Workers' Party and Polish Socialist Party during 1945-48 recognized the origins of German imperialism in its class structure and advocated demilitarization and unification of Germany. The Peasant and Labor parties, on the other hand, attributed the German danger to traditional German nationalism and advocated the permanent division of Germany. C. M. Nowak

2007. Wolański, Marian S. STANOWISKO POLSKICH UGRUPOWAŃ POLITYCZNYCH WOBEC UTWORZENIA DWU PAŃSTW NIEMIECKICH [The attitudes of Polish political groupings to the creation of two German states]. *Śląski Kwartalnik Hist. Sobótka [Poland] 1980 35(4): 587-605.* Views the reaction of the Polish Workers' Party, as well as the other official parties, the Democratic Party (SD) and the Peasant Party (SL), to the creation in 1949 of two German states, stressing their instant support for the left-wing parties in East Germany and condemnation of West Germany's revisionism.

2008. Żarnowski, Janusz; with commentary by Góra, Władysław et al. KLASA ROBOTNICZA A RUCH ROBOTNICZY [Working class and labor movement]. *Z Pola Walki [Poland] 1984 27(1-2): 21-34.* Assesses the role of intellectuals among working-class activists in the formation and development of the 20th-century Polish worker movement. Although the early worker parties, the Proletariat Party and the Social Democracy of the Kingdom of Poland and Lithuania (SDKPiL), were formed and led by members of the intelligentsia, working-class participation at all levels was increased by the 1905 and 1917 Russian revolutions. Between 1945 and the 1960's the Polish United Workers Party claimed many high-ranking activists and officials of proletarian origins, although a reversal of this trend occurred in the 1970's. The latter, creating a crisis of identification between class and movement, was one of the factors which contributed to the 1980 upheaval. Comments, pp. 115-147. Secondary sources; 10 notes. Russian and English summaries. M. Hernas

2009. Ziemski, Franciszek. RADY NARODOWE W WOJEWÓDZTWIE ŚLĄSKO-DĄBROWSKIM, 1944-47 [The national councils in the Silesian and Dąbrowa Górnicza voivodship, 1944-47]. *Kwartalnik Hist. [Poland] 1974 81(4): 818-840.* A detailed account of the transitional period in which the underground national councils created chiefly by the Polish Workers' Party (PPR) turned from clandestine activity against the Germans to a political and administrative role after the collapse of the occupation in Silesia. Discusses the organization of the councils and background in the area, especially the struggle of the PPR against the Peasant Party and the pro-capitalist elements in the population. Based on documentary materials from the voivodship and central archives; 6 tables, 62 notes. H. Heitzman-Wójcicka

2010. Ziviak, Yosef. MISMEKHEY SIN'A: SHLOSHA PIRSUMIM PNIM-MIFLAGTIYIM SHEL P.Z.P.R. [Documents of hatred: three internal party documents of the PZPR]. *Shvut [Israel] 1973 1: 145-156.* There were vast numbers of anti-Semitic publications in Poland following the Six-Day War. Not only were such tracts encouraged by the ruling party, but in April and December 1968 the Polish United Workers' Party (PZPR) issued three anti-Semitic tracts of its own for distribution among Party officials. The anti-Semitic policy also manifests itself in the education of members of the youth movement and of Party members. There was no change in Polish policy under the new leadership of the early 1970's. Based on the three tracts and secondary sources; 66 notes. M. Feingold

2011. —. FROM THE PRISONS OF POLAND: TWO ACTIVISTS TELL WHAT HAPPENED AFTER MARTIAL LAW. *Dissent 1983 30(1): 56-74.*

Moszcz, Gustaw. INTRODUCTION, *pp. 56-57.* The rank-and-file membership of the Polish United Workers' Party and the outlawed Solidarity union "concur in their views as to the most viable solution for Poland's political situation."

—. WITOLD'S STORY, *pp. 57-66.* Reminiscences of a Polish United Workers' Party secretary of his arrest and imprisonment after the December 1981 declaration of martial law in Poland.

—. HANNA'S STORY, *pp. 66-74.* A senior official in the Solidarity union's Warsaw branch recalls her arrest and imprisonment, 1981-82.

2012. —. THE KUBIAK REPORT. *Survey [Great Britain] 1982 26(3): 87-107.* The Kubiak Report, named after commission chairman Hieronim Kubiak, was written by the Party Commission appointed at the extraordinary Ninth Party Congress of Poland on 2 September 1981 to examine the causes of the recurring crises in Poland. The commission submitted its conclusions—that the fundamental reasons for the crises of 1956, 1979, and 1980 were the Party's methods of rule and not subversive actions by the West—to General Wojciech Jaruzelski's Politburo in July 1982. The Kubiak Report was a highly embarrassing document to the Jaruzelski regime and highlighted Jaruzelski's personal failures as a leader as well as the moral bankruptcy of his regime. Includes excerpts from the Kubiak Report. L. J. Klass

2013. —. PRZEMÓWIENIE TOW. WIESŁAWA NA PLENARNYM POSIEDZENIU KC PPR W DN. 3 CZERWCA 1948 ROKU [Comrade Wiesław's speech at a plenum of the Central Committee of the Polish Workers' Party, 3 June 1948]. *Zeszyty Hist. [France] 1975 (34): 54-71.* Approximate text of a speech delivered by Władysław Gomułka (using his resistance sobriquet "Wiesław") at a June 1948 Central Committee plenum on uniting the Polish Workers' Party and the Polish Socialist Party.

2014. —. SPRAWOZDANIE CKKP PZPR ZA OKRES OD VIII ZJAZDU DO IX NADZWYCZAJNEGO ZJAZDU PZPR [Report of the Central Commission of Party Control of the Polish United Workers' Party for the period from the 8th to the 9th Party Congress]. *Nowe Drogi [Poland] 1981 (8): 83-92.* A report to the Polish party congress of 1981 concerning expulsions from the party, prepared by the Central Commission of Party Control.

2015. —. SPRAWOZDANIE CKR PZPR ZA OKRES OD VIII ZJAZDU DO IX NADZWYCZAJNEGO ZJAZDU PZPR [Report of the Central Auditing Board of the Polish United Workers' Party for the period from the 8th to the 9th Party Congress]. *Nowe Drogi [Poland] 1981 (8): 93-101.* A report to the Polish party congress of 1981, presented by the Central Auditing Board, and discussing control systems ensuring proper use of funds, complaints received during the year, and results of its investigations.

2016. —. SPRAWOZDANIE KC PZPR ZA OKRES OD VIII ZJAZDU DO IX NADZWYCZAJNEGO ZJAZDU PZPR [Report of the Central Committee of the PWUP for the period from the 8th to the 9th Extraordinary Party Congress]. *Nowe Drogi [Poland] 1981 (8): 53-82.* The Central Committee report to the 9th Extraordinary Congress of the Polish United Workers' Party of 1981, giving an account of its political activities in relation to the directives of the 8th Congress.

2017. —. SPRAWOZDANIE Z POSIEDZENIA RADY GOSPODARCZEJ KC PPR OBRADUJĄCEJ W DNIACH 21 I 22 LIPCA 1946 R. W WARSZAWIE [A report on the meeting of the Economic Council of the Central Committee of the Polish Workers' Party, Warsaw, 21-22 July 1946]. *Z Pola Walki [Poland] 1981 24(3-4): 257-286.* A transcript of the main speech and the debate at a session of the Economic Council of the Polish United Workers' Party in 1946 on trade, prices, and the private sector in industry. The main speech was delivered by Hilary Minc, the Minister for Trade and Industry. Stefan Jędrychowski, the Minister for Foreign Trade and Fishery, argued for the abolition of the private sector. Władysław Mazur, a secretary in the Central Committee of the Party, argued for the continuation of the private sector. The discussion also involved Zygmunt Modzelewski, a deputy minister for foreign affairs. The first publication of a document held at the Central Archives of the Central Committee of the Polish United Workers' Party. Introductory comment by Władysław Mroczkowski and Tadeusz Sierocki; 28 notes. E. Jaworska

2018. —. WALKA IDEALOGICZNA PRZECIWKO ANTYKOMUNIZMOWI W DZIEDZINIE HISTORII RUCHU ROBOTNICZEGO I ZADANIA PARTYJNYCH CZASOPISM HISTORYCZNYCH [An ideological struggle against anticommunism in the field of history of the workers' movement and the tasks of Party historical periodicals]. *Z Pola Walki [Poland] 1974 68(4): 3-22.* The peaceful coexistence of countries of different social systems raises the importance of ideological struggle. The field of this struggle is also a science of history, especially the history of the workers' movement. The anticommunist centers publish many books and specialized periodicals aimed at falsifying the ideology of Marxism-Leninism, the history of the international worker and communist movement, the history of particular parties, and of socialist countries. Anticommunist trends are visible in bourgeois and rightist-social democratic historiography as well as in literature originated in extreme leftist and Maoist circles. The article is an analysis of general trends in anticommunist penetration in the field of the history of Polish and international workers' movement. Shortened from a paper presented by the *Z Pola Walki* editorial board to an international conference of Party historical periodicals, Warsaw on 9-11 April 1974. J

2019. —. WYJAŚNIENIE SEKRETARZA GENERALNEGO KC PPR WŁADYSŁAWA GOMUŁKI W ZWIĄZKU Z JEGO REFERATEM I PROJEKTEM REZOLUCJI BIURA POLITYCZNEGO [Explanation by Władysław Gomułka, Secretary General of the Central Committee of the Polish Workers' Party, regarding his report and a Politburo draft resolution]. *Zeszyty Hist. [France] 1975 (34): 71-85.* On 15 June 1948, Władysław Gomułka defended certain points he made in the report he delivered at the Polish Workers' Party plenum of 3 June 1948 following a letter on the report from the Polish Workers' Party Politburo.

Romania

2020. Abinov, M. V. 50 LET RUMYNSKOI KOMMUNISTICHESKOI PARTII [Fifty years of the Rumanian Communist Party]. *Voprosy Istorii KPSS [USSR] 1971 (7): 152-156.* Discusses the papers read at a scholarly conference at the Institute for Marxism-Leninism on 5 May 1971 dealing with the history of the Rumanian Communist Party.

2021. Alexsandrescu, Ion. RABOTNICHESKO-SELSKIIAT SUIUZ I NEGOVOTO RAZVITIE PREZ PERIODA 1944-1947 G [The worker-peasant alliance and its development, 1944-47]. *Izvestiia na Inst. po Istoriia na BKP [Bulgaria] 1972 27: 456-473.* This paper, given at a joint conference of Bulgarian and Rumanian party historians, held in Bucharest in November 1970, deals with relations between the Rumanian Communist Party and allied peasant parties, as well as the growth of the Party's influence in rural areas.

2022. Alexandrescu, Ion. CONCEPŢIA ŞI ACTIVITATEA P.C.R. ŞI A GUVERNULUI DEMOCRAT PRIVIND RELAŢIILE ECONOMICE EXTERNE ALE ROMÂNIEI (1945-1948) [The conception and activity of the PCR and the democratic government on Rumania's foreign economic relations, 1945-48]. *Anale de Istorie [Rumania] 1972 18(6): 96-107.* Analyzes the correctness and wisdom of the policies established by the Petru Groza regime and the National Conference of the Communist Party in October 1945, in bringing about Rumanian economic recovery after the devastation of World War II, a succession of bad harvest years, and strong efforts by foreign capitalists to dominate the nation's economy. The programs advocated by the National Liberals and the National Peasant Party would have subordinated Rumania to foreign financial interests, ignoring the fact that a nation must control its own economy. The author demonstrates the steady progress made in achieving a favorable balance of trade down to 1948, the growth of foreign commerce, and the expanding horizons of Rumania's trade relations. The era of the Sovroms is described as inadequate and nonequitable from the political and economic point of view, especially at a time when Rumania was formulating a new type of economic relations conceived as a factor in the defense and consolidation of the independence and sovereignty of the country. Table, 26 notes. G. J. Bobango

2023. Anrod, Werner. ZUM IDEOLOGISCHEN WANDEL IN DER POLITIK RUMÄNIENS [On ideological change in Rumanian politics]. *Zeitschrift für Politik [West Germany] 1973 20(4): 361-374.* Argues that the surprisingly independent diplomatic and economic policies of Rumania in the 1960's were not sudden changes, but logically followed long-range theoretical, ideological, and historical trends in Rumanian Communist development. Analyzes internal change in the Rumanian Communist Party and concomitant foreign economic policy changes. Rumania has not been willing to conform to Soviet economic plans inside the Comecon framework, but has tried to open world markets for international trade, especially with Asia. Describes how Rumania proceeds with

an independent economic policy while often using contradictory orthodox jargon. Based on Nicolae Ceausescu's writings and speeches, official journals, and on secondary works; 45 notes.
J. B. Street

2024. Antoniuk, D. I. VIDNYI POLITICHESKII I GOSUDARSTVENNYI DEIATEL' RUMYNII [An eminent politician and statesman from Romania]. *Voprosy Istorii KPSS [USSR] 1981 (11): 89-92.* In honor of the 80th anniversary of the birth of Gheorghe Gheorghiu-Dej, describes his working career from the age of 11, the development of his political ideas, his involvement in the Communist Party, his activity during World War II and efforts in the postwar years, and his work for friendship and coordination with the USSR. 24 notes.
L. Smith

2025. Ardeleanu, Ion. EVENIMENTI ISTORICE [Historical events]. *Magazin Istoric [Romania] 1982 16(12): 2-3, 29.* Recapitulates Nicolae Ceaușescu's progress report to the Plenum of the Central Committee of the Romanian Communist Party, October 1982.

2026. Ardeleanu, Ion. MARXISM-LENINISMUL CREATOR, FUNDAMENTUL POLITICII P.C.R. ÎN LUPTA PENTRU FORMAREA CONȘTIINȚEI SOCIALISTE A OAMENILOR MUNCII DIN ROMÂNIA [Creative Marxism-Leninism, basis of the policy of the Rumanian Communist Party in the effort to shape the socialist consciousness of Rumanian workers]. *Anale de Istorie [Rumania] 1974 20(5): 40-45.* Shows the importance of the ideological program and norms of ethics and socialist equity adopted by the 1971 plenary session of the 10th congress of the Rumanian Communist Party. Rumanian society demands the formation of a new advanced moral superiority and social consciousness, dedicated to progress. The need remains for extirpating vestiges of parasitism and petty-bourgeois egoism remaining from the pre-1944 society, and convince all of the duty and honor of work and the subordination of narrow private interests to those of society in general. To this end the Party is dedicating strenuous efforts, the success of which are already apparent in the masses' broader ideological horizons. Secondary documents; 11 notes.
G. J. Bobango

2027. Ardeleanu, Ion. MUZEUL DE ISTORIE A PARTIDULUI COMUNIST, A MIȘCĂRII REVOLUȚIONARE ȘI DEMOCRATICE DIN ROMÂNIA LA A 25-A ANIVERSARE [The Museum of the History of the Communist Party, and of the revolutionary and democratic movement in Rumania, on its 25th anniversary]. *Anale de Istorie [Rumania] 1973 19(3): 199-204.* Celebrates 25 years of the Party Museum in Bucharest, 1948-73, reviewing its major themes, special projects, and varied displays, and the profound impressions left on countless visitors reminded of the struggles not only of the Communist Party, but of the entire Rumanian people. 7 notes.
G. J. Bobango

2028. Ardeleanu, Ion and Popișteanu, Cristian. THE RCP CONGRESSES—IMPORTANT MOMENTS IN THE ROMANIAN PEOPLE'S HISTORY. *Romania [Romania] 1979 4(4): 3-21.* Reviews the 1st through 12th Communist Party Congresses, showing the development of the workers' movement, 1893-1921, and the 1st Congress Nicolae Ceaușescu's leadership of the Communist Party has ushered in a "Golden Age" of Romanian history and has modernized Romania's social and economic goals.

2029. Ardeleanu, Ion. TINERETUL SUB FLAMURA DE LUPTĂ A PARTIDULUI COMUNIST ROMÂN [Youth under the Romanian Communist Party's banner of struggle]. *Magazin Istoric [Romania] 1982 16(3): 2-7, 17.* An address on the 60th anniversary of the founding of the Romanian Union of Communist Youth out of the struggle of the various socialist groups 1918-22 and its activities through 1948.

2030. Bacon, Walter M., Jr. ROMANIA: VALUE TRANSFORMATIONS IN THE MILITARY. *Studies in Comparative Communism 1978 11(3): 237-249.* By 1955 only 10% of the army cadres were officers who had been active before 1944. Although in theory the Rumanians are now in the period of "system consolidation," political education continues in part because of the present relationship with the Soviet Union. The adoption of a territorial defense strategy challenged the monopoly of the armed forces over weapons and so required the special subordination of the armed forces to the Communist Party. 39 notes.
D. Balmuth

2031. Bălteanu, B. EȘUAREA ÎNCERCĂRILOR MONARHIEI ȘI A REACȚIUNII INTERNE DE A RASTURNA REGIMUL DEMOCRAT-POPULAR (6 MARTIE 1945-IANUARIE 1946) [The failure of attempts by the monarchy and by internal reactionary forces to overturn the popular-democratic regime, 6 March 1945-January 1946]. *Studii: Rev. de Istorie [Rumania] 1957 10(6): 17-37.* Presents the London Council of Foreign Ministers, called to discuss the Rumanian question in December 1945, as a victory for the Soviet-backed Rumanian Communist Party and the Rumanian masses, and as a defeat for the British and American-backed bourgeoisie and monarchy. Great Britain and the United States recognized the Rumanian government in February 1946.

2032. Bărbulescu, C. MIȘCAREA REVOLUȚIONARĂ A TINERETULUI DIN ROMÂNIA IN PERIOADA AUGUST 1944-MARTIE 1949 [The revolutionary movement of Rumanian youth in the period August 1944-March 1949]. *Analele Inst. de Istorie a Partidului de pe Lingă C.C. al P.C.R. [Rumania] 1965 (5): 68-86.* The Union of Communist Youth (UTC), a Marxist-Leninist revolutionary organization, played an important role in educating and mobilizing workers, peasants, and students to fight against the oppression of the Ion Antonescu regime in Rumania. Under the leadership of the Rumanian Communist Party many young people gave their lives in the cause of their nation's independence and sovereignty. Following the successful armed uprising of August 1944, UTC members took part in the establishment of a democratic government, economic reform, and agrarian land redistribution, and continued to strive for the political, economic, and social progress of the Rumanian socialist state. Primary and secondary sources; 55 notes.
P. T. Herman

2033. Bărbulescu, C. PARTIDUL UNIC MUNCITORESC: EXPRESIE A DESĂVÎRȘIRII UNITĂAȚII POLITICE, IDEOLOGICE ȘI ORGANIZATORICE A CLASEI MUNCITOARE DIN ROMÂNIA [A single workers' party: expression of the development of the political, ideological, and organizational unity of the Rumanian working class]. *Analele Inst. de Studii Istorice și Social-Politice de pe Lîngă C.C. al P.C.R. [Rumania] 1968 14(1): 16-26.* Despite the founding of the Rumanian Communist Party in 1921, the nation's labor union movement lacked unity due to the continued existence of "reformist" social democratic groups. This split lasted until the creation of the United Workers' Front in April 1944, formed to bring about an anti-fascist insurrection. The climax of cooperation came at the 1948 Congress, which saw the merger of the Communist and the Social Democratic Party, producing the Rumanian Workers' Party, a union based on class principles, without political or ideological deals or compromises, but based on organic unity. Only after this could the working class fulfil its mission as the leading class of society in the building of a socialist system. 2 notes.
G. J. Bobango

2034. Barbulescu, Constantin. CONFERINȚA NAȚIONALĂ A P. C.R. DIN OCTOMBRIE 1945—EVENIMENT IMPORTANT ÎN DEZVOLTAREA PARTIDULUI ȘI A ȚĂRII [The National Conference of the Rumanian Communist Party in October 1945: important event in the development of the Party and the country]. *Anale de Istorie [Rumania] 1970 16(5): 80-92.* The National Party Conference formulated the basic goals for constructing the Rumanian socialist state. Reconstruction from the war, the development of industry, transportation, agriculture, education, and the revamping of life in city and village were the goals. Cooperation with the Plowman's Front and other socialist elements was then a necessity, as was internal consolidation and unification of the Party itself. Since 1945 class exploitation has disappeared in economic and political life. Secondary sources; 7 notes.
G. J. Bobango

2035. Beer, Klaus P. DIE INTERDEPENDENZ VON GESCHICHTSWISSENSCHAFT UND POLITIK IN RUMÄNIEN VON 1945 BIS 1980. DIE HISTORIOGRAPHIE ÜBER DEN ZEITRAUM 1918-1945 [The interdependence of the science of history and politics in Romania, 1945-80: historiography on the period 1918-45]. *Jahrbücher für Geschichte Osteuropas [West Germany] 1984 32(2): 241-274.* Until the mid-1950's Romanian historiography conformed to a Marxist-Leninist *Weltanschauung* and reflected a pro-Soviet interpretation. With Romania's political and economic emancipation from Moscow in 1964 came "de-Russification" of the Romanian Communist Party, the state and economic apparatus, intellectual life, and naturally also of historiography. Although the Romanian Party leadership did not change its ideological views, it raised the national factor to equal status with class struggle. Historiography of the late 1970's shows no regard for Soviet sensitivities and has rehabilitated the Romanian past and its leaders. The reversion to the national cultural values and traditions of the pre-Communist era is a politically directed process although it is erroneous to conclude that the Party has diverted from Marxist-Leninist fundamentalism or moved toward the acceptance of intellectual freedom. Based on a survey of Romanian historiography; 174 notes. S. A. Welisch

2036. Bolintineanu, Alexandru. INDEPENDENŢA ŞI SUVERANITATEA NAŢIONALĂ: COORDONATE MAJORE ACTUALE ALE POLITICII PARTIDULUI COMUNIST ROMÂN [Independence and national sovereignty: major parameters of current Romanian Communist Party policy]. *Rev. de Istorie [Romania] 1979 32(8): 1515-1529.* Examines the definition of independence and national sovereignty presented in Romanian Communist Party documents and the works of Party Secretary and Romanian President Nicolae Ceauşescu. Describes Party actions in accordance with these definitions in its foreign relations, including joint declarations with other countries and UN activities. 25 notes. French summary. R. O. Khan

2037. Bolintineanu, Alexandru. ROLUL PARTIDULUI ÎN ELABORAREA POLITICII EXTERNE A ROMÂNIEI SOCIALISTE [The Party's role in the elaboration of foreign policy in socialist Romania]. *Revista de Istorie [Romania] 1981 34(4): 667-680.* During its first 60 years, the Romanian Communist Party devoted special attention to foreign affairs. The principles according to which Romania should regulate its foreign relations were given by the Party as follows: Romania should pursue the affirmation of justice and peace in international affairs, should help guarantee the freedom of Europe and the rest of the world, and help create a new international economic and political system. Stresses the important contributions of the Romanian president, Nicolae Ceauşescu, in the establishment and realization of these guidelines. 34 notes. French summary. P. D. Herman

2038. Botoran, Constantin and Unc, Gheorghe. PARTIDUL COMUNIST ROMAN IN FRUNTEA ACŢIUNILOR PE SOLIDARITATE CU LUPTA REVOLUŢIONARA A POPORULUI CHINEZ [The Rumanian Communist Party in the vanguard of actions for solidarity with the Chinese people's revolutionary struggle]. *Anale de Istorie [Rumania] 1971 17(4): 51-65.* Assesses the support given by the Rumanian workers' movement to the Chinese people in their struggle for national and social emancipation and examines relations between the two countries' Communist Parties. Considers that, historically, Rumania has shown solidarity by supporting Chinese criticism of both Japanese militarism and the presence of imperialist powers in China. Based on contemporary periodicals; 46 notes. R. O. Khan/S

2039. Bozga, Vasile. SOOTNOSHENIE MEZHDU PROMYSHLENNOST'IU I SEL'SKIM KHOZIAISTVOM V SVETE DOKUMENTOV XII-GO S"EZDA RUMYNSKOI KOMMUNISTICHESKOI PARTII [Industry and agriculture in light of the decisions of the 12th Romanian Communist Party Congress]. *Rev. Roumaine des Sci. Sociales: Série des Sci. Econ. [Romania] 1982 26(1-2): 107-125.* Discusses the changes in the ratio between industry and agriculture in the socialist economy of Romania.

2040. Budrigă, V. ADUNAREA DE LA CLUJ DIN 13 MARTIE 1945 ŞI REUNIREA TRANSILVANIEI DE NORD CU ROMÂNIA [The 13 March 1945 meeting at Cluj and the reunification of northern Transylvania with Rumania]. *Analele U. Bucureşti: Seria Ştiinţe Sociale [Rumania] 1969 18(2): 115-126.* Examines the reunification of northern Transylvania and Rumania in March 1945 and the question of the annulment of the 1940 Vienna Dictate, which the Axis powers had imposed on Rumania, infringing the nation's right to territorial integrity. The 13 March 1945 meeting at Cluj formally restored the area that had been annexed from Rumania: this victorious act was the result of the struggle of the Rumanian people under the direction of the Rumanian Communist Party to resist the fascist yoke. The reintegration of the area contributed to its economic, cultural, and social development. The Vienna Dictate was nullified on 10 February 1947 at the peace treaty signed in Paris by Rumania and the Allied powers, when the border between Rumania and Hungary was redefined. Based on archives, newspapers, and secondary sources; 51 notes. P. T. Herman

2041. Burks, R. V. THE ROMANIAN NATIONAL DEVIATION: AN ACCOUNTING. *Continuity 1981 (2): 63-104.* Since the late 14th century, Eastern Europe has been ruled or dominated by external powers. Only a brief respite brought about by the collapse of the Central Powers after World War I interrupted this pattern, but after World War II the area became a focus for contention between the USSR and the United States. Throughout this sorry past, Eastern Europeans never regarded their foreign rulers as legitimate representatives of their interests. Romania deviated from most Eastern European powers by testing the dominant Soviet regime, and enjoying a measure of success. A variety of elements allowed this, including the Sino-Soviet rift. Native politicians were also able to counter Moscow's influence within the Romanian Communist Party. Close analysis reveals a thin thread of nationalism which allowed Romanians to quietly yet effectively defy the Soviet conception of the future of Eastern Europe. In the end the Romanian Communist Party evolved into a national movement. W. A. Wiegand

2042. Busuioc, Aneta. TRĂSĂTURI ALE ACTIVITĂŢII IDEOLOGICE A PARTIDULUI COMUNIST ROMÂN ÎN ETAPA ACTUALĂ [Characteristics of the ideological activity of the Rumanian Communist Party at the current stage]. *Anale de Istorie [Rumania] 1974 20(3): 78-90.* Shows the perfect dialectical unity between theory and practice as elaborated and applied by the Rumanian Communist Party and its dedicated, enlightened leadership. The development of a permanent political-ideological activity is an objective necessity in the entire period of constructing a multilaterally developed socialist state, since the building of socialism is an ongoing revolutionary process and must respond to the particular exigencies of place and time. Based on the works of Marx, Engels, and N. Ceauşescu; 22 notes. G. J. Bobango

2043. Ceauşescu, Ilie and Olteanu, Constantin. EVOLUŢIA FORŢELOR ARMATE ROMÂNE ÎN PROCESUL TRANFORMĂRILOR REVOLUŢIONAR-DEMOCRATICE [The evolution of the Rumanian armed forces during the revolutionary-democratic transformations]. *Anale de Istorie [Rumania] 1977 23(5): 29-42.* After the antifascist insurrection of 23 August 1944, the Rumanian Communist Party exerted every effort to democratize the Rumanian military, to place progressive elements in the cadres and officer corps, and to purge it of reactionary bourgeois forces. The goal was to establish "an organic, indestructible connection between the army and the people." A series of measures produced a new military organization, a complete program of reeducation, the right to vote for members of the army for the first time, and aimed at the creation of a new "citizen-soldier" and a system of territorial mobilization able to respond to any threat to the nation's independence. In the 1946 elections, the military gave 90% of its vote to the Democratic Parties Bloc, showing clearly its new progressive and democratic orientation. Thus the army became a vital component in the ensemble of forces acting for the realization of the vital aspirations of the masses. Based on Communist Party archives, *Scînteia,* military dossiers, and army journals; 33 notes. G. J. Bobango

2044. Ceauşescu, Nicolae. CUVÎNTAREA TOVARĂŞULUI NICOLAE CEAUŞESCU LA ADUNAREA SOLEMNĂ CONSACRATĂ ANIVERSĂRII SEMICENTENARULUI UNIUNII TINERETULUI COMUNIST [The speech of comrade Nicolae Ceauşescu given at the solemn meeting dedicated to the 50th anniversary of the Union of Communist Youth]. *Anale de Istorie*

[Rumania] 1972 18(2): 3-13. Founded in 1922, the Union of Communist Youth was active in the struggle against fascism and many of its members died during World War II. Since then it has played an important part in the reconstruction of the economy and the building of a new society. It is the first organization to receive the Victoria Socialismului award. M. Daly

2045. Ceaușescu, Nicolae. EROIC DRUM DE LIPTE, JERTFE ȘI VICTORII [The heroic road of struggles, sacrifices, and victories]. *Magazin Istoric [Romania] 1979 13(11): 2-5.* Extracts from works of Nicolae Ceaușescu, arranged to form a continuous history of Communist Party successes in Romania from 1921 to 1981.

2046. Ceaușescu, Nicolae. 60 DE ANI DE SLUJIRE DEVOTATĂ A POPORULUI DE LUPTĂ PENTRU DREPTATE SOCIALĂ ȘI LIBERTATE NAȚIONALĂ, PENTRU CONSTRUIREA SOCIALISMULUI ȘI RIDICAREA BUNĂSTĂRII MASELOR, PENTRU INDEPENTA PATRIEI, COLABORARE INTERNAȚIONALĂ ȘI PACE [60 years of dedicated work for the people, of struggle for social justice and national freedom, for the building of the socialist society and raising the well-being of the masses, for Romania's independence, international collaboration and peace]. *Anale de Istorie [Romania] 1981 27(3): 3-35.* Summarizes the Romanian Communist Party's contribution to building up the country. 2 tables. J. P. H. Myers/S

2047. Ceterchi, Ion. CONCEPȚIA PARTIDULUI COMUNIST ROMÂN CU PRIVIRE LA ROLUL STATULUI SOCIALIST ÎN ÎNFĂPTUIREA SOCIETĂȚII SOCIALISTE MULTILATERAL DEZVOLTATE ȘI ÎNAINTARII ȚĂRII SPRE COMUNISM [The Romanian Communist Party's concept of the role of the socialist state in effecting a multilaterally developed socialist society and directing the country toward Communism]. *Anale de Istorie [Romania] 1981 27(4): 16-32.* Expounds contemporary Romanian Communist Party ideology concerning the role of the socialist state in bringing about a socialist society, drawing principally on the works of Nicolae Ceaușescu, president of the Romanian Socialist Republic and secretary-general of the Romanian Communist Party. Stresses the state's task of organizing the nation's socioeconomic activities and defending the nation's revolutionary achievements, independence, sovereignty, and territorial integrity. Outlines the role of the principal organs of the state and its activities on the international level. 10 notes. R. O. Khan

2048. Chiriță, Gr. CONTRIBUȚII LA CRONOLOGIA PRIMEI ETAPE A REVOLUȚIEI POPULARE DIN ROMÎNIA (23 AUGUST 1944-30 DECEMBRIE 1947) [Contributions to the chronology of the first stage of Rumania's popular revolution, 23 August 1944-30 December 1947]. *Studii: Rev. de Istorie [Rumania] 1959 12(4): 325-359.* A chronological survey of events in Rumania, 1944-47, stressing the activities of the Rumanian Communist Party.

2049. Ciobanu, Elena. MIHAIL GH. BUJOR (1881-1964) [Mihail Gh. Bujor, 1881-1964]. *Anale de Istorie [Rumania] 1971 17(2): 139-142.* Born in Iași to a family of civil servants, Mihail Bujor wanted to join the Social Democratic Party at the age of 16, but had to wait until he finished his high school education two years later. Between 1902 and 1917 he became known throughout Rumania as a publicist, propagandist, and organizer of the workers' movement, leader of the Socialist Union, and coeditor of *Viitorul social* [The Social Future]. During the October Revolution he wrote the newspaper *Lupta* [The Struggle] in Odessa and organized Rumanian revolutionary detachments in southern Russia. He knew V. I. Lenin and was a resistance leader against the Germans in the Ukraine. When Bujor returned to Rumania he was arrested and condemned to death, then to forced labor for life. Released after 14 years, often in solitary at Doftana prison, he was again imprisoned in 1937. His prison poems reveal his courage and devotion to the cause of the people and their freedom. Released after 1944, Bujor became a member of the Presidium of the Grand National Assembly, and was chosen to various honorary offices. G. J. Bobango

2050. Coman, Ion. SESIUNEA ȘTIINȚIFICĂ JUBILIARĂ A ACADEMIEI DE ÎNVĂȚĂMÎNT SOCIAL-POLITIC "ȘTEFAN GHEORGHIU" DE PE LÎNGĂ C.C. AL P.C.R. [The jubilee session of the Stefan Gheorghiu Academy of the Rumanian Communist Party]. *Anale de Istorie [Rumania] 1971 17(3): 240-241.* Comments on the presentations of the 50th anniversary of the founding of the Rumanian Communist Party, detailing the Party's instrumental role in organizing and leading the working class and building the edifice of the socialist state. Papers included Janeta Brill's, "The Socialist Movement in Our Country: Component Part of the International Workingclass Movement," Gheorghe Moldoveanu's "On the Ideological Activity of the P.C.R. from 1921 to 1924," and Ion Coman's, "Aspects of the Participation of the P. C.R. in the Political Life of the Country, 1921-1928," and many others given between 30 March and 28 April 1971. G. J. Bobango

2051. Constantinescu-Iași, Petre. SEMNIFICAȚIA ISTORICĂ A CREĂRII PARTIDULUI COMUNIST ROMÂN PENTRU DEZVOLTAREA SOCIETĂȚII IN PATRIA NOASTRĂ [The historical significance of the creation of the Rumanian Communist Party for the development of Rumanian society]. *Anale de Istorie [Rumania] 1971 17(1): 3-14.* Details the high points of the history of the Communist Party from its founding in 1921 to the 10th Party Congress (1970). G. J. Bobango

2052. Copoiu, Nicolae. OMUL ȘI MILITANTUI: GHEORGHE CRISTESCU [The man and the militant: Gheorghe Cristescu]. *Magazin Istoric [Romania] 1982 16(10): 18-19, 44.* Eulogizes Gheorghe Cristescu, first Secretary General of the Romanian Communist Party, who survived, aged 89, to attend the celebrations in 1971 of its first half century.

2053. Copoiu, Nicolae. SIXTY YEARS SINCE THE MAY 1921 CONGRESS: THE PLACE OF THE WORKING-CLASS PARTY IN ROMANIA'S MODERN HISTORY. *Rev. Roumaine d'Études Int. [Romania] 1981 15(3): 231-242.* The Romanian Social Democratic Workers' Party, founded in the late 19th century and later called the Socialist Party, became in May 1921 the Communist Party of Romania. During the interwar period its two main objectives were the restoration of the organizational, political and ideological unity of the working class and the fight against fascism. It was in the forefront of the events of August 1944, and the main actions of that time were carried out by Communists or under their guidance. This powerful political force, which has dominated the country's political scene since 1944, has grown on the very soil of the country. Its history is not distinct from the modern history of the country itself. 8 notes. J. V. Coutinho

2054. Covaci, Maria. EUFROSINA NICULESCU-MIZIL (1902-1954) [Eufrosina Niculescu-Mizil, 1902-54]. *Anale de Istorie [Rumania] 1971 17(1): 175-177.* Eufrosina Cotor, daughter of a poor peasant family in Neamț had a difficult childhood and left her village for Bucharest in 1918, seeking work unsuccessfully. By 1919 a member of the Socialist Youth Union, she was mobilizing strikes, writing articles demanding workers' rights, and calling on women to unite in the struggle against oppression. She led the transport workers during the 1920 general strike, and became a delegate to the 1921 founding congress of the Communist Party at age 19. Arrested and tried in the famous Dealul Spirei investigations, she spent months in prison. By 1922 she married the militant revolutionary Gh. Niculescu-Mizil and eventually raised six children. She took part in the Red Assistance effort against the fascist dictatorship and the liberation of 23 August 1944. G. J. Bobango

2055. Dan, Martian. RUMANIA'S YOUNG BUILDERS OF SOCIALISM. *World Marxist R. [Canada] 1973 16(2): 100-107.* The role of youth movements in the rise of communism in Rumania.

2056. Dima, Romus. MOMENTE ALE LUPTEI REVOLUȚIONARE A MASELOR POPULARE DIN OLTENIA ÎN PERIOADA AUGUST 1944-NOIEMBRIE 1946 [The revolutionary struggle of the workers in Oltenia, August 1944-November 1946]. *Anale de Istorie [Romania] 1981 27(3): 110-124.* Basing its

program on lines laid down by Nicolae Ceaușescu after the victory of 23 August 1944, the Communist Party of Oltenia, at a conference in Craiova in September, set about ridding the country of its political, social, and economic past. The work continued throughout 1945 until, with the fresh elections in November 1946, a definitive stage had been reached in the creation of the new state. Based mainly on the press and Romanian archival material; 50 notes.
J. P. H. Myers

2057. DuBois, Pierre. LA POLITIQUE ETRANGERE ROUMAINE DE 1944 A 1947 [Romanian foreign policy, 1944-47]. *Rev. d'Hist. Moderne et Contemporaine [France] 1982 29(July-Sept): 411-441.* From the overthrow of Ion Antonescu's (1882-1946) dictatorship in August 1944 to the abdication of King Michael in December 1947, Romanian foreign policy was circumscribed by the Soviet military presence and the gradual concentration of power into the hands of the pro-Soviet section of the Communist Party. Foreign Minister Gheorghe Tatarescu (1892-1957) was unpopular, distrusted by the Communists, and trapped in the division of the Balkans which placed Romania firmly in the Soviet orbit. Romania obtained the revisions of frontiers she wanted, but was not granted the status of cobelligerent, and Tatarescu got little help from the Americans or British. Good relations were established with other east European states, including Yugoslavia, but the replacement of Tatarescu by Ana Pauker in November 1947 meant that Romanian policy became firmly based on the idea of mutually hostile eastern and western blocs. 145 notes. D. J. Nicholls

2058. Dumitriu, Dumitru. AGRARIAN POLICY OF RUMANIAN CP. *World Marxist Rev. 1972 15(5): 43-50.* Discusses economic, trade, and technological aspects of the agricultural policy of the Communist Party in Rumania, 1966-70's.

2059. Emtsova, R. S. and Shcherbakov, Iu. N. O TRADITSIIAKH SOVMESTNOI BOR'BY POD ZNAMENEM PROLETARSKOGO INTERNATSIONALIZMA [The traditions of collaborative struggle under the banner of proletarian internationalism]. *Voprosy Istorii KPSS [USSR] 1971 (5): 68-81.* Surveys the close ties between Soviet and Rumanian Communists, 1917-70, confirming the international character of Soviet communism in the interest of world peace and security.

2060. Emtsova, R. S. 60-LET RUMYNSKOI KOMMUNISTICHESKOI PARTII [60 years of the Romanian Communist Party]. *Voprosy Istorii KPSS [USSR] 1981 (7): 144-148.* A meeting organized by the Union of Soviet Friendship Societies and the Soviet-Romanian Friendship Society took place on 6 May 1981 at the Central Committee of the Communist Party of the Soviet Union Institute of Marxism-Leninism in honor of the 60th anniversary of the foundation of the Romanian Communist Party. Participants included M. V. Zimianin, V. I. Konotop, G. A. Kiselev, P. A. Rodionov, and D. I. Antoniuk, and discussions were held on the history of the Romanian Communist Party, its beginnings, development, aims, and difficulties, its links with and assistance from the Communist Party of the Soviet Union, and its continued efforts toward the construction of socialism on a Marxist-Leninist basis. L. Smith

2061. Fătu, Mihai. POLITICA DE ALIANȚE A PARTIDULUI COMUNIST ROMÂN ÎN LUPTA PENTRU INSTAURAREA ȘI CONSOLIDAREA PUTERII DEMOCRAT-POPULARE (1944-1947) [The alliance policy of the Rumanian Communist Party in the struggle for establishing and strengthening the people's democratic power]. *Anale de Istorie [Rumania] 1973 19(5): 3-18.* Presents facts about the tactics of the Rumanian Communist Party on the question of political alliances during the period from the August 1944 antifascist victory to the December 1947 proclamation of the People's Republic.
Romanian Scientific Abstracts 11:423

2062. Fischer, Mary Ellen. THE ROMANIAN COMMUNIST PARTY AND ITS CENTRAL COMMITTEE: PATTERNS OF GROWTH AND CHANGE. *Southeastern Europe 1979 6(1): 1-28.* Analyzes the patterns of growth and change in the Romanian Communist Party since World War II with emphasis on the period since 1965. The Party has become the dominant political force, an indigenous Romanian party which includes national minorities in representative proportions. Therefore, present problems of recruitment and promotion result from the composition and structure of the entire Romanian population. Based on official publications of the Communist Party; 7 tables, 77 notes. J. M. Lauber

2063. Fischer-Galati, Stephen. THE COMMUNIST TAKEOVER OF RUMANIA: A FUNCTION OF SOVIET POWER. *Studies on the Soviet Union [West Germany] 1971 11(4): 281-291.* Installation of a Communist regime in Rumania was the work of the Red Army. The local Communists actually hindered the process. King Michael cut all ties with Germany in 1945 and declared the nation to be on the side of the Allies. A local Communist group formed a new government, making necessary a lengthy process of undermining the king and the native government and eventually replacing them with trusted Communists selected by Moscow. Secondary sources; 11 notes. V. L. Human

2064. Gahany, Anneli Ute. PERSONENKULT UND KULTPERSON [Personality cult and cult person]. *Osteuropa [West Germany] 1978 28(8): 714-718.* Since the beginning of the 1960's the cult which has grown around the Rumanian leader Nicolae Ceaușescu has been applied by the Rumanian Communists as a unifying instrument.

2065. Georgescu, Ion. IACOB SCHASCHEK (1894-1970) [Jacob Schaschek, 1894-1970]. *Anale de Istorie [Rumania] 1971 17(2): 146-149.* Jacob Schaschek, a tailor from Lugoj, joined the Social Democratic Party (PSD) in 1915, helped organize major strikes during 1919, and attempted to radicalize the PSD. A delegate to the 1921 congress which created the Rumanian Communist Party, he was arrested for the third time and imprisoned after the Dealul Spirei trials. By the end of the 1920's his work throughout Predeal and in the Banat brought him five more prison sentences, the last for his widespread proselytizing for the Workers-Peasants Bloc. He led the early 1930's strikes in Lugoj, stood out in the antifascist struggles by his work for the Patriotic Defenders, and lived to see the triumph of his cause in 1944. He was decorated with the Order of Tudor Vladimirescu in the Party's 45th anniversary.
G. J. Bobango

2066. Georgescu, Titu. IOAN GH. OLTEANU (1881-1968) [Joan Gh. Olteanu, 1881-1968]. *Anale de Istorie [Rumania] 1971 17(3): 197-199.* Born in a village near Brașov, Joan Gh. Olteanu became active in the "România muncitoare" [Rumanian Workers] in Bucharest by 1907, and for the rest of his life was active in the working-class movement, participating in major strikes and demonstrations and supporting the creation of the Communist Party of Rumania. Imprisoned after the Dealul Spirei trials for his participation in the 1920 general strike, he was freed in 1929 and continued his syndicalist activity. President of the "Solidarity" syndicate until 1933, leader in the Workers' Assistance and the Unitary Syndicate groups, antifascist organizer and speaker at countless mass meetings, Olteanu lived to see the victory of his ideals in 1944 and to be honored in his old age. G. J. Bobango

2067. Gheorghiu-Dej, Gheorghe. A XV-A ANIVERSARE A ELIBERĂRII ROMÎNIEI DE SUB JUGUL FASCIST [The 15th anniversary of Rumania's liberation from fascist oppression]. *Studii: Rev. de Istorie [Rumania] 1959 12(4): 5-20.* The text of a speech by Gheorghe Gheorghiu-Dej before the Great National Assembly, 22 August 1959, praising the achievements of socialist Rumania.

2068. Ghimeș, Gheorghe. P.C.R., CONTINUATOR AL TRADIȚIILOR REPUBLICANE, CONDUCĂTOR AL LUPTEI ANTIMONARHICE [The Rumanian Communist Party, champion of republican traditions and leader of the struggle against the monarchy]. *Anale de Istorie [Rumania] 1972 18(5): 26-36.* At its first congress in 1921, the Rumanian Communist Party (RCP) called for the abolition of the monarchy as part of its struggle against the bourgeois-landowner regime. During the unrest of 1923 the Party campaigned against King Ferdinand I and later King Carol II, blaming the latter for the violent suppression of workers in 1933. The Communist opposition grew with Carol II's intransigence, the territorial losses of August 1940, the fascist dictatorship of Ion Antonescu, and the entry of Rumania into World War II. After August 1944, the monarchy was temporarily retained, providing a degree of stability while the people consolidated their power. 25 notes. M. Daly

2069. Gilberg, Trond. CEAUŞESCUS "KLEINE KULTUR-REVOLUTION" IN RUMÄNIEN [Ceauşescu's "little cultural revolution" in Rumania]. *Osteuropa [West Germany] 1972 22(10): 717-728.* In Rumania, the requirements of rapid modernization often favor the technician over the party functionary. To counteract this tendency and reinforce his own leadership, Party Secretary Nicolae Ceauşescu in 1971 launched a campaign which revived the Communist Party's ideological control over education and industry. Far more limited in scope than the Chinese Cultural Revolution, Ceauşescu's "consciousness-raising" has apparently achieved its initial objective. 36 notes. R. E. Weltsch

2070. Gilberg, Trond. POLITICAL LEADERSHIP AT THE REGIONAL LEVEL IN ROMANIA: THE CASE OF THE JUDET PARTY, 1968-1973. *East European Q. 1975 9(1): 97-111.* Uses the appointment of party secretaries in new territorial units in 1968 to analyze the Rumanian party leaders. These appointees were Party line apparatchiki whose most common feature was their close association with party chief, Nicolae Ceausescu. Based on official Rumanian sources; 2 tables. C. R. Lovin

2071. Giugariu, Sandina. SIMPOZIUM, POSVIASHCHENNYI 60-LETNEI GODOVSHCHINE OBRAZOVANIIA RUMYNSKOI KOMMUNISTICHESKOI PARTII [Symposium honoring the 60th anniversary of the founding of the Romanian Communist Party]. *Rev. Roumaine d'Études Int. [Romania] 1981 15(5): 495-498.* Reports proceedings of this symposium sponsored by the Romanian Association of International Law and International Relations (ADIRI). The five papers dealt with Romanian political and economic achievements of the post-World War II era in the national and international arenas, especially the personal involvement and contributions of President Nicolae Ceauşescu. N. Frenkley

2072. Iacos, Ion and Mamina, Ion. SEMNIFICAŢIILE UNEI DEZBATERI: PROCESUL GREVIST ÎN ROMÂNIA [The results of a debate: the development of the strike movement in Rumania]. *Anale de Istorie [Rumania] 1971 17(4): 38-50.* Reports on a conference of members of a number of Rumanian historical and sociopolitical institutions, held by the *Anale de Istorie* in 1971. The delegates analyzed the relationship of the strike movement to the class struggle and its international sociopolitical significance. They considered the promotion of national and international workers' solidarity and the rejection of middle-class mysticism and individualism. They also stressed that the workers' movement had been stimulated by the foundation of the Rumanian Communist Party, and showed that there had been a greater discussion of the aims and methods of the strike movement since 1944. 2 notes. R. O. Khan

2073. Inoan, Mihai and Duţu, Alexandru. TRANSFORMAREA REVOLUŢIONARĂ A ARMATEI ROMÂNE ÎN ANII EDIFICĂRII NOII ORÎNDUIRI Î ŢARA NOASTRĂ [The revolutionary transformation of the Rumanian army during the construction of the new order in our country]. *Rev. de Istorie [Rumania] 1977 30(12): 2163-2183.* Traces the reorganization of the Rumanian army after World War II on the model of the Soviet Red Army and the works of V. I. Lenin, together with elements of Rumanian military tradition. The continuity of the army was maintained, but it was gradually transformed into a socialist army parallel to developments in government and according to the program of the Rumanian Communist Party. Table, 55 notes. R. O. Khan

2074. Ionescu, Vasile. CONTRIBUŢII PRIVIND CUNOAŞTEREA MUNCII ORGANIZAŢIILOR DE PARTID DIN JUDEŢELE BAIA, BOTOŞANI, CÎMPULUNG, DOROHOI, RĂDĂUŢI, SUCEAVA ÎN ANII 1944-1947 [Contributions on the work of Party organizations in Baia, Botoşani, Cimpulung, Dorohoi, Radauţi, and Suceava districts, 1944-47]. *Anale de Istorie [Rumania] 1975 21(5): 121-127.* Outlines the creation of local Communist Party networks in the principal factories, villages, rural districts, cultural and educational institutes of northern Moldavia. Before 1944 a District Party Committee for northern Moldavia supervised the six counties indicated, until individual *judeţe* (district) committees sprang up. Then the North Moldavian Regional Organization replaced the district mode, with its seat at Suceava. Lack of industry in this region meant small numbers of workingmen and thus peasants predominated in the local cells, many only partly proletarian in nature. Lax standards for membership were often applied, and difficulties encountered. Economic growth and the work of the United Workers' Front overcame these problems by 1947. The regional grouping was disbanded in favor of direct contact between county committees and the PCR Central Committee. Based on district archival sources; 47 notes. G. J. Bobango

2075. Ionescu, Vasile G. PARTIDUL SOCIAL-DEMOCRAT ŞI PROBLEMA UNITĂŢII DE ACŢIUNE A CLASEI MUNCITOARE ÎN ANII 1944-1948 [The Social Democratic Party and the problem of unity of action of the working class, 1944-48]. *Anale de Istorie [Rumania] 1973 19(3): 102-117.* Relates the internal struggle within the Rumanian Social Democratic Party (PSD) by the left-wing forces seeking to unite the PSD with the Communist Party. The result by 1947 was the Single Workingmen's Front, which contained a PSD purged of its right-wing, retrogressive elements. A critical test of who would control the PSD's evolution came with the syndical elections of 1946 and the question of whether candidates would be listed in common with the Communists and other democratic organizations represented in the Groza government. Constantin Titel-Petrescu's leadership of the opposition to political collaboration by the time of the PSD 18th Party Congress, which voted full participation henceforth in the Democratic Parties Bloc coalition, was thus unable to delay the historic necessity for a single working-class organization. Elements inimical to the interests of the workers and large masses were removed, and the old fratricidal struggle between Socialists and Communists ceased. Based on PCR archives and newspapers; 57 notes. G. J. Bobango

2076. Ioniţă, Elisabeta. DIN TRADIŢIILE MIŞCĂRII MUNCITOREŞTI ŞI ALE P.C.R. DE EDUCARE ŞI ORGANIZARE A CELOR MAI TINERE VLĂSTARE [The traditions of the labor movement and the PCR in educating and organizing their youth]. *Anale de Istorie [Rumania] 1974 20(2): 102-111.* Young people and youth organizations were instrumental in the struggles, growth, and success of the labor and Communist movement since 1909. The author recounts the dedicated participation of young people and the evolution of their associations, especially the Young Communists of the 1920's, the support of youth at the barricades during the strikes of 1933, the Red Scholar movement of the 1930's, and the manner in which Rumanian youth fought the military-fascist dictatorship, many of them arrested, imprisoned, even condemned to death. Today the Pioneers continue the heroic traditions of Rumanian youth. 39 notes. G. J. Bobango

2077. Ioniţă, Elisabeta et al. EXPOZIŢIA "MOMENTE DIN ISTORIA U.T.C." [The exhibition, Moments from the history of the Union of Communist Youth]. *Anale de Istorie [Rumania] 1972 18(3): 169-173.* To mark the 50th anniversary of the foundation of the Union of Communist Youth, the Museum of the History of the Communist Party in Bucharest arranged an exhibition of documents, photographs, and other items concerning important events in the union's history and of the role of youth in socialist construction in Rumania. M. Daly

2078. Ioniţă, Elisabeta. TRADIŢII DE LUPTĂ EROICĂ ALE TINERETULUI SUB CONDUCEREA PARTIDULUI COMUNÍST ROMÂN. DOCUMENTE [Traditions of heroic struggle of the youth led by the Romanian Communist Party: documents]. *Revista de Istorie [Romania] 1982 35(4): 511-532.* In honor of the 60th anniversary of the Union of Communist Youth, the author presents a collection of documents that reflects the struggles and achievements of the revolutionary youth movement in Romania. Numerous documents describe Nicolae Ceauşescu's early activities as leader of the Union of Communist Youth and later as leader of the Romanian Communist Party. 6 notes. French summary. P. D. Herman

2079. Ioniţă, Gh. I. and Chiper, Ioan. MIŞCAREA REVOLUŢIONARĂ DIN ANII 1917-1923 ÎN ISTORIOGRAFIA ROMÂNEASCĂ DIN ULTIMUL DECENIU [The revolutionary struggle of 1917-23 in Rumanian historiography of the last decade]. *Analele U. Bucureşti: Istorie [Rumania] 1974 23(1): 203-209.* Rumanian historiography on the 1917-23 period has made significant progress in the last ten years. The authors list the most important books that have appeared. Particular effort has been made by Rumanian historians to collect important documents. These have been followed by studies exploring the newly organized materials. The 50th anniversary of the Rumanian Communist Party in 1971 was marked by the appearance of numerous works as was the 100th anniversary of Lenin's birth. Two other emphases of recent historiography on this era have been biographies of revolutionary militants and the study of local and regional revolutionary activities. The chief impressions given by these works concern the dynamism of the revolutionary movement in Rumania and the importance of the founding and leadership of the Rumanian Communist Party. 5 notes. P. E. Michelson

2080. Ioniţă, Gheorghe I. ACTIVITATEA TEORETICĂ DESFĂŞURATĂ DE P.C.R. ÎN PERIOADA INTERBELICĂ PENTRU APĂRAREA UNITĂŢII NAŢIONALE, A INDEPENDENŢEI ŞI SUVERANITĂŢII ŢĂRII [The PCR's theoretical activity in the interwar era for the defense of national unity and of the independence and sovereignty of the country]. *Anale de Istorie [Rumania] 1975 21(4): 53-73.* Surveys Communist theoretical writings between the wars, along with a chronological overview of Communist Party program documents, manifestos, and proclamations on the struggle against Hitlerism, the defense of the nation's independence, and the union of all progressive forces against the royalist dictatorship. Rumanian labor solidarity with the Czechoslovaks and other victims of fascist aggression is clearly evident. Based on party archives and other primary sources; 61 notes.
G. J. Bobango

2081. Ioniţă, Gheorghe I. CERCETAREA ISTORIEI CONTEMPORANE A ROMÂNIEI ÎN ULTIMUL SFERT DE VEAC [Contemporary historical research in Rumania, 1944-69]. *Anale de Istorie [Rumania] 1969 15(6): 38-51.* Stresses how postwar Rumanian historiography, under the aegis of the Communist Party has altered traditional historical writing by founding historical study on a Marxist-Leninist basis. While "uncritical" works continue to appear occasionally, the progress and output of the past 25 years is important, with its emphasis on Party history, labor and peasant movements, and the history of syndicalism. Lists major publications of the Party Institute of History, and the Institute of Historical, Social-Political Studies since 1965, while suggesting areas of research still relatively untapped. Elaborates the goals of Rumanian historical research as outlined by the 1969 10th Party Congress. 8 notes.
G. J. Bobango

2082. Ioniţa, Gheorghe I. CLASA MUNCITOARE: FORŢA SOCIALĂ FUNDAMENTALĂ A ISTORIEI CONTEMPORANEA ROMÂNIEI [The working class: the fundamental social force in Rumania's contemporary history]. *Anale de Istorie [Rumania] 1971 17(5): 3-24.* Surveys the political maturation and activities of the Rumanian working class from 1846 until the formation of the Communist Party in 1921, and examines the class conflict waged by the working and peasant classes, under Party leadership from 1921. Party activities, 1918-39, illustrate working class success against fascism and its defense of Rumanian territorial integrity, and sovereignty. The unification of antifascist forces, 1939-45, the establishment of a socialist state in 1944, and Rumania's social and industrial progress, is cited as proof of the working class's dominance, advanced achievement, and the Party's dutiful leadership. Based on contemporary Rumanian historiography, particularly works of President Nicolae Ceauşescu; 2 tables, notes.
R. O. Khan/S

2083. Ioniţă, Gheorghe I. LUCREŢIU PĂTRĂŞCANU—UN OM, O EPOCĂ, UN CUNOSCĂTOR ŞI UN IUBITOR DE ISTORIE [Lucreţiu Pătrăşcanu—a man, an era, an expert and lover of history]. *Revista de Istorie [Romania] 1980 33(11): 2145-2168.* Presents a general survey of the life, activity, and work of Communist and revolutionary fighter Lucreţiu Pătrăşcanu on the 80th anniversary of his birth. Particular attention is given to Pătrăşcanu's conception of history, his socioeconomic studies, and his activity as publicist and academician. The article lists and discusses Pătrăşcanu's works in his many fields of endeavor. 57 notes. French summary. T. Z. Herman

2084. Ioniţă, Gheorghe I. PARTIDUL COMUNIST ROMÂN, INIŢIATORUL, CONDUCATORUL SI DINAMIZATORUL PROCESULUI DE EDIFICARE A SOCIETĂŢII SOCIALISTE MULTILATERAL DEZVOLTATE [The Romanian Communist Party: initiator and leader of the building process of the socialist society multilaterally developed]. *Revista de Istorie [Romania] 1981 34(4): 639-665.* Examines the most important events of the Romanian Communist Party in the consolidation of a socialist society multilaterally developed as discussed during the 10th Congress of the Party in 1969 and the plenary sessions of the Central Committee in 1971. Presents the important contributions made by the Secretary of the Communist Party and President of Socialist Romania, Nicolae Ceauşescu, toward the accomplishment of the Party's historic tasks. Based on secondary sources; 30 notes. French summary.
P. D. Herman

2085. Ioniţă, Gheorghe I. ROLUL ŞTIINŢEI ISTORICE ÎN ACTIVITATEA POLITICO-IDEOLOGICĂ ŞI CULTURAL-EDUCATIVĂ A P.C.R. [The role of historical science in the Rumanian Communist Party's political-ideological and cultural-educational activity]. *Anale de Istorie [Rumania] 1975 21(1): 92-110.* Romanian Scientific Abstracts 12:1083

2086. Jowitt, Kenneth. AN ORGANIZATIONAL APPROACH TO THE STUDY OF POLITICAL CULTURE IN MARXIST-LENINIST SYSTEMS. *Am. Pol. Sci. Rev. 1974 68(3): 1171-1191.* Specifies an analytic approach to Marxist-Leninist sociopolitical systems that integrates regime and sociocultural units. This approach rests on a structural conception of political culture, a conception that stresses the informal adaptive quality of political culture, and that includes behavioral as well as attitudinal patterns. The author also analyzes the paradoxical character of development in Soviet-type systems; development that simultaneously reinforces and undermines traditional-peasant political cultures at the community, regime, and elite levels. Finally, this pattern of development is examined in the context of a single Soviet-type regime and society, the Rumanian. J

2087. Karpeshchenko, E. D. and Spivakovski, E. I. IZ ISTORII INTERNATSIONAL'NYKH SVIAZEI RUMYNSKOGO PROLETARIATA (OBZOR RUMYNSKOI ISTORIOGRAFII ZA 1968-1971 GG) [The international relations of the Rumanian proletariat: an examination of Rumanian historiography, 1968-71]. *Novaia i Noveishaia Istoriia [USSR] 1972 (4): 53-70.* The Rumanian socialist movement has a long and distinguished history as the work of Rumanian historians, 1968-71, illustrates. Rumanian socialists took part in the Paris Commune, 1871, and the First International. During the 1880's and 1890's the Rumanian socialist movement was beset by reformist errors, but the formation of the Rumanian Socialist Workers' Party in 1893 was a notable achievement. The movement fought against reformism and gained international prestige. In 1908 the Social Democratic Party of Rumania was formed and subsequently opposed involvement in World War I. Rumanian workers enthusiastically greeted the Russian Revolution, and hailed the "Declaration of the rights of the nations of Russia" as a model for the self-determination of nations. Rumanian socialists maintain close international links, and are guided by Marxist-Leninism. Based on Lenin's works, and Rumanian secondary sources; 105 notes. A. J. Evans/S

2088. King, Robert R. THE BLENDING OF PARTY AND STATE IN RUMANIA. *East European Q. 1979 12(4): 489-500.* Discusses in detail the Romanian ideological contribution to Marxism-Leninism, referred to as the blending of party and state. In general, this concept has been implemented by having officials hold similar offices in the Communist Party and in the government. Councils have also been combined so the same body serves a similar function for both the party and state. Some results not anticipated are already occurring; e.g., the expansion of the party to include more people. Published documents; 20 notes. C. R. Lovin

2089. Kushnir-Mikhailovich, Klara. MUZEI ISTORII RUMYNSKOI RABOCHEI PARTII [The Museum of the History of the Rumanian Workers' Party]. *Voprosy Istorii KPSS [USSR] 1962 (4): 230-236.* Describes the holdings of the Museum of the History of the Communist Party in Bucharest, founded in 1954.

2090. Lache, Ştefan. ALEGERILE DIN NOIEMBRE 1946 ŞI SEMNIFICAŢIA PRIMULUI PARLIAMENT DEMOCRATIC DIN ROMÂNIA [The elections of November 1946 and the significance of Rumania's first democratic parliament]. *Anale de Istorie [Rumania] 1971 17(5): 59-70.* Emphasizes the importance of the 1946 elections in establishing working-class democracy, and returning a parliament which closely reflected the character of the government set up on 6 March 1945. This reinforcement of the power of the revolutionary government permitted the popular expansion of Communist Party influence. The 1946 parliament passed anticapitalist economic measures and a People's Republic was declared on 30 December 1947 after the elimination of middle-class parliamentary representatives and the abolition of the monarchy. 52 notes. R. O. Khan/S

2091. Liveanu, Vasile. DIN LUPTA PARTIDULUI COMUNIST ROMÎN PENTRU UNITATEA CLASEI MUNCITOARE [The Rumanian Communist Party's struggle for working-class unity]. *Studii: Rev. de Istorie [Rumania] 1959 12(4): 71-115.* Describes the formation of the Rumanian Workers' Party resulting from the absorption by the Workers' Unique Front of left-wing Social Democrats under the influence of the Rumanian Communist Party.

2092. Liveanu, Vasile. PARTICULARITĂŢI ALE STRATEGIEI POLITICE A PARTIDULUI COMUNIST ROMÂN ÎN REVOLUŢIA POPULARĂ. REVENDICĂRILE IMEDIATE ŞI OBIECTIVUL FINAL [Specifics of the political strategy of the Rumanian Communist Party in the popular revolution: immediate aims and the final objective]. *Studii: Rev. de Istorie [Rumania] 1971 24(3): 581-607.* Touching the seldom-discussed need for separating short-term tactics from long-range strategy, shows how the Party subordinated its ultimate goals to eradicate all elements of fascism, 1944-48, reversing the Vienna Diktat, etc. Collaboration with bourgeois and leftist parties created, in the National Democratic Front, a political instrument for gaining control of state policy. Avoiding premature action was vital. Based on *Scînteia* and Party archives; 118 notes. G. J. Bobango

2093. Liveanu, Vasile. PARTIDUL COMUNIST ROMÂN ŞI MONARHIA (1944-1947) [The Rumanian Communist Party and the monarchy, 1944-47]. *Studii: Rev. de Istorie [Rumania] 1972 25(6): 1229-1255.* Analyzes the strategy and tactics of the Communist Party during the period of its collaboration with the monarchy, when it sought the king's support against the fascist Ion Antonescu (1882-1946). The Party promised at that time to keep the monarch's prerogatives intact as long as he did not oppose the work of democratic reorganization and social justice for which the Communist Party strove. Although hoping to come to power by constitutional means, the Petru Groza government nevertheless readied an armed force of 70,000 men in case the king refused to cooperate with the 6 March 1945 government alignment. It was obvious by the end of 1947 that due to Rumania's bourgeois-democratic transformations, the monarchy had lost its social and political base and thus had to be eliminated. Based on archives of the Rumanian Communist Party and contemporary issues of the *Jurnalul de dimineaţă*; 116 notes. Résumé in French. G. J. Bobango

2094. Liveanu, Vasile. ROLUL PARTIDULUI COMUNIST ROMÂN ÎN PREGĂTIREA INSURECŢIEI NATIONALE ANTIFASCISTE ARMATE (ÎN LUMINA IZVOARELOR PUBLICATE ÎN ANII 1944-1947) [The Rumanian Communist Party's role in preparing the antifascist armed national insurrection in light of sources published during 1944-47]. *Rev. de Istorie [Rumania] 1974 27(8): 1145-1165.* The information provided by the representatives of noncommunist parties attests to the premier role played by the Rumanian Communist Party in preparing and launching the uprising (August 1944). Based on speeches, memorial articles by the leaders and militants of various political parties, information supplied to the press by participants, the transcripts of war crimes trials, etc. Romanian Scientific Abstracts 12:409

2095. Matichescu, Olimpiu. TOVARĂŞA ELENA CEAUŞESCU: EMINENTĂ PERSONALITATE A VIEŢII NOASTRE POLITICE ŞI ŞTIINŢIFICE [Comrade Elena Ceauşescu: an eminent personality in our political and scientific life]. *Rev. de Istorie [Romania] 1979 32(1): 11-20.* Laudatory biography of Elena Ceauşescu, wife of the current president of Romania, Nicolae Ceauşescu. Before World War II she led the committee responsible for the reorganization of the Union of Communist Youth in Romania. During the war she helped Communist and antifascist detainees to keep contact with the resistance and revolutionary movement. For her devotion to the Communist cause she received rapid promotion in the Party during the 1970's. She has assisted her husband in his foreign policy, especially in his international peacekeeping efforts. A chemist, she has actively sought to stimulate Romania's scientific life. R. O. Khan

2096. Matichescu, Olimpiu and Georgescu, Elena. 80 DE ANI DE LA PRIMA SĂRBĂTOAREA A ZILEI DE 1 MAI (1890-1970) [The 80th anniversary of the first celebration of 1 May, 1890-1970]. *Anale de Istorie [Rumania] 1970 16(3): 56-71.* Traditionally May Day was the day when contracts were renewed and new working conditions negotiated in the United States. In many European centers demonstrations took place on 1 May 1890, and the Second International chose that date as the festival of the international proletariat. In 1905 in Rumania, workers were forbidden to demonstrate in the streets, though propaganda in favor of celebrating May Day increased with the creation of the Rumanian Communist Party in 1921. With the rise of fascism, increasingly repressive measures were taken against the celebration of May Day, but since 1945 it has been observed as a demonstration of national unity. 27 notes. M. Daly

2097. Mitran, Ion. ACTIVITATEA PARTIDULUI COMUNIST ROMÂN DUPĂ CEL DE-AL IX-LEA CONGRES—PERIOADA CEA MAI FERTILĂ ÎN REALIZĂRI [The activity of the Rumanian Communist Party (PCR) after the ninth congress: a period of the highest accomplishment]. *Anale de Istorie [Rumania] 1974 20(4): 57-64.* The adoption of a new constitution and the proclamation of the Socialist Republic of Rumania, along with the program of multilateral socialist development laid down in 1965 by the ninth congress of the PCR opened "a new period in the socialist development of the country." There followed not simple quantitative economic growth, but the building of an industrial establishment, unitary and complex, of a qualitatively new kind, along with an improvement in the quality of life. The author gives special attention to the leading role of the Party as it seeks to form new men through raising cultural horizons and the inculcation of advanced attitudes regarding the family, work, and society. G. J. Bobango

2098. Mocuta, Stefan. TOWARD SOCIAL HOMOGENEITY. *World Marxist Rev. [Canada] 1976 19(12): 51-59.* Considers the historical setting in Rumania in the Communist Party's creation since 1938 of the material, economic, and social conditions which are the prerequisites for social homogeneity and the classless society.

2099. Muşat, Mircea and Hurmuzache, Ştefan. CONCEPŢIA TOVARĂŞULUI NICOLAE CEAUŞESCU PRIVIND ISTORIA UNICĂ ŞI UNITARĂ A POPORULUI ROMÂN [Comrade Nicolae Ceauşescu's outlook on the unique and unitary history of the Romanian people]. *Revista Arhivelor [Romania] 1984 46(1): 7-19.* Nicolae Ceauşescu's views on the importance of history as the unifying factor in the emergence of Romania as a united state, after centuries of mass struggle, were given at the 12th Party Conference in June 1982.

2100. Muşat, Mircea. LA SIGNIFICATION DE LA RÉVOLUTION DE LIBÉRATION SOCIALE ET NATIONALE, ANTIFASCISTE ET ANTI-IMPÉRIALISTE D'AOÛT 1944 DANS L'ÉVOLUTION DE LA ROUMANIE CONTEMPORAINE [The significance of the revolution of social and national, antifascist and anti-imperialist liberation of August 1944 in the evolution of contemporary Romania]. *Rev. Roumaine d'Hist. [Romania] 1979 18(3): 441-456.* The antifascist revolution of 23 August 1944 was the culminating point of decades of struggle by the Romanian proletariat led by the Communist Party. From the uprising of the railroad and petroleum workers in 1933, to the pact of Ţebea which coalesced the major progressive political and economic forces of the country in 1935, to the vast antifascist demonstrations of 1 May 1939, the working class aimed to eliminate the dictatorial, fascist-oriented conservative-bourgeois regime. Current economic data clearly shows the progress made since the triumph of socialism.
G. J. Bobango

2101. Muşat, Mircea T. MOMENTE DE MARE SEMNIFICAŢIE ISTORICĂ ALE LUPTEI REVOLUŢIONARE ŞI PROGRESISTE DIN ROMÂNIA [Moments of great historic significance in the revolutionary and progressive struggle in Rumania]. *Anale de Istorie [Rumania] 1973 19(1): 65-78.* Recalls three significant events in the history of the Rumanian working class struggle against exploitation, fascism, and fractionist elements within the Communist Party. Focuses on the railwaymen's and petroleum workers' strikes of 1933 and the Griviţa confrontation. At the same time, the Plowman's Front was being launched in Hunedoara, stimulated by the heroic action of the urban workers, who were soon collaborating with other groups in a common antifascist platform centered on the 1935 Ţebea Accord with the Madosz. Reviews the struggle of the Rumanian Communist Party for the unity of all progressive forces, culminating in the creation of the United Workers Front by 1944 and the forging of a single political party of the working class in February 1948. These events help demonstrate that "one of the conditions for the successful construction of socialism is the creation of political, organizational, and ideological unity."
G. J. Bobango

2102. Muşat, Ştefan. CONSIDERAŢII PRIVIND DEZVOLTAREA ISTORIOGRAFIEI MIŞCĂRII MUNCITOREŞTI ŞI A P. C.R. DUPĂ 23 AUGUST 1944 [The development of the historiography of the labor movement and of the Rumanian Communist Party since 23 August 1944]. *Anale de Istorie [Rumania] 1972 18(3): 11-31.* Historiography has played an important part in the ideological work of the Rumanian Communist Party since 1944. Rumanian historians have studied the class struggle, the evolution of society as a continuous historical process, and the formation and development of the working class and the labor union movement. Focuses on the spread of Marxism in the 19th century, the economic and social data of the late 19th-early 20th centuries, and the foundation of the Rumanian Communist Party. 34 notes. Article to be continued.
M. Daly

2103. Neagu, Marin. DEMOCRAŢIA ŞI PARTIDELE POLITICE. PARTIDUL COMUNIST ROMÂN—PROMOTORUL DEZVOLTĂRII DEMOCRAŢIEI SOCIALISTE ÎN ROMÂNIA [Democracy and political parties: the Rumanian Communist Party—promoter of the development of socialist democracy in Rumania]. *Anale de Istorie [Rumania] 1971 17(1): 60-78.* Demonstrates, with the help of Raymond Aron's *Democratie et totalitarisme* (1965) the unscientific nature of bourgeois propaganda which insists that only multiparty regimes can be democratic. The nature of two-party systems in England and the United States is such that there is no essential difference between parties; to win votes, moreover, both adopt the politics of the center. Socialism and democracy are not contradictory, but reciprocal, conditions. Socialist democracy is a continually developing process, a gradual deepening and strengthening of the path to socialism. It differs from country to country, according to the peculiarities of each nation's history, economy, and level of socialist construction. Parties are only manifestations of the class struggle. Socialist democracy unites all classes in common goals, thus there is a need for only a single party, dedicated to the people's progress. Secondary sources, especially the works of Lenin and N. Ceauşescu; 22 notes. G. J. Bobango

2104. Nedeianu, T. PROCLAMAREA REPUBLICII POPULARE ROMÂNE [The proclamation of the Rumanian People's Republic]. *Analele U. Bucureşti: Istorie [Rumania] 1973 22(1): 79-86.* The proclamation of the Rumanian People's Republic in 1947 was one of the most important moments in the worker's struggle to transform Rumania. It was achieved in two stages: the first stage was the popular democratic revolution, 1944-47; the second stage was the socialist revolution of 1947. In both stages the leading force was the Rumanian Communist Party. Various machinations of the old line parties and the king were in the end thwarted by the rapid revolutionary, economic, and sociopolitical transformation of the country. With the ouster of the Gheorghe Tătărăşcu faction in November 1947, power passed completely into the hands of the people, the last step in the successful division and annihilation of the bourgeois and reactionary forces. Based on archives of the Rumanian Communist Party and the Arhivele Statului, Bucharest, and printed sources; 43 notes. P. E. Michelson

2105. Nichita, Paraschiva. LA ORA 0, MINUS 30 MINUTE [Zero minus 30]. *Magazin Istoric [Rumania] 1975 9(3): 6-9.* Describes events leading to the Rumanian Communist Party coming to power on 6 March 1945. J. M. McCarthy

2106. Nichiţelea, Pamfil. COORDONATE ALE POLITICII CULTURALE A PARTIDULUI COMUNIST ROMÂN ÎN PERIOADA REVOLUŢIEI ŞI CONSTRUCŢIEI SOCIALISTE [Coordinates of the Rumanian Communist Party's cultural policy in the period of the revolution and socialist construction]. *Anale de Istorie [Rumania] 1974 20(5): 46-57.* Surveys the philosophy and objectives whereby the Rumanian Communist Party leadership has gradually raised the ideological and political level of consciousness of the working classes through its cultural policies. The author reviews the progress made in all areas of state education, the victory over illiteracy, the reorganization of scientific and cultural institutions, the new organizational basis for the Rumanian Academy, and the high literacy and cultural goals projected by the 10th Party Congress, the National Conference of 1972, and the Central Committee's Plenary Session in 1973. Table, 16 notes.
G. J. Bobango

2107. Nicolae, Ionel; Nichiţelea, Pamfil; and Popescu, Al. I.. ROMÂNIA ÎN ANII REVOLUŢIEI ŞI CONSTRUCŢIEI SOCIALISTE [Rumania in the years of revolution and socialist construction]. *Studii: Rev. de Istorie [Rumania] 1972 25(6): 1271-1289.* Reviews events which laid the foundations for socialist construction, and recounts events and decisions until "the complete and definitive triumph of socialism in 1962" which the Communist Party took in meeting many new and difficult problems. Special attention is given to the post-1965 period, opened by the ninth Congress of the PCR, wherein "the rigorous scientific direction of the mechanisms of social life" were developed, alongside directives for the scientific elaboration of economic processes. A chronological treatment presents the most important stages in overall national development, 1966-70, climaxing with the National Party Conference of July 1972. Based on secondary reports and Party documents, including the writings of N. Ceauşescu; 25 notes. Résumé in French.
G. J. Bobango

2108. Olteanu, Constantin. MUTAŢII CALITATIVE INTERVENITE ÎN DEZVOLTARE PUTERII ARMATE ÎN PERIOADA DUPĂ CONGRESUL AL IX-LEA AL P.C.R. [Qualitative changes in the development of the armed forces after the 9th Congress (1965) of the Romanian Communist Party]. *Rev. de Istorie [Romania] 1979 32(12): 2241-2259.* Notes significant improvements in the condition of the armed forces in Romania since the 9th Communist Party Congress and the coming to power of Nicolae Ceauşescu, stressing the defensive nature of Romanian military plans. Based on the notion that the nation's defense is the task of the whole people, the national defense was thoroughly reorganized, particularly by augmenting the army with popular units. Instruction

and equipment have been improved and modernized and Communist Party organizations have played an important role in political and moral instruction. 35 notes. French summary.
R. O. Khan

2109. Olteanu, Constantin. POLITICA PARTIDULUI COMMUNIST ROMÂN DE LICHIDARE A EXPLOATĂRII CAPITALISTE ÎN ROMÂNIA [The policy of the Rumanian Communist Party of eliminating capitalist exploitation in Rumania]. *Anale de Istorie [Rumania] 1974 20(2): 64-74.* Evaluates Communist Party measures for the building of socialism and for the removal of conditions which made exploitation possible implemented since it seized power. Emphasizes the sixth and seventh party congresses (1948 and 1955) and the five-year plans for 1950-65, providing statistical material to demonstrate the progress under each phase. Gives special attention to agricultural collectivization and to the distribution of kulakism. With the success of cooperativism in rural Rumania, the peasantry has become a new, homogeneous, socialist class. By 1959 the Grand National Assembly could announce the end of the final vestiges of exploitation in the country. Based on government and Party statistics and records; 21 notes.
G. J. Bobango

2110. Paraschiva, Nichita. CONSIDERAŢII PRIVIND INSTAURAREA PUTERII DE STAT MUNCITOREŞTI-ŢĂRĂNEŞTI, DE TIP SOCIALIST, ÎN ROMÂNIA [Considerations on the installation of workers-peasants state power, of a socialist type in Rumania]. *Anale de Istorie [Rumania] 1972 18(6): 13-23.* Reviews political evolution between the August 1944 overthrow of the Ion Antonescu regime and the abolition of the monarchy in 1947. Originally holding only a single ministerial position in the Democratic Bloc government headed by General Constantin Sănătescu, the workers parties such as the PCR and the Social Democrats advanced to control four departments in the reformed coalition early in 1945 and with the installation of the Petru Groza regime by March, the revolutionary-democratic power of the masses finally began to prevail. The full elimination of fascist elements, the assault on the exploiting classes, and the redistribution of land to the peasants was initiated. The final steps came after the great electoral victory of November 1946 for the Democratic Parties Bloc, when the last of the bourgeois parties, the National Liberals and the National Peasants, were eliminated. With all its support gone, the anachronistic monarchy was toppled by the Petru Groza-Gh. Gheorghiu-Dej democratic alignment. The year 1948 brought the creation of truly representative organs of the state, such as the Grand National Assembly and local workers' councils. 27 notes. G. J. Bobango

2111. Paraskiva, Nikita. POLITIKATA NA SUIUZI NA RUMUNSKATA KOMUNISTICHESKA PARTIIA PREZ 1944-1948 G [The Rumanian Communist Party's policy of alliances, 1944-48]. *Izvestiia na Inst. po Istoriia na BKP [Bulgaria] 1972 27: 411-436.* This paper, given at a joint Bulgarian-Rumanian conference of party historians held in Bucharest in November 1970, studies the evolution of Communist Party relations with allied groups in the People's Democratic Front from 1944 up to the establishment of exclusive Communist power in December 1947.

2112. Petculescu, Constantin. IN THE FRONT RANKS OF THE REVOLUTIONARY FORCES. *Romania [Romania] 1982 7(3): 2-19.* The founding in 1932 of the Union of Communist Youth and of the Union of Communist Students Associations in 1957 were Romanian landmarks in the triumph of young socialist intellectuals.

2113. Petric, Aron. POLITICA P. C. R. DE TRANSFORMARE SOCIALISTĂ A AGRICULTURII [The policy of the Rumanian Communist Party for the socialist transformation of agriculture]. *Anale de Istorie [Rumania] 1972 18(1): 75-87.* The Rumanian Communist Party realized the importance of worker-peasant solidarity in its struggle for power and, although being illegal, played a leading role in the Worker-Peasant Front during the 1929-33 crisis. Since 1944 it has regarded socialist construction in industry and agriculture as a single process. Collectivization, begun in July 1949 and completed in March 1962, has raised the living standards of both workers and peasants, while the state has given much financial support to agriculture and put new scientific and technological developments at its disposal. 14 notes. M. Daly

2114. Petric, Aron and Ţuţui, Gheorghe. PROBLEME ALE REVOLUŢIEI DEMOCRAT-POPULARE ÎN ROMÂNIA [Problems of the popular democratic revolution in Rumania]. *Studii şi Articole de Istorie [Rumania] 1972 (18): 15-23.* Describes the transformation of Rumania into a socialist people's republic under post-World War II conditions, emphasizing the role of the Rumanian Communist Party.

2115. Petric, Aron. PROCLAMAREA REPUBLICII POPULARE ROMÂNE ŞI SEMNIFICAŢIA SA ISTORICĂ [The proclamation of the Rumanian People's Republic and its historical significance]. *Studii: Rev. de Istorie [Rumania] 1972 25(6): 1143-1157.* Presents the political and military measures taken by the Communist Party and democratic government of Rumania, 1946-47, for abolishing the monarchy and preventing a grouping of royalist and reactionary forces around the Hohenzollern throne. Cooperation with the monarchy was necessary for a short time for its eventual overthrow. Numerous comments in the foreign press, especially in France, testify to the welcome reception accorded the new democratic and socialist order. Based on contemporary newspaper sources, some state archival materials, and secondary sources; 42 notes. Résumé in French. G. J. Bobango

2116. Pope, Earl A. CHURCH-STATE RELATIONS IN ROMANIA. *Kyrkohistorisk Årsskrift [Sweden] 1977 77: 291-297.* By the 1970's interest in religion in Rumania had increased without resulting in tension with the state. Apparently religion and communism were not necessarily incompatible. 47 notes.

2117. Popescu, Eufrosina. PROCLAMAREA REPUBLICII POPULARE ROMÂNE ŞI SEMNIFICAŢIA ISTORICĂ A ACESTUI EVENIMENT [The proclamation of the Rumanian People's Republic and the historical importance of this event]. *Studii şi Articole de Istorie [Rumania] 1973 (21): 41-47.* Describes the establishment of a People's Republic in Rumania, stressing the role of the Rumanian Communist Party, and examines the democratic nature of Dr. Petru Groza's government, formed on 6 March 1945.

2118. Popescu-Puţuri, Ion. ÎNDEMN LA CREAŢIE [Stimulus to creation]. *Anale de Istorie [Romania] 1981 27(5): 3-22, (6): 13-30.* Part 1. Applauds the role of the Romanian Communist Party in investigating new developments in sociopolitical theory and the country's socioeconomic achievements. Compares aspects of Romania's economic growth with other East European countries and stresses its consistently high level and improving productivity. Notes that innovative attitudes have been characteristic of the socialist movement in Romania throughout its history. Part 2. Correlates the Party's creative attitude toward the practical application of Marxist-Leninist theory with passages from the works of Karl Marx, Friedrich Engels, and V. I. Lenin. Notes the various Romanian Communist Party congresses at which significant ideological reforms were instituted. Table, 55 notes. R. O. Khan

2119. Popescu-Puţuri, Ion. INSURECŢIA NAŢIONALĂ ANTIFASCISTĂ DIN AUGUST 1944—INCEPUT AL REVOLUŢIEI POPULARE IN ROMÂNIA [The national antifascist insurrection of August 1944: beginning the popular revolution in Rumania]. *Anale de Istorie [Rumania] 1974 20(3): 11-23.* Describes the meaning of the great popular uprising of 1944, the liquidation of the bourgeois regime, and the national regeneration of the Rumanian people. The Communist Party replaced reactionary mayors, prefects, and priests who opposed the popular will; eliminated the National Liberal and the National Peasant Party; nationalized the principal means of production by 1948, giving expropriated land to the peasantry; and seized local organs of power. Late in 1945, the Petru Groza government and the National Conference of the Communist Party elaborated a vast program of economic development. Social homogeneity grew with the modification of class relations. G. J. Bobango

2120. Popescu-Puţuri, Ion. LE PARTI COMMUNISTE ROUMAIN FACE AUX ALLIANCES POLITIQUES ET AU PROBLÈME DE L'UNITÉ DU MOUVEMENT OUVRIER, 1921-1948 [The Rumanian Communist Party, political alliances, and the problem of uniting the workers movement, 1921-48]. Comité Natl. des Hist. de la République Socialiste de Roumanie. *Nouvelles Etudes d'Hist.* (Bucharest: Editura Academiei Republicii Socialiste, 1975): 209-220. A detailed study of the growth of the Communist movement in Rumania, the Party's activities among the workers, its role during the war, and the achievement of its ambitions in the immediate postwar era. Among other topics the author stresses the antifascist activities of the Marxist groups and the lead taken by Communists in opposing government policies in the interwar years.
S. D. Spector

2121. Popescu-Puţuri, Ion. LUPTA MULTI-SECULARĂ A POPORULUI ROMÂN PENTRU APĂRAREA DREPTULUI DE LIBERTATE SOCIALĂ ŞI NAŢIONALĂ P.C.R. CONTINUATORUL TRADIŢIILOR DE LUPTĂ PENTRU SUVERANITATEA ŞI INDEPENDENŢA POPORULUI ROMÂN [The Rumanian people's age-old struggle for social and national freedom: the Rumanian Communist Party continues the traditional fight for Rumanian sovereignty and independence]. *Anale de Istorie [Rumania] 1975 21(3): 23-44.* Chronological presentation of the Rumanian people's struggle for freedom, national unity, and independence. The traditions of struggle of the Rumanian people have been taken over by the workers' movements and its revolutionary party. RSA (12:1132)

2122. Popescu-Puţuri, Ion. O UNICĂ ŞI UNITARĂ ISTORIE A POPORULUI ROMÂN [The unique and united history of the Romanian people]. *Magazin Istoric [Romania] 1982 16(11): 2-4.* A gloss on Nicolae Ceauşescu's address on 1-2 June 1982 to the Plenum of the Central Committee of the Communist Party stressing the essential unity of the Romanian people throughout history.

2123. Popescu-Puţuri, Ion. PARTIDUL REVOLUŢIONAR AL CLASEI MUNCITOARE A ADUS ROMÂNIA ÎN PAS CU VIITORUL [The revolutionary party of the working class set Romania on its road to the future]. *Anale de Istorie [Romania] 1981 27(2): 3-40.* Based on secondary sources, 26 notes.

2124. Popescu-Puturi, Ion. THE PARTY OF THE WORKING CLASS—ITS ORGANIZATION AND PLACE IN ROMANIAN HISTORY. *Romania [Romania] 1981 6(1): 12-47.* Unlike all other political parties and groupings that played a part in Romania's social and political life over the years and whose program evinced the limitations of the social classes they represented, the revolutionary party of the working class—now known as the Communist Party of Romania—has been the most advanced political force of the time, an exponent and promoter of the vital aims of the entire Romanian people since the party's beginnings as the Socialist Party in 1893.

2125. Popescu-Puţuri, Ion. PROGRAMUL P.C.R. DESPRE INDEPENDENŢA NAŢIONALĂ A ROMÂNIEI CA PERMANENŢĂ A ISTORIEI POPORULUI NOSTRU [The program of the Rumanian Communist Party on Rumanian national independence: a permanent feature of the history of our people]. *Anale de Istorie [Rumania] 1977 23(1): 15-38.* In celebrating the 100th anniversary of the declaration of Rumanian national independence, the author shows that independence has been the tradition of the Rumanian people since the earliest times. Reviews major moments of the struggle against Ottoman and Habsburg domination, such as the battles of the medieval princes to create autonomous feudal *voievodates*, the drawing up of the *Supplex* in 1791, the union of the principalities and the winning of autonomy under Alexandru I. Cuza, and the war for independence in 1877-78. The working-class political party has always been in the forefront of the conquest of freedom and the defense of the state. In the 20th century the union of all progressive forces under the Communist Party has been the backbone of opposition to all imperialist forces threatening the nation. Based on the 1975 Program of the Rumanian Communist Party; 56 notes. G. J. Bobango

2126. Popescu-Puţuri, Ion. UNITY: TRADITION OF THE ROMANIAN WORKING-CLASS MOVEMENT. *Romania [Rumania] 1978 3(1): 112-138.* Discusses events leading up to the February 1948 Congress which proclaimed the merging of the Rumanian Communist and Socialist Parties whose joint task was to lead Rumanian working-class society toward complete socialism.

2127. Popesku-Putsur', Ion. 30 LET SO DNIA OSVOBOZHDENIIA RUMYNII OT FASHISTSKOGO GOSPODSTVA [Thirty years since the liberation of Rumania from fascist domination]. *Voprosy Istorii KPSS [USSR] 1974 (8): 45-54.* On 23 August 1944 the Rumanian Communist Party led a popular front in overthrowing the fascist regime of Ion Antonescu (1882-1946). Subsequently, the Party's leadership brought Rumania significant economic, scientific, cultural, educational, and international achievements.
L. E. Holmes

2128. Popisteanu, Cristian. "NOUL GUVERN A DEPUS JURAMINTUL" ["A new government has been sworn in"]. *Magazin Istoric [Rumania] 1975 9(3): 14-15.* Describes the installation of the Communist government in March 1945. 2 notes.
J. M. McCarthy

2129. Potapov, V. I. RUMYNSKOI KOMMUNISTICHESKOI PARTII—60 LET [The Romanian Communist Party (RCP) is 60 years old]. *Voprosy Istorii KPSS [USSR] 1981 (5): 107-110.* The RCP was founded 8 May 1921 under the influence of the October Russian Revolution. It has always inspired the Romanian people to great deeds of socialist construction. Lenin had a great influence on the Party, which has always been Marxist-Leninist. The RCP struggled against the rising tide of 1930's fascism, but in vain. On 23 August 1944, thanks to the Soviet army's victories, the RCP staged an uprising that marked the beginning of the national revolution. March 1945 saw the first democratic government in Romanian history. The USSR has given great economic aid in transforming Romania from a backward agrarian society to an industrial society. Based on histories of the Communist party of the Soviet Union and the RCP; 4 notes. A. J. Evans

2130. Puia, Ilie. INFLUENŢA PARTIDULUI COMUNIST ROMÂN ASUPRA UNOR PERIODICE SOCIAL-ECONOMICE BURGHEZE ÎN PERIOADA INTERBELICĂ [The influence of the Rumanian Communist Party on bourgeois socioeconomic periodicals in the interwar period]. *Studii: Rev. de Istorie [Rumania] 1971 24(3): 525-536.* Surveys the National Peasant Party publication *Independenţa economică* (Economic Interdependence), founded by economists V. Madgearu and I. Raducanu, which offered its columns to a variety of progressive writers and viewpoints, 1918-47. Among these, Lucreţiu Pătrăşcanu, Miron Constantinescu, Ştefan Voicu, Roman Moldovan, and G. Vlădescu-Răcoasa contributed often, advancing historical materialism in articles, reviews, and studies ranging from Romania's agrarian crisis, to the nation's place in the world economy, to the contradictions of the capitalist order and the threat of fascist economic imperialism. Primary sources; 44 notes.
G. J. Bobango

2131. Puiu, Alexandru. LA COLLABORAZIONE ECONOMICA DELLA RUMANIA CON I PAESI SOCIALISTI [Rumania's economic cooperation with the Socialist countries]. *Est-Ovest [Italy] 1973 4(2): 55-76.* Analyzes Rumania's foreign trade and economic cooperation with other Communist countries, 1965-71.

2132. Răducu, Constantin. VALORIFICAREA TRADIŢILOR PROGRESISTE: IMPERATIV MAJOR ÎN ENDUCAREA PATRIOTICĂ REVOLUŢIONARĂ A MASELOR [The appreciation of progressive traditions: a major imperative in the revolutionary and patriotic education of the masses]. *Anale de Istorie [Romania] 1981 27(4): 33-50.* Stresses the important role of Romanian folkloric traditions and customs in developing the spiritual qualities of the nation and maintaining the continuity of the national character. Analyzes the patriotic ideals communicated by the traditional ballads, legends, proverbs, tales, sculpture, wood-carving, pottery, folk costumes, and other folk art forms. Emphasizes the need to distinguish and maintain the more progressive and positive traditions and notes the Romanian Communist Party's recognition of these traditions in advancing socialism and the labor movement. 15 notes. R. O. Khan

2133. Radulescu, Gheorghe. RUMUŃSKA PARTIA KOMUNISTYCZNA W 55 ROCZNICĘ POWSTANIA [The Communist Party of Rumania on its 55th anniversary]. *Nowe Drogi [Poland] 1976 (6): 86-90.* Recounts the main developments in the Rumanian Communist Party.

2134. Rațiu, Alexander and Virtue, William. *Stolen Church: Martyrdom in Communist Romania.* Huntington, Ind.: Our Sunday Visitor, 1979. 192 pp.

2135. Redulescu, Ilie. NAUCHNYI KHARAKTER POLITIKI RUMYNSKOI RABOCHEI PARTII [The scientific character of the policies of the Rumanian Workers' Party]. *Voprosy Istorii KPSS [USSR] 1961 (4): 80-94.* Studies the scientific approach to policies characteristic of the Rumanian Workers' Party since its creation in 1921, with particular reference to the period since the formation of a democratic government in Rumania in 1945.

2136. Rotman, Liviu, et al. MĂRTURII ALE UNUI TRECUT GLORIOS DE LUPTĂ REVOLUŢIONARĂ: LOCURI ISTORICE LEGATE DE LUPTA P.C.R. ŞI A ORGANIZAŢIILOR SALE DE MASĂ [Witnesses of a glorious past of revolutionary struggle: historic places related to the struggle of the P.C.R. and its mass organizations]. *Anale de Istorie [Rumania] 1971 17(3): 174-196.* A listing of streets, addresses, buildings, and other places having historic significance for the Rumanian Communist Party. Indicate whether the site is still standing and changes of name.
G. J. Bobango

2137. Sbârnă, Gheorghe. CREAREA ŞI ACTIVITATEA UNIUNII TINERETULUI MUNCITORESC (1947-1949) [The creation and activity of the Union of Working Youth, 1947-49]. *Rev. de Istorie [Romania] 1979 32(5): 825-841.* Founded under the aegis of the Romanian Communist Party in 1947 the Union of Working Youth has been important in the Party's mobilization of youth in the solution of the problems of democracy and the establishment of socialism in postwar Romania. It continued the work of the wartime Union of Communist Youth, its membership drawn largely from young factory workers. By 1949, it grouped all youth organizations together. 38 notes. French summary. R. O. Khan

2138. Schultz, Lothar. DIE ZWEITE LANDESKONFERENZ DER RUMÄNISCHEN KP [The second national conference of the Rumanian Communist Party]. *Osteuropa [West Germany] 1973 23(1): 21-28.* The conference of 19-21 July 1972 supplied an occasion for Communist Party Secretary Nicolae Ceauşescu to push his policies for Rumanian industrialization, for closer integration of Party and state organs, and for more responsive local government. He also reaffirmed Rumania's independent initiatives in Balkan and international politics. 19 notes; additional documentation on pp. A56-A64. R. E. Weltsch

2139. Scurtu, I. POZIŢIA P.C.R. FAŢĂ DE PARTIDELE "ISTORICE" ÎN TIMPUL GUVERNULUI RĂDESCU [The position of the Rumanian Communist Party toward the "historical" parties during Rădescu's government]. *Analele Universităţii Bucureşti: Seria Ştiinţe Sociale-Istorie [Rumania] 1966 15: 167-84.* Nicolae Rădescu's goverment was the third reactionary government of Rumania after the armed antifascist insurrection of 1944. The Rumanian Communist Party (RCP) cooperated with the bourgeois parties on the basis of a common program accepted by the National Peasant Party and the National Liberal Party. At the same time the RCP conducted a widespread political campaign to unmask the leaders of the "historical" parties opposed to revolutionary changes and win the masses to the cause of the revolution. On 6 March 1945 the new government of Petru Grosa, representing democratic power, put an end to the state apparatus that favored the bourgeois landowners. Primary and secondary sources; 117 notes.
P. T. Herman

2140. Şerbănescu, Ion. PERSPECTIVELE DEZVOLTĂRII POLITICE A ROMÂNIEI ÎN DEZBATERILE DE IDEI DIN ANII 1944-1947 [Rumanian political developments in the ideological debates of 1944-47]. *Studii: Rev. de Istorie [Rumania] 1971 24(3): 609-626.* Although the fundamental strategy for instituting a bourgeois-democratic revolution in Rumania had been formulated by the 5th Congress of the Rumanian Communist Party (PCR) in 1931, conditions after the revolution of 23 August 1944 called for a reassessment of plans and modalities. The major political groupings consisted of Marxism-Leninism, social democracy, liberalism of the C.I.C. Brătianu-Gh. Tătărăscu variety, and the Iuliu Maniu camp's peasantism. The most lucid and far-sighted was the Communists' Marxism-Leninism. 42 notes. G. J. Bobango

2141. Şerbănescu, Ion. ŞTIINŢA ROMÂNEASCA ÎN ANII REVOLUŢIEI POPULAR DEMOCRATICE [Romanian science during the years of the people's democratic revolution]. *Revista de Istorie [Romania] 1981 34(4): 715-728.* Examines the conception of the Communist Party of the increasingly important role played by intellectuals in general and scientists in particular in the revolutionary transformation of Romanian society. The Party became more and more aware of the state of mind and the desire expressed by a large category of intellectuals to serve their country. During the 12th congress of the Communist Party a program for the development of scientific and technological research was discussed and approved. Based on archives of the Central Committee of the Romanian Communist Party and secondary sources; 40 notes.
P. D. Herman

2142. Sheviakov, A. A. VNESHNIAIA POLITIKA RUMYNII V PERIOD MIUNKHENA [Rumania's foreign policy in the Munich period]. *Voprosy Istorii [UUSR] 1970 (12): 71-83.* Analyzes Soviet-Rumanian and Rumanian-German relations in the years immediately preceding World War II, demonstrating the intensification of the reactionary, anti-Soviet foreign policy line followed by bourgeois Rumania since the establishment of a monarchist dictatorship and Nazi Germany's demand for the partition of Czechoslovakia. Stresses that the Rumanian rulers attempted to thwart the USSR's attempts to safeguard the national interests of Czechoslovakia and illustrates Rumania's efforts to maintain its pro-Hitler position without severing its traditional ties with Britain and France. The failure of Rumania's pro-Munich policy was the logical result of the anti-Soviet course steered by the Rumanian rulers.

2143. Simion, Aurică. CREŞTEREA ROLUL CONDUCĂTOR AL PARTIDULUI ÎN VIAŢA SOCIETĂŢII ÎN PERIOADA CONSOLIDĂRII CONSTRUCŢIEI SOCIALISTE [The growth of the Party's leading role in the period of the consolidation of the building of socialism]. *Anale de Istorie [Rumania] 1978 24(3): 47-62.* Discusses the Rumanian Communist Party's role in national life following the rise to power of Nicolae Ceauşescu, 1965-70.

2144. Sonea, Gavril. ADEZIUNEA ŞI SPRIJINUL MASELOR POPULARE ÎN ÎNFĂPTUIREA ACTULUI REVOLUŢIONAR AL NAŢIONALIZĂRII PRINCIPALELOR MIJLOACE DE PRODUCŢIE [Adherence and support by the popular masses to the revolutionary act of nationalizing the principal means of production]. *Anale de Istorie [Rumania] 1973 19(4): 48-57.* Relates the importance of the 1948 act of nationalization, the concrete steps taken by the masses for the successful nationalization of the principal means of production, and the role of the Rumanian Communist Party in its elaboration and implementation.
Romanian Scientific Abstracts 11:406

2145. Spălăţelu, Ion. AN EXAMPLE OF PATRIOTISM, REVOLUTIONARY FIGHT AND DEDICATION. *Romania [Romania] 1983 8(1): 6-39.* A life of Nicolae Ceauşescu, Romanian Communist Party chief since 1965.

2146. Stroia, M. NOI LUCRĂRI DESPRE ISTORIA U. T. C. [New works on the history of the Communist Youth Union]. *Rev. de Istorie [Rumania] 1974 27(8): 1239-1245.* Surveys publications issued to celebrate the 50th anniversary of the Union's foundation: C. Bărbulescu et al's *File de Istoria U. T. C.* (Bucharest: Editura Politică, 1972); Constantin Petculescu's *Crearea Uniunii Tineretului*

Comunist (Bucharest: Editura Politică, 1972); *O tribună de luptă. Presa tineretului revoluționar din România* (Bucharest, 1972); C. Petculescu et al's *Tineretului Comunist în acțiune* (Bucharest: Editura Științifică, 1972); and *Așa a fost ieri* (Bucharest, 1972).

2147. Surpat, Gheorghe. CONTRIBUTIA PARTIDULUI COMUNIST ROMÂN LA DEZVOLTAREA TEOREI ȘI PRACTICII REVOLUTIEI ȘI CONSTRUCȚIEI SOCIALISTE [The Rumanian Communist Party's contribution to developing the theory and practice of revolution and the building of socialism]. *Anale de Istorie [Rumania] 1978 24(2): 17-39.* Surveys the theoretical and practical promotion of socialism by the Rumanian Communist Party, especially since the rise to power of Nicolae Ceaușescu.

2148. Surpat, Gheorghe. DEZBATEREA PROGRAMULUI P.C.R. DE CĂTRE ÎNTREGUL PARTID ȘI POPOR, EXPRESIE A PROFUNDULUI DEMOCRATISM AL ORÎNDUIRII NOASTRE [The debate on the Party's program by the whole party and people, an expression of the profound democracy of our system]. *Anale de Istorie [Rumania] 1974 20(5): 31-39.* Elaborates on the nationwide meetings, conferences, debates, discussions in the press, on the județe, town, and municipal level of the programs and documents to be adopted by the 11th Congress of the Rumanian Communist Party (PCR), centering on directives for the 1976-80 five-year plan aimed at creating a multilaterally developed socialist society and advancing Rumania toward communism. Stresses the "real and all-inclusive nature of the socialist democracy" which characterizes Rumanian society, and how this will be deepened in the years ahead. A great advance in this direction was the creation of the Socialist Unity Front in 1968, a powerful demonstration of the deep social consciousness, unity, and homogeneity of the broad masses of the people, and a symbol of their support for the enlightened leadership of the Rumanian Communist Party, a political force now numbering some 2.4 million workers, peasants, and intellectuals, some of the most advanced workingmen in all spheres of activity. From Party program documents; 3 notes. G. J. Bobango

2149. Surpat, Gheorghe. EXPERIENȚA P. C. R. ÎN ASIGUREA ROLULUI CONDUCĂTOR AL CLASEI MUNCITOARE ÎN REVOLUȚIA ȘI CONSTRUCȚIA SOCIETĂȚII SOCIALISTE [The experience of the Romanian Communist Party in ensuring the leading role of the working class in revolution and the construction of a socialist society]. *Anale de Istorie [Romania] 1981 27(1): 33-50.* Based on secondary sources; 15 notes.

2150. Surpat, Gheorghe. ÎNTĂRIREA CONTINUA A UNITĂȚII MORAL-POLITICE ȘI COEZIUNII ÎNTREGULUI POPOR ÎN PROCESUL EDIFICĂRII SOCIETĂȚII SOCIALISTE MULTILATERAL DEZVOLTATE ÎN ROMÂNIA [The continuous strengthening of the moral and political unity and cohesion of the entire people during the process of building a multilaterally developed socialist society in Romania]. *Anale de Istorie [Romania] 1981 27(5): 23-41.* Surveys the socialist transformation of life in Romania under the leadership of the Romanian Communist Party since shortly after World War II, tracing the installation of the Communist administration and distinguishing two distinct phases of socialist development—before and after the accession of Nicolae Ceaușescu as secretary-general of the Romanian Communist Party in 1965. Stresses the broad range of socialist achievements, especially in the latter period, and notes the major changes in the structure of Romanian society since World War II. Outlines the role of the Front for Democracy and Socialist Unity, created in 1968, to ensure the organized participation of the whole nation in developing the society. Table, 13 notes. R. O. Khan

2151. Surpat, Gheorghe. PARTIDUL COMUNIST ROMÂN: MARELE ARCHITECT AL ROMÂNIEI SOCIALISTE [The Romanian Communist Party: the great architect of socialist Romania]. *Magazin Istoric [Romania] 1979 13(12): 5-9.* Demonstrates the leading role played by the Communist Party in directing progress and social advance in Romania after 1944.

2152. Surpat, Gheorghe. PARTIDUL COMUNIST ROMÂN: PROMOTOR AL LUPTEI ÎMPOTRIVĂ IDEOLOGIEI PARTIDELOR BURGHEZE ÎN ANII REVOLUȚIEI POPULARE [The Rumanian Communist Party: promoter of the struggle against the middle class political parties' ideology during the people's revolution]. *Anale de Istorie [Rumania] 1971 17(5): 42-58.* Analyzes the Communist Party's political campaign against the National Liberal Party and the National Peasant Party following the 1944 insurrection. Discusses how the Party's program served contemporary national economic interests and became established, despite the opposition's insistence that the working class would be unsatisfactory as the dominant social force, and its rejection of the universal applicability of Marxism. Based on contemporary political publications. 34 notes. R. O. Khan

2153. Surpat, Gheorghe. SEMNIFICAȚIA ISTORICĂ A PLENAREI C.C. AL P.C.R. DIN 3-4 MARTIE 1949 ÎN ORGANIZAREA ȘI DEZVOLTAREA PE BAZE SOCIALISTE A AGRICULTURII ROMÂNEȘTI [The historic significance of the Central Committee Plenary of the Romanian Communist Party on 3-5 March, 1949 in organizing and developing Romanian agriculture on a socialist basis]. *Anale de Istorie [Romania] 1979 25(1): 20-40.* The Romanian Communist Party outlined its fundamental long-range policy for the collectivization of Romanian agriculture at the Central Committee Plenary session of March, 1949, a program for passing from small-scale production based on private property to large-scale socialist production, based on collective ownership. Two vital elements of the program were the coordination of agricultural growth with the nation's industrial development, and a massive education program to demonstrate the benefits of the new order to the peasantry. Data showing the great successes registered in Romanian agriculture over the past thirty years are presented, with discussion of the manner in which successive Party meetings and congresses refined and perfected the original 1949 designs. Based on statistical annuals, official bulletins, secondary works; 51 notes. G. J. Bobango

2154. Surpat, Gheorghe. TREI DECENII DE DEZVOLTARE A ROMÂNIEI PE COORDONATELE SOCIALISMULUI [Three decades of development in Rumania on the coordinates of socialism]. *Anale de Istorie [Rumania] 1974 20(1): 121-135.* Documents the progress in Rumanian society 30 years after the national antifascist insurrection of August 1944. Central to Rumania's prosperity has been the creation of a socialist economy which has raised the standards and quality of life for all, and a political system in which all power belongs to the people through elected spokesmen in the Grand National Assembly and the political instrumentality of the Socialist Unity Front. In the forefront has been the Rumanian Communist Party. Presents statistical data illustrating significant progress in industry, agriculture, salaries, education, scientific and cultural life, women's rights, housing, rights of minorities, and the gradual equalizing and homogenization of all classes and social categories. Under the guidance of the current five-year plan and the 1972 Tenth Party Congress, progress on all fronts in the immediate years ahead will be even more striking. From the *Statistical Annual*; 2 tables, 10 notes. G. J. Bobango

2155. Tejchman, Miroslav. UPEVNĚNÍ SOCIALISMU A MATERIÁLNĚTECHNICKÉ ZÁKLADNY NOVÉ SPOLEČNOSTI V RUMUNSKU V LETECH 1965-1969 [The strengthening of socialism and technological bases of the new society in Romania, 1965-69]. *Slovanský Přehled [Czechoslovakia] 1984 70(6): 472-477.* During the 9th Congress of the Romanian Communist Party, important priorities were agreed upon for the next five-year plan and for a reorganization of Party and state administration. As a result of the changes made and the policies followed, by 1969 the chemical industry and machine production showed an increase in productivity of 66%. These economic gains were clearly reflected in the higher standard of living achieved by the Romanians by the 1970's, which was also connected with successful trading arrangements, not only with the Eastern European countries but also with the Western nations. 13 notes. B. Reinfeld

2156. Tejchman, Miroslav. 60 LET RUMUNSKÉ KOMUNISTICKÉ STRANY [60 years of the Romanian Communist Party]. *Slovanský Přehled [Czechoslovakia] 1981 67(5): 439-443.* Cites the achievements of the Communist Party, starting with its championship of the working class in 1920, progressive politics throughout the period between the wars, organization of the uprising in 1944 against the fascists, and its role at the head of Romanian development since the war. Its most recent project, heralded as a great conservation plan, is the five-year plan announced in 1980, focusing on industrial development that will be energy efficient. 3 notes. B. Reinfeld

2157. Tudor, Gheorghe. ROLUL CONDUCĂTOR A PARTIDULUI COMUNIST ROMÂN ÎN ETAPA EDIFICĂRII SOCIETAŢII SOCIALISTE MULTILATERAL DEZVOLTATE [The leading role of the Romanian Communist Party at the stage of building the multilateral developed socialist society]. *Rev. de Istorie [Romania] 1979 32(2): 199-209.* Attempts to define the role of the Romanian Communist Party in leading the development of socialist society in Romania and the means by which it executes this role, especially noting its increasing integration in every aspect of Romanian life. Analyzes the documents of the 10th and 11th Party congresses and national congresses in 1972 and 1977 from which emerges the overall concept that at the present stage of Romanian society the best way to increase the Party's leading role is to extend yet further its integration into Romanian society. 31 notes. French summary. R. O. Khan

2158. Ţuţui, Gh. OCTOMBRIE 1945: UN MOMENT AL VIITORULUI [October 1945: a moment for the future]. *Magazin Istoric [Romania] 1980 14(10): 11-12, 15.* From 16-22 October 1945, a year after the liberation of Romania, the Communist Party, legal for the first time in 20 years, held a decisive conference in which it laid down a program as crucial for the immediate future as in its turn was to be the later conference in 1965.

2159. Ţuţui, Gheorghe. DEZVOLTAREA LEGĂTURILOR P.C.R. CU MASELE ÎN PREMII ANI AI REPUBLICII [The development of the bonds between the Rumanian Communist Party and the masses during the first years of the republic]. *Rev. de Istorie [Rumania] 1977 30(12): 2185-2205.* The first unified economic, social, and political policy of the Communist Party, after the war, was based on a fundamental restructuring of the party to reinforce its contact with the people. Various solutions were found to involve them more directly in government, especially important being the role of the Union of Communist Youth, the labor unions, and other public organizations. Other political parties also had to be eliminated. 47 notes. R. O. Khan

2160. Ţuţui, Gheorghe. DEZVOLTAREA PARTIDULUI COMUNIST ROMÂN ÎN ANII 1944-1948 [Development of the Rumanian Communist Party (PCR), 1944-48]. *Anale de Istorie [Rumania] 1970 16(6): 3-15.* Describes the reorganization, internal strengthening, and enormous growth of the PCR following the historic act of 23 August 1944. Stresses the importance of the National Conference of October 1945, in laying the ideological and political foundations for building a socialist state, and its strategy for winning the parliamentary elections of 1946. Other plenary sessions of the Party were instrumental in combatting national chauvinism and revisionism. Based on Party archives and *Scînteia;* 37 notes. G. J. Bobango

2161. Ţuţui, Gheorghe. DIN ACTIVITATEA POLITICĂ-IDEOLOGICĂ DESFĂŞURATĂ DE P.C.R. PRIVIND CARACTERUL ŞI PERSPECTIVELE PUTERII DE STAT ÎN ANII 1945-1947 [On the political-ideological activity developed by the PCR as to the character and perspectives of state power, 1945-47]. *Anale de Istorie [Rumania] 1972 18(6): 24-36.* Evaluates the ideological struggle against the forces of bourgeois reaction for the support of the popular masses during the critical period of creating a popular democracy in Rumania. Views this period of founding the people's republic not as a mere extension of bourgeois democracy, but as a transition to a form of the politial organization of society based on a new set of class relations. Summarizes the high points in the campaign waged by the workers' representatives, the leaders of the Communist and Social Democratic parties, in writings by Lotar Rădăceanu, Petru Groza, Ştefan Voicu, and Gheorghe Gheorghiu-Dej, while stressing the role of the National Conference of the PCR in October 1945. The exploitative policies of the previous regime were unmasked, thus bringing new clarifications on how democracy was to be extended to the greatest number of citizens. The Brătianu-led National Liberals and the National Peasant Party under Iuliu Maniu launched a vicious propaganda campaign against the new order, but could not prevent the increasingly rapid transfer of power to the workers and peasants or the passage of state power to the masses. 32 notes. G. J. Bobango

2162. Ţuţui, Gheorghe. EDINNIIAT RABOTNICHESKI FRONT-OSNOVA NA SUIUZNATA POLITIKA, PROVEZHDANA OT RKP V GODINITE NA NARODNODEMOKRATICHESKATA REVOLIUTSIIA [The united workers' front: the basis of the policy of alliances followed by the Rumanian Communist Party in the years of the popular democratic revolution]. *Izvestiia na Inst. po Istoriia na BKP [Bulgaria] 1972 27: 437-455.* This paper, given at a joint conference of Bulgarian and Rumanian party historians held in Bucharest in November 1970, deals with the development of the united workers' front and the establishment of a revolutionary democratic government and a popular democratic structure, leading in February 1948 to the creation of a united Communist Party.

2163. Ţuţui, Gheorghe. FRONTUL UNIC MUNCITORESC—TEMELIA ALIANŢELOR POLITICE PROMOVATE DE P.C.R. ÎN ANII 1944-1948 [The United Workers' Front—foundation of the political alliances promoted by the P.C.R. in the years 1944-48]. *Anale de Istorie [Rumania] 1974 20(2): 39-50.* Reports the process whereby the Rumanian Communist Party and the Social Democratic Party gradually coalesced in the years following the great national antifascist uprising of August 1944. The agreement by the central committees of both parties to collaborate in the United Workers Front as of 2 October 1944, was instrumental in furthering a gradual rapprochement which led to electoral cooperation in the Democratic Parties Bloc during the 1946 elections. Although the revolutionary demands of the times turned many of the Social Democrats to a more radical ideology, some rightists refused to conform to the historic necessities. Only when these were eliminated from control of the P.S.D. could a true merger between the two progressive, democratic parties take place. By February 1948 the union was accomplished and the working class had a united organization to fulfill its historic mission. In the meantime other fusions were occurring, such as that of the National Peasants' Party and the Plowman's Front, as all the forces interested in the construction of socialism reached a new, higher level of action. Based on newspapers and secondary works; 18 notes. G. J. Bobango

2164. Ţuţui, Gheorghe. PARTIDELE POLITICE DEMOCRATICE DIN ROMÂNIA ÎN PERIOADA DE DUPĂ 23 AUGUST 1944 [Democratic political parties in Rumania after 23 August 1944]. *Anale de Istorie [Rumania] 1969 15(6): 3-18.* Traces the Rumanian Communist Party's tactical coalition with the nonsocialist leftist party factions led by Gheorghe Tătărăscu and Anton Alexandrescu, which produced the National Democratic Bloc. By 1945 this evolved into the National Democratic Front, and was the basis for the leftists' participation in the 1946 parliamentary elections, under the banner of the Democratic Parties Bloc. The election mandate brought a powerful shift of political forces toward the proletariat and its allies, making possible in 1947 the union of workers and peasants groups into the Rumanian Workers' Party. Soon the Petru Groza-Gheorghe Gheorghiu-Dej regime could outlaw all bourgeois parties, and purge the Tătărăscu elements, the National Peasants, and the Plowman's Front from the government. The 1952 Constitution recognized the Rumanian Workers' Party as the only legitimate party. 37 notes. G. J. Bobango

2165. Ţuţui, Gheorghe and Tudor, Gheorghe. PLENARELE COMITETULUI CENTRAL AL PARTIDULUI COMUNIST ROMÂN (1948-1977) [The Plenary Sessions of the Central Committee of the Rumanian Communist Party, 1948-77]. *Rev. de Istorie [Rumania] 1977 30(11): 2061-2080.* Surveys all the Rumanian Communist Party Central Committee Plenary Sessions, 1948-77, briefly summarizing the principal debates and decisions of each.

Stresses the increasing role of the Central Committee especially since 1965, describing its organization and activities. Table, 16 notes. R. O. Khan

2166. Voitec, Ştefan. ÎNTĂRIREA FRONTULUI UNIC MUNCITORESC PRIN CREAREA SINDICATELOR UNITE—SEPTEMBRIE 1944 [Strengthening the United Workers' Front through the creation of the United Syndicates]. *Anale de Istorie [Rumania] 1974 20(4): 48-56.* The Commission for Organizing a United Labor Movement resulted from the meeting of the Rumanian Communist Party and the Social Democratic Party 1 September 1944. By January 1945, at the first congress of the General Trade Union Confederation unions in factories throughout the country represented more than half a million workers. The congress adhered closely to the new program of the United Democratic Front. Such unity of action of all progressive working-class forces helped significantly to bring about the ultimate union of the PCR and the Social Democrats in 1948. All this was the product of a strong union tradition going back to the turn of the century. 11 notes. G. J. Bobango

2167. Zaharescu, Barbu. PROGRAM FOR COMPREHENSIVELY DEVELOPED SOCIALISM: SUMMING UP THE 11TH CONGRESS OF THE RUMANIAN COMMUNIST PARTY. *World Marxist R. 1975 18(2): 94-103.* Analyzes Rumania's economic development and presents the party's future plans as discussed at the 1975 congress.

2168. Zaharia, Gheorghe and Surpat, Gheorghe. DE LA REPUBLICA POPULARĂ LA REPUBLICA SOCIALISTĂ. CONDUCEREA OPEREI DE EDIFICARE A SOCIALISMULUI ÎN CONCEPŢIA ŞI PRACTICA P.C.R. [From the popular republic to the socialist republic: leadership in the work of building socialism in the concept and practice of the PCR]. *Anale de Istorie [Rumania] 1972 18(6): 37-51.* Highlights the significant steps of eliminating the capitalist-bourgeois order and transforming Rumania to its present advanced stage of constructing a multilaterally developed socialist state. Focuses on the leading role of the 6th, 9th, and 10th Communist Party Congresses, the astounding progress made in industrializing the country, the gradual resolution of the centuries-old agrarian problem climaxing with the completion of collectivization in 1962, and the scientific, cultural, artistic, and educational progress made since 1948. The Party conceives the state as fundamental to socializing the nation and bringing the working class to its historic fulfillment. Parallelism is being eliminated by creating organs which are both Party and state organs, such as the Council of Culture and Socialist Education. Under the leadership of the Communist Party, the necessary premises are being laid for the eventual transition to the highest phase of the new order, that of communism, which will result from the increasing use of state power. Secondary sources; 3 notes. G. J. Bobango

2169. —. CONDIŢIILE SOCIALE-POLITICE ŞI IMPORTANŢA FĂURIRII DE CĂTRE PARTID A UNIUNII TINERETULUI COMUNIST [Sociopolitical conditions and the importance of the creation of the Union of Communist Youth by the Party]. *Revista de Istorie [Romania] 1982 35(4): 533-557.* On 19 November 1981 a debate was organized by the School of National History and the Ştefan Gheorghiu Academy as part of the scientific and educational activities celebrating the anniversary of the Union of Communist Youth. Presents a shortened version of the lectures delivered by Ion Apostol, Ioan Bălgrădean and Gheorghe I. Ioniţă, among others. Sociopolitical conditions during the years following the establishment of the Romanian national state favored an intense process of organization and development that led to the creation of the organization of Communist youth. P. D. Herman

2170. —. [LUCRETIU PATRASCANU]. *Magazin Istoric [Rumania] 1975 9(11): 6-12.*

Popişteanu, Cristian. TÎNĂR COMUNIST [Young Communist], *pp. 6-8.* Lucretiu Patrascanu (1900-75) joined the Rumanian Communist Party in October 1919 at age 19. His observations on the Weimar Republic while studying in Germany, 1922-23, especially affected his thought. 3 notes.

Dandara, Livia. PROFESOR UNIVERSITAR [University professor], *pp. 9-11.* In pursuit of his candidacy for the chair of theoretical economics at the University of Bucharest, Patrascanu submitted an extensive curriculum vitae which serves as a prime source for reconstructing his teaching career.

Savu, A. G. ISTORIC MARXIST [Historic Marxist], *pp. 11-12.* Patrascanu's achievements as an economist justify his being hailed as a resolute fighter for socialist humanism. J. M. McCarthy.

2171. —. MĂRTURII ISTORICE REFERITOARE LA VIAŢA ŞI ACTIVITATEA REVOLUŢIONARĂ A TOVARĂŞULUI NICOLAE CEAUŞESCU [Historical testimony on the life and revolutionary activity of comrade Nicolae Ceauşescu]. *Anale de Istorie [Rumania] 1973 19(1): 25-64.* A photographic portfolio commemorating Nicolae Ceauşescu's 40 years of involvement and leadership in the workers' movement, covering his life from entry into Communist activity at 15 to his present position as Secretary-General of the Rumanian Communist Party and President of the Council of State of the Socialist Republic of Rumania. Published on the occasion of his 55th birthday. Primary sources. G. J. Bobango

2172. —. PARTIDUL COMUNIST ROMÂN—CONDUCĂTORUL OPEREI DE CONSTRUIRE A SOCIALISMULUI ÎN ŢARA NOASTRĂ ÎN PERIOADA 1948-1962 [The Rumanian Communist Party: leader in the socialist construction of our country, 1948-62]. *Anale de Istorie [Rumania] 1972 18(5): 97-127.* Examines the importance of the creation of a single Marxist-Leninist Party in the construction of socialism in Rumania through the nationalization of production, the establishment of a unified socialist economy, the improvement in the workers' living standards, and the growth of education and culture. The continual strengthening of the Party as the vanguard of the working class has made it the leading political force in the nation. Biblio. M. Daly

2173. —. PARTIDUL COMUNIST ROMÂN ÎN ETAPA FĂURIRII SOCIETĂŢII SOCIALISTE MULTILATERAL DEZVOLTATE [The Rumanian Communist Party at the stage of constructing the multilaterally developed socialist society]. *Anale de Istorie [Rumania] 1973 19(2): 174-192.* Part of the series "For the Assistance of Students of the PCR and the Working Class Movement in Rumania," a set of five lectures elaborating on the goals, programs, and work of the 9th and 10th Congresses of the PCR in 1965 and 1969, the Plenary Session of the Central Committee in 1971, and the National Party Conference of 1972. Includes "The Policies of Perfection of Life and Social Leadership, Organizing and Planning the National Economy," "Deepening the Development of Socialist Democracy," "The Rumanian Communist Party—Leading Political Force in the Work of Raising the Multilaterally Developed Socialist Society," and "The National Conference—Brilliant Affirmation of the Party's Capacity to Fill the Leading Role in Our Society." G. J. Bobango

2174. —. P.C.R. ÎN FRUNTEA LUPTEI MASELOR PENTRU TRANSFORMĂRI REVOLUŢIONARE FUNDAMENTALE ÎN SOCIETATEA ROMÂNEASCA (1944-1947) [The Rumanian Communist Party leading the masses' struggle for revolutionary change in Rumanian society, 1944-47]. *Anale de Istorie [Rumania] 1978 24(5): 130-151.* Describes the possibilities open to the Rumanian Communist Party to transform Rumania into a socialist state after the antifascist uprising of August 1944 and how they were exploited.

2175. —. SESIUNE ŞTIINŢIFICĂ JUBILIARĂ CU TEMA: "LOCUL ŞI ROLUL TINERETULUI ÎN VIAŢA SOCIAL-POLITICĂ A ROMÂNIEI" DEDICATĂ ANIVERSĂRII A 50 DE ANI DE LA CREAREA U.T.C. [The anniversary scientific conference on the place and role of young people in the sociopolitical life of Rumania dedicated to the 50th anniversary of the foundation of the Union of Communist Youth]. *Anale de Istorie [Rumania] 1972 18(2): 153-174.* This jubilee conference was held at the Musuem of the History of the Communist Party in Bucharest on 15-17 March 1972. It was organized by the Central Committtee of the Union of Communist Youth, the Academy of Social and Political Science, and the Ministry of Education. It was attended by delegates from Communist bloc countries. Includes a list of participants, summaries of papers given, and the text of telegrams sent to the Central Committee of the Union of Communist Youth and to Nicolae Ceauşescu. M. Daly

2176. —. SESIUNEA ŞTIINŢIFICĂ JUBILIARĂ ÎN CINSTEA CELEI DE-A 25-A ANIVERSĂRI A PROCLAMĂRII REPUBLICII [Jubilee scientific session in honor of the 25th anniversary of the proclamation of the republic]. *Anale de Istorie [Rumania] 1973 19(1): 187-193.* Summarizes the papers presented 22 December 1972 at the Rumanian Atheneum conference celebrating a quarter-century of the Rumanian People's Republic. Papers by Aron Petric, Ervin Hutira, Ioan Ceterchi, Dumitru Mazilu, Alexandru Tănase, and others clearly showed how the Rumanian Communist Party elevated the people's republican and antimonarchist tradition to a higher level, and carried out a successful change to a new form of state in which all power is held by the working classes. These papers stressed the humanistic nature of socialist democracy, and the constant dialogue carried on between Party and people that created new modalities of Marxist structures and economic accomplishment. Ion Tutoveanu emphasized the fundamental military concepts of the Communist Party, or the defense of the nation by the entire people, and Nicolae Ecobescu documented Rumanian foreign policy. G. J. Bobango

Yugoslavia

2177. Aleksic, Milan. GROWING COOPERATION. *World Marxist R. [Canada] 1974 17(7): 110-116.* Reports on Yugoslavia's support for the economic integration of Communist countries especially under auspices of Comecon, 1947-73.

2178. Bezdanov, Stefan. VOSPITUVANIETO I OBRAZOVANIETO VO DOKUMENTITE I REVOLUCIONERNATA AKCIJA NA KPJ/SKJ (1919-1979) [Upbringing and education in the documents and revolutionary action of the Communist Party of Yugoslavia-League of Communists of Yugoslavia, 1919-79]. *Istorija [Yugoslavia] 1981 17(1): 201-231.* Documents from congresses and conferences from 1919-79 show that the Communist Party of Yugoslavia, later reconstituted as the League of Communists of Yugoslavia, regarded the upbringing and education of youth as an integral part of the class struggle and a priority task in the ideological and political development of the working class.

2179. Biber, Dušan. NARODNOOSVOBODILNI BOJ V JUGOSLAVIJI ZA SVOBODO IN LJUDSKO OBLAST [National liberation struggle for liberty and popular government in Yugoslavia]. *Prispevki za Zgodovino Delavskega Gibanja [Yugoslavia] 1978-79 18-19(1-2): 53-62.* Discusses the strategy and tactics of the Yugoslav Communist Party and the National Liberation Movement in the struggle for liberation and the seizure of power. J/S

2180. Blagoev, S. M. K VOPROSU O KONSTITUIROVANII FEDERATIVNOI NARODNOI RESPUBLIKI IUGOSLAVII [The founding of the Federal People's Republic of Yugoslavia]. *Sovetskoe Slavianovedenie [USSR] 1975 (6): 70-82.* Examines some aspects of the people's revolution in Yugoslavia, particularly the solution of the nationality question. The task of an effective struggle to liberate the country from the fascists demanded the unification of all the Yugoslav people. The Communist Party's national liberation war had as its goal not only the expulsion of the fascists, but a change in the status of all nationalities in Yugoslavia. The second session of the anti-fascist *veche* of the national liberation of Yugoslavia, 29-30 November 1943, resolved that Yugoslavia be built on democratic federal principles, a federal union of equal nationalities which would guarantee the equal rights of Serbs, Croatians, Slovenians, Macedonians, and Montenegrans. On 29 November 1945, the birth of the new national state, the Federal People's Republic of Yugoslavia, was proclaimed. Based mostly on secondary sources; 43 notes. L. Kalinowski

2181. Bodrožić, Milica. NAUČNI SKUP "60 GODINA KPJ (SKJ), SKOJ-A I REVOLUCIONARNIH SINDIKATA" [The conference "60 years of the Communist Party of Yugoslavia (the League of Communists of Yugoslavia), of the League of Communist Youth of Yugoslavia, and of the revolutionary trade unions"]. *Vojnoistorijski Glasnik [Yugoslavia] 1980 31(1): 303-305.* Discusses papers presented at a conference in Leskovac, 8-9 February 1980, organized by the Leskovac National Museum. The main aim of the conference was to review the activities of the Communist Party and the Youth League in Southern Serbia from 1918-47. All the reports are to be published in the *Leskovački Zbornik.* J. Bamber

2182. Brković, Savo. O NEKIM KONSTATACIJAMA U MATERIJALIMA I (OSNIVAČKOG) KONGRESA KP CRNE GORE [Statements made in the material presented to the 1st (founding) Congress of the Communist Party of Montenegro]. *Istorijski Zapisi [Yugoslavia] 1966 19(3): 543-563.* Refutes some facts and dates in the reports submitted at the 1st (founding) Congress of the Communist Party of Montenegro, 4-7 October 1948, relating to the history of the Communist movement in Montenegro, 1920-42.

2183. Campbell, John C. JUGOSLAVIA: CRISIS AND CHOICE. *Foreign Affairs 1963 41(2): 384-397.* Discusses the impact on Yugoslavia's foreign policy of worsening economic relations with other Communist countries and with the European Economic Community, 1950's-62.

2184. Canapa, Marie-Paule. AUTOGESTION ET POUVOIR EN YOUGOSLAVIA [Self-management and authority in Yugoslavia]. *Rev. d'Etudes Comparatives Est-Ouest [France] 1983 14(4): 5-29.* Examines the effect of worker self-management on the authority of the Communist Party and the government relative to decision-making and the legitimacy of power.

2185. Carlton, David and Schaerf, Carlo, ed. *South-Eastern Europe after Tito: A Powder-Keg for the 1980s?* New York: St. Martin's, 1983. 211 pp.

2186. Carter, April. *Democratic Reform in Yugoslavia: The Changing Role of the Party.* Princeton: Princeton U. Pr., 1982. 285 pp.

2187. Cohen, Lenard J. PARTISANS, PROFESSIONALS, AND PROLETARIANS: ELITE CHANGE IN YUGOSLAVIA, 1952-78. *Can. Slavonic Papers [Canada] 1979 21(4): 446-478.* The direction of Yugoslavian socialism in the post-Tito era may be determined by examining changes in membership of the Central Committee of the Communist Party. Analysis of the elite, 1952-78, reveals a shift from a unified group of professional revolutionaries and politicians to younger members from diverse social, educational, and occupational backgrounds. The resultant trend toward decentralization, rapid modernization, and increased nationalist sentiments of the 1960's was checked by Tito in 1972 with extensive purging of the Central Committee. The reinstatement of older Party and military representatives halted the fusion of nationalists with the traditional elite, yet a balance between political continuity and adaptation to social modernization remains to be achieved. Primary sources, 7 tables, 47 notes. French abstract.

2188. Denitch, Bogdan. NOTES ON THE RELEVANCE OF YUGOSLAV SELF-MANAGEMENT. *Pol. and Soc. 1973 3(4): 473-489.* Discusses worker self-management in Yugoslavia and its evolution since the expansion of the Communist Party in the 1940's.

2189. Denitch, Bogdan. THE USE OF SPECIALISTS IN POLICYMAKING IN YUGOSLAVIA. *Studies in Comparative Int. Development 1978 13(2): 77-87.* The use of non-Communists as military and political specialists at top policy levels in Yugoslavia began during World War II. This condition existed because the Party cadres lacked necessary skills. Since the war, the Party has viewed science, technology, and higher education as the formula for modernization, and Communist Party membership has become necessary for a serious political career. This has led to the development of a bureaucracy that is top-heavy with university educated personnel. Education has become a necessity for upward social mobility within the Party and state. The result is exaggerated influence by academicians and the potential for development of new elites. Table, 3 ref. S. A. Farmerie

2190. Djilas, Milovan. *Tito: The Story from Inside.* New York: Harcourt Brace Jovanovich, 1980. 185 pp.

2191. Djurović, Borislav. KLASNA OSNOVA SAVEZA KOMUNISTA JUGOSLAVIJE [The class basis of the Communist League of Yugoslavia]. *Zbornik za Društvene Nauke [Yugoslavia] 1977 (63): 7-16.* Studies Josip Tito's concept of the relationship between Party and class. From the Communist Party Congress in Zagreb in 1952, Tito insisted on a firm connection between the Communist Party and the working class, emphasizing the need for the Communist League to strengthen the class spirit and class influence of the workers. 24 notes. A. C. Niven/S

2192. Doneska-Trenchevska, Dzhurdzhevka. UCHILISHNITE EMISII PO ISTORIIA NA RADIO SKOPIE I 60-GODISHNINATA OD OSNOVANIETO NA KPJ ODNOSNO SKJ [Radio Skopje's school programs on history and the 60th anniversary of the Communist Party of Yugoslavia, later the League of Communists of Yugoslavia]. *Istorija [Yugoslavia] 1979 15(1): 191-195.* Describes the content of special programs broadcast by Radio Skopje in 1979 to mark the 60th anniversary of the formation of the Communist Party of Yugoslavia, which later became the League of Communists of Yugoslavia.

2193. Figa, Jozef. "Legitimacy and Self-Management in Socialist Yugoslavia: Contradictions and Reconciliations in Yugoslav Society." U. of New Hampshire 1984. 384 pp. *DAI 1984 45(5): 1544-1545-A.* DA8419552

2194. Genest, Jean. L'AUTOGESTION [Self-management]. *Action Natl. [Canada] 1974 64(3): 239-265.* A new brand of socialism based on the participation of workers in the management of enterprises appeared in Yugoslavia in 1950 and has been incorporated by various Communist parties, notably in France.

2195. Hadžibegovic, Ilijas. DRUGI (VUKOVARSKI) KONGRES KPJ 1920 [The second (Vukovar) congress of the Communist Party of Yugoslavia, 1920]. *Godišnjak Društva Istoričara Bosne i Hercegovine [Yugoslavia] 1968-69 18: 309-311.* Discusses the proceedings of, and papers presented at the second (Vukovar) congress of the Communist Party of Yugoslavia, 1920, 22-23 June 1970, on the occasion of the 50th anniversary of the 1920 congress.

2196. Kasaš, Aleksandar. JEDINSTVENI SINDIKATI RADNIKA I NAMEŠTENIKA VOIVODINE U PERIODU OD 1945. DO 1948. GODINE [The United Trade Unions of Workers and Employees of Voivodina, 1945-48]. *Zbornik za Istoriju [Yugoslavia] 1981 (23): 31-62.* The trade unions of Voivodina were reconstituted under the directives of the Communist Party even prior to the end of the war, in January 1945. For the next several months their activities were directed toward the immediate needs of the war-ravaged countryside. From war's end to April 1947 the trade unions participated in several ways in the efforts of national reconstruction; in April 1947 the adoption of the first national Five-Year Plan made ample place for the activities of the unions in fulfilling the plan goals, shockwork, and rationalization of production. 108 notes. P. J. Adler

2197. Končar, Ranko. KONSTITUISANJE JEDINSTVENIH SINDIKATA VOJVODINE 1945 [The founding of united labor unions in Vojvodina in 1945]. *Zbornik za Istoriju [Yugoslavia] 1977 16: 23-35.* By 1945, the Communist Party of Yugoslavia recognized the need to unite the working class, organize social security, raise workers' political and cultural awareness, and mobilize them for the task of the nation's economic recovery. The author explores the political, military, and economic circumstances in Vojvodina before the First Conference of the United Labor Unions of Vojvodina on 6 May 1945 and union activities during 1945. Based on documents from the Vojvodina Archives and secondary sources; 46 notes. J. Bamber

2198. Končar, Ranko. PRILOG PITANJU KONCENCIJE KPJ PREMA DRUŠTVENO-EKONOMSKOM RAZVOJU JUGOSLAVIJE U PERIODU "REVOLUCIONARNOG ETATISMA" [On the concept of the Communist Party of Yugoslavia concerning the socioeconomic development of Yugoslavia in the period of "revolutionary state socialism"]. *Zbornik za Istoriju [Yugoslavia] 1980 (21): 69-78.* In view of the subjective conditions of the development of the Communist Party in Yugoslavia as well as the objective conditions of the immediate postwar period, a certain intertwining of the Party with the bureaucracy of the state was to be expected. This did in fact occur, and at times to a degree which might justify the term "revolutionary state socialism" during the years 1945 to 1949. P. J. Adler

2199. Kreger, S. "Das Jugoslawische Parteiorgan 'BORBA' als Spiegel der Beziehungen Jugolawiens zum Ostblock sowie der Entstalinisierung nach dem Kominformkonflikt in den Jahren 1948-1953" [The Yugoslav Party organ *Borba* (The struggle) as a mirror of the Yugoslav relation to the East and of the destalinization after the conflict with the Cominform, 1948-53]. U. of Vienna [Austria] 1980. 135 pp. *DAI-C 1983 43(3): 440; 8/2014c.*

2200. Markovich, Stephen C. WHEN TO AID COMMUNIST COUNTRIES. *East Europe 1972 21(9): 7-10.* The 1948 Yugoslavian break with the USSR, helped by US aid, was unique among Communist countries. Geography, hesitant Soviet reaction, an army, and a Communist Party of Tito's own creation enabled him to defy the Soviets, who successfully crushed similar movements in Poland and Hungary in 1956 and in Czechoslovakia in 1968. E. W. Jennison, Jr.

2201. Markovich, Stephen C. WHITHER THE LEAGUE OF COMMUNISTS? *Can. Slavonic Papers [Canada] 1980 22(1): 92-98.* In 1952, the Sixth Party Congress, under Tito's leadership, agreed that the Party and the state in Yugoslavia would begin to wither away. In 1971, after some considerable reduction in the Party's power, Tito restored its authority. This proved to be a major source of confusion in the 1970's. The quandary over the Party's role stems from two dilemmas: the conflict between the role of the Party and the role of the self-management system, and the contradiction between the role of the Party in theory and the role of the Party in practice. 12 notes. J. F. Harrington, Jr.

2202. Miller, Robert F. and Merrill, E. Vance. YUGOSLAV CENTRAL COMMITTEE MEMBERSHIP: WHAT THE FIGURES SHOW. *Politics [Australia] 1979 14(1): 71-81.* Comparisons of the 1974 and 1978 Party central committee membership reflect an increasing conservatism, if not immobilism, as the system prepares for the post-Tito era. The authors isolate a set of particular demographic and occupational characteristics which distinguish a core elite of holdovers, who manifest these conservative tendencies to an even greater degree than the general CC memberships. It turns out that Party and government job incumbencies, as well as a long record of Party membership and participation in the World War II partisan movement, are considerably more important than nationality in predicting core elite status. The tendency toward "Old Guardism" had become especially strong by 1978. Secondary sources; 12 notes. J/S

2203. Miller, Robert F. THE 12TH CONGRESS OF THE LEAGUE OF COMMUNISTS OF YUGOSLAVIA: THE SUCCESSION PROCESS CONTINUES. *Australian Outlook [Australia] 1982 36(3): 11-18.* An observer at the 12th Congress of the League of Communists of Yugoslavia (the first without Tito), which took place in Belgrade, 26-29 June 1982, summarizes the background to and proceedings of the meetings. Problems that had emerged were ethnic rivalries, especially an outburst among Albanians in Kosovo, Serbia; economic weakness, including declining real incomes, unemployment, and inflation; and the failure of nonalignment in foreign policy. The congress reflected well balances within the country.

Serbs continued to dominate the Presidium; the Presidium had become somewhat weaker in comparison with the Central Committee in the absence of a real successor to Tito; solutions to economic problems were vague and rhetorical; and the party had emerged as more confederal, which accorded with the realities of provincial nationalism. Based on Yugoslav publications; 29 notes.
W. D. McIntyre

2204. Muravchik, Joshua. THE INTELLECTUAL ODYSSEY OF MILOVAN DJILAS. *World Affairs 1983 145(4): 323-346.* Yugoslavian Communist Milovan Djilas broke consecutively with Stalin, Tito, Lenin, and ultimately with Marx, and ended up as an "existential humanist," who saw ideologies—closed systems of thought and action—as the problem, where man sought political answers to questions that were more spiritual than political; his heresy led to dismissal from his offices in the Yugoslav government and imprisonment.

2205. Neal, Fred Warner. YUGOSLAV COMMUNIST THEORY. *Am. Slavic and East European Rev. 1960 19(1): 42-62.* Though Communist theory in both the USSR and Yugoslavia are based in Marxist political theory and Leninist political theory, Yugoslavia differs in its national form of socialism, theory on transition from capitalism, proletarian internationalism, role of the state party, and dictatorship of the proletariat, ownership, localized socialism, and beliefs about the relation of democracy to socialism.

2206. Nemes, János. A SZOCIALISTA JUGOSZLÁVIA ÉS A JKSZ EGYSÉGÉÉRT [For socialist Yugoslavia and the Yugoslavian League of Communists]. *Társadalmi Szemle [Hungary] 1972 27(3): 39-43.* An analysis of the League of Communists' 2d Party Conference, 1970, with reference to its main aims and tasks.

2207. Nikiforov, L. COOPERATION IN THE INTERESTS OF SOCIALISM. *Int. Affairs [USSR] 1974 (2): 22-25.* Asserts the importance of unity among Communist countries for the development of world socialism and particularly discusses the evolution of Soviet-Yugoslav cooperation since the Belgrade Declaration (1955).

2208. Očak, Ivan. JUGOSLAVENSKI INTERNACIONALISTI U SSSR-u POSLIJE GRAĐANSKOG RATA [Yugoslav internationalists in the USSR after the civil war]. *Rad Jugoslavenska Akademija Znanosti i Umjetnosti: Društveni Znanosti [Yugoslavia] 1969 356(15): 75-108.* Investigates the careers of the so-called Yugoslav internationalists who had been participants in the October Revolution and the civil war, who after 1921 stayed in the Soviet Union and worked in the Red Army, the Communist Party, and other Soviet political organizations.

2209. Pacor, Mario. ORIENTAMENTI DELLA STORIOGRAFIA JUGOSLAVA SULLA RESISTENZA [The orientations of Yugoslavian historiography toward the resistance]. *Movimento di Liberazione in Italia [Italy] 1964 (76): 71-86.* Summarizes Yugoslavian political history, 1918-46, emphasizing the role of the Yugoslavian Communist Party in organizing the resistance, in the liberation, and in the subsequent socialist revolution. Surveys postwar Yugoslavian historiography on the period, particularly since the rigorous and extensive organization of research after the late 1950's, and considers archival sources. The frequently subjective historiography of the first postwar years has evolved into a more scientific and critical approach. Lists principal Yugoslavian works on this period with Italian title translations. Biblio.
R. O. Khan

2210. Petranović, Branko. IZVORI ZA ISTORIJU KPJ (HEURISTIĆKO-METODOLOŠKI OSVRT) [Source materials for the history of the Yugoslavian Communist Party: a heuristic and methodological sketch]. *Istorijski Glasnik [Yugoslavia] 1978 (1-2): 39-47.* The history of Communists in Yugoslav lands must be approached in the context of the varying situations of the Communist Party as a sociopolitical force. In the opening phase of its existence, a brief period of legality was followed by a decade and a half of underground existence under intense government persecution. The documentation of the Party is sketchy for most of this period, and must be supplemented extensively by documents drawn from official and bourgeois sources. During the second world war, the Party entered a different phase of open resistance to the invaders and their pawns; documentation of Party activity again has gaps caused by external conditions, but may be supplemented by the occupiers' records. In the period since 1945, the Party occupied a quite different position in public life, and the documents for the study of Party activity can now be segregated according to the sector and nature of its program.
P. J. Adler

2211. Petranović, Branko. ZAPISNICI MESNE (GRADSKE) KONFERENCIJE KPS BEOGRADA 1945-1951. KAO ISTORIJSKI IZVOR [Stenographic transcripts of the city conference in Belgrade of the Communist Party of Serbia, 1945-51, as historical sources]. *Istorijski Glasnik [Yugoslavia] 1979 (1-2): 57-72.* Four city conferences held by the Communist Party of Serbia in Belgrade, 1945-51, dealt with party organizational structure, economic conditions, and social priorities. 5 notes.
P. J. Adler

2212. Petrovski, Dancho. "TRKALEZNA MASA" PO POVOD 40-GODISHNINATA OD ODRZHUVANIETO NA POKRAINSKATA KONFERENTSIIA NA KPJ VO MAKEDONIIA [Round Table on the 40th anniversary of the Provincial Conference of the Communist Party of Yugoslavia for Macedonia]. *Istorija [Yugoslavia] 1980 16(2): 254-259.* Describes the proceedings at a round table seminar held at the Mito Hadzhivasilev-Iasmin Marxist Center in Skopje in September 1980.

2213. Popov, Jelena. ORGANIZACIJA KOMUNISTIČKE PARTIJE JUGOSLAVIJE U VOJVODINI 1945-1948 [The organization of the Communist Party of Yugoslavia in the Vojvodina, 1945-48]. *Zbornik za Istoriju [Yugoslavia] 1979 (19): 61-96.* In the period immediately after World War II, the Communist Party in the Vojvodina underwent substantial gains in membership and changes in its class structure. The majority of the membership was of Serb nationality, with Hungarians a distant second. Most of the new members were peasants, and by 1948 they still constituted a bare majority of the total membership, but they were losing ground to the workers. It is noteworthy that the postwar immigrants from other regions of Yugoslavia included a higher proportion of Party members than the autochthonous population of whatever nationality. Based on published Yugoslav sources; tables, 98 notes.
P. J. Adler

2214. Prpic, George J. COMMUNISM AND NATIONALISM IN YUGOSLAVIA. *Balkan Studies [Greece] 1969 10(1): 23-50.* Nationalist pressures present since at least 1920 and continued Croatian claims of linguistic and cultural suppression by Serbia threaten the unity of Yugoslavia and the organization of the Communist Party.

2215. Rakas, Milan. PREPARATIONS FOR 10TH CONGRESS OF YUGOSLAV LEAGUE OF COMMUNISTS. *World Marxist R. [Canada] 1974 17(4): 131-136.* In an interview Milan Rakas, editor-in-chief of *Kommunist*, describes preparations for the 10th Congress of the League of Communists of Yugoslavia (scheduled 27-30 May 1974) and his newspaper's support of the LCY.

2216. Ramet, Pedro. POLITICAL STRUGGLE AND INSTITUTIONAL REORGANIZATION IN YUGOSLAVIA. *Political Science Quarterly 1984 99(2): 289-301.* Organizational instability has been a constant factor in Yugoslav politics since the postwar imposition of a Communist regime. Expectations that the 1982 Twelfth Party Congress would resolve the tensions between the federal government and its constituent republics were unfounded because the Party's attempt to maintain unity has been frustrated by rival policy opponents who seek to promote their program through institutional reorganization, and because Yugoslav Party congresses have primarily served as reflections of current policy debates rather than arbiters of Communist strategy. Based on Foreign Broadcast Information Service, Daily Report articles, Yugoslav newspaper articles, and secondary sources; 46 notes.
R. M. Gray

2217. Remington, Robin Alison. YUGOSLAVIA: THE PARTISAN VANGUARD. *Studies in Comparative Communism 1978 11(3): 250-264.* In Yugoslavia the Communist Party was weakened by efforts to establish self-managing organs, then by decentraliza-

tion, and finally in the 1970's by Tito's reassertion of charismatic authority in the face of nationalism. The Party and army were closely allied until the era of experiments. With Tito's restored authority, political influence over the army has increased and the Yugoslav defense minister now sits on the Presidium of the League of Communists. The Party itself has not been cohesive in presenting values which might be accepted by the military. 25 notes.
D. Balmuth

2218. Sandulowicz, Marek. KSZTAŁTOWANIE SIĘ WŁADZY LUDOWEJ W JUGOSLAWII 1941-1946 [Formation of people's power in Yugoslavia, 1941-46]. *Z Pola Walki [Poland] 1981 23[i.e., 24](1): 46-67.* Surveys the process of transformation of the movement for national liberation in Yugoslavia at the end of World War II into a social and political revolution. Under the leadership of the Communist Party, committees for future administration were established in the liberated territories, which developed into a dense network. At the end of the war the new state was forced to compromise with bourgeois forces, but its legal foundations are in compliance with the Marxist-Leninist doctrine. Secondary sources; 23 notes. Russian and English summaries. M. Hernas

2219. Seroka, J. H. THE PARTY, NATIONAL CRISES, AND LEGISLATIVE BEHAVIOR IN SOCIALIST YUGOSLAVIA. *East European Quarterly 1984 18(1): 73-92.* In 1973 constitutional changes and policies made at the 10th Congress of the League of Communists of Yugoslavia, reflected the need for fundamental changes in the processes of social reform in order to maintain the integrity and legitimacy of the Yugoslav state. There were three issues which specifically concerned the Party apparatus: developmental inequalities, the resurgence of ethnic tensions, and the acceptance of legitimate authority. Yugoslav legislatures are dynamic organizations actively concerned about some of the major issues of Yugoslav political life. The federal legislature maintains a powerful professional component, but it has tried to open up the system to all sectors of society. Legislative reforms appear to be successful in channeling conflict; and the Party has not surrendered control over major policy issues to the legislature. 64 notes.
G. L. Neville

2220. Singleton, F. YUGOSLAVIA TAKES STOCK. *Critique [Great Britain] 1978-79 (10-11): 173-180.* Discusses the changes in Yugoslav Communist Party policy from its Fifth Congress in July 1948; the Yugoslavs, though expelled from the Cominform, still felt themselves allied to Stalin.

2221. Sohn, S. "Die 'Praxis'-Gruppe (Darstellung ihrer Konzeption und Versuch einer Kritischen Auseinandersetzung)" [The Praxis-Group: explanation and critical review of its conception]. U. of Vienna 1982. 340 pp. *DAI-C 1984 45(3): 690; 9/2820c.*

2222. Stojanović, Stanislav. SKJ I MEDJUNARODNI RADNIČKI POKRET [The League of Communists of Yugoslavia and the international workers' movement]. *Politička Misao [Yugoslavia] 1975 12(4): 55-70.* Because the League of Communists of Yugoslavia has been firmly committed to nonalignment, 1960-75, its international relations include all progressive movements and cannot be limited to superficial contacts with other Communist parties. 6 notes. S. Košak

2223. Tito, Josip Broz. ŠEZDESET GODINA REVOLUCIONARNE BORBE SAVEZA KOMUNISTA JUGOSLAVIJE [Sixty years of the revolutionary struggle of the League of Communists of Yugoslavia (LCY)]. *Vojnoistorijski Glasnik [Yugoslavia] 1979 30(2): 11-39.* Speech given on the occasion of the 60th anniversary of the LCY, founded in 1919 as the Socialist Workers' Party of Yugoslavia (Communist). Lists crucial landmarks in the Party's history, among them the creation of the People's Front in 1935; the Party's role in the coup d'état of 27 March 1941 in Belgrade; the organization of armed resistance during World War II, culminating in the second session of the Anti-Fascist Council of the National Liberation of Yugoslavia on 29 November 1943, which abolished the monarchy and proclaimed the new Yugoslavia; the break with the Cominform in 1948; the dissolution of state enterprises and the introduction of worker self-management in 1950; and the constitution of 1974 and the Law of Associated Labor, replacing representative by direct democracy. Concludes with a survey of Yugoslavia's foreign relations and its role in the nonaligned movement.
S. Košak

2224. Tito, Josip Broz. SHEESET GODINI REVOLUTSIONERNA BORBA NA SOIUZOT NA KOMUNISTITE NA JUGOSLAVIIA [Sixty years of revolutionary struggle by the Communist League of Yugoslavia]. *Istorija [Yugoslavia] 1979 15(1): 7-44.* Reviews the Communist Party's development and achievements since its formation in 1919. Reproduction of a report by Josip Broz Tito in the Macedonian edition of *Komunist,* 20 April 1979.

2225. Todorović, Aleksandar. ULOGA SKJ U RAZVOJU SAMOUPRAVNIH ODNOSA I RADNIČKESVESTI [The role of the League of Communists of Yugoslavia in the development of self-management and of the workers' awareness]. *Zbornik za Društvene Nauke [Yugoslavia] 1969 54: 5-32.* Traces the development of the working class resulting from industrialization on Yugoslav territory: in Slovenia after 1848, in Croatia, Bosnia and Herzegovina by the end of the 19th century, and in Serbia at the beginning of the 20th century. Outlines the rise of working class consciousness in Europe as reflected particularly in the idea of self-management, which began to develop in England in 1833-34. Although the development of the Yugoslav working class came much later, the League of the Communists of Yugoslavia was able to develop workers' awareness and implement the idea of of self-management. 42 notes.
S. Košak

2226. Vujičić, Gojko. TITO—VOJNA MISAO I DJELA (IZBOR IZ VOJNIH DJELA) [Tito—military ideas and achievements: a selection of his military works]. *Vojnoistorijski Glasnik [Yugoslavia] 1983 34(1): 313-315.* Reviews *Tito—Military Ideas and Achievements: A Selection of His Military Works* (1982). It examines the politics of the Yugoslav Communist Party between 1936 and 1941, the Yugoslav national liberation struggle between 1941 and 1945, and the Yugoslav system of national defense between 1945 and 1979. A. J. Evans

2227. Walkin, Jacob. YUGOSLAVIA AFTER THE TENTH PARTY CONGRESS. *Survey [Great Britain] 1976 22(1): 55-73.* Little in the way of fundamental political change has occurred as a result of the 10th Yugoslav Party Congress in May 1974. The self-management system has been retained, the role of the police has been reduced, and the republics have more autonomy. The author doubts that a return to secrecy at the party center would be feasible. Based on personal observations and interviews, and contemporary press and magazine accounts; 17 notes.
R. B. Valliant

2228. Willoughby, Charles A. THE CROATIAN SLAUGHTERHOUSE. *East Europe 1975 24(2): 18-20.* Following World War II, Communists massacred thousands of Croatian, Slovenian, and Serbian anti-Communists. From the author's *Operation Slaughterhouse: Eyewitness Accounts of Postwar Massacres in Yugoslavia* (Philadelphia: Dorrance & Company).

2229. Zaninovich, M. George. YUGOSLAV SUCCESSION AND LEADERSHIP STABILITY. *Studies in Comparative Communism 1983 16(3): 179-190.* The smooth leadership change in Yugoslavia was facilitated by the existence of a collective presidency, a board of 15, by the purge of the ambitious, the strengthening of the home guard, emphasis on the need to moderate dissent during a time of crisis, the growth of the membership of the Communist League and its major role in the army, and an emphasis on popular participation through the Socialist Alliance, workers' control, and labor associations. The prospect is for smooth changes in leadership henceforth. 8 notes. D. Balmuth

2230. —. [IS YUGOSLAVIA LENINIST?]. *Studies in Comparative Communism 1977 10(4): 403-411.*

Johnson, A. Ross. IS YUGOSLAVIA LENINIST?, *pp. 403-407.* Response to an earlier article by William Zimmerman. The institutional pluralization seen by Western observers in the 1960's was often the result of political conflict among republican Party organizations. In 1971 Tito forced replacement of the Party leadership in Croatia and after 1971 the Yugoslav League of Communists asserted its "guiding role" in contrast to the "leading role" stated in 1952-53. The "guiding role" meant influence. Zimmerman saw a Leninist model for the Party in the 1970's, but ignored the federal character of the Party as well as the fact that the central Party apparatus is not the exlusive decisionmaking body. A unitary *nomenklatura* system has not been reinstituted but central government bodies have become a forum for reconciling conflicting republican economic interests. Many republican presidents are not members of the Party Executive Committee and most are republican rather than Yugoslav political figures. The prospect for succession is competition among personalities and institutions including the Party. The political system will play a role. 9 notes.

Zimmerman, William. REJOINDER, *pp. 408-411.* Emphasizing general agreement with Johnson, notes that the Party will not tolerate views differing from those of the League. The role of the central Party apparatus in the succession will be preeminent. 6 notes. D. Balmuth

2231. —. PREGLED ISTORIJE SAVEZA KOMUNISTA JUGOSLAVIJE [A survey of the history of the League of Communists of Yugoslavia]. *Istorijski Zapisi [Yugoslavia] 1964 17(2): 191-390.* A special issue which summarizes the papers presented at a conference organized by the Historical Commission of the Central Committee of the League of Communists of Montenegro, the Institute of History, and the Historical Society of Montenegro, held 15-16 April 1964. The conference discussed *Pregled Istorije Saveza Komunista Jugoslavije* [A Survey of the History of the League of Communists of Yugoslavia].

Western Europe

General

2232. Adilov, V. A.; Cherkasov, R. F.; and Stepanov, M. I. V CHEST' IUBILEEV KOMMUNISTICHESKIKH PARTII [In honor of Communist Party jubilees]. *Voprosy Istorii KPSS [USSR] 1981 (6): 143-151.* In honor of the 60th anniversary of the Italian Communist Party, a conference took place on 16 March 1981 at the Central Committee of the Communist Party of the Soviet Union Institute of Marxism-Leninism, organized by the Institute with the Central Committee's Academy of Social Sciences and the Academy of Sciences' Institute of International Workers' Movements. A. E. Egorov presided over the proceedings, emphasizing in his introductory speech the importance of recognizing anniversaries of foreign Communist Parties and maintaining and strengthening links with them. Papers were read by P. A. Rodionov, R. Trivelli, V. A. Bogorad, and G. S. Filatov. A similarly organized conference was held in the same institute under the guidance of A. E. Egorov on 25 March in honor of the 60th anniversary of the Portugese Communist Party, and papers were read by M. P. Mchedlov, V. I. Koval', and Carlos Aboim Ingles. L. Smith

2233. Albrecht-Carrié, René. CAN THE WEST REGAIN THE INITIATIVE? *South Atlantic Q. 1963 62(2): 159-168.* Assesses economic growth, political change, and shifts in the balance of power throughout Great Britain and Western Europe, 1945-60, and speculates on whether Western foreign policy actions can become initiative rather than reaction to Communism.

2234. Albright, David E., ed. *Communism and Political Systems in Western Europe.* Boulder, Colo.: Westview Pr., 1979. 379 pp.

2235. Andersen, Palle. 50 LET KOMPARTII DANII [Fifty years of the Danish Communist Party]. *Voprosy Istorii KPSS [USSR] 1969 (11): 9-102.* Outlines the history of the Communist Party in Denmark, emphasizing its links wth the socialist states of Eastern Europe.

2236. Andrzejewski, Marek. ZARYS DZIEJÓW RUCHU ROBOTNICZEGO W SZWAJCARII [The worker movement in Switzerland]. *Z Pola Walki [Poland] 1982 25(3-4): 77-101.* Sketches the emergence and development of the worker movement in Switzerland, formed under the influence of German socialism and Bakuninian anarchism during the 1870's. Switzerland, the asylum of exiled Russian and German left-wing activists, quickly developed radical parties of its own. In 1921 the split over Comintern resulted in the emergence of the Communist Party of Switzerland, declared illegal in 1940. Legal again since 1945, the party's importance has diminished, although the Socialist Party of Switzerland has permanent cabinet members, and has had, on average, 25% of the votes. 76 notes. Russian and English summaries. M. Hernas

2237. Arkes, Hadley. DEMOCRACY AND EUROPEAN COMMUNISM. *Commentary 1976 61(5): 38-47.* Bringing the Communist parties of Italy and France into their respective governments is apparently an idea "whose time has come." A number of books have recently appeared suggesting that the Communist parties of Western Europe deserve to be treated as legitimate parts of the political order and therefore legitimate claimants to a role in government. According to Irving Howe, the greater "looseness" in the Communist parties of the West is not enough reason to suppose that they have genuinely accepted the terms of parliamentary democracy. The coming to power of Communists in Italy and France would itself be taken as the sign of a new dynamic at work in Europe. Their ascension would establish worldwide expectations about a new structure of power in the world. Primary and secondary sources. S. R. Herstein

2238. Arnal, Oscar L. A MISSIONARY "MAIN TENDUE" TOWARD FRENCH COMMUNISTS: THE "TEMOIGNAGES" OF THE WORKER-PRIESTS, 1943-1954. *French Historical Studies 1984 13(4): 529-556.* Between 1943 and 1954 more than 100 French and Belgian worker priests immersed themselves in proletarian life and cooperated on practical programs with Communist labor leaders. Suppressed by Catholic conservatives in 1954, the movement was revived by popular demand less than 10 years later. In the first three decades of its existence it brought tangible advancements for the working classes and served to improve the image of the Catholic Church. Private papers of René Boudot, personal interviews, and published sources; 64 notes. J. R. Vignery

2239. Arnot, Robin Page. 50 LET ZHURNALA *LEIBOR MANSLI* [Fifty years of the journal *Labor Monthly].* *Voprosy Istorii KPSS [USSR] 1971 (7): 116-119.* Reviews the history and policies of the British periodical, 1921-60's.

2240. Aslanov, R. M. and Bolotin, B. A. MAOIST GROUPINGS IN THE WEST SUFFER IDEOLOGICAL AND POLITICAL DEFEAT. *Far Eastern Affairs [USSR] 1980 (3): 118-130.* Pro-Peking Maoist groupings remain small sects, having no influence on the working class and masses in Western Europe, because Maoist maxims are unsuitable for Europe, while Europe's Communist parties consistently grow.

2241. Bartolini, Stefano. PER UN'ANALISI DEI RAPPORTI TRA PARTITI SOCIALISTI E COMUNISTI IN ITALIA E FRANCIA [Analysis of the relations between the Socialist and Communist Parties in Italy and France]. *Riv. Italiana di Scienza Pol. [Italy] 1976 6(3): 439-480.* Since World War II, electoral development on the Left has progressed similarly in Italy and France, although the electoral advantage of the Communists in Italy more closely parallels that of the Socialists in France. The author analyzes the institutional and political factors that have influenced the ideological competition on the Left in each country. The more important political element is the potential for competition between the two parties. The analysis of the parties' internal participation leads to a comparison of the internal participation within each party, the mobility of its elite, and the ability to achieve electoral mobilization. A third level of analysis considers the attitudes and behaviors of electorates toward the parties, particularly levels of party identification and perceptions of party legitimacy. J/S

2242. Beer-Jergitsch, Lilli. GESPRÄCH MIT FRAU LEOPOLDINE MÜNICHREITER (JÄNNER 1970) [Conversation with Mrs. Leopoldine Münichreiter (January 1970)]. *Zeitgeschichte [Austria] 1980 7(8): 277-287.* Recollections by the wife of an Austrian leftist who participated in the 1934 revolt in Austria and was finally executed. Mrs. Münichreiter found asylum in the USSR after a spectacular escape with her three children. Details her further life in Soviet Russia and her return to Austria in 1946.
G. E. Pergl

2243. Bellamy, Joan. THE STRUGGLE AGAINST RACISM IN BRITAIN. *World Marxist R. [Canada] 1974 17(3): 97-105.* Outlines the growth of racial discrimination in Great Britain after World War II and recent efforts by Britain's Communist Party and labor unions to combat such discrimination.

2244. Bezrukova, M. I. POLITICHESKAIA KARIKATURA I SATIRA KHERLUFA BIDSTRUPA [Herluf Bidstrup's political caricature and satire]. *Skandinavskii Sbornik [USSR] 1971 16: 224-240.* Discusses the contributions of Danish artist Herluf Bidstrup, who received the International Lenin Prize for his work in "strengthening peace among peoples." Bidstrup's works include book illustrations and posters, travel sketches, drawings, comic strips, and caricatures, but he is best known for his political illustrations, which emphasize antifascism, democracy, and peace. Bidstrup's activities in the postwar period were related closely to *Land og Folk* [Land and People], the central organ of the Danish Communist Party. Illus., 56 notes.

2245. Blum, Jean. KOMMUNISTICHESKOI PARTII BEL'GII: 50 LET [The Communist Party of Belgium: 50 years]. *Voprosy Istorii KPSS [USSR] 1971 (9): 100-106.* Surveys the history of the Party and prints six previously published statements that reflect its concern for peace.

2246. Bogorad, V. A. and Matveev, R. F. NEKOTORYE PROBLEMY ORGANIZATSIONNO-PARTIINOI RABOTY NA PREDPRIIATIAKH V STRANAKH KAPITALA [Some problems of organizational-Party work in enterprises of capitalist countries]. *Voprosy Istorii KPSS [USSR] 1974 (6): 33-47.* Since 1945 Communist parties in Western nations, mainly through their all-important factory cells as well as labor unions, have increasingly exercised ideological, political, and organizational leadership. The Party has been particularly successful in France and Italy. Based primarily on French, Italian, and Soviet periodical literature; 47 notes.
L. E. Holmes

2247. Bogorod, V. A. and Sokolov, R. N. IUBILEIAM KOMMUNISTICHESKIKH PARTII POSVIASHCHAETSIA [Dedications to anniversaries of Communist Parties]. *Voprosy Istorii KPSS [USSR] 1981 (3): 141-148.* Reports a 1980 Institute of Marxist-Leninism conference to celebrate the 60th anniversary of the French Communist Party and observes that 8 January 1981 was the 60th anniversary of the founding of the Luxembourg Communist Party. A. J. Evans

2248. Campbell, John C. THE MEDITERRANEAN CRISIS. *Foreign Affairs 1975 53(4): 605-624.* Discusses the need for clear-thinking policy formation in the Mediterranean basin. Examines the Arab-Israeli conflict and the dispute between Greece and Turkey over Cyprus. In the eastern Mediterranean, detente with Russia has led to detente on NATO's flank between Greece and Turkey, neither of whom are following US leadership. The third problem is the Communist Party in southern Europe. The Portuguese party under Alvaro Cunhal is a Moscow-line party; Portuguese nonalignment with Western defense would be a serious blow to the European balance. Spain and Italy have moderate, coalition-oriented parties, but within the government they could sabotage NATO, the Community, and the balance in the Mediterranean. Note. C. W. Olson

2249. Christensen, Jorn. COMMUNIST PARTY OF DENMARK AFTER ITS CONGRESS: CONFIDENCE AND OPTIMISM. *World Marxist Rev. 1977 20(4): 50-55.* Examines setbacks experienced by Denmark's Communist Party due to the Social-Democratic government's movement toward state-monopoly capitalism, 1973-77.

2250. Dankelmann, Ottfried. DER SOWJETISCHE BEITRAG ZUR BEFREIUNG EUROPAS VOM FASCHISMUS UND DIE ENTWICKLUNG DER WESTEUROPÄISCHEN ARBEITERBEWEGUNG (1943-49) [The Soviet contribution to the liberation of Europe from fascism and the development of the Western European worker movement, 1943-49]. *Martin-Luther-U. Halle-Wittenberg. Wissenshaftliche Zeitschrift. Gesellschafts- und Sprachenwissenschaftliche Reihe [East Germany] 1976 25(2): 23-28.* The growth of postwar European communism was inspired by the Russian contribution to the defeat of fascism and to the heavy losses sustained by European Communist parties in World War II. For example, 75,000 French Communists died in the Resistance, but after the war the French Communist party grew in number to 650, 000. Russian influence, at its peak in 1945, began to dwindle in Europe with the rise of social democracy. 18 notes.
A. Alcock

2251. Demertzis, Efstratios. "Factionalism in the Greek Communist Party." New York U. 1979. 198 pp. *DAI 1980 40(11): 5988-A.* 8010277

2252. Dimov, Nencho. IDEINO POLITICHESKA EVOLIUTSIIA NA ZAPADNOEVROPEISKATA SOTSIALDEMOKRATSIIA PREZ PURVATA POLOVINA NA 70-TE GODINI [The intellectual and political evolution of Western European Social Democracy in the first half of the 1970's]. *Istoricheski Pregled [Bulgaria] 1978 34(4): 3-27.* Studies the revitalization of theoretical activity and the modernization of the ideology of Democratic Socialism in the Socialist and Social Democratic parties of Austria, Germany, Sweden, France, and Belgium and in the Socialist International since 1970. Interprets this tendency as an attempt by right-wing leaderships to strengthen the attack on Marxism-Leninism in an era of mounting capitalist crisis, but notes also a countertendency, particularly in France and Belgium, for activists to question the monopoly-capitalist system and to seek cooperation with Communist parties.
F. A. K. Yasamee

2253. Domdey, Karl-Heinz. EUROPÄISCHE SICHERHEIT UND WIRTSCHAFTLICHE BEZIEHUNGEN ZWISCHEN DEN SOZIALISTISCHEN UND KAPITALISTISCHEN STAATEN EUROPAS [European security and economic relations among capitalist and Communist countries in Europe]. *Wissenschaftliche Zeitschrift der Humboldt-U. zu Berlin. Gesellschafts- und Sprachwissenschaftliche Reihe [East Germany] 1970 19(4): 415-433.* Analyzes the attempts to achieve peaceful, antidiscriminatory economic competition by strengthening the economic, scientific and technological cooperation among Communist and Western European states, 1959-69.

2254. Dominique, Pierre. LES "EUROPES" D'HIER ET CELLE D'AUJOURD'HUI [The "Europes" of yesterday and today]. *Écrits de Paris [France] 1973 (322): 40-45.* Views the Communist peril to Western Europe in the perspective of the unifying movements—Roman, Christian, and republican—which have dominated the European continent in earlier periods.

2255. Doorselaer, R. van. KOMMUNISTISCHE PARTIJ VAN BELGIË [The Communist Party of Belgium]. *Spiegel Hist. [Netherlands] 1981 16(4): 207-209.* The Communist Party of Belgium experienced a significant advance due to its role in the Resistance in World War II, but the Cold War contributed to its decline in the 1950's. Its fortunes since then have largely depended upon its identification with the Soviet Union and events in Central Europe. Primary sources; 3 illus. C. W. Wood, Jr.

2256. Dutschke, Rudi. AGAINST THE POPES: HOW HARD IT IS TO DISCUSS BAHRO'S BOOK. *Int. J. of Pol. 1980 10(2-3): 186-212.* Uses Rudolf Bahro's critique of existing communism (attacking the "popes"—the orthodox Communist leaders) as the basis of discussion. Since Russian communism arose in a country in the Asiatic mode of production, it developed into bureaucratic tyranny and state slavery. The capitalist West (wage slavery) and the communist East (state slavery) are united in opposition to change in the status quo. NATO and the Warsaw Pact act in consonance to block the road to socialism. Socialist class struggle in Western Europe will fail without democratic initiative in Russian and Eastern Europe. 10 ref. R. E. Noble

2257. Fedorov, V. G. NA SLUZHBE NARODU (K 60-LETIIU OSNOVANIIA KOMPARTII FINLANDII) [In the service of the people: the 60th anniversary of the founding of the Finnish Communist Party]. *Voprosy Istorii KPSS [USSR] 1978 (8): 108-112.* A short history of the Communist Party of Finland, founded in 1918, using Finnish sources.

2258. Fedorov, V. G. SOROK PIAT' LET BOR'BY ZA INTERESY TRUDOVOGO NARODA FINLIANDII [Forty five years of struggle for the interests of the working people of Finland]. *Voprosy Istorii KPSS [USSR] 1963 (8): 91-95.* Describes the formation and growth of the Communist Party of Finland, 1918-63, and mentions the names of several of its leaders.

2259. Fedorov, V. G. VETERAN KOMMUNISTICHESKOI PARTII FINLIANDII: K 80-LETIIU SO DNIA ROZHDENIIA V. PESSI [A veteran of the Communist Party of Finland: on the 80th birthday of V. Pessi]. *Voprosy Istorii KPSS [USSR] 1982 (3): 92-95.* Ville Pessi was born on 24 March 1902 to a proletariat family in Kaukol. He joined the Communist youth movement in 1919 and was the secretary of the Socialist Union of Finnish Youth from 1925 to 1927, when it was banned. He joined the Finnish Communist Party in 1924, heading the Party from 1935. During the war he was arrested and tortured. After the war he tirelessly promoted socialism in Finland. He was a member of the coalition government in 1966 and never renounced true socialist principles. He fought for Finnish-Soviet friendship and attended several Party congresses in the USSR. Based on Ville Pessi's *Selected Articles and Speeches;* Moscow, 1978; 20 notes. A. J. Evans

2260. Fidas, George C. THE EVOLUTION OF CYPRIOT COMMUNISM. *Studies in Comparative Communism 1973 6(4): 437-444.* Reviews T. W. Adams's *AKEL: The Communist Party of Cyprus* (Stanford, 1971). Communism is a modernizing force in developing society; in incompletely developed societies, a mass movement; and in developed societies, an electoral party. The party, originally reformist, was bolshevized in the 1940's. It now represents many groups and won about 40% of the vote in the 1970 elections. This electoral success belies the notion that communism is an alien ideology. The party has accommodated itself to Cypriot society and seeks recruits from all classes. It has always been somewhat independent of Moscow. D. Balmuth

2261. Flores, Marcello. STORIA E POLITICA NELLE MEMORIE DE JULES HUMBERT-DROZ [History and politics in the memoirs of Jules Humbert-Droz]. *Italia Contemporanea [Italy] 1976 28(125): 61-84.* Reviews and evaluates the four-volume memoirs of Jules Humbert-Droz, a militant Swiss socialist (Neuchâtel, 1969-73). Provides a concise biography of Humbert-Droz and describes the context of many of his interpretations as set forth in his memoirs. Based on Humbert-Droz's memoirs and other secondary sources; 72 notes. M. T. Wilson

2262. Forsberg, Ture. COMMUNISTS AND THE TRADE UNIONS. *World Marxist R. [Canada] 1973 16(3): 89-94.* Attitudes toward trade unions expressed by Sweden's Left Party—Communist (Vaensterpartiet Kommunisterna) at its 23d congress (1972).

2263. Friend, J. W. THE ROOTS OF AUTONOMY IN WEST EUROPEAN COMMUNISM. *Problems of Communism 1980 29(5): 28-43.* Firm Stalinist control over the international Communist movement began to wane with Stalin's death and subsequent desanctification under Nikita Khrushchev. Yet, Western European parties remained reluctant to express views independent from Moscow until the Sino-Soviet split and the 1968 invasion of Czechoslovakia. Today, the Soviets exercise diplomatic influence over Western parties, which have full autonomy but do not constantly assert it, since in practice they agree with the Soviets much of the time. Based on numerous French, Italian, and Spanish Communist Party studies; 46 notes. J. M. Lauber

2264. Gasperoni, Ermenegildo. V AVANGARDE BOR'BY TRUDIASHCHIKHSIA SAN'MARINO [In the vanguard of the struggle of the workers of San Marino]. *Voprosy Istorii KPSS [USSR] 1981 (8): 103-106.* Ermenegildo Gasperoni, President of the Communist Party of San Marino, recalls his own personal struggle as a Communist and the formation and development of his party. Gasperoni left San Marino in 1924 and spent the next 16 years in contact with Communist organizations throughout Europe, including a lengthy period with the international brigades during the Spanish civil war. He returned to San Marino in 1940 with the intention of establishing a Communist Party there. A San Marino section of the Italian Communist Party had been set up in 1921, but it was not until after Gasperoni's return that an independent party was set up in the republic on 7 July 1941. The Party had 50 activists by 1944 and was the only political party in San Marino. It became legal in 1945, and by 1957 more than one in 10 of the republic's 14,000 population were members. The San Marino Communist Party became the party of government in the elections of 1978. J. Bamber

2265. Gilberg, Trond. PATTERNS OF NORDIC COMMUNISM. *Problems of Communism 1975 24(3): 20-35.* Explores the fortunes of the Communist parties in Norway, Denmark, and Iceland and the reasons behind their differences. The last decade has seen a significant upswing of political radicalism in Western Europe, especially in those Nordic states that have developed furthest along the path of industrialization and the welfare state. However, with the exception of Iceland, the traditional Communist parties have been unable to reap any rewards from this phenomenon. Primary sources; 51 notes. J. M. Lauber

2266. Goldsmith, Maurice. *Sage: A Life of J. D. Bernal.* London: Hutchinson, 1980. 256 pp.

2267. Graber, Michael. UNEQUAL PARTNERSHIP. *World Marxist Rev. 1975 18(10): 61-68.* Foreign investment in Austria, notably in the form of multinational corporations, requires action on the part of the Austrian Communist Party in the 1970's.

2268. Greene, Thomas. NON-RULING COMMUNIST PARTIES AND POLITICAL ADAPTATION. *Studies in Comparative Communism 1973 6(4):331-361.* Communist sympathies in states with nonruling Communist parties are the result of major political events such as civil wars rather than social and economic conditions. Revisionists appear when political competition to the Communists increases. During the French Fifth Republic, adoption of single-member constituencies forced the Party into cooperation with other parties. In Italy, the Communists compete vigorously with the Christian Democrats for votes. Nonruling Communist parties adapt to changed conditions. They now respond to their supporters' views about social opportunities and privilege. The major parties have thus become interest groups that have helped to integrate their supporters into the existing social structure. 3 tables, 38 notes. D. Balmuth

2269. Gudager, E. SLAVNYI IUBILEI [Splendid jubilee]. *Voprosy Istorii KPSS [USSR] 1963 (10): 107-111.* Charts the history of Norway's Communist Party, from its creation in 1923 to its emergence as a mass party after World War II. The author stresses the strength of the anti-Communist forces in Norway.

2270. Gurovich, P. V. UIL'IAM GALLAKHER—REVOLIUTSIONER-INTERNATSIONALIST [William Gallacher, revolutionary and internationalist]. *Novaia i Noveishaia Istoriia [USSR] 1977 (5): 94-108, (6): 83-94.* Part I. William Gallacher (1881-1965), a leader of the shop stewards' revolt on the Clyde, headed their 1915 strike, disregarding the World War I truce between trade unions and government. Despite repeated arrests, he organized antiwar demonstrations and workers' strikes, welcomed the October 1917 Revolution in Russia and attended the Second Congress of the Comintern in Petrograd in 1920.

Under Lenin's influence, he relinquished his ultraleftist ideology, joined the Communist Party, and successfully campaigned for the merger of the Communist Parties of Scotland and England. Together with other members of the Political Bureau of the Communist Party of Great Britain, he was arrested in October 1925. After his release in September 1926, he continued his political activity and agitation on behalf of workers, skillfully dodging police surveillance. Photo. 98 notes. Part II. Describes Gallacher's struggle for British workers during the economic crisis of 1929-33 and subsequent political activity. He joined the Communist drive for a United Front against factional deviations, supported the resolutions of the 7th Comintern Congress (1935) against reaction and fascism, and was the first Communist elected to the British Parliament. He opposed the British Laborite policy of nonintervention in the Spanish Civil War and Neville Chamberlain's surrender of Czechoslovakia to Hitler. He defended USSR foreign policy during the so-called Phony War, backed Britain's war effort after Hitler's attack on the Soviet Union (June 1941), condemned British post-World War II anti-Soviet policy and supported anticolonial liberation movements. Though defeated in the Parliamentary elections of 1950, Gallacher continued his political work for the Communist Party and was elected Party Chairman in 1956, a position he held until 1963. 82 notes. N. Frenkley

2271. Haapakoski, Pekka. BREZHNEVISM IN FINLAND. *New Left R. [Great Britain] 1974 (86): 29-49.* Traces the history of the Finnish Communist Party, its limited participation in the Finnish government in 1944-48 and 1966-71, and since 1968 the rise within it of a neo-Stalinist minority popular with radical students and workers.

2272. Hakovirta, Harto and Patokallio, Pasi. BRIDGE-BUILDING BETWEEN OPPOSED ECONOMIC SYSTEMS: NOTES ON THE FINNISH PERFORMANCE. *Co-Existence [Great Britain] 1974 11(1): 1-20.* Discusses Finland's political and economic cooperation with Communist countries from the 1950's-70's, emphasizing the applicability of capitalism to international trade.

2273. Hakovirta, Harto and Patokallio, Pasi. EAST-WEST ECONOMIC COOPERATION: IS THERE A FINNISH MODEL? *Cooperation and Conflict [Norway] 1975 10(1/2): 33-50.* Recent developments in East-West relations have in some connections given impetus to discussions on the role of small and neutral countries in furthering cooperative processes, for instance, through providing examples. The authors examine the Finnish position and performance in this context, with special emphasis on economic cooperation. Through a comparative analysis it is found that Finland is exceptional in many respects, and that, in the light of the criteria adopted, she qualifies with reservations as a model. In empirical terms this means that Finland has been exceptionally active in trading with the socialist countries, in initiating new forms of economic cooperation, and in overall responsiveness. The possible implications of the Finnish model for East-West cooperation in the future are also taken up for discussion. J

2274. Handy, Thomas Hughes. "British Communist Party Propaganda on Domestic Affairs: 1944-1950." U. of Texas, Austin 1979. 359 pp. *DAI 1979 40(3): 1664-1665-A.* 7920124

2275. Hänninen, Olavi. COLLABORATION OF FINLAND'S WORKING-CLASS PARTIES: EXPERIENCE AND PROBLEMS. *World Marxist R. 1975 18(2): 25-33.* Discusses programs of the Communist Party and the Social Democrats in the 1970's.

2276. Hansen, Michael Seidelin. DEBAT: NOGLE METODISKE OVERVEJELSER OM STUDIET AF KOMMUNISTISKE PARTIERS HISTORIE [Debate: some methodological considerations on the study of the history of Communist Parties]. *Meddelelser om Forskning i Arbejderbevaegelsens Hist. [Denmark] 1981 (17): 40-51.* A discussion of the methodological problems encountered in studying the history of Communist Parties, especially in France and, to a lesser extent, Italy, and shows the lessons that Denmark can draw from this.

2277. Hodgson, John H. FINNISH COMMUNISM AND ELECTORAL POLITICS. *Problems of Communism 1974 23(1): 34-45.* Analyzes Finnish Communism and its electoral policies since World War II in light of their apparent acceptance of a transition to socialism via the ballot box. Finland is an interesting and important case study of the possibilities and problems facing a Communist party committed to a "peaceful path" to socialism. Prospects for the rest of this decade seem to indicate that they will be able to gain at most only a token share of power. Based on primary and secondary sources; 60 notes. J. M. Lauber

2278. Hodgson, John H. FINNISH COMMUNISTS AND THE "OPPORTUNISM OF CONCILIATION". *Studies in Comparative Communism 1973 6(4): 397-404.* The Finnish Communist Party split in the 1920's when rightists opposed emigrant influence on policy formation. Despite pressure in the late 1920's from a young leftist group, the Party moved to the right, although not as much as the Italian Communists. What restrained the move to the right was Finland's proximity to the USSR. While a leftist group within the Party still exists, the present official leadership under Aarne Saarinen is rightist and believes in a parliamentary transition to socialism. 35 notes. D. Balmuth

2279. Holmberg, H. O. "Folkmakt, Folkfront, Folkdemokrati. De Svenska Kommunisterna och Demokratifrågen 1943-1977" [People's power, popular front, people's democracy: Swedish Communists and the problem of democracy, 1943-77]. Uppsala U. [Sweden] 1982. 242 pp. *DAI-C 1983 44(2): 297; 8/1295c.*

2280. Holmberg, Håkan. *Folkmakt, Folkfront, Folkdemokrati: De Svenska Kommunisterna och Demokratifrågan, 1943-1977* [National power, popular front, People's democracy: Swedish Communism and questions of democracy, 1943-77]. (Studia Historica Upsaliensia, no. 122.) Uppsala: Acta U. Upsaliensis, 1982. 242 pp. English summary.

2281. Horbik, V. O. ANHLIYS'KI ULTRA: PAST AND PRESENT [The English fringe: past and present]. *Ukrains'kyi Istorychnyi Zhurnal [USSR] 1974 (12): 95-100.* Discusses the anti-communist activities of extreme right-wing groups and individuals in Great Britain, 1932-72, such as the League for Freedom, the Monday Club, the National Front, Fascists, Oswald Mosley, and Enoch Powell.

2282. Horbyk, V. O. and Kornilova, V. O. NASH KALENDAR: 60-RICHCHYA KOMPARTII VELYKOBRYTANII [Our calendar: the 60th anniversary of the Communist Party in Great Britain]. *Ukraïns'kyi Istorychnyi Zhurnal [USSR] 1980 (7): 121-123.* Reviews the history of the Communist Party in Great Britain, established in London 31 July-1 August 1920.

2283. Horn, Gyula. NYUGAT-EURÓPAI VÁLTOZÁSOK [Changes in Western Europe]. *Társadalmi Szemle [Hungary] 1978 33(6): 77-87.* Surveys the causes of the economic crisis of Western Europe, 1974-78, and its impact on Western societies with special reference to the activity of the Communist Parties.

2284. Ialamov, Ibrakhim. NOVI TENDENTSII V RAZVITIETO NA TURSKOTO RABOTNICHESKO DVIZHENIE PREZ 60-TE I 70-TE GODINI [New tendencies in the development of the Turkish workers' movement during the sixties and the seventies]. *Izvestiia na Inst. po Istoriia na BKP [Bulgaria] 1979 41: 265-300.*

2285. Iivonen, Jyrki. VELJEYTTÄ RAJOJEN [Fraternity across borders]. *Politiikka [Finland] 1985 27(1): 16-27.* Traces relations between the Communist Party of the Soviet Union and the Finnish Communist Party from 1918 to 1984. Based on newspapers, books, and articles in Finnish, Russian, and English: 17 notes, biblio. English summary. R. G. Selleck

2286. Janicki, Janusz. DETERMINANTY WPŁYWÓW WYBORCZYCH ZACHODNIOEUROPEJSKICH PARTII KOMUNISTYCZNYCH W LATACH 1956-1974 [Determinants of the electoral influence of Western European Communist Parties in the period 1956-74]. *Z Pola Walki [Poland] 1979 22(3): 81-109.* Examines the effect on Communist voting in Western European countries of relative national economic development, social policy, political development, domestic issues, Communist programs and strategy, and events in Eastern Europe. Based on standard Western statistical works, contemporary periodicals, and secondary sources; 2 tables, 68 notes. Russian and English summaries. J/S

2287. Kaeselitz, Hella. DIE NACHKRIEGSPOLITIK DER KOMMUNISTISCHEN PARTEIEN ENTWICKELTER KAPITALISTISCHER LÄNDER EUROPAS [The postwar policies of Communist parties in the developed capitalist countries in Europe]. *Beiträge zur Gesch. der Arbeiterbewegung [East Germany] 1980 22(5): 643-656.* During World War II the membership of the Communist parties in Western Europe increased. After 1945 these Communist parties tried to create an alliance among the working classes. An essential strategic point was unity in the struggle for democracy and socialism. An important aim of the imperialist bourgeoisie after World War II was the reversal of the influence of the Communist Party. Communists who had held governmental offices in France, Italy, Belgium, Luxembourg, Austria, Finland, Denmark, and Iceland were relieved of their positions during 1945-48. These factors, combined with the Cold War and the economic and political effects of the Marshall Plan, caused a decline in Communist Party membership. Secondary sources; 48 notes. G. L. Neville

2288. Kaeselitz, Hella. DIE WICHTIGSTEN ETAPPEN DES KAMPFES DER KOMMUNISTISCHEN PARTEIEN KAPITALISTISCHER LÄNDER EUROPAS FÜR FRIEDEN UND EUROPÄISCHE SICHERHEIT NACH 1945 [The most important states in the struggle of the Communist Parties in capitalist countries in Europe for peace and European security since 1945]. *Zeits. für Geschichtswissenschaft [East Germany] 1982 30(10-11): 996-1007.* Discusses the activities of the Communist Parties in Western Europe since 1945 to maintain and strengthen peace and to promote international detente and disarmament. The most important stages in this struggle have been: the victory over fascism; the development of the world peace movement in the late 1940's and early 1970's. Renewed international tension during the 1970's and the threat of nuclear war led to the continued efforts of the European Communist Parties to promote international peace, detente and disarmament. G. L. Neville

2289. Kahn, Peggy. AN INTERVIEW WITH FRANK WATTERS. *Bull. of the Soc. for the Study of Labour Hist. [Great Britain] 1981 (43): 54-67.* A transcription of an interview between the author and Frank Watters (b. 1920), a Scottish coal miner, who remained in Scotland as a miner and Communist organizer until 1953, when he went to the Yorkshire coalfields as a full-time organizer for the Communist Party of Great Britain.

2290. Kapluk, Manfred. 60 LET BOR'BY ZA SOTSIALIZM [60 years of struggle for socialism]. *Voprosy Istorii KPSS [USSR] 1978 (12): 113-120.* The German Communist Party founded in West Germany in 1968 inherited the great tradition of the Communist Party of Germany (banned in 1956) and carries on in its struggle for the interests of the German working class and democracy.

2291. Karasawidis, Lefteris. STRATEGIA I TAKTYKA KOMUNISTYCZNEJ PARTII GRECJI W LATACH WOJNY DOMOWEJ (1946-1949) [The strategy and tactics of the Communist Party of Greece in the civil war, 1946-49]. *Z Pola Walki [Poland] 1981 24(3-4): 65-91.* In the early stages of the civil war, 1946-1947, the Communist Party of Greece sought to develop a guerrilla movement and to engage in legal political activity. Later, 1948-1949, it focused entirely on armed struggle hoping for popular support and international aid. The revolution failed because of British and American military superiority and the absence of a classical revolutionary situation. Based on Greek sources; 97 notes. E. Jaworska

2292. Karvonen, Timo. BOR'BA FINSKIKH KOMMUNISTOV ZA UKREPLENIE DOBROSOSEDSKIKH OTNOSHENII MEZHDU FINLIANDIEI I SOVETSKIM SOIUZOM [The struggle of Finnish Communists for strengthening neighborly relations between Finland and the Soviet Union]. *Voprosy Istorii KPSS [USSR] 1975 (9): 57-70.* Describes Soviet-Finnish relations since the 1948 Friendship Treaty. Under two successive Presidents, Juho Kusti Paasikivi and Urho Kaleva Kekkonen, Finland has expanded its cultural, economic, and political relations with the USSR. In the face of bourgeois opposition, including demands for entry into the Common Market, this has occurred because of the efforts of the Finnish Communist Party and broadly based organizations such as the Finland-Soviet Union Society and Proponents of Peace in Finland. Based on Finnish archival materials, memoirs, and periodical literature; 40 notes. L. E. Holmes

2293. Karvonen, Toivo. KOMPARTIIA FINLIANDII V BOR'BE ZA DRUZHBU FINSKOGO I SOVETSKOGO NARODOV [The Finnish Communist Party in the struggle for friendship between the Finnish and Soviet peoples]. *Voprosy Istorii KPSS [USSR] 1965 (2): 53-61.* On the 20th anniversary of the Russo-Finnish war, summarizes the Finnish Communist Party's attempts to bring about friendship between Finland and the USSR from the 1920's to 1960.

2294. Kendall, Walter. THE COMMUNIST PARTY OF GREAT BRITAIN. *Survey [Great Britain] 1974 20(1): 118-131.* A short history of the British Communist Party from its founding by the Communist International to the present day. The party is mostly middle class and has a transient membership around a solid core. An updated extract from Witold S. Sworakowski, ed., *World Communism: A Handbook 1918-1965* (Palo Alto, California: Hoover Inst., 1973). R. B. Valliant

2295. Kerrigan, Peter. KOMMUNISTICHESKAIA PARTIIA VELIKOBRITANII I PROBLEMY PROFSOIUZNOGO DVIZHENIIA [The Communist Party of Great Britain and problems in the labor union movement]. *Voprosy Istorii KPSS [USSR] 1961 (1): 88-110.* Describes the relationship between the Communist Party and labor unions and organizations in Great Britain since 1920 arguing that the unions should build on the British tradition of class struggle and international workers' solidarity.

2296. Khristakudis, Apostolos. PROBLEMITE NA "TRETIIA SVIAT" V IDEOLOGIIATA I POLITIKATA NA OBSHTOGRÜTSKOTO SOTSIALISTICHESKO DVIZHENIE (PASOK) [The problems of the Third World in the ideology and politics of the Pan-Hellenic Socialist Movement (PASOK)]. *Izvestiia na Instituta po Istoriia na BKP [Bulgaria] 1983 (48): 355-365.* Since its founding in 1974 the Pan-Hellenic Socialist Movement under Andreas Papandreou has adopted a progressive anti-imperialist, anticolonialist attitude toward the developing nations of Latin America, Asia, and Africa. PASOK opposes Western European and US military and political interference in the Third World, but supports socialist movements there, and views the USSR sympathetically. PASOK urges a radical change in the world economy in favor of the Third World. PASOK, however, displays inconsistencies, especially in its view of events in Cambodia and Afghanistan. The party's analysis of the superpowers and hegemony does not always differentiate clearly between the USSR and the United States. 42 notes. A. J. Evans

2297. Kitsikis, Dimitri. GREEK COMMUNISTS AND THE KARAMANLIS GOVERNMENT. *Problems of Communism 1977 26(1): 42-56.* Examines the strategy and tactics of the newly legalized Greek Communist forces against the background of their behavior during prior years and in the context of the reestablishment of parliamentary democracy in Greece. Based on primary and secondary Greek and English language sources; 2 tables, 33 notes. J. M. Lauber

2298. Kitsikis, Dimitri. LE MOUVEMENT COMMUNISTE EN GRÈCE [The Communist movement in Greece]. *Études Int. [Canada] 1975 6(3): 334-354.* Examines the difficulty of trying to adapt an international, urban, Western communism to a nationalist, peasant, non-Western European culture and points out the obstacles to implanting communism in the midst of an essentially petit bourgeois society which espouses fascism. Outlines the growth of the Greek Communist Party from 1918 to 1974 and discusses the Constantine Karamanlis regime. 40 notes. J. F. Harrington, Jr.

2299. Kol'cov, P. S. EIN WAHRER SOLDAT DER REVOLUTION: OTTO KUUSINEN [A true soldier of the revolution: Otto Kuusinen]. *Beiträge zur Gesch. der Arbeiterbewegung [East Germany] 1982 24(5): 737-745.* Traces the life, career, and political activities of the Finnish Communist leader Otto Kuusinen (1881-1964). The author pays particular attention to his activities in the Finnish Social Democratic Party, 1904-18, as a leader in the Finnish revolution of 1918, his flight to Russia in 1918, his work to establish the Communist Party in Finland in 1918, and his role within the international Communist movement, 1921-40. In addition the author discusses his activities within the Soviet Union, his writings on Marxism-Leninism, and his work as a member of the Academy of Sciences in the USSR. Secondary sources; 28 notes. G. L. Neville

2300. Kousoulas, D. George. THE GREEK COMMUNISTS TRIED THREE TIMES—AND FAILED. *Studies on the Soviet Union [West Germany] 1971 11(4): 264-280.* Reviews the failure of three Communist efforts to seize power in Greece. World War II saw the usual pattern unfold once more—a popular front resistance which gradually became Communist-dominated. No doubt the party could have grabbed power in early 1944, but desisted, on orders from Moscow. Later in the year an outright revolt was unleashed, but party tactics were defective. The party then turned to a lengthy guerrilla war, but lacked popular support. The Greek army with American military aid developed effective techniques for fighting guerrillas. Secondary sources; 28 notes. V. L. Human

2301. Krähe, Martin. DIE HALTUNG DER KOMMUNISTISCHEN PARTEIEN WESTEUROPAS ZU DEN DIREKTWAHLEN FÜR DAS EUROPAPARLAMENT IM JUNI 1979 [The attitude of the West European Communist Parties to direct elections for the European Parliament in June 1979]. *Wiss. Zeits. der Wilhelm-Pieck-Universität Rostock. Gesellschafts- und Sprachwissenschaftliche Reihe [East Germany] 1979 28(10): 693-697.* Reviews the ideas and objectives of the German, French, and Italian Communist Parties for the European parliamentary elections, June 1979.

2302. Krahenbuhl, Margaret. THE TURKISH COMMUNISTS: SCHISM INSTEAD OF CONCILIATION. *Studies in Comparative Communism 1973 6(4): 405-413.* Irreconcilable differences within the Turkish Communist Party have continued. In the 1920's, rightists associated themselves with the Kemalist revolution and were ousted from the party. During the years of illegality, the party avoided splits. But in the 1960's, the party split into those pledged to evolutionary change and leftists who adopted terrorism. The split continued until a military coup in Turkey in 1971 cracked down on the leftists. 10 notes. D. Balmuth

2303. Kuranov, G. G. SOROK PIAT' LET BOR'BY ZA INTERESY TRUDIASHCHIKHSIA AVSTRII [Forty-five years of struggle for the interests of the workers of Austria]. *Voprosy Istorii KPSS [USSR] 1963 (10): 103-107.* Explores the history of the Austrian Communist Party, its policies, is relations with social democracy, its work during World War II, and its development into a mass party.

2304. Kuranov, I. N. KOMMUNIST, INTERNATSIONALIST, PATRIOT [Communist, internationalist, and patriot]. *Voprosy Istorii KPSS [USSR] 1982 (10): 109-112.* Commemorates the 80th birthday of I. Bilen (b. 1902), Secretary-General of the Communist Party of Turkey. Bilen's political life started in about 1920 in Istanbul, where he was working as a motor mechanic. He joined the groups of young men who were helping in the country's liberation struggle against the forces of the Entente and internal reaction. He became a member of the newly formed Communist Party in 1922 and a year later was sent to the USSR for training. Bilen was active in the Turkish labor movement in the 1930's and played a key role in the anti-imperialist front in World War II. He became Secretary-General of the Party in 1974 and since then has forcefully led Turkey's Communists in their fight against repression and for social justice. 18 notes. J. Bamber

2305. Kuranov, I. N. V BOR'BE ZA KORENNYE INTERESY TURETSKOGO NARODA [In the struggle for the fundamental interests of the Turkish nation]. *Voprosy Istorii KPSS [USSR] 1980 (9): 107-110.* Commemorates the 60th anniversary of the foundation of the Communist Party of Turkey (CPT). The first Communist organizations were founded in 1918 in major cities and the Party was established in July 1920. Describes the history of the Party's struggle for democracy and social justice and against US imperialism. In recent years the Party has suffered severe terrorist attacks from neofascist nationalist organizations. The CPT is an important unit of the international Communist movement and has participated in all major events organized by the movement. 13 notes. V. Sobell

2306. Lane, Tony. A MERSEYSIDER IN DETROIT. *Hist. Workshop J. [Great Britain] 1981 (11): 138-153.* Stan Coulthard (b. 1898) describes his emigration from Birkenhead, near Liverpool, to the United States in 1922, his dreams of going to college to become a dentist, his experiences in the Detroit car plants and dairies, his activities as a union organizer, his return to Merseyside in 1935, and his activities in the British Communist Party, 1935-50. The author's introduction examines Coulthard's life and career, the background to emigration from Liverpool, 1820-1950, and the links between Liverpool and labor organizations in the United States and lists other British union organizers in Detroit, 1930's-40's. Secondary sources; 41 notes. G. L. Neville

2307. Lange, Peter and Vannicelli, Maurizio, ed. *The Communist Parties of Italy, France, and Spain: Postwar Change and Continuity: A Casebook.* Casebook Series on European Politics and Society, no. 1. Winchester, Mass.: Allen & Unwin, 1981. 385 pp.

2308. Laulajainen, Pertti. THE COMMUNIST DEFEAT IN THE 1948 FINNISH ELECTION: NOTES ON THE IMPACT OF ORGANIZATION. *Scandinavian Political Studies [Norway] 1984 7(1): 39-53.* Socioeconomic factors had no significant impact on the defeat of the Communist Party in the 1948 elections in Finland; the rapid increase in industrial population in some regions weakened social control, however, and eased the operation of the Social Democratic Party's organization of party agents.

2309. Lavau, Georges. LES PARTIS COMMUNISTES EN FRANCE ET EN ITALIE [The Communist parties in France and Italy]. *Etudes [France] 1982 356(6): 757-768.*

2310. Lavretski, I. R. KATOLICHESKOE RABOCHEE DVIZHENIE I POLITIKA KOMMUNISTICHESKIKH PARTII [The Catholic workers' movement and the policy of Communist Parties]. *Voprosy Istorii KPSS [USSR] 1961 (1): 144-155.* Charts the relationship between the Catholic workers' movement and European Communist Parties with particular reference to France and Italy in the post-war period, arguing that Communist policy has always been to work closely with the Catholic workers' movement.

2311. Lazaridis, Takis. KOMPARTIIA GRETSII—DETISHCHE RABOCHEGO KLASSA [The Communist Party of Greece: child of the working class]. *Voprosy Istorii KPSS [USSR] 1982 (9): 77-88.* Greece's small but strong working class created the Socialist Workers' Party of Greece in 1918. In 1920 this joined the Comintern and about five years later was renamed the Communist Party of Greece. It continued to represent workers' interests despite military dictatorship and repression in the late 1920's and rapidly increased its membership. The Communist Party, in keeping with its traditional proletarian principles, led the fight against the rise of fascism in the 1930's and organized the national liberation struggle in World War II. Since then it has consistently tried to lead Greece out of the sphere of influence of American imperialism. The Party has constantly grown in strength and stature; in the elections of

1981 it polled more than 10% of the votes and became the third largest party in parliament. Based on official documents of the Communist Party of Greece, Athens; 18 notes. J. Bamber

2312. Leonhard, Wolfgang. POSITIONEN UND TENDENZEN DER WESTEUROPÄISCHEN KOMMUNISTEN [Positions and tendencies of Western European Communists]. *Osteuropa [West Germany] 1980 30(1): 3-20.* While the Communist parties of Ireland, West Germany, Austria, Finland, Greece, and Portugal kept their pro-Soviet ideology through the 1960's and 1970's, the Communist parties of Great Britain, Sweden, Denmark, Iceland, Belgium, Italy, and Spain in the late 1950's began to revise communism, stressing the special characters of national economic, cultural, and political developments, a revision that became known as Eurocommunism.

2313. Lindkvist, K. "Program och Parti: Principprogram och Partiideologi inom den Kommunistiska Rörelsen i Sverige 1917-1972" [Program and Party: principle program and Party ideology of the Communist Party of Sweden, 1917-72]. Lund U. [Sweden] 1982. 248 pp. *DAI-C 1983 44(1): 70; 8/366c.*

2314. Lindop, Fred. INTERVIEW WITH HARRY WATSON. *Bull. of the Soc. for the Study of Labour Hist. [Great Britain] 1979 (39): 73-77.* Harry Watson (b. 1907), a lighterman from 1922-71, was president of the London based Watermen's, Lightermen's, Tugmen and Bargemen's Union (WLTBU), 1959-71, and a member of the Communist Party of Great Britain from 1941 onwards. In an interview he talks about working conditions for lightermen, labor union organization, and his activities in the CPGB.

2315. Liu, William H. WEST EUROPEAN SOCIALISTS AND COMMUNISTS: THEIR UNEASY ALLIANCES AND CONFLICTS. *Issues and Studies [Taiwan] 1976 12(6): 16-36.* Discusses the patterns of Communism and socialism throughout Western Europe and the USSR in the 1970's, examining basic differences as they relate to Marxist thought, class struggle, and capitalism; examines the rise of socialism concurrently with trade unions, 1900-76.

2316. Liubimov, D. A. GORDON MAKLENNAN [Gordon McLennan]. *Voprosy Istorii KPSS [USSR] 1975 (5): 119-121.* A biographical sketch of Gordon McLennan. In 1942 McLennan became a member of the Executive Committee of Great Britain's Young Communist League, was elected a member of the British Communist Party's Executive Committee in 1957, and has served as its General Secretary since 1965. Based on Communist newspapers, especially *Morning Star* and *Pravda*; 11 notes. L. E. Holmes

2317. Liubimov, D. Sh. UIL'IAM GALLAKHER [William Gallacher]. *Voprosy Istorii KPSS [USSR] 1972 (1): 115-117.* Surveys the political life of William Gallacher (1881-1965), a leading figure of the Communist Party of Great Britain and member of Parliament, 1935-50.

2318. Mahon, John. EIN LEIDENSCHAFTLICHER KÄMPFER FÜR DIE ARBEITERKLASSE. HARRY POLLITT [A passionate fighter for the working class: Harry Pollitt]. *Beiträge zur Geschichte der Arbeiterbewegung [East Germany] 1972 14(5): 819-825.* In 1918-20 Harry Pollitt played an important part in the "hands off of Soviet Russia" movement. He became one of the most important leaders of the British Communist Party, organizing in the 1920's the minority movement in the British trade unions, which opposed the reformist policy of the right-wing trade union leaders. Pollitt's greatest achievement was the organization of a British battalion of volunteers for the Spanish Civil War and the establishment of a broad antifascist front in Britain. Secondary sources; 9 notes. R. Wagnleitner

2319. Matkovsky, N. V. VAZHNAIA ISTORICHESKAIA VEKHA V ANGLIISKOM RABOCHEM DVIZHENII: K 50-LETIU OBRAZOVANIA KOMMUNISTICHESKOI PARTII VELIKOBRITANII [A historical landmark in the British workers' movement: the 50th anniversary of the formation of the Communist Party of Great Britain]. *Voprosy Istorii KPSS [USSR] 1970 (8): 92-99.* Traces the history of the Communist Party of Great Britain from its beginnings and emphasizes its relationship with the Labour Party.

2320. McClain, Charles J., Jr. FROM IDEOLOGY TO UTOPIA: ERNST FISCHER IN RETROSPECT. *J. of Contemporary Hist. [Great Britain] 1977 12(3): 565-594.* Originally a Social Democrat, Ernst Fischer joined the Austrian Communist Party in 1934 and rose rapidly to top leadership ranks. He remained a leading theoretician until Khrushchev's iconoclasm of 1956. He then tried to diagnose the disease of Stalinism and evolve a new Marxist-Leninist vision. He was expelled from the party in 1969 and died in 1972. Fischer thought that socialist artists and writers could learn much from their capitalist colleagues, especially those whose productions involved protest against existing conditions. Socialist realism "did not refer to a style, but to an attitude... of commitment to the working class and knowledge of the discoveries of Marx, Engels and Lenin." He also held that a coalition of technically skilled workers and intellectuals was destined to replace the proletariat as the vanguard of the socialist movement. In full accord with the Czech reforms, he vigorously protested the Soviet invasion of Czechoslovakia in 1968. 74 notes. M. P. Trauth

2321. McCrackin, Bobbie Humenny. "The Etiology of Radicalization Among American and British Communist Autobiographers." Emory U. 1980. 450 pp. *DAI 1980 41(4): 1751-A.* 8021288

2322. McHugh, John and Ripley, B. J. THE NEATH BY-ELECTION, 1945: THE TROTSKYISTS IN WEST WALES. *Llafur: J. of the Soc. for the Study of Welsh Labour Hist. [Great Britain] 1981 3(2): 68-78.* The Neath by-election of 15 May 1945 was the first occasion on which a British Trotskyist party contested a Parliamentary election. Examines the reasons for the Revolutionary Communist Party's decision to fight the seat in January 1945, and considers the importance of the parallel "shadow" campaign between the Trotskyists and the local Communist Party for influence over sections of the Neath and South Wales working class. The Trotskyists failed because they were unable to lay down an alternative to the revolutionary socialist tradition already established by the Communist Party. Based on newspaper articles and secondary sources; 49 notes. G. L. Neville

2323. Middlemas, Keith. *Power and the Party: Changing Faces of Communism in Western Europe.* London: Andre Deutsch, 1980. 400 pp.

2324. Mikhailov, M. CONCERNING EXCHANGES AND CONTACTS. *Int. Affairs [USSR] 1973 (5): 64-68.* Asserts that cultural exchanges between Western nations and communist countries should be conducted with due respect for the sovereignty and laws of each country and maintains that proclamations from the United States and Western Europe, 1970-73, claiming greater freedom of speech than that of socialist countries, are bourgeois propaganda.

2325. Morris, Ronald. T. ISLWYN NICHOLAS, 1903-1980. *Llafur: J. of the Soc. for the Study of Welsh Labour Hist. [Great Britain] 1981 3(2): 28-31.* Provides a summary of the life and career of Thomas Islwyn Nicholas (1903-80), and examines the influence of his father T. E. Nicholas and the socialist dentist D. Ernest Williams (1870-1956). Traces his career as a dental mechanic, his involvement with the Labour Movement, and his membership in the British Communist Party from 1921. Describes his atheism, his visit to the USSR in 1935 and his adherence to Soviet communism, his arrest and imprisonment for his left-wing pacifist views in 1940, his writings—particularly his research on David Ivon Jones (1883-1924), one of the founders of the South African Communist Party—his shift to agnosticism, and his association with the New Street Unitarian Meeting House in Aberystwyth. G. L. Neville

2326. Mosolov, V. G. BOEVOI AVANGARD TRUDIASHCHIKHSIA [The militant vanguard of laborers]. *Voprosy Istorii KPSS [USSR] 1979 (2): 140-142.* A summary of speeches delivered by the Director and Deputy Director of the Institute of Marxism-Leninism and by G. Farakos, member of the Politburo of the

Greek Communist Party, at a special meeting of the Institute of Marxism-Leninism, 16 November 1978, honoring the 60th anniversary of the Greek Communist Party. L. E. Holmes

2327. Mosolov, V. G. 60-LETIE KOMMUNISTICHESKOI PARTII DANII [The Communist Party of Denmark: 60 years]. *Voprosy Istorii KPSS [USSR] 1980 (2): 156-158.* The November 1979 celebration of Danish communism was opened by A. G. Egorov, director of the Institute of Marxism-Leninism. It included tributes to Danish solidarity with Vietnam, Chile, and Uruguay; discussions on the anti-Common Market campaign; and protests against NATO nuclear installations in Europe. M. R. Colenso

2328. Neck, Rudolf. ÖSTERREICHS RÜCKKEHR ZUR DEMOKRATIE [Austria's return to democracy]. *Österreich in Geschichte und Literatur [Austria] 1965 9(9): 455-461.* The Austrian election of 1945 occurred despite the long absence of democratic elections and postwar economic problems. Its most important result was the defeat of the Communist Party. Biblio.

2329. Nerlund, I. NEKOTORYE VOPROSY MEZHDUNARODNOGO ZNACHENIIA ISTORICHESKOGO OPYTA KPSS [The international significance of the historical experience of the CPSU]. *Voprosy Istorii KPSS [USSR] 1963 (9): 59-68.* Mentions the links between the Danish and Russian workers' movements in the prerevolutionary period. Focuses mainly on the development of Denmark's Communist Party, emphasizing the lessons that have been learned from the history and politics of the Soviet Communist Party.

2330. Nikitin, N. V. DZHON GOLLAN [John Gollan]. *Voprosy Istorii KPSS [USSR] 1971 (7): 119-122.* Surveys the political activities of Gollan, general secretary of the Communist Party of Great Britain, 1926-70.

2331. Nirhano, Anna-Maija. DAS VOLKSARCHIV: ZENTRALARCHIV DER KOMMUNISTISCHEN UND DER VOLKSDEMOKRATISCHEN BEWEGUNG IN FINNLAND [The people's archive: the Central Archive of the Communist and People's Democratic Movement in Finland]. *Archivmitteilungen [East Germany] 1978 28(3): 99-102.* Traces the origins, aims, contents, and system of the people's archive from its foundation in 1956 to the time of its reorganization in 1973-74. Also traces the development of the left wing in Finland from 1909 to ca. 1970.

2332. Nørlund, Ib. THE SEARCH FOR NEW WAYS AND FIDELITY TO PRINCIPLE. *World Marxist R. [Canada] 1974 17(12): 52-59.* Analyzes Communist Party political activities in Denmark, 1958-74.

2333. Northedge, F. S. and Wells, Audrey. *Britain and Soviet Communism: The Impact of a Revolution.* London: Macmillan, 1982. 280 pp.

2334. O'Riordan, M. and Sinclair, B. IRISH COMMUNISTS AND TERRORISM. *World Marxist Rev. [Canada] 1976 19(10): 87-96.* Examines the political activities, 1950-76, of both Northern and Southern Irish; examines terrorism and maintains that the Communist Party has little faith in it as a means of national liberation.

2335. O'Riordan, M. THE OCTOBER REVOLUTION, LENIN, IRELAND. *World Marxist Rev. [Canada] 1977 20(9): 21-24.* The great examples of what followed from the October Revolution (proof of the ability of the working class to govern, the end of unemployment, the development of industrial and military strength, and guarantees of human rights and national identity) are a source of confidence to the Communist Party of Ireland and the Irish people in their struggle for independence since 1916.

2336. Ortak, Selim. ZNAMENATEL'NAIA DATA V ISTORII RABOCHEGO DVIZHENIA TURTSII: K 50-LETIU OBRAZOVANIA KOMMUNISTICHESKOI PARTII TURTSII [A historic date in the history of the Turkish workers' movement: the 50th anniversary of the founding of the Communist Party of Turkey]. *Voprosy Istorii KPSS [USSR] 1970 (11): 121-123.* Outlines the history of the Turkish Communist Party since its formation, in 1920, and the labor movements prior to that date.

2337. Papaioannou, Ezekias. AN ALLIANCE TESTED BY HISTORY. *World Marxist Rev. 1976 19(11): 3-10.* Discusses the 50th anniversary celebration of the Communist Party of Cyprus (AKEL) stressing the continual support for the Party from the USSR.

2338. Paris, Marie-Alix. LE MOUVEMENT COMMUNISTE EUROPÉEN À L'AUTOMNE 1977 [The European Communist movement in the fall of 1977]. *Défense Natl. [France] 1977 33(12): 25-34.* Analyzes the way Western Europeans' concept of communism has antagonized the USSR in its opposition to the Soviet model. Examines the development of European communism, 1972-77, and exchanges between European and Soviet Communists during this period.

2339. Peck, Edward. THE UNITED NATIONS AND THE PROBLEM OF GREECE AND ITS NEIGHBORS, 1946-1951. *Indiana Social Studies Q. 1980 33(1): 90-104.* Examines the roles of the UN Special Commission of Investigation and the Special Committee on the Balkans (UNSCOB) in the post-World War II struggle in Greece between communism and nationalism and concludes that the UN activities, while of little actual consequence, did maintain the focus of world attention on the situation.

2340. Pospelov, B. V. PODRYVNAIA DEIATEL'NOST' MAOISTOV PROTIV MIROVOGO KOMMUNISTICHESKOGO DVIZHENIIA [Subversive activity of the Maoists against the world Communist movement]. *Voprosy Istorii KPSS [USSR] 1978 (2): 40-51.* Quoting Leonid Brezhnev's condemnation of Maoism at the 25th Communist Party Congress in 1977, the author examines the activities of Maoist groups on the fringe of Communist Parties throughout the world, with some emphasis on West Germany, France, and the Maoist Forum in Rome earlier in 1977.

2341. Pruessen, Ronald W. GREEK TRAGEDY, AMERICAN TRAGEDY. *Rev. in Am. Hist. 1983 11(2): 273-278.* Reviews Lawrence S. Wittner's *American Intervention in Greece, 1943-1949* (1982), which argues that US foreign policy was guided by the belief that Greece was "one of the many fronts in the struggle with the international Communist conspiracy."

2342. Radzikowski, Piotr. KOMUNIŚCI RFN I AUSTRII WOBEC EUROPEJSKIEJ WSPÓLNOTY GOSPODARCZEJ (1957-1980) [West German and Austrian Communists and the European Economic Community, 1957-80]. *Przegląd Zachodni [Poland] 1983 39(2): 139-153.* At the time the European Economic Community (EEC) was formed, socialists and Communists in West Germany and Austria strongly opposed joining the supranational European organization. In West Germany, the socialists soon changed their mind and became ardent supporters. Austrian socialists were tempted to join and support the EEC, but found that this would be against the neutrality of their country. Communists in both countries steadfastly remained in opposition. In West Germany, the Communist Party was soon made illegal, but kept issuing its warnings. When the EEC turned out to be a success, both Communist Parties supported participation in elections to the European parliament, hoping that that body would diminish the power of bureaucracies, but warned against the diminution of sovereignty of member nations. Based on reports of respective Communist Parties and secondary publications; 35 notes. M. Krzyzaniak

2343. Reisberg, Arnold. ICH DIENE DER ARBEITERKLASSE [I serve the working class]. *Beiträge zur Geschichte der Arbeiterbewegung [East Germany] 1979 21(4): 593-602.* Provides a detailed biography of Johann Köplenig (1891-1968), a leader of the Austrian Communist Party for over 40 years. A cobbler's apprentice, he became a Social Democrat, served in World War I, became a prisoner of war in revolutionary Russia, and returned home to help organize Austrian communism. Fighting the Anschluss, Köplenig led the resistance movement in the underground. After liberation he became a leader of Austria's Communist movement and of the international workers' movement. 21 notes. G. E. Pergl

2344. Rudnik, D. Ia. KOMMUNISTICHESKAIA PARTIIA BEL'GII [The Communist Party of Belgium]. *Voprosy Istorii KPSS [USSR] 1981 (9): 99-101.* A number of small and disparate Communist groups in Belgium came together in 1920 to form the Belgian Communist Party. These units had previously done much to further the interests of the working class, but they failed to understand the need for a united political struggle. Shortly after the Party was established, a left-wing faction founded a rival Communist Party with a stricter Marxist line. Both parties applied for membership in the Comintern and they amalgamated in 1921. This united party contributed much to the fight against fascism before and during World War II. It was subjected to vicious repressions in the 1940's and 1950's. Since then it has worked unceasingly for peace and progress but it has often been hampered by internal organizational difficulties. 5 notes. J. Bamber

2345. Rykin, V. S. NA POZITSIIAKH PROLETARSKOGO INTERNATSIONALIZMA (K 60-LETIIU KOMMUNISTICHESKOI PARTII LIUKSEMBURGA) [In the ranks of the international proletariat (60 years of the Luxembourg Communist Party)]. *Voprosy Istorii KPSS [USSR] 1981 (1): 99-102.* Outlines the history of the Luxembourg Communist Party (CPL) since its founding in 1921. The Party was formed by a group of socialists who were dissatisfied with a decision taken at the Socialist Party Congress not to join the Comintern. The Party was subjected to a great deal of repression in its early years and was only saved from being declared illegal by the positive outcome of a 1937 referendum. The Party was able to capitalize on its war-time resistance activities by winning 5 seats in the 1945 parliament. It reached a peak in 1968 when it obtained 15% of the vote in elections in that year. Recent elections have seen a drop in the CPL's share of the vote as a result of a general swing to the right in the country. 7 notes.
A. Brown

2346. Saarinen, Aarne. LEADING FORCE OF DEMOCRATIC DEVELOPMENT. *World Marxist R. [Canada] 1975 17(11): 38-43.* Relates the history of Communist Party political activities in Finland, 1918-74.

2347. Saarinen, Aarne. THE STRATEGIC AIM OF THE FINNISH COMMUNISTS. *World Marxist Rev. 1975 18(9): 93-95.* Good relations with the USSR and the Finnish Communist Party's ideological consistency account for the Party's increased participation in the government of Finland.

2348. Salles, René. LE PARTI COMMUNISTE DE GRANDE-BRETAGNE ET LES ÉLECTIONS [The British Communist Party and the elections]. *Rev. Française de Sci. Pol. [France] 1977 27(3): 407-427.* A study of modern British elections shows that the Communist Party of Great Britain, having evolved from British communism which has its roots in industrial rather than parliamentary political activity, has little influence in British politics.

2349. Savko, V. S. V BOR'BE ZA MIR I SOTSIAL'NYI PROGRESS: K 60-LETIIU KOMMUNISTICHESKOI PARTII DANII [The struggle for peace and social progress: commemorating the 60th anniversary of the Danish Communist Party]. *Voprosy Istorii KPSS [USSR] 1979 (11): 115-119.* Reviews the history and development of the Danish Communist Party from its formation soon after the Russian Revolution to the present day. While tracing the Party's origins in Denmark to the discontent of the previous century, the author emphasizes the Party's pacifist traditions, in particular its wartime opposition to fascism and its postwar opposition to NATO, and its continuing struggle against the government's domestic and international policies, including membership in the European Economic Community. It has found support in the country's trade unions and student community. 5 notes.
J. S. S. Charles

2350. Schmölz, Franz-Martin. DAS UNAUFHÖRLICHE TRAUMA [The endless trauma]. *Zeitgeschichte [Austria] 1974 1(4): 97-99.* Review article on Ernst Fischer's *Das Ende einer Illusion. Erinnerungen 1945-1955* (Vienna, 1973) and analyzes Fischer's ideological development and conflicts with the Austrian Communist Party. Review article. R. Wagnleitner

2351. Selle, Per. THE NORWEGIAN COMMUNIST PARTY IN THE IMMEDIATE POSTWAR PERIOD. *Scandinavian Pol. Studies [Norway] 1982 5(3): 189-216.* The temporary sharp increase in Norwegian Communist Party strength in 1946 was typical and due to political tradition and organizing effort.

2352. Serfaty, Simon. AN INTERNATIONAL ANOMALY: THE UNITED STATES AND THE COMMUNIST PARTIES IN FRANCE AND ITALY, 1945-1947. *Studies in Comparative Communism 1975 8(1/2): 123-146.* In France, after 1945, American influence did not play a major role in the ouster of Communists from the Ramadier government. By 1947 the Communists themselves found their position intolerable. Moreover, de Gaulle wanted their ouster. Ramadier made the move, which pleased the United States in order to stem Gaullism. In Italy, US influence was greater. De Gasperi was aware of the US position, that substantial US economic aid was contingent on the ouster of the Communists. But their ouster also suited De Gasperi's position. In fact, the United States and De Gasperi were using each other. 65 notes.
D. Balmuth

2353. Serfaty, Simon. THE U.S. AND THE COMMUNIST PARTIES OF ITALY AND FRANCE: NO UNCERTAIN PAST BUT STILL AN UNCERTAIN FUTURE. *Towson State J. of Int. Affairs 1979 14(1): 1-8.* The French and Italian Communist Parties are neither so dominated by the USSR nor undemocratic as they once were, but neither are they as legitimate, national, or institutionally normal as they may wish to be or as some recent commentators have claimed they are.

2354. Shemenkov, K. A. ZAKALENNAIA V BOR'BE ZA INTERESY TRUDOVOGO NARODA [Hardened in the struggle for the interests of toiling people]. *Voprosy Istorii KPSS [USSR] 1978 (12): 120-124.* Briefly surveys the history of the Communist Party of Greece on the occasion of the 60th anniversary of the Party's founding.

2355. Shemenkov, K. A. 50 LET BOR'BY ZA INTERESY NARODA [Fifty years of struggle in the interests of the people]. *Voprosy Istorii KPSS [USSR] 1976 (8): 125-130.* Describes Communist activity under Ezekias Papaioannu in Cyprus and Cypriot conflicts with British colonists and the Turks, 1920-74.

2356. Shishov, O. O. TAKTYKA KOMPARTII KAPITALISTYCHNYKH KRAIN U ROBOTI SERED PROHRESYVNOI MOLODI [The tactics of the Communist Parties in capitalist countries in their work with progressive youth]. *Ukrains'kyi Istorychnyi Zhurnal [USSR] 1973 (6): 39-46.* Discusses the growth of leftwing, Marxist ideology among youth in capitalist countries such as France and Germany since 1967, presenting the Soviet view of such Communist political education.

2357. Shmatov, I. P. V STROIU BORTSOV ZA INTERESY TRUDOVOGO NARODA (K 80-LETIIU SO DNIA ROZHDENIIA POCHETNOGO PREDSEDATELIA KOMMUNISTICHESKOI PARTII LIUKSEMBURGA DOMINIKA URBANI) [In the ranks of fighters for the interests of the laboring people: on the 80th anniversary of the honorary president of the Luxembourg Communist Party, Dominique Urbani]. *Voprosy Istorii KPSS [USSR] 1983 (3): 115-118.* Traces the career of Dominique Urbani from his participation in the first Communist groups in Luxembourg in 1919 to his work as president of the party. 11 notes. G. Dombrovski

2358. Siegbahn, Bo. KOSACVAL FÖRR OCH NU [Cossack elections then and now]. *Svensk Tidskrift [Sweden] 1977 64(3): 127-134.* Compares and describes the Social Democratic election defeats of 1928 and 1976, called "Cossack elections" because on both occasions the Communist threat was a main issue. In 1928 the Social

Democrats were in opposition but hoped to gain a majority with help from the Communists, with whom they made an agreement. After their defeat the Social Democratic leaders strongly criticized the actions of the communists. In 1976 the labor unions were the main difficulty, for they insisted on pressing proposals for the nationalization of industry. After the election the Social Democratic leaders exhibited much bitterness toward other political parties but failed to fully recognize their own faults. U. H. Bartels

2359. Sinisalo, T. HALF-CENTURY STRUGGLE FOR THE FRIENDSHIP WITH THE USSR. *Int. Affairs [USSR] 1973 (1): 20-26.* Examines the evolution of relations between Finland and the USSR, 1920's-70's, discussing the Communist Party of Finland's attempt to combat anti-Soviet attitudes in the 1930's and early 1940's.

2360. Sinisalo, Taisto. COMMUNISTS IN THE FINNISH DIET. *World Marxist Rev. 1972 15(5): 30-38.* Discusses the distribution of the Communist Party, the Social Democratic Party and the Democratic Alliance of the People of Finland in the Diet of Finland, 1945-72.

2361. Smith, Charles Roger. "Winston Churchill and the Rise of Totalitarianism: Statesmanship and the Challenge of Modern Tyranny." Catholic U. of Am. 1983. 416 pp. *DAI 1983 43(10): 3409-A.* DA8304644

2362. Starobin, Joseph R. THE IDENTITY CRISIS OF WEST EUROPEAN COMMUNISTS. *Dissent 1975 22(3): 251-260.*

2363. Stehle, Hansjakob. *Eastern Politics of the Vatican, 1917-1979.* Smith, Sandra, transl. Athens: Ohio U. Pr., 1981. 466 pp.

2364. Stocker, Hans. DEN REVISIONISMUS VOLLENDEN: DIE CHANCEN DES SOZIALISMUS IN WESTEUROPA [Bringing revisionism to its end: the chances of socialism in Western Europe]. *Frankfurter Hefte [West Germany] 1980 35(12): 13-21.* Responsiveness to revisionist democratic socialist principles helped the Italian and Spanish Communists become acceptable to the greatest number of voters since the late 1960's, while the return to centralist principles weakened the French Communists in the 1970's.

2365. Tannahill, R. Neal. LEADERSHIP AS A DETERMINANT OF DIVERSITY IN WESTERN EUROPEAN COMMUNISM. *Studies in Comparative Communism 1976 9(4): 349-368.* The background of leaders of Western European Communist parties shows that working-class leaders are more pro-Soviet than middle-class leaders who tend toward independence. University graduates and intellectuals are more innovative and more difficult to discipline. Organization men tend to be pragmatic and union militants nonrevolutionary. Older leaders are usually wedded to older policies. In the 1950's, the new line of coalition with socialists brought to power a new leadership. Participation in government is often associated with a leaning toward reformist policies. Leaders without strong personal ties to the USSR have shown some independence of Moscow. 88 notes. D. Balmuth

2366. Tarschys, Daniel. THE UNIQUE ROLE OF THE SWEDISH CP. *Problems of Communism 1974 23(3): 36-44.* Intrepets the unique role of the Swedish Communist Party since 1970 when it furnished the parliamentary support for maintaining the Social Democratic Party in power. The Communist Party's peripheral position in the political spectrum greatly reduces its ability to maneuver in Parliament or put a price on its votes. It does exercise a certain degree of influence on the general perception of political problems and the limits of choice. 6 notes. J. M. Lauber

2367. Timmermann, Heinz. DIE EUROPAPOLITISCHE KONFERENZ WESTEUROPÄISCHER KOMMUNISTISCHER PARTEIEN IN BRÜSSEL [The policy conference of Western European communist parties in Brussels]. *Osteuropa [West Germany] 1974 24(6): 442-453.* The Western European communist "summit" of 26-28 January 1974 reemphasized the growing communist pressure for a share in power, but generally agreed on maintaining dialogues with social-democratic and liberal-progressive groups. A majority favored working within the framework of the European Economic Community. The outcome displeased the Soviet communist leadership, since it disregarded Moscow's immediate objectives. 33 notes. R. E. Weltsch

2368. Timmermann, Heinz. WESTEUROPAS KOMMUNISTEN [Western Europe's Communists]. *Schweizer Monatshefte [Switzerland] 1975 55(9): 702-723.* A vital question in Europe today is whether Western Communist parties, especially those of Italy, France, and Spain, are truly independent of Moscow and are evolving in a democratic direction.

2369. Tschernowa, Tamara. EINIGE BEMERKUNGEN ZUR HALTUNG DER KOMMUNISTISCHEN PARTEI ÖSTERREICHS BEZÜGLICH DER FREMDARBEITERPOLITIK (1970-1975) [Remarks on the attitude of the Communist Party of Austria on policy regarding foreign workers, 1970-75]. *Wissenschaftliche Zeitschrift der Wilhelm-Pieck-Universität Rostock. Gesellschaftswissenschaftliche Reihe [East Germany] 1982 31(1-2): 65-70.* Documents of the Communist Party of Austria and reports in the press expose the discrimination practiced against foreign workers as well as their solidarity with the Austrian working class.

2370. Urbany, Dominique. THIRTY YEARS IN PARLIAMENT: REMINISCENCES. *World Marxist Rev. [Canada] 1976 19(1): 83-93.* The head of the Communist Party of Luxembourg reflects on parliamentary politics, 1945-75.

2371. Van Geyt, Louis. COMMUNAL AND POWER CRISIS IN BELGIUM. *World Marxist R. [Canada] 1974 17(9): 73-82.* The Communist Party advocates forming a democratic federal republic in Belgium to solve the nation's economic problems and ease ethnic tensions between the Flemish and Walloon populationns.

2372. Vermaat, J. A. Emerson. THE KGB AND THE WEST EUROPEAN PEACE MOVEMENTS. *Midstream 1984 30(5): 7-12.* Describes the efforts of the International Department of the Communist Party of the Soviet Union to plan and support Western European peace movements.

2373. Vermaat, J. A. Emerson. MOSCOW FRONTS AND THE EUROPEAN PEACE MOVEMENT. *Problems of Communism 1982 31(6): 43-56.* The Soviet Union has waged a "peace" campaign in recent years aimed at preventing the modernization of the West European defense system. Moscow has activated the Soviet front organizations and utilized the organizational structure of several Western European Communist parties in order to interact with indigenous peace groups and, thereby, influence public opinion in the West. Based on official Soviet and West European newspaper and periodical literature; 64 notes. J. M. Lauber

2374. Vree, Dale. COALITION POLITICS ON THE LEFT IN FRANCE AND ITALY. *R. of Pol. 1975 37(3): 286-316.* Despite the many political, social, cultural, and religious similarities of postwar Italy and France, the dialogue between Communists and Catholics in the two countries has differed because "the Italian Communists need their Catholics but the French Communists do not need theirs." Although the situation is changeable, the French Communists dominate their Catholic allies while in Italy, the Catholics dominate their Communist allies. Secondary sources. L. Ziewacz

2375. Whetten, Lawrence L. *New International Communism: The Foreign and Defense Policies of Latin European Communist Parties.* Lexington, Mass.: Lexington Books, 1982. 262 pp.

2376. White, Stephen. REVOLUTIONARIES AND PARLIAMENT: THE BRITISH CASE. *Co-existence [Great Britain] 1974 11(2): 173-176.* Questions whether revolutionaries should contest Parliamentary elections in Great Britain as was done between 1969 and 1974 in view of the low number of votes received by the Communist Party and other Leftist political parties.

2377. Winter, E. OTNOSHENIE VATIKANA K SOVETSKOMU SOIUZU [The Vatican's attitude to the Soviet Union]. *Voprosy Istorii [USSR] 1972 9: 39-51.* Examines the basic propositions set forth by the author in Volume Three of his *Russia and Papacy* focusing on the Vatican's attitude to Soviet Russia for the period since the victory of the Great October Socialist Revolution to our days. Drawing on a wealth of factual material, the author shows how and under what circumstances the policy pursued by the Vatican for over half a century gradually underwent an evolution from open hostility and engineering a crusade against the USSR to normalizing relations with the Soviet Union and other socialist countries. Underlines that it is only the Vatican's tactics that undergoes changes according to circumstances that take place; as far as its strategy, it remains unchanged. J

2378. Wolf, Ioop. BOGATAIA ISTORIIA—NEPRERYVNAIA BOR'BA [Abundant history, permanent struggle]. *Voprosy Istorii KPSS [USSR] 1978 (11): 31-40.* A member of the Politburo of the Communist Party of Netherlands surveys the difficult path this Party has trodden and sees a brighter future for it due to the new unity forged at its 26th Congress.

2379. Zagladin, N. V. NOVYE ASPEKTY IDEOLOGICHESKOI STRATEGII IMPERIALIZMA SSHA V OTNOSHENII KOMMUNISTICHESKO O DVIZHENIIA ZAPADNOI EVROPY [New aspects of the ideological strategy of US imperialism in relation to the Communist movement in Western Europe]. *Voprosy Istorii KPSS [USSR] 1979 (9): 83-93.* In the 1970's, the European Communist parties strengthened their positions and as a result the anti-Communist, Cold War ideology was undermined. A new strategy was adopted by the United States that insisted developed capitalist countries lacked a suitable environment for the development of socialism and argued that the Communist parties had changed their politics and rejected orthodox Marxism in favor of social democracy. To reinforce this ideological strategy a program has been formulated by the United States to weaken the economies of countries where Communist parties are in power. Secondary sources; 40 notes. L. Waters

2380. Zagladina, Kh. T. KOMPARTIIA IRLANDII V BOR'BE ZA INTERESY TRUDIASHCHIKHSIA, ZA NATSIONAL'NYI I SOTSIAL'NYI PROGRESS [The Communist Party of Ireland strives for the welfare of the workers and national and social progress]. *Voprosy Istorii KPSS [USSR] 1983 (6): 79-89.* Discusses the history and activity of the Irish Communist Party, 1909-82, emphasizing its role in the struggle for national independence and its part in the current fight for a unified Ireland. 36 notes. R. Kirillov

2381. Zaharieva, Luba. AVSTRIISKATA KOMUNISTICHESKA PARTIIA I VUNSHNATA POLITIKA NA AVSTRIA (KRAIA NA 60-TE I PURVATA POLOVINA NA 70-TE GODINI) [The Austrian Communist Party and Austria's foreign policy, the end of the 1960's and the first half of the 1970's]. *Izvestiia na Inst. po Istoriia na BKP [Bulgaria] 1979 40: 157-193.* Survey of the part played by the Austrian Communist Party in the relaxation of the international relations since the end of the 1960's. Based on documents of Austrian Communist Party congresses and writings in the party daily *Volkstimme* and the periodical *Weg und Ziel.*

2382. Zaitsev, V. P. GARRI POLLIT: K 80-LETIU SO DNIA ROZHDENIA [Harry Pollitt: the 80th anniversary of his birth]. *Voprosy Istorii KPSS [USSR] 1970 (11): 123-126.* Summarizes the career of Harry Pollitt, his involvement with labor unions and the Communist Party of Great Britain, and his talents as a writer.

2383. Zakravsky, Peter. DIE INDUSTRIELLEN SCHUHARBEITER IM KAMPF UM IHREN KOLLEKTIVVERTRAG. EIN STREIKPORTRÄT (3.3.1948-3.5.1948) [The industrial shoeworkers in their struggle for a collective contract: portrait of a strike, 3 March 1948-3 May 1948]. *Zeitgeschichte [Austria] 1981 8(9-10): 349-365.* The workers in the Austrian shoe industry staged a nine-week strike in 1948 which does not fit the overall pattern of arbitration in Austrian labor relations. While the strike was a success, it had serious ramifications within the Austrian Trade Union Federation (ÖGB). It was used by moderate trade union leaders to exclude Communists from union leadership, an act that must be seen in the context of the Marshall Plan negotiations. Primary and secondary sources; 72 notes. M. Geyer

2384. Zhilin, P. A. AVANGARNAIA ROL' KOMMUNISTOV V BOR'BE S FASHIZMOM I NEONATSIZMOM [The vanguard role of the Communists in the struggle against fascism and neo-Nazism]. *Voprosy Istorii KPSS [USSR] 1979 (9): 50-60.* The establishment of fascist dictatorships in Europe was the direct result of the policies of the right opportunist leaders of Social Democracy and their hostility to the Communists. After the breakdown of the Moscow negotiations in August 1939, engineered by England and France, it was already too late to stop the rise of fascist aggression. The lessons of history indicate that a strong Soviet Union and socialist system is a major factor in insuring success in the struggle against fascism and neo-Nazism. 30 notes. L. Waters

2385. —. THE INSTITUTE OF CONFLICT STUDIES. *Critique [Great Britain] 1978 (9): 129-134.* Looks at the origins, structure, and operations of the British Institute of Conflict Studies, formed in 1970, and the source of a widely distributed anticommunist report, *The Attack on Higher Education* (1976).

2386. —. IRELAND: CONCRETE CLASS ANALYSIS ESSENTIAL TO UNDERSTAND STRUGGLE. *Progressive Labor 1973 9(2): 71-88, (3): 46-62.* Part I. "Traces the roots of the current struggles by analysing the class forces shaped by the uneven development of capitalism exemplified by Ireland." Part II. "Deals with Ireland since Partition. An appendix on the Communist movement in Ireland is included." J

2387. —. NO RETURN TO POWER POLITICS. *World Marxist R. [Canada] 1974 17(5): 57-61.*
Fuernberg, Friedl. RESPECT NEUTRALITY, *pp. 57-58.*
Knutsen, Martin Gunnar. NO NATO FOR NORWAY, *pp. 58-59.*
Karkabi, Zahi. ADVANCES TOWARD PEACE, *pp. 59-61.*
Outlines the primary foreign policy objectives of the Communist Party in Austria, Norway, and Israel.

France

2388. Abosch, Heinz. DIE FRANZÖSISCHE LINKSUNION IST TOT [The French United Left is dead]. *Schweizer Monatshefte [Switzerland] 1979 59(5): 346-351.* The break of the political alliance between the French Communists and Socialists, who closely cooperated after 1968, was already imminent in the formative period, as shown by the example of the failure in the 1930's, because the Communists realized that they were doomed to be the junior partner.

2389. Adereth, Maxwell. *The French Communist Party (PCF): A Critical History (1920-84): From Comintern to "the Colours of France."* Manchester, England: U. of Manchester Pr., 1985. 326 pp.

2390. Adorean, George. PARTIDUL COMUNIST FRANCEZ LA 50 DE ANI DE EXISTENŢĂ [50 years of the French Communist Party]. *Anale de Istorie [Rumania] 1971 17(1): 124-135.* Founded in December 1920 at Tours, the French Communist Party (PCF) is the heir of the revolutionary and socialist tradition of France. Surveys the internal struggles in the French Socialist Party before 1914, centering on the party's stand toward war and revisionism. The syndicalist elements continued to dissent over control and methods to be used, and the lack of democratic centralism kept the party disunited, a conglomerate of departmental federations and local autonomous sections, lacking cohesion. Years were required for the PCF to mature and defeat sectarianism. Under Maurice Thorez, 1930-64, the party was present in all essential stages of France's national life, including the Popular Front and the Resistance. By the 19th Congress in 1970, the groundwork for a socialist France had been laid. Reprints a communication from the PCF in which French leaders are interviewed on party history and goals. G. J. Bobango

2391. Angelelli, J. P. SUR UNE REPUBLIQUE DÉFUNTE... [On a defunct republic]. *Écrits de Paris [France] 1975 (352): 45-50.* A review article on *La Quatrième République* (Paris: Pr. U. de France, 1975) by Paul Courtier, dwelling on the strong anti-Communism in France in the late 1940's.

2392. Antiukhina-Moskovchenko, V. I. MARSEL KASHEN-REVOLIUTSIONER LENINSKOI SHKOLY [Marcel Cachin: a revolutionary in the Leninist mould]. *Novaia i Noveishaia Istoriia [USSR] 1970 (1): 39-53, (2): 115-132, (4): 77-96.* Marcel Cachin (1869-1958), the French Communist leader, was deeply affected by his visit to Russia in the spring of 1917. He strove to present a true picture of the USSR immediately after the October Revolution, when the government of France was especially hostile to the Bolsheviks. He called for a cessation of French intervention in the Russian Civil War, and for diplomatic recognition of the USSR. Throughout his subsequent life Cachin remained a firm believer in proletarian internationalism and a constant suporter of the USSR. 228 notes. L. Smith/D. N. Collins/S

2393. Antonian, Armen. THE FRENCH COMMUNIST PARTY AND THE GOVERNMENT OF FRANÇOIS MITTERRAND (1981-1983). *Proceedings of the Annual Meeting of the Western Society for French History 1983 11: 405-416.* Examines the cooperation of the French Communist Party with the Socialist government of President François Mitterrand. From May 1981 to March 1982 the Communist Party worked to eliminate dissension within itself as it gave cautious support to the government. From March 1982 to March 1983 the Communists were firm allies of Mitterrand. Beginning in March 1983 their allegiance to the government weakened. They gradually disassociated themselves from Mitterrand's unpopular austerity program and from his foreign policies. Based on newspapers and other printed sources; 48 notes. T. J. Schaeper

2394. Aviv, Isaac. THE FRENCH COMMUNIST PARTY FROM 1958 TO 1978: CRISIS AND ENDURANCE. *West European Pol. [Great Britain] 1979 2(2): 178-197.* Accounts for the stability of the French Communist Party in the face of recurrent crises from 1958 to 1978.

2395. Aviv, Isaac. LE PCF DANS LE SYSTÈME FRANÇAIS DES ANNÉES 1930 À LA FIN DE LA IVe RÉPUBLIQUE [The Communist Party (PCF) in the French political system: from the 1930's to the end of the Fourth Republic]. *Mouvement Social [France] 1978 104: 75-94.* The extraordinary stability of the French Communist Party has been due to French cultural stability. J/S

2396. Bedarida, François. UN VOYAGE À L'INTÉRIEUR DU PARTI [A trip to the interior of the Party]. *Esprit [France] 1975 (2): 201-205.* Review article on the book by André Harris and Alain de Sédouy *Voyage á l'interieur du Parti communist* (Paris: Le Seuil, 1975). The author sees it as a positive contribution but concludes that those making a trip to the interior will need other guidebooks as well. 2 notes. G. F. Jewsbury

2397. Benoit, Lucien. VOICE OF HONOR AND CONSCIENCE; 70TH ANNIVERSARY OF "L'HUMANITÉ." *World Marxist R. [Canada] 1974 17(4): 127-131.* Relates the history of the French Communist Party's daily newspaper *L'Humanité* from 1904 to 1974.

2398. Berg, Helene and Sukhanov, Viktor. COMMUNISTS IN AGRICULTURE (LETTERS FROM FRANCE). *World Marxist Rev. [Canada] 1972 15(5): 51-58.* Discusses the unemployment of farmers due to alleged agricultural monopoly in villages in France, 1956-72, emphasizing population problems and the activities of the Communist Party.

2399. Billoux, F. WHEN WE WERE MINISTERS. *World Marxist R. 1975 18(8): 59-65.* Discusses the participation of the Communist Party in France's government, 1944-47.

2400. Billoux, François. CHLEN POLITBIURO FKP: O PIATIDESIATILETII FRANTSUZSKOI KOMMUNISTICHESKOI PARTII [From the FCP Politburo: the 50th anniversary of the French Communist Party]. *Voprosy Istorii [USSR] 1971 (1): 44-54.* Traces the 50-year road traversed by the Communist Party of France. The author stresses that the French Communist Party owes its origin to the objective processes taking place in the French working-class movement, to the powerful impact made on the latter by the October Revolution in Russia. The article brings out the significance of Lenin's ideas, of the Bolshevik Party's organizational and programmatic principles for the activity of the French Communists. Guarding the purity of Marxism-Leninism, the French Communist Party wages an irreconcilable struggle against bourgeois ideology, against Right and "Left" opportunism. It has made its distinctive contribution to the elaboration of important theoretical questions of the proletarian struggle, notably the formation of a broad popular front, the possibility of averting another war, the paths of transition to socialism, the working-class allies, etc. An inalienable feature of the French Communist Party is its unflinching fidelity to the principles of proletarian internationalism. It consistently strives to enhance the unity of the working class, to form a close alliance of all the anti-imperialist forces and to repel the offensive launched by the monopolies against the working people's standard of living and fundamental democratic rights. J

2401. Blume, Ilse. DIE FRANZÖSISCHE KOMMUNISTISCHE PARTEI UND DIE INTELLIGENZ [The French Communist Party and the intelligentsia]. *Zeitschrift für Geschichtswissenschaft [East Germany] 1976 24(1): 24-41.* In addition to the cooperation in the 1930's-40's with the traditionally left-wing French intelligentsia, the French Communist Party tried to attract the scientific-technical and pedagogic intelligentsia in the 1960's and 1970's. This strategy is combined with a complicated ideological struggle against various technocratic, social reformist, and left radical theories as well as against the bourgeoisie which tries to continue its political domination over the intelligentsia. Based on printed documents, secondary literature, journals, and newspapers; 78 notes. R. Wagnleitner

2402. Boccara, Paul. APROPOS CRISIS OF STATE-MONOPOLY CAPITALISM. *World Marxist Rev. [Canada] 1972 15(11): 120-129.* Discusses the economic policy of the French Communist Party for solving France's problems of inflation and unemployment, 1966-72.

2403. Bongiovanni, Bruno. PARTITO COMUNISTA FRANCESE E STORIOGRAFIA NEGLI ANNI SETTANTA [The French Communist Party and historiography in the 1970's]. *Belfagor [Italy] 36(6): 677-695.* Recent historians have documented the internal politics of the French Communist Party during World War II and after, throwing light on many of the twists of the party line by situating them in a net of complex historical interdependence.

2404. Brossollet, Guy. LE PARTI COMMUNISTE FRANÇAIS ET LA CHINE [The French Communist Party and China]. *R. de Défense Natl. [France] 1968 24(6/7): 1076-1089.* Traces modern China's "Long March" to development, which justifies certain differences between European and Chinese socialism, offers theoretical reflections on the nature of Maoism as compared to orthodox Marxism, and outlines the major points of controversy between Peking and Moscow today. Stresses the originality of the Chinese "model" of socialism. Based on Roger Garaudy's *Le Problème Chinois* (Paris: Seghers, 1967) and secondary sources; 33 notes. S. Sevilla

2405. Broyer, Philippe; Cassan, Didier; and DaLage, Olivier. LES CANDIDATS COMMUNISTES AUX ÉLECTIONS LÉGISLATIVES DE 1973 ET 1978 [Communist candidates in the 1973 and 1978 parliamentary elections]. *Rev. Française de Sci. Pol. [France] 1979 29(2): 213-229.* A statistical comparative analysis of Communist candidacies in the 1973 and 1978 French parliamentary elections shows a strong trend toward younger candidates, more women candidates and only slight changes in social composition as a result of a deliberate political choice to preserve the original traits of the Communist Party.

2406. Calmy, Christophe. LA GUERRE DES GAUCHES [The war of the Left]. *Histoire [France] 1978 (1): 92-93.* Examines the conflict between the Socialist Party and the Communist Party in France, 1920-78.

2407. Campbell, Ian. THE FRENCH COMMUNISTS AND THE UNION OF THE LEFT: 1974-76. *Parliamentary Affairs [Great Britain] 1976 29(3): 246-263.* Leading up to the 1974 presidential elections, the leaders of the French Socialists and Communists agreed to a Common Program and common presidential candidate. Since the 1974 elections the Union of the Left has deteriorated. The author details the background and substance of the union, and the influences which have brought about its deterioration. Among some factors involved are grass-roots rebellion among young Communist militants against concessions, the Portuguese Socialist-Communist situation, and the Socialist attempts to build an industrial base in the unions comparable to the Communists'. The struggle has strengthened the Socialists under François Mitterand, but has created still unresolved problems for Communist leader Georges Marchais. 11 notes. J. C. Holsinger

2408. Carpinelli, Francesco Saverio. IL CONCETTO DI CLASSE E PARTITO IN JEAN PAUL SARTRE [The concept of class and the party in Jean Paul Sartre]. *Pensiero Pol. [Italy] 1975 8(2): 171-202.* Clarifies the development and evolution of Sartre's concept of social classes and the organization of the working class. Sartre approached the political and social world on psychological-moral terms and in a more subjective than objective manner, particularly in his earlier writings. His analysis remained at odds with the socio-historical conception of the working class of Marx and many Marxists by emphasizing the role of the individual. The working class cannot act to overthrow society without a strong and highly organized party, according to Sartre. The author follows closely the vicissitudes in Sartre's relationship with the French Communist Party throughout his lifetime. This rarely satisfying relationship (for both sides) split perhaps conclusively with Sartre's support, in May 1968, of the Gauchistes, who created in Sartre's words "the sketch for a new relationship between the political and the moral, the possibility of a new political experience, a refusal of integration." Based on the writings of Jean Paul Sartre and secondary sources; 76 notes. M. T. Wilson

2409. Castoriadis, Cornelius. THE FRENCH COMMUNIST PARTY: A CRITICAL ANATOMY. *Dissent 1979 26(3): 315-325.* Surveys the French Communist Party line from its rigid Stalinism of the 1940's and 1950's to its alleged democratization between 1972 and 1977. The changes are more apparent than real, for the Party has retained a self-perpetuating totalitarian structure.

2410. Charlton, Sue Ellen M. DERADICALIZATION AND THE FRENCH COMMUNIST PARTY. *Rev. of Pol. 1979 41(1): 38-60.* In Robert C. Tucker's analysis of a Communist party, any radical movement that exists without achieving its goals, undergoes deradicalization. This theory outwardly describes the French Communist Party in the 1970's but alone does not explain the behavior of the Communists. Internal and external conditions have forced the Party to alter its radical principles and tactical doctrine. Tucker's view that deradicalization is an irrevocable process seems to be confirmed in France. However, future events do not preclude a stalling effort to create a middle ground between bourgeois electoralism and Stalinist isolation. 43 notes. L. Ziewacz

2411. Cherkasov, R. F. V BOR'BE ZA INTERESY TRUDIASHCHIKHSIA, ZA MIR I SOTSIAL'NYI PROGRESS [In the struggle for the interests of the laboring masses, for peace and social progress]. *Voprosy Istorii KPSS [USSR] 1980 (12): 99-102.* Briefly relates the history of the French Communist Party from its founding in 1920. Discusses the lessons that should have been learned from events in 1958 and problems in the relationship between the Socialist and Communist parties. Based on sources in French and Russian; 16 notes. D. N. Collins

2412. Cogniot, Georges. BOR'BA FRANTSUZSKIKH KOMMUNISTOV PROTIV ANTIKOMMUNIZMA I ANTISOVETIZMA [The struggle of French Communists against anti-Communism and anti-Sovietism]. *Voprosy Istorii KPSS [USSR] 1975 (12): 33-44.* As the economic situation in capitalist countries such as France worsens, the rightist circles escalate their attacks on the Communist Party. Apologists for monopoly capitalism, often prompted by American pressure including that from the Central Intelligence Agency, attack the policies of the French Communist Party which seeks to unite all classes and left parties against monopolistic oligarchy, induce the French Socialist Party to cease cooperation with the Communist Party, and distort the role the French Communist Party and the Soviet Union played in helping France during and after World War II. Based on recent articles published in the French press; 18 notes. L. E. Holmes

2413. Courtieu, P. TOWARD AN ALLIANCE OF THE FRENCH PEOPLE. *World Marxist R. 1975 18(2): 15-24.* Notes the objectives of the Communist Party in France in the 1970's.

2414. Courtieu, Paul. THE FRENCH CP FIGHTS FOR POPULAR UNITY. *World Marxist R. [Canada] 1973 16(3): 82-89.* The 20th Congress of France's Communist Party urged political cooperation with the Socialist Party to bring about social reform.

2415. Cranston, Maurice. THE IDEOLOGY OF ALTHUSSER. *Problems of Communism 1973 22(2): 53-60.* Investigates the ideas of Louis Althusser, who has emerged as the only philosopher of eminence remaining on the Central Committee of the French Communist Party since the expulsion of Roger Garaudy. Centers on Althusser's concept of the "epistemological break" and the essential role that ideology plays in all societies. Based on Althusser's works; 21 notes. J. M. Lauber

2416. Dauphin-Meunier, Achille. RENÉ BELIN ET LE SYNDICALISME CONSTRUCTIF [René Belin and constructive unionism]. *Écrits de Paris [France] 1977 (366): 14-20.* Describes the activities of French posts and telegraph union leader, René Belin (1898-1977), who throughout his union career assiduously avoided entanglements with the Communists.

2417. Defrosière, Maria. COUP DE PRAGUE MANQUÉ OU DEFFÉRÉ? [The "coup de Prague," failed or deferred?]. *Écrits de Paris [France] 1976 (359): 66-71.* Explains why the Communist uprising on 1 May 1947 in France, popularly referred to as the coup de Prague, failed to materialize as anticipated, holding open the possibility of its eventual reoccurrence.

2418. Derville, Jacques and Croisat, Maurice. LA SOCIALISATION DES MILITANTS COMMUNISTES FRANÇAIS: ELÉMENTS D'UNE ENQUÊTE DANS L'ISÈRE [Socialization of the French Communist militants: elements of an inquiry in the Isère department]. *Rev. Française de Sci. Pol. [France] 1979 29(4-5): 760-790.*

2419. Domenach, Jean-Marie; Ozouf, Jacques; Winock, Michel; and Lavau, Georges. FRENCH COMMUNISTS: CHANGE OR STAGNATION? *Dissent 1975 22(3): 238-250.* "The discussion focuses on the problem of Communist-Socialist relations in France, on whether the Communist Party has begun significantly to change, and especially on the reasons for the recent series of attacks the French Communists have launched against the Socialists."

2420. Domergue, Raymond. FOI ET RÉVOLUTION: L'ITINÉRAIRE DE "FRÈRES DU MONDE" [Faith and revolution: the itinerary of *Frères du Monde*]. *Esprit [France] 1978 (9): 40-58.* Studies the history, contents, and directions of the Communist magazine *Frères du Monde,* during its 15-year existence, 1959-74.

2421. Dornier, Antoine. PRAGUE PARMI NOUS [Prague among us]. *Esprit [France] 1979 (1): 90-104.* Reviews and comments on the attitudes of the French Communist Party toward Czechoslovakia and on the so-called normalization in Prague since 1968.

2422. Drozdov, E. A. SOIUZ LEVYKH SIL VO FRANTSII I ZNACHENIE EGO OPYTA [The significance of the alliance of the French Left]. *Novaia i Noveishaia Istoriia [USSR] 1982 (5): 32-52.*

Discusses the problems of building the class and political alliances of the Left, democratic forces in France in the 1970's and the lessons the French Communists have drawn from this experience. Also analyzes the new conditions for the struggle for democratic changes, and consolidation of the working-class movement after the government of the Left forces, with the participation of Communists, came to power. J/S

2423. Drozdov, E. A. VIDNYI RUKOVODITEL' FRANTSUZSKOGO RABOCHEGO DVIZHENIIA: K 90-LETIIU SO DNIA ROZHDENIIA BENUA FRASHONA [A prominent leader of the French workers movement: on the 90th anniversary of the birth of Benoit Frachon]. *Voprosy Istorii KPSS [USSR] 1983 (5): 108-111.* Charts the career of working-class Communist Benoit Frachon and assesses his contribution to the French trades union movement, particularly during the events of 1968. 9 notes. G. Dombrovski

2424. Dubar, Claude; Gayot, Gérard; and Hédoux, Jacques. SOCIABILITE MINIERE ET CHANGEMENT SOCIAL A SALLAUMINES ET A NOYELLES-SOUS-LENS (1900-1980) [Miner sociability and social change in Sallaumines and in Noyelles-sous-Lens, 1900-80]. *Rev. du Nord [France] 1982 64(253): 363-463.* Sociological and historical study of sociability and social change in Sallaumines and Noyelles-sous-Lens, Pas-de-Calais, between the beginning of the 20th century and the late 1970's. Owing to the constraints of the coal mining industry, these two cities have become very similar since World War I in their demography and socio-professional structure; but at the same time, they never ceased to claim a different collective identity, in the miners' fights, in the participation in associative life and in elections—60 years of socialism in Noyelles, 40 years of communism in Sallaumines. Noyelles-sous-Lens has sustained an associative life relatively independent of the socialist municipal power and mining traditions, and its people evolved a memory of the past and an idea of the future where miners' housing estates and the mine are progressively giving way to the little tertiary town in the outskirts of the big agglomeration of Lens. Sallaumines has "nested" in the coal: the mine has always occupied the totality of the communal space; the village, destroyed in 1914, was never reconstructed, and the Communist city council has attempted since 1935 to mobilize all the population and the associations to defend coal mining, the pits, and the miners. In Sallaumines, it is painful to think of reconversion because the memory and the future of coal have taken hold of the individual and collective representations. Based on interviews, local organizational and governmental records, and a survey questionnaire. J/S

2425. Dubief, H.; Garmy, R.; and Kriegel, A. LEGS HÉLÈNE BRION [The Hélène Brion legacy]. *Mouvement Social [France] 1963 (44): 93-100.* A study of the documents of Hélène Brion (1882-1962), including dossiers, correspondence, clippings, and an extensive collection of newspapers (*La Bataille Syndicaliste*, *La Vérité*). Hélène Brion is remembered as a teacher, member of the Communist Party, feminist, and member of the teacher's union since its formation. Her notes trace her development toward socialism, revolutionary unionism, and militant feminism, and describe harsh repression from the Clemenceau administration. 10 notes. S. Sevilla

2426. Duclos, Jacques. LENIN I FRANTSUZSKOE RABOCHEE DVIZHENIE [Lenin and the French workers' movement]. *Voprosy Istorii KPSS [USSR] 1970 (1): 31-57.* Discusses how Leninism has decisively influenced the French Communist Party and criticizes ideological deviations and tactical errors of the Socialist Party in France.

2427. Duclos, Jacques. VII KONGRESS KOMINTERNA I NARODNYI FRONT VO FRANTSII [The seventh Comintern Congress and the French Popular Front]. *Voprosy Istorii KPSS [USSR] 1965 (8): 38-47.* A member of the French Communist Party refers to the importance of the seventh Comintern Congress of 1935 in helping to unite anti-fascist movements.

2428. Duhamel, Luc. INTERPRETING MOSCOW'S AIMS WITHIN THE COMMUNIST RANKS. *Internat. Perspectives [Canada] 1974 (4): 15-18.* Discusses the significance of the USSR's policy of detente with the West to the French Communist Party.

2429. Emanuilov, Emanuil G. UCHASTIETO NA KOMUNISTI VUV FRENSKOTO PRAVITELSTVO (1944 - 1947 G.) [The participation of Communists in the French government, 1944-47]. *Istoricheski Pregled [Bulgaria] 1972 28(4): 3-21.* A description and analysis of the participation of the French Commurist Party and Communist leaders, particularly Maurice Thorez, Jacques Duclos, Ambroise Croizat, and Francois Billoux, in the governments and politics of France after World War II. The Communist Party attempted to create coalition governments with other democratic parties in the interest of the lower classes. Although Communists participated in a number of coalitions in the years discussed, US intervention in domestic French affairs and the anti-Communist position of the French Socialist Party led to the triumph of the bourgeois parties and the exclusion of the Communists in 1947. Based on documents in *Journal Officiel*, the contemporary French press, and memoirs; 109 notes. F. B. Chary

2430. Fedoseev, P. N. V. I. LENIN I ISTORICHESKII PUT' FRANTSUZSKOI KOMMUNISTICHESKOI PARTII [Lenin and the historical path of the French Communist Party]. *Novaia i Noveishaia Istoriia [USSR] 1971 (2): 3-17.* V. I. Lenin's writings show his role in establishing the French Communist Party. He wanted to bring French socialists into the fold of the Comintern and split off opportunist elements. The Communist Party of France implemented Marxist-Leninist theory during its 50-year history. However, during the political troubles of the 1960's anti-Soviet views appeared among the party leadership. Revisionists on the right deny the leading role of the working class and its revolutionary party, while leftists accuse the working class of losing their revolutionary spirit and the Communist Party of bureaucracy and sectarianism. Paper given to a conference in Paris on the 50th anniversary of the French Communist Party. Based on primary and secondary sources; 38 notes. E. R. Sicher

2431. Fejto, François. SUR L'EVOLUTION DU PARTI COMMUNISTE FRANÇAIS [On the evolution of the French Communist Party]. *Études Int. [Canada] 1975 (3): 355-362.* Examines the reasons for the evolving Communist-Socialist alliance in France, 1970-75. Secondary sources; 15 notes. J. F. Harrington, Jr.

2432. Figer, Leo. O NEKOTORYKH UROKAKH POLITICHESKOI BOR'BY PROTIV TROTSKIZMA VO FRANTSII [Lessons from the political struggle against Trotskyism in France]. *Voprosy Istorii KPSS [USSR] 1972 (5): 70-77.* Notes the difficulties and achievements of the French Communist Party in its battles against Trotskyites, 1935-71.

2433. Fine, Keitha Sapsin. "The French Communist Party: The Theory of State Monopoly Capitalism and the Practice of Class Politics, 1958-1978." Tufts U. 1979. 531 pp. *DAI 1979 39(12): 7496-A.* 7913069

2434. Flavien, Jean. FRENCH FARMERS AND THE FCP PROPOSALS. *World Marxist Rev. [Canada] 1972 15(5): 58-61.* Discusses economic aspects of the Communist Party's agricultural policy for independent farmers in France in 1971, including the roles of monopolies and the Common Market.

2435. Flavien, Jean. TOPIC OF THE DAY: THE PEASANTRY. *World Marxist R. [Canada] 1975 18(4): 90-96.* Focuses on the relation between agricultural reform, peasants, and the Communist Party in France.

2436. Friedrich, Paul J. LÉGITIMITÉ ET REPRÉSENTATION [Legitimacy and representation]. *Esprit [France] 1975 (2): 206-217.* Examines the question of how far the Communist Party of France has evolved in the recent past, and at what levels that evolution has taken place. Most studies have concentrated only on the symptoms of evolution, but not on the causes. The author considers the problems of legitimacy of power and the Communist Party's drive for representation among the workers, the Party's views on political power, the major problems of adjusting Leninist ideology to French conditions, and the question of how far the Party can change and still remain Communist. 7 notes. G. F. Jewsbury

2437. Friend, Julius W. SOVIET BEHAVIOR AND NATIONAL RESPONSES: THE PUZZLING CASE OF THE FRENCH COMMUNIST PARTY. *Studies in Comparative Communism 1982 15(3): 212-235.* Conflict between the French Communist Party and the Soviet Communists since the late 1950's has involved Thorez's criticism of Khrushchev, French Communist criticism of Soviet actions in Czechoslovakia, and the increasing independence of the French Communists as they sought political power in France and to this end tried to be critical of the Soviets. Relations have eased in the 1980's as the French party has adjusted to the ouvrieriste tradition which simultaneously rejects reform and compromise in France and sees the Soviets as a paragon of revolution. The French party remains ambivalent toward Soviet policies. 41 notes.
D. Balmuth

2438. Frolkin, M. M. SLAVNYI SYN TRUDOVOI FRANSII (DO 80-RICHCHIA Z DNIA NARODZHENNIA ZHAKA DIUKLO) [A renowned son of the workers of France: the 80th anniversary of the birth of Jacques Duclos]. *Ukrains'kyi Istorychnyi Zhurnal [USSR] 1976 (10): 130-133.* Examines the life and work of French Communist Party leader Jacques Duclos (1896-1975).

2439. Gait, Maurice. MOSCOU ET LES ÉLECTIONS FRANÇAISES [Moscow and the French elections]. *Écrits de Paris [France] 1973 (322): 3-13.* The USSR may not have desired victory for the Socialist-Communist coalition in the 1973 French elections because a new government would end a system that has worked to the benefit of Soviet interests.

2440. Glasneck, Johannes. DIE BEDEUTUNG DER LEHREN DER PARISER KOMMUNE FÜR DIE STRATEGIE UND TAKTIK DER FRANZÖSISCHEN KOMMUNISTISCHEN PARTEI [The importance of the doctrine of the Paris Commune for strategy and tactics of the French Communist Party]. *Martin-Luther-Universität Halle-Wittenberg. Wissenschaftliche Zeitschrift. Gesellschafts- und Sprachwissenschaftliche Reihe [East Germany] 1972 21(4): 5-18.* Both the people's front policies during the 1930's and early 1970's and the Party's attempt to attract intellectuals and white-collar workers, 1945-72, reflect the experience of the Paris Commune.

2441. Godchau, Jean-François and Dreyfus, Michel. UN ARTICLE SCANDALEUX [A scandalous article]. *Rev. Française de Sci. Pol. [France] 1980 30(1): 140-147.* A rebuttal to Jean-François Kesler's "Le Communisme de gauche en France (1927-1947)" *[Rev. Française de Sci. Pol.* 1978 28(4)]. Chastises Kesler for his lack of comprehension of the ideas and development of left-wing communism, particularly Trotskyism, many factual errors, and inconclusive information obtained from biased sources; includes a short rejoinder by Kesler.

2442. Godlewski, Tadeusz. PARTIA KOMMUNISTYCZNA W SYSTEMIE POLITYCZNYM POWOJENNEJ FRANCJI (1944-1947) [The Communist Party in the political system of postwar France, 1944-47]. *Z Pola Walki [Poland] 1978 21(2): 103-137.* Although the French Communist Party was the main force in the resistance and in postwar elections gained over one-fourth of the vote, its positions within the government were restricted. The principles of bourgeois democracy—when considering the Communists—were applied selectively. As members of the government, the Communist ministers introduced practice of consultation of intentions and decisions with social and professional organizations; they were particular about protection of interests of the poorest social groups. Calling for intensification of productive efforts the party was opposed to the resignation of working masses. Their professional and political activities were appreciated as conditions for solution of economic difficulties of the postwar period and simultaneously as a basis for effective realization of democratic change.
J/S

2443. Goldberg, Richard. "The International Relations of the French Communist and Socialist Parties: 1968-1975." U. of Massachusetts 1982. 352 pp. *DAI 1982 43(4): 1282-A.* DA8219809

2444. Gras, Christian. ALFRED ROSMER ET LE MOUVEMENT REVOLUTIONNAIRE INTERNATIONAL [Alfred Rosmer and the international revolutionary movement]. *Mouvement Social [France] 1971 (74): 9-18.* Studies Alfred Rosmer, an important French militant and member of the international revolutionary movement. Rosmer's career, evolving from revolutionary syndicalism through communism to Trotskyism and anti-Stalinism, raised such issues as reform versus revolution; the relationship between unions and political parties on the national and international level; the social makeup of proletarian organizations; and the connection between the Communist International and general historical events. Focuses on Rosmer's association with Trotsky, their different analysis of Stalinism and Rosmer's position as an anti-Stalinist communist. Based on archives, newspapers and secondary sources.
P. M. Arum

2445. Guérin, Jeanyves. ENTRE LE SOCIALISME IDEAL ET LE COMMUNISME REEL (1945-1952) [Between ideal socialism and actual communism, 1945-52]. *Esprit [France] 1983 (1): 57-72.* Describes the various attitudes of postwar French intellectuals toward communism as a solution to totalitarianism and their reaction to mounting Soviet oppression.

2446. Hável, József. VÁLSÁG ÉS KIÚTKERESÉS A FRANCIA POLITIKÁBAN [Crisis and the search for a way out in French politics]. *Társadalmi Szemle [Hungary] 1979 34(7-8): 123-129.* Describes the impact of industrial crisis on society and the activity of the French Communist Party.

2447. Heller, John Davis. "French Communist Party, Credible Reformist Party?" University of Southern California 1984. *DAI 1985 45(11): 3442-A.*

2448. Hincker, Francois. THE PERSPECTIVE OF THE FRENCH COMMUNIST PARTY. *Marxist Perspectives 1978 1(2): 124-137.* Examines the development and current political philosophy of the French Communist Party in light of the development of the labor movement in France and the growth of capitalism, 1945-77.

2449. Hirsch, J. P. "LA SEULE VOIE POSSIBLE": REMARQUES SUR LES COMMUNISTES DU NORD ET DU PAS-DE-CALAIS DE LA LIBÉRATION AUX GRÈVES DE NOVEMBRE 1947 ["The only possible course": comments on the Communists of the Nord and of Pas-de-Calais from the liberation to the strikes of November 1947]. *Rev. du Nord [France] 1975 57(227): 563-578.* Explores the evolution in military Communist Party strategy in postwar northern France, including the secretiveness and isolationist politics it was forced to adopt in the hard social battle. One of nine articles in this issue on the political problems of 1944-47.

2450. Hors'kyi, V. M. ROZROBKA FRANTSUZ'KOIU KOMMUNISTYCHNOIU PARTIIEIU AHRARNO-SELIANS'KOHO PYTANNIA NA SUCHASNOMU ETAPI [The French Communist Party's solutions to the problems of agriculture and the peasantry in recent times]. *Ukrains'kyi Istorychnyi Zhurnal [USSR] 1973 (7): 84-92.* Discusses agricultural development in France, 1965-72, and the policies of the French Communist Party.

2451. Howorth, Jolyon. FOUR LESSONS IN COMMUNIST INTROSPECTION. *Bull. of the Soc. for the Study of Labour Hist. [Great Britain] 1980 (40): 67-71.* A review article that considers: Louis Althusser's *Ce Qui Ne Peut Plus Durer dans le Parti Communiste* (1978), Paul Laurent's *Le PCF comme Il Est* (1978), Alexandre Adler, Francis Cohen, Maurice Decaillot, Claude Frioux, and Léon Robel's *L'URSS et Nous* (1978), and Maurice Goldring's *L'Accident* (1978). These four essays reveal the dilemma facing the French Communist Party (PCF) since their defeat in the 1978 elections.

2452. Jacquot, Sylvie. LE PARTI COMMUNISTE FRANÇAIS: LA FIN DU GHETTO? [The French Communist Party: no more ghetto?]. *Études [France] 1973 338(2): 163-186.* After 20 years of exclusion, deliberately ignored and distrusted by the political forces that could have been its allies, the French Communist Party, has established a strong structure, financial stability, an effective press, a policy of democratic centralism, and a stable electorate. Having demonstrated a capacity for adaptation, it now prepares to assume a new role in the political system, determined to become in 1973, or 1976, the opposition party. Primary and secondary sources; 4 tables, 27 notes. R. K. Adams

2453. Jäger, Wolfgang. DIE KOMMUNISTISCHE PARTEI FRANKREICHS: WANDEL IN DER KRISE? [The Communist Party in France: change in crisis?]. *Politische Vierteljahresschrift [West Germany] 1979 20(1): 16-29.* The Communist party reached its height of power during the Fourth Republic, when it accounted for a quarter of the voters. Since 1958, however, its support has eroded. Its alliance with the socialists and left radicals in the Union of the Left in 1972 changed nothing. With the other parties of the alliance it pledged support for a démocratie avancée, but the Party broke with the coalition in 1977, unable to go in the direction of social democracy. The Party cannot be designated as Eurocommunist. 76 notes. S. Bonnycastle

2454. Jeantet, Claude. L'HEURE DE VÉRITÉ ET LE BARRAGE ANTICOMMUNISTE [The moment of truth and the anti-Communist dam]. *Ecrits de Paris [France] 1974 (342): 17-22.* Comments on a televised confrontation between the Interior Minister Michel Poniatowski, a liberal, and Communist leader Jacques Duclos. P. Rabineau

2455. Jenson, Jane and Ross, George. THE UNCHARTED WATERS OF DE-STALINIZATION: THE UNEVEN EVOLUTION OF THE PARTI COMMUNISTE FRANÇAIS. *Pol. & Soc. 1980 9(3): 263-298.* The French Communist Party (PCF) entered contemporary Eurocommunism through a process of incremental but uneven change. Its Stalinized version of Bolshevism gave way in the 1960's and 1970's to a theory of state monopoly capitalism leading to a socialist state without the proletarian dictatorship. However, as the internal structure of the party changed very little from the 1930's, the contradictions within the party itself led to the breakup of the French Union of the Left in 1977 and the party's electoral disaster in March 1978. Based on PCF congress records and reports; 46 notes. D. G. Nielson

2456. Jenson, Jane and Ross, George. *The View from Inside: A French Communist Cell in Crisis.* Berkeley: University of California Press, 1985. 346 pp.

2457. Johancsik, János. A FRANCIA KOMMUNISTÁK TÖRTÉNETI FOLYÓIRATÁRÓL (1976-1981) [Historical journal of the French Communists, 1976-81]. *Párttörténeti Közlemények [Hungary] 1983 29(4): 217-222.* Critical reflections, historicobiographical studies, and descriptions of national and international workers' movements are covered by *Cahiers d'Histoire,* the official quarterly publication of the Scientific Institute of the French Communist Party. Several noteworthy articles are described to demonstrate the increase in depth and quality during the past six years of publication. T. Kuner

2458. Judt, Tony. UNE HISTORIOGRAPHIE PAS COMME LES AUTRES [A historiography unlike others]. *European Studies Rev. [Great Britain] 1982 12(4): 445-478.* The interest of scholars in French Communists began almost immediately after they split from the Socialists in December 1920. The French Communists have a remarkably impoverished intellectual inheritance in comparison with Communist Parties in other western European countries. The first period of historical writing extends from the late 1930's to the end of the 1950's and consists mostly of memoirs. In the second period, from 1960 to the early 1970's, attempts at analytical accounts of the Party's origins and development emerged. The most recent attempts include a new generation of memoirs and early efforts at synthesis. Since 1964, Anne Kriegel has dominated historical scholarship of the party. A critical examination of her ideas along with those of other writers reveals her to be the most authoritative interpreter of the Party today. 59 notes. J. G. Smoot

2459. K. L. DOŚWIADCZENIA FRONTU LUDOWEGO WE FRANCJI [Experiences of the Popular Front in France]. *Nowe Drogi [Poland] 1976 321(2): 144-148.* Compares the Popular Front strategy of the French Communist Party in the 1930's and the party's current alliance politics in France. The principal difference between the French Popular Front strategy and the party's contemporary coalition politics is that whereas in the 1930's the choice in France was between democracy and fascism, today the effort is directed at attaining a "developed democracy" based on a "broad alliance of the French nation" supporting a "government of democratic unity." The author regards the French Popular Front experience as a source of inspiration and guidance to Communist parties struggling in capitalist countries today. Primary and secondary sources; 7 notes. W. J. Lukaszewski

2460. Kaganova, R. I. FRANTSUZSKAIA KOMMUNISTICHESKAIA PARTIIA NA SOVREMENNOM ETAPE [The French Communist Party at its present stage]. *Novaia i Noveishaia Istoriia [USSR] 1973 (5): 20-39.* Analyzes the aims of the French Communist Party (FCP), 1968-72, with reference to the 1972 joint program of the Communists and Socialists. Discusses the FCP's analysis of modern state-monopolistic capitalism, the problem of youth unemployment, and the strike movement, and considers the FCP's views on the forms of transition to a socialist revolution, particularly the links between the struggles for democracy and for socialism. Describes France's transition to socialism and the solidarity shown by the USSR. 35 notes. C. R. Pike

2461. Kahn, Jacques. INTERNATIONAL MONOPOLY. *World Marxist Rev. [Canada] 1972 15(8): 73-80.* Discusses the roles of the Common Market and the Communist Party during the economic crises of state-monopoly capitalism in France, 1968-72.

2462. Kanet, Roger E. THE SOVIET UNION, THE FRENCH COMMUNIST PARTY AND AFRICA, 1945-1950. *Survey [Great Britain] 1976 22(1): 74-92.* During 1945-50, the USSR had no direct contacts with Africa. While following an essentially Maoist policy of appealing to all patriotic elements in a struggle against the imperialists, it was forced to work through the Communist Party of France, which for reasons of its own, supported the Rassemblement Democratique African, a bourgeois-nationalist organization. When the Soviet Union tried to pursue a strictly Communist policy, the bourgeois-nationalists broke away and Soviet policy ended in failure. Secondary sources; 75 notes. R. B. Valliant

2463. Kelly, M. LOUIS ALTHUSSER AND THE PROBLEMS OF A MARXIST THEORY OF STRUCTURE. *Pro. of the Royal Irish Acad. Section C [Ireland] 1978 78(7): 199-212.* In the early 1960's leading French Communist academician Louis Althusser suggested that Karl Marx lacked an adequate theory of structure and undertook to supply a philosophical theory from structuralism. The author details Althusser's adaptation of Marxism to structuralism and evaluates Althusser's success. In 1966 the French Central Committee took public note of the impact Althusser's ideas were having on Communist students. As a result, Althusser consented to reassess his position. Subsequent editions of his works such as *Reading Marx* have been reedited, and he by and large abandoned his earlier attempt to redefine Marx. 11 notes. J. C. Holsinger

2464. Kesler, Jean-François. LE COMMUNISME DE GAUCHE EN FRANCE (1927-1947) [Left-wing Communism in France, 1927-47]. *Rev. Française de Sci. Pol. [France] 1978 28(4): 740-757.* Because Trotskyism in France is linked with Bolshevism in the USSR, from the outset left-wing French Communism has split into many different factions and has had to play off one faction against the other.

2465. Kriegel, Annie. LA DIMENSION INTERNATIONALE DU PCF [The international dimension of the French Communist Party]. *Pol. Étrangère [France] 1972 37(5): 639-671.* Analyzes the complex relations between the international Communist movement and the Western Communist parties, by examining the development of the French Communist Party, 1914-72.

2466. Kriegel, Annie. LE PARTI COMMUNISTE FRANÇAIS, LA RÉSISTANCE, LA LIBÉRATION ET L'ÉTALISSEMENT DE LA QUATRIÈME RÉPUBLIQUE (1944-1947) [The French Communist Party, the Resistance, the Liberation, and the founding of the Fourth Republic, 1944-47]. *Storia e Politica [Italy] 1975 14(1-2): 255-265.* Distinguishes three periods in the evolution of the Communist Party after the liberation of France: 1) June-November 1944, attempts to win sole power; 2) November 1944-January 1946, cooperation with Socialists and Catholics under de Gaulle's leadership; and 3) 1946-47, popular front strategy of Cooperation with Socialists to 1947, when Communists were dismissed from the government. A. Canavero

2467. Kriegel, Annie. L'HISTORIOGRAPHIE DU COMMUNISME FRANÇAIS: PREMIER BILAN ET ORIENTATION DE RECHERCHES [Historiography of French Communism: first results and orientation of research]. *Mouvement Social [France] 1965 (53): 130-142.* Presents a plan for writing the complex history of the French Communist Party. Archival material from the International and French Communist Parties is limited. No definitive history has yet been written. Research should determine whether the French Communist Party was the party of the worker, what place it held in the workers' movement, and the factors and consequences of the insertion of the party into the international movement. H. D. Nycz

2468. Kwiatek, Leszek. NA ŁAMACH CZASOPISMA "LES CAHIERS DU COMMUNISME" [From the journal *Les Cahiers du Communisme*]. *Nowe Drogi [Poland] 1983 (8): 176-183.* A survey of the 1982 volume of the monthly of the French Communist Party with special emphasis on articles criticizing the capitalist system and life in capitalist society.

2469. Labbé, Dominique. LE DISCOURS COMMUNISTE [Communist language]. *Rev. Française de Sci. Pol. [France] 1980 30(1): 46-77.* A lexicographic analysis of the language of the French Communist Party (PCF), based on the adopted political resolutions of the four latest PCF conferences (1972-1979). Attempts to understand Communist political ideology through the evolution of the content of their discourse during this time. Analyzes each resolution as a thematic unit, rather than solely through the word by word approach.

2470. Lavau, Georges. L'HISTORIOGRAPHIE COMMUNISTE [Communist historiography]. *Esprit [France] 1978 (3): 3-19.* Explains the intellectual working process of the French Communist Party through a critical analysis of the *Manuel d'histoire du Parti communiste français* (1964) and the two volumes of *L'Histoire du réformisme en France* (1976).

2471. Lavrenov, V. V. FRANTSUZSKOI KOMMUNISTICHESKOI PARTII: 50 LET [The French Communist Party is 50 years old]. *Voprosy Istorii KPSS [USSR] 1971 (2): 150-153.* Outlines papers presented at a conference of Soviet historians and leading representatives of the French Communist Party, concerning the history of the latter, held in Moscow in December 1970.

2472. Levine, Andrew. REVIEW ARTICLE: BALIBAR, ON THE DICTATORSHIP OF THE PROLETARIAT. *Pol. and Soc. 1977 7(1): 69-83.* Review essay on E. Balibar's *Sur la dictature du prolétariat.* Balibar's is a classical but rearguard expression of this basic concept in Marxist and Leninist theory of revolution. Balibar's work was issued in response to what he considered the wrongheaded decision of the French Communist Party at its 22d Congress in 1976 to formally abandon as historically superceded the concept of the dictatorship of the proletariat. Secondary sources; 17 notes. D. G. Nielson

2473. Libbey, Kenneth R. THE FRENCH COMMUNIST PARTY IN THE 1960'S: AN IDEOLOGICAL PROFILE. *J. of Contemporary Hist. [Great Britain] 1976 11(1): 145-165.* The French Communist Party (PCF), despite its strongly orthodox ideological background, has been under pressure to relax its ideological posture in order to accommodate itself to a hostile political environment. Generally the PCF has tolerated limited cooperation with other leftist parties and has demonstrated flexibility in pursuit of its goals. Its acceptance of a Marxist rather than a Leninist approach has earned it the contempt of more revolutionary groups but has enhanced the unity of the French Left. Primary and secondary sources; 22 notes. B. A. Block

2474. Lindenau, Gisela. ENTWICKLUNG DER AKTIONSEINHEIT VON FKP UND FSP 1969-1975 [Development of active unity by French Communist Party and French Socialist Party, 1969-75]. *Beiträge zur Geschichte der Arbeiterbewegung [East Germany] 1979 21(6): 855-871.* Analyzes the attempts to unify the Left in France. The presidential campaign of 1974 tested the unity. Based on published documents; 38 notes. G. E. Pergl/S

2475. Loth, Wilfried. FRANKREICHS KOMMUNISTEN UND DER BEGINN DES KALTEN KRIEGES. DIE ENTLASSUNG DER KOMMUNISTISCHEN MINISTER IM MAI 1947 [French Communists and the beginning of the Cold War: the dismissal of Communist ministers in May 1947]. *Vierteljahrshefte für Zeitgeschichte [West Germany] 1978 26(1): 9-65.* Contrary to most popular interpretations, it was neither US pressure nor a Moscow-ordered Communist attack that brought the May 1947 dismissal of Communists from France's post-World War II tripartite coalition government of Socialists, Communists, and Christian Democrats (MRP). Neither Communists nor Socialists initially regarded the break as permanent, but simply as the result of rank-and-file pressures against the Communist leadership's Moscow-inspired policy of stabilizing production and reasserting French world power at any cost and thus against the government's reconstruction policy. Only subsequent international developments made Communist isolation permanent. Based on memoirs, most notably Vincent Auriol's recently published journal, Socialist Party records, and secondary works. 100 notes. D. Prowe

2476. Loth, Wilfried. FRANKREICHS LINKE IN VORMARSCH UND KRISE [The Left in France in advance and crisis]. *Schweizer Monatshefte [Switzerland] 1978 58(1): 7-19.* Analyzes the ideological development of the French Communist Party after the occupation of Czechoslovakia in 1968 and the working out of a common political program with the French Socialist Party in the early 1970's. Based on newspapers and secondary sources; 13 notes. R. Wagnleitner

2477. Loth, Wilfried. SOZIALISTEN UND KOMMUNISTEN IN FRANKREICH. ZWISCHENBILANZ EINER STRATEGIE [Socialists and Communists in France: interim results of a strategy]. *Europa Archiv [West Germany] 1975 30(2): 39-50.* The French Socialist-Communist alliance in the 1970's strengthened the socialist partner and promoted internal Communist contradictions.

2478. Lottman, Herbert R. "ONE ALWAYS COMES BACK TO JEWISH LIFE": ODYSSEY OF AN EX-COMMUNIST. *Present Tense 1975 2(4): 58-62.* Biography of Annie Kriegel explaining how she came to reject communism, with references to her current work on socialism and Zionism.

2479. Maj, Kazimiera. *CAHIERS D'HISTOIRE DE L'INSTITUT MAURICE THOREZ:* PRZEGLĄD ZAWARTOŚCI ZA LATA 1975-1979 [*Cahiers d'Histoire de l'Institut Maurice Thorez:* review of contents, 1975-79]. *Z Pola Walki [Poland] 1980 23(4): 230-236.* A quarterly on the French and international Communist movements, the *Cahiers* encourages contributions from other countries, but French authors and topics predominate: the French Communist Party, origins of the French workers' movement, class struggle, political economy, the agrarian question, colonies, and the French Revolution. Since 1978, the Institut Maurice Thorez has also published a supplement for results of research in progress. Reviews some of its articles. I. Lukes

2480. Mari, Giovanni. LOUIS ALTHUSSER [Louis Althusser]. *Belfagor [Italy] 1980 35(4): 407-442.* Discusses the main themes in the theoretical work of the French Marxist philosopher Louis Althusser in the context of discussions within the French Communist Party during the past 20 years.

2481. Messmer, Pierre. SOCIALISTES ET COMMUNISTES FACE À L'ARME NUCLEAIRE [The Socialist and Communist position on nuclear arms]. *Nouvelle Rev. des Deux Mondes [France] 1978 (1): 3-20.* Although French foreign policy since 1939 has shown that national independence depends on an independent defense policy based on nuclear capacity, the Communists have only recently espoused an independent foreign policy while the Socialists continue to depend on foreign alliances.

2482. Mikhailov, Iu. L. UROKI FEVRALIA (K 30-LETIIU ANTIFASHISTSKIKH VYSTUPLENII FRANTSUZKOGO PROLETARIATA V FEVRALE 1934 G.) [The lessons of February: on the 30th anniversary of the antifascist demonstrations of the French proletariat in February 1934]. *Voprosy Istorii KPSS [USSR] 1964 (2): 104-110.* The antifascist struggles of 1934 to 1936 taught the French Communist Party to support the economic demands of French workers and to defend republican legality and democratic institutions, principles which were subsequently applied particularly in 1958 against the Secret Army (OAS).

2483. Milhau, Jacques. THEORETICAL ACTIVITY OF THE FRENCH COMMUNIST PARTY. *World Marxist Rev. 1975 18(9): 96-105.* Scholarship on Marxism is flourishing in France thanks to the support of the French Communist Party.

2484. Milza, Pierre. LA GUERRE FROIDE À PARIS: "RIDGWAY LA PESTE" [The Cold War in Paris: "Ridgway the plague"]. *Histoire [France] 1980 (25): 38-47.* On 28 May 1952 thousands of militant Communists demonstrated against the nomination of General Matthew B. Ridgway as head of NATO, because he had been accused—wrongly—of waging bacteriological warfare in the Korean War. Large-scale repression of the Communist Party followed the demonstrations. J

2485. Mirov, A. O. BOR'BA KOMMUNISTOV FRANTSII PROTIV KOLONIAL'NOI VOINY V INDOKITAE (K VOPROSU O PARLAMENTSKOI TAKTIKE FKP) [The French Communists' struggle against the colonial war in Indochina and the French Communist Party's parliamentary tactics]. *Narody Azii i Afriki [USSR] 1974 (1): 60-70.* Describes the attempts of the French Communist Party, mainly through its members of the National Assembly, to oppose France's colonial aggression against Vietnam in the late 1940's and early 1950's.

2486. Moch, Jules. LA GAUCHE ET LE PROGRAMME COMMUN [The Left and the common program]. *Nouvelle Rev. des Deux Mondes [France] 1976 (9): 517-525.* Compares the Socialist-Communist electoral alliance forged in 1972 with the French Popular Front of the 1930's and cites postwar Czechoslovakian experience with Communist coalition behavior as a warning to French voters in 1978.

2487. Moch, Jules. LES GAUCHES ET LA FORCE DE FRAPPE [The Left and nuclear power]. *Nouvelle Rev. des Deux Mondes [France] 1977 (9): 586-594.* The Communist Party's support of atomic weapons is a political maneuver which denies the facts that France's geographical position, its production capacity in comparison to other countries, and the high cost of nuclear arms make them strategically useless.

2488. Moss, Bernard H. WORKERS AND COMMUNISTS IN FRANCE. *Science & Society 1984 48(3): 350-359.* Reviews George Ross's *Workers and Communists in France: From Popular Front to Eurocommunism* (1982). Ross assesses the shifting relations between France's General Confederation of Labor (CGT) and the French Communist Party (PCF). His bias in favor of the Eurocommunist orientation of the two organizations in the 1960's and 1970's distorts his rendering of earlier years, while his opposition to Leninist strategies detract from some of his assessments. Nonetheless, the volume is "the most accurate and complete account of the contemporary PCF and CGT available." Secondary sources; 19 notes. R. E. Butchart

2489. Murphy, Francis J. MILESTONES OF CHRISTIAN-MARXIST DIALOGUE IN FRANCE. *J. of Ecumenical Studies 1978 15(1): 139-151.* Dialogue between French Christians and Communist officials has been quite lively and amicable, and the French Communist Party actively seeks Christian members. The author analyzes recent Party policy and Christian reaction to it, 1937-77. J. A. Overbeck

2490. Neufeld, Karl H. GEMEINWOHL UND GESCHICHTE [Common wellbeing and history]. *Stimmen der Zeit [West Germany] 1978 196(10): 715-717.* The French Jesuit philosopher Gaston Fessard (1897-1978) analyzed the ideological heritage of Hegel and Marx in an attempt to begin a dialogue between the Catholic Church and Communist countries.

2491. O'Donnell, Paddy. LUCIEN SEVE, ALTHUSSER AND THE CONTRADICTIONS OF THE PCF. *Critique [Great Britain] 1981 (15): 7-29.* Examines the importance of psychology to Marxist philosophy and the debate on this matter between Lucien Sève and Louis Althusser within the Communist Party of France.

2492. Pelachaud, Guy. "ZERO GROWTH": IDEOLOGY AND POLITICS. *World Marxist R. [Canada] 1975 18(6): 72-80.* The Communist Party in France insists that the solution to economic problems is not Malthusian theory, but control of monopolies.

2493. Pfister, Thierry. DE L'INACTION À L'UNITÉ D'ACTION [From inaction to unity of action]. *Rev. Pol. et Parlementaire [France] 1971 73(825): 5-12.* Studies the development of written platforms and plans of action for the organization of unity among the Socialists and Communists in France, 1969-71. Until then, the rhetorical tendencies of the French Left led to frequent factional disputes and resulted in almost complete inaction. In 1969 the United Socialist Party drafted 17 propositions, and the 1970 congress of the French Democratic Confederation of Workers (CFDT) wrote propositions on technology and democracy and 1972 objectives. The French Communist Party's *For Advanced Democracy, for Socialist France* defines the Communist role in the national evolution. The author outlines the objectives of these groups and offers a unification plan for Left strategy. S. Sevilla

2494. Pitts, Jesse R. THE COMMUNIST PARTY AS THE SORCERER'S APPRENTICE IN THE EVENTS OF MAY 1968. *Pro. of the Ann. Meeting of the Western Soc. for French Hist. 1974 2: 386-401.* Low worker militancy and the resulting possibility of failed strikes, as well as the desire to avoid violence that would invite state repression caused the Communist Party of France and the Communist-controlled General Confederation of Labor (CGT) to exercise caution in the 1960's. However in May 1968, the Communists "saw in the weakening of governmental authority and prestige created by the student disorders, an occasion to develop a noninsurrectional general strike which would force the State and the Employer's Confederation to grant substantial wage increases." When order was restored after the carefully planned month-long strike, the CGT secured a 14% wage increase, but the Communist Party was blamed for the disorder and suffered heavy election defeats. 63 notes. T. Simmerman

2495. Platone, François and Ranger, Jean. LE PARTI COMMUNISTE FRANÇAIS ET L'AUDIO-VISUEL: EN VOULOIR OU PAS [The French Communist Party and the use of audiovisual techniques: desirable or not]. *Rev. Française de Sci. Pol. [France] 1979 29(2): 184-202.* Examines the use of audiovisual materials by the Communist Party to influence the public and as a factor in Party organization. More recently, emphasis has been placed on the Party's literature.

2496. Plissonnier, Gaston. THE FRENCH FARMER: CHANGES AND PERSPECTIVES. *World Marxist R. [Canada] 1974 17(6): 85-92.* Describes the Communist Party's program for the solution of the economic difficulties encountered by small farmers in France since the 1950's.

2497. Rice-Maximin, Edward; Wall, Irwin (commentary). THE UNITED STATES AND THE FRENCH COMMUNISTS 1945-1949 (A STUDY BASED UPON STATE DEPARTMENT DOCUMENTS). *Pro. of the Ann. Meeting of the Western Soc. for French Hist. 1981 9: 387-398, 400-401.* The United States saw the French Communists as a major foe in the years immediately following World War II. Although the State Department usually overestimated this threat, American policy nevertheless was rather sophisticated and successful. By 1949 the Communists had been expelled from the government, and their labor movement was isolated and divided. Rather than support Charles de Gaulle, the United States encouraged the non-Communist Left. Despite its setbacks, the French Communist Party in 1949 still posed a danger to the economic stability of the country. Based on State Department documents in the National Archives and on printed primary sources; 28 notes. Comments, pp. 400-401. T. J. Schaeper

2498. Rice-Maximin, Edward. THE UNITED STATES AND THE FRENCH LEFT, 1945-1949: THE VIEW FROM THE STATE DEPARTMENT. *Journal of Contemporary History [Great Britain] 1984 19(4): 729-747.* The US State Department was very apprehensive about the power of the French Communist Party and tried to thwart its coming to power. To this end, there was collusion between the US embassy in Paris and the Socialist Party as the United States sought to split the labor groups into competing factions. Other than this, the United States was relatively passive, while remaining concerned about the Communists. Based on materials in the US National Archives; 37 notes. M. P. Trauth

2499. Robrieux, Philippe. LE RENVOI DES MINISTRES COMMUNISTES [The dismissal of the Communist ministers]. *Historama [France] 1984 (1): 42-50.* Analyzes the behavior of the French Communist Party during the term of the 4th Republic Socialist Premier Paul Ramadier who, in 1947, dismissed the Communist ministers because of the embarrassing situation created by the latters' attempts to profit by the power of the government to which they belonged without endorsing its policies but following exactly Moscow's political line.

2500. Ross, George. THE CONFÉDÉRATION GENÉRALE DU TRAVAIL IN EUROCOMMUNISM. *Pol. and Soc. 1979 9(1): 33-60.* Like other Communist parties in Western Europe since the 1960's, the French Communist Party has become nationalized, casting off its earlier Soviet orthodoxy. In the process it has tried to form new links with the largest French labor union, the General Confederation of Labor (CGT) and alliances with other unions which in the present Eurocommunist era represent the social classes most hurt by state monopoly capitalism. The attempt to promote a cross-class alliance has resulted in an attenuation of the party's call to socialism and an increase in its nationwide appeal for antimonopoly reforms. 40 notes. D. G. Nielson

2501. Roth, Jack J. THE "REVOLUTION OF THE MIND": THE POLITICS OF SURREALISM RECONSIDERED. *South Atlantic Q. 1977 76(2): 147-158.* Originally a French artistic movement, surrealism moved into French politics only after the Rif War of 1925. Led by André Breton, the surrealists had a love-hate affair with the French Communist Party which lasted until World War II. Sigmund Freud and the young Karl Marx fascinated the surrealists; this fascination prevented their absorption into the French Left. The surrealists remained faithful to the Freudian revolution of the individual mind and the rejection of the primacy of history. In this, they most resemble Herbert Marcuse and the New Left of the 1960's. 20 notes. W. L. Olbrich

2502. Rudnik, D. Ia. BORETS ZA INTERESY TRUDIASHCHIKHSIA (K 60-LETIIU SO DNIA ROZHDENIIA GENERAL'NOGO SEKRETARIA FKP TOVARISHCHA ZHORZHA MARSHE) [Fighter for the interests of the working people: the 60th birthday of comrade Georges Marchais, General Secretary of the Communist Party of France (PCF)]. *Voprosy Istorii KPSS [USSR] 1980 (6): 119-123.* Georges Marchais was born into a working-class family in Normandy in 1920. In 1935 he moved to Paris and for several years worked in an aviation factory. He joined the Communist Party at 27 and held a number of important posts within it. Since the 20th Congress of the Communist Party of France in 1972, he has been the party's General Secretary. Secondary sources; 14 notes. G. Dombrovski

2503. Sartre, Jean Paul; Lévy, Benny, interviewer. THE LAST WORDS OF JEAN-PAUL SARTRE. *Dissent 1980 27(4): 397-422.* Reprints in English translation an extended interview given by Sartre to his secretary and collaborator Benny Lévy in which Sartre reviews a host of problems, from his attitudes toward hope and despair to his earlier collaboration with the Communists in France.

2504. Sedykh, V. N. VAL'DEK ROSHE (K 60-LETIIU SO DNIA ROZHDENIIA) [Waldeck Rochet: on the 60th anniversary of his birth]. *Voprosy Istorii KPSS [USSR] 1965 (4): 82-86.* A brief laudatory biography of the general secretary of the French Communist Party, Waldeck Rochet (b. 1905).

2505. Sharma, T. R. BETWEEN THE DEVIL AND THE DEEP SEA: THE CASE OF COMMUNISTS IN FRANCE. *Political Science Review [India] 1983 22(4): 316-347.* Explores the relationship of the French Communist Party with the Socialist Party over the past 60 years. The ebb and flow of the relationship has hinged on such historic forces as the rise of Nazi Germany, World War II, and the Algerian Revolution. Generally, when the relations of the two parties have been close, the Communist Party has lost much of its ideological underpinning. Similarly, the Socialist Party usually gained from the Communist Party's tradition of anticlerical attitudes, ties with the Soviet Union, and extra-parliamentary means of gaining power. 4 tables, 55 notes. J. F. Riddick

2506. Shilov, V. S. BOR'BA PARTII BO FRANTSII PO VOPROSU O VYHODE IZ VOENNOI ORGANISATSII SEVEROATLANTICHESKOGO BLOKA [The struggle of the Party in France over the departure from the military organization of the North Atlantic Block]. *Novaia i Noveishaia Istoriia [USSR] 1974 (1): 153-163.* Economic changes in France in the 1960's allowed France's exit from NATO which produced conflicts among imperialist governments. Between 1959 and 1960 the French Socialists, Radicals, and Communists united against "individual power" and grew in strength. Two main political trends existed; the middle class political parties, and the Communist and noncommunist opposition. The Communist Party defended the workers' rights against limitations of freedom, and demanded France's withdrawal from NATO. The noncommunist left criticized the government's social, economic, and agrarian policies. The Democratic Center, formed in 1966, defended the rights of the middle classes. The decision to leave NATO strengthened the French Communist Party. 66 notes. L. Smith

2507. Sommer, René. "PAIX ET LIBERTÉ:" LA QUATRIÈME RÉPUBLIQUE CONTRE LE PC ["Peace and Liberty:" the Fourth Republic against the French Communist Party]. *Histoire [France] 1981 (4): 26-35.* The Peace and Liberty movement, founded in 1950 by the socialist Fourth Republic to combat Moscow propaganda spread by French Communists, testified to the anxiety created in France by Communist initiatives in the early 1950's.

2508. Subileau, Françoise. LES COMMUNISTES PARISIENS EN 1977 [The Parisian Communists in 1977]. *Rev. Française de Sci. Pol. [France] 1979 29(4-5): 791-811.* A comparison of statistics compiled in 1974 and 1977 indicates that Party members are increasingly of a high sociocultural level, that the process of recruiting militants has evolved and that the membership apparatus has become stronger.

2509. Thorez, Maurice. V AVANGARDE BOR'BY TRUDIASHCHIKHSIA MASS: K 40-LETIIU FRANTSUZSKOI KOMMUNISTICHESKOI PARTII [In the forefront of the struggle of the working class: commemorating the 40th anniversary of the French Communist Party]. *Voprosy Istorii KPSS [USSR] 1960 (5): 30-48.* Traces the history of socialism in France, 1914-60, and the struggle of the French Communist Party against capitalism, imperialism, and fascism.

2510. Tiersky, Ronald. THE FRENCH COMMUNIST PARTY AND DETENTE. *J. of Internat. Affairs 1974 28(2): 188-205.* Although the French Communist Party would not break with Moscow short of a sell-out, they do use the Sino-Soviet rift and the US-USSR detente as leverage for independence. French Communists, themselves torn by "government" versus "vanguard" roles, support left-wing unity on both national and European levels. The Soviets are justifiably satisfied with the independent foreign policies of the French regime and Communists. R. D. Frederick

2511. Tiersky, Ronald. FRENCH COMMUNISM IN 1976. *Problems of Communism 1976 25(1): 20-47.* Explores the state of French Communism today in light of the reassessment by the French Communist Party (PCF) of its goals and strategy, made necessary by events in Chile in 1973, Portugal in 1974, and Indochina in 1975. Centers on the future of the alliance made in June 1972 between the PCF and the Socialist parties, an alliance that is destined to suffer many stresses and strains. Based on primary and secondary French and English sources; 98 notes. J. M. Lauber

2512. Tiersky, Ronald. LE P. C. F. ET LA DÉTENTE [The French Communist Party and detente]. *Esprit [France] 1975 (2): 218-241.* Studies the complex relations of the Communist Party of France with the policy of detente on three levels: the tension between the roles of the Communist Party as a national party of the oppositional vanguard and as a party of government; the rapport between the French Party and the Communist Party of the Soviet Union in their roles as revolutionary parties of the international movement; and the tensions created by the interpenetrations of national and international images. The Soviets jealously defend their world power interests and at the same time try to remain preeminent in the international movement of their fraternal parties. In the process, they are constrained to refuse to consider seriously the strategic interests of the other parties, such as the French Communist Party. The problem for the French Party is how to improve on this Soviet strategy of profiting from the mystique of proletarianism while working to pursue their own narrower, political aims. 46 notes. G. F. Jewsbury

2513. Timmermann, Heinz. DIE FRANZÖSISCHE KOMMUNISTISCHE PARTEI ZWISCHEN STAGNATION UND WANDEL [The French Communist Party between stagnation and change]. *Politische Studien [West Germany] 1971 22(199): 451-467.* An examination of the French Communist Party in the light of its 19th Congress held in February, 1970. Deals with the Party's internal situation, social composition, leadership changes, and policy evaluation as reflected in congress debates. Despite the PCF's importance in the international communist movement and domestic politics, the debates reflected disappointment with internal stagnation and the united front strategy and represented defensive consolidation in the wake of a series of domestic and international crises. The PCF is limited in political mobility by its unresolved succession problem and a tenuous balance between traditionalists and modernists. 35 notes. F. H. Eidlin

2514. Timmermann, Heinz. FRANKREICHS KOMMUNISTEN: WANDEL DURCH MITARBEIT [The French Communists: change through cooperation]. *Europa Archiv [West Germany] 1973 28(9): 300-310.* After 1958, French Communists moved away from their strict orientation toward Soviet communism and slowly began to promote an autonomous, primarily nationally inclined, foreign policy that enabled the Party to ally with French socialists in the beginning of the 1970's.

2515. Valentin, Marie-Renée. LES GREVES DES CHEMINOTS FRANÇAIS AU COURS DE L'ANNEE 1947 [Strikes in the French railway industry, 1947]. *Mouvement Social [France] 1985 (130): 55-80.* In May 1947 the Communist ministers were ousted from the French government. In the following months two strikes interfered with rail transport. The strike that broke out in June in the Paris region, and later spread throughout the entire network, was caused by the tightening of food rationing. In November, work stoppages broke out simultaneously in Marseille, in the north, and in the Paris region, as a result of the actions of Communist militants. The movement then spread throughout France. J/S

2516. Varfolomeeva, R. S. MORIS TOREZ: KOMMUNIST, SYN NARODA FRANTSII [Maurice Thorez: Communist, son of the people of France]. *Novaia i Noveishaia Istoriia [USSR] 1979 (3): 70-90, (4): 92-110.* Part I. Maurice Thorez was born in 1900 in a Northern French mining town. His father was a foundry worker, his uncle worked in the mines, and he himself began work in the mines at age 14. The Russian Revolution of 1917 inspired him and he began spreading Communist doctrine among the workers in his region. In December 1920 the French Communist Party was formed. Thorez became a member of its central committee in 1924 and in 1934, a Party member of parliament. He worked to establish a Popular Front government, to oppose nonintervention in Spain and to organize working people against fascism. Rather than serve in the army during the war he spent five years from 1939-44 living in Moscow and working for Comintern. Part II. Thorez was a pragmatist in French politics. He spoke out consistently on various topics. In the early 1950's he said categorically that French Communists would not fight against the USSR and that war was not inevitable. He led the opposition to French involvement in Algeria, Tunisia, Syria, and Vietnam. Communist fortunes fluctuated at the polls: 186 (of 622) seats won in 1946 to defeat in 1957, and recovery in 1962, when Communists and other parties of the Left gained 150 seats. Thorez attributed peace in Europe to Franco-Soviet friendship, which he always promoted, especially in cultural exchanges. He died 11 June 1964. 105 notes. L. J. Seymour

2517. Vaucelles, Louis de. LE XXIIe CONGRÈS DU PARTI COMMUNISTE FRANČAIS [The 22d Congress of the French Communist Party]. *Études [France] 1976 344: 535-551.* Analyzes the workings of the Communist Party in France today, including the role of the workers, the social plan, relations with other political parties, and the adherence to Leninism in the party, on the occasion of the Party congress in Paris, 4-8 February 1975.

2518. Villard, Claude. SŬZDAVANE NA FRENSKATA KOMUNISTICHESKA PARTIIA [The founding of the French Communist Party]. *Izvestiia na Inst. po Istoriia na BKP [Bulgaria] 1971 25: 179-193.* Founded in France in 1920 and inspired by the Great October Socialist Revolution, the Party has constantly struggled for socialism, combatting antisocialist machinations and false theories.

2519. Wall, Irwin M. *French Communism in the Era of Stalin: The Quest for Unity and Integration, 1945-1962.* (Contributions in Political Science, 97.) Westport, Conn.: Greenwood, 1983. 268 pp.

2520. Wall, Irwin M. THE FRENCH COMMUNISTS AS A GOVERNMENT PARTY, 1944-1947. *Pro. of the Ann. Meeting of the Western Soc. for French Hist. 1973 (1): 427-442.* The Communist Party of France has rarely, if ever, advocated the destruction of the French administrative bureaucracy. The Communists in their ministerial efforts consistently sought "pragmatic, efficient, demonstrable achievement in the short term." During 1944-47 the party had "the chance to participate, expand its political influence, and, through legal means, carve out a semi-permanent niche for itself in the newly-fashioned social order." Primary and secondary sources; 44 notes. L. S. Frey

2521. Wall, Irwin M. FRENCH COMMUNISM AND ITS HISTORIANS. *J. of European Studies [Great Britain] 1973 3(3): 255-267.* Surveys major historical controversies about the history of the Communist Party of France up to its 50th anniversary in 1970.

2522. Wall, Irwin M. THE FRENCH COMMUNISTS AND THE ALGERIAN WAR. *J. of Contemporary Hist. [Great Britain] 1977 12(3): 521-543.* Jean Paul Sartre criticized the French Communist Party's handling of the Algerian war as early as January 1957. Traditionally, Communists are supposed to support unconditionally all movements of national liberation against imperialist powers. The French Communist Party (PCF) favored the autonomy of Algeria in union with France, or even peace at any price. In 1959, when de Gaulle announced his willingness to accept self-determination, the PCF experienced an inner crisis of dissension. The PCF, despite some martyrs in the civil war, deserved little credit for its general role. 67 notes. M. P. Trauth

2523. Winock, Michel. THOREZ OU LE COMMUNISME D'APPAREIL [Thorez or the communism of the *apparat*]. *Esprit [France] 1975 (10): 517-529.* Reviews Philippe Robrieux's *Maurice Thorez: Vie secrète et vie publique* (Fayard), noting its importance as a source on French communism, 1920's-60's.

2524. Wolf, Marc. CHOIX DE SOCIÉTÉ OU ÉLECTION DE QUARTIER? LES ÉLECTIONS LÉGISLATIVES DE 1973 À LILLE [Choice of society or district election? The 1973 parliamentary elections in Lille]. *Rev. Française de Sci. Politique [France] 1975 25(2): 259-290.* A detailed analysis of the results of 96 polling stations during the 1973 parliamentary elections in Lille, and an examination of the electoral rolls (socio-occupational category, age, abstention) indicate that the Communist Party is on the whole less well established in the working classes and lower social strata in Lille than is the Socialist Party. However, the influence of the latter varies considerably from one district to another. Most of the progress made by the Socialist Party in 1973 was due to votes won from the lower class supporters of the majority, without there being any shift from the center. Finally, an analysis of the 1974 Presidential elections confirms that the Left in Lille is more solidly established among the lower classes than at national level, but is underrepresented among the wealthier classes. J

2525. Zaborov, M. A. OPYT PARIZHSKOI KOMMUNY I BORBA KOMMUNISTICHESKIKH PARTII BURZHUAZNYKH STRAN ZA DEMOKRATIIU I SOTSIALIZM V SOVREMENNYKH USLOVIIAKH [The experience of the Paris Commune and the struggle of the Communist parties in the capitalist countries for democracy and socialism in present-day conditions]. *Voprosy Istorii [USSR] 1971 (3): 95-107.* The author highlights the significance of the historical experience of the world's first proletarian revolution for the activity of the Communist and Workers' parties in present-day conditions. Drawing primarily on the works of French Marxists, he shows how in their fight for democracy and socialism the Communists turn to the history of the Paris Commune in order to explain to the masses the essence of the proletarian state as a state of the new type and to expose the anti-popular character of bourgeois democracy. A close analysis of the experience of the Paris Commune shows the utter insolvency of the attempts made by the authors of diverse social-reformist and revisionist conceptions to distort the essence of the Paris Commune with a view to discrediting the teaching on the socialist revolution and the dictatorship of the proletariat. The author arrives at the conclusion that the experience of the Commune of 1871 has lost none of its significance and urgency for the Communist parties now upholding the fundamental interests of the working masses. J

2526. —. *CRS À MARSEILLE* ET LE *JOURNAL* DE VINCENT AURIOL [*CRS À Marseille* and the *Journal* of Vincent Auriol]. *Mouvement Social [France] 1975 (92): 49-91.*

Gallissot, René. L'ILLUSION RÉPUBLICAINE: SOCIALISTES ET COMMUNISTES EN 1947. RÉFLEXION SUR *CRS À MARSEILLE* ET LE *JOURNAL* DE VINCENT AURIOL [The republican illusion: Socialists and Communists in 1947. Reflection on *CRS à Marseille* et le *Journal* de Vincent Auriol], *pp. 49-74.*

Agulhon, Maurice and Barrat, Fernand. AU DOSSIER DES *CRS À MARSEILLE* [*CRS à Marseille* revisited], *pp. 75-91.*

A reconfirmation of the main thesis of *CRS à Marseille 1944-1947* (1970). There were many Communist militants in the police forces because of the special conditions of the Liberation period. Their weakness in the 12 November riot in Marseilles resulted from a variety of factors although they did not take part in revolutionary plan. Based on new evidence and testimonies collected after the book's publication. J/S

2527. —. LETTRE ULTRA SECRETE AUX CADRES DU PC [A top secret letter to the Communist Party officials]. *Historama [France] 1984 (1): 52-53.* The previously unpublished text, with editorial comments, of a top secret letter of 9 June 1968 from French Communist Party leader Gaston Plissonnier to Party officials repudiating official disapproval of the Soviets' military intervention in Czechoslovakia, expressed two weeks earlier by French Communist Party General Secretary, Waldeck Rochet.

Italy

2528. Agnoletti, Enzo Enriques. TROPPO DEBOLE E TROPPO FORTE [Too weak and too strong]. *Ponte [Italy] 1976 32(9): 971-974.* Discusses the background to the Italian Communist Party's unofficial participation in the Andreotti government following the national elections in 1976.

2529. Alfieri, Vittorio Enzo. RICORDO DI BENEDETTO CROCE A VENT'ANNI DALLA SCOMPARSA [Benedetto Croce 20 years after his death]. *Risorgimento [Italy] 1973 25(2): 115-128.* Marks the 20th anniversary of the death of Italian philosopher and critic Benedetto Croce (1866-1952), with a special emphasis on the political changes in Italy before, during, and after Fascism as they affected Croce's life and work. Cites Croce's angry reply of 21 June 1944 to charges of Italian Communist Party leader Palmiro Togliatti that he "collaborated openly" with Fascism against Marxism and communism. Traces broad lines of his philosophical development with respect to other European philosophers. C. Bates

2530. Allum, Percy and Mannheimer, Renato. IL VOTO DEL PARTITO COMUNISTA NEL DOPOGUERRA: IL CASO DI NAPOLI [The Communist Party vote since the war: the case of Naples]. *Ann. dell'Istituto Giangiacomo Feltrinelli [Italy] 1981 21: 313-360.* Electoral data on postwar Naples show a real reversal of prevailing political forces. At liberation Naples was decidedly oriented to the right-wing and moderate forces; from 1975 the left-wing parties have tallied an absolute majority in four successive elections. A study of the Communist vote reveals the image of a party with a solid and stable social and territorial base among the working classes, with a progressive extension toward new strata of middle and upper-middle classes. 9 tables, 33 notes, 3 charts.

J. V. Coutinho

2531. Amendola, Giorgio. RIFLESSIONI SU UNA ESPERIENZA DI GOVERNO DEL PCI (1944-1947) [Reflections on an experience of the PCI in the government, 1944-47]. *Storia Contemporanea [Italy] 1974 5(4): 701-736.* A leading group in the resistance, the Italian Communist Party (PCI) was included in the Italian government beginning in 1944. This was the period when the feeling of unity among all anti-Fascists was still strong, for the war was still on and the north of Italy was occupied by the Nazis. The author traces the intricate political maneuvering of the postwar years which resulted in the Communists' leaving the government in 1947 amid a growing confrontation over economic policy at home and against the background of the beginning of the Cold War abroad. J. C. Billigmeier

2532. Anderlini, Fausto. LA CELLULA [The cell]. *Ann. dell'Istituto Giangiacomo Feltrinelli [Italy] 1981 21: 185-226.* Describes the role of the cell in the postwar organizational history of the Italian Communist Party in the context of the transition from a bolshevist organizational model to Palmiro Togliatti's "new party," a party of the masses, of struggle, and of government. Changes in the social and political life of the country have made of the cell a transitional form in which contradictory currents of socialization from below and regimentation from above, Western socialist tradition and Soviet bolshevist tradition, gradualistic and revolutionary tendencies, and emphasis on masses and on cadres coexist in the same historical milieu. 9 tables, 67 notes, 7 charts.

J. V. Coutinho

2533. Andreucci, Franco and Sylvers, Malcolm. THE ITALIAN COMMUNISTS WRITE THEIR HISTORY. *Sci. and Soc. 1976 40(1): 28-56.* Since the 1960's the Italian Communist Party has allowed and even encouraged a relatively objective historiography of its past. The previously hagiographic accounts of its early history, ignoring or obscuring party and personality errors in fact and judgment, have gradually been superseded by historical analyses which are less colored by distortion. The pioneering works are the *Storia del Partito comunista italiano* by Paolo Spriano and the *Opere* of Palmiro Togliatti, edited by Ernesto Ragioneri. N. Lederer

2534. Andreucci, Franco. SULL'OPERA DI ERNESTO RAGIONIERI: STORIA DEL MOVIMENTO OPERAIO E STORIOGRAFIA DEL PARTITO [On the work of Ernesto Ragionieri: history of the workers' movement and historiography of the party]. *Italia Contemporanea [Italy] 1981 33(142): 113-125.* Ernesto Ragionieri (d. 1975) in his publications about the Italian Communist Party, was dedicated to writing serious history rather than a glorification of the party. One central question that exercised Ragionieri in the 1950's and 1960's was why so many Italians were joining the party. Ragionieri's work on the party, on the workers' movement, and on Palmiro Togliatti, represent important contributions to the study of Italian history. Primary sources; 38 notes. E. E. Ryan

2535. Angotti, Thomas R. and Dale, Bruce S. BOLOGNA, ITALY: URBAN SOCIALISM IN WESTERN EUROPE. *Social Policy 1976 7(1): 4-11.* Urban renewal in Bologna, 1971-75, involves citizen political participation in the decisionmaking, allows residents to retain their homes, increases the services available to residents, preserves the architecture and historical character of the environment, and receives financial aid from the Communist local government.

2536. Barbagallo, Roberta and Cazzola, Franco. LE ORGANIZZAZIONI DI MASSA [The mass organizations]. *Ann. dell'Istituto Giangiacomo Feltrinelli [Italy] 1981 21: 801-823.* Describes the role played in the last 35 years by certain parapolitical organizations which have variously linked themselves with the battles and programs of the Left, and especially with the Communist Party. Among them have been the Italian Women's Union, the Cultural and Recreational Association, the former National Farmers' Association, the National Association of Partisans, and the Partisans for Peace. Examines how far these organizations were able to create a political consciousness and to what extent they were able to mediate demands from specific groups to political institutions. 35 notes. J. V. Coutinho

2537. Barkan, Joanne. THE ITALIAN COMMUNISTS: ANATOMY OF A PARTY. *Radical Am. 1978 12(5): 26-48.* Discusses the Italian Communist Party (PCI) since the end of World War II. The Communist Party was transformed from a class-oriented, mass party to a socially-heterogeneous electoral force. The Party's organizational strength declined through the 1960's, but it subsequently gained strength again. Also examines the traditionally weak links between the PCI and the most politically advanced and militant sectors of Italian society.

2538. Barkan, Joanne. ITALY: WORKING CLASS DEFEAT OR PROGRAM FOR TRANSITION? *Monthly Rev. 1977 29(6): 26-38.* Criticizes Max Gordon and Carl Marzani (see *Monthly Revue,* June 1977) for their support of the Italian Communist Party, showing how the Party's policy of "historic compromise" has alienated much of the working class.

2539. Bechelloni, Giovanni and Buonanno, Milly. IL QUOTIDIANO DEL PARTITO: *L'UNITA* [The Party daily *l'Unità*]. *Ann. dell'Istituto Giangiacomo Feltrinelli [Italy] 1981 21: 861-877.* Explores the complex and many-sided functions performed by the Communist daily in Italian political and cultural life, from the point of view of style and quality. A first part examines questions of method and research hypotheses, while a second part analyzes the results of a mini-survey among readers in a Southern area. 6 tables, 8 notes. J. V. Coutinho

2540. Bennett, Roy. CRISIS IN ITALY: THE STRATEGY OF COALITIONS. *Social Policy 1975 6(3): 53-58.* Discusses the prospects for social change in Italy during the 1970's, including the roles played by the Communists, Socialists, and Christian Democratic Party.

2541. Berner, Wolfgang. DIE SYSTEMKRISE IN ITALIEN [The crisis of the political system in Italy]. *Aussenpolitik [West Germany] 1970 21(11): 697-705.* The postwar strength of the Communist Party helps account for the Italian political crises, 1945-70.

2542. Berta, Giuseppe. LE CONFERENZE OPERAIE [Workers' conferences]. *Ann. dell'Istituto Giangiacomo Feltrinelli [Italy] 1981 21: 721-743.* The workers' conferences of the Communist Party were the result of the crisis in the relations between the Party and the workers, which reached a peak in the mid-1950's. Since then they have served to consolidate the Party's link with the working class, to bring out and institutionalize its specific class character. Shows how this theme has been given various expressions in successive conferences. 63 notes. J. V. Coutinho

2543. Bertolo, Gianfranco; Curti, Roberto; and Guerrini, Libertario. ASPETTI DELLA QUESTIONE AGRARIA E DELLE LOTTE CONTADINE NEL SECONDO DOPOGUERRA IN ITALIA: 1944-1948 [Aspects of the agrarian question and of peasant struggles in the postwar period in Italy: 1944-48]. *Italia Contemporanea [Italy] 1974 26(117): 3-47.* The debate on the agrarian question in Italy during the immediate postwar period centered around the great themes of agricultural reform and the *patti agrari* (presents extracted by landowners in addition to the agreed rent). The Communists played the leading role in the struggle for agrarian reform. In the course of the peasant struggle, the issue of land property itself grew in importance. After 1948 there developed a new coalition of forces united in the anticapitalist struggle. 130 notes, chronology. J. C. Billigmeier

2544. Bibes, Geneviève. LE PARTI COMMUNISTE ITALIEN [The Italian Communist Party]. *Études [France] 1976 344: 517-534.* Analyzes the political and economic stands of the Italian Communist Party, whose influence in the postwar era is growing in the local and the federal governments, studying its international and domestic policy.

2545. Bibes, Geneviève. LE PARTI COMMUNISTE ITALIEN DANS L'ANTICHAMBRE DU POUVOIR [The Italian Communist Party in the antechamber of power]. *Défense Natl. [France] 1979 35(May): 65-79.* Considers the background to the crucial role played by the Italian Communist Party in the vicissitudes of politics in Italy, 1978-79. Based on Italian newspaper reports; 10 notes.

2546. Bogorad, V. A. ANTONIO GRAMSHI (K 80-LETIYU SO DNIA ROZHDENIYA) [Antonio Gramsci: on the 80th anniversary of his birth]. *Voprosy Istorii KPSS [USSR] 1971 (1): 108-110.* Outlines the career of the former leader of Italy's Communist Party.

2547. Bordone, Sandro. IL CONTRASTO SINO-SOVIETICO E LA POLEMICA TRA PCI E PCC [The Sino-Soviet conflict and the polemic between the Italian Communist Party and the Chinese Communist Party]. *Politico [Italy] 1979 44(2): 282-315.* The Italian Communist Party, which under the leadership of Palmiro Togliatti was committed to finding a "national path" to socialism, sought to mediate between China and the USSR after the split following the revelations of the 20th Soviet Party Congress (1956). Resisting Soviet pressures for the convocation of a world conference of Communist parties to officially condemn the Chinese, the PCI maintained a critical position toward China that was consistent with its developing general political line. The Chinese simply regarded the Italian Party as revisionist. J/S

2548. Bordone, Sandro. IL PCI E LA CRISI CINESE (1969-1977) [The Italian Communist Party (PCI) and the Chinese crisis, 1969-77]. *Politico [Italy] 1982 47(3): 561-600.* The Sino-Soviet rift put the Italian Communist Party in the precarious position of attempting to maintain good relations with both countries and to promote a balanced view of the differences between the USSR and

China without abdicating its responsibility to apply rigorous Marxist-Leninist principles in assessing official actions within and between the two red giants. J/S

2549. Borsellino, Nino. CARLO SALINARI [Carlo Salinari]. *Belfagor [Italy] 1982 37(3): 285-298.* Discusses the thought of Carlo Salinari (1919-77), literary critic, member of the Communist Party, and resistance activist.

2550. Botti, Alfonso. POLITICA TOGLIATTIANA E "CORRENTE POLITECNICO": RELIGIONE, DC, QUESTIONE CATTOLICA [Togliatti's policies and *Corrente Politecnico:* religion, Christian Democracy, and the Catholic question]. *Ponte [Italy] 1980 36(7-8): 709-722.* Discusses two ways for the Left to deal with religion, the Christian Democratic Party, and the Catholic question: Palmiro Togliatti's method as head of the Italian Communist Party (pragmatic, oriented toward facilitating the Catholics' move into the Party), and E. Vittorini's approach in *Politecnico* (a theoretical, intellectual approach leading to a new integration between Christianity and Communism, distinguishing between the Church and religion) which leads to proposing a Third Christianity.

2551. Broadhead, H. S. TOGLIATTI AND THE CHURCH, 1921-1948. *Australian J. of Pol. and Hist. [Australia] 1972 18(1): 76-91.* Surveys the background to the policy of Palmiro Togliatti, the Moscow-trained leader of the Italian Communist Party, in the immediate post-World War II years. Building on the tradition of Antonio Gramsci, who, in the 1920's, had attacked Fascism but not Catholicism, Togliatti supported the Christian Democrat motion at the Italian Constituent Assembly in 1947 favoring the 1929 Lateran Treaty which had regulated Italian Church-State relations. Togliatti's motives were tactical. He aimed at winning the 1948 elections and wanted to avoid being a target for Catholic denunciation. The tactics failed; the Pope mobilized anti-Communist forces and broader issues of the Cold War had their influence. Based on newspapers and monographs. W. D. McIntyre

2552. Bujor, Nicu. PALMIRO TOGLIATTI—EMINENT MILITANT AL MIŞCĂRII COMUNISTE ŞI MUNCITOREŞTI ITALIENE ŞI INTERNAŢIONALE [Palmiro Togliatti: eminent militant of the Italian and international communist and workers' movement]. *Anale de Istorie [Rumania] 1973 19(2): 168-173.* Brief biographical sketch of Palmiro Togliatti (1893-1964), cofounder of the Italian Communist Party, opponent of Mussolini's fascist regime, secretary in 1935 of the Communist International, deputy in the Italian Parliament, and vice president of the Council of Ministers in the late war years. His funeral in Rome brought a turnout of a million people, and he was eulogized by the working-class leadership all over the world. Togliatti's importance lies in his emphatic belief that each socialist and communist party must act in an autonomous fashion, grounding its policies on the concrete situation and level of development in each country. G. J. Bobango

2553. Camerlenghi, Enio and Principe, Ilario. LOTTE CONTADINE, TERRA E COMMUNISTI IN CALABRIA [Peasant struggles, land, and Communists in Calabria]. *Ponte [Italy] 1977 33(10): 1133-1145.* Two separate articles look at a recent book by Paolo Cinanni *Lotte per la terra e comunisti in Calabria* (Milan: Feltrinelli, 1977) and discuss land reform and the development and behavior of the Communist Party in Calabria between 1943 and 1953.

2554. Catalano, Franco. LE *LEZIONI SUL FASCISMO* DI TOGLIATTI [Togliatti's *Lessons on Fascism]. Movimento di Liberazione in Italia [Italy] 1973 25(111): 89-105.* The lectures delivered by Palmiro Togliatti (1893-1964) before small groups of the outlawed Italian Communist Party, were published as *Lezioni sul fascismo* (Rome: Editori Riuniti, 1970). The Communists' failure, first in Italy and then in Germany forced their leaders to reexamine earlier assessments and miscalculations, defining Fascism and its unforeseen success. Much of Togliatti's argumentation hinges upon the political character and revolutionary leanings of the lower middle class. Theorists of the Italian Communist Party had overlooked that the masses, especially the rural population, held nationalist and conservative views. Togliatti admitted some of the errors committed by the Party in the 1920's, but maintained that the lower middle class had a revolutionary spirit of its own. H. W. L. Freudenthal

2555. Cazzola, Franco. CONSENSO E OPPOSIZIONE NEL PARLAMENTO ITALIANO. IL RUOLO DEL PCI DALLA I ALLA IV LEGISLATURA [Consensus and opposition in the Italian Parliament: the role of the Communist Party from the first to the fourth legislature]. *Riv. Italiana di Scienza Pol. [Italy] 1972 2(1): 71-96.* Analyzes the development, 1947-72, of the competition in Parliament between the majority parties and the Communist opposition. Considers a sample of laws in their procedure through the Chamber of Deputies. From the analysis of the data, it is clear that Communist opposition cannot be identified—at least judging by the statements of principle with the abstract goals of a neo-capitalist society. The Italian Communist Party (PCI) disagrees with the "abstract aims" of the system, accepting however not only its instruments of decision, but also the policy implemented by it. In fact, the PCI often admits adhering explicitly, though with some regret, to this policy. J

2556. Cerroni, Umberto. ITALIAN COMMUNISM'S HISTORIC COMPROMISE. *Marxist Perspectives 1978 1(1): 126-145.* Maintains that the sectarianism which has characterized Italian politics since World War II must be abandoned in favor of a unitary, national, and responsible policy.

2557. Chubb, Judith. NAPLES UNDER THE LEFT: THE LIMITS OF LOCAL CHANGE. *Comparative Pol. 1980 13(1): 53-78.* Discusses the historical background and climate that enabled the Communist Party (PCI) to come to power in Naples in 1975, and the difficulties it subsequently faced in maintaining its power base given the economic structure of the city, the weakness of the local economy, the limits of local power, and the crisis of local finance. The 1980 election results showed a general return to clientelism throughout southern Italy. This was not the case with Naples, indicating that the Communist Party has weathered the storm and has made some progress in administering the city. Based on an interview with the Assessor of Economic Planning (PCI), an unpublished paper, doctoral dissertation; 4 tables, 36 notes. M. A. Kascus

2558. Civardi, Marisa Bottiroli. UN'ANALISI ECOLOGICA DEL VOTO POLITICO: IL CASO DELLA LOMBARDIA [An ecological analysis of political voting: the case of Lombardy]. *Politico [Italy] 1983 48(1): 55-90.* Discusses probable links between transformations in the socioeconomic structures of Lombardy from 1946 to the 1970's and electoral behavior. Analyzes elections of 1953, 1963, 1972 and 1976, chosen mainly for their proximity to the census years, in terms of 61 indicators, divided into four groups, demographic, economic, sociocultural, and socioeconomic. Step-wise multiple regression analyses were run for the Communist Party, the Christian Democratic Party, and the Socialist Party. A quite clear specularity has emerged between PCI and DC and a substantial inadequacy of the methodology applied to explain the vote to PSI. J/S

2559. Collotti, Enzo, ed. ARCHIVIO PIETRO SECCHIA (1945-1973) [The Pietro Secchia archives, 1945-73]. *Ann. dell'Istituto Giangiacomo Feltrinelli [Italy] 1978 19: 7-751.* Publishes with a lengthy introduction the papers of Pietro Secchia, veteran Stalinist member of the Italian Communist Party, consisting of an autobiographical survey by Secchia, diaries, and correspondence together with accounts of his travels. Secchia was a keen observer, but never an objective one. He was loyal to the USSR, and was deeply disturbed by the Sino-Soviet conflict. He was a close associate of Palmiro Togliatti. 647 notes. J. C. Billigmeier

2560. Cotta, Maurizio. CLASSE POLITICA E ISTITUZIONALIZZAZIONE DEL PARLAMENTO: 1946-1972. [The political elite and the institutionalization of the Italian parliament: 1946-72]. *Riv. Italiana di Scienza Pol. [Italy] 1976 6(1): 71-110.* With the help of a number of indicators such as the mean tenure and age of retirement of members, the stability of parliamentary leaders, the steps of their political career and the rate of turnover, the author examines the unity and stability of the Italian parliament. The institution has failed to parliamentarize the Communist Party, the legislature is fragmented, and the governing parties lack stable leadership. Thus the Italian parliament is not well equipped to face the Communist Party challenge. Based on data provided by a study of members of the Italian parliament, 1946-72. J/S

2561. Craver, Earlene. THE REDISCOVERY OF AMADEO BORDIGA. *Survey [Great Britain] 1974 20(2/3): 160-175.* A short account of the role of Amadeo Bordiga (1889-1970) in the formation of the Italian Communist Party. Bordiga was one of the leading organizers of the Party but was expelled in 1930 for refusing to heed Comintern directives. Thereafter he became an "unperson" in Communist literature. In the 1960's the New Left rediscovered him while searching for a "new heroic model with which to confront the official Communist Party's hero," Antonio Gramsci. They have praised him for his attempt to find a "revolutionary theory-praxis adapted to conditions in the West" and his opposition to any kind of united front. Based on the author's unpublished doctoral dissertation; 59 notes. R. B. Valliant

2562. Dankert, Jochen and Kretzschmar, Heinz. ITALIEN UND DIE SOZIALISTISCHEN LÄNDER EUROPAS [Italy and the socialist countries of Europe]. *Dokumentation der Zeit [East Germany] 1972 24(6): 22-28.* Chronic economic problems threaten the political domination of monopoly capitalism in Italy. Consequently, while Italy follows NATO's lead politically, it seeks closer economic relations with the Warsaw Pact countries, exporting mainly finished products and importing fuel and raw materials. Rome has normal diplomatic relations with all East European states except East Germany, which regards Italy as an agent of Willy Brandt's *Ostpolitik.* There is growing pressure to recognize the GDR and to participate in a European security conference. Based on newspaper reports and government documents; 7 tables. R. J. Bazillion

2563. De Rosa, Giuseppe. DIE KOMMUNISTISCHE PARTEI ITALIENS [The Communist Party of Italy]. *Stimmen der Zeit [West Germany] 1976 194(6): 363-376.* Traces the roots of the Italian Communist Party's present independent stance to its earlier leadership under Gramsci and Togliatti and its experience as an illegal party under Fascism. Its democratic features, its rejection of the Leninist elite party, and its greater readinesss to form alliances with other parties, now on a basis of equality, and to appeal to other classes than the proletariat prompt the question whether the Italian Communist Party is indeed different from others and is sincere in its statements about a unique Italian way to socialism. The author expresses some scepticism, noting that Communists once in power have never permitted democracy. R. Stromberg

2564. DeGiorgi, Fulvio. "CULTURA E REALTA" TRA COMUNISMO E TERZA FORZA [*Cultura e Realtà* between communism and the third force]. *Italia Contemporanea [Italy] 1981 33(145): 59-75.* Promoted by Felice Balboa, Mario Motta, Giorgio Ceriani Sebregondi, and Franco Rodano, the Italian periodical *Cultura e Realtà* [Culture and reality] made its first appearance May-June 1950. The group of Catholic Communists supporting it aimed to oppose Zhdanovian Communist orthodoxy. A study of the articles published in the review indicates that its originality lay in its critique of historicism. Publication ceased after four issues. The major motive for the cessation arose from the growing isolation in which Catholics in the Italian Communist Party found themselves. Primary sources, including oral testimony received from the principals by the author; 71 notes. E. E. Ryan

2565. DeMarco, Paolo. LE CONFERENZE MERIDIONALI [The Southern conferences]. *Ann. dell'Istituto Giangiacomo Feltrinelli [Italy] 1981 21: 745-765.* Postwar Communist leadership in the Mezzogiorno has consistently defended the peculiarity and specificity of conditions in their region. This led them to seek alliances with all progressive, including bourgeois, forces against the reactionary backlash instead of looking for a revolutionary alliance between peasants and workers. Subsequent events have confirmed the southern leadership's view and have led to an increased interest in and changed attitude toward southern problems in the Communist party. 4 tables, 23 notes. J. V. Coutinho

2566. DiPalma, Giuseppe. THE AVAILABLE STATE: PROBLEMS OF REFORM. *West European Pol. [Great Britain] 1979 2(3): 149-165.* Characterizes Italian postwar politics, particularly the relationship between the Christian Democrats and the Communist Party.

2567. D'Onofrio, Edoardo. V AVANGARDE BOR'BY ITAL'IANSKOGO NARODA ZA MIR, DEMOKRATIIU I SOTSIALIZM [In the vanguard of the struggle of the Italian people for peace, democracy, and socialism]. *Voprosy Istorii KPSS [USSR] 1961 (3): 77-93.* Traces the history of the Italian Communist Party from its foundation in 1921, through the antifascist struggles of the 1930's and 1940's to the 1950's, with particular reference to the relationship between the Communist Party and the Italian Socialist Party.

2568. Dorros, Sybilla Green. ANTONIO GRAMSCI: THEORETICIAN OF THE ITALIAN LEFT. *Philippine Social Sci. and Humanities Rev. [Philippines] 1978 42(1-4): 109-163.* Discusses recent Marxist efforts to popularize the political theory of Antonio Gramsci, a co-founder of Italy's Communist Party. Secondary sources; 80 notes, biblio. M. Mtewa/S

2569. Draganov, Dragomir. KOMUNISTICHESKATA PARTIA I USTANOVIAVANE NA REPUBLIKA V ITALIA [The Communist Party and the establishment of a republic in Italy]. *Izvestiia na Inst. po Istoriia na BKP [Bulgaria] 1979 40: 115-155.* Survey of the fight of the Italian Communist Party from April 1945 to June 1946 for the establishment of a republic in Italy.

2570. Earle, John. THE ITALIAN ECONOMY: A DIAGNOSIS. *World Today [Great Britain] 1976 32(6): 214-221.* Discusses economic crises, foreign debts and devaluation of the lira in Italy in 1975, emphasizing the differing economic policies of the Christian Democratic Party and the Communist Party.

2571. Eisenhammer, J. S. THE ITALIAN GENERAL ELECTION OF 1983. *Electoral Studies [Great Britain] 1983 2(3): 280-285.* The principal consequence of this election has been the decline in the hold of the two major political parties from an all-time high in 1976 when the Christian Democratic Party and the Communist Party together accounted for 73% of the popular vote, they now represent a little over 62%; the most notable effect has been increased volatility at the center of the political spectrum.

2572. Fabbri, Fabio. LA COOPERAZIONE: 1945-1956. [Cooperatives, 1945-56]. *Ann. dell'Istituto Giangiacomo Feltrinelli [Italy] 1981 21: 825-859.* Traces the development of the cooperative idea and of the interest in cooperatives in the Italian Communist Party in the early postwar years. Interest in cooperatives was never very strong among Communists, who considered them reformist mechanisms within capitalism and at best "schools for socialism," although the contrary opinion found expression and support and organization of cooperatives would have fit well with postwar Party efforts to transform itself from a party of cadres into a mass party. 184 notes. J. V. Coutinho

2573. Fanti, Guido. L'ESPERIENZA EMILIANA [The experience of Emilia-Romagna]. *Problemi di Ulisse [Italy] 1974 13(78): 70-78.* Examines how Emilia-Romagna, with its Communist administration, used the new institutional prerogatives brought about by the regional reform of 1970.

2574. Faragó, Jenő. TARTÓS KRÍZIS ÉS POLITIKAI KÖVETKEZMÉNYEI OLASZORSZÁGBAN [The long-lasting crisis and its political consequences in Italy]. *Társadalmi Szemle [Hungary] 1979 34(7-8): 130-138.* Views the movements of Italian polity from the 1976 elections onward with special regard to the growing influence of the Communist Party.

2575. Favre, Pierre. LE MODÈLE LÉNINISTE D'ARTICULATION PARTI-SYNDICATS-MASSES: LE PARTI COMMUNISTE ITALIEN ET L'UNITÉ SYNDICALE [The Leninist model of relations among the party, the unions, and the masses: the Italian Communist Party and trade union unity]. *Rev. Française de Sci. Pol. [France] 1975 25(3): 433-472.* The "Leninist model" of sociopolitical organization elucidates governing relations among Communist parties, trade union movements, and the masses in the Western countries. In 1920, these relations were incorporated in an "initial model" defined by Lenin and having the following characteristics: the Party is present in the enterprise solely through the medium of the trade unions; Communist nuclei must be formed in all unions; the unions remain an autonomous form of proletarian action. The subsequent positions adopted by the Comintern and the conditions of application of its directives gradually led to the definition of a "derived model": the Party must be present as such in enterprises in the form of Communist cells; it sets up "nuclei" in only one union over which it has tight control. By way of example, the influence of such a model is singled out in the process of trade union unification in progress in Italy since the end of the 1960's. The fact that the Italian Communist Party conforms to the derived Leninist model is one of the causes of the current unification, but the fact that the derived model is called in question by union unity has not caused it to disappear. J

2576. Fedele, Marcello. LA DINAMICA ELETTORALE DEL PCI: 1946-1979 [Electoral dynamics of the Italian Communist Party, 1946-79]. *Ann. dell'Istituto Giangiacomo Feltrinelli [Italy] 1981 21: 293-312.* The growth of the Communist vote in Italy in the last 30 years does not reflect a change in the relation between electorate and society, which as far as social composition is concerned has remained substantially the same. It reflects rather a change in the relation between the two permanent components of Party's electorate, the area vote and the militant vote. While the latter has thinned, the former has become weightier and more decisive. 13 tables, 31 notes. J. V. Coutinho

2577. Femia, Joseph V. *Gramsci's Political Thought: Hegemony, Consciousness, and the Revolutionary Process.* New York: Oxford U. Pr., 1981. 303 pp.

2578. Ferrante, Gianni. INTERSCAMBIO DI DIRIGENTI TRA PARTITO E SINDACATO [Interchange of leaders between the Communist Party and labor union]. *Ann. dell'Istituto Giangiacomo Feltrinelli [Italy] 1981 21: 673-691.* Studies some of the characteristics of the ways in which Communist militants pass from experience in Party organs to union experience in the General Confederation of Labor (CGIL), and vice versa. For a time the Party furnished the cadres to the union but there has lately been a tendency in the opposite direction, with a resulting greater autonomy of the union. 29 notes, 3 charts. J. V. Coutinho

2579. Ferrari, Lilliana. GLI STATUTI DELL'AZIONE CATTOLICA DEL 1946 [The 1946 rules of the Catholic Action group]. *Italia Contemporanea [Italy] 1978 30(130): 57-83.* Discusses the new statutes of the Italian Catholic Action group put forward in 1946 which arose out of the church's perception that her most immediate postwar enemy was the Communist Party. It was decided to make the Catholic Action group permanent and its function was to focus Christian Democrat policy with the result that their current role is defined as that of defender of the Church from the modern world. Based on the statutes of the Italian Catholic Action group and secondary sources; 87 notes. C. E. King

2580. Filatov, G. S. GAZETE ITAL'IANSKIKH KOMMUNISTOV—SOROK LET [The Italian Communist Party newspaper after 40 years]. *Voprosy Istorii KPSS [USSR] 1964 (2): 95-98.* Traces the main events in the history of Italy between 1924 and 1964 as reflected in the pages of the Communist Party newspaper *l'Unità*.

2581. Flores, Marcello. DIBATTITO INTERNO SUL MUTAMENTO DELLA STRUTTURA ORGANIZZATIVA, 1946-1948 [Internal debate on changing the organizational structure, 1946-48]. *Ann. dell'Istituto Giangiacomo Feltrinelli [Italy] 1981 21: 35-61.* In the immediate postwar period, in the context of Palmiro Togliatti's call for a "new party," a party of the people and of government, lively debates took place within the Communist Party. The main organizational themes in the debate were the relation between centralism and decentralization and the equilibrium to be maintained between a party of cadres and a party of the masses. The enormous increase in membership and popular participation in political action led the party toward an ever stronger link with society. 103 notes. J. V. Coutinho

2582. Fonta, Ilie. NEOFASCISMUL ÎN ITALIA [Neofascism in Italy]. *Revista de Istorie [Romania] 1981 34(10): 1919-1939.* Analyzes the causes of the reactivation of organizations and political parties with a Nazi and neofascist orientation in capitalist countries, especially Italy, after World War II. Their objectives were the destruction of democracy, the annulment of workers' rights and of the Italian Communist Party, and other political or professional organizations of the working classes. The Italian Communist Party and other democratic political forces took political and juridical measures in order to weaken and later eliminate neofascism and violence from the Italian political scene. Based on secondary sources; 50 notes. French summary. T. Z. Herman

2583. Franchi, Paolo. L'ORGANIZZAZIONE GIOVANILE: 1968-1979 [The youth organization, 1968-79]. *Ann. dell'Istituto Giangiacomo Feltrinelli [Italy] 1981 21: 783-800.* In the postwar period youth unrest in Italy expressed itself in explosive fashion at least three times, in 1960, 1968, and 1977. Each time the youth movements developed outside, often against, the Communist Party and its youth organization. This fact provoked an internal reappraisal in the youth federation leading to a more or less open conflict with the Party. The conflict was resolved or patched up by canvassing among the less politicized sectors of the movements and by adopting some of their themes, after a careful sifting, and to the extent that they did not conflict with the Communist political tradition. The results in organizational terms were not always positive. Membership continues to decline. 20 notes. J. V. Coutinho

2584. Fraser, John. ENRICO BERLINGUER ET LA TRANSITION VERS LA TRANSITION [Enrico Berlinguer and the transition toward transition]. *Études Int. [Canada] 1975 6(3): 318-333.* Analyzes Berlinguer's role in the dramatic rise of the Italian Communist Party, emphasizing particularly his contributions to Italian communism. Discusses the Italian Communist Party in terms of the class struggle, the nature of the present crisis in Italy, the Communist solution to the problems of Aldo Moro's government, and the future of the party. 13 notes. J. F. Harrington, Jr.

2585. Galante, Severino. SULLE *CONDIZIONI* DELLA DEMOCRAZIA PROGRESSIVA NELLA LINEA POLITICA DEL PCI (1943-1948) [On the conditions of "progressive democracy" in the political line of the Italian Communist Party (PCI), 1943-48]. *Politico [Italy] 1975 40(3): 455-474.* Asserts that progressive democracy failed because the PCI underestimated the strength of capitalism. The failure of the theory of progressive democracy, seen in the defeat of the left wing in the 1948 elections, was not tied to the downfall of the hypothesis of national economic self-sufficiency, which fell through in 1945. Neither was it caused by the outbreak of the cold war which buried Communist illusions about the future of the wartime Grand Alliance. Its failure was due to Italy's unitary policy, which denied systems of mass democracy anticipated by the resistance, and to popular struggles after the war. J/S

2586. Gallerano, Nicola. L'ORGANIZZAZIONE DEL PARTITO NEL MEZZOGIORNO: 1943-1947 [Party organization in the South, 1943-47]. *Ann. dell'Istituto Giangiacomo Feltrinelli [Italy] 1981 21: 1061-1086.* In the context of a debate on the role of the Communist Party in Southern Italy in the 1940's concerning the relative merits of Party organization and participation in spontaneous peasant revolts, the author argues that the mediation of the Party, if not adequate, was that which was historically possible given the conditions, the level of consciousness, and the restrictions imposed by the Party line. Based on material in the Party archives; 75 notes. J. V. Coutinho

2587. Galli, Gino. IL PARTITO E LE AMMINISTRAZIONI LOCALI: IL CASO DELL'UMBRIA (1944-1979) [The Party and local administration: the case of Umbria (1944-79)]. *Ann. dell'Istituto Giangiacomo Feltrinelli [Italy] 1981 21: 553-579.* Studies the presence of Communist Party political personnel in the local bodies of Umbria, beginning with a description of the communes in terms of the social composition of the population: industrial and agricultural workers, artisans and merchants, employees, teachers, and professionals. Describes the relative influence of the Communist, Socialist, and Social Democratic parties. Communist personnel is described in terms of sex, age, and education. 26 tables, 18 notes. J. V. Coutinho

2588. Galli, Gino. "UNITA"—50 YEARS. *World Marxist R. [Canada] 1974 17(2): 117-119.* In an interview Gino Galli, deputy head of the Press and Propaganda Department, Communist Party of Italy, covers the current status and editorial policy of the Communist newspaper *Unità.*

2589. Garner, Larry and Garner, Roberta. PROBLEMS OF THE HEGEMONIC PARTY: THE PCI AND THE STRUCTURAL LIMITS OF REFORM. *Sci. & Soc. 1981 45(3): 257-273.* Examines and critiques the present strategy of the Italian Communist Party (PCI) of trying first to attain Italian political hegemony as a prelude to finally gaining state power. This strategy of a transitional period, according to Italian Marxists, is necessary because advanced capitalist countries do not react in a serious crisis the same revolutionary way that developing countries do. Workers of advance capitalist countries, however, might be willing to gamble with socialism if greater publicity were given to the successful evolution of Eastern European socialism to the point where it now stands for full employment, high standards of living, and an inflation-free economy. 18 notes.

2590. Garner, Lawrence. A CHANGE IN ITALY'S CHOIRMASTER? *Current History 1984 83(492): 160-163, 181-183.* A genuine political change in Italy is impossible so long as the Communist Party is excluded from the set of potential government parties. Despite the debut of a Socialist premier, Bettino Craxi of the Italian Socialist Party (PSI), in 1983, the Communists remain outside the ruling circle.

2591. Gazzo, Emanuele. RÜCKWIRKUNGEN DER DIREKTWAHL ZUM EUROPÄISCHEN PARLAMENT AUF DIE INNENPOLITIK DER MITGLIEDSTAATEN. ITALIEN: MÖGLICHE ÄNDERUNGEN DER PARTEIENKONSTELLATION [Repercussions of the direct elections for the European Parliament on the domestic politics of the member states. Italy: possible changes of the constellation of parties]. *Europa Archiv [West Germany] 1978 33(24): 805-811.* The domestic political development of Italy in the 1960's and 1970's shows that the Italian Communists have slowly developed a realistic and positive attitude toward the EEC, which, if they adopt an even more positive policy, will enable them to participate in the Italian government.

2592. Ghini, Celso. GLI ISCRITTI AL PARTITO E ALLA FGCI. 1943-1979 [Members of the Party and the Italian Young Communist Federation (FGCI), 1943-79]. *Ann. dell'Istituto Giangiacomo Feltrinelli [Italy] 1981 21: 227-292.* Describes the fluctuations in the membership of the Party and its youth federation. Examines geographical and class origin, sex, education, occupation of members, the role of women and workers in the Party and the innovational structures introduced in the postwar construction of the "new party." 16 tables, 35 notes. J. V. Coutinho

2593. Ghini, Celso. IL COMITATO REGIONALE [The regional committee]. *Ann. dell'Istituto Giangiacomo Feltrinelli [Italy] 1981 21: 121-126.* The Italian Communist Party's regional committees were revived in 1947, after the breakup of the resistance coalition and the unity governments. Traces the history of these committees and the problems they gave rise to, chief among them being the sifting off of the more capable militants from the section to the region. 5 notes. J. V. Coutinho

2594. Gianotti, Renzo. L'ORGANIZZAZIONE DEL PARTITO ALLA FIAT MIRAFIORI: 1941-1980 [Party organization at the FIAT Mirafiori plant: 1941-80]. *Ann. dell'Istituto Giangiacomo Feltrinelli [Italy] 1981 21: 1105-1115.* Deals with the founders, leaders, membership, and activities of the Communist Party section at the FIAT plant at Mirafiori. 2 notes. J. V. Coutinho

2595. Ginsborg, Paul. THE COMMUNIST PARTY AND THE AGRARIAN QUESTION IN SOUTHERN ITALY, 1943-1948. *History Workshop Journal [Great Britain] 1984 (17): 81-101.* In the wake of Mussolini's fall in 1943, the opportunity existed to build a democratic and reformist movement of significant proportions in Italy. In particular, the proposed agrarian reforms of the Communist minister of agriculture Fausto Gullo could have transformed peasant-landlord relations in southern Italy. The resistance, peasant militancy, and the partial discrediting of the ruling class created exceptional historical circumstances for reform. But the Communist Party chose to solidify its narrow, leadership-based alliance with the Christian Democrats rather than devote itself to the mass mobilization necessary for significant reform. K. Fones-Wolf

2596. Golden, Miriam Anna. "Austerity and Its Opposition: Italian Working Class Politics in the 1970's." Cornell U. 1983. 529 pp. *DAI 1983 43(12): 4024-A.* DA8309483

2597. Good, Martha H. THE ITALIAN COMMUNIST PARTY AND LOCAL GOVERNMENT COALITIONS. *Studies in Comparative Communism 1980 13(2-3): 197-219.* Since 1951 Communist local government strategy in Italy has been to form coalitions where necessary in order to rule. Prior to 1960 Socialists willingly joined such coalitions. After 1960 the Communists indicated they would join with any antifascist party, but Christian Democratic coalitions with socialists weakened the Communist Party. The historic compromise of 1975 led Communists to form open coalitions in order to attract new allies; the Socialists after 1975 favored coalitions with the Left if possible. The pursuit of coalitions in local government has altered the image of the party, but in 1978 the Communists lost in partial local elections. 59 notes. D. Balmuth

2598. Gori, Neri. L'ORGANIZZAZIONE DEL PCI A FIRENZE (1945-1971) [The organization of the PCI in Florence, 1945-71]. *Rassegna Italiana di Sociologia [Italy] 1974 15(3): 387-442.* Describes some of the characteristics of the ideological formation and organizational history of the Italian Communist Party (PCI) in Florence after World War II.

2599. Grazioso, Innocenzo. *L'UNITÀ* E LA CINA [*L'Unità* and China]. *Mondo Cinese [Italy] 1981 9(2): 9-39; 1982 10(1): 47-77.* Part 1. Examines coverage of China and of the relationship between the Italian and Chinese Communist parties in *l'Unità,* the Italian Communist newspaper, July 1945 to October 1949. Part 2. Coverage extends to 1953. J/S

2600. Grishina, R. P. "LEKTSII O FASHIZME" P. TOL'IATTI I NEKOTORYE VOPROSY IZUCHENIIA FASHIZMA V STRANAKH TSENTRAL'NOI I IUGO-VOSTOCHNOI EVROPY [P. Togliatti's *Lectures on Fascism* and some aspects of study dealing with fascism in the countries of Central and Southeast Europe]. *Sovetskoe Slavianovedenie [USSR] 1976 (6): 17-24.* In 1970, the Italian Communist Party published Palmiro Togliatti's lectures on fascism, given January-April 1935 in Moscow. These lectures, translated into Russian by V. A. Bogorad, a specialist in Italian history and the history of Italian workers and the Communist movement, were published in 1974. Togliatti's observations regarding the characteristic features of the fascist party go beyond the Italian example. The author describes how they can be used in the study of the regimes of the countries of Central and Southeast Europe in the interwar period. 6 notes. L. Kalinowski

2601. Hall, John Russell. "Antonio Gramsci, Italian Communism and Education." Michigan State U. 1980. 196 pp. *DAI 1980 41(3): 966-A.* 8020704

2602. Hegge, Per Egil. ITALIENERNES NASJONALKOMMUNISME [Italian national communism]. *Internasjonal Politikk [Norway] 1976 (4): 815-821.* Since the 1950's, the Italian Communist Party has developed a specifically Italian character, though it is careful to emphasize the debt it owes to Marx, Engels, and Lenin.

2603. Hellman, Stephen. GENERATIONAL DIFFERENCES IN THE BUREAUCRATIC ELITE OF ITALIAN COMMUNIST PARTY PROVINCIAL FEDERATIONS. *Can. J. of Pol. Sci. [Canada] 1975 8(1): 82-106.* Because so much control over upward mobility remains in the hands of the older generation of Party functionaries, the younger and more radical Party members are likely to be promoted very selectively. 6 tables, 2 figs., 42 notes. R. V. Kubicek

2604. Hellman, Stephen. THE ITALIAN CP: STUMBLING ON THE THRESHOLD? *Problems of Communism 1978 27(6): 31-48.* The Italian Communist Party (PCI) made substantial gains in the general elections of 1976 and moved quickly to capitalize on their increased leverage in the political system. The Christian Democratic government bowed to the inevitable and granted the PCI certain political offices long denied. Recently, however, the PCI has run into a number of serious difficulties, which seem to stem in part from overall political strategy, organizational and ideological issues, and PCI-Socialist Party relations. Communist momentum appears to have slackened, but the strength of the PCI has by no means been seriously deflated. Based on PCI publications and secondary sources; 3 tables, fig., 32 notes. J. M. Lauber

2605. Hick, Alan. KEEPING EURO-LEFT: THE ITALIAN COMMUNIST PARTY AND THE EUROPEAN "THIRD WAY." *Contemporary Rev. [Great Britain] 1982 241(1399): 58-63.* Contrasts British Labour Party policy on the European Economic Community (EEC) in recent years to that of the Italian Communist Party, which regards the EEC as the most appropriate transnational political apparatus for launching a joint European socialist campaign.

2606. Hine, David. SOCIALISTS AND COMMUNISTS IN ITALY—REVERSING ROLES? *West European Pol. [Great Britain] 1978 1(2): 144-160.* From 1966 to 1977 the Italian Socialist Party (PSI) has abandoned its attempt to isolate the Communist Party and instead has sought to reintegrate it into the group of so-called democratic parties, a process which has culminated in the PSI's proposal for a socialist alternative government to replace Christian Democratic rule. The Communist response has been to accept the legitimacy thus bestowed, but to use it to impose its own solution—a grand coalition of Communists, Socialists, and Christian Democrats.

2607. Ilardi, Massimo. SISTEMA DI POTERE E IDEOLOGIA NEL PCI: LE CONFERENZE NAZIONALI D'ORGANIZZAZIONE [Power system and ideology in the Italian Communist Party: the national organizational conferences]. *Ann. dell'Istituto Giangiacomo Feltrinelli [Italy] 1981 21: 3-33.* Initiates an inquiry into the history and structure of the organization of the Italian Communist Party, testing a hypothesis regarding a link between change, power, and organization. Applies the hypothesis to the comprehension of certain politico-historical periods of the Communist organization as it has been developed by the national conferences of Florence (1947), Rome (1955), and Naples (1964) and the Central Committee conference of December 1976. 89 notes. J. V. Coutinho

2608. Kaplan, Jim. INTRODUCTION TO THE REVOLUTIONARY LEFT IN ITALY. *Radical Am. 1973 7(2): 1-5.* An introduction to a special issue on the working class movement in Italy, giving a brief history of the Communist Party and the more radical revolutionary Left (1960's-73).

2609. Kelly, Craig Allen. "The Anti-Fascist Resistance and the Shift in Political-Cultural Strategy of the Italian Communist Party 1936-1948." University of California, Los Angeles 1984. 243 pp. *DAI 1984 45(6): 1841-A.* DA8420196

2610. Kertzer, David I. *Comrades and Christians: Religion and Political Struggle in Communist Italy.* New York: Cambridge U. Pr., 1980. 304 pp.

2611. Kertzer, David I. THE LIBERATION OF EVELINA ZAGHI: THE LIFE OF AN ITALIAN COMMUNIST. *Signs 1982 8(1): 45-67.* Evelina Zaghi, one of the first women of Bologna to be called a political leader, rose in the Communist hierarchy of her area. Her political and economic egalitarianism came from her working-class background and in no way rejected the traditional role of women. While women tend to be less activist today, there is a continuing interest in women's participation in political issues. Based on an interview with Zaghi; 13 notes. S. P. Conner

2612. Komolova, Nelli Pavlovna and Filatov, Georgii Semenovich. PAL'MIRO TOL'IATTI: VYDAIUSHCHIISIA DEIATEL' ITAL'IANSKOGO I MEZHDUNARODNOGO KOMMUNISTICHESKOGO DVIZHENIIA [Palmiro Togliatti: an outstanding figure of the Italian and international Communist movements]. *Novaia i Noveishaia Istoriia [USSR] 1980 (4): 75-92, (5): 74-84, (6): 85-106.* Part I. Togliatti (1893-1964) joined the Italian Socialist Party in 1914. After the war he and other young socialists joined a new newspaper, *Ordine Nuovo,* in 1919. In 1921 the Italian Communist Party was formed and Togliatti became chief editor of the Party's newspaper. Thereafter he and his fellow Communists faced intense persecution by Mussolini's Fascist government, and in 1926 Togliatti began a forced exile that lasted 18 years. Part II. Deals with the years of the Spanish Civil War and World War II. Togliatti fought in Spain, helping the Spanish Communists as a Comintern representative. In 1939 he was arrested in France while carrying a false passport. He escaped to the USSR, where he broadcast messages to Italy under the name of Mario Correnti. Part III. Summarizes Togliatti's participation in the reconstruction of Italy after World War II and his attempts to bring a Communist-led government to power. Based on published documents, speeches, newspaper and secondary accounts in Russian and Italian; autograph, 4 photos, 210 notes. D. N. Collins

2613. Kopkind, Andrew. MODEL CITY. *Working Papers for New Soc. 1976 4(2): 32-40.* Discusses the role of the Communist Party in the fiscal management, politics, local government, and labor unions of Bologna, Italy in the 1970's, and describes the standard of living of the working class.

2614. Krylov, A. A. LUIDZHI LONGO [Luigi Longo]. *Voprosy Istorii KPSS [USSR] 1975 (3): 116-119.* A biographical sketch of Luigi Longo, member of the Italian Communist Party since its inception in 1921; active participant in the struggle against Italian fascism, in the Spanish Civil War, and in post-1943 Italian politics; General Secretary from 1964 to 1972 and since 1972 Chairman of Italy's Communist Party. Based on secondary works and published memoirs; 9 notes. L. E. Holmes

2615. LaMalfa, Ugo. COMMUNISM AND DEMOCRACY IN ITALY. *Foreign Affairs 1978 56(3): 476-488.* Italy is in the midst of a profound social and economic crisis. Further chaos can be avoided only by the admission of the Communist Party (PCI) into the national governing process. The PCI has evolved remarkably in recent years; adherence to Leninism and the monolithic Moscow line has given way to new flexibility and a willingness to operate within traditional democratic guidelines. M. R. Yerburgh

2616. Lanchester, Fulco. I DELEGATI AI CONGRESSI NAZIONALI [The delegates to the national congresses]. *Ann. dell'Istituto Giangiacomo Feltrinelli [Italy] 1981 21: 619-672.* Studies the policies of delegate selection in relation to the policies of cadre selection and training as they evolve in time in response to intra-Party and national factors. The process is followed from level to level and attention is given to the influence of geographical differences. 33 tables, 132 notes. J. V. Coutinho

2617. Lanchester, Fulco. LA NASCITA DEL "PARTITO NUOVO" IN UNA ZONA PARTIGIANA: IL PCI DELL'OLTREPÒ PAVESE [The birth of the "New Party" in a partisan zone: the PCI in the Pavian regions beyond the Po]. *Italia*

Contemporanea [Italy] 1975 27(3): 169-194. The building of a "New Party" was one of the essential elements of Communist strategy in 1944. When Mussolini fell in July 1945, the Italian Communist Party (PCI) in the region of Pavia was a small, rigidly organized, clandestine network. But soon it sought to expand and become a mass party. It did this by working hard within the partisan movement, forming many Resistance units itself. It also held back its own extremists and cooperated with the two other large anti-Fascist parties, the Socialists and the Christian Democrats. 4 reproductions, 56 notes. J. C. Billigmeier

2618. Lange, Peter and Vannicelli, Maurizio. CARTER IN THE ITALIAN MAZE. *Foreign Policy 1978-79 (33): 161-173.* The Carter administration is continuing Henry A. Kissinger's policy of opposing participation of the Italian Communist Party (PCI) in the government of Italy. Italy's social and economic problems probably cannot be solved without Communist participation. America must adopt a policy more consistent with Italian realities, recognizing that the Italian people must decide the future of the PCI. A policy of "critical coexistence" (accepting the legitimacy of the PCI while continuing to disagree with it) would serve this purpose, and would encourage the party to continue its independent evolution. T. L. Powers

2619. Lange, Peter. CRISIS AND CONSENT, CHANGE AND COMPROMISE: DILEMMAS OF ITALIAN COMMUNISM IN THE 1970S. *West European Pol. [Great Britain] 1979 2(3): 110-132.* Discusses the outward political successes and inward tension of the Italian Communist Party and its decisionmaking during the crisis of the 1970's.

2620. Lanzardo, Liliana. I CONSIGLI DI GESTIONE NELLA STRATEGIA DELLA COLLABORAZIONE [The Management Councils within the strategy of cooperation]. *Ann. della Fondazione Giangiacomo Feltrinelli [Italy] 1974-75 16: 325-365.* A few days before the liberation of the North of Italy (April 1945), the North Italian Committee of National Liberation (CLNAI) issued a decree entrusting Management Councils elected by the workers with administrative tasks in the factories. The General Confederation of Industrial Employers (*Confindustria*) and its president, Angelo Costa, were against them. Nevertheless, the councils began to work in some firms such as FIAT, Montecatini, ILVA, and Alfa Romeo. Their tasks were quite technical. They neither endangered private enterprise nor limited the property of the industries. Until 1948 the Management Councils collaborated with the factory owners. But after the elections of April 1948 and the heavy losses of the Italian left wing, they changed, as the Communists attempted to use the Management Councils to support their positions. In a short time the Management Councils were eliminated. 40 notes. A. Canavero

2621. Longo, Luigi. A POWERFUL FORCE FOR CHANGE. *World Marxist Rev. [Canada] 1976 19(4): 12-20.* The author, a Communist Party official in Italy, describes the revolutionary activities of his party from the 1920's to 1975.

2622. Macaluso, Emanuele. LE CONFERENZE AGRARIE [The agrarian conferences]. *Ann. dell'Istituto Giangiacomo Feltrinelli [Italy] 1981 21: 1087-1103.* Since 1967 the Communist Party has held four national agrarian conferences, attended by hundreds of delegates from grass-roots organizations and many scholars and guests from both inside and outside the Party. These conferences have had the double effect of deepening and enriching the agrarian Party line adopted from the beginning, and of enabling the Party to contribute to the elaboration of a national agrarian policy through the Party organization, the parliament, the labor organizations, the farmers' associations, and through universities and research institutes. 44 notes. J. V. Coutinho

2623. Maestri, Ezio G. PARTITI E SISTEMA PENSIONISTICO IN ITALIA. UN'ANALISI DELL'AZIONE PARLAMENTARE DELLA DC E DEL PCI (1953-1975) [Political parties and the pension system in Italy: an analysis of the Christian Democratic and Communist parliamentary activity, 1953-75]. *Riv. Italiana di Sci. Pol. [Italy] 1984 14(1): 125-159.* Discusses the distribution of pension benefits among different social groups defined according to their labor market position and the role of party competition, strikes, and legislative production concerning the pension system in explaining the levels and nature of the bills introduced by Christian Democratic and Communist members of parliament. By means of regression techniques, determines the combined impact of the three factors, showing that party competition has been a prominent variable in explaining party action in the pension field. J/S

2624. Margiocco, Mario. *Stati Uniti e PCI, 1943-1980* [The United States and the Italian Communist Party, 1943-80]. Bari: Laterza, 1981. 327 pp.

2625. Mariani, Laura. TANTE ALTRE CON ISIDE, MARCELLINA E ROSA LUXEMBURG: STORIA DI UNA RICERCA SULLE DETENUTE POLITICHE NEL CARCERE DI PERUGIA (1927-1950) [And so many others with Iside Viana, Marcellina Oriani, and Rosa Luxemburg Panichi: the story of a research on women political prisoners in Perugia (1927-50)]. *Memoria: Riv. di Storia delle Donne [Italy] 1981 (2): 89-102.* Presents the development of a research on the Communist women who in successive waves were imprisoned in Perugia from Fascist times to the immediate postwar period. The work was motivated by a personal quest for female identity, a theoretical interest in a critique of revolutionary orthodoxy, and a practical concern with the possibility of an effective process of transformation. Biblio. J. V. Coutinho

2626. Martinelli, Renzo. GLI STATUTI DEL PCI: 1921-1979 [The statutes of the Italian Communist Party: 1921-79]. *Ann. dell'Istituto Giangiacomo Feltrinelli [Italy] 1981 21: 63-82.* Analyzes the fundamental statutory texts of the Italian Communist Party from its inception to the present. They are grouped in three main periods: the initial period, 1921-29, the immediate postwar period, 1945-48, and the period from 1956 to 1975 leading to the statute of 1979. Underlines the link between the statutory text and the effective political activity of the Party during those periods. 48 notes. J. V. Coutinho

2627. Marx, Lily Elena. KOMMUNISTISCHE PARTEI UND GEWERKSCHAFTEN IN ITALIEN [The Communist Party and trade unions in Italy]. *Frankfurter Hefte [West Germany] 1981 36(1): 25-32.* In the 1950's Palmiro Togliatti was already developing the new concept for the Italian Communist Party toward the trade unions that would lead to the merging of the three major Italian trade union confederations in 1980.

2628. Massari, Oreste. LA FEDERAZIONE [The federation]. *Ann. dell'Istituto Giangiacomo Feltrinelli [Italy] 1981 21: 127-151.* The federation as a link between the grass roots and the directing center is an innovation of the Communist Party with reference to the Socialist tradition. From the statutory point of view, its structure was fixed in the postwar period. Its history is discussed in the context of the formation of the "new party" and of decentralization. 3 tables, 55 notes. J. V. Coutinho

2629. Massari, Oreste. LA SEZIONE [The section]. *Ann. dell'Istituto Giangiacomo Feltrinelli [Italy] 1981 21: 153-183.* The section is characteristic of the tradition of the socialist labor movement, that is, of a movement without a strong organizational structure at the central and middle levels, and engaged mainly in electoral and propagandistic activities. The assumption of this model created difficulties in a party organized on antithetical lines. Discusses these problems, in the context of the "new party," and especially in the period 1956-79. 10 tables, 82 notes. J. V. Coutinho

2630. Miller, James E. TAKING OFF THE GLOVES: THE UNITED STATES AND THE ITALIAN ELECTIONS OF 1948. *Diplomatic Hist. 1983 7(1): 35-55.* Analyzes American intervention to insure pro-Western election results. The United States first concentrated on supporting Prime Minister Alcide DeGasperi, the Christian Democratic leader, and extending economic aid. DeGasperi responded by excluding leftists from the government and curbing inflation. When a Communist victory seemed imminent, the United States instituted a massive propaganda campaign, covert funding of pro-American parties, covert arms shipments, Central Intelligence Agency operations, and other measures. Although Catholic Church activities, overt economic aid, and effective campaigning determined the Christian Democrats' victory, the United States was convinced of the efficacy of direct, covert intervention, even though such intervention thwarted long-term stability. Based on State Department and National Security Council records and other primary sources; 77 notes. T. J. Heston

2631. Monteleone, Renato. GAETANO PERILLO: LA VITA [Gaetano Perillo: life]. *Movimento Operaio e Socialista [Italy] 1976 22(1-2): 3-7.* A political biography of Gaetano Perillo (1897-1975), founder of the journal *Movimento Operaio e Socialista* and its director until his death. He first joined the Italian Socialist Party in 1922, and later the Italian Communist Party. His political activity centered in a cork cooperative in Campasso, where he organized his fellow workers. He suffered continual arrest and harassment, along with the entire party after the March on Rome. In 1925, he became the secretary of the Ligurian Federation of the PCI. In 1934 he was expelled from the Party because of accusations made by police infiltrators that he was a Trotskyist. Isolated, he continued political work until he reentered the Party in 1942 and then remained an active member until his death. M. T. Wilson

2632. Monti, Aldo. NORBERTO BOBBIO E L'ITALIA CIVILE CHE SCOMPARE [Norberto Bobbio and civil Italy that is disappearing]. *Belfagor [Italy] 1980 35(1): 1-20.* Analyzes the debate between the liberal scholar Norberto Bobbio and the Italian Communist Party, 1930's-70's, on the issue of democracy.

2633. Moscati, Ruggero. NOTA SULLA "SVOLTA" DEL GIUGNO 1947 [A note on the "turn" of June 1947]. *Storia Contemporanea [Italy] 1974 5(4): 569-590.* The Communists and their allies, the Nenni Socialists, withdrew from the Italian coalition government in the spring of 1947. The author gives a detailed account of the events that led up to that historic withdrawal, and emphasizes the tremendous personal role played by the Christian Democratic Prime Minister, Alcide De Gasperi (1881-1945), who enjoyed the support not only of the largest bloc of Italian voters but also of the United States. Note. J. C. Billigmeier

2634. Mottura, Giovanni and Pugliese, Enrico. AGRICOLTURA, MERCATO DEL LAVORO E POLITICA DEL MOVIMENTO OPERAIO [Agriculture, labor market, and the politics of the workers' movement]. *Ann. della Fondazione Giangiacomo Feltrinelli [Italy] 1974-75 16: 367-408.* Censures postwar Communist policies toward the peasants of Southern Italy. From 1943 they began to occupy uncultivated lands. In 1944 a law allowed these lands to be held by peasant associations which promised to cultivate them. In spite of this law, the occupations of cultivated lands continued. The Communists were against these unlawful actions. The opposition of the Communist Party led to the defeat of the peasants' movement and allowed the Christian Democrats to gain political power in rural Italy. Based on secondary works; 63 notes. A. Canavero

2635. Murav'eva, N. A. and Blinova, E. P. ITAL'IANSKAIA KOMPARTIIA V AVANGARDE DEMOKRATICHESKOGO DVIZHENIIA ZHENSHCHIN [The Italian Communist Party in the vanguard of the democratic women's movement]. *Voprosy Istorii KPSS [USSR] 1966 (1): 30-39.* Surveys progress toward female emancipation in Italy, emphasizing the role of Communists, 1943-46.

2636. Naumov, V. K. LUIDZHI LONGO: K 70-LETIIU SO DNIA ROZHDENIIA [Luigi Longo: to commemorate the 70th anniversary of his birth]. *Voprosy Istorii KPSS [USSR] 1970 (3): 106-111.* Examines the career and political views of Luigi Longo, General Secretary of the Italian Communist Party, particularly his participation in the struggle against fascism.

2637. Neubert, Harald. DIE POLITISCHE ENTWICKLUNG ITALIENS IN DEN ERSTEN MONATEN NACH DER BEFREIUNG VOM FASCHISMUS [The political development of Italy in the first months after the liberation from fascism]. *Zeitschrift für Geschichtswissenschaft [East Germany] 1975 23(10): 1117-1134.* After the defeat of fascism the Italian Communist Party (PCI) continued to cooperate with the Committees for National Liberation (CLN). However, the government of Ferruccio Parri, formed in June 1945 and based on the CLN, was unable to carry out necessary political, social, and economic reforms, chiefly because of the increasing opposition of the bourgeois parties, backed by the Western occupation forces. The PCI did not resist the fall of the Parri government in November 1945 because Italy was not yet ready for socialist revolution. 54 notes. J. T. Walker

2638. Neubert, Harald. PALMIRO TOGLIATTI—REVOLUTIONÄRER ARBEITERFÜHRER UND INTERNATIONALIST [Palmiro Togliatti: revolutionary leader of workers and internationalist]. *Einheit [East Germany] 1974 29(8): 951-959.* In the 1930's Palmiro Togliatti (1893-1964) enforced Leninist principles against resistance within the Communist Party of Italy. As secretary of the Comintern executive he greatly influenced its ideological development in the 1930's and 1940's.

2639. P. A. A POLITICAL AND PHILOSOPHICAL INTERVIEW. *New Left R. [Great Britain] 1974 (86): 3-28.* Interview with Italian Marxist philosopher Lucio Colletti (b. ca 1925) probes his ideological relationship to the Italian Communist Party, Jean Jacques Rousseau, Friedrich Engels, Karl Marx, Maoism, his epistemological positions, and his vision for the future of Marxism.

2640. Pallante, Pierluigi. IL PARTITO COMUNISTA ITALIANO E LA QUESTIONE DI TRIESTE NELLA RESISTENZA [The Italian Communist Party and the question of Trieste in the Resistance]. *Storia Contemporanea [Italy] 1976 7(3): 481-504.* Luigi Longo claimed in December 1953 that the Italian Communist Party had defended the Italian character of Trieste in the closing months of World War II and in the postwar period. He was correct in the sense that the PCI had always emphasized the Italian nationality of the city and region, but not in a political sense. The PCI never claimed Trieste and Venezia Giulia as part of the Italian state. In fact, the PCI, desirous of close cooperation with the Yugoslav Communists, had avoided directly opposing Tito's demand for Trieste. Class struggle was more important than nationality. 82 notes. J. C. Billigmeier

2641. Parks, Tim. THE ITALIAN COMMUNISTS: AN HISTORIC COMPROMISE. *Contemporary Rev. [Great Britain] 1984 245(1425): 186-190.* Considers the development of the Italian Communist Party between 1944 and 1984 with reference to the so-called historic compromise between the Communists and the Christian Democratic Party between 1976 and 1979, Eurocommunism, and the Party's attitude toward the USSR.

2642. Pasquino, Gianfranco. LA DEMOCRACIA ITALIANA EN UN PERIODO DE CAMBIO [Italian democracy in a period of change]. *Rev. de Estudios Pol. [Spain] 1980 (13): 105-143.* An analysis of the postwar Italian political system and the causes of its instability. Distinctions must be made between instability derived from rapid turnovers in political power, electoral inconsistency, and lack of organized parties, and that owing to the complexity of problems to be resolved and the magnitude of change to be realized. The former are only superficial. It is the latter type of instability which characterizes contemporary Italian politics. Specifically, the integration of the Communist Party and the working class into the system is the fundamental factor in the current Italian political crisis. 2 tables, 53 notes. N. A. Rosenblatt

2643. Pasquino, Gianfranco. UNE CRISE QUI VIENT DE LOIN [A crisis that goes far back]. *Esprit [France] 1976 44(11): 534-553.* Discusses Italy's political, economic, and social crisis, which dates back to the establishment of the republican regime after the fall of Fascism in 1945. Shows that in order to solve the crisis the Italian political system should be restructured to allow the Communist Party participation in the government.

2644. Piombino, Giancarlo. REALISMO E CONTRADDIZIONI NELLA RELAZIONE DE BERLINGUER AL CONGRESSO DEL PCI [Realism and contradiction in the speeches of Berlinguer at the Congress of the Italian Communist Party]. *Civitas [Italy] 1975*

26(5): 21-38. Analyzes the recent congress of the Italian Communist Party, the speeches of General Secretary Enrico Berlinguer, and the Party's recent move toward broad political collaboration.
J/S

2645. Platone, Rossana. STORIA DELLA SEZIONE "ITALIA" DI ROMA: 1944-1979 [History of the "Italia" section of Rome, 1944-79]. *Ann. dell'Istituto Giangiacomo Feltrinelli [Italy] 1981 21: 1141-1152.* The Italia district of Rome, centered on the area between the Via Nomentana and the Via Tiburtina, rose during the Fascist years to house bureaucrats of every grade. Villa Torlonia, Mussolini's residence, was situated in the district. During the immediate postwar years it had a rich section, a middle-income, and a small popular section. Describes the founding, membership, and activities of a section of the Communist Party in the district. 4 tables, note. J. V. Coutinho

2646. Poggi, Giancarlo. IL PARTITO E LE AMMINISTRAZIONI LOCALI: IL CASO DELL'EMILIA [The Party and local administration: the case of Emilia]. *Ann. dell'Istituto Giangiacomo Feltrinelli [Italy] 1981 21: 581-618.* Attempts to determine, in the selection and functioning of Communist Party local administrators, certain characteristics of the relation between Party and administration in Emilia-Romagna. Focuses on the relation between selection of the political class and the social and political demand, with special reference to the class composition of the politicians and the policy of alliances. Around this theme other topics are examined: party-state integration at the local level, the use of state institutions and the professionalization and bureaucratization of political initiative. 11 tables, 59 notes. J. V. Coutinho

2647. Porcu, Sebastiano. LE PARTI COMMUNISTE ITALIEN ET L'ADMINISTRATION LOCALE À BOLOGNE (1945-1977) [The Italian Communist Party and local government in Bologna, 1945-77]. *Rev. Française de Sci. Pol. [France] 1979 29(1): 33-52.* The Communist Party's long rule in Bologna has adapted to local socioeconomic conditions.

2648. Portelli, Hugues. LA LONGUE MARCHE DU PARTI COMMUNISTE ITALIEN. [The long march of the Italian Communist Party]. *Esprit [France] 1976 44(11): 554-567.* Analyzes the evolution of the Italian Communist Party since the 1920's and shows that, if it is to participate openly in the government, it should enhance its credibility and convince the Church and the Italian economic forces that cooperation and coexistence with a liberal Communist Party are to their best advantage.

2649. Putnam, Robert D. INTERDEPENDENCE AND THE ITALIAN COMMUNISTS. *Int. Organization 1978 32(2): 301-350.* The recent growth in Italian Communist Party (PCI) influence on national policy making has been accompanied by a reversal of the party's traditional opposition to Italian participation in NATO and the European Communities. This reversal is due to Italy's increasingly irreversible involvement in the network of economic interdependence that links the Western economies. PCI leaders have come to recognize and accept the political consequences of interdependence. Other important factors contributing to the policy shift are: 1) changes in Italian public opinion that made opposition to Italy's Western alignment increasingly costly for the PCI; and 2) constraints imposed by the PCI's need to seek alliances with non-Communists, both in Italy and elsewhere in Western Europe.
J

2650. Quazza, Guido. OMAGGIO A TERRACINI [Homage to Terracini]. *Italia Contemporanea [Italy] 1976 28(124): 107-113.* On the occasion of the bestowal of honorary citizenship of Torino to a militant of the Italian Communist Party, Umberto Terracini, 6 June 1976, the author recalls Terracini's unique relationship with the working class of that city. Terracini had a long and difficult career as a militant of the Italian Socialist Party and then the Italian Communist Party. In 1926 he was condemned to prison where he remained until his release in 1943. In that same year, Terracini was expelled from the Party because of his continued insistence on independent judgments and anticonformist thinking. He later returned to the Party, and as a professional revolutionary has been known for his passionate defense of the youth of the New Left.
M. T. Wilson

2651. Quercioli, Elio. FOR A GOVERNMENT OF DEMOCRATIC CHANGE. *World Marxist Rev. [Canada] 1972 15(7): 68-77.* Reports on the 13th Congress of the Italian Communist Party (Milan, 13-17 March 1972) and reviews the progress of the electoral struggle with the Christian Democratic Party in Italy, 1968-72.

2652. Rossi, Michele. NEO-FASCISM IN ITALY. *World Marxist R. [Canada] 1975 18(4): 22-31.* The Communist Party in Italy is trying to check the advance of Fascism.

2653. Rossi, Michele. RIGHT-CENTER CABINET MUST BE OVERTHROWN. *World Marxist R. [Canada] 1973 16(1): 84-89.* The political policy of Italy's Communist Party is to overthrow the government's rightist efforts to destroy democratic growth.

2654. Ruscoe, James. *On the Threshold of Government: The Italian Communist Party, 1976-81.* New York: St. Martin's, 1983. 293 pp.

2655. Salvetti, Patrizia. LA STAMPA D'ORGANIZZAZIONE PERIODICA: 1945-1979 [The periodical press, 1945-79]. *Ann. dell'Istituto Giangiacomo Feltrinelli [Italy] 1981 21: 879-896.* Analyzes the function, characteristics, and evolution of the Italian Communist Party's press organs in relation to postwar Party activities. Only periodicals with national circulation are included, and they are studied from the point of view of organizational issues. 72 notes.
J. V. Coutinho

2656. Salvetti Palazzi, Patrizia. ALCUNE CONSIDERAZIONI SUL PCI E LA SVOLTA DI SALERNO [Some considerations concerning the PCI and the change of direction at Salerno]. *Storia e Politica [Italy] 1973 12(2): 305-318.* The USSR recognized the Badoglio government and reopened regular diplomatic relations with Italy on 14 March 1944. Some days later, the Italian Communist Party (PCI) made an about-face, turning from a doctrine of revolution and resistance to everything not purely anti-Fascist to one of cooperation with the government and, eventually, participation in it. This was the first step in the PCI's evolution from a working-class based revolutionary party to a political party with wide appeal in the democratic arena. 34 notes. J. C. Billigmeier

2657. Santarelli, Enzo. ALFONSO LEONETTI [Alfonso Leonetti]. *Belfagor [Italy] 1983 38(3): 299-308.* Describes the career of one of the leading figures of Italian Marxism and his relations with the Communist Party, particularly after 1960.

2658. Sassoon, Donald. *The Strategy of the Italian Communist Party: From the Resistance to the Historic Compromise.* New York: St. Martin's, 1981. 259 pp.

2659. Scalpelli, Adolfo. DOCUMENTI SULL'ORGANIZZAZIONE DEL PCI IN UNE BRIGATA PARTIGIANA [Documents on the organization of the PCI in a partisan brigade]. *Movimento di Liberazione in Italia [Italy] 1966 (85): 56-72.* Presents 11 documents, letters, and minutes concerning the "Leo De Biasi" partisan brigade of Belluno in 1945. Documents show the care partisans took in accepting new members and the necessity they felt for self-criticism. The brigade was part of the Belluno Federation of the Italian Communist Party (PCI). Primary sources. C. Collon

2660. Scalpelli, Adolfo. MEMORIE DI MILITANTI COMUNISTI [Memoirs of Communist militants]. *Italia Contemporanea [Italy] 1974 26(116): 111-128.* On the 50th anniversary of the Italian Communist Party (PCI), the author discusses a considerable number of memoirs written by old Communists. The figures of Antonio Gramsci and Palmiro Togliatti loom large in the pages of those reminiscences. The memoirs add a personal dimension to the "objective" events with which they deal. The author points out that such unofficial, free-wheeling autobiographies would be unthinkable in Eastern Europe, or even in other Western European Communist parties; that they appear is evidence of the uniqueness of the PCI among Communist parties. J. C. Billigmeier

2661. Schilardi, Gianni. ORIGINE E SVILUPPO DEL PARTITO A GALATINA [Origin and development of the Party in Galatina]. *Ann. dell'Istituto Giangiacomo Feltrinelli [Italy] 1981 21: 1117-1139.* Galatina was a large agricultural center in the province of Terra d'Otranto, which before the Fascist period comprised the territories of the present provinces of Lecce, Brindisi, and Taranto. Describes the growth of the Communist Party in this city, which had known the Socialist Party since the 1890's and many economic and social changes since then. 53 notes. J. V. Coutinho

2662. Sebastiani, Chiara. ORGANI DIRIGENTI NAZIONALI: FUNZIONI, ANALISI E DATI [National leadership organs: their functions, data and analysis]. *Ann. dell'Istituto Giangiacomo Feltrinelli [Italy] 1981 21: 83-119.* Studies the structure and function of the national leadership organs of the Italian Communist Party, using both empirical indicators and a formal-institutional analytical concept. Seeks to illuminate "latent" functions of these organs through a comparative historical analysis. 40 notes, 3 tables, 3 charts. J. V. Coutinho

2663. Sebastiani, Chiara. ORGANI DIRIGENTI NAZIONALI: COMPOSIZIONE, MECCANISMI DI FORMAZIONE E DI EVOLUZIONE: 1945-1979 [National leadership organs: composition and training and development mechanisms, 1945-79]. *Ann. dell'Istituto Giangiacomo Feltrinelli [Italy] 1981 21: 387-444.* Focuses on the Italian Communist Party's directing organs and their evolution in the postwar period. It studies the Central Committee, the Direction and the Secretariat of the Party in sociological terms, in terms of structure, historical evolution, social composition, models of authority, and continuity and change. 71 notes, 7 tables, 4 charts. J. V. Coutinho

2664. Segre, Sergio. THE "COMMUNIST QUESTION" IN ITALY. *Foreign Affairs 1976 54(4): 691-707.* Examines the three cycles of Italian political history since 1945, the role of the Communist Party, and the Party's domestic and international goals. PCI General Secretary Enrico Berlinguer's "historic compromise" calls for "convergence and collaboration among all the democratic and popular forces" in Italy in order to avoid a Left-Right confrontation as occurred earlier in Chile. The Communist Party's success at the polls (18.9% in 1946 to 35.3% in 1975) increased not only its prestige but its credibility as a responsible governing force. The author, himself a Communist, is aware of the new sources of Party strength and indicates that the separate path it has taken from Moscow is irrevocable. 6 notes. C. W. Olson

2665. Seidelman, Raymond. PROTEST THEORIES AND THE LEFT IN POWER: ITALIAN CITIES UNDER COMMUNIST RULE. *West European Politics [Great Britain] 1984 7(3): 43-63.* A theory that social protest pay be diffused by timely reforms was contradicted by the experiences of the Italian Communist Party (PCI) in response to protests in three cities that it controlled after 1975: Florence, Naples, and Turin.

2666. Seidelman, Raymond. URBAN MOVEMENTS AND COMMUNIST POWER IN FLORENCE. *Comparative Pol. 1981 13(4): 437-459.* Discusses the performance of the Italian Communist Party (PCI) in control of Florence's city government, focusing on the effects of the Party's policy initiatives on its own organization and urban movements in Florence. Decentralization of urban government to popularly elected neighborhood councils has been a major Communist initiative. The political and social transformation sought by the Communists in Florence has been inhibited by the party's own reforms, and this is seen as indicative of the problems that the party will face at the national level. Based on questionnaires, interviews, and newspapers; 37 notes. M. A. Kascus

2667. Seidelman, Raymond Michael. "Neighborhood Communism in Florence: Goals and Dilemmas of the Italian Road to Socialism." Cornell U. 1979. 422 pp. *DAI 1979 39(11): 6945-6946-A.* 7910778

2668. Serfaty, Simon. THE ITALIAN COMMUNIST PARTY AND EUROPE: HISTORICALLY COMPROMISED? *Atlantic Community Q. 1977 15(3): 275-287.* The growth of the Italian Communist Party (PCI) and the related decline of the Christian Democratic Party (DC) "has been the result of the steady and progressive deterioration of the administrative, economic and social fabric of Italy" and "has not been the result of a growing support for communist ideology proper." J/S

2669. Serfaty, Simon and Gray, Lawrence, ed. *The Italian Communist Party: Yesterday, Today, and Tomorrow.* Contributions in Political Science, no. 46. Westport, Conn.: Greenwood, 1980. 256 pp.

2670. Serri, Rino. L'ORGANIZZAZIONE GIOVANILE: 1945-1968 [The youth organization, 1945-68]. *Ann. dell'Istituto Giangiacomo Feltrinelli [Italy] 1981 21: 767-781.* In the immediate postwar years there was no independent Communist youth organization but only a national unitary youth front. The Communist organization was revived in 1949 in the context of the increased class conflict and the Cold War. It did not have much success, though the Party succeeded in establishing some rapport with youth. Analyzes internal and external factors influencing events during the period under study. 21 notes. J. V. Coutinho

2671. Smirnov, G. P. ITAL'IANSKAIA KOMMUNISTICHESKAIA PARTIIA (K 60-LETIIU SO DNIA OSNOVANIIA) [The 60th anniversary of the founding of the Italian Communist Party]. *Voprosy Istorii KPSS [USSR] 1981 (1): 95-98.* Outlines the basic features of the development of the Italian Communist Party since its creation in 1921, emphasizing its essential unity despite certain recurrent internal contradictions. The Party owed its origins to the workers' disenchantment with the ineffective polices of the Italian Socialist Party. Initially the Party was in the hands of Bordiga who was critical of Lenin and caused a split in the rank and file. The majority of the workers rallied around Togliatti and Gramsci in 1926. Thereafter the Party adopted a strong anti-Fascist policy, becoming more internationally oriented in the 1930's. World War II forced the Communists to become more inward looking and they played a big part in organizing the resistance. After the war Togliatti attempted to widen the Party's appeal and it has played a major role in initiating much needed reforms. 4 notes. A. Brown

2672. Smirnov, G. P. PAL'MIRO TOL'IATTI—BORETS ZA MIR, DEMOKRATIIU I SOTSIALIZMA: K 90-LETIIU SO DNIIA ROZHDENIIA [Palmiro Togliatti—fighter for peace, democracy, and socialism: on the 90th anniversary of his birth]. *Voprosy Istorii KPSS [USSR] 1983 (3): 111-114.* Traces the biography of prominent Italian Communist Palmiro Togliatti, his activities in Spain during the Civil War; his stay in the USSR, 1940-44; and examines the main themes of his speeches and writings. 12 notes. G. Dombrovski

2673. Smith, E. Timothy. THE FEAR OF SUBVERSION: THE UNITED STATES AND THE INCLUSION OF ITALY IN THE NORTH ATLANTIC TREATY. *Diplomatic Hist. 1983 7(2): 139-155.* Italy, with the largest Communist Party in the West, was brought into NATO primarily to prevent its communization through subversion. Initially, most Europeans opposed Italian participation because Italy was not a North Atlantic nation, because it might prove to be a military liability, and because it could use the alliance to circumvent the arms limitation clauses of the 1946 peace treaty. France supported Italy due to its territorial proximity. After Italy requested membership, the other allies left the decision to the United States. After considerable debate, the United States supported Italy in order to bolster that nation's pro-Western politicians. Based on US State Department records and other primary sources; 73 notes. T. J. Heston

2674. Sodaro, Michael J. THE ITALIAN COMMUNISTS AND THE POLITICS OF AUSTERITY. *Studies in Comparative Communism 1980 13(2-3): 220-249.* The Italian Communist Party's (PCI) move to adopt austerity in the mid-1970's met opposition from rank-and-file union members. The 1976 election results indicate that the party's call for worker restraint did not produce electoral results. Still, the anti-inflation policy of the PCI, directly opposite to that of the Communist Party of France (PCF), appears to be a permanent accommodation of the party to Italy's difficulties. The policy was the basis for the party's arrangement with the Christian Democrats. 66 notes. D. Balmuth

2675. Spriano, Paolo. LA POLITICA DEL PARTITO COMUNISTA ITALIANO DALLA RESISTENZA ALLA REPUBBLICA [Italian Communist Party policy from Resistance to Republic]. *Storia e Politica [Italy] 1975 14(1-2): 266-281.* Italian Communists accepted the tactic of the national fronts against the Germans and Fascists. Therefore they cooperated not only with Socialists, but also with Catholics and Liberals. For the unity of the national front, the Communists set aside the choice between monarchy and republic until the referendum of 2 June 1946. A. Canavero

2676. Spriano, Paolo. LE RIFLESSIONI DEI COMUNISTI ITALIANI SULLE SOCIETA DELL' EST E IL "SOCIALISMO REALE" [The reflections of Italian Communists on the society of the East and "real socialism"]. *Studi Storici [Italy] 1982 23(1): 51-74.* Surveys Italian Communist criticism of socialist government activities in countries such as Poland and Czechoslovakia from 1967 to the present. The survey demonstrates the need for a new synthesis of ideas to make possible a genuine and complete critique of those activities. This synthesis must take into account the relationship between socialism and democracy, and between the laboring class and others in a socialist society. Such a synthesis would be valuable for every group that is dedicated to the ideal of socialism. Primary sources; 55 notes. E. E. Ryan

2677. Stehle, Hansjakob. THE ITALIAN COMMUNISTS ON THE PARLIAMENTARY PATH TO POWER. *World Today [Great Britain] 1978 34(5): 175-183.* Chronicles the growth in political power of the Communist Party in Italy's Parliament as witnessed by concessions made by the ruling Christian Democrats, 1976-78.

2678. Stehle, Hansjakob. ITALIEN: NOCH EINMAL EIN "KLEINER KOMPROMISS." DIE WACHSENDE MITBETEILIGUNG DER KOMMUNISTEN AN DER MACHT [Italy, once again a "small compromise": the Communists' growing power participation]. *Europa Archiv [West Germany] 1978 33(7): 213-220.* Since the election success of the Communists in 1976, the Italian Christian Democratic Party has negotiated two agreements with the Communist Party which has brought it into almost full participation in government decisionmaking.

2679. Stehle, Hansjakob. TOGLIATTI, STALIN UND DER ITALIENISCHE KOMMUNISMUS 1943-1948 [Togliatti, Stalin, and Italian communism, 1943-48]. *Quellen und Forschungen aus Italienischen Arch. und Bibliotheken [Italy] 1982 62: 319-335.* The policies of the Italian Communist Party after World War II were largely determined by their relation to Stalin. Palmiro Togliatti followed his directive to compromise and construct an antifascist democracy. Since he expected this policy to continue, believing the constitution of 1948 was the only means to Italian unity, the Cold War caught him by surprise. The more he professed his adherence to the republic, the more he was distrusted. His "Italian way" was caught between the increasing dependence of the Christian Democrats on the United States and events in Eastern Europe, and ultimately led to the isolation of his party within Italy. 27 notes. Italian abstract. T. F. Mayer

2680. Stern, Alan J. THE ITALIAN CP AT THE GRASS ROOTS. *Problems of Communism 1974 23(2): 42-54.* Explores the subject of popular support and organization of the Italian Communist Party (PCI), focusing on the so-called "Red Belt" of Emilia-Romagna, Tuscany, and Umbria. The apparent stagnation in the growth of the PCI that appeared by the 1972 elections would seem to be ready to change when and if the PCI decides to champion social reforms in the structure of Italian society. Based on primary and secondary sources; map, table, 28 notes. J. M. Lauber

2681. Stern, Alan J. RUDIMENTARY POLITICAL BELIEF SYSTEMS IN FOUR ITALIAN COMMUNITIES. *J. of Pol. 1975 37(1): 235-261.* A comparative study of the political ideas of party militants in four Italian towns, selected to isolate socioeconomic setting and partisan domination as independent variables. Finds no regular association of economic or administrative environment and belief patterns. Among Christian Democratic local elites, there are some indications of beliefs serving to identify goals for community policies. But for the Communist activists, political ideas serve three personal needs. They are cultural and historical placement, surrogate education, and social ties. The flexibility of the national organization of the Communist Party is hampered by the strong commitments of this grass-roots leadership to established political ideas. The article calls attention to the desirability of studying the way other individuals use political beliefs to serve their personal needs. J

2682. Tarrow, Sidney. ITALIAN COMMUNISM: THE OLD AND THE NEW. *Dissent 1977 24(1): 54-60.* Traces the periods of crisis in the Communist Party of Italy since its inception in 1920, concluding that the "historical compromise" strategy of the present secretary, Enrico Berlinguer, is not a sharp break with the party's past.

2683. Tempestini, Attilio. INDIPENDENTI DI SINISTRA E PCI. UN PRIMO CONFRONTO DEL LORO COMPORTAMENTO LEGISLATIVO [The independent Left and the PCI: a first comparison of their legislative behavior]. *Riv. Italiana di Scienza Pol. [Italy] 1978 8(1): 113-134.* Among the parliamentary groups in the Italian Senate, there is an original and interesting one: the Independent Left. This group does not correspond, as in general do the others, to a party active in the country, and it is composed almost in its entirety by senators elected as "independent,"—i.e., not registered in the lists of the Italian Communist Party (PCI). The author explores the relation between the activities of the Independent Left and that of the PCI by examining the votes on the laws, creating a classification of the cases in which the votes don't coincide. Concludes that the Independent Left's existence is profitable for the PCI. J

2684. Timmermann, Heinz. DIE ITALIENISCHEN KOMMUNISTEN UND IHRE AUSSENPOLITISCHE KONZEPTION [The Italian Communists and their foreign political concept]. *Europa Archiv [West Germany] 1971 26(21): 751-760.* By the late 1950's, the Italian Communists had developed an independent policy line promoting an end to the status quo of the Cold War.

2685. Timmermann, Heinz. DIE KPI: PROFIL EINER EUROKOMMUNISTISCHEN PARTEI IN DER REGIERUNGSMEHRHEIT [The CPI: profile of a Euro-Communist party in a government majority]. *Osteuropa [West Germany] 1978 28(5): 415-428, (6): 511-523.* Part I. Discusses the social structure of the Italian Communist Party, and the Italian Communist labor unions and related organizations, 1946-76. Part II. After 1956, the Italian Communist Party's program was revised to demand democratic economic progress, political decisions for the whole people, political democracy, the establishment of a socialist state, and a more positive policy concerning NATO.

2686. Todero, Frigyes. LOS PARTIDOS Y LAS ELECCIONES EN ITALIA [Parties and elections in Italy]. *Estudios Pol. [Mexico] 1977 3(11): 47-62.* An analysis of changing political forces in Italy, 1946-76. Postwar Italian politics has been a contest between the Christian Democratic Party and the Communist Party. Enjoying the support of the Church, the Christian Democratic Party had maintained power without an electoral majority. Parliamentary elections of 1976, in which left-wing parties garnered pluralities in both the Senate and Chamber of Representatives, broke the traditional domination of the Christian Democrats, forcing them to take Communists and other left-wing political groups into the government. The rising strength of the Italian Left reflected increasing urbanization and industrialization. Based on seven studies of Italian politics; 10 tables. F. J. Shaw, Jr.

2687. Toniolo, D. "Il Compromesso Storico: Un Tentativo di Collaborazione tra Marxisti e non Marxisti" [The historic compromise: a collaboration attempt between Marxists and non-Marxists]. Pontificia U. Gregoriana [Vatican] 1979. 523 pp. *DAI-C 1981 41(3): 469; 5/3212c.*

2688. Tullio-Altan, Carlo. ATTEGGIAMENTI POLITICI E SOCIALI DEI GIOVANI IN ITALIA [Political and social attitudes of Italian youth]. *Riv. Italiana di Scienza Pol. [Italy] 1973 3(3): 581-609.* Supports the hypothesis of a deep gap between the ethical, political, and ideological values proposed by the Communist Party (PCI) and the strongly traditional cultural structure prevailing in Italian society. According to research on a representative sample of 7,530 14- to 25-year-old youths, the great majority of them are still bound to traditional values and reveal conservative attitudes in politics. This phenomenon is much more widespread among working class people and peasants than among the middle strata and in economically backward southern regions than in northern industrialized regions. Such a situation, in addition to explaining the relative failure of the PCI in its attempts to reach power democratically, also throws light on many features which are typical of Italian society. Finally, it poses serious problems for the parties representing sizable working class sectors, the PCI and the Christian Democrats above all, which must therefore reconcile the need for profound social reforms with the danger of losing touch with their traditional electorate, thus opening the way to undemocratic outcomes. J

2689. Urban, George. "HAVE THEY REALLY CHANGED?" A CONVERSATION WITH ALTIERO SPINELLI. *Encounter [Great Britain] 1978 50(1): 7-27.* Interview with Altiero Spinelli, an important member of the group that aided in the establishment of the European Economic Community, in which he discusses his recent move toward Communism, what communism means for Italy, and the present nature of Eurocommunism, 1976-78.

2690. Urban, Joan Barth. ITALIAN COMMUNISM AND THE "OPPORTUNISM OF CONCILIATION," 1927-1929. *Studies in Comparative Communism 1973 6(4): 362-396.* The gradualist strategy of the Italian Communist Party in the 1920's was opposed by a youthful faction headed by Luigi Longo. Under Stalin's aegis, the Comintern condemned Palmiro Togliatti for conciliating rightists. While ostensibly accepting this ruling, the Party refused to expel rightists and remained loyal to its leaders. In recent years the Party has accepted the goal of a pluralist socialist society and also condemned Soviet intervention in Czechoslovakia. Just as the party refused to support a purge of rightists in the 1920's, it has rejected a purge of leftists in the 1960's. 125 notes. D. Balmuth

2691. Urban, Joan Barth. MOSCOW AND THE PCI: KTO KOVO? *Studies in Comparative Communism 1980 13(2-3): 99-167.* Relations between the Communist Party of Italy (PCI) and the Party in the USSR since 1968 have been marked by increased Italian insistence on a "third way." Criticism of Soviet foreign and domestic policy has been interspersed with periods of reconciliation especially in the 1976 Berlin conference. Enrico Berlinguer was in Beijing (Peking) in April 1980 and the PCI was denouncing the invasion of Afghanistan. PCI policy has been dictated in part by domestic policy needs. The party now seems headed toward a left-of-center coalition. 204 notes. D. Balmuth

2692. Urban, Joan Barth. SOCIALIST PLURALISM IN SOVIET AND ITALIAN COMMUNIST PERSPECTIVE: THE CHILEAN CATALYST. *Orbis 1974 18(2): 482-510.* Discusses the attitudes of the Communist Party in Italy and the USSR, particularly in relation to the situation in Chile, 1970-73.

2693. Urban, Joan Barth. SOVIET POLICIES AND NEGOTIATING BEHAVIOR TOWARD NONRULING COMMUNIST PARTIES: THE CASE OF THE ITALIAN COMMUNIST PARTY. *Studies in Comparative Communism 1982 15(3): 184-211.* From the late 1960's, the Soviet Communist Party (CPSU) and the Italian Communists (PCI) have been in conflict on a number of issues: the PCI's "Historic compromise" and acceptance of pluralism, the Czech invasion, relations with the Chinese Communists, and Soviet actions in Afghanistan and Poland. The Soviets used polemic as well as concessions to win PCI support for its foreign policy. But when the PCI denounced Soviet actions in Poland and suggested that Soviet and American foreign policies were similar, *Pravda* denounced the "blasphemy" of the PCI. Now that the Soviets have support among national liberation movements, they may be less concerned about the support of the largest European Communist party. 70 notes. D. Balmuth

2694. Vasil'ev, G. V. PAL'MIRO TOL'IATTI [Palmiro Togliatti]. *Voprosy Istorii KPSS [USSR] 1963 (3): 83-87.* Examines the career of Palmiro Togliatti, his participation in the Italian socialist and Communist movements, and his contribution to the struggle for peace.

2695. Vasil'ev, S. D. V CHEST' 50-LETIIA ITAL'IANSKOI KOMPARTII [In honor of the 50th anniversary of the Italian Communist Party]. *Voprosy Istorii KPSS [USSR] 1971 (3): 150-153.* Outlines papers read at a conference of Soviet historians and leading members of the Italian Communist Party devoted to the history of the Italian Party, and held in Moscow in January 1971.

2696. Webb, A. J. K. THE EVOLUTION OF THE ATTITUDE OF THE ITALIAN COMMUNIST PARTY TOWARDS THE EUROPEAN ECONOMIC COMMUNITY. *Millennium [Great Britain] 1984 13(1): 45-56.* Traces the stages by which the Italian Communist Party moved from its initial hostility toward the European Economic Community to a state of complete acceptance. National, pragmatic, and ideological factors influenced this transformation, but the first two were of greater importance and determined the framework within which ideology was applied.

2697. Weber, Maria. QUINDICI ANNI DEL MOVIMENTO MARXISTA-LENINISTA IN ITALIA [Fifteen years of the Marxist-Leninist Movement in Italy]. *Mondo Cinese [Italy] 1977 5(3): 59-69.* Follows the tumultuous history of the Italian Marxist-Leninist Movement whose origins date from 1962. In that year Palmiro Togliatti severely criticized the Chinese delegation to the 10th congress of the Italian Communist Party. In response to this polemic several Marxist-Leninists formed their first newspaper in Padua called *Viva Il Leninismo.* The ensuing history of this movement is punctuated by continuous factionalism, purges, and schisms. This movement does, however, represent the first serious attempt to adopt Maoism in Italy. Based on documents of the Marxist-Leninist Movement and secondary sources; 29 notes. M. T. Wilson

2698. Wilson, David Luke. "The Italian Communist Party in Italian Politics, 1944-1948." Stanford U. 1979. 307 pp. *DAI 1980 40(9): 5147-A.* 8006372

2699. Wollemborg, Leo J. ITALO-COMMUNISM: THE COURSE OF "WESTERNIZATION." *Freedom at Issue 1978 (48): 12-18.* Traces the beginnings of the Westernization of the Communist Party of Italy (PCI) back to Antonio Gramsci in the 1930's and Palmiro Togliatti in the late 1940's and to Luigi Longo today, but points out that there are both domestic and Soviet pressures to be less accommodating to other Italian political parties.

2700. Yugov, L. ITALIAN POLICY AND RELAXATION IN EUROPE. *Int. Affairs [USSR] 1972 (10): 48-52.* Examines the relationship between internal political conflicts involving the Italian Communist Party and the conservative Christian Democrats and Italy's foreign policy toward the United States and NATO, 1960's-70's.

2701. Zanotti-Karp, Angela. ITALY'S NEW COMMUNISTS. *Worldview 1974 17(5): 41-45.* Discusses ideology, the youth movement, and working-class and intellectual participation in the Communist Party in Italy since 1968.

2702. Zülch, Rüdiger. DAS ITALIENISCHE PARTEIENSYSTEM UND DER "HISTORISCHE KOMPROMISS" [The Italian party system and the "historical compromise"]. *Zeitschrift für Politik [West Germany] 1975 22(4): 367-380.* Discusses the history and structure of the Italian party system in light of the proposed "historic compromise," a coalition between the Christian Democrats and the Italian Communists.

2703. —. DE GASPERI YESTERDAY AND TODAY. *Italy. Documents and Notes [Italy] 1975 24(2): 115-130.* A retrospective look at Alcide De Gasperi's leadership, praising him especially for his decision in 1947 to exclude the Socialists and Communists from the government.

2704. —. [DIALOGUE BETWEEN THE ROMAN CATHOLIC CHURCH AND ITALIAN COMMUNISM]. *Marxist Perspectives 1979 2(3): 90-117.*

Genovese, Eugene D. EDITOR'S NOTE, *pp. 90-91.*

Marzani, Carl. INTRODUCTION, *pp. 91-97.*

Betazzi, Luigi. CONCERN FOR THE FUTURE OF ITALY, *pp. 98-103.*

Berlinger, Enrico. THE IDEAL INSPIRATION OF THE PCI, *pp. 103-113.*

—. *OSSERVATORE ROMANO.* CONSIDERATION AND REFLECTION, *pp. 113-117.*

Presents documents originally published in 1977 that express the increasing dialogue between the Roman Catholic Church and the Italian Communist Party (PCI), a dialogue whose beginnings go back to changes in the attitudes of Pope John XXIII in 1958 and PCI General Secretary Palmiro Togliatti in 1954.

2705. —. IN DEFENSE OF THE ITALIAN CP. *Monthly Rev. 1977 29(2): 1-24.*

Marzani, Carl, *pp. 1-8.*

Gordon, Max, *pp. 8-15.* Refute comments in articles entitled "The New Revisionism," *Monthly Rev.* 28 (2,6), and defend the goals and actions of the Communist Party in Italy.

Sweezy, Paul M. and Magdoff, Harry, THE EDITORS REPLY, *pp. 15-24.*

2706. —. ÖTVENÉVES AZ OLASZ KOMMUNISTA PÁRT [The Italian Communist Party is 50 years old]. *Társadalmi Szemle [Hungary] 1971 26(2): 58-60.* Describes Party history in Italy, 1921-69.

West Germany

2707. Bachman, Kurt. GEORGI DIMITROV ZHIVEE V ISTORIIATA I NASTOIASHTETO [Georgi Dimitrov lives in history and in the present]. *Izvestiia na Inst. po Istoriia na BKP [Bulgaria] 1982 46: 317-327.* The Communist Party in West Germany has learned much from Georgi Dimitrov and his works and activities during the decades of struggle against fascism and reaction.

2708. Badia, Gilbert. LE PARTI COMMUNISTE ALLEMAND. DEUTSCHE KOMMUNISTISCHE PARTEI (D.K.P.) [The German Communist Party (DKP)]. *Rev. d'Allemagne [France] 1970 2(2): 251-263.* In spring 1968, a new party was formed in West Germany: the *Deutsche Kommunistische Partei* [German Communist Party]. It replaced the old *Kommunistische Partei Deutschlands,* which was outlawed in the early 1950's. While fully Communist in ideology, the new Party tried to give the impression of being different from the old. 47 notes. J. C. Billigmeier

2709. Ezhov, Vsevolod Dmitrievich. GERMANSKAIA KOMMUNISTICHESKAIA PARTIIA: OBRAZOVANIE, TSELI, PUT' BOR'BY [The Communist Party of West Germany: its formation, aims, and struggle]. *Novaia i Noveishaia Istoriia [USSR] 1980 (4): 23-39.* The formation of a legal Communist Party in West Germany was agreed to in 1968, reflecting the easing of Cold War tensions. Outlawed by the Adenauer government in 1956, it had continued to exist and function. The Party pursues the aims of socialism and antimonopolism in West Germany and opposes the massive expenditure on militarism and NATO. It favors closer links with East Germany and the USSR but is under constant attack from reactionary elements. It is international in outlook and an active participant in the international Communist movement. 55 notes.

J. S. S. Charles

2710. Fisch, Horst. 15 JAHRE DKP. KAMPF UM FRIEDEN UND SOZIALEN FORTSCHRITT [15 years of the German Communist Party: the struggle for peace and social progress]. *Beiträge zur Gesch. der Arbeiterbewegung [East Germany] 1983 25(5): 647-658.* Traces the evolution and development of the German Communist Party, which was established in the German Federal Republic in September 1968. The author examines the party's role and responsibilities in West Germany, 1968-83, and its origins in the 19th-century German revolutionary tradition. Discusses its trade union and political activities and the conditions that produced its legalization in the late 1960's, party ideology and activities, and its increased membership. Based on Communist Party documents and other primary and secondary sources; 22 notes.

G. L. Neville

2711. Fromme, Friedrich K. SE DÉFENDRE CONTRE LES ENNEMIS DE LA CONSTITUTION [Self-defense against the enemies of the constitution]. *Documents [France] 1976 31(6): 80-91.* Outlines the growth of communism in the German Communist Party and the Communist League in West Germany, 1945-74, discussing their threat to the existing democratic and liberal order.

2712. Hajdú, János. BELPOLITIKAI ERŐPRÓBA AZ NSZK-BAN [Internal trial of strength in West Germany]. *Társadalmi Szemle [Hungary] 1972 27(1): 47-52.* Investigates financial and economic policy in West Germany, 1966-71, with reference to the Communist Party's position in 1971 and West Germany's policy toward Eastern Europe.

2713. Hub, Rudolf. GESCHICHTE DER KPD IN SCHULGESCHICHTSBÜCHERN IN DER BRD [The history of the German Communist Party in history textbooks in the German Federal Republic]. *Beiträge zur Gesch. der Arbeiterbewegung [East Germany] 1980 22(4): 574-587.* Examines West German history textbooks written during the 1970's and their treatment of the history of the German Communist Party (KPD). He considers the place and value of the history of the German Communist Party in West German textbooks; the treatment of the November Revolution 1918-19 and the founding of the KPD, the Party's struggles during the Weimar years, and its attitude to fascism and war. All the themes considered in West German textbooks work against a change of society; they are unscientific and falsified and present an imperialist picture of history. Based on 96 history and sociology textbooks published beween 1970 and 1978 and secondary sources; 65 notes. G. L. Neville

2714. Jaworski, Ludwik. RUCH KOMUNISTYCZNY W NIEMCZECH ZACHODNICH W LATACH 1945-1968 [The Communist movement in West Germany, 1945-68]. *Z Pola Walki [Poland] 1977 20(1): 69-93.* The Communist Party of Germany (KPD) revived after the triumph of the USSR and other states of the anti-Nazi coalition. The defeat of fascism created conditions for deep social and economic transformations to be realized on ruins of the Third Reich according to resolutions of the Potsdam Conference. The author discusses subsequent activities of the KPD in Western occupation zones, the Cold War policy of Western powers, and the anti-Communist attitude of the rightist leadership of the Social Democratic Party (SPD). After the establishment of the Federal Republic of Germany in 1949, the activities of Communists faced greater and greater obstacles. An anti-Communist campaign led by the Christian Democratic Party resulted in a judgment issued on 17 August 1956 by the Federal Constitutional Tribunal in Karlsruhe banning activities of the Communist Party of Germany. Being declared illegal, the Communist Party was again forced to go underground. During this period the party realized numerous propaganda actions and campaigns and continued the struggle for the reinstatement of its legality. Positions won by KPD among working class and in progressive public opinion enabled the party in 1968 to establish itself legally as the German Communist Party (DKP). J/S

2715. Kimura, Seiji. DOITSU RENGO KYŌWA KOKU NI OKERU SAIKIN NO KYŌSANTŌSHI KENKY TO SHIRYŌ JŌKYŌ [Recent studies on the history of the Communist Party and the state of its historical documentation in West Germany]. *Shigaku Zasshi [Japan] 1970 79(11): 68-79.*

2716. Klemm, Annemarie. CHARAKTER UND WIRKSAMKEIT DES DEMOKRATISCHEN AKTIONS- UND WAHLBÜNDNISSES ZUR BUNDESTAGWAHL 1969 IN DER BRD [Character and effectiveness of the Democratic Action and Election Alliance of 1969 in West Germany]. *Beiträge zur Geschichte der Arbeiterbewegung [East Germany] 1978 20(1): 100-110.* In the late 1960's democratic forces in West Germany increased their pressure on the "grand coalition" and its reactionary monopolistic policies. In 1968 a wide spectrum of progressives, led by the reconstituted German Communist Party, united in the Democratic Action and Election Alliance to contest the 1969 parliamentary election. The program of the alliance called for recognition of East Germany, a pacific foreign policy, and democracy and socialism in West Germany. Despite limited electoral success, the alliance was effective in ending the grand coalition, forcing a more realistic foreign policy, and introducing crucial issues into the political debate. Based on newspapers, journals, and secondary works; 20 notes. J. B. Street

2717. Korolev, B. I. KAK "OSTFORSHUNG" FAL'SIFITSIRUET PROGRAMMU KPSS [How *Ostforschung* falsifies the Communist Party of the Soviet Union (CPSU) program]. *Istoriia SSSR [USSR] 1963 7(2): 180-204.* Review article. Takes issue with Soviet studies by West German imperialist ideologues, in particular Boris Meissner's *Das Parteiprogramm der KPdSU 1903-1961* (1962) and Günther Wagenlehner's "Das neue Programm der KPdSU" *(Osteuropa,* 1962 12(1-2): 25-42). 43 notes. N. Frenkley

2718. Mietkowska-Kaiser, Ines. DIE "GEISTIGE OSTFRONT": WESTDEUTSCHE POLITISCH-IDEOLOGISCHE ZENTREN DER PSYCHOLOGISCHEN KRIEGFÜHRUNG [The "intellectual Eastern front": West German political-ideological centers of psychological warfare]. *Jahrbuch für Geschichte der Sozialistischen Länder Europas [East Germany] 1970 14(2): 137-165.* Provides a background to the founding, organization, financing, membership, areas of specialization, and goals of 11 leading research institutes in West Germany devoted to Eastern European and Soviet studies. Argues that these institutes are controlled by the West German State and that they pursue anti-Communist psychological warfare against the socialist bloc. Based on published parliamentary documents, government press bulletins, journals, and secondary sources; 64 notes. J. B. Street

2719. Moryganov, I. V. BOEVOI AVANGARD RABOCHEGO KLASSA F.R.G. [The militant vanguard of the West German working class]. *Voprosy Istorii KPSS [USSR] 1964 (1): 69-73.* The history of the German Communist Party since 1919 shows that despite having been subject to terror and unrestrained anti-Communist propaganda it remains a vital fighting force showing the strength of the idea of communism in Germany. 8 notes.

2720. Papenko, N. S. DO ISTORII STVORENNIA NIMETS'KOI KOMUNISTYCHNOI PARTII [The creation of the German Communist Party]. *Ukrains'kyi Istorychnyi Zhurnal [USSR] 1978 (11): 114-117.* The West German Communist Party's birth as a legal Marxist-Leninist political organization began in fall 1968 under difficult conditions due to the strengthened positions of imperialism and militarism. Banned in 1956, the Party campaigned clandestinely for legalization. In the program documents for the first legal congress in 1969, the Party stated what needed to be done to strengthen socialism and protect the workers' economic and political rights. 21 notes. V. Packer

2721. Probst, Ulrich. DIE KOMMUNISTISCHEN PARTEIEN DER BUNDESREPUBLIK DEUTSCHLAND [The Communist parties of the German Federal Republic]. *Zeits. für Pol. [West Germany] 1979 26(1): 59-96.* Surveys the West German Left, including details about radicals and radicalism, Communist parties and movements, and other political parties.

2722. Ruch, Ursula. DIE ANTIKOMMUNISTISCHE VERFÄLSCHUNG DES REALEN SOZIALISMUS DURCH DEN TROTZKISMUS [The anticommunist falsification of real socialism by Trotskyism]. *Martin-Luther-Universität Halle-Wittenberg. Wissenschaftliche Zeitschrift. Gesellschafts- und Sprachwissenschaftliche Reihe [East Germany] 1975 24(4): 5-15.* The renaissance of Trotskyism in West Germany in the 1960's-70's is interpreted as part of the anticommunist intellectual strategy directed against the USSR. R. Wagnleitner

2723. Rykin, V. S. GERBERT MIS [Herbert Mies]. *Voprosy Istorii KPSS [USSR] 1979 (3): 121-124.* A biographical sketch of Herbert Mies (1929-), member of the German Communist Party since 1945 and chairman of the Communist Party of West Germany since 1973. Mies has consistently fought for the existence of a Communist Party in West Germany, for the preservation of socialism in the countries of East Europe, and for detente. Based on published documents; 7 notes. L. E. Holmes

2724. Vogelsang, Thilo. EINFÜHRUNG IN DIE PROBLEMATIK [Introduction to the issues]. *Vierteljahrshefte für Zeitgeschichte [West Germany] 1973 21(2): 166-170.* Introduces an issue examining the main topics of historiography on the immediate postwar period in West Germany. The worldwide anti-Hitler coalition was replaced by the formation of an anti-Communist bloc. The majority of the people soon found themselves in agreement with the Western Allies who promised political stability. The anti-Communist bias further contributed to the restorative disposition and fostered the consciousness of continuity among the compromised middle class. 4 notes. U. Wengenroth

2725. Yergin, Angela Stent. WEST GERMANY'S SÜDPOLITIK: SOCIAL DEMOCRATS AND EUROCOMMUNISM. *Orbis 1979 23(1): 51-71.* Analyzes the German Social Democratic Party's relations with Western Communist parties during the 1970's.

Iberian Peninsula

2726. Aguado Sánchez, Francisco. EL TORNO AL BANDOLERISMO COMUNISTA: HACIA UNA HISTORIA GENERAL DEL MISMO [On communist banditry: toward a history of the movement]. *Rev. de Estudios Hist. de la Guardia Civil [Spain] 1972 5(9): 115-156, (10): 77-159.* Studies attempts at armed revolt in Spain between 1943 and 1952 by the Maquis, an exclusively Communist Party organization and so-called in imitation of the French movement. Portrays Spain's Republican exiles in France who participated in the Forces Françaises de l'Intérieur as the Agrupación de Guerrilleros Españoles. Infiltration through frontier passes began in October 1944. Crossover zones and episodes of the struggle in various provinces as well as the Agrupación de Guerrilleros del Centro y Extremadura are examined. The author gives statistics on the Guardia Civil's acts of suppression, noting that 624 corps members died along with more than 5,000 insurgents. A. L. (IHE 87446)

2727. Ardiaca, Pere. RECORD DE L'AMIC JOSEP MOIX [Remembrance of a friend, Joseph Moix]. *Serra d'Or [Spain] 1974 16(176): 33-35.* Evokes the political personality of Josep Moix i Regàs (b. 1898), who died in Prague in 1973. He was one of the directors of the Sabadell Local Union Federation—affiliated with the National Confederation of Labor (CNT), and in 1937 with the General Workers' Union (UGT)—mayor of Sabadell, director general of labor in the government of the Generalitat, and as a member of the Unified Socialist-Communist Party of Catalonia, named labor minister by Juan Negrín. M. Cl. (IHE 95894)

2728. Avramova, Bistra; Venetsanopoulos, Vasilis; and Kadulin, Vladimir. AVANTE, CAMARADA, AVANTE! PORTUGUESE SPEAK OF THEIR LIFE, THEIR COUNTRY, THEIR REVOLUTION. *World Marxist R. 1975 18(3): 57-84.* Discusses politics, economic conditions, and the Communist Party since 1974 in Portugal.

2729. Avtonomov, A. S. PERESMOTR KONSTITUTSII PORTUGALII [Revision of the Portuguese constitution]. *Sovetskoe Gosudarstvo i Pravo [USSR] 1983 (12): 90-96.* The Portuguese constitution of 1976, reflecting immediate postrevolutionary political groupings, was revised in succeeding years under pressure from right-wing parties, but democratic opposition headed by the Portuguese Communist Party prevented the achievements of the April 1974 revolution from being destroyed.

2730. Brown, Douglas. IBERIAN COMMUNISM. *Int. Rev. [Great Britain] 1974 (3): 49-54.* Discusses the growing influence of communism in the politics of Spain and Portugal, 1958-70's, emphasizing the role of the military and attitudes toward revolution.

2731. Camiller, Patrick. THE ECLIPSE OF SPANISH COMMUNISM. *New Left Review [Great Britain] 1984 (147): 122-128.* Reviews Santiago Carrillo's *Memoría de la Transición* (1983), Fernando Claudín's *Santiago Carrillo: Crónica de un Secretario General* (1983), and Manuel Azcárate's *Crisis del Eurocomunismo* (1982). They consider the declining influence of the Communist Party of Spain.

2732. Cunhal, A. PORTUGAL'S NEW ROAD. *World Marxist R. 1975 18(3): 23-28.* Discusses the economic conditions, politics, and the role of the Communist Party since the 1974 revolution.

2733. Cunhal, Alvaro. THE GREAT OCTOBER AND THE WORLD REVOLUTIONARY PROCESS. *World Marxist Rev. 1977 20(12): 14-22.* Traces the inspiration derived from the USSR's October Revolution by the Communists in Portugal and traces the history of the Portuguese Communist Party.

2734. Danilenko, V. N. and Iastrzhembski, S. V. GOSUDARSTVENNO-PRAVOVOE RAZVITIE PORTUGALII POSLE 25 APRELIA 1974 G. [The development of the state and legal system in Portugal after 25 April 1974]. *Sovetskoe Gosudarstvo i Pravo [USSR] 1978 (2): 115-120.* Describes the political situation in Portugal after the overthrow of the fascist dictatorship on 25 April 1974: the political differences between military and civilian interests and left- and right-wing parties; the democratic program of the Portuguese Communist Party; the socioeconomic and electoral reforms under the five provisional governments; and the abortive attempts of rightists, supported by capitalist countries, to undermine the progress achieved by the Communist Party, the working class, and left-wing military forces. Discusses the constitution of 1976 with its deliberate ambiguities and compromises, and the results of the parliamentary and presidential elections of April and June 1976 respectively. 22 notes. N. Frenkley

2735. Fasting, Christian. PORTUGALS KOMMUNISTISKE PARTI [Portugal's Communist Party]. *Samtiden [Norway] 1975 84(1): 24-28.* Outlines the history of the Portuguese Communist Party from 1921 to the present. R. G. Selleck

2736. García Cotarelo, Ramón. LA VICISITUDES DEL COMUNISMO ESPAÑOL Y SU HISTORIOGRAFÍA [The vicissitudes of Spanish communism and its historiography]. *Rev. de Estudios Pol. [Spain] 1978 (3): 133-141.* Reviews Joan Estruch's *Historia del PCE (1) (1920-1939)* (1978), Pelai Pagés's *Historia del Partido Comunista de España* (1978), and Fernando Claudín's *Documentos de una Divergencia Comunista* (1978), which deal with the "Stalinism" of the Spanish Communist Party, and find it not so much a product of the Civil War as of the conditions of clandestine activity and repression within which the Party has had to operate.
N. A. Rosenblatt

2737. Gelautz, B. I. "Die Rolle der Demokratie in Theorie und Politik der Komunisten in Spanien" [The role of democracy in the theory and policy of Spanish Communists]. U. of Vienna 1982. 478 pp. *DAI-C 1984 45(3): 689; 9/2814c.*

2738. Georgiev, Tsonko. POLITIKATA NA ISPANSKATA KOMUNISTICHESKA PARTIIA ZA SVALIANETO NA FRANKIZMA PREZ PURVATA POLOVINA NA 70-TE GODINI [The policies of the Spanish Communist Party in the decline of Francoism during the first half of the 1970's]. *Izvestiia na Inst. po Istoriia na BKP [Bulgaria] 1982 (47): 354-368.* From 1970 to 1975 the Spanish Communist Party fought against Franco's dictatorship, for democratic freedoms, social justice, and international policies of peaceful coexistence. 44 notes.

2739. Grayson, George W. PORTUGAL AND THE ARMED FORCES MOVEMENT. *Orbis 1975 19(2) 335-378.* Discusses the 1974 coup d'etat by young officers of the Armed Forces Movement in Portugal and the threat of dictatorship by the Communist Party.

2740. Grayson, George W. PORTUGAL AND THE FUTURE. *Current Hist. 1975 68(403): 109-113.*

2741. Hammond, John L. PORTUGAL'S COMMUNISTS AND THE REVOLUTION. *Radical Hist. Rev. 1980 (23): 140-161.* Discusses the support by the Portuguese Communist Party (PCP) for the Armed Forces Movement's 1974 coup and the PCP's growing power up to and following the failed right-wing coup of March 1975.

2742. Hermet, Guy. LE PARTI COMMUNISTE D'ESPAGNE: LA SORTIE DU GHETTO? [The Communist Party of Spain: Leaving the ghetto?]. *Études Int. [Canada] 1975 6(3): 363-374.* Discusses the history of the Spanish Communist Party since the Popular Front emphasizing its relationship with the anarcho-syndicalists, workers' movements, and the middle class. Examines the party's role vis-à-vis the other forces opposing Franco and notes its liberal stance within the world Communist movement. 13 notes.
J. F. Harrington, Jr.

2743. Hermet, Guy. LE PORTUGAL, DE LA "RÉVOLUTION" À LA "REMISE EN ORDRE" [Portugal, from revolution to reorganization]. *Défense Natl. [France] 1976 32(4): 67-78.* Presents the background to the situation which ended Portuguese military-Communist adventurism on 25 November 1975, highlighting the lessons to be learned from it, and clarifying the reasons for its failure.

2744. Höch, Rudolf. RICHTUNGSSTREIT IM UNTERGRUND: DIE KOMMUNISTISCHE PARTEI SPANIENS UND IHR VERHÄLTNIS ZUR SOWJETISCHEN KP [Conflict over direction in the underground: the Communist Party of Spain and its relationship to the Soviet Communist Party]. *Frankfurter Hefte [West Germany] 1972 27(2): 81-84.* In the last 10 years the Communist Party of Spain has shown independence from the USSR, sympathizing publicly with Soviet dissidents sentenced to jail, condemning the Warsaw Pact invasion of Czechoslovakia, and excluding pro-Soviet members from the Party's central committee.

2745. Iastrzhembski, S. V. PORTUGAL'SKAIA KOMMUNISTICHESKAIA PARTIIA I NIZOVYE ORGANIZATSII TRUDIASHCHIKHSIA [The Portuguese Communist Party and local organizations of laborers]. *Voprosy Istorii KPSS [USSR] 1979 (6): 82-91.* Describes the Communist Party's role in three forms of local organizations created after the Portuguese revolution of 25 April 1974 and examines the functions of workers' committees, tenant committees, and popular assemblies. Often under the Party's leadership, workers' committees established control over factories and contributed to the nationalization of industry. Tenant committees took control of prices charged for housing and food. The Party encourages each local organization to adopt tactics designed to meet local needs, seeks to create tenant committees where there are

none, and rejects attempts by anarchists and Maoists to use popular assemblies as replacements for organs of state power. Based on published documents and periodical literature; 37 notes.
L. E. Holmes

2746. Iastrzhembski, S. V. VO GLAVE SIL MIRA I PROGRESSA [At the head of the forces of peace and progress]. *Voprosy Istorii KPSS [USSR] 1981 (3): 105-108.* The Portuguese Communist Party was founded 6 March 1921 in Lisbon and early contended with anarcho-syndicalism, a politically ignorant population, and from 28 May 1926 a dictatorial regime which turned fascist in 1929. Reviews Portuguese history since 1976 and the CP's stalwart part in educating workers and peasants, and in the forming of a progressive constitution. The party continues to grow, but rightist forces have regrouped. The worsening economic situation causes workers to see the value of the CP's socialist policies. Based on *Avante,* A. Cunhal's works, and the programs of the PCP; 20 notes.
A. J. Evans

2747. Iwiński, Tadeusz. FASZYZM HISZPAŃSKI I JEGO PRZECIWNICY [Spanish fascism and its enemies]. *Nowe Drogi [Poland] 1975 (12): 147-158.* Surveys the history of Francisco Franco's regime, 1939-75, its growing difficulties, and the growth of legal and illegal opposition parties, especially the Spanish Communist Party.

2748. Iwiński, Tadeusz. PORTUGALSKA PARTIA KOMUNISTYCZNA (1921-1978). ZARYS DZIAŁALNOŚCI I STRATEGII [Communist Party of Portugal, 1921-78: an outline of activities and strategy]. *Z Pola Walki [Poland] 1979 22(1): 81-109.* Discusses the history and problems of strategy of the Portuguese Communist Party (PCP), now one of the strongest in Western Europe. In its half century the PCP accumulated exceptionally rich and varied experiences in the long period of struggle against the fascist regime and the short but stormy and complicated recent period of legal activities, when the party participated in governmental cabinet.
J/S

2749. Kukushkin, Iu. M. BOR'BA PORTUGAL'SKIKH KOMMUNISTOV ZA OBEDINENIE DEMOKRATICHESKIKH SIL DLIA SVERZHENIIA FASHIZMA [Portuguese Communist Party in the struggle for democracy]. *Novaia i Noveishaia Istoriia [USSR] 1975 (1): 46-66.* The history of the Portuguese Communist Party reveals the growth and strengthening of the revolutionary consciousness of the Portuguese proletariat, its transformation into the main force in the struggle against fascism and for the restoration of democratic freedoms. The author makes an attempt to highlight the many years' struggle waged by the Portuguese Communist Party for antifascist unity, directed toward the overthrow of the fascist regime of Salazar and Caetano. This struggle led to the victory of democratic forces.
J

2750. Kukushkin, Y. M. KRAKH FASHISTSKOI DIKTATURY V PORTUGALII [The downfall of the fascist dictatorship in Portugal]. *Voprosy Istorii [USSR] 1975 (3): 96-116.* "Examines the economic and political reasons that led to the emergence of a revolutionary situation in Portugal, traces the gradual rise and spread of the 'captains' movement' and the process of its subsequent development into the Armed Forces Movement, and dwells on the democratic reforms carried out by the Provisional Revolutionary Government since the victory of the democratic revolution on April 25, 1974. The author analyzes the struggle carried on by the democratic forces against the reactionary elements who are doing everything they can to disrupt the revolutionary process, the policy steadfastly pursued by the Portuguese Communist Party with the aim of consolidating the democratic forces and promoting closer unity between the people and the Armed Forces Movement. The article also sums up the results of the Seventh Extraordinary Congress of the Portuguese Communist Party and the progress made in the nation-wide preparations for elections to the Constituent Assembly."
J

2751. Macleod, Alex. PORTRAIT OF A MODEL ALLY: THE PORTUGUESE COMMUNIST PARTY AND THE INTERNATIONAL COMMUNIST MOVEMENT, 1968-1983. *Studies in Comparative Communism 1984 (1): 31-52.* The Portuguese Communists supported Soviet policies in Afghanistan, Poland, and Czechoslovakia and also served as important spokesmen for communism in the former Portuguese African colonies. The second largest Communist Party in Western Europe controls 16-20% of the Portuguese electorate. The issues on which the Portuguese Communists support the USSR are not considered important by the voters who support the Portuguese Communists. 83 notes.
D. Balmuth

2752. Martin, Benjamin. SPANISH SOCIALISTS IN POWER. *Dissent 1984 31(1): 116-120.* Describes the decline of the Union of the Democratic Center (UCD) and the Communist Party (PCE), and the rise to power of the Socialist Workers' Party in the national elections of 28 October 1982, with the strength and will to govern despite the challenges of a restless military clique and economic problems.

2753. Maxwell, Kenneth. THE COMMUNISTS AND THE PORTUGUESE REVOLUTION. *Dissent 1980 27(2): 194-206.* Discusses the unrest within the Portuguese military that toppled the government, the development of the Communist Party, and the rising strength of the Socialists between 1974 and 1980.

2754. Mendes, Catarina. THE DAWN OF FREEDOM. *World Marxist R. [Canada] 1974 17(7): 95-98.* Analyzes the problems, government activities, and the Communist Party's role following the military coup d'etat in Portugal in April 1974.

2755. Mendes, Catarina. PORTUGAL CASTS OFF FASCISM. *World Marxist R. [Canada] 1974 17(6): 25-28.* Reports on the causes of Portugal's revolution in April 1974 and the Communist Party's participation.

2756. Meshcheriakov, M. T. DOLORES IBARRURI [Dolores Ibarruri]. *Voprosy Istorii KPSS [USSR] 1975 (12): 118-122.* A biographical account of Dolores Ibarruri (b. 1895), member of the Spanish Communist Party since its inception in 1920. Ibarruri served the party as an organizer, publicist, and official-member of the Central Committee since 1930, in 1935 candidate member of the Executive Committee of the Comintern, and party chairperson since 1960. Since 1939 she has lived in exile. Based on *Pravda* and memoirs by Ibarruri; 4 notes.
L. E. Holmes

2757. Meshcheriakov, M. T. PUT' BOR'BY I POBED [Path of struggle and victories]. *Voprosy Istorii KPSS [USSR] 1963 (4): 138-141.* Traces the career of the Spanish Communist, Dolores Ibarruri, 1913-63, concentrating on her part in the Civil War.

2758. Meshcheriakov, Marklen T. KHULIAN GRIMAU (K 60-LETIIU SO DNIA ROZHDENIIA) [Julián Grimau García: the 60th anniversary of his birth]. *Voprosy Istorii KPSS [USSR] 1971 (2): 96-97.* Outlines the career of a former leader of the Spanish Communist Party.

2759. Mujal-León, Eusebio. *Communism and Political Change in Spain.* Bloomington: Indiana U. Pr., 1983. 288 pp.

2760. Mujal-Leon, Eusebio. THE PCE IN SPANISH POLITICS. *Problems of Communism 1978 27(4): 15-37.* Reviews the failure of the Spanish Communist Party (PCE) to shape Spain's political transition to the post-Franco era and the impact of that failure on the party's fortunes. Explores future possibilities of a PCE role in the politics of the Spanish Left. Based on primary Spanish language sources; 52 notes.
J. M. Lauber

2761. Mujal-León, Eusebio. THE SOVIET AND SPANISH COMMUNIST PARTIES: POLICIES, TACTICS, NEGOTIATING BEHAVIOR. *Studies in Comparative Communism 1982 15(3): 236-265.* The Soviet Communists have used polemic against the Spanish Communist Party (CPE) and its Secretary General, Santiago Carrillo. They have concentrated on the leaders although occasionally the Soviets have supported efforts to create rival parties. The Eurocommunist position of the CPE became most clear in the mid-1970's. Carrillo faced opposition within the leadership, which tried to establish pluralism within the Party as well as strong pro-Soviet sentiment. By the late 1970's, the CPE had become less anti-Soviet, in part because it has done poorly at elections and has come to rely heavily on pro-Soviet groups in Spain. 92 notes. D. Balmuth

2762. Mujal-Leon, Eusebio M. THE PCP AND THE PORTUGUESE REVOLUTION. *Problems of Communism 1977 26(1): 21-41.* Analyzes the various responses of the Portuguese Communist Party (PCP) to the changing situation in Portugal since the military coup of 30 April 1974. Also projects possible future patterns of PCP participation in Portugal's political process and prospects for internal change in the PCP toward a more pluralistic, accommodating stance typical of other major West European Communist parties. Based on primary and secondary Portuguese and English language sources; 56 notes. J. M. Lauber

2763. Mujal-Leon, Eusebio M. SPANISH COMMUNISM IN THE 1970'S. *Problems of Communism 1975 24(2): 43-55.* The Spanish Communist Party (PCE) has emerged since the late 1960's as the best organized opposition force within Spain and will probably play a significant role in the post-Franco era. Since the Portuguese revolution of 1974, the Soviet Union has increased its backing of the PCE with the belief that Spain has entered a transitional period with respect to its political structure. Primary sources; 68 notes. J. M. Lauber

2764. Preston, Paul. THE DILEMMA OF CREDIBILITY: THE SPANISH COMMUNIST PARTY, THE FRANCO REGIME AND AFTER. *Government and Opposition [Great Britain] 1976 11(1): 65-83.* Examines the struggle of the Spanish Communist Party for popular credibility, particularly its competition with the Portuguese party and its efforts to move toward a policy of democratic socialism, 1970's.

2765. Schmitter, Philippe. LE PARTI COMMUNISTE PORTUGAIS ENTRE LE "POUVOIR SOCIAL" ET LE "POUVOIR POLITIQUE" [The Portuguese Communist Party between "social power" and "political power"]. *Études Int. [Canada] 1975 6(3): 375-388.* Graphically demonstrates the courage and persistence of the party leadership in Portugal under the dictatorship of Salazar, enabling the party to record a 10% opposition vote in the 1969 elections. Although traditionally a minimalist party, the Portuguese CP is becoming more active in infiltrating non-Communist social organizations. 4 tables, 29 notes. J. F. Harrington, Jr.

2766. Shelton, Richard L. "The Partido Comunista Português (PCP): The Development of the Communist Party in Portugal, 1921-1976." Saint Louis University 1984. 253 pp. *DAI 1984 45(6): 1861-A.* DA8418697

2767. Sukhanov, V. I. "REVOLIUTSIIA GVOZDIK" V PORTUGALII ["The Revolution of Carnations" in Portugal]. *Novaia i Noveishaia Istoriia [USSR] 1978 (4): 113-124.* Describes the coup d'etat of 24-25 April 1974, popularly called Revolution of Flowers or Carnations, executed by the Armed Forces Movement and actively supported by the Communist Party headed by Alvaro Cunhal. Several abortive coups were attempted by fascists and deviationist leftist factions, supposedly to thwart an imaginary Communist threat to freedom while actually designed to strengthen the political clout of General (later President) António de Spínola. Spínola's flight to Spain in March 1975 and the formation of the Supreme Revolutionary Council demonstrated to counterrevolutionaries at home and in Western Europe that enemies of socialism had little hope of winning the support of the masses in Portugal. 29 notes. Article to be continued. N. Frenkley

2768. Vladimirov, V. P. DOLORES IBARRURI: K 75-LETIU SO DNIA ROZHDENIA [Dolores Ibarruri: on the 75th anniversary of her birth]. *Voprosy Istorii KPSS [USSR] 1970 (12): 122-123.* Traces the career of Dolores Ibarruri, a leading figure in the Spanish Communist Party, emphasizing her struggle against fascism in the 1930's.

2769. Vladimirov, V. P. 50 LET BOR'BY ZA INTERESY TRUDIASHCHIKHSIA ISPANII [Fifty years of struggle on behalf of Spanish workers]. *Voprosy Istorii KPSS [USSR] 1970 (4): 109-112.* Traces the history of the Spanish Communist Party on the 50th anniversary of its formation, its struggle against fascism and its underground activities.

2770. Zapirain, Sebastian. FREEDOM FOR CAMACHO AND HIS COMRADES. *World Marxist R. [Canada] 1973 16(5): 81-83.* Communist Party of Spain pleas for the release of the labor leader Marcelino Camacho and nine others associated with him.

3. COMMUNISM IN CHINA

General

2771. Aage, Hans. POLITISK HOLDNINGSPÅVIRKNING I DEN KINESISKE FOLKREPUBLIK OG SOCIOLOGISK TEORI [The shaping of political attitudes in the People's Republic of China, and sociological theory]. *Statsvetenskaplig Tidskrift [Sweden] 1973 76(3): 185-198.* Examines the purposes, techniques, and results of thought reform as used by the Chinese Communist Party since 1942. Through distinctive methods of mass political education, the Chinese have achieved not only major shifts in political attitudes, but also a new motivational basis for the human efforts required in economic development. Sociological theories which assume attitudes to be determined by structural factors cannot account for Chinese developments. Attitudes appear to be independent variables capable of autonomous change under proper conditions. George C. Homans' interaction theory seems best to account for this phenomenon. Based on western sources; biblio.
R. G. Selleck

2772. Adelman, Jonathan R. THE IMPACT OF CIVIL WARS ON COMMUNIST POLITICAL CULTURE: THE CHINESE AND RUSSIAN CASES. *Studies in Comparative Communism 1983 16(1-2): 25-48.* Differences are clear in the situation of the Bolsheviks and the Chinese Communists prior to their civil wars as well as in the character of those struggles. Nevertheless, both the Soviet and Chinese Communist Parties reverted to many of the ideas and attitudes of the civil war in later years. The Chinese reversion occurred during the Great Leap Forward and the Cultural Revolution; the Soviet reversion came when Stalin led the transformation of the 1930's. 58 notes. D. Balmuth

2773. Altaiskii, M. L. IDEOLOGIIA I POLITIKA MAOIZMA NA SLUZHBE ANTIKOMMUNIZMA [The ideology and policies of Maoism in the service of anti-Communism]. *Voprosy Istorii KPSS [USSR] 1975 (1): 66-78.* Since the 1930's and especially since the early 1960's anti-Sovietism has been the pivot of Mao Tse-tung's doctrine. Maoists claimed China as the center of the international revolutionary movement as early as the 1930's, failed to actively pursue war with Japan in 1941, discredited socialism in the USSR, reprinted in the Chinese press Western reactionary attacks on the Soviet Union, sought to create schisms among socialist nations and Communist parties, and pursued many policies designed to disrupt detente between the USSR and West. Based on Soviet and Chinese periodical literature; 35 notes. L. E. Holmes

2774. Badour, William. LA CHINE ET L'URSS: LIENS ENTRE POLITIQUE INTERNE ET POLITIQUE EXTERNE [China and the Soviet Union: linkages between internal and external politics]. *Études Internationales [Canada] 1972 3(4): 473-484.* Briefly reviews Sino-Russian rivalry since the 17th century and focuses on the relations between the two Communist parties, 1921-72. Special emphasis is given to pro-Moscow elements in the Chinese Communist Party, notably Kao Kang, Peng Teh-huai, and Lin Piao. Mao Tse-tung's unalterable opposition to Soviet influence in China has resulted in Peking's evolving toward a distinctly independent Communist model. Primary and secondary sources; 25 notes.
J. F. Harrington, Jr.

2775. Bandyopadhyaya, J. TRIUMPHS AND TRAGEDIES OF MAOISM IN CHINA. *China Report [India] 1973 9(2): 20-30.* Rapid economic development, increased military capability, including development of nuclear arms, and strong nationalistic feelings have all profited the advance of Chinese communism, yet the masses have been forced to cede numerous personal rights and relinquish power to strongly centralized totalitarian government, 1949-72.

2776. Bartke, Wolfgang; Jarke, Waldtraut, transl. OLD CADRES FROM THE SEVENTH AND EIGHTH CENTRAL COMMITTEES WHO HAVE BEEN ELECTED TO THE TENTH CENTRAL COMMITTEE. *Chinese Studies in Hist. 1975 9(1): 38-42.* Members of the seventh Central Committee of the Chinese Communist Party, elected in 1945, have shown amazing political endurance: 41% were elected to the 1973 10th Central Committee. These men had proven themselves in the early military and political struggles to liberate China. Of the members of the eighth Central Committee, elected in 1956, only 31% survived the turmoil of the Cultural Revolution. These figures suggest that the Cultural Revolution was a power struggle between new and old leaders in China. 2 tables. J. W. Leedom

2777. Bedeski, Robert E. THE EVOLUTION OF THE MODERN STATE IN CHINA: NATIONALIST AND COMMUNIST CONTINUITIES. *World Pol. 1975 27(4): 541-568.* The modern state is a theoretical concept and a historical phenomenon which can be examined as force, power, and authority. The foundations of the modern state in China were laid by the Nationalist regime in Nankin after 1927. The Kuomintang's efforts in unification and treaty renegotiation greatly facilitated the labors of the Communists when they came to power. State development since 1949 reflects Nationalist influence in constitutionalization, party role, status of the army, and even world outlook. If the Nationalist and Communist periods are viewed as a continuum, state evolution in modern China appears as a rough recapitulation of the European state's development. J

2778. Bedeski, Robert E. LEADERSHIP ROLES IN MODERN CHINA: THE KUOMINTANG AND COMMUNIST EXPERIENCES. *Studies in Comparative Communism 1974 7(1/2): 53-63.* In the face of the squabbles of imperial powers, the Kuomintang sought unity by force and built railroads and roads and ended internal tariffs. But without a mass base, Chiang Kai-shek lost out to the Communists and especially their army. The subsequent conflict between army and Party led to the fall of P'eng Te-huai in 1959 and then Lin Piao. Just as under the Kuomintang, conflicts have arisen among leader, Party, and the army. The army's role will continue to be important. 5 notes. D. Balmuth

2779. Benton, Gregor. CHINESE COMMUNISM AND DEMOCRACY. *New Left Review [Great Britain] 1984 (148): 57-73.* Although the Communist revolution in China was genuine, the socialism it established lacked democratic qualities which would have made it more successful. Traces the progressive bureaucratization of Communism in China during the revolutionary movements of Mao Zedong through the Yan'an period of resistance to the Japanese military occupation during World War II, the defeat of the Nationalists, and Mao's rule to the beginnings of Deng Xiaoping's reforms.

2780. Bianco, Lucien. ESSAI DE DÉFINITION DU MAOÏSME [Toward a definition of Maoism]. *Ann.: Écon., Soc., Civilisations [France] 1979 34(5): 1094-1108.* "Maoism" refers to the last two decades (circa 1957-76) of Mao Tse-tung's life, the period during which "Maoism" became as popular a term as "Leninism" or "Stalinism." While Mao's earlier activity embodied a kind of revolutionary model (a peasant and military strategy) for the Third World, his late and intellectually more ambitious and original constructions missed the historical rendezvous between Leninism and the Third World. Indeed, Mao's originality, instead of arising from a Third World environment (where one would have expected it to lie), did rather belong to the more abstract realm of revolution: it could be called an attempt at permanent revolution. Such a temptation has been costly for the Chinese revolution, and did not create any practical outlet from the blind alleys of Leninism. 18 notes.
J

2781. Bianco, Lucien. "FU-CHIANG" AND RED FERVOR. *Problems of Communism 1974 23(5): 2-9.* Tries to determine how much of the Chinese Communist course since 1949 represents the traditional quest for *fu-chiang* (wealth and power), and what accomplishments are clearly of a different order. 5 notes. J. M. Lauber

2782. Bloodworth, Dennis. *The Messiah and the Mandarins: Mao Tsetung and the Ironies of Power.* New York: Atheneum, 1982. 331 pp.

2783. Bobrow, Davis B.; Chan, Steve; and Kringen, John A. *Understanding Foreign Policy Decisions: The Chinese Case.* New York: Free Pr., 1979. 242 pp.

2784. Botton Beja, Flora. WANG MENG Y LA NUEVA NARRATIVA CHINA [Wang Meng and the new Chinese fiction]. *Estudios de Asia y Africa [Mexico] 1984 19(2): 193-201.* After its publication in 1956, Wang Meng's (b. 1935) short story, "A Young Newcomer to the Organization Department," was a bold attack against the Communist Party's cadres. Wang was confined in northeastern Xinjiang province until his rehabilitation and return to Beijing in 1978. In his stories published between 1978 and 1982, he maintained his old thematic concern for everyday life of the Party's petty cadres conveyed through modern narrative techniques, not always accepted by Chinese readers and authorities. After 1982, he showed a greater awareness of ideological correctness and accuracy in his social criticism of the regime. 18 notes. C. Pasadas-Ureña

2785. Brahm, Heinz. SOWJETISCHE INTELLEKTUELLE ÜBER DIE "CHINESISCHE GEFAHR" [Soviet intellectuals on the "Chinese danger"]. *Osteuropa [West Germany] 1978 28(2): 150-166.* In semi-official publications Soviet intellectuals suggest that Soviet-Chinese differences since the 1950's have been useful to the Russian and Chinese systems as a means of diverting attention from internal problems within the USSR and China.

2786. Brugger, William. *China: Liberation and Transformation, 1942-1962.* New York: Barnes & Noble, 1981. 288 pp.

2787. Brugger, William. *China: Radicalism to Revisionism, 1962-1979.* New York: Barnes & Noble, 1981. 275 pp.

2788. Byczkowski, Włodzimierz. DRAMAT KOMUNISTÓW CHIŃSKICH [The drama of the Chinese Communists]. *Nowe Drogi [Poland] 1976 (7): 146-153.* Discusses changes in the political line of the Communist Party of China since its founding.

2789. Caldwell, James Timothy. "Elite Specialization, Bureaucracy and Modernization: The Case of China 1949-1969." U. of Texas, Austin 1980. 204 pp. *DAI 1981 41(11): 4821-A.* 8109139

2790. Camilleri, Joseph. *Chinese Foreign Policy: The Maoist Era and Its Aftermath.* Seattle: U. of Washington Pr., 1981. 311 pp.

2791. Chai, Trong R. THE COMMUNIST PARTY OF CHINA: THE PROCESS OF INSTITUTIONALIZATION. *Asian Affairs [Great Britain] 1980 11(1): 43-54.* Challenges the general view that the Communist Party of China maintained its leadership, organization, and ideology and became increasingly powerful after its conquest of China. Analyzes the meetings of the Chinese Central committees of 1956, 1969, 1973, and 1977, using the three measures of institutionalization (boundary, stabilization, and autonomy) to determine if the party has become more institutionalized since it came to power. The leaders of the Ninth Central Committee Meeting in 1969 were victims of the Cultural Revolution, which significantly disrupted a pattern of increasing institutionalization. Secondary sources; 2 tables, 19 notes. S. H. Frank

2792. Chai, Trong R. COMMUNIST PARTY CONTROL OVER THE BUREAUCRACY: THE CASE OF CHINA. *Comparative Pol. 1979 11(3): 359-370.* Discusses the Chinese State Council, 1949-69, with special attention to the efficacy of Party control of the State Council during the 1960's. For the purposes of the study, party is defined as the groups led by Mao Zedong (Mao Tse-tung). Findings do not support the conventional belief of Party dominance of the bureaucracy, as reflected in the power of its leaders, in Communist systems. Based on the analysis of turnover patterns of ministers and commission chairmen of 38 ministries; table, 3 graphs, 21 notes. M. A. Kascus

2793. Chai, Winberg. THE IMPACT OF IDEOLOGY UPON PUBLIC POLICY IN MAINLAND CHINA. *Issues & Studies [Taiwan] 1970 6(9): 32-36.* Discusses the close association of ideology and public policy in the Chinese Communist Party since its creation in 1921.

2794. Chang, Parris. THE ANTI-LIN PIAO AND CONFUCIUS CAMPAIGN: ITS MEANING AND PURPOSES. *Asian Survey 1974 14(10): 871-886.*

2795. Chang, Parris H. THE EVOLUTION OF THE CCP SINCE 1949. *Korea & World Affairs [South Korea] 1984 8(1): 104-131.* The Chinese Communist Party experienced steady increase in membership after 1949 but Maoist rule by fiat and the rise to political prominence of the People's Liberation Army in the wake of the Cultural Revolution of the late 1960's limited its influence.

2796. Chang, Tsai-yu. HSIEN TSUNG-T'UNG CHIANG KUNG TI FAN-KUNG SSU-HSIANG [The Late President Chiang Kai-shek's Thoughts on Communism]. *Shih-ta Hsüeh-pao (Bulletin of National Taiwan Normal University) [Taiwan] 1984 29: 1-23.* President Jiang Jieshi (Chiang Kai-shek) was the prophet for all anti-Communists. In his three most celebrated works on Communism, he probed deeply into the evils of Communism and advocated the theory of the unity of spirit and material as the best antidote to Marx's historical materialism. He argued that the greatest threat to world peace was Chinese Communism and the best way to remove this threat was to drive the Communists out of mainland China. Therefore it was a mistake for the anti-Communist countries to align themselves with Communist China in opposition to the USSR. Based on published writings, speeches, and interviews of President Jiang Jieshi; 32 notes. R. C. Houston

2797. Chang Ching-li. CCP's TREATMENT OF THE "FIVE CATEGORIES OF ELEMENTS." *Issues & Studies [Taiwan] 1980 16(3): 13-27.* Even before the Communists came to power, they labeled and began to persecute "five elements" of the population: landlords, rich peasants, counterrevolutionaries, bad elements, and rightists. Those tagged as of these elements suffered death, imprisonment, surveillance, forced labor, or deprivation of rights. After years of erratic progress in removing the rightist label, the government removed all labels in 1979. Among resulting gains to the regime are political stability and the release of formerly stigmatized experts to participate in modernization. But these elements continue to be targets of control and will still resist Communist rule. Based on statements of Communist Party officials, Party documents, and reports from the *Renmin Ribao* [People's Daily]; 30 notes. J. A. Krompart

2798. Chang Chi-p'eng. THE CCP'S POLICY TOWARD RELIGION. *Issues & Studies [Taiwan] 1983 19(9): 55-70.* The Chinese Communists have a long history of both opposition to religion and a declared policy of religious freedom. In recent years they have been tolerant of religion as part of their united front policy, designed to promote internal stability and external relations with nations where religion plays a strong role. Nevertheless, their ultimate goal is to eliminate all religions from China. Based on the works of Marx, Engels, Lenin, and Mao and editorials from the *People's Daily;* 17 notes. J. A. Krompart

2799. Chao Hung-Tzu. THE NATURE OF CHINESE COMMUNISM. *Issues & Studies [Taiwan] 1983 19(11): 12-35.* The beginnings of Communism in China can be traced into the 19th century when Chinese intellectuals espoused its doctrines in their reaction to the impact of the West. Marxism-Leninism is, however, incapable of achieving stability in China because of its inherent defects. 36 notes. J. A. Krompart

2800. Cheek, Timothy. DENG TUO: CULTURE, LENINISM AND ALTERNATIVE MARXISM IN THE CHINESE COMMUNIST PARTY. *China Q. [Great Britain] 1981 (87): 470-492.* Deng Tuo (Deng Yunte), purged and driven to suicide during China's Cultural Revolution, suffered for his opposition to Mao Zedong. A long-time Communist Party member, Deng resisted Mao for the latter's non-Leninist willingness to place will above objective reality. Deng's current rehabilitation is a further indication of Mao's reduced place in contemporary Chinese hagiography. Based primarily on Deng's writings and other Chinese materials; 111 notes.
J. R. Pavia, Jr.

2801. Cheek, Timothy. THE FADING OF WILD LILIES: WANG SHIWEI AND MAO ZEDONG'S *YAN'AN TALKS* IN THE FIRST CPC RECTIFICATION MOVEMENT. *Australian Journal of Chinese Affairs [Australia] 1984 (11): 25-58.* The Yan'an rectification movement was a successful strategy of the Congress of the Communist Party of China to bring art and literature under Party control, and it purged dissenters such as Wang Shiwei who advocated cosmopolitan and individualistic ideas.

2802. Chen, Theodore H. E. THE MAOIST MODEL OF EDUCATION: THEORY IN PRACTICE. *Asian Affairs: An Am. Rev. 1976 4(1): 41-61.* Traces problems facing Chinese educators from the establishment of the Republic in 1911. Cites the impact of foreign education models, the search for a uniquely Chinese model, and the rapid emergence of Chinese nationalism. More recently, Soviet influences and revisionism were followed by the emergence of a Chinese model during the Cultural Revolution and the current rivalry between radical Maoist ideologues and moderate, pragmatic educators, bureaucrats, and technocrats. Explores the objectives, standards, curricula, administration and organization, and the socioeconomic and political repercussions of the Maoist model. Primary and secondary sources; 25 notes. R. B. Mendel

2803. Chen, Vincent. THE SIGNIFICANCE OF MASS CAMPAIGN IN MAINLAND CHINA. *Issues & Studies [Taiwan] 1971 7(10): 56-60.* Discusses how the Chinese Communist Party has used mass movements.

2804. Cheng, Peter P. THE CPC CONSTITUTION: 1956 VS. 1969. *Issues & Studies [Taiwan] 1972 8(4): 68-73.* Compares the Chinese Communist Party's 1956 and 1969 constitutions.

2805. Cheng Chu-yuan. LEADERSHIP CHANGES AND ECONOMIC POLICIES IN CHINA. *J. of Int. Affairs 1978 32(2): 255-273.* While paying lip service to Mao's revolutionary line, the moderate post-Mao leaders have proclaimed economic policies that vitiate principles and institutions held sacrosanct by Maoists in recent years. This turnabout is the sequel to a continued struggle carried on between the revolutionists and pragmatists for leadership within the Chinese Communist Party. If the new economic policies, which constitute a return to the "revisionist line" advocated by the pragmatists in the past, are successfully implemented, they will bring about a fundamental change in the socioeconomic structure of China. Diagram, 66 notes. V. Samaraweera

2806. Cheng Hsueh-chia. ON *HUNG-SE WU-TAI* (*THE RED STAGE*). *Issues & Studies [Taiwan] 1973 9(4): 68-81.* Describes the life of the former Communist political writer Li Ang from the late 1920's to 1947, and discusses the historical accuracy of his *Hung-se Wu-tai* [Red Stage] (ca. 1942), a novel of the Communist Party's early growth in China.

2807. Chey, Myung JUNGKONGAE ISSUHSUHEY JUNGCHIJUK SOOKCHUNG [Political purges in Communist China]. *J. of Asiatic Studies [South Korea] 1973 16(2): 91-138.* Analyzes struggles to overcome "anti-party" groups which the Chinese Communist Party faced after the 1949 unification of China. The three anti-party factions were that led by Kao Kang and Jao Shu-shih during 1954-55; the right-wing opportunist faction which tried to replace the general direction of the Party, and the capitalist roaders behind Liu Shao-ch'i. 171 notes. Y. C. Ro

2808. Chiang Hsin-li. A REFUTATION OF THE MAOISTS' "ON SLAVE SOCIETY." *Issues and Studies [Taiwan] 1974 10(15): 45-58.* Discusses historical misconceptions in the Maoist analysis of the transition from slavery to feudalism in ancient China; the interpretation, based on historical materialism, was first proposed by Kuo Mo-jo in 1952.

2809. Chien T'ieh. THE CCPCC MILITARY COMMISSION: ITS DEVELOPMENT AND RESPONSIBILITIES. *Issues and Studies [Taiwan] 1978 14(5): 45-64.* The history of the Communist Party's Military Commission (1924-78), China's highest policymaking body for military affairs and high command for military operations.

2810. Chien T'ieh. A HISTORICAL PERSPECTIVE ON THE MILITARY REGIONS OF THE CHINESE COMMUNISTS. *Issues and Studies [Taiwan] 1975 11(1): 29-41.* Discusses the history and administrative structure of Communist Party military organizations in China from 1927 to the 1970's.

2811. Chien T'ieh. A HISTORY OF THE RED FOURTH FRONT ARMY: BASED ON THE STUDY OF "HWANGAN-MACHENG CADRES." *Issues and Studies [Taiwan] 1976 12(12): 26-38.* Traces the origins of the Red Fourth Front Army in Hwangan and Macheng counties (Hupeh) in China 1920-59, and its eventual transformation into the politically powerful Second Field Army, now sometimes referred to as the "Hwangan-Macheng Cadres."

2812. Ch'in Yung-fa. THE ECONONOMIC AND POLITICAL SIGNIFICANCE OF CHINESE COMMUNIST PRODUCTION AND EXPORTATION OF DANGEROUS DRUGS. *Issues & Studies [Taiwan] 1972 8(6): 11-29.* Discusses the Chinese Communist Party's policy 1928-1972 of producing dangerous drugs for the illicit narcotics trade.

2813. Ch'iu K'ung-yüan. "BOURGEOIS RIGHTS" AND PEOPLE'S LIVELIHOOD IN MAINLAND CHINA. *Issues and Studies [Taiwan] 197 13(8): 7-25.* Since 1958, open debates have raged within the Chinese Communist Party on abolishing or restricting civil rights in China. While the power struggle goes on within the Party, the people of China suffer, particularly the peasants, because it is their rights that are being debated and opposed. The ruling members of the Party constitute a truly privileged class and possess rights they do not desire to forego. Secondary sources; 77 notes.
A. N. Garland

2814. Ch'iu Kung-yuan. PROSPECTS FOR THE INTELLIGENTSIA IN COMMUNIST CHINA. *Issues and Studies [Taiwan] 1975 11(1): 75-90.* Discusses the Communist Party's policies regarding intellectuals, 1955-70's.

2815. Choi, Eui-Chul. "Mao Zedong, Zhou Enlai and the Bureaucracy." U. of Illinois, Urbana-Champaign 1982. 532 pp. *DAI 1982 43(3): 911-A.* DA8218447

2816. Chou Tzu-ch'iang. AN ANALYSIS OF THE CHINESE COMMUNIST MILITARY AREA SYSTEM. *Issues & Studies [Taiwan] 1972 8(5): 35-49.* Discusses the Chinese Communist Party's area system of military organization which was developed between the 1930's and 1972.

2817. Chou Tzu-ch'iang. ELEMENTS OF CHINESE CULTURE IN MAO TSE-TUNG'S WORKS. *Issues & Studies [Taiwan] 1973 9(6): 35-56.* Mao Tse-tung's works, 1926-66, reveal his acceptance of communism from European culture and his distortion of China's traditional culture.

2818. Chou Wei-ling. PLANNING THE CHINESE COMMUNIST TRADE UNION, CYL AND WOMEN'S FEDERATION CONGRESSES. *Issues and Studies [Taiwan] 1975 11(8): 58-71.* Describes the steps in the reorganization of the labor unions, the Communist Youth League, and the Women's Federation in China, after the disruption of the Cultural Revolution.

2819. Chu, Leonard L. PRESS CRITICISM AND SELF-CRITICISM IN COMMUNIST CHINA: AN ANALYSIS OF ITS IDEOLOGY, STRUCTURE, AND OPERATION. *Gazette: Int. J. for Mass Communication Studies [Netherlands] 1983 31(1): 47-61.* The ritual of criticism and self-criticism in the Chinese press is purported to function as a control mechanism to curb possible abuses by the Communist Party and by the government. However, the control of all media is firmly in Party hands in China, including the content of published criticism. The result is that the practice is merely a propaganda instrument for those in power.
D. Powell

2820. Chu Wen-lin. PEIPING'S INTERNAL CONTROVERSY ON MILITARY IDEOLOGY. *Issues and Studies [Taiwan] 1974 10(14): 18-44.* Discusses ideological conflicts within the Communist Party regarding the role of the military and the concept of people's war in China.

2821. Coleman, Gordon K. A. CHINESE COMMUNIST PARTY ORGANIZATION AND LEADERSHIP: 1949-1969. *Internat. R. of Hist. and Pol. Sci. [India] 1972 9(3): 1-32.* Two purposes inspire political activity in mainland China: national integration and the attainment of world leadership. For purposes of administration and implementation, ideological and organizational structures are similar in both the state and the party. Intellectual and ideological roles are utilized to complement and to challenge each other with a view toward development. Secondary sources; 3 tables, 7 charts, 47 notes.
E. McCarthy

2822. Crook, David. FROM LAMA TEMPLE TO COMMUNE BRIGADE. *Eastern Horizon [Hong Kong] 1977 16(2): 39-41.* Contrasts the present situation in the Tibetan autonomous district of Ngawa (Aba) in modern China, with conditions in 1940. The old temple, where senior lamas once exploited junior monks and the general population, is now the headquarters of the Happy Peasant Commune. Land reform was instituted gradually, in keeping with the Communist policy of giving special consideration to national minorities. Most monks and lamas joined the commune and only one Grand Lama was executed. Based on the author's visits to the area in 1940 and 1976.
T. Sassoon

2823. Crozier, Brian. COMPETITIVE SUBVERSION IN EAST ASIA. *Asian Affairs [Great Britain] 1976 63(3): 277-284.* Analyzes the competition between the USSR and China for political control of Asia in the 20th century. Although the Chinese Communist Party was a creation in 1920 of Lenin's Comintern, by the time of World War II Mao Tse-tung and others were effectively controlling the operation of that organization. The entry of the Soviet Union into the war against Japan in the final week of that struggle clearly assisted the Chinese Communists in their fight with the Nationalists which continued far beyond World War II. Compares the efforts of Russian and Chinese Communist leaders to gain control in India, Burma, Indonesia, Malaya, the Philippines, and Vietnam. Analyzes the Sino-Soviet conflict as it emerged between 1957 and 1960. Communist efforts in many Asian countries were supported by rebel forces guided by a nationalist ideology rather than by Communist dogma.
S. H. Frank

2824. Curtin, Katie. WOMEN AND THE CHINESE REVOLUTION. *Internat. Socialist R. 1974 35(3): 7-11, 25-39.*

2825. Davin, Delia. THE IMPLICATIONS OF SOME ASPECTS OF C.C.P. POLICY TOWARD URBAN WOMEN IN THE 1950'S. *Modern China 1975 1(4): 363-378.* Marxist classics explained the inferior role of women as the result of their being detached from productive labor. Early Chinese Communist policy supported this but in the mid-1950's the emphasis changed. Women were then told to fulfill themselves in the home and through their families. This continued until the Great Leap. Based on Chinese and English sources; 13 notes.
J. R. Pavia, Jr.

2826. Davis-Friedmann, Deborah. *Long Lives: Chinese Elderly and the Communist Revolution.* (Harvard East Asian Series, no. 100.) Cambridge, Mass.: Harvard U. Pr., 1983. 140 pp.

2827. Deal, David M. "THE QUESTION OF NATIONALITIES" IN TWENTIETH CENTURY CHINA. *Journal of Ethnic Studies 1984 12(3): 23-53.* Compares the policies of the Nationalists and Communists toward China's ethnic minorities, from the Provisional Constitution of 1912 to the mid-1960's. The Nationalists anticipated much of the Communists' minority theory, as both parties were deeply influenced by the Soviet Union and both faced a common problem: the presence of some fifty ethnic minorities making up 6% of the population and scattered throughout sensitive border regions such as Mongolia, Tibet, Kwangsi, and Korea. Ultimately assimilation of minorities and the creation of a new, unified Chinese "community" were goals of both governments, but there has never been a simple solution. Secondary sources; 123 notes.
G. J. Bobango

2828. Demarchi, Franco. LA STABILIZZAZIONE DEL POTERE NELLA CINA POPOLARE [The stabilization of power in China]. *Mondo Cinese [Italy] 1974 2(8): 3-37.* Analyzes from a sociological point of view the stabilization of power by the Chinese Communist Party, both in terms of the evolution of Mao's thought, and internal events. The author considers the political economy, the changes of foreign politics, and the great internal debates, especially the criticism of Lin Piao and Confucius. He points out the influence of the concepts of Mao, concepts that are antibureaucratic and fundamentally marked by a great faith in the self-determination of the masses. It is shown that since the *Report* of 1927 until the Conference at Lushan in 1970, Mao Tse-tung had fought for his conviction that the masses are capable of "taking the direction everywhere."
J

2829. Dirlik, Arif. THE PREDICAMENT OF MARXIST REVOLUTIONARY CONSCIOUSNESS: MAO ZEDONG (MAO TSE-TUNG), ANTONIO GRAMSCI, AND THE REFORMULATION OF MARXIST REVOLUTIONARY THEORY. *Modern China 1983 9(2): 182-211.* Revolutionary consciousness, or the ability to understand and change social reality, was a central theme of Mao Zedong's Marxism. Mao sinified Marxism to the extent that he adopted it to China's circumstances, but his nationalism was also a result of his Marxism. The characteristics of Mao's philosophy of the role of the Communist Party in China, involving a leadership of various classes with an understanding of the national culture, bears close comparison to Antonio Gramsci's concept of hegemony. Seen in this light, the Cultural Revolution was at its inception true to Mao's Marxism, only later to be diverted from its intended course. Based on sources in English; 5 notes, 25 ref.
K. W. Berger

2830. Dittmer, Lowell. CHINESE COMMUNIST REVISIONISM IN COMPARATIVE PERSPECTIVE. *Studies in Comparative Communism 1980 13(1): 3-40.* Liu Shaoqi (Liu Shao-ch'i) represented revisionism in the Chinese Communist Party, i.e., emphasis on materialism, bureaucracy, skills instead of voluntarist ideas and ideology. Revisionism appears when a socialist movement seizes power, becomes nationalist, and seeks to industrialize the country. The radical or nonrevisionist view may survive because of new recruits to the Party during the Cultural Revolution. Also radicalism may reappear because material incentives will produce oppostion and because Mao's ideas give little support to revisionism. Secondary sources; 77 notes.
D. Balmuth

2831. Dixon, John. THE WELFARE OF PEOPLE'S LIBERATION ARMY VETERANS AND DEPENDANTS IN CHINA, 1949-1979. *Armed Forces and Soc. 1983 9(3): 483-494.* Despite some reluctance on the part of peasants, the Communist Party succeeded in providing minimal income support, employment opportunities, some housing, and self-help programs for disabled veterans and for dependants of revolutionary martyrs based on minimal state aid and maximum local contributions. 56 notes.
R. Grove

2832. Domes, Jürgen. THE MODEL FOR REVOLUTIONARY PEOPLE'S WAR: THE COMMUNIST TAKEOVER OF CHINA. *Studies on the Soviet Union [West Germany] 1971 11(4): 469-486.* The Communist takeover of China required 22 years to complete. The author discusses factors contributing to the Nationalists' collapse. American diplomatic ineptness forced the Kuomintang to seek armistice in the midst of a victorious drive; arms supplies were cut off when needed most. World War II wrecked the Chinese economy. Runaway inflation encouraged corruption and alienated popular support. Chiang's strategy was outdated; his military maneuvers played into Communist hands. Secondary sources; 32 notes. V. L. Human

2833. Domes, Jürgen. THE PATTERN OF POLITICS. *Problems of Communism 1974 23(5): 20-25.* Investigates elements of continuity and change in politics within the Chinese Communist Party and in Communist rule generally. All political differences in the past 25 years have revolved essentially around the proper approach to economic and social development. The major question for the future is whether China will follow the general transition of other revolutionary governments from charismatic to institutionalized rule. 4 notes. J. M. Lauber

2834. Domes, Jurgen. THE RELATIONSHIP BETWEEN PARTY, ARMY, AND GOVERNMENT IN COMMUNIST CHINA. *Issues and Studies [Taiwan] 1976 12(8): 41-63.* Discusses politics in China and the difficulty which has been experienced in gaining organizational stability especially among the leadership factions, 1956-76; speculates on the interrelationship of the Communist Party, the army, and the functioning of the national government during this period.

2835. Dorris, Carl E. PEASANT MOBILIZATION IN NORTH CHINA AND THE ORIGINS OF YENAN COMMUNISM. *China Q. [Great Britain] 1976 (68): 697-719.* Yenan, far from being the origin of "Yenan Communism" was a symbolic center profiting from the experience of resistance bases in North China. Secure from Japanese attack, Yenan drifted toward commandism and bureaucracy until, in 1943, more successful mobilization methods, developed in the face of Japanese resistance, were adopted and spread as "Yenan Communism." Based on Chinese and English sources; 45 notes. J. R. Pavia, Jr.

2836. Dreyer, June Teufel. ETHNIC RELATIONS IN CHINA. *Ann. of the Am. Acad. of Pol. and Social Sci. 1977 433: 100-111.* Due to their strategic location and their occupation of some of China's most valuable lands, the ethnic minorities of the Chinese People's Republic have occupied the attention of the central government to a far greater degree than would be expected from their relatively insignificant six percent of the total population. The Chinese Communist Party inherited an ethnic cleavage pattern of some salience from prior governments and has been trying to deal with it through alternating policies of tolerance for ethnic particularism with policies repressive of these particularities. The tension between these two policies forms an ongoing theme in China's leadership struggles and can be traced to two different statements by Mao Tse-tung on the proper handling of ethnic problems. The debate between proponents of the two different policies can be expected to go on, though domestic and international constraints seem to portend a continuation of the moderate measures presently in force. The leadership's dissatisfaction with the status of nationalities relations should not be allowed to obscure the Party's successes in dealing with its ethnic minorities. J

2837. Duke, Marvin L. THE MILITARY DOCTRINE OF RED CHINA. *Marine Corps Gazette 1967 51(2): 18-24.* Analyzes the military doctrine of the Chinese Communist Party, 1927-67.

2838. Esherick, Joseph W. and Perry, Elizabeth J. LEADERSHIP SUCCESSION IN THE PEOPLE'S REPUBLIC OF CHINA: CRISIS OR OPPORTUNITY. *Studies in Comparative Communism 1983 16(3): 171-177.* Bureaucratic rule has replaced heroic rule in China. The transition was only completed in 1982 with the choice of Hu Yaobang as general secretary. Mao Zedong opposed bureaucracy, but the new program encourages efficient bureaucracy. 19 notes. D. Balmuth

2839. Felber, Roland. KONTINUITÄT UND WANDEL IM VERHÄLTNIS DES MAOISMUS ZUM KONFUZIANISMUS. ÜBER HISTORISCHE VORAUSSETZUNGEN DER KAMPAGNE ZUR KRITIK AN LIN BIAO UND KONFUZIUS IN CHINA [Continuity and change in the relationship of Maoism and Confucianism: the historical assumptions of the campaign of criticism against Lin Piao and Confucius]. *Zeitschrift für Geschichtswissenschaft [East Germany] 1975 23(6): 686-699.* Chinese Communist leaders once praised Confucius because some of his teachings resembled Maoism, though other aspects of Confucianism ran counter to the tenets of Mao Tse-tung. During the 1960's, opponents of government policies made good use of the teachings of Confucius. Consequently, the government later launched an anti-Confucius campaign to discredit opponents of the Cultural Revolution. Ultimately, anti-Confucian arguments were even used against Lin Piao, allegedly the originator of the Mao cult. Because of these varied uses of Confucianism, the present regime in China no longer refers to him in its propaganda. 60 notes. J. T. Walker

2840. Fitzgerald, Stephen. COMMUNIST CHINA AND THE EDUCATION OF OVERSEAS CHINESE YOUTH: THE END OF AN ERA. *Papers on Far Eastern Hist. [Australia] 1970 2: 63-95.* Examines the reason for Communist rejection of traditional Chinese government policy concerning the education of, and relations with, Chinese emigrants.

2841. Fond, Richard. A DEMOGRAPHIC ESTIMATE OF CHINESE COMMUNISM'S COST TO HUMAN LIFE. *Issues & Studies [Taiwan] 1972 8(4): 56-67.* Estimates the number of deaths attributable to Chinese Communist Party activities from 1949 to 1970.

2842. Friedman, Edward. ON MAOIST CONCEPTUALIZATIONS OF THE CAPITALIST WORLD SYSTEM. *China Q. [Great Britain] 1979 (80): 806-837.* China, as a developing socialist state in a world dominated by mature capitalist units, of necessity developed a nationalist response to the international system. While partially explaining China's split from Moscow, this has also forced China into a role that is not always socialistic. Based largely on Chinese press materials and western commentaries; 52 notes. J. R. Pavia, Jr.

2843. Fyfield, J. A. *Re-educating Chinese Anti-Communists.* New York: St. Martin's, 1982. 125 pp.

2844. Gawlikowski, Krzysztof. IDEOLOGIA KPCH A KLASYCZNA FILOZOFIA CHIŃSKA STOSUNEK KPCH DO FILOZOFII KLASYCZNEJ I JEGO HISTORYCZNE UWARUNKOWANIA [The ideology of the Chinese Communist Party and classical Chinese philosophy: the attitude of the Chinese Communist Party to classical philosophy and its historical premises]. *Studia Filozoficzne [Poland] 1976 (6): 35-65.* Describes the acceptance of Marxism by Chinese society and the links of Marxism with the formation of national and class awareness as well as with the changes in the interpretation of national heritage, 1920-76.

2845. Ghosh, S. K. WHO COMMANDS THE GUN: PARTY OR ARMY. *China Report [India] 1972 8(1-2): 19-29.* Chronicles events, 1950's-72, which indicate the rift between the People's Liberation Army and the Chinese Communist Party, culminating in the 1971 campaign by the Party to reassert power over the PLA, and the eventual fall of Lin Piao.

2846. Ginsburg, Norton. THE NEW-OLD CHINA. *Center Mag. 1976 9(3): 52-61.* Describes the Communist Party's attempts to reform agriculture and promote industrialization in China, 1949-75.

2847. Glunin, V. I.; Grigorev, A. M.; Kukuškin, K. V.; and Jurev, M. F. DIE INTERNATIONALE KOMMUNISTISCHE BEWEGUNG UND DIE KOMMUNISTISCHE PARTEI CHINAS [The international Communist movement and the Communist Party of China]. *Beiträge zur Geschichte der Arbeiterbewegung [East Germany] 1972 14(3): 405-422.* Lenin developed a concept for the development of close contacts and relations between the Communist and national liberation movements in the East which was used as a model for the cooperation between the Comintern and the Communist Party of China. In the revolutionary movement of the 1920's-40's the Comintern played an important part, helping in the formation of the Chinese Red army, establishment of the principles of its relation to the people, and working out of its strategy and tactics. The victory of the Chinese revolution was the result of the alliance of the forces of the international Communist movement with the national liberation movement, especially the peasant movement of China. The development of the Chinese Communist Party in the last years has shown that the self-isolation from the international Communist movement led to grave mistakes, a continuous crisis in the party, and the loss of its revolutionary achievements. Based on printed documents and secondary literature; 34 notes.

R. Wagnleitner

2848. Glunin, V. I.; Grigoriev, A. M.; Kukushkin, K. V.; and Yuriev, M. F. MEZHDUNARODNOE KOMMUNISTICHESKOE DVIZHENIE I KOMMUNISTICHESKAIA PARTIIA KITAIA [The international Communist movement and the Communist Party of China]. *Voprosy Istorii [USSR] 1971 (8): 43-58.* Drawing on documentary materials and the latest works produced by Marxist historians, the authors examine the important role played by the interaction of the international Communist movement and the Communist Party of China in formulating the strategy and tactics of the Chinese revolution in its different stages. The article subjects to a critical analysis the various bourgeois and Maoist conceptions of the history of the CPC, convincingly showing the identifical approach manifested by bourgeois and Maoist historiography in their assessment of the major developments in the history of the CPC, particularly in their efforts to counterpose the history of the CPC to the international Communist movement. The close contact maintained by the CPC with the international Communist movement and its struggle up to the end of the 1950's within the ranks of the world revolutionary movement enabled the Communist Party of China to neutralize the nationalist forces. The crisis developments in the Chinese People's Republic and in the Communist Party of China are attributable to the Chinese leaderships's departure at the close of the 1950's and in the early 1960's from the coordinated line of the international Communist movement with regard to domestic and foreign policy problems. J

2849. Godwin, Paul H. B. CHINA: THE GUERRILLA EXPERIENCE. *Studies in Comparative Communism 1978 11(3): 265-277.* Where communism came to power after a civil war, conflict between the military and the Party is less likely. After 1954 the Chinese army was in the system maintenance period. The military commission, through which the Party controlled the army, was really the military committee of the Politburo. Coercion was used in the two military purges of Marshal P'eng and of Lin Piao. The purges were not the result of disloyalty to the Party but of conflicts within the Party. 11 notes. D. Balmuth

2850. Goodman, David S. G. THE PROVINCIAL FIRST PARTY SECRETARY IN THE PEOPLE'S REPUBLIC OF CHINA, 1949-1978: A PROFILE. *British J. of Pol. Sci. [Great Britain] 1980 10(1): 39-74.* Traces the increase in the importance of the position of first secretary of a provincial committee of the Chinese Communist Party between the years 1949 and 1978.

2851. Gregor, William J. THE POLITICAL PROBLEM OF THE PEOPLE'S ARMY. *Military Rev. 1975 55(4): 3-14.* Both the Bolsheviks and the Chinese Communists conceived of the nation-in-arms, or people's militia, as the protector of democratic-socialistic precepts rather than a governmental institution. In each case, however, political considerations forced them to abandon this theory in favor of viewing the nation-in-arms as the guarantor of the government, regardless of the government's form. Primary and secondary sources; 8 illus., 39 notes. J. K. Ohl

2852. Grigor'ev, A. PODRYVNOI KURS MAOISTOV V AZII I AFRIKE [The undermining policies of the Maoists in Asia and Africa]. *Aziia i Afrika Segodnia [USSR] 1976 (2): 24-27.* Analyzes the policies of the Chinese government in Africa and Asia and shows how the Maoists try unsuccessfully to drive a wedge between the peoples of these continents and the socialist countries.

2853. Gupta, Krishna Prakash. CHINESE TRADITION OF INTERNATIONAL RELATIONS. *China Report [India] 1971 7(4): 2-11.* Discusses the possibility of detente between China and the United States in the context of China's traditional ideologies of Marxism-Leninism and Maoism, 1949-71.

2854. Gupta, Krishna Prakash. LIBERAL ARTS EDUCATION IN CHINA. *China Report [India] 1971 7(5): 18-25.* Discusses the effect of Maoism on educational reform in the liberal arts in China, emphasizing teaching, curricula, and the institutional structure of colleges and universities, 1956-71.

2855. Gupta, Krishna Prakash. MARXISM-LENINISM, MAO TSE-TUNG THOUGHT: VISIONS AND REVISIONS. *China Report [India] 1974 10(5-6): 19-37.* Discusses the extent to which Marxism and Leninism played an important role in the modernization of China juxtaposed with the philosophy of Mao Tse-tung; assesses the blend of the three which has yielded the communism known in China, 1927-74.

2856. Gupta, Krishna Prakash. "SOCIETY AS A FACTORY": MAOIST APPROACH TO SOCIAL SCIENCES. *China Report [India] 1972 8(3): 36-58.* Study of the social sciences in China is not strictly an academic discipline, but rather strategic studies of manipulated change along Maoist lines, as opposed to Marxist-Leninist or Soviet methods of socialist reform, based on Chinese values and the tradition of China's highly structured social system, 1930's-70's.

2857. Han Lih-wu. CHINESE CULTURE ON TRIAL. *Issues & Studies [Taiwan] 1973 9(12): 10-17.* Discusses the development of culture in China since ca. 600 B.C. and the challenge of communism to traditional values.

2858. Heaton, William. ULANFU: SKETCH OF A MONGOLIAN CAREER THROUGH CRISIS. *Canada-Mongolia Rev. [Canada] 1978 4(1): 63-69.* Examination of Ulanfu's career discloses the relationship of minorities and career progress in the Chinese Communist Party, the significance of patronage in the upper echelons of the Communist Party, and the overall issue of career progress in the CCP. Secondary sources; 10 notes.

J. F. Harrington, Jr.

2859. Hirano, Tadashi. CHUGOKU KYŌSANTŌ NO KŌNICHI MINZOKU TŌITSU SENSEN SEISAKU NO HATTEN: "HANSHŌ KŌNICHI" KARA "RENSHŌ KŌNICHI" E NO TENKAN NO IGI NI TSUITE [The development of the policies of the national united front of the Chinese Communist Party in opposition to Japan: the significance of the change from an anti-Japanese policy which opposed Chiang Kai-shek to an anti-Japanese policy cooperating with him]. *Rekishi Hyōron [Japan] 1974 (3): 108-127.*

2860. Hoffmann, Rainer. DAS MAOISTISCHE MODELL DER ENTWICKLUNG [The Maoist model of development]. *Frankfurter Hefte [West Germany] 1976 31(11): 24-33.* Analyzes the development model represented by China under Mao Tse-tung, one which has as its basis the use of the masses as both planners and agents of economic development.

2861. Hoffmann, Rainer. DER MAOISMUS: ANMERKUNGEN ZUM MAOISTISCHEN MODELL DER GESELLSCHAFT [Maoism: observations on the Maoist model of society]. *Internationales Asienforum [West Germany] 1979 10(1-2): 67-83.* Discusses the role, influence, and political philosophy of the Chinese leader Mao Zedong (1893-1976) in the historical context of the Chinese revolution, 1949-79. Topics include Mao's special relationship with the aspirations of the rural masses, urban-rural development, Party leadership via mass-line politics based on the socioeconomic characteristics of Maoism, the Maoist concept of controlled social conflict, youth in the postrevolutionary climate of the 1960's, the failure of Maoism, and the anti-Maoist policies pursued by the new Chinese leadership since 1976.

2862. Honig, Emily. SOCIALIST REVOLUTION AND WOMEN'S LIBERATION IN CHINA—A REVIEW ARTICLE. *Journal of Asian Studies 1985 44(2): 329-336.* It was once popular for Western scholars to view the liberation of women as one of the most dramatic accomplishments of the Chinese revolution. This article reviews three recently published studies that present a more sanguine view of the impact of the policies adopted by the Chinese Communist Party (CCP) on women's lives. Throughout its history (with the possible exception of the 1920's) the CCP has failed to commit itself to the achievement of gender equality. To have done so would have alienated male peasants, the most important constituency of the CCP. Patriarchy, rather than being dismantled, has been perpetuated and reinforced in China. This argument is substantiated by an analysis of Party policy and political campaigns. The extent to which these policies and campaigns reflect social reality is a task that future scholars will have to confront. J/S

2863. Houn, Franklin W. THE EIGHTH CENTRAL COMMITTEE OF THE CHINESE COMMUNIST PARTY: A STUDY OF AN ELITE. *Am. Pol. Sci. Rev. 1957 51(2): 392-404.* Surveys age, geographic origin, education, occupation, length of affiliation, and intra-Party work of members of the 8th Central Committee members, concluding that ruling officials of the Chinese Communist Party constitute an upper middle-class elite, 1927-56.

2864. Hsing Kuo-ch'iang. CADRE POLICY: A CCP DILEMMA. *Issues and Studies [Taiwan] 1979 15(12): 52-71.* The cadres have played a prominent role in the People's Republic of China since 1949, and now problems surrounding the cadres, especially their debates over the ideological line, are an obstruction to the Four Modernizations the regime hopes to achieve.

2865. Hsing Kuo-ch'iang. A STUDY OF THE MOVEMENT TO "CRITICIZE REVISIONISM AND RECTIFY THE STYLE OF WORK." *Issues & Studies [Taiwan] 1973 9(7): 28-36.* Since 1947 large-scale criticism and rectification movements in China, instead of consolidating Communist Party leadership, have caused frequent political purges, which will continue until revisionism is clearly defined.

2866. HSü Ch'ing-lan. SOCIAL PSYCHOLOGICAL CHANGES IN MAINLAND CHINA. *Issues & Studies [Taiwan] 1972 8(4): 36-44.* Discusses how changes in social psychology in China since 1949 have resulted from Communist Party activities. Based on talks given at the 1971 Sino-Japanese Conference on Mainland China.

2867. Hsu Kuang. WOMEN'S LIBERATION THROUGH STRUGGLE. *Chinese Studies in Hist. 1974 7(4): 100-108.* A Chinese woman relates her contributions (1937-73) to the destruction of feudalism in China and to the realization of women's rights through Communism.

2868. Hsüan Mo. PARTY CONSOLIDATION: TENG'S FINAL STRUGGLE. *Issues & Studies [Taiwan] 1984 20(1): 12-25.* Ever since Yenan, "Party consolidation" and "Party rectification" campaigns have been used by the CCP faction in power to eliminate rival elements. The current campaign, initiated in 1983, is not just aimed at eradicating ideological, work style, and organizational impurities but is also designed to quell anti-Deng factions. Based on the writings of Mao and other Mainland publications; 14 notes. J. A. Krompart

2869. Huai Yuan. WANG MING, MAO TSE-TUNG AND THE SOVIET UNION. *Issues and Studies [Taiwan] 1974 10(8): 82-89.* Discusses the political rivalry in the Chinese Communist Party, 1931-45, between Mao Tse-tung and Wang Ming following the latter's death in Moscow, 1974.

2870. Jacoby, Russell. STALINISM AND CHINA. *Radical Am. 1976 10(3): 7-24.* The official Chinese version of the split between the USSR and China has been accepted without reservation by most parts of the American Left. This has also had the effect of rendering Stalinism acceptable to the Left. The Chinese Revolution and Maoism, however, diverged from the Russian model in at least three areas: the role of the peasants, political organization, and economic organization and industrialization. N. Lederer

2871. Johnson, Chalmers. PEASANT NATIONALISM REVISITED: THE BIOGRAPHY OF A BOOK. *China Q. [Great Britain] 1977 (72): 766-785.* Fifteen years after the publication of his controversial *Peasant Nationalism and Communist Power,* the author faces his many critics with the insistence that he would change nothing of substance in the work. Based on *Peasant Nationalism* and Chinese and English works printed since 1962; 35 notes. J. R. Pavia, Jr.

2872. Joseph, William Allen. "Impatient Revolutionaries: The Critique of Ultra-Leftism and Chinese Politics, 1958-1980." Stanford U. 1981. 471 pp. *DAI 1981 42(2): 836-837-A.* 8115800

2873. Joshi, Gopa. THE CYL: A LINK BETWEEN THE PARTY AND THE YOUTH 1957-79 (II). *China Report [India] 1980 16(4): 3-17.* Continued from a previous article (see entry 33B:3325). Between 1957 and 1966, a time of struggle within the Party leadership itself, Communist Youth League First Secretary Hu Yaobang, by focusing on ideological education as a means of mobilizing youth for socialist construction, took a line similar to that adopted by chairman Mao Zedong. During the Cultural Revolution, however, Mao bypassed the CYL, for although it had assisted in rusticating youth, a target of the Great Leap Forward period, it had also managed to alienate many, especially its more intellectual members. After the 9th Congress of the Communist Party of China, reconstruction of the CYL on Maoist lines was planned, but after Mao's death the problem of rusticated students again became a major one. Primary sources; 55 notes. E. L. Keyser

2874. Kao Hsiang-kao. [CURRENT ECONOMIC SITUATION IN MAINLAND CHINA]. *Issues & Studies [Taiwan] 1971 7(9): 50-62, (10): 67-82.* PART I. GROWTH RATE AND RELATED PROBLEMS. Computes China's economic growth rate, 1952-70, and evaluates growth rate statistics published by the Communist Party. PART II. INDUSTRIAL DEVELOPMENT. Describes the industrial development of China, 1950's-70.

2875. Keith, Ronald C. "EGALITARIANISM" AND "SEEKING THE TRUTH FROM THE FACTS" IN THE PEOPLE'S REPUBLIC OF CHINA. *Dalhousie Review [Canada] 1983 63(2): 322-340.* The concept of "egalitarianism" has again been repudiated by the Chinese Communist Party leadership as inconsistent with the Party's tradition of empirical analysis and investigation and as conflicting with Mao's 1941 directive "to seek the truth from the facts." The concept is viewed as "an attempt to level the socioeconomic distinctions between men, and as an attempt to promote an equal distribution of goods in society," and is thus a problem of lingering "feudalism" in modern socialist society in China. The issue of "egalitarianism" is extremely sensitive as it relates to the Cultural Revolution attack on the Party leadership for having advocated Liu Shaoqu's "theory of productive forces." 49 notes. L. J. Klass

2876. Khot, Nitin. MAOISM *IN EXTREMIS,* LIUISM IN COMMAND: ECONOMIC MODERNIZATION AS STRATEGY IN CLASS STRUGGLE IN CHINA. *China Report [India] 1979 15(6): 53-80.* A study of the ideologies, strategies, and relationships between the two main political factions within the Chinese Communist Party, each struggling to gain the upper hand in the socialist economic development of the country, here called "Liuists" and "Maoists." Each area of the economy has become a battleground in the seesaw of power over the last three decades. Present Liuist attacks on the previous Maoist policies and the policies of the Gang of Four are really a cover for the demobilization of radical socialism in China. For a structure that worked it is substituting "gilded mediocrity." 114 notes. R. V. Ritter

2877. Koloskov, B. T. MAOISTSKIE FAL'SIFIKATSII I PRAVDA ISTORII [Maoist falsifications and the truth of history]. *Voprosy Istorii KPSS [USSR] 1974 (2): 60-72.* Recent Maoist interpretations of Chinese history ignore the positive role the Comintern

and USSR played in advancing the interests of the Chinese people. Soviet historical scholarship has correctly emphasized the adventurist and dictatorial nature of Mao Tse-tung's policies from the 1920's to the "Cultural Revolution" and the present. Based on published documents and Soviet historical studies; 47 notes.
L. E. Holmes

2878. Kooiman, D. HET DILEMMA WU-WANG CHRISTENEN IN NIEUW CHINA [The Wu-Wang dilemma: Christians in the new China]. *Wereld en Zending [Netherlands] 1974 3(5): 387-401.* Describes the reactions, represented by Wu Yao-tsung and Wang Ming-tao, of Christians in China to the Communist government in 1949, and traces the history of their theological and political differences from 1920.

2879. Kovalev, E. F. A NEW STEP IN THE STUDY OF SINO-SOVIET RELATIONS BETWEEN 1945 AND 1970. *Soviet Studies in Hist. 1973-74 12(3): 71-87.* Argues that Soviet policy toward the People's Republic of China has been totally correct and consistent with the principles of Marxism-Leninism, while finding the view that Soviet models were simply imposed and were not integrated into the special conditions existing in China completely erroneous; chauvinistic Maoism continues to distort China's attitude toward the USSR. Based on *Sovetsko-kitaiskie otnosheniia, 1945-1970. Kratkii ocherk* [Soviet-Chinese relations, 1945-1970: a short sketch] (Moscow, 1972) by O. B. Borisov and B. T. Koloskov.

2880. Kraus, Richard Curt. THE LIMITS OF MAOIST EGALITARIANISM. *Asian Survey 1976 16(11): 1081-1096.* Examines Maoist thought on egalitarianism and the action taken, 1949-75 toward removing inequality in China.

2881. Kroker, Eduard J. M. DER MAOISMUS—EINE CHINESISCHE VARIANTE DES MARXISMUS [Maoism—a Chinese variation of Marxism]. *Stimmen der Zeit [West Germany] 1973 191(12): 820-834.* Stresses the differences between Maoism and orthodox Marxist-Leninist conceptions of the party, revolution, and social class. Maoism does not regard the party as inseparable from the dictatorship of the proletariat. The Maoist party is subject to limitations by "the masses" as represented by the chairman. The Cultural Revolution destroyed the party's claim to infallibility. Mao's concept of the revolutionary class places more stress on the peasants and less on technological rationalization. Based on Mao's writings.
R. Stromberg

2882. Kroker, Eduard J. M. EHE UND FAMILIE IN DER CHINESISCHEN WELT [Marriage and family in the Chinese world]. *Stimmen der Zeit [West Germany] 1982 200(3): 147-160.* Maoism secularized marriage, separated it from the traditional Chinese concept of ancestors, and broke the continuity of the formerly cosmic transcendental order, a policy that can be analyzed with the help of decrees and laws on marriage, the elderly, family planning, and divorce between 1949 and the wedding laws of 1980.

2883. Kubarov, B. SOCIAL-CHAUVINISM IN PEKING'S POLICIES. *Int. Affairs [USSR] 1974 (3): 66-77.* Analyzes the historical roots and current characteristics of China's socialist ideology and finds it to be nationalistic and contrary to the unity and cohesion of international communism.

2884. Kun, Joseph C. PEKING AND WORLD COMMUNISM. *Problems of Communism 1974 23(6): 34-43.* Explores the claim that China set itself up as a separate center of the international Communist movement in the decade after 1961. It is obvious that by 1974 Peking has done nothing to guide the Marxist-Leninist splinter parties that appeared throughout the world in support of the Chinese. Primary and secondary sources; 29 notes.
J. M. Lauber

2885. Kung Teh-liang. A BRIEF REVIEW OF CCP ACTIVITIES DURING THE PAST FIFTY YEARS. *Issues & Studies [Taiwan] 1972 7(10): 31-39, (11): 53-63, (12): 78-89.* Part I. Discusses the national congresses held by China's Communist Party and the party's organizational changes, 1921-71. Part II. Discusses the methods used by the Party, 1921-71, to overthrow the Nationalists and convert China to socialism. Part III. Examines the battles between political factions in the Party, 1921-71.

2886. Kung Teh-liang. THE CHINESE COMMUNIST U.S. POLICY. *Issues & Studies [Taiwan] 1971 7(9): 13-25.* Discusses the foreign policy of the Chinese Communist Party toward the United States from 1922 to 1971.

2887. K'ung Te-liang. CCP VERSUS THE ARMY. *Issues & Studies [Taiwan] 1973 9(10): 38-47.* Reviews relations between the Communist Party of China and its military forces, 1930's-72.

2888. Kuo, Warren. THE EVOLUTION OF THE CHINESE COMMUNIST PARTY. *Issues and Studies [Taiwan] 1975 11(2): 2-26.* Discusses the political evolution of the Communist Party in China from 1922 to the 1970's, emphasizing the ideology that has made the CCP a threat to world peace.

2889. Kuo, Warren. THE POLITICAL POWER STRUCTURE IN MAINLAND CHINA. *Issues and Studies [Taiwan] 1978 14(6): 20-31.* Lacking a democratic basis and fixed organization, the Communist Party has been a one-man or—since 1976—an oligarchic dictatorship.

2890. Lambert, Geoffrey. "Trends in the Circulation of the Chinese Communist Elite: The State Council, 1949-1973." U. of Minnesota 1979. 230 pp. *DAI 1980 40(9): 5169-A.* 8006635

2891. Larev, V. I. PRIRODA I KORNI MAOISTSKOGO ANTI-SOVETIZMA [The nature and roots of Maoist anti-Sovietism]. *Voprosy Istorii KPSS [USSR] 1975 (10): 84-96.* A critical analysis of the views of Mao Tse-tung, domestic and foreign policies of Communist China, and Sino-Soviet relations. The retreat of China from socialist policies to those of chauvinism, racism, military expansion, and creation of a military-bureaucratic dictatorship has occurred as a result of general problems of backwardness and Mao Tse-tung's attitudes, including his hatred of the Soviet Union. Based on Vladimir Il'ich Lenin's *Collected Works*, published documents, and published speeches of Mao Tse-tung; 56 notes.
L. E. Holmes

2892. Lazarev, V. I. IZ ISTORII SGOVORA MAOISTSKIKH LIDEROV S IMPERIALISTAMI SSHA [From the history of collusion of Maoist leaders with imperialists of the United States]. *Voprosy Istorii KPSS [USSR] 1980 (10): 74-86.* Surveys the history of collusion between Mao Zedong and the United States from the early 1930's with special emphasis on the period from 1936 to the 1950's. Mao sought American military and economic assistance through Edgar Snow in 1936 and other Americans invited to Yenan. Promises to break relations with Moscow and alter the political program of the Chinese Communist Party continued during World War II, as Mao looked primarily to the United States for help. In 1949 Zhou Enlai (Chou En-lai) asked for US assistance so that China could follow an independent course, a proposal that foundered because of internal opposition, Soviet aid, and Korea. Later, however, a series of anti-Soviet deals were struck with the United States as Chinese policy increasingly represented the petit bourgeois nature of Maoist leadership. Based on memoirs and published documents; 56 notes.
L. E. Holmes

2893. Lazarev, V. I. KOMPARTIIA KITAIA: PROSHLOE I NASTOIASHCHEE [The Chinese Communist Party, past and present]. *Voprosy Istorii KPSS [USSR] 1981 (7): 105-114.* In recognition of the 60th anniversary of the foundation of the Communist Party of China, analyzes the past and present and predicts the future of the Party. Considers the background and beginnings, the membership, the early attitudes and policies, the response to the Great October Socialist Revolution, and relations with the new Soviet government, the involvement in the Chinese Revolution and subsequent changes in policies and attitudes toward other countries and other Communist Parties, the deterioration of relations with the Communist Party of the Soviet Union, the importance of Maoism, and the necessity of friendly relations with the USSR for the united promotion of socialism and world peace. Based mainly on Soviet and Chinese newspaper articles; 71 notes. L. Smith

2894. Leader, Shelah Gilbert. THE COMMUNIST YOUTH LEAGUE AND THE CULTURAL REVOLUTION. *Asian Survey 1974 14(8): 700-771.* Explains the downfall of the Communist Youth League (CYL), the divergence of the current organization from its antecedent, and thus, the impact of the Cultural Revolution on it.

2895. Leonidov, K. and Mikhailov, Y. MAOISTS' ANTI-POPULAR ECONOMIC POLICY. *Int. Affairs [USSR] 1975 (2): 34-43.* Attacks Maoist economic policy as formulated by the 9th and 10th Congresses of the Communist Party of China (1969, 1973). Pursuance of such policies not only violate China's present economic requirements but also have produced disastrous results in the past, namely 1958-59 and 1966-69. More importantly, however, Maoist economic policy provides clear evidence of Maoism's anti-working class outlook, distortion of the bases of socialism, continuing militarism, and anti-Soviet and antisocialist line. Fig., 10 notes. D. K. McQuilkin

2896. Levine, Norman. NON-MARXIST ELEMENTS IN THE COMMUNISM OF MAO. *Asian Thought and Soc. 1976 1(3): 307-332.* Explores the reasons for the dissimilarities in Maoism and Marxism.

2897. Leys, Simon. THE DEATH OF LIN BIAO. *Dissent 1983 30(3): 317-321.* Presents an account, by an anonymous Chinese author, revealing the deadly and unscrupulous power struggles within Communist Chinese leadership, as exemplified by the alleged murder of Mao Zedong loyalist, General Lin Biao.

2898. Li Ming-hua. AN ANALYSIS OF THE RECONSTRUCTION OF TRADE UNIONS ON THE MAINLAND. *Issues & Studies [Taiwan] 1973 9(12): 35-44.* Discusses the Chinese Communist Party's relations with labor unions in China since 1921 with emphasis on the Party's reconstruction of the unions in 1973.

2899. Li T'ien-min. BIOGRAPHIES OF CHINESE COMMUNIST PERSONALITIES. *Issues and Studies [Taiwan] 1977 13(1): 77-90.* Reviews various collections of biographical writings on important members of the Chinese Communist Party and the effect which they have had as instruments of propaganda as well as informative sources for the outside world, 1949-72.

2900. Li T'ien-min. MAO'S LEGACY AND COMMUNIST CHINA IN TRANSITION. *Issues and Studies [Taiwan] 1976 12(12): 1-10.* Examines the history of political power struggles in China, 1935-76, as they have related to the regime of Mao Tse-tung; discusses the legacy of unceasing struggle and of military presence in the political arena which Mao left to the Communist Party.

2901. Li T'ien-min. ON LIN PIAO'S "ILLICIT RELATIONS WITH FOREIGN COUNTRIES." *Issues & Studies [Taiwan] 1973 9(6): 24-34.* An examination of Lin Piao's career, 1938-71, fails to substantiate charges made by the Communist Party of China after he was purged that he had had illicit relations with the USSR.

2902. Li Yu-ning. THE VICISSITUDES OF CHINESE COMMUNIST HISTORIOGRAPHY: CH'Ü CH'IU-PAI FROM MARTYR TO TRAITOR. Fogel, Joshua A. and Rowe, William T., ed. *Perspectives on a Changing China: Essays in Honor of Professor C. Martin Wilbur on the Occasion of his Retirement* (Boulder, Colo.: Westview Pr., 1979): 237-258. Traces the activities of Qiu Qiubo (Ch'ü Ch'iu-pai, 1899-1935) in the Chinese Communist movement, including years as chief of the Chinese Party Politburo and member of the Comintern Executive Committee (ECCI) in the 1920's. Left with the rear guard when the Long March began, he was captured and executed by the Guomindang (Kuomintang) in 1935. Revered as a martyr by the Chinese Communists, though with recognition of his political "errors," until 1960, he became the object of progressively more abusive and formulaic attacks as an enemy and traitor with the onset of the Cultural Revolution, largely perhaps because of his Russian and Comintern connections. Based in part on the author's dissertation. 36 notes.

2903. Liao Gailong; Kwan Oi-va, transl. HISTORICAL EXPERIENCES AND OUR ROAD OF DEVELOPMENT. *Issues & Studies [Taiwan] 1981 17(10): 65-94, (11):81-110, (12): 79-104.* Reproduces a 1980 report of a researcher (Liao Gailong) for the Chinese Communist Party Central Committee to the National Party-School Forum. Part 1. Outlines Party history since 1949. Part 2. Overemphasis on class struggle was a major cause of the Cultural Revolution. Analyzes mistakes that marred the later years of Mao Zedong's brilliant work for China's revolution. Part 3. Analyzes the new course of development selected by China's Party Central Committee. J. A. Krompart

2904. Lien Chan. OBSERVATIONS ON COMMUNIST CHINA'S ORGANIZATIONAL STRUCTURE AND BUREAUCRATIC STYLE. *Issues and Studies [Taiwan] 1979 15(7): 63-76.* The democracy and centralism of the Communist Party are in conflict with the traditional Chinese mode of operation.

2905. Lin Chen. MAINLAND PEOPLE AGAIN RESIST COMMUNISTS' ECONOMIC OPPRESSION. *Issues & Studies [Taiwan] 1970 6(9): 47-59.* Describes the resistance of mainland Chinese to the Communist Party's economic policy, 1952-70.

2906. Lindsay, Michael. AN ANALYSIS OF THE PEOPLE'S REPUBLIC OF CHINA. *Asia Q. [Belgium] 1975 (2): 153-174.* When Chinese Communism has adhered too strongly to the Marxist-Leninist dogmas it has not been successful. The Communist Party exploits the masses and it is unlikely that there will be a new revolution until the masses demand equal rights with the rulers. Resentment against the exploitation of the masses by the Party will continue to manifest itself only in rebellions, not revolutions, until a revolutionary theory offering a workable system of democratic government develops. F. Birch

2907. Lonshchakov, G. THE XINHUA AGENCY: AN INSTRUMENT OF SUBVERSIVE ACTIVITIES OVERSEAS. *Far Eastern Affairs [USSR] 1981 (3): 132-138.* Traces the history of the Xinhua Press Agency, the official news and propaganda agency of the Communist Party of China, from 1938 to 1981, commenting on changes in the goals, structure, and nature of the agency brought about by China's break with the USSR in the 1960's.

2908. MacInnis, Donald E. IMPLICATIONS OF CHINA'S REVOLUTIONARY FORCE FOR THEOLOGY AND MISSION. *Foundations 1974 17(4): 311-320.* Discusses the displacement of Christianity by Marxism in China since 1950 and the lessons to be drawn for missionaries dealing with developing nations in 1973.

2909. Mackerras, Colin. "PARTY CONSOLIDATION" AND THE ATTACK ON "SPIRITUAL POLLUTION." *Australian Journal of Chinese Affairs [Australia] 1984 (11): 175-186.* Party consolidation called for by an October 1983 Communist Party of China session included a crackdown on crime, checks on infiltration of foreign ideologies, and selective replacement of certain government officials.

2910. Madsen, Richard P. MASS MOBILIZATION IN MAO'S CHINA. *Problems of Communism 1981 30(6): 69-76.* Reviews Charles P. Cell's *Revolution at Work: Mobilization Campaigns in China* (1977) and Thomas P. Bernstein's *Up to the Mountains and Down to the Villages: The Transfer of Youth from Urban to Rural China* (1977). Insofar as mass campaigns coincided with the moral vision of the Chinese people, the Maoist version of politics enjoyed wide popular acceptance in the 1950's but subsequently became increasingly alien to the Chinese populace. 7 notes. J. M. Lauber

2911. Maksimov, Nikolai. PROTIV TEORIIATA NA MAOIZMA [Against the theory of Maoism]. *Izvestiia na Instituta po Istoriia na BKP [Bulgaria] 1975 33: 155-193.* This study, aimed at preparing potential Party lecturers on the history of Maoism, surveys the main points in anti-Maoist polemics. Includes philosophical, economic, and political criticism of the activities of Mao and other leaders since their anti-Soviet policy turn of 1958. Because the Chinese learned dialectics from secondary Stalinist sources, not directly from Marxist classics, the contradictions within the Maoist eclectic dialectic led to confusion about 19th-century liberalism, reformism, and utopian socialism. Based on Chinese secondary sources; 160 notes. C. S. Masloff

2912. Maloney, Joan M. WOMEN IN THE CHINESE COMMUNIST REVOLUTION: THE QUESTION OF POLITICAL EQUALITY. Berkin, Carol R. and Lovett, Clara M., ed. *Women, War & Revolution* (New York: Holmes & Meier, 1980): 165-181. Presents a background to the Chinese Communist revolution from the formation of the Soviet Woman's Bureau in 1917. Focuses on the difficulty of mobilizing peasant women to the cause of women at the grass-roots level, which was largely due to the hostility of the Nationalist government.

2913. Mammitzsch, Ulrich H. WOMEN'S EMANCIPATION IN CHINA: REFLECTIONS ON RECENT TRENDS IN THE PERCEPTION OF THE PROCESS. *J. of Ethnic Studies 1980 8(3): 77-108.* The question of women in modern China has not only been inextricably linked to the larger issues of the Chinese revolution but also to issues of women's emancipation of a more general nature, such as the ideological stance and exaggerated claims of the Chinese Communist Party leadership, a condition which forced students to rely on incomplete and manipulated information. Examines the Chinese feminist-socialist position and its shifting congruence and incongruence with nationalist-revolutionary goals, analyzing Claudie Broyelle's *Women's Liberation in China* (1977), Shelah Gilbert Leader's "The Emancipation of Chinese Women," in *World Politics* 1973 26(1), and other recent studies. G. J. Bobango

2914. Martin, Helmut. *Cult & Canon: The Origins and Development of State Maoism.* White Plains, N.Y.: M. E. Sharpe, 1982. 233 pp.

2915. Max, Rolf and Schobe, Werner. ZUR POLITIK DER GEGENWÄRTIGEN CHINESISCHEN FÜHRUNG GEGENÜBER DER ARBEITERKLASSE IN DER VR CHINA [On the policy of the present Chinese leadership toward the Chinese working class]. *Beiträge zur Geschichte der Arbeiterbewegung [East Germany] 1974 16(2): 206-224.* Since 1949 the proportion of rural to urban Communist Party members in the People's Republic of China has changed from 9:1 to nearly 1:1 through the policy of combining the roles of worker, farmer, and soldier. Mao Tse-tung recognized in the Chinese a people who were ready to follow a progressive leader. Through training and industrialization at local levels the present political leadership has brought the Chinese people into the ranks of the international working class. Based on Chinese journals and secondary works; 57 notes. G. H. Libbey

2916. Meisner, Maurice. MAOIST UTOPIANISM AND THE FUTURE OF CHINESE SOCIETY. *Internat. J. [Canada] 1971 26(3): 535-555.* "Whereas in communist countries generally, Marxist utopian goals have tended to become ritualistic in nature and function soon after the revolutionary victory, in China this has not been the case." Traces the transformation of Mao the pragmatist revolutionary to Mao the utopian prophet. 23 notes. E. P. Stickney

2917. Meisner, Maurice. *Marxism, Maoism, and Utopianism: Eight Essays.* Madison: U. of Wisconsin Pr., 1982. 255 pp.

2918. Meisner, Mitch. IDEOLOGY AND CONSCIOUSNESS IN CHINESE MATERIAL DEVELOPMENT. *Pol. and Soc. 1975 5(1): 1-31.* Traces the experiences of the "model" collective Tachai Production Brigade, asserting they are illustrative of the transition to socialism in modern China. Analyzes the roles of ideology and consciousness in this transformation as found in the concept of a unity of theory and practice in Maoism. Primary and secondary sources; 54 notes. D. G. Nielson

2919. Melnick, A. James. SOVIET PERCEPTIONS OF THE MAOIST CULT OF PERSONALITY. *Studies in Comparative Communism 1976 9(1-2): 129-144.* The cult of Mao is seen by Soviet scholars to be a continuation of Confucianism. In 1963 the Soviets first charged that the Chinese were developing their own cult of personality. Analysis of the origins of the cult has led the Soviets to the position that cults may arise because of peculiar conditions. The USSR sees the cult as diminishing in importance since the end of the Cultural Revolution and find potential in China for the elimination of the cult. 58 notes. D. Balmuth

2920. Meserve, Walter J. and Meserve, Ruth. COMMUNIST CHINA'S WAR THEATER. *J. of Popular Culture 1972 6(2): 313-324.* Since 1929 the Communist Party in China has used the theater as a propaganda tool for winning support for war.

2921. Metzger, Thomas A. CHINESE COMMUNISM AND THE EVOLUTION OF CHINA'S POLITICAL CULTURE: A PRELIMINARY APPRAISAL. *Issues and Studies [Taiwan] 1979 15(8): 51-63.* Discusses modernization and Marxism in relation to Chinese tradition since 1949.

2922. Miller, Joseph Thomas. "The Politics of Chinese Trotskyism: The Role of a Permanent Opposition in Communism." U. of Illinois, Urbana-Champaign 1979. 334 pp. *DAI 1980 40(10): 5576-5577-A.* 8009111

2923. Mohanty, Manoranjan. THE FUTURE OF CHINESE POLITY. *China Report [India] 1974 10(5-6): 91-101.* Examines politics and political organization in China, 1925-74. What appears to Westerners as chaos was actually a learning through struggle and upheaval. Examines the decentralization of power in the Communist Party and discusses Chinese class perspective, mass line, Party leadership, and ideological education, 1949-74.

2924. Mohanty, Manoranjan. MAO, DENG AND BEYOND: DIALECTICS OF THE EARLY STAGE OF SOCIALISM. *China Report [India] 1984 20(4-5): 123-132.* The problems faced by China in its efforts at socialist construction related to three forces—the growth of mass consciousness, the mechanism of modern technology, and the pressures of the world capitalist system. Mao Zedong sought to grapple with these forces by breaking with the capitalist framework of the industrial revolution. Deng Xiaoping's approach was a critique of Mao's, working within the framework of the industrial revolution and a people's democratic state. Secondary sources; 22 notes. J. Powell

2925. Mos'ko, G. N. NARODNOE OPOLCHENIE (MIN'BIN) V POLITICHESKOI ZHIZNI K. N. R. [The National Home Guard or *min'bin* in the political life of China]. *Narody Azii i Afriki [USSR] 1978 (6): 105-112.* The National Home Guard was created in China in the second half of the 1920's by the Communist Party for the struggle against internal counterrevolution. The author discusses the three stages of its history: from its creation to the formation of the Chinese People's Republic in 1949; China's period of transition to socialism, 1949-57; and the period, 1958-60. Toward the mid-1950's, however, the militia had become obsolete as a weapon of class struggle within the country. Biblio.
S. R. Gudgin

2926. Murphey, Rhoads. *The Fading of the Maoist Vision: City and Countryside in China's Development.* New York: Methuen, 1980. 169 pp.

2927. Myers, Ramon H. THE CONTEST BETWEEN TWO CHINESE STATES. *Asian Survey 1983 23(4): 536-552.* The violence between the Chinese Communist and the Nationalist parties ended in 1949, but a contest continued over which model of political and economic development should decide the future of the nation of China. The Communist Party could neither achieve economic modernization nor convince the Nationalists to unite with them without radically changing the relationship between state and society. Based on documents and radio broadcasts. M. A. Eide

2928. Nikiforov, V. N. RABOCHEE DVIZHENIE I VOZNIKNOVENIE KOMPARTII KITAIA V OTRAZHENII SOVETSKOI ISTORIOGRAFII [The workers' movement and the establishment of the Communist Party of China in Soviet historiography]. *Voprosy Istorii KPSS [USSR] 1982 (1): 123-132.* The writings of Soviet scholars on the Chinese workers' movement that appeared in the 1920's were marred by overemphasis on the role of the proletariat in the general development of Chinese society. Later work achieved a more balanced evaluation of the strength and significance of the workers' movement and of the events connected with the founding of the Chinese Communist Party. By the late 1960's, research work was of a high standard and made full use of Comintern archive documents. Soviet historians reject the theory put forward by bourgeois scholars that China proves the incorrectness of Marxism-Leninism. Based on secondary sources; 83 notes. G. Dombrovski

2929. Nobel, Genia. DIE ANTIMARXISTISCHE POLITIK DES MAOISMUS [The anti-Marxist policy of Maoism]. *Einheit [East Germany] 1972 27(2): 198-210.* Reviews the development of Maoism in China: the "period of regulation" (1961-65), the "cultural revolution," the consolidation of Maoist dictatorship and its attempt to gain international recognition, and the contrast between Maoist chauvinistic "great power policy" and China's low economic development. The latent crisis of the Maoist regime was mainly caused by the misinterpretation of Marxist principles by political leadership. 14 notes. G. E. Pergl

2930. Onate, Andrew D. *Chairman Mao and the Chinese Communist Party.* Chicago: Nelson-Hall, 1979. 289 pp.

2931. Papoian, A. VELIKII OKTIABR' I KITAI [The October Russian Revolution and China]. *Aziia i Afrika Segodnia [USSR] 1982 (10): 26-27, 36.* Describes the significance of the October Revolution for China and discusses political, diplomatic, military, and economic aid rendered to China by the USSR and other socialist countries.

2932. Peng, Shu-tse. *The Chinese Communist Party in Power.* London: Monad, 1980. 508 pp.

2933. Peyrefitte, Alain. DE CONFUCIUS À MAO TSE-TUNG [From Confucius to Mao Tse-tung]. *Rev. des Travaux de l'Acad. des Sci. Morales et Politiques et Comptes Rendus de ses Séances [France] 1974 127(1): 143-165.* Describes Maoist thought as a synthesis of Taoist methodology, "elitist" Confucianism, anti-individualistic concepts from the ancient School of Laws, and Marxist doctrines. The Chinese hierarchy's recent attacks on Confucianism indicate a shift in emphasis to the authoritarian and totalitarian elements of Mao's philosophy. This implies a return to a more revolutionary style, perhaps even a renewal of the Cultural Revolution. Though official secrecy obscures what is happening in China, we can conclude that despite internal tensions the regime exerts totalitarian control and that the figure of Mao Tse-tung will dominate all philosophical debates. J. R. Vignery

2934. Pfeffer, L. and Eber, A. ZUR HERAUSBILDUNG UND ENTWICKLUNG EINER BESONDEREN SCHICHT ZWISCHEN ARBEITERKLASSE UND BAUERNSCHAFT IN DER VR CHINA UND IHRE ROLLE IN DER MAOISTISCHEN POLITIK [On the formation and development of a special strata between working class and peasantry in the People's Republic of China and its role in the Maoist policy]. *Beiträge zur Geschichte der Arbeiterbewegung [East Germany] 1974 16(3): 398-413.* The development of a distinct class between industrial workers and farmers is unique to China among the Communist nations. This class rose from a country which was in 1948 still partly feudal and partly colonial. Maoist policy included this class, which divides its labor between agriculture and industry, because China was unable to industrialize rapidly enough to absorb into industry the farmers displaced by more extensive and intensive agricultural methods. China's allowance for this class marks its ideological differences from the mainstream of Marxist-Leninist thought and practice. Based on works of Marx, Engels, and Lenin and secondary works; 61 notes. G. H. Libbey

2935. Possony, Stefan T. MAOIST CHINA AND HEROIN. *Issues & Studies [Taiwan] 1971 8(2): 21-46.* Discusses the Chinese Communist Party's participation in heroin smuggling, 1938-71.

2936. Prybyla, Jan S. THE ECONOMIC SYSTEM OF THE PEOPLE'S REPUBLIC OF CHINA. *Asian Thought & Society 1984 9(25): 3-29.* Describes China's struggle with poverty following the Communist triumph in 1949 and the destruction of traditional institutionalized societal interrelationships and economic structure, with dramatic reductions in private ownership of industry, commerce, handicrafts, and agriculture, during the construction of China's Soviet-style socialization.

2937. Record, Jane Cassels and Record, Wilson. TOTALIST AND PLURALIST VIEWS OF WOMEN'S LIBERATION: SOME REFLECTIONS ON THE CHINESE AND AMERICAN SETTINGS. *Social Problems 1976 23(4): 402-414.* Considers the women's liberation movements in China and the United States with primary reference to the ideological context and discusses issues such as liberation within capitalism and Maoism, the role of the state vis-à-vis the household, and private institutions, and its role in opening new doors. Consideration of ideological forces should be at the center of attempts to analyze developments in China. A. M. Osur

2938. Reed, John Harland. "Brass Butterflies or the Thoughts of Mao Tse Tung: The Sociology of Schistosomiasis Control in China." Cornell U. 1979. 280 pp. *DAI 1979 39(11): 6979-A.* 7910827

2939. Richter, Harald. CHEN WANGDAO: EIN ABRISS SEINES LEBENS UND WERKES [Chen Wangdao: a synopsis of his life and work]. *Oriens Extremus [West Germany] 1980 27(1): 61-72.* Chen Wangdao (Ch'en Wang-tao) (1890-1977), late rector of Fudan University, Shanghai, was a pioneer of the Chinese Communist Party, having been active in the May Fourth Movement of 1919. He studied law, literature, and philosophy at several universities in China and Japan. He translated the Communist Manifesto into Chinese, but his main interests lay in political journalism and education. Based on Chen's own works and secondary sources; 100 notes. A. H. Menicant

2940. Rickett, W. Allyn. THE NEW CONSTITUTION AND CHINA'S EMERGING LEGAL SYSTEM IN PERSPECTIVE. *Journal of the Hong Kong Branch of the Royal Asiatic Society [Hong Kong] 1982 22: 99-117.* The almost continual state of turmoil existing in China in this century as well as traditional Chinese disregard of individual human rights culminated in the Cultural Revolution and the antirightist movement, which proved a disaster for China's budding judicial profession and its concern for civil rights. In the post-Mao period, however, there have been increasing written safeguards for human rights, culminating in the adoption on 4 December 1982 by the National People's Congress of a new constitution that extended further guarantees for the protection of individual citizens against the arbitrary abuse of Party and state power. 19 notes. L. J. Klass

2941. Rozman, Gilbert. SOVIET REINTERPRETATIONS OF CHINESE SOCIAL HISTORY: THE SEARCH FOR THE ORIGINS OF MAOISM. *J. of Asian Studies 1974 34(1): 49-72.* A critical review of Soviet Chinese studies, 1960-74, and in particular Soviet interpretation of Chinese social history. Soviet historians isolated reasons for the failure of socialism in China after 1955. Socialism could have been secured if development had proceeded at a slower pace during 1949-55. Soviet historians assumed a well-understood course of development from 1920 to 1949, which actually does not fit the Chinese reality. They viewed the period between 1840 and 1919 in a very negative light, arguing that China

trailed England and France by hundreds of years in the coming of capitalism, and that prior to 1840 feudalism reigned along with a willingness to grant blind obedience to rulers. 67 notes, biblio.
R. V. Ritter

2942. Sabattini, M. OSSERVAZIONI SULLA "VIA CINESE" [Observations on the "Chinese way"]. *Pensiero Pol. [Italy] 1975 8(1): 54-62.* By the recent contacts of American and European experts with Chinese life, the traditional view of an immobile, static country has given way to the realization that the "revolution" is still in progress. Comparative analysis of the theoretical bases of Russian and Chinese socialism affirms Mao's concern for the interrelationship of social and political dogma with the realities of practice in effecting the cultural revolution. In 1958 Mao rejected Soviet models, finalizing his own directives on agrarian reform, industrialization, and the connections between urban and rural life. This has resulted in the development of a flexible Chinese citizenry.
S. Ruffo-Fiore

2943. Samuelsson, K. G. EXIT LIU SHAO-CHI [Exit Liu Shao-chi]. *Kungliga Krigsvetenskaps Akademiens Handlingar och Tidskrift [Sweden] 1969 173(8): 482-489.* An account of the conflict associated with Chinese domestic policy, 1956-68, especially between Mao Tse-tung and Liu Shao-chi. Mao Tse-tung gradually gained control over the Communist Party, one of the reasons for his victory being his use of the youth movement to further his policies during the Cultural Revolution, 1966-68. Secondary sources; note, biblio. U. G. Jeyes

2944. Sanders, William Vernon. "Maoist Labor Incentives." Pennsylvania State U. 1981. 195 pp. *DAI 1982 42(7): 3250-A.* 8129210

2945. Sapozhnikov, B. ANTIMARKSISTSKAIA PRAKTIKA MAOIZMA V VOPROSAKH VOENNOGO STROITEL'STVA [The anti-Marxist practice of Maoism in the development of the armed forces]. *Voenno-Istoricheskii Zhurnal [USSR] 1972 (9): 93-97.* Examines changes which have taken place in the social structure of China and in the organization of the Chinese People's Army, drawing attention to the potential threat to the USSR which they represent.

2946. Scalapino, Robert A. THE STRUGGLE OVER HIGHER EDUCATION: REVOLUTION VERSUS DEVELOPMENT. *Issues and Studies [Taiwan] 1976 12(7): 1-8.* Examines political factions in the Chinese Communist Party, some favoring the advancement of economic development and growth (which predominated, 1949-57) and those favoring advancement of higher education (which is presently gaining popularity); examines the differences of opinion and the political power underlying these factions.

2947. Scalapino, Robert A. THE STUDY OF CHINESE COMMUNISM: AN AMERICAN POLITICAL SCIENTIST'S VIEWS. *Issues and Studies [Taiwan] 1974 10(5): 2-9.* Discusses attitudes in political science theory toward the study of communism in China since 1945.

2948. Schenk-Sandbergen, L. C. SOME ASPECTS OF POLITICAL MOBILIZATION IN CHINA. *Modern Asian Studies [Great Britain] 1973 7(4): 677-689.* Examines the character of mass political mobilization by the Chinese Communists from the 1920's to the 1960's.

2949. Schram, Stuart R. TO UTOPIA AND BACK: A CYCLE IN THE HISTORY OF THE CHINESE COMMUNIST PARTY. *China Q. [Great Britain] 1981 (87): 404-439.* The 60 years of Chinese Communist Party existence reflect a tension between periods in which utopia was held to be realizable in the near future, if not already achieved, and those in which reality forced a retreat. The failure of Mao's last 20 years greatly limits utopianism in China today. Based largely on Chinese materials, especially "Resolution on Certain Questions in the History of our Party since the Founding of the People's Republic"; 72 notes. J. R. Pavia, Jr.

2950. Schwartz, Benjamin. MODERNIZATION & MAOIST VISION: SOME REFLECTIONS ON CHINESE COMMUNIST GOALS. *Dissent 1974 21(2): 237-248.* Discusses the broad goals and motivations of the Chinese Communist leadership, including modernization, nationalism, collectivism and education. Published Fall 1965; reprinted as one of 21 articles on *Dissent*'s 20 years of publication.

2951. Sih, Paul K. T. CONFUCIANISM AS AN ANTITOXIN FOR MAOISM. *Issues & Studies [Taiwan] 1972 8(5): 29-34.* Discusses the incompatibility of Maoism and Confucianism in Communist China.

2952. Sirvent G., Carlos A. SOCIEDAD, PODER POLÍTICO Y BUROCRACIA: CHINA 1949-1969 [Society, political power, and bureaucracy: China, 1949-69]. *Rev. Mexicana de Ciencia Pol. [Mexico] 1972 18(68): 55-62.* Discusses the gap between the Chinese bureaucracy and the people, the relationship between the Communist Party and the masses, and the major movements, 1949-69.

2953. Škvařil, Jaroslav. KOŘENY A ZDROJE IDEOLOGIE MAOISMU [Roots and resources of Maoism]. *Hist. a Vojenství [Czechoslovakia] 1981 30(4): 126-140.* Maoism, anti-Marxist, anti-Leninist, and hostile to contemporary revolutionary movements, controls all basic aspects of daily life in China on the pretext of national necessity. Fundamentally petit-bourgeois in its nature, Maoism is bellicose, expansionist, chauvinistic, despotic, militaristic, bureaucratic, dictatorial, and deeply inimical to scientific socialism. The chauvinistic goals of the regime are camouflaged by pseudo-Marxist phraseology, and thin revolutionary slogans cover the roots of Maoism. Based on published works; 22 notes.
G. E. Pergl/S

2954. Sladkovski, M. THE ROLE OF PROLETARIAN INTERNATIONALISM IN THE CPC'S FORMATION AND ACTIVITY. *Far Eastern Affairs [USSR] 1981 (3): 111-122.* Briefly traces the history of proletarian international movements from 1847 to the present; discusses the political history of China prior to the founding of the Communist Party of China (CPC), and closely examines the role of the Comintern and other Soviet proletarian groups in the founding and growth of the CPC from its birth in 1921 to China's break with the USSR in the 1960's.

2955. Spae, J. DE THEOLOGIE EN DE NIEUWE MAOISTISCHE MENS [Theology and the new Maoist man]. *Wereld en Zending [Netherlands] 1974 3(5): 322-337.* Analyzes the attitudes and assumptions behind, and characteristics of Maoism over the past 50 years and outlines the problems facing the Christian Church in Maoist China.

2956. Tan Chung. CULTURAL LEGACY AND COMMUNIST REVOLUTION. *China Report [India] 1974 10(5-6): 50-60.* Examines traditional social organization in China and the role of Confucianism. The "personality cult" surrounding Confucius necessitates an attack on Confucian values so that communism may triumph.

2957. Tao, L. S. CRIMINAL JUSTICE IN COMMUNIST CHINA. *Issues and Studies [Taiwan] 1977 13(6): 15-42, (7): 19-50.* Part I. Reviews the development of law in China, 1949-77, investigates the patterns of criminal justice administration under the Communists, and examines the role of the courts and other law enforcement institutions in relation to the Party. Part II. Reviews conditions in the Chinese Communist judiciary, 1958-77, where judges, although not necessarily Party members, are subject to political and governmental pressures.

2958. Taraki, Bariman. INSTITUTIONALIZATION AND BUREAUCRACY IN CHINA: THE RELEVANCE OF THE MAOIST EXPERIENCE. *Studies in Comparative Int. Development 1978 13(1): 100-124.* Describes positivistic and normative views and the Maoist theory of institutionalization. Examines in the Chinese context restoration and old values, restoration and bureaucratization, restoration as revisionism, and restoration and the Party. Secondary sources; 10 notes, 88 ref. S. A. Farmerie

2959. Teiwes, Frederick C. *Politics & Purges in China: Rectification and the Decline of Party Norms, 1950-1965.* White Plains, N.Y.: M. E. Sharpe, 1979. 729 pp.

2960. Townsend, James R. CHINESE POPULISM AND THE LEGACY OF MAO TSE-TUNG. *Asian Survey 1977 17(11): 1003-1015.* Whereas in traditional China virtue was thought to reside in an intellectual elite reigning over the ignorant masses, the creed of contemporary China is populist, namely, that virtue resides in the common people. Mao Tse-tung, by his incessant rebellion against authority, his advocacy of the mass line, decentralized administration, and egalitarianism, greatly contributed to this remarkable transformation of Chinese society. Mao's populism has always been in conflict with the Chinese Communist Party's determination to exercise centralized control over the country. G. M. Alexander

2961. Treadgold, Donald W. CHINESE COMMUNISM. *Asian Affairs: An Am. Rev. 1977 4(4): 232-254, (5): 317-341.* Part I. DOMESTIC TURMOILS. Intersperses personal impressions of seven provinces (Hopei, Kiangsu, Hupei, Honan, Shensi, Hunan, Kwangtung), Peking, and Shanghai during a January 1977 visit with explanatory historical data, 1922-77. Discusses the impact of traditional China, Mao Tse-tung, Stalin, Chou En-lai, the Hungarian Revolution and Imre Nagy (1956), and the Gang of Four on social, economic, educational, artistic, religious domestic development. Describes the politicization of all areas of Chinese society. Based on primary anecdotal and secondary source material; 3 notes. Part II. FOREIGN PROSPECTS. Traces the Sino-Soviet relationship from the break with the Kuomintang (mid-1920's) to the present. Analyzes Chinese adaptations of Soviet experiences and their foreign policy in general. Discusses Chinese nationalism as a secular religion as well as its social, cultural, and military effects. Based on personal experiences, other primary sources (including the anecdotal) and secondary sources; 7 notes. R. B. Mendel

2962. Trivière, Léon. LA CHINE ET SES DIRIGEANTS [China and its leaders]. *Études [France] 1973 339(6): 643-665.* Outlines the ten crises, 1927-73, of the Chinese Communist Party which altered and affected the political direction of Mao's cultural revolution, and the influence of these past problems on the elections of the 24-28 August 1973 10th National Congress of the Party.

2963. Ts'ai, Shih-Shan H. CHINESE IMMIGRATION THROUGH COMMUNIST CHINESE EYES: AN INTRODUCTION TO THE HISTORIOGRAPHY. *Pacific Hist. R. 1974 43(3): 395-408.* A bibliographic and critical study of all Communist works available outside of mainland China on Chinese immigration to the United States. They focus on three aspects: "the motives and processes of Chinese immigration; the background of a series of treaties and laws by which the United States managed the immigration; and the reasons for the anti-Chinese movement.... Though we might not accept their Marxist analyses, we must recognize that the Communist Chinese researchers have added a considerable array of new data to the study of Chinese immigration." 43 notes.

R. V. Ritter

2964. Ts'ai Yu-ch'en. HU YAO-PANG: HIS CAREER AND PROSPECTS. *Issues & Studies [Taiwan] 1981 17(11): 8-21.* Hu Yaobang (Hu Yao-pang, b. 1915) has been active in the Communist Party since his early teens. Since his post-Cultural Revolution rehabilitation, he has contributed to high-level Party actions, including the de-Maofication campaign. In June 1981 he was appointed Party Chairman. Hu's chances to succeed Deng Xiaoping (Teng Hsiao-p'ing) depend on whether Deng and his followers can improve the Chinese economy. J. A. Krompart

2965. Ts'ao, Ignatius J. H. [AI SSU-CH'I].

AI SSU-CH'I: THE APOSTLE OF CHINESE COMMUNISM—PART ONE: HIS LIFE AND WORKS. *Studies in Soviet Thought [Netherlands] 1972 12 (1): 2-36.* Discusses the life and political philosophy of Communist Party theorist Ai Ssu-ch'i in China, 1935-66.

AI SSU-CH'I'S PHILOSOPHY—PART TWO: DIALECTICAL MATERIALISM. *Studies in Soviet Thought [Netherlands] 1972 12 (3): 231-244.* Discusses the influence of Marxism-Leninism on Ai Ssu-ch'i from the 1930's to the 1950's.

2966. Tseng Yung-hsien. THE ORGANIZATION OF THE CHINESE COMMUNIST PARTY: ITS CHARACTERISTICS. *Issues and Studies [Taiwan] 1975 11(5): 66-76.* Discusses the organizational structure of China's political system as a reflection of the thought of Mao Tse-tung, 1926-70's, and its relationship to traditional notions of Marxism-Leninism.

2967. Twardy, Tomasz. SINOCENTRYZM JAKO PODSTAWA MAOIZMU [Sinocentrism as the basis of Maoism]. *Nowe Drogi [Poland] 1974 (12): 53-61.* Considers the ancient Chinese concept of the *Middle Kingdom* as a factor behind the current chauvinistic policy of Mao Tse-tung.

2968. Uehara, Kazuyoshi. CHGOKU SHAKAI SHUGI KENKY NO GENJŌ TO KADAI [The present situation and tasks of studies on Chinese socialism]. *Rekishi Hyōron [Japan] 1976 (318): 34-49.* Reviews the present situation and tasks of the studies on Chinese socialism on the basis of the general situation of studies on socialism in Japan. The author proposes tasks to clarify the stages of development of the Chinese socialism and the essence of Maoism as viewed by scientific and independent study in Japan. The essence of Maoism is the principle of equality characteristic of small producers which is conditioned by the stage of underdeveloped socialism. Suggests that the communism aimed at by Mao is to realize "equal division" in society, building on the wartime communism of the Yenan era. Lastly, the author emphasizes, from the standpoint of his study on the problems of workers in the Great Leap Forward period, the need to throw light on the actual condition of the proletariat in the building of Chinese socialism. 46 notes.

H. Takatsuna

2969. Van Slyke, Lyman P. THE UNITED FRONT IN CHINA. *J. of Contemporary Hist. [Great Britain] 1970 5(3): 119-135.* Despite weak Comintern influence over the Chinese Communist Party (CCP) and Mao Tse-tung, the CCP moved toward a united front policy beginning in 1935. It was oriented toward conditions in China rather than international Soviet interests and focused on cooperation with the Nationalist Party against Japanese invaders and gaining mass popular support. The united front was continued for the latter purpose through the civil war and is still nominally an official policy of the CCP. Primary and secondary sources; 12 notes. B. A. Block

2970. Volti, Rudi. ORGANIZATIONS AND EXPERTISE IN CHINA. *Administration and Soc. 1977 8(4): 423-458.* Discusses the role of technological expertise in the Chinese bureaucracy, and its political, economic, and social organization in the 1960's and 1970's and how technology fits in with Maoist ideology.

2971. Walder, Andrew G. ORGANIZED DEPENDENCY AND CULTURES OF AUTHORITY IN CHINESE INDUSTRY. *J. of Asian Studies 1983 43(1): 51-76.* Examines an "institutional culture of authority" that has come to characterize Chinese industrial enterprises. This institutional culture is shaped by a pattern of organized dependency inherent in the economic relationship of employees to enterprises, and also in systems of reward and control that link the opportunities of employees to their behavior and attitudes. This institutional culture is manifested in widespread ritualism in political meetings, exercise of low voice by subordinates, the creation of patron-client networks linking the Party to selected employees, and the everyday cultivation of personal connections for individual gain. J

2972. Walder, Andrew G. SOME IRONIES OF THE MAOIST LEGACY IN INDUSTRY. *Australian J. of Chinese Affairs [Australia] 1981 (5): 21-38.* Discusses the Maoist experiment, 1957-76, concluding that the changes that took place in this period were precisely opposite the Maoists' intentions; the problems characteristic of Soviet-style systems were intensified rather than diminished.

2973. Walker, Richard L. THE HUMAN COST OF COMMUNISM IN CHINA. *Issues & Studies [Taiwan] 1971 7(12): 16-30, 8(1): 61-76.* Estimates the deaths, the number of refugees, and the destruction of culture caused by the Chinese Communist Party, 1921-71.

2974. Wang, John Ming-Kae. "A History of Chinese Communist Drama (1937-1972)." Southern Illinois U., Carbondale 1979. 118 pp. *DAI 1980 40(8): 4303-A.* 8004101

2975. Wang Chien-min. THE CHINESE COMMUNIST PARTY: A CRITICAL REVIEW COVERING 1921-1971. *Issues & Studies [Taiwan] 1971 7(10): 40-55.* A history of China's Communist Party emphasizing Mao Tse-tung's rise to power despite Stalin's early dominance of the party.

2976. Wang Hsueh-wen. CHINA'S TRADITIONAL CULTURE AND CHINESE COMMUNIST CULTURAL POLICY. *Issues and Studies [Taiwan] 1973 10(3): 33-45.* Communist proletarian culture advocates a radical destruction of China's ethical, Confucian heritage and criticizes it for deriving its basis from the class struggle.

2977. Wang Hsueh-wen. CHINESE COMMUNISTS' DESTRUCTION AND EXPLOITATION OF ANCIENT BOOKS AND ARTIFACTS (PART II). *Issues & Studies [Taiwan] 1973 9(12): 65-77.* Continued from a previous article. Describes the Communist Party's destruction of antiquities and books and artifacts in China, 1949-71, and Communist attempts to preserve such cultural artifacts since 1971.

2978. Wang Hsueh-wen. MAOIST RECTIFICATION OF THE YOUNG COMMUNIST LEAGUE. *Issues & Studies [Taiwan] 1970 7(2): 29-38.* Discusses how Maoists in China attempted to control the Young Communist League through ideological rectification of its members, 1957-70.

2979. Wang Hsueh-wen. A SURVEY OF PEIPING'S YOUTH RUSTICATION PROGRAM. *Issues and Studies [Taiwan] 1979 15(6): 65-80.* Discusses the policy of the Communist Party of China in sending educated urban youth to the countryside in order to integrate them with peasants and workers.

2980. Wang Hsüeh-wen. THE YENAN EXPERIENCE AND THE "EDUCATIONAL REVOLUTION". *Issues & Studies [Taiwan] 1972 8(6): 68-74.* Discusses the educational policy of the Communist Party in China from the 1930's to 1971.

2981. Wang Ming. THE FATE OF THE "LONELY MONK." *Issues and Studies [Taiwan] 1975 11(5): 104-113.* Excerpts from the memoirs of Wang Ming (Ch'en Shao-yü), long-time leader of the internationalist wing of the Chinese Communist Party, who died in Moscow 27 March 1974. This segment is devoted to an attack on the political errors since the 1920's that have made Mao Tse-tung a "lonely monk." Article to be continued.

2982. Weber, Maria. IL CONTROLLO DEL "FUCILE": POLITICI E MILITARI IN CINA [Control of the rifle: politicians and soldiers in China]. *Politico [Italy] 1976 41(3): 430-448.* Examines the political role of the army in China. Discusses the history of the soldier figure in the Middle Kingdom; warlord politics and the rise to power of the Red Army; relations between the Chinese Communist Party and the People's Liberation Army after the revolution; coalitions between civil and military groups; the direct intervention of the People's Liberation Army during the Cultural Revolution, and the political and structural effects deriving from the inability of the party to control the army and its various factions. The Chinese army controls the balance of power in the Maoist system but the weakness of the military lies in its factionalism. J/S

2983. Weiss, Ruth. "THE BEST COMPUTER CANNOT CALCULATE THESE GAINS!"—A PERSONAL BALANCE SHEET. *Eastern Horizon [Hong Kong] 1976 15(1): 49-58.* China made great strides under the leadership of Mao Tse-tung (1893-1976). The author draws upon personal knowledge from 1933 to assess the improvements, but concedes that it is impossible to really measure the impact of communism on the personal lives of the Chinese—the only impact that really matters. She details the propaganda use of the examples of the Taching oil field development and the greatly increased production of the Tachai commune to spur further effort from the Chinese people. L. C. Wilson

2984. White, Gordon. *Party and Professionals: The Political Role of Teachers in Contemporary China.* White Plains, N.Y.: Sharpe, 1981. 359 pp.

2985. White, Lynn T., III. CHINESE INTELLECTUALS AND PARTY POLICY. *Issues & Studies [Taiwan] 1984 20(10): 11-30, (11): 12-32.* The Chinese Communist Party policy toward intellectuals has a long history of alternating encouragement and repression. The regime seeks to kindle intellectuals' enthusiastic support, but the lower intelligentsia still suffers poor housing and low wages, and all intellectuals fear the sudden loss of status that could follow future political shifts. In recent years the Party and government have claimed to bear a high regard for intellectuals, but official pronouncements and campaigns have disclosed wariness and ambiguity toward them. The political potential of the intellectuals can be an important factor in resolving this contradiction. Based on newspapers and periodicals; 163 notes. J. A. Krompart

2986. White, Lynn T., III. LOCAL AUTONOMY IN CHINA DURING THE CULTURAL REVOLUTION: THE THEORETICAL USES OF AN ATYPICAL CASE. *Am. Pol. Sci. Rev. 1976 70(2): 479-491.* Explores the extent to which Shanghai and its subordinate units have been politically independent of higher authorities in the Chinese government. Evidence from the fifties and early sixties suggests increasing managerial and cultural independence at the city level. Evidence from the early Cultural Revolution, however, suggests conceptual problems in the connection of usual notions of autonomy with substantive issue areas, and in their connection with local and central patterns of factions. The slow reconstruction of a local Communist Party hierarchy in Shanghai was paralleled by a decentralization of some commercial and industrial decisions. Shanghai's role as a model in Party rebuilding increased the fully national role of the city's top leadership. Analysis of autonomy, power, or dependence in administrative units is affected when strong local leaders acquire national ambitions. J

2987. Yahuda, Michael. POLITICAL GENERATIONS IN CHINA. *China Q. [Great Britain] 1979 (80): 793-805.* Five political "generations" exist in contemporary China. First are the older cadres, currently the leadership group, who share with the second—the older intellectuals—the distinction of having been the primary targets of the Cultural Revolution. The 1950's generation, from 35 to 55 years old, represent those trained in the earlier Soviet period, while a "lost generation," 20's to 30's, were politicized during the Cultural Revolution. Finally, the new generation consists of youths emerging from middle school to face doubtful futures. Based largely on western commentaries; 23 notes. J. R. Pavia, Jr.

2988. Yakimova, Y. SOCIO-PSYCHOLOGICAL CONCEPTS OF MAOISM IN US SINOLOGY. *Far Eastern Affairs [USSR] 1982 (1): 132-143.* Regardless of the interpretations of American sinologists, from the 1960's until today, the core of China's ruling ideology is still Maoism and is hostile to socialism.

2989. Yang Lu-hsia. THE CHINESE COMMUNIST MILITIA. *Issues & Studies [Taiwan] 1973 9(9): 48-57, (10): 71-76.* Parts I and II. According to the Chinese Communist Party armed struggle is the key to political power. Since 1927, in the course of army construction, the Communists have expanded both the regular Red Army and the local militias.

2990. Yao Meng-hsüan. THE CLASS VIEWPOINT AND CLASS CHARACTER OF THE CHINESE COMMUNISTS: THEIR THEORY OF PARTY-BUILDING AND ORGANIZATION. *Issues & Studies [Taiwan] 1984 20(3): 25-40.* The Communist Party of China was established on V. I. Lenin's concept of a "class party" of proletarian members preparing for violent revolution. Chinese Communists still uphold this theory of party-building even though the Party has always been heterogeneous and has often needed to use united front tactics. The present policy of integrating intellectuals into the common effort does not change this historical nature of the Party. Based on the works of Lenin, Stalin, and Mao and media reports from China; table, 23 notes. J. A. Krompart

2991. Yen, Joseph Chen-ying. AN HISTORICAL SURVEY OF CHINESE COMMUNISTS POLITICAL INFLUENCE ON THE THEATRE. *Issues and Studies [Taiwan] 1976 12(1): 31-68.* Details of Mao Tse-tung's May 1942 "Talks at the Yenan Forum on Literature and Art," in which Mao stressed that "the arts are indispensable for the revolutionary machine," reveal the philosophical foundations for contemporary Chinese theater. The subsequent 1949 National Congress of Writers and Artists and similar organizations illustrate the Communist Party's implementation and constant rethinking of Mao's ideas. Even the 1956 "Let a Hundred Flowers Bloom" campaign, which encouraged diversity of expression, served to expose the "unreformed" individuals, who were then purged. Since the Cultural Revolution, the eight theatrical works created under the direction of Mao's wife have become the models for China's artistic expression. Primary and secondary sources; 103 notes. J. C. Holsinger

2992. Yin, J. THE SOVIET CHARGE OF THE MISCHIEVOUS BEHAVIOR OF PEIPING. *Issues & Studies [Taiwan] 1972 9(3): 72-78.* From approximately 1963 to 1970 the USSR's Communist Party blamed China's cultural heritage for the poor public policies of the Chinese Communist Party.

2993. Yin Ching-yao. THE BITTER STRUGGLE BETWEEN THE KMT AND THE CCP. *Asian Survey 1981 21(6): 622-631.* Reviews the relationship between the Chinese Communist Party and the Nationalists (Guomindang) since 1920. Today China is not really interested in cooperation with the Guomindang (Kuomintang, or KMT), but wishes Taiwan to be reunified with the mainland regime. The mainland Chinese will be content with peaceful means to this goal only when they are weak. When they are strong they will use force. Secondary sources. J. Powell

2994. Yin Ch'ing-yao. MAO TSE-TUNG'S VIEW OF WAR. *Issues & Studies [Taiwan] 1973 9(5): 63-71.* Mao Tse-tung's thoughts on war are the product of Communist theories and are not the result of traditional culture in China dating back to the 6th century B.C.

2995. Yin Ch'ing-yao. ON COMMUNIST NEGOTIATIONS. *Issues & Studies [Taiwan] 1980 16(2): 13-29.* Mutually acceptable compromise is the ostensible goal of international negotiations. Communists, however, enter both peace and trade negotiations only when they feel they can profit, negotiating to gain concessions without war, play for time, and other objectives. They use such tactics as wooing neutrals to isolate anti-Communists and turn negotiations into opportunities for propaganda, boycott, and sabotage, as the examples of the USSR and China indicate. Based on writings of Lenin, Mao, Jiang Jieshi (Chiang Kai-shek), and others and contemporary news accounts from the *New York Times, Wen Hui Pao,* etc; 27 notes. J. A. Krompart

2996. Ying Kuei-fang. THE BIRTH CONTROL MOVEMENT ON THE CHINESE MAINLAND. *Issues and Studies [Taiwan] 1974 10(5): 80-89.* Discusses the Communist Party's policies toward birth control, family planning and late marriage in China, 1953-70's.

2997. Young, Graham. CONTROL AND STYLE: DISCIPLINE INSPECTION COMMISSIONS SINCE THE 11TH CONGRESS. *China Q. [Great Britain] 1984 (97): 24-52.* To restore order to the Chinese Communist Party after the chaos of the Cultural Revolution, Discipline Inspection Committees (DIC) were reestablished by the 11th Party Congress in 1977. The DIC's were charged with reform of Party style, factionalism, privileges and corruption, discipline, etc. but seem to lack the resources and authority necessary for real Party reform. Based largely on articles appearing in *Renmin Ribao (People's Daily)* and Chinese radio broadcasts; 124 notes. J. R. Pavia, Jr.

2998. Young, Graham. VANGUARD LEADERSHIP AND CULTURAL REVOLUTION ACTIVISM. *Australian J. of Chinese Affairs [Australia] 1980 (3): 41-66.* Throughout 1968 it was claimed that Party-building was consistent with and a continuation of the earlier stages of the Cultural Revolution, but in the post-Cultural Revolution period many of the Cultural Revolution standards persisted, often embraced by people recently risen to positions of authority. They continued to generate problems for the leading role of the Party.

2999. Zagoria, Donald S. MAO'S ROLE IN THE SINO-SOVIET CONFLICT. *Pacific Affairs [Canada] 1974 47(2): 139-153.* Argues that throughout most of the history of the Chinese Communist Party it has been divided into "internationalist" and "nativist" factions which have been more or less sympathetic to Russian views and policies. Mao Tse-tung has been rather consistently in the "nativist" camp. Mao has consistently opted for a more "Titoist" (independent or nationalist) policy. Examines the current conflict of factions in the Chinese Communist Party and seeks to explain how these different factions may view relations with the Soviet Union after Mao's death. Stresses the decisive role of Chinese internal politics as opposed to ideological factors in explaining the Sino-Soviet conflict. From a paper delivered at the International Conference on Peace and Security in Asia, 21-24 January 1974, at Kyung Nam University, Korea. 33 notes. S. H. Frank

3000. Zhou Enlai. *Selected Works of Zhou Enlai.* Vol. 1. Beijing: Foreign Languages Pr., 1981. 486 pp.

3001. Zvada, Jan. MAOISMUS—HISTORICKÉ, GNOZEOLOGICKÉ A SOCIÁLNÍ KOŘENY JEHO VZNIKU A POLITICKÉHO VÝVOJE [Maoism: the historical, conceptual and social roots of its origin and political development]. *Československý Časopis Hist. [Czechoslovakia] 1979 27(3): 321-350.* Mao Zedong (1893-1976) built his ideology and government on Chinese petit-bourgeois traditions, while he manipulated a hardline Leninism to secure his revolutionary credentials. Based on a politically unstable peasantry—eclectic, changeable, and non-Marxist in its policies—Maoism represents a victory of China's Sinocentric past over its revolutionary present. Instead of national liberation and class-conscious proletarian internationalism it has proclaimed Chinese world hegemony and has opened the way to imperialist influences. 30 notes. R. E. Weltsch

3002. —. CHANG AI-P'ING—NEW VICE-PREMIER OF THE STATE COUNCIL. *Issues & Studies [Taiwan] 1980 16(12): 77-83.* Zhang Aiping (Chang Ai-p'ing) of Sichuan (Szechuan) province, joined the Chinese Communist Party in 1928. Since 1934 he has served in various military capacities and was made a full general in 1955. He lost power during the Cultural Revolution but was reinstated in 1972. He was made a vice-premier of the State Council in the September 1980 leadership reshuffle and is likely to be named National Defense Minister in the near future. J. A. Krompart

3003. —. CHANG CHING-FU—MINISTER IN CHARGE OF THE STATE ECONOMIC COMMISSION. *Issues & Studies [Taiwan] 1982 18(5): 78-83.* Zhang Jingfu (Chang Ching-fu), who was active in the Chinese Communist Party in the 1930's, has held many responsible offices, particularly in Anhui (Anhwei) province. Persecuted during the Cultural Revolution, he resumed his career in

1974. In 1982 Zhang was appointed State Councilor and put in charge of the State Economic Commission. Based on Mainland media sources; 11 notes. J. A. Krompart

3004. —. CH'EN YUNG-KUEI—A POLITBURO MEMBER OF THE 10TH CCP CENTRAL COMMITTEE. *Issues and Studies [Taiwan] 1974 10(5): 90-93.* Discusses the political career of Communist Party Central Committee and Politburo member Ch'en Yung-kuei in China from 1956-73, including a list of his writings and speeches.

3005. —. CHI TENG-K'UEI—A MEMBER OF THE CCP CENTRAL COMMITTEE POLITBURO. *Issues and Studies [Taiwan] 1977 13(10): 70-73.* Traces the career of Chi Teng-k'uei, who was reelected to China's Communist Party Central Committee Politburo at the Eleventh Party Congress (1977). Nothing is known about Chi's early career; his public activities can be traced back only to 1957. Chi gained much power during the Cultural Revolution, but he later lost authority and was held in custody for four months. Chi became an alternate member of the Politburo in 1969, where he kept a close connection with the Gang of Four until he began to antagonize them in 1975. W. R. Hively

3006. —. CH'IAO HSIAO-KUANG AND THE HANDLING OF LEFTOVER PROBLEMS IN KWANGSI. *Issues & Studies [Taiwan] 1984 20(9): 80-86.* Qiao Xiaoguang (Ch'iao Hsiao-kuang) has served the Chinese Communist Party at least since 1949. Most of his posts have been in Guangxi (Kwangsi) Province. One of the few high provincial-level officials to survive the repudiation of leftists following the Cultural Revolution, Qiao, 1st Secretary in Guangxi since 1977, is under pressure as the Party focuses on Guangxi in its policy of eliminating leftist remnants. Based on Mainland media reports; 9 notes. J. A. Krompart

3007. —. CH'IN CHI-WEI—COMMANDER OF THE PEKING MILITARY REGION. *Issues & Studies [Taiwan] 1984 20(7): 112-115.* Qin Jiwei (Ch'in Chi-wei, b. 1914), a military associate of Deng Xiaoping (Teng Hsiao-p'ing), was appointed commander of the important Beijing Military Region in 1980 and alternate Politburo member of the Central Committee of the Chinese Communist Party in 1982. Qin, a party member since 1930, had a distinguished military and administrative career, interrrupted only when he was purged during the Cultural Revolution. 6 notes.
J. A. Krompart

3008. —. THE CHINA DEMOCRATIC LEAGUE AND ITS CHAIRMAN SHIH LIANG. *Issues & Studies [Taiwan] 1984 20(5): 74-80.* Shi Liang (Shih Liang, b. 1900) has played a strong role in Communist united front programs since the 1930's. Forced from party office during the Cultural Revolution, she has recently regained high posts, including the chair of the China Democratic League, which was infiltrated by the Communists prior to 1949 and maintained ever since as a national "democratic party."
J. A. Krompart

3009. —. CHU HSÜEH-FAN—NEW VICE CHAIRMAN OF THE NPC STANDING COMMITTEE. *Issues & Studies [Taiwan] 1982 18(3): 78-84.* Zhu Xuefan (Chu Hsüeh-fan, b. 1902) has been associated with the Chinese Communist Party since 1938. Long involved in the workers movement, he is considered a "democratic parties and groups" member. Zhu was appointed Vice Chairman of the National People's Congress Standing Committee in December 1981. Based on media reports from China; 14 notes.
J. A. Krompart

3010. —. CH'U WU—VICE CHAIRMAN OF THE NATIONAL COMMITTEE OF THE CPPCC. *Issues & Studies [Taiwan] 1984 20(1): 98-104.* Chu Wu (Ch'u Wu, b. 1898) is a longtime member of the CCP who studied in Russia in the 1920's and 1930's. He has held many responsible political posts. In June 1983 he was made a vice chairman of the 6th National Committee of the Chinese People's Political Consultative Conference.
J. A. Krompart

3011. —. A DOCUMENT OF THE CENTRAL COMMITTEE OF THE CHINESE COMMUNIST PARTY *CHUNG-FA* (1980) NO. 25. *Issues and Studies [Taiwan] 1980 16(11): 70-93.* A translation of documents circulated to party members by the Chinese Communist Party Central Committee on 9 March 1980. The first describes how and why the resolution to rehabilitate Liu Shaoqi (Liu Shao-ch'i, 1898-1973) is to be presented at all levels of the Party so that the understanding of it will be ideologically correct. The second document describes in detail how Liu was wrongly labeled a traitor to both Party and nation by the Gang of Four and repudiates each piece of false evidence used to accuse him of crimes. The Central Committee resolved to remove the slanderous labels that had been imposed on Liu. J. A. Krompart

3012. —. FALSIFIERS OF WORLD HISTORY. *Far Eastern Affairs [USSR] 1979 (4): 25-43.* Report of a seminar on Maoist interpretations of history, after about 1960, which, especially in Russian history, were distortions intended to justify Chinese expansionism.

3013. —. FENG WEN-PIN—VICE-PRESIDENT OF THE CCP CENTRAL PARTY SCHOOL. *Issues & Studies [Taiwan] 1982 18(9): 103-107.* Feng Wenbin (Feng Wen-pin, b. 1919), one of several cadres being promoted for their experience in the youth movement, has worked for the Party since 1931. Although he was removed from his post in the General Office of the Central Committee in 1982, he has remained Vice President of the Central Party School and holds office in units researching Party history. Based on Mainland media reports; 9 notes. J. A. Krompart

3014. —. FOUR SECRETARIES OF THE CCP PROVINCIAL-LEVEL COMMITTEES. *Issues & Studies [Taiwan] 1983 19(6): 97-100.* Among recently appointed secretaries of CCP Provincial Committees are Wang Fang of Zhejiang (Chekiang) and Su Yiran (Su I-jan) of Shandong (Shantung), both of whom have had public security experience and have served the regime from its early years. Han Peixin (Han P'ei-hsin) of Jiangsu (Kiangsu) and Li Lian (Li Li-an) of Heilongjiang (Heilungkiang) have been politically active since the Cultural Revolution. Han has light industry experience and Li has held a variety of Party posts. J. A. Krompart

3015. —. [FURTHER DISCUSSION ON "A FACTIONALISM MODEL FOR CCP POLITICS"]. *China Q. [Great Britain] 1976 (65): 98-117.*

Tsou, Tang. PROLEGOMENON TO THE STUDY OF INFORMAL GROUPS IN CCP POLITICS, *pp. 98-114.* Presents an appreciative but critical commentary to A. J. Nathan's earlier article (see abstract 20B:1646). The criticisms focus on a preference for informal group rather than faction as the basis of Communist Party politics in China and on Nathan's assumption that the inability of any one faction to gain total power is a fundamental rule of the game. 20 notes.

Nathan, Andrew J. REPLY, *pp. 114-117.* Stresses the formality of what Tsou would call informal and the historical failure of any single faction (or informal group) to maintain power in spite of many attempts to do so. Note. J. R. Pavia, Jr.

3016. —. HU YAO-PANG'S CLANSMEN FROM THE COMMUNIST YOUTH LEAGUE. *Issues & Studies [Taiwan] 1982 18(4): 71-79.* Discussses eight men with important positions in the Communist Chinese hierarchy. These and a number of others were once associated with the Communist Youth League, in which Hu Yaobang (Hu Yao-pang) was active during the 1950's and 1960's. This large following should support Hu's rise to increased power.
J. A. Krompart

3017. —. HUANG HUA—NEW VICE-PREMIER OF THE STATE COUNCIL. *Issues & Studies [Taiwan] 1980 16(11): 61-69.* Huang Hua, of Hebei (Hopeh) province, was a student at Yenching University in 1935. In 1936 he joined the Chinese Communist Party. Since that time, he has served the Party continuously, most often in external propaganda, foreign affairs, and diplomatic positions for which his acquaintance with the Yenching staff initially qualified him. He weathered the Cultural Revolution, was appointed foreign minister in 1976, and, in September 1980, became a vice-premier of the State Council, a combination indicating high status and carrying heavy responsibilities. J. A. Krompart

3018. —. [THE IMPORTANCE OF TENG YING-CH'AO]. *Chinese Studies in Hist. 1980 14(1): 85-103.*

Li Yu-ning. EDITOR'S NOTE: TENG YING-CH'AO, *pp. 85-92.* Teng (Deng Yingchao) has been politically active for well over 50 years as a leader of the women's movement in China. Her commitment to Chinese nationalism and the Chinese Communist Party has directed her life.

Teng Ying-ch'ao. REMEMBRANCES OF THE MAY FOURTH MOVEMENT, *pp. 93-103.* Deng was heavily involved in the May Fourth Movement of 1919. She supported the New Culture movement and became a recognized leader of the "new tide" group. She was a founding member of the Chüeh-wu she (Juewu she) and by the middle 1920's had settled on communism as her ideological basis for action. A. C. Migliazzo

3019. —. LI CHING-CH'ÜAN—A LIBERATED CADRE. *Issues and Studies [Taiwan] 1975 11(8): 82-86.* Traces the career of Li Ching-ch'üan, former Poliburo member, purged during the Cultural Revolution, and rehabilitated ("liberated") in 1973 to take a place on the Communist Party Central Committee.

3020. —. LIN HU-CHIA—FIRST SECRETARY OF THE CCP PEKING MUNICIPAL COMMITTEE. *Issues & Studies [Taiwan] 1980 16(3): 94-98.* Lin Hujia (Lin Hu-chia), born in 1917 in Shandong (Shantung), joined the Chinese Communist Party in 1937. Throughout the 1950's Lin held government and Party posts in Zhejiang (Chekiang). In 1959 he was labeled a right opportunist. He was returned to official duties in 1972 and, in 1976, worked in Shanghai to eliminate the Gang of Four power base there. In 1978 Lin replaced Tianjin (Tientsin) and Beijing (Peking) officials being attacked in wall posters and became First Party Secretary of the CCP Beijing Municipal Committee in October 1978. Based on mainland newspaper and news agency reports; 16 notes.
J. A. Krompart

3021. —. NIEH JUNG-CHEN: VICE-CHAIRMAN OF THE CCPCC MILITARY AFFAIRS COMMISSION. *Issues and Studies [Taiwan] 1977 13(2): 94-100.* Biography of Nieh Jung-chen (1899-) and his work in China, 1926-77, which eventuated his position as vice-chairman of the Military Affairs Commission of the Communist Party Central Committee.

3022. —. PAI JU-PING—FIRST SECRETARY OF THE CCP SHANTUNG PROVINCIAL COMMITTEE. *Issues & Studies [Taiwan] 1982 18(10): 93-98.* Bai Rubing (Pai Ju-ping, 1916-) is one of the two provincial secretaries retaining their posts after the fall of the Gang of Four. Bai, who has had important assignments since 1949, specializes in finance. In 1977 he was elected a member of the 11th CCP Central Committee and deputy for Shandong to the 5th National People's Congress. Based on Mainland media reports; 9 notes. J. A. Krompart

3023. —. THE "REVOLUTIONARY COMMITTEE OF THE KUOMINTANG" AND ITS CHAIRMAN WANG K'UN-LUN. *Issues & Studies [Taiwan] 1984 20(4): 92-98.* Wang Kunlun (Wang K'un-lun, b. 1902), active in pro-Communist political groups since the 1920's, joined the Revolutionary Committee of the Kuomintang, a Communist united front "democratic party," in 1949. Ousted from the post of deputy mayor of Peking in the Cultural Revolution, he was elected to several high offices, including chair of the 6th RCK Central Committee, in 1983. Based on mainland media reports; 7 notes. J. A. Krompart

3024. —. SU YÜ—VICE-CHAIRMAN OF THE STANDING COMMITTEE OF THE FIFTH PEOPLE'S CONGRESS. *Issues & Studies [Taiwan] 1981 17(3): 69-77.* Su Yu (Su Yü, 1907-) joined the Chinese Communist Party in 1927. From 1927 to 1949 he served in the Communist military forces and rose to the rank of corps commander. Since 1949 he has held high military and political posts. He was investigated as a possible counterrevolutionary during the Cultural Revolution but did not lose his status. Su was elected an additional vice-chair of the Standing Committee of the Fifth National People's Congress in September 1980. Based on Mainland documents, publications, and news services; 14 notes.
J. A. Krompart

3025. —. T'IEH YING—CHAIRMAN OF THE CHEKIANG PROVINCIAL ADVISORY COMMISSION. *Issues & Studies [Taiwan] 1984 20(10): 84-92.* Tie Ying (T'ieh Ying), who became chairman of the Zhejiang (Chekiang) Provincial Advisory Commission in 1983, began his career in Chinese Communist military units during the Sino-Japanese War and rose rapidly in the Chekiang Party organization during the 1960's. After surviving the Cultural Revolution, Tie became a supporter of Hua Guofeng (Hua Kuo-feng). Tie is now being charged by officials of the Deng (Teng) regime with resistance to the new rural policy and the Party rectification campaign. Based on Chinese media reports; 28 notes.
J. A. Krompart

3026. —. WANG EN-MAO: NEWLY APPOINTED FIRST SECRETARY OF THE CCP KIRIN PROVINCIAL COMMITTEE. *Issues and Studies [Taiwan] 1977 13(5): 87-93.* Wang En-mao (b. 1912), a strong man in the northwest, has had a history of opposition to Mao Tse-tung going back to 1935, but his abilities and leadership experience have permitted him to maintain significant positions of power such as the new one he achieved in March 1977.

3027. —. WANG EN-MAO—REAPPOINTED FIRST SECRETARY OF THE CCP SINKIANG UIGHUR AUTONOMOUS REGIONAL COMMITTEE. *Issues & Studies [Taiwan] 1982 18(2): 58-66.* Wang Enmao (Wang En-mao, b. 1912), a military man of substantial experience in Xinjiang (Sinkiang) province, was reappointed to the position of First Secretary of the Sinkiang Uighur Autonomous Regional Committee in December 1981. He is expected to continue to exert a unifying influence on the disparate groups and nationalities of Northwest China. Based on Mainland media reports; 15 notes. J. A. Krompart

3028. —. WANG FANG—NEWLY APPOINTED SECRETARY OF THE CCP CHEKIANG PROVINCIAL COMMITTEE. *Issues & Studies [Taiwan] 1983 19(8): 67-71.* Wang Fang, active in Zhejiang (Chekiang) Province since the 1950's, has been appointed secretary of the Provincial Committee of the Chinese Communist Party. A supporter of Deng Xiaoping (Teng Hsiao-p'ing), Wang benefitted from the 1983 reorganization of provincial Party leadership. Based on Chinese media reports; 19 notes. J. A. Krompart

3029. —. WEI KUO-CH'ING—FIRST SECRETARY OF THE CCP KWANGTUNG PROVINCIAL COMMITTEE. *Issues and Studies [Taiwan] 1976 12(4): 104-107.* The elevation of Wei Kuo-ch'ing to first secretary of the Provincial Communist Party and chairman of the Revolutionary Committee in Kwangtung is only the latest in a long series of advancements for Wei. Beginning as a company commander in the army of the Nationalist Government in 1929, Wei later associated himself with the Communists—serving as a Communist representative when in 1946 General George C. Marshall tried to mediate between the Nationalists and Communists. Wei's 29 October 1975 appointment was Peking's attempt to handle some discord in the province.
J. C. Holsinger

3030. —. WEN MIN-SHENG—MINISTER OF POSTS AND TELECOMMUNICATIONS. *Issues & Studies [Taiwan] 1981 17(11): 76-80.* Wen Minsheng (Wen Min-sheng, b. 1916), whose forte is undercover and confidential work, has held responsible Party posts since 1930. Purged in the Cultural Revolution, he later had assignments in Manchuria, and in 1981 was appointed Minister of Posts and Telecommunications. Based on Chinese media reports; 13 notes. J. A. Krompart

3031. —. YANG CHING-JEN—NEWLY APPOINTED VICE PREMIER OF THE STATE COUNCIL. *Issues & Studies [Taiwan] 1980 16(10): 74-78.* Yang Jingren (Yang Ching-jen, b. 1918), who has a Moslem background, joined the Communist Party in 1937, served in the war against Japan, and held a variety of Party posts, mostly dealing with Moslems in China or foreign relations with the

Arab world, until he lost power and was denounced during the Cultural Revolution. His rapid rise after the fall of the Gang of Four seems to indicate the interest of the current leaders in promoting relations with minorities. J. A. Krompart

3032. —. YANG SHANG-K'UN—NEW VICE-CHAIRMAN OF THE NPC STANDING COMMITTEE. *Issues & Studies [Taiwan] 1981 17(1): 72-77.* Yang Shangkun (Yang Shang-k'un) of Sichuan (Szechwan) province, joined the Chinese Communist Party in 1926 and spent his early years as a Party member in Moscow. After returning to China in 1930, he held increasingly responsible Party and Red Army posts. A member of the Deng Xiaoping (Teng Hsiao-p'ing) faction, he lost power during the Cultural Revolution. He was liberated in December 1978 and subsequently took up high Party posts in Guangdong (Kwangtung) province. In September 1980, he was made secretary-general and a vice-chairman of the Fifth National People's Congress Standing Committee. Based on Mainland publications; 12 notes. J. A. Krompart

3033. —. YEH CHIEN-YING: THE ACTING FIRST VICE CHAIRMAN OF CCP MILITARY AFFAIRS COMMISSION. *Issues and Studies [Taiwan] 1976 12(11): 92-99.* Political and military biography of Yeh Chien-ying, 1925-76, now acting First Vice Chairman of the Chinese Communist Party Military Affairs Commission and initially considered a possible successor to Mao Tse-tung as premier of the State Council.

1945-1956

3034. Buhite, Russell D. MISSED OPPORTUNITIES? AMERICAN POLICY AND THE CHINESE COMMUNISTS, 1949. *Mid-America 1979 61(3): 179-188.* It has been argued that the United States missed opportunities to establish friendly relations with Chinese Communists in 1949. Two such possibilities were an overture by Zhou Enlai (Chou En-lai) and an invitation to John Leighton Stuart to visit Beijiug (Peking). State Department officials doubted Chou's sincerity and were also concerned with American domestic reaction. The Chinese were constrained by their Marxist-Leninist ideology as well as Soviet pressure to treat America as an enemy. It is not clear if such opportunities existed in reality. Based on State Department records, *Foreign Relations of the United States,* other primary and secondary sources; 30 notes. J. M. Lee

3035. Chan, F. Gilbert, ed. *China at the Crossroads: Nationalists and Communists, 1927-1949.* A Westview Replica Edition. Boulder, Colo.: Westview, 1980. 267 pp.

3036. Chin, Luke Kai-hsin. "The Politics of Drama Reform in China after 1949—Elite Strategy of Resocialization." New York U. 1980. 337 pp. *DAI 1980 41(2): 782-783-A.* 8017552

3037. Crook, Isabel and Crook, David. *Ten Mile Inn: Mass Movement in a Chinese Village.* Asia Library. New York: Pantheon, 1979. 264 pp.

3038. Cunningham, William J. THE COMMUNIST PARTY OF CHINA AND THE UNITED NATIONS, 1943-1950. *Asia Q. [Belgium] 1972 (3): 191-201.* Examines the evolution of Chinese Communist Party attitudes toward the UN from the Moscow Declaration on postwar collective security until the beginning of the Korean War. Divides this seven-year period into three phases: the adjournment of the San Francisco Conference in June 1945; the proclamation of the People's Republic of China; and the final period ending in June, 1950. The author believes that Peking's attitude toward the UN shows cautious but growing acceptance of the organization, and a willingness to participate in it. Based on newspapers, government documents, radio transcripts, and secondary sources; 18 notes. G. M. White

3039. Dubinsky, A. M. PEREGOVORY "SOIUZNICHESKOI GRUPPY NABLIUDATELEI" SSHA S RUKOVODSTVOM KPK [The negotiations conducted by the US "Allied Group of Observers" with the CPC leadership]. *Voprosy Istorii [USSR] 1979 (1): 71-81.* The author traces the activity of the American "allied group of observers," which arrived in Yenan in July 1944 and entered in contact with Mao Tse-tung and his closest entourage. The special line of the CPC leadership in the person of Mao Tse-tung (whose anti-Sovietism was already manifested at that time) attracted the attention of American diplomats who tried to prevent the development of the national-liberation revolution in China into the socialist revolution and to bar China's orientation on the Soviet Union. But the whole course of the Chinese revolution in 1945-49 thwarted the designs of American politicians. 47 notes. J

3040. Evans, Harriet. ORGANIZACION DE MASAS Y PARTICIPACION POPULAR EN EL MEDIO RURAL CHINO [Mass organization and popular participation in China's countryside]. *Estudios de Asia y Africa [Mexico] 1982 17(1): 1-25.* Studies the period of land reform and early cooperativization from the point of view of popular participation and organization as part of the process of transformation of consciousness and the practice of political hegemony. The success of this period was due to the Communist Party's skill in combining the peasants' self-interest with the more global goals of the socialist revolution, but chiefly to the constant effort to achieve local and popular understanding of and participation in centrally planned policies. 10 notes, biblio. J. V. Coutinho

3041. Farquhar, Mary. REVOLUTIONARY CHILDREN'S LITERATURE. *Australian J. of Chinese Affairs [Australia] 1980 (4): 61-84.* Surveys Communist Party literature for children in China.

3042. Garsombke, Thomas Walter. "A Causal-Effect Analysis of Resource-Constrained Conditions and Political Influences on Policy Formation and Program Development of a Higher Educational Institution—Yan'an University." Northeastern University 1984. 206 pp. *DAI 1985 45(9): 2772-A.* DA8425983

3043. Goldstein, Steven M. CHINESE COMMUNIST POLICY TOWARD THE UNITED STATES: OPPORTUNITIES AND CONSTRAINTS, 1944-1950. Borg, Dorothy and Heinrichs, Waldo, ed. *Uncertain Years: Chinese-American Relations, 1947-1950* (New York: Columbia U. Pr., 1980): 235-278. Mao Zedong's (Mao Tse-tung) "lean to one side" speech of June 1949 was not a benchmark in China's foreign policy, marking the end of a period of open-ended policy allowing for rapprochement with the United States, but a confirmation of the hard line that the Chinese Communists had been following since 1946.

3044. Gupta, Bhabani Sen. AN ASPECT OF THE CHINA CRISIS, 1945-47. *China Report [India] 1971 7(4): 30-43.* Discusses US inability to understand the political needs of Chinese Communists, 1945-47, emphasizing the roles of President Harry S. Truman, Chiang Kai-shek and Mao Tse-tung.

3045. Harris, Peter. A HISTORY OF THE CHINESE COMMUNIST PARTY, 1921-1949. *J. of Oriental Studies [Hong Kong] 1974 12(1-2): 104-108.* A review of Jacques Guillermaz's *A History of the Chinese Communist Party, 1921-1949* (London: Methuen, 1972). Mao Tse-tung was a great Chinese leader who combined the traditional experiences of Chinese popular insurrections with modern revolutionary tactics. He helped create China's Communist Party as a vehicle to mobilize and discipline the Chinese. The increasingly favorable international situation from 1931 to 1945 enormously assisted the Party. It was successful because of its military ability, ideology, organization, propaganda, and the quality of its personnel. International factors and Chinese social and economic dislocations led to Communist victory in 1949. J. Sokolow

3046. Jackal, Patricia Stranahan. CHANGES IN POLICY FOR YANAN (YENAN) WOMEN, 1935-1947. *Modern China 1981 7(1): 83-112.* During the Second United Front period (1937-41) the major concern of the Chinese Communist Party was mobilization of the population against the Japanese. Women's liberation was a secondary consideration, and women were urged to participate in production in order to achieve equality, but what kind of production and how it would further their equality was never fully defined. The ineffectiveness of this approach, combined with a policy to make the Border Regions self-sufficient, led to a better defined production role (primarily textile production) for women. By the end of 1945, the economic situation of both the Border Regions and women had greatly improved, and as the Party broadened its base among the population as it prepared for civil war, women were brought into full participation in social and economic affairs. Based on primary and secondary sources in English and Chinese; 43 notes, 25 ref. K. W. Berger

3047. Jackal, Patricia Stranahan. "Development of Policy for Yenan Women, 1937-1947." U. of Pennsylvania 1979. 268 pp. *DAI 1980 40(10): 5550-A.* 8009422

3048. Jacobs, Dan N. *Borodin: Stalin's Man in China.* Cambridge: Harvard U. Pr., 1981. 368 pp.

3049. Joshi, Gopa. THE CYL: A LINK BETWEEN THE PARTY AND THE YOUTH 1949-56 (I). *China Report [India] 1980 16(3): 15-26.* In 1946 the Communist Party of China transformed the relatively independent Communist Youth League (CYL) into the New Democratic Youth League (NDYL), an adjunct of the Party. After occupying itself from 1949 to 1952 with organizational problems, the NDYL played a crucial role during the first Five-Year Plan in developing heavy industry. Internal problems such as admission policy, outmoded ideas, and poor education made the NDYL less effective in the process of agricultural cooperativization and ideological education. Primary sources; 54 notes. Article to be continued. E. L. Keyser

3050. Joshi, Gopa. THE ROLE OF STUDENTS IN THE CHINESE REVOLUTIONARY MOVEMENT, 1919-49. *China Report [India] 1973 9(1): 23-31.* Contrasts the attitudes of the Kuomintang and the Chinese Communist Party toward youth movements in China, 1919-49, and the impact of students in each group. Students supported the CCP because it was partial to youth participation and because national sovereignty in the fight against the Japanese invasion of Manchuria was of importance to the CCP.

3051. Lai Tse-han and Hsiao Hsin-huang. HSIEN-TAI CHUNG-KUO CH'ENG-HSIANG TS'E-LUEH CHIH FEN-HSI: 1911-1949 [An analysis of urban and rural strategies in modern China: 1911-49]. *Ssu yü Yen (Thought and Word) [Taiwan] 1981 18(6): 75-84.* The 19th-century impact of the West brought China into a worldwide modernization system and caused the cities to assume political importance at the expense of the 80% of the population that live in rural areas. The Nationalists sought to promote rural development but were hampered by ignorance, civil strife, and foreign invasion. Contrary to general belief, the Chinese Communists' rise to power was not heavily based on a strong emphasis on agriculture. Their early power base was in the cities. Based on Chinese documents; biblio. J. A. Krompart

3052. Ledovski, A. M. TAINYE KONTAKTY MAOISTOV I AMERIKANSKOI DIPLOMATII V 1949 GODU [The Maoists' clandestine contacts with American diplomacy in 1949]. *Voprosy Istorii [USSR] 1980 (10): 75-89.* Highlights the clandestine contacts between US diplomacy and the Mao Zedong group in 1949 on the eve of the victorious Chinese Revolution. Washington tried to use nationalist elements in the Communist Party of China in order to save the Guomindang (Kuomintang) regime from utter defeat and to retain the positions of American imperialism in China. Mao Zedong and his closest associates were prepared to go to great lengths to seize political power in the country and strike a bargain with American imperialism for the sake of attaining their selfish aims. This conspiracy was thwarted by the victorious development of the people's revolution, which enjoyed broad international support from the forces of democracy and socialism and which relied on the USSR's internationalist assistance. J

3053. Levine, Steven I. INTRODUCTION. Borg, Dorothy and Heinrichs, Waldo, ed. *Uncertain Years: Chinese-American Relations, 1947-1950* (New York: Columbia U. Pr., 1980): 181-183. Outline of scholars' major approaches to Chinese Communist Party foreign policy in order to provide a context for papers by Michael Hunt and Steven M. Goldstein that emerged from the Conference on Chinese-American Relations, Mt. Kisco, New York, 1978.

3054. Levine, Steven I. A NEW LOOK AT AMERICAN MEDIATION IN THE CHINESE CIVIL WAR: THE MARSHALL MISSION AND MANCHURIA. *Diplomatic Hist. 1979 3(4): 349-375.* Chronicles George C. Marshall's efforts to mediate between the Nationalists and Communists to form one government. Marshall believed that only through political reform could a Communist takeover in China be prevented. He gave up on the Guomindang (Kuomintang) as a vehicle for reform and hoped that an American-style nonpartisan government made up of reformers from both Chinese factions could be formed. He failed to resolve China's political crisis but succeeded in removing China as an area of conflict in Soviet-American relations, keeping the USSR's political influence at a minimum by providing only limited American support for the Nationalists. 88 notes.

3055. Long, Charles H. THE LIBERATION OF THE CHINESE CHURCH: A MEMOIR OF THE REVOLUTION FROM A MISSIONARY POINT OF VIEW. *Hist. Mag. of the Protestant Episcopal Church 1980 49(3): 249-280.* Autobiographical account of Charles H. Long's trip to China in 1946 as a missionary of the Protestant Episcopal Church. Recounts what it was to be part of "the end of the missionary era," to observe first-hand the Communist revolution as it occurred. He shared briefly in the life of the Chinese church during its liberation from dependency and privilege over a three-year period. The liberation of the church began long before the arrival of the Communists, beginning when the Chinese clergy during World War II squarely faced the fact that they might never again be able to depend on American support. The "greatest obstacle to our coming back to China will not be the Communists but the Chinese Church itself." H. M. Parker, Jr.

3056. Meyer, Hektor. *Die Entwicklung der Kommunistischen Streitkräfte in China von 1927 bis 1949: Dokumente und Kommentar* [The development of Communist military forces in China, 1927-49: documents and commentary]. (Beiträge zur Auswärtigen und Internationalen Politik, no. 8.) Berlin, West Germany: Walter de Gruyter, 1982. 594 pp.

3057. Mori, Kazuko. CHUGOKU KAKUMEI TO AJIA NO "REISEN" KOZO [The Chinese revolution and the structure of the Cold War in Asia]. *Rekishigaku Kenkyū [Japan] 1975: 190-200.* Locates the Chinese revolution of 1949 and the establishment of the People's Republic of China in the structure of the Cold War between the United States and the USSR, 1945-49. Attempts to inquire into the inner logic of how the Chinese people crushed the American cold war policy in Asia with the victory of the Chinese revolution. The author seeks in the Chinese Communist Party at that time a freedom from the ideology and the myths of the Cold War system and a realistic recognition of the concrete appearance of the Cold War in China. Sets high value on the international understanding of the Chinese Communist Party. The "paper tiger" theory of Mao Tse-tung in 1946 decided the international character of the Chinese revolution and contributed greatly to its development. Based on the *Jie fang ri bao, Ren min ri bao, Qun zhong, Wen hui bao,* and other sources. M. Uchiyama

3058. Müller, Eva. EINIGE BEMERKUNGEN ZUM PROBLEM DER DARSTELLUNG UND SELBSTDARSTELLUNG DES PRODUCTIONSARBEITERS IN DER LITERATUR DER VOLKSREPUBLIK CHINA WÄREND DER JAHRE 1949 BIS 1975 [Some remarks on the problem of the representation and self-representation of the industrial worker in the literature of the People's Republic of China, 1949-57]. *Wissenschaftliche Zeitschrift der Humboldt-Universität zu Berlin [East Germany] 1974 23(2): 163-166.* Discusses the manner in which Chinese fiction mirrored social and economic change and the development of communist society in China between 1949 and the 1960's. Many literary examples are cited to illustrate the growth of industry and its effect on the lives and thought of the people of each period. Writers were at first slow to deal with the industrial worker but before the 1960's a considerable literature with that theme developed; thereafter Mao's theory

of union between revolutionary realism and revolutionary romanticism and his general attitude toward the arts sharply limited the publication of really meaningful fiction. 17 notes.
M. Faissler

3059. Pantsov, A. LIFE GIVEN TO THE STRUGGLE FOR FREEDOM (SEVENTY-FIVE YEARS SINCE THE BIRTH OF BO GU). *Far Eastern Affairs [USSR] 1983 (1): 122-129.* After winning leadership of the Chinese Communists in 1934 at age 24, Bo Gu (Po Ku; real name Chin Bangxian—Ch'in Pang-hsien) organized the unified front against the Japanese invasion as the Communists' liaison officer in negotiations with the Nationalists. He died in a 1946 airplane accident.

3060. Pe Li. DEVELOPMENTS OF THE SOCIALIST CONSTRUCTION OF THE MAOISTS. *Issues and Studies [Taiwan] 1972 8(11): 39-50, (12): 47-56.* Traces the socialist economic development policy of the Communist Party in Maoist China, in the 1950's, especially emphasizing peasant-oriented agricultural, industrial, and transportation projects.

3061. Pickler, Gordon K. THE USAAF IN CHINA, 1946-47. *Air U. R. 1973 24(4): 69-74.* Discusses the Army Air Force's airlift of Communist officials and their staffs and families from Nanking and other Nationalist cities to the Communist capital of Yenan in 1947. Based on interviews and secondary sources; 5 photos, 4 notes.
J. W. Thacker, Jr.

3062. Price, Jane L. REVOLUTION, NATION-BUILDING, AND CHINESE COMMUNIST LEADERSHIP EDUCATION DURING THE SINO-JAPANESE WAR. Fogel, Joshua A. and Rowe, William T., ed. *Perspectives on a Changing China: Essays in Honor of Professor C. Martin Wilbur on the Occasion of his Retirement* (Boulder, Colo.: Westview Pr., 1979): 197-216. Describes the extensive educational complex erected by the Chinese Communist Party during the Sino-Japanese War. The most influential institution was the Kangda (K'ang-ta) school, or Anti-Japanese Military and Political College, led by Lin Biao (Lin Piao) and Lo Ruiqing (Lo Juich'ing), with 8,000 students in its fifth (1938) class. Kangda stressed military and united front issues for processing nationalist intellectuals and advanced peasants into leadership functions in the Communist-led movement. Specialist schools—the Natural Sciences Research Institute, the Lu Hsun Academy of Arts—were eventually gathered in the Yenan University, aimed at supplying technical experts for the governing of liberated areas. The hint of a "red-expert" controversy in the two types of schools was met by the 1942 *zhengfeng (cheng-feng)* rectification movement, guided by cadres from the Central Party School and other Party schools. 67 notes.

3063. Radtke, K. W. DE OORLOG TEGEN JAPAN EN DE BURGEROORLOG [The war against Japan and the class war]. *Spiegel Hist. [Netherlands] 1981 16(6): 341-349.* An overview of events in China between the Japanese invasion of 1937 and the Communist victory in 1949, with an emphasis on those factors contributing to Communist success. Secondary sources; 14 illus.
C. W. Wood, Jr.

3064. Reardon-Anderson, James. *Yenan and the Great Powers: The Origins of Chinese Communist Foreign Policy, 1944-1946.* New York: Columbia U. Pr., 1980. 216 pp.

3065. Reglar, Steve. THE DEVELOPMENT OF THE CHINESE APPROACH TO SOCIALISM: CHINESE REFORMS AFTER THE DENUNCIATION OF STALIN. *J. of Contemporary Asia [Sweden] 1980 10(1-2): 181-214.* Concentrates on China in the period immediately following the 20th Congress of the Communist Party of the Soviet Union (CPSU) and leading to the launching of the Great Leap Forward. The mid-1950's was a period of crisis for the model of administration and development laid down by Joseph Stalin. The development of the Chinese approach to socialist transformation, which became embodied in the Great Leap Forward, was a response to internal contradiction stemming from the 1st Five Year Plan, in which the Soviet model of development was adopted, and to the Chinese perception of the external events which shook the socialist world—Nikita Khrushchev's secret speech denouncing Stalin, and the Hungarian and Polish rebellions. Secondary sources; 149 notes.
J. Powell

3066. Shaw, Yu-ming. JOHN LEIGHTON STUART AND US-CHINESE COMMUNIST RAPPROCHEMENT IN 1949: WAS THERE ANOTHER "LOST CHANCE IN CHINA"? *China Q. [Great Britain] 1982 (89): 74-96.* The failure of Ambassador John Leighton Stuart to meet with Mao Zedong and Chou Enlai in the summer of 1949 has been regretted as a "lost chance" for Sino-American rapprochement. However, Stuart did contact Mao and Chou through an intermediary, Zhen Mingshu (Chen Ming-shu) during that summer. The stumbling blocks of continued US support for the Nationalists and China's "leaning to one side" prevented any agreement and make the "lost chance" an unlikely thesis. Based largely on Stuart's dispatches in *Foreign Relations of the United States, 1949;* 56 notes.
J. R. Pavia, Jr.

3067. Shue, Vivienne. *Peasant China in Transition: The Dynamics of Development toward Socialism, 1949-1956.* Los Angeles: U. of California Pr., 1980. 394 pp.

3068. Sladkovski, M. IN LIBERATED MANCHURIA. *Far Eastern Affairs [USSR] 1980 (4): 39-53.* Describes Manchuria, liberated by the Soviet Army in 1945. Only in Manchuria was the People's Army of China able, with Soviet assistance, to hold a vast territory, making it its main military and economic stronghold for a strategic offensive against US-backed Guomindang (Kuomintang) troops in mid-1947.

3069. Sukharchuk, G. D. AGRARNOE ZAKONODATEL'STVO KPK I KNR (1946-1950) [Agrarian legislation of the Communist Party of China, 1946-50]. *Narody Azii i Afriki [USSR] 1980 (3): 44-54.* Unlike other socialist countries, China has a vast marginal population comprising hundreds of millions of paupers who play a destabilizing role in socioeconomic development. The Communist Party was faced with the dilemma of whether to partition land to maximize overall agricultural production or feed its neediest masses. Land reforms enacted by the CPC at different stages of the revolution, 1946-50, were frequently contradictory and achieved only compromise solutions. Table, 36 notes. English summary.
N. Frenkley

3070. Tanaka, Kyoko. THE CIVIL WAR AND RADICALIZATION OF CHINESE COMMUNIST AGRARIAN POLICY, 1945-1947. *Papers on Far Eastern Hist. [Australia] 1973 (8): 49-114.* Examines the process of radicalization of Communist policy toward the peasants, arguing that this political change was essential for the survival of the Communist Party in China.

3071. Tanaka, Kyoko. MAO AND LIU IN THE 1947 LAND REFORM: ALLIES OR DISPUTANTS? *China Q. [Great Britain] 1978 (75): 566-593.* In 1945, with a new struggle before it, the Chinese Communist Party sought to strengthen its base with a land reform campaign which would make every peasant a proprietor. Initially unaware of a land shortage that would make this impossible, Liu Shao-chi led the Party to search for hidden wealth and dishonest cadres. Though this was later presented as a major struggle between Liu and Mao Tse-tung, both men seem to have agreed on this policy at the time. Chinese materials and secondary Western sources; 109 notes.
J. R. Pavia, Jr.

3072. Tanaka, Kyōko. NAISEN TO CHKYŌ TOCHI SEISAKU NO TENKAN [The land reform policy of the Chinese Communist Party: its transformation during the civil war]. *Ajia Kenkyū [Japan] 1978 24(4): 1-24, 25(1): 1-26.* Examines the land reform policies of the Chinese Communist Party (CCP) which rapidly became radical after Japan's surrender in 1945, and discusses the factors that led to the success of the mass mobilization by the CCP in the civil war. The land reform was initiated in the fall of 1945, and demanded that traitors should return their excessive profits and pay for damages. It aimed at transforming the social position of farmers at promoting the farmers' enthusiasm and at obtaining support from non-Party members and intellectual leaders, through inspiring nationalism. 121 notes. M. Nakayama/S

3073. Tanaka, Kyōko. SENGO CHKYŌ TOCHI KAIKAKU NO KYSHINKA—1947-NEN "TOCHIHŌ DAIKŌ" NI TSUITE [Radicalism in Chinese Communist land reform: the 1947 general rules of land law of China]. *Shakaikeizaishigaku (Socio-Economic Hist.) [Japan] 1980 46(2): 44-62.* The 1947 General Rules of Land Law of the Chinese Communist Party, designed to provide every peasant with an equal amount of land, was ultimately a disastrous plan because of the low land to population ratio in Northern China, leaving poor peasants still poor and resulting in a work stoppage.

3074. Tanaka, Kyōko. TOCHI KAIGI TO SEITŌ: NAISENKI NI OKERU CHKYŌ KYSHINSHUGI NO ICHI-SOKUMEN [The land congress and Party consolidation: one phase of radicalism in the Chinese Communist Party during the period of the civil war]. *Ajia Kenkyū [Japan] 1982 28(3-4): 97-130.* After the termination of the anti-Japanese war, the Chinese Communist Party precipitated full-scale civil war in 1947-48, and soon came to assert a more radical land policy. This was derived from the unfavorable military conditions at the outset of the civil war. The Communist Party took a pessimistic view of conditions for land reform at that time, and therefore conducted a very strict thought struggle and Party consolidation movement through the national and local land congresses and cadres' congress. As a result, there spread such an extreme radicalism that middle- and low-level landowners were seen in the very worst light, and poor or employee farmers were treated with utmost generosity. Due to the evil influence perceived in this attitude and to more favorable military circumstances, the Party's land policy was moderated in 1948. Based on Party newspapers, the writings of Mao Zedong, and Party documents; 117 notes. E. Honno

3075. Teiwes, Frederick C. THE ORIGINS OF RECTIFICATION: INNERPARTY PURGES AND EDUCATION BEFORE LIBERATION. *China Q. [Great Britain] 1976 (65): 15-53.* Differences in Chinese Communist Party response to internal dissent were not the result of the personal or ideological views of Mao and his opponents but rather the outcome of objective conditions. These conditions are identified as external hostility or internal leadership cleavage which led to forceful internal control and security or internal leadership unity which produced the rectification, i.e., persuasion approach. Primary and secondary materials in Chinese and English; 94 notes. J. R. Pavia, Jr.

3076. Thomas, S. Bernard. *Labor and the Chinese Revolution: Class Strategies and Contradictions of Chinese Communism, 1928-48.* (Michigan Monographs in Chinese Studies, no. 49.) Ann Arbor: U. of Michigan, Center for Chinese Studies, 1983. 341 pp.

3077. Tozer, Warren W. LAST BRIDGE TO CHINA: THE SHANGHAI POWER COMPANY, THE TRUMAN ADMINISTRATION AND THE CHINESE COMMUNISTS. *Diplomatic Hist. 1977 1(1): 64-78.* A study of the American-owned Shanghai Power Company during 1949-50 indicates that the United States "was primarily responsible for closing the Open Door in China. The People's Republic of China (PRC) not only appeared willing to tolerate American firms for the short term but sought to establish some type of relationship with the United States.... The Truman administration, pursuing a policy of containment, refused to deal with the Chinese Communists, except on its own terms, and attempted to control trade with the PRC in order to force compliance with American demands." Based primarily on the Boise Cascade Corporation Archives; 55 notes. G. H. Curtis

3078. Tucker, Nancy Bernkopf. AN UNLIKELY PEACE: AMERICAN MISSIONARIES AND THE CHINESE COMMUNISTS, 1948-1950. *Pacific Hist. Rev. 1976 45(1): 97-116.* Between 1948 and 1950 the Chinese Communists pursued a policy of toleration of religion, including foreign missionaries. The outbreak of the Korean War ended the policy. The toleration policy was more fully observed in urban than in rural areas. Protestants were better treated than Catholics. American missionaries were divided in their response to Chinese Communists: Catholics and fundamentalist Protestants were hostile but modernist Protestants were more likely to believe cooperation was possible. Other missionaries who decided to cooperate were motivated by the desires of Chinese Christians and by a concern to protect their churches' property holdings in China. Some missionaries also attempted to influence American policy. Many lobbied in 1949 for an end to American aid to the Kuomintang and for recognition of the Communist government. Based on manuscripts in church archives, published primary sources, and published and unpublished secondary works; 66 notes. W. K. Hobson

3079. Wang Chien-min. THE HISTORICAL LESSONS OF KMT-CCP NEGOTIATIONS. *Issues and Studies [Taiwan] 1974 10(10): 71-87.* Analyzes the peace negotiations between China's Communist Party and the Kuomintang, 1922-49.

3080. Wang Hsueh-wen. [A STUDY OF CHINESE COMMUNIST EDUCATION DURING THE YENAN PERIOD]. *Issues & Studies [Taiwan] 1971 7(5): 50-63, (6): 75-90, (7): 77-91, 8(2): 90-102, (3): 96-103; 1972 (4): 74-86, (5): 86-98.* PART I. CHINESE COMMUNISTS' YENAN SPIRIT AND EDUCATIONAL TRADITION. Notes the continuing importance of the Yenan Period (1937-47) to China's Communist Party, particularly the educational tradition established during the era. PART II. THEORY AND POLICY OF YENAN EDUCATION. (See abstract 19B:1563). PART III. THE SYSTEM AND POLICIES OF YENAN EDUCATION. Outlines the educational system, methods, and policies developed by the Party, 1938-46. PART IV. HIGHER EDUCATION DURING THE YENAN PERIOD. Reviews the history of the first eight training classes at the Party's Anti-Japanese Military and Political College, 1936-41, and describes the administrative organization of the school. PART V. HIGHER EDUCATION DURING THE YENAN PERIOD (CONT'D.) Discusses the educational objectives, principles, and method; learning method; recruitment regulations; teaching staff; and funding of the Anti-Japanese College. PART VI. HIGHER EDUCATION DURING THE YENAN PERIOD (CONT'D.) Describes several of the Party's institutions of higher education operating, 1937-44. PART VII. CHINESE COMMUNIST CADRE EDUCATION OF THE YENAN PERIOD. Considers the education of Party members, 1937-42.

3081. Yang, Reynold J. S. THE CHINESE PEOPLE'S POLITICAL CONSULTATIVE CONFERENCE AND THE "DEMOCRATIC" PARTIES. *Issues & Studies [Taiwan] 1980 16(12): 53-76.* Describes the formation and composition of 11 of the so-called democratic parties that proliferated after the 1912 revolution and eventually came to support the Chinese Communists during the 1935-49 period, when the Communist Party pushed for unity and a coalition government in opposition to the Guomindang (Kuomintang). Mao's writings of the period fully describe this policy. The Communist Party treated each of these parties differently to gain its ends, and the September 1949 meeting of the Political Consultative Conference of the Chinese People finally nullified their real participation in government. Based on the writings of Mao Zedong and other Chinese publications; 69 notes. J. A. Krompart

1956-1965

3082. Das, Naranarayan. PEKING'S CAMPAIGN AGAINST CRITICS. *China Report [India] 1976 12(4): 28-41.* Continued from a previous article. The anti-rightist campaign was part of a long-standing Party policy of using intellectuals to build socialism but not allowing them to hold positions of power. In addition, the Party wishes to woo middle-of-the-roaders from the rightist influence. The author describes the process of attacks, the general charges, as well as the punishment for convicted offenders. The leftists' counter charges are also detailed. The attacks were intended to reform errant rightists while cleansing the Party of undesirable elements. 93 notes. S. F. Benfield

3083. Das, Naranarayan. 'RIGHTIST' DISSENT IN CHINA DURING 1957-58. *China Report [India] 1974 10(1-2): 36-54.* Examines Communist definitions of the term "rightist," notes several individuals accused of "rightism" (Lin Hsi-ling, Chang Pochun, Lo Lung-chi, et al.), observes that they were essentially concerned with individual freedom and democratic rights and opposed blind imitation of the Soviet Union, and concludes that despite their acceptance of the leadership of the Communist Party they asserted their right to point out its deviations and to criticize the shortcomings of its members.

3084. Eckstein, Alexander. ON THE ECONOMIC CRISIS IN COMMUNIST CHINA. *Foreign Affairs 1964 42(4): 655-668.* Discusses the economic depression in China caused by the failure of the Communist Party's plan for the Great Leap Forward, 1958-60.

3085. Goodman, David S. G. LI JINGQUAN AND THE SOUTH-WEST REGION, 1958-66: THE LIFE AND "CRIMES" OF A "LOCAL EMPEROR." *China Q. [Great Britain] 1980 (81): 66-96.* In the debate over whether Chinese power was centralized or decentralized between 1958 and 1966, those favoring decentralization make much of the denunciation of Li Jingquan (Li Ching-ch'uan), a leading Communist Party figure in the southwest from 1952 to 1967. Charged with having followed an independent policy and of having become a "local emperor," Li is seen as proof of decentralization. Study of the charges against Li, however, suggest he was not independent of Beijing. Such innovation as did take place in China's southwest may have been inspired by national rather than regional politics. Based primarily on Chinese radio and press reports; 150 notes. J. R. Pavia, Jr.

3086. Halperin, Morton H. and Lewis, John Wilson. COMMUNIST CHINA ARMY-PARTY RELATIONS. *Military Rev. 1967 47(2): 71-78.* Resolutions adopted in 1958 by the Chinese Communist Party reflect deprofessionalization of the military, reliance on revolutionary strategy based on the People's War, and promotion of nuclear weapons.

3087. Mos'ko, G. OB IDEOLOGICHESKOI OBRABOTKE MAOISTAMI LICHNOGO SOSTAVA KITAISKOI ARMII V 1959-1965 GG [Maoist ideological indoctrination of the staff of the Chinese army, 1959-65]. *Voenno-Istoricheskii Zhurnal [USSR] 1976 (7): 101-105.* Outlines methods used by the Maoists to effect the ideological indoctrination of the military general staff of China's army, 1959-65.

1965-1976

3088. Bakešová, Ivana. KULTURNÍ REVOLUCE NA PEKINGSKÉ UNIVERSITĚ II [The Cultural Revolution at Beijing University. Part 2]. *Slovanský Přehled [Czechoslovakia] 1984 70(6): 516-524.* Continued from an earlier article. Deals with the radicalization of the Cultural Revolution as it was exported from Beijing to Shanghai, where it met resistance within the Party. By the beginning of 1967 the extremist factions began a self-criticism of the progress of the revolution, and more moderate opinion prevailed within the councils of the Communist Party. The educational system began to recover from the assaults on the professorial profession in the 1970's, when examinations were reinstated. Based largely on the press of the Red Guards; 56 notes. B. Reinfeld

3089. Bartke, Wolfgang; Jarke, Waldtraut, transl. THE NEW CENTRAL COMMITTEE OF THE CHINESE COMMUNIST PARTY. *Chinese Studies in Hist. 1975 9(1): 3-37.* In 1973 the 10th Congress of the Chinese Communist Party elected a new central committee, with far more civilian members than its predecessors. The new ideal is a politically active worker, not a military man. The Politburo also has a larger provincial staff, reflecting a move toward unifying the country through the national government. There are new tensions in the central committee, particularly in the Cultural Group, which has become an organ for leftist agitation. The armed forces have not been appeased with their diminished role in government. The new central committee does show that the Cultural Revolution has given China new leaders, even if it is too early to see new policies. Chart, 7 tables. J. W. Leedom

3090. Bartke, Wolfgang; Jarke, Waldtraut, transl. THE 195 MEMBERS OF THE TENTH CENTRAL COMMITTEE OF THE CCP. *Chinese Studies in Hist. 1975 9(1): 43-91.* Provides short biographies of all 195 members of the 10th Central Committee of the Chinese Communist Party, elected in 1973. J. W. Leedom

3091. Bertricau, Adrien. LA POLITIQUE INTERIEURE CHINOISE [Chinese internal policy]. *Rev. de l'Est [France] 1973 4(4): 127-149.* Traces China's domestic policy since the Cultural Revolution. Examines the place of the army relative to the increasingly important revolutionary committees and criticizes its technocratic professionalization. The army has remained subordinate to the political power, despite temptation during the Cultural Revolution. The reorganization of the Party has been a keystone of the power struggle, and the committees, set up in 1967, were to see it through the transition. They survived the debate over the role of the Party (1971-72) due to the influence of important committee members. The Ninth Party Congress (April 1969) decreed a reorganization aimed at injecting new blood at all Party levels. Recent consolidation has put Party, committees, and army under a "unified command," but present institutions are likely to be reexamined as the era of the "founding fathers" comes to an end. J/S

3092. Borisov, O. and Il'in, M. MAOISTSKAIA "KUL'TURNAIA REVOLIUTSIIA" [The Maoist Cultural Revolution]. *Voprosy Istorii [USSR] 1973 (11): 81-102; (12): 78-100.* Demonstrates the sum and substance of the events associated with the so-called cultural revolution in China and the main causes that gave rise to this "revolution," as well as the character of the evolution undergone by Maoism during the past few years. Illustrates the utter groundlessness and futility of the attempts made by Mao Tse-tung and his group in conjunction with bourgeois and revisionist theoreticians and scientists to rehabilitate Maoism and to justify the policy pursued by Mao Tse-tung and his followers, clearly showing that the "cultural revolution" was the result of an acute economic, political, and ideological crisis of Maoism. Traces the main springs of the sociopolitical development of China over the past decade, which precipitated the sharp crisis and determined the spasmodic character of this development. Analyzes the materials of the 9th and 10th congresses of the Chinese Communist Party. Characterizes the complex internal struggles going on within the Maoist top leadership, tracing the evolution of the Mao group from "pseudo-Leftist" slogans to downright betrayal of the interests of world socialism, and efforts toward an alliance with the most reactionary and aggressive imperialist circles on the basis of rabid antisocialism and anti-Sovietism. Having objectively aligned itself with the ultrareactionary anti-Communist forces and with Right and "Left" revisionism, Maoism has become one of the most dangerous ideological and political enemies of the international Communist movement, of scientific socialism. J

3093. Borisov, O. and Koloskov, B. PEKING'S FOREIGN POLICY AFTER THE 10TH CONGRESS OF THE CPC. *Int. Affairs [USSR] 1974 (7): 32-44.* Criticizes China's foreign policy toward the USSR, the United States, and developing nations following the 10th Congress of the Chinese Communist Party in 1973.

3094. Borisow, O. and Iljin, M. MAOISTOWSKA "REWOLUCJA KULTURALNA" [The Maoist Cultural Revolution]. *Nowe Drogi [Poland] 1974 2(297): 94-106, 3(298): 125-132, 4(299): 132-141.* Part I: Surveys and strongly criticizes China's Cultural Revolution, 1958-69, and identifies Maoism with anticommunism and revisionism. Part II: Considers the period 1969-73 and critically assesses the cult of Mao's personality and the destructive effects of the Revolution on Chinese government, education, and national culture. Part III: Examines the period 1971-73, emphasizing the militarization of China's economy and social and political life, and its anti-Soviet foreign policy, asserting that China's socialism is neutralized by its military-bureaucratic dictatorship.

3095. Brosseau, Maurice. "The Cultural Revolution in Chinese Industry." U. of Chicago 1982. *DAI 1982 43(6): 2120-A.*

3096. Brown, Cheryl Luvenia. "Restoring a One-Party Regime in China: A Study of Party Branches, 1964-1978." U. of Michigan 1983. 501 pp. *DAI 1984 45(1): 289-A.* DA8402250

3097. Bryan, Derek. CHANGING SOCIAL ETHICS IN CONTEMPORARY CHINA. *Pol. Q. [Great Britain] 1974 45(1): 49-57.* The concrete achievements of the Cultural Revolution have been the ending of external and internal oppression, the maintenance of peace and security, a minimum standard of living, protection against the forces of nature, and the development of industry and agriculture. More important though is the creation of a unique philosophy of communist man. Primary and secondary sources; 11 notes. L. Brown

3098. Burton, Barry. THE CULTURAL REVOLUTION'S ULTRALEFT CONSPIRACY: THE "MAY 16" GROUP. *Asian Survey 1971 11(11): 1029-1053.* Examines efforts to purge the Chinese Communist Party of conservative elements, notably intellectuals in the People's Liberation Army, Wang Li, Chi'i Pen-yü, Kuan Feng, Hu Hsin, Chao I-ya, and Lin Chieh, known as the "May 16" group because of the date on the circular issued which directed that the Party "drag out the small handful of capitalist-roaders in the army."

3099. Chang, Kuo-Sin. REFLECTIONS ON THE TENTH PARTY CONGRESS. *Asian Affairs 1973 1(2): 80-90.* Analyzes the Chinese Communist Party's Congress of 24-28 August 1973.

3100. Chang, Parris H. MAO TSE-TUNG AND HIS GENERALS. *Military Rev. 1973 53(9): 19-27.* During the early stages of the Cultural Revolution Mao Tse-tung used the People's Liberation Army as a powerful political instrument in his attack on the bureaucracy of the Chinese Communist Party. In the process, however, the Party's control over the PLA weakened, and since 1970 he has followed a policy of "divide and rule, check and balance" to reassert Party control. Primary and secondary sources; 7 illus., 10 notes. J. K. Ohl

3101. Chang Chen-pang. AN ANALYSIS OF THE CULTURAL REVOLUTION FACTION. *Issues and Studies [Taiwan] 1974 10(14): 45-57.* Discusses the role of the political faction headed by Mao Tse-tung's wife Chiang Ch'ing in the internal politics of the Communist Party during and after the Cultural Revolution in China.

3102. Chang Ching-wen. THE FOURTH NATIONAL PEOPLE'S CONGRESS—AN ANALYSIS OF THE PERSONNEL APPOINTMENT. *Issues and Studies [Taiwan] 1975 11(2): 50-54.* Discusses key Communist Party personnel appointments at the Fourth National People's Congress in Peking, China in 1975.

3103. Chang Chun. DEVELOPMENT OF HYDROELECTRIC PRODUCTION ON THE CHINESE MAINLAND. *Issues and Studies [Taiwan] 1975 11(6): 44-59.* Discusses resources for hydroelectric power stations in China in the 1970's, including aspects of Communist Party energy policy.

3104. Chaudhuri, Ranjit. REVOLUTION AND REVISIONISM IN CHINA. *China Report [India] 1971 7(1): 16-26.* Discusses ideological conflicts of revolution versus revisionism in Maoist doctrine in the Communist Party of China during the Cultural Revolution, 1967-69.

3105. Cheng, Peter P. AN ANALYSIS OF THE 1965-68 ATTACKS ON LIU SHAO-CHI'S EARLY CAREER. *Issues & Studies [Taiwan] 1971 7(12): 55-77.* Evaluates Liu Shao-chi's career in China's Communist Party, 1920-49, in the light of attacks made upon him in 1965-68.

3106. Chi, Wen-shun. SUN YEH-FANG AND HIS REVISIONIST ECONOMICS. *Asian Survey 1972 12(10): 887-900.* Analyzes Sun Yeh-Fang's revisionist economic ideas and their clash with those of the Maoists.

3107. Chiang Chen-ch'ang. THE CULTURAL REVOLUTION AND THE IDENTITY CRISIS IN MAINLAND CHINA. *Issues & Studies [Taiwan] 1984 20(4): 12-29.* Political education of citizens in Communist China was successful until the Cultural Revolution weakened confidence in government and the Party. To regain popular trust, the Communists are emphasizing patriotism and national identity rather than Marx's internationalism, but youths, whose major life experience is the Cultural Revolution, remain alienated. Based on mainland media reports; 38 notes. J. A. Krompart

3108. Chiao Chien. NEW WINE IN OLD BOTTLES: SOME CHARACTERISTICS OF THE STUDY OF MAO TSE-TUNG'S THOUGHT MOVEMENT IN THE SIXTIES. *J. of the Chinese U. of Hong Kong [Hong Kong] 1975 3(1): 207-216.* Identifies and describes six traditional elements persisting in the Study of Mao Tse-tung's Thought Movement in the sixties: studying with both "heart" and "mind," learning well rather than more, morality as the prime concern of learning, self-examination or criticism, practice or application, and model emulation. Traditional method may often be used to transmit new and revolutionary ideas or ideology, and "putting new wine in old bottles" may very well be a common phenomenon in culture change. J

3109. Chintamani, C. RECONSTRUCTION OF MASS ORGANIZATIONS IN CHINA: WHO CONTROLS LABOUR UNIONS NOW? *China Report [India] 1973 9(4): 3-6.* In 1973 the All-China Federation of Labor Unions was under the firm control of Chiang Ch'ing and Yao Wen-yuan after having undergone a great purge which included the expulsion of Liu Shao-ch'i, while the Communist Youth League now seems to have recovered from the Red Guard takeover and has been reactivated.

3110. Chintamani, C. REVIVAL OF THE YOUTH LEAGUE. *China Report [India] 1971 7(1): 27-29.* Discusses the Communist Party's attempt to revive the Communist Youth League in China in the 1970's, including the policies of Chairman Mao Tse-tung.

3111. Chou Pai-yun. MAO'S EDUCATIONAL IDEOLOGY: A PROBE OF THE "COUNTERATTACK AGAINST THE RIGHT DEVIATIONIST WIND." *Issues and Studies [Taiwan] 1976 12(5): 28-41.* General examination of Maoism's attitudes toward education and Chinese leaders' educational plans, 1961-76.

3112. Chou Wei-ling. THE MAY 7 CADRE SCHOOL: A STUDY OF ITS RECENT SITUATION. *Issues and Studies [Taiwan] 1976 12(9): 16-27.* Discusses the background of the May 7 Cadre School, 1966-76, which aims at the training and education of cadres as a means to perpetuate the proletarian dictatorship, and discusses the evolution of its goals, its rotation of instruction, the organization and training of students and instructors, and certain drawbacks inherent in the system.

3113. Chou Wei-ling. THE STATUS OF THE PROVINCIAL CYL COMMITTEES. *Issues and Studies [Taiwan] 1973 10(1): 52-65 (2): 77-87.* Part I. Explains the motivation of China's Communist Youth League as a means of supervision and control of youth; describes the league's disintegration in 1966 and reorganization at a provincial level in 1972. Part II. Discusses the Maoist political foundations of the provincial Communist Youth League Committees and the organizational structure of the provincial and municipal committees, following the convention of the league's congresses in 1973.

3114. Chu Wen-lin. AN ANALYSIS OF THE 29 NEW CCP COMMITTEES AT THE PROVINCIAL LEVEL. *Issues & Studies [Taiwan] 1971 8(2): 47-65.* Discusses the Chinese Communist Party's organization of new committees to direct the provincial branches of the party. Article to be continued.

3115. Chuan Tsun. THE LIN PIAO INCIDENT AND ITS EFFECT ON MAO'S RULE. *Issues & Studies [Taiwan] 1972 8(5): 21-28.* Discusses the Lin Piao purge of 1972, compares it to other purges in the Chinese Communist Party, and analyzes its impact on Mao Tse-tung and various political factions in the party.

3116. Coccopalmerio, Domenico. LINEAMENTI DEL MARXISMO-LENINISMO [An outline of Marxism-Leninism]. *Mondo Cinese [Italy] 1973 1(1): 66-81.* Discusses Maoism, and clarifies the relation between it and the historical and cultural reality of China. The Communist Party is the vertex and the center of gravity of society and political power; Chinese society is divided into six strata, but the distinctions between them are not rigid and fixed. The Cultural Revolution sought to produce "a higher level of interiorization of values and ideals of socialism according to the thought of Mao Tse-Tung". J/S

3117. Dansoko, Amath and Pahad, Essop. MAOISM SELF-EXPOSED IN AFRICA. *World Marxist Rev. [Canada] 1976 19(4): 75-80.* In breaking with Marxism-Leninism and allying itself with the forces of reaction, imperialism, and racism since the early 1960's, China has betrayed the cause of revolution and freedom in Africa in pursuing its anti-Soviet foreign policy.

3118. Deshingkar, G. D. THE CONSTRUCTIVE PHASE. *China Report [India] 1971 7(2): 34-40.* Discusses the economic, industrial, political, and foreign policies outlined in the Chinese Communist Party's Five-Year Plan, 1969-71.

3119. Domes, Jurgen. THE "GANG OF FOUR" AND HUA KUO-FENG: ANALYSIS OF POLITICAL EVENTS IN 1975-76. *China Q. [Great Britain] 1977 (71): 473-497.* Seven groups within the Chinese Communist Party leadership have struggled over five policy issues since 1973. Shifting alliances among the seven have resulted in the 6 October 1976 arrest of the Gang of Four and brought the opportunist Hua Kuo-feng to the position of chairman. Based on Chinese language broadcasts and publications; table, 79 notes. J. R. Pavia, Jr.

3120. Fanchelieu, Lucien and Zafanolli, W. UNE ÉQUATION MAOISTE: UN PLUS UN=UN [A Maoist equation: one plus one=one]. *Esprit [France] 1978 (9): 40-58.* Traces the ever-changing political orientation of Teng Hsiao-p'ing throughout his political career.

3121. Fang Chün-kuei. THE VICISSITUDES AND THE STATUS OF THE CCP CENTRAL POLITBURO MEMBERS. *Issues and Studies [Taiwan] 1972 8(8): 35-39.* Discusses the selection of Politburo members of the Communist Party in China, by the Ninth Congress (1969) and the variations in their status based on order of listing in public appearances, 1969-72.

3122. Feng, Hai. THE CULTURAL REVOLUTION AND THE RECONSTRUCTION OF THE CHINESE COMMUNIST PARTY. *Asia Q. [Belgium] 1972 (4): 303-320.* Aided by the army and the Red Guard movement, Mao Tse-tung won the Communist Party power struggle against the administration of Liu Shao-ch'i and Têng Hsiao-p'ing during 1965-67. The revolutionary committees, the central committee set up by the 9th Party congress, and Party organizations at all levels founded after the congress were based on a combination of the army, cadres, and mass delegates. Mao saw his role as mediator in the struggle and balancer of these forces. Based on government documents, newspapers, and secondary sources; 4 charts, 14 notes. G. M. White

3123. Garver, John William. "China's Decision for Rapprochement with the United States, 1969-1971." U. of Colorado, Boulder 1979. 462 pp. *DAI 1980 40(8): 4736-A.*

3124. Goodstadt, Leo. DEMOCRACY V. DYNASTIES. THE ELEVENTH CONGRESS OF THE CHINESE COMMUNIST PARTY. *Round Table [Great Britain] 1977 (268): 337-344.* Traces the development of Chinese politics since the Cultural Revolution. Parallels recent events in China and India, concerning the domination of one family and its subsequent replacement by men who captured power away from the family's own stronghold. Examines the attitude of the 11th Congress to the Gang of Four, the attempts to prevent the emergence of local or national despots by guaranteeing the right to petition and complain, and the efforts to coordinate production and democratic remuneration. C. Anstey

3125. Gupta, Krishna Prakash. CHINA'S THEORY AND PRACTICE OF INTERVENTION. *China Report [India] 1971 7(6): 12-27.* Discusses issues of morality, law, and Marxism-Leninism in China's foreign policy toward India and Bangladesh, 1960's-70's.

3126. Gupta, Krishna Prakash. TSINGHUA EXPERIENCE AND HIGHER EDUCATION IN CHINA. *China Report [India] 1971 7(1): 2-14.* Discusses the influences of Maoism in higher education curricula at Tsinghua University in China, 1966-71.

3127. Halimarski, Andrzej. WOKÓŁ OSTATNICH WYDARZEŃ W CHRL [Recent events in the People's Republic of China]. *Nowe Drogi [Poland] 1976 (5): 156-169.* Gives an historical account of the crisis of Maoism.

3128. Hiniker, Paul J. THE CULTURAL REVOLUTION REVISITED: DISSONANCE REDUCTION OR POWER MAXIMIZATION. *China Q. [Great Britain] 1983 (94): 282-303.* Though the Cultural Revolution can be seen as a power struggle it may also be approached as an attempt at reduction of cognitive dissonance. Confronted with the obvious failure of the Great Leap, devoted Maoists could only intensify their support of the ideology that produced the failure and claim class enemies to have been the cause of the economic chaos. 54 notes. J. R. Pavia, Jr.

3129. Hook, Brian. THE CAMPAIGN AGAINST LIN PIAO AND CONFUCIUS. *Asian Affairs [Great Britain] 1974 61(3): 311-316.* Describes the campaign of criticism launched in China in the spring of 1974 linking the name of the former Defense Minister, Lin Piao, with that of the sage, Confucius. This activity stems from remarks attributed to Chairman Mao Tse-tung at the Tenth National Party Congress in Peking. Confucius is attacked as representing the ancient declining slave-owning aristocracy and Lin Piao is regarded as a modern-day "traitor" to the progressive forces. Many similarities exist between the Cultural Revolution and the new villification of Lin Piao: street posters, criticism of a new revolutionary Shansi opera, and quasi-historical debates. Lin Piao allegedly advocated the line of the "Soviet revisionist renegade clique" as being superior to the Maoists agricultural views epitomized by the "Tachai" brigade. The new anti-Lin campaign represents a consolidation of the gains made in the Cultural Revolution in terms of a synthesis of Leninism and national reality that Mao sought at its outset. Based on the author's observations during the third tour of the Royal Central Asian Society in the People's Republic of China; 14 notes. S. H. Frank

3130. Horbachov, B. M. VYKORYSTANNIA MAOISTAMY ZBROINYKH SYL KYTAIU V "KUL'TURNII REVOLIUTSII" [The use made by Maoists of the armed forces of China in the Cultural Revolution]. *Ukrains'kyi Istorychnyi Zhurnal [USSR] 1976 (4): 103-110.* Exposes the anti-scientific approach of the Chinese leadership to the role of the army as a serious departure from Marxism-Leninism, illustrating the disastrous effects of this by the events of the Cultural Revolution, when the army carried out police functions and became an anti-popular tool of Maoist policy.

3131. Hu Chang. CCP'S MEDICAL AND HEALTH POLICY SINCE THE CULTURAL REVOLUTION. *Issues & Studies [Taiwan] 1971 7(7): 71-76.* Analyzes the impact of Maoism on the medical reforms and public health policies of China's Communist Party, 1968-71.

3132. Iurkov, S. POLITIKA PEKINA V OTNOSHENII STRAN SOTSIALIZMA [Peking's policies toward the socialist bloc]. *Mezhdunarodnaia Zhizn' [USSR] 18(10): 23-33.* Surveys new developments in Chinese foreign policy toward the USSR and its socialist allies, 1969-71, following changes instituted at the 9th Congress of the Chinese Communist Party.

3133. Joyaux, François. À PROPOS D'UN ARTICLE DE LIN BIAO [Regarding an article by Lin Piao]. *R. de Défence Natl. [France] 1967 23(3): 445-451.* Studies Lin Piao's definition of what is "orthodox" in modern Chinese communism and attempts to prove the universal nature of the thought of Mao Tse-tung. Examines the themes of Mao's writings on Chinese Marxism-Leninism and China's essential objectives. Stresses contradictions in Lin Piao's effort to transform internal politics into principles of international politics to provide a doctrinal basis for the "liberation" of China. Secondary sources; 27 notes. S. Sevilla

3134. Kakkar, Ranjana. THE ROLE OF THE PLA DURING THE CULTURAL REVOLUTION. *China Report [India] 1977 13(5): 29-36.* Studies the circumstances which led the People's Liberation Army (PLA) to undertake a political role. Mao Tse-tung, under the influence of Liu Shao-chi acquiesced impatiently in slower paced revolution until Mao decided to revitalize the revolution and turned to the PLA for assistance. In the face of intra-Party factionalism, the PLA was the only intact organization. The PLA was not a radical revolutionary force but was a moderating and stabilizing force in the midst of anarchy. Civil war in China was averted through compromise agreements with many regional and local military commanders. 23 notes. R. V. Ritter

3135. Kessen, William. AN AMERICAN GLIMPSE OF THE CHILDREN OF CHINA: REPORT OF A VISIT. *Social Science Research Council Items 1974 28(3): 41-44.* Describes education under Communism in China in 1973.

3136. King, Ambrose Yeo-Chi. A VOLUNTARIST MODEL OF ORGANIZATION: THE MAOIST VERSION AND ITS CRITIQUE. *British J. of Sociol. [Great Britain] 1977 28(3): 363-374.* Discusses the historical and cultural significance of the Cultural Revolution in China, 1966.

3137. Kintner, William R. THE ESSENCE OF STRATEGY: SOVIET AND CHINESE COMMUNIST STYLE. *R. Militaire Générale [France] 1971 (9): 477-487.* The success of the grand strategies of the USSR and of the People's Republic of China has been due to the integration and mutual support of political and psychological action and military force, together with the maintenance of the initiative and a persistency of commitment. Three Western schools of thought have produced analyses of communist strategy supporting this thesis. Western strategies have been defensive and difficult to maintain. Moreover, Western public opinion can be manipulated by the Communists, but the reverse is not true. The West must restore its spirit and purpose, weakened by the nihilistic alienation of the youth, "the insatiable materialism of the rest of the population," and moral decline. J. S. Gassner

3138. Kitts, Charles. THE GREAT PROLETARIAN CULTURAL REVOLUTION. *Issues & Studies [Taiwan] 1970 6(11): 29-35.* Mao Tse-tung used the Cultural Revolution, 1966-69, to regain his dominance in China's Communist Party.

3139. Koloskov, B. VNUTRENNIAIA I VNESHNIAIA POLITIKA MAOIZMA: PRIAMYE I OBRATNYE SVIAZI [The internal and foreign policy of Maoism: direct links and feedbacks]. *Mirovaia Ekonimika i Mezhdunarodnye Otnosheniia [USSR] 1976 (6): 42-55, (7): 34-45.* Part I. Analyzes the impact of China's cultural revolution on economic life and foreign policy, with reference to the "economic thaw" which oriented Communist China toward the West. Part II. Discusses the causes and results of the September Crisis of 1971 in China with an analysis of the decisions of the 10th Extraordinary Congress of the Communist Party of China.

3140. Kramers, R. P. WERKELIJKHEID EN VISIE—CHINA 1974 [Vision and reality: China, 1974]. *Wereld en Zending [Netherlands] 1974 3(5): 356-386.* Describes the author's visit to China in 1974, examining social and educational ideas in Maoist China and discussing the growing campaign against Lin-Piao and Confucius.

3141. Krasucki, Ludwik. WALKA Z KONFUCJUSZEM: TŁO I CHARAKTER [The struggle against Confucius: background and character]. *Nowe Drogi [Poland] 1974 (6): 71-83.* Discusses the work and thought of Confucius in old China and indicates how the anti-Confucius campaign, 1972-73, is yet another phase in the crisis brought about by Maoism which is hindering China's march toward true communism. W. H. Zawadzki

3142. K'ung Te-liang. AN ANALYSIS OF THE CCP'S TENTH NATIONAL CONGRESS. *Issues and Studies [Taiwan] 1973 10(1): 17-30.* Analyzes internal problems of China's Communist Party, citing the differences in the 10th National Congress. 1973, from previous congresses, unusual secrecy in procedures, and changes in political leadership as indicators of future instability.

3143. Kung Te-liang. IDEOLOGICAL RECTIFICATION ON THE CHINESE MAINLAND. *Issues & Studies [Taiwan] 1970 7(2): 24-28.* Discusses the renewed effort of China's Communist Party to purge party members of false ideological positions during 1969-70.

3144. Kuo, Warren. VIEWS ON THE STUDY OF CHINESE MAINLAND PROBLEMS. *Issues & Studies [Taiwan] 1973 9(4): 82-85.* Discusses the preparation needed by scholars before they begin research on the Communist Party in China.

3145. Kuriyama, Yoshihiro. A JAPANESE "MAOIST": NIIJIMA ATSUYOSHI. *Asian Survey 1976 16(9): 846-854.* A short biography of Niijima Atsuyoshi, a China scholar in Japan who helped in developing diplomatic relations between China and Japan and who subscribes to the type of people-to-people diplomacy used in China; examines Atsuyoshi's defense of the Chinese Communist Party, 1960's-76.

3146. Lee, Hung Yung. MAO'S STRATEGY FOR REVOLUTIONARY CHANGE: A CASE STUDY OF THE CULTURAL REVOLUTION. *China Q. [Great Britain] 1979 (77): 50-73.* Bureaucratization of the Chinese Communist Party (CCP) led Mao Zedong (Mao Tse-tung) to launch the Cultural Revolution. Counting on symbol manipulation to reach a consensus, Mao soon found it necessary to support first one faction and then another as unexpected alliances and desires surfaced. Mao's unique position as formal and charismatic (informal) leader allowed him this approach. Based on Chinese materials and Western commentaries; fig., 73 notes. J. R. Pavia, Jr.

3147. Li Chiu-i. POLICY ENFORCEMENT ORGANS OF THE CCP CENTRAL COMMITTEE: PERSONNEL STATUS. *Issues and Studies [Taiwan] 1974 10(11): 48-56.* Discusses the personnel status of policy enforcement administrators in the Communist Party Central Committee during and after the Cultural Revolution in China, 1967-70's.

3148. Li Chiu-i. A STUDY OF THE EVOLUTION OF THE CADRE POLICY. *Issues and Studies [Taiwan] 1977 13(2): 66-78.* Chronicles the evolution of Mao Tse-tung's cadre system as a way of dealing with political factions in China's Communist Party; examines the distribution of power within the cadres, 1966-67.

3149. Li Ming-hua. THE ESTABLISHMENT AND DECLINE OF THE CENTRAL LEADERSHIP POWER OF THE CCP. *Issues and Studies [Taiwan] 1973 10(3): 46-54.* A decline in political leadership authority has continually weakened the Communist Party Central Committee and the political power of Mao Tse-tung in China since the Cultural Revolution.

3150. Li T'ien-min. CHOU EN-LAI: AFTER THE FOURTH NATIONAL PEOPLE'S CONGRESS. *Issues and Studies [Taiwan] 1975 11(5): 3-10.* Discusses the role of Chou En-lai in political power struggles within the Communist Party before, during and after the 1975 Fourth National People's Congress in China, 1973-75.

3151. Li T'ien-min. CONFLICTS BETWEEN THE CCP AND THE PLA AND BETWEEN MAO AND LIN. *Issues & Studies [Taiwan] 1972 8(6): 48-56.* Discusses how conflicts from 1968 to 1971 between the Chinese Communist Party and the army led to Mao Tse-tung's attempts to purge Lin Piao.

3152. Li T'ien-min. CRITICISM OF LIN PIAO'S MILITARY LINE: A MAOIST MOVEMENT. *Issues and Studies [Taiwan] 1975 11(8): 20-34.* Discusses the Maoist propaganda campaign against the military strategy of Lin Piao in China, 1971-73.

3153. Li T'ien-min. THE CULTURAL REVOLUTION FACTION: ITS PAST AND FUTURE. *Issues and Studies [Taiwan] 1976 12(8): 83-93.* Discusses the emergence of the Cultural Revolution faction within the Communist Party in China, 1966-76; headed by Chiang Ch'ing, its members include ranking Party, government, and possibly army officials.

3154. Li T'ien-min. LIN PIAO'S SITUATION. *Issues & Studies [Taiwan] 1971 8(2): 66-74.* Discusses the growing influence of Lin Piao in the Chinese Communist Party during the Cultural Revolution, 1966-71.

3155. Lieberthal, Kenneth. THE FOREIGN POLICY DEBATE IN PEKING AS SEEN THROUGH ALLEGORICAL ARTICLES, 1973-76. *China Q. [Great Britain] 1977 (71): 528-554.* Though the currently disgraced Gang of Four is denounced solely for having sought personal power, real disputes over policy can be seen in allegorical articles published during 1973-76. While the radicals recognized an external threat, they insisted the greater danger lay within China at the highest level of the Communist Party. Two moderate factions insisted the threat was military, differing only in their willingness to make concessions to the USSR, but agreeing on the necessity for material incentives to win support in China. Based on research conducted at the Rand Corporation and nine articles from the Chinese press; 73 notes. J. R. Pavia, Jr.

3156. Lien Chan. NEGOTIATION IN COMMUNIST CHINA'S FOREIGN POLICY TOWARD THE UNITED STATES. *Issues and Studies [Taiwan] 1975 11(2): 27-49.* Discusses the role of negotiations in China's diplomacy and foreign policy toward the United States in the 1960's and 70's, emphasizing aspects of Maoism.

3157. Lin Kuo-hsiung. ON THE REVOLUTIONARY DIPLOMACY OF THE CHINESE COMMUNISTS. *Issues and Studies [Taiwan] 1973 10(3): 55-66.* Explains China's revolutionary diplomacy as part of the general strategy of communism toward world revolution through proletarian internationalism; discusses the impact of President Nixon's visit on this policy.

3158. Liu, William H. UNIVERSITY ADMINISTRATION IN POST-CULTURAL REVOLUTION CHINA. *China Report [India] 1974 10(1-2): 27-35.* Before the Cultural Revolution, Party control of university administration appeared to be advisory and indirect, but since 1970 the Communist Party University Committee has increasingly asserted its authority over all aspects of university life and has become the *de facto* ruling organ responsible directly to the Party's Central Committee.

3159. Liu Mao-nan. ON THE LIN PIAO INCIDENT. *Issues & Studies [Taiwan] 1972 8(6): 41-47.* Discusses the purging of Lin Piao in 1971 and 1972 by Maoists in the Chinese Communist Party.

3160. Liu Mao-nan. RECENT DEVELOPMENTS OF THE MOVEMENT TO CRITICIZE REVISIONISM AND RECTIFY THE STYLE OF WORK. *Issues & Studies [Taiwan] 1971 8(1): 38-44.* Discusses how the Communist Party in China reemphasized Maoism, 1967-71, in order to reform revisionists and conservatives.

3161. Mohanty, Manoranjan. CONTINUING THE REVOLUTION. *China Report [India] 1972 8(3): 4-7.* Struggle within China, 1971-72, centered around strengthening collective Communist Party leadership, expunging revisionism, and extending CCP control over the People's Liberation Army.

3162. O'Leary, Greg. ULTRA-LEFTISM AND LIN PIAO. *J. of Contemporary Asia [Sweden] 1974 4(2): 151-169.* Analyzes the implications of Lin Biao's downfall and the campaign against the "Ultra-Leftists" (now "Ultra-Rightists") in China by examining the role of the PLA, elitism, and economic and foreign policy. Lin's ultra-leftist commitments, i.e., a politically strong army, the idea of the "great man" over the masses, the emphasis on the electronic industry, the confrontation of two principal enemies (USSR and US), fell into disfavor. In each case, Lin and the Ultra-Leftists failed to determine the "correct stage" of historical development. G. W. Manning

3163. Ott, Richard. ČÍNSKÁ MLÁDEŽ A MAOISMUS [Chinese youth and Maoism]. *Hist. a Vojenství [Czechoslovakia] 1976 25(3): 156-169.* The changing attitudes of China's political leaders from 1965 to the present on the nation's youth. Three directives promulgated in 1968 directed young intellectuals to remote regions of China for reeducation; the objective was to halt any further political and economic damage resulting from the Cultural Revolution. This government program of rustication bred dissatisfaction among the young people concerned. During and after the 10th Communist Party Congress (1973) emphasis was put on training youth cadre to become the bearers of Mao's ideas in the Communist Party and in local and works administration. 28 notes. L. Short

3164. Price, R. F. CHINESE TEXTBOOKS, FOURTEEN YEARS ON. *China Q. [Great Britain] 1980 (83): 535-550.* In spite of changing policies, Chinese textbooks appear to have changed very little in form, content, or style. Where Confucian filial piety served as a rationale in the past, the paternalism of the Chinese Communist Party acts as a contemporary, not too dissimilar, replacement. Based on Chinese language readers of 1978 and earlier texts of 1964; 3 tables, 88 notes. J. R. Pavia, Jr.

3165. Sabrosky, Alan Ned. FOREIGN POLICY IMPLICATIONS OF THE CHINESE POLITICAL SUCCESSION. *Asian Affairs: An Am. Rev. 1974 2(1): 29-37.* Analyzes the succession to Mao Tse-tung in terms of the three major factions in Chinese Communist leadership: the professional Party cadres (Mao Tse-tung, Chou En-lai), militant Red Guard Maoists (Wang Hung-wen, Li Teh-sheng), and the politicized Army cadres (Lin Piao). Details the proceedings and implications of the Tenth Party Congress (Peking, 24-28 August 1973). Primary and secondary sources; 4 notes. R. B. Mendel

3166. Saywell, William G. CHINA CONFRONTS THE TENSIONS OF MAOISM AND MODERNIZATION. *Internat. Perspectives [Canada] 1974 (1): 3-7.*

3167. Scalapino, Robert A. THE CCP'S PROVINCIAL SECRETARIES. *Problems of Communism 1976 25(4): 18-35.* Examines the changes that took place in the ranks of the provincial secretaries of the Communist Party in China between 1970 and 1975. The changes reflect continuing political instability that will certainly be projected into the post-Mao period. Based on Chinese and English language sources; map, table, 11 notes. J. M. Lauber

3168. Scharping, Thomas. CHINAS ZWEITE KULTURREVOLUTION: DIE KRITIK AN LIN PIAO UND KONFUZIUS IM SPIEGEL DER WANDZEITUNGEN [China's second Cultural Revolution: the critique of Lin Piao and Confucius as seen in the wall-newspapers]. *Int. Asienforum [West Germany] 1976 7(1/2): 22-53.* The 10th Congress of the Chinese Communist Party in August 1973 started a new move to the Left with another mass movement against "revisionism" and the motto "Critique of Lin Piao and Confucius"; its progress can be followed in the wall newspapers which appear in the great cities of China.

3169. Schiffrin, Harold Z. MILITARY AND POLITICS IN CHINA: IS THE WARLORD MODEL PERTINENT? *Asia Q. [Belgium] 1975 (3): 193-206.* Contemporary Chinese army leaders are heavily involved in politics but this does not justify arguments that warlordism is reemerging. The army intervened during the Cultural Revolution and in so doing stabilized politics and reasserted

Party authority rather than increasing its power. In the absence of ideological or Party crises it is premature to talk of the resurgence of warlordism. F. D. Birch

3170. Semyonov, Y. THE BITTER FRUIT OF MAOISM: "CULTURAL REVOLUTION" AND PEKING'S POLICY. *Int. Affairs [USSR] 1976 (9): 36-47.* The Cultural Revolution of Maoist China has fostered internal dissent, restricted cultural and technological growth, caused political unrest, and served as political stepping stones for degenerate opportunists who purported to promote the economic and social development of China, 1965-75.

3171. Sinha, Mira. BANGLA DESH FROM THE CHINESE PERSPECTIVE. *China Report [India] 1971 7(6): 29-38.* Discusses elements of Maoism in China's diplomacy and foreign policy toward India, Pakistan, and Bangladesh, 1969-71.

3172. Sinha, Mira. FOREIGN POLICY: SPELLING OUT THE MAOIST VISION. *China Report [India] 1974 10(5-6): 123-141.* China's new Maoist proletarian revolutionary line, as formulated since 1969, identifies major world contradictions and a consequent strategic principle, relying on the international Communist movement, national liberation movements, the united front, and peaceful coexistence.

3173. Sung, George C. S. CHINA'S REGIONAL POLITICS: A BIOGRAPHICAL APPROACH. *Asian Survey 1975 15(4): 346-365.* Makes a statistical analysis of secretaries elected to Chinese Communist Party provincial committees in 1970-71.

3174. Tang, Peter S. H. MAO TSETUNG THOUGHT SINCE THE CULTURAL REVOLUTION. *Studies in Soviet Thought [Netherlands] 1973 13(3-4): 265-278.* A paean of praise for recent "Mao thought." Besides producing such masterpieces as "The Yellow River Concerto" and the film "The Red Detachment of Women," China under Maoism has made "remarkable progress on all fronts," revitalized Marxist-Leninist thought and waged "fearlessly insatiable battle" against revisionism. R. Stromberg

3175. Ts'ao, Ignatius J. H. "LEGALISM" REASSESSED BY THE LATTER-DAY MAOISTS. *Asian Thought and Soc. 1976 1(3): 291-306.* Discusses Mao's use of ideological mobilization as a method for seizing and maintaining political power, and the reassessment of Mao's policies by Maoists toward the end of his political career.

3176. Ts'ao, Ignatius J. H. STUDY NOTES OF MARXIST "CLASSICS" AND THE *RED FLAG* 1971-1972. *Studies in Soviet Thought [Netherlands] 1973 13(3-4): 279-310.* Articles in *Red Flag,* the theoretical journal of the Central Committee of the Chinese Communist Party, 1971-72, reflect study of the Marxist classics of Karl Marx, Friedrich Engels, and V. I. Lenin, support Mao's philosophy of continuing class struggle under socialism, emphasize the importance of an ideological superstructure, and oppose economism or crude historical materialism. The purpose is to justify the Cultural Revolution, Chinese policy toward the USSR, and attack revisionists such as Liu Shao-ch'i. R. Stromberg

3177. Tsou, Tang. MAO TSE-TUNG THOUGHT, THE LAST STRUGGLE FOR SUCCESSION, AND THE POST-MAO ERA. *China Q. [Great Britain] 1977 (71): 498-527.* Mao Tse-tung's contention that "in the contradiction between theory and practice, practice *generally* plays the principal and decisive role" accurately expressed his own pragmatic application of Marx and Lenin. But it also provided his successors with a flexible dogma adaptable to factional strife. The leftists, currently out of power, drew upon Mao Tse-tung thought to place principal before practice while the current victors championed practicality. Having won, they then labeled the Gang of Four ultrarightists to more easily explain the disruption of the Party and economy that has followed the Cultural Revolution. Based on Chinese periodicals and journals; 84 notes. J. R. Pavia, Jr.

3178. Vostokov, D. VNESHNIAIA POLITIKA KNR POSLE IX S"EZDA KPK [Chinese foreign policy after the 9th Congress of the Chinese Communist Party]. *Mezhdunarodnaia Zhizn' [USSR] 1971 18(12): 31-43.* Examines expansionism in Chinese foreign policy following the 9th Chinese Communist Party Congress, 1969.

3179. Wang, Yun. THE CPSU'S RECENT REPUDIATION OF MAOIST IDEOLOGY AND POLICY. *Issues & Studies [Taiwan] 1970 6(11): 46-56, (12): 41-46.* Describes the position taken by the USSR's Communist Party, 1966-70, on Maoism, and on China's Cultural Revolution and repudiation of a unified international communist movement.

3180. Wang Hsueh-wen. THE MAOISTS' CRITICISM OF WANG YANG-MING. *Issues and Studies [Taiwan] 1975 11(5): 55-65.* Discusses the role of class struggle in Maoists' ideological campaign against Ming Dynasty Confucian philosopher Wang Yang-ming in China in the 1970's.

3181. Wang Hsueh-wen. THE MAOISTS' CRITICISM OF TUNG CHUNG-SHU. *Issues and Studies [Taiwan] 1974 10(11): 24-34.* Discusses political and ideological factors in Maoists' propaganda campaign to criticize philosopher Tung Chung-shu (179-104 B.C.) in China in 1974, emphasizing his alleged acceptance of feudalism.

3182. Wang Hsueh-wen. PEKING AND TSINGHUA UNIVERSITIES: 1966-1976. *Issues and Studies [Taiwan] 1977 13(6): 75-90.* Gives short histories of both schools and concludes that if Maoist thinking prevails, these institutions will become doctrinaire establishments and decline drastically in quality.

3183. Watson, Andrew. THE TENTH NATIONAL CONGRESS OF THE CHINESE COMMUNIST PARTY. *Critique [Great Britain] 1973 1(2): 83-88.* Gives background to the Tenth National Congress of the Chinese Communist Party (24 August-28 August 1973), focusing on the Party's attempts to reunify itself following the Lin Piao conspiracy.

3184. Yao Meng-hsien. SOME QUESTIONS CONCERNING THE CHINESE COMMUNIST INTERNAL STRUGGLE. *Issues & Studies [Taiwan] 1973 9(10): 48-60, (11): 67-79.* Part I. Discusses the purge of Lin Piao and the controls placed on the army by the Chinese Communist Party, 1970-71. Part II. QUESTIONS CONCERNING MAO TSE-TUNG'S SUCCESSORS.

3185. Yeh Hsiang-chih. PEIPING'S INTERNAL CRISIS AND ITS FOREIGN POLICY. *Issues & Studies [Taiwan] 1972 8(4): 30-35.* Discusses how the continuing political crisis in the Communist Party has affected China's foreign policy since 1967. Based on talks given at the 1971 Sino-Japanese Conference on Mainland China.

3186. Ying Kuei-fang. THE CURRENT WOMEN'S MOVEMENT ON THE CHINESE MAINLAND. *Issues and Studies [Taiwan] 1974 10(10): 50-63.* Discusses the political motives of the women's movement in China's Communist Party, 1968-70's, stressing criticism of Confucianism and Lin Piao.

3187. Young, L. C. and Ford, S. R. GOD IS SOCIETY: THE RELIGIOUS DIMENSION OF MAOISM. *Sociol. Inquiry [Canada] 1977 47(2): 89-98.* Maoism as a politico-religious form emerged in a society in the process of disintegration. It became crystallized as a response to the demands of rapid modernization. The Maoist belief system centers around the concept "people," the ultimate sacred reality. Its ethic emphasizes ceaseless service to others, individual asceticism, and intensive practical activity as necessary to the achievement of social salvation and collective immortality. A number of ritual parallels are identified between Maoism and contemporary Christianity: the worship service and ministry, the initiation process, sin and atonement, and various initiative rituals. From an evolutionary perspective, both primitive and ultra-modern elements are identified in Maoism. J

3188. Zhelokhovtsev, A. N. SOBYTIIA 5 APRELIA 1976 G. V KITAISKOI LITERATURE [The events of 5 April 1976 in Chinese literature]. *Narody Azii i Afriki [USSR] 1980 (2): 52-63.* Studies the changed interpretations by the Chinese Politburo of the demonstrations on Tiananmen (T'ien-an-men), Square in Beijing (Peking) on 5 April 1976. The event was described then as anti-Maoist, but those who were arrested have more recently been rehabilitated, and the current appraisal stresses the revolutionary aspects of the meeting. The author quotes verses, songs, and articles about the event, signed or anonymous, written at the time and published after November 1978. 39 notes. English summary. C. Pichelin

3189. —. CCP CENTRAL COMMITTEE DOCUMENT—CHUNG-FA NO. 21 (1974). *Issues and Studies [Taiwan] 1975 11(1): 101-104.* Discusses and presents a restricted Communist Party Central Committee document dealing with cadres, economic conditions and industrial and agricultural production in China in 1974.

3190. —. CHIA CH'I-YÜN: A LIBERATED CADRE. *Issues and Studies [Taiwan] 1977 13(3): 106-111.* Reviews the career of Chia Ch'i-yün, former First Secretary of the Chinese Communist Party Yunnan Provincial Committee, from 1966, when he opposed the pro-Mao faction in the Cultural Revolution, to February 1977, when he was dismissed from all his posts.

3191. —. THE GENERAL POLITICAL DEPARTMENT'S "REQUEST FOR INSTRUCTIONS CONCERNING THE PROPOSAL TO REVOKE THE SUMMARY OF THE FEBRUARY 1966 FORUM ON THE WORK IN LITERATURE AND ART IN THE ARMED FORCES." *Issues & Studies [Taiwan] 1984 20(9): 87-92.* Translations of two 1979 documents of the CCP Central Committee and General Political Department which seek revocation of Chung-fa ('66) No. 211, "Summary of the February 1966 Forum on the Work in Literature and Art in the Armed Forces," a Cultural Revolution document reputed to have been authored by Jiang Qing (Chiang Ch'ing) and other disgraced officials. Because of Mao's part in the creation of the "Summary" and its other politically sensitive associations, the 1979 documents include a request that this revocation not be publicized. J. A. Krompart

3192. —. "STUDY MATERIAL FOR THE NEW YEAR CONCERNING THE INTERNATIONAL SITUATION." *Issues and Studies [Taiwan] 1972 8(9): 71-75.* Reprints one of five articles of an internal Chinese Communist Party document, this one titled "Corruption and Ruin are Prevailing in Capitalist World Headed by the United States."

3193. —. WU TEH—FIRST SECRETARY OF THE CCP PEKING MUNICIPAL COMMITTEE. *Issues and Studies [Taiwan] 1974 10(1): 88-90.* Sketches the political career of Wu Teh as first secretary of the Communist Party Municipal Committee in Peking, China during and after the Cultural Revolution, 1966-74.

1976-Present

3194. Andreyev, K. ANTI-SOVIETISM AND ANTI-COMMUNISM: IDEOLOGY AND PRACTICE OF MAOISM. *Int. Affairs [USSR] 1976 (7): 33-42.* Following the Cultural Revolution, Chinese foreign policy abandoned the principles of proletarian internationalism in favor of great-power chauvinism and hegemonism and actively pursued a line of strident anti-Sovietism, 1970's.

3195. Barnett, A. Doak. POST-MAO CHINA: ON A NEW COURSE. *SAIS Rev. 1983 3(1): 147-160.* Since 1977 it appears that China has embarked on a course that emphasizes stability rather than struggle; the new policy also displays some disillusionment with the Party and its bureaucracy.

3196. Bartke, Wolfgang and Schier, Peter. *China's New Party Leadership: Biographies and Analysis of the Twelfth Central Committee of the Chinese Communist Party.* Armonk, N.Y.: M. E. Sharpe, 1985. 289 pp.

3197. Benton, Gregor. THE FACTIONAL STRUGGLE IN THE CHINESE COMMUNIST PARTY. *Critique [Great Britain] 1977 (8): 100-123.* The year 1976 saw a partial resolution of the chronic crisis of leadership in favor of the restored and strengthened moderate faction, although internal divisions of various sorts continue to threaten the new ruling group's stability and wide sectors of ordinary Chinese are growing impatient for real change.

3198. Borisov, O. THE 26TH CPSU CONGRESS AND SOME PROBLEMS OF STUDYING THE HISTORY OF CHINA. *Far Eastern Affairs [USSR] 1981 (4): 3-11.* Describes how the resolutions of the 26th Congress of the Communist Party of the Soviet Union, 1981, contain the main fundamental precepts for a Marxist-Leninist history of the People's Republic of China.

3199. Botton Beja, Flora. EL DECIMO CONGRESO NACIONAL DE LA LIGA DE LA JUVENTUD COMUNISTA DE CHINA: INFORME Y COMENTARIOS [The 10th National Congress of the Young Communist League of China: report and commentary]. *Estudios de Asia y Africa [Mexico] 1980 16(3): 549-558.* The congress marked a stage in the new policy of reviving the mass organizations, which had been neglected in the last 12 years, and mobilizing them in the service of modernization programs. However, the problems of China's youth were only superficially touched upon, and it is not likely that the young people will find much guidance or support in the league. J. V. Coutinho

3200. Brugger, William. *China since the "Gang of Four."* New York: St. Martin's, 1980. 281 pp.

3201. Cherkasski, L. E. "OBLICHITEL'NAIA" POEZIIA V SOVREMENNOM KITAE ["Accusatory" poetry in contemporary China]. *Narody Azii i Afriki [USSR] 1982 (2): 87-95.* Reviews the development between 1976 and 1980 of so-called accusatory poetry in China. It started with the appearance of poems on wall posters on Tiananmen Square (the Gate of Heavenly Peace) in Beijing. Its anti-Maoist stance was originally supported by the authorities, who saw it as a potentially useful tool in their fight against the followers of the late Defense Minister Lin Biao. Examples of the genre are Ai Tsin's "On the Crest of the Wave," in which he likens demagogic politicians to jackals, and "History Will be the Judge" by Yan Mu, who attacks bureaucracy. Secondary sources; 28 notes. J. Bamber

3202. Chiang Chen-ch'ang. THE NEW LEI FENGS OF THE 1980S. *Issues & Studies [Taiwan] 1984 20(5): 22-42.* Lei Feng (1940-62), who died in an accident, was extolled as a model hero, selflessly subservient to the party. Eclipsed by the politics of the 1971-81 decade, the "Lei Feng spirit" is again being publicized and new heroes have been created to arouse enthusiasm for service and ideology. This campaign of the Deng (Teng) regime has not achieved great success. Based on Chinese writings and media reports; 41 notes. J. A. Krompart

3203. Chiang Hsin-li. THE "THEORETICAL STRUGGLE" ON THE CHINESE MAINLAND: THE NEW PHASE. *Issues and Studies [Taiwan] 1979 15(2): 36-66.* Examines the ideological struggle between factions of the Chinese Communist Party following the death of Mao Zedong (Mao Tse-tung) in 1976.

3204. Ch'iu K'ung-yüan. PROCEEDINGS OF THE ELEVENTH CCP CONGRESS: AN ANALYSIS. *Issues and Studies [Taiwan] 1977 13(10): 1-12.* The 11th Chinese Communist Party National Congress was a showdown between the new power holders and the Cultural Revolution faction. As expected, the new power holders won a victory by reshuffling the Party and the Politburo. Mao was worried before his death about a coup d'etat by rightists and about the future of the Cultural Revolution. He had good reason to worry; this Congress implies the possibility of endless tumult. Such a temporary compromise among the new power holders, based on their common efforts to overthrow the Gang of Four, could hardly have been fruitful. Based on congress proceedings, news reports, and other sources; 33 notes. W. R. Hively

3205. Clarke, Christopher M. CHINA'S REFORM PROGRAM. *Current History 1984 83(494): 254-256, 273.* Elaborates key factors involved in maintaining the success of China's reform program as Party leadership passed to younger hands.

3206. Clubb, O. Edmund. CHINA AFTER MAO. *Current Hist. 1977 73(429): 49-53, 86.* Revision and reinterpretation of Communist philosophy and the political line espoused by Mao Tse-tung have brought about a less revolution-oriented brand of communism.

3207. Das, Naranarayan. CHINA'S NEW CONSTITUTION: TRIUMVIRATE ON TRIAL. *China Report [India] 1984 20(4-5): 47-54.* Under the 1982 constitution of China, the state and the Party are formally differentiated. The remaining member of the triumvirate, the People's Liberation Army, is under the direction of the newly created Central Military Commission, and owes allegience neither to the Party nor to the state. These three institutions will invariably experience contradictory aspirations along with varying and unequal popular support. Primary sources; 18 notes. J. Powell

3208. Deng Xiaoping TENG HSIAO-P'ING'S SPEECH AT THE SECOND PLENARY SESSION OF THE 12TH CENTRAL COMMITTEE OF THE CHINESE COMMUNIST PARTY. *Issues & Studies [Taiwan] 1984 20(4): 99-111.* A translation of Deng Xiaoping's (Teng Hsiao-p'ing) October 1983 speech on ideological threats to the Party and the regime. The Party at all levels must take effective measures against economic criminals and other undesirable elements. Problems of ideological pollution, especially erroneous viewpoints in academe and literature and art circles, must also be addressed. J. A. Krompart

3209. Domes, Jürgen. CHINA IN 1977: REVERSAL OF VERDICTS. *Asian Survey 1978 18(1): 1-16.* On 6 October 1976 the military-bureaucratic-complex in China overthrew the central leadership of the cultural revolutionary left and established control over the state administrative, military, and Party machine. By 1977 this coup d'etat had brought about the return of pre-Cultural Revolution policies and personnel, many of whom had been either purged or criticized during the Cultural Revolution of the 1960's. Examines the significance of the reversal in the public image of Teng Hsiao-p'ing, who now holds the third position in the Chinese Communist Party, in the light of a decade of political developments in China. Also analyzes the 11th Central Committee of the Communist Party in terms of these changes. Based on newspapers and interviews; 5 tables, 40 notes. M. Feingold/S

3210. Esposito, Bruce J. CHINA: THE SIXTH NATIONAL PEOPLE'S CONGRESS: A REVIEW. *Asian Thought & Soc. 1983 8(24): 225-230.* The 1983 Chinese People's Congress featured a review of successes and shortcomings followed by plans and predictions for the future, still extolling Maoism as a guiding principle.

3211. Gold, Thomas B. "JUST IN TIME!": CHINA BATTLES SPIRITUAL POLLUTION ON THE EVE OF 1984. *Asian Survey 1984 24(9): 947-974.* China's 1984 campaign against "spiritual pollution" was engineered by Deng Xiaoping to purge unsupportive members of the Chinese Communist Party and to stem decreasing popular respect for the Party. The campaign, which concentrated on prevailing humanism and a sense of alienation, was short-lived because it disturbed social stability, frightened potential investors away, and threatened China's efforts toward modernization. Originally presented to the California Regional China Seminar, Berkeley, 1984; 64 notes. L. J. Howell

3212. Goodman, David S. G. THE SECOND PLENARY SESSION OF THE 12TH CCP CENTRAL COMMITTEE: RECTIFICATION AND REFORM. *China Q. [Great Britain] 1984 (97): 84-90.* A three-year rectification program was announced at the 12th Congress of the Communist Party of China in September of 1982. Its implementation followed the October 1983 meeting of the Party Central Committee and is to be directed at the Party alone. Ideological unity and strengthened Party discipline are among the goals of the campaign, but it remains to be seen if rectification will serve merely to strengthen Deng Xiaoping. Drawn substantially from the *Beijing Review;* 18 notes. J. R. Pavia, Jr.

3213. Hook, Brian. CHINA AFTER CHAIRMAN MAO: THE NEW LEADERSHIP AND THE 11TH NATIONAL CONGRESS OF THE COMMUNIST PARTY OF CHINA. *Contemporary Rev. [Great Britain] 1978 232(1347): 169-178.* Examines Chinese politics between the death of Chairman Mao, in September 1976, and early 1978 and the outcome of the power struggle.

3214. Hsing Kuo-ch'iang. COMPOSITION OF THE ELEVENTH CCPCC. *Issues and Studies [Taiwan] 1977 13(1C): 13-59.* Analyzes the membership of the Politburo and the Central Committee elected by the 11th Chinese Communist Party Congress. The deaths of Mao Tse-tung and other Politburo members and the purge of the "Gang of Four" left nine vacancies in the Politburo. One more full member was added. The author includes a roster of the 201 full members and the 132 alternate members. It appears that the Party hierarchy intends to govern by the barrel of the gun and to continue suppressing the remnants of the "Gang of Four." W. R. Hively

3215. Hsing Kuo-ch'iang. AN EVALUATION OF THE CHINESE COMMUNIST CADRE PROBLEMS. *Issues & Studies [Taiwan] 1980 16(9): 44-61.* Lack of a workable cadre system due to an environment of political struggle, ideological differences, friction between old and new cadres, favoritism, and bribery is a chronic problem for the Chinese Communists. Top party leaders have initiated a discipline system and established principles for political conduct but the government is not stable enough to effectively achieve a long-range solution to this problem. A paper presented to the 9th Sino-American Conference, Taipei, 1980. Based on Mainland documents and the statements of Party leaders; 47 notes. J. A. Krompart

3216. Hsüan Mo. DISCRIMINATION AGAINST KNOWLEDGE AND INTELLECTUALS. *Issues & Studies [Taiwan] 1983 19(7): 29-39.* At the 1983 Peking observance of the centenary of Karl Marx's death, Hu Yaobang (Hu Yao-pang) devoted the greater part of his speech to current CCP policies toward intellectuals. Although he emphasized that Marxism values both general and scientific knowledge and included intellectuals in the working class, he also reaffirmed that workers and peasants are the basic force in Chinese society. Based on Mainland publications and the works of Marx and Engels; 6 notes. J. A. Krompart

3217. Hu Yao-pang. HU YAO-PANG'S SPEECH DELIVERED AT THE "MEETING ON ISSUES CONCERNING THE IDEOLOGICAL FRONT." *Issues & Studies [Taiwan] 1984 20(1): 105-124.* A translation of Hu Yaobang's (Hu Yao-pang) August 1981 speech in which he discusses Deng Xiaoping's (Teng Hsiao-p'ing) July 1981 talk on ideology. Deng urged comrades to strengthen Party control of ideology, especially in literature and art. In rectifying the current weakness in ideological control emphasis should be on identifying historical causes and future methods and not on placing blame on individuals. J. A. Krompart

3218. Hu Yao-pang. PROBLEMS CONCERNING THE PURGE OF K'ANG SHENG: HU YAO-PANG'S SPEECH AT THE CENTRAL PARTY SCHOOL (COMPLETE SPEECH). *Issues & Studies [Taiwan] 1980 16(6): 74-100.* A translation of a speech by Hu Yaobang (Hu Yao-pang) in China at the Central Party School, 9 November 1978. Hu described the actions and alignments of loyal and subversive Communist Party members from the 1930's to the present and discussed misuses of power perpetrated by Kang Sheng (K'ang Sheng, 1899-1975) late head of central security. An investigation just completed at the time of the speech indicated that Kang was a Trotskyite, a counterrevolutionary, and a coconspirator with the Gang of Four, guilty of many serious crimes, including falsification of evidence against loyal party members and the murder of Li Zongren (Li Tsung-jen, 1890-1975). J. A. Krompart

3219. Huang, I-shu. LITERARY SCENE IN POST-MAO CHINA. *China Report [India] 1984 20(4-5): 55-66.* During the Cultural Revolution Mao Zedong abandoned his policy of "letting a hundred flowers bloom and a hundred schools of thought contend." The post-Mao leadership again granted creative freedom to writers as long as their work served the cause of socialism. The attitude of the Chinese Communist Party toward literary freedom changed frequently. The new liberalization will at least cause controversies concerning the degree of deviation tolerated by the state. Primary sources; 27 notes. J. Powell

3220. Johnston, Alastair I. CHANGING PARTY-ARMY RELATIONS IN CHINA, 1979-1984. *Asian Survey 1984 24(10): 1012-1039.* Between 1979 and 1984 Deng Xiaoping labored to reduce the influence of the People's Liberation Army (PLA) in Chinese Communist Party (CCP) affairs, while strengthening the national security independence of the PLA from the machinations of CCP politics. To overcome elements of resistance to his policies within the PLA, Deng pushed for personnel changes and institutional restructuring within the PLA. 56 notes. L. J. Howell

3221. Kirchrue, Ewalt R. VERSCHLUSSACHE: WAHLKAMPF 1980: EIN INTERNER BERICHT ZUR LAGE DER STUDENTBEWEGUNG IN CHINA [A closed matter: the elections of 1980: an internal report on the state of the student movement in China]. *Internationales Asienforum [West Germany] 1984 15(3-4): 301-324.* Prints a German translation of a secret internal report on the election campaign held at a branch of Beijing University in November 1980. It examines the difficulties of the Communist Party organization in coping with the demands of the politically conscious youth for democratic reforms.

3222. Kuo, Warren. FACTIONAL DISSENSION IN COMMUNIST CHINA. *Issues & Studies [Taiwan] 1980 16(9): 11-23.* Describes the recent history of Chinese Communist Party factionalism, reviewing both Western and Chinese scholarship on the subject. Lucian W. Pye views this factional struggle as one primarily for power rather than over policy or doctrine. Recent strife has centered among the factions of Hua Guofeng (Hua Kuo-feng), Ye Jianying (Yeh Chien-ying), and Deng Xiaoping (Teng Hsiao-p'ing). Based on writings of Mao Zedong; 7 notes. J. A. Krompart

3223. Kuo, Warren. POWER STRUGGLE AND POLICY-LINE STRUGGLE AMONG THE CURRENT CHINESE COMMUNIST LEADERS. *Issues and Studies [Taiwan] 1979 15(5): 9-21.* Discusses the ideological struggle among the leaders of the Chinese Communist Party since the coup d'état of 1976 against the Gang of Four.

3224. Kuo, Warren. REFORMING THE CHINESE COMMUNIST LEADERSHIP SYSTEM. *Issues & Studies [Taiwan] 1981 17(6): 11-23.* Describes the 1980 Party leadership changes and gives a brief history of Chinese Communist Party leadership systems. Although reform of the leadership system was the supposed objective of recent changes, the fall of the Hua Guofeng (Hua Kuo-feng) faction was the result. Deng Xiaoping (Teng Hsiao-p'ing) has called for reforms to counter misuse of authority, overconcentration of power, and other abuses. Because of the pervasiveness of the political power struggle, there can be little hope of their succeeding. A paper presented at the tenth Sino-American Conference on Mainland China, Berkeley, California, 16-18 June 1981. Based on Taiwan and Mainland publications of official speeches and other documents; 19 notes. J. A. Krompart

3225. Latham, Richard J. "Comprehensive Socialist Reform: The Case of China's Third Plenum Reforms." U. of Washington 1984. 588 pp. *DAI 1984 45(5): 1513-A.* DA8419163

3226. Lee Tsung-ying. EASTERN DIARY. *Eastern Horizon [Hong Kong] 1981 20(8): 1-6.* Examines the substitution of Hu Yaobang for Hua Guofeng as the Chairman of the Communist Party of China, detailing Hua's political career and the reasons for his fall from power, and analyzes the resolution that disposed of Hua and discussed Mao Zedong's role in Chinese history and the impact of the Cultural Revolution.

3227. Leng, Shao-chuan. CRIMINAL JUSTICE IN POST-MAO CHINA. *China Q. [Great Britain] 1981 (87): 440-469.* Though the new legal codes that went into effect 1 January 1980 promise a more secure and less arbitrary system of criminal justice and greater defense of individual rights against state power, much remains to be achieved in this area. The government can still detain offenders in labor camps for as long as four years without a trial and the Communist Party continues to exert its influence over judicial actions. Based primarily on Chinese materials; 144 notes.
J. R. Pavia, Jr.

3228. Murthy, Sheela. RESTORING THE ROLE OF INTELLECTUALS. *China Report [India] 1984 20(4-5): 67-84.* The attitude of the Chinese Communist Party to intellectuals was inconsistent. Though intellectuals helped usher in the revolution, they suffered greatly during the anti-Rightist campaign and the Cultural Revolution. From early 1981, the Party attempted to grant them freedom of expression and to enlist their support for fulfilling the task of the four modernizations. Secondary sources; 68 notes. J. Powell

3229. Nethercut, Richard D. DENG AND THE GUN: PARTY-MILITARY RELATIONS IN THE PEOPLE'S REPUBLIC OF CHINA. *Asian Survey 1982 22(8): 691-704.* Deng Xiaoping's (Teng Hsiao-p'ing) appointment, at age 77, to head the Chinese Communist Party's Military Commission underscores the current importance and sensitivity of Party-military relations. Deng appears to be dedicated to consolidating Party and government control over the People's Liberation Army (PLA), curtailing its traditional role in politics, and eventually modernizing and reforming PLA forces. Objections have been raised to his plans, and he has had to make some concessions to the military opposition, but predictions are that he will be able to make progress toward his goals. Based on radio broadcasts, newspapers, and speeches. M. A. Eide

3230. Novozybkov, V. AN IMPORTANT EVENT IN THE PRC'S POLITICAL LIFE (ON RESULTS OF A SESSION OF THE NATIONAL PEOPLE'S CONGRESS). *Far Eastern Affairs [USSR] 1983 (4): 47-59.* The sixth convocation of the National People's Congress, held 6-21 June 1983 in Beijing, had on its agenda the following important issues: economic reform; ideological and foreign policy directives; administrative reform; personnel changes; Communist Party personnel changes and hints of a possible Party purge in the near future; and general tenor of antagonism toward the USSR and support for the United States and other NATO countries.

3231. Pairault, Thierry. LA POLITIQUE ÉCONOMIQUE CHINOISE DU Ier PLENUM DU XIe CONGRÈS (AOÛT 1977) À LA VEILLE DU 3eRET PLENUM (DÉCEMBRE 1978) [Chinese economic policy from the First Plenum of the XI Congress of the Chinese Communist Party (August 1977) to the eve of the Third Plenum (December 1978)]. *Rev. d'Études Comparatives Est-Ouest [France] 1979 10(3): 91-129.*

3232. Powles, Cyril H. CHRISTIANITY IN CHINA TODAY: A PERSONAL VIEW. *Hist. Mag. of the Protestant Episcopal Church 1981 50(2): 197-209.* The Chinese experience of contemporary Christianity poses a number of questions that might stimulate Christians in the West to examine fundamental assumptions about their mission, structure, and traditional modes of thinking about church, ministry, sacraments, and God's activity in history. The collapse of Nationalist China in 1949 was not the end of Chinese Christianity; it was the end of Western Christianity in China. Chinese Christians came to admire the Communist leaders because they gave up security and social standing in order to take the side of the downtrodden peasants and workers. The experiences of the revolution have helped the Chinese Christians change from the middle-class orientation they inherited from the Western missionary movement. Today's church identifies with the lower class, as Jesus did. Based largely on recent articles, pamphlets, studies, and letters; 29 notes.
H. M. Parker, Jr.

3233. Rosen, Stanley. PROSPERITY, PRIVATIZATION, AND CHINA'S YOUTH. *Problems of Communism 1985 34(2): 1-28.* The sweeping reforms introduced in December 1978 have had a

profound impact on the work of China's Communist Youth League (CYL). The ensuing elevation of higher education and technical expertise at the expense of ideology has crippled youth work in China and left CYL cadres confused, uncertain, and demoralized. Once a primary channel of party recuitment and political socialization, the CYL is now considered by most youth as irrelevant to both their careers and China's current modernization drive. Based on publications of the Chinese Communist Youth League; 2 tables, 127 notes.
J. M. Lauber

3234. Scalapino, Robert A. THE CONTINUING STRUGGLE OVER DEMAOIFICATION. *Issues & Studies [Taiwan] 1980 16(7): 23-36.* The Deng Xiaoping (Teng Hsiao-p'ing) faction in China, seeking to avoid political and ideological chaos and to gain freedom to eliminate old Maoists and choose new directions, continues to portray Maoism as the foundation of the state but criticizes Mao himself as fallible. For internal political considerations, Mao's errors are regarded as dating from 1956. Since the 1950's were a time of Sino-Soviet amity, this line has implications for China's future foreign policy. Presented to the Ninth Sino-American Conference on Mainland China, Taipei, 10-13 June 1980. Based on Mainland documents and periodical publications; 13 notes.
J. A. Krompart

3235. Škvařil, Jaroslav. VNITŘNÍ POLITIKA SOUČASNÉHO ČÍNSKÉHO VEDENÍ. HLAVNÍ RYSY VNITROPOLITICKÉHO VÝVOJE ČLR V OBDOBÍ 1976-1979 [Internal politics of contemporary Chinese leadership: main characteristics of internal development in China, 1976-78]. *Hist. a Vojenství [Czechoslovakia] 1980 29(2): 101-130.* Chinese domestic policy during the last three years was a further step away from the principles of pure Marxism and socialism. The deep contradictions between objective needs of population and the anti-popular military-bureaucratic regime were clearly visible. The 1977 party convention stressed the worship of Mao and of his ideology, which is based on petit bourgeois nationalism and pursues chauvinist and hegemonic goals under the disguise of "real" Marxism. Based on official records and printed sources; table, 70 notes. G. E. Pergl

3236. Suharchuk, Gregorii D. MODERNIZATION IN CHINA AND FOREIGN POLICY. *Asian Survey 1984 24(11): 1157-1162.* Chinese attempts to modernize its industries and economy during the early 1980's called for the importation of Western technology without undesirable Western ethical and political ideas. This was not found to be possible, and China began to examine the writings of Marx, Engels, and Lenin with the purpose of reviewing the course of Chinese Communism. The results of such a review have had strong implications for the conduct of Chinese foreign policy.
L. J. Howell

3237. Tang, Tsou. THE HISTORIC CHANGE IN DIRECTION AND CONTINUITY WITH THE PAST. *China Q. [Great Britain] 1984 (98): 320-347.* Reviews *Deng Xiaoping Wenxuan (1975-1982)* [Selected works of Deng Xiaoping, 1975-82] (1983). The 47 pieces, 39 of which appear for general distribution for the first time, illustrate Deng's authority and his role in redirecting China, especially in reforming the army and the Communist Party. 127 notes.
J. R. Pavia, Jr.

3238. Teng Ying-ch'ao. "BE STEADFAST IN IMPROVING THE WORK STYLE OF THE PARTY." *Issues & Studies [Taiwan] 1984 20(11): 87-99.* A translation of a February 1981 speech by Deng Yingchao (Teng Ying-ch'ao) of the Chinese Communist Party Central Committee's Commission for Inspection of Discipline, in which she described the commission's prodigious work to rectify wrongfully conducted past court cases and exhorted Party leadership cadres to vigorously oppose bureaucratism and other lapses of discipline. J. A. Krompart

3239. Vetter, Horst F. DIE TRANSFORMATION DER REVOLUTION: POLITISCHE VERÄNDERUNGEN IM CHINA NACH MAO ZEDONG [The transformation of the revolution: political changes in China after Mao Zedong]. *Internationales Asienforum [West Germany] 1979 10(1-2): 85-101.* Compares the Maoist era with the educational policy of the new leadership as well as the present social spirit and shows how fundamentally present-day political practice is departing from revolutionary Maoism.

3240. Wang, Shu-shin. HU YAOBANG: NEW CHAIRMAN OF THE CHINESE COMMUNIST PARTY. *Asian Survey 1982 22(9): 801-822.* Hu Yaobang (Hu Yao-pang), a participant in the Chinese Communist movement for 54 years and a protegé of Deng Xiaoping (Teng Hsiao-p'ing), became the new chairman of the Chinese Communist Party in June 1981. As Deng's heir apparent, Hu now plays a leading role in China's decisionmaking process. Hu will mobilize all positive factors to push Deng's political line and modernization program forward; however, because of his adherence to the "absolute" leadership of the Party and because of China's backward environment, he may not be able to achieve Deng's goals fully. Based on newspapers and documents; 76 notes.
M. A. Eide

3241. Wu An-chia. THE CCP REAPPRAISAL OF CH'IN SHIH HUANG. *Issues and Studies [Taiwan] 1978 14(12): 27-47.* The Gang of Four launched a campaign to criticize Lin Piao and Chou En-lai for their alleged Confucianism while exalting Mao Tse-tung for having surpassed the Legalism of anti-Confucianist Ch'in Emperor Shih Huang Ti (259-210 B.C.), viewed by the Gang as antireactionary. After the Four were removed in October 1976 the Chinese Communist Party (CCP) has emphasized the negative aspects of Ch'in's tyrannical rule.

3242. Wu An-chia. THE MOVEMENT TO "ELIMINATE IDEOLOGICAL POLLUTION." *Issues & Studies [Taiwan] 1984 20(3): 11-24.* In October 1983 the Communist Party of China initiated an unprecedented movement to eliminate "ideological pollution." Aimed at undesirable views, such as "capitalist ideologies" which have entered China with Western technology, this nationwide effort attacks antisocialist tendencies and vigorously asserts Marxist thought. The results, however, are often at odds with other Beijing policies, including the Four Modernizations, and threaten to jeopardize China's foreign relations. Based on published sources from China; 26 notes. J. A. Krompart

3243. Yao Meng-hsuan. THE PARTY POLICY LINE DEBATE AND THE POLITICAL OUTLOOK IN COMMUNIST CHINA. *Issues and Studies [Taiwan] 1979 15(9): 13-41.* The Second Plenary Session of the Fifth National People's Congress (NPC) and the Second Session of the Fifth Political Consultative Conference of the Chinese People (CPPCC) met in Beijing in the summer of 1979, and the reports and speeches emanating from those meetings indicate that both the NPC and the CPPCC are merely rubber stamps for the Communist Party.

3244. —. THE CCP CENTRAL COMMITTEE'S INSTRUCTIONS CONCERNING THE IMPROVEMENT OF POLITICAL AND JUDICIAL WORK (JANUARY 13, 1982). *Issues & Studies [Taiwan] 1984 20(10): 93-103.* A translation of "Instructions Concerning the Improvement of Political and Judicial Work," issued by the Central Committee of the Chinese Communist Party on 13 January 1982. This document calls upon all Party committees to strengthen the Party leadership role in society, increase control over public security, reform political and judicial systems, etc., in order to combat juvenile crime and other rural and urban civil disorders.
J. A. Krompart

3245. —. DECISION OF THE CCP CENTRAL COMMITTEE AND THE STATE COUNCIL ON CRACKING DOWN ON SERIOUS CRIME IN THE ECONOMIC SPHERE (APRIL 13, 1982). *Issues & Studies [Taiwan] 1984 20(2): 102-115.* Translates the "Decision on Cracking Down on Serious Crime in the Economic Sphere" jointly issued by the Chinese Communist Party (CCP) Central Committee and the State Council, 13 April 1982. This document acknowledges that the incidence of economic crimes (smuggling, bribery, theft of state property, etc.) has risen dramatically, and exhorts all elements of the population to unite against these abuses. J. A. Krompart

3246. —. DECISION ON FURTHER PROMOTION OF EDUCATION AMONG STAFF MEMBERS AND WORKERS. *Issues & Studies [Taiwan] 1984 20(5): 81-91.* The CCP Decision on Further Promotion of Education Among Staff Members and Workers, issued 20 February 1981, describes the need for education, especially technical education, of staff and workers in support of the national economy and outlines how this program should be implemented. J. A. Krompart

3247. —. A DOCUMENT OF THE CCP CENTRAL COMMITTEE *CHUNG-FA* (1982) NO. 12. *Issues & Studies [Taiwan] 1983 19(9): 95-105.* Until social classes are eliminated, it is vital to foster unity with elements outside the Party and to avoid the leftist error of believing the Party alone can handle everything.

J. A. Krompart

3248. —. A DOCUMENT OF THE CCP CENTRAL COMMITTEE *CHUNG-FA* (1982) NO. 19. *Issues & Studies [Taiwan] 1983 19(8): 72-90.* A translation of Chongfa (Chungfa) No. 19 (1982), a statement of the current Chinese Communist Party policy on religion. All comrades are exhorted to bring domestic religious factions into a united front for the building of a modern socialist state and to respect religion until it naturally expires. J. A. Krompart

3249. —. *A Great Trial in Chinese History: The Trial of the Lin Biao and Jiang Qing Counter-revolutionary Cliques, Nov. 1980-Jan. 1981.* New York: New World, 1981. 521 pp.

3250. —. HUO SHIH-LIEN—FIRST SECRETARY OF THE CCP SHANSI PROVINCIAL COMMITTEE. *Issues & Studies [Taiwan] 1981 17(9): 81-85.* Little is known of the early years of Huo Shilien (Huo Shih-lien), Communist Party First Secretary for Shanxi (Shansi) Province since the fall of 1980. He has held Party posts since at least 1937, many of them in the northwest, and was purged during the Cultural Revolution. His present post, which is at the center of the Dazhai (Tachai) model commune controversy, is a sensitive one in national politics. J. A. Krompart

3251. —. LA RIFORMA DELLA STRUTTURA ECONOMICA [Reform of the economic structure]. *Mondo Cinese [Italy] 1984 12(4): 49-73.* Prints a translation of the program approved by the Central Committee of the Communist Party to reform the Chinese economy in October 1984. The new program focuses on rural development and modernization of the cities. Economic productivity is to be linked to technology, industrial growth, and trade. The document notes the errors of the past and the importance of the Communist Party in directing economic reform. Italian translation of the decision of the Central Committee of the Communist Party of China, 20 October 1984; 3 notes.

3252. —. SOME NEW FACES ON THE 12TH CCP CENTRAL COMMITTEE. *Issues & Studies [Taiwan] 1983 19(2): 72-77, (3): 79-83.* Part 1. Brief biographies of five new Central Committee members who are scientific and technical specialists, several of whom were victims of the Cultural Revolution: mining engineer Yu Hongen (Yü Hung-en); nuclear engineers Jiang Xinxiong (Chiang Hsin-hsiung) and Peng Shilu (P'eng Shih-lu); petroleum engineer Zhao Zongnai (Chao Tsung-nai); and radio specialist Li Huifen. Part 2. Four new members of the CCP Central Committee are representative of current party policy to promote competent younger cadres. Automobile plant technician Wang Zhaoguo (Wang Chao-kuo, b. 1941); Hu Jintao (Hu Chin-t'ao, b. 1943), a graduate of Tsinghua University; Yang Di (Yang Ti, b. 1923), with a background in public security, and educator Xing Zhikang (Hsing Chih-k'ang, b. 1931) all rose to prominence since the late 1970's. Based on Mainland media reports; 11 notes. J. A. Krompart

3253. —. TENG LI-CH'ÜN—DIRECTOR OF THE POLICY RESEARCH OFFICE OF THE CCPCC SECRETARIAT. *Issues & Studies [Taiwan] 1981 17(10): 62-64.* Deng Lichun (Teng Li-ch'ün), of Hunan province, is a leading Communist writer and theoretician in China and has the confidence of those currently in power. Now in his sixties, Deng was active in the Party at least as early as 1935. He was purged during the Cultural Revolution. Since 1980 he has directed the Party Central Committee Research Office.

J. A. Krompart

4. COMMUNISM IN ASIA AND THE PACIFIC AREA

General

3254. Ali, Mehrunnisa. THE CHANGING STANCE OF ASEAN TOWARDS ITS COMMUNIST NEIGHBOURS. *Pakistan Horizons [Pakistan] 1976 29(2): 33-58.* Describes the international factors of the 1970's which have led to a thaw in the relations between the Association of Southeast Asian Nations (ASEAN) and their Communist neighbors.

3255. Pokataeva, T. S. KOMMUNISTICHESKIE PARTII STRAN IUGO-VOSTOCHNOI AZII V BOR'BE ZA NATSIONAL'NUIU NEZAVISIMOST' I DEMOKRATIIU: 1948-1962 GG [Communist Parties of the countries of Southeast Asia in the struggle for national independence and democracy, 1948-62]. *Voprosy Istorii KPSS [USSR] 1962 (5): 61-78.* Surveys the history of the Communist Parties of India, Indonesia and Ceylon, finding that their influence has grown steadily since 1948.

3256. Roucek, Joseph S. THE ROLE OF COMMUNIST GUERRILLAS IN FAR EAST AND SOUTH-EAST ASIA. *Asia Q. [Belgium] 1972 (2): 157-166.* Analyzes the methods used by Communists guerrillas in the Philippines, Malaya, Indonesia, North Vietnam, Cuba, Cyprus, Laos, and Ceylon which resulted from decolonization following World War II. Guerrilla warfare goes through three phases: 1) organization of the countryside; 2) a rising tempo of guerrilla action against local and regional government; and 3) open warfare until the central government is toppled. Based on a study of the Philippine Defense Committee, newspapers, and secondary sources; 21 notes. G. M. White

3257. Wheeler, Geoffrey. NATIONALISM VERSUS COMMUNISM IN ASIA. *Asian Affairs [Great Britain] 1977 64(1): 38-47.* Reviews the nature, progress, and relative effects of the influences of nationalism and Soviet Communism on South, Southwest, and Central Asia during and after the breakup between 1918 and 1947 of the Ottoman, Russian, and British empires. The European idea of nationalism first became apparent in the second half of the 19th century in British India. It envisaged a single Indian nation which would proceed to independence by way of dominion status. Of the non-Arab Middle East countries only Turkey and Israel became true successor states of the Ottoman Empire. Although Georgia, Armenia, and Azerbaidzhan became independent of csarist rule, they were overrun by the Red Army in 1922 and incorporated into the Soviet Union. Of the Central Asian communities only the Kazakhs displayed any semblance of national cohesion. Transcaucasia, Turkestan, and the Steppe region passed under Soviet control as synthetic national republics. Secondary sources; 4 notes.

S. H. Frank

3258. Wimbush, S. Enders. THE POLITICS OF IDENTITY CHANGE IN SOVIET CENTRAL ASIA. *Central Asian Survey [Great Britain] 1985 3(3): 69-78.* Both Lenin and Stalin saw the problem of reconsolidation of Russian influence in Central Asia and the strengthening of the Communist Party in the region as one of overcoming the "Muslim problem." After 1923, Stalin indicated that Islam would not be allowed to remain as an alternative identity system within the new Soviet empire, and Communism and Islam have been engaged in ideological warfare ever since. The Islamic Revolution in Iran and the Soviet invasion of Afghanistan have prompted heightened attention to Islam in Soviet Central Asia, and the Soviets have begun a new anti-Islamic campaign which is focusing on Sufism in Central Asia and the Caucasus. Presented at a conference on "Central Asian Identity and the Study of Central Asia" held at the University of Wisconsin at Madison on 18-19 November 1983. 12 notes. L. J. Klass

South Asia

3259. Adie, W. A. C. MAKE WAR OR DO BUSINESS? *China Report [India] 1971 7(2): 7-10.* Discusses military and ideological obstacles in India's foreign relations and negotiations with China, 1957-71, emphasizing the role of Maoism.

3260. Balogh, András. AZ INDIAI KOMMUNISTÁK HARCA A FÜGGETLENSÉGÉRT ÉS A TÁRSADALMI HALADÁSÉRT AZ ORSZÁG GYARMATI IDŐSZAKÁBAN [The struggle of Indian Communists for independence and social progress in the colonial period]. *Párttörténeti Közlemények [Hungary] 1979 25(1): 174-195.* Describes Indian Communists' contribution to Indian independence in August 1947 and their activities in the new conditions to eliminate the colonial heritage and form a democratic society.

I. Hajdú

3261. Bennigsen, Alexandre. THE SOVIET UNION AND MUSLIM GUERILLA WARS, 1920-1981: LESSONS FOR AFGHANISTAN. *Conflict 1983 4(2-4): 301-324.* Claims that the lessons learned from Soviet-Moslem wars should have been applied to Afghanistan. The USSR should divide the enemy, win over crucial indigenous groups, create a strong local Communist Party apparatus, field a Moslem national army, and establish Afghan national Communism.

3262. Bhattacharyya, Jnanabrata. AN EXAMINATION OF LEADERSHIP ENTRY IN BENGAL PEASANT REVOLTS, 1937-1947. *J. of Asian Studies 1978 37(4): 611-635.* Examines leadership entry in peasant rebel movements in Bengal from 1937 to 1947. These rebellions were organized by the Communist Party of India (CPI) and received their support from the masses of Hindu peasants, with smaller numbers of Christians and animists. These people were not only socially oppressed by the landowning *zamindars,* but were also religiously marginal in largely Moslem Bengal. The government was not repressive toward the rebels; the Moslem-dominated Bengali ministry was middle-class and reformist, and worked with the peasant organizations to achieve land reform. British authorities arrested Communist leaders for antiwar activities in 1940-41, but released them when they switched to support of the war effort after Germany's attack on the Soviet Union in June 1941. Communist guerrillas then fought against the Japanese in areas which the latter had occupied. After the war, there were more rebellions. None ever threatened the provincial order because of the marginality of the populations involved. 127 notes.

J. C. Billigmeier

3263. Broekmeijer, M. W. J. M. THE FUTURE OF COMMUNISM IN SOUTH ASIA. *Asia Q. [Belgium] 1974 1: 43-63.* Looks at the foreign policy of the USSR and China and investigates the growth of Communist movements within India, Pakistan, and Bangladesh. Discusses how politics and strategy play important roles. India and Bangladesh are vulnerable to a Chinese attack which would cut off the USSR from South Asia. The author concludes that while it is too late to neutralize the Indian Ocean, it must remain a shared lake where the West and the USSR can operate on an equal basis to protect their interests. 20 notes.

G. M. White

3264. Bulatov, Iu. A. KOMMUNISTICHESKAIA PARTIIA I MOLODEZHNOE DVIZHENIE V INDII [The Communist Party and the youth movements in India]. *Narody Azii i Afriki [USSR] 1978 (3): 105-110.* The 1960's witnessed the growing attempts of Indian young people and students to defend their rights. This change from the indifference of the 1950's to the activism of the 1960's presented the Indian Communist Party with the task of giving the young a correct political orientation and raising their ideological consciousness. The methods chosen have included seminars, symposia and conferences, and the creation of Marxist youth organizations (e.g., the Pan-India Federation of Youth and the Pan-India Federation of Students) and drawing the young into the Party. Based on Indian newspapers, Communist Party reports, and secondary sources. J. M. Chambers

3265. Chintamani, C. INDIAN COMMUNISTS ON BANGLADESH: A REVIEW. *China Report [India] 1972 8(3): 19-24.* Examines the influence of three branches of the Communist Party of India (CPI) in Bangladesh: the CPI itself, the CPI (Marxist), and the CPI (Marxist-Leninist). Although Bangladesh has sovereignty, 1972, it is still economically and socially dependent and requires a strong Communist Party dedicated to Marxism-Leninism.

3266. Damodaran, K. MEMOIR OF AN INDIAN COMMUNIST. *New Left Rev. [Great Britain] 1975 93: 35-59.* Presents an interview with Indian Communist K. Damodaran, emphasizing the growth and development of the Communist Party in India, 1929-75.

3267. Das, Amritananda. THE BENGAL NAXALITE PREDICAMENT: THEORY VS. PRACTICE OF MAOISM. *China Report [India] 1970 6(6): 30-35.* Discusses political and ideological factors in the Maoist Naxalite movement in west Bengal 1962-70, including the role of the Communist Party.

3268. Dhanagare, D. N. THE POLITICS OF SURVIVAL: PEASANT ORGANIZATIONS AND THE LEFT-WING IN INDIA, 1925-46. *Sociol. Bull. [India] 1975 24(1): 29-54.* Examines workers' and peasants' parties in the 1920's and a variety of *kisan sabahas* (peasant organizations) in the 1930's and 1940's in India. Analyzes their formation, development, leadership, and ideology. M. N. Roy founded the Communist Party in India following the Second Congress of the Communist International in Moscow in the summer of 1920. When the Communist Party was banned in India, however, it organized the Workers' and Peasants' Party in Bengal, Bombay, United Provinces, and Punjab. Urban industrial workers from the trade unions who made up these parties had little to do with peasants until the 1930's. During the late 1930's and World War II the *kisan sabahas* set up by the Communist Party of India followed a united front strategy and cooperated with the Congress Party and other antiestablishment forces. Even the left wing of the Congress Party and other political organizations found it difficult to cooperate effectively with the organizations created by the Communist Party. Secondary sources; 16 notes, biblio. S. H. Frank

3269. Ganguly, S. M. M. N. ROY: A BIBLIOGRAPHICAL STUDY. *Indian Arch. [India] 1975 24(2): 21-46.* Outlines the sources for research on M. N. Roy (1887-1954), born Narendranath Bhattacharya, the Indian proponent and theorist of communism in developing nations. Lists bibliographies of Roy's publications and notes unpublished correspondence, speeches, and manuscripts available in the M. N. Roy Archives of the Nehru Memorial Museum Library in Delhi. Various journals and newspapers associated with Roy are described. Significant conference proceedings, reports, messages, government publications, archival material, and biographies are identified. Chronology of Roy's career and bibliography of published material appended. 9 notes.

S. C. Strom

3270. Gordon, Leonard A. RADICAL BENGALIS: ALLIANCES AND ANTAGONISMS. *South Asian R. [Great Britain] 1972 5(4): 341-344.* Reviews *Radical Politics in West Bengal* by Marcus F. Franda (MIT Press, 1971). Considers this the best available study of radical politics in West Bengal, especially in its skillful analysis of post-independence developments among Communist party factions. Finds the pre-1947 Bengali history a mixture of misconceptions, errors of fact, and internal contradictions. Challenges Franda's thesis that the *bhadralok* (leaders of the Bengali renaissance) turned to communism in the 1930's from frustration at the rise of new Moslem leaders who gained political eminence. Challenges that Subhas Chandra Bose was ever the "undisputed leader of the *bhadralok.*" Praises Franda's descriptions of the "brokers" who linked the radical parties to the rural masses of Bengal.

S. H. Frank

3271. Gupta, Harmala Kaur. A NOTE ON THE UNITED FRONT. *China Report [India] 1980 16(1): 7-14.* Unlike the Communist Party of China under the leadership of Mao Zedong, the Communist Party of India has failed to apply united front strategy successfully. The Communist Party of India has persisted in trying to apply the strategy conceived as appropriate for the more developed capitalist countries of Europe advanced by the Third Congress of the Comintern, a strategy that China tried during the 1920's and, under Mao's leadership, abandoned. The united front in India has subsequently become a tactic for playing off one faction of the bourgeoisie against another. Based on *The Communist International 1919-1943: Documents;* 23 notes. E. L. Keyser

3272. Haynes, John E. "KEEPING COOL ABOUT KABUL": THE *WASHINGTON POST* AND THE *NEW YORK TIMES* COVER THE COMMUNIST SEIZURE OF AFGHANISTAN. *World Affairs 1983 145(4): 369-383.* The violent 1978 military takeover of Muhammed Daoud's dictatorship by Nur Muhammed Taraki and his Communist People's Democratic Party and the 1979 Russian invasion and installation of Babrak Karmal as the new PDP leader were alternately reported by both the *Washington Post* and the *New York Times* as a Russian-backed coup and as a benign nationalistic agrarian reform movement; reports on Islamic guerrilla resistance also varied.

3273. Heeger, Gerald. THE SOURCES OF COMMUNIST POLITICAL POWER IN KERALA. *Studies on the Soviet Union [West Germany] 1971 11 (4): 573-590.* The election of 1957 saw the establishment of a Communist government in Kerala, India. The party has long been strong in this populous, well-educated, but poverty-stricken state where ideologies pit the propertied class against those without property. The Congress Party entered the campaign in disarray and had recently undertaken an unpopular program to redraw state lines at Kerala's expense. The Communist regime was voted out two years later, having proved itself equally incapable, but the party retains a strong economic base. Secondary sources; table, 41 notes. V. L. Human

3274. Hunter, Thelma. INDIAN COMMUNISM AND THE KERALA EXPERIENCE OF COALITION GOVERNMENT, 1967-69. *J. of Commonwealth Pol. Studies [Great Britain] 1972 10(1): 45-70.* Analyzes the reasons for the fall of the united front coalition government in Kerala, 1969, with particular reference to Indian Communism.

3275. Iurlova, E. S. BOR'BA KOMMUNISTICHESKOI PARTII INDII ZA PRAVA I INTERESY TRUDIASHCHIKHSIA ZHENSHCHIN [The struggle of the Communist Party of India for the rights and interests of working women]. *Narody Azii i Afriki [USSR] 1981 (2): 110-117.* Describes the Communist Party of India (CPI) from its beginnings in 1925, through the 1930's and 1940's when it organized mass demonstrations of women (many of whom had studied Marxist-Leninism in jail), to the present day. The Party's organization at all levels is detailed. The December 1953-January 1954 3d Party Congress demanded equal pay for women and equal rights in property, inheritance, marriage, and divorce. In June 1954 the National Federation of Indian Women was formed. Communist women, braving social disapproval, are struggling for their own rights and are strengthening the struggle for democracy and progress. Based on the CPI congress reports and the Indian press; 37 notes. A. J. Evans

3276. Jeffrey, Robin. INDIA'S WORKING-CLASS REVOLT: PUNNAPRA-VAYALAR AND THE COMMUNIST "CONSPIRACY" OF 1946. *Indian Econ. and Soc. Hist. Rev. [India] 1981 18(2): 97-122.* In October 1946 an organized working-class group in Travancore, India led an armed revolt against the government. This was the only example in Indian history of an armed attempt at proletarian revolution, despite the fact that the Indian proletariat had always been oppressed and that Travancore was remote from

any decisive location in the then current struggle. The Communists were active in the situation and saw it as a glorious chapter in the freedom struggle. The anti-Communists charged that the people in the struggle were sacrificed for the reputation of the Communist Party. Traces the development of the insurrection, which shows that the Indian Communists correctly identified the causes of mass discontent but were unable to channel that discontent into revolution. Based on government records and other contemporary accounts and secondary works including Communist publications; 98 notes.
J. V. Groves

3277. Jeyasingham, Shakuntala Jean. JANATHA VIMUKTHI PERAMUNA. *South Asian Studies [India] 1974 9(1/2): 1-16.* The Janatha Vimukthi Peramuna, led by Rohana Wijeweera, was a splinter from the pro-Peking Communist Party of Sri Lanka. The JVP was organized in 1966; it staged an unsuccessful coup d'etat in 1971. A party of "petit bourgeois intelligensia," it received little support from either the peasants or organized labor.
J. C. English

3278. Johari, J. C. THE POLITICAL IDEAS OF A BENGAL NAXALITE REVOLUTIONARY: CHARU MAJUMDAR. *Pacific Community [Australia] 1971 (9): 43-51.* Enumerates the Maoist principles (peasant revolt, annihilation of police, military, capitalists and profiteers, etc.) that have been present in the program of Naxalite Communists led by Chairman Charu Majumdar, 1967-71.

3279. Khlebnikov, L. V. and Aksenov, Iu. D. SUGISVARA ABEIAVARDENA VIKREMASINGKHE [Sugisvara Abeiavardena Vikremaskingkhe]. *Voprosy Istorii KPSS [USSR] 1976 (4): 115-119.* Reviews the life of S. A. Vikremasingkhe, Chairman of the Sri Lanka Communist Party, on the 75th anniversary of his birth, stressing his loyalty to Moscow.

3280. Khlebnikov, L. V. V BOR'BE ZA NATSIONAL'NOE OSVOBOZHDENIE I SOTSIAL'NYI PROGRESS (K 40-LETIIU KOMPARTII SHRI LANKI) [In the struggle for national liberation and social progress: on the 40th anniversary of the Communist Party of Sri Lanka]. *Voprosy Istorii KPSS [USSR] 1983 (8): 133-137.* Since its formation in 1943, the Communist Party of Sri Lanka has played an important role in the country's political life. Communists participated in the struggle for independence, and supported both the establishment of diplomatic relations with the USSR and the signing of the agreement on economic, technical, and cultural cooperation between the two countries. The Party has admitted the tactical errors committed during the 1970's and, following its new policies, has developed into an important political force capable of influencing current events. Secondary sources; 3 notes.
G. Dombrovski

3281. Klatt, Werner. CASTE, CLASS AND COMMUNISM IN KERALA. *Asian Affairs [Great Britain] 1972 59 (3): 275-287.* Surveys the history and culture of Kerala. The first democratically elected Communist government in the world was elected in Kerala in 1957, and the failure of the Congress Party to enact reforms led to a second Communist victory 10 years later. The lingering problem of land reform restricts further development of this potentially productive area. Based on an address at the Royal Central Asian Society, 28 June 1972.
S. H. Frank

3282. Krishnan, N. K. THE INITIATIVE IS IN THE HANDS OF LEFT AND DEMOCRATIC FORCES. *World Marxist R. [Canada] 1973 16(4): 60-68.* Outline of Communist Party of India's successes since 1969.

3283. Krishnan, N. K. A SHARP TURN. *World Marxist Rev. 1975 18(10): 33-43.* Given the sickness of world capitalism and the strength of Soviet-led world socialism, the Communist Party of India is making progress in the 1970's.

3284. Lerski, George J. TROTSKYISM IN SRI LANKA. *Studies in Comparative Communism 1977 10(1-2): 109-132.* The reformist socialist party in Sri Lanka, the Lanka Sama Samaja (LSSP), founded in 1935, was controlled by Trotskyists. In 1940, the Trotskyists expelled the Stalinists from the Party on the issue of adherence to the Comintern. During World War II, leaders of the Party were interned. After the war, the Trotskyists became the main parliamentary opposition to the government of independent Ceylon. Eventually, some leaders of the Trotskyists joined the government of Sirimavo Bandaranaike and under Mrs. Bandaranaike, ex-Trotskyists and ex-Stalinists have cooperated. In 1971, leftists alienated by this cooperation attempted an unsuccessful revolt. 62 notes.
D. Balmuth

3285. Lieten, Georges K. THE SCOPE FOR PEOPLE'S DEMOCRACY IN INDIAN STATES—THE CASE OF KERALA. *J. of Contemporary Asia [Sweden] 1978 8(4): 513-530.* India's bourgeoisie used policies of appeasement, compromise, and enticement in its struggles with the proponents of landlordism and imperialism. The election of a Communist government in Kerala in 1957 forced the Indian central government to abandon the policy of camouflage. The Kerala Communist government conducted meaningful agricultural, educational, industrial, and labor reforms between 1957 and 31 July 1959, when the central government imposed President's rule. The period of Communist control revealed a number of positive and negative things about the party, but above all it deepened the class struggle. Based mainly on periodical sources; 66 notes.
R. H. Detrick

3286. Majeed, Akhtar. POLITICAL VIOLENCE OF, AMONG AND AGAINST THE COMMUNISTS IN INDIA. *Indian J. of Pol. [India] 1977 11(2): 147-158.* Describes the struggles between factions of the Communist Party of India, 1946-75, following the Party's decisions in 1945 on revolutionary aims and tactics.

3287. Mitter, Swasti. SONARPUR: A PEASANTS' VIEW OF THE CLASS WAR. *South Asian Rev. [Great Britain] 1975 8(4): 323-342.* Analyzes the complex interaction of conflicting ideologies and interests among the landlords, various strata of peasantry, and political leaders. Between 1967 and 1970, a small rural area of 109 villages called Sonarpur in the 24 *parganas* in West Bengal formed a part of a statewide "struggle for land" movement launched under the leadership of the Communist Party of India (Marxist). This revolt received almost equal publicity to that given to the Naxalbari Rebellion of 1967. Most of the land of the "branded" *jotdars* (landlords) was forcibly seized by the year 1969 and redistributed among the poor peasants. Red flags were unfurled everywhere to symbolize the liberation of peasants from the *sammatra badi* (feudal exploitation). Based on field interviews and secondary sources; 10 notes.
S. H. Frank

3288. Namburiripad, E. M. S. KOMMUNISTICHESKAIA PARTIIA I AGRARNYI VOPROS V INDII [The Communist Party and the agrarian issue in India]. *Voprosy Istorii KPSS [USSR] 1961 (5): 91-103.* Criticizes the agricultural policy of the Indian first and second Five-Year Plans, 1951-61.

3289. Nayyar, Deepak. SOUTH ASIA'S ECONOMIC RELATIONS WITH THE SOCIALIST COUNTRIES. *South Asian R. [Great Britain] 1974 7(3): 237-241.* Discusses the net gains to India and Pakistan arising from their trade with the Soviet Union and Eastern Europe as revealed in two books: Asha L. Datar's *India's Economic Relations with the USSR and Eastern Europe, 1953-69* (Cambridge U. Press, 1972), and Michael Kidron's *Pakistan's Trade with the Eastern Bloc Countries* (London: Praeger, 1972). Both studies are pessimistic about the future prospects of growth in trade between South Asia and the socialist countries of Eastern Europe even though this exchange almost quadrupled during the 1960's. Aid from the Communist bloc accounted in quantitative terms to only 8% of the total foreign aid received by India, 1951-68.
S. H. Frank

3290. Noorani, A. G. THE DANGE LETTERS. *Survey [Great Britain] 1979 24(2): 160-174.* The publication of the prison letters by S. A. Dange, for 50 years one of the leading figures of the Communist Party of India, has aroused considerable controversy centering on their impact on the party, their contents, authenticity, and implications. 38 notes.
V. Samaraweera

3291. Nossiter, Thomas J. *Communism in Kerala: A Study in Political Adaptation.* Berkeley: U. of California Pr. for the Royal Inst. of Int. Affairs, 1983. 426 pp.

3292. Pavier, Barry. *The Telengana Movement, 1944-51.* New Delhi: Vikas, 1981. 208 pp.

3293. Pillai, K. Raman. THE CPI ON INDIA'S FOREIGN RELATIONS. *India Q.: J. of Int. Affairs [India] 1969 25(3): 229-253.* Discusses the Communist Party of India's positions on foreign policy problems, 1953-60's, emphasizing nonalignment, foreign aid from the United States and Great Britain, and relations with Pakistan and China.

3294. Polonskaia, L. R. and Shastitko, P. M. ADZHOI GKHOSH [Ajoy Ghosh]. *Voprosy Istorii [USSR] 1969 (6): 149-157.* Biography of Ajoy Kumar Ghosh (1909-62), Indian freedom fighter and leader of the anticolonial and antireligious movements. He founded an underground student organization in Allahabad in 1927, joined the Communist Party in 1931, which he served as secretary general of the Central Committee from 1951 until his death. Ghosh adhered to Leninist principles on national liberation, considered peaceful coexistence with democratic countries vital for India, and supported the pro-USSR orientation of the Indian Communist Party. 26 notes. N. Frenkley

3295. Riley, Parkes. POVERTY, LITERACY AND THE COMMUNIST VOTE IN INDIA. *Asian Survey 1975 15(6): 543-558.* A statistical analysis of the 1950's-70's shows the connections between increased literacy and Communist government in Kerala.

3296. Roy, A. K. NATIONALIST AND COMMUNIST FORCES AT CROSS-ROADS IN BANGLA DESH. *United Asia [India] 1971 23(3): 164-171.* In 1970, Sheikh Mujibur Rahman, Awami League leader, was able to rally conflicting shades of opinion behind the single issue of Bengali nationalism, so that leftist leaders such as Maulana Bashani came out in support of the Awami League. Muhammad Toha broke with the National Awami Party and organized the hardcore Maoist extremists as the East Pakistan Communist Party (Marxist-Leninist), which took advantage of the Awami League's ineffective efforts to conduct the war of liberation.

3297. Samaraweera, Vijaya. SRI LANKAN MARXISTS IN ELECTORAL POLITICS, 1947-1977. *J. of Commonwealth and Comparative Pol. [Great Britain] 1980 18(3): 308-324.* Examines support for the Communist Party and Lanka Sama Samaja Party in electoral politics in Sri Lanka between 1947 and 1977, and analyzes their results in the eight national and regional general elections in this period. The year 1947 was the apex of their achievement and 1977 the nadir, performance in intervening elections varying with the number of candidates and alliances with the Sri Lanka Freedom Party (SLFP), which generally benefited the SLFP more. Analysis of election results suggests that traditional explanations of their support, especially their supposed basis in urban rather than rural areas, should be modified. Based on electoral data and secondary works; 3 tables, 43 notes. D. J. Nicholls

3298. Sardesai, Srinivas. UNHOLY ALLIANCE OF INDIA'S RIGHT AND "LEFT". *World Marxist Rev. [Canada] 1976 19(4): 66-74.* Discusses how right- and left-wing political parties have attacked the Communist Party in India, 1971-76.

3299. Sen Gupta, Bhabani. COMMUNISM AND INDIA: A NEW CONTEXT. *Problems of Communism 1981 30(4): 33-45.* Since the defeat of Indira Gandhi's ruling Congress Party in 1977, there have been important shifts in relations between India's two major Communist parties, between these and the Indian political system, between the respective Communist groups and the Communist Party of the Soviet Union and the Chinese Communist Party, and between India and the USSR and China. Most striking has been the new political cooperation between the two major Indian Communist Parties in their opposition to Indira Gandhi since her return to power in January 1980. Based on Indian periodical press literature and newspaper accounts; 69 notes. J. M. Lauber

3300. Sharma, T. R. THE INDIAN COMMUNIST PARTY SPLIT OF 1964: THE ROLE OF FACTIONALISM LEADERSHIP RIVALRY. *Studies in Comparative Communism 1978 11(4): 388-409.* Regional differences based on population density, literacy, and size of average land holdings affected the Indian Communist Party split; high density states were leftist and were against alliances between the Communists and the Congress Party. Personal issues were important as leftists opposed S. A. Dange as party chairman and opposed rightist control of the party. The leftists set up parallel party organizations and became independent in 1964. The Soviets supported the Dange faction and the leftists gravitated toward China. 54 notes. D. Balmuth

3301. Sharma, Yogindra. THE SOURCES OF STRENGTH OF A REVOLUTIONARY PARTY. *World Marxist Rev. [Canada] 1976 19(11): 44-54.* Discusses the Communist Party of India, 1950's-76, as an instrument for the realization of democracy and socialism in India; examines difficulties met in attempting to mold the Party into a monolithic whole in a country as heterogeneous as India.

3302. Swarup, Rama. THE MAOISTS IN INDIA. *Issues & Studies [Taiwan] 1970 7(3): 15-20.* Discusses the activities of India's Communist Party (Maoist) groups and their split into pro- and anti-Peking factions, 1967-68.

3303. Tabibi, L. "Die Afghanische Landreform von 1979: Ihre Vorgeschichte und Konsequenzen" [The 1979 Afghan land reform: its previous history and consequences]. Free University of Berlin [West Germany] 1981. 236 pp. *DAI-C 1985 46(3): 615; 46/2955c.*

3304. Talbot, I. A. THE GROWTH OF THE MUSLIM LEAGUE IN THE PUNJAB 1937-1946. *J. of Commonwealth and Comparative Pol. [Great Britain] 1982 20(1): 5-24.* Argues that the progress of the Punjab Moslem League between 1937 and 1944 was rather slow and that its attempts to bypass the unionist rural elite by appealing directly to villagers were unsuccessful. However, after many supporters abandoned the Unionist Party in 1944 and 1945, the league was able to grow. In the important 1946 elections the league acquired much support; landlords used their economic and social influence to persuade tenants to vote for the league, which had promised to help villagers over their wartime economic difficulties. Secondary works. A. Alcock

3305. Talwar, S. N. EVE OF INDIAN INDEPENDENCE: THE CPI AT CROSSROADS. *Indian Pol. Sci. Rev. [India] 1983 17(2): 163-171.* During World War II the Communist Party of India (CPI) allied itself with British imperialism and against the Quit India Movement that was laboring to free India from British rule. Divisions within the Party, uncertainty in its political directions, and lack of support from the Soviet Union all hampered the CPI in exercising leadership in the independence struggle. By 1947 the party was completely out of touch with the Soviets and advocating support of the Mountbatten plan, which the Soviets opposed. 37 notes. L. J. Klass

3306. Taylor, Robert H. THE BURMESE COMMUNIST MOVEMENT AND ITS INDIAN CONNECTION: FORMATION AND FACTIONALISM. *J. of Southeast Asian Studies [Singapore] 1983 14(1): 95-108.* Indian Communist and nationalist movements were a major source of similar movements in Burma, but with some ambivalence about the connection due to ethnic tensions caused by the Bengalese presence in Burma. Communist ideology made its first substantive appearance in Burma in the 1930's, and actual Party formation developed only after the 1300 Revolution (1938-39). Faced with the Japanese invasion, political factions resulted, splintering Burmese Communists into several different groups. These factions remained after the war, and the end result was that after Britain's withdrawal the Communists had little influence on the formation of the new state. 65 notes. P. M. Gustafson

3307. Tharamangalam, Joseph. THE COMMUNIST MOVEMENT AND THE THEORY AND PRACTICE OF PEASANT MOBILIZATION IN SOUTH INDIA. *J. of Contemporary Asia [Sweden] 1981 11(4): 487-498.* Despite the readiness with which poor peasants participate in labor unions and support communism when they are organized, India's three Communist Parties, since World War II and the gaining of India's independence, have failed to exploit this readiness, perhaps because of the Marxist-Leninist notion that the peasants should be led by and subordinate to the proletariat and thus constitute a marginal group combined with the peasants' real tactical weakness and concern for human rights as well as for economic issues. 11 notes. E. L. Keyser

3308. Varkey, Ouseph. THE CPI-CONGRESS ALLIANCE IN INDIA. *Asian Survey 1979 19(9): 881-895.* At the time of the formation of the Communist Party of India (CPI) in 1925, the Indian National Congress was the only powerful national movement in India. The CPI's attitude toward the Congress Party fluctuated between contemptuous hostility and eagerness for cooperation. In the late 1960's a partnership developed between the two parties, which with varying intensity persisted well into the 1970's. In the late 1970's, however, there has been a major shift in CPI tactics, stressing the need for unity of the two Communist parties and for a united front of leftist parties to oppose both the Janata Party and Mrs. Gandhi's Congress Party. 3 tables, 35 notes. M. A. Eide

3309. Veits, G. N. GOSUDARSTVENNYI SEKTOR INDII: SOVERSHENSTVOVANIE MEKHANIZMA UPRAVLENIIA [The state sector in India: perfecting the mechanism of management]. *Narody Azii i Afriki [USSR] 1974 (6): 105-113.* Examines the strengthening of the state sector of industry in India during the third Five-Year Plan, 1966-74, a policy actively supported by the Indian Communist Party and opposed by right-wing politicians.

3310. Volodin, V. MAOISM: FROM "ULTRA-REVOLUTIONARINESS" TO A BLOC WITH REACTION. *Int. Affairs [USSR] 1976 (4): 101-107.* Accuses the Chinese Communist Party of interference in the Communist Party of India and claims that Maoists encouraged a split in the Indian Party in order to control it. The Indian Party has continued to splinter, causing confusion and hostility, for Maoism is essentially a petit bourgeois nationalistic trend fundamentally inconsistent with the interests of the working masses.

3311. Vykhukholev, V. V. VERNYI SYN INDIISKOGO NARODA (K 70-LETIIU SO DNIA ROZHDENIIA CHANDRY RADZHESHVARA RAO) [The faithful son of the Indian nation: on the 70th birthday of Chandra Rajeshwara Rao]. *Voprosy Istorii KPSS [USSR] 1984 (6): 115-118.* Sketches the biography of the General Secretary of India's Communist Party, Chandra Rajeshwara Rao (b. 1914). Leader of the Indian movement for national liberation in the 1930's, he became elected to the Party's Central Committee in 1948. During the 1964 rift within the Party, Rao took an unwavering Marxist stance against revisionist trends. 19 notes. M. Hernas

3312. Weidemann, Diethelm. ZUR BEDEUTUNG DER REGIONALEN FORMIERUNG DER ARBEITERKLASSE IN SÜDASIEN IM KAMPF GEGEN IMPERIALISMUS UND EINHEIMISCHE REAKTION [The significance of the formation of the working class in South Asia in the fight against imperialism and the native reactionary forces]. *Wissenschaftliche Zeitschrift der Humboldt-Universität zu Berlin [East Germany] 1974 23(2): 134-137.* In India, Sri Lanka (Ceylon), and Burma the proletariat now begins to constitute a class, in Pakistan and Bangladesh progress has been made in that direction, while in Nepal only the first steps have been taken. Everywhere proletarians live and work in depressed conditions. The formation of a broad workers' movement is opposed by the native bourgeoisie, residual imperialist advantage, and the influence of Maoism, a real enemy of Marxian communism. M. Faissler

3313. Wheeler, Geoffrey. ENCOUNTERS WITH COMMUNISM IN ASIA: PERSONAL RECOLLECTIONS. *Asian Affairs [Great Britain] 1977 64(3): 306-312.* Reviews the encounters of British and Russian agents operating in Asia. In 1926 the author was appointed military attaché to the British Consulate General in Mashhad, in northern Persia. Discusses the subversive activities of Soviet OGPU agents attempting to influence members of the Persian government. In 1929 Russian agents also undertook to infiltrate Anglo-Iranian oil company operations in south Persia. The author worked against these efforts from Iraq. In the 1930's M. N. Roy was the major activist for Central Asia, India, and Afghanistan. During World War II British agents struggled against Indian Communists who attempted to gain advantage during the British preoccupation in Europe. In 1946 Russian efforts in northern Iran were only marginally successful. Concludes that traditional Asian suspicions and fears of Russian intentions forestalled most Communist efforts in Central Asia. Lecture to the Royal Society for Asian Affairs, June 1977. S. H. Frank

3314. Wijeweera, Rohan. SPEECH TO THE CEYLON CRIMINAL JUSTICE COMMISSION, 2 NOVEMBER 1973. *New Left R. [Great Britain] 1974 (84): 85-104.* Rohan Wijeweera, leader of Ceylon's Chinese-oriented Communist Party (the Janatha Vimukthi Peramuna), defended himself against charges of conspiracy and rebellion by arguing that his party neither condoned violence nor attempted to revolt in 1971.

3315. Wright, Theodore P., Jr. INDIAN MUSLIM POLITICS AND THE CHALLENGE OF COMMUNISM. *Asian Thought & Soc. 1983 8(24): 218-224.* Muslim Communists in India, first drawn together to oppose the British, were sharply split by the Indian Communist Party's pro-Pakistan policies and the USSR intervention in Afghanistan.

3316. Yoshida, Mitsuyoshi. TELANGANA TOSO NO TENKAI TO SONO HAIKEI [The background and development of the Telangana struggle in India]. *Rekishigaku Kenkyū [Japan] 1975 (425): 13-33.* Investigates the process and the background of the Telangana struggle, which developed in Hyderabad State, India, 1946-51. Studies on the Indian peasant movements have greatly progressed in Japan recently. Delay of those studies was restricted by the shortage of historical materials and the existence of many languages in India, and the lack of earnest study on the Telangana struggle. The author fully analyzes such materials as *People's Age,* which was the organ of the Indian Communist Party. Concludes that the anti-Nizam united front movement included wide-range social strata aimed at the overthrow of the absolute rule of the Nizam and was based on the peasant struggle to end the rule of the big landlord system. Based on *People's Age,* and secondary sources; 4 diagrams, 101 notes. M. Uchiyama

3317. —. CPI(ML), INDIA DOCUMENTS AND DISCUSSION. *J. of Contemporary Asia [Sweden] 1974 4(4): 509-536.* Reprints nine documents which originally appeared in the *Weekly Frontier* (India) in 1974, giving the full text of each and analyzing their implications for the Communist Party of India (Marxist-Leninist).

Southeast Asia

3318. An, Tai Sung. TURMOIL IN INDOCHINA: THE VIETNAM-CAMBODIA CONFLICT. *Asian Affairs: An Am. Rev. 1978 5(4): 245-256.* Traces and examines the historical roots of Khmer (Cambodian)-Vietnamese conflict from before the artificial, ambiguous, French-colonial-imposed boundary separating Cambodia from Vietnam to the present. Discusses the national interests of each, their presumed common ideological base, their relations with neighboring states, and Chinese, Soviet, and American exploitation of Indochinese nationalism. Based on speeches, newspapers, political journals, and government-induced propaganda statements; 20 notes. R. B. Mendel

3319. Anand, J. P. CHINA MENDS FENCES WITH BURMA. *China Report [India] 1977 13(2): 23-29.* Burma, which gained independence in January 1948, became the first non-Communist country to recognize China in December 1949. Since then the two countries have cooperated from time to time in operations against Kuomintang remnants along their common frontier. But another force operating in this area, the Communist Party of Burma and its tribal allies, has caused friction. Anti-Chinese riots in Burma sparked by the Maoist activities of Burma's Chinese minority occasioned a complete diplomatic break in 1967. In 1970 the breach was healed, and Chairman Ne Win, Burmese head of state, terminated the American military aid program which had aided Burma against the Chinese-supported insurgents. At present Chinese policy is characterized by friendliness to Burma coupled with unconcealed support for the CPB. 32 notes. L. W. Van Wyk

3320. Bass, Jerome R. THE PKI AND THE ATTEMPTED COUP. *J. of Southeast Asian Studies [Singapore] 1970 1(1): 96-105.* Stresses the complexities of the "abortive Communist coup" label applied to the September 30 movement in Indonesia, 1965, and presents diverse commentaries on the controversial movement. Among arguments put forward regarding the ambiguous motives and machinations of elements within the army and the Indonesian Communist Party (PKI) there is a division between an assessment of PKI relative weakness and a minimal estimation of the Party's involvement in the coup on the one hand, and between an assessment of PKI strength and maximal involvement in the coup on the other. Based on secondary sources; 48 notes. K. C. Snow

3321. Bauer, Heinz. EIN HISTORISCHER SIEG DES VIETNAMESISCHEN VOLKES UND DER INTERNATIONALEN SOLIDARITÄT [An historic victory of the Vietnamese people and international solidarity]. *Einheit [East Germany] 1973 28(3): 266-272.* Discusses the historical significance of the conclusion of the Paris Agreement of 27 January 1973 which ended US participation in the Vietnam War. Notes the failure of US policy and contrasts it with that of the Communists. The Vietnamese triumphed because they were led by a battle-tested Marxist-Leninist workers' party which embodied the best traditions of the Vietnamese national war of liberation and of proletarian internationalism. The victory of the Vietnamese was also a common victory for all anti-imperialist forces, with whose assistance the Vietnamese showed the US imperialists the limits of their power. F. H. Eidlin

3322. Bögös, László. A KAMBODZSAI NÉP GYÖZELME [The victory of the people of Cambodia]. *Társadalmi Szemle [Hungary] 1979 34(3): 85-92.* The revolt of the people against Pol Pot started in 1977, and within two years, when the Communist Party consolidated its ranks against his clique, it achieved complete victory.

3323. Boonprasat-Lewis, Nantawan. "In Search of an Integral Liberation: A Study on the Thai Struggle for Social Justice from a Christian Perspective—The Contemporary Thai Farmers' Movement as a Case Study." Princeton Theological Seminary 1982. 344 pp. *DAI 1982 43(3): 838-A.* DA8218349

3324. Burgess, L. K. GESTAPU—TEN YEARS AFTER. *Naval War Coll. Rev. 1976 28(3): 65-75.* The 1965 abortive coup by the Communist Party of Indonesia against the established political order was a unique and extremely important event in Asian history. Although it was totally unsuccessful and was suppressed in less than two days, the consequences included a massive and bloody elimination of Indonesian Communists and their sympathizers. The author describes the revolution and its aftermath and examines the objectives of the revolutionary leaders, the means they used, and how and why they failed. In so doing, he discusses many problems inherent in the Indonesian Communist Party. J

3325. Buttinger, Joseph. THE COLONIAL HERITAGE IN VIETNAM. *Dissent 1974 21(2): 249-252.* The colonial regime imposed on Vietnam by France provided the social and economic conditions that nurtured the inevitable success of communism. Published Fall 1965; reprinted as one of 21 articles in *Dissent*'s 20th anniversary issue.

3326. Chandler, David P. KAMPUCHEA: END GAME OR STALEMATE? *Current History 1984 83(497): 413-417, 433-434.* Chronicles Communist parties and movements in Cambodia and political factions operating during military occupation by Vietnam.

3327. Chandler, David P. REVISING THE PAST IN DEMOCRATIC KAMPUCHEA: WHEN WAS THE BIRTHDAY OF THE PARTY? *Pacific Affairs [Canada] 1983 56(2): 288-300.* In September 1976, many of the early leaders of the Cambodian Communist movement, such as Keo Meas, Suan Nan, and Non Suan, were arrested and after lengthy interrogations, during which they wrote confessions, executed. One of Keo Meas's written confessions titled "1951 or 1960" discussed the founding of the Communist Party of Kampuchea (CPK). By late 1976, the country's leadership appears to have wanted to disassociate itself from its past Vietnamese Communist heritage and to rewrite history to make it appear that Communism came to Kampuchea in 1960 when the CPK was founded. Within approximately two years of this decision, independent Kampuchea disappeared. Ironically its demise may also have saved the lives of many Cambodians. Under the current regime the Party's birthday is still a moveable feast. Based on Cambodian documents; 36 notes. R. H. Detrick

3328. Cheah Boon Kheng. SOME ASPECTS OF THE INTERREGNUM IN MALAYA (14 AUGUST-3 SEPTEMBER 1945). *J. of Southeast Asian Studies [Singapore] 1977 8(1): 48-74.* Chaotic social conditions, conflict between Chinese and Malayans, rumors of Chinese invasion, and the presence of a nominal British force kept the Malayan Communist Party from attempting a coup d'etat following Japanese surrender at the end of World War II, 1945.

3329. Christie, C. J. MARXISM AND THE HISTORY OF NATIONALIST MOVEMENTS IN LAOS. *J. of Southeast Asian Studies [Singapore] 1979 10(1): 146-158.* Unlike Vietnam, there has not been in Laos a symbiotic link between nationalism and Marxism-Leninism since 1945. The conservative nationalist elite was dependent on foreign support, first from the French and then the Americans, allowing the Pathet Lao to attack them as puppets of neocolonial power, and the scale and destructiveness of American intervention after 1962 gave credence to this claim, even though the Pathet Lao were themselves dependent on North Vietnam. Laos is thus exceptional in the general history of Marxism and Third World independence movements, but shows that the greatest advantage in Marxism for nationalist movements is the approach to the minorities question, usually ignored by conservative nationalists. Based on secondary works; 46 notes. D. J. Nicholls

3330. Clutterbuck, Robert L. ANTI-COMMUNIST AGENT IN MALAYA. *Marine Corps Gazette 1964 48(8): 32-35.* Describes the exploits of an anti-communist citizen of Malaya who served as a British agent against communist insurgents in his country.

3331. Colebrook, Joan. PRISONERS OF WAR. *Commentary 1974 57(1): 30-37.* Discusses American public opinion and Communist propaganda about treatment of prisoners of war in the Korean War and the Vietnam War.

3332. Diem, Bui. A NEW KIND OF WAR IN SOUTHEAST ASIA. *Asian Affairs: An Am. Rev. 1979 6(5): 273-281.* Observations of a former Vietnamese ambassador to the United States analyzes the historical roots of conflict among the nations of Southeast Asia. The Vietnamese invasion of Cambodia and the retaliatory Chinese invasion of Vietnam were turning points in the history of world communism in terms of the balance of power. The dominant factor is no longer East versus West, but Chinese versus Soviet communism, with Vietnamese nationalism as the fulcrum between Southeast Asia and the rest of the world. Primary sources. R. B. Mendel

3333. Dinh, Tran Van. VIETNAM IN THE YEAR OF THE DRAGON: REUNIFICATION, REUNION, AND SOCIALIST RECONSTRUCTION. *Monthly Rev. 1976 28(1): 19-33.* Since the liberation army entered Saigon in 1975, the process of reconciliation has proceeded peacefully and efficiently. "The history of the two Indochina wars proved to all Vietnamese beyond any doubt that territorial division was part and parcel of foreign aggressions." The successful reintegration of the South with its 20 years of economic reliance on the United States demands continual retraining and reeducation. Ho Chi Minh once said, "Unity, unity, greater unity, accomplishment, accomplishment, greater accomplishment." If Vietnam's 45 million inhabitants remember those words, then the nation's viability is almost assured. M. R. Yerburgh

3334. Drugov, A. Iu. K 50-I GODOVSHCHINE KOMPARTII INDONEZII [The 50th anniversary of the Communist Party of Indonesia]. *Voprosy Istorii KPSS [USSR] 1970 13(5): 85-90.* Describes the development of the Indonesian Communist Party, 1920-70, and its struggle not only against Dutch colonialists but against right and left-wing opportunism since the country's independence.

3335. Duiker, William J. *The Communist Road to Power in Vietnam.* (Special Studies on South and Southeast Asia.) Boulder, Colo.: Westview, 1981. 393 pp.

3336. Duncanson, Dennis J. THE CONQUEST OF INDOCHINA. *World Today [Great Britain] 1975 31(6): 226-231.* Reviews the political and military strategy by which the Indochina Communist Party by 1975 achieved dominion over Cambodia and Laos, as well as all of Vietnam.

3337. Duncanson, Dennis J. VIETNAM: FROM BOLSHEVISM TO PEOPLE'S WAR. *Studies on the Soviet Union [West Germany] 1971 11(4): 443-468.* Traces the establishment of the Communist Party in Vietnam, the training of Ho Chi Minh as a writer in France, where he came to understand the psychology of democratic peoples, and conditions in Vietnam which made the takeover there unique. Ho converted normal Communist procedures into a war of anticolonialism, first against France and then against the United States. Ho recognized the absurdity of attempting to defeat stronger armies in the field, and therefore cleverly played on the feelings of Western peoples to win by propaganda the victory he could not win by arms. Secondary sources; 94 notes. V. L. Human

3338. Fessen, Helmut. DIE POLITIK DER KOMMUNISTISCHEN PARTEI INDONESIENS GEGENÜBER DEN BAUERN 1945 BIS 1965 [The policy of the Communist Party of Indonesia toward the peasants, 1945-65]. *Mitteilungen des Inst. für Orientforschung [East Germany] 1971-72 17(3): 398-425.* The agricultural policy of the Indonesian Communist Party, especially after the formulation of its agricultural program in 1954, led the Party into direct conflict with the parties of the landowners during the land reform in 1960 and eventually into illegality.

3339. Filipi, Mario. DILEME INDONEŽANSKE KOMMUNISTIČKE PARTIJE [Dilemmas of the Communist Party of Indonesia]. *Politička Misao [Yugoslavia] 1972 9(2-3): 255-272.* Analyzes the activities of the Communist Party of Indonesia since its foundation in 1920, and shows that the Party is now virtually nonexistent.

3340. Furuta, Motoo. INDOCHINA KYŌSANTŌ KARA MITTSU NO TŌ E: 1948-51 NEN NO VIETNAM KYŌSANSHUGISHA NO TAI CAMBODIA LAOS SEISAKU [From the Indochinese Communist Party to three separate parties: Vietnamese Communists' policies toward Cambodia and Laos in 1948-51]. *Ajia Kenkyū [Japan] 1983 29(4): 42-78.* Analyzes why Vietnamese Communists separated the Indochinese Communist Party into the three parties—one each in Vietnam, Laos and Cambodia—while fighting against the return of French power into Indochina after World War II. Although they saw the need of cooperation with Communists in Laos and Cambodia under the intensification of the conflict between the West and the East, they also recognized that the economic system and the party organization of those two countries were not as developed as that of Vietnam. The task and characteristics of the revolution should be, therefore, different according to each stage. Thus, they separated the party into three, making the former members of the Vietnamese Workers' Party in Laos and Cambodia the "advisers" to new parties. Based on unpublished primary sources kept in Vietnam; 91 notes. E. Motono

3341. Gershman, Carl. AFTER THE DOMINOES FELL. *Commentary 1978 65(5): 47-54.* Describes the repression and slaughter in Southeast Asia after the fall of Vietnam. South Vietnam is now a totalitarian state, life is equally harsh in Laos, and Cambodia has experienced even greater savagery than its neighbors. Communism is a system based on terror and total power which requires the individual to surrender his soul. J. Tull

3342. Goodman, Allan E. and Franks, Lawrence M. THE DYNAMICS OF MIGRATION TO SAIGON, 1964-1972. *Pacific Affairs [Canada] 1975 48(2): 199-214.* Reports on the dynamics of rural migration to the cities in South Vietnam, 1964-72. Guerrilla warfare sought to drive the peasant masses into the cities, but the major impact was in the middle-sized cities and provincial towns, not Saigon. Unlike the migrants to Saigon of the 1950's, few villagers and farmers came to the city with the expectation that their stay would be short. Over three million migrants applied for the Land Development and Hamlet Building Program. One half million people planned resettlement from Saigon—20% more than the number who migrated there during the war years. The victorious People's Revolutionary Government did not force an exodus from the cities as happened in Cambodia. Based on extensive interviews in Saigon and Gia Dinh province and secondary sources; 4 tables, 18 notes. S. H. Frank

3343. Gunawan, B. POLITICAL MOBILIZATION IN INDONESIA: NATIONALISTS AGAINST COMMUNISTS. *Modern Asian Studies [Great Britain] 1973 7(4): 707-715.* Examines the role and strategy of the Indonesian Communist Party in politics from the struggle for independence to its suppression in 1965.

3344. Heaton, William R. CHINA AND SOUTHEAST ASIAN COMMUNIST MOVEMENTS: THE DECLINE OF DUAL TRACK DIPLOMACY. *Asian Survey 1982 22(8): 779-800.* There has been a gradual process of Chinese downgrading of support for insurgent Communist parties in Southeast Asian countries. The rise of Deng Xiaoping (Teng Hsiao-p'ing) and the growth of Soviet and Vietnamese "hegemonism" in Southeast Asia are major reasons. In essence, China has progressively disassociated itself from the Communist-led insurgencies in Southeast Asia because of a perceived need to secure ASEAN support on the Indochina question. The efforts have not been remarkably successful, and it appears that the issue of dual track diplomacy will continue to complicate Chinese foreign policy. Based on radio broadcasts; 47 notes. M. A. Eide

3345. Ho Tai Yan. THE GESTAPU COUP OF 1965. *J. of the Hist. Soc., U. of Singapore [Singapore] 1976-77: 33-36.* Assesses the evidence on the Indonesian Communist Party's involvement in the Gestapu coup d'etat in Indonesia in 1965.

3346. Hosmer, Stephen T.; Kellen, Konrad; and Jenkins, Brian M. THE FALL OF SOUTH VIETNAM. *Conflict 1980 2(1): 1-8.* Summarizes a 1975 Rand Corporation report, based on interviews of South Vietnamese civilian and military leaders, concerning US policy, 1972-75, especially the Paris Accords, as the most prominent among several anterior causes of the suddenness of the fall of South Vietnam to Communism in April 1975.

3347. Hunt, David. REMEMBERING THE TET OFFENSIVE. *Radical Am. 1977-78 11(6)-12(1): 79-96.* The Tet Offensive of 1968 was the turning point in the effort of the National Liberation Front of South Vietnam to take power in the country. It also inspired the political Left in many countries, including the United States, and provided a major step forward for socialism. The Offensive was a remarkable military achievement as well as a political victory in that it was based on highly effective coordination of many small units scattered throughout the country and located inside enemy urban strongholds. The confidence of the Vietnamese middle class was severely shaken by the Offensive, while large sections of the nation were, at least temporarily, successfully placed under NLF control. The large losses in men suffered by the NLF did not basically diminish its insurgent capabilities. N. Lederer

3348. Il'ichev, B. I. SLAVNYE STRANITSY ISTORII BOR'BY KOMPARTII INDONEZII [Glorious pages from the history of the struggle of the Indonesian Communist Party]. *Voprosy Istorii KPSS*

[USSR] 1963 (2): 137-140. Summarizes some of the articles and speeches of the president of the Indonesian Communist Party, 1951-61, Dwipa Nusantara Aidit.

3349. Jaguaribe, Helio. EL VIETNAM Y LOS ESTADOS UNIDOS [Vietnam and the United States]. *Estudios Int. [Argentina] 1975 8(31): 3-18.* Discusses post-World War II Vietnam, the reasons for US intervention, the place of the US in the world order, and the victory of Communism in Vietnam.

3350. Johnson, George and Feldman, Fred. CONTRIBUTION TO A DEBATE: ON THE NATURE OF THE VIETNAMESE COMMUNIST PARTY. *Int. Socialist Rev. 1973 34(7): 4-9, 63-90.* Traces the development of the Vietnamese Communist Party in the struggle against French colonialism, 1930's-70's, and analyzes the Vietnamese Party's relations with China and the USSR.

3351. Kelabora, Lambert. RELIGIOUS INSTRUCTION POLICY IN INDONESIA. *Asian Survey 1976 16(3): 230-248.* Religious education in secular schools was a controversial issue in Indonesia, 1940-71. The presence of Communist armed forces formed the most powerful secular force in the country, whose presence in politics weighed heavily against the Moslems. The Moslems argued that religious instruction had saved the country from communism. "The domination of the political scene by non-Islamic groups usually leads to non-compulsory religious instruction while the victory of the Islamic forces brings about a compulsory religious instruction policy." 41 notes. E. P. Stickney

3352. Kiernan, Ben. CONFLICT IN THE KAMPUCHEAN COMMUNIST MOVEMENT. *J. of Contemporary Asia [Sweden] 1980 10(1-2): 7-74.* Discusses the ideologies of a chauvinist group led by Pol Pot, whose major concern has been the rapid development of Cambodia into an industrial country with great strength for national defense, and the group now led in Pnompenh by President Heng Samrin, consisting of people attracted to the Vietnamese socialist model. These different approaches are reflected in the magazine *Tung Padevat* and a 1973 *Summary of Annotated Party History.* Based on a paper presented at the 10th Anniversary Conference of the J. of Contemporary Asia at Stockholm, 23-25 August 1979; 214 notes. J. Powell

3353. Lance, Michel. LE DÉGAGEMENT DE LA ROUTE HAIPHONG-HANOI 20 DÉCEMBRE 1946-7 JANVIER 1947 [Reopening the Haiphong-Hanoi highway 20 December 1946 - 7 January 1947]. *R. Militaire Générale [France] 1971 (6): 43-65.* On 19 December 1946, Vietminh units launched a surprise attack in the Haiphong-Hanoi area, seizing a number of key points along the east-west highway which links the two cities. French forces in Haiphong counterattacked, taking the offensive against Haiduong, midway between Haiphong and Hanoi. After seizing Haiduong, they moved west toward Hanoi while a unit from Hanoi moved east to link up with them. Based on personal reminiscences of a participating officer; map. J. S. Gassner

3354. Leclerc, Jacques. B BLASON DE LA RÉVOLUTION: SENS ET CONTRE-SENS DANS LE DISCOURS D'AIDIT, 1962-1963 [Blazon of the Revolution: meaning and counter-meaning in Aidit's speech, 1962-63]. *Rev. Française de Sci. Pol. [France] 1978 28(3): 441-458.* Part II. Continued from a previous article. Criticizes the 1963 speech of the chairman of the Indonesian Communist Party, D. N. Aidit, and stresses his use of new metaphoric statements.

3355. Leclerc, Jacques. B LA CLANDESTINITE ET SON DOUBLE A PROPOS DES RELATIONS D'AMIR SJARIFUDDIN AVEC LE COMMUNISME INDONESIEN (II) [The underground and its double à propos the relations of Amir Sjarifuddin with Indonesian Communism, part 2]. *Asian Thought & Soc. 1981 6(17-18): 156-166.* Continued from an earlier article. Discusses the overt and covert activities in the formation and attempted fusion of the Indonesian Socialist Party and the Popular Socialist Party, their role in Indonesian politics, and their relationship to world communism.

3356. Leclerc, Jacques. A BLASON DE LA RÉVOLUTION: SENS ET CONTRE-SENS DANS LE DISCOURS D'AIDIT, 1962-1963 [Escutcheon of the revolution: sense and countersense in the speeches of Aidit, 1962-63]. *Rev. Française de Sci. Pol. [France] 1978 28(2): 349-375.* Part I. Examines the speeches made by the chairman of the Communist Party of Indonesia, D. N. Aidit, 1962-63. Article to be continued.

3357. Leclerc, Jacques. A LA CLANDESTINITÉ ET SON DOUBLE: À PROPOS DES RELATIONS D'AMIR SJARIFUDDIN AVEC LE COMMUNISME INDONÉSIEN (I) [The underground and its double: Amir Sjarifuddin's relations with Indonesian communism, Part I]. *Asian Thought and Soc. 1981 6(16): 36-48.* Biography of Amir Sjarifuddin, one of the founders of Indonesia's independence and a Protestant who, among the Communists, had rebelled against Dutch colonialism. Article to be continued.

3358. Lo Shih-fu. THE CAUSES AND EFFECTS OF NAW SENG'S DEATH AS VIEWED FROM THE INTERNAL STRIFE OF THE BURMESE COMMUNIST PARTY. *Issues and Studies [Taiwan] 1972 8(11): 28-38.*

3359. Lo Shih-fu. COMMUNIST DEVELOPMENTS IN BURMA. *Issues and Studies [Taiwan] 1970 6(8): 42-50.* Sketches the history of the Burmese Communists, 1932-70. The Marxists under Thakin Than Tun and Thakin Soe have been active since the early period of Burmese nationalism. They formed the nucleus of the Thakin Party and the Anti-Fascist Peoples Freedom League (AFPFL). They also instigated the assassination of Aung San and seven other ministers in 1947. Before 1949, the Burmese Communists were primarily under the influence of the Communist Party of the Soviet Union through the Indian party. Since 1949, however, the Chinese have dominated through the Red and White Flag guerrillas and the Kachin rebels. The Ne Win government's general success in combating the Communists is more the result of Sino-Soviet factionalism than of successful anti-Communist activities. Based on news reports and secondary sources; 28 notes. L. J. Stout

3360. Long, Nguyen and Kendall, Harry H. *After Saigon Fell: Daily Life under the Vietnamese Communists.* Berkeley: U. of California, Inst. of East Asian Studies, 1981. 164 pp.

3361. Lulei, Wilfried. DIE ENTSTEHUNG DER DEMOKRATISCHEN REPUBLIK VIETNAM [The origin of the Democratic Republic of Vietnam]. *Zeitschrift für Geschichtswissenschaft [East Germany] 1970 18(6): 804-809.* From the 1930's, the Communist Party of Vietnam was the main force in the anticolonial struggle because of its small but well-organized structure and because it was confronted only by a weak bourgeois opposition. When the French started the war against the Viet Minh in 1946, the anticolonialists had already established such an efficient administration that made it impossible for the colonialists to win the war. Based on secondary literature; 12 notes. R. Wagnleitner

3362. Maclear, Michael. *The Ten Thousand Day War: Vietnam, 1945-1975.* New York: St. Martin's, 1981. 368 pp.

3363. Mallin, Jay. TERRORISM AS A POLITICAL WEAPON. *Air U. R. 1971 22(5): 45-52.* Discusses 20th-century terrorism, especially Communist terror in the Vietnam War.

3364. Mans, R. S. N. THE NEW CONFLICT. *Marine Corps Gazette 1968 52(10): 22-26.* Examines the evolution of communist insurgency in Southeast Asia since World War II.

3365. Marsot, Alain-Gérard. THE CRUCIAL YEAR: INDOCHINA 1946. *J. of Contemporary Hist. [Great Britain] 1984 19(2): 337-354.* The year 1946 was a turning-point in French relations with Indochina. When General Charles de Gaulle resigned and the Socialist government was busy writing the Constitution of the Fourth Republic, Ho Chi Minh called for Vietnamese independence. Factions in France began pushing for a war of reconquest. Events climaxed on the night of December 19-20 when Vietminh elements attacked the French forces in Hanoi and massacred civilians. The next day, December 21, Ho Chi Minh called for all-out insurrection and took to the jungle. The war was on. Based on published sources and an interview with Georges Bidault, French Premier in 1946; 33 notes. M. P. Trauth

3366. McWilliams, Edmund. VIETNAM IN 1982: ONWARD INTO THE QUAGMIRE. *Asian Survey 1983 23(1): 62-72.* During 1982 there was a continuing economic crisis and a military and political stalemate in Kampuchea (Cambodia), which provided a sobering backdrop for the 5th Vietnamese Communist Party Congress. As the congress convened, the food supply was inadequate; medical care for the general population was poor; and production in both heavy and light industries had fallen as the cost of Soviet oil increased. Vietnam's position in Kampuchea led to increasing political isolation. This isolation, coupled with deteriorating economic performance, engendered increasing dependence on the USSR. M. A. Eide

3367. Mikheev,Iu. Ia. and Kudinov, V. P. MARKSISTSKO-LENINSKII AVANGARD LAOSSKOGO NARODA (K 25-LETIIU SOZDANIA NARODNO-REVOLIUTSIONNOI PARTII LAOSA) [The Marxist-Leninist vanguard of the Laotian people: 25 years of the People's Revolutionary Party of Laos]. *Voprosy Istorii KPSS [USSR] 1980 (3): 114-118.* The Communist Party of Indochina was the voice of Marxism-Leninism in Vietnam, Laos, and Cambodia in 1930. A Laos section formed in 1936 to organize Laotian revolutionary activity. In 1955 the People's Party of Laos arose under the guidance of the Soviet and the Vietnamese Communist parties. It was renamed the People's Revolutionary Party of Laos in 1972. M. R. Colenso

3368. Mosolov, V. G. KOMPARTII INDONEZII—60 LET [The Communist Party of Indonesia is 60 years old]. *Voprosy Istorii KPSS [USSR] 1980 (8): 151-154.* Reports on the proceedings and abstracts papers presented at a session commemorating the 60th anniversary of the founding of the Communist Party of Indonesia. The seminar was organized by the Institute of Marxism-Leninism attached to the Central Committee of the Communist Party of the Soviet Union (CPSU) in cooperation with the Academy of Social Sciences of the Central Committee of the CPSU. V. Sobell

3369. Nguyen, Van Canh and Cooper, Earle. *Vietnam under Communism, 1975-1982.* Stanford, Calif.: Hoover Inst. Pr., 1983. 312 pp.

3370. Nikitin, A. S. STOIKII MARKSIST-LENINETS (K 75-LETIIU SO DNIA ROZHDENIIA GENERAL'NOGO SEKRETARIA TSK KPV LE ZUANA) [A steadfast Marxist-Leninist: on the 75th anniversary of the birthday of the General Secretary of the Communist Party of Vietnam, Le Duan]. *Voprosy Istorii KPSS [USSR] 1982 (4): 108-111.* Le Duan, born 7 April 1907, was the right-hand man of Ho Chi Minh. He learned the love of work from his carpenter father and of study from his mother. During his youth, Vietnam was swept by the antimonarchist movement. He joined the Communist Party in 1930, and in 1931 was imprisoned for a 20-year term by the colonial power. He was released in 1936 and continued revolutionary work. He was elected a member of the Party's permanent committee in 1939. The Democratic Republic of Vietnam was proclaimed 2 September 1945, and liberation wars were fought against France and the United States. China's betrayal is described. Le Duan was present at all the struggles and victories of Vietnam. He became a member of the Politburo in 1951 and General Secretary of the Party in 1976. He is an optimist, ardent Marxist-Leninist, patriot, internationalist, and friend of the USSR. Based on the collected works of Le Duan and Soviet sources; 19 notes. A. J. Evans

3371. Osborne, Milton. MAKERS OF THE 20TH CENTURY: HO CHI MINH. *Hist. Today [Great Britain] 1980 30(Nov): 40-46.* Traces Ho Chi Minh's political commitment from 1917-23, when he joined the French Communist Party, through experiences in the USSR, Hong Kong, and southern China, to Vietnam, where he led the Communists and helped found the Vietnam Independence League (Viet Minh) in 1941, maintaining political influence until his death.

3372. Pike, Douglas. COMMUNIST VS. COMMUNIST IN SOUTHEAST ASIA. *Int. Security 1979 4(1): 20-38.* Reviews events in Southeast Asia since 1975 and perceives that there are now three major Communist Asian powers as well as large non-Communist nations all attempting to establish power bases and stability in the area. But old antagonisms—many antedating the colonial era—are making themselves apparent in much of the region.

3373. Prizzia, Ross. THAILAND: NEW SOCIAL FORCES AND RE-EMERGING SOCIALIST PRINCIPLES. *Asia Q. [Belgium] 1975 (4): 343-365.* Socialism has had an unprecedented popular appeal in Thailand in recent years, although it has had a long history. The Communist Party of Thailand has existed since 1925. From the mid-1960's it took on an increasingly revolutionary stance, and from 1968 there was an increase in rebellion along with a unification of factions under the title People's Liberation Army of Thailand. The student revolution of 1973 catalyzed insurgency. Recent attempts to prevent insurgency may have occurred too late, although the new democracy may lead to compromise and agreement. F. Birch

3374. Quinn, Kenneth M. POLITICAL CHANGE IN WARTIME: THE KHMER KRAHOM REVOLUTION IN SOUTHERN CAMBODIA, 1970-1974. *Naval War Coll. Rev. 1976 28(4): 3-31.* When the Khmer Communists finally defeated the Cambodian government in April 1975, little was known in the West about this movement. Following their capture of Phnom Penh, it was clear that a forced evacuation of that city was one of the new regime's first steps. The revolutionary process now apparently underway in Cambodia began in some parts of the country as early as 1971. An examination of the experience of southern Cambodia from 1971 to 1974 explains how a small but dedicated force was able to impose a revolution on a society without widespread participation of the peasantry. J

3375. Quinn, Kenneth Michael. "The Origins and Development of Radical Cambodian Communism." U. of Maryland 1982 277 pp. *DAI 1983 44(6): 1913-A.* DA8323577

3376. Rodulfo, A. M. ETHNIC AND RELIGIOUS MINORITIES IN SOUTH-EAST ASIA. *Pacific Community [Australia] 1970 (5): 3-16.* Since the 1950's communism has taken advantage of the two main aspects of the minorities problem in Southeast Asia (the "primitives" on the one hand and the large minorities of advanced cultures such as the Chinese and the Indians on the other) by offering such people respect and continuity of ethnic identity, and those Southeast Asian countries that wish to resist the advance of communism must learn to do likewise.

3377. Roth, David F. POLITICAL CHANGES IN ASIA AFTER VIETNAM: SOME THOUGHTS AND ALTERNATIVES TO DOMINOES. *Asia Q. [Belgium] 1977 (1): 3-16.* Defines the domino theory, examines the acceleration of Soviet-Chinese rivalry with its impacts on national political stability in Asia after Vietnam, and government changes in Southeast Asia prior to the Vietnam War which even when they were triggered by events outside the region interacted with an independent set of factors within each nation, namely, military dissatisfaction, communal competition, existing leadership bids to power maintenance, and student-mobilized socioeconomic frustration. It is difficult to conclude that any of the assumptions posited by "domino theorists" are conclusive. Based on government documents and other primary and secondary sources; 20 notes. G. M. White

3378. Rotter, Andrew Jon. "The Big Canvas: The United States, Southeast Asia and the World: 1948-1950." Stanford U. 1981. 502 pp. *DAI 1982 42(8): 3724-A.* 8202033

3379. Sergeev, A. S. SOTSIALISTICHESKII VIETNAM. *Novaia i Noveishaia Istoriia [USSR] 1977 (5): 160-173.* Reviews Vietnamese history since the establishment in Hanoi, 1945, of the Democratic Republic of Vietnam. Contrasts the peaceful socioeconomic development of North Vietnam after partition in 1954 with the drawn-out struggle for liberation in the South. Soviet-Vietnamese friendship, based on common ideological tenets of Marxism-

Leninism, led to the creation of the Communist Party of Vietnam in 1930, helped the Vietnamese struggle for independence against the French and Americans, and provided economic and technological aid for postwar reconstruction of a united Vietnam. 26 notes. N. Frenkley

3380. Shee, Poon Kim. INSURGENCY IN SOUTHEAST ASIA. *Problems of Communism 1983 32(3): 45-55.* Communist insurgencies in the countries of the Association of Southeast Asian Nations (ASEAN) have not prospered in the period following establishment of Communist rule in Kampuchea, Laos, and South Vietnam. This reflects internal weaknesses in the insurgencies, the resistance of local cultures to Communist activities, and the absence or decline of external assistance. Based on publications and radio broadcasts of the ASEAN countries; 68 notes. J. M. Lauber

3381. Shinde, B. E. OUTLINE HISTORY OF KAMPUCHEAN COMMUNISM 1930-78. *China Report [India] 1982 18(1): 11-47.* A review of the nature and course of the Communist Party of Cambodia prior to the invasion by Vietnam. The Party began in 1930 and for the next 26 years was carefully controlled by the Communist Party of Vietnam. Early strains between the two were apparent. Then the tie was broken, and the Cambodian Party went its own way. Prince Sihanouk was won over, and his support permitted war to be waged against the Lon Nol regime. Vietnam invaded Cambodia to regain its traditional control. Tales of Pol Pot's savagery and repression continue because all sources of data have come under the control of the Vietnamese regime. 305 notes. V. L. Human

3382. Shurygin, V. A. SLAVNYI PUT' [The glorious path]. *Voprosy Istorii KPSS [USSR] 1961 (4): 193-197.* Provides historical background to the pamphlet *Forty Years of the Indonesian Communist Party* (1960) tracing the history of socialism in Indonesia, 1905-60.

3383. Simon, Sheldon W. CAMBODIA: BARBARISM IN A SMALL STATE UNDER SIEGE. *Current Hist. 1978 75(442): 197-201, 227, 228.* Rule by the Cambodian Communist Party since 1975 has meant collectivization and terrorization of Cambodians and the likelihood of continued war with Vietnam.

3384. Sinuraja, Thomas. V. I. LENIN, KOMINTERN I KOMMUNISTICHESKAIA PARTIIA INDONEZII [V. I. Lenin, the Comintern, and the Communist Party of Indonesia]. *Voprosy Istorii KPSS [USSR] 1980 (1): 44-51.* A survey of the history of the Indonesian Communist Party. Upon its creation, the Party followed the Leninist directions set by the Executive Committee of the Comintern by emphasizing national liberation and democratic reforms. Inexperienced Party members, however, supported a premature revolution in 1926. It failed and once again the Party cooperated with nationalist organizations achieving a significant degree of popularity during the 1950's and early 1960's. Rejection of the united front severely damaged the Party's reputation, and the army coup of 1965 hobbled it. Since then, the leadership has returned to an emphasis on forming a front of national unity and demanding general democratic reforms. 4 notes. L. E. Holmes

3385. Sinuraja, Tomas. INDONESIAN COMMUNISTS CONTINUE STRUGGLE. *World Marxist Rev. [Canada] 1972 15(6): 64-73.* Discusses the Communist Party of Indonesia from its founding in 1920 to its present underground political activities.

3386. Smith, R. B. *An International History of the Vietnam War. Vol. I: Revolution versus Containment, 1955-61.* New York: St. Martin's, 1984. 301 pp.

3387. Stebbins, C. W. FRANCES FITZGERALD, *FIRE IN THE LAKE: THE VIETNAMESE AND THE AMERICANS IN VIETNAM;* DOUGLAS PIKE: *THE ORGANIZATION AND TECHNIQUES OF THE NATIONAL LIBERATION FRONT OF SOUTH VIETNAM;* FRANK N. TRAGER, *WHY VIETNAM? J. of Oriental Studies [Hong Kong] 1976 14(2): 186-190.* American works on Vietnam have been hampered by emotionalism and an inability to perceive events from a Vietnamese perspective. Pike's *Viet Cong* (1966) tried to prove that the success of the Viet Cong was due to its excellent organization and use of communications among South Vietnamese peasants. Trager's *Why Vietnam?* (1966) presented the traditional Cold War argument about containing Communism. Fitzgerald's *Fire in the Lake* (1972) tried to account for the success of the Communists by arguing that they were adept at translating their ideology into terms which peasants could understand and appreciate. Her study is more sophisticated than the others and effectively downplays emotionalism while it employs a Vietnamese perspective. J. Sokolow

3388. Stuart-Fox, Martin. TENSIONS WITHIN THE THAI INSURGENCY. *Australian Outlook [Australia] 1979 32(2): 182-197.* A survey of the divisions within the Communist movement of Thailand from the 1930's, concentrating on the impact of China's and Vietnam's attitude to Cambodia in the 1970's. The Thai Communist Party began with Thai Chinese rather than ethnic Thais. Recently Vietnam's relations with the Thai Government have been served by cutting aid to the insurgents. Based on newspapers and journals; 99 notes. W. D. McIntyre

3389. Suryanarayan, V. MALAYAN COMMUNISM AT THE CROSSROADS. *China Report [India] 1974 10(4): 60-76.* Reviews the history of the Malayan Communist Party from 1940 to 1974, noting that the MCP is made up chiefly of Malaysian Chinese, but China's decision (against the wishes of the MCP) to establish diplomatic relations with Malaysia seems to have undercut the power and prestige of the MCP.

3390. Tao, Van. VE TRI THUC VIET NAM TRONG CACH MANG XA HOI CHU NGHIA [Vietnamese intellectuals in the socialist revolution]. *Nghien Cuu Lich Su [Vietnam] 1981 (6): 6-15.* After 20 years of socialist revolution, the corps of Vietnamese intellectuals is numerous and stable, something never seen previously. This was achieved by the formation of new intellectuals and the reformation of intellectuals of previous regimes, led by the Vietnam Communist Party and the proletarian state. This development and maturation are the expression of lawful character of the Vietnamese socialist revolution. J/S

3391. Tixier, René. IL ÉTAIT UN PAYS NOMMÉ CAMBODGE [There was a country named Cambodia]. *Écrits de Paris [France] 1977 (369): 43-48.* Describes the destruction by the Khmers Rouges of a country and a culture since the fall of Phnom Penh 18 April 1975, in order to show the destructive potential of a Communist takeover.

3392. Toai, Doan Van and Chanoff, David. LEARNING FROM VIET NAM. *Encounter [Great Britain] 1982 59(3-4): 19-26.* Discusses the lessons the West, especially the American Left can learn from recent Vietnamese history, with special attention to the necessity of learning to differentiate between Communist rhetoric and Communist reality.

3393. Turley, William S., ed. *Vietnamese Communism in Comparative Perspective.* Special Studies on South and Southeast Asia. Boulder, Colo.: Westview, 1980. 271 pp.

3394. Van Alstyne, Richard W. THE VIETNAM WAR IN HISTORICAL PERSPECTIVE. *Current Hist. 1973 65(388): 241-246, 273-274.*

3395. Van Der Kroef, Justus M. THE WAGES OF AMBIGUITY: THE 1965 COUP IN INDONESIA, ITS ORIGINS AND MEANING. *Studies on the Soviet Union [West Germany] 1971 11(4): 487-515.* The failure of the 1965 Communist coup in Indonesia was a consequence of contradictions within the party's tactics and policies. Having enjoyed phenomenal growth under the semiofficial support of President Sukarno, the party wavered between traditional Communist methods and new ways. The coup exacerbated these ambiguities and was easily put down. Secondary sources; 63 notes. V. L. Human

3396. VanderKroef, Justus M. COMMUNISM IN BURMA: ITS DEVELOPMENT AND PROSPECTS. *Issues and Studies [Taiwan] 1979 15(3): 44-64.* The Burmese Communist Party was not founded until 1939; by 1979 it was but one of several regional movements operating against the Rangoon government.

3397. vanderKroef, Justus M. INDONESIA, COMMUNIST CHINA AND THE P.K.I. *Pacific Community [Australia] 1970 (5): 27-42.* Since diplomatic relations between Indonesia and the People's Republic of China (PRC) were severed in 1967, China allegedly attempted to subvert the Suharto government (according to Indonesia), and the Indonesians have pursued a policy of persecuting members and suspected members of the Indonesian Communist Party (PKI), especially if the alleged Communists are ethnic Chinese (according to the PRC).

3398. vanderKroef, Justus M. THE INDONESIAN MAOISTS: DOCTRINES AND PERSPECTIVES. *Asian Thought and Soc. 1976 1(1): 2-17.* Discusses the emergence of Indonesian Maoism since the abortive coup of 30 September 1965, and its analysis of Party tactics and concerns.

3399. VanderKroef, Justus M. LE VIETNAM AU KAMPUCHEA: LA STRATEGIE DE CONSOLIDATION [Vietnam in Kampuchea: The strategy of consolidation]. *Etudes Int. [Canada] 1984 15(2): 291-309.* Discusses Vietnam's consolidation of power in Kampuchea. Hanoi sent 40,000 Party officials and professionals along with 100,000 Vietnamese farmers to resurrect an economy destroyed by the Pol Pot regime. 45 notes. J. F. Harrington

3400. VanDerKroef, Justus M. RELIGION, ETHNICITY AND COMMUNIST TACTICS IN SOUTHEAST ASIA'S PLURAL SOCIETIES. *Plural Societies [Netherlands] 1976 7(4): 3-26.* Discusses the diverse religious and ethnic groups of Southeast Asia. Although the Communist Party recognizes the divergent groups, Southeast Asians wishing to ally themselves with Communism must accept ethnic and other identities as transitory.

3401. vanderKroef, Justus M. SOVIET-INDONESIA RELATIONS AND THE P.K.I. *Pacific Community [Australia] 1970 (4): 311-325.* Reviews Soviet-Indonesian relations, 1956-69, concluding that, while the USSR promised in 1969 not to interfere in Indonesian affairs, it continued a long-standing policy, openly supporting the now outlawed Indonesian Communist Party (PKI), although it dared not go too far in antagonizing the Suharto government because the USSR wanted to recover the considerable amount of money owed it by Indonesia, the chronic delinquency of the latter notwithstanding.

3402. Van Der Kroef, Justus M. THE 1965 COUP IN INDONESIA: THE CIA'S VERSION. *Asian Affairs: An Am. Rev. 1976 4(2): 117-131.* The US Central Intelligence Agency report (1968) on the 1965 Gestapu affair, Gerakan Tige Pulu September, the attempted coup d'etat by the Thirty September Movement against the Indonesian government, covers planning, recruitment, "established facts," interrogation irregularities, extent of military involvement, and Communist Chinese involvement. 13 notes. R. B. Mendel

3403. Vasilkov, Ye. KAMPUCHEA: THE MAOIST "EXPERIMENT" THAT FAILED. *Far Eastern Affairs [USSR] 1979 (3): 41-51.* Kampuchea was a testing ground for remodeling society along Maoist lines, exterminating three million Cambodians in the process, 1950's-79.

3404. Volodin, A. S. and Zelentsov, V. A. VDOKHNOVITEL' I ORGANIZATOR POBED V'ETNAMSKOGO NARODA [The inspiration and organizer of the victories of the Vietnamese people]. *Voprosy Istorii KPSS [USSR] 1980 (2): 114-118.* The Vietnamese Communists progressed from fragmented representation in the Revolutionary Youth Association of Vietnam and two other organizations to consolidation into a Vietnamese Communist Party under Ho Chi Minh in 1930. After struggles against French colonialists the First Congress of the Indochinese party convened in March 1935. Ho returned in February 1940 as leader of the anti-Japanese resistance, and in September 1945 the Democratic Republic of Vietnam was proclaimed. The anti-French campaigns, 1946-54, and resistance to American aggression after 1965 ended in 1973 with the Paris accord. Full independence followed in 1975. A 30-day confrontation with China occurred in 1979. M. R. Colenso

3405. Vongvichit, Phoumi. THIRTY YEARS OF STRUGGLE, SECOND YEAR OF FREEDOM. *World Marxist Rev. [Canada] 1976 19(11): 81-89.* Examines the war over Communism in Laos 1945-76, focusing on US foreign policy.

3406. Weatherbee, Donald E. COMMUNIST REVOLUTIONARY VIOLENCE IN THE ASEAN STATES. *Asian Affairs: An Am. Rev. 1983 10(3): 1-17.* Surveys the Communist Party and its activities in Thailand, Malaysia, Singapore, Indonesia, and the Philippines. Determines that the most capable Communist Party is that in the Philippines. Attributes this to its isolation, self-reliance, leadership, and the dysfunction of Ferdinand Marcos's administration. Concludes that "urban terrorism" is the face of the future in the Association of Southeast Asian Nations (ASEAN) countries. 18 notes. R. B. Mendel

3407. White, Christine. PEASANT MOBILIZATION AND ANTI-COLONIAL STRUGGLE IN VIETNAM: THE RENT REDUCTION CAMPAIGN OF 1953. *J. of Peasant Studies [Great Britain] 1983 10(4): 187-213.* While Vietnam seems to present an unusually successful case of coordination of national liberation struggle and peasant revolution, the relationship between these two aspects of the movement has been very complex, and the national and class struggles have had contradictory as well as complementary aspects. Following a summary of two poles of a debate on the topic within the Vietnamese Communist movement in the 1930's and 1940's, the relationship between the independence struggle and social revolution during 1953, the year in which the Communist Party introduced mass mobilization for class struggle for the first time, is analyzed. J

3408. White, Christine Katherine Pelzer. "Agrarian Reform and National Liberation in the Vietnamese Revolution: 1920-1957." Cornell U. 1981. 531 pp. *DAI 1981 41(12): 5235-A.* 8111002

3409. Willmott, W. E. ANALYTICAL ERRORS OF THE KAMPUCHEAN COMMUNIST PARTY. *Pacific Affairs [Canada] 1981 54(2): 209-227.* On 27 September 1977, Pol Pot delivered a speech announcing the existence of the Kampuchean Communist Party (KCP) and tracing its rise to power. The speech is the most detailed statement available of the KCP view of Khmer history and society. Pol Pot described Kampuchean history in Stalinist terms. He contended that until the formation of the KCP in 1960 the peasant masses could not overcome exploitation because they were following an incorrect political line. Pol Pot's analysis of Kampuchean history is erroneous. The fact that the existence of the KCP was hidden, 1960-77 is evidence that the peasantry did not support the KCP. KCP repression and the successful 1978 Vietnamese invasion of Kampuchea resulted from Pol Pot's faulty assumption that the peasant-landlord relationship was the basic contradiction in Khmer society during the 1960's. French and English sources; 59 notes. R. H. Detrick

3410. —. LA CONSTRUCCIÓN DEL SOCIALISMO EN LA REPÚBLICA DEMOCRÁTICA DE VIET NAM Y LA GUERRA DE DESTRUCCIÓN YANQUI CONTRA SU ECONOMÍA [The building of socialism in the Democratic Republic of Vietnam and the Yankee war of destruction against its economy]. *Investigación Econ. [Mexico] 1973 32(128): 849-880.* Describes the economic development of North Vietnam during war or relative peace, 1930's-72.

East Asia and the Pacific Area

3411. Ahn Byung-joon. SOUTH KOREA AND THE COMMUNIST COUNTRIES. *Asian Survey 1980 20(11): 1098-1107.* Since its establishment in 1948 the Republic of Korea (ROK) has had no formal relations with any of the Communist countries, but with the exception of North Korea there are few areas of direct conflict between the ROK and the Communist countries. The armistice ending the Korean War in 1953 did not lay the groundwork for improved relations between North and South Korea. Until this situation changes, South Korea is not likely to go beyond its current policy of probing contacts with a few Communist nations. Based on newspapers and secondary sources; 8 notes. M. A. Eide

3412. Andreyev, V. and Osipov, V. RELATIONS OF THE USSR AND THE EUROPEAN SOCIALIST COUNTRIES WITH THE DPRK IN THE 1970'S. *Far Eastern Affairs [USSR] 1982 (1): 52-62.* During the 1970's North Korea was a trading partner of all the European socialist nations, who are unified in their desire for the departure of foreign troops and Korean unification.

3413. Apollonova, E. A. 60 LET KOMMUNISTICHESKOGO DVIZHENIIA V AVSTRALII [60 years of the Australian Communist movement]. *Voprosy Istorii KPSS [USSR] 1980 (11): 108-112.* A brief outline of the development of the Communist Party in Australia on its 60th anniversary, describing the Australian Party's support for Russian policy in Afghanistan and its rising authority among the workers. Based on published works in Russian and English; 17 notes. D. N. Collins

3414. Barkowski, Jürgen. DIE HERAUSBILDUNG UND ENTWICKLUNG DER MONGOLISCHEN ARBEITERKLASSE [The formation and development of the Mongolian working class]. *Wissenschaftliche Zeitschrift der Humboldt-Universität zu Berlin [East Germany] 1974 23(2): 138-142.* A sympathetic account of the transformation of nomadic Mongolia into a Communist state. Influenced by the October Revolution and relying on Soviet aid and Lenin's thesis that industrialization is not a prerequisite for communism, the Mongolians began their revolution in 1921. By 1940 there were, in effect, two Mongolias, one still nomadic and the other with some industry, trained Communist cadres, and a steadily improving standard of living. By 1974 Mongolia was a full-blown Communist state, a partner in world communism, with the working class in the vanguard, state planning, state or cooperative industry, general literacy, and such advantages as modern housing. Mongolian and Russian sources; 16 notes. M. Faissler

3415. Barranco, Vicente F. SEOUL 1948: PAGES FROM A KOREAN DIARY. *Asian and Pacific Q. of Cultural and Social Affairs [South Korea] 1978 10(2): 3-12.* Inherent distrust of Korean Communists under Soviet direction caused South Koreans to take a strong nationalist and anti-Communist stand after World War II. The electric power monopoly of Soviet-occupied North Korea, anti-United States and anti-United Nations radio broadcasts denouncing efforts at Korean unification, and the existence of an underground Communist "People's Republic" in South Korea in 1945, contributed to the South Korean abhorrence of any coalition with the Communists. A. C. Migliazzo

3416. Batochir, L. RUKOVODSTVO MNRP SOTSIALISTICHESKIM PREOBRAZOVANIEM SEL'SKOGO KHOZIAISTVA [The guidance of the Mongolian People's Revolutionary Party in the socialist transformation of agriculture]. *Voprosy Istorii KPSS [USSR] 1971 (3): 83-92.* Outlines the development of socialist agriculture in Mongolia, largely since 1947.

3417. Bednov, Iu. V. 50 LET KOMMUNISTICHESKOI PARTII FILIPPIN [The 50th anniversary of the Filipino Communist Party]. *Voprosy Istorii KPSS [USSR] 1980 (11): 156-158.* An account of a meeting 26 August 1979 in the Institute of Marxism-Leninism in the USSR to commemorate the 50th anniversary of the establishment of a Communist Party in the Philippines, discussing the history of the Party, the expulsion of a Maoist faction in 1967, and the internationalism of the Filipino Party from the 1930's onward. D. N. Collins

3418. Berton, Peter. THE JAPANESE COMMUNISTS' RAPPROCHEMENT WITH THE SOVIET UNION. *Asian Survey 1980 20(12): 1210-1222.* On 24 December 1979, the Japanese Communist Party (JCP) concluded a summit meeting with the Communist Party of the USSR, ending 15 years of strained relations between the two Communist parties. The Soviet Union benefited in public relations by obtaining this summit agreement with one of the largest nonruling Communist parties. The position of the JCP was strengthened in the pro-Soviet Communist camp but its prospects of improved relations with China were diminished, as was its image as an independent Japanese political party. Based on Japanese and Russian newspapers; 29 notes. M. A. Eide

3419. Berton, Peter. THE SOVIET AND JAPANESE COMMUNIST PARTIES: POLICIES, TACTICS, NEGOTIATING BEHAVIOR. *Studies in Comparative Communism 1982 15(3): 266-287.* The Japanese Communist Party sided with the Chinese in the early 1960's, but the relationship then deteriorated. By 1979, relations between the Japanese and Soviet Communists had normalized. Then the Japanese Communists condemned the invasion of Afghanistan. At a meeting between Japanese and Soviet leaders in December 1979, the Japanese brought up the question of the "Northern Territories," areas taken over by the Soviets after the war, but the Soviets refused to consider the question open to discussion. 61 notes. D. Balmuth

3420. Blackmur, Douglas. THE ALP INDUSTRIAL GROUPS IN QUEENSLAND. *Labour History [Australia] 1984 (46): 88-108.* The Australian Labor Party (ALP) industrial groups in Queensland arose as a response to Communist Party of Australia (CPA) influence on trade union activity in 1940's. The ALP groups soon became connected with Catholic labor activists, and after a brief period of hegemony in the labor union sphere splintered during the 1950's as a result of leadership ineffectiveness. 96 notes. L. J. Howell

3421. Blake, Audrey. THE EUREKA YOUTH LEAGUE: A PARTICIPANT'S REPORT. *Labour Hist. [Australia] 1982 (42): 94-105.* Discusses the socialist youth movement in Australia from 1930 to 1952. The Young Communist League of the 1920's was succeeded in 1939 in Victoria by the League of Young Democrats; when this was banned by the Menzies government in 1940, it became the Eureka Youth League in 1941. The EYL had strong links with the Communist Party and was especially popular among young women. Based on the author's personal experience. J. Powell

3422. Bowden, Tim. THE MAKING OF AN AUSTRALIAN COMMUNIST: RUPERT LOCKWOOD. *Politics [Australia] 1974 9(1): 10-21.* Reproduces a 1973 interview with journalist Rupert Lockwood in which he discusses the political events of the 1930's which converted him to communism; his activities as an Australian Communist, 1939-65; his rejection of the Communist Party in 1969, which was influenced by the USSR's Stalinist politics; his personal experiences in the Soviet Union, 1965-68; and the Warsaw Pact invasion of Czechoslovakia, 1968. C. A. McNeill

3423. Chiou C. L. and Tsiu-shuang Han. IDEOLOGY AND POLITICS IN THE 1966-1967 SPLIT BETWEEN THE COMMUNIST PARTIES OF CHINA AND JAPAN. *Studies in Comparative Communism 1978 11(4): 361-387.* In part the split between the Japanese and Chinese Communists resulted from Japanese involvement in Chinese political affairs. The joint statement of the parties in 1966 was drawn up by the Liu-Teng faction and was critical of revisionism. Mao demanded more explicit criticism of the Soviet leaders and the Japanese refused. Soon after came the attacks on Liu and Teng and then attacks on the Japanese Communists. 68 notes. D. Balmuth

3424. Chu, John. A COMPARISON OF TWO SYSTEMS OF SELECTING TALENTS. *Issues and Studies [Taiwan] 1973 10(2): 38-44.* Compares contemporary systems of talent selection in the United States and Communist China, praising the American dream of equal opportunity and condemning the tyranny of Communism.

3425. Coolidge, T. Jefferson, Jr. KOREA: THE CASE AGAINST WITHDRAWAL. *Asian Affairs: An Am. Rev. 1976 4(2): 71-84.* Analyzes the consequences of US withdrawal for the Republic of

Korea as a nation (military security, political stability, humanitarian concerns); US-Asian relations; and Soviet, Communist Chinese, and North Korean reactions. Primary sources; 3 notes.

R. B. Mendel

3426. Copper, John Franklin. THE JAPANESE COMMUNIST PARTY'S RECENT ELECTION DEFEATS: A SIGNAL OF DECLINE? *Asian Survey 1979 19(4): 353-365.* In the election of December 1976 the Japanese Communist Party (JCP) lost over half of its seats in the House of Representatives and in July 1977 the party lost four additional seats in the House of Councillors. Subscriptions to the party's newspaper declined as did membership in its affiliate organizations. These factors suggest that the Party's growth has peaked at least temporarily. 42 notes.

M. A. Eide

3427. Cumings, Bruce G. KIM'S KOREAN COMMUNISM. *Problems of Communism 1974 23(2): 27-41.* Investigates the specifically Korean aspects of the brand of communism developed in North Korea under Kim Il-sung. It has been decidedly nationalistic and self-reliant in tone and practice, and has involved an exceptionally high degree of politicization of the country's social organization. Since the Korean War, Pyongyang has even set itself up as a model for other emerging societies in the sphere of economic development. Based on primary and secondary sources; 72 notes.

J. M. Lauber

3428. Curthoys, Ann and Merritt, John, ed. *Australia's First Cold War, 1945-1953. Vol. 1: Society, Communism and Culture.* Winchester, Mass.: Allen & Unwin, 1985. 243 pp.

3429. Damdinsuren, S. ROL' KOMINTERNA V UKREPLENII MNRP NA PRINTSIPAKH MARKSIZMA-LENINIZMA I PROLETARSKOGO INTERNATSIONALIZMA [The role of the Comintern in strengthening the principles of Marxism-Leninism and proletarian internationalism in the Mongolian People's Republic]. *Voprosy Istorii KPSS [USSR] 1978 (1): 56-67.* An account of the part played by the Comintern from 1920 in building up Mongolian cadres to insure the success of Communism in that underdeveloped country.

3430. Durdin, Tillman. PHILIPPINE COMMUNISM. *Problems of Communism 1976 25(3): 40-48.* Examines the international and domestic factors affecting the fortunes of a divided Philippine Communist movement. The tactics used by the government are a combination of manipulation of the various Communist groups and their sponsors and a concerted effort at military suppression of the insurgent arm of the Peking-oriented group. Primary and secondary sources; map, 22 notes.

J. M. Lauber

3431. Emmerson, John K. THE JAPANESE COMMUNIST PARTY AFTER FIFTY YEARS. *Asian Survey 1972 12(7): 564-580.*

3432. Falkenheim, Peggy L. EUROCOMMUNISM IN ASIA: THE COMMUNIST PARTY OF JAPAN AND THE SOVIET UNION. *Pacific Affairs [Canada] 1979 51(1): 64-77.* Analyzes the relationship of the Communist Party in Japan to the Communist Party in the USSR from 1964 to 1978. The Russian Party discipline under Khrushchev, although less rigid than during the Stalin era, tended to react to dissident Japanese activities more strongly, often with less provocation, than did Chairman Brezhnev. Tensions between the Communist parties increased as Japan continued to side with China in international disputes. Ongoing questions about fishing rights and the Kurile Islands exacerbated these tensions. Secondary sources; 39 notes.

S. H. Frank

3433. Farrell, Frank. EXPLAINING COMMUNIST HISTORY. *Labour Hist. [Australia] 1977 (32): 1-10.* Details the attempts made by members of the Communist Party of Australia to relate their own history and to explain the accession to its leadership.

3434. Fessen, Helmut. ZUR FRAGE DER HISTORISCHEN MISSION DER ARBEITERKLASSE IN DEN ÖKONOMISCH SCHWACH ENTWICKELTEN LÄNDERN SÜDOSTASIENS [On the problem of the historic mission of the working class in the economically weak countries of Southeast Asia]. *Wissenschaftliche Zeitschrift der Humboldt-Universität zu Berlin [East Germany] 1974 23(2): 127-133.* Real proletarians, few in numbers in all Southeast Asia, are village and family oriented, separated from each other by differences of race, by the effects of colonialism, and the varieties of religion. Although after World War II and independence Marxist parties existed everywhere, their weakness, lack of ideology, and the strong forces facing them prevented their assuming leadership anywhere. The author outlines Communist efforts in Burma, Malaya, and the Philippines. Some indications of Communist leadership in social reforms may lead toward socialism, especially in Burma, but no one road to a Communist state seems likely for the whole area in the near future. 28 notes, biblio.

M. Faissler

3435. Hammond, Thomas T. THE COMMUNIST TAKEOVER OF OUTER MONGOLIA: MODEL FOR EASTERN EUROPE? *Studies on the Soviet Union [West Germany] 1971 11(4): 107-144.* Outer Mongolia is important in the history of world Communization not only because it represented the first successful spread of revolution beyond the borders of the Soviet Union, but also because the methods used became models for subsequent takeovers in post-World War II Eastern Europe. A revolutionary party was established, a provisional government and native army were organized on Soviet soil, and the Red Army invaded to prepare the way for the exile native regime to assume power. The Soviet Union retained the positions of real power and gradually solidified its hold. Secondary sources; 122 notes.

V. L. Human

3436. Han Bae-ho. NAMBOOKHAN EUY CHUNGCHI CHAEJAE EUY BYKYO SUSUL (I) [Toward a comparative analysis of the South and North Korean political systems]. *J. of Asiatic Studies [South Korea] 1971 14(3): 1-48.* Analyzes the distinctive characteristics of the South and North Korean political systems, examining the political elite, political groups, authority structures, and policies. The political elites formed under Japanese rule within the nationalist and communist movements. The author describes the ideologies, social and psychological characteristics, structures, and strategic differences of the movements. 82 notes. Article to be continued.

Y. C. Ro

3437. Itoh, Hiroshi. COMPARATIVE INQUIRY INTO THE FAILURE OF THE JAPANESE COMMUNIST PARTY. *Asian Thought and Soc. 1979 4(11): 189-204.* Unlike in China, the Communist Party in Japan has not been successful, 1950's-70's, because of the opposition of all other political parties, the strength of non-Communist opposition parties, public perception of the Party as a conspiratorial group, and the recent decline in economic growth.

3438. Johnston, Craig. THE COMMUNIST PARTY OF AUSTRALIA AND THE PALESTINIAN REVOLUTION, 1967-1976. *Labour Hist. [Australia] 1979 (37): 86-100.* The Palestinian-Israeli conflict presented the Communist Party of Australia (CPA) with an insoluble dilemma in theory and practice. The CPA, traditionally with a prominent Jewish membership, in 1948 and 1967 supported the existence of Israel. After 1970 policy began to alter, especially in Victoria where support for the UN Resolution 242 was strong. In 1973, the CPA sided with Egypt and Syria. Yet, in 1974 a clear stand in opposition to Israel proved impossible to achieve. In 1975 the CPA national committee supported a call for a conference in Geneva to initiate the Israeli withdrawal from territory occupied in 1967. The national conference refused to deal with the issue and again the CPA failed to formulate a position of the Arab-Israeli conflict. Based heavily on the *Tribune* (Sydney); 90 notes.

D. F. Schafer

3439. Kaul, Man Mohini. THE MARCOS REGIME IN THE PHILIPPINES. *India Q. [India] 1978 34(3): 313-327.* Examines the Communist and Moslem opposition to the government of Ferdinand Marcos in the Philippines. In 1942, when the People's Anti-Japanese Army, later styled the Hukbalahap or Huks, organized, their membership was not entirely Communist. After independence, however, they rose in an insurrection that was suppressed only in 1950 under the leadership of Ramón Magsaysay. In 1957 the Communist Party was legally banned. In 1968 José Ma Sison founded Kabataang Makabayan, a coalition of militant student groups which later became the New People's Army. Islam came to the Philippines in 1380 but was turned back by the Spanish conquerors in 1542 except in Mindanao. After independence, the Christian-dominated government tried to force religious and political assimilation on the Moslems. By 1972 a militant Moro National Liberation Front was active and supported by Libya. Although closely tied to the United States by military and trade agreements, Marcos was unable to bring American intervention in the Philippines to counter his Communist and Moslem enemies. Based on secondary sources; 78 notes. S. H. Frank

3440. Kho, David S. "The Transition to Communism in North Korea (1953-1970): A Critical Analysis." York University [Canada] 1981. *DAI 1985 45(8): 2642-2643-A.*

3441. Kim, Hak-joon. THE RISE OF KIM CHONG-IL: IMPLICATIONS FOR NORTH KOREA'S INTERNAL AND EXTERNAL POLICIES IN THE 1980'S. *J. of Northeast Asian Studies 1983 2(2): 81-92.* Kim Jong-il has the power base and is virtually certain to succeed his father as North Korea's leader, but his policy intentions remain unclear and he faces some Party opposition.

3442. Kim, Hong N. DERADICALIZATION OF THE JAPANESE COMMUNIST PARTY UNDER KENJI MIYAMOTO. *World Pol. 1976 28(2): 273-299.* The phenomenal growth of the Japanese Communist Party's electoral strength during a period of unprecedented economic growth and prosperity (1961-74) clearly deviates from Benjamin's and Kautsky's "curvilinear theory" of the economic development and strength of Communist parties. Nor does it conform to Lipset's hypothesis that there exists an inverse correlation between the economic growth and the strength of Communist parties. The recent growth in the JCP's organizational strength and electoral successes should be ascribed to the overall deradicalization of the party which has taken place since 1961. The findings of this study substantiate theories on deradicalization of the Marxist movement advanced earlier by Robert Michels and more recently by Robert C. Tucker, who hypothesized that there exists an inverse correlation between the deradicalization of a revolutionary party and its "worldly success." His findings also confirm Triska's and Finley's hypothesis that deradicalized Communist parties in the developed countries would become not significantly different from other non-Communist parties either in structure or functions. J

3443. Kim, Hong N. THE JCP'S PARLIAMENTARY ROAD. *Problems of Communism 1977 26(2): 19-35.* Examines the quest for power of the Japanese Communist Party (JCP) and its strategy in recent years, emphasizing its electoral performance. Analyzes the factors behind the JCP's electoral debacle of 5 December 1976 and the implications of recent developments for the JCP's future course and prospects. Based on primary and secondary Japanese and English language sources; 99 notes. J. M. Lauber

3444. Kim, Samuel S. BOOK REVIEW—RESEARCH ON CONTEMPORARY COMMUNISM: THE KOREAN CASE. *J. of Korean Affairs 1975 5(1): 52-68.* Reviews Robert A. Scalapino and Chong-sik Lee's *Communism in Korea* (U. of California Pr., 1973), dealing with political, educational, ideological, and socioeconomic characteristics of Korea, 1918-72.

3445. Kim, Samuel S. RESEARCH ON KOREAN COMMUNISM: PROMISE VERSUS PERFORMANCE. *World Pol. 1980 32(2): 281-310.* Review article on six recent books on North Korean communism. Examines the performance of current scholarship on North Korean politics in light of the promise of the comparative study of communism, identifying key normative, conceptual, and methodological problems that plague the current lines of inquiry in the field, probing the areas of substantive strengths, weaknesses, and gaps in our present knowledge about the North Korean political system, focusing on two issues of normative and policy importance to both domestic and foreign policy—legitimacy and *chuch'e.* 36 notes. J/S

3446. Kim Nam Sik. BOOKHAN EUY KONGSANHUA KWAJUNG KWA KEIKEUP NOSUN [The communization process and class line in North Korea]. *J. of Asiatic Studies [South Korea] 1971 14(3): 95-142, (4): 127-172.* Part I. The process of the application and realization of the class-struggle in North Korea. The setting up and the practices of the North Korean Communist Party's class line were intrinsically related to the communization process. Korean communization passed through the periods of the democratic revolution, the transition to socialism, and the building of socialism. 2 tables, 72 notes. Part II. Describes the activities of the Communist Party during the period of the basic building of socialism, 1953-60, to change the revolutionary democratic base to a socialist one, to create a socialist economy, and to establish a socialist social order. 151 notes. Y. C. Ro

3447. Koh, B. C. THE IMPACT OF THE CHINESE MODEL ON KOREA. *Asian Survey 1978 18(6): 626-643.* China's Communist government was the product of a revolution, whereas the Democratic People's Republic of Korea was installed during the Soviet occupation after World War II. Yet Mao Tse-tung's modifications of Marxism were echoed by Kim Il-sung, and the Communist parties of both nations share the same pyramidal hierarchy. Both Mao and Kim cultivated myths about themselves, and relied heavily on indoctrinating their people with the "correct" ideology. Following China's lead, North Korea has adopted policies increasingly independent of the Kremlin. Admitting China's enormous influence, Korea has shaped many Marxist tenets to suit peculiarly Korean problems. 31 notes. J. W. Leedom

3448. Kovalenko, I. STRUGGLE OF THE COMMUNIST PARTY OF JAPAN FOR DEMOCRATIC REFORMS. *Far Eastern Affairs [USSR] 1980 (2): 52-71.* Describes the growth and unification of the Communist Party of Japan, which has expressed and defended the interests of the masses against the Liberal Democratic Party, the representative of monopoly capital.

3449. Kovalenko, I. I. KOMMUNISTICHESKAIA PARTIIA IAPONII V BOR'BE PROTIV LEVOGO EKSTREMIZMA [The Communist Party of Japan in the struggle against Leftist extremism, 1950-55]. *Narody Azii i Afriki [USSR] 1981 (1): 40-52.* In the early 1950's the Party, overestimating the revolutionary situation worked for armed insurrection, a damaging mistake. After the peace treaty with the United States (1952), there was greater realism, taking account of the very complicated national peculiarities and conditions and the presence in Communist parties generally of persons affected by bourgeois ideology. Based on Japanese Communist publications. E. S. Kirby

3450. Kovalenko, I. I. OPYT BOR'BY IAPONSKIKH KOMMUNISTOV ZA SOZDANIE MASSOVOI AVANGARDNOI PARTII [The struggle by the Japanese Communists to create a mass avant-garde party]. *Voprosy Istorii KPSS [USSR] 1980 (7): 33-45.* The meeting between the representatives of the Communist Party of the Soviet Union (CPSU) and the Communist Party of Japan in December 1979 showed that despite disagreements on minor issues both parties hold consonant views on a large number of key problems. The history of the Japanese Party's efforts at building up its membership is a valuable lesson for the whole international communist movement. Currently the Party has 440,000 members and its goal is one million members. Based on the Japanese press and documents published by the Communist Party of Japan; 27 notes. V. Sobell

3451. Kovalenko, Ivan I. KOMMUNISTICHESKOE DVIZHENIE V IAPONII V PERVYE POSLEVOENNYE GODY [The Communist movement in Japan during the early postwar years]. *Voprosy Istorii [USSR] 1980 (8): 72-84.* Describes the struggle of progressive forces led by the Japanese Communist Party (JCP) for the democratization and demilitarization of Japan following surrender. Traces the reestablishment of the Communist Party, highlights its achievements, and analyzes its early difficulties. These difficulties were caused not only by the repressive actions of the American occupation forces and Japanese reactionaries, but also by the mistakes committed in formulating the party's strategic course in the harsh conditions created by the occupation. J/S

3452. Krauss, Ellis S. THE URBAN STRATEGY AND POLICY OF THE JAPANESE COMMUNIST PARTY: KYOTO. *Studies in Comparative Communism 1979 12(4): 322-350.* The Japanese Communist Party has grown in strength since 1966 because of its policy of building alliances with other leftist groups and its support of local interests. In Kyoto the strategy resulted in great local strength, about 25% of the votes in local elections. Its power has brought no significant variation in local expenditures except that personnel expenditures for teachers, strong supporters of the party, are higher than elsewhere. The 1979 election showed an end of growth. Based on newspaper accounts; 82 notes. D. Balmuth

3453. Kudinov, V. P. KOMMUNISTY V RABOCHEM DVIZHENII NOVOI ZELANDII [Communists in the New Zealand labor movement]. *Voprosy Istorii [USSR] 1981 (12): 66-80.* Survey of the New Zealand Communist movement over the 60 years of its existence—from the establishment in 1921 of the Communist Party of New Zealand (CPNZ) to the present. The party was popular among the working masses when it pursued a Marxist-Leninist course. However, when, in the 1960's, it shifted to the positions of ultraleftism and Maoism and followed Beijing's divisive policies in the international Communist movement, it lost worker support and became a narrow sectarian organization. The Socialist Unity Party of New Zealand formed in 1966 continued the Marxist-Leninist internationalist traditions of the former CPNZ in the labor movement. It is widely represented in New Zealand trade unions and enjoys support and prestige among the progressive forces in New Zealand and the international Communist and workers' movement. J

3454. Kudinov, V. P. RABOCHEE DVIZHENIE I KOMMUNISTY NOVOI ZELANDII [The working-class movement and Communists of New Zealand]. *Voprosy Istorii KPSS [USSR] 1981 (2): 98-101.* Discusses the development of New Zealand socialism and Communism from the founding of the miner's union-based Federation of Labor in 1911 until the present day. A group of miners formed the New Zealand Marxist Association in 1918 and sent the secretary to America to obtain information and literature on the Russian revolution. The Communist Party was founded in 1921 and could claim 2,500 members by 1946. During the second world war the Communist Party helped provide the Soviet Union with much-needed medicine and clothing. In the 1960's the Communist Party lost influence among the trade unions and became isolated from the labor movement. A new party with a Marxist-Leninist basis was formed, calling itself the Socialist Unity Party of New Zealand. 10 notes. A. Brown

3455. Kudinov, V. P. 60-LETIE KOMMUNISTICHESKOGO DVIZHENIIA V AVSTRALII [Sixtieth anniversary of the Australian Communist movement]. *Voprosy Istorii [USSR] 1980 (12): 69-81.* Discusses the history of the Australian Communist movement, covering the founding of the Communist Party of Australia in 1920 and its consistent internationalist Marxist-Leninist policy up to the mid-1960's, and the founding of the Socialist Party of Australia in 1972, which has worked for Left unity, international working-class and Communist solidarity against imperialism and for peace and socialism. J/S

3456. Lee, Changsoo. CHOSOREN: AN ANALYSIS OF THE KOREAN COMMUNIST MOVEMENT IN JAPAN. *J. of Korean Affairs 1973 3(2): 3-32.* Gives background on the political action by Koreans in Japan since 1945 and analyzes Chosoren, a quasi-government agent of the North Korean regime.

3457. Lee, Tosh. TOKYO METROPOLITAN ASSEMBLY ELECTION: 1973. *Asian Survey 1974 14(5): 478-488.* The election was "primarily a showdown" between the Liberal-Democratic Party and the Japan Communist Party.

3458. Lee Joong-Koon. NORTH KOREAN FOREIGN TRADE IN RECENT YEARS AND THE PROSPECTS FOR NORTH-SOUTH KOREAN TRADE. *J. of Korean Affairs 1974 4(3): 18-32.* Discusses political factors in North Korean trade with Communist countries and Europe in the 1960's and 1970's and the prospects for trade between North and South Korea.

3459. Lkhamsuren, B. OPYT STANOVLENIIA I UKREPLENIIA MNRP KAK PARTII MARKSISTSKO-LENINSKOGO TIPA [The experience of the formation and strengthening of the Mongolian People's Revolutionary Party (MPRP) as a Party of Marxist-Leninist type]. *Voprosy Istorii KPSS [USSR] 1975 (7): 31-43.* With the help of the USSR and the Comintern, the Mongolian People's Revolutionary Party united the Mongolian peasantry and workers in a struggle for national independence and socialism. It successfully completed the transition of Mongolia from feudalism to socialism, bypassing capitalism in the process; rejected left and right opportunism, including contemporary Maoism; and cooperated with authentic Marxist-Leninist parties throughout the world. Based on published primary and secondary sources; 22 notes. L. E. Holmes

3460. Lo Shih-fu. DISTURBANCES IN THE PHILIPPINES AND THE STRATEGY OF THE PHILIPPINE COMMUNISTS. *Issues & Studies [Taiwan] 1971 8(2): 75-83.* Analyzes the subversive activities of the Communist Party in the Philippines from 1941 to 1970.

3461. Lo Shih-fu. THE MORO REBELLION: ITS HISTORY AND BACKGROUND. *Issues and Studies [Taiwan] 1973 10(1): 41-51.* Traces the historical roots of the Moro secessionist movement in the Philippines from the introduction of Islam in 1450. The contemporary power struggle is more than a religious and national conflict, as it is directly supported by the Communist Party in Peking as well as Manila.

3462. Luther, Hans U. GOVERNMENT CAMPAIGNS IN SOUTH KOREA: EXORCISM AND PURIFICATION OF NATURE AND PEOPLE. *Internationales Asienforum [West Germany] 1980 11(1-2): 61-77.* Describes and analyzes several different government campaigns that have been promoted in South Korea since 1961 to mobilize the people and to implement "social discipline" in order to increase labor productivity, promote nation building and maintain anti-Communist indoctrination.

3463. McCalman, Janet. THE BRODNEY PAPERS. *Labour Hist. [Australia] 1981 (40): 95-96.* The papers of A. T. "Bob" Brodney and his wife, May Francis, have been placed in the Manuscripts Collection of the La Trobe Library. May Francis's collection is the larger, covering such topics as World Wars I and II anticonscription campaigns, trade unions, labor movement, the Communist Party in Melbourne, and considerable biographical material. Bob's collection includes biographical material, material on the Communist Party, labor litigations, spies and revolutionaries, intellectual activities in Sydney and Melbourne, and an autobiographical tape recording. Radical literature is well represented. The papers are a major addition to the labor archives of Australia. D. F. Schafer

3464. Merrill, John. THE CHEJU-DO REBELLION. *J. of Korean Studies 1980 2: 139-197.* The island of Cheju has a long history of weak government control and periodic rebellions. The last traditional rebellion occurred in 1901, caused by the establishment of a new tax administration and the introduction of Catholicism there. The most appalling rebellion, however, began on 3 April 1948, and was led by Communist guerrilla bands. Only by 1953 were the last remnants of the guerrillas eliminated. During the rebellion about 10% of the island's population was killed. Only in the 1960's did the island finally begin to recover. Based on Korean, Communist, and American archival and secondary sources; 156 notes. H. S. Marks

3465. Minis, A. GEGEN DIE MAOISTISCHE KONZEPTION VON DER ARBEITERKLASSE UND ZUR ROLLE DER ARBEITERKLASSE IN DER MONGOLISCHEN VOLKSPARTEI [Against the Maoist conception of the working class and on the role of the working class in the Mongolian Peoples' Party]. *Beiträge zur Geschichte der Arbeiterbewegung [East Germany] 1974 16(5): 816-820.* According to V. I. Lenin the working class is the pivotal social group. This interpretation of Marxism rejects the primacy of the peasantry as proposed by Mao Tse-tung; the combination of worker and peasant only weakens the working-class ideology as it removes the Chinese from the international movement. Mao's error is made apparent by the 500 percent increase in the working-class sector of Chinese society over the past three decades. Secondary materials; note. G. H. Libbey

3466. Mirov, A. IUBILEI MONGOL'SKIKH KOMMUNISTOV [Jubilee of the Mongolian Communists]. *Aziia i Afrika Segodnia [USSR] 1981 (3): 25-26.* Shows key political, economic, and cultural achievements in Mongolia in 1976-80.

3467. Morris, Stephen J. A SCANDALOUS JOURNALISTIC CAREER. *Commentary 1981 72(5): 69-77.* Reviews the career and autobiography of Australian journalist Wilfred Burchett and claims that Burchett's political reportage in various countries has consistently corresponded with the ideology of the Australian Communist Party.

3468. Mortimer, Rex. UNRESOLVED PROBLEMS OF THE INDONESIAN COUP. *Australian Outlook [Australia] 1971 25(1): 94-101.* Reviews Arnold C. Brachman's *The Communist Collapse in Indonesia* (Singapore: Donald Moore for Pacific Press, 1970). The thesis that the Communist Party was responsible for the abortive coup in Indonesia in 1965 has weaknesses. Brachman places the coup in an international context and attempts to establish that Sukarno gave prior approval for it. The book has more errors, misstatements, and distortions than are acceptable. Secondary sources; 11 notes. E. Plumridge

3469. Nam, Koon Woo. THE PURGE OF THE SOUTHERN COMMUNIST IN NORTH KOREA: A RETROSPECTIVE VIEW. *Asian Forum 1973 5(1): 43-54.* Discusses the purges of the South Korean Communists carried out by Kim Il-sung, the North Korean Premier and Chairman of the Korean Workers' Party, indicating that the charges against South Korean communists were groundless. The mass purges of South Korean communists had important effects upon the subsequent development of North Korean communism. 44 notes. R. B. Orr

3470. Nastiuk, M. I. and Minaiev, O. I. 60-RICHCHIA VYZVOLENNIA ZABAIKALLIA TA DALEKOHO SKHODU VID INTERVENTIV I BILOHVARDIITSIV [The 60th anniversary of the liberation of Trans-Baikal and the Far East from interventionists and the White Guards]. *Ukrains'kyi Istorychnyi Zhurnal [USSR] 1982 (10): 145-149.* Discusses the 60th anniversary of the liberation of the Trans-Baikal and the Far East from the Japanese and the White Guards. This region played the role of a buffer between the USSR and Japan. Gives a brief history of the struggle in the region and shows the development of the military and the growth of Communist partisan groups and the Communist Party. L. Djakowska

3471. Nesterov, A. ARMIIA TRUDOVOGO NARODA [The army of the working people]. *Voenno-Istoricheskii Zhurnal [USSR] 1982 (4): 70-72.* On 25 April 1932, the Korean Communists, led by Kim Il-sung, founded the first units of the army which was to fight against the Japanese in the 1930's and in World War II and thus contributed to the creation of the Korean People's Democratic Republic. Between 1950 and 1953 the soldiers of the Korean army fought bravely against American forces in the Korean War, as a result of which the plans of the imperialists were thwarted and Korea preserved its independence. Based on secondary sources; 5 notes. G. Dombrovski

3472. Openshaw, Roger. "A SPIRIT OF BOLSHEVISM": THE WEITZEL CASE OF 1921 AND ITS IMPACT ON THE NEW ZEALAND EDUCATIONAL SYSTEM. *Pol. Sci. [New Zealand] 1981 33(2): 127-139.* Discusses the impact of the 1921 sedition trial of college student Hedwig Weitzel on New Zealand's educational system from 1921 to 1981, commenting on the political atmosphere in New Zealand during the 1920's with respect to communism.

3473. Park, Jae Kyu. FACTIONS AND POWER RELATIONS IN THE NORTH KOREAN COMMUNIST REGIME. *Asian Forum 1973 5(2): 60-78.* Analyzes the origins of political factions in the North Korean Communist Party, and their relations with Kim Il-sung. Secondary sources; 17 tables, 23 notes. R. B. Orr

3474. Prybyla, Jan S. *HSIA-FANG*: THE ECONOMICS AND POLITICS OF RUSTICATION IN CHINA. *Pacific Affairs [Canada] 1975 48(2): 153-172.* Analyzes the practice of *hsia-fang* in the People's Republic of China which in 1961-63 sent some 20 million urban dwellers to the countryside and in 1969-73 moved over 8 million urban youths to work on farms and rural projects. Its objectives were mainly economic, the prevention and reduction of intellectual unemployment in the cities. But *hsia-fang* included strong elements of ideological reeducation and punishment. Moreover, this practice also tended to shift allegiances away from the family unit. This transfer of the young and relatively well-educated also helped to raise the level of technical and other skills necessary to modernize agricultural production. These *hsia-fang* activities of manual labor and contact with the peasant masses vary from *lao-kai* farms (concentration camps) to vacation-type retreats. Notes the rising level of dissatisfaction and frustration among rusticated young intellectuals. Based on field study in China in 1974 and secondary sources; 40 notes. S. H. Frank

3475. Pye, Lucian W. SCHOLARSHIP PENETRATES THE LAST HOLD-OUT OF STALINISM. *Freedom at Issue 1974 (26): 10-13.* Reviews Robert A. Scalapino's and Chong-Sik Lee's *Communism in Korea, the Movement* and *Communism in Korea, the Society* (Berkeley: U. of California Pr., 1972), dealing with communism, totalitarianism, economics, and politics in North Korea, 1950's-70's.

3476. Rohlen, Thomas P. VIOLENCE AT YOKA HIGH SCHOOL: THE IMPLICATIONS FOR JAPANESE COALITION POLITICS OF THE CONFRONTATION BETWEEN THE COMMUNIST PARTY AND THE BURAKU LIBERATION LEAGUE. *Asian Survey 1976 16(7): 682-699.* Examines the effects which a split in the Buraku Liberation League (partially supported by the Socialists and partially supported by the Communists) had on national politics, especially the withdrawal of candidacy of Tokyo's leftist governor, Ryokichi Minobe, and the eruption of violence in a high school in Tajima in 1974 over the rights of Burakumin students.

3477. Rosenberg, David A. COMMUNISM IN THE PHILIPPINES. *Problems of Communism 1984 33(5): 24-46.* There has been a considerable revival in the fortunes of the Maoist-oriented Communist Party of the Philippines (CPP), along with its New People's Army and its political coalition, the National Democratic Front. This is due largely to a shift among a new generation of radical leaders toward a Filipino version of "people's war"; to a lack of other means to express popular grievances; and to a decline in the Marcos government's political authority in the year since the assassination of Benigno Aquino. The CPP may yet pose a significant threat to the Marcos, and to post-Marcos Philippine authorities. Based on newspapers and government studies both in the United States and the Philippines; 80 notes. J. M. Lauber

3478. Ross, Jeffrey A. THE MONGOLIAN PEOPLE'S REPUBLIC AS A PROTOTYPICAL CASE FOR THE DEVELOPMENT OF A COMPARATIVE POLITICS OF COMMUNIST SYSTEMS. *Canada-Mongolia Rev. [Canada] 1978 4(1): 1-15.* Extends Thomas Hammond's work, which used Mongolia to study the means and effects of revolution in Communist countries. Quickly reviews the history of Mongolia since the 17th century, noting especially the role of factionalism and foreign dependence. Secondary sources; 43 notes. J. F. Harrington, Jr.

3479. Santamaria, B. A. "THE SPLIT." *Australian Q. [Australia] 1971 43(2): 98-103.* Reviews Robert Murral's *The Split: Australian Labour in the Fifties* (The Cheshire Group) on the presence of communists in the Australian labor movement.

3480. Scheidig, Robert E. A COMPARISON OF COMMUNIST NEGOTIATING METHODS. *Military Rev. 1974 54(12): 79-89.* Compares and analyzes Communist peace negotiating methods in Korea and Vietnam.

3481. Suh, Dae-sook. *Korean Communism 1945-1980: A Reference Guide to the Political System.* Honolulu: U. Pr. of Hawaii, 1981. 592 pp.

3482. Tamginski, I. I. IZ ISTORII BOR'BY KOMMUNISTICHESKOI PARTII IAPONII PROTIV PRAVOGO OPPORTUNIZMA (1945-1950 GG.) [The Japanese Communist Party's struggle against right-wing opportunism, 1945-50: a historical survey]. *Narody Azii i Afriki [USSR] 1980 (3): 55-65.* The defeat of Japan's fascist-military regime enabled the reborn Communist Party to become a leader in the people's drive for democracy and national independence, despite repression by the Japanese government and American occupation forces. However, inefficient party leadership, parochialism, underrating of the importance of ideology in cadre training, and errors of strategy and tactics in the fight against right deviationists caused intraparty discord and led to a party split in 1950. 30 notes. N. Frenkley

3483. Taxubayev, A. PEOPLE'S MONGOLIA: NEW HORIZONS. *Int. Affairs [USSR] 1976 (10): 67-75.* Reports on economic growth, agricultural development, and increased participation in international relations on the part of Mongolia, 1970-76, as reported at the 17th Congress of the Mongolian People's Revolutionary Party, 1976.

3484. Tsedental, Iumzhagiin. SOTSIALISTICHESKAIA DEISTVITEL'NOST' MONGOLII: VOPLOSHCHENIE IDEI LENINA [The socialist reality of Mongolia: the embodiment of the ideas of Lenin]. *Voprosy Istorii KPSS [USSR] 1970 (4): 34-45.* Traces the influence of V. I. Lenin's ideas on the formation of the People's Revolutionary Party and the 1921 Revolution in Mongolia, as well as the country's progress since that time.

3485. Tsymbal, S. M. MONGOL'SKOI NARODNO-REVOLIUTSIONNOI PARTII—60 LET [The Mongolian People's Revolutionary Party is 60 years old]. *Voprosy Istorii KPSS [USSR] 1981 (5): 146-151.* A February 1981 Moscow conference celebrated the March 1921 founding of the Mongolian People's Revolutionary Party (MPRP). Bourgeois historians slander the MPRP, as they are unable to understand real socialism in practice. The MPRP, helped by the Communist Party of the Soviet Union (CPSU) and the Soviet people, showed that it is possible to pass directly from feudalism to socialism. The relations between the MPRP and the CPSU are a model of the relations between new style parties. The Soviet and Mongolian peoples are linked by economic and political ties and by deep mutual affection. Based on MPRP and CPSU conference reports; 5 notes. A. J. Evans

3486. VanderKroef, Justus M. AUSTRALIAN COMMUNISM: THE SPLINTERING PRISM. *J. of Internat. Affairs 1974 28(2): 206-218.* Though small and badly fragmented, Australian communism is powerful in labor and intellectual circles. Detente is unimportant and ignored. R. D. Frederick

3487. VanderKroef, Justus M. CLASS STRUCTURE AND ECONOMIC DEVELOPMENT IN INDONESIAN AND PHILIPPINE COMMUNISM: A COMPARATIVE ANALYSIS. *Asian Thought and Soc. 1976 1(3): 266-290.* Compares the class structure and development of Indonesian society under the influence of the Indonesian Communist Party (PKI) with that of communism in the Philippines.

3488. VanderKroef, Justus M. PHILIPPINE COMMUNIST THEORY AND STRATEGY: A NEW DEPARTURE? *Pacific Affairs [Canada] 1975 48(2): 181-198.* Analyzes the theories and strategies of the Maoist-oriented Communist Party of the Philippines, Marxist-Leninist (CPP-ML), and the older Moscow-oriented Communist Party of the Philippines (PKP), 1973-75. The Marcos government's accelerating interest in improving its relations with China and the USSR made it easier for these groups to carry on their efforts than had been the case for decades. The extraordinary organizational and tactical stress in the CPP-ML in the North and the Moslem insurgents in the South suggests that the Chinese do not really exercise a controlling role. Indeed, the Moslem rebellion is advantageous as a tactical irritant but may prove dangerous to both the CPP-ML and the PKP if its successes continue. Secondary sources; 23 notes. S. H. Frank

3489. VanderKroef, Justus M. THE PHILIPPINE MAOISTS. *Orbis 1976 16(4): 892-897.* Discusses the role of the New People's Army in the Philippines since 1969.

3490. Vrevski, V. and Ivanov, V. THE SOVIET POSITION ON QUESTIONS OF NORMALIZING POLITICAL RELATIONS AND OF DEVELOPING ECONOMIC RELATIONS IN THE PACIFIC OCEAN REGION. *Soviet Studies in Hist. 1983 21(4): 87-115.* As a leading Pacific Ocean power, the USSR has a vital interest in working for peace and stability throughout the vast Pacific Area. On numerous occasions, the Soviet Union has demonstrated its commitments to a normalization of relationships among the countries of the Pacific. If a "Pacific Ocean Association" of peace loving states is to develop along lines beneficial to all parties, the United States and other capitalistic countries must clearly show that they are not committed to the economic isolation of the socialist countries. 22 notes. M. R. Yerburgh

3491. Wagner, Jeffrey P. SANO MANABU AND THE JAPANIZATION OF MARXISM-LENINISM. *Asian Profile [Hong Kong] 1979 7(3): 231-248.* Discusses the political career and thought of Sano Manabu, leader of the Japanese Communist Party, 1927-32. During the years 1932 and 1933 he denounced the Japanese Communist Party and was "reborn" as a Japanese nationalist. Throughout his career he retained his agreement with Marxist-Leninist doctrine and continued to support liberation movements, but he discarded the Marxist notions of economic determinism and reaffirmed the necessity of the Japanese emperor system and Japanese nationalism. Secondary sources; 65 notes. J. Powell

3492. Warhurst, John. CATHOLICS, COMMUNISM AND THE AUSTRALIAN PARTY SYSTEM. *Politics [Australia] 1979 14(2): 222-242.* Critics of Robert G. Menzies and other observers have claimed that he owed his success in seven elections between 1949 and 1963 to his astute use in election campaigns of the "Communist bogey." Between 1949 and 1958 a realigning electoral era took place in Australia, with realignment occurring at different times in different states. The realignment took place because a significant number of Catholic voters transferred their allegiance from the Australian Labor Party to other parties, in a movement of which the emergence of the Democratic Labor Party represents only one part. This transfer was the result of a complex process in which the communism issue played a significant role, so that the conventional explanation, based largely on socioeconomic factors to the neglect of the issue, has distorted our understanding of this period. J

3493. Yamamoto, Kiyoshi. SENGO KIKI NI OKERU "TAISHJI" UNDŌ [The "mass demonstration" movements during the postwar crisis]. *Shakai Kagaku Kenkyū [Japan] 1975 26(6): 72-115.* Discusses the mass demonstration movements that occurred between 15 August 1945, the end of the Pacific War, and 20 May 1946, the day the Mass Movement Prohibition statement was issued by Douglas MacArthur. Examines the guiding principles of the movement—especially of the "food struggle" by the Communist Party—the organization of the movement, its actions and its historical significance. 3 tables, notes. Y. Ishihara

3494. Yu, Lydia N. THE JAPAN COMMUNIST PARTY. *Japan Q. [Japan] 1974 21(3): 265-272.* Politics in Japan "now seem to be at the threshold of a major change" and of all the indicators of this change "the growing strength of the Japanese Communist Party (JCP)... seems to be the most interesting." There have been five significant turning points in the history of the postwar Japanese Communist Party: the 1949 general election; the eighth congress held in July 1961; the tenth congress of October 1966; the eleventh congress of July 1970; and the general election of 1972. Throughout the years since 1949, the JCP has proclaimed its independence from any foreign intervention, a policy of peaceful revolution, the manipulation of economic problems, and the creation of "a coalition government through parliamentary means." It does seem "the best that the JCP could hope for is its participation in a coalition government." A. N. Garland

3495. —. [AUSTRALIA'S MAOISTS]. *J. of Commonwealth Pol. Studies [Great Britain] 1971 9(1): 68-69.*

McQueen, Humphrey. SOME COMMENTS ON 'AUSTRALIA'S MAOISTS.' *p. 68.* Continued from a previous article by Justus M. VanderKroef. Criticizes Justus M. VanderKroef's paper concerning the Communist Party of Australia and suggests that his sources are inadequate and that much of his analysis is erroneous.

VanderKroef, Justus M. A REJOINDER. *p. 69.* Refutes Humphrey McQueen's criticism, denies that he has used anti-Communist sources, and reaffirms his original position.

3496. —. [MINOR PROTAGONISTS]. *Politics [Australia] 1973 8(1): 97-112.* Mayer, Henry, ed. *Labor to Power: Australia's 1972 Election* (Angus & Robertson, 1973).

McIntyre, Angus. THE NARCISSISM OF MINOR DIFFERENCES: THE ELECTORAL CONTEST IN SYDNEY BETWEEN THE COMMUNIST PARTY OF AUSTRALIA AND THE SOCIALIST PARTY OF AUSTRALIA, pp. 97-104.

Richards, Mike and Edwards, Max. GUARDIANS OF ETERNAL TRUTHS: THE LEAGUE OF RIGHTS AND THE ELECTION, pp. 105-110.

Harcourt, David. AN ASSAULT ON THE JEW-DEMOCRATIC NUT-MAD HOUSE, pp. 111-112.

5. COMMUNISM IN AFRICA AND THE MIDDLE EAST

General

3497. Cooley, John K. THE SHIFTING SANDS OF ARAB COMMUNISM. *Problems of Communism 1975 24(2): 22-42.* Explores the interaction between the political fortunes of the Arab Communists and the ups and downs in the relations between the Arab governments and Moscow. Uses the four key Arab countries of Egypt, Syria, Iraq, and Lebanon as case studies to illustrate different aspects of this interaction. Primary and secondary sources; 47 notes. J. M. Lauber

3498. Gavrilov, Iurii Nikolaevich. PROBLEMY FORMIROVANIIA AVANGARDNOI PARTII V STRANAKH SOTSIALISTICHESKOI ORIENTATSII [Problems in the formation of vanguard parties in socialist-oriented countries]. *Narody Azii i Afriki [USSR] 1980 (6): 10-23.* Logical evolution of anti-imperialist Third World liberation movements leads to the formation of a Communist vanguard based on the ideology of scientific socialism, which eventually gains control of the mass movement: Angola, Benin, Congo, Ethiopia, Mozambique, South Yemen. Major impediments to the development of vanguard parties arise from the absence of an indigenous progressive intelligentsia, the survival of residual capitalism, and foreign and domestic exploitation. 53 notes. N. Frenkley

Africa

3499. Agnoletti, Enzo Enriques. SUDAN, UNA BANCAROTTA [The Sudan: a case of bankruptcy]. *Ponte [Italy] 1971 27(8/9): 884-887.* Comments on the civil war in the Sudan. Unlike other Arab nations, in the Sudan the Communist Party and labor movement, thanks to the culture and personal qualities of their leaders, have gained respect. The author attacks the Italian Communist Party (PCI) organ *L'Unità* for its equivocal position on the Sudan and for its failure to criticize Soviet passivity in the affair. The PCI had previously claimed to be independent of the USSR. C. Bates

3500. Arnold, A.-S. DIE HERAUSBILDUNG VON SOZIALEM PROGRAMM UND ANTIIMPERIALISTISCHER BÜNDNISKONZEPTION DER "VOLKSBEWEGUNG FÜR DIE BEFREIUNG ANGOLAS" (MPLA) [The development of social program and anti-imperialist alliance concept of the Popular Movement for the Liberation of Angola (MPLA)]. *Wissenschaftliche Zeitschrift der Karl-Marx-U. Leipzig. Gesellschafts- und Sprachwissenschaftliche Reihe [East Germany] 1976 25(6): 597-605.* In 1956 the Communist Party of Angola managed to establish a close cooperation with national democratic forces, which resulted in the founding of the MPLA, which based its national revolutionary strategy on a dialectical understanding of the systems of colonialism and imperialism.

3501. Botman, Selma. "Oppositional Politics in Egypt: The Communist Movement, 1936-1954." Harvard University 1984. 594 pp. *DAI 1985 45(7): 2223-A.* DA8419302

3502. Botoran, Constantin and Istrate, Silvia. LOCUL ȘI ROLUL CLASEI MUNCITOARE DIN ȚĂRILE AFRICANE ÎN LUPTA PENTRU ELIBERAREA NAȚIONALĂ ȘI CONSOLIDAREA INDEPENDENȚEI [The place and role of the working class of African countries struggling for national liberation and the consolidation of independence]. *Anale de Istorie [Romania] 1981 27(6): 114-142.* Describes the poor economic status and working conditions for African workers after World War II, the emergence of worker movements in various African countries, and the conduct of the ensuing liberation struggles. Notes the varying responses of the colonial powers and the importance of Communist parties in particular countries as a revolutionary political force. Describes the postindependence problems of various countries, particularly after 1960, often resulting from their colonial heritage. Traces the emergence of new social structures and stresses the positive organizational contribution of Communist parties. 132 notes. R. O. Khan

3503. Camera d'Afflitto, Isabella. LA "MAGIALLAH" DELL'UNIVERSITA ISLAMICA DI AL-AZHAR FRA TRADIZIONE E RIVOLUZIONE (1930-1970) [The *Magiallah* of the Islamic University of Al-Azhar between tradition and revolution (1930-70)]. *Ann. della Facoltà di Sci. Pol.: Lingua, Letteratura, Civiltà [Italy] 1980-81 17: 125-139. Magiallah,* official organ of the university, illustrates the role of that religious institution in support of the anti-communist campaign in Nasser's Egypt.

3504. Clough, Michael. EXPLORING AFROCOMMUNISM. *Problems of Communism 1984 33(6): 70-74.* A review of Carl G. Rosberg and Thomas M. Callaghy's, ed., *Socialism in Sub-Saharan Africa* (1979), David Ottaway and Marina Ottaway's *Afrocommunism* (1981), Allen Issacman and Barbara Issacman's *Mozambique: From Colonialism to Revolution, 1900-1982* (1983), Michael Wolfers and Jane Bergerol's *Angola in the Frontline* (1983), and M. Crawford Young's *Ideology and Development in Africa* (1982). It is not yet clear whether "Afrocommunism" constitutes a qualitative departure from earlier "African socialism," or is only a new manifestation of populism. 7 notes. J. M. Lauber

3505. Contu, Giuseppe. LE DONNE COMUNISTE E IL MOVIMENTO DEMOCRATICO FEMMINILE IN EGITTO FINO AL 1965 [Communist women and the women's liberation movement in Egypt up to 1965]. *Oriente Moderno [Italy] 1975 55(5-6): 237-247.*

3506. Dyba, Marian. SUDAŃSKA PARTIA KOMUNISTYCZNA 1946-1958 [The Sudanese Communist Party 1946-58]. *Z Pola Walki [Poland] 1974 17(65): 185-213.* Deals with problems connected with the Sudanese Communist Party from 1946 to 17 November 1958 when the reactionary coup d'état changed the conditions of activity of Sudanese Communists. The role played by the Party in the struggle against British colonialism is presented against the social and economic background of the Sudan. J/S

3507. Eppstein, John. THE FATE OF PORTUGUESE AFRICA. *World Survey [Great Britain] 1975 (83): 1-17.* Discusses the Communist Party's assumption of power in Guinea and Mozambique and its struggle to control Angola following the revolution in Portugal in 1974.

3508. Giblin, Jim. THE IMAGE OF THE LOYAL AFRICAN DURING WORLD WAR II AND ITS POSTWAR USE BY THE FRENCH COMMUNIST PARTY. *Can. J. of African Studies [Canada] 1980 14(2): 319-326.* Both Gaullist and Vichyite literature on wartime French African colonies south of the Sahara created false images of African loyalty to France and overlooked the real autonomy of African political interests and actions. In the postwar period the French Communist Party failed to examine actual conditions in the colonies and used the wartime propaganda to formulate a colonial policy which did not recognize the changes then transforming colonial Africa. 29 notes.

3509. Goldberg, Ellis Jay. "Tinker, Tailor, and Textile Worker: Class and Politics in Egypt 1930-1954." U. of California, Berkeley 1983. 450 pp. *DAI 1984 45(3): 932-A.* DA8413402

3510. Henze, Paul B. COMMUNISM AND ETHIOPIA. *Problems of Communism 1981 30(3): 55-74.* Despite Communist rhetoric and some early radical social measures, the regime of Ethiopian leader Mengistu Haile-Mariam is finding Marxist solutions and Soviet-bloc influence of decreasing relevance to the domestic and foreign problems facing Ethiopia. Traditional nationalism and resurgent Christianity and Islam are strong obstacles to the Marxist ideology. Furthermore, the military leadership shows no haste to develop a genuine revolutionary party. Based on international newspaper accounts; 62 notes. J. M. Lauber

3511. Hura, V. K. Z ISTORII DIIAL'NOSTI MAROKKANS'KOI KOMPARTII [The work of the Moroccan Communist Party]. *Ukrains'kyi Istorychnyi Zhurnal [USSR] 1974 (1): 74-79.* Highlights the work of Morocco's Communist Party 1956-73, and discusses the influence of the Soviet Communist Party.

3512. Irkhin, Iu. V. ZHURNAL *THE AFRICAN COMMUNIST* [The journal *The African Communist*]. *Voprosy Istorii [USSR] 1981 (3): 152-157.* The *African Communist,* which has appeared since 1959, is the theoretical organ of the South African Communist Party, published since 1960 in London. It contains articles by leading activists of communist, workers and freedom movements in Africa, by progressive scholars of West European countries, and by Soviet Africanists. Contemporary problems of the African countries are considered in the context of world history. The sharpening national liberation struggles in southern Africa are analyzed, as well as imperialist neocolonialist policies. 6 notes. A. Brown

3513. Kiracofe, Clifford A., Jr. THE COMMUNIST TAKEOVER OF MOZAMBIQUE: AN OVERVIEW. *J. of Social, Pol. and Econ. Studies 1982 7(1-2): 115-128.* The Moscow-guided transformation of the National Liberation Movement into a Marxist-Leninist party, and the 1974-75 armed takeover threatens international mining and access to strategic minerals in South Africa, and hence the world economy.

3514. Kiracofe, Clifford A., Jr. THE COMMUNIST TAKEOVER OF ANGOLA. *J. of Social, Pol. and Econ. Studies 1981 6(4): 417-437.* Discusses the background of the takeover of Angola in 1975 by the Popular Movement for the Liberation of Angola (MPLA), with special attention to the role of Soviet and Cuban forces.

3515. Lacina, Karel. BOJ POKROKOVÝCH SIL JIŽNÍ AFRIKY PROTI POLITICE APARTHEIDU A JEHO ODRAZ V SOUDOBÉ POLITICE RASISTŮ [The struggle against apartheid policy by the progressive forces in South Africa and its reflection in the current policy of the racists]. *Československý Časopis Historický [Czechoslovakia] 1985 33(1): 25-50.* Surveys the struggle of South Africa's nonwhite majority for human, political, and economic rights, 1949-79. After 1961, the brutal countermeasures by the government forced the African National Congress into subversive activities. Nevertheless, resistance throughout the 1970's has become more coordinated and militant, thanks to the help of the Communist Party and the Revolutionary Council which, since 1969, have enlisted a broadly popular front in the fight. Based on Communist and other publications; 83 notes. Russian and English summaries. R. E. Weltsch

3516. Legum, Colin. SUDAN'S THREE-DAY REVOLUTION: "PEOPLE'S UPRISING" FAILS TO RALLY THE PEOPLE. *Africa Report 1971 16(7): 12-15.* The Communist-led revolution of July 1971 destroyed the influence of the Sudan Communist Party, resulted in an open break between the Sudan regime and the Soviet bloc, and strengthened China's position in Khartoum.

3517. Makarov, A. A. AVANGARD REVOLIUTSIONNIKH SIL IUZHNOI AFRIKI [The vanguard of the revolutionary forces of Southern Africa]. *Voprosy Istorii KPSS [USSR] 1981 (7): 101-104.* In honor of the 60th anniversary of the foundation of the Communist Party of South Africa, considers the history and development of the Party (declared illegal by the South African government), the background and nature of its membership, the development of political awareness and policies, the specific difficulties encountered in relation to the South African regime, the Party's importance in relation to and cooperation with other Communist Parties in capitalist and imperialist states, and the importance of relations with and aid and guidance from the Soviet Communist Party and government for further efforts toward peace, friendship, and socialism. Based on *The African Communist* and newspaper articles; 6 notes. L. Smith

3518. Manchkha, P. I. KOMMUNISTY, REVOLIUTSIONNYE DEMOKRATY I NEKAPITALISTICHESKII PUT' RAZVITIIA V STRANAKH AFRIKI [Communists, revolutionary democrats and the noncapitalist path of development in countries of Africa]. *Voprosy Istorii KPSS [USSR] 1975 (10): 57-69.* An analysis of postcolonial black Africa. By their political, economic, cultural, and social policies, revolutionary democratic parties in Africa now represent the bulk of the population, striving toward a noncapitalist development. Despite difficulties created by repression and socioeconomic backwardness, Communist parties do exist in Africa as the vanguard of anti-imperialist and anticapitalist efforts. Communists must deal with anticommunism in the guise of theories of "special African socialism" or "specific black psychology." Based on published primary sources and V. I. Lenin's *Collected Works*; 15 notes. L. E. Holmes

3519. Manchkha, P. I. KOMPARTII STRAN AFRIKI NA SOVREMMENOM ETAPE BORBY ZA SOTSIALNII PROGRESS [The Communist Parties of African countries at the present stage of the struggle for social progress]. *Voprosy Istorii KPSS [USSR] 1981 (6): 84-95.* Considers some of the major problems of international Communist and national liberation movements, with particular reference to Africa, noting that the history of such areas is usually considered as part of the general history of the Arabian East. Discusses the general problems encountered by Communist Parties in capitalist countries, the problems particular to the nations in question, and the importance of maintaining and strengthening links with the Soviet Communist Party, which provides valuable aid and examples for the achievement of vital socialist goals such as the achievement of economic independence and the overthrow of capitalism and imperialism. Based on published Soviet and African works; 27 notes. L. Smith

3520. Manchkha, P. I. PEREDOVOI OTRIAD REVOLIUTSIONNOGO DVIZHENIIA NA IUGE AFRIKI (K 20-LETIIU OSNOVANIIA KOMMUNISTICHESKOI PARTII LESOTO) [An advanced detachment in the revolutionary movement in Southern Africa: on the 20th anniversary of the founding of the Communist Party of Lesotho]. *Voprosy Istorii KPSS [USSR] 1982 (5): 112-115.* The Russian Revolution was the greatest political event of the 20th century; it inspired nations great and small. The Communist Party of Lesotho was formed under its influence. The evolution of Lesotho, which, until 4 October 1966, was the colonial Basutoland, is described, as are its present difficulties, especially with the Republic of South Africa. The Party was banned in 1970, but even in illegality it continues to struggle to improve the workers' lot. It is Marxist-Leninist, permeated with proletarian internationalism, and imbued with love of the USSR. It is assured of Soviet support. Based on Soviet and Lesotho historical sources; 15 notes. A. J. Evans

3521. Marks, J. B. BREAKING THE SHACKLES. *World Marxist Rev. 1972 15(5): 124-130.* Discusses the author's activities in the Communist Party of South Africa from the 1920's, the influence of Marxism-Leninism on the thought of party founder D. I. Jones, and apartheid.

3522. Mikhailov, A. M. 60 LET KOMMUNISTICHESKOGO DVIZHENIIA V EGIPTE [Sixty years of the Communist movement in Egypt]. *Voprosy Istorii KPSS [USSR] 1981 (8): 106-109.* In August 1921, against the background of a national liberation struggle against British imperialism, the Progessive forces in Egypt set up the Egyptian Socialist Party. This joined the Comintern in 1922 and became the Egyptian Communist Party. The Party immediately started to play a leading role in the Egyptian workers' movement, but was subjected to repression. A particularly bad period was from 1928-36, when the Party was decimated. Two Communist organizations, the Egyptian Movement for National Liberation and Ash-

Sharara (the Spark), were active in mobilizing the Egyptian masses in World War II. The Communist movement played a similar role in the war against Israel in 1967. The Party was outlawed after the death of President Nasser in 1970, and since then has worked illegally to form a progressive government. 2 notes. J. Bamber

3523. Mulira, James. NATIONALISM AND COMMUNIST PHOBIA IN COLONIAL UGANDA, 1945-1960. *Mawazo [Uganda] 1983 5(1): 3-16.* The leaders of Ugandan independence movements attempted to gain the aid of Communist countries to further their political aims. The British colonial administration, the press, and the Catholic Church took advantage of these efforts to allege Communist infiltration and conspiracy in Uganda, even though no factual evidence was ever available to them. The effect of this propaganda on future politics in Uganda has proved to be far-reaching. 49 notes. C. Pasadas-Ureña

3524. Nagy, J. László. A KOMMUNISTA MOZGALOM ÉS A NEMZETI FELSZABADÍTÓ MOZGALOM KAPCSOLATA ALGÉRIÁBAN (1943-1947) [Connections between the Communist movement and the national liberation movement in Algeria, 1943-47]. *Párttörténeti Közlemények [Hungary] 1982 28(2): 145-169.* The Algerian Communist Party was greatly concerned about the damage to the image of the French Communist Party if it were to take the position of opposing French rule in Algeria. This unfortunate attitude did not make the party very popular in Algeria. Realizing its error in 1945, the Communist Party introduced its new policy in complete support of nationalist forces. 62 notes.
T. Kuner

3525. Nkozi, Z. PIATIDESIATAIA GODOVSHCHINA IUZHNO-AFRIKANSKOI KOMMUNISTICHESKOI PARTII [The 50th year of the South African Communist Party]. *Voprosy Istorii KPSS [USSR] 1971 (7): 113-115.*

3526. Pegushev, A. M. UCHENYE SOTSIALISTICHESKIKH STRAN O PROBLEMAKH NATSIONAL'NOGO DVIZHENIIA V AFRIKE [Scholars of the socialist countries on problems of national liberation movements in Africa]. *Narody Azii i Afriki [USSR] 1980 (5): 169-179.* The 3d Symposium of Historians and Africanists of Socialist Countries entitled History of the National Liberation Movement in Africa: The Problem of Leadership and the fourth meeting of the working group History of Africa and the National Liberation Movement in Africa took place in September, 1979 in Leipzig. Participants came from Czechoslovakia, East Germany, Hungary, Poland, and the USSR. These meetings served to increase the collaboration among Africanists from the Socialist countries. Cites previous symposiums on similar subjects (Budapest in 1977 and Varna in 1975), publications resulting there from, and other primary sources; 9 notes. S. J. Talalay

3527. Rabesahala, Gisele. MADAGASCAR REVOLUTIONARY DEMOCRATS. *World Marxist Rev. [Canada] 1972 15(9): 119-125.* Discusses the role of the revolutionary democratic Independence Congress Party (AKFM) in the struggle against neocolonialism in Madagascar, 1946-70's.

3528. Ramaro, Elie. LA RÉUNION ENTRE LE DÉPARTEMENT ET LA NATION [Réunion: between department and nation]. *Rev. Française d'Études Pol. Africaines [France] 1972 (77): 38-50.* A historical perspective and report on the modern status of Réunion Island, a French territory since 1638, and a department of France since 1946. Outlines its development from prison island to an important economic and strategic French foothold in the Indian Ocean. Describes Réunion's social and ethnic groups as they evolved from slaves, landowners, traders, etc., during the rapid population increase of the colonial period. Exports of sugar, rum, vanilla, and perfume products dominate the island's economy and determine French policy toward Réunion. Separatist movements reflect internal strife and the participation of the French Communist Party, which became the Communist Party for Autonomy. Based on newspaper articles and other published sources; 27 notes.
S. Sevilla

3529. Solodovnikov, V. G. SOVETSKAIA AFRIKANISTIKA MEZHDU XXIV I XXV SEZDAMI KPSS [Soviet African studies between the 24th and 25th Congresses of the CPSU]. *Narody Azii i Afriki [USSR] 1976 (2): 8-19.* The 24th Party Congress foretold the events that took place in Africa: the further development of national liberation movements into social revolutions and the crash of the colonial system. The author describes the research which has been done between the two Party Congresses by the Institute of Africa at the Academy of Sciences of the USSR, whose research tries to answer such questions as how to overcome economic backwardness and how to use Africa's resources and productive forces. The researchers also point out the detrimental effect of foreign monopolies on the economies of the new states and the advantages of state control over them. The institute is also studying sociopolitical and ideological processes and social and class changes in contemporary African society. Also mentions some of the research done by other institutes and institutions of higher education. Primary sources; 5 notes. L. Kalinowski

3530. Tomaszewski, Władysław. KRAJE SOCJALISTYCZNE NA RYNKU AFRYKAŃSKICH KRAJÓW ROZWIJAJĄCYCH SIĘ [Socialist countries in the markets of the developing nations of Africa]. *Ekonomista [Poland] 1974 (2): 415-425.* Examines the socialist countries' share of the African market since the 1960's.

3531. Weinberg, Eli. *Portrait of a People: A Personal Photographic Record of the South African Liberation Struggle.* London: Int. Defence & Aid Fund for South Africa, 1981. 198 pp.

3532. Woodward, Peter. NATIONALISM AND OPPOSITION IN SUDAN. *African Affairs [Great Britain] 1981 80(320): 379-388.* A review of the history and nature of the liberation movement in Sudan. The argument that the Communist-dominated revolutions of southern Africa must take place in other African states demands a look at their history here. Both the Sudan Communist Party and the revolt in southern Sudan have caused problems of violence, but neither seems to have a great deal of faith in mass participation and armed struggle. The core of future problems here may be racial and religious, rather than class, oriented. 12 notes.
V. L. Human

3533. Zakaria, Ibrahim. THE STRUGGLE OF THE SUDANESE COMMUNISTS. *World Marxist Rev. 1977 20(4): 55-62.* Sketches the activities of the Sudanese Communist Party, 1946-77.

The Middle East

3534. Bator, Wolfgang and Bator, Angelika. DER KAMPF DER PALÄSTINENSISCHEN WIDERSTANDSBEWEGUNG [The fight of the Palestinian resistance movement]. *Dokumentation der Zeit [East Germany] 1970 (9): 13-18.* Reviews the history and development of the Palestinian Liberation Organization (PLO) with its groups: Palestinian Liberation Army (PLA), the Al-Fatah, the Al-Saiqa, the Popular Front of Liberation (PFLP), and Arabian Liberation Front (ALF). The Al-Fatah recently developed its own military-political conception. Communist parties in Arab states support the struggle as expressed in international conferences in Berlin and Moscow. 48 notes. G. E. Pergl

3535. Chaoui, Nicolas. THE ANTI-IMPERIALIST FRONT AND THE ARAB LIBERATION MOVEMENT. *World Marxist R. [Canada] 1974 17(8): 30-37.* Events in the Middle East show that the Arab national liberation movement must join Communist countries and the world's working class in order to defeat capitalistic imperialism.

3536. Dadiani, L. I. KOMMUNISTICHESKAIA PARTIIA IZRAILIA V BOR'BE ZA MIRNUIU I DEMOKRATICHESKUIU AL'TERNATIVU DLIA STRANY [The Communist Party of Israel in a struggle for a peaceful and democratic alternative for the country]. *Voprosy istorii KPSS [USSR] 1973 (5): 52-63.* The ruling Zionist groups in Israel have pursued an imperialist policy that has led to the continued threat of war, lower real wages, and the cre-

ation in Israel of a police state. The Israeli Communist Party provides the alternative of creating a united front dedicated to a return to the borders of 4 June 1967; the Palestinian refugees a choice of either returning to their homeland or accepting compensation; liquidation of Israel's dependence on America and foreign monopolies; equality between Arabs and Jews in Israel; and more economic benefits for the Israeli working class. Based on materials in the *Information Bulletin* of the Israeli Communist Party; 31 notes.
L. E. Holmes

3537. Edelstein, Meir. THE 1965 SPLIT IN MAKI AND THE CPSU. *Soviet Jewish Affairs [Great Britain] 1974 4(1): 23-38.* Describes how the Israeli Communist Party divided between 1963 and 1965 over the Arab-Israeli conflict despite the USSR's efforts to maintain unity in the party.

3538. Flores, Alexander. THE PALESTINE COMMUNIST PARTY DURING THE MANDATORY PERIOD: AN ACCOUNT OF SOURCES AND RECENT RESEARCH. *Peuples Mediterranéens-Mediterranean Peoples [France] 1980 (11): 57-84.* Analyzes the history of the Communist Party during the 1920's and subsequent writings.

3539. Gallissot, René. ENTRE LA NATION ARABE LE COMMUNISME ET LA PATRIE LIBANAISE: L'HISTOIRE DU MOUVEMENT SYNDICAL AU LIBAN DE JACQUES COULAND [The Arab nation, Communism, and Lebanese nationalism: *L'Histoire du mouvement syndical au Liban* by Jacques Couland]. *Pensée [France] 1974 (176): 128-132.* Reviews Jacques Couland's *L'Histoire du mouvement syndical au Liban* [The history of the labor movement in Lebanon] (Paris: Editions Sociales, 1970) which traces the conflict between Marxism, pan-Arabic consciousness, and nationalism in the Lebanese labor movement. The first labor parties and unions were established in 1919 and 1921 under Communist influence. From 1926 through 1936, the movement became reformist and nationalist, and, during the era of the Popular Front and World War II, it was tolerated. Because of its role in the resistance and subsequent struggle for independence, the movement was granted legal recognition by the newly established Lebanese government in 1946.
A. W. Novitsky

3540. Goldberg, Giora. ADAPTATION TO COMPETITIVE POLITICS: THE CASE OF ISRAELI COMMUNISM. *Studies in Comparative Communism 1980 14(4): 331-351.* Communists in Israel have never won more than 5% of the vote. Of the two Communist parties, Maki and Rakah, only Rakah has survived since the mid-1970's. Rakah's strategy unites Jewish with the dominant Arab groups. In parliament, Rakah has acted as a custodian of procedure and provided favors for its Arab constituents. Since the triumph of Likhud, Rakah has been less successful in securing favors for its clients. The Soviets would like to prevent the party from becoming an Arab nationalist party. In the 1981 election, two-thirds of the Arab vote moved away from Rakah to support the Alignment. In the 1977 election more than half of the Arab vote went to the Communist front. 33 notes.
D. Balmuth

3541. Greilsammer, Alain. COMMUNISM IN ISRAEL: 13 YEARS AFTER THE SPLIT. *Survey [Great Britain] 1977-78 23(3): 172-192.* Discusses the recent progress of Communist parties in Israel. The monolithic party split in 1965 and two factions emerged: the New Communist List (RAKAH), generally more pro-Soviet and predominantly composed of Arabs; and the Israeli Communist Party (MAKI), more nationalistic and entirely made up of Jews. The differences between the two were extreme and they have remained quite separate. The MAKI has steadily declined in power, as measured by electoral success, whereas the RAKAH has improved its performance. This success has been attributed to Israeli foreign policy and to the policies of the Begin government. 70 notes.
V. L. Human/S

3542. Hottinger, Arnold. ARAB COMMUNISM AT LOW EBB. *Problems of Communism 1981 30(4): 17-32.* With the single exception of South Yemen, Arab communism is at a low ebb of power and influence. In several Arab countries, there appears to be no organized Communist movement at all. In most others, the existing Communist parties are proscribed and forced to lead a clandestine existence. In a few cases, the parties are legal, but they are closely controlled by the ruling regimes. However, given the volatile nature of the Arab world, one may expect new opportunities for Arab communism to exploit. In responding, they will have to deal with the growing force of Islamic fundamentalism. Based on numerous Western and Arab newspaper accounts; 36 notes.
J. M. Lauber

3543. Khenin, David. ISRAEL AFTER THE OCTOBER WAR. *World Marxist R. [Canada] 1974 17(2): 96-102.* Communists in Israel argue that the October War (1973) showed the bankruptcy of the Israeli policy of securing defensible borders through annexation of Arab land.

3544. Maurer, Marvin. QUAKERS AND COMMUNISTS: VIETNAM AND ISRAEL. *Midstream 1979 25(9): 30-35.* Discusses efforts of Quakers, Communists, and others to undermine Israel in the 1970's as they undermined Vietnam in the 1960's.

3545. Mounayer, Michel. SYRYJSKA PARTIA KOMUNISTYCZNA ZARYS DZIEJÓW [The Communist Party of Syria: an outline of its history]. *Z Pola Walki [Poland] 1979 22(1): 199-212.* The Communist Party of Syria was founded on 28 October 1924. In May 1930, the first Congress of the Party took place. Between 1947 and 1954 the Party was illegal and as a result of the union between Egypt and Syria in 1958 the Party was banned again, until 1961. In 1976 the Communist Party agreed to cooperate with the ruling Baath party, insisting on some autonomy and risking a degree of persecution. The leading figure in the Syrian Communist movement remains Khalid Bakdash, Party member since 1930. Based on Syrian Communist press articles and the writings of Khalid Bakdash; 38 notes.
E. Jaworska

3546. Mroué, Karim. THE ARAB NATIONAL-LIBERATION MOVEMENT. *World Marxist R. [Canada] 1973 16(2): 65-72.*

3547. Muhammed, Aziz. THE SOCIALIST COMMUNITY IS OUR DEPENDABLE ALLY. *World Marxist R. [Canada] 1975 18(1): 53-61.* Discusses ties between Communist countries and the developing nations, particularly Iraq.

3548. Nechkin, G. N. POLVEKA BOR'BY I ISPYTANII [A half century of struggle and trials]. *Voprosy Istorii KPSS [USSR] 1984 (3): 135-139.* A survey of the history of the Iraq Communist Party on the occasion of the 50th anniversary of its formation. The Party has constantly in its years of struggle tried to advance the cause of socialism, international revolution, the Palestinians, and friendship with the USSR. Based on sources in Arabic and Russian; 12 notes.
D. N. Collins

3549. Potomov, Iu. S. and Nikolaev, V. N. V BOR'BE ZA INTERESY NARODA [In the struggle for the interests of the people]. *Voprosy Istorii KPSS [USSR] 1982 (6): 85-88.* Commemorates the 70th birthday of Nikola Shawi, president of the Lebanese Communist Party. Shawi joined the joint Lebanese-Syrian Communist Party in the 1920's and in the 1930's headed its Beirut organization and edited a Party newspaper. Jailed by the French mandate authorities from 1940 to 1941, he founded the independent Lebanese CP in 1944 and became secretary of the Central Committee. In 1947 the Party went underground. In the 1950's Shawi was prominent in campaigns against the Bagdad Pact and the entry of US Marines into Lebanon in 1958. Both then and since, his career has shown him to be a tireless defender of the working class and of the USSR.
F. A. K. Yasamee

3550. Rouleau, Eric. REVOLUTIONARY SOUTHERN YEMEN. *Monthly R. 1973 25(1): 25-42.* Describes the National Liberation Front, its history as a revolutionary force, and the social, economic, and military problems faced by South Yemen.

3551. Schnall, David. ORGANIZED COMMUNISM IN ISRAEL. *Midstream 1978 24(7): 26-36.* Discusses the internal conflicts over social and ideological issues of the Communist parties in Palestine and Israel, 1917-77.

3552. Seliger, Kurt. RAKACH UND MAKI. DIE ZWEI KOMMUNISTISCHEN PARTEIEN ISRAELS [RAKAH and MAKI: the two Communist Parties of Israel]. *Osteuropa [West Germany] 1976 26(4): 251-253.* In 1965 the Communist Party of Israel split into two factions, the Israeli Communist Party (Miflaga Komunistit Yisraelit—MAKI) and the New Communist List (Reshima Komunistit Chadasha—RAKAH); MAKI called the Nasser regime in Egypt reactionary and supported the Israeli military action in the 1967 war; RAKAH, relying chiefly on Arab voters, was pro-Arab and was supported by Moscow.

3553. Slann, Martin W. IDEOLOGY AND ETHNICITY IN ISRAEL'S TWO COMMUNIST PARTIES: THE CONFLICT BETWEEN MAKI AND RAKAH. *Studies in Comparative Communism 1974 7(4): 359-374.* Since 1965 the Israeli Communist Party has been divided into two parties, Maki (since 1973, Moked) and Rakah. Moked is the Jewish Communist Party while Rakah, whose leaders are both Jewish and Arab, has recruited its major support from Arabs. Most Israeli Arabs vote for moderate Arab or Jewish parties, but Rakah, which is accepted by the USSR and opposes Israel's existence, has attracted more Arab votes than any single party. Since the split, Moked has moved closer to the position of other Jewish dominated parties. 3 tables, 57 notes.
D. Balmuth

3554. Slepov, N. B. V BOR'BE ZA MIR, DEMOKRATIIU I SOTSIAL'NYI PROGRESS [In the struggle for peace, democracy, and social progress]. *Voprosy Istorii KPSS [USSR] 1979 (6): 110-114.* Surveys the history of the Communist Party of Palestine-Israel from its formation in 1919 and describes the Party's plans for a comprehensive plan to bring peace, equal rights, prosperity, and security to both Arabs and Jews in the Middle East. This plan will free the area of Zionism, racism, and dependence on imperialism and foreign monopolies. Based on published documents and periodical literature; 16 notes. L. E. Holmes

3555. Stefankin, V. A. RASISTSKAIA SUSHCHNOST' IDEOLOGII SIONISTSKIKH PRAVITELEI IZRAILIA [The racist essence of the ideology of the Zionist leaders of Israel]. *Narody Azii i Afriki [USSR] 1979 (3): 22-32.* Reviews the Israeli Communist Party's struggle against the Zionist reality of their government. Analyzes Zionism and gives examples of the government's Zionist policies and treatment of the Arabs. 48 notes. V. A. Packer

3556. Steinkühler, Manfred. THE ITALIAN COMMUNIST PARTY AND THE MIDDLE EASTERN CONFLICT. *Wiener Lib. Bull. [Great Britain] 1972 26(26-27): 9-12.* Discusses the involvement of the Italian Communist Party in the settlement of the Middle East crisis, 1967.

3557. Touma, Emile. PROGRAM FOR A PEACE FRONT. *World Marxist Rev. [Canada] 1972 15(11): 83-88.* Discusses the Middle Eastern peace policy of Israel's Communist Party, 1967-72.

3558. Vavilov, A. I. VERNYI SYN BORIUSHCHEGOSIA NARODA (K 70-LETIIU KH. BAGDASHA) [A true son of a fighting people: the 70th birthday of Kh. Bagdash]. *Voprosy Istorii KPSS [USSR] 1982 (11): 129-132.* Briefly records the life and exploits of Khalid Bagdash (b. 1912), the general secretary of the Syrian Communist Party. He was first elected to the post in 1937. From time to time the Party became illegal, but by 1977 Bagdash was able to serve openly as a member of the Syrian parliament. The Syrian Communist Party closely supported Leonid Brezhnev's initiatives toward peace in the Middle East. Bagdash was granted the Order of the October Revolution in 1972. Several references to the press in Russian and Arabic; 4 notes. D. N. Collins

3559. Vilner, Meir. PEACE IN THE MIDDLE EAST: SHEET ANCHOR FOR ISRAEL. *World Marxist Rev. 1977 20(4): 32-40.* Discusses efforts of Israel's Communist Party toward democracy, equal rights for Arabs, and an independent state for the Palestinians, 1967-77.

3560. Yata, Ali. CHANGE IN WORLD RELATIONS AND THE NATIONAL LIBERATION MOVEMENT. *World Marxist R. [Canada] 1974 17(5): 35-42.* The progress of the Arabs in the Middle East since 1973 suggests that the continuing cooperation between communism and national liberation movements can strengthen socialism and peace by limiting capitalist tendencies toward war.

3561. Yodfat, Aryeh. B''RITH HAMOATZOTH BEN KUMMUNISTIM L'BATYAM BSURIA [The Soviet Union between Communists and Ba'athists in Syria]. *Hamizrah Hehadash [Israel] 1972 22(1): 1-24.* Describes the Soviet dilemma in Syria: should the USSR support local communist parties or the party in power which is friendly to the USSR but may persecute local communists?
F. Rosenthal

3562. —. COMMUNIST FIGHTER. *World Marxist R. [Canada] 1974 17(8): 129.* Obituary for Parviz Hekmatdju (1921-74), Central Committee member of the People's Party of Iran.

3563. —. THE SOVIET ATTITUDE TO THE PALESTINE PROBLEM. *J. of Palestine Studies [Lebanon] 1972 2(1): 187-212.* Offers three documents, 1970-72, which elucidate the attitudes of the USSR and the Syrian Communist Party on the Palestinian problem, following a dispute within the highly nationalistic Syrian Party which was referred to the Soviet Party, 1970-1972.

6. COMMUNISM IN LATIN AMERICA

General

3564. Berríos, Rubén. LA EMPRESA TRANSIDEOLOGICA Y LAS RELACIONES ECONOMICAS ESTE-OESTE-SUR [Transideological enterprise and East-West-South economic relations]. *Estudios Int. [Chile] 1982 15(57): 88-103.* Discusses the recent evolution of enterprise and trade between East, West, and developing nations of Latin America, underlining the compromises of communism, socialism, and capitalism.

3565. Blanksten, George I. CUBA, CHILE, AND THE CRISIS OF DEMOCRACY. *Secolas Ann. 1973 4: 11-15.* Compares Cuba and Chile in the context of the decentralization of the Communist movement and the state of value analysis in political science. One of eight papers on Cuba and Chile read at the annual meeting of the Southeastern conference on Latin American Studies.

3566. Burke, Arleigh. TARGET FOR COMMUNIST CONQUEST. *Marine Corps Gazette 1964 48(9): 25-28.* Examines Cuban efforts to subvert American interests in Latin America, 1954-64.

3567. Camejo, Peter. A CRITIQUE AND SOME PROPOSALS, WHY GUEVARA'S GUERRILLA STRATEGY HAS NO FUTURE. *Int. Socialist Rev. 1972 33(10): 10-17, 30-39.* The revolutionary strategy of rural guerrilla warfare is inappropriate in most Latin American countries in the 1970's.

3568. Dabagian, E. S. LITERATURA PO ISTORII KOMMUNISTICHESKOGO I RABOCHEGO DVIZHENIIA V STRANAKH LATINSKOI AMERIKI: ISTORIOGRAFICHESKII OBZOR [Literature on the history of the communist and workers' movements in the countries of Latin America: a historiographical survey]. *Voprosy Istorii KPSS [USSR] 1962 (1): 164-176.* Surveys sources relating to 20th-century Communist Parties and movements in Latin America, a subject not fully examined by Marxist historians.

3569. Delgado, Alvaro. LATIN AMERICA'S PRIESTS IN REVOLT. *World Marxist R. [Canada] 1973 16(3): 68-75.* Catholic priests are beginning to aid the movement toward communism in Latin America.

3570. Fuchs, Jaime. STRUCTURAL CRISIS AND CONTRADICTIONS IN LATIN AMERICA. *World Marxist Rev. [Canada] 1972 15(5): 62-70.* Discusses the role of the Communist Party in the movement for change in the socioeconomic structure of Latin American countries from the 1950's to the 1970's, emphasizing the need for agricultural reform and the destructive effects of US monopolies.

3571. Gilbert, Guy J. SOCIALISM AND DEPENDENCY. *Latin Am. Perspectives 1974 1(1): 107-123.* The main thrust of the criticism of dependency theory has focused on the hypothesis that dependency is a universal phenomenon making any alternative for Latin American development impossible. Neither the Soviet Union nor China penetrate and exploit other socialist countries through the vehicle of ownership of foreign capital, nor have they attempted to maintain weaker countries as suppliers of cheap raw materials. The political elites of the Latin American socialist countries are to varying degrees subservient to the Soviet Union or China, but this is based not on the wealth of these two powers nor on their penetration in the economic and social life of these countries of Latin America. Instead influence is through common ideological and practical considerations and/or party bureaucracy. Thus, in the socialist sphere we do not find the functional equivalent of the dependence relation found within the capitalist sphere. A

3572. Grenier, Richard. THE CURIOUS CAREER OF COSTA-GAVRAS. *Commentary 1982 73(4): 61-71.* Discusses the anti-Americanism and pro-Communism of Greek-born French filmmaker Constantin Costa-Gavras since 1964, noting his inability to separate fact from fantasy in dealing with the US role in Latin America.

3573. Kaeselitz, R. DIE GESCHICHTE DER KOMMUNISTISCHEN PARTEIEN LATEINAMERIKAS UND IHRE VERFÄLSCHUNG DURCH BORIS GOLDENBERG [The history of the Communist parties in Latin America and its falsification by Boris Goldenberg]. *Lateinamerika [East Germany] 1972 (Fall): 43-49.* Refutes the viewpoint expressed by West German historian Boris Goldenberg in his book about South American Communism and sees it as a distortion of actual events. 4 notes.

3574. Kudachkin, M. F. KOMMUNISTICHESKIE PARTII LATINSKOI AMERIKI V AVANGARDE ANTIIMPERIALISTICHESKOI BOR'BY [The Communist Parties of Latin America in the forefront of the anti-imperialist struggle]. *Novaia i Noveishaia Istoriia [USSR] 1971 (5): 15-27.* The end of the 1960's saw a sharpening of the economic and social crisis in Latin America. US influence declined and some reformist politicians became interested in noncapitalist development. More Communist Parties than ever before could operate legally, and the proportion of workers in their ranks increased. Their political programs aimed to bring about a democratic, agrarian, and anti-imperialist revolution, and for this they hoped to ally with other political forces and social groups. Based on Party programs, reports and newspaper articles; 21 notes. C. I. P. Ferdinand

3575. Livingstone, Neil C. DEATH SQUADS. *World Affairs 1983-84 146(3): 239-248.* Since the 1950's, anti-Communist terrorism in Latin America has been characterized by the appearance of death squads that have often been allied to conservative governments.

3576. Nadra, F. THE REVOLUTIONARY AWAKENING IN LATIN AMERICA. *Int. Affairs [USSR] 1977 (12): 49-56.* Traces the growth of revolutionary movements in Latin America and particularly in Argentina. The Mexican revolution of 1910-17 was the most important event on the continent after the wars for independence, but it failed. Communist parties appeared in Latin America under the impact of the October Revolution in Russia and class struggle intensified. The Cuban revolution opened a new phase in the struggle and dispelled the myth of geographical fatalism. Cuba was host for the significant Conference of Latin American Communist Parties in 1975. The conference's final document proves the validity of proletarian internationalism. W. R. Hively

3577. Needler, Martin C. DETENTE: IMPETUS FOR CHANGE IN LATIN AMERICA? *J. of Internat. Affairs 1974 28(2): 219-228.* The question of direct action vs. legalism and intransigence vs. collaboration and their relations to other leftist groups have caught Latin American Communists between the authoritarian right and the insurrectionary left. Older leaders work within their systems while younger members fail at urban and rural guerrilla war. Cuba is honored, as Chile once was, for its independence of the United States, but internal movements in each nation overshadow international events such as detente. R. D. Frederick

3578. Ramos, Dionisio Bejarano and Soler, Miguel Angel. BUILDING UP STRENGTH. *World Marxist R. [Canada] 1973 16(3): 95-100.* Discussion between the general secretaries of the Communist parties of Paraguay and Honduras on socialism in Latin America.

3579. Shokina, I. E. DIE LATEINAMERIKANISCHEN KOMMUNISTEN ÜBER DIE ROLLE DER NATIONALISTISCHEN "POPULISTISCHEN" MASSENBEWEGUNGEN IN DER ANTI-

IMPERIALISTISCHEN EINHEIT [Latin America's Communists on the role of nationalist "populist" mass movements in the anti-imperialist unity]. *Lateinamerika [East Germany] 1975 (Fall): 5-16.* Evaluates the birth of different nationalist factions engaged in the anti-imperialist movement and generating trends toward socialism in Latin America. 17 notes.

3580. —. LATIN AMERICA: EXPERIENCE AND LESSONS OF REVOLUTIONARY STRUGGLE; INTERNATIONAL SEMINAR. *World Marxist R. [Canada] 1974 17(5): 95-109.* Reports on a 1974 seminar among Latin American Communists concerning the revolutionary movement in Latin America.

South America

3581. Angell, Alan. CLASSROOM MAOISTS: THE POLITICS OF PERUVIAN SCHOOLTEACHERS UNDER MILITARY GOVERNMENT. *Bull. of Latin Am. Res. [Great Britain] 1982 1(2): 1-20.* Since the advent of a reformist military government in 1968, public sector unions, of which the schoolteachers are the most important, have assumed a significant political role, associated with the growth of a Maoist left. The schoolteachers' union was in constant opposition to the military government from 1968 to 1980. This article is an attempt to answer some questions about the social and economic background of its membership and about its aims and activities. 39 notes. J. V. Coutinho

3582. Angell, Alan. MAOISTAS DE SALON DE CLASE: LA POLITICA DE LOS MAESTROS BAJO EL GOBIERNO MILITAR PERUANO [Classroom Maoists: teacher political action under the Peruvian military government]. *Foro Int. [Mexico] 1982 23(1): 58-81.* Analyzes the growth and political activity of the Sindicato Único de Trabajadores de la Educación Peruana [Single Union of Workers in Peruvian Education] (SUTEP), a Maoist teachers union in Peru. Based on interviews with Peruvian educators and secondary sources; 39 notes. Article first published in the *Bulletin of Latin American Research* May 1982. D. A. Franz

3583. Antonov, Iu. A. CHEST' I SOVEST' BRAZIL'SKOGO NARODA (K 80-LETIIU SO DNIA ROZHDENIIA LUISA KARLOSA PRESTESA) [The honor and conscience of the Brazilian people: the 80th birthday of Luis Carlos Prestes]. *Voprosy Istorii KPSS [USSR] 1978 (1): 95-99.* Traces the career of L. C. Prestes (b. 1898), general secretary of the Brazilian Communist Party. From a military background, Prestes spent much of his life in exile, leading a party that was mostly illegal but still able to exert force in Brazilian politics.

3584. Antonov, Iu. A. V AVANGARDE BOR'BY ZA DEMOKRATIIU I SOTSIAL'NYI PROGRESS: K 60-LETIIU BRAZIL'SKOI KOMMUNISTICHESKOI PARTII [In the forefront of the struggle for democracy and social progress: on the 60th anniversary of the Brazilian Communist Party]. *Voprosy Istorii KPSS [USSR] 1982 (3): 88-91.* The pre-1922 class struggles in Brazil and the Great October Socialist Revolution of 1917 led to the formation of the Brazilian Communist Party on 25 March 1922. In November 1935 the Vargas government banned the Communist Party-inspired front against fascism, imperialism, and latifundism. In May 1940 the entire leadership of the Brazilian Communist Party (PCB) was arrested. Legalized in 1945, the PCB received 10% of the votes in that year's election. In the 1974 election the BCP persuaded 62% of the voters to vote against official government candidates. The PCB struggles for progress and maintains close ties with the Communist Party of the Soviet Union. Based on *Pravda* and selections from *Documentos do Partido Comunista Brasileiro,* Lisbon, 1976; 15 notes. A. J. Evans

3585. Barnard, Andrew. CHILEAN COMMUNISTS, RADICAL PRESIDENTS AND CHILEAN RELATIONS WITH THE UNITED STATES, 1940-1947. *J. of Latin Am. Studies [Great Britain] 1981 13(2): 347-374.* Economic and financial ties formed the bases for US interest in Chile and the framework within which these foreign relations were conducted during the 1940's. In 1940, 1946, and 1947, Radical presidents in Chile broke ties with the Communist Party of Chile (PCCh). The PCCh suspected US influence behind these breaks. However, changes in domestic and international circumstances, not US suggestion, prompted the action in 1940. The break in 1946 can be explained in exclusively Chilean terms. In 1947, the US State Department, as part of its Cold War policy, did indeed place pressure on President Gabriel González Videla to break with the PCCh. For his own political reasons, however, González Videla found the action acceptable. Based largely on British Foreign Office Records, US Department of State Archives, and contemporary newspapers; 134 notes. M. A. Burkholder

3586. Castillo, Rene. LESSONS AND PROSPECTS OF THE REVOLUTION. *World Marxist R. [Canada] 1974 17(8): 107-116.* Analyzes the actions which the Communist Party and other democratic elements in Chile must take in order to depose the country's military junta.

3587. Castillo, Rene. LESSONS AND PROSPECTS OF THE REVOLUTION. *World Marxist R. [Canada] 1974 17(7): 83-95.* A letter by the author, a member of Chile's Communist Party, analyzes reasons for the defeat of the leftist Popular Unity alliance in the 1973 military coup d'etat.

3588. Castro, Sofia de. FASCISM AND THE "REPRESENTATIVE DEMOCRACY" TACTIC. *World Marxist Rev. [Canada] 1976 19(11): 101-107.* Examines the reactionary military coup in Brazil in 1964 and the Communist Party's resistance to it.

3589. Chrenko, H. AKTUELLE PROBLEME DER BÜNDNISPOLITIK DER PERUANISCHEN KOMMUNISTISCHEN PARTEI [Current problems of the alliance policy of Peru's Communist Party]. *Lateinamerika [East Germany] 1974 (Fall): 39-46.* Discusses the political changes in Peru since 1968 and their effects on state control of the economy. 6 notes.

3590. Dias, Giocondo. DZIAŁALNOŚĆ KOMUNISTÓW BRAZYLIJSKICH [The activities of Brazilian Communists]. *Nowe Drogi [Poland] 1983 (7): 114-118.* An analysis of the internal and external sociopolitical situation in Brazil by the general secretary of the Central Committee of the Brazilian Communist Party.

3591. Dulles, John W. F. THE BRAZILIAN LEFT: EFFORTS AT RECOVERY, 1964-1970. *Texas Q. 1972 15(1): 134-185.* The 31 March 1964 coup that forced João Goulart out of office turned some Communists to urban guerrilla warfare and kidnapping. The failure of these activities gained supporters for the Russian-backed program of peaceful revolution. Primary and secondary sources; 142 notes. R. H. Tomlinson

3592. Ellner, Steve. "Acción Democrática-Partido Comunista de Venezuela: Rivalry on the Venezuelan Left and in Organized Labor, 1936-1948." U. of New Mexico 1979. 230 pp. *DAI 1980 40(12): 6388-A.* 8012544

3593. Fazio, Hugo. THE DARK NIGHT WILL END. *World Marxist R. 1975 18(5): 128-133.* Discusses economic conditions and the Communist Party in Chile, 1974-75.

3594. Figueroa, Humberto. INTERNATIONAL SOLIDARITY IN ACTION. *World Marxist Rev. [Canada] 1976 19(11): 89-91.* A 60th birthday tribute to Luis Corvalán, leader in the Chilean Communist Party and symbol of liberation against the fascist regime which overthrew Salvador Allende in 1973.

3595. Fuenmayor, Juan Bautista. *Historia de la Venezuela Política Contemporánea* [The history of contemporary Venezuelan politics]. 9 vol. Caracas: n.p., 1976-82.

3596. Furci, Carmelo. THE CHILEAN COMMUNIST PARTY (PCCH) AND ITS THIRD UNDERGROUND PERIOD, 1973-1980. *Bull. of Latin Am. Res. [Great Britain] 1983 2(1): 81-95.* Examines the developments within the Chilean Communist Party after the fall of Salvador Allende, especially the party's analysis of the Allende years, the post-1973 party structure both in Chile and in exile, and its present strategy for a return to democracy in Chile. The crucial difference between this period and the party's two earlier underground periods is the enormous number of its members in exile, and the different experiences and difficulties in communication resulting from this division. 60 notes. J. V. Coutinho

3597. Furci, Carmelo. *The Chilean Communist Party and the Road to Socialism.* London: Zed, 1985. 204 pp.

3598. Gamutilo, V. A. IZDANIE TRUDOV V. I. LENINA V ARGENTINE [The publication of V. I. Lenin's works in Argentina]. *Novaia i Noveishaia Istoriia [USSR] 1970 (2): 194-197.* The Argentinian Communist Party, founded in 1918, began publishing Lenin's works in the same year, and subsequently Lenin's writings appeared in *La Internacional, La Juventud Communista, La Companera,* and *La Obteva.* In September 1930 repressions and prohibitions were introduced against the socialist press, but the Communist Party continued publishing illegally. Lenin's collected works were first published during the 1940's, and again by Kartago publishers between 1957 and 1964. Many of Lenin's brochures were produced by the Anteo publishing house during the period 1945-57. 17 notes. L. Smith

3599. Goncharov, V. M. KHERONIMO ARNEDO AL'VARES (K 75-LETIIU SO DNIA ROZHDENIIA) [Heronimo Arnedo Alvarez on his 75th birthday]. *Voprosy Istorii KPSS [USSR] 1972 (10): 107-109.* Surveys the history of Argentina's Communist Party, 1925-70, through the life of Alvarez (b. 1897).

3600. Goncharov, V. M. PEDRO SAAD [Pedro Saad]. *Voprosy Istorii KPSS [USSR] 1979 (5): 129-131.* A biographical sketch of Pedro Saad (b. 1909), member of the Communist Party of Ecuador since 1934 and of its Executive Committee since 1938. He has served as the Party's General Secretary since 1952.
L. E. Holmes

3601. Goncharov, V. M. RODOLFO GIOLDI: REVOLIUTSIONER LENINSKOI SHKOLI [Rodolfo Ghioldi: a revolutionary of the Lenin school]. *Novaia i Noveishaia Istoriia [USSR] 1972 (6): 59-71.* Examines the life of Rodolfo Ghioldi, from his birth in Buenos Aires on 21 January 1897, to when he received the Order of the October Revolution in the Kremlin on the 28 June 1972. Describes: his early life; his entry into the university library at Buenos Aires; his early interest in sociopolitical literature; his active political involvement from the age of 16; his work for the Communist Party of Argentina; his arrest and imprisonment in 1935 in Brazil; his return to Argentina; the Argentinian coup d'etat of June 1943; his nomination for the presidency; the attempts made on his life; his work as a deputy of the Constitutional Assembly of Argentina; and his journey to the USSR. Based on articles in *Pravda,* and secondary works. 35 notes. L. Smith

3602. Goncharov, V. M. VIKTORIO KODOVIL'IA—REVOLIUTSIONER, INTERNATSIONALIST, PATRIOT [Victorio Codovilla, revolutionary, internationalist, patriot]. *Novaia i Noveishaia Istoriia [USSR] 1979 (1): 68-82, (2): 100-115.* Part I. The life and work of Victorio Codovilla (1894-1970), a leader of the Communist Party. Germany attacked the USSR in 1941, Codovilla returned illegally from exile in Chile to Argentina and organized a solidarity movement in support of the Soviet Union. In 1954 he was the main proponent of the view that the Communist Party should play a leading role in a broad democratic opposition against Argentinian dictatorship. In the immediate postwar years Codovilla called for support for some of Juan Peron's reformist measures. Codovilla was imprisoned and constantly persecuted by the reactionary authorities. Part II. The establishment of Latin America's first socialist state in Cuba raised new hopes for all the progressive forces in the area. The Argentine Party expressed its sympathies with Cuba and Codovilla went there in 1964. Argentina lived through yet another of its structural crises and the government ruthlessly followed International Monetary Fund strictures. Codovilla advocated cooperation with left-wing Peronists and fought for internal party unity. He organized against US imperialism and the Vietnam War and sided with the USSR against China. He died in Moscow in April 1970 after a long illness. 62 notes.
V. Sobeslavsky

3603. Gonzalez, Julio. AGAINST THE DICTATORSHIP. *World Marxist R. [Canada] 1975 18(4): 97-104.* Portrays the role of the Communist Party toward the liberation of Uruguay, 1973-75.

3604. Gugushkin, V. A. K 50-LETIIU BRAZIL'SKOI KOMMUNISTICHESKOI PARTII [The 50th anniversary of the Brazilian Communist Party]. *Voprosy Istorii KPSS [USSR] 1972 (3): 101-106.*

3605. Hackethal, Eberhard. ZUM KAMPF DER KOMMUNISTISCHEN PARTEI CHILES UM DIE EINHEIT DER ARBEITERKLASSE UND DIE ANTIIMPERIALISTISCHE VOLKSEINHEIT (1956-69) [The struggle of the Communist Party of Chile for unity of the working class and anti-imperialist unity of the people, 1956-69]. *Beiträge zur Geschichte der Arbeiterbewegung [East Germany] 1973 15(5): 739-756.* The Communist Party of Chile opposed simplified theories of the sudden introduction of the dictatorship of the proletariat and the dogmatic application of the armed guerrilla warfare. It aimed instead at winning a majority of the supporters of the Christian Democrats, increasingly disillusioned by the policies of the government. To realize the united front policy of a broad people's front, the Party first had to develop and improve its agrarian theories. Cooperation with the Socialist Party of Chile and involvement in the trade unions prepared the ground for a united front. In the sixties this resulted in the development of a Communist mass movement and the foundation of the Popular Unity in 1969. Primary and secondary sources; 91 notes.
R. Wagnleitner

3606. Henderson, James D. ANOTHER ASPECT OF THE *VIOLENCIA. Secolas Ann. 1980 11: 120-136.* Examines the strong anti-Communist nature of Colombia's *Violencia,* 1940's-65.

3607. Jordan, David C. PERON'S RETURN, ALLENDE'S FALL AND COMMUNISM IN LATIN AMERICA. *Orbis 1973 17(3): 1025-1052.* Discusses Latin American politics concerning Juan Peron and Argentina, Salvador Allende and Chile, and communism in the 1970's.

3608. Kohen, A. CLAVES PARA LA COMPRENSIÓN DE UNA ÉPOCA: 1945-1955 [Keys toward understanding an epoch: 1945-55]. *Lateinamerika [East Germany] 1977 (Aut): 5-35.* The role of the Communists in combatting Juan Perón and "peronismo" in Argentina is fitted into the larger context of the cold war between the United States and the USSR. "Peronismo" failed to take into account the economic realities and needs of the Argentinian people, and as a result it failed to mobilize the working class. In the 1973 return of Perón, the left-wing peronistas responded to the economic consciousness of the workers. Secondary sources; 26 notes.
D. R. Stevenson

3609. Kolomijez, G. N. DIE KOMMUNISTISCHE PARTEI ARGENTINIENS IM KAMPF FÜR EINE NATIONALE DEMOKRATISCHE FRONT [The Communist Party of Argentina in the struggle for a national democratic front]. *Lateinamerika [East Germany] 1972 (Fall): 55-60.* An overview of Argentina's political development since the 1970 emergence of the national movement. 3 notes.

3610. Korolev, Iu. N. BOR'BA ZA EDINSTVO RABOCHEGO KLASSA V CHILI (1956-1970 GG.) [The struggle for the unity of the working class in Chile, 1956-70]. *Voprosy Istorii [USSR] 1973 (1): 62-77.* Highlights the acute political and ideological struggle attending the emergence and consolidation of the United Trade Union Centre of Chile—a powerful organization of the country's working population uniting about one million workers, office employees and peasants. Analyzes the peculiarities in the structure of the Chilean working class and its organizations, and emphasizes the outstanding role played by the Chilean Communist Party in the struggle to achieve labour unity. The unity of the Chilean working class provided the groundwork for the establishment of a broad alliance of democratic and anti-imperialist forces, on the basis of which there emerged a coalition of the Left political parties—the Popular Unity Bloc, which gained victory in the presidential elections of September 1970. The country's working class is the chief motive force which directs the process of revolutionary transformations taking place in Chile. J

3611. Kozlov, Iu. K. BOEVOI RUKOVODITEL' URUGVAISKIKH KOMMUNISTOV (K 70-LETIIU SO DNIA ROZHDENIIA PERVOGO SEKRETARIA TSK KOMPARTII URUGVAIA RODNEIA ARISMENDI) [Militant leader of the Uruguayan Communists: on the 70th birthday of Rodney Arismendi, First Secretary of the Central Committee of the Communist Party of Uruguay]. *Voprosy Istorii KPSS [USSR] 1983 (3): 118-121.* Charts the political career of Rodney Arismendi, particularly his participation in the Communist youth movement and his parliamentary work. Examines his writings on various aspects of the struggle for socialism. Note. G. Dombrovski

3612. Kozlov, Iu. K. GUSTAVO MACHADO [Gustavo Machado]. *Voprosy Istorii KPSS [USSR] 1978 (7): 121-124.* A biographical sketch of Gustavo Machado (b. 1898), Latin American revolutionary and one of the founders and leaders of the Communist Party of Venezuela. Machado helped organize radical groups and Communist parties throughout Latin America. Despite frequent arrests and exile, Machado served the Venezuelan Communist Party as a member of the Secretariat, parliamentary delegate, and from 1971 as chairman. Based on published documents and secondary sources; 3 notes. L. E. Holmes

3613. Kudachkin, M. F. KOMPARTIIA CHILI V BOR'BE ZA EDINSTVO I POBEDU NARODNYKH ANTIIMPERIALISTICHESKIKH SIL [The Chilean Communist Party in the struggle for the unity and victory of popular anti-imperialist forces]. *Voprosy Istorii KPSS [USSR] 1971 (2): 47-60.* Outlines the growth of these forces in Chile since 1952, but concentrates both on events between 1967 and Salvador Allende's election as president in September 1970, and on the role of the Chilean Communist Party.

3614. Kudachkin, M. F. KOMPARTIIA CHILI V BOR'BE ZA EDINSTVO NATSIONAL'NYKH SIL [The Chilean Communist Party in the struggle to unify national forces]. *Voprosy Istorii KPSS [USSR] 1964 (2): 54-65.* Discusses the long-term attempts of the Chilean Communist Party to develop a strategy of popular electoral alliances to combat the forces of the right.

3615. Kudachkin, M. F. LUIS KORVALAN: VIDNYI DEIATEL' KOMMUNISTICHESKOGO DVIZHENIIA [Luis Corvalán: a prominent figure in the Communist movement]. *Voprosy Istorii KPSS [USSR] 1976 (9): 101-106.* Describes the revolutionary work of the Secretary General of the Chilean Communist Party under Salvador Allende.

3616. Kudachkin, M. F. OPYT BOR'BY KOMPARTII CHILI ZA EDINSTVO LEVYKH SIL I REVOLIUTSIONNYE PREOBRAZOVANIIA [The struggle of the Chilean Communist Party for unity of leftist forces and revolutionary transformation]. *Voprosy Istorii KPSS [USSR] 1974 (5): 48-60.* From its election in 1970, the Chilean government of Popular Unity headed by Salvador Allende attempted by legal and peaceful means to transform Chilean society and economy. But such a complete transformation was precluded by opposition forces in the congress, reliance on the old state apparatus by the new government, the opposition's use of illegal means including an armed coup, and failure to create armed units capable of defending the revolution. Based on published Chilean and Soviet sources; 20 notes. L. E. Holmes

3617. Llanos, M. A. Huesbe and Shaver, Barbara M. ALLENDE: THE COMMUNIST STRATEGY IN CHILE. *North Dakota Q. 1977 45(2): 6-23.* Chronicles the political career of Salvador Allende Gossens, 1932-71, in Chile focusing on his involvement with the Communist Party.

3618. Lovas, Gyula. FASIZMUS ÉS AZ OSZTÁLYHARC ÚJ FELTÉTELEI CHILÉBEN [Fascism and the new conditions of class struggle in Chile]. *Társadalmi Szemle [Hungary] 1974 29(3): 73-80.* Describes the military dictatorship that replaced Salvador Allende's progressive government and outlines the tactics and revised program of the Chilean Communist Party and its allies after the coup.

3619. Maidana, Antonio. KOMMUNISTY PARAGVAIA VO GLAVE PROGRESSIVNYKH SIL V BOR'BE PROTIV VOENNOI DIKTATURY [Paraguay's Communists at the head of progressive forces in the struggle against the military dictatorship]. *Voprosy Istorii KPSS [USSR] 1978 (3): 81-92.* Survey of the history of the Communist Party of Paraguay from its founding in 1928, with primary attention devoted to its most recent past. Paraguay has been victimized by the combined forces of foreign capital, foreign- and native-owned latifundia, and the military dictatorship of Alfredo Stroessner. Paraguay's Communist Party proposes a popular program of sweeping political, economic, cultural, and social changes for the democratization of the nation's life. 16 notes. L. E. Holmes

3620. Martin, Markos. V AVANGARDE BOR'BY RABOCHEGO KLASSA (K 60-LETIIU SO DNIA OSNOVANIIA KOMMUNISTICHESKOI PARTII ARGENTINY) [In the vanguard of the working class struggle: the 60th anniversary of the founding of the Argentine Communist Party]. *Voprosy Istorii KPSS [USSR] 1978 (1): 99-101.* A tribute to the Communist Party of Argentina, founded in 1918, claiming substantial and increasing popular support, but nonetheless an underground, or at best semilegal party for most of its existence.

3621. Martinez Codo, Enrique. COMMUNIST GUERRILLAS IN ARGENTINA. *Marine Corps Gazette 1965 49(9): 43-49.* An account of communist insurgency in Argentina during 1964.

3622. Melis, Antonio. BRASILE: QUALI INTERESSI DIFENDE LA TORTURA [Brazil: the interests torture upholds]. *Ponte [Italy] 1970 26(6): 661-666.* Examines government torture in Brazil since 1964. Attacks the US neocolonialism of the Alliance for Progress, notably in the Amazon region, with its precious metals and radioactive minerals. Regrets that the Brazilian Communist Party sought the support of enlightened bourgeois elements such as Don Helder Câmara, since liberal governments are doomed to fail in oligarchic countries and revolutionary change is called for. Secondary sources; 8 notes. C. Bates

3623. Montes, Jorge. BOR'BA KOMMUNISTICHESKOI PARTII CHILI ZA EDINSTVO NARODA (K 50-LETIIU KOMPARTII CHILI) [The struggle of the Communist Party of Chile for the unity of the people on the 50th anniversary of the Party of Chile]. *Voprosy Istorii KPSS [USSR] 1972 (1): 51-57.* Reviews the Party's history from the mid-1930's to the late 1960's, with emphasis on the united front campaign of 1936-45 against fascism.

3624. Palacios, Jorge. *Chile: An Attempt at "Historic Compromise."* Birmingham, Ala.: Banner, 1979. 525 pp.

3625. Pastorino, Enrique. STOP THE TERROR! *World Marxist R. [Canada] 1974 17(7): 108-110.* In 1974 Uruguay's rulers used terror to defeat the Communist Party and the revolutionary movement.

3626. Paz Gimeno, Luis M. HOW THE CHILEAN COMMUNIST PARTY WON THE PRESIDENTIAL ELECTIONS. *Pacific Community [Australia] 1971 (9): 8-14.* Views the career of Salvador Allende and the Chilean Communist Party from 1958 to 1970 as a gradual movement from initial defeat to eventual political victory, obtained essentially through the technique of infiltrating a broad spectrum of political, military, judicial, educational, and other institutions in the country.

3627. Peterson, Harries-Clichy. PERU'S SUCCESSFUL COUNTERINSURGENCY. *Marine Corps Gazette 1968 52(7): 30-33.* Describes the Peruvian Government's campaign to suppress communist insurgency, 1961-65.

3628. Prado, Jorge del. THE REVOLUTION CONTINUES. *World Marxist R. [Canada] 1973 16(1): 64-72.* Peru is moving inexorably toward communism.

3629. Prestes, L. C. THE COMMUNISTS' HISTORICAL OPTIMISM. *World Marxist Rev. [Canada] 1976 19(10): 17-26.* Briefly outlines historical events in Brazil, 1964-75, which supply a political background for Communist Party operations today; extensive discussion of the 25th CPSU Congress.

3630. Prieto, Roberto. FIVE WEEKS IN JUNTA TORTURE CHAMBERS; LETTER TO THE EDITOR. *World Marxist R. [Canada] 1974 17(2): 109-112.* A Communist Party member describes his imprisonment after the 1973 military coup in Chile.

3631. Rodriguez, Enrique. URUGUAY AFTER THE COUP. *World Marxist R. [Canada] 1974 17(5): 135-142.* Describes the 1973 military coup in Uruguay and the resulting changes in political strategy adopted by the Uruguayan Communist Party.

3632. Rybalkin, I. E. POD ZNAMENEM BOR'BY ZA INTERESY NARODA [Under the banner of the struggle for the people's interests]. *Voprosy Istorii KPSS [USSR] 1980 (1): 115-119.* Surveys the history of the Bolivian Communist Party from its formation in 1950 to its cooperation with other parties in successfully opposing a military coup in 1980. Published documents; 15 notes.
L. E. Holmes

3633. Rybalkin, I. E. 60 LET BOR'BY ZA INTERESY NARODA (K IUBILEIU KOMMUNISTICHESKOI PARTII CHILI) [60 years of struggle for the people's interests: the Communist Party of Chile]. *Voprosy Istorii KPSS [USSR] 1982 (1): 109-112.* From its founding in January 1922, the Communist Party of Chile has taken an active part in the struggle to defend the interests of the working masses. In response to the difficult political conditions in which it has had to work, the Party has altered its tactics. In 1981, it adopted a manifesto which analyzed events in the country since the establishment of the military government in 1973 and recognized that violence could not be avoided in the fight against oppression. At the same time the Chilean Communists emphasize that their aims are peace, democracy, and socialism. Based on secondary sources; 22 notes. G. Dombrovski

3634. Saxlund, Ricardo. THE QUIET HEROISM OF THE REVOLUTIONARY. *World Marxist Rev. [Canada] 1977 20(2): 70-78.* Discusses the continuing struggle of the Communist Party in Uruguay, through examination of letters and statements of relatives of political prisoners, or those active in the cause, 1970-1977.

3635. Schmirgeld, J. LA POLÍTICA DE ALIANZAS Y DE FRENTES DEMOCRÁTICOS ANTIIMPERIALISTAS EN LA ARGENTINA [The policy of alliance and the democratic anti-imperialist fronts in Argentina]. *Lateinamerika [East Germany] 1974 (Fall): 47-58.* Explains the causes of the current socioeconomic crisis in Argentina and presents a Communist solution. 22 notes.

3636. Seron, Jorge Barria. THE CHILEAN PEASANT MOVEMENT. *Cahiers Int. d'Hist. Écon. et Sociale [Italy] 1978 8: 156-165.* Analyzes peasant movements in Chile, 1810-1973. These were affected by the gradual process of territorial occupation, semifeudal labor organization, and a slow process of urbanization. A massive popular movement began in the 1920's as a corollary to local and world conditions. The first political program containing peasant claims was issued in 1923 by the newly-founded Communist Party. The First National Peasant Congress was held in 1939 and this resulted in the formation of the National Peasant Federation. In 1940 the organization of peasant labor unions was permitted, and in 1967 union strength was split between Christian Democrats and Marxists. 5 notes, biblio. F. X. Hartigan

3637. Shokina, I. E. LA CLASE OBRERA ARGENTINA CONTEMPORÁNEA Y EL PERONISMO [The working class in Argentina today and Peronism]. *Lateinamerika [East Germany] 1974 (Fall): 59-70.* Explains the problem of Peronism in Argentina's working class movement and why Communists see it as the main obstacle to unity. 23 notes.

3638. Shragin, Victor. *Chile, Corvalán, Struggle.* Sviridov, Yuri, transl. Moscow: Progress, 1980. 202 pp.

3639. Sierra, Sergio. INTERNATIONAL ASPECTS OF THE URUGUAYAN DRAMA. *World Marxist Rev. [Canada] 1976 19(12): 86-94.* Examines the growth of the Communist Party in Uruguay as both a weapon against a fascist regime and a method of presenting anti-imperialism sentiments, 1972-76.

3640. Soares, Alberto. LENINSKOE UCHENIE O PARTII I KOMPARTIA URUGVAIA [Leninist teaching about the Party and the Communist Party of Uruguay]. *Voprosy Istorii KPSS [USSR] 1970 (10): 48-58.* Outlines the history of the Uruguayan Communist Party and its consistent adherence to Leninism.

3641. Suarez, Alberto. BOR'BA KOMPARTII URUGVAIA ZA USILENIE VLIIANIIA V MASSAKH [The struggle of the Uruguayan Communist Party to strengthen its influence on the masses]. *Voprosy Istorii KPSS [USSR] 1963 (5): 42-52.* Traces the history of the Uruguayan Communist Party, 1956-62, mentioning the decisions of congresses and agitational campaigns and evaluates the popular front forged with other left forces.

3642. Suarez, Alberto. THE OLIGARCHY OF THE PEOPLE. *World Marxist R. [Canada] 1973 16(2): 77-85.* The revolution of socialism is being assisted by Uruguay's Communist Party. Part of the continuing series "Political Portrait of Latin America."

3643. Teitelboim, Volodia. PRELUDE TO FUTURE VICTORIES. *World Marxist R. [Canada] 1974 17(3): 83-90.* Analyzes the revolutionary strategy of Chile's Communist Party and the lessons of the 1973 coup d'etat.

3644. Teitelboim, Volodia. REFLECTIONS ON THE 1,000 DAYS OF POPULAR UNITY RULE. *World Marxist Rev. [Canada] 1977 20(1): 50-62.* Assesses the rule of Popular Unity in Chile and studies the methods and devices of the counterrevolutionary forces in order to eventually return Chile to popular rule.

3645. Vasquez, Pedro. AN ANTI-DICTATORIAL FRONT IN THE MAKING. *World Marxist R. [Canada] 1974 17(4): 82-87.* Paraguay's Communist Party is leading a growing anti-dictatorial front against the country's ruler, Alfredo Stroessner.

3646. Vasquez, Pedro. UNITY AGAINST THE DICTATORSHIP. *World Marxist R. [Canada] 1975 18(6): 32-37.* Discusses the Communist Party in Paraguay since 1971.

3647. Vieira, Gilberto. NEW FACES OF ANTI-COMMUNISM. *World Marxist Rev. [Canada] 1972 15(11): 99-108.* Describes the development of ultra-Left and Zionist forms of anticommunism in the world at large and traces ultras' activity in Colombia and traditional and official anticommunist repression up to 1972.

3648. Viejra, E. BOR'BA URUGVAISKIKH KOMMUNISTOV V USLOVIIAKH PODPOL'IA I REPRESSII DIKTATURY [The struggle of Uruguayan Communists as an underground movement during dictatorial repression]. *Voprosy Istorii KPSS [USSR] 1976 (12): 95-99.* Despite arrests of many Communists and a general repression of the Communist Party since October 1975 the Party retains its ideological and organizational strength as well as unity. Its struggle to uphold its principles, especially the creation of an anti-fascist front, has been inspired by the Party's previous success in the face of repression following the military coup of June 1973. 2 notes. L. E. Holmes

3649. Viktorov, A. V. 60-LETIE KOMMUNISTICHESKOI PARTII URUGVAIA [60 years of the Uruguayan Communist Party]. *Voprosy Istorii KPSS [USSR] 1981 (1): 149-153.* Describes the proceedings and papers presented at a conference held at the Institute of Marxism-Leninism in Moscow to mark the 60th anniversary of the founding of the Communist Party of Uruguay (CPU). The conference opened with a general report on the history of the CPU followed by a report on the CPU's role as the vanguard of the working classes. The first secretary of the Communist Party of Uruguay, Rodney Arismendi, gave a personalized account of the development of the Party in his country. A. Brown

Central America, Mexico, and the Caribbean

3650. Acciaris, Ricardo. NICARAGUA-PAYS SOCIALISTES: VERS UNE CONSOLIDATION DES LIENS ECONOMIQUES? [Nicaragua and the socialist countries: toward a consolidation of economic ties?]. *Problèmes d'Amérique Latine [France] 1984 (74): 104-126.* On the basis of socialist and Western data assesses the strength of Nicaragua's economic ties with Soviet bloc countries, the future of which depends on many variables.

3651. Behrendt, R.; Herold, M.; Luscher, M.; and Müller, G. INTERNATIONALES KOLLOQUIUM DER SEKTION LATEINAMERIKANWISSENSCHAFTEN DER WILHELM-PIECK-UNIVERSITÄT ROSTOCK: 30 JAHRE MONCADA: HISTORISCHER PLATZ UND AKTUELLE BEDEUTUNG DER KUBANISCHEN REVOLUTION [International colloquium of the Latin American studies section of the Wilhelm Pieck University at Rostock: 30 years of Moncada: historical location and actual significance of the Cuban Revolution]. *Lateinamerika [East Germany] 1983 (Spr): 144-157.* Compares the Cuban revolution with the socialist revolutionary movements in Europe and the national liberation movements in Africa and Latin America. Looks at the roles of the farm worker and the soldier in the Cuban revolution and analyzes the wider possibilities of revolution in the western hemisphere based on the Cuban success.
D. R. Stevenson

3652. Bejarano, Dionisio Ramos. SOMETHING NEW IN HONDURAS? *World Marxist R. [Canada] 1973 16(5): 67-71.* Honduras' Communist Party analyzes the achievements of the military regime in social reform and economic development.

3653. Braden, Spruille. CUBA: THE SOVIETS' FOURTH STEP TOWARD WORLD CONQUEST. *East Europe 1975 24(3): 7-9, 28.* Warns of the menace of communism in Cuba, its spread to Latin America, and the dangers of a naive US foreign policy.

3654. Cole, Johnetta B. AFRO-AMERICAN SOLIDARITY WITH CUBA. *Black Scholar 1977 8(8-10): 73-80.* Ties between the two communities began in the 19th century with the revolution which broke out in 1868, and have continued to the present. Currently the Afro-American people oppose US aggressions against Cuba and support the revolution which will bring equality to the Cuban people. Primary and secondary sources; 8 notes.
B. D. Ledbetter

3655. Crain, David A. GUATEMALAN REVOLUTIONARIES AND HAVANA'S IDEOLOGICAL OFFENSIVE OF 1966-1968. *J. of Inter-Am. Studies and World Affairs 1975 17(2): 175-205.* Following Cuba's successful revolution, Fidel Castro attempted to build a Latin American revolution, based on an independent Marxist approach. Castro supported armed intervention in other governments and actually intervened in the operations of Communist parties throughout Latin America. The Guatemalan Labor Party, a Communist organization whose Castroite faction inhibited the party's growth, became disturbed over Castro's activity. After the death of Che Guevara, however, Castro backtracked on the hemisphere-wide revolution and became more conciliatory toward America's Communist parties. Based on Cuban and Guatemalan documents and secondary sources; 24 notes, biblio.
J. R. Thomas

3656. Cruz, Vladimir de la. EL PRIMER CONGRESO DEL PARTIDO COMUNISTA DE COSTA RICA [The first congress of the Costa Rican Communist Party]. *Estudios Sociales Centroamericanos [Costa Rica] 1980 9(27): 25-63.* Examines the roots of worker and Communist activity in Costa Rica, the 1931 founding of the Communist Party, and its growth and spread. Based upon newspapers and secondary sources; 60 notes. T. D. Schoonover

3657. Darusenkov, O. CUBA ON THE ROAD TO SOCIALISM. *Int. Affairs [USSR] 1976 23(3): 49-53.* Report on Cuban socialist development on the conclusion of the First Congress of the Communist Party of Cuba 17-22 December 1975. Praises Cuba's social and economic progress, the strengthening of relations between Cuba and the Soviet bloc, the growing importance of Cuba as the leader of the anti-imperialist struggle in Latin America, and the CPC's strong adherence to a pro-Soviet line. D. K. McQuilkin

3658. Duch, Juan. POLVEKA BOR'BY (50-LETIIU MEKSIKANSKOI KOMMUNISTICHESKOI PARTII) [Half a century of struggle: the 50th anniversary of the Mexican Communist Party]. *Voprosy Istorii KPSS [USSR] 1969 (12): 82-87.* Outlines the history of the Communist Party in Mexico.

3659. Emel'ianov, Iu. V. KONGRESS S.SH.A. I REVOLIUTSIONNAIA KUBA [The US Congress and revolutionary Cuba]. *Voprosy Istorii [USSR] 1978 (3): 55-69.* Drawing on his close study of the US Congressional records, the author traces the progress of Congress debates on the Cuban question, which reflect the differences existing between the various groups within the US ruling circles and the evolution of US policy toward Cuba. The discussion of the different variants of American policy in the Senate and the House of Representatives revealed the existence in the US Congress of a group of realistic-minded politicians who clearly realized the futility of the US administration's anti-Cuban policy and from the very outset were fully aware of the need to recognize the fact of the revolutionary changes effected in Cuba. At the same time other Congressmen, complying with the will of the monopolies which had made big investments in the economy of prerevolutionary Cuba, the military-industrial circles and counter-revolutionary émigrés, took the initiative in organizing hostile acts against Cuba and openly demonstrated their vigorous opposition to any normalization of relations with it.

3660. Gallo, Patrick J. CASTRO AND THE CUBAN REVOLUTION. *Riv. di Studi Politici Int. [Italy] 1974 41(1): 81-98.* Discusses the aims of the Cuban Revolution of 1959, the effect of US policy, how Fidel Castro became a Communist, and whether he promised one revolution but gave another.

3661. Garza Elizondo, Humberto. LA OSTPOLITIK DE MEXICO: 1977-1982 [Mexican Ostpolitik: 1977-82]. *Foro Internacional [Mexico] 1984 24(3): 341-357.* Evaluates Mexican foreign policy regarding socialist states under the José López Portillo government as inconsistent and incongruent. D. A. Franz

3662. Goldenberg, Boris. RADICALIZATION OF A LATIN-AMERICAN STATE: THE ESTABLISHMENT OF COMMUNISM IN CUBA. *Studies on the Soviet Union [West Germany] 1971 11(4): 536-548.* The Castro regime in Cuba is unique. Castro sought neither mass support nor the appearance of it when he was contesting for the reins of power. His government is a top-directed totalitarian dictatorship, but tries to avoid unnecessary harshness. Many of the more radical decisions were taken by groups without asking Castro's support. Castro feels obliged to be further Left than the European Communist states, and yet he was not a Communist when he came to power. His posture is essentially one of self-sufficiency and independence. Secondary sources.
V. L. Human

3663. Grigulevich, I. R. DAVID AL'FARO SIKEIROS: SOLDAT, KHUDOZHNIK, KOMMUNIST [David Alfaro Siqueiros: soldier, artist, communist]. *Novaia i Noveishaia Istoriia [USSR] 1980 (1): 92-106.* Continued from earlier article. Siqueiros's life from his imprisonment and trial in 1962 through the award of Mexico's National Arts Prize in 1966 to his 1973 visit to the USSR. Based on published works in Russian and Spanish; 19 notes.
D. N. Collins

3664. Handal, Schafik Jorge. WALKA REWOLUCYJNA W SALWADORZE [The revolutionary struggle in El Salvador]. *Nowe Drogi [Poland] 1983 (7): 110-113.* The general secretary of the Communist Party of El Salvador writes on the current revolutionary struggle against US imperialism.

3665. Kirkpatrick, Jeane. U.S. SECURITY & LATIN AMERICA. *Commentary 1981 71(1): 29-40.* The ideology embodied in Zbigniew Brzezinski's *Between Two Ages,* the two Linowitz reports, and *The Southern Connection,* a report issued by the Institute for Policy Studies Ad Hoc Working Group on Latin America, all of which abandoned the Monroe Doctrine for a global, rather than hemispheric, approach, determined the Carter administration's policy toward Latin America; the resulting commitment to "change" in Latin America has led to a Cuban-backed takeover in Nicaragua, the probability of another in El Salvador, and, but for a military coup, the accession of Hernan Siles Zuazo, strongly Communist- and Castro-connected, in Bolivia.

3666. Kruger, Alexander. EL SALVADOR'S MARXIST REVOLUTION. *J. of Social, Pol. and Econ. Studies 1981 6(2): 119-139.* The Salvadorean guerrilla organizations that make up the leadership of El Salvador's revolutionary movement came into being through various subdivisions within the Communist Party during the last decade. Although invited to participate in the elections, the guerrillas refused because their popular support has fallen.

3667. León, César A. de LA GRAN REVOLUCIÓN DE OCTUBRE Y PANAMÁ [The Great October Revolution and Panama]. *Casa de las Américas [Cuba] 1977 18(105): 18-31.* The Russian Revolution plays a significant role in Latin America's struggle against capitalist imperialism. Panamanian independence coincided with the development of American imperialism, which exploited the masses with the support of the Panamanian bourgeoisie. Working-class parties in the 1920's organized to combat imperialism. The 1930's witnessed the founding of the Communist Party and the University of Panama. World War II brought more capital into the country and a greater number of American soldiers. Improved conditions did not resolve socioeconomic problems. The anti-imperialism struggle culminated in the 1964 insurrection to regain control of the Canal Zone, which was aided by a sympathetic national guard. Additional victories came with a labor code and a democratic constitution in 1972 and the abrogation of the Hay-Bunau-Varilla Treaty in 1977. The Communist Party deserves credit for these changes but the Panamanians must be aware of the continued threat of capitalist imperialism. H. J. Miller

3668. Leonard, Thomas M. THE UNITED STATES AND COSTA RICA, 1944-1949: PERCEPTIONS OF POLITICAL DYNAMICS. *Secolas Ann. 1982 13: 17-31.* Examines US perceptions of Costa Rica's Communist Party in terms of the United States's early Cold War policy, and gives a background to Costa Rica's social, economic, and political order from the 1920's.

3669. Matsulenko, V. PROVAL AGRESSII PROTIV KUBY [The failure of aggression against Cuba]. *Voenno-Istoricheskii Zhurnal [USSR] 1970 (3): 25-38.* Condemns US financed counterrevolutionary activity in socialist Cuba and describes events leading to the crisis of 1962 and eventual US political defeat.

3670. Menges, Constantine C. CENTRAL AMERICA AND THE UNITED STATES. *SAIS Rev. 1981 (2): 13-33.* Examines the historical background of the current situations in El Salvador and Nicaragua (including US involvement) to illuminate the need for greater understanding of the political purposes, structures, and actions of three competing forces: the reformist moderates, the Communist Party, and the extreme right.

3671. Nadezhdin, E. M. KOMMUNISTICHESKAIA PARTIIA SAL'VADORA: PIAT'DESIAT LET BOR'BY [The Communist Party of El Salvador: 50 years of struggle]. *Voprosy Istorii KPSS [USSR] 1980 (3): 119-122.* The short-lived Arturo Araújo government in El Salvador fell to Maximiliano Hernández Martínez in 1931 and junta rule began, vigorously suppressing left-wing revolt. The Third Communist Party Congress in 1948 adopted the National Unity Program, and mass activization followed, boosted in 1959 by Cuba's victory. The National Opposition Union (UNO) coalition (1971), a Communist Party initiative, included the National Democratic Union, the Christian Democratic Party, and the National Revolution Movement. Despite UNO advances in the 1972 presidential elections, Colonel Molina of the Partido de Conciliación Nacional achieved power. In 1964 and 1975 the Communist Party participated in the international conferences of Latin American and Caribbean countries. M. R. Colenso

3672. Padilla, Rigoberto. THE COLLAPSE OF BOURGEOIS REFORMISM AND THE COMMUNIST ALTERNATIVE: ON THE RESULTS OF THE THIRD CONGRESS OF THE COMMUNIST PARTY OF HONDURAS. *World Marxist Rev. 1977 20(11): 62-67.* Traces the battle waged by the Communist Party of Honduras between 1972 and 1977 against the political and economic tyranny of the reformist, bourgeois-reformist, ultra-rightist, and oligarchic elements seeking to gain hegemony in the national government.

3673. Paredes, Milton Rene. THE PARTY BEGINS WITH ITS BASIC UNIT, THE NUCLEUS. *World Marxist R. [Canada] 1975 18(4): 78-84.* Discusses the Communist Party in Honduras, 1954-75.

3674. Robbins, Carla Anne. "The Cuban Threat." U. of California, Berkeley 1982. 501 pp. *DAI 1983 43(8): 2781-A.* DA8300633

3675. Rodriguez, Miguel. TWENTY-FIVE TRYING YEARS. *World Marxist R. [Canada] 1974 17(9): 25-33.* Traces the revolutionary struggle of Guatemala's Communist Party, the Party of Labor, 1944-74.

3676. Scalpelli, Adolfo. VITTORIO VIDALI E LA GUERRA ANTIFASCISTA [Vittorio Vidali and the anti-Fascist war]. *Italia Contemporanea [Italy] 1974 26(114): 111-114.* During 1942-46, Vittorio Vidali, Italian Communist refugee, lived in Mexico and wrote a weekly column for the newspaper *El Popular.* These weekly comments have now been collected and published in Italian as *La guerra antifascista* (Milan: 1973). They reflect the changing pattern of realities during World War II, developing themes of international solidarity of labor, the need for a second front to relieve the Soviet Union, and the danger of right-wing influence in the United States and Latin America. J. C. Billigmeier

3677. Schneider, Ronald M. GUATEMALA: AN ABORTED COMMUNIST TAKEOVER. *Studies on the Soviet Union [West Germany] 1971 11(4): 516-535.* The Arbenz regime in Guatemala represented the first historical instance of a leader becoming a Communist after assuming power. The party was small and inexperienced, but competent. The time-honored technique of establishing coalition governments and then taking control of them was implemented. A US-backed exile invasion and a simultaneous internal uprising undid Arbenz. The subsequent history of Guatemala has not been more glorious thereby. The Arbenz experience was invaluable to the Communists in Cuba when Castro came to power. Secondary sources; 21 notes. V. L. Human

3678. Souza, Ruben Dario. ANTIIMPERIALISTICHESKAIA BOR'BA V PANAME I ZADACHI KOMMUNISTOV [The anti-imperialist struggle in Panama and the tasks of Communists]. *Voprosy Istorii KPSS [USSR] 1972 (10): 49-57.* Reviews the growth of the National Party of Panama and its struggles against US-supported reactionary governments, 1925-70.

3679. Souza, Rubén Darío. PANAMA CHOOSES THE ROAD. *World Marxist R. [Canada] 1973 16(3): 50-56.* Explores the Communist Party's struggle against imperialism.

3680. Thomas, Hugh. THE U.S. AND CASTRO, 1959-1962. *Am. Heritage 1978 29(6): 26-35.* Fidel Castro, a caudillo, needed and used the support of Cuban Communists from the beginning of his revolution. Until the revolution, the United States played a negligible role in Cuba. Castro's background and personality combined with strong anti-Americanism to lead to his public declaration in 1961 of his Marxist position. 7 illus. J. F. Paul

3681. Torres, Pedro Gonzales. DICTATOR VERSUS PEOPLE. *World Marxist R. [Canada] 1973 16(4): 68-73.* The working class struggle against the dictatorship of Araña Osorio of Guatemala continues. Part of continuing series "Political Portrait of Latin America."

3682. Tsaregorodtsev, V. A. AGUSTIN FARABUNDO MARTI [Agustín Farabundo Martí]. *Voprosy Istorii [USSR] 1981 (8): 185-188.* Freedom fighter and Communist Agustín Farabundo Martí (1890-1932) was instrumental in inspiring and motivating the Farabundo Martí Front of National Liberation in El Salvador. Armed resistance to the Martínez dictatorship started in 1932, following Farabundo Martí's death by military tribunal decree. Maximiliano Martínez was finally removed in 1944, but the liberation struggle continued, directed by the Communist Party working in the underground. Active resistance by the liberation front continues to this day, with Agustín Farabundo Martí as its banner in the fight against internal reaction and US imperialism. Primary sources, 18 notes. V. A. Packer

3683. Vértes, Imre. EGY GYŐZTES FORRADALOM PÉLDÁJA ÉS TANULSÁGAI (KUBAI TESTVÉRPÁRTUNK ELSŐ KONGRESSZUSÁRÓL) [The example and lessons of a victorious revolution: on the 1st Congress of our fraternal Party in Cuba]. *Társadalmi Szemle [Hungary] 1976 31(2): 66-71.* The 1st Congress of the Communist Party of Cuba, 17-22 December 1975, was a historic signpost on the road to socialism spearheaded by the 200,000-strong Communist Party of Cuba, emphasizing the country's role in supporting the Latin American peoples' anti-imperialist endeavors and the continent's Communist movement.

3684. Wesson, Robert, ed. *Communism in Central America and the Caribbean.* Stanford: Hoover Inst. Pr., 1982. 177 pp.

3685. —. ENTREVISTA A RIGOBERTO PADILLA, VICESECRETARIO GENERAL DEL PARTIDO COMUNISTA DE HONDURAS [Interview with Rigoberto Padilla, General Vicesecretary of the Communist Party of the Honduras]. *Am. Latina [USSR] 1978 (4): 71-87.* Born in 1929 Padilla became a revolutionary in 1948 or 1949. For a time he toyed with the reformist ideas of various liberal groups but he soon became disillusioned with them and turned into a dedicated Communist. He saw that communism was the only solution for the problems of his country and the whole region. In spite of severe and prolonged persecution, the Honduran Communist Party has survived and will eventually triumph. J. D. Barnard

7. COMMUNISM IN THE UNITED STATES AND CANADA

The United States - General

3686. Alexander, Robert J. SCHISMS AND UNIFICATIONS IN THE AMERICAN OLD LEFT, 1953-1970. *Labor Hist. 1973 14(4): 536-561.* Analyzes the continued schisms since 1953 within the Socialist Labor Party, the Socialist Party, the Communist Party, and the Trotskyists. The long practice in the Old Left of splitting and then attempting to reunify remained prevalent as a result of conflicting leadership, developments within the international movement, and doctrinal issues. No new element appeared as a result of the schisms. Based upon party publications. 39 notes. L. L. Athey

3687. Appatov, S. I. IDEOLOGICHNI ASPEKTY ZOVNISHN'O POLITYCHNTKH DOKTRYN SSHA PISLIA DRUGOI SVITOVOI VIYNY [Ideological aspects of foreign policy doctrines of the United States after World War II]. *Ukrains'kyi Istorychnyi Zhurnal [USSR] 1978 (5): 134-140.* American foreign policy was based on ideologies of hatred toward Communism in general and against the USSR in particular. The author cites many Soviet and US writers who have warned the US administration to be more flexible toward Communist states. Based on H. A. Arbatow's *Ideological Struggle in Present International Relationships* and others; 12 notes. H. M. Diuk

3688. Baxandall, Rosalyn Fraad. THE GOD THAT FLOURISHED, AN AMERICAN HERO. *Radical History Review 1984 (28-30): 407-412.* Reviews the autobiography of a Croatian-born American Leninist, *Steve Nelson, American Radical* (1981). Nelson coauthored the book with James Barrett and Rob Ruck. A practical though committed Communist, Nelson is influenced more by his immigrant-worker background than by Marxist theory. An optimistic, self-educated man interested in humanitarian socialism, he is little concerned with answering for apparent inconsistency over the years in the US and Soviet Communist parties. Illus.

3689. Beck, Kent M. THE ODYSSEY OF JOSEPH FREEMAN. *Historian 1974 37(1): 101-120.* Uses detailed examination of Joseph Freeman's autobiography, *An American Testament* (New York: 1936), and the remainder of his voluminous publications, to trace the career of a Communist whose path from Greenwich Village to Paris, to Moscow, and home again was followed by other 20th-century American intellectuals concerned about how to create a just economic order and how to liberate the individual from society. 125 notes. N. W. Moen

3690. Breindel, Eric M. THE STALINIST FOLLIES. *Commentary 1982 74(4): 46-49.* Looks at the responses of American Communists, and former Communists, to USSR invasions and Stalinist terror, especially Paul Robeson, Susan Sontag, Paul Robeson, Jr., Jessica Mitford, Pete Seeger, and Steve Nelson; observes the difficulty of a true Communist to find fault with any of the decisions of Joseph Stalin or his successors.

3691. Buhle, Paul. PAUL NOVICK: A RADICAL LIFE. *Radical Am. 1983 17(5): 74-75.* Paul Novick worked on the *Morgan Freiheit*, a Yiddish Communist newspaper, from its founding in 1922. Since 1939, he has been its editor. Novick and the paper actively link an aging Yiddish community with their roots, their radicalism, and the present. When the paper was founded there were many like it. It has survived party-line shifts and the decline of the native-language press. Based on oral history materials of the American Left at the Tamiment Institute. C. M. Hough

3692. Diggins, John P. BUCKLEY'S COMRADES: THE EX-COMMUNIST AS CONSERVATIVE. *Dissent 1975 22(4): 370-386.* Discusses the ex-radicals and ex-Communists who turned conservative and joined William F. Buckley, Jr.'s *National Review* (1950's-70's).

3693. Duke, David C. ANNA LOUISE STRONG AND THE SEARCH FOR A GOOD CAUSE. *Pacific Northwest Q. 1975 66(3): 123-137.* Committed to humanitarian causes throughout her life, Anna Louise Strong initially received inspiration from Industrial Workers of the World activities and the Seattle General Strike of 1919. But it was in the USSR of the 1920's and 1930's that she found a new sense of achievement as organizer and writer. Never a doctrinaire Marxist and never fully recognized for her achievements in the Soviet Union, Ms. Strong gradually developed an affection for the Maoist brand of communism. Her praise of the Chinese model led to deportation from the Soviet Union in 1948. Though subsequently exonerated of the charges, she chose life in China as an activist writer until her death in 1970. Based on primary and secondary sources; 2 photos, 67 notes. M. L. Tate

3694. Duke, David C. SPY SCARES, SCAPEGOATS, AND THE COLD WAR. *South Atlantic Q. 1980 79(3): 245-256.* Traces the paths of two American women, Agnes Smedley (d. 1950) and Anna Louise Strong (1885-1970), from the post-World War I period until their respective deaths. Smedley was quite enamored by the Communist movement in China, Strong by the Communist takeover in Russia. Strong was later deported from the USSR for not adhering precisely to the Communist line—a very disenchanting experience for her. Both became scapegoats for Americans and Russians who were looking for excuses for the failures that marked their Cold War ventures. Based on the Strong Papers, University of Washington Libraries, Seattle; Strong Papers, Swarthmore College Peace Collection, and the writings of Agnes Smedley; 28 notes. H. M. Parker, Jr.

3695. Fenyo, Mario D. TROTSKY AND HIS HEIRS: THE AMERICAN PERSPECTIVE. *Studies in Comparative Communism 1977 10(1-2): 204-215.* American Trotskyists such as Novack and Rodney deal with Marxist thought. Cannon's *History of American Trotskyism* is the best source on Trotskyism. Trotskyists have presented their views on socialist countries. Mandel, a Belgian Trotskyist, writes on economics and Soviet foreign policy. Trotskyists continue to express their views on race and feminism. 5 notes, biblio. D. Balmuth

3696. Feuer, Lewis S. BERTRAM DAVID WOLFE 1896-1977. *Survey [Great Britain] 1977-78 23(1): 194-201.* Bertram David Wolfe, author of *Three Who Made a Revolution,* lost his position as a teacher in New York shortly after becoming a radical socialist and lived as an underground revolutionary for the next 13 years. Influential in both the Mexican and American Communist Parties, Wolfe supported Jay Lovestone and represented the American Communist Party on the Executive Committee of the Communist International. Disenchantment with Communism turned Wolfe to Spanish literature and he took a masters' degree in the subject in 1931 from Columbia University. Wolfe subsequently served in a number of teaching posts and finally accepted an appointment as a Fellow of the Hoover Institution. D. R. McDonald

3697. Fisher, Sethard. MARXIST PRESCRIPTIONS FOR BLACK AMERICAN EQUALITY. *Phylon 1984 45(1): 52-66.* Reviews the position of the Communist Party and the Socialist Workers Party on equality for blacks in the United States, and discusses Marxist interpretations of blacks' struggle in revolutionary context. Primary sources; 23 notes.

3698. Glazer, Nathan. JEWISH INTELLECTUALS. *Partisan Rev. 1984-85 51-52(4-1): 674-679.* Glazer explores the attraction of communism and socialism, as universals, to Jewish intellectuals and how the result contributed to literary modernism. Although many Jewish intellectuals contributed to the *Partisan Review*, the magazine had little to say about Jews, Jewishness, or Judaism. D. K. Pickens

3699. Hall, Gus. THE BAROMETER POINTS TO STORMY WEATHER. *World Marxist Rev. [Canada] 1976 19(4): 20-31.* Sees a rise and decline of the United States between 1876 and 1975, and predicts that revolutionary movements will continue to grow through the Bicentennial.

3700. Hudson, Hosea. *Black Worker in the Deep South.* New York: Internat., 1972. 130 pp.

3701. Karmarkovic, Alex. AMERICAN EVANGELICAL RESPONSES TO THE RUSSIAN REVOLUTION AND THE RISE OF COMMUNISM IN THE TWENTIETH CENTURY. *Fides et Hist. 1972 4(2): 11-27.* Evangelical Christians took little note of the Russian Revolution in the years immediately following 1917; although later they unanimously perceived both communism and the Soviet Union as implacable, even satanic, threats to America and Christianity. Evangelical opposition took little cognizance of communism's economic or political thrust, emphasizing rather its spiritual aspects—militant antireligion, materialism, and violence. To counter communism they have advocated an aroused, enlightened, and religiously recommitted Christianity. Based on primary and secondary sources; 43 notes. R. Butchart

3702. Koroleva, A. P. NEGRITIANSKIE VYSTUPLENIIA 1960-KH GODOV V SSHA [The Negro disturbances of the 1960's in the United States]. *Voprosy Istorii [USSR] 1973 (12): 123-138.* Surveys the unrest and disturbances in black urban districts of American cities during the summers of the 1960's. Chronicles various disturbances, describes the development and organization of black movements, the reaction of business to the turmoil, the government's response at various levels, and the position of the American Communist Party in the crisis. Based on news reports; 85 notes.

3703. LaPointe, Richard Terry. "Ideology and Organization in Teacher Unionism." U. of California, Los Angeles 1976. 254 pp. *DAI 1976 37(1): 156-157-A.*

3704. Latham, Earl. FROM LEFT TO RIGHT. *Rev. in Am. Hist. 1977 5(1): 106-111.* Review article prompted by John P. Diggins, *Up from Communism: Conservative Odysseys in American Intellectual History* (New York: Harper & Row, 1975), which discusses Max Eastman, John Dos Passos, Will Herberg, and James Burnham, and why these at-first radical leftists became staunch anti-Communists.

3705. Leon, D. H. REVIEW: WHATEVER HAPPENED TO THE AMERICAN SOCIALIST PARTY? A CRITICAL SURVEY OF THE SPECTRUM OF INTERPRETATIONS. *Am. Q. 1971 23(2): 236-258.* A review of recent publications dealing with socialism and the socialist movement in America, including Communists, Social Democratics, Trotskyites, Maoists, and any other avowedly socialist political party. The political failure of American socialism is due to the success of American capitalism. After an examination of a variety of explanations for socialist failure, notes that there is a general feeling that America has achieved the chief values of socialism through its other parties. "The Party was defeated but its program was (more or less) fulfilled." This argument, however, contains major flaws because it is not equivalent to a claim that the basic socialist program has been adopted. 35 notes. R. V. Ritter

3706. Mostovets, N. V. GENRI UINSTON [Henry Winston]. *Voprosy Istorii KPSS [USSR] 1981 (4): 98-101.* A biographical sketch of Henry Winston, a prominent official in the Communist Party of the United States. Winston was born in Mississippi in 1911, joined the Communist Party in 1933, was arrested in 1948, was imprisoned in 1956, and was elected the Party's national chairman in 1964. Based on newspaper accounts; 7 notes. L. E. Holmes

3707. Mostovets, N. V. GENRI UINSTON—NATSIONAL'NYI PREDSEDATEL' KOMMUNISTICHESKOI PARTII SSHA [Henry Winston: national chairman of the Communist Party of the United States]. *Novaia i Noveishaia Istoriia [USSR] 1981 (3): 108-122, (4): 86-98.* Part 1. Henry Winston is currently chairman of the Communist Party. Discusses Winston's career from his earliest days as the son of a Mississippi sawmill worker, his entry into the party during the Depression, his visit to Moscow, his military service, his five years in the underground followed by five in jail, and his release in 1961. Part 2. After his release from prison, Winston went with his family to Moscow. He returned to the United States in 1964 to renew his political activity. Due partly to his efforts, the authority of the Communist Party increased, especially among young people involved in Vietnam War protests. An important theoretician, Winston wrote several works on American imperialism. He is a true Marxist-Leninist and a reliable supporter of the USSR. Based on the Soviet press and Winston's works; photo, 37 notes. J. P. H. Myers/V. Sobell

3708. Novack, George. JAMES P. CANNON, 1890-1974: A TRIBUTE. *Internat. Socialist R. 1974 35(9): 6-9.* An obituary and tribute to James P. Cannon, founder and leader of American Trotskyism.

3709. Novack, George. MAX SHACHTMAN: A POLITICAL PORTRAIT. *Internat. Socialist R. 1973 34(2): 26-29, 44.*

3710. Parenti, Michael. *The Anti-Communist Impulse.* New York: Random, 1969. 333 pp.

3711. Park, Seong Mo. "Reinhold Niebuhr's Perspective on Marxism." Drew U. 1976. 522 pp. *DAI 1976 37(5): 2971-2972-A.*

3712. Passent, Daniel. O ROBOTNIKU AMERYKANSKIM [About the American worker]. *Nowe Drogi [Poland] 1975 (8): 126-136.* Surveys the US working class with reference to the workers' conditions, political attitudes, reaction to the Vietnam War, which emphasizes the important fact that the Communist Party of the United States is becoming a working-class party.

3713. Pastusiak, Longin. SYTUACJA SPOLECZNA W USA [The social situation in the United States of America]. *Nowe Drogi [Poland] 1972 (282): 80-92.* Believes the United States is internally divided to an extent unknown since the Civil War. The Vietnam War intensified many of the cleavages and radicalized solutions to the social conflict. Among the negative aspects of that war cited are: the alienation of a large part of the youth and Negro populations, the militarization of the economy, an external trade deficit, and the deterioration of the dollar. The rise in the cost of living is stimulated by demands for higher wages. Notes other social ills: insufficient social security coverage for the elderly, decaying cities, and an inadequate medical insurance system. The recent revival of the Communist Party is aimed at remedying many of those ills. 3 notes. T. N. Cieplak

3714. Pittman, John. ROZHDENNAIA POD VOZDEISTVIEM VELIKOGO OKTIABRIA [Born under the influence of Great October]. *Voprosy Istorii KPSS [USSR] 1979 (9): 61-70.* In the decades prior to World War I, class struggle in the United States sharpened and the clash between the opportunist and revolutionary currents in the socialist movement led in 1919 to the creation of two Communist parties. Disillusioned members of the Socialist Party of America under the leadership of John Reed founded the Communist Labor Party of America and another group under Charles E. Ruthenburg organized the Communist Party of America. In 1920 the two groups merged, adopting the name, Workers Party of America. In 1924, despite harsh government persecution, the Communists succeeded in launching the *Daily Worker* newspaper. Secondary sources; 25 notes. L. Waters

3715. Potiekhin, O. V. KOMUNISTYCHNA PARTIIA SSHA V BOROT'BI ZA INTERESY TRUDIASHCHOI MOLODI [The Communist Party in the struggle for the interests of the working youth]. *Ukrains'kyi Istorychnyi Zhurnal [USSR] 1974 (4): 36-45.* In dealing with youth problems, the Communist Party since 1960 has drawn from the experience of the Soviet Communist Party and Soviet Komsomol organizations, often urging young Americans to strive for fuller participation in public and political life.
V. Bender

3716. Richmond, Al. *A Long View from the Left: Memoirs of an American Revolutionary.* Boston: Houghton Mifflin, 1973. 447 pp.

3717. Roth, Henry and Friedman, John S. ON BEING BLOCKED AND OTHER LITERARY MATTERS. *Commentary 1977 64(2): 27-38.* Discusses Roth's childhood in New York City, his student days at City College of New York, his authorship of *Call It Sleep,* his membership in the Communist Party, his growing sympathy for Israel, and his eventual reunion with Judaism.
D. W. Johnson

3718. Rubin, Charles. *The Log of Rubin the Sailor.* New York: Internat., 1973. 358 pp.

3719. Ruggiero, Josephine A. RESEARCH ON SOCIAL CLASS AND INTOLERANCE IN THE CONTEXT OF AMERICAN HISTORY AND IDEOLOGY. *J. of the Hist. of the Behavioral Sci. 1979 15(2): 166-176.* This article examines the trends reported in empirical investigations of the relationship between social class and intolerance over the last three decades in the light of American history and ideology. Two key studies are cited as landmark works: *The Authoritarian Personality* [by T. W. Adorno, et al.] and *Communism, Conformity, and Civil Liberties* [by Samuel A. Stouffer]. The author notes that findings from both works, as well as conclusions drawn from related studies, have been interpreted as supporting an essentially negative view of the lower classes with regard to tolerance of nonconformity. A brief critique of research findings is presented.
J

3720. Schwartz, Harvey. HARRY BRIDGES AND THE SCHOLARS: LOOKING AT HISTORY'S VERDICT. *California Hist. 1980 59(1): 66-79.* Appraises Harry Bridges and his controversial career as leader of the International Longshoremen's and Warehousemen's Union. Retired since 1977, Bridges first gained national attention with his leadership of the international longshoremen's strike and the San Francisco general strike of 1934. For 19 years afterward, the federal government tried to deport Bridges, a native of Australia, but failed to prove his Communist connections. The charge of Communist sympathizer-member has long been attached to Bridges, whose outspoken views have included consistent pro-Soviet statements, approval of Communist unionists, cooperation with Communists, endorsement of the general strike, opposition to American entry in the Korean War, and support of Henry Wallace in 1948. Scholars have varied widely in their assessment of Bridges, from supporting his union activities to condemning his pro-Communist views. Recent scholarly efforts have shown more moderation, and recognize that his view of labor unity was practical, traditional in method, and international in outlook. Calls the question of his relationship to the Communist Party beside the point. Photos, 43 notes.
A. Hoffman

3721. Shi, David E. *Matthew Josephson, Bourgeois Bohemian.* New Haven: Yale U. Pr., 1981. 314 pp.

3722. Simmons, Jerold. THE ORIGINS OF THE CAMPAIGN TO ABOLISH HUAC, 1956-1961, THE CALIFORNIA CONNECTION. *Southern Calif. Q. 1982 64(2): 141-157.* Traces the efforts to create a national movement to abolish the House Un-American Activities Committee (HUAC). The chief impetus came from organizations based in Southern California, the Southern California Civil Liberties Union, and the Citizens Committee to Preserve American Freedoms (CCPAF), following HUAC investigations of the film industry. During 1956-60 national organizations were reluctant to challenge HUAC. But in 1959-60, HUAC made some key blunders in accusing California teachers and college students who were protesting HUAC hearings of Communist infiltration. A HUAC-produced film, *Operation Abolition,* aroused protest because it distorted facts. Frank Wilkinson of the CCPAF, aided by influential HUAC opponent Aubrey Williams, successfully established the National Committee to Abolish HUAC, which utilized CCPAF staff to create a constituency urging congressmen to vote for the demise of HUAC. Pressure mounted in the 1960's, and in 1975 HUAC was finally ended. 42 notes.
A. Hoffman

3723. Smith, Tom W. THE POLLS: AMERICAN ATTITUDES TOWARD THE SOVIET UNION AND COMMUNISM. *Public Opinion Q. 1983 47(2): 227-292.* Reviews national surveys conducted by 14 American survey organizations in order to chart American attitudes toward the USSR and Communism. The relatively neutral feelings of Americans for the Soviets during the detente era of the early 1970's was a sharp contrast to those during the Cold War era of the 1950's. Since 1973 these neutral feelings declined because of the Soviet arms buildup, Russian-Cuban activities in Africa, the Soviet invasion of Afghanistan, and tensions in Poland. 5 notes.
J. Powell

3724. Stein, Harry. BEFORE THE COLORS FADE: MARX'S DISENCHANTED SALESMAN. *Am. Heritage 1971 23(1): 58-61, 100-102.* Earl Russell Browder, general secretary of the Communist Party of the United States (1930-45), in an interview shortly after his 80th birthday stated that in the 1930's the American Communist Party was not anti-American and in fact quietly supported the policies of Franklin Roosevelt. The labor movement was the Party's main activity and its members were trade-unionists first, communists second. Browder also expressed opinions on other subjects from civil rights to Richard Nixon. Illus.
B. J. Paul

3725. Vaganov, Iu. F. VERNYI SYN AMERIKI [A true son of America]. *Voprosy Istorii KPSS [USSR] 1981 (5): 154-158.* The Central Committee of the Communist Party of the Soviet Union held a conference 4 March 1981 to commemorate the 100th anniversary of the birth of William Z. Foster, an American who battled tirelessly for workers' rights. The son of a poor working family, he was an excellent communist, Trades Unionist, and organizer of the masses, and he brimmed with human qualities. He wrote about US politics, economics, and race problems and proved US capitalism was doomed. Foster struggled for friendship between the United States and the USSR. Based on Soviet sources, and Foster's works; 4 notes.
A. J. Evans

3726. Viktorov, A. V. 60-LETIE KOMMUNISTICHESKOI PARTII SSHA [The 60th anniversary of the Communist Party of the USA]. *Voprosy Istorii KPSS [USSR] 1979 (11): 155-157.* Summarizes the proceedings of a meeting on 30 August 1979 at the Institute of Marxism-Leninism in Moscow. The speakers praised the work of the Party, emphasizing the difficult, even hostile, circumstances in which it has promoted international communism and the cause of the working people, and pursued antiracist, anticapitalist, and pacifist policies. Note.
J. S. S. Charles

3727. Voigt, Wolfgang. NEUERE LITERATUR DER KOMMUNISTISCHEN PARTEI DER USA [Recent literature of the Communist Party of the United States]. *Zeitschrift für Geschichtswissenschaft [East Germany] 1974 22(6): 621-627.* Reviews 17 publications by US Communist authors on the development of the Communist Party USA since World War II, on the US intervention in Indochina, and on the race problem.

3728. Wiener, Jon. THE COMMUNIST PARTY TODAY AND YESTERDAY: AN INTERVIEW WITH DOROTHY HEALY. *Radical Am. 1977 11(3): 25-45.* The Communist Party has been quite successful in recruiting young blacks and Chicanos. Minority groups, however, despite Angela Davis and others, have as little freedom of maneuver as other elements within the Party. Gus Hall has been a detriment to the Party in his hard-line allegiance to the policies of the USSR, his vulgarization of Marxist theory, and his exaggeration of Party strength and potential growth in membership and influence. The West Coast branch has always been more open to discussion and dissent than eastern elements of the party. Dorothy Healy's campaign for tax assessor of Los Angeles County in

1966 displayed an attention to local issues resulting in considerable non-Party support for her candidacy. Based on information derived from active Party membership between 1928 and 1973 and on observation since that date. N. Lederer

3729. —. [DÉTENTE, DEMOCRACY AND ALEKSANDR SOLZHENITSYN]. *Society 1975 13(1): 14-47, 95.*

Solzhenitsyn, Aleksandr. DETENTE AND DEMOCRACY, *pp. 14-34.*

Simirenko, Alex. A NEW TYPE OF SOVIET RESISTANCE?, *pp. 35-37.*

Gurtov, Melvin. RETURN TO THE COLD WAR, *pp. 37-38.*

Turgeon, Lynn. IN DEFENSE OF DÉTENTE, *pp. 38-39.*

Etzioni, Amitai. INTERVENING IN THE SOVIET UNION, *pp. 39-40.*

Lowenthal, Richard. THE PROPHET'S WRONG MESSAGE, *pp. 40-44.*

Birnbaum, Norman. SOLZHENITSYN AS PSEUDO-MORALIST, *pp. 44-45.*

Horowitz, Irving Louis. AN AMNESTY INTERNATIONAL OF ONE, *pp. 45-47, 95.*

Presents Alexander Solzhenitsyn's views in 1975 on repression in Communist countries since 1918 and on detente between Communist and Western nations, and commentaries on those views.

3730. —. ONCE UPON A SHOP FLOOR: AN INTERVIEW WITH DAVID MONTGOMERY. *Radical Hist. Rev. 1980 (23): 37-53.* Interview with Communist militant David Montgomery, a factory worker, union organizer, and active Communist during the 1950's who turned to scholarship in the 1960's to become a foremost radical historian; his credits include *Beyond Equality* (1967) and *Workers Control in America* (1979).

3731. —. VELIKII OKTIABR' GLAZAMI PROGRESIVNYKH AMERIKANTSEV [Great October through the eyes of progressive Americans]. *Novaia i Noveishaia Istoriia [USSR] 1977 (4): 40-49.* Translates 10 American documents which illustrated the American Communist attitude toward the October Revolution, 1917. They date from 1918 to 1975, and all refer to the importance of Russia's example for the United States. One is a resolution adopted by the American Communist Party in 1920 calling for aid to Soviet workers; another calls on American workers to celebrate 7 November 1924; and another extols V. I. Lenin's significance for the present day. 6 notes. D. N. Collins

3732. —. [WOMEN IN THE LEFT]. *Feminist Studies 1979 5(3): 432-461.*

Trimberger, Ellen Kay. WOMEN IN THE OLD AND NEW LEFT: THE EVOLUTION OF A POLITICS OF PERSONAL LIFE, *pp. 432-450.* Compares the autobiographies of Peggy Dennis, *The Autobiography of an American Communist: A Personal View of a Political Life, 1925-1975* (Berkeley: Lawrence Hall & Co., 1977), and Elinor Langer, "Notes for the Next Time, A Memoir of the 1960's," *Working Papers* Fall, 1973: 48-83. Focuses on how changes in class and generation in the American family structure changed the culture of personal relations for women active in the Old Left (in Peggy Dennis's case the American Communist Party, as the wife of Eugene Dennis, one of the top leaders from 1938 to 1961) and the New Left (Langer was active in the Students for a Democratic Society in the 1960's). Delineates the differences in the Old and New Left movements, particularly the conflicts Dennis and Langer experienced in their expectations for their personal life as political activists. 54 notes.

Dennis, Peggy. A RESPONSE TO ELLEN KAY TRIMBERGER'S ESSAY, "WOMEN IN THE OLD AND NEW LEFT," *pp. 451-461.* Critical response to Trimberger's analysis of Dennis's autobiography, Trimberger's theory and interpretations of Dennis's life as a member of the Old Left are incorrect. Points out basic differences of opinion based on Dennis's belief that time, socioeconomics, Communist Party ideology, and views of women provide the context necessary for understanding how Communist ideology "determined the Old Left's views of the world and itself," and "the quality and the impact of that unique, total, long-pull commitment Communists had to that ideology and that organization." Trimberger failed to consider this context. (Followed by a brief afterword by Trimberger.) G. L. Smith

The United States - 1945-1965

3733. Adams, John G. *Without Precedent: The Story of the Death of McCarthyism.* New York: Norton, 1983. 285 pp.

3734. Alexander, Milnor. POLITICAL REPRESSION IN THE USA. *Can. Dimension [Canada] 1976 11(6): 16-22.* Discusses 1946-50's repression of political radicals, the Communist Party, and ordinary citizens by the House Committee on Un-American Activities, by Congress in such legislation as the International Security Act of 1950 (the McCarran Act) and the McCarran-Walter Immigration Act of 1952, and by state loyalty oaths.

3735. Alley, Rewi. SOME MEMORIES OF ANNA LOUISE STRONG. *Eastern Horizon [Hong Kong] 1970 9(2): 7-19, (3): 45-55.* Part I. Reviews the early life and works of American Communist Anna Louise Strong. The Russian Revolution of 1917 altered her political conceptions forever. A dedicated journalist, she patrolled the world, striving always to get the facts behind often-manufactured headlines, and she soon became a fierce and indomitable figure in world affairs. Her reporting of the Chinese Revolution in the 1920's was one of the few accurate accounts available at the time. She spent many years in the United States and the Soviet Union, but China remained her first love. In 1958, she returned to Peking to stay. Part II. After settling permanently in China in 1958, she continued to write and to lecture. Death came in 1970 when she was 85. Anna Louise Strong's career remains unique for its devotion and intensity. Her efforts on their behalf will never be forgotten by the humble peoples of the world. 2 photos. V. L. Human

3736. Anderson, Helen Esther Fleischer. "Through Chinese Eyes: American China Policy, 1945-1947." U. of Virginia 1980. 302 pp. *DAI 1980 41(5): 2247-A.* 8024048

3737. Andrew, William D. FACTIONALISM AND ANTI-COMMUNISM: FORD LOCAL 600. *Labor Hist. 1979 20(2): 227-255.* The House Committee on Un-American Activities hearings of 1952 provided a powerful rationale for the United Auto Workers to create an administratorship for Ford Local 600, but the history of the local reveals that factionalism and anti-Reuther activities in the local were important elements in the decision. Based on UAW proceedings, newspapers, and HUAC hearings; 70 notes. L. L. Athey

3738. Anicas, J. LIETUVIU KLERIKALINE EMIGRACIJA IR REAKCINIAI KAPITALISTINIU ŠALIU REŽIMAI 1945-1975 [The Lithuanian clerical emigration and reactionary regimes in the capitalist countries, 1945-1975]. *Lietuvos TSR Mokslu Akademijos. Darbai. Serija A: Visuomenes Mokslai [USSR] 1976 (4): 39-49.* The right wing of the emigration, the clergy, aligned itself with McCarthyism in the United States and with other antidemocratic regimes such as Franco and Salazar. 53 notes. A. E. Senn

3739. Arroyo, Luis Leobardo. "Industrial Unionism and the Los Angeles Furniture Industry, 1918-1954." U. of California, Los Angeles 1979. 302 pp. *DAI 1980 40(7): 4190-4191-A.*

3740. Baldasty, Gerald J. and Winfield, Betty Houchin. INSTITUTIONAL PARALYSIS IN THE PRESS: THE COLD WAR IN WASHINGTON STATE. *Journalism Q. 1981 58(2): 273-278, 285.* Examines press coverage of the Washington State Committee on Un-American Activities and its investigation of Communist influence at the University of Washington during the 1940's. The newspapers under study exhibited some degree of hostility toward the implicated faculty members. These negative feelings were reflected in the contents of the stories themselves, the placement of the stories, and the sources consulted. 4 tables, 27 notes. J. S. Coleman

3741. Baral, Jaya Krishna. US INVOLVEMENT IN VIETNAM: FROM COLD WAR TO 1960. *China Report [India] 1976 12(3): 28-52.* The 1950's saw heightened tensions and solidification of American policy toward world Communism. America's Asian policy in general and Vietnam policy in particular were linked directly to the US policy of containment in Europe. The failure of this policy is attributed to several factors: the United States' perception of Communism as monolithic in nature, the domino theory, and a "Europe first" policy. 92 notes. S. F. Benfield

3742. Belfrage, Cedric. *The American Inquisition, 1945-1960.* Indianapolis: Bobbs-Merrill, 1973. 316 pp.

3743. Belknap, Michael R. THE FIGHT FOR THE RIGHT TO COUNSEL. *Ohio Hist. 1976 85(1): 28-48.* Studies the political-constitutional issues facing the Cleveland Bar Association in the early 1950's as it attempted to defend individuals having alleged Communist associations. Based on manuscript, contemporary comments, and secondary sources; 2 illus., 50 notes. T. H. Hartig

3744. Belknap, Michal R. JOE MUST GO. *Rev. in Am. Hist. 1979 7(2): 256-261.* Review article prompted by Donald F. Crosby's *God, Church, and Flag: Senator Joseph R. McCarthy and the Catholic Church, 1950-1957* (Chapel Hill: U. of North Carolina Pr., 1978) and David Oshinsky's *Senator Joseph McCarthy and the American Labor Movement* (Columbia: U. of Missouri Pr., 1976).

3745. Belknap, Michal Robert. "The Smith Act and the Communist Party: A Study in Political Justice." U. of Wisconsin 1973. 673 pp. *DAI 1974 34(10): 6555-6556-A.*

3746. Bethune, Beverly Moore. "The New York City Photo League: A Political History." U. of Minnesota 1979. 220 pp. *DAI 1980 40(9): 4787-A.*

3747. Biskind, Peter. THE PAST IS PROLOGUE: THE BLACKLIST IN HOLLYWOOD. *Radical Am. 1981 15(3): 59-65.* Commentary on the recent literature on the House Committee on Un-American Activities and the blacklist of the Hollywood 10, focusing on Victor Navasky's *Naming Names* (1980). The key strategy was as evident in the movie industry of the 1950's as it was during the Vietnam War: have the good dissidents turn against the bad, uncooperative ones. This betrayal would bind them more securely to the center of the political spectrum. 6 illus. C. M. Hough

3748. Borisov, A. DNO ANTIKOMMUNIZMA V SSHA [The nadir of anti-Communism in the United States]. *Mezhdunarodnaia Zhizn' [USSR] 1970 17(10): 60-65.* A catalog of American anti-Communist activity, starting from Congressional Resolution No. 111, 17 July 1959, declaring the third week in July "Captive Nations Week"; the growth of ultrareactionary influence on US foreign policy being ascribed to the military-industrial complex, abetted by other groups, emigrant and irredentist, whose policy is hardly that of peaceful coexistence.

3749. Bykov, Vil'. UIL'IAM FOSTER: STRANITSY ZHIZNI I BOR'BY (II. V BOR'BE ZA DELO KOMMUNIZMA) [William Foster: pages from his life and struggle (II. In the struggle for the cause of Communism)]. *Novaia i Noveishaia Istoriia [USSR] 1973(5): 70-84.* Continued from a previous article. Describes a visit to Moscow in the spring of 1921 by William Z. Foster (d. 1961), leader of the American League of Trade Union Propaganda, particularly his attendance at the Third Congress of the Comintern and the International Congress of Red Trade Unions. Describes Foster's pro-Soviet attitude, his book *The Russian Revolution,* and his arrest by American police on 6 August 1922. Concludes with an assessment of Foster's contribution as a leading American Communist from the late 1920's until his death. 52 notes. C. R. Pike

3750. Camp, Helen Collier. "'Gurley:' A Biography of Elizabeth Gurley Flynn, 1890-1964." Columbia U. 1980. 674 pp. *DAI 1982 43(5): 1650-A.* DA8222357

3751. Carleton, Don E. MC CARTHYISM IN HOUSTON: THE GEORGE EBEY AFFAIR. *Southwestern Hist. Q. 1976 80(2): 163-176.* Dr. George Ebey became deputy superintendent of the Houston Independent School District in 1952 just as the city was going through a stage of militant anti-Communism and anti-liberalism led by the Minute Women and school business manager Hubert L. Mills. Ebey had worked for liberal social causes in California and Oregon in the 1940's and the Minute Women accused him of Communist associations. A board investigation did not prove the charges but did show Ebey's background as too liberal for the board's conservative majority, which terminated his contract in 1953. Primary sources; 32 notes. J. H. Broussard

3752. Carleton, Don Edward. "A Crisis of Rapid Change: The Red Scare in Houston, 1945-1955." U. of Houston 1978. 324 pp. *DAI 1979 40(2): 1024-A.*

3753. Centola, Kathleen Gefell. "The American Catholic Church and Anti-Communism, 1945-1960: An Interpretive Framework and Case Studies." State U. of New York, Albany 1984. 642 pp. *DAI 1984 45(5): 1497-A.* DA8414608

3754. Ceplair, Larry and Englund, Steven. *The Inquisition in Hollywood: Politics in the Film Community, 1930-1960.* Garden City, N.Y.: Anchor, 1980. 536 pp.

3755. Charney, George. OUT OF THE COMMUNIST PAST. *Dissent 1968 15(5): 436-441.* The author, once an American Communist, left the party in 1958.

3756. Clark, Wayne Addison. "An Analysis of the Relationship between Anticommunism and Segregationist Thought in the Deep South, 1948-1964." U. of North Carolina, Chapel Hill 1976. 254 pp. *DAI 1977 37(8): 5297-A.*

3757. Connolly, Peter M. THE EARLY FIFTIES: ANOTHER LOOK. *Dissent 1977 24(4): 436-438.* However intensely one may believe that American Communism was a moral and intellectual disaster, it must be acknowledged that history presents some American Communists of the early 1950's as martyrs to their beliefs, and that in retrospect their absolute right to their opinions must be defended by those who care about human rights.

3758. Crandell, William F. "A Party Divided against Itself: Anticommunism and the Transformation of the Republican Right, 1945-1956." Ohio State U. 1983. 428 pp. *DAI 1983 44(4): 1179-A.* DA8318339

3759. Crosby, Donald F. *God, Church, and Flag: Senator Joseph R. McCarthy and the Catholic Church, 1950-1957.* Chapel Hill: U. of North Carolina Pr., 1978. 307 pp.

3760. Crosby, Donald F. THE JESUITS AND JOE MC CARTHY. *Church Hist. 1977 46(3): 374-388.* Discusses Jesuits during the Communist hunt of Senator Joseph R. McCarthy. There were repeated attempts to link McCarthy with the Jesuits, or paradoxically to link them with the Senator's opponents. The national Jesuit weekly *America* became embroiled in one bitter argument. Illustrates the intense nature of the dispute over McCarthy and the position of the order in the Catholic Church and in the nation's intellectual life. 48 notes. M. Dibert

3761. Dawson, Nelson L. UNEQUAL JUSTICE: MCCARTHY AND HISS. *Midstream 1981 27(4): 13-16.* Compares the treatment of Joseph R. McCarthy and Alger Hiss in history textbooks, with special attention to the liberal bias in these books that dangerously makes Communism appear as just another political option in a pluralistic world.

3762. Denisoff, R. Serge and Reuss, Richard. THE PROTEST SONGS AND SKITS OF AMERICAN TROTSKYISTS. *J. of Popular Culture 1972 6(2): 407-424.* Discusses the songs and skits produced by American Trotskyists, 1928-50's.

3763. Diamond, Arlyn. A LEGACY. *Massachusetts R. 1975 16(3): 588-591.* Calls Michael and Robert Meeropol's *We Are Your Sons: The Legacy of Ethel and Julius Rosenberg, Written by Their Children* (Boston: Houghton Mifflin Co., 1975) a good work that incorporates prison letters to the sons and an account of how the youngsters adjusted to a life without parents. The book is more a social history of American radicalism than a psychological study. Based on primary and secondary sources; 4 notes.
M. J. Barach

3764. Diamond, Sigmund. ON THE ROAD TO CAMELOT. *Labor Hist. 1980 21(2): 279-290.* Reprints the questions of Congressman John F. Kennedy to (among others) Robert Buse, President of United Automobile Workers of America, Local 248 (UAW-CIO), from the hearings of the House Committee on Education and Labor on 1 March 1947. Suggests that Kennedy tried to link the 1946-47 Allis-Chalmers strike in Milwaukee, Wisconsin, to the Communist Party. 6 notes. L. L. Athey/S

3765. Diggins, John P. *Up from Communism: Conservative Odysseys in American Intellectual History.* New York: Harper and Row, 1975. 522 pp.

3766. Dorsey, John Thomas. "The Courtroom Drama in Postwar Germany and America." U. of Illinois, Urbana-Champaign 1979. 218 pp. *DAI 1980 40(8): 4582-A.*

3767. Drynina, N. I. SLAVNYI SYN AMERIKI (K 60-LETIIU SO DNIA ROZHDENIIA IUDZHINA DENNISA) [A glorious son of America: the 60th birthday of Eugene Dennis]. *Voprosy Istorii KPSS [USSR] 1964 (8): 82-85.* Since joining the Communist Party at the age of 23, Eugene Dennis has fought for the realization of its socialist and internationalist ideals.

3768. Dulles, Eleanor Lansing. FOOTNOTE TO HISTORY: A DAY IN THE LIFE OF SENATOR JOE MCCARTHY. *World Affairs 1980 143(2): 156-162.* Describes a meeting between Senator Joseph R. McCarthy and Secretary of State John Foster Dulles on 1 April 1953 over the senator's well-publicized efforts to put an end to trade with the Communist countries, China in particular, as it involved the ships of non-Communist nations, those of Greece especially.

3769. Ewig, Rick. MCCARTHY ERA POLITICS: THE ORDEAL OF SENATOR LESTER HUNT. *Ann. of Wyoming 1983 55(1): 9-21.* Despite his own conviction that communism was a rising threat to the United States, Wyoming's Senator Lester Hunt ardently opposed the opportunistic, "red-baiting" tactics of Senator Joseph R. McCarthy. Pressure by McCarthyites, indecision over whether to seek reelection, failing health, and a morals charge against his son, contributed to Hunt's 1954 suicide. Based on newspapers and archival collections; 8 photos, 76 notes. M. L. Tate

3770. Fetzer, James. THE CASE OF JOHN PATON DAVIES, JR. *Foreign Service J. 1977 54(11): 15-22.* An anti-Communist campaign of the 1950's wrongly accused John Paton Davies, Jr., of having connections with the Communist Party and eventually drove him from the Foreign Service in 1954.

3771. Feuer, Lewis S. THE FELLOW-TRAVELLERS. *Survey [Great Britain] 1974 20(2/3): 206-210.* A review article of David Caute's *The Fellow Travellers: A Postscript to the Enlightenment* (New York: Macmillan, 1973). The fellow travelers were less "children of the Enlightenment," as Caute argues, than "heirs to the Platonic aspiration toward the status of philospher-king." Whatever their occupation, "they responded warmly to the notion that their kind were ruling in the Soviet Union." The book is weakest in its discussion of the American fellow travelers. All were superior to the Communist Party members intellectually, and they were aware (but never said so publicly) that if they joined the Party it would mean submitting to the mediocre. This was a "freedom" they recommended only to others. R. B. Valliant

3772. Fischel, Jacob Robert. "Harry Gideonse: The Public Life." U. of Delaware 1973. 569 pp. *DAI 1974 34(10): 6177-A.*

3773. Freed, Norman. COMMUNISTS AND "NEW LEFT" IDEAS. *Communist Viewpoint [Canada] 1971 3(5): 43-50.* "The various "new left" trends, because of their unscientific approach, generalize the appearance of the contradictions and paradoxes of our time and therefore come up with pseudo-revolutionary theories."

3774. Freeland, Richard M. *The Truman Doctrine and the Origins of McCarthyism: Foreign Policy, Domestic Politics, and Internal Security, 1946-1948.* New York: Knopf, 1972. 419 pp.

3775. Freeman, Joshua Benjamin. "The Transport Workers Union in New York City, 1933-1948." Rutgers U. 1983. 917 pp. *DAI 1983 44(5): 1548-A.* DA8320472

3776. Fried, Richard M. COMMUNISM AND ANTI-COMMUNISM: A REVIEW ESSAY. *Wisconsin Mag. of Hist. 1980 63(4): 309-321.* A review essay of *The Romance of American Communism* by Vivian Gornick, *The Great Fear: The Anti-Communist Purge under Truman and Eisenhower* by David Caute, *Crisis on the Left: Cold War Politics and American Liberals, 1947-1954,* by Mary Sperling McAuliffe, *God, Church, and Flag: Senator Joseph R. McCarthy and the Catholic Church, 1950-1957,* by Donald F. Crosby, and *Perjury: The Hiss-Chambers Case* by Allen Weinstein, all published in 1978. 7 photos, 22 notes.
N. C. Burckel

3777. Fried, Richard M. MCCARTHYISM WITHOUT TEARS: A REVIEW ESSAY. *Wisconsin Mag. of Hist. 1982-83 66(2): 143-146.* Reviews Thomas C. Reeves's *The Life and Times of Joe McCarthy: A Biography* (1982), which reassesses McCarthy's personality and motivations. 20 notes. N. C. Burckel

3778. Friedman, Lester. THE ENEMY WITHIN? *J. of Pol. & Military Sociol. 1982 10(2): 327-330.* Reviews Victor S. Navasky's *Naming Names* (1980), a history of the House Un-American Activities Committee and its 1947 inquiry into Communist infiltration in the film industry. J. Powell

3779. Gardner, David P. BY OATH AND ASSOCIATION: THE CALIFORNIA FOLLY. *J. of Higher Educ. 1969 40(2): 122-134.* The dismissal of 36 members of the University of California faculty in 1950 for refusing to sign loyalty oaths showed "how unavailing it is to seek to know another man's mind by oath and his intentions by association."

3780. Garrigues, George L. THE GREAT CONSPIRACY AGAINST THE *UCLA BRUIN. Southern California Q. 1977 59(2): 217-230.* Describes how the *Daily Bruin,* the student newspaper at the University of California, Los Angeles, was smeared with the charge of Communism, undercut by the university administration, and deprived of its independent editorial position. Although only one identifiable Communist ever held a position on the paper, the *Daily Bruin* had an undeserved reputation in the McCarthy era for being Communist-controlled. Certain administrators and journalism professors, infected with the paranoia of the period, succeeded in ousting liberal editors and replacing them with conservatives and in compelling applicants for the editor's position to run for the post as if it were a student body political office. There also were pressures to require a code of ethics, limit the length of opinion articles, and ban political advertising. On 7 December 1954, administrators placed control of the paper with the student council. A student protest, unusual for the era, failed when UC President Robert Sproul rejected its appeal. Not until 1963 did the *Daily Bruin* succeed in removing itself from the influence of the student council. The incident is a case study of the sacrifice of academic freedom for college journalism in the McCarthy era. Primary sources; 43 notes. A. Hoffman

3781. Ghosh, Partha S. FROM RED SCARE TO [MC CARTHYISM]: BUILDING OF NATIONAL IMAGES: THE AMERICAN EXPERIENCE. *China Report [India] 1978 14(5-6): 27-46.* Changes in US anti-Communism, first against the USSR and then against the People's Republic of China as well, 1917-50, were due to shifting economic and political interest in the United States.

3782. Gill, Glenda E. CAREERIST AND CASUALTY: THE RISE AND FALL OF CANADA LEE. *Freedomways 1981 21(1): 15-27.* Biography of black actor Canada Lee (d. 1952), born Leonard Lionel Cornelius Canegata, focusing on his career in American theater, 1934-46, and his career in films, 1944-52; probes by the House Committee on Un-American Activities and the Federal Bureau of Investigation destroyed his career.

3783. Glazer, Nathan. AN ANSWER TO LILLIAN HELLMAN. *Commentary 1976 61(6): 36-39.* In *Scoundrel Time*, Lillian Hellman's memoir of her 1952 appearance before the House Committee on Un-American Activities, she criticizes intellectuals and journals who did not defend her and the other witnesses who refused information to the Committee and subsequently lost jobs or were jailed. Many of today's younger scholars feel that the congressional committees investigating Communism conducted unjustified attacks on freedom of speech and thought. The question remains what actions were necessary and proper against domestic Communism and what actual threat the movement represented within the United States. If responsible intellectuals in the early fifties had written and spoken about domestic Communism would there have been any role left for congressional committees? Did they abdicate their responsibility to tell the truth and inform the public? Based on personal experience. S. R. Herstein

3784. Goldfield, Michael. THE DECLINE OF THE COMMUNIST PARTY AND THE BLACK QUESTION IN THE U.S.: HARRY HAYWOOD'S *BLACK BOLSHEVIK*. *Rev. of Radical Pol. Econ. 1980 12(1): 44-63.* Harry Haywood's autobiography is reviewed with special attention focused upon the Communist Party's approach to the black question. Haywood's charge that the CP degenerated into Browderism (accommodation to nonrevolution as well as neglect of racism and its revolutionary potential) is assessed without coming to a conclusion. Haywood's analytic framework is rejected, but his kernels of insight are welcomed, as the black question is deemed to be an inadequate vantage point of analysis. 71 notes. D. R. Stevenson

3785. Grechukhin, A. A. UIL'IAM Z. FOSTER (K 100-LETIIU SO DNIA ROZHDENIIA) [The centennial anniversary of the birth of William Z. Foster]. *Voprosy Istorii KPSS [USSR] 1981 (2): 94-97.* Biographical sketch of the American socialist William Z. Foster (1881-1961). Foster was born in Taunton, Massachusetts, and joined the American Socialist Party in 1901 after having done a variety of unskilled work. He was expelled from the party in 1909 and in 1912 founded the North America Trade Union League. Although the League only lasted for two years, Foster remained active in the trade union movement. He met Lenin at the 3d Comintern Congress in 1921 and joined the American Communist Party in the same year. He was its chairman for nearly 30 years. He published many works in his lifetime, including *History of the Communist Party of the United States.* Foster was frequently harassed by officials and imprisoned 11 times. He died in Moscow and is buried in Chicago. 13 notes. A. Brown

3786. Griffith, Robert. THE POLITICS OF ANTI-COMMUNISM: A REVIEW ARTICLE. *Wisconsin Mag. of Hist. 1971 54(4): 299-308.* Reviews books on McCarthyism which interpret and reinterpret the politics of anti-Communism, 1950's-71.

3787. Griffith, Robert. *The Politics of Fear: Joseph R. McCarthy and the Senate.* Lexington: U. of Kentucky Pr., 1970. 362 pp.

3788. Griffith, Robert and Theoharis, Athan, eds. *The Specter: Original Essays on the Cold War and the Origins of McCarthyism.* New York: New Viewpoints, 1974. 368 pp.

3789. Group, David Jacob. "The Legal Repression of the American Communist Party, 1946-1961: A Study in the Legitimation of Coercion." U. of Massachusetts 1979. 274 pp. *DAI 1980 40(10): 5601-A.*

3790. Gupta, Surendra K. AMERICA'S CHINA POLICY AND MCCARTHYISM: THE CASE OF JOHN CARTER VINCENT. *China Report [India] 1981 17(5): 35-42.* Reviews Gary May's study of McCarthyism, *China Scapegoat: The Diplomatic Ordeal of John Carter Vincent* (1979) and the current resurgence of extremist anti-Soviet feeling in the United States. The account of Vincent's ordeal, ending in his unjust humiliation, may serve to remind Americans of the dangers of extremism. 7 notes. J. Cushnie

3791. Harper, Alan D. THE ANTIRED DECADE REMEMBERED. *Rev. in Am. Hist. 1979 7(1): 128-133.* Review article prompted by Michael R. Belknap's *Cold War Political Justice: The Smith Act, the Communist Party, and American Civil Liberties* (Westport, Conn.: Greenwood Pr., 1977), Vivian Gornick's *The Romance of American Communism* (New York: Basic Books, 1977) and Mary Sperling McAuliffe's *Crisis on the Left: Cold War Politics and American Liberals, 1947-1954* (Amherst: The U. of Massachusetts Pr., 1978).

3792. Harper, Alan D. *The Politics of Loyalty: The White House and the Communist Issue, 1946-1952.* Westport, Conn.: Greenwood, 1969. 318 pp.

3793. Hartgen, Stephen Anthony. "The Interpretation of the Chinese Communist Revolution, 1945-1949: By Four American Daily Newspapers." U. of Minnesota, 1976. 437 pp. *DAI 1977 37(10): 6119-A.*

3794. Hausknecht, Murray. INFORMERS AND OTHER VILLAINS: A DISCUSSION OF VICTOR NAVASKY'S BOOK *NAMING NAMES. Dissent 1981 28(2): 173-177.* Reviews Victor Navasky's *Naming Names* (1980), which deals with McCarthyism and the investigations of the House Committee on Un-American Activities (HUAC), making use of sociological theories to analyze people who were informers on suspected Communists during the HUAC era.

3795. Haynes, John E. COMMUNISTS AND ANTI-COMMUNISTS IN THE NORTHERN MINNESOTA CIO, 1936-1949. *Upper Midwest Hist. 1981 1: 55-73.* In Minnesota the Communist Party's moderate program found favor with some liberals and radicals, creating the so-called Popular Front, and becoming a powerful force in the Farmer-Labor Party and the local Congress of Industrial Organizations. Forces outside the region, the Hitler-Stalin pact, German invasion of Russia, and the Cold War, forced the Popular Front into less popular positions after 1948, permitting anti-Communists to gain power. Based on labor records in the Minnesota Historical Society; 55 notes. G. L. Olson

3796. Haynes, John Earl. "Liberals, Communists, and the Popular Front in Minnesota: The Struggle to Control the Political Direction of the Labor Movement and Organized Liberalism, 1936-1950." U. of Minnesota 1978. 904 pp. *DAI 1978 39(2): 1059-A.*

3797. Haynes, John Earl. THE 'RANK AND FILE' MOVEMENT IN PRIVATE SOCIAL WORK. *Labor Hist. 1975 16(1): 78-98.* In New York City the downward pressures on wages and the increase in case loads in private social work agencies stimulated a "Rank and File" movement among social workers. Three goals emerged: unionization of social workers, reformation of social work practices, and radical political action. Although resistance by the private agencies was important, the decline of the movement began

with its shifts in political action caused by the influence of Communists among rank and filers. Based on papers in the Social Welfare History Archives and on *Social Work Today*; 44 notes.
L. L. Athey

3798. Hellman, Lillian. *Scoundrel Time.* Boston: Little, Brown, 1976. 155 pp.

3799. Henrickson, Gary Paul. "Minnesota in the 'McCarthy' Period: 1946-1954." U. of Minnesota 1981. 231 pp. *DAI 1982 42(12): 5165-A.* DA8211485

3800. Hertz, Howard Lee. "Writer and Revolutionary: The Life and Works of Michael Gold, Father of Proletarian Literature in the United States." (Volumes I and II) U. of Texas, Austin 1974. 879 pp. *DAI 1975 35(8): 5406-A.*

3801. Holmes, Thomas Michael. "The Specter of Communism in Hawaii, 1947-53." U. of Hawaii 1975. 406 pp. *DAI 1976 36(9): 6264-A.*

3802. Hook, Sidney. AN AUTOBIOGRAPHICAL FRAGMENT: THE STRANGE CASE OF WHITTAKER CHAMBERS. *Encounter [Great Britain] 1976 46(1): 78-89.* Discusses the role of Whittaker Chambers as a witness in the 1949 trial which convicted Alger Hiss of perjury concerning espionage on behalf of the Communist Party.

3803. Hook, Sidney. THE CASE OF ALGER HISS. *Encounter [Great Britain] 1978 51(2): 48-55.* Analyzes research by Allen Weinstein in *Perjury: The Hiss-Chambers Case* (New York: Alfred A. Knopf); due to the evidence Weinstein changed his mind and concluded that, without a doubt, Alger Hiss was guilty of espionage and treason despite his persistent denials.

3804. Hook, Sidney. THE COMMUNIST PEACE OFFENSIVE. *Partisan Rev. 1984-85 51-52(4-1): 692-711.* Sidney Hook recalls a "Cultural and Scientific Conference for World Peace" in New York City organized by a group of American Stalinists; they plotted against Hook and other people from the democratic center, preventing them from taking part in the program. Appendix.
D. K. Pickens

3805. Hook, Sidney. DAVID CAUTE'S FABLE OF "FEAR & TERROR": ON "REVERSE MC CARTHYISM." *Encounter [Great Britain] 1979 52(1): 56-64.* In British author David Caute's fantasy *The Great Fear: The Anti-Communist Purge under Truman and Eisenhower* (New York: Simon and Schuster) liberal US anti-Communists emerge as the major villains. He calls Communist Party members mere "Leftists," refuses to admit Soviet control over the Communist Party, USA, thinks Communist Party membership not a legitimate issue in security risk and espionage cases, treats facts and quotations cavalierly and selectively, and ignores not only the arguments of the anti-Communist liberals he criticizes but also the Korean War, the danger of war with the USSR, and the genuine Fifth Column activity of the CPUSA. 5 notes.
D. J. Engler

3806. Hook, Sidney. LILLIAN HELLMAN'S *SCOUNDREL TIME. Encounter [Great Britain] 1977 48(2): 82-91.* Reviews Lillian Hellman's *Scoundrel Time* (Little, Brown and Company, 1976), dealing with her experiences and observations on civil rights abuses during the era of McCarthyism and extreme anti-communism from 1951-53.

3807. Horwitz, Gerry. BENJAMIN DAVIS, JR., AND THE AMERICAN COMMUNIST PARTY: A STUDY IN RACE AND POLITICS. *UCLA Hist. J. 1983 4: 92-107.* Traces the career of Benjamin Davis, Jr., a leading official in the American Communist Party in the 1940's-50's. Born to a black middle-class Georgia family and educated at Amherst and Harvard Law School, Davis was radicalized when he represented Angelo Herndon in the 1930's during Georgia's political prosecution of Herndon. Davis joined the American Communist Party and became an organizer rather than an intellectual revolutionary. During World War II, Davis followed the party line of defeating fascism before attacking domestic discrimination. Elected to the New York City Council, he found it difficult to reconcile his party membership with elective office. He gained political strength as a Democrat, but his Communist connections brought increasing unpopularity. Convicted of violating the Smith Act, he served a term in prison. Davis remained active in Communist affairs until his death in 1964, balancing party allegiance and political activism. 43 notes.
A. Hoffman

3808. Howe, Irving. LILLIAN HELLMAN AND THE MC CARTHY YEARS. *Dissent 1976 23(4): 378-382.* Presents a critique of Lillian Hellman, her book *Scoundrel Time* (Boston: Little, Brown, 1976), and Garry Wills' introduction to the book which concerns aspects of the McCarthy years.

3809. Ingalls, Robert P. *Point of Order: A Profile of Senator Joe McCarthy.* New York: Putnam's Sons, 1981. 160 pp.

3810. Isserman, Maurice. THE 1956 GENERATION: AN ALTERNATIVE APPROACH TO THE HISTORY OF AMERICAN COMMUNISM. *Radical Am. 1980 14(2): 42-51.* A study of the Communist Party constituency in America, practical political strategies, and theoretical formulations before, during, and immediately after the Hungarian Revolution in 1956. The Communist Party USA was by no means a "single-celled organism"; rather it was very complex and reflected great diversity. By no means were members subject, like automatons, to top level party leadership. Many left the Party after the Revolution because they could no longer accept the USSR's model of socialism. American socialism "must be built on the country's democratic traditions and institutions." 4 photos, 13 notes.
R. V. Ritter

3811. Jaffe, Philip J. AGNES SMEDLEY: A REMINISCENCE. *Survey [Great Britain] 1974 20(4): 172-179.* Details Agnes Smedley's early attraction to radicalism, her life in China, dismissal by Chu Teh whom she worshipped, and her relationship to Richard Sorge, the Soviet spy, in Tokyo which later caused her much trouble in the five years preceding the McCarthy era and finally drove her to England where she died.
R. B. Valliant

3812. Jaffe, Philip J. THE VARGA CONTROVERSY AND THE AMERICAN CP. *Survey [Great Britain] 1972 18(3): 138-160.* Reexamines the controversy generated in the Communist Party by Eugene Varga's *Changes in the Economics of Capitalism as a Result of the Second World War (1945)* and his un-Marxist views of capitalism. Violent attacks against Varga, the Department of Justice's announcement to plan a "dramatic round-up of dozens of communist leaders and alleged fellow travellers," and Andrei Zhdanov's radical speech in 1947 on the international situation led to the American Communist Party's endorsement of a proposed third party in the presidential campaign of 1948. Based on memoirs and secondary materials; 5 notes.
B. L. Fenske

3813. Johnson, Ralph H. and Altman, Michael. COMMUNISTS IN THE PRESS: A SENATE WITCH-HUNT OF THE 1950S REVISITED. *Journalism Q. 1978 55(3): 487-493.* In the mid-1950's the US Senate Internal Security Subcommittee conducted investigative hearings on the alleged influence of Communists in the press. Although the hearings were without legislative purpose, they raised issues regarding the rights of congressional witnesses. During the period, the US Supreme Court ruled on those rights, especially in *Watkins* v. *United States* (US, 1957) and *Barenblatt* v. *United States* (US, 1959), and usually decided against persons accused of being Communists. Newspaper publishers often fired employees for associating with Communists and in general were slow to recognize and debate the threat to constitutional rights posed by the hearings and court decisions. 38 notes.
R. P. Sindermann, Jr.

3814. Johnson, Ronald W. ORGANIZED LABOR'S POSTWAR RED SCARE: THE UE IN ST. LOUIS. *North Dakota Q. 1980 48(1): 28-39.* Discusses the antiradical attacks on District 8 of the United Electrical, Radio and Machine Workers of America (UE) in St. Louis, Missouri, as an example of the antiradical, anti-

Communist conflicts within the Congress of Industrial Organizations (CIO) during the late 1940's by liberal and right-wing people in organized labor.

3815. Johnson, Ronald Wayne. "The Communist Issue in Missouri: 1946-1956." U. of Missouri, Columbia 1973. 267 pp. *DAI 1974 35(2): 1014-A.*

3816. Josephson, Harold. EX-COMMUNISTS IN CROSSFIRE: A COLD WAR DEBATE. *Historian 1981 44(1): 69-84.* Historical emphasis on the politics of McCarthyism and the Cold War era has obscured the contemporaneous public debate over the role of ex-Communists. That debate helps place ex-Communist testimony in the evolution and ultimate prominence of anti-Communism in US policy. Former Communists provided a rationale for domestic red-baiting and witch-hunting; their accusations served as a focal point for both the supporters and opponents of the government's loyalty and security programs. Government officials, conservatives, intellectuals and liberals responded to the ex-Communist portrayal of a world endangered by a massive conspiracy of evil in ways which served their own interests and cause. Based on primary sources; 47 notes. R. S. Sliwoski

3817. Kanfer, Stefan. *A Journal of the Plague Years.* New York: Atheneum, 1973. 306 pp.

3818. Kaspi, André. "MACCARTHYSME": LA PEUR AMÉRICAINE [McCarthyism: American fear]. *Histoire [France] 1980 (27): 18-26.* At the height of the Cold War, an obscure politician named Joseph R. McCarthy made Americans believe that they were the victims of a universal Communist conspiracy. J

3819. Katz, Jonathan. THE FOUNDING OF THE MATTACHINE SOCIETY: AN INTERVIEW WITH HENRY HAY. *Radical Am. 1977 11(4): 27-40.* Henry Hay was a prominent figure in the founding of the Mattachine Society in 1950, an organization that remained the principal homosexual rights group until the late 1960's. His recruiting efforts for the society were spurred on by his own deep involvement in Communist Party activities and his belief that homosexuals would become a major target of McCarthyite attacks. The involvement of Hay and other early organizers of the society in politically extremist activities generated additional public hostility toward the society as well as criticism from otherwise responsive homosexuals. The original purpose of the society and of the Foundation which spearheaded the group's activities was to identify homosexuals as a self-conscious group, confident of their place in history and working collectively as a positive force in relationship to the heterosexual majority. Hay left the society and dissolved the Foundation in 1953 when he became convinced that internal dissension was masking the original intent of the society. N. Lederer

3820. Keeran, Roger. *The Communist Party and the Auto Workers Unions.* Bloomington: Indiana U. Pr., 1980. 340 pp.

3821. Keeran, Roger R. EVERYTHING FOR VICTORY: COMMUNIST INFLUENCE IN THE AUTO INDUSTRY DURING WORLD WAR II. *Sci. and Soc. 1979 43(1): 1-28.* The decline of Communist influence within the United Automobile Workers of America during World War II can only partially be traced to the group's support for incentive pay and the no-strike clause; both of which were highly popular among many workers. In these matters the Communists were acting in accordance with the "win-the-war" philosophy of the UAW and CIO leadership. The waning of Communist power owed a great deal to the general anti-labor and rightwing political influences that gained strength during the war and to the confusion within Party ranks over Earl Browder's post-Teheran policies. Communists remained influential among black workers and despite the election of Walter Reuther in 1946 were by no means a negligible force in the UAW in the immediate post-war period. Printed primary and secondary sources. N. Lederer

3822. Keil, Hartmut. ERKLÄRUNGSVERSUCHE ZUM MC CARTHYISMUS-STAND DER FORSCHUNG NACH ZWEI JAHRZEHNTEN [Attempts at explanation as to McCarthyism—State of research after two decades]. *Zeitschrift für Politik [West Germany] 1974 21(2): 168-183.* Discusses the rise and fall of Joseph R. McCarthy, red-baiting senator of the early 1950's, and the historian's view of him 20 years later.

3823. Keil, Hartmut. LIBERALE UND MCCARTHY: ZUR MCCARTHYISMUS-REZEPTION IN DEN FÜNFZIGER JAHREN [Liberals and McCarthy: on the reception of McCarthyism in the 1950's]. *Amerikastudien/Am. Studies [West Germany] 1974 19(2): 220-241.* This essay explores the liberals' understanding of McCarthyism and points out the political context and consequences of their attitude. The censuring of Senator Joseph R. McCarthy, expressed in terms of personal integrity and political expediency, is chosen as a typical example of their superficial level of analysis. Their reaction to McCarthy, as reflected in liberal periodicals, is placed in the context of developments after World War II, when the initial impetus for reorientation and reform within liberal ranks was blocked by the cold war and when, as a result, the "anti-communist left" emerged as the representative liberal force of the 50's. The resultant political views, more than anything else, help explain the ambivalent liberal attitude toward McCarthyism. Thus, liberals agreed with Marxists and communists in their analysis of McCarthyism as showing fascist symptoms; they did not, however, share the latter's interpretation that McCarthyism was an indication of emerging fascist structures, but characterized it instead as the reprehensible conduct of an individual politician, or of marginal groups at best. On the other hand—notwithstanding allegations by conservatives to the contrary—liberals and the right wing agreed in principle on the issue of anti-communism. As a consequence, they restricted the discussion of McCarthyism to the question of the appropriate methods to be used in the fight against communism. Their lack of principled opposition in this issue contributed to a gradual undermining of their position on civil liberties. It was McCarthy's crude methods and the right-wing theory of the "Communist conspiracy"—a stereotype also used by liberals—that served liberals as a means of dissociating themselves from the McCarthyists, by characterizing McCarthyism as a paranoid social splinter movement that had to be analyzed not within the theoretical framework of pluralistic society, but of mass society. By the time of the Senate's censure of McCarthy, the common anti-communist stand had left its mark on political, legal and social institutions. The Senate's action, while reprimanding an individual Senator, did not abolish previously conceded encroachments on civil liberties. J

3824. Klehr, Harvey. FEMALE LEADERSHIP IN THE COMMUNIST PARTY OF THE UNITED STATES OF AMERICA. *Studies in Comparative Communism 1977 10(4): 394-402.* In 1921 representation of women on the Central Committee was small; in the 1930's it rose and in 1959 and 1961, 10 women were in the party leadership, the largest number ever. Women took an average of 15.4 years from admission to the party to membership in the Central Committee while men took 11.6 years. Jews constituted the single largest ethnic group among Party leaders but took the longest time to reach Central Committee membership, presumably because of a Party effort to present a less Jewish image. Few women were members of the many committees connected with the Central Committee. On some committees however, the percentage of women reflected the female percentage of the Party. The fact that the Party was heavily foreign-born may have affected the careers of women since many of the foreign cultures placed women in a subordinate posistion. Communists were not notably more successful than other associations in bringing women into leadership positions despite an ideological commitment. 3 tables, fig., 6 notes. D. Balmuth

3825. Klehr, Harvey. IMMIGRANT LEADERSHIP IN THE COMMUNIST PARTY OF THE UNITED STATES OF AMERICA. *Ethnicity 1979 6(1): 29-44.* Until the late 1930's, the leadership of the Communist Party was dominated by immigrants. In addition, these immigrants were disproportionately Eastern European, especially Russian. The leadership also contained a relatively high proportion of Jews. This foreign emphasis probably inhibited the party's appeal to the general American population and helped to tag the party as un-American and subversive. Covers ca. 1921-61. 7 tables, fig., biblio. T. W. Smith

3826. Klehr, Harvey. MARXIST THEORY IN SEARCH OF AMERICA. *J. of Pol. 1973 35(2): 311-331.* Marxist theory has never effectively assimilated the American experience. Reasons for this include the American worker's "lack of class-consciousness" and "peculiar backwardness," and the Marxist view that the United States was essentially a colony of Europe with a totally different historical experience. America was a capitalist country from its birth. The Communist Party USA failed to develop an effective theory of "American exceptionalism" and spent most of its effort on "protection of the Soviet homeland." America has never been placed into the "great puzzle" Marx and Engels "claimed to have unraveled." 60 notes. A. R. Stoesen

3827. Klehr, Harvey. SEEING RED "SEEING RED." *Labor History 1985 26(1): 138-143.* Reviews *Seeing Red: Stories of American Communists,* a 1983 documentary motion picture by James Klein and Julie Reichart. The movie provides a sympathetic portrayal of the political activities of a small group of Americans who joined the Communist Party in the 1930's and had mostly left the Party by the late 1950's. The movie is a "major disappointment," however. "The Communists are not entirely representative, their recollections are presented in a confusing way and Reichart and Klein have dramatically and seriously distorted the historical record." L. F. Velicer

3828. Klehr, Harvey. THE STRANGE CASE OF ROOSEVELT'S "SECRET AGENT": FRAUDS, FOOLS, & FANTASIES. *Encounter [Great Britain] 1982 59(6): 84-91.* Discusses the life, political role, and possible mental instability of Josephine Truslow Adams, who allegedly served as a liaison between Franklin D. Roosevelt and Communist Party leader Earl Browder during World War II; notes postwar interest in her allegations.

3829. Klehr, Harvey E. *Communist Cadre: The Social Background of the American Communist Party Elite.* Stanford, Calif.: Hoover Inst. Pr., 1978. 141 pp.

3830. Klíma, Vladimír. DUBOISUV PANAFRIKANISM [DuBois's Pan-Africanism]. *Nový Orient [Czechoslovakia] 1983 38(5): 138-143.* The development of modern Pan-Africanism could be found in the life and work of W. E. B. Du Bois (1868-1963) who joined the US Communist Party in 1961.

3831. Koch, Lene. ANTI-COMMUNISM IN THE AMERICAN LABOR MOVEMENTS. REFLECTIONS ON THE COMMUNIST EXPULSIONS IN 1949-1950. *Am. Studies in Scandinavia [Norway] 1981 13(2): 93-110.* The Congress of Industrial Organizations (CIO) developed a consistent political stance closely allied with the Democratic Party's position. This position evolved partially in response to the Communists within the CIO and partly as a result of the ouster of the Communists from the CIO in 1949 and 1950. 37 notes. E. E. Krogstad

3832. Kudrin, A. A. KOMPARTIIA SSHA ZHIVET I BORETSIA [The US Communist Party lives and fights]. *Voprosy Istorii KPSS [USSR] 1963 (3): 47-58.* Traces the postwar history of the US Communist Party, describing its congresses and its daily struggle against the forces of reaction.

3833. Lapitskii, M. I. and Mostovets, N. V. IUDZHIN DENNIS: ZHIZN', OTDANNAIA BOR'BE [Eugene Dennis: a life dedicated to struggle]. *Novaia i Noveishaia Istoriia [USSR] 1984 (3): 81-98.* Continued from a previous article. During the Cold War, a number of laws were passed in the United States directed against Communist organizations. One of the first victims of McCarthyism was Eugene Dennis, the general secretary of the American Communist Party. He was brought to trial in 1947 and imprisoned for one year. In 1949 he received another sentence along with other National Committee members of the American Communist Party. In 1955 he was released from a third sentence, and until his death in 1961 he fought revisionism within the American Communist Party. Secondary sources; 48 notes. S. F. Jones

3834. Leab, Daniel J. HOW RED WAS MY VALLEY: HOLLYWOOD, THE COLD WAR FILM, AND *I MARRIED A COMMUNIST. J. of Contemporary Hist. [Great Britain] 1984 19(1): 59-88.* During the 1940's-60's, the Hollywood film industry reflected shifting US political attitudes concerning the Soviet Union and Communism. The film *I Married a Communist* illustrates efforts during the Cold War to uncover subversion in American business and government. The movement toward detente, however, made this theme out-of-date. Primary sources; 53 notes. M. P. Trauth

3835. Leathers, Dale G. FUNDAMENTALISM OF THE RADICAL RIGHT. *Southern Speech J. 1968 33(4): 245-258.* The Radical Right's assertion that Communists control the United States is based on beliefs, not on fact.

3836. Ledeen, Michael. HISS, OSWALD, THE KGB AND US. *Commentary 1978 65(5): 30-36.* Discusses information from Allen Weinstein's *Perjury: The Hiss-Chambers Case* and Edward J. Epstein's *Legend: The Secret World of Lee Harvey Oswald.* In both instances, experts were extremely unwilling to accept evidence of KGB espionage. Indeed, a mood of anti-anti-Communism has developed, which may only now be yielding to a more realistic appraisal of the KGB's intelligence ability and the lack of American expertise in counterintelligence. J. Tull

3837. Lee, R. Alton. "NEW DEALERS, FAIR DEALERS, MISDEALERS, AND HISS DEALERS": KARL MUNDT AND THE INTERNAL SECURITY ACT OF 1950. *South Dakota Hist. 1980 10(4): 277-290.* Senator Karl Mundt (1900-74) of South Dakota contributed more to the enactment of the Internal Security Act (US, 1950), popularly called the McCarran Act, than has been credited to him. In 1947 Mundt was the first congressman to call for the registration of Communists and members of front organizations. Hearings on this proposal, labeled the Mundt-Nixon bill, were held in 1948. In 1949 Mundt suggested that a Subversive Activities Control Board should be part of any internal security legislation. Due to Mundt's persistence and organization, the Internal Security Act, which included his proposals, was passed in 1950. Based on the Karl Mundt Papers at the Karl E. Mundt Library, Dakota State College, Madison, South Dakota, and other primary sources; illus., 2 photos, 30 notes. P. L. McLaughlin

3838. Levine, Norman. THE MARXIAN EXPLOITATION OF BLACKS. *Montclair J. of Social Sci. and Humanities 1973 2(2): 89-105.* Blacks in America are neither a revolutionary proletariat (Marxian) nor a national liberation movement (Maoist).

3839. Levitt, Morton and Levitt, Michael. *A Tissue of Lies: Nixon vs. Hiss.* New York: McGraw-Hill, 1979. 353 pp.

3840. Long, Edward R. EARL WARREN AND THE POLITICS OF ANTI-COMMUNISM. *Pacific Hist. Rev. 1982 51(1): 51-70.* As both attorney general and governor of California during the 1940's-50's, Earl Warren accepted the goals and sometimes the tactics of anti-Communist politics, disregarding civil liberties. Although in 1950 he expressed disapproval of Senator Joseph R. McCarthy's tactics, he agreed that the nation should be protected against security risks. When it suited his political interests, Warren labelled certain individuals as Communists and supported antisubversive legislation. His proposal of a loyalty oath for all California state employees contributed to his gubernatorial election in 1950. His hatred of Communism subsided by the end of the 1950's, when tensions between the United States and the USSR relaxed. Based on Warren papers, oral history records, and other primary sources; 83 notes. R. N. Lokken

3841. Long, Edward Robert. "Loyalty Oaths in California, 1947-1952: The Politics of Anti-Communism." U. of California, San Diego 1981. 193 pp. *DAI 1981 42(4): 1762-A.* 8120534

3842. Longaker, Richard. EMERGENCY DETENTION: THE GENERATION GAP, 1950-1971. *Western Pol. Q. 1974 27(3): 395-408.* The Emergency Detention Act, Title II of the McCarran Internal Security Act (1950-71), provided for potential incarceration of Communists and political saboteurs in detention camps.

3843. Lyons, Paul Harold. "The Communist as Organizer: The Philadelphia Experience, 1936-1956." Bryn Mawr Coll. 1980. 255 pp. *DAI 1981 41(12): 5263-A.* 8106984

3844. MacKinnon, Jan and MacKinnon, Steve. AGNES SMEDLEY (1892-1950). *Eastern Horizon [Hong Kong] 1980 19(8): 20-23.* American author Agnes Smedley was committed to proletarian internationalism, worked with Indian nationalists in the United States, spent years as a correspondent in China and associated with the Chinese Communists and with satirist Lu Xun (Lu Hsün).

3845. Maland, Charles J. *ON THE WATERFRONT* (1954): FILM AND THE DILEMMAS OF AMERICAN LIBERALISM IN THE MCCARTHY ERA. *Am. Studies in Scandinavia [Norway] 1982 14(2): 107-127.* The film *On the Waterfront* represented the political and personal dilemma of its director, Elia Kazan, a noted liberal in the McCarthy era. Kazan rewrote the script shortly after his second testimony before the House Un-American Activities Committee, to whom he identified individuals he knew to be members of the Communist Party before 1937. Shunned by many of his friends in the industry, Kazan worked out his own concerns in the film: to be an artist with a social conscience at a time when criticism of American society was suspect; to maintain the liberal commitment to labor unions when organized labor was politically unpopular; and to resist the Communist menace while suffering the notoriety of being an informer. Secondary sources.
R. E. Goerler

3846. Markowitz, Norman D. THE MC CARTHY PHENOMENON. *Rev. in Am. Hist. 1977 5(1): 112-117.* Review article prompted by Richard M. Fried's *Men Against McCarthy* (New York: Columbia U. Pr., 1976), which discusses the trend among scholars to question Senator Joseph R. McCarthy's anti-Communism during 1950-54.

3847. McAuliffe, Mary S. DWIGHT D. EISENHOWER AND WOLF LADEJINSKY: THE POLITICS OF THE DECLINING RED SCARE. *Prologue 1982 14(3): 109-127.* Discusses the Wolf Ladejinsky case as an episode in the politics of loyalty-security during the 1st Eisenhower administration. The Agriculture Department dismissed Ladejinsky, a leading expert on Asian land reform, as a security risk. The slowness of Eisenhower and his administration to respond opened the administration's loyalty-security program to serious criticism and contributed to Eisenhower's reputation as an inept, indecisive leader. Based on newspapers, correspondence, Dwight D. Eisenhower Papers, and Mollenhoff Papers; 8 photos, 95 notes. M. A. Kascus

3848. McAuliffe, Mary S. LIBERALS AND THE COMMUNIST CONTROL ACT OF 1954. *J. of Am. Hist. 1976 63(2): 351-367.* The Communist Control Act (1954), drafted and supported by liberals, illustrates how deeply McCarthyism penetrated American society. When Senator Hubert H. Humphrey and others defended the Act as a civil libertarian measure, they failed to comprehend the basic dangers of the Red Scare. Joseph R. McCarthy's technique of guilt by association had caught liberals as well as radicals. Liberals wanted to silence their enemies on the right while limiting the catch to Communist Party members. The Act thus confirms liberals' acquiescence to and participation in the post-World War II Red Scare. Based on the *Congressional Record,* interviews, newspapers, and other sources; 57 notes. W. R. Hively

3849. McDougall, Daniel John. "McCarthyism and Academia: Senator Joe McCarthy's Political Investigations of Educators, 1950-54." Loyola U. of Chicago 1977. 372 pp. *DAI 1977 38(4): 1936-1937-A.*

3850. Melby, John F. THE MARSHALL MISSION IN RETROSPECT: A REVIEW ARTICLE. *Pacific Affairs [Canada] 1977 50(2): 272-277.* Review article prompted by *Marshall's Mission to China, December 1945-January 1947: The Report and Appended Documents,* with an introduction by Lyman P. Van Slyke. The official report to President Truman of the fruitless effort of General George C. Marshall to avert a civil war in China was written by Philip D. Sprouse, who also wrote the same section in the China White Paper. S. H. Frank

3851. Mogensen, Henrik. OVERSIGTER: MCCARTHYISMEN OG MCCARTHY [Surveys: McCarthyism and McCarthy]. *Hist. Tidsskrift [Denmark] 1980 80(2): 500-524.* Analyzes American domestic politics in the 1950's from the position that there is a clear difference between Joseph R. McCarthy and McCarthyism, between the man and the movement. McCarthyism, which began in early 1950, peaked during 1952-53, and ended in December 1954, was an umbrella name for many small reactionary conservative factions, was never a political organization, and was only a sign of the times. McCarthy was McCarthyism's flagbearer but was not identical with it. A historiographical review. 43 notes.
P. D. Walton

3852. Morris, Robert Christian. "Era of Anxiety: An Historical Account of the Effects of and Reactions to Right Wing Forces Affecting Education during the Years 1949 to 1954." Indiana State U. 1976. 382 pp. *DAI 1977 38(4): 1937-A.*

3853. Mostovets, N. V. DEIATEL'NOST' KOMPARTII SSHA V USLOVIIAKH RAZRIADKI MEZHDUNARODNOI NAPRIAZHENNOSTI [The activity of the Communist Party of the USA in conditions of detente]. *Voprosy Istorii KPSS [USSR] 1974 (7): 40-53.* The American Communist Party, under the leadership of Gus Hall and Henry Winston, has recently enjoyed greater authority among the American working class. Through election campaigns and the media, party leaders have explained to American workers the nation's economic difficulties and have exposed attempts by right-wing elements including George Meany to disrupt detente by impeaching Richard Nixon. Secondary sources; 39 notes.
L. E. Holmes

3854. Murdock, Steve. CALIFORNIA COMMUNISTS—THEIR YEARS OF POWER. *Sci. and Soc. 1970 34(4): 478-487.* Since 1930 the Communist Party in California has influenced state politics and labor unions and organizations. California has always had a rich history of radical thought by international organizers, utopian colonists, and literary figures. Between 1930 and the early 1950's, the party exerted an influence far beyond its membership registration. Based on secondary sources and interviewers. W. Marr

3855. Nagy, Alex. "Federal Censorship of Communist Political Propaganda and the First Amendment: 1941-1961." U. of Wisconsin 1973. 394 pp. *DAI 1974 35(1): 490-491-A.*

3856. Nass, Deanna Rose. "The Image of Academic Freedom Conveyed by Select Scholarly Journals of the McCarthy Era." (Volumes I and II) Columbia U. 1979. 455 pp. *DAI 1980 40(10): 5560-A.*

3857. Navasky, Victor S. *Naming Names.* New York: Viking, 1980. 482 pp.

3858. O'Brien, Kevin John. "*Dennis v. U.S.:* The Cold War, The Communist Conspiracy and the F.B.I." Cornell U. 1979. 701 pp. *DAI 1979 40(6): 3492-A.*

3859. O'Reilly, Kenneth. "The Bureau and the Committee: A Study of J. Edgar Hoover's FBI, the House Committee on Un-American Activities, and the Communist Issue." Marquette U. 1981. 641 pp. *DAI 1982 42(9): 4120-A.* DA8203775

3860. O'Reilly, Kenneth. *Hoover and the Un-Americans: The FBI, HUAC, and the Red Menace.* Philadelphia: Temple U. Pr., 1983. 411 pp.

3861. Painter, Nell and Hudson, Hosea. HOSEA HUDSON: A NEGRO COMMUNIST IN THE DEEP SOUTH. *Radical Am. 1977 11(4): 7-23.* A worker in basic industry in Birmingham, Alabama in the 1920's, Hosea Hudson remained apolitical until drawn into politics through the agitation over the Scottsboro Boys trial in the early 1930's. He became involved in clandestine Communist Party work and has remained an active member of the party until the present. As a political radical, Hudson was involved in Deep South campaigns to organize the unemployed through welfare marches and demonstrations at social welfare offices. His politically extremist activities caused him to lose a succession of factory jobs once his involvement became known. Based on extensive oral interviews with Hudson. N. Lederer

3862. Peterson, F. Ross. *Prophet Without Honor: Glen H. Taylor and the Fight for American Liberalism.* Lexington: U. Pr. of Kentucky, 1974. 216 pp.

3863. Phillips, William. WHAT HAPPENED IN THE FIFTIES. *Partisan Rev. 1976 43(3): 337-341.* Taking issue with Lillian Hellman's *Scoundrel Time,* comments on the pitfalls of revisionist history. In the process he defends the *Partisan Review* by making distinctions between the anti-Communism of the Left and of the Right. D. K. Pickens

3864. Pierce, Robert Clayton. "Liberals and the Cold War: Union for Democratic Action and Americans for Democratic Action, 1940-1949." U. of Wisconsin, Madison 1979. 445 pp. *DAI 1979 40(6): 3495-3496-A.*

3865. Polsby, Nelson W. DOWN MEMORY LANE WITH JOE MCCARTHY. *Commentary 1983 75(2): 55-59.* The historiography of McCarthyism since the 1950's, may be divided into those who believed McCarthyism to be an elite phenomenon of the Republicans or of the Democrats and those who see it as a mass phenomenon.

3866. Prickett, James Robert. "Communists and the Communist Issue in the American Labor Movement, 1920-1950." U. of California, Los Angeles 1975. 488 pp. *DAI 1976 36(8): 5499-A.*

3867. Radosh, Ronald and Milton, Joyce. *The Rosenberg File: A Search for the Truth.* New York: Holt, Rinehart & Winston, 1983. 608 pp.

3868. Reeves, Thomas C. MC CARTHYISM: INTERPRETATIONS SINCE HOFSTADTER. *Wisconsin Mag. of Hist. 1976 60(1): 42-54.* Traces the historiography of McCarthyism since the "status politics" interpretation of Richard Hofstadter, published in 1954. Reviews the contributions of sociologists, such as Daniel Bell, David Riesman, Nathan Glazer, Talcott Parsons, and Seymour Martin Lipset; political scientists, such as Nelson Polsby, Earl Latham, and Michael Paul Rogin; a group of "New Left" historians, such as Athan Theoharis, Richard Freeland, and Norman Markowitz; and liberals, such as Alonzo Hamby. Concludes with a plea for more scholarly biographies of McCarthyites and those who opposed them, monographs on the Americans for Democratic Action and the American Civil Liberties Union, and studies of the extent of the Second Red Scare. 4 photos, 45 notes. N. C. Burckel

3869. Reuss, Richard A. AMERICAN FOLKSONGS AND LEFT-WING POLITICS: 1935-56. *J. of the Folklore Inst. 1975 12(2/3): 89-111.* Discusses accusations of Communist Party and leftist ideological influence in lyrics of American folk songs 1935-56, including the works of Woody Guthrie.

3870. Ricks, John. "MR. INTEGRITY" AND MCCARTHYISM: ROBERT A. TAFT, SR. AND JOSEPH R. MCCARTHY. *Cincinnati Hist. Soc. Bull. 1979 37(3): 175-190.* Discusses why Senator Taft, a Republican presidential hopeful in 1952, supported Senator Joseph R. McCarthy's anti-Communism.

3871. Ricks, John Addison, III. " 'Mr. Integrity' and McCarthyism: Senator Robert A. Taft and Senator Joseph R. McCarthy." U. of North Carolina, Chapel Hill 1974. 215 pp. *DAI 1975 36(1): 493-A.*

3872. Rovere, Richard. INSIDE THE GREAT FEAR. *Civil Liberties Rev. 1978 5(1): 44-46.* Reviews David Caute's *The Great Fear: The Anti-Communist Purge Under Truman and Eisenhower* (New York: Simon and Schuster, 1978), discussing Joseph R. McCarthy.

3873. Salmond, John A. "THE GREAT SOUTHERN COMMIE HUNT": AUBREY WILLIAMS, THE SOUTHERN CONFERENCE EDUCATIONAL FUND, AND THE INTERNAL SECURITY SUB COMMITTEE. *South Atlantic Q. 1978 77(4): 433-452.* A detailed account of the Senate Internal Security Subcommittee, headed by Eastland of Mississippi, and the hearings held in New Orleans in March 1954 at which time Aubrey W. Williams, president of the Southern Conference Educational Fund Inc., was queried and harassed regarding Communists in the SCEF. The hearing emphasized that in the McCarthy era the pursuit of subversion too easily turned into the harassment of domestic dissenters; in this instance it was the uncompromising advocates of integration in a region girding itself for the battle against what would be the most serious challenge yet to its social structure, the anticipated Supreme Court decision outlawing public school segregation. Suggests that Eastland had very much in his mind the need to destroy the credibility of those white southerners who opposed the prevailing system. Based on two collections of Aubrey Williams's papers—one in the Roosevelt Library, the other in the possession of Mrs. Anita Williams—, contemporary newspaper accounts and interviews; 43 notes. H. M. Parker, Jr.

3874. Sanders, Jane. *Cold War on the Campus: Academic Freedom at the University of Washington, 1946-64.* Vancouver: U. of British Columbia Pr., 1977. 94 pp.

3875. Scalapino, Robert A. BALANCE OF WEAKNESS, EAST AND WEST. *Freedom at Issue 1977 (43): 16-20.* Discusses international balance of power as a balance of weakness, comparing weaknesses among Communist countries (primarily in the area of material and cultural fields) and democratic countries (lying primarily in organizational and ideological areas).

3876. Schebera, Jürgen. GERHART EISLER IM KAMPF GEGEN DIE USA-ADMINISTRATION: DOKUMENTE AUS DEN JAHREN 1946/1947 [Gerhart Eisler and his struggles against the US administration: documents from 1946-47]. *Beiträge zur Gesch. der Arbeiterbewegung [East Germany] 1982 24(6): 843-866.* In 1941, the Austrian-born Communist and journalist Gerhart Eisler was one of a group of German Communists allowed to travel to Mexico after being freed from a French internment camp. However, Gerhart had to make the trip to Mexico via New York. Upon his arrival in New York, US authorities prohibited his journey to Mexico and he had to stay in the United States. He worked as an antifascist journalist for the German-language weekly, *German American,* and wrote for American Communist newspapers and periodicals. In 1945, Eisler applied to return to Germany and was granted an exit visa in 1946. However, during 1946-47, he was tried for subversive activities and imprisoned until 1949. He managed to escape to England aboard a Polish ship. Reproduces the text of a radio broadcast given by Eisler in December 1946, and Eisler's statement to the House Committee on Un-American Activities in Washington, February 1947. Based on original documents in the possession of Hilde Eisler; 19 notes. G. L. Neville

3877. Schebera, Jürgen. GERHART EISLER IM KAMPF GEGEN DIE USA-ADMINISTRATION: DOKUMENTE AUS DEN JAHREN 1946/1947 [Gerhart Eisler and his struggles against the US administration: documents from 1946-47]. *Beiträge zur Gesch. der Ärbeiterbewegung [East Germany] 1982 24(6): 843-866.* In 1941, the Austrian-born Communist and journalist Gerhart Eisler was one of a group of German Communists allowed to travel to Mexico after being freed from a French internment camp. However, Gerhart had to make the trip to Mexico via New York. Upon his arrival in New York, US authorities prohibited his journey to Mexico and he had to stay in the United States. He worked as an antifascist journalist for the German-language weekly, *German American,* and wrote for American Communist newspapers and periodicals. In 1945, Eisler applied to return to Germany and was granted an exit visa in 1946. However, during 1946-47, he was tried for subversive activities and imprisoned until 1949. He managed to escape to England aboard a Polish ship. Reproduces the text of a radio broadcast given by Eisler in December 1946, and Eisler's statement to the House Committee on Un-American Activities in Washington, February 1947. Based on original documents in the possession of Hilde Eisler; 19 notes. G. L. Neville

3878. Schebera, Jürgen. HANNS EISLER IM VERHÖR [Hanns Eisler cross-examined]. *Beiträge zur Geschichte der Arbeiterbewegung [East Germany] 1975 17(4): 652-672.* Reprints (in German translation) selections from the cross-examination of Hanns Eisler before the House Committee on Un-American Activities in 1947. A progressive composer of socialist leanings, Eisler was forced to leave Germany in 1933. From that time he was active in antifascist circles of German emigrant writers. By 1947 his socialist philosophy and the anti-Communist hysteria in the United States led to charges that he was a Soviet agent. 40 notes. G. H. Libbey

3879. Schneier, Edward V. WHITE-COLLAR VIOLENCE AND ANTICOMMUNISM. *Society 1976 13(3): 33-37.* Describes the vigilantism of the House Committee on Un-American Activities in the 1950's against the Communist Party.

3880. Schrecker, Ellen. ACADEMIC FREEDOM AND THE COLD WAR. *Antioch Rev. 1980 38(3): 313-327.* Discusses pre-Cold War events in 1940 and 1941 as well as events during the 1950's; US colleges and universities, contrary to popular belief, had anti-Communist policies and denied jobs to or purged faculty members who were, or would not deny being, Communist Party members.

3881. Scobie, Ingrid Winther. JACK B. TENNEY AND THE "PARASITIC MENACE": ANTI-COMMUNIST LEGISLATION IN CALIFORNIA, 1940-1949. *Pacific Hist. R. 1974 43(2): 188-211.* A study of Jack B. Tenney's career in the California legislature and Senate, 1940-49, as leader of an energetic crusade to search out subversives and to urge passage of antisubversive legislation. These activities he carried out as chairman of the Joint Fact-Finding Committee on Un-American Activities in California, which he dominated until 1949. For several years his fears and appeals made sense to millions of Californians, but as his proposed safeguards affected more people and controlled more institutions, increasing numbers began to question his methods and strong opposition brought about the relinquishing of his committee post in 1949. 56 notes. R. V. Ritter

3882. Scobie, Ingrid Winther. "Jack B. Tenney: Molder of Anti-Communist Legislation in California, 1940-49." U. of Wisconsin 1970. 279 pp. *DAI 1974 34(10): 6575-6576-A.*

3883. Selcraig, James Truett. "The Red Scare in the Midwest, 1945-1955: A State and Local Study." U. of Illinois, Urbana-Champaign 1981. 303 pp. *DAI 1981 42(6): 2824-A.* 8127686

3884. Shain, Russell E. HOLLYWOOD'S COLD WAR. *J. of Popular Film 1974 3(4): 334-350.* Discusses Hollywood's portrayal of Communists during the Cold War.

3885. Shields, Art. BOEVOI AVANGARD TRUDIASHCHIKHSIA S.SH.A. [The militant avant-garde of the American workers]. *Voprosy Istorii KPSS [USSR] 1964 (9): 81-85.* Outlines the history of the Communist Party of the United States from its founding in 1919 with particular emphasis on the period since 1945.

3886. Sigal, Clancy. HOLLYWOOD DURING THE GREAT FEAR. *Present Tense 1982 9(3): 45-48.* Discusses the impact on the Hollywood Jewish community of McCarthyism, blacklisting, and the investigations of the House Committee on Un-American Activities, focusing on the position of Jews, including the author, who worked in the movie industry.

3887. Skinner, James M. CLICHE AND CONVENTION IN HOLLYWOOD'S COLD WAR ANTI-COMMUNIST FILMS. *North Dakota Q. 1978 46(3): 35-40.* Films during 1947-52 promoted anti-Communism because of film-makers' political beliefs and as a reaction to scrutiny from the House Committee on Un-American Activities.

3888. Small, Melvin. HOLLYWOOD AND TEACHING ABOUT RUSSIAN AMERICAN RELATIONS. *Film and Hist. 1980 10(1): 1-8.* Examines the changing view of the USSR and Communism evidenced in a selection of American films from 1939 to 1966.

3889. Smith, Ronald A. THE PAUL ROBESON-JACKIE ROBINSON SAGA AND A POLITICAL COLLISION. *J. of Sport Hist. 1979 6(2): 5-27.* In 1949, the House Committee on Un-American Activities asked Jackie Robinson (1919-72) to help eliminate Paul Robeson's (1898-1976) leadership role among blacks by criticizing Robeson's statements that blacks would refuse to fight against the USSR. Robeson helped to desegregate baseball, and it was ironic that later Robinson, the first black to play in the Major Leagues in the 20th century, agreed to counter Robeson's pro-Soviet viewpoints. Robinson desegregated baseball under white terms, while Robeson fought for human rights under free political terms. The attacks on Robeson were part of the Cold War hysteria. Both men fought in their own ways for equal rights for blacks. 2 illus., 100 notes. M. Kaufman

3890. Sorenson, Dale. THE LANGUAGE OF A COLD WARRIOR: A CONTENT ANALYSIS OF HARRY TRUMAN'S PUBLIC STATEMENTS. *Social Sci. Hist. 1979 3(2): 171-186.* Content analysis reveals little change in the rhetoric of President Harry S. Truman's public statements concerning the USSR and domestic communism during 1945-50. Public opinion changed relatively independently of the president's public statements. This finding rejects the revisionist theory that Truman's rhetoric played a major role in increasing the Red Scare hysteria of the 1950's McCarthy era. Based on the published papers of Harry S. Truman; 6 graphs, 19 notes. L. K. Blaser

3891. Sorenson, Dale Rich. "The Anticommunist Consensus in Indiana, 1945-1958." Indiana U. 1980. 242 pp. *DAI 1980 41(3): 1191-A.* 8020040

3892. Spector, Bert Alan. " 'Wasn't That a Time?' Pete Seeger and the Anti-Communist Crusade, 1940-1968." U. of Missouri, Columbia 1977. 290 pp. *DAI 1982 42(9): 4122-A.* DA8205424

3893. Spector, Susan Jane. "Uta Hagen: The Early Years, 1919-1951." New York U. 1982. 405 pp. *DAI 1983 43(7): 2160-A.* DA8227232

3894. Starobin, Joseph R. *American Communism in Crisis, 1943-1957.* Research Institute on Communist Affairs, Columbia University. Cambridge, Mass.: Harvard U. Pr., 1972. 331 pp.

3895. Stein, Judith. BLACK, RED... AND SOMETIMES GREEN. *Rev. in Am. Hist. 1979 7(2): 247-255.* Review article prompted by Harry Haywood's *Black Bolshevik: Autobiography of an Afro-American Communist* (Chicago: Liberator Pr., 1978) and Richard Wright's *American Hunger* (New York: Harper & Row, 1944, 1977).

3896. Steinberg, Peter Lincoln. "The Great 'Red Menace': U. S. Prosecution of American Communists, 1947-1951." New York U. 1979. 528 pp. *DAI 1979 40(5): 2844-2845-A.*

3897. Steinberg, Philip Arthur. "Communism, Education, and Academic Freedom: Philadeplphia, A Case Study." Temple U. 1978 335 pp. *DAI 1978 39(4): 2101-2102-A.*

3898. Suber, Howard. POLITICS AND POPULAR CULTURE: HOLLYWOOD AT BAY, 1933-1953. *Am. Jewish Hist. 1979 68(4): 517-534.* The politics of hysteria and repression that overtook the United States found an easy scapegoat in Hollywood for the fearful, the demagogic, political adventurers, union busters, and latent anti-Semites, as much as fellow travelers and crypto-Communists. Makes clear that long-term labor union and political conflicts in the film industry contributed significantly to the second Red Scare of 1947 with its "Hollywood Ten" and its blacklist. Based on interviews, court depositions and other primary sources; photo, 32 notes. F. Rosenthal

3899. Theoharis, Athan, ed. *Beyond the Hiss Case: The FBI, Congress, and the Cold War.* Philadelphia: Temple U. Pr., 1982. 423 pp.

3900. Theoharis, Athan G. MCCARTHYISM: A BROADER PERSPECTIVE. *Maryland Hist. 1981 12(2): 1-7.* A historiographical essay urging scholars to avoid simplistic labeling of Cold War scholars. Material unclassified since 1975 reveals that McCarthyism was rooted in institutions of the Executive Branch. Secondary sources, 15 notes. G. O. Gagnon

3901. Thomas, Lately. *When Even Angels Wept: The Senator Joseph McCarthy Affair—A Story Without a Hero.* New York: Morrow, 1973. 654 pp.

3902. Walker, Thomas Joseph. "The International Worker's Order: A Unique Fraternal Body." U. of Chicago 1983. *DAI 1984 44(7): 2218-A.*

3903. Wertheim, Larry M. NEDRICK YOUNG, ET AL. V. MPAA, ET AL.: THE FIGHT AGAINST THE HOLLYWOOD BLACKLIST. *Southern California Q. 1975 57(4): 383-418.* Traces the efforts to obtain an official judgment against the blacklisting of writers, actors, and directors by the motion picture industry. The famous Hollywood Ten actually included over 200 artists adversely affected by the Hollywood blacklist from 1948 until—for some—the 1970's. The litigation endured numerous obstacles, including lack of funds, the difficulty of proving the existence of an official blacklist, and adverse court decisions. Further hampering the effort was the view of some blacklisted writers such as Dalton Trumbo who held that everyone had suffered and that there could only be victims. Trumbo, disgusted with the legal maneuvering involved in the courts, called for individual rather than collective effort. The entire campaign was characterized by a lack of collective support, reluctance to reignite the controversy, and self-interest. The case, which began in 1960 with demands for $7.65 million in damages, was settled out of court in 1965 for $100,000. Suggests not only that Communists made no impression in Hollywood before 1947, but also that the blacklistees demonstrated a clear lack of radicalism in their efforts to reinstate themselves in the motion picture industry. Based on correspondence, documents, and other primary sources, and published records; 129 notes. A. Hoffman

3904. Whitlatch, Michael David. "The House Committee on Un-American Activities' Entertainment Hearings and Their Effects on Performing Arts Careers." Bowling Green State U. 1977. 343 pp. *DAI 1978 38(9): 5132-5133-A.*

3905. Williams, Roger M. A ROUGH SUNDAY AT PEEKSKILL. *Am. Heritage 1976 27(3): 72-79.* In 1949 Paul Robeson, black singer-actor and advocate of Communist causes, tried to give a concert in Peekskill, New York. The ensuing confrontation between his leftist supporters and local townspeople was a prologue to the anti-Communist McCarthyite movement. 8 illus. B. J. Paul

3906. Wolfe, Gary K. *DR. STRANGELOVE, RED ALERT,* AND PATTERNS OF PARANOIA IN THE 1950'S. *J. of Popular Film 1976 5(1): 57-67.* Discusses patterns of paranoia in American thought and focuses on Stanley Kubrick's *Dr. Strangelove* and Peter George's 1958 novel *Red Alert,* which inspired it, as a representative of the 1950's fear of communism, assassination, and nuclear holocaust.

3907. Wreszin, Michael. MCCARTHYISM: MEDIA MANIPULATION, PARTISAN POLITICS, OR INSTITUTIONAL COMPLICITY? *Rev. in Am. Hist. 1982 10(2): 250-254.* Review essay of Edwin R. Bayley's *Joe McCarthy and the Press* (1981) and Michael O'Brien's *McCarthy and McCarthyism in Wisconsin* (1980).

3908. Yablonsky, Mary Jude. "A Rhetorical Analysis of Selected Television Speeches of Archbishop Fulton J. Sheen on Communism—1952-1956." Ohio State U. 1974. 226 pp. *DAI 1975 35(11): 7434-7435-A.*

3909. Younger, Irving. WAS ALGER HISS GUILTY? *Commentary 1975 60(2): 23-37.* Reexamines the circumstances, issues, evidence, and personalities surrounding the Alger Hiss case of the late 1940's and early 1950's.

3910. Zimring, Fred R. NOTES AND DOCUMENTS: COLD WAR COMPROMISES: ALBERT BARNES, JOHN DEWEY, AND THE FEDERAL BUREAU OF INVESTIGATION. *Pennsylvania Mag. of Hist. and Biog. 1984 108(1): 87-100.* Presents eight documents illustrating how anti-Communist liberals John Dewey and Albert Barnes collaborated with the FBI in discrediting such left-wing liberals as author Barrows Dunham. Based on FBI files, Dunham's private papers, interviews, newspapers, and secondary works; 21 notes. T. H. Wendel

The United States - 1965-1985

3911. Adler, Mortimer. DECLARATION V. MANIFESTO. *Center Mag. 1976 9(5): 38-43, 45-48.* Discusses political, economic, and ideological differences between democracy and communism in the 1960's and 70's, emphasizing the role of libertarian values.

3912. Aptheker, Herbert. KRIZIS AMERIKANSKOGO OBSHCHESTVA I POLITIKA KOMPARTII SOEDINENNYKH SHTATOV [The crisis of American society and the policy of the Communist Party of the United States]. *Voprosy Istorii KPSS [USSR] 1979 (7): 71-80.* The United States experiences a financial, political, and moral crisis. Its population suffers from inflation, unemployment, a shocking level of illiteracy, inadequate housing and health care, racism, and excessive military expenditures by the government. Efforts by the Communist Party to correct these problems and to create a left-center coalition have made the Party the most influential leftist force in the United States. Based on periodical literature; 3 notes. L. E. Holmes

3913. Bollinger, Klaus. DER KRIEG DES USA—IMPERIALISMUS GEGEN DIE NEGERBEVOLKERUNG [War of US imperialism against the Negro population]. *Deutsche Aussenpolitik [East Germany] 1968 13(1): 45-50.* Two wars waged by US imperialism were exposed by the events of 1967. The first was against the Vietnamese nation and the second was against the American black population. The black problem overflowed US borders and became an international enigma. Emphasizes the need to unify America's working class with the black people's movement. White chauvinism must be abandoned because it is an instrument of political schism. Active black and white unity, as declared by America's Communist Party, is the only possibility for future defeat of bourgeois and capitalist racist ideology. Secondary sources; 12 notes. G. E. Pergl

3914. Bozeman, Adda B. UNDERSTANDING THE COMMUNIST THREAT. *Society 1977 15(1): 92-96.* Communism threatens the active pursuit of international human rights; as far as American political pursuits are concerned, human rights presently are guaranteed in neither domestic nor international law, are not values shared throughout the world, are legitimate concerns, and are legitimate policy propositions.

3915. Bryant, Pat. JUSTICE VS. THE MOVEMENT. *Radical Am. 1980 14(6): 7-22.* Events after the November 1979 Klan shooting of Communist Workers' Party members in Greensboro, North Carolina, bring the work of the federal government's Community Relations Service into question. From its founding in 1964 to 1966 (when transferred from the Commerce to the Justice Department) it served its legislated purpose to assist the civil rights movement. Since then, and increasingly in the 1970's, it has played a role akin to intelligence collection for the FBI and divided and distracted the local and national civil rights groups from concerted action in communities throughout the nation. Based primarily on interviews in communities like Greensboro and with Community Relations Service representatives; 5 illus. C. M. Hough

3916. Dixler, Elsa. THE AMERICAN COMMUNIST PARTY AND THE REVOLUTION. *Am. Behavioral Scientist 1977 20(4): 567-578.* Examines the Communist Party USA; no truly revolutionary party may exist in the United States without considering the meaning of revolution in an American context, 1970's.

3917. Donner, Frank. LET HIM WEAR A WOLF'S HEAD: WHAT THE FBI DID TO WILLIAM ALBERTSON. *Civil Liberties R. 1976 3(1): 12-22.* In 1964 William Albertson was expelled from the Communist Party for being an informer for the Federal Bureau of Investigation. Presents evidence that the FBI was guilty of fabricating the evidence in order to disrupt the Communist Party. Describes the actions of the FBI, the gullible reaction of the Communist Party, the violation of Albertson's civil rights, and the suffering it caused him and his family.

3918. Eastland, Terry. THE COMMUNISTS AND THE KLAN. *Commentary 1980 69(5): 65-67.* The confrontation between the Ku Klux Klan and the Communist Workers' Party (then the Workers' Viewpoint Organization) in November 1979 in Greensboro, North Carolina, proceeded from the class relations of industrial North Carolina and from the deliberate ideological intentions of the Communists.

3919. Farsoun, Karen; Farsoun, Samih; and Ajay, Alex. MID-EAST PERSPECTIVES FROM THE AMERICAN LEFT. *J. of Palestine Studies [Lebanon] 1974 4(1): 94-119.* The American Left, comprised of the Communist Party of the United States (including Marxist, Maoist, and Trotskyite factions and offshoots), the Workers World Party, the Progressive Labor Party, and social democrat groups, though traditionally pro-Israeli, began to recognize the inequities in the Arab-Israeli conflict and to support the Arabs after the Six-Day War of 1967.

3920. Gershman, Carl. TOTALITARIAN MENACE. *Society 1980 18(1): 9-15.* Discusses divergencies in attitudes toward Communism between the Social Democrats-USA and Michael Harrington of the Democratic Socialist Organizing Committee since the split of the socialist movement in 1972, emphasizing detente and the Soviet invasion of Afghanistan in 1979.

3921. Geschwender, James A. MARXIST-LENINIST ORGANIZATION: PROGNOSIS AMONG BLACK WORKERS. *J. of Black Studies 1978 8(3): 279-298.* The rise and fall (1968-71) of the League of Revolutionary Black Workers in the Detroit automobile industry provides a model for predicting possible future developments in Marxist-Leninist black workers' organizations in the United States. Most actual or potential black industrial workers share the characteristics of the league's members, except their history of radicalism. From a 1972 peak, black workers' groups declined to token levels by 1976 because of the discriminatory discharge of black workers in a declining national economy. When the economy revives, black workers' organizations can thrive by combining Marxist class theory with black nationalism. Based on published government documents and secondary sources; 2 tables, biblio. R. G. Sherer

3922. Gordon, George N. *Communications and Media: Constructing a Cross-Discipline.* New York: Hastings, 1975. 209 pp.

3923. Huntley, Richard Thomas. "Events and Issues of the Angela Davis Dismissal." U. of Southern California 1976. *DAI 1977 37(9): 5630-5631-A.*

3924. Ilké, Fred Charles. ON NEGOTIATING WITH COMMUNIST POWERS. *Foreign Service J. 1971 48(4): 21-25, 55-57.*

3925. Institute for Southern Studies. THE THIRD OF NOVEMBER. *Southern Exposure 1981 9(3): 55-67.* Reviews the televised murders of five Communist Workers' Party demonstrators in Greensboro, North Carolina, on 3 November 1979 by members of the Ku Klux Klan and Nazi Party and the acquittal one year later of the six men charged with the crime.

3926. Kiernan, Bernard P. *The United States, Communism, and the Emergent World.* Bloomington: Indiana U. Pr., 1972. 248 pp.

3927. Krebs, Edward S. HISTORY OF THE UNITED STATES-CHINA PEOPLE'S FRIENDSHIP ASSOCIATION OF ATLANTA. *West Georgia Coll. Studies in the Social Sci. 1983 22: 101-109.* Founded by three Maoist students in 1972, just prior to their own journey to China; the association is now active in promoting student exchange.

3928. Mostovets, N. V. NOVYE CHERTY RABOCHEGO DVIZHENIIA I DEIATEL'NOSTI KOMPARTII SSHA [New characteristics of the workers' movement and activity of the Communist Party in the USA]. *Voprosy Istorii [USSR] 1977 (12): 51-63.* Reviews the American political and economic scene, 1977, based on American periodical sources, and stemming from remarks by Brezhnev at the 25th Party Congress. (This coincided with the US Bicentennial celebrations.) The new characteristics appear to lie in the strengthening of trade union activities.

3929. O'Brien, Jim. AMERICAN LENINISM IN THE 1970S. *Radical Am. 1977-78 11-12(6-1): 27-62.* In recent years American Leninism has been shaped by the influence of the US Communist Party, the student revolts of the 1960's and, ideologically, the American working class. The position of the Communist Party as the dominant Leninist group remains without serious challenge, but aspirants to the position continue to arise, including such entities as the Socialist Workers Party, the Workers World Party, International Socialists, Progressive Labor Party, Revolutionary Communist Party and Communist Party (Marxist-Leninist). The long and severely tried existence of the Communist Party as the major Leninist organization seems unlikely to be supplanted, given the problems plaguing other organizations. This includes the wasteful absorption of membership in doctrinal discussion and conflict, shaky ideological positions, extremely small numbers, and the proliferation of organizations. N. Lederer

3930. Parenti, Michael and Kazdin, Carolyn. THE UNTOLD STORY OF THE GREENSBORO MASSACRE. *Monthly Rev. 1981 33(6): 42-50.* Examines the role played by agents of the law in the murder of five Communist Workers' Party leaders in 1979 in Greensboro, North Carolina, and in the acquittals in 1980 of the Klansmen and American Nazis charged with the murders; singles out Bernard Butkovitch, an agent of the Bureau of Alcohol, Tobacco, and Firearms, Edward Dawson, a former FBI informant, Detective Cooper of the Greensboro police, and District Attorney Michael Schlosser as partly responsible for the killings and acquittal.

3931. Pittman, John. AMERICAN COMMUNISTS ON THE WAYS OF THEIR COUNTRY'S PROGRESS. *World Marxist R. 1975 18(11): 65-75.* Analyzes US foreign and domestic policy in the light of the positions of the US Communist Party (CPUSA) in the 1970's.

3932. Potiekhin, O. V. SPADSHCHYNA AMERYKANS'KOI REVOLIUTSII 18 ST. I SUCHASNA MOLOD' SSHA [The heritage of the American Revolution and modern youth in the United States]. *Ukrains'kyi Istorychnyi Zhurnal [USSR] 1976 (8): 92-97.* Describes how today's youth are more interested in returning to the principles of the American Revolution and its democratic traditions as expressed in the Declaration of Independence and the Bill of Rights, stressing the influence of the American Communist Party on this progressive phenomenon.

3933. Reed, Adolph L., Jr. STRATEGY FOR A COMMUNIST AGENDA: CIVIL RIGHTS EQUALS SOCIAL REVOLUTION. *Phylon 1976 37(4): 334-342.* Henry Winston, National Chairman of the Communist Party USA, wrote *Strategy for a Black Agenda* (1973). He views Martin Luther King, Jr., as an enlightened national bourgeois democrat who was developing toward socialism. The fundamental theoretical weakness of the book is a "failure to appreciate that, especially for political theory, interpretation of the past is important only insofar as it facilitates interpretation of the present and thus some possibility for prediction and control of the future." 5 notes. E. P. Stickney

3934. Rothchild, John. AMERICAN COMMUNES: VOLUNTARY MAOISM. *Washington Monthly 1975 7(4): 16-23.* The commune movement in America achieved widespread attention in the 1960's and continues to prosper in the 1970's without the same public notice.

3935. West, James. KOMMUNISTY SSHA—ZA MIR, PROTIV UGROZY IADERNOI VOINY [Communists in the USA struggle for peace and against nuclear war]. *Voprosy Istorii KPSS [USSR] 1983 (6): 68-78.* The Communist Party in the United States has condemned Ronald Reagan's domestic and foreign policies and the arms race, and has participated in the growing peace movement. Based on published works; 18 notes. R. Kirillov

3936. Williams, Irene. WOMEN IN THE DARK TIMES: THREE VIEWS OF THE ANGELA DAVIS TRIAL. *San José Studies 1978 4(1): 35-43.* Review article on the Angela Davis trial, 1970; prompted by Angela Davis's *With My Mind On Freedom: An Autobiography,* Bettina Aptheker's *The Morning Breaks,* and Mary Timothy's *Jury Woman.*

3937. Winston, Henry. THE BURDEN OF THE BICENTENNIAL. *World Marxist Rev. [Canada] 1976 19(7): 71-79.* Inflation, unemployment, and other social problems caused by the crisis of capitalism in America in 1976 have led to the Communist Party's attempt to participate in the national elections.

3938. —. JOINT COMMUNIQUE OF THE VIITH CONFERENCE OF THE WORLD ANTI-COMMUNIST LEAGUE. *Ukrainian R. [Great Britain] 1974 21(3): 7-12.* Presents resolutions from this meeting in Washington, D.C., in April 1974.

3939. —. RESPONSES TO HAKI MADHUBUTI (DON L. LEE). *Black Scholar 1975 6(5): 40-53.*

Salaam, Kalamu Ya. RESPONSE, *pp. 40-43.* This and the following article reply to Haki R. Madhubuti's recent article about New Left attacks on black nationalism. Provides this extension of Madhubuti's thesis: "There are those of us who are black and who *refuse* to voluntarily integrate ... we will exercise our right to be what we are: Black and Afrikan (born in America)."

Smith, Mark. RESPONSE, *pp. 44-53.* Provides "a defense of Marxism-Leninism" in response to Madhubuti's statement, "As far as we are concerned communism and capitalism are the left and right arms in the same white body." D. J. Engler

Canada

3940. Abella, Irving Martin. *Nationalism, Communism, and Canadian Labour: The CIO, the Communist Party, and the Canadian Congress of Labour, 1935-1956.* Toronto: U. of Toronto Pr., 1973. 256 pp.

3941. Avakumovic, Ivan. *The Communist Party in Canada: A History.* Toronto: McClelland and Stewart, 1975. 309 pp.

3942. Azhaev, V. PERSPEKTIVY ANTIIMPERIALISTICHESKOI BOR'BY I NOVAIA DEMOKRATICHESKAIA PARTIIA KANADY [Perspectives for anti-imperialist struggle in the Canadian New Democratic Party]. *Mirovaia Ekonomika i Mezhdunarodnye Otnosheniia [USSR] 1982 (12): 109-113.* The party seeks to make Canadian capitalism more efficient; the Canadian Communist Party on the other hand seeks to build socialism.

3943. Beeching, W. C. FARMERS IN THE ANTI-MONOPOLY STRUGGLE. *Communist Viewpoint [Canada] 1973 5(2): 19-27.*

3944. Bilets'ka, I. B. ROZROBKA KOMPARTIYEYU KANADY STRATEHIYI I TAKTYKY BOROT'BY ZA STVORENNYA ANTYMONOPOLISTYCHNOYI KOALITSIYI [The development of the Communist Party of Canada, its strategy and tactics in the struggle to create an antimonopolistic coalition]. *Ukrains'kyi Istorychnyi Zhurnal [USSR] 1981 (4): 114-120.* Discusses the problems faced by the Communist Party of Canada, including the influence of the United States, its racial composition, and its unemployment problems. Considers how it has strived to achieve communism in Canada, giving details of the work it has done and the congresses and meetings held, and discusses the antimonopolistic movement, 1921-69. L. Djakowska

3945. Bowen, Roger. DEATH OF AN AMBASSADOR. *Can. Dimension [Canada] 1981 15(6): 31-34.* Explains why Canadian diplomat E. Herbert Norman was accused of being a Soviet spy by the US Senate Subcommittee on Internal Security; these irresponsible charges in the 1950's were a primary cause of Norman's death in 1957, in effect, a "murder by slander."

3946. Bowen, Roger W., ed. *E. H. Norman: His Life and Scholarship.* Toronto: U. of Toronto Pr., 1984. 206 pp.

3947. Buck, Tim. *Yours in the Struggle: Reminiscences of Tim Buck.* William Beeching and Phyllis Clarke, ed. Toronto: NC, 1977. 414 pp.

3948. Comeau, Robert. LA CANADIAN SEAMEN'S UNION (1936-1949): UN CHAPITRE DE L'HISTOIRE DU MOUVEMENT OUVRIER CANADIEN [The Canadian Seamen's Union, 1936-49: a chapter in the history of the Canadian labor movement]. *Rev. d'Hist. de l'Amérique Française [Canada] 1976 29(4): 503-538.* During the depression period of the 1930's and the decade of the 1940's, the Canadian Seamen's Union contributed to the growth of Canadian syndicalism. Its activities illustrated the inherent polarization among militant workers who wanted to improve working conditions in the face of collusion among the shipowners, the federal government, and the corrupt directors of an international union. Discusses the important role of the militant Communists. Based on journals, newspapers, and published monographs; 73 notes. L. B. Chan

3949. Demers, Claire. COMMUNISTS AND THE DEFENSE OF DEMOCRACY. *Communist Viewpoint [Canada] 1971 3(2): 50-58.* Section 98 of the Criminal Code, the Padlock Law, and the Public Order Act of Canada violate civil rights. From a symposium on 50 years of the Canadian Communist Party's thought and action.

3950. Dewhurst, Alfred. COMMUNISTS AND THE FIGHT FOR PEACE. *Communist Viewpoint [Canada] 1971 3(2): 44-49.* From a symposium on 50 years of the Canadian Communist Party's thought and action.

3951. Dewhurst, Alfred. NEW PROGRAM OF THE COMMUNIST PARTY OF CANADA. *World Marxist R. [Canada] 1972 15(3): 52-61.* The 21st convention of the Communist Party of Canada (27-29 November 1971) updated the 1962 draft of the Party program and celebrated the Party's 50th anniversary. The New Program says that monopoly in Canada is both US and Canadian. It rebukes revisionist and Chinese attacks on Marxism-Leninism and calls for a 32-hour week, earlier retirement, higher pensions, women's rights, and tax reform, in addition to the following positions: 1) nationalization of energy and natural resources industries, 2) a new Canadian constitution with English and French binational organization and self-determination, and 3) independent foreign policy with reduced military spending and withdrawal from Canadian-US defense agreements. S. J. O'Neil

3952. Dubois, Maria. THE FEMINISTS, THE FUZZ AND THE COMMUNISTS. *Communist Viewpoint [Canada] 1971 3(2): 38-43.* The Women's Liberation Movement can learn from the Communist Party the true source of their exploitation. From a symposium on 50 years of the Canadian Communist Party's thought and action.

3953. Endicott, Stephen. *James G. Endicott: Rebel out of China.* Toronto: U. of Toronto Pr., 1980. 421 pp.

3954. Fournier, Marcel. *Communisme et Anticommunisme au Québec (1920-1950)* [Communism and anti-Communism in Quebec, 1920-50]. Montréal: Albert Saint-Martin, 1979. 167 pp.

3955. Fraser, John D. INTELLECTUALS AND THE PARTY. *Communist Viewpoint [Canada] 1973 5(3): 30-35.*

3956. Hammond, Sam. ROLE AND PLACE OF YOUTH IN OUR SOCIETY. *Communist Viewpoint [Canada] 1971 3(4): 35-40.* Youth occupies a vital place in society; the Young Communist League is the "guardian of the working class ideology together with and on behalf of the Communist Party among the youth."

3957. Harris, George. COMMUNISTS AND THE "HUNGRY THIRTIES." *Communist Viewpoint [Canada] 1971 3(2): 28-32.* In the 1930's the Communist Party helped the unemployed in Canada to organize, and still promotes the unity of labor. From a symposium on 50 years of the Canadian Communist Party's thought and action.

3958. Hill, Elizabeth and Freed, Norman. COMMUNISTS AND THE WORKING AND STUDENT YOUTH. *Communist Viewpoint [Canada] 1971 3(2): 33-37.* The Young Communist League (YCL) is fighting for the unity of youth in English and French Canada. From a symposium on 50 years of the Canadian Communist Party's thought and action.

3959. Kashtan, William. COMMUNIST STRATEGY AND TACTICS. *Communist Viewpoint [Canada] 1971 3(2): 8-13.* From a symposium on 50 years of the Canadian Communist Party's thought and action.

3960. Kashtan, William. THE FEDERAL ELECTION AND THE ROAD AHEAD. *Communist Viewpoint [Canada] 1973 5(1): 5-18.*

3961. Kashtan, William. NEW FEATURES OF COMMUNIST PARTY DRAFT PROGRAM. *Communist Viewpoint [Canada] 1971 3(4): 5-11.* The 1962 draft program has been amended, reworked, and updated.

3962. Kashtan, William. WHAT THE CANADIAN BAROMETER INDICATES. *World Marxist R. 1973 16(4): 50-60.* The Communist Party's political policies and election tactics, 1972-73.

3963. Kenny, Robert S. 125TH ANNIVERSARY OF COMMUNIST MANIFESTO. *Communist Viewpoint [Canada] 1973 5(2): 14-18.*

3964. Klymasz, Robert B. V. D. BONCH-BRUEVICH AND THE LENIN CONNECTION IN NEW WORLD FOLKLORISTICS. *J. of Am. Folklore 1980 93(369): 317-324.* Vladimir Dmitrievich Bonch-Bruevich (1873-1955) was both folklorist of Canada's Russian Dukhobor sect and Party faithful in the USSR under V. I. Lenin. Bruevich canvassed every Dukhobor household to obtain a complete collection of Dukhobor psalms. 22 notes.

W. D. Piersen

3965. Kolasky, John. *The Shattered Illusion: The History of Ukrainian Pro-Communist Organizations in Canada.* Toronto: Martin, 1979. 255 pp.

3966. Lembcke, Jerry. THE INTERNATIONAL WOODWORKERS OF AMERICA IN BRITISH COLUMBIA, 1942-51. *Labour [Canada] 1980 6(Aut): 113-148.* From 1942 to 1951, the British Columbia District Council of the International Woodworkers of America (IWA) was embroiled in a battle for political control between a left-wing "Red Bloc" and an anticommunist "White Bloc." By the early 1950's, the left wing had been defeated. The secession of the left-led British Columbia District from the International in 1948 was a last-ditch attempt to preserve the district's autonomy. The rank-and-file did not abandon its communist leaders but was forcefully separated from its leaders by the anticommunist movement within the Canadian Congress of Labour-Congress of Industrial Organizations (CCL-CIO) and by the repressive power of the state. J/S

3967. Magnuson, Bruce. COMMUNISTS AND THE WORKING CLASS. *Communist Viewpoint [Canada] 1971 3(2): 14-20.* From a symposium on 50 years of the Canadian Communist Party's thought and action.

3968. Magnuson, Bruce. TRADE UNIONS AND INDEPENDENCE OF CANADA. *World Marxist R. [Canada] 1975 18(12): 77-86.* The Communist Party of Canada has encouraged a recent move by the Canadian Labour Congress to adopt a more militant and reform-oriented position.

3969. Magnuson, Bruce. TURNING POINT IN BATTLE FOR LABOR UNITY. *World Marxist R. [Canada] 1973 16(7): 91-100.* The Communist Party in Canada calls for unity within the labor union movement and an end to US domination in economic affairs.

3970. McEwen, Tom. *The Forge Glows Red: From Blacksmith to Revolutionary.* Toronto: Progress, 1974. 261 pp.

3971. Naumov, D. M. NATSIONAL'NI PROBLEMY KANADS'KOI KONFEDERATSII [National problems of the Canadian Confederation]. *Ukrains'kyi Istorychnyi Zhurnal [USSR] 1969 (9): 92-100.* Examines the causes and nature of national problems, particularly French Canadians', but also smaller national groups', which have been critical of the government since the late 19th century, and suggests possible solutions, stressing the role of the Communist Party.

3972. Nikolaiev, M. V. V BOR'BE ZA INTERESY TRUDIASHCHIKHSIA: K 60-LETIIU KOMPARTII KANADY [In the struggle for the interests of the working people: the 60th anniversary of the Canadian Communist Party]. *Voprosy Istorii KPSS [USSR] 1982 (2): 116-118.* Retraces the history of the Communist Party of Canada, including its first congress in 1921 and first leaders. After suffering great repression and bans during the 30's, the Party grew in authority briefly after the Second World War, then became prey to revisionist groups inside it in the 50's, and fell under the influence of Chinese and US imperialism in the 60's. It is now gradually returning to its founding principles of Marxism-Leninism and representing the interests of the working people. Note.

V. A. Packer

3973. Petryshyn, Jaroslav. "A. E. Smith and the Canadian Labour Defense League." U. of Western Ontario 1977. *DAI 1978 38(9): 5642-5643-A.*

3974. Rasporich, Anthony. TOMO ČAČIĆ: REBEL WITHOUT A COUNTRY. *Can. Ethnic Studies [Canada] 1978 10(2): 86-94.* Surveys the career of Tomo Čačić (1896-1969), Croatia-born radical Communist labor organizer in the western United States and western Canada. In Ontario he was a Communist Party organizer and newspaperman until his arrest and imprisonment. In 1934, he was deported to England; soon he escaped to Moscow. After three years he enlisted in the Spanish Civil War. He returned to Yugoslavia in 1941 and fought there with the Partisans throughout the war. After the war he continued his interest in the Canadian radical cause. Primary sources; 50 notes. R. V. Ritter

3975. Riddell, John and Fidler, Dick. THE TORONTO CONVENTION: A STEP FORWARD FOR CANADIAN TROTSKYISM. *Int. Socialist Rev. 1973 34(7): 10-13.* Discusses and presents Trotskyists' resolutions at the 1973 meeting of the Canadian League for Socialist Action regarding Canada's relationship to US imperialism and class struggle in Quebec.

3976. Ross, William. INDUSTRIAL DEVELOPMENT OF THE WEST. *Communist Viewpoint [Canada] 1973 5(4/5): 6-10.* The industrialization of Western Canada and the new resultant national policies will benefit the Communist Party.

3977. Smykov, F. N. V CHEST' IUBILEIA KOMPARTII KANADY [In honor of the anniversary of the Communist Party of Canada]. *Voprosy Istorii KPSS [USSR] 1982 (5): 153-157.* The Communist Party of Canada has suffered banning and persecution. But as the Party's General Secretary William Kashton said, the Party is a great Marxist-Leninist institution in spite of mistakes it may have made. It is resolutely proletarian internationalist, and many of its members perished in the antifascist struggle. The party is firmly committed to friendship with the USSR. Based on *Pravda;* 2 notes. A. J. Evans

3978. Stewart, William. COMMUNISTS AND THE FIGHT ON TWO FRONTS. *Communist Viewpoint [Canada] 1971 3(2): 59-66.* Discusses the struggle against right opportunism and left petty-bourgeois revolutionism. From a symposium on 50 years of the Canadian Communist Party's thought and action.

3979. Stewart, William. MAOISM IN CANADA. *Communist Viewpoint [Canada] 1973 5(2): 9-13.*

3980. Stewart, William. ONTARIO ELECTION. *Communist Viewpoint [Canada] 1971 3(5): 20-25.* Appraises a coming election in terms of political power distribution between the NDP, the Tories, the Liberals, and the Communist Party.

3981. Stewart, William. THERE IS SUCH A PARTY. *Communist Viewpoint [Canada] 1973 5(6): 36-42.* Response to a "Draft Paper" entitled "On Democracy: Whither Waffle" by Treat Hull, Don Lake, and Judy Skinner.

3982. Swankey, Ben. COMMUNISTS AND THE NDP. *Communist Viewpoint [Canada] 1973 5(3): 15-26.* Discusses the New Democratic Party in Canada, 1961-73.

3983. Sydney, Mark. EDUCATION AT THE CROSSROADS. *Communist Viewpoint [Canada] 1971 3(4): 28-34.* Summarizes the report of the Ontario Committe of the Communist Party of Canada on the problems facing post-secondary education in Ontario.

3984. Tishkov, V. A. KANADA 70-KH GODOV [Canada in the 1970's]. *Novaia i Noveishaia Istoriia [USSR] 1980 (1): 139-153.* Sketches developments in Canada during the 1970's from the heady days of the early Trudeau era through economic crisis to the collapse of the concept of a just society. Focuses on the growing class struggle and the rise in Quebec nationalism, especially the Canadian Communist Party's attitude on separatism. The author approves of the Canadian decision not to stock US nuclear warheads on Canadian soil. Based on Soviet published accounts; 12 notes, biblio. D. N. Collins

3985. Turk, James L. SURVIVING THE COLD WAR: A STUDY OF THE UNITED ELECTRICAL WORKERS IN CANADA. *Can. Oral Hist. Assoc. J. [Canada] 1980 4(2): 16-28.* Discusses anti-Communism among Canada's workers from 1940 to 1959, especially the dislodgement of Communists and other left-wingers from key positions, and details resistance within the United Electrical, Radio and Machine Workers' Union to such assaults; mentions the role of oral history in studies of labor history and of the Cold War.

3986. Wagner, J. Richard. CONGRESS AND CANADIAN-AMERICAN RELATIONS: THE NORMAN CASE. *Rocky Mountain Social Sci. J. 1973 10(3): 85-92.* Congress' role in the investigation of a Communist espionage case involving E. Herbert Norman, a Canadian diplomat.

3987. Walsh, Sam. COMMUNISTS AND THE FRENCH-CANADIAN NATION. *Communist Viewpoint [Canada] 1971 3(2): 21-27.* The Communist Party supports the struggle of the French Canadians of Quebec for self-determination. From a symposium on 50 years of the Canadian Communist Party's thought and action.

3988. Walsh, Sam. FOR A MASS FEDERATED PARTY OF THE WORKING PEOPLE IN QUEBEC. *Communist Viewpoint [Canada] 1973 5(6): 25-36.* Since October, 1970, large sections of the working class have felt the need to create a mass, federated party of the working people in Quebec, independent of the bourgeois and petty-bourgeois parties.

3989. Weir, John. COMMUNISTS AND CANADIAN DEMOCRATIC TRADITIONS. *Communist Viewpoint [Canada] 1971 3(2): 67-73.* The Communist Party of Canada has always defended democracy. From a symposium on 50 years of the Canadian Communist Party's thought and action.

3990. Weisbord, Merrily. *The Strangest Dream: Canadian Communists, Spy Trials, and the Cold War.* Toronto: Dennys, 1983. 255 pp.

3991. Yeomans, Donald K. THE ORIGIN OF NORTH AMERICAN ASTRONOMY: SEVENTEENTH CENTURY. *Isis 1977 68(243): 414-425.* Summarizes the astronomical studies of John Winthrop, Jr., Samuel Danforth, Increase Mather, Nathaniel Mather, Thomas Brattle, John Foster, Jeremiah Horrox, and others in 17th-century New England. 47 notes. M. M. Vance

8. COMMUNISM IN THE WORLD SINCE 1945: HISTORIOGRAPHY, BIBLIOGRAPHY, AND AN OVERVIEW

3992. Adelman, Jonathan R., ed. *Communist Armies in Politics.* Boulder, Colo.: Westview, 1982. 225 pp.

3993. Adelman, Jonathan R. LESSONS OF THE RUSSIAN & CHINESE CIVIL WARS FOR THE DEVELOPMENT OF COMMUNIST ARMIES. *Military Affairs 1979 43(3): 139-143.* Analyzes the similarities and differences between the Communist armies in the Russian Civil War, 1918-21, and the Chinese Civil War, 1946-49. Both shared a low level of military technology in tanks, aircraft, naval power, and transportation and supply systems. Differences involved the nature and size of the proletarian and Party strata in the army, the degree of decentralization of command, the effectiveness and degree of institutionalization of the armies, and the mechanisms of social control within the armies. 44 notes.
A. M. Osur

3994. Adelman, Jonathan R., ed. *Terror and Communist Politics: The Role of the Secret Police in Communist States.* Boulder, Colo.: Westview, 1984. 292 pp.

3995. Alexander, Robert J. IMPACT OF THE SINO-SOVIET SPLIT ON LATIN AMERICAN COMMUNISM. *Texas Q. 1972 15(1): 35-74.* Since Latin American Communist parties have played an integral part in the international Communist movement, the Sino-Soviet conflict has had major implications for Latin America: Communist parties have divided into groups loyal to Moscow (peaceful revolution), Peking (violent revolution), and most recently Havana. Soviet leadership has remained strong, however, especially after the unsuccessful use of violence by Venezuelan rebels in the early 1960's. Primary and secondary sources; 47 notes.
R. H. Tomlinson

3996. Anikeev, V. V. and Usikov, R. A. OBZOR IZDANI PARTIINYKH ARKHIVOV [Survey of publications of Party archives]. *Voprosy Istorii KPSS [USSR] 1972 (2): 113-122.* Discusses numerous archival collections organized and catalogued in the late 1960's by the Central Party Archive of the Institute of Marxism-Leninism and republican Institutes of Party History dealing with V. I. Lenin and the history of the Communist Party.

3997. Astaf'ev, G. V. and Narochnitski, A. L. LZHEISTORIIA NA SLUZHBE VELIKODERZHAVNYKH ZAMYSLOV PEKINA [Pseudohistory in the service of the great power aims of Peking]. *Novaia i Noveishaia Istoriia [USSR] 1973 (1): 82-91.* The Maoists, believing that world war is inevitable, have produced domestic chaos, and abandoned Marxism-Leninism and proletarian internationalism, justifying their chauvinistic course with pseudo-Marxist arguments. They see capitalism, not as being imperialistic, but as the politics of plunder, and assail the Soviet Union's help to national liberation movements. They say that the Russian Revolution was merely a phase in the world's development, and not something qualitatively new. The Maoists disregard the people's natural affinity to socialism and Communism, and ignore, or slander, the success of the USSR. Based on a series of articles in the Chinese Communist Party journal *Khunntsi,* on the works of Lenin, and the researches of Soviet historians; 10 notes. A. J. Evans/S

3998. Atkinson, James D. AMERICAN MILITARY POLICY AND COMMUNIST UNORTHODOX WARFARE. *Marine Corps Gazette 1958 42(1): 20-25.* Assesses the problems of the United States in combatting Communist guerrilla warfare with conventional military tactics, with comments on the Communists' theories and implementation of guerrilla warfare in China, Yugoslavia, Greece, Malaya, and Africa since 1941.

3999. Atkinson, James D. AMERICAN MILITARY POLICY AND COMMUNIST UNORTHODOX WARFARE. *Marine Corps Gazette 1958 42(1): 20-25.* Assesses the problems of the United States in combating Communist guerrilla warfare with conventional military tactics, with comments on the Communists' theories and implementation of guerrilla warfare in China, Yugoslavia, Greece, Malaya, and Africa since 1941.

4000. Avreiski, Nikola. SUVETSKATA ISTORICHESKA NAUKA ZA DEINOSTA NA V.I. LENIN V KOMINTERNA [Soviet historiography and the activity of V. I. Lenin in the Comintern]. *Izvestiia na Inst. po Istoriia na BKP [Bulgaria] 1981 44: 81-117.* Discusses V. I. Lenin's part in the activities of the Communist International as outlined in the investigations of the Soviet historians since 1920.

4001. Basmanov, M. I. KOMMUNISTY I SOVREMENNOE ANTIVOENNOE DVIZHENIE [Communists and the contemporary antiwar movement]. *Voprosy Istorii KPSS [USSR] 1983 (8): 82-94.* During the 1970's-80's, the international Communist movement has been increasingly prominent in the struggle for peace. The peace movement can be successful only if it has a clear program of action and a common political platform uniting all antiwar forces. Communists are prepared to work alongside all individuals and groups who are sincerely committed to the cause of peace. Secondary sources; 50 notes. G. Dombrovski

4002. Belfiglio, Valentine J. ISRAEL, THE UNITED STATES, AND THE THIRD WORLD. *Int. Problems [Israel] 1977 16(3-4): 35-42.* Considers the use of the UN General Assembly as a platform from which Third World and Communist countries may confront Israel and the United States.

4003. Berenshtein, L. Iu. KRYTYKA SIONISTS'KYKH FAL'SYFIAKATSII ISTORII VELYKOI ZHOVTNEVOI SOTSIALISTYCHNOI REVOLIUTSII [Critique of Zionist falsifications of the history of the Great October Socialist Revolution]. *UKrains'kyi Istorychnyi Zhurnal [USSR] 1978 (1): 128-134.* Singles out the American Jewish Congress and the World Zionist Organization as the main propagators of anti-Communist works through organs such as academic journals, newspapers, and the media, notably *Voice of America, Radio Liberty* and the British Broadcasting Corporation. Refutes their claims that the Bolsheviks seized power by chance, that the October events were an isolated phenomenon, that the Revolution did not improve the lot of the Jews, and in particular, that Simon Petlyura (1879-1926) expressed the true will of the Ukrainian people. Reaffirms the greatness of the October Revolution and the successful development of Communism in the USSR. Secondary sources; 49 notes. V. A. Packer

4004. Bespalov, N. E. RABOCHII KLASS SSSR NA SOVREMENNOM ETAPE V OSVESHCHENII ANGLO-AMERIKANSKOI BURZHUAZNOI ISTORIOGRAFII [The Soviet working class at the current stage of development as viewed in Anglo-American historiography]. *Istoriia SSSR [USSR] 1981 (1): 180-191.* Refutes point by point misinformation in some 25 British and American studies published 1960-79. Their claims that the Communist Party of the USSR has become an "elitist" party engaged in a process of "deproletarization" by discriminating against rank-and-file workers and depriving them of leadership roles within the party and trade unions are distortions. 82 notes. N. Frenkley

4005. Bohinia, L. P. and Musiienko, V. V. ZNACHENNIA REFERATU NA SEMINARS'KYKH ZANIATTIAKH Z ISTORII KPRS [The importance of the preparation and discussion of papers submitted at seminars devoted to the history of the CPSU]. *Ukrains'kyi Istorychnyi Zhurnal [USSR] 1975 (9): 108-113.*

4006. Bordone, Sandro. LA NORMALIZZAZIONE DEI RAPPORTI TRA PCC E PCI [The normalization of relations between the Chinese and Italian Communist parties]. *Politico [Italy] 1983 48(1): 115-158.* Since Mao's death the Chinese have showed an increasing interest in the phenomenon of Eurocommunism and a greater readiness for dialogue. The PCI, though critical of Peking's anti-Soviet policy, expressed satisfaction in the new Chinese acceptance of pluralism as the basis of autonomy, independence, and equality. The resumption of relations occurred officially with the visit of the Secretary of the PCI to China in April 1980. J/S

4007. Braunthal, Julius. *History of the International.* Vol. 3: *1943-1968.* Ford, Peter and Mitchell, Kenneth, transl. Boulder, Colo.: Westview, 1980. 600 pp.

4008. Brown, H. Haines. THE IMPACT OF MARXISM. Parker, Harold T., ed. *Problems in European History,* (Durham, N.C.: Moore Publ., 1979): 191-209. Reviews Marxism's basic ideas, emphasizing that Marxist theory is an evolving discipline, designed to enable man to consciously and rationally shape his own history. Discusses the Second International (1889-1914), which abandoned the search for a genuine revolutionary praxis, preferring to pursue limited working-class goals within the framework of bourgeois democracy. This led to the collapse of socialist internationalism in 1914. A historic conference at Zimmerwald, Switzerland (1915), attended by Lenin and Rosa Luxemburg, heralded the Marxist success in Russia and the founding of the Third International. Discusses interwar Marxist efforts and the postwar rise of Eurocommunism, insisting that the latter, in seeking a revolutionary praxis short of a dictatorship of the proletariat, remains radically distinct from the fundamentally faulty approach of the Second International. Ref. L. W. Van Wyk

4009. Budwig, Eckhardt. SÜDOSTASIEN UNTER DEM ROTEN DOPPELSTERN [South East Asia under the red double star]. *Österreichische Osthefte [Austria] 1962 4(5): 369-375.* South East Asia reflects the dualism between the USSR and China. While the Communist Parties of China, North Vietnam, and Albania demanded an offensive against colonialism and imperialism, the USSR translated the policy of world revolution into the official world power policies of the Russian state. 3 notes. R. Wagnleitner

4010. Bunce, Valerie and Echols, John M., III. POWER AND POLICY IN COMMUNIST SYSTEMS: THE PROBLEM OF "INCREMENTALISM". *J. of Pol. 1978 40(4): 911-932.* While incrementalism is seen as the best description of the nature of both elite decisionmaking and policy change in democratic states, it is hypothesized as a major determinant in Communist states as well. Ideological activism may have characterized the Stalin and Khrushchev era, but has subsided as the revolutionary transformation was completed. Examination of health, welfare, education, and total budgetary expenditures from 1950 to 1973 in four Communist states (Soviet Union, German Democratic Republic, Poland, and Romania) and four Western states (United States, Sweden, Great Britain and Federal Republic of Germany) supports the hypothesis of incrementalism as a major factor in both systems. Based on primary and secondary sources; 6 tables, 47 notes. A. W. Novitsky

4011. Burks, R. V. VERGLEICHENDE KOMMUNISMUSFORSCHUNG IN AMERIKA [Comparative research on communism in the United States]. *Osteuropa [West Germany] 1979 29(4): 275-289.* In the 1960's and the 1970's US comparative communism research concentrated on Stalinism as revolution from above, technical rationality and communism, and Asian, Italian and French communism.

4012. Chekhutov, A. RAZVITIE FINANSOVO-EKONOMICHESKOGO SOTRUDNICHESTVA SOTSIALISTICHESKIKH I OSVOBODIVSHIKHSIA STRAN [The development of financial and economic cooperation of socialist and liberated nations]. *Mirovaia Ekonomika i Mezhdunarodnye Otnosheniia [USSR] 1981 (4): 50-62.* Covers a wide range of problems associated with the establishment of economic relations between the Socialist countries and the newly liberated countries of Asia, Africa, and Latin America.

4013. Childs, David, ed. *The Changing Face of Western Communism.* New York: St. Martin's, 1980. 286 pp.

4014. Choudbury, Deba Prosad. AMERICAN RESPONSE TO THE INDIA-CHINA CONFLICT IN THE HIMALAYA. *Quarterly Review of Historical Studies [India] 1983 23(1): 5-12.* The United States, accustomed to thinking of a monolithic Communist menace to all non-Communist countries, was slow to recognize that the USSR was not behind China's attack on India in 1962. US objections to military aid for India were that the aid would likely be used against Pakistan, rather than China, that it would alienate friendly Pakistan without altering India's place in the nonaligned movement, that India's toleration of Communists in its government would constitute a security risk for the United States, and that India's good foreign relations with the USSR were intolerable. 31 notes. R. Grove

4015. Clarke, Roger A. THE STUDY OF SOVIET-TYPE ECONOMIES: SOME TRENDS AND CONCLUSIONS. *Soviet Studies [Great Britain] 1983 35(4): 525-532.* Western analyses of Soviet-type economies reveal that industrial growth rates for the USSR have often been overstated. With the exception of Hungary, planned, centralized economies of the Soviet persuasion face a gloomy future. 26 notes. M. R. Yerburgh

4016. Clemens, Walter C., Jr. THE IMPACT OF DETENTE ON CHINESE AND SOVIET COMMUNISM. *J. of Internat. Affairs 1974 28(2): 133-157.* The current detente yields positive results by means of increased East-West trade, controlled arms race, and guaranteed US noninvolvement in a Sino-Soviet war. Driven by reasons of state, party leaders in Moscow and Peking cite Lenin as the ideological justification for detente's institutionalization. Yet the security of their persons, regimes, and blocs continues to take priority; domestic stability has remained unaffected. For all the celebration of detente, the future is more dependent upon the outcome of the struggles for succession in Peking and Moscow. R. D. Frederick

4017. Clubb, O. Edmund. MAOISM VERSUS KHRUSHCHEVISM: TEN YEARS. *Current Hist. 1974 65(385): 102-105, 135.* Recounts the ideologies, conflicts, and strategies of Maoism and Khrushchevism, 1963-73.

4018. Croll, Elizabeth J. WOMEN IN RURAL PRODUCTION AND REPRODUCTION IN THE SOVIET UNION, CHINA, CUBA, AND TANZANIA: SOCIALIST DEVELOPMENT EXPERIENCES. *Signs 1981 7(2): 361-374.* Collectivization as a tenet of socialist economic development should free women economically by removing patriarchal authority patterns. While women have been recruited into agriculture, they are paid less, maintaining a strong sexual division of labor. Although they were promised state aid in reducing domestic tasks, women instead have fallen under the "double burden" of domestic work and employment. The women's revolution appears to have been lost within the socialist revolution to the detriment of women. 11 notes. S. P. Conner

4019. Djilas, Milovan. *Rise and Fall.* New York: Harcourt Brace Jovanovich, 1985. 382 pp.

4020. Djurović, Borislav. NEKA GLEDIŠTA O AGRARNIM ODNOSIMA U SOCIJALISTIČKIM ZEMLJAMA [Some views on agrarian relations in socialist countries]. *Zbornik za Društvene Nauke [Yugoslavia] 1977 1(62): 165-175.* Discusses characteristic views in Western, Yugoslav, and Soviet literature concerning the socialization of agriculture, collective farms, collectivization in general, and social relations on kolkhoz-type farms during the period 1918-77. Western authors stress the antipeasant nature of collectivization. Yugoslav theories consider the nature of social transformation and make a case for gradual development of social ownership without violent infringements on individual ownership. Soviet writers insist that the only correct socialist transformation is that of the Soviet type; anything else is regarded as a deviation from the Party line. 40 notes. A. C. Niven

4021. Dobriansky, Lev E. REFLECTIONS ON THE "20TH." *Ukrainian Q. 1979 35(4): 348-359.* Reviews the history and development of Captive Nations Week and the Captive Nations List in the 20th year of their existence. 14 notes.

K. N. T. Crowther

4022. Dobrokhotov, V. Ia. O NEKOTORYKH VOPROSAKH METODOLOGII ISTORII KPSS [On some problems in the methodology of the history of the CPSU]. *Voprosy Istorii KPSS [USSR] 1977 (7): 103-107.* One of a series of articles published in 1976 and 1977 on methods and methodology of Marxist scholarship on the history of the Communist Party of the Soviet Union. The author regards Communist partisanship *(partiinost')* historicism, and relevance as the fundamental principles of historical scholarship. 8 notes. L. E. Holmes

4023. Donneur, Andre P. PARTIS COMMUNISTES ET PARTIS SOCIALISTES: QUATRE EXPERIÉNCES DE COLLABORATION [Communist Parties and Socialist Parties: four experiences of collaboration]. *Études Int. [Canada] 1976 7(4): 542-571; 1977 8(1): 3-42.* Part I. FRONT UNIQUE ET FRONT POPULAIRE [United Front and Popular Front]. Reviews socialist-communist collaboration in France, 1921-38, particularly the United Front years, 1921-23, and the Popular Front of 1934-38. The United Front was a socialist concept accepted by the Communists, while the Popular Front stemmed from the French Communist Party declaration of May 1934 which called for a common stance against fascism. Part II. FRONT NATIONAL ET UNION DE LA GAUCHE [National Front and Union of the Left]. Emphasizes the National Front, 1943-47, and the Union of the Left since 1965. Examines the effectiveness of other national front movements in Yugoslavia, Albania, Greece, Poland, Rumania, Hungary, Bulgaria, Czechoslovakia, Italy, and France. Studies the new left coalitions in Finland, France, Italy, Spain, Portugal, and Chile which grew out of the spirit of the 20th Party Congress in 1956. 143 notes.

J. F. Harrington, Jr.

4024. Dunaevski, V. A.; Zaborov, M. A.; and Rasputnis, B. I. NEKOTORYE VOPROSY SOVETSKOI ISTORIOGRAFII SOVREMENNOGO KOMMUNISTICHESKOGO I RABOCHEGO DVIZHENIIA KAPITALISTICHESKIKH STRAN [Some questions of the Soviet historiography of the present-day Communist and working-class movement in the capitalist countries]. *Novaia i Noveishaia Istoriia [USSR] 1978 (4): 21-34.* Deals with the main trends in the studies of the history of the current Communist and working-class movement in the capitalist countries of Europe and North America and gives a brief analysis of latest Soviet publications on this subject. J

4025. Eskandari, Iradj and Bilen, I. ANTI-COMMUNISM BEATING A RETREAT. *World Marxist R. [Canada] 1974 17(8): 116-122.* Discusses the Communist Party's efforts to combat anti-Communist propaganda in Turkey and Iran during the 1960's-70's.

4026. Fejto, François. LE MOUVEMENT COMMUNISTE INTERNATIONAL: L'ÉVOLUTION DES RELATIONS ENTRE LES PARTIS COMMUNISTES [The international Communist movement: the evolution of relations among Communist parties]. *Études Internationales [Canada] 1972 3(4): 451-472.* Examines Moscow's attempts to retain hegemony within the world Communist movement. Discusses the forces of unity and disunity within the movement and notes especially the discontent caused by some of the USSR's foreign policy views and internal politics. Gives considerable attention to the relations of the Communist parties in the satellite states, Western Europe, and East Asia toward Moscow and one another. Primary and secondary sources; 37 notes.

J. F. Harrington

4027. Fejtö, François. MAOISMO E TITOISMO. AFFINITÀ E DIVERGENZE [Maoism and Titoism: similarities and differences]. *Comunità [Italy] 1972 26(166): 204-214.* Despite the fact that Tito and the Chinese communists appeared to occupy polar extremes in the controversy surrounding Khrushchev and Soviet revisionism, there are basic similarities between the two parties. In contrast to the Russians, both Yugoslavian and Chinese communists found their greatest strength from among the intellectuals and peasants rather than the urban proletariat. They made use of nationalist, anti-imperialist propaganda in a war of national liberation and managed to forge their revolutionary victories in spite of the pessimistic prognostications of Stalin. Translation of an essay appearing in the forthcoming *Les avatars de l'internationalisme prolétarien. Introduction à la problématique du marxisme-léninisme contemporain* (Paris: Casterman). 9 notes. E. J. Craver

4028. Fleron, Frederic J., Jr. TECHNOLOGY AND COMMUNIST CULTURE: BELLAGIO, ITALY, AUGUST 22-28, 1975. *Technology and Culture 1977 18(4): 659-665.* Summarizes the five major approaches taken by 20 scholars at this conference on the problem of technology transfer from capitalist countries to communist countries. C. O. Smith

4029. Fochler-Hauke, Gustav. BEDEUTUNG UND ZIELE DER KOMMUNISTISCHEN "KOEXISTENZ-POLITIK" [Significance and goals of the Communist coexistence policy]. *Sudetenland [West Germany] 1971 13(4): 242-247.* Describes diplomacy of the USSR and other Communist nations since World War II. The International Conference of Workers' and Communist Parties (1969) indicated that Communists accept coexistence with the secret intent of overthrowing capitalism. R. G. Penney/S

4030. Fomin, Vasili T. FASHIZM I NOVYE FORMY IMPERIALISTICHESKOI REAKTSII [Fascism and new forms of imperialist reaction]. *Novaia i Noveishaia Istoriia [USSR] 1984 (4): 230-232.* The swing in the late 1970's-early 1980's toward conservatism and the ultraright in capitalist countries shows that, in conditions of detente, imperialism cannot compete with socialism and has to revert to Cold War politics. American preachers of anticommunism, the so-called "new right" financed by the American military-industrial complex, propagate racism and oppose detente and disarmament. Similar movements are growing in Great Britain, and some 80 neofascist organizations exist in Germany. Abridged text of paper presented at an international conference, Sofia, 15-16 December 1983. Secondary sources; 12 notes, appendix.

N. Frenkley

4031. Frank, Pierre. *The Fourth International: The Long March of the Trotskyists.* Schein, Ruth, transl. New York: Pathfinder, 1979. 189 pp.

4032. Fruck, Horst. ZUR LÖSUNG DER BODENFRAGE IN DEN SOZIALISTISCHEN LÄNDERN [The land reform solution in the Communist countries]. *Wissenschaftliche Zeitschrift der Humboldt-U. zu Berlin. Gesellschafts- und Sprachwissenschaftliche Reihe [East Germany] 1968 17(6, Supplement): 1-47.* Discusses Marxist-Leninist agricultural reforms in the USSR, Mongolia, Eastern Europe, China, Vietnam, and North Korea; 1917-68.

4033. Galkin, I. S. LENINIZM—OSNOVA USPEKHOV MIROVOGO KOMMUNISTICHESKOGO DVIZHENIIA [Leninism: the basis for success of the international Communist movement]. *Vestnik Moskovskogo Universiteta, Seriia 9: Istoriia [USSR] 1961 16(6): 3-15.* Discusses Leninist theories of class struggle, his strategy for world revolution based on mass working-class support, and the implementation of Lenin's (1870-1924) ideas of centralized leadership in the Communist parties of Europe, Asia, Africa, and Latin America. Though Communist movements in different countries are faced with different problems, the basic principles and aims of Leninism remain the same whether applied to social revolutions or colonial wars of liberation. Based on Soviet Party programs and documents; 47 notes. N. Frenkley

4034. Görtemaker, Manfred. AMERIKANISCH-SOWJETISCHE BEZIEHUNGEN AM SCHEIDEWEG [American-Soviet relations on a decisive point]. *Osteuropa [West Germany] 1982 32(12): 969-982.* Reports on the increasing tensions in US foreign policy toward Communist countries, and on developments in Afghanistan and Poland in the context of that policy.

4035. Greene, Thomas H. A COMPARATIVE NOTE ON THE STUDY OF NON-RULING COMMUNIST PARTIES. *Studies in Comparative Communism 1973 6(4): 455-459.* The Communist parties of Japan, Cyprus, Venezuela, and Australia indicate that Communist parties are not a monolithic group. One should not deal with discrete parties but compare at least two from similar societies. Tests should deal with the origins, strength, continuity, organization, recruitment, ideology, and sociology of the voter as well as the party's adaptive capabilities. D. Balmuth

4036. Grey, Robert D. LENINISM, THE SOVIET UNION, AND PARTY DEVELOPMENT IN CUBA AND ETHIOPIA. *Northeast African Studies 1980-81 2-3(3-1): 171-181.* Compares the similarities in the processes by which revolutionary leadership came to power in Cuba and Ethiopia as well as in the subsequent evolution of the two regimes. Before coming to power both revolutionary movements lacked any coherent political and ideological strategy for taking over the country. Both were vague about their mission and moderate in their goals. Neither was a tightly organized political party, and neither resembled Communist political parties. The "halting nature" of Party development in Cuba and Ethiopia suggests that in both countries the incentives for Party development are weak while the obstacles are strong. Secondary sources; 31 notes. G. L. Neville

4037. Grünwald, Leopold. ZUR GESCHICHTE DER "GESCHICHTE DER KPDSU" [On the history of the *History of the CPSU*]. *Osteuropa [West Germany] 1973 23(6): 430-441.* Compares the Stalinist history of the Soviet Communist Party (1938) with the official versions of 1959, 1962, and 1972. The Soviet leaders cannot dispense with Joseph Stalin's basic framework, which they consider necessary for their own legitimacy. Their refusal to face up to the past has come under attack by Spanish, Italian, and other Communists. 60 notes. R. E. Weltsch

4038. Haberl, Othmar Nikola. JUGOSLAWISCHE ARBEITEN ZUR GESCHICHTE DER INTERNATIONALEN ARBEITER-BEWEGUNG [Yugoslav writings on the history of the international labor movement]. *Int. Wiss. Korrespondenz zur Gesch. der Deutschen Arbeiterbewegung [West Germany] 1979 15(3): 443-470.* Reviews the phases of Yugoslav historiography on the international labor movement, handbooks and aids, works on the history of the 1st and 2d Internationals, the history of the Comintern, the history of the international labor movement after 1945, the Soviet-Yugoslav conflict, the conferences of the communist and labor parties, the Chinese Revolution and the Soviet-China conflict, reform communism and Eurocommunism and the reevaluation of proletarian internationalism.

4039. Hammond, Thomas T. THE HISTORY OF COMMUNIST TAKEOVERS. *Studies on the Soviet Union [West Germany] 1971 11(4): 1-45.* An overview of the histories and methods of Communist takeovers. Several of the original Bolshevik revolutionary methods have been retained; others have been discarded and new methods introduced. Early Soviet efforts to export revolution were failures, causing the Party to turn inward. The rise of Fascism renewed revolutionary ardor and introduced the Popular Front technique. World War II produced Communist regimes wherever the Red Army penetrated. Successful revolutions in China and Cuba marked the high tide of Soviet expansionism. At present, the Communist bloc of nations is rent with internal schisms, causing hesitation at the prospect of adding additional nations to the Red list. Secondary sources; 58 notes. V. L. Human

4040. Heerdegen, Helga. ZUR METHODOLOGIE UND THEORIE DER GESCHICHTE DER KPDSU [The methodology and theory of the history of the Communist Party of the Soviet Union]. *Zeitschrift für Geschichtswissenschaft [East Germany] 1977 25(12): 1441-1447.* The history of the Communist Party of the Soviet Union requires a special methodology, the basic principles of which are partisanship and historicity. Soviet historians decided at the 25th Congress of the Party in 1976, that research should focus on: the economic tasks of the Party; its leadership in the developed Socialist society; Party structure; and the relationship of the Party to both the Socialist bloc and Western Nations. 28 notes. J. T. Walker

4041. Henry, E. PROFESSIONAL'NYI ANTI-KOMMUNIZM [Professional anticommunism]. *Mirovaia Ekonomika i Mezhdunarodnye Otnosheniia [USSR] 1980 (3): 131-141.* Traces tactics of anti-Communist movements since the 19th century.

4042. Herz, Martin F. HOW THE COLD WAR IS TAUGHT. *Social Educ. 1979 43(2): 118-122.* Coverage of the Cold War in American history textbooks for secondary schools is biased, inaccurate, and inadequate, in treating Communism favorably and US policy unfavorably; even if students reach the end-of-the-book Cold War section before the end of the school year, their textbooks misrepresent or ignore crucial facts about Communism, World War II, the Korean War, the Vietnam War, and US policy. D. J. Engler

4043. Hirszowicz, Maria. *The Bureaucratic Leviathan: A Study in the Sociology of Communism.* New York: New York U. Pr., 1980. 208 pp.

4044. Hobday, Charles. *Communist and Marxist Parties of the World.* Santa Barbara, California: ABC-CLIO, 1986. 529 pp.

4045. Hollander, Paul. PILGRIMS ON THE RUN: IDEOLOGICAL REFUGEES FROM PARADISE LOST. *Encounter [Great Britain] 1981 57(4): 8-21, (5): 41-49.* Analyzes the motives and methods of Western intellectuals' pilgrimages to Russia, China, Vietnam, and Cuba since the 1930's. Critical of their own societies, they were in search of utopias, not noticing the oppressiveness of these societies, and often later emerged as "ideological refugees" when their Communist paradise lost its luster.

4046. Holmes, Leslie, ed. *The Withering Away of the State?: Party and State under Communism.* Chicago: Sage, 1981. 294 pp.

4047. Horowitz, Irving Louis. CAPITALISM, COMMUNISM AND MULTINATIONALISM. *Society 1974 11(2): 32-43.* Multinational corporations have altered the dimensions of the ideological struggle between capitalism and Communism.

4048. Isaienko, Zh. I. VELYKYI ZHOVTEN': POCHATOK NOVOHO ETAPU V POZVYTKU MIZHNARODNOHO KOMUNISTYCHNOHO I ROBITNYCHOHO RUKHU [Great October: the beginning of a new era in the development of the international communist and workers' movement]. *Ukrains'kyi Istorychnyi Zhurnal [USSR] 1968 2(83): 43-49.* Describes the influence of the October Revolution on the establishment and strengthening of world communist parties, 1917-68.

4049. Iskrov, M. V. O NEKOTORYKH PROBLEMAKH SOZDANIIA OCHERKOV ISTORII MESTNYKH PARTIINYKH ORGANIZATSII [Some problems on the creation of notes on the history of local Party organizations]. *Voprosy Istorii KPSS [USSR] 1980 (9): 147-154.* Local Party organizations were responsible for the success of the Bolshevik revolution in 1917 and today, under conditions of mature socialism, they ensure the democratic nature of the Soviet political system. To date the affiliates of the Institute of Marxism-Leninism at the Central Committee of the Soviet Communist Party have produced 95 notes on the history of local Party organizations; this work supersedes that undertaken in the 1960's.

Discusses certain methodological difficulties faced by the researchers. Based on local Party organizations' histories, Party Congress documents, and Lenin's works; 8 notes. V. Sobell

4050. Iurchuk, V. I. INSTYTUTU ISTORII PARTII PRY TSK KOMPARTII UKRAINY—60 ROKIV [The Party History Institute of the Central Committee of the Communist Party of the Ukraine is 60 years old]. *Ukrains'kyi Istorychnyi Zhurnal [USSR] 1981 (2): 16-27.* The Party History Institute at the Central Committee of the Communist Party of the Ukraine, a branch of the Institute of Marxism-Leninism of the Central Committee of the CPSU, marked its 60th anniversary on 13 February 1981. The history of the development of this academic research establishment, its propagation of the theoretical legacy of the founders of Marxism-Leninism, and its work on problems of the history of the CPSU and the Communist Party of the Ukraine are surveyed. Primary CPSU sources; 26 notes. I. Krushelnyckyj

4051. Johnston, Whittle. RADICAL REVISIONISM AND THE DISINTEGRATION OF THE AMERICAN FOREIGN POLICY CONSENSUS. *Orbis 1976 20(1): 179-206.* The doctrine guiding US foreign policymakers today is under heavy attack, particularly from the radical revisionists who are "eager to recast the definition of American interest in molds at fundamental variance with those of past doctrines." It is apparent from the presentations they have made regarding the Cold War that the radical revisionists have determined "to flatten the complexities of collective experience into conformity with the strictures of a preconceived ideology, and take as their goal supplanting the intrinsic corruption of society by a new and revolutionary ethic." The radical revisionists "have degraded scholarship for the purpose of ideological argumentation," as is amply demonstrated in the writings of William Appelman Williams, an early revisionist. What is needed is the formulation of adequate alternative perspectives, and a major effort to let the people of this country know that the tendency of the radical revisionists is acceptance of the Russian faith, because for them, "Marxism-Leninism offers rational coherence and universal comprehensiveness, ultimate meaning and daily guidance." A revised version of a paper originally presented at a conference held at the University of Virginia, 14-16 August 1975. 24 notes. A. N. Garland

4052. Kabuzenko, V. F. DEIATEL'NOST' KPSS PO RAZVITIIU TRUDOVOI AKTIVNOSTI RABOCHEGO KLASSA V VOSSTANOVITEL'NYI PERIOD 1921-1925 GG. ISTORIOGRAFICHESKI OBZOR [The activity of the CPSU in developing the labor activism of the working class in the reconstruction period, 1921-25: a historiographical survey]. *Voprosy Istorii KPSS [USSR] 1972 (4): 113-121.*

4053. Kaeselitz, Hella. ZU DEN ANTIMONOPOLISTISCH-DEMOKRATISCHEN ALTERNATIVPROGRAMMEN DER KOMMUNISTISCHEN PARTEIEN ENTWICKELTER KAPITALISTISCHER LÄNDER ENDE DER FÜNFZIGER/ANFANG DER SECHZIGER JAHRE [The antimonopolist-democratic alternative programs of the Communist Parties of developed capitalist countries at the end of the fifties and the beginning of the sixties]. *Beiträge zur Geschichte der Arbeiterbewegung [East Germany] 1977 19(1): 29-42.* Communist parties in established capitalist countries found it necessary by about 1960 to plan for several steps in the progress toward socialism, rather than toward immediate revolutionary change. Karl Marx recognized that some changes could be made when workers gathered sufficient power to enforce them. Lenin viewed this as extending democracy to its ultimate end. In Great Britain, France, Italy, Japan, and the United States plans were formulated to achieve a peaceful changeover to socialism. 50 notes. G. H. Libbey

4054. Kanet, Roger E. SOVIET AND AMERICAN BEHAVIOUR TOWARD THE DEVELOPING COUNTRIES: A COMPARISON. *Can. Slavonic Papers [Canada] 1973 15(4): 439-461.* Both the USSR and the United States employ the same general types of foreign policy when focused on particular areas. In the Middle East and South Asia both supply military and economic assistance. They differ in that there are local Communist parties willing to support Soviet foreign policy goals in Asia and Africa. However, in the past ten years these have been plagued by power struggles between pro-Soviet and pro-Chinese elements, reducing their effectiveness. Since the mid-1960's both the United States and the USSR have tended to reduce their commitments to the developing world. 8 tables, 30 notes. E. P. Stickney

4055. Kaplan, Morton A. ROBERT STRAUSZ-HUPÉ: SCHOLAR, GENTLEMAN, MAN OF LETTERS. *Orbis 1970 14(1): 58-70.* Robert Strausz-Hupé's scholarly views have been misinterpreted by his liberal critics because of his rhetoric. His collaborative book *Protracted Conflict* (Harper & Row, 1959) presents a fairly accurate diagnosis of Soviet behavior, but the rhetoric has obscured its meaning. Strausz-Hupé's tone is caused by experiences in Europe between the wars when his warnings of the dangers of Nazi Germany were ignored. He feels that rhetoric is necessary to alert the public to the dangers of Communism. 2 notes. M. C. Lewis

4056. Karcz, Jerzy F. *The Economics of Communist Agriculture: Selected Papers.* Wright, Arthur W., ed. Studies in East European and Soviet Planning, Development, and Trade, no. 25. Bloomington, Ind.: Int. Development Inst., 1979. 494 pp.

4057. Kashtan, William. POSITIVE CHANGES IN THE WORLD AND NEW POSSIBILITIES IN THE REVOLUTIONARY STRUGGLE. *World Marxist R. 1975 18(6): 3-13.* Discusses detente between the United States and the Soviet Union and the role of Communist and Workers' Parties in anti-imperialism.

4058. Kerst, Kenneth A. CPSU HISTORY RE-REVISED. *Problems of Communism 1977 26(3): 17-32.* Examines the writing of Communist Party history under the Brezhnev regime. The barrenness that now characterizes Party historiography suggests the present leadership's total lack of confidence in the Khrushchevian assumption that the Party as an institution could withstand critical examination. Based on primary and secondary Russian and English language sources; 41 notes. J. M. Lauber

4059. Kim, G. F. MAOIZM I NATSIONAL'NO-OSVOBODITEL'NOE DVIZHENIE [Maoism and the national liberation movement]. *Voprosy Istorii [USSR] 1975 (9): 89-101.* Analyzes the policy pursued by the People's Republic of China in Asia, Africa, and Latin America with the aim of imposing its hegemony on the peoples of these continents. Particular attention is devoted to a close examination of the Maoists' activity in the developing countries spearheaded against the Soviet Union which works steadfastly and consistently to strengthen the national sovereignty and to promote the social progress of the peoples of Asia, Africa, and Latin America. The author makes it abundantly clear that the Maoists' actions are basically aimed at undermining the alliance of the national-liberation movement with the socialist world system. To achieve this purpose the Maoists are entering into blocs with the most reactionary forces and ultra-Left adventurist elements within the developing countries. J

4060. Kir'ian, M. VOENNYE VOPROSY V DOKUMENTAKH KPSS I SOVETSKOGO GOSUDARSTVA [Military questions in Soviet government and Communist Party documents]. *Voenno-Istoricheskii Zhurnal [USSR] 1981 23(11): 85-87.* Discusses the contents of an annotated bibliographical index of Soviet government and Communist Party documents, 1917-79, pertaining to the activities of the Party and the state in dealing with the structuring, organizing, and equipping of the Soviet armed forces. 3 notes. A. Brown

4061. Klimov, Iu. M. SOVREMENNYI TROTSKIZM NA SLUZHBE ANTIKOMMUNIZMA [Contemporary Trotskyism in the service of anticommunism]. *Voprosy Istorii KPSS [USSR] 1975 (9): 71-83.* A description and critique of the activity of Trotskyist organizations in Europe and Latin America, especially in France and Chile, from about 1960 to 1975. Trotskyists objectively serve the interests of the bourgeoisie by rejecting the USSR as just another superpower, opposing peaceful coexistence, rejecting a coalition of anti-imperialist forces, and in general, attempting to penetrate as many youth and protest movements as possible. Based on secondary works and Communist as well as Trotskyite periodical literature; 48 notes. L. E. Holmes

4062. Koch, Ute. ÜBERSICHT ZU PUBLIKATIONEN UND UNTERSUCHUNGEN ZUR GESCHICHTE DES KOMSOMOL IN DER SOWJETUNION SEIT 1970 [A survey of publications and investigations into the history of the Komsomol of the Soviet Union appearing since 1970]. *Wissenschaftliche Zeitschrift der Wilhelm-Pieck-Universität Rostock, Gesellschafts- und Sprachwissenschaftliche Reihe [East Germany] 1976 25(1): 71-75.* A bibliographical essay relating to Russian-language conferences and publications since 1970 on the history of the Soviet Young Communist League (Komsomol). The movement serves as a model for the Free German Youth (FDJ) organization of the German Democratic Republic. 25 notes. English summary. J. A. Perkins

4063. Krivoguz, I. M. ISTORICHESKII OPYT I SOVREMENNYE PROBLEMY UCHASTIIA KOMMUNISTOV V PRAVITEL'STVAKH NESOTSIALISTICHESKIKH STRAN [The historical experience and contemporary problems of participation of Communists in governments of nonsocialist countries]. *Voprosy Istorii KPSS [USSR] 1975 (6): 43-56.* Communists have and should continue to participate in nonsocialist governments as long as the party follows the guidelines set forth by Karl Marx and V. I. Lenin—retention of Communist unity, independence, and goals. Participation and its extent depends on the relative progressiveness of the government, conditions of participation, and general Party aims given each nation's history and stage of development. The author provides examples of successful and, to a lesser degree, unsuccessful participation from the revolutions of 1848, Paris Commune, United Fronts of the 1920's and 1930's, and post-World War II Europe to more recent developments in India, Indonesia, Cuba, Chile, and Portugal. Based on secondary works, periodical literature, and Lenin's *Collected Works*; 60 notes. L. E. Holmes

4064. Krivoruchenko, V. K. NEKOTORYE VOPROSY NAUCHNOI RAZRABOTKI ISTORII LENINSKOGO KOMSOMOLA [Some issues in the scientific development of the history of the Leninist Young Communist League]. *Voprosy Istorii KPSS [USSR] 1974 (11): 94-104.* Reviews the treatment of the Young Communist League in the works of Party leaders and Party historians and in memoirs, popular studies, textbooks, journal articles, and document collections published in the Soviet Union, 1957-74. 60 notes. L. E. Holmes

4065. Kryvoruchenko, V. K. DOKUMENTY VLKSM: ZHIVYE SVIDETELI EGO ISTORII [Documents of the Young Communist League: living witnesses of its history]. *Sovetskie Arkhivy [USSR] 1978 (5): 68-73.* Views the publication of collections of documents on the history and activities of the Young Communist League since its formation in 1917.

4066. Kuz'min, V. I. OBOBSHCHENIE V DOKUMENTAKH PARTII ISTORICHESKOGO OPYTA SOTSIALISTICHESKOI REKONSTRUKTSII SOVETSKOI EKONOMIKI [Party document summaries of the historical experience of socialist reconstruction of the Soviet economy]. *Voprosy Istorii KPSS [USSR] 1981 (5): 111-119.* Reviews Communist Party analyses of the history of the USSR and its lessons, including collectivization of agriculture, which ensured food surpluses and inspired the peasantry to great deeds, and the world wars, a hard school from which much has been learned. History also shows the importance of keeping the Party free of opportunist and other undesirable elements. Based on the *CPSU in Resolutions and Decisions, Pravda,* and Brezhnev's works; 80 notes. A. J. Evans

4067. Lekin, Valeri V. MEZHDUNARODNYI BANK EKONOMICHESKOGO SOTRUDNICHESTVA: K 20-LETIIU DEIATEL'NOSTI [The International Bank for Economic Cooperation: 25 years of its activity]. *Voprosy Ekonomiki [USSR] 1984 (1): 127-134.* Since 1964 the International Bank for Economic Cooperation has provided internal and external banking for its members, which are Bulgaria, Hungary, the German Democratic Republic, Poland, Romania, the USSR, Czechoslovakia, Cuba (since 1974), and Vietnam (since 1977). Based on surveys of the International Bank for Economic Cooperation; 2 tables, 3 notes.

4068. Lerner, Warren. *A History of Socialism and Communism in Modern Times: Theorists, Activists, and Humanists.* Englewood Cliffs, N.J.: Prentice-Hall, 1982. 253 pp.

4069. Leshukov, A. S. NEKOTORYE VOPROSY BOR'BY MARKSISTOV-LENINTSEV PROTIV ANARKHISTSKOI PSEVDOREVOLIUTSIONNOSTI [Aspects of the Marxist-Leninist struggle against pseudorevolutionary anarchism]. *Voprosy Istorii KPSS [USSR] 1979 (12): 52-62.* Examines the development of anarchist movements, anti-Marxist and pseudorevolutionary in character, attacks anarchist concepts, and demonstrates the basic directions of Communist opposition to anarchism. Particular reference is made to Italy and West Germany's extreme-left and terrorist groups, and to the efforts of Communists to prevent the spread of anarchist influence among the young. 48 notes. J. S. S. Charles

4070. Lotsek, Gerkhard. OSNOVNYE TENDENTSII I NAPRAVLENIIA ISTORIOGRAFII V FRG [Basic tendencies and directions in West German historiography]. *Novaia i Noveishaia Istoriia [USSR] 1970 (4): 153-161.* An East German view of contemporary West German historical studies, listing works published, and institutions established, to counter East German Marxist-Leninist historiography. The currents of historical writing are divided into pseudoliberal, conservative-nationalist, openly Neo-Nazi, and right social democrat. The works mentioned all date from the 1960's. Secondary works; 37 notes. D. N. Collins

4071. Lowenthal, Richard. CAN COMMUNISM OFFER AN ALTERNATIVE WORLD ORDER? SOME LESSONS OF 20TH-CENTURY POLITICS. *Encounter [Great Britain] 1977 48(4): 17-26.* Leninist communism changed the USSR and China into superpowers while failing utterly as a revolutionary force in the West and thus divided the world. Although it is one of the major historical forces of our time it is not a portent of a world to come.

4072. Lubski, A. V. and Pronshtein, A. P. O NEKOTORYKH VOPROSAKH METODOLOGII ISTORII KPSS [Problems in the methodology of the history of the CPSU]. *Voprosy Istorii KPSS [USSR] 1977 (6): 103-108.* Discusses the methods, methodology, and historiography of Marxist scholarship on the history of the Communist Party of the Soviet Union. Based on a critique of articles recently published in *Voprosy Istorii KPSS;* 28 notes. L. E. Holmes

4073. Madzharov, A. S. K VOPROSU O KLASSIFIKATSII MEMUAROV PO ISTORII KPSS [On the question of the classification of the memoirs on the history of the CPSU]. *Vestnik Leningradskogo Universiteta [USSR] 1976 (8): 27-33.* The memoirs of participants have great significance for research in the history of the Communist Party of the Soviet Union (CPSU). Their immense number and importance has led researchers to propose various ways to classify the memoirs. The author attempts to establish some bases for such a classification. 30 notes. G. F. Jewsbury

4074. Maiorov, S. M. NOVOE IZDANIE UCHEBNIKA "ISTORIIA KPSS" [A new edition of the textbook *A History of the Communist Party of the USSR]. Voprosy Istorii KPSS [USSR] 1970 (3): 102-107.* Reviews the third edition of B. N. Ponamorev et al., eds., *A History of the Communist Party of the USSR* (1969) indicating amendments to previous editions.

4075. Malenbaum, Wilfred. MODERN ECONOMIC GROWTH IN INDIA AND CHINA: THE COMPARISON REVISITED, 1950-1980. *Econ. Development and Cultural Change 1982 31(1): 45-84.* Compares economic growth in India and China between 1950 and 1980, discussing structural change, industrial growth, agricultural growth, and prospects for the future. Agricultural growth and more effective worker involvement are needed for economic growth to accelerate. Based on published sources; 8 tables, 25 notes. J. W. Thacker, Jr.

4076. Mančev, Krastjo. ANTIFAŠISTICKÝ ODBOJ A OTÁZKA MOCI NA BALKÁNĚ [The antifascist struggle and the question of power in the Balkans]. *Slovanský Přehled [Czechoslovakia] 1980 66(2): 102-111.* As a result of the German-Italian offensive in the spring of 1941 the Balkan nations lost independence and suffered from shortages of all kinds. Most of the bourgeois leadership went into exile in England, and the masses fought against the occupation. For them, the USSR represented moral and material help. The Communists were at the forefront of antifascist organizations. This internal strength combined with the fact that Russian troops crossed three of the Balkan countries as they marched west made the climate in the Balkans receptive to the ideas of socialism. Only in Greece was the opposition of emigré groups to a Communist takeover of overriding importance. But this was primarily due to the fact that the Greeks were not yet entering the socialist phase of the revolution, but only the bourgeois-democratic one. In all the other lands the partisans felt closely allied to the Soviet Union and socialist ideas. 24 notes. B. Reinfeld

4077. Marshall, Paul and Welton, Mike. A GUIDE TO CHRISTIAN-MARXIST DIALOGUE. *Can. Dimension [Canada] 1979 13(5): 50-52.* Lists sources on the relationship of theologians and communists, and their increasing intermingling in the 1970's.

4078. Martini, Mauro, ed. MOSCA NOVEMBRE 1960, POLACCHI E CINESI A CONFRONTO [Moscow, November 1960: Polish-Chinese confrontation]. *Ponte [Italy] 1981 37(11-12): 1166-1179.* Gives the text of two conversations between the Chinese Communists, led by Liu Shaoqi and the Poles, led by Władysław Gomułka, on matters that provoked the open schism between the Chinese and Soviet Parties at the 1960 congress. The Chinese were unable to convince the Poles, who had already taken the Soviet side.

4079. Marushkin, B. I. PROTIV ANTIKOMMUNISTICHESKIKH KONTSEPTSII ISTORII SSSR [Anti-Communist conceptions of the history of the USSR]. *Prepodavanie Istorii v Shkole [USSR] 1973 (6): 19-26.* Describes the recent attempts of American historians to undermine the achievements of the October Revolution in their historiography of the Bolshevik takeover, and the denigration of Soviet economic, nationality, and cultural policies.

4080. Mattick, Paul. ECONOMICS, POLITICS, AND THE AGE OF INFLATION. *Int. J. of Pol. 1978 8(3): vii-viii, 3-143.* Provides six articles written between 1973 and 1978 from an "independent Marxist" viewpoint. One deals with the Great Depression and New Deal; the others focus on various, but related, aspects of the world economic and politicsl crisis of the 1970's. "Bourgeois" economic theory is bankrupt, unable to explain the causes of the crisis or point the way to a solution. A root cause is the inability of capitalism, on a world scale, to generate sufficient profits to fuel the necessary accumulation to keep the system going. Nor do the so-called socialist states such as the USSR offer a way out; they are a form of state capitalism which, like the mixed economies, maintains a class society and exploits the workers. Capitalism and the political state, in whatever form, are powerless to resolve the crisis. R. E. Noble

4081. McIntyre, Angus. THE TRAINING OF AUSTRALIAN COMMUNIST CADRES IN CHINA 1951-1961. *Studies in Comparative Communism 1978 11(4): 410-423.* The Australian Communists considered Chinese training less formal and more flexible than Soviet training, but this did not prevent them from breaking with the Chinese and becoming pro-Soviet in the late 1950's. Nonetheless, Chinese trained Communists organized the break between the Communist Party of Australia and the USSR in 1970 possibly because their Chinese training allowed them to dissociate the cause of Communism from that of the USSR. 47 notes. D. Balmuth

4082. Mikhailov, I. M. OSVESHCHENIE ISTORICHESKOGO OPYTA BOR'BY LENINSKOI PARTII PROTIV TROTSKIZMA V SOVETSKOI LITERATURE [Elucidation of the historical experience of the battle by the Leninist party against Trotskyism in Soviet literature]. *Voprosy Istorii KPSS [USSR] 1981 (7): 115-123.* Taking into account the Western imperialist use of Trotsky's theories as a weapon against the revolutionary Marxist-Leninist outlook of the working class, analyzes the most important Soviet works on the problem of Trotskyism in Soviet literature, including K. D. Shalagin's *The Bolsheviks' Struggle with Trotskyism (1907-14),* B. I. Makarov's *Criticism of Trotskyism on the Questions of the Construction of Socialism in the USSR,* K. V. Gusev's *V. I. Lenin's Struggle against Petit Bourgeois Revolutionism and Adventurism,* and V. M. Ivanov's *The Communist Party in the Struggle against Anti-Leninist Tendencies and Groups in the Period of the Construction of Communism, 1921-29.* 46 notes. L. Smith

4083. Miller, Robert F. WRITING ABOUT COMMUNISM. *Australian J. of Pol. and Hist. [Australia] 1975 21(3): 167-171.* A review of four books: *The Communist Party in Canada: A History* by Ivan Avakumovic (Toronto, 1975); *The Politics of Modernization in Eastern Europe: Testing the Soviet Model* ed. by Charles Gati (New York and London, 1974); *Bureaucracy and Revolution in Eastern Europe* by Chris Harman (London, 1974); and *Organizacija i Funkcije Javne Uprave: Osnovne Uporedne i Istorijske Karakteristike* [The organization and function of public administration: basic comparative and historical characteristics] by Aleksandar Stojanović (Belgrade, 1972). The author compares the books, each of which respectively illustrates four different analytical perspectives—viz., that of the traditional political and historical scholar; that of the current Western (mainly American) scholar striving for scientific objectivity in the comparative analysis of communist systems; that of the Western New Left critiques of existing socialist systems; and finally, the sympathetic but critical analyses of insiders (mainly Yugoslavs) who seek basically nonrevolutionary change to enhance the humanistic and popular elements of their societies. Secondary sources; 4 notes. R. G. Neville

4084. Moch, Jules. DISSECTION DU COMMUNISME [Dissecting communism]. *Nouvelle Rev. des Deux Mondes [France] 1977 (3): 544-555, (4): 26-38, (5): 272-282, (6): 519-540.* Part I. COMMUNISME ET CIVILISATION [Communism and civilization]. Reviews the record of communism in the USSR, emphasizing civil rights violations. Part II. FISSURES ET BRÈCHES [Fissures and breaches]. Outlines the breakdown in international Communist unity: the Yugoslav rupture; China's evolution as early as 1920; the rebellions in Hungary, Poland, and Czechoslovakia; and the separate paths taken by Communist parties in France and other capitalist countries. Part III. FORCE APPARENTE ET FAIBLESSES RÉELLES [Apparent strength and actual weaknesses]. Part IV. À PROPOS DU LIVRE DE JACQUES FAUVET ET ALAIN DUHAMEL [Jacques Fauvet and Alain Duhamel's book]. Analyzes *History of the French Communist Party.*

4085. Mond, Georges. MONOPOLE OU CONCENTRATION DE LA PRESSE DANS LES PAYS SOCIALISTES [Monopoly or concentration of the press in socialist countries]. *Rev. d'Études Comparatives Est-Ouest [France] 1975 6(2): 193-216.* The means of communications in 14 communist countries is almost entirely monopolized, the hold over television, radio, films, and the diffusion of news being total. The origin of this current toward concentration is that authority in socialist countries generally prefers concentration and centralization of the press, partly because it is more effective in reducing competition between rival enterprises engaged in mass media or because such a system seems easier to handle, being more independent of numerous human, regional, and national factors. Moreover, a concentrated press is more capable of smoothing over political issues. The economic concentration of the occidental press (the political effects of which are important) is comparable to the political and administrative concentration of the socialist press, which has important, although secondary, economic effects. The latter system leads to almost total monopoly of information, while the former, also open to criticism, nevertheless permits more diversified coverage and plurality of opinion. J/S

4086. Möschner, Günter and Steinke, Volker. WISSENSCHAFTLICHE KONFERENZ ZUM THEMA "KAMPFGEMEINSCHAFT SED-KPDSU" [Scientific conference on the common struggle of the Socialist Unity Party of Germany and the Soviet Communist Party]. *Beiträge zur Geschichte der Arbeiterbewegung [East Germany] 1976 18(4): 710-712.* Reviews the lectures and discussions of the conference of the Commission of German and Soviet Historians, Leipzig, April 1976, which analyzed cooperation between the Communist parties of Germany and the USSR since 1946. R. Wagnleitner

4087. Nakajima, Mineo. SOREN KYŌSANTŌ 20 KAI TAIKAI TO CHGOKU KYŌSANTŌ [The 20th Congress of the CPSU and the Chinese Communist Party]. *Rekishigaku Kenkyū [Japan] 1980 (478): 27-34.* An attempt to identify the origin of the Sino-Soviet confrontation through analyzing how the 20th Congress of the Soviet Communist Party influenced the Chinese Communist Party. Stalin worship was the result of the maturity of the Soviet society as a highly industrialized one, and met the needs of the social class that had grown up in the Soviet period. The Chinese Communist Party, however, did not recognize this background and interpreted the Stalin issue based simply upon its own experiences of revolutionary struggle. Thus, it committed the contradictory act of simultaneously defending Stalin and establishing Mao Tse-tung worship. Such differences in viewpoint led to the real confrontation. Based on *Jên-min Jih-pao, Hung-ch'i, Pei-jing Chou-pao, Mao Tse-tung Hsüan-chi,* and *Mao Tsu-tung Ssu-hsiang Wan-sui;* 29 notes. E. Honno

4088. Nelson, Daniel and White, Stephen, ed. *Communist Legislatures in Comparative Perspective.* Albany, N.Y.: State U. of New York Pr., 1982. 201 pp.

4089. Neubert, Harald. INTERNATIONALES UND NATIONALES IM WELTREVOLUTIONÄREN PROZESS [International and national features in the world revolutionary process]. *Beiträge zur Geschichte der Arbeiterbewegung [East Germany] 1976 18(5): 778-787.* Discusses the development of proletarian internationalism in the Communist parties of Europe, Asia, and Africa since 1945. Based on printed documents and secondary literature; 25 notes. R. Wagnleitner

4090. Oldberg, Ingmar. PARTIMÄSSIGHET OCH HISTORISM: SOVJETMARXISTISKA BÖCKER OM NORGE OCH DANMARK UNDER ANDRA VÄRLDSKRIGET [Party policy alignment and historicism: Soviet Marxist books on Norway and Denmark during World War II]. *Hist. Tidskrift [Sweden] 1981 (1): 62-77.* Historical research in socialist countries like the USSR must regard history as class struggle and support the present Communist Party policies. However, a survey and analysis of one Polish and three Soviet monographs on Scandinavia during World War II shows that the simultaneous demand for historicism allows for varying interpretations of both Party policies and historical events and that the approach varies in individual socialist countries. 24 notes, 25 ref. H. C. Andersen

4091. Palm, Charles G. and Reed, Dale. *Guide to the Hoover Institution Archives.* Bibliographical Series, no. 59. Stanford, Calif.: Hoover Inst., 1980. 418 pp.

4092. Paret, Peter and Shy, John W. GUERRILLA WAR AND US MILITARY POLICY: A STUDY. *Marine Corps Gazette 1962 46(1): 24-32.* Comments on the nature of Communist guerrilla warfare as practiced by Mao Zedong and Che Guevara and suggests how the United States may combat it.

4093. Pletsch, Carl E. THE THREE WORLDS, OR THE DIVISION OF SOCIAL SCIENCE LABOR, CIRCA 1950-1975. *Comparative Studies in Soc. and Hist. [Great Britain] 1981 23(4): 565-90.* Addresses the artificiality of dividing the world into the three spheres: of free, Communist, and developing nations, and the implications of this for social scientists. The three worlds concept emerged simultaneously with Communism research, area studies, and government contracted social studies activities following World War II. The governing dimensions underlying this division are traditional or modern and ideological or free. Modernization is a constituent of the structural relationship among the underlying terms. Social science labor is apportioned by the several disciplines among the three worlds. A new conceptualization of the globe to replace the three worlds is suggested but no paradigm is presented. 33 notes, fig. S. A. Farmerie

4094. Podhoretz, Norman. WHY *THE GOD THAT FAILED* FAILED.... *Encounter [Great Britain] 1983 60(1): 28-34.* The six ex-Communist authors of *The God That Failed,* while conceding that practical Marxism and brutality are inseparable, continued to seek utopias that reject Western practices.

4095. Roberts, Dick. APOLOGISTS FOR STALIN'S CRIMES: THE *GUARDIAN'S* SERIES ON TROTSKYISM. *Internat. Socialist R. 1973 34(8): 24-35 and (10): 18-28.* Reviews events of the Russian and Chinese revolutions and the genesis of the Trotskyist schism in reply to a series on Trotskyism that ran in the New York Maoist weekly the *Guardian.*

4096. Rosenberg, William G. and Young, Marilyn B. *Transforming Russia and China: Revolutionary Struggle in the Twentieth Century.* New York: Oxford U. Pr., 1982. 397 pp.

4097. Roy, Asish Kumar. MAOISM: INDIAN COMMUNIST MOVEMENT AND PEASANTRY—AN OVERVIEW. *China Report [India] 1977 13(6): 31-41.* A study of comparative communism related to agrarian problems in India and China. The Indian and Chinese Communist parties both began in the early 1920's, but the lot of the rural proletariat differed in the two countries. The poor peasants were central in the movement in China, but in India they did not get the attention given the industrial proletariat, though the situation of the peasants was worse. Maoism kept the revolutionary movement alive in India by encouraging the more radical elements of the Party. This resulted in successive radical split-offs and three Communist parties in India. But the Indian parties "did not really conform to Mao Tse-tung's method of achieving a creative synthesis of the universal truth of Marxism-Leninism and the concrete reality in each country." 26 notes. R. V. Ritter

4098. Roy, Asish Kumar. PEKING AND THE LEFT COMMUNISTS IN INDIA: A STUDY OF THEIR IDEOLOGICAL DIFFERENCES. *China Report [India] 1977 13(5): 16-28.* Studies developments within the Communist Party of India (CPI) and the more radical Communist Party of India (Marxist) [CPI(M)] vis-à-vis interference from the Communist Party of China (CPC), 1964-66. The CPI(M)'s commitment to a peaceful transition to socialism through the parliamentary process was a sell-out to Maoists and provoked their repeated attacks. The CPC incited rebels in the CPI(M) to break off from the neorevisionist CPI(M). The new splinter group formed the third Communist party in India, the Communist Party of India (Marxist-Leninist) in 1969. 41 notes. R. V. Ritter

4099. Sagnes, Jean. "PARTI COMMUNISTE" ET "PARTI SOCIALISTE": GENESE D'UNE TERMINOLOGIE ["Communist Party" and "Socialist Party": the birth of a terminology]. *Rev. Française de Sci. Pol. [France] 1982 32(4-5): 795-809.* Describes the formulation of the Communist philosophy in the 19th century, the French labor movement to the early 20th century and the founding of various Communist states throughout the world.

4100. Santsevych, A. V. DEIAKI PYTANNIA DZHERELOZNAVCHOHO ANALIZU DOKUMENTIV CPRS [The scientific analysis of historical sources: CPSU documents]. *Ukrains'kyi Istorychnyi Zhurnal [USSR] 1978 (4): 60-68.* Lively discussion of the methodology of the analysis of historical sources took place between historians, 1976-77, in particular of the works of the founders of Marxism-Leninism, Communist Party documents and materials, and speeches by Party and state workers. 20 notes. V. Packer

4101. Scalapino, Robert A. IN THE AGE OF NATIONAL COMMUNISM: THE INTERNATIONAL ORDER AND COMMUNISM IN NORTHEAST ASIA. *J. of Asiatic Studies [South Korea] 1977 20(2): 1-18.* Reviews the development of national communism in China, North Korea, and Japan, and the current role of the

USSR in northeast Asia. Paper presented at the Conference on Triangular Relations of Mainland China, the Soviet Union, and North Korea, Seoul, 23-25 June 1977. M. Elmslie

4102. Schapiro, Leonard B. ANTISEMITISM IN THE COMMUNIST WORLD. *Soviet Jewish Affairs [Great Britain] 1979 9(1): 42-52.* Examines anti-Semitism in the USSR and Eastern Europe from 1913 to the present. Official anti-Semitism, disguised as anti-Zionism, has been increasing recently to serve government interests, although Romania and Hungary have maintained considerable independence on this issue. Traditional Russian nationalism rooted in Russian Orthodox Christianity is generally free of anti-Semitism.

4103. Schuchardt, Ingrid. DER ANTIKOMMUNISMUS DER "REVOLTE" DES HERBERT MARCUSE [The anticommunism of the "revolt" of Herbert Marcuse]. *Wissenschaftliche Zeitschrift der Friedrich-Schiller-Universität Jena. Gesellschafts- und Sprachwissenschaftliche Reihe [East Germany] 1979 29(2): 269-278.* Herbert Marcuse's theories on revolution and revolt are analyzed as nihilistic and anticommunist, most clearly evident in his criticism of the aggressiveness of the socialist systems. 44 notes.
R. Wagnleitner

4104. Schulz, Donald E. and Adams, Jan S., ed. *Political Participation in Communist Systems.* Pergamon Policy Studies on International Politics. New York: Pergamon, 1981. 334 pp.

4105. Sharapov, G. V. BOR'BA KOMPARTII KAPITALISTICHESKIKH STRAN ZA INTERESY KREST'IANSTVA [Communist parties' struggle in capitalist countries on behalf of peasants]. *Voprosy Istorii KPSS [USSR] 1965 (10):17-29.* Discusses the actions and words of Communist parties in capitalist countries, including the United States and Canada, intended to help the peasantry in poor regions of the world, 1960-65.

4106. Sheikh, Ahmed. COMPARATIVE STUDY OF THE SOVIET AND THIRD WORLD POLITICAL SYSTEMS. *Pol. Sci. Rev. [India] 1972 11(4): 273-299.* Presents a developmental typology for the comparative study of Soviet Russian and Third World political systems. Many Communist governments which are actively engaged in modernization and industrialization can be fruitfully compared with non-Communist developing nations at various stages of modernization. The commonality of nationalist and socialist attitudes, the desire to modernize, the rejection of Western political models, and the authoritarian roles of national governments operate in many similar ways. Analyzes the economic, sociopolitical, and ecological factors in early 20th-century Russia and identifies similarities in modern India, Pakistan, Ghana, and the Philippines. Outlines a typology of development based on historic factors and institutional characteristics. Secondary works; 37 notes, biblio.
S. H. Frank

4107. Sheldon, Charles H. PUBLIC OPINION AND HIGH COURTS: COMMUNIST PARTY CASES IN FOUR CONSTITUTIONAL SYSTEMS. *Western Pol. Q. 1967 20(2, part 1): 341-360.* Identifies the relationship between public opinion and high court decisions by studying the constitutional interpretations of the Communist Party by the courts of Canada, Australia, the Federal Republic of Germany, and the United States during the 1950's.

4108. Sibilev, N. G. VLIIANIE USPEKHOV MIROVOGO SOTSIALIZMA NA SOTSIAL-DEMOKRATIIU [The influence of world socialism's successes on Social Democrats]. *Voprosy Istorii KPSS [USSR] 1976 (4): 72-84.* Suggests that the successes of the world socialist camp, especially the USSR, have pushed European Social Democrats into modernizing their ideas, 1960-76, though they still hold unacceptable reformist views.

4109. Simon, Róbert. AZ ISZLÁM "VÁLASZAI" AZ EURÓPAI "KIHÍVÁSOKRA" [Islam's answers to European challenges]. *Magyar Tudomány [Hungary] 1981 26(9): 661-672.* Islamic nations have historically been sympathetic to the Communist movement. The 1905 Russian revolution influenced the 1906 Iranian revolution and the 1911-12 Chinese revolution and in India strengthened the Congress movement. Asian nations were in close contact with the Third International after the 1917 Russian revolution. A cohesive Communist party in the Middle East and North Africa was difficult to attain because these nations were involved in internal class wars and in fighting colonialism. Lenin advanced the theory after 1917 that communism in the Middle East was possible without first building an independent bourgeois nation, provided that the Soviet Communist Party aided the effort. In the Arab world, the Moslem coalition has been more important for Communist political success than has statehood. Any successful movement there depends on Moslem support. 30 notes. A. M. Pogany

4110. Simons, William B., ed. *The Constitutions of the Communist World.* Alphen aan den Rijn, Netherlands: Sijthood & Noordhoof, 1980. 644 pp.

4111. Smyser, W. R. *The Independent Vietnamese: Vietnamese Communism between Russia and China, 1956-1969.* (Papers in International Studies, Southeast Asia, no. 55.) Athens: Ohio U., Center for Int. Studies, 1980. 143 pp.

4112. Spirin, L. M. O NEKOTORYKH VOPROSAKH RAZRABOTKI TEORETICHESKIKH I METODOLOGICHESKIKH PROBLEM ISTORIOGRAFII ISTORII KPSS [Several issues in the analysis of theoretical and methodological problems of the historiography of the CPSU]. *Voprosy Istorii KPSS [USSR] 1979 (1): 106-114.* Classifies, periodizes, and reviews Soviet historiography on the Communist Party of the USSR, examining 10 types of historiographical studies and seven main groups of historiographical sources. Soviet writing on Party history occurred in four stages: from the mid-1890's to October 1917; from 1917 to the mid-1930's; from the second half of the 1930's to the end of the 1950's; and from the end of the 1950's to the present. During the last stage, historians overcame dogmatism and subjective evaluations produced by the cult of personality of the previous period. From the mid-1960's, Soviet historians rejected tendencies that had begun earlier in the decade to diminish the successes of socialist construction and retreat from interpretations based on the principle of class struggle. Soviet secondary works; 44 notes.
L. E. Holmes

4113. Staar, Richard F., ed.; Wesson, Robert, introd. *Yearbook on International Communist Affairs 1982: Parties and Revolutionary Movements.* Stanford: Hoover Inst. Pr., 1982. 576 pp.

4114. Starr, Richard F. CHECKLIST OF COMMUNIST PARTIES IN 1984. *Problems of Communism 1985 34(2): 90-101.* This list gives information on the major Communist parties and movements recognized by Moscow as well as a number of revolutionary democratic parties viewed by the Kremlin as being at a less developed political stage. Based on data collected from Soviet published sources, *The New York Times, The Washington Post,* and the Foreign Broadcast Information Service, *Daily Report: Soviet Union;* table; 47 notes. J. M. Lauber

4115. Tabachnikov, B. Ia. PO STRANITSAM *ARCHIVUM RUCHU ROBOTNICZEGO* [The pages of *Archivum Ruchu Robotniczego*]. *Voprosy Istorii [USSR] 1979 (6): 151-158.* Reviews the collection of documents released and published since 1973 by the Central Archive of the Central Committee of the Polish United Workers' Party in the series entitled *Archivum Ruchu Robotniczego.* To date the archive has published five volumes, each containing seven to 15 documents and three to four notes on the thematic holdings of the archive. The documents concern the history of the Polish and Russian working class and the international working-class movement. Chronologically they cover the 20th century. 9 notes. V. Sobeslavsky

4116. Tangpoonsinthana, Chantanee. THAILAND AND MAINLAND CHINA, 1975-1980. *Issues & Studies [Taiwan] 1983 19(11): 73-96.* Both internal and external factors, such as intra-party conflicts in the Thai Communist Party and Thai perceptions of Vietnam's expansionism, have affected Thai-Chinese relations since their formalization in 1975. These political factors have had a greater impact than trade and other economic activities. 2 tables, 82 notes. J. A. Krompart

4117. Tarrow, Sidney. TRANSFORMING ENEMIES INTO ALLIES: NON-RULING COMMUNIST PARTIES IN MULTIPARTY COALITIONS. *J. of Pol. 1982 44(4): 924-954.* Communists have participated in liberal democratic regimes during three distinct periods: in the 1930's during the Popular Front of France and Spain; immediately after World War II in Finland, France, and Italy; and during the period of detente in Finland, 1966-71, 1975-79; Chile, 1970-73; and Italy, 1976-79. Over time, the significance of international events has yielded to domestic political issues, especially income policy, in creating these coalitions. Most such attempts at sharing power have resulted in the communists' return to opposition. Opponents who had been considered captives of capital were turned briefly into difficult allies almost impossible to defeat. Communist participation in coalitions has led to only modest gains or tragic reversals for the working class. Such coalitions generally welcomed communists as the left wing while socialists occupied the center. 7 notes, biblio. A. W. Novitsky

4118. Therborn, Göran. *Science, Class, and Society: On the Formation of Sociology and Historical Materialism.* London: Verso, 1980. 461 pp.

4119. Titarenko, S. L. O NEKOTORYKH NAPRAVLENIIAKH FAL'SIFIKATSII ISTORII I POLITIKI KPSS V SOVREMENNOI BRUZHUAZNOI ISTORIOGRAFII [The falsification of the history and policy of the CPSU in contemporary bourgeois historiography]. *Voprosy Istorii KPSS [USSR] 1971 (9): 46-57.* Criticizes the interpretations and methodology of several Western historians' accounts of the Communist Party since 1918.

4120. Titarenko, S. L. VYNUZHDENNYE PRIZNANIIA I LZHIVYE VERSII IDEOLOGOV BURZHUAZII [Forced confessions and false versions of bourgeois ideologists]. *Voprosy Istorii KPSS [USSR] 1968 (10): 94-103.* Shows that bourgeois ideologists have used the 50th anniversary of the October Revolution to make false claims about the supposed failings and deviations of Soviet communism.

4121. Titov, A. EIGHTY YEARS OF OTTO BRAUN'S BIRTH. *Far Eastern Affairs [USSR] 1980 (4): 141-147.* A biographical look at Otto Braun, a veteran of the German and international working-class movement, who fought fascism, was a true friend of the Soviet Union, and took part in the Chinese people's struggle for national and social liberation.

4122. Trager, Frank N. WARS OF NATIONAL LIBERATION: IMPLICATIONS FOR U.S. POLICY AND PLANNING. *Orbis 1974 18(1): 50-105.* Discusses communist concepts of wars of national liberation developed during 1859-1972 and their implications for US foreign policy.

4123. Tuan Chia-feng. SCHISM IN THE INTERNATIONAL COMMUNIST MOVEMENT. *Issues & Studies [Taiwan] 1982 18(1): 64-86.* The Chinese Communist Party, the Communist Party of the USSR, and the Eurocommunists are individually strong but have mutually irreconcilable differences. None offers a viable solution to the problem of world peace. Based on Mainland and Soviet publications; 66 notes. J. A. Krompart

4124. Unger, Leopold. WIDZIANE Z BRUKSELI [The view from Brussels]. *Kultura [France] 1983 (3): 70-81.* Examines links between the secret services of the East European countries, notably the USSR and Bulgaria, and political assassinations in the West, such as Leon Trotsky's and his son's and the attempt on the life of Pope John Paul II in 1981.

4125. Urban, G. R. *Communist Reformation: Nationalism, Internationalism and Change in the World Communist Movement.* New York: St. Martin's, 1979. 335 pp.

4126. Vinogradov, N. P. IZUCHENIE V SSSR ISTORII KOMMUNISTICHESKOGO I RABOCHEGO DVIZHENIIA V KITAE [The study in the USSR of the history of the Communist and workers' movements in China]. *Voprosy Istorii KPSS [USSR] 1961 (2): 167-173.* Surveys Soviet historiography on the Communist and workers' movement in China, finding that a substantial amount of work was published, 1950-60.

4127. Wagner, Wolfgang. L'URSS, LA RDT, GLI ALTRI STATI SOCIALISTI E LA CONFERENZA PER LA SICUREZZA EUROPEA [The USSR, East Germany, the other Communist countries, and the European Security Conference]. *Riv. di Studi Politici Int. [Italy] 1971 38(2): 282-292.*

4128. Wells, E. F. BEFORE WE BURN IT DOWN! *Freeman 1973 23(1): 25-30.* Draws attention to the economic and social failures of the communist states in China, Cuba, and the Soviet Union and suggests that the rebels of the New Left should investigate the alternatives before destroying capitalist society. D. A. Yanchisin

4129. Weremowicz, Elzbieta. NOWE RADZIECKIE PUBLIKACJE O TROCKIZMIE [New Soviet publications on Trotskyism]. *Nowe Drogi [Poland] 1973 (8): 97-101.* Reviews the renewed Soviet attempts to analyze the political activities of Leon Trotsky and his followers.

4130. Wesson, Robert G. *The Aging of Communism.* New York: Praeger, 1980. 168 pp.

4131. Westoby, Adam. *Communism since World War II.* New York: St. Martin's, 1981. 514 pp.

4132. Whitfield, Stephen J. INNOCENTS ABROAD. *Rev. in Am. Hist. 1982 10(3): 424-430.* Reviews *Paul Hollander's Political Pilgrims: Travels of Western Intellectuals to the Soviet Union, China, and Cuba 1928-1978* (1981), which examines the reasons why Western intellectuals have extolled the virtues of Communist societies while refusing to live in them.

4133. Whiting, Allen S. SINO-SOVIET RELATIONS: WHAT NEXT? *Annals of the American Academy of Political and Social Science 1984 (476): 142-155.* China's three demands for normalization of Sino-Soviet relations are not likely to win Soviet compliance. Only a modest reduction of the 480,000 Soviet troops opposite China is possible, but not removal of the 125 SS-20 missiles and 60 Backfire bombers, which have regional and global strategic significance. No Soviet concessions on Afghanistan, Vietnam, or Cambodia are expected. Ideology is no longer an issue between Moscow and Beijing as during Mao's time, but conflicts in national interest deadlock negotiations. Meanwhile, increased Sino-Soviet trade and travel reflect improved state relations. A further improvement could serve US interests in Korea, Indochina, and arms control without jeopardizing US and allied security interests elsewhere. Sino-Soviet relations are, however, basically independent of American influence and should not determine Sino-American relations. J

4134. Zeisler, Kurt. GENESIS UND FUNKTIONEN DER GEGENWÄRTIGEN IMPERIALISTISCHEN "KOMMUNISMUSFORSCHUNG" [Origin and functions of the present imperialist research on Communism]. *Zeitschrift für Geschichtswissenschaft [East Germany] 1973 (10): 1157-1181.* Analyzes the economic, political, and ideological background of American and West German research on communism. Secondary literature; 62 notes. R. Wagnleitner

4135. Zieliński, Eugeniusz. INSTYTUCJA REFERENDUM W PAŃSTWIE SOCJALISTYCZNYM [The institution of the referendum in the socialist state]. *Państwo i Prawo [Poland] 1965 20(2): 232-240.* Analyzes the provisions for referendums provided in the constitutions of the USSR, Mongolia, Albania, Bulgaria, Rumania, Hungary, East Germany, and Yugoslavia since 1936.

4136. Zimbler, Brian L. PARTNERS OR PRISONERS? RELATIONS BETWEEN THE PCF AND CPSU, 1977-1983. *Studies in Comparative Communism 1984 (1): 3-29.* The Communist Party of the Soviet Union (CPSU) and the French Communist Party (PCF) have used each other for their own purposes. Since 1960 the French Communists have shown more independence from the Soviets, moving first in the direction of Eurocommunism and then away from it. Since the late 1970's, they have to some extent exchanged their own support for Soviet policy in Afghanistan and Poland and their abandonment of Eurocommunism for Soviet tolerance of the alliance of the PCF with the Socialists. The PCF chose this alliance to arrest their declining electoral power. 168 notes.

D. Balmuth

4137. —. [THE AMERASIA PAPERS]. *Issues and Studies [Taiwan] 1970 6(8): 18-41.*

Tung Kung-hsuan. LESSONS FROM THE "AMERASIA PAPERS", *pp. 18-26.* Summarizes American foreign policy toward China, 1943-46. The failure of the US government to fully prosecute the *Amerasia* case as espionage is attributed to the switch in US China policy from support of Chiang Kai-shek to tacit support of the Communists. This change was brought about through the efforts of the "old China hands"—John Patton Davies, John Stewart Service, John Carter Vincent, and others—who undermined Ambassador Hurley's and General Wedemeyer's efforts as well as misdirecting General Marshall's mission. *The Amerasia Papers* rectify the mistaken image created by the 1949 *White Paper* and provide a lesson that today's policymakers should not ignore. Based on *The Amerasia Papers: A Clue to the Catastrophe of China* (compiled by Anthony Kubek for the US House Internal Security Subcommittee, 15 February 1970).

Yin Ching-yao. THE '*AMERASIA PAPERS*' AS A CHINESE SEES IT, *pp. 27-41.* Reviews Soviet policy toward China and its influence on the Chinese and American Communist parties. Communist tactics of subversion through manipulation of democratic institutions are examined in the light of the *Amerasia* case and the rise of the "China experts" in the American government. Because of the distorted reports of Davies, Service and other China hands, the United States unwittingly helped the Communists in the crucial postwar period. This bitter experience was an exception to normal Sino-American relations but should enable both countries to sharpen vigilance in the future. Based on secondary sources; 6 notes. L. J. Stout

4138. —. BRIEF INFORMATION ON COMMUNIST AND WORKERS' PARTIES. *World Marxist R. [Canada] 1975 18(6): 38-41.* Comments on the Communist Party in Turkey since 1918, the African Independence Party of Senegal since 1957, and the Communist Party of the Dominican Republic since 1944.

4139. —. CHILE, FRANCE AND ITALY: A DISCUSSION. *Government and Opposition [Great Britain] 1972 7(3): 389-408.* Discusses the political and ideological role of the Communist Party and leftists in Chile, France and Italy in the 1970's.

4140. —. DOKUMENTY I STAT'I PO ISTORII KPSS I MEZHDUNARODNOGO KOMMUNISTICHESKOGO I RABOCHEGO DVIZHENIIA, OPUBLIKOVANNYE V ZHURNALAKH, UCHENYKH ZAPISKAKH, SBORNIKAKH, I TRUDAKH V NOIABRE 1974 G. [Documents and articles on the history of the Communist Party and the international communist and workers' movement, published in journals, scholarly papers, collections and monographs, November 1974]. *Voprosy Istorii KPSS [USSR] 1976 (1): 141-147.* A list by categories of Soviet publications on Party history and the history of the Communist and workers' movement, published in November 1974. L. E. Holmes

4141. —. DOKUMENTY I STAT'I PO ISTORII KPSS I MEZHDUNARODNOGO KOMMUNISTICHESKOGO I RABOCHEGO DVIZHENIIA, OPUBLIKOVANNYE V ZHURNALAKH, UCHËNNYKH ZAPISKAKH, SBORNIKAKH I TRUDAKH V NOIABRE 1965 G [Documents and articles on the history of the Communist Party of the USSR and the international Communist and workers' movement, published in November 1965]. *Voprosy Istorii KPSS [USSR] 1966 (1): 143-148.* A bibliography divided into five sections: V. I. Lenin, the period before the October Revolution, the period after the October Revolution, local Party organizations, and the international Communist and workers' movements.

4142. —. DOKUMENTY I STAT'I PO ISTORII KPSS I MEZHDUNARODNOGO KOMMUNISTICHESKOGO I RABOCHEGO DVIZHENIIA, OPUBLIKOVANNYE V ZHURNALAKH, UCHENYKH ZAPISKAKH, SBORNIKAKH I TRUDAKH [Documents and articles on the history of the CPSU and of the international Communist and workers' movement, published in journals, academic notes, collections, and transactions]. *Voprosy Istorii KPSS [USSR] 1979 (4): 138-142.* A bibliography of materials on Party history and on the international and workers' movement received by the Institute of Marxism-Leninism in December, 1978.

L. E. Holmes

4143. —. K ITOGAM OBMENA MNENIIAMI PO NEKOTORYM VOPROSAM PERIODIZATSII ISTORII KPSS [The results of the exchange of views on questions of the periodization of Soviet Communist Party history]. *Voprosy Istorii KPSS [USSR] 1972 (11): 103-115.* An essay on contemporary approaches of Soviet historians to the issue of periodization of Party history, an issue still to be carefully studied.

4144. —. NEKOTORYI VOPROSY RAZVITIIA ISTORIKO-PARTIINOI NAUKI [Some problems of the development of historical party science]. *Voprosy Istorii KPSS [USSR] 1976 (2): 70-86.* A survey of achievements in the field of Communist Party history from 1971 to 1975, including recent publications of the works of Marx and Lenin, the published comments on Party history by L. I. Brezhnev, the work of special conferences and of such organizations as the Institute of Marxism-Leninism, and most importantly, recently published studies of the Party's activity and ideology from its inception to the contemporary period. Based on contributions to Party history published since 1971; 66 notes. L. E. Holmes

4145. —. O NEKOTORYKH VOPROSAKH METODOLOGII ISTORII KPSS [Problems in the methodology of the history of the CPSU]. *Voprosy Istorii KPSS [USSR] 1977 (5): 97-104.*

Duchenko, N. V., *pp. 97-100.* Discusses the methodology of Marxist scholarship on the history of the Communist Party of the Soviet Union. The principle of Party loyalty requires of the historian a conscious defense of the interests of the proletariat.

Zlobin, V. I., *pp. 100-104.* The author supports the principle of Party loyalty; however, no distinct historical methodology exists for the study of Party history. Based on the published works of Marx, Engels, Lenin, and Leonid Brezhnev; 20 notes.

L. E. Holmes

4146. —. PATH OF PROGRESS; DEPUTY HEADS OF GOVERNMENT OF SOCIALIST COUNTRIES ON RESULTS AND PROSPECTS OF CMEA. *World Marxist R. [Canada] 1974 17(1): 76-95.* Deputy heads of Communist governments in Eastern Europe, Cuba, and Mongolia note the benefits of the Council for Mutual Economic Assistance (Comecon) and the ways to improve cooperation among its members.

4147. —. PROBLEMY ISTORIOGRAFII ISTORII KPSS PERIODA RAZVITOGO SOTSIALIZMA [Problems of the historiography of the history of the CPSU for the period of developed socialism]. *Voprosy Istorii KPSS [USSR] 1981 (11): 101-121.* Reports on a 25 May 1981 meeting on problems of the historiography of the Communist Party of the USSR during the period of the development of socialism. Participants included A. P. Kosulnikov, N. N. Maslov, N. A. Barsukov, P. S. Koltsov, and V. S. Lelchuk. Topics discussed included the growing role of historiography, the content and significance of conceptions of the development of socialism, the leading role of the Party, the Party and the working class in the conditions of the development of socialism, and the activity of local Party organizations. Based on conference material, the 26th Party Congress, and secondary works; 41 notes. L. Smith

4148. —. SPISKI TEM DISSERTATSII, ZASHCHISHCHENNYKH V 1970G NA SOISKANIE UCHENOI STEPENI KANDIDATA ISTORICHESKIKH NAUK PO RAZDELU "ISTORIIA KOMMUNISTICHESKOI PARTII SOVETSKOGO SOIUZA" [Lists of dissertations on the history of the CPSU defended in 1970 for the degree of Candidate of Historical Sciences]. *Voprosy Istorii KPSS [USSR] 1971 (10): 155-158.* Lists 76 theses dealing with the history of the Communist Party of the USSR, almost all covering aspects of the post-1917 period, as well as one thesis treating the history of the Communist Party of East Germany.

4149. —. SPISKI TEM DISSERTATSII, ZASHCHISHCHENNYKH V 1964 I 1965 GG NA SOISKANIE UCHENOI STEPENI KANDIDATA ISTORICHESKIKH NAUK PO RAZDELU ISTORII KOMMUNISTICHESKOI PARTII SOVETSKOGO SOIUZA [Lists of theses defended 1964-65 for the degree of candidate of historical sciences in the history of the Communist Party of the Soviet Union]. *Voprosy Istorii KPSS [USSR] 1966 (4): 151-158.* Lists dissertation topics submitted 1964-65 under chronological headings covering the period 1894-1958.

4150. —. TEMY DOKTORSKIKH DISSERTATSII ODOBRENNYE OTDELOM KOORDINATSII NAUCHNO-ISSLEDOVATEL'SKOI RABOTY V OBLASTI ISTORII KPSS INSTITUTA MARKSIZMA-LENINIZMA PRI TSK KPSS [The themes of doctoral dissertations in the field of the history of the CPSU approved by the Department for the Coordination of Scientific Research Work of the CPSU Institute of Marxism-Leninism]. *Voprosy Istorii KPSS [USSR] 1971 (3): 153-155.* Lists 56 doctoral theses dealing with the history of the Communist Party of the USSR and its republican and regional party organizations, almost all of which concentrate on the post-1917 period.

4151. —. VON HELSINKI NACH MADRID: DIE ENTWICKLUNG DER OST-WEST-WIRTSCHAFTSBEZIEHUNGEN IM HINBLICK AUF DIE KSZE-KORB II-BESCHLÜSSE [From Helsinki to Madrid: the development of East-West economic relations with regard to the decisions of the Conference on Security and Cooperation in Europe, Basket 2]. *Osteuropa Wirtschaft [West Germany] 1980 25(3): 165-198.* Examines the development of the East-West trade system after 1975, now shadowed by the Soviet invasion of Afghanistan, and the US reaction to the invasion.

SUBJECT INDEX

In ABC-CLIO's Subject Profile Index (ABC-SPIndex), each index entry is a complete profile of the abstract and consists of one or more subject, geographic, and biographic terms followed by the dates covered in the article. The index terms are rotated so the complete subject profile is cited under each of the terms. No particular relationship between any two terms in the profile is implied; terms within the profile are listed in alphabetical order following the first term.

Cities, towns, and other small geographical subdivisions are normally listed in parentheses following their respective countries, e.g., "Brazil (Minas Gerais)." However, certain regions of divided, disputed, changed, or indeterminate sovereignty do appear as leading terms listed alphabetically in the index, e.g., "Alsace-Lorraine."

The terms "Book" and "Dissertation" have been added to help the reader distinguish between an entry that refers to a single book or dissertation and an entry that refers to bibliographic lists of books or dissertations.

Terms beginning with an arabic numeral are listed after the letter Z. Chronology of a particular article appears at the end of the string of index descriptors. In the chronological descriptor, "c" stands for century, i.e., "19c" means "19th century."

The last number in the index string, in italics, in each individual index profile refers to the entry number in the book.

A

B

C

D

E

F

G

H

I

J

K

L

N

O

P

S

T

U

V

W

X

Y

Z

AUTHOR INDEX

A

B

C

D

E

F

J

K

S

Z

LIST OF PERIODICALS

A

Acta Historica [Hungary]
Acta Politica [Netherlands]
Acta Poloniae Historica [Poland]
Acta Universitatis Carolinae Philosophica et Historica [Czechoslovakia]
Action Nationale [Canada]
Administration & Society
Africa Report
African Affairs [Great Britain]
Agrártörténeti Szemle [Hungary]
Air University Review
Ajia Kenkyū [Japan]
America Latina [Union of Soviet Socialist Republic]
American Behavioral Scientist
American Heritage
American Jewish History
American Journal of Political Science
American Political Science Review
American Quarterly
American Slavic and East European Review (see Slavic Review)
American Studies in Scandinavia [Norway]
Amerikastudien/American Studies [German Federal Republic]
Anale de Istorie [Romania]
Analele Institutului de Istorie a Partidului de pe Lîngă C.C. al P.C.R. (see Anale de Istorie) [Romania]
Analele Universității București: Istorie [Romania]
Annales d'Etudes Internationales (see Annals of International Studies = Annales d'Etudes Internationales) [Switzerland]
Annales: Economies, Sociétés, Civilisations [France]
Annales Universitatis Scientiarum Budapestinensis de Rolando Eötvös Nominatae: Sectio Historica [Hungary]
Annales Universitatis Scientiarum Budapestinensis de Rolando Eötvös Nominatae: Sectio Philosophica et Sociologica [Hungary]
Annali della Facoltà di Scienze Politiche: Lingua, Letteratura, Civiltà [Italy]
Annali dell'Istituto Giangiacomo Feltrinelli [Italy]
Annals of International Studies = Annales d'Etudes Internationales [Switzerland]
Annals of the American Academy of Political and Social Science
Annals of the Ukrainian Academy of Arts and Sciences in the U.S.
Annals of Wyoming
Année Politique et Economique (ceased pub 1975) [France]
Antioch Review
Archeion [Poland]
Archiv für Sozialgeschichte [German Federal Republic]
Archivmitteilungen [German Democratic Republic]
Armed Forces & Society
Asia Quarterly (ceased pub 1980) [Belgium]
Asian Affairs [Great Britain]
Asian Affairs: An American Review
Asian Forum (ceased pub 1981)
Asian Profile [Hong Kong]
Asian Studies Professional Review
Asian Survey
Asian Thought and Society
Atlantic Community Quarterly
Aussenpolitik [German Federal Republic]
Australian Journal of Chinese Affairs [Australia]
Australian Journal of Politics and History [Australia]
Australian Outlook [Australia]
Australian Quarterly [Australia]
Aziia i Afrika Segodnia [Union of Soviet Socialist Republic]

B

Balcanica: Storia, Cultura, Politica [Italy]
Balkan Studies [Greece]
Beiträge zur Geschichte der Arbeiterbewegung [German Democratic Republic]
Belfagor: Rassegna di Varia Umanità [Italy]
Biuletyn Żydowskiego Instytutu Historycznego w Polsce [Poland]
Black Scholar
Bohemia [German Federal Republic]
Brigham Young University Studies
British Journal of Political Science [Great Britain]
British Journal of Sociology [Great Britain]
Bulgarian Historical Review = Revue Bulgare d'Histoire [Bulgaria]
Bulgarian Review [Brazil]
Bulletin of Latin American Research [Great Britain]
Bulletin of the Society for the Study of Labour History [Great Britain]

C

Cahiers Internationaux d'Histoire Economique et Sociale [Italy]
California History
Canada-Mongolia Review = Revue Canada-Mongolie (ceased pub 1979) [Canada]
Canadian Dimension [Canada]
Canadian Ethnic Studies = Etudes Ethniques au Canada [Canada]
Canadian Journal of African Studies = Revue Canadienne des Etudes Africaines [Canada]
Canadian Journal of History of Sport = Revue Canadienne de l'Histoire des Sports [Canada]
Canadian Journal of History of Sport and Physical Education (see Canadian Journal of History of Sport = Revue Canadienne de l'Histoire des Sports) [Canada]
Canadian Journal of Political Science = Revue Canadienne de Science Politique [Canada]
Canadian Oral History Association Journal = Journal de la Société Canadienne d'Histoire Orale [Canada]
Canadian Review of Studies in Nationalism = Revue Canadienne des Etudes sur le Nationalisme [Canada]
Canadian Slavonic Papers = Revue Canadienne des Slavistes [Canada]
Canadian-American Review of Hungarian Studies (see Hungarian Studies Review) [Canada]
Canadian-American Slavic Studies
Casa de las Américas [Cuba]
Časopis Matice Moravské [Czechoslovakia]
Center Magazine
Central Asian Survey [Great Britain]
Česká Literatura [Czechoslovakia]
Československý Časopis Historický [Czechoslovakia]
China Quarterly [Great Britain]
China Report [India]
Chinese Studies in History
Church History
Cincinnati Historical Society Bulletin (see Queen City Heritage)
Civil Liberties Review (ceased pub 1979)
Civitas [Italy]
Civitas [Switzerland]
Co-Existence [Great Britain]
Colorado Quarterly
Commentary
Communist Viewpoint [Canada]
Comparative Political Studies
Comparative Politics
Comparative Studies in Society and History [Great Britain]
Comunità [Italy]
Conflict
Contemporary Review [Great Britain]
Continuity
Cooperation and Conflict [Norway]
Critique [Great Britain]
Current History

D

Dalhousie Review [Canada]
Défense Nationale [France]
Deutsche Aussenpolitik [German Democratic Republic]
Diplomatic History
Dissent
Documents [France]
Dokumentation der Zeit (ceased pub 1972) [German Democratic Republic]
Donauraum [Austria]

E

East Central Europe
East Europe (ceased pub 1975)
East European Quarterly
Eastern Horizon (ceased pub 1981) [Hong Kong]
Economic Development and Cultural Change
Ecrits de Paris [France]
Einheit [German Democratic Republic]
Ekonomika Sovetskoi Ukrainy [Union of Soviet Socialist Republic]
Ekonomista [Poland]
Electoral Studies [Great Britain]
Encounter
Esprit [France]
Est-Ovest [Italy]
Estudios de Asia y Africa [Mexico]
Estudios Internacionales [Chile]
Estudios Políticos [Mexico]
Estudios Sobre la Unión Soviética (ceased pub 1972) [German Federal Republic]
Estudios Sociales Centroamericanos [Costa Rica]
Ethnicity (ceased pub 1981)
Etudes [France]
Etudes Balkaniques [Bulgaria]
Etudes Historiques (see Etudes Historiques Hongroises) [Hungary]
Etudes Historiques Hongroises [Hungary]
Etudes Internationales [Canada]
Europa Archiv [German Federal Republic]
Europa Ethnica [Austria]
European History Quarterly [Great Britain]
European Studies Review (see European History Quarterly) [Great Britain]

F

Far Eastern Affairs [Union of Soviet Socialist Republic]
Feminist Studies
Fides et Historia
Film & History
Foreign Affairs
Foreign Policy
Foreign Service Journal
Foro Internacional [Mexico]
Foundations: A Baptist Journal of History and Theology (superseded by American Baptist Quarterly)
Frankfurter Hefte [German Federal Republic]
Freedom at Issue
Freedomways (suspended pub 1986)
Freeman
French Historical Studies

G

Gazette: International Journal for Mass Communication Studies [Netherlands]
German Yearbook of International Law [German Federal Republic]
Godishnik: Natsionalen Muzei na Revoliutsionnoto Dvizhenie [Bulgaria]
Godišnjak Društva Istoričara Bosne i Hercegovine [Yugoslavia]
Government and Opposition [Great Britain]

H

Hadtörténelmi Közlemények [Hungary]
Hamizrah Hehadash [Israel]
Histoire [France]
Historama [France]
Historian
Historical Magazine of the Protestant Episcopal Church
Historické Štúdie [Czechoslovakia]
Historický Časopis [Czechoslovakia]
Historie a Vojenství [Czechoslovakia]
Historisk Tidskrift [Sweden]
Historisk Tidsskrift [Denmark]
History Teacher
History Today [Great Britain]
History Workshop Journal [Great Britain]
Hungarian Studies Review [Canada]

I

Iberian Studies [Great Britain]
India Quarterly: Journal of International Affairs [India]
Indian Archives [India]
Indian Economic and Social History Review [India]
Indian Journal of Politics [India]
Indian Political Science Review (suspended pub 1985) [India]
Indiana Social Studies Quarterly (superseded by International Journal of Social Education)
Internasjonal Politikk [Norway]
International Affairs [Great Britain]
International Affairs [Union of Soviet Socialist Republic]
International Journal [Canada]
International Journal of Politics
International Organization
International Perspectives [Canada]
International Problems [Israel]
International Review (ceased pub 1975) [Great Britain]
International Review of History and Political Science (ceased pub 1981) [India]
International Security

International Socialist Review
International Studies |India|
Internationale Spectator |Netherlands|
Internationale Wissenschaftliche Korrespondenz zur Geschichte der Deutschen Arbeiterbewegung |German Federal Republic|
Internationales Asienforum |German Federal Republic|
Investigación Económica |Mexico|
Isis
Issues & Studies |Taiwan|
Istoricheski Pregled |Bulgaria|
Istoricheskie Zapiski |Union of Soviet Socialist Republic|
Istoriia SSSR |Union of Soviet Socialist Republic|
Istorija: Spisanie na Sojuzot na Drushtvata na Istoricharite na SR Makedonija |Yugoslavia|
Istorijski Glasnik |Yugoslavia|
Istorijski Zapisi |Yugoslavia|
Italia Contemporanea |Italy|
Italy: Documents and Notes |Italy|
Izvestiia na Instituta po Istoriia na BKP |Bulgaria|
Izvestiia na Instituta za Istoriia (pub suspended 1975-78) |Bulgaria|
Izvestiia Sibirskogo Otdeleniia Akademii Nauk SSSR. Seriia Istorii, Filologii i Filosofii |Union of Soviet Socialist Republic|

J

Jahrbuch für Geschichte |German Democratic Republic|
Jahrbuch für Geschichte der Sozialistischen Länder Europas |German Democratic Republic|
Jahrbuch für Geschichte der UdSSR und der Volksdemokratischen Länder Europas (see Jahrbuch für Geschichte der Sozialistischen Länder Europas) |German Democratic Republic|
Jahrbuch für Volkskunde und Kulturgeschichte |German Democratic Republic|
Jahrbuch für Wirtschaftsgeschichte |German Democratic Republic|
Jahrbücher für Geschichte Osteuropas |German Federal Republic|
Japan Quarterly |Japan|
Jednota Annual Furdek
Journal of American Folklore
Journal of American History
Journal of Asian Studies
Journal of Asiatic Studies (Asea Yon'gu) |South Korea|
Journal of Black Studies
Journal of Common Market Studies |Great Britain|
Journal of Commonwealth & Comparative Politics |Great Britain|
Journal of Commonwealth Political Studies (see Journal of Commonwealth and Comparative Politics) |Great Britain|
Journal of Contemporary Asia |Sweden|
Journal of Contemporary History |Great Britain|
Journal of Ecumenical Studies
Journal of Ethnic Studies
Journal of European Studies |Great Britain|
Journal of Folklore Research
Journal of Higher Education
Journal of Interamerican Studies and World Affairs
Journal of International Affairs
Journal of International and Comparative Studies (see Potomac Review)
Journal of Korean Affairs (ceased pub 1977)
Journal of Latin American Studies |Great Britain|
Journal of Library History, Philosophy, & Comparative Librarianship
Journal of Northeast Asian Studies
Journal of Oriental Studies |Hong Kong|
Journal of Palestine Studies
Journal of Peasant Studies |Great Britain|
Journal of Political and Military Sociology
Journal of Political Science
Journal of Politics
Journal of Popular Culture
Journal of Social and Political Studies (see Journal of Social, Political and Economic Studies)
Journal of Social, Political and Economic Studies
Journal of Southeast Asian Studies |Singapore|
Journal of Sport History
Journal of the Chinese University of Hong Kong (ceased pub 1979) |Hong Kong|
Journal of the Folklore Institute (see Journal of Folklore Research)
Journal of the History of Biology |Netherlands|
Journal of the History of the Behavioral Sciences
Journal of the History Society, University of Singapore |Singapore|
Journal of the Hong Kong Branch of the Royal Asiatic Society |Hong Kong|
Journal of the Royal United Services Institute for Defence Studies |Great Britain|
Journal of World Trade Law |Switzerland|
Journalism Quarterly

K

Kleio |Netherlands|
Komunikaty Mazursko-Warmińskie |Poland|
Korea & World Affairs |South Korea|
Közgazdasági Szemle |Hungary|
Kultura |France|
Kultura i Społeczeństwo |Poland|
Kungliga Krigsvetenskaps Akademiens Handlingar och Tidskrift |Sweden|
Kwartalnik Historii Ruchu Zawodowego |Poland|
Kwartalnik Historyczny |Poland|
Kyrkohistorisk Årsskrift |Sweden|

L

Labor History
Labour = Travail |Canada|
Labour History |Australia|
Lateinamerika |German Democratic Republic|
Latin American Perspectives
Latvijas PSR Zinątņu Akadēmijas Vēstis |Union of Soviet Socialist Republic|
Levéltári Közlemények |Hungary|
Lietuvos TSR Mokslų Akademijos. Darbai. Serija A: Visuomenės Mokslai |Union of Soviet Socialist Republic|
Llafur: Journal of the Society for the Study of Welsh Labour History |Great Britain|

M

Macedonian Review |Yugoslavia|
Magazin Istoric |Romania|
Magyar Könyvszemle |Hungary|
Magyar Tudomány |Hungary|
Marine Corps Gazette
Martin-Luther-Universität Halle-Wittenberg. Wissenschaftliche Zeitschrift. Gesellschafts- und Sprachwissenschaftliche Reihe |German Democratic Republic|
Marxist Perspectives (ceased pub 1980)
Maryland Historian
Massachusetts Review
Mawazo |Uganda|
Meddelelser om Forskning i Arbejderbevaegelsens Historie (see Arbejderhistorie) |Denmark|
Medjunarodni Problemi |Yugoslavia|
Memoria: Rivista di Storia delle Donne |Italy|
Mezhdunarodnaia Zhizn' (see International Affairs edition) |Union of Soviet Socialist Republic|
Michigan Academician
Mid-America
Midstream
Militärgeschichte |German Democratic Republic|
Military Affairs
Military Review
Millennium: Journal of International Studies |Great Britain|
Mirovaia Ekonomika i Mezhdunarodnye Otnosheniia |Union of Soviet Socialist Republic|
Mitteilungen des Instituts für Orientforschung |German Democratic Republic|
Modern Age
Modern Asian Studies |Great Britain|
Modern China
Mondo Cinese |Italy|
Montclair Journal of Social Sciences and Humanities (ceased pub 1974)
Monthly Review
Morskoi Sbornik |Union of Soviet Socialist Republic|
Mouvement Social |France|
Movimento di Liberazione in Italia (see Italia Contemporanea) |Italy|
Movimento Operaio e Socialista |Italy|

N

Narody Azii i Afriki |Union of Soviet Socialist Republic|
Nationalities Papers
Naval War College Review
Neue Politische Literatur |German Federal Republic|
New Hungarian Quarterly |Hungary|
New Left Review |Great Britain|
New World Review
Nghien Cuu Lich Su |Vietnam|
Norsk Militaert Tidsskrift |Norway|
North Dakota Quarterly
Northeast African Studies
Nouvelle Revue des Deux Mondes (see Revue des Deux Mondes) |France|
Novaia i Noveishaia Istoriia |Union of Soviet Socialist Republic|
Nový Orient |Czechoslovakia|
Nowe Drogi |Poland|
Nuestro Tiempo (IHE) |Spain|
Nuova Antologia |Italy|

O

Ohio History
Økonomi og Politik |Denmark|
Orbis
Oriens Extremus |German Federal Republic|
Oriente Moderno |Italy|
Österreich in Geschichte und Literatur |Austria|
Österreichische Osthefte |Austria|
Osteuropa |German Federal Republic|
Osteuropäische Rundschau (ceased pub 1973) |German Federal Republic|
Osteuropa-Wirtschaft |German Federal Republic|
Ostkirchliche Studien |German Federal Republic|

P

Pacific Affairs |Canada|
Pacific Community (ceased pub 1971) |Australia|
Pacific Historical Review
Pacific Northwest Quarterly
Paedagogica Historica |Belgium|
Pakistan Horizon |Pakistan|
Państwo i Prawo |Poland|
Papers on Far Eastern History |Australia|
Parameters
Parliamentary Affairs |Great Britain|
Partisan Review
Párttörténeti Közlemények |Hungary|
Patma-Banasirakan Handes. Istoriko-Filologicheskii Zhurnal |Union of Soviet Socialist Republic|
Pennsylvania Magazine of History and Biography
Pensée |France|
Pensiero Politico |Italy|
Peuples Méditerranéens-Mediterranean Peoples (see Mediterranean Peoples = Peuples Méditerranéens) |France|
Phylon
Plural Societies |Netherlands|
Polish Review
Polish Western Affairs = Pologne et les Affaires Occidentales |Poland|
Political Quarterly |Great Britain|
Political Science |New Zealand|
Political Science Quarterly
Political Science Reviewer
Political Studies |Great Britain|
Politička Misao |Yugoslavia|
Politico |Italy|
Politics |Australia|
Politics & Society
Politiikka |Finland|
Politique Etrangère |France|
Politische Studien |German Federal Republic|
Politische Vierteljahresschrift |German Federal Republic|
Polity
Ponte |Italy|
Právněhistorické Studie |Czechoslovakia|
Prepodavanie Istorii v Shkole |Union of Soviet Socialist Republic|
Present Tense
Prispevki za Zgodovino Delavskega Gibanja |Yugoslavia|
Problèmes d'Amérique Latine |France|
Problemi di Ulisse |Italy|
Problems of Communism
Problems of the Peoples of the USSR |German Federal Republic|
Proceedings of the Annual Meeting of the Western Society for French History
Proceedings of the Royal Irish Academy. Section C |Republic of Ireland|
Progressive Labor
Prologue: the Journal of the National Archives
Prmyslové Oblasti (ceased pub?) |Czechoslovakia|
Przegląd Historyczny |Poland|
Przegląd Zachodni |Poland|
Public Administration |Great Britain|
Public Opinion Quarterly

Q

Quarterly Review of Historical Studies |India|
Queen City Heritage
Quellen und Forschungen aus Italienischen Archiven und Bibliotheken |German Federal Republic|

R

Rad Jugoslavenska Akademija Znanosti i Umjetnosti: Društveni Znanosti [Yugoslavia]
Radical America
Radical History Review
Rassegna Italiana di Sociologia [Italy]
Rekishi Hyôron [Japan]
Rekishigaku Kenkyû [Japan]
Review (Fernand Braudel Center)
Review of Politics
Review of Radical Political Economics
Reviews in American History
Revista Arhivelor [Romania]
Revista de Estudios Históricos de la Guardia Civil (IHE) [Spain]
Revista de Estudios Internacionales (supersedes Revista de Política Internacional) [Spain]
Revista de Estudios Políticos [Spain]
Revista de Istorie [Romania]
Revista de Política Internacional (superseded by Revista de Estudios Internacionales) [Spain]
Revista Mexicana de Ciencia Política (see Revista Mexicana de Ciencias Políticas y Sociales) [Mexico]
Revista Mexicana de Ciencias Políticas y Sociales [Mexico]
Revue d'Allemagne [France]
Revue de Défense Nationale (see Défense Nationale) [France]
Revue de l'Est (see Revue d'Etudes Comparatives Est-Ouest) [France]
Revue Dějin Socialismu (ceased pub 1970) [Czechoslovakia]
Revue des Deux Mondes [France]
Revue des Travaux de l'Académie des Sciences Morales et Politiques & Comptes Rendus de ses Séances (see Revue des Sciences Morales & Politiques) [France]
Revue d'Etudes Comparatives Est-Ouest [France]
Revue d'Histoire de l'Amérique Française [Canada]
Revue d'Histoire Moderne et Contemporaine [France]
Revue du Nord [France]
Revue Française de Science Politique [France]
Revue Française d'Etudes Politiques Africaines [France]
Revue Militaire Générale (ceased pub 1973) [France]
Revue Politique et Parlementaire [France]
Revue Roumaine des Sciences Sociales: Série des Sciences Economiques [Romania]
Revue Roumaine d'Etudes Internationales [Romania]
Revue Roumaine d'Histoire [Romania]
Risorgimento [Italy]
Rivista di Studi Politici Internazionali [Italy]
Rivista Italiana di Scienza Politica [Italy]
Rocky Mountain Social Science Journal (see Social Science Journal)
Romania: Pages of History [Romania]
Round Table (suspended pub 1982) [Great Britain]

S

SAIS Review
Samtiden [Norway]
San José Studies
Sborník Historický [Czechoslovakia]
Sborník Prací Filosofické Fakulty Brněnské University: Řada Historická [Czechoslovakia]
Scandinavian Political Studies [Norway]
Schweizer Monatshefte [Switzerland]
Science & Society
Search: Journal for Arab and Islamic Studies
Secolas Annals
Serra d'Or (IHE) [Spain]
Shakai Kagaku Kenkyû [Japan]
Shakaikeizaishigaku (Socio-Economic History) [Japan]
Shigaku Zasshi [Japan]
Shih-ta Hsüeh-pao = Bulletin of National Taiwan Normal University [Taiwan]
Shirin [Japan]
Shvut [Israel]
Signs: Journal of Women in Culture and Society
Skandinavskii Sbornik [Union of Soviet Socialist Republic]
Śląski Kwartalnik Historyczny Sobótka [Poland]
Slavic Review: American Quarterly of Soviet and East European Studies
Slezský Sborník [Czechoslovakia]
Slovakia
Slovanské Štúdie [Czechoslovakia]
Slovanský Přehled [Czechoslovakia]
Social Education
Social Forces
Social Policy
Social Problems
Social Science History
Social Science Journal
Social Science Research Council Items
Social Sciences [Union of Soviet Socialist Republic]
Society
Sociological Bulletin [India]
Sociological Inquiry
Sotsiologicheskie Issledovaniia [Union of Soviet Socialist Republic]
Soundings (Nashville, TN)
South Asian Review (ceased pub 1975) [Great Britain]
South Asian Studies [India]
South Atlantic Quarterly
South Dakota History
Southeastern Europe
Southern California Quarterly
Southern Exposure
Southern Speech Communication Journal
Southern Speech Journal (see Southern Speech Communication Journal)
Southwestern Historical Quarterly
Sovetskie Arkhivy [Union of Soviet Socialist Republic]
Sovetskoe Gosudarstvo i Pravo [Union of Soviet Socialist Republic]
Sovetskoe Slavianovedenie [Union of Soviet Socialist Republic]
Soviet Jewish Affairs [Great Britain]
Soviet Military Review [Union of Soviet Socialist Republic]
Soviet Studies [Great Britain]
Soviet Studies in History
Soviet Union
Spiegel Historiael [Netherlands]
Sprawy Międzynarodowe [Poland]
Ssu yü Yen = Thought and Word [Taiwan]
Statsvetenskaplig Tidskrift [Sweden]
Stimmen der Zeit [German Federal Republic]
Storia Contemporánea [Italy]
Storia e Politica (suspended pub 1984) [Italy]
Studi Storici [Italy]
Studia Albanica [Albania]
Studia Filozoficzne [Poland]
Studia Historica Slovaca [Czechoslovakia]
Studia Nauk Politycznych [Poland]
Studies in Comparative Communism [Great Britain]
Studies in Comparative International Development
Studies in Soviet Thought [Netherlands]
Studies on the Soviet Union (ceased pub 1971) [German Federal Republic]
Studii: Revistă de Istorie (see Revista de Istorie) [Romania]
Studii şi Articole de Istorie [Romania]
Studime Filologjike [Albania]
Studime Historike [Albania]
Sučasnist [German Federal Republic]
Sudetenland [German Federal Republic]
Südost-Forschungen [German Federal Republic]
Survey [Great Britain]
Svensk Tidskrift [Sweden]
Századok [Hungary]

T

Társadalmi Szemle [Hungary]
Technology and Culture
Texas Quarterly (ceased pub 1978)
Történelmi Szemle [Hungary]
Towson State Journal of International Affairs

U

UCLA Historical Journal
Ukrainian Quarterly
Ukrainian Review [Great Britain]
Ukrains'kyi Istorychnyi Zhurnal [Union of Soviet Socialist Republic]
United Asia [India]
Upper Midwest History

V

Valkanika Symmeikta [Greece]
Vestnik Leningradskogo Universiteta: Seriia Istorii, Iazyka i Literatury [Union of Soviet Socialist Republic]
Vestnik Moskovskogo Universiteta: Istoriko-Filologicheskaia Seriia (superseded by Vestnik Moskovskogo Universiteta, Seriia 9: Istoriia) [Union of Soviet Socialist Republic]
Vierteljahrshefte für Zeitgeschichte [German Federal Republic]
Voenno-Istoricheskii Zhurnal [Union of Soviet Socialist Republic]
Vojnoistorijski Glasnik [Yugoslavia]
Voprosy Ekonomiki [Union of Soviet Socialist Republic]
Voprosy Filosofii [Union of Soviet Socialist Republic]
Voprosy Istorii KPSS [Union of Soviet Socialist Republic]

W

Washington Monthly
Wereld en Zending [Netherlands]
West European Politics [Great Britain]
West Georgia College Studies in the Social Sciences
Western Political Quarterly
Wiener Library Bulletin (ceased pub 1983) [Great Britain]
Wilson Quarterly
Wisconsin Magazine of History
Wissenschaftliche Zeitschrift der Friedrich-Schiller-Universität Jena. Gesellschafts- und Sprachwissenschaftliche Reihe [German Democratic Republic]
Wissenschaftliche Zeitschrift der Ernst-Moritz-Arndt- Universität Greifswald. Gesellschaftswissenschaftliche Reihe [German Democratic Republic]
Wissenschaftliche Zeitschrift der Humboldt Universität zu Berlin. Gesellschaftswissenschaftliche Reihe [German Democratic Republic]
Wissenschaftliche Zeitschrift der Karl-Marx-Universität Leipzig. Gesellschafts- und Sprachwissenschaftliche Reihe [German Democratic Republic]
Wissenschaftliche Zeitschrift der Universität Rostock. Gesellschafts- und Sprachwissenschaftliche Reihe (see Wissenschaftliche Zeitschrift der Wilhelm-Pieck-Universität Rostock. Gesellschaftswissenschaftliche Reihe) [German Democratic Republic]
Wissenschaftliche Zeitschrift der Wilhelm-Pieck-Universität Rostock. Gesellschaftswissenschaftliche Reihe [German Democratic Republic]
Working Papers for a New Society (see Working Papers Magazine)
World Affairs
World Marxist Review [Canada]
World Politics
World Survey [Great Britain]
World Today [Great Britain]
Worldview

Z

Z Pola Walki [Poland]
Zapiski Historyczne [Poland]
Zbornik Matice Srpske za Društvene Nauke [Yugoslavia]
Zbornik za Društvene Nauke (see Zbornik Matice Srpske za Društvene Nauke) [Yugoslavia]
Zeitgeschichte [Austria]
Zeitschrift für Geschichtswissenschaft [German Democratic Republic]
Zeitschrift für Politik [German Federal Republic]
Zeszyty Historyczne [France]

LIST OF ABSTRACTERS

A

Adams, R. K.
Adler, P. J.
Alcock, A.
Aldrich, R.
Alexander, G. M.
Andersen, H. C.
Andrews, H. D.
Anstey, C.
Aoki, Y.
Armstrong, A.
Arum, P. M.
Athey, L. L.

B

Balmuth, D.
Bamber, J.
Barach, M. J.
Barnard, J. D.
Bartels, U. H.
Bates, C.
Bazillion, R. J.
Bender, V.
Benfield, S. F.
Berger, K. W.
Billigmeier, J. C.
Birch, F. D.
Blaser, L. K.
Block, B. A.
Bobango, G. J.
Boehnke, S.
Bonnycastle, S.
Broussard, J. H.
Brown, A.
Brown, L.
Burckel, N. C.
Burkholder, M. A.
Butchart, R. E.

C

Cameron, D. D.
Canavero, A.
Chambers, J. M.
Chan, L. B.
Charles, J. S. S.
Chary, F. B.
Chojecki, Z. K. L.
Cieplak, T. N.
CK-AU
Cleyet, G. P.
Coleman, J. S.
Colenso, M. R.
Collins, D. N.
Collon, C.
Conner, S. P.
Coutinho, J. V.
Craver, E. J.
Cregier, D. M.
Crowther, K. N. T.
Curtis, G. H.
Cushnie, J.

D

Daly, M.
Dejevsky, N.
Detrick, R. H.
Dibert, M.
Diuk, H.
Djakowska, L.
Dombrovski, G.
Dunn, E.
Dunn, S. P.

E

Eid, L. V.
Eide, M. A.
Eidlin, F. H.
Elmslie, M.
Engler, D. J.
English, J. C.
Evans, A. J.

F

Faissler, M.
Farmerie, S. A.
Feingold, M.
Feintuck, L. J.
Fenske, B. L.
Ferdinand, C. I. P.
Fones-Wolf, K.
Foxcroft, Gy. and N. H.
Frank, S. H.
Franz, D. A.
Frederick, R. D.
Frenkley, N.
Freudenthal, H. W. L.
Frey, L. S.
Fritze, R. P.

G

Gagnon, G. O.
Garland, A. N.
Gassner, J. S.
Geyer, M.
Glatfelter, R. E.
Glovins, G. A.
Goerler, R. E.
Gray, R. M.
Grove, R.
Groves, J. V.
Gudgin, S. R.
Gustafson, P. M.

H

Hajdú, I.
Harahan, J. P.
Harrington, J. F.
Hartig, T. H.
Hartigan, F. X.
Heitzman-Wojcicka, H.
Herman, P. D.
Herman, P. T.
Herman, T. Z.
Hernas, M.
Herritt, G.
Herstein, S. R.
Heston, T. J.
Hetzron, R.
Hidas, P. I.
Hively, W. R.
Hobson, W. K.
Hoffman, A.
Holland, B.
Holmes, L. E.
Holsinger, J. C.
Honno, E.
Hont, I.
Hough, C. M.
Houston, R. C.
Howell, A. W.
Howell, L. J.
Human, V. L.

I

Imura, Y.
Ishihara, Y.

J

Jackson, S. G.
Jaworska, E.
Jennison, E. W.
Jeszenszky, G.
Jewsbury, G. F.
Jeyes, U. G.
Johnson, D. W.
Jones, S. F.

K

Kabdebo, T.
Kalinowski, L.
Karacs, I.
Kascus, M. A.
Kaufman, M.
Keyser, E. L.
Khan, R. O.
Kimmel, B.
King, C. E.
Kipp, J. W.
Kirby, E. S.
Kirillov, R.
Klass, L. J.
Kommer, D. J.
Koppel, T.
Košak, S.
Kowalski, W.
Krogstad, E. E.
Krompart, J. A.
Krushelnyckyj, I.
Krzyzak, L. A.
Krzyzaniak, M.
Kubicek, R. V.
Kuner, T.

L

Lauber, J. M.
Law, D. G.
Layton, R. V.
Ledbetter, B. D.
Lederer, N.
Lee, J. M.
Leedom, J. W.
Lewis, M. C.
Libbey, G. H.
Lindgren, R. E.
Linkfield, T. P.
Liptai, S.
Lloyd, D. S.
Logoreci, A.
Lokken, R. N.
Long, J. W.
Lovin, C. R.
Lukaszewski, W. J.
Lukes, I.

M

Manning, G. W.
Marks, H. S.
Marr, W.
Masloff, C. S.
Maxted, L. R.
Mayer, T. F.
McCarthy, E.
McCarthy, J. M.
McDonald, D. R.
McIntyre, W. D.
McLaughlin, P. L.
McLendon, E. M.
McNeill, C. A.
McQuilkin, D. K.
Mendel, R. B.
Menicant, A. H.
Michelson, P. E.
Migliazzo, A. C.
Miller, H. J.
Mina, A.
Moen, N. W.
Moody, C.
Moody, L. C.
Motono, E.
Mtewa, M.
Munro, G. E.
Murdoch, D. H.
Myers, J. P. H.

N

Naçi, G-D. L.
Nakayama, M.
Neville, G. L.
Neville, R. G.
Nicholls, D. J.
Nielson, D. G.
Niven, A. C.
Noble, R. E.
Novitsky, A. W.
Nowak, C. M.
Nycz, H. D.

O

Ohl, J. K.
Olbrich, W. L.
Olson, C. W.
Olson, G. L.
O'Neil, S. J.
Orchard, G. E.
Orr, R. B.
Osur, A. M.
Overbeck, J. A.

P

Pach, B. R.
Packer, V. A.
Palat, M. K.
Parker, H. M.
Parker, T.
Pasadas-Ureña, C.
Paul, B. J.
Paul, J. F.
Pavia, J. R.
Penney, R. E.
Pentland, N. S. T.
Pergl, G. E.
Perkins, J. A.
Petrzilkova, M.-M.
Pichelin, C.
Pickens, D. K.
Piersen, W. D.
Pike, C. R.
Plumridge, E.
Pogany, A. M.
Powell, D.
Powell, J.
Powers, T. L.
Presland, J. H. H.
Prowe, D.

R

Rabineau, P.
Read, C. J.
Reid, W. S.
Reinfeld, B.
Richardson, T. P.
Riddick, J. F.
Ritter, R. V.
Ro, Y. C.
Rosenblatt, N. A.
Rosenthal, F.
Ruffo-Fiore, S.
Ryan, E. E.

S

Samaraweera, V.
Sassoon, T.
Sather, L. B.
Sbacchi, A.
Schaeper, T. J.
Schafer, D. F.
Schmidt, L. H.
Schoonover, T. D.
Schuetz, A.
Seitz, R.
Selleck, R. G.
Senn, A. E.
Sevilla, S.
Seymour, L. J.
Shaw, F. J.
Sherer, R. G.
Shields, H. S.
Short, L.
Sicher, E. R.
Simmerman, T.
Sindermann, R. P.
Sliwoski, R. S.
Smith, C. O.
Smith, G. L.
Smith, L.
Smith, T. W.
Smoot, J. G.
Snow, G. E.
Snow, K. C.
Sobell, V.
Sobeslavsky, V.
Sokolow, J.
Soos, E. E.
Spade, D. F.
Spector, S. D.
Spira, T.
Standley, A. E.
Stevenson, D. R.
Stickney, E. P.
Stoesen, A. R.
Stout, L. J.
Street, J. B.
Strnad, A. A.
Strom, S. C.
Stromberg, R. N.
Swiecicka-Ziemianek, M.
Szamuely, H.
Szilassy, S.

T

Takatsuna, H.
Talalay, S. J.
Tate, M. L.
Taylor, P. R.
Taylorson, P. J.
Thacker, J. W.
Thomas, J. R.
Tomlinson, R. H.
Trauth, M. P.
Troebst, S.
Tudor, F. P.
Tull, J.
Tulloch, G. S.
Turk, E. L.
Twyman, L. G. G.

U

Uchiyama, M.

V

Valliant, R. B.
Vance, M. M.
Velicer, L. F.
Vignery, J. R.
Vilums, R.

W

Wagnleitner, R.
Walker, J. T.
Walton, P. D.
Ware, R. J.
Waters, L.
Watson, D. H.
Welisch, S. A.
Weltsch, R. E.
Wendel, T. H.
Wengenroth, U.
White, G. M.
Wiegand, W. A.
Wilczek, J. M.
Williams, J.
Wilson, L. C.
Wilson, M. T.
Wojcicka, H. Heitzman
Wood, C. W.
Wurster, H. W.
Wyk, L. W. Van

Y

Yanchisin, D. A.
Yasamee, F. A. K.
Yerburgh, M. R.
Young, W. F.

Z

Zawadzki, W. H.
Ziewacz, L. E.